Majority and Minority

Majority and Minority

The Dynamics of Race and Ethnicity in American Life

Sixth Edition

Edited by

Norman R. Yetman
The University of Kansas

Allyn and Bacon

Boston   London   Toronto   Sydney   Tokyo   Singapore

Series Editor: Sarah L. Kelbaugh
Editor-in-Chief, Social Sciences: Karen Hanson
Editorial Assistant: Jennifer Muroff
Executive Marketing Manager: Suzy Spivey
Cover Administrator: Jenny Hart
Composition Buyer: Linda Cox
Manufacturing Buyer: Meghan Cochran
Production Coordinator: Deborah Brown
Editorial-Production Service: Anne Rebecca Starr

Library of Congress Cataloging-in-Publication Data

Majority and minority : the dynamics of race and ethnicity in American
   life / edited by Norman R. Yetman. — 6th ed.
      p.   cm.
   Includes bibliographical references (p. 523).
   ISBN 0-205-14569-8
   1. United States—Race relations.   2. United States—Ethnic
relations.   3. Minorities—United States.   I. Yetman, Norman R.,
1938–
E184.A1M256   1998
305.8'00973—dc21   98-20954
                                                                        CIP

Printed in the United States of America

10 9 8 7 6 5 4 3 2 1   03 02 01 00 99 98

For

Lucile Darling Yetman
and
Aidan Cole Yetman-Michaelson

May he and his generation
realize the dreams
she shared with us.

Contents

Preface

The life of the six editions of *Majority and Minority* has been bracketed by two presidential commissions on American race relations. In July 1967, in the wake of three summers of progressively more intense racial disorders that devastated cities throughout the United States, President Lyndon Johnson appointed a commission to investigate the causes of this unrest and to recommend public policies to address the conditions that spawned them. Less than a year later—February 29, 1968—the President's Commission on Civil Disorders—named the Kerner Commission after its chair, Illinois Governor Otto Kerner—issued its report. The Commission's basic conclusion was succinctly stated on the first page of the report: "Our nation is moving toward two societies, one black, one white—separate and unequal. . . . What white Americans have never fully understood—but what the Negro can never forget—is that white society is deeply implicated in the ghetto." The report continued, "White institutions created it, white institutions maintain it, and white society condones it. . . . White racism is essentially responsible for the explosive mixture which has been accumulating in our cities since the end of World War II." The assassination of Martin Luther King, Jr., the symbol of the black freedom movement, less than two months later provided a tragic affirmation of the Kerner Commission's conclusions.

The idea for *Majority and Minority* was conceived within this context. Hoy Steele and I were both young and idealistic. Hoy, an ordained Methodist minister, had received a divinity degree from Union Theological Seminary in New York and was a graduate student in American Studies at the University of Kansas. I, a Methodist PK (preacher's kid), was fresh out of graduate school and had joined the University of Kansas faculty two years earlier. The academic interests in race and ethnicity in American life that Hoy and I shared were intimately interwoven with our personal commitments to the realization of a society free of social inequality and social injustice—the dream of which Martin Luther King, Jr., so eloquently spoke. The impact of that tumultuous and turbulent era and the sense of urgency it inspired shaped our approach to the first edition of *Majority and Minority,* and the indelible imprint of those events and the perspectives with which we approached them can be seen in each subsequent edition. We sought to emphasize the *practical,* as well as the theoretical, need for a fundamental understanding of the dynamics of racial and ethnic relations. We were convinced that analysis and understanding are irrelevant unless they are complemented by action to alter existing systems of inequality.

The context within which this sixth edition of *Majority and Minority* appears reflects the old adage, "The more things change, the more they stay the same"—it is both dramatically different and strikingly similar to the state of race relations thirty years ago. Although the dynamics of race and ethnicity in American life have been transformed in many ways, glaring racial inequalities and intergroup conflicts persist. This paradox is reflected in the most recent presidential commission on American race relations. Thirty years after President Johnson's appointment of the Kerner Commission, President Bill Clinton appointed another commission to assess the state of race relations in American life. However, the President's charge to this commission—that it examine how to achieve equality and civility in a *multiracial* society—reflected one of the dramatic changes in the thirty years since Johnson appointed the Kerner Commission. American society has become more diverse, more genuinely multiracial and multicultural than ever before in its history, and this reality has increasingly challenged the appropriateness of the biracial model of two societies, black and white, that the Kerner Commission described. Yet the chair of the commission appointed by President Clinton, the distinguished African American historian John Hope Franklin, rejected the focus on multiracialism and instead argued that any discussion of issues of race in American society would have to begin by confronting the divide between black and white because, he contended, "that is where this country cut its teeth." Although many of the most contentious issues today differ from those three decades ago, the persistence of racial and ethnic inequality and conflict has not diminished. Rather, it has remained deeply ingrained in American life, and the concerns that undergirded the first edition of *Majority and Minority* remain as urgent today as in 1970.

The basic assumption that has informed each edition of *Majority and Minority* has been that the study of racial and ethnic relations should focus primarily on patterns of differential power and intergroup conflict. I have retained this orientation. However, as before, I have sought to respond both to the changing realities of race in American society and to the changing perspectives with which race relations have been interpreted. Foremost among the factors that have influenced my conceptualization, selection, and organization of materials has been the continued—indeed, increased—salience of and scholarly attention devoted to race and ethnicity throughout the world. Events in Bosnia, Rwanda, the Middle East, Northern Ireland, South Africa, Québec, and Sri Lanka—to name but a few places—as well as the heightened prominence of ethnicity in many quarters of American life, demonstrate that ethnic and racial identities are not superficial or fleeting phenomena in the modern world. On the contrary, these realities demonstrate that race and ethnicity are crucial to understanding the dynamics of modern societies in general and of the United States in particular.

Given the voluminous—and growing—literature on ethnic relations throughout the world, it would be impossible to provide the necessary breadth and depth of analysis to cover these phenomena worldwide. Consequently, I have once again restricted coverage to issues concerning race and ethnicity in American life. However, my focus on American society does not imply a lack of concern for comparative issues, nor should it reinforce the parochial perspective from which many American students view race and ethnicity. As many of the selections emphasize, American racial and ethnic relations today cannot be adequately comprehended apart from a transnational perspective that sees the United States linked in a broader global economy. When I was deciding which articles to include in this edition, my main criterion was that they simultaneously explore both some aspect of race and ethnicity in the United States and address broader conceptual issues. Therefore, most articles address intergroup relations in general, but use racial and ethnic relations from the United States as examples. I hope in this way to increase the volume's conceptual breadth and to keep it attractive to students of race and ethnicity in American life.

One of the continuing objectives of this edition is to familiarize students with the *range* of conceptual perspectives or ways of interpreting American racial and ethnic relations. Of the twenty-seven selections included, I have retained five from previous editions—including classics by Berreman, Gordon, Gans, and Wilson. Above all, I have sought to include selections that address the inevitable comparisons among the categories comprising what Hollinger has termed the American "ethnoracial pentagon"—American Indians, European Americans, African Americans, Latinos, and Asian Americans—and to emphasize the similarities and differences in conceptual perspectives in interpreting the location of different ethnoracial categories in American life.

The primary audience for whom *Majority and Minority* is intended is upper-division undergraduates or graduate students; it is not intended as an introduction to the field. In most instances I have reprinted selections in their entirety in order to preserve the integrity of an author's argument and to enable readers to situate a selection in the broader discourse on and literature of race and ethnicity. To facilitate student interest and comprehension, I have edited several of the more difficult selections with an eye toward emphasizing their central conceptual issues, and, because of space limitations, I have omitted footnotes in a few cases. Moreover, I have expanded the essays considerably, introducing each part to provide a context within which to consider each selection and to alert students to some of the salient issues that the selections raise.

I have retained both the strong structural and historical perspectives of previous editions. My organization of the materials has at times been arbitrary, but I have sought to provide at least a modicum of coherence to the order in which they are presented. Part 1 is designed to provide a definitional and conceptual overview for the entire volume and to stress the emphasis on structure and differential power that has informed my selection of materials throughout. I have tried to provide the historical depth necessary for understanding the various ways in which different ethnic and racial groups have adapted to American society. Although Part 2 is explicitly devoted to historical perspectives, the historical dimension is stressed throughout the book. Subsequent sections build on the conceptual and historical bases established in Part 2. Part 3 focuses on patterns of ethnic integration in the American experience, particularly engaging the contentious issue of identifying which models are appropriate for explaining differences in attainment of status and power among the categories that comprise the American "ethnoracial pentagon." Part 4 examines the way in which the ethnic composition of American society and the dynamics of American racial and ethnic relations are being transformed today, especially by immigration throughout the world. It also discusses the implications of these changes for the future of ethnicity in American life. Finally, to assist readers, I have included a Statistical Appendix that provides an overview of historical and contemporary statistical data on American racial and ethnic groups. As always, I am eager to receive feedback on this edition, so I invite readers to contact me at norm@falcon.cc.ukans.edu.

Acknowledgments

As usual, I'm indebted to numerous individuals, especially the many students with whom I have tried out the ideas, organization, and selections that make up this edition. I'm deeply indebted to Karen Hanson and Sarah Kelbaugh, my editors at Allyn and Bacon, for their continued support and forbearance for my numerous delays in getting this edition into production, and to Anne Starr, for her superb skills in guiding the book through production. Thanks also to the reviewers: Peter Adler, University of Denver; Richard Alba, State University of New York at Albany; Gerry Cox, University of Wisconsin at LaCrosse; Anjelika Hoeher, State University of New York Agricultural and Technical College at Cobleskill; and Carol Stix, Pace University. Numerous individuals—Penny Fritts, Matt Hayes, Pat Johnston, David Katzman, Tim Larsen, Pam LeRow, Pam Levitt, Pat Mazumdar, Terri Rockhold, Bill Tuttle, and a whole bunch of Yetmans—Anne Yetman, Doug Yetman, Jill Yetman-Michaelson, and Jeremy Yetman-Michaelson —assisted me in the research, writing, and editing process.

And, finally, although he didn't actually push any paper or help me organize the chaos of my study (indeed, as he crawled around my office floor, at times he made it worse), my two-year-old grandson, Aidan Cole Yetman-Michaelson, has brought incredible—indeed, inexpressible—joy to my life and has reinforced the sense of urgency that we create for him and his generation a more humane social order. To him, and to the memory of my mother, Lucile Darling Yetman, who, with her exuberance, dogged determination, intense commitments, passion for learning, and increasing resolve to expand the boundaries of her worlds, set an example through eighty-nine years of how to live life to its fullest, this edition is dedicated.

N. R. Y.

List of Contributors

Richard D. Alba is Professor of Sociology and Public Policy at the State University of New York at Albany.

James R. Barrett is Chair and Professor of History at the University of Illinois, Urbana.

Frank D. Bean is Ashbel Smith Professor of Sociology at the University of Texas, Austin.

Gerald D. Berreman is Professor of Anthropology at the University of California, Berkeley.

Stephen Cornell is Professor of Sociology at the University of California, San Diego.

Nancy A. Denton is Associate Professor of Sociology at the State University of New York, Albany.

Ashley W. ("Woody") Doane, Jr., is Associate Professor of Sociology at the University of Hartford.

Karl Eschbach is Assistant Professor of Sociology at the University of Houston.

Joe R. Feagin is Graduate Research Professor of Sociology at the University of Florida.

Herbert J. Gans is Robert Lynd Professor of Sociology at Columbia University.

Milton M. Gordon is Emeritus Professor of Sociology at the University of Massachusetts.

David A. Hollinger is Professor of History at the University of California, Berkeley.

Pierrette Hondagneu-Sotelo is Associate Professor of Sociology at the University of Southern California.

David R. James is Associate Professor of Sociology at Indiana University.

Russell A. Kazal is a doctoral candidate at the University of Pennsylvania.

Marlene Kim is Assistant Professor of Labor Studies and Employment Relations at Rutgers University.

Ivan Light is Professor of Sociology at the University of California, Los Angeles.

Don Mar is Associate Professor of Economics at San Francisco State University.

Douglas S. Massey is Chair and Dorothy Swain Thomas Professor of Sociology at the University of Pennsylvania.

Joane Nagel is Chair and Professor of Sociology at the University of Kansas.

John U. Ogbu is Professor of Anthropology at the University of California, Berkeley.

Alejandro Portes is Madison Professor of Sociology at Princeton University.

David Roediger is Professor of History and Chair of American Studies at the University of Minnesota.

Roger Rouse is Assistant Professor of Anthropology at the Residential College, the University of Michigan.

Saskia Sassen is Professor of Sociology at the University of Chicago.

C. Matthew Snipp is Professor of Sociology at Stanford University.

Marta Tienda is Professor of Sociology and Public Affairs at Princeton University.

Roger Waldinger is Professor of Sociology at the University of California, Los Angeles.

Mary C. Waters is Professor of Sociology at Harvard University.

William Julius Wilson is Malcolm Wiener Professor of Social Policy at Harvard University.

Norman R. Yetman is Chancellors Club Teaching Professor of American Studies and Sociology at the University of Kansas.

Min Zhou is Associate Professor of Sociology at the University of California, Los Angeles.

Introduction: Definitions and Perspectives

1

Among the most dramatic social phenomena of the past quarter century has been the resurgence of racial and ethnic rivalries, tensions, and hostilities throughout the world. Prejudice, discrimination, conflict, and violence based on racial and ethnic distinctions are widely found throughout the world today—among black, white, colored, and Indian in South Africa; between English-speaking and French-speaking people in Canada; between Islamic Arabs and black Christians in the Sudan; between East Indians and blacks in Guyana; between Kurds and Iraqis in Iraq; between Tamils and Sinhalese in Sri Lanka; between Chinese and Malays in Malaysia; between Hutu and Tutsi in Burundi and Rwanda; and between Krahn, Gio, and Mano ethnic groups in Liberia. In the last few decades, more people have died in ethnic conflicts around the world than in the Korean and Vietnam wars combined.

Indeed, the political ferment that was created by the dramatic political changes throughout eastern Europe during the late 1980s unleashed a resurgence of historic ethnic and national rivalries and antagonisms. The disintegration of the Soviet Union was reinforced by interethnic conflicts, such as those between the Armenians and Azerbaijanis, as well as by demands from numerous other nationalities, such as Lithuanians, Latvians, Estonians, Georgians, ethnic Poles, and Ukrainians, for greater ethnic autonomy and even independence. Even after the breakup of the Soviet Union, Russia has continued to be the site of numerous conflicts—in 1992 alone involving more than 180 ethnic clashes, and in 1994, 1995, and 1996 a bloody war to prevent nationalist rebels in the province of Chechnya from declaring their independence.

Slavic nationalism, which earlier in the century had provided the spark that ignited World War I, resurfaced with a vengeance. In the former Yugoslavia, conflicts among the country's several nationalities—Serbs, Croatians, Slovenes, Bosnians, Montenegrins, Macedonians, and Albanians—led to the nation's dissolution and to one of the most bitter and deadly conflicts among European peoples in the post–World War II era, resulting in the death of over 250,000 people and the displacement of more than 2 million (Cohen 1994). Since 1992, Bosnian Serbs have used a reign of terror, including rape, murder, torture, and intimidation, to expel forcibly hundreds of thousands of

Croats and, especially, Muslims from their homes and villages in Bosnia-Herzegovena. They characterized their efforts to eliminate non-Serbians from territories under their control as "ethnic cleansing," thereby adding a new and horrifically precise term to the lexicon of human ethnic conflict.

Prior to the fall of Rumanian strongman Nicolae Ceauşescu in 1989, approximately two million Hungarians living in Rumania were subject to forced assimilation, the closing of Hungarian schools and social organizations, the suppression of the Hungarian language, and discrimination against those Hungarians who tried to retain their ethnic identity. Similar accusations of forced assimilation were raised by the Turkish minority in Bulgaria, where ethnic tensions led to the forced removal of thousands of Muslim Turks to Turkey.

These examples demonstrate how widespread and deeply rooted ethnic conflict is throughout our world today. In this section we consider some basic definitions and some of the conceptual approaches that have been used to comprehend the dynamics of racial and ethnic relations, especially in the United States.

Ethnic, Racial, and Caste Categories

Ethnicity

The word *ethnic* is derived from the Greek word *ethnos,* meaning "people." An ethnic group is *socially defined* on the basis of its *cultural* characteristics. Ethnicity, the sense of identification with and membership in a particular ethnic group, implies the existence of a distinct culture or subculture in which people perceive themselves and are perceived by others to be bound together by a common origin, history, values, attitudes, and behaviors—in its broadest sense, a sense of peoplehood—and are so regarded by other members of the society. Ethnic groups may differ in cultural characteristics as diverse as eating habits, family patterns, sexual behaviors, modes of dress, standards of beauty, political orientations, economic activities, religions, languages, and recreational patterns. As Joane Nagel points out in Article 2 ("Constructing Ethnicity"), "ethnicity is constructed out of the material of language, religion, culture, appearance, ancestry, or regionality."

This conception of ethnicity resembles what Robert N. Bellah and his colleagues have termed "communities of memory," in which people share an identity rooted in a collective history, tradition, and experience that can be both heroic and painful. However, a community of memory is not simply cultural, involving shared beliefs and ideas; it is sustained through social relations, by participation in the life of the community. Such participation, which Bellah has termed "practices of commitment," "define the patterns of loyalty and obligation that keep the community alive" (Bellah et al. 1985:152–155). In American society, Mexican Americans, Italian Americans, Jewish Americans, Polish Americans, Filipino Americans, and white Anglo-Saxon Protestant Americans can all be considered ethnic groups, however broad and diverse their internal composition.

For example, in 1970 Lewis Killian argued that, because of their distinctive history, cultural characteristics, language, and identity, white Southerners represented an important ethnic category that had seldom previously been considered "ethnic." During Jimmy Carter's 1976 presidential campaign, Patrick Anderson, one of Carter's chief aides, described the ethnic dimensions of the Carter candidacy and the sense of ethnic identity it evoked.

> *Perhaps you have to be a Southerner to understand what [Jimmy Carter's candidacy] means to some of us. There is a great sense of personal pride and personal vindication involved, a sense that after losing for a long, long time, our side is finally going to win one. I imagine that Jews and blacks will feel the same way when one of their own finally gets a shot at the White House.*
> *The emotions involved run deep, and are hard to communicate, but I think they must be considered by anyone who wants to understand why young Southerners . . . are driving themselves so relentlessly on Governor Carter's behalf. They are motivated, I think, not only by the personal ambition that afflicts us all, but by personal affection for the candidate, by political commitment to certain goals, and by* a regional pride that has its roots many generations in the past. *(Anderson 1976:21, emphasis added)*

Ethnic groups are inherently ethnocentric, regarding their own cultural traits as natural, correct, and superior to those of other ethnic groups, who are perceived as odd, amusing, inferior, or immoral. Donald Noel (1968) has suggested that ethnocentrism is a necessary, but not sufficient, condition for the emergence of ethnic stratification. According to Noel, a dominant-subordinate relationship between two mutually ethnocentric groups cannot develop unless the groups are competing for the same scarce resources and, most important, one group possesses superior power to impose its will on the other.

Race

The terms *race* and *ethnicity* are often used interchangeably, but for analytic purposes they should be distinguished. Whereas an *ethnic group* is distinguished by *cultural* characteristics, *race* refers to a social category that is defined on the basis of *physical* characteristics. However, the term *race* is meaningless in a biological sense, because there are no "pure" races: the racial categories found in each society are social constructs or conventions; the characteristics that distinguish one racial group from another are arbitrary and thus are *socially defined and constructed.* As Berreman contends in Article 1 ("Race, Caste, and Other Invidious Distinctions"), "systems of 'racial' stratification are social phenomena based on social rather than biological facts." A group is defined as a race when certain physical characteristics are selected for special emphasis by members of a society. As Berreman notes, the definition of a group as a race is not a function of biological or genetic differences between groups, but of society's perceptions that such differences are real and that they are important—that they are related to or reflect other apparently innate mental, emotional, and moral differences, such as intelligence.

The term *race* has been an extremely loose, variable, and imprecise concept; it has been used to refer to linguistic categories (Aryan, English-speaking), to religious categories (Hindu, Jewish), to national categories (French, Italian), and to mystical, quasi-scientific categories (Teutonic). The wide range of social categories that have been considered "races" reinforces the notion that racial designations are artificial; they serve the function of separating certain social categories on the basis of an arbitrary selection or identification of specific physical or biologically transmitted characteristics. Because of the imprecision with which the term *race* has been used, some scholars have chosen to dispense with it, preferring to subsume what have previously been termed "races" under the broad category of ethnic groups.

Many groups possess physically identifiable characteristics that do not become the basis for racial distinctions. Thus, the criteria selected to make racial distinctions in one society may be overlooked or considered insignificant or irrelevant by another. For instance, in much of Latin America skin color and the shape of the lips—important distinguishing criteria in the United States—are much less significant than are hair texture, eye color, and stature. A person considered black in Georgia or Michigan might be considered white in Peru or the Dominican Republic (Pitt-Rivers 1967).

Many examples of the arbitrary, socially (and politically) defined nature of American racial categories can be found throughout American history. In 1926 three members of the National Association of Colored People (NAACP) asked the distinguished defense lawyer Clarence Darrow to defend a Detroit black man who had been accused of murdering a member of a white mob that was threatening his home. Arthur Spingarn, a dark-skinned man of Puerto Rican descent, described the case to Darrow, who replied,

> "Yes. I know full well the difficulties faced by your race."
> "I'm sorry, Mr. Darrow," replied Spingarn, "but I'm not a Negro."
> Darrow turned to Charles Studin, another member of the committee, and said, "Well, you understand what I mean."
> "I am not colored either," replied Studin.
> The third man had blond hair and blue eyes. "I would not make that mistake with you," Darrow told him.
> "I am a Negro," replied Walter White, secretary of the NAACP.
> Darrow jumped out of bed. "That settles it," he cried. "I'll take the case." (Stone 1943:470, quoted in Katzman 1973:82)

This example demonstrates that racial identity is not primarily a matter of skin color or is not based simply on physical appearance. It is, much more significantly, based on the social categories to which people are assigned. Although there may be some perceived biological basis for the distinctions we make, the criteria that we use and the range of people that we include in each category are arbitrary, irrational, and frequently illogical.

Marvin Harris (1964) has identified two socially defined "rules" that determine the racial categories into which people in the United States will be placed. First is the "one-drop rule," through which anyone who has *any* African ancestry, no matter how remote, will be classified as "black." The other is the "rule of hypodescent," by which people of multiracial backgrounds will be unable to claim membership in the dominant "race" but will automatically be placed in the minority racial category. As Barbara Fields has pointed out, these "rules" lead to the absurd racial convention "that considers a white woman capable of giving birth to a black child but denies that a black woman can give birth to a white child" (Fields 1982:149).

The operation of these "rules" and the socially defined nature of American racial categories are vividly demonstrated by laws in the United States prohibiting interracial marriages. Until 1967, when the Supreme Court ruled in *Loving v. Virginia* that such laws were unconstitutional, many states stipulated that any person with one-fourth or more African ancestry (that is, with one black grandparent) was legally defined as "black" and therefore prohibited from marrying someone "white."[1] However, some states enacted even more restrictive definitions of race. Indeed, the variability in state laws defining racial categories underscores the arbitrary nature of such classifications. If "race" is a "natural," invariable, and clearly biological phenomenon, then one's race should not change simply by crossing a state line into another state.

A recent court case in Louisiana illustrates the operation of the "one-drop rule" and the "rule of hypodescent." Susie Guillory Phipps, a light-skinned woman with Caucasian features and straight black hair, found that her birth certificate classified her as "colored." Mrs. Phipps, who contended that she had been "brought up white and married white twice," challenged a 1970 Louisiana law declaring that anyone with at least one-thirty-second "Negro blood" was legally black. Under this law an individual who had *one* great-great-great-grandparent who was black (and thus had one-thirty-second "black" and thirty-one–thirty-seconds "white" ancestry) was legally defined as black. Although the state's lawyer conceded that Phipps "looks like a white person," the state strenuously maintained that her racial classification was appropriate, and this interpretation was upheld by Louisiana's supreme court. However, Louisiana later repealed the law (Trillin 1986).

The arbitrary, irrational, and socially constructed nature of racial and ethnic categories and identities is also revealed by circumstances in which individuals change categories; if racial categories are "real," people should be unable to escape classification within them. The story of Gregory Howard Williams, the dean of the Ohio State University School of Law, is instructive in this regard. Williams grew up in Virginia believing that he was white. He was ten when his parents' marriage and his father's businesses failed, and he and his brother moved with their father to his hometown of Muncie, Indiana. On the bus ride to Muncie, his father told him and his brother, "Life is going to be different from now on. In Virginia you were white boys. In Indiana you're going to be colored boys. I want you to remember that you're the same today that you were yesterday. But people in Indiana will treat you differently" (Williams 1995:33). In Muncie he was thrust into the black segment of a racially segregated community, and his book describes the difficulties he encountered trying to negotiate "life on the color line" between black and white (Williams 1995). Thus, racial identity is not fixed, immutable, or unchanging.

The former South African system of apartheid, or racial separation, provides one of the most vivid examples of the way in which racial classifications are social, not biological, categories that are arbitrarily imposed. Under apartheid, which was established in 1950 and formally abolished in 1991, all people were required to be classified into one of four legally defined racial categories—white, black, colored, and Indian. The racial categories into which people were arbitrarily placed determined many features of their lives, including whether they could vote or own land, what jobs they could hold, which schools they could attend, where they could live, eat, or play, and whom they could love and marry. As in the case of Gregory Williams, the arbitrary and irrational nature of such categories is revealed in circumstances in which an individual's legal racial classification—and the entire range of opportunities that flowed from that classification—were changed. In 1988 a South African news-paper reported,

> Nearly 800 South Africans became officially members of a different race group last year. They included 518 coloreds who were officially reclassified as white, 14 whites who became colored, 7 Chinese [who are classified as "honorary whites"] who became white, 2 whites who became Chinese, 3 Malays [who are classified as colored] who became white, 1 white who became Indian, 50 Indians who became colored, 54 coloreds who became Indian, 17 Indians who became Malay, 4 coloreds who became Chinese, 1 Malay who became Chinese, 89 blacks who became colored, 5 coloreds who became black. (Usy 1988:27)

Because consciousness of race is so pronounced in the United States, most Americans are placed in a specific racial category by cultural conventions and everyday discourse—the "common sense" understandings that are widely shared among the American people. These categories are reinforced, as well, by discussions such as this one, which, by attaching labels to arbitrarily identified groups of people, serve to heighten the perception of the categories themselves and thus, ironically, to legitimize the notion that race is a "real"—biologically based—phenomenon and thus to obscure its socially constructed, contingent, and emergent nature.

The Variability of "Racial" Distinctions

Racial distinctions are not restricted to skin pigmentation alone but can involve other visible physical characteristics as well. An excellent example is found in the small African countries of Burundi and Rwanda, which during the past quarter century have experienced waves of intergroup violence and conflict in which the principal biological distinction between political antagonists has been stature.

Burundi and Rwanda are neighboring, landlocked countries of central Africa, situated between the republics of Zaire, Uganda, and Tanzania. During their colonial periods, which ended in 1962, both were controlled by the Belgians. As in several other African countries, independence from European colonialism brought deep-rooted ethnic rivalries to the surface. In 1972 a wave of government-sponsored violence swept through Burundi. An estimated 100,000 Hutus—3.5 percent of the population—were killed in 1972, and more than 100,000 more in subsequent massacres in 1988, 1993, and 1996 by the country's Tutsi-dominated military. A comparable annihilation in the American population would mean the deaths of about 9 million people. But the numbers killed in Burundi pale in comparison to the slaughter that occurred in neighboring Rwanda in 1994, where more than 750,000 people—nearly 10 percent of all Rwandans—were murdered by the Hutu-dominated Rwandan government, and over a million more were made homeless; subsequently, more than 2 million Hutus then fled Rwanda after Tutsi rebels gained power.

The genocide in Burundi and Rwanda reflects the rivalry of the countries' two major racial groups: the Tutsi and the Hutu. The Tutsi, originally a tall and slender people among whom men average six feet in height, make up only about 15 percent of Burundi's population and less than 10 percent of the population of Rwanda. For centuries before the arrival of European colonial powers, the Tutsi had held the Hutu, a people of shorter stature, in a form of serfdom (the term *Hutu* itself means "subject" or "servant"). During the colonial period the Belgians magnified and exaggerated the social divisions of a Tutsi aristocracy and a Hutu servant class. When independence was achieved in 1962, many Hutu were hopeful that, because they represented the overwhelming numerical majority of the populations of both countries, the promise of majority rule would bring an end to Tutsi domination. However, Hutu frustration in Burundi grew in the years following independence as the more politically powerful Tutsi effectively blocked Hutu efforts to change the status quo.

In 1972 the Tutsi-dominated government of Burundi responded with a wave of violence to allegations of a Hutu revolt against Tutsi control. In many villages, all Hutu of any wealth, community influence, or educational level above grade school were systematically shot or beaten to death. The killing was selective, aimed at all influential Hutu. The objective of the annihilation of the Hutu elites was to crush any Hutu threat to Tutsi power. The Tutsi sought to eliminate "not only the rebellion but Hutu society as well, and in the process lay the foundation of an entirely new social order" (Lemarchand 1975:575). This wave of genocide ensured Tutsi political and economic power in Burundi and led to the systematic exclusion of Hutu from the army, civil service, the university, and high schools. In 1988, 1993, and 1996 the long-simmering tension between these two groups flared once again into violent conflict. At least 5,000 more people were killed in another Hutu uprising and the Tutsi reprisal that followed, and more than 50,000 Hutu fled to the neighboring country of Rwanda, where Hutu are the tribal majority (Brooke 1988; Perlez 1988; Friedman 1996).

In Rwanda, on the other hand, freedom from colonial Belgian rule led to a bloody but successful Hutu-led revolt against Tutsi political domination. But exiled Tutsi leaders continued to seek to regain political power; and, fearful that they would succeed, Hutu extremists in the Rwandan government used Rwandan President Haabyarimana's death in a plane crash in April 1994 as a pretext to begin their campaign of genocide. Government-sponsored death squads roamed the country, using guns, clubs, and machetes to annihilate all opposition—primarily Tutsi but including any Hutus who protected Tutsi or protested against government policies (Smith 1995). The result was one of the most savage massacres of people since the Holocaust perpetrated by Nazi Germany during the 1930s and 1940s.

Although numerous writers have argued that racial and ethnic distinctions did not *cause* the waves of genocide that have swept Burundi and Rwanda, the savage conflict between Tutsi and Hutu in these two troubled countries not only demonstrates how racial and ethnic divisions continue to provide the basis for bloodshed and violence throughout the modern world but also suggests that, because of the principal criterion upon which the distinctions between Hutu and Tutsi were originally based—the physical characteristic of stature—this violent conflict between the two peoples can be considered racial.

As the racial/ethnic conflict in Burundi and the caste status of the *Burakumin* in Japan (which we will discuss more fully later) demonstrate, in real life, race, ethnicity, and caste are intimately related, and distinctions between them are difficult to make. Indeed, there has been considerable debate among social scientists concerning whether race relations are different in kind from ethnic relations or whether race relations can appropriately be subsumed under the broad rubric of ethnicity. Because in American society *racial* conflicts—those based on physical, rather than cultural, differences—have generally been more intense than ethnic conflicts, there has been a tendency to attribute a preeminence to the study of race relations. However, as many examples throughout the world in the past quarter century demonstrate— the enduring conflict between Protestants and Catholics in Northern Ireland or the violent tensions that have characterized the former Yugoslavia in the post-Soviet era, for example—ethnic differences are capable of eliciting antagonisms and loyalties comparable in intensity and tenacity to those based on racial distinctions. In an extensive comparative analysis of a wide range of ethnically divided societies in Asia, Africa, and the Caribbean, Horowitz (1985) has contested the assumption that *race* relations are somehow qualitatively different from intergroup relations based on language, religion, or putative common ancestry or origins. Such a notion, he contends, is based on two unwarranted premises—that racial distinctions arouse "uniquely intense emotions and loyalties" and that such distinctions "serve as unusually reliable signs of individual identity. . . . Neither of these assumptions," he argues, "can be supported" (Horowitz 1985:42).

Given that it is difficult to establish conclusively that *racial* and *ethnic* phenomena can be qualitatively distinguished, it is appropriate to adopt an inclusive definition of ethnicity that emphasizes the different criteria—physical differences, language, religion, and putative common ancestry or origins—used to distinguish groups. Such an inclusive definition is consistent with Berreman's emphasis that the crucial feature of such phenomena is that group differences are *attributed* to ascriptive characteristics. In other words, I am arguing that *racial* characteristics, which are perceived to be so crucial to the distinctions used in American society, represent only one of several possible criteria that can be used to allocate people to different ethnic categories. Therefore, in subsequent discussion, this book treats "racial" relations as one dimension of ethnic relations and uses the terms *ethnic* and *ethnicity* in this broader and more inclusive sense.

Primordial and Situational Explanations

Why have people used racial and ethnic distinctions so frequently throughout history to rank a society's members? Why have racial and ethnic differences so often demarcated the lines of intergroup conflict? Two broad explanatory models have been advanced: the primordialist (or nonrational) perspective and the social constructionist (or rational or situational) perspective. The former model conceptualizes racial and ethnic identities and distinctions as *essentialist*—that is, they are perceived to be biologically based, present at birth, instinctive, innate, and unchangeable, "attachments [that] seem to flow more from a sense of natural affinity than from social interaction" (Burgess 1978:266). A constructionist position, on the other hand, locates the sources of ethnicity in the structure and dynamics of human societies. From this perspective, race and ethnicity are functional, pragmatic, emergent, and constantly evolving and changing phenomena, "a rational group response to social pressures and a basis for group action, especially where no other exists. . . . Ethnicity [is] a strategy chosen to advance individual [and group] interest as the situation dictates" (Burgess 1978:267).

Pierre van den Berghe has been one of the most prominent and articulate advocates for what has been broadly termed a primordialist perspective, one that sees racial and ethnic distinctions as deeply rooted in the basic nature of human sociality. He contends that kin selection and its corollary, nepotism, are the basic principles on which societies have been based for most of human existence; and that ethnic and racial distinctions are merely extensions of kinship principles. The pervasiveness of ethnic distinctions and ethnocentrism in human societies suggests that these phenomena are instrumental in establishing group boundaries. Most preliterate societies, for example, employ cultural—ethnic—markers such as language or body adornment, rather than physical—racial—ones, for the simple reason that they rarely encounter other peoples who are physically distinguishable from themselves. Racial distinctions, van den Berghe argues, are the consequence primarily of large-scale migrations, which have occurred only relatively recently in human history:

> Humans, like other animals, are selected to favor kin, and whatever does a quick, easy and accurate job of differentiating kin and non-kin will be used. In most cases, and until recently, cultural criteria have been predominantly used. Physical criteria became salient only after large, strikingly different-looking populations found themselves in sudden and sustained contact. (van den Berghe 1978c:407–408)

A social constructionist approach to race and ethnicity, on the other hand, emphasizes that definitions of ethnic and racial categories are *socially* defined phenomena, the boundaries and content of which are constantly being renegotiated, revised, and redefined. From this perspective, an ethnic identity is neither "natural" nor inherent in the nature of the group itself; rather it is socially constructed, a reflection and product of broader social factors and competing individual and group interests. As Nagel points out in "Constructing Ethnicity" (Article 2), "Ethnicity is created and recreated as various groups and interests put forth competing visions of the ethnic composition of society and argue over which rewards or sanctions should be attached to which ethnicities." Nagel especially emphasizes the role of state and political factors in eliciting, heightening, and reinforcing ethnicity as an organizational resource around which competition for resources and power can be played out. She contends that ethnicity may be *resurgent* (involving the revitalization of historic identities) or *emergent* (involving the creation of newly formed groups). Her primary objective is to identify the conditions under which *ethnic mobilization,* "the process by which a group organizes along ethnic lines in pursuit of group ends," occurs. Her analysis suggests that the state possesses a capacity—one frequently ignored by students of race and ethnicity—to shape ethnic relations and to generate ethnic awareness and identification, either intentionally or unintentionally. Her basic thesis is that because ethnicity in the modern world is a largely political phenomenon, because it arises out of the political structures and policies of the modern nation-state, it is unlikely that its significance will diminish in the near future. The implication is that, as the power of the American state continues to expand and penetrate all sectors of modern life, the salience of ethnicity is unlikely to diminish in the future. The constructionist model, therefore, "constitutes an argument for the durability, indeed, the inevitability, of ethnicity in modern societies." Nagel's argument, therefore, has special relevance to Part 4, in which we shall consider more fully the future of race and ethnicity in American life.

As noted before, a constructionist perspective is useful not only in explaining the persistence of historic ethnic distinctions and conflicts but also in identifying the factors that contribute to both the *resurgence* of ethnic identities and the emergence of new forms of ethnic identity throughout the world. One of the most interesting of these has been the development of *panethnicity,* which refers to situations in which peoples of several previously distinct tribal, national, ethnic, or racial groups come to identify or be identified on the basis of a broader, more inclusive ethnic category.

For example, historians of European American ethnic groups have pointed out that a sense of national identity was in many instances not fully developed among many immigrants; rather, identity with a nation emerged only after they had lived in the United States for some time. For example, during the late nineteenth and early twentieth centuries people who emigrated from Italy to the United States often did not think of themselves as Italians; rather, they drew their primary identities from the villages or region of the country from which they hailed. Their consciousness of themselves as Italians emerged only as a consequence of their encounter with American society (Vecoli 1964). Similarly, William Yancey and his colleagues (1976) contend that among many European immigrant groups, a sense of ethnicity was produced, not as a result of the cultural baggage—shared cultural characteristics—or of a shared sense of ethnic identity that people brought with them, but rather by external factors—the conditions they confronted in their settlements in the United States. In such circumstances ethnic identity was always "emergent," that is, it represented a response to the common conditions in the cities in which the people settled. Among these conditions were "common occupational positions, residential stability and concentration, and dependence on common institutions and services, [which were] in turn directly affected by the process of industrialization."

Moreover, as both Doane (Article 3) and Barrett and Roediger (Article 6) argue, the very category of "white" has been socially constructed and has over time come to include groups (such as the Irish, Italians, Jews, Poles) that had previously been placed in other, or "inbetween," racial categories. In 1985 Lieberson identified from his analysis of 1980 census data, the emergence in American society of a new ethnic category: *unhyphenated whites,* whose European national origins are so obscure or so mixed that their only ethnic identity is in reference to American society. Since then, issues of ethnic identity among people of European descent and, in particular, the question of what it means to be "white"—seldom previously considered in studies of American race relations—have become the focus of a wide range of scholarly studies. These scholars see "whiteness" as a racial category that, like any other, has changed, acquired new meaning, and subsumed different groups over time. The basic questions with which these scholars (for example, Ignatiev 1995; Frankenberg 1993; Saxton 1990; Roediger 1991, 1994) are concerned are how to explain both the process by which these changes occurred and the social consequences of these changes for defining race in American life. Doane points out that the failure to consider the impact of "whiteness" "leaves the dominant group as the hidden center of race and ethnic relations in the United States [that] plays a key role in the persistence and reproduction of [dominant] group hegemony." This perspective was recently reinforced by the response of Derrick Bell, a prominent African American legal scholar, to President Bill Clinton's appointment of a national commission to initiate a national dialogue on race. The critical question that the commission—and, by implication, all Americans—should address, Bell argued, is, "What does it really mean to be white, not as a matter of pride in cultural heritage, but as social and economic facts of life in the United States?" (Bell 1997:19).

Thus each of the five broad categories that comprise what Hollinger (Article 4) has termed the American *"ethnoracial pentagon"* (American Indians, African Americans, Europeans, Asians, and Hispanics) are panethnic—that is, they subsume within them a broad range of cultural, national, linguistic, regional, tribal, religious, and generational groups. Although such categories give the illusion of cultural homogeneity (thus simultaneously reinforcing and redefining the structure of ethnic relations in American society), they ignore or obscure considerable internal diversity, conflict, and mutual antagonism within each category. For example, Espiritu (1992) notes that the Asian American category is comprised of diverse and often antagonistic national elements, including Chinese, Japanese, Korean, Vietnamese, Thai, Khmer, and Asian Indian. Joane Nagel points out in Article 2 how the terms *American Indian* and *Native American* are consequences of their minority status in American society and obscure the substantial tribal (ethnic) differences among them. Similarly, the terms *Hispanic* or *Latino,* which two decades ago were not even part of the common language, are increasingly employed to subsume into one category several extremely diverse ethnic categories. Although such distinctions are employed by social scientists, journalists, business people, and ultimately the people themselves, Cynthia Enloe (1981) has contended that the state has played a crucial role in defining these arbitrary social categories: "The state employs ethnic categories to suit its administrative-political needs. In so doing it requires individuals subject to certain laws to respond as 'Hispanics' or 'Indians' or 'Filipinos.' "

Examination of the U.S. census and the controversy over the categories to be used when the next decennial census is taken in 2000, reflect the fluid, arbitrary nature of American concepts of race and ethnicity. The racial categories used in each census, which the United States Constitution specifies is to be collected every ten years, are inevitably the result, not of a "scientific" and rational classification system but instead of arbitrary decisions that reflect primarily the social, cultural, and political assumptions of the day and governmental efforts to standardize them (see Wright 1994; Snipp 1997). The categories used in the 1980 and 1990 censuses were established by Statistical Directive 15, issued by the Office of Management and Budget in 1977. This bureaucratic definition officially recognizes four general racial categories in the United States: American Indian, Asian, Black, and White; people are also classified as Hispanic or non-Hispanic. As a consequence of this federal government definition, "the identities of Americans were fixed in five broad groupings. Those racial and ethnic categories that were dreamed up almost twenty years ago were not neutral in their effect. By attempting to provide a way for Americans to describe themselves, the categories actually began to shape those identities. The categories became political entities, with their own constituencies, lobbies, and vested interests. What was even more significant, they caused people to think of themselves in new ways—as members of 'races' that were little more than statistical devices" (Wright 1994:52–53).

Thus the census itself reflects the changing dynamics and meaning of race and ethnicity in American life. Because numerous governmental policies and practices address issues of racial classification, the racial categories to be used in the 2000 census has been the source of great acrimony and divisiveness. Numerous groups argued that the categories be changed to benefit their particular interests. For example, the National Council of La Raza urged that Hispanics be considered a race, not simply an ethnic group. Native Hawaiians have petitioned to be included under the category of American Indians/Native Americans rather than as Asians. And one of the heated controversies over the census to be administered in the year 2000 concerns pressures from an increasingly large group of people who are the children of interracial unions to have available a new category—"Multiracial"—a procedure that would have the effect of creating a new racial category in the United States (Wright 1994). Given the extent to which existing racial categories affect public policy (for example, in determining the boundaries for Congressional districts or in testing for racial discrimination in mortgage-lending practices), the consequences of any such change could be profound.

On the other hand, as intermarriage and the number of people acknowledging mixed racial ancestry have recently increased, the arbitrariness of racial categories has become increasingly apparent, as many people have recognized the difficulties of placing themselves or others in the existing categories. Indicative of this increasing recognition of the illogic of racial categories was the 1995 *Newsweek* cover story, "What Color Is Black?" in which it answered its own question with the assertion that "It is every conceivable shade and hue from tan to ebony—and suddenly a matter of ideology and identity as much as pigmentation" (*Newsweek* 1995:64).

As a result of demographic, cultural, social, and economic factors that we will explore throughout this book, increasing numbers of Americans, especially those with multiracial backgrounds, are rejecting requirements that they choose one single racial category on census forms, on school enrollment forms, and on job, loan, and mortgage applications. Increasingly, people are calling either for the elimination of official racial distinctions altogether or for the creation of a "multiracial" category that will not force individuals to choose between two or more racial identities. This situation has been epitomized by the golfing phenom Tiger Woods, whose 1997 victory at the prestigious Masters tournament was hailed by many sports commentators as the first such win by an African American. But because his mother was Thai, some Asian Americans contended that he was the first Asian American to win the tournament. Yet Woods, who also claims Caucasian and American Indian ancestry, coined the term "Cablinasian" to reflect his multiple backgrounds (Leland and Beals 1997; White 1997).

Some critics have gone even further and contend that, whatever public policy benefits may derive from having the Census Bureau continue to categorize the American people on the basis of race, those benefits are far outweighed by the negative consequences of continuing their use. One of the principal objections is that governmental racial categories contribute to a *self-fulfilling prophecy*, which refers to a situation that is inaccurately or falsely defined but, because it is believed to be true, produces behavior that makes the original belief come true. Thus, sociologist Orlando Patterson has criticized the Census Bureau decision to retain racial categories on the 2000 census, contending that, by contributing to the perception that these racial categories are real, the categories themselves only furthered racial division. "Distinguishing between race and ethnicity is an ingrained part of America's racial ideology. The racial categories maintained by the Census Bureau can only perpetuate the idea that there is such a thing as racial purity and that people in the United States have essential biological differences" (Patterson 1997:A21).

Ethnicity and Social Stratification

Societies differ in the extent to which they permit and encourage *social mobility*—the movement of persons from one social stratum to another. An *open system of stratification* is one in which few obstacles exist for people who are changing social positions;

achievement is unaffected either by the constraints of disadvantaged social origins or by the privileges of advantaged social rank. All people, regardless of birth status (sex, race, religion, ethnicity, social background), have genuinely equal opportunity to change positions and move up or down in the stratification. The greater the degree of social mobility, the more open the class system is. In an open class system, emphasis is placed on achievement.

By contrast, a *closed system of stratification* allows virtually no social mobility; children inherit their parents' social position. In a closed system, people's places in a social hierarchy are fixed or ascribed (that is, on the basis of qualities such as race, ethnicity, social background, or sex, over which they have no control). In a closed system, little possibility exists for social mobility. People are born into a position and cannot, under normal circumstances, move out of it.

The most rigid and closed of all stratification systems is a *caste system,* a system of social inequality characterized by rigidly separated social categories in which an individual's status is birth-ascribed, inherited, immutable, permanent, and fixed. A caste system is endogamous, which means that people must marry within their own caste. A person who does not marry within her or his caste will probably be punished severely. Intimate contact, such as eating with someone of a different caste, is prohibited. Typically elaborate systems of rituals and customs are developed to limit interaction between members of different castes. However, no stratification system is totally closed or totally open; virtually all societies display both ascription and achievement in some form (Tumin 1969).

The traditional Indian caste system, the basis of organizing Indian society since the fifth century B.C., is usually cited as the classic example of caste. The system can be divided into five broad strata, each of which contains thousands of internal distinctions based primarily on occupation. At the top of the hierarchy stand the *Brahmans,* the priests, scholars, and teachers of basic religious principles, who provided religious support and legitimation for the social order (Mayer and Buckley, 1970). Occupying the lowest and most despised position are the *Harijans,* a term meaning "people of God," which was popularized by Mohandas Gandhi. These people are the outcastes, whom Indians believe fall outside the caste system. They are frequently called "untouchables" because they are not permitted to touch members of the upper castes. Indians believe that they can be contaminated even if an outcaste's shadow touches their clothing, food, or person. Outcastes are so despised that in rural areas, they are frequently barred from villages during the parts of the day when they would cast long shadows and would therefore be more likely to contaminate other villagers.

Since 1949 discrimination on the basis of caste has been outlawed in India, and the coming of modernity to that nation has undermined and disrupted the traditional caste system, especially in large metropolitan areas. In the modern Indian world of bureaucracies, factories, and schools, contact among castes has increased. Despite these changes, however, the Indian caste system persists, especially in the rural areas, where 75 percent of the Indian population lives. In rural villages people still find it unthinkable to marry someone from another caste. How deeply the caste system is rooted and how harshly its rules are enforced is illustrated by a recent incident in a rural Indian village in which a sixteen-year-old girl, her eighteen-year-old lover, and a friend who had tried to help them elope were lynched by relatives and neighbors. The young woman was a *Jat,* the dominant caste in the region, while the young men were outcastes. The deaths of all three were decreed by the *Jat*-dominated village council after the young woman refused to give up her lover (Crossette 1991:60).

A caste system is not unique to India. For example, the Japanese *Burakumin*—Japan's "invisible race"—represent another excellent example of a caste system without apparent racial distinctions. Physically indistinguishable from other Japanese, the *Burakumin* are acknowledged to be completely Japanese, but of such lowly social origins that they are economically and socially discriminated against and are considered mentally inferior by the rest of Japanese society; marriages between *Burakumin* and members of the upper caste are considered a tragedy and are strongly discouraged (DeVos and Wagatsuma 1966).

The contemporary *Burakumin* are descendants of the untouchable *eta* caste. The degree to which the *eta* were despised by the rest of Japanese society is revealed in the name itself: *eta* means "filth abundant." Under the feudal system of Tokugawa Japan, from the seventeenth to the nineteenth centuries, the *eta* occupied an outcaste status below the four superior castes (the ruling caste of warriors and administrators, the peasants, the artisans, and the merchants) that constituted Japanese society. The *eta* were discriminated against in every aspect of their lives, and a number of laws were enacted to reinforce their inferior status. For example, as outcastes they were restricted to the dirtiest, most defiling, and least desirable occupations (such as being butchers, leatherworkers, grave tenders, and executioners). They were legally segregated from the rest of the Japanese people and forced to live in isolated ghettos. Moreover, they were required to walk barefoot and to wear special clothing that identified them as *eta*. Because they were considered innately inferior and "impure," their marriages were restricted to other *eta;* intermarriages with non-*eta* were virtually nonexistent.

The *eta* were legally "emancipated" during the mid–nineteenth century, and the laws that had formerly restricted their lives and discriminated against them were formally abolished. Although emancipation provided legal freedom, discrimination against the outcasts (subsequently known as *Burakumin,* or "village people") has persisted. Among the popular prejudices about the *Burakumin* that persisted well into the twentieth century were the following:

> *One rib is lacking; they have a dog's bone in them; they have distorted sexual organs; they have defective excretory systems; if they walk in the moonlight their necks will not cast shadows, and, they being animals, dirt does not stick to their feet when they walk barefoot. (Quoted in Neary 1986:558)*

Today there are an estimated one to three million *Burakumin* living in Japan, a nation of 123 million. During the past quarter century the status of the *Burakumin* has begun to change. The Japanese government has enacted legislation designed to end the cycle of poverty and discrimination against them and to improve their living conditions, and it has invested heavily in social programs designed to improve *Burakumin* neighborhoods. As a consequence, *Burakumin* are no longer restricted to their traditional occupations, and their access to housing outside traditional neighborhoods has increased.

Despite such signs of improvement, the socioeconomic status of *Burakumin* lags considerably behind that of the rest of the Japanese population. *Burakumin* family income is only 60 percent of the national average; they are often the "last hired and first fired." Single parent households are twice as common as in the nation as a whole, and *Burakumin* welfare rates are seven times those of the overall population. *Burakumin* children are characterized by lower IQ scores than are non-*Burakumin,* and their rates of college attendance are only about half that of other Japanese. And they are still more likely to live in overcrowded slum ghettoes (Kristoff 1995; Fallows 1990).

Although deeply ingrained prejudices against the *Burakumin* have begun to decline, traditional negative stereotypes persist. The *Burakumin* continue to be viewed by most Japanese as "mentally inferior, incapable of high moral behavior, aggressive, impulsive, and lacking any notion of sanitation or manners" (Wagatsuma 1976:245). The power of these stereotypes and the fear they elicit are reflected in the importance still attached to family registration records, which certify "proper" social backgrounds. Until recently, such records were frequently required in connection with applications for jobs, loans, and admissions to schools. Above all, it was not unusual for families to undertake exhaustive investigations of the lineages of their children's prospective spouses to ensure that their families would not be "contaminated" by *eta* origins. Although such searches have declined in recent years, few public figures are today willing to admit having had *Burakumin* ancestry (Kristoff 1995).

During the twentieth century, the *Burakumin* have organized social movements to protest the discrimination they have continued to encounter in employment, education, and housing. Recently, the militant *Burakumin* Liberation League has become a potent political force by using techniques of direct harassment and intimidation against those who do not share its views of the *Burakumin* plight. As a consequence, the publishers of Japanese books, magazines, and newspapers, fearful of disruptions of their offices and homes by *Burakumin* "direct action" squads, have adopted an unwritten policy of not mentioning the *Burakumin* in their publications (Fallows 1990).

The example of the *Burakumin* is instructive in two respects. First, upper-caste Japanese attribute the *Burakumin's* undesirable traits to biological—innate and inherited—factors, yet no physical characteristics can be detected between them. Second, there are remarkable similarities between the stereotypes of the *Burakumin* and those of subordinate groups in other racially stratified systems. As Donald Horowitz has pointed out, "Whether or not there is an attempt to deny the common humanity of the subordinate group, the stereotype of such a group generally depicts it as irremediably slow, violent, lazy, unmannered, and dirty" (Horowitz 1985:27). Thus, caste and racially stratified systems function in a similar manner. De Vos and Wagatsuma, on the basis of their analysis of the *Burakumin,* support Berreman's contention that racial and caste systems are analytically comparable: "From the viewpoint of comparative sociology or social anthropology, and from the viewpoint of human social psychology, racism and caste attitudes are one and the same phenomenon" (De Vos and Wagatsuma, 1966).

The Japanese *Burakumin* represent a caste system without racial distinctions as Americans usually think of them. However, as this example suggests, systems of racial stratification are closely related to caste systems. Indeed, Berreman contends that all systems of racial or ethnic stratification and caste are qualitatively comparable—that is, both are based on notions of birth-ascribed and immutable characteristics that are believed to determine one's status.

Racial factors—that is, physical characteristics such as skin color, hair texture, height, or the shape of the nose, eyes, or lips—can serve as the basis for status distinctions in a caste system; however, a caste system can also be organized without reference to distinguishable physical characteristics so long as social categories are distinguished on the basis of traits believed to be birth-ascribed.

As we will note more fully in Part 2, the structure of relations between blacks and whites in the United States historically—during more than two centuries of slavery and nearly a century and a half of "freedom"—has resembled a caste system in which hereditary factors (physical features such as skin color, hair texture, lip form) have determined one's status at birth; in which marriage between members of the different castes was legally prohibited; and in which opportunities for members of the lower caste have been circumscribed. African Americans have been relegated to an inferior status, and their access to political representation, education, employment, and housing has been restricted. Moreover, throughout the South especially, interpersonal relations between black and white were governed by what was known as the "etiquette of race relations," which required patterns of deference by the subordinate caste (blacks) to the dominant caste (whites). Although the legal basis for the caste system has been eliminated by judicial rulings and by federal legislation during the last half century, the issue of how closely black-white relations today resemble a caste system remains controversial.

Because ethnicity has frequently been associated with relations of dominance and subordination and thus to a society's system of stratification, there has been a tendency to equate ethnic relations with majority-minority relations. However, the relationship between ethnicity and a system of social ranking is not invariable or inevitable. In other words, it is possible for groups that are ethnically distinct and even in conflict to coexist without a system of dominant-subordinate relationships developing among them. However, because a ranking system involving relations of dominance and subordination has been so prominent a feature of ethnic relations, both today and in the past, in societies throughout the world, we will examine some of the key features of majority-minority relations.

Majority-Minority Relations

The centrality of ethnicity to many of the recent social and political upheavals in Eastern Europe serves as a reminder that the term *minority group* was originally derived from the European experience. Use of the term *minority* emerged in the context of the rise of nationalism and the nation-state in late-eighteenth-century and early-nineteenth-century Europe. In that context, it was used to characterize national or ethnic groups that had become subordinate to the peoples of another national or ethnic group through the imposition of, or the shifts in, political boundaries. Although in the past two centuries many commentators have predicted that "minority" concerns, issues, identities, and conflicts would wane as societies modernized, the extent to which long-simmering ethnic conflicts have emerged and resurfaced in the past decade reflects the tenacity of racial and ethnic identities, the significance of ethnic boundaries in organizing intergroup competition for scarce resources, and, hence, the continuing significance of majority-minority relations in human societies.

Although the term *minority* was widely used in Europe throughout the nineteenth century, it was adopted in the United States only after World War I, primarily in response to the publicity given to issues involving European minorities that were addressed in the negotiations that ended the war (Gleason 1991:393). However, in the United States the term developed a different meaning than in Europe. As Gunnar Myrdal commented in his monumental book *An American Dilemma,* "The minority peoples of the United States are fighting for status within the larger society; the minorities of Europe are mainly fighting for independence from it" (Myrdal 1944:50, quoted in Gleason 1991:397). Gleason contends that the way in which the social scientific concept of minority evolved in the United States reflected implicit American cultural and political assumptions about the nature of minorities—i.e., that minorities are the consequence of exclusion by majorities from the mainstream of American society and that, once tolerated and accepted as equals, minorities will (and should) ultimately disappear. Implicit in this conception is a notion of the majority's victimization of the minority and the idea that the goal of social policy should be to remove the barriers to their inclusion (Gleason 1991).

However, in numerous circumstances throughout the world, minorities do not seek inclusion into but rather separation from the society of which they are a part. What has typically characterized the definition of minority by American sociologists, however, is the assumption that members of a minority group seek inclusion into a society but are typically excluded from full participation in it; that they are the object of discrimination by the majority group; and that their life chances, when compared with those of the majority group, are circumscribed. Although many American minority groups have sought and do seek full admission to American society, it is important to recognize that the goal of minorities is not necessarily integration into a society's mainstream.

Nevertheless, American social scientists have generally used the terms *majority* and *minority* to refer to systems of structured social inequality in which racial and ethnic criteria play a critical role in the system's ranking system. The term *minority* has been applied with greatest frequency to subordinate groups characterized by hereditary membership and endogamy—racial, caste, and ethnic groupings (for example, Williams 1964:304; Wagley and Harris 1958:4–101). A minority or *subordinate group* occupies an inferior position of prestige, wealth, and power in a society.

However, it is important to recognize that the distinctive feature of majority-minority relations—group differences in power—is not restricted to racial and ethnic relations alone, but can characterize other forms of social relations. Therefore, a more inclusive definition of minority, one not restricted to racial and ethnic relations, is appropriate. Joseph B. Gittler's comprehensive definition is consistent with this approach: "Minority groups are those whose members experience a wide range of discriminatory treatment and frequently are relegated to positions relatively low in the status structure of a society" (Gittler 1956:vii). This definition retains the crucial elements of the term's original meaning: the reference to a distinct group or social category occupying a subordinate position of prestige, privilege, and power.

The term *minority* does not refer to the numerical size of a group. Occasionally a so-called minority group will represent a numerical majority of the total population. For example, in South Africa today, blacks are a numerical majority (69 percent) of the total population; but, despite the formal abolition of the repressive system of apartheid and the accession to political power by the predominantly black African National Congress, blacks are still dramatically underrepresented in higher-status occupations in the South African economy, while those individuals who have experienced occupational mobility and increased affluence still encounter social discrimination and exclusion from informal social networks that are frequently essential to economic advancement (Daley 1997). Similar situations existed historically in some areas of the American South and in most colonial situations. For example, in 1910, although African Americans represented more than 55 percent of the population of Mississippi and South Carolina, they were completely excluded from all political offices in these two states.[2] Numerical superiority, therefore, does not necessarily ensure majority status.

Many commentators have suggested that the terms *majority* and *minority* be replaced by *dominant* and *subordinate* to represent more accurately the differences in power. However, because *majority* and *minority* have been so widely used, I will use them here with the understanding that the crucial feature of the minority's status is its inferior social position, in which its interests are not effectively represented in the political, economic, and social institutions of the society. I will use the term *dominant* as a synonym for *majority,* and *subordinate* for *minority.*

Minorities and Conflict

Many different dimensions, such as race, ethnicity, and religion, have been used to distinguish a minority from the majority. However, ethnic, racial, or religious differences do not automatically generate conflict and social inequalities. Culturally, religiously, or racially distinct groups may coexist without a system of ethnic inequality developing (Horowitz 1985). Majority-minority relations do not appear until one group is able to impose its will on another. By definition, minority groups are subordinate segments of the societies of which they are a part. Once people perceive ethnic differences and ethnic groups and then compete against each other, the crucial variable is power.

Power is the ability of one group to realize its goals and interests, even in the face of resistance. This power may be derived from the superior size, weapons, technology, property, education, or economic resources of the dominant group. Hence, minority groups are categories of people that possess imperfect access to positions of equal power, prestige, and privilege in a society. Superior power is crucial not only to the establishment of a system of ethnic stratification but also to its maintenance and perpetuation. Having obtained control of a society's institutions, a majority group generally strives to solidify and consolidate its position.

Although conflict is not always overt, continuous, or apparent in a social system based on structured inequality, the potential for conflict is continually present. The extent to which conflict or stability are manifested itself is related to social structure. Pierre van den Berghe (1967) contrasted the patterns of race relations characteristic of two structurally different types of societies. Under the *paternalistic* type, characteristic of a traditional, preindustrial, predominantly agricultural society, race relations are highly stable, and conflict is submerged—a function of both the mechanisms of social control used by the dominant group and of the symbiotic nature of relations between dominant and subordinate groups. On the other hand, race relations in a *competitive* setting—an urbanized and highly industrialized society characterized by a complex division of labor—are less likely to remain stable. Overt conflict, initiated by both the dominant and the subordinate groups, frequently erupts.

However, even in the most stable situations, dominant groups view minority groups as potentially threatening to their position. This fact is nowhere more apparent than in the American slave system, which exemplifies van den Berghe's paternalistic type of race relations. Proponents of slavery—the so-called "peculiar institution"—frequently justified slaveholding on the grounds of the slave's docility, dependence, improvidence, and fear of freedom. Simultaneously, however, they saw slaves as "a troublesome presence" (Stampp 1956), they initiated elaborate mechanisms (such as patrols, passes, and legal prohibitions against literacy and the possession of weapons) to reduce resistance to the slave regime, and they employed brutal sanctions to discourage noncompliance with the prescribed subordinate roles.

The social inequalities inherent in majority-minority relations are, as Berreman points out in Article 1, symbolically expressed in the institutionalized patterns of interpersonal relations between dominant and subordinate group members. Social interaction among majority and minority group members is never among status equals; as noted above, it consistently involves what was known in the American context as "the etiquette of race relations," which involved restrictions on such activities as eating, touching, terms of address, marriage, sexual conduct, and social contact generally. Although the patterns of deference that the slave system demanded persisted long after slavery was legally abolished, the American slave regime vividly exemplified this point. One primary objective of slave socialization was to implant in slaves a sense of personal inferiority. Slaves were taught to "know their place," to recognize the difference between the status of master and slave. Whites interpreted any impudence on the part of slaves as an effort to reject their subordinate role. Frederick Douglass, the great nineteenth-century African American leader, recalled that slaves could be labeled disobedient and punished for a variety of actions, including "the tone of an answer; in answering at all; in not answering; in the expression of countenance; in the motion of the head; in the gait, manner and bearing of the slave" (Stampp 1956:145).

As events during the Black Protest Movement of the 1960s in the United States demonstrated, attempts by a minority group to alter traditional relationships between dominant and subordinate groups and to achieve autonomy and equality of status are strenuously resisted by the majority group. Allen D. Grimshaw has summarized the history of changes in black-white relations by pointing out that

> The most savage oppression, whether expressed in rural lynching and pogroms or in urban race riots, has taken place when the Negro has refused to accept a subordinate status. The most intense conflict has resulted when the subordinate minority group has attempted to disrupt the accommodative pattern or when the superordinate group has defined the situation as one in which such an attempt is being made. (Grimshaw 1959:17)

Efforts to alter the relative power of the majority and the minority thus inevitably involve conflict between the two groups, with the subordinate group attempting to decrease the inequalities in the system through a wide variety of means, including violence; and with the dominant group resorting to a multiplicity of techniques, also including violence (both legal and extralegal) to prevent such changes from occurring.

Majorities and Institutional Power

The discussion thus far has suggested that the concept of minority group must always be considered in relation to a majority, or dominant, group. Although this conclusion may appear self-evident, until the 1970s only a meager amount of the voluminous research on racial and ethnic relations had been devoted to the characteristics and attributes of the majority group and the mechanisms by which the relationships between majority and minority are created, maintained, and altered. A notable exception was the work of Robert Bierstedt. In "The Sociology of Majorities," published half a century ago, Bierstedt wrote the following:

> It is the majority . . . which sets the culture pattern and sustains it, which is in fact responsible for whatever pattern or configuration there is in a culture. It is the majority which confers upon folkways, mores, customs, and laws the status of norms and gives them coercive power. It is the majority which guarantees the stability of a society. It is the majority which requires conformity to custom and which penalizes deviation—except in ways in which the majority sanctions and approves. It is the majority which is the custodian of the mores and which defends them against innovation. And it is the inertia of majorities, finally, which retards the processes of social change. (Bierstedt 1948:709)

Writing nearly fifty years later, Doane (Article 3) similarly emphasizes the "hidden" nature of dominant group identity, assumptions, and privilege:

> The hidden nature of dominant group identity and the normalization of cultural, political, and economic dominance tend to obscure the advantages that accrue to dominant group members. This taken-for-granted aspect of dominant group privilege, when coupled with the removal of formal barriers to subordinate group advancement, leads to the denial of ethnicity or race as a meaningful social force amid the promotions of ideologies of individualism.

Bierstedt's and Doane's insistence that the analysis of majority-minority relations focus on the characteristics of the dominant group, not on those of the minority, reflects one of the major themes of this book. From this perspective, the principal focus of inquiry should be on the nature of "white" ethnic identity and the manner in which the dominant group controls the institutions of the society. As Preston Wilcox has argued, "Much of what has been written as sociology would suggest that . . . minorities suffer problems because of their unique characteristics rather than [because of] the systems which impinge upon them and the sanctioning of these systems by dominant groups" (Wilcox 1970:44).

Lack of recognition of the importance of societal patterns of institutional control has meant that, as John Horton (1966) has pointed out, sociologists and laypeople alike frequently define social problems as a minority group's deviation from dominant societal norms and standards; seldom do they themselves critically examine the society's institutions, values, and social processes. The importance of an institutional approach to the analysis of mass protest and violence in America was forcefully articulated in 1969 by the Violence Commission, which was appointed by President Lyndon Johnson to examine and explain the mass protest that swept the country during the turbulent 1960s. Mass protest, the Commission contended,

> must be analyzed in relation to crises in American institutions. . . . [It] is an outgrowth of social, economic, and political conditions. Recommendations concerning the prevention of violence which do not address the issue of fundamental social, economic, and political change are fated to be largely irrelevant and frequently self-defeating. (Skolnick 1969:3)

In other words, both the sources of, and the solutions to, problems of majority-minority conflict are institutional. Thus, the most realistic approach to their analysis must focus primarily on the majority group and the institutional structures that they created, and continue to operate and control.

Examination of the ways that majority group members typically approach inter-group conflict demonstrates the importance of an institutional perspective. As noted before, the majority determines whether a problem even exists—witness the classic statement advanced by proponents of the status quo in communities throughout America: "We have no problems here. Our [insert appropriate minority group residing in the community] are happy." Whether or not one perceives social conditions as a problem depends on one's position within the social structure. As the Violence Commission noted, whether or not one classifies behavior as violent depends on whether one is challenging the existing institutional arrangements or is seeking to uphold them (Skolnick 1969:3–4).

In an important article examining the functions of racial conflict, Joseph Himes (1966) has pointed out that conflict may have positive consequences: it can force the dominant group to be aware of, come to grips with, and respond to societal inequities. Himes argues that organized social conflict alters traditional power relations and the traditional etiquette of race relations. As the minority group develops the ability to mobilize power against the dominant group's interests, traditional race relations change to the point where minority grievances can be more realistically discussed and addressed. During the late 1950s and early 1960s, African Americans, denied change through institutionalized political channels (voting, for example), used mass protest to mobilize power against the dominant group's entrenched interests. Nonviolent protest and conflict were integral strategies of power in the civil rights movement. Martin Luther King, Jr., one of history's most articulate advocates of the weapon of nonviolence, perceived that it represented a means of effecting a redistribution of power:

> Nonviolent direct action seeks to create such a crisis and foster such a tension that a community which has constantly refused to negotiate is forced to confront the issue. It seeks so to dramatize the issue that it can no longer be ignored. (King 1964:81)

If the dominant group acknowledges social problems at all, they invariably ascribe them to the characteristics of the subordinate group rather than to defects in the social system controlled by the majority group. For many years, discussion of black-white relations in America was described as the "Negro problem," a stance explicitly challenged by Gunnar Myrdal in his classic work, *An American Dilemma* (1944). Today, most white Americans deny that opportunities for black Americans are limited, and perceive that blacks themselves are primarily responsible for the conditions in which they find themselves (Schumann 1969; Kluegel and Smith 1982; Schuman, Steeh, and Bobo 1985).

This interpretation is also implicit in the idea of cultural deprivation (Baratz and Baratz 1970), or what Maxine Baca Zinn (1989) has termed the "cultural deficiency model" for explaining poverty and, especially, what has recently been termed the *underclass*—the most impoverished segment of American society. Found primarily in the nation's inner cities, the underclass is characterized by high unemployment, school dropouts, academic failures, out-of-wedlock births, female-headed families, welfare dependence, homelessness, and serious crime. According to the cultural deficiency model, these characteristics are attributable primarily to the internal deficiencies and instabilities of the minorities—primarily black and Hispanic—that make up the underclass. That is, cultural, family, and community and neighborhood factors, not the inadequate economic and educational opportunities, are the primary causes of the social dislocations experienced by the underclass. The cultural deficiency model focuses on the characteristics of minorities and deflects attention from the institutional factors that impinge upon them. In short, the emphasis in such a model is on the symptom rather than on the disease.

The resolution of intergroup conflict also reflects power differentials, for conflicts tend to be resolved within limits acceptable to the majority group. Efforts to alter the pattern of inequalities are therefore restricted to methods defined as legitimate or appropriate by the majority group, a requisite that seldom poses a threat to the continued functioning of the existing system. The history of American Indian encounters with white Americans provides an excellent example of this pattern. Indian-white problems were almost invariably defined from the perspective of whites and generally involved the refusal of Native Americans to accede to white demands for cultural assimilation or for the cession of their lands. Native American values, needs, and desires were seldom, if ever, a consideration in the solution of such confrontations. According to the humanitarian Thomas Jefferson, if Indians did not conform to white cultural patterns, the only viable solution was their forcible removal.

The role of the majority group in delimiting the context within which solutions to problems of intergroup conflict can be reached is exemplified by the analysis and recommendations of the 1968 Kerner Commission report and the nation's reactions to it. Charged by President Lyndon Johnson with investigating the causes of the civil disorders that rent the nation for several years during the 1960s, the Commission concluded, as we shall note later, that the primary explanation was white racism. Moreover, it argued that, given the sustained and pervasive effects of racism, "there can be no higher priority for national action and no higher claim on the nation's conscience" than the elimination of racism from American society (National Advisory Commission on Civil Disorders 1968:21, 203). However, it warned that implementation of its recommendations would necessitate "unprecedented levels of funding and performance." Because implementation of these terms were politically unpopular with the dominant group, the response to the Kerner report—both officially and unofficially— was to discredit or (perhaps more significant) to ignore its findings.

Because the conclusion that white racism was primarily responsible for the intense racial conflicts of the 1960s was unacceptable to most white Americans, the Commission's report demonstrated that majority solutions to social problems seldom entail basic alterations of the society's institutional patterns. On the one hand, the Kerner Commission indicted American institutions as the primary source of the racism that permeates the society. On the other hand, most of its recommendations involved changing blacks to conform to these institutions rather than substantially altering the institutions themselves. Such an approach, involving what Horton (1966) has termed an *order model* of social problems, slights the basic institutional sources of racial inequality in American society, a subject that we will explore more fully in Parts 3 and 4.

Prejudice, Discrimination, and Racism

Prejudice and discrimination are important elements in all majority-minority relations. The term *prejudice* derives from two Latin words, *prae* "before" and *judicum* "a judgment." It denotes a judgment before all the facts are known. According to Gordon Allport, *prejudice* is "an avertive or hostile attitude toward a person who belongs to a group, simply because he [or she] belongs to that group, and is therefore presumed to have the objectionable qualities ascribed to the group" (Allport 1958:8). Prejudice thus refers to a set of rigidly held negative attitudes, beliefs, and feelings toward members of another group.

Prejudice often involves an intense emotional component. Thus, many white Americans consciously and rationally reject the myths of African American inferiority but react emotionally with fear, hostility, or condescension in the presence of African Americans. The forms of prejudice range from unconscious aversion to members of the out-group to a comprehensive, well-articulated, and coherent ideology, such as the ideology of racism.

Discrimination, on the other hand, involves unfavorable treatment of individuals because of their group membership. Prejudice and discrimination should not be equated. Prejudice involves attitudes and internal states, whereas discrimination involves overt action or behavior. Discrimination may be manifested in a multitude of ways: mild slights (such as Polish jokes); verbal threats, abuse, and epithets; intimidation and harassment (such as threatening phone calls); defacing property with ethnic slurs, graffiti, or symbols; unequal treatment (such as refusing to hire or promote qualified applicants); systematic oppression (such as slavery); or outright violence (vandalism, arson, terrorism, lynching, pogroms, massacres).

Because sociologists are primarily concerned with human behavior, the focus in this book is on discrimination. Clearly, however, a close relationship frequently exists between prejudice and discrimination. Consequently, an extensive amount of research has been carried out concerning the nature and causes of prejudice. Attitude surveys conducted in the United States since the 1940s have shown a significant decline in antiblack prejudice; increasingly, white Americans have come to support broad principles of racial integration and equal treatment in public accommodations, employment, public transportation, schools, housing, and marriage. For example, in 1942, 32 percent of whites agreed that whites and blacks should attend the same schools; by 1982, this figure was 90 percent. When asked in 1958 whether they would object to sending their children to schools in which half the children were black, nearly half (47 percent) responded affirmatively; by 1997, this figure had declined to 12 percent. In 1944, 45 percent thought that blacks should have as good a chance as whites to get any kind of job; and by 1972, 97 percent agreed. The percentage approving integration in public transportation rose from 46 percent in 1942 to 88 percent in 1970. Moreover, whites have indicated increasing willingness to participate personally in desegregated settings. In 1958, four-fifths of whites said they would move if blacks moved into their neighborhood "in great numbers"; in 1997, those indicating they would move declined to 12 percent. Finally, whereas only 4 percent of whites said they approved of interracial marriages in 1958, more than three-fifths (61 percent) expressed their approval in 1997 (Schuman, Steeh, and Bobo 1985; Hochschild

1995; Gallup Poll Social Audit 1997). These changes are a result of two factors. First, they reflect attitude changes among individuals over their lifetimes. Second, younger people generally exhibit less racial prejudice than their elders, and as younger, more tolerant cohorts have replaced older, more prejudiced ones, overall racial prejudice has declined (Firebaugh and Davis 1988).

However, among white Americans, the same striking agreement on how to combat discrimination or segregation does not appear. Although today white Americans endorse broad principles of nondiscrimination and desegregation in important areas of American life, they are much less likely to support policies for translating these principles into practice. For example, despite the strong support among white Americans for the principle of integrated education, the percentage of whites who felt that the federal government should ensure that black and white children attend the same schools declined between the 1960s and 1980s. Moreover, widespread white opposition was raised to busing as a means of desegregating schools (Schuman, Steeh, and Bobo 1985).

The substantial gap between white people's support for broad principles of equality and their support for specific programs to implement these principles indicates the complexity of racial attitudes. The relationship between prejudicial attitudes and discriminatory behavior is equally complex. Prejudice does not always produce discrimination, although it has frequently been treated as the cause of discrimination. An individual, however, may be prejudiced without *acting* in a discriminatory manner. In recent years it has become less fashionable to express racial prejudice publicly. Overt forms of discrimination, such as exclusion from public accommodations, jobs, and colleges and universities—behaviors that in the past were tolerated by most whites—are now often prohibited by law and condemned by public opinion.

The distinction between prejudice and discrimination and the interrelationship between these two phenomena were first systematically developed by Robert Merton (1949) in his classic article, "Discrimination and the American Creed." "Prejudicial attitudes," Merton argued, "need not coincide with discriminatory behavior." Merton demonstrated the range of possible ways in which prejudice and discrimination interact by distinguishing among four types of individuals:

1. The unprejudiced nondiscriminator—the all-weather liberal
2. The unprejudiced discriminator—the fair-weather liberal
3. The prejudiced nondiscriminator—the fair-weather bigot
4. The prejudiced discriminator—the all-weather bigot

The unprejudiced nondiscriminator consistently adheres to the American creed of equality for all in both belief and practice. The unprejudiced discriminator, on the other hand, internalizes and may even articulate the ideals of the American creed but may acquiesce to group pressures to discriminate. Similarly, the prejudiced nondiscriminator conforms to social pressures not to discriminate despite harboring prejudices toward ethnic minorities. Finally, the prejudiced discriminator is, like the unprejudiced nondiscriminator, consistent in belief and practice, rejecting the American creed and engaging in personal discrimination.

Merton's discussion was critical to the recognition that whether prejudice becomes translated into discriminatory behavior depends on the social context. From this perspective it becomes impossible to understand the dynamics of majority-minority relations by examining prejudice alone; prejudice is most appropriately considered not as a causal factor but as a dependent variable. As Richard Schermerhorn has cogently suggested, prejudice "is a product of situations, historical situations, economic situations, political situations; it is not a little demon that emerges in people because they are depraved" (Schermerhorn 1970:6).

Thus, discrimination is much more likely to occur in a social setting in which acts of ethnic and racial bias are accepted or are not strongly condemned. This principle was underscored in a study undertaken at Smith College, where in 1989 racial tensions erupted after four black students received anonymous hate messages. Researchers asked students how they felt about these incidents. Before a student could answer, a confederate, arriving at the same time, would respond by strongly condemning or strongly justifying the incidents. The researchers found that the students' opinions were strongly influenced by the opinions they heard expressed by the confederates. Hearing others express strongly antiracist opinions produced similar sentiments, whereas students who first heard expressions more accepting of racism offered "significantly less strongly antiracist opinions" (Blanchard, Lilly, and Vaughn 1991:105). Clearly, the social climate affects whether personal prejudices are translated into discriminatory acts; to explain the dynamics of ethnic and racial relations fully, it is necessary to analyze the historical, cultural, and institutional conditions that have preceded and generated them.

During the past quarter century, the conceptualization of American race relations has undergone several significant changes. These changes have been profoundly influenced by the changing nature of race relations in the United States. Before the advent of the Black Protest Movement during the 1950s, social scientists focused their attention primarily on racial attitudes, because prejudice was thought to be the key to understanding racial and ethnic conflict. This perception of the essential dynamics of race relations is perhaps best illustrated in Myrdal's classic *An American Dilemma,* in which he defined race prejudice as "the whole complex of valuations and beliefs which are behind discriminatory behavior on the part of the majority group . . . and which are contrary to the egalitarian ideals in the American Creed" (Myrdal 1944:52). This model of race relations was predicated on the assumption that racial conflict in the United States was a problem of ignorance and morality that could best be solved by changing—through education and moral suasion—the majority's prejudicial attitudes toward racial minorities. "A great majority of white people in America," Myrdal wrote, "would be better prepared to give the Negro a substantially better deal if they knew the facts" (Myrdal 1944:48).

The black protest era of the 1950s and 1960s challenged the assumption that change in the patterns of racial inequality in American society could be brought about through a reduction in prejudicial attitudes alone. Sociologists and social activists focused increasingly on the dynamics of discrimination and sought means of eliminating discriminatory behavior. The numerous forms of direct protest, such as nonviolent sit-ins, boycotts, and voter registration drives, were tactics designed to alter patterns of discrimination. In keeping with this emphasis on discrimination were the legislative efforts undertaken to secure enactment of the Civil Rights Act of 1964, which outlawed discrimination in public accommodations and employment, and the 1965 Voting Rights Act, which provided federal support to ensure that African Americans had the right to vote throughout the South.

However, the greatest racial unrest of the black protest era occurred after these legislative victories had been achieved. Whereas the earlier civil rights phase of the Black Protest Movement had been directed primarily against public discrimination and especially its manifestations in the South, the outbreak of urban riots in northern cities focused attention on the nature of racial inequalities affecting African Americans throughout the entire nation. For several summers during the late 1960s, the nation was torn with racial strife. Parts of cities were burned, property damage ran into the millions of dollars, and the toll of dead—primarily, although not exclusively, blacks—numbered almost a hundred (National Advisory Commission on Civil Disorders 1968:116). In July 1967 President Lyndon Johnson appointed a national commission (the Kerner Commission) to investigate the causes of these urban riots. In 1968 the commission issued its report, which concluded the following:

> What white Americans have never fully understood—but what the Negro can never forget—is that white society is deeply implicated in the ghetto. White society condones it. . . . Race prejudice has shaped our history decisively in the past; it now threatens to do so again. White racism is essentially responsible for the explosive mixture which has been accumulating in our cities since the end of World War II. (National Advisory Commission on Civil Disorders 1968:203)

Racism

Especially because the Kerner Commission concluded that the ultimate responsibility for the racial disorders of the 1960s should be attributed to "white racism," the term has been widely invoked to explain racial inequalities and conflict in American society. However, the term is extremely imprecise and ambiguous. This imprecision enabled President Johnson, who had created the Kerner Commission, to ignore its findings, and his successor, Richard Nixon, to condemn and deny them. Consequently, the term *racism* is in urgent need of clarification.

First, *racism* is a general term, subsuming several analytically distinct phenomena —prejudice and several forms of discrimination. Stokely Carmichael and Charles Hamilton distinguished between *individual* racism and *institutional* racism:

> Racism is both overt and covert. It takes two closely related forms: individual whites acting against individual blacks and acts by the total white community against the black community. . . . The second type is less overt, far more subtle, less identifiable in terms of specific individuals committing the acts. But it is no less destructive of human life. . . . When white terrorists bomb a black church and kill five black children, that is an act of individual racism, widely deplored by most segments of the society. But when in that same city, Birmingham, Alabama—five hundred black babies die each year because of the lack of proper food, shelter, and medical facilities, and thousands more are destroyed and maimed physically, emotionally, and intellectually because of the conditions of poverty and discrimination in the black community, that is a function of institutional racism. (Carmichael and Hamilton 1967:4)

However, as I will note more fully later, prejudicial attitudes are causal factors in Carmichael and Hamilton's conceptualization of institutional racism. Moreover, they do not distinguish between psychological and sociological factors in its operation.

Another problem in the use of the word *racism* is that although it lumps together all forms of racial oppression, it is not sufficiently inclusive. It does not encompass majority-minority situations based on criteria other than race—criteria such as religion, tribal identity, ethnicity, or gender. Therefore, in the following discussion, I have analytically distinguished the terms *racism, prejudice,* and *discrimination.*

The term *racism* has traditionally referred to an *ideology*—a set of ideas and beliefs—used to explain, rationalize, or justify a racially organized social order. There are two essential parts of racism: its content and its function. Racism is distinguished from ethnocentrism by insistence that differences among groups are biologically based. The in-group is believed to be innately superior to the out-group, and members of the out-group are defined as being "biogenetically incapable of ever achieving intellectual and moral equality with members of the ingroup" (Noel 1972:157). Howard Schuman has offered a commonly accepted definition of racism:

> *The term racism is generally taken to refer to the belief that there are clearly distinguishable human races, that these races differ not only in superficial physical characteristics, but also innately in important psychological traits; and finally that the differences are such that one race (almost always one's own, naturally) can be said to be superior to another. (Schuman 1969:44)*

Racism's primary function has been to provide a rationale and ideological support —a moral justification—for maintaining a racially based social order. In other words, the assertion of the innate "natural" superiority or inferiority of different racial groups serves to justify domination and exploitation of one group by another. As Manning Nash has written, "no group of [people] is able systematically to subordinate or deprive another group of [people] without appeal to a body of values which makes the exploitation, the disprivilege, the expropriation, and the denigration of human beings a 'moral' act" (Nash 1962:288). In addition, not only does an ideology of racism provide a moral justification for the dominant group of their positions of privilege and power, but it also discourages minority groups from questioning their subordinate status and advancing claims for equal treatment.

Van den Berghe (1967:16–181) has suggested three major sources of Western racism. First, racism developed as a justification of capitalist forms of exploitation, particularly slavery in the New World. As Noel has argued, "As slavery became ever more clearly the pivotal institution of Southern society, racism was continually strengthened and became an ever more dominant ideology" (Noel 1972:162).

Second, racism was congruent with late nineteenth-century Darwinian notions of stages of evolution and survival of the fittest, and with the idea of Anglo-Saxon superiority. According to these doctrines, those people in inferior social positions were destined to their station because they were least evolved or least fit in the struggle for existence. In 1870 Francis A. Walker, United States Commissioner of Immigration, characterized the immigrants from southern and eastern Europe in the following manner:

> *They are beaten men from beaten races: representing the worst failures in the struggle for existence. Centuries are against them, as centuries were on the side of those who formerly came to us. They have none of the ideas and aptitudes which fit men to take up readily and easily the problem of self-care and self-government. (Quoted in Saveth 1948:40)*

The third explanation of racism, van den Berghe argues, is paradoxically related to the egalitarian ideas of the Enlightenment, which were expressed in the Declaration of Independence:

> *Faced with the blatant contradiction between the treatment of slaves and colonial peoples and the official rhetoric of freedom and equality, Europeans and white North Americans began to dichotomize humanity between men and submen (or the "civilized" and the "savages"). The scope of applicability of the egalitarian ideals was restricted to "the people," that is, the whites, and there resulted . . . regimes such as those of the United States or South Africa that are democratic for the master race but tyrannical for the subordinate groups. The desire to preserve both the profitable forms of discrimination and exploitation and the democratic ideology made it necessary to deny humanity to the oppressed groups. (van den Berghe 1967:17–18)*

As noted before, there has been a substantial decline in professions of racist attitudes among white Americans in the past half century; especially since 1970, white Americans have increased their approval of racial integration (Schuman, Steeh, and Bobo 1985; Gallup Poll Social Audit 1997). In 1942 only 42 percent of a national sample of whites reported that they believed blacks to be equal to whites in innate intelligence; since the late 1950s, however, around 80 percent of white Americans have rejected the idea of inherent black inferiority. The Kerner Commission was therefore misleading in lumping all white antipathy toward blacks into the category of racism.

Rather than believing that African Americans are genetically inferior, whites often employ a *meritocratic ideology* to explain the substantial gap that continues to separate black and white income, wealth, and educational attainment. The basic element in a meritocratic ideology is the assumption of equality of opportunity—that all people in the United States have equal chances to achieve success, and that inequalities in the distribution of income, wealth, power, and prestige reflect the qualifications or merit of individuals in each rank in society. In other words, in a meritocratic society, all people are perceived to have an equal opportunity to succeed or fail—to go as far as their talents will take them—and the system of social ranking that develops is simply a "natural" reflection of each person's abilities or merit. Affluence is perceived as the result of the personal qualities of intelligence, industriousness, motivation, and ambition, while the primary responsibility for poverty rests with the poor themselves. Therefore, in this aristocracy of talent, those in the upper strata deserve the power, prestige, and privileges that they enjoy, while those lower in the social ranking system are placed according to their ability. Such a belief system is not inherently racist, but rather is a general judgment about human nature that can be applied to all sorts of human conditions or groups. However, it can have racist effects when it is used to explain racial inequalities in the United States without recognizing or acknowledging the external disabilities (such as prejudice and discrimination) that racial minorities experience. Thus, by this definition, African Americans are still considered inferior people; otherwise, they would be as well-off as whites. (See Hochschild 1995 for an excellent discussion of the conflicting perceptions of whites and blacks regarding opportunity in American society.)

If the term *racism* referred merely to the realm of beliefs and ideology and not to behavior or action, its relevance for the study of race relations would be limited. To restrict the meaning of racism to ideology would be to ignore the external constraints and societally imposed disabilities—rooted in the power of the majority group—confronting a racial minority. If one group does not possess the power to impose its belief system on another, ethnic stratification cannot occur (Noel 1968). During the late 1960s and 1970s, when critics charged that the ideology of Black Power was "racism in reverse," African American spokespersons responded that their critics failed to consider the components of differential power that enabled the ideology of white supremacy to result in white domination:

> There is no analogy—by any stretch of definition or imagination—between the advocates of Black Power and white racists. Racism is not merely exclusion on the basis of race but exclusion for the purpose of subjugating or maintaining subjugation. The goal of the racists is to keep black people on the bottom, arbitrarily and dictatorially, as they have done in this country for over three hundred years. (Carmichael and Hamilton 1967:47)

Recently Feagin and Vera (1995) have taken a similar stance against the contention that "black racism" is equally as critical an issue as white racism. They contend that "black racism does not exist" because

> Racism is more than a matter of individual prejudice and scattered episodes of discrimination. There is no black racism because there is no centuries-old system of racialized subordination and discrimination designed by African Americans to exclude white Americans from full participation in the rights, privileges and benefits of this society. Black (or other minority) racism would require not only a widely accepted racist ideology directed at whites but also the power to systematically exclude whites from opportunities and rewards in major economic, cultural, and political institutions. (Feagin and Vera 1995:ix–x)

Therefore, the crucial component of a definition of racism is behavioral. Racism in its most inclusive sense refers to actions on the part of a racial majority that have discriminatory effects, preventing members of a minority group from securing access to prestige, power, and privilege. These actions may be intentional or unintentional. This broader conception of racism therefore entails discrimination as well as an ideology that proclaims the superiority of one racial grouping over another.

As noted earlier, *discrimination* refers to the differential treatment of members of a minority group. Discrimination in its several forms comprises the means by which the unequal status of the minority group and the power of the majority group are preserved. In the ensuing discussion, I distinguish between *attitudinal* discrimination, which refers to discriminatory practices attributable to or influenced by prejudice, and *institutional* discrimination, which cannot be attributed to prejudice, but instead is a consequence of society's normal functioning. Both of these types can be further elaborated according to the sources of the discriminatory behavior. In reality, these types are at times interrelated and reinforce each other. Seldom is discrimination against a minority group member derived from one source alone.

Attitudinal Discrimination

Attitudinal discrimination refers to discriminatory practices that stem from prejudicial attitudes. The discriminator either is prejudiced or acts in response to the prejudices of others. Attitudinal discrimination is usually direct, overt, visible, and dramatic. Despite increasing white acceptance of principles of nondiscrimination and racial segregation, ethnic minorities, especially African Americans, continue to be confronted with incidents of attitudinal discrimination. In "The Continuing Significance of Race" (Article 20), Feagin distinguished five categories of such discrimination: avoidance, rejection, verbal attacks, physical threats and harassment, and physical attacks. Despite increasing verbal acceptance by whites of the principles of nondiscrimination and racial integration, African Americans have been confronted with attitudinal discrimination in almost every public aspect of their lives. Many of these discriminatory acts appear trivial, insignificant, and unimportant to white observers: a white couple's crossing the street to avoid walking past a black male, a "hate stare," receiving poor service at restaurants, stores, and hotels. Many whites also trivialize discrimination that takes the form of racial and ethnic slurs and epithets. Incidents of this kind are seldom reported in the press, yet they are demeaning realities to which minorities of all social classes are consistently exposed.

Much more dramatic incidents of discrimination are reported almost daily in the news media. For example, the brutal beating of Rodney King, a black motorist, by members of the Los Angeles Police Department in 1991 was captured on videotape, was widely publicized, and drew widespread attention to the vulnerability of blacks to police harassment. The subsequent acquittal of four police officers who had been videotaped beating him unleashed the most destructive American urban disorders of the twentieth century. Yet the King incident was only one of 15,000 complaints of police brutality filed with the federal government between 1985 and 1991 (Lewis 1991). Moreover, during the 1980s and 1990s hundreds of incidents of discrimination, intimidation, harassment, and vandalism as well as physical attacks against racial and religious minorities were reported. These included the burning of over 65 black churches in 1995 and 1996 alone; although investigators concluded that there was no evidence of an organized national racist conspiracy, they did find that racial hatred was a motive in most cases (Sack 1996; Butterfield 1996).

Similarly, cases of racial discrimination in education, in housing, in public accommodations, and in the workplace continue to be widely reported. Some of the most widely publicized cases of discrimination in the workplace and in public accommodations involved nationally prominent corporations—Denney's, Shoney's, Avis, Circuit City, and Texaco (*Time* 1987; Ehrlich 1990; U.S. Commission on Civil Rights 1990; Jaffe 1994; Feagin and Vera 1995; Eichenwald 1996; Myerson 1997). Yet these cases were among only the most widely publicized; between 1990 and 1993 the Equal Employment Opportunity Commission (EEOC), the federal agency responsible for enforcing civil rights laws in the workplace, resolved an average of 4,636 cases in favor of individuals charging racial discrimination. In most instances, however, discrimination is extremely difficult to prove, and the burden of filing charges and the recourse to legal remedies are so cumbersome and time-consuming that many people are discouraged from pursuing them. Nevertheless, by 1995 the EEOC had a back log of about 100,000 cases charging racial discrimination in employment alone (Kilborn 1995; Myerson 1997).

Thus, despite the enactment of antidiscrimination legislation and contrary to white perceptions that discrimination has been eradicated and that, as a consequence of affirmative action programs, minorities receive preferential treatment in hiring, recent "bias studies" have demonstrated that African Americans and Hispanics continue to experience discrimination. In a study of employment discrimination, for example, pairs of white and black men with identical qualifications applied for 476 jobs advertised in Washington and Chicago newspapers. Whereas 15 percent of the white applicants received job offers, only 5 percent of the black applicants did. Moreover, white applicants advanced further in the hiring process and in the Washington area were much less likely to receive rude, unfavorable, or discouraging treatment than were their black counterparts. These findings were similar to an earlier study of the hiring experiences of Hispanics and Anglos in Chicago and San Diego in which whites were three times as likely both to advance further in the hiring process and to receive job offers as were Hispanic applicants (Turner, Fix, and Struyk 1991).

What are the consequences of these continuing encounters with attitudinal discrimination? In his study involving interviews with African Americans throughout the United States (Article 20), Feagin found that despite antidiscrimination legislation and changing white attitudes, even middle-class blacks remain vulnerable to discrimination and that incidents of discrimination against them are far from isolated. Instead, they are *cumulative;* that is, a black person's encounters with discrimination are best described as a "lifelong series of such incidents."

The cumulative impact of constant experiences of discrimination—what writer Ellis Cose (1993) has characterized as "soul-destroying slights"—and the energy expended in dealing with them was clearly articulated by one of the respondents in Feagin's study:

> . . . if you can think of the mind as having one hundred ergs of energy, and the average man uses fifty percent of his energy dealing with the everyday problems of the world—just the general kinds of things—then he has fifty percent more to do creative kinds of things that he wants to do. Now that's a white person. Now a black person also has one hundred ergs: he uses fifty percent the same way a white man does, dealing with what the white man has [to deal with], so he has fifty percent left. But he uses twenty-five percent fighting being black, [with] all the problems of being black and what it means. Which means he really only has twenty-five percent to do what the white man has fifty percent to do, and he's expected to do just as much as the white man with that twenty-five percent. . . . So, that's kind of what happens. You just don't have as much energy left to do as much as you know you really could if you were free, [if] your mind were free.

Anthony Walton, an African American who grew up in a comfortable middle-class home in the Chicago suburbs, has referred to these "petty, daily indignities that take such a toll on the psyches of American blacks" as a "black tax," "the tribute to white society that must be paid in self-effacement and swallowed pride" (Walton 1996:7).

Attitudinal discrimination does not always occur in so virulent or so direct a manner. It may be manifested less dramatically merely by the acceptance by members of the dominant group of social definitions of traditional subordinate group roles. Malcolm X, the charismatic black protest leader who was assassinated in 1965, recalled how his well-intentioned white high school English teacher, Mr. Ostrowski, was bound by cultural norms concerning the "proper" caste roles for blacks:

> I know that he probably meant well in what he happened to advise me that day. I doubt that he meant any harm. . . . I was one of his top students, one of the school's top students—but all he could see for me was the kind of future "in your place" that almost all white people see for black people. . . . He told me, "Malcolm, you ought to be thinking about a career. Have you been

giving it any thought?" . . . The truth is, I hadn't. I have never figured out why I told him, "Well, yes, sir, I've been thinking I'd like to be a lawyer." Lansing certainly had no lawyers—or doctors either—in those days, to hold up an image I might have aspired to. All I really knew for certain was that a lawyer didn't wash dishes, as I was doing.

Mr. Ostrowski looked surprised, I remember, and leaned back in his chair and clasped his hands behind his head. He kind of half-smiled and said, "Malcolm, one of life's first needs is for us to be realistic. Don't misunderstand me, now. We all here like you, you know that. But you've got to be realistic about being a nigger. A lawyer—that's no realistic goal for a nigger. You need to think about something you can be. You're good with your hands—making things. Everybody admires your carpentry shop work. Why don't you plan on carpentry? People like you as a person— you'd get all kinds of work." (Malcolm X 1966:36)

Here we should recall Merton's distinction between the prejudiced discriminator and the unprejudiced discriminator. According to the definition advanced earlier, discrimination involves differential treatment of individuals because of their membership in a minority group. The term has traditionally referred to actions of people who arbitrarily deny equal treatment (for example, equal opportunity to obtain a job or to purchase a home) to minority group members because of their own personal prejudices. Such is the behavior of the prejudiced discriminator or all-weather bigot.

But discrimination can occur without the discriminator's necessarily harboring prejudices. As Merton points out, an unprejudiced discriminator—the fair-weather liberal—can discriminate simply by conforming to existing cultural patterns or by acquiescing to the dictates of others who are prejudiced. Such discrimination can be attributed to the actor's conscious or unconscious perception of the negative effects that nondiscriminatory behavior will have. An employer or a realtor may genuinely disclaim any personal prejudice for having refused a minority group member a job or home. Perhaps the person felt constrained by the negative sanctions of peers, or by the fear of alienating customers. In this case, the discriminatory actor's judgment would be based on the prejudicial attitudes of a powerful reference group. Although the heart and mind of the actors in our hypothetical situations may be devoid of any personal prejudice, nevertheless, the consequences—no job, no home—for the minority-group applicant are no different than if they were old-fashioned, dyed-in-the-wool bigots.

Attitudinal discrimination remains an important component of intergroup relations. One of the most prominent examples is the world of sports, which is perceived by most Americans to be devoid of racism. Although there have been substantial— even overwhelming—changes in the racial composition of sports teams during the past half century, the persistence of racial stacking (the placement of black and white players in certain positions, such as quarterback or wide receiver, in which they are stereotyped as best suited), the omission of African Americans from leadership and outcome-control positions, and the relative dearth of African Americans in second-team positions, indicate that discrimination is still a factor in player selection. The effects of attitudinal discrimination are even more pronounced at management levels: while African Americans are overrepresented in player roles, there is still a dearth of African-American executives, managers, and coaches (Yetman and Eitzen 1982; Jaynes and Williams 1989:95–98; Center for the Study of Sport in Society 1998).

Communication, including the mass media and everyday conversation, provides one of the most important means by which negative images and the powerlessness of minorities are (often unconsciously) perpetuated. Geneva Smitherman-Donaldson and Teun van Dijk contend that the process of communication and discourse "essentially reproduces and helps produce the racist cognitions and actions of and among the white majority" (1988:18). They use the term *symbolic racism* to refer to communications that preserve or justify racist acts and policies:

> *Even more than physical racism (or sexism for that matter), symbolic racism allows for subtlety, indirectness, and implication. It may, paradoxically, be expressed by the unsaid, or be conveyed by apparent "tolerance" and egalitarian liberalism. Whereas the racial slur, the graffiti, or the old movie may be blatantly racist, many other present-day types of talk may communicate racism in a more veiled way.*
>
> *In everyday talk, underlying ethnic prejudices may indirectly appear in "innocent" stories about a black neighbor, or about a Turkish immigrant worker cleaning the office. Although such stories claim to tell the "facts," describe how "they" did it (wrong) again, or generally imply that "they" are stupid, lazy, welfare-cheats, criminal, or lack motivation to learn, the storyteller may, at the same time, emphasize that he has nothing against "them," and they are his "best friends." Yet the stories, spreading quickly in families, schools, or neighborhoods, and occasionally greatly magnified by media reproduction, contribute to the fundamental communication and reproduction of racism in society. (Smitherman-Donaldson and van Dijk 1988:18)*

Symbolic racism is manifested in a variety of communication contexts. Popular magazines and children's literature have been among the most conspicuous purveyors of racial stereotypes. Although social scientists have pointed out the racially biased nature of these publications for decades, a 1965 study found that of 5,206 children's trade books published from 1962 through 1964, only 349, or 6.7 percent, included one or more blacks (Larrick 1965:63–65; Berelson and Salter 1946; Klineberg 1963; Teague 1968). Moreover, Tom Engelhardt (1971) has shown that the cultural stereotypes in American movies reinforce those found in other media forms. All positive, humanitarian virtues remain with whites: even if they represent the dregs of Western society, "any White is a step up from the rest of the world." Nonwhites, on the other hand, are depicted as alien intruders, helpless, dependent, or less than human. When they do assume center stage, they do so as villains—"the repository for evil." Hune (1977) has demonstrated how stereotypes of Asian Americans have been reinforced and legitimated by the omission, distortion, or misrepresentation of the role of racial and ethnic minorities in the nation's history books (see also Henry 1967 and Stampp et al. 1968). Hune argues the assumptions of leading intellectuals—social scientists and historians in particular—have influenced policies and practices toward both European and Asian immigrants. Therefore, whether undertaken consciously or unconsciously, intentionally or unintentionally, perpetuation of these symbolic biases serves to reflect and reinforce cultural beliefs in the racial inferiority of nonwhites.

Institutional Discrimination

Both forms of attitudinal discrimination just defined are ultimately reducible to psychological variables: the actor is prejudiced, defers to, or is influenced by the sanctions of a prejudiced reference group or the norms of a racially biased culture. Institutional discrimination, on the other hand, refers to organizational practices and societal trends that exclude minorities from equal opportunities for positions of power and prestige. This discrimination has been labeled "structural" by some scholars (*Research News* 1987:9). Institutional or structural discrimination involves "policies or practices which appear to be neutral in their effect on minority individuals or groups, but which have the effect of disproportionately impacting on them in harmful or negative ways" (Task Force on the Administration of Military Justice in the Armed Forces 1972:19). The effects or consequences of institutional discrimination have little relation to racial or ethnic attitudes or to the majority group's racial or ethnic prejudices.

The existence of institutional inequalities that effectively exclude substantial portions of minority groups from participation in the dominant society has seldom been considered under the category of discrimination. According to J. Milton Yinger, discrimination is "the persistent application of criteria that are arbitrary, irrelevant, or unfair by *dominant standards,* with the result that some persons receive an undue advantage and others, *although equally qualified,* suffer an unjustified penalty" (Yinger 1968:449, italics added). The underlying assumption of this definition is that if all majority-group members would eliminate "arbitrary, irrelevant, and unfair criteria," discrimination would, by definition, cease to exist. However, if all prejudice—and the attitudinal discrimination that emanates from it—were somehow miraculously eliminated overnight, the inequalities rooted in the normal and impersonal operation of existing institutional structures would remain. Therefore, the crucial issue is not the equal treatment of those with equal qualifications but rather is the access of minority-group members to the qualifications themselves.

Consider the following additional examples of institutional discrimination:

- An employer may be genuinely willing to hire individuals of all races but may rely solely on word-of-mouth recommendations to fill job vacancies. If Hispanics had previously been excluded from such employment, they would be unlikely to be members of a communications network that would allow them to learn about such vacancies.
- Jury selection is supposedly color-blind in most states, with jurors randomly selected from lists of registered voters. However, because they are more likely to be poor and geographically mobile (and thus ineligible to vote), blacks are less frequently selected as jurors. Similarly, a recent study found that, because a disproportionate number of black males are in prison or have been convicted of a felony, 14 percent of black men—nearly 1.5 million of a total voting age population of 10.4 million—are ineligible to vote, thus substantially diluting African American political power (Butterfield 1997).
- City commissions are often selected on either an at-large or a district basis. In at-large elections, all voters select from the same slate of candidates. By contrast, when elections are conducted on a district basis, the city is divided into geographically defined districts, and a resident votes only for candidates within his or her district. When an ethnic or a racial group constitutes a numerical minority of a city's population, its voting power is likely to be diluted and its representation in city government is likely to be lower than its proportion of the population under an at-large system of voting. Thus, under an at-large system, a city with a population that is 40 percent black could have no black representation on the city commission if voting followed racial lines. Because of patterns of residential seg-

regation, this situation would be much less likely in a system organized on a district basis.

- In Minnesota a judge ruled unconstitutional a law that punished possession of crack more severely than possession of comparable amounts of powdered cocaine. Testimony indicated that crack is used mainly by blacks, whereas whites are much more likely to use cocaine. Although there was general agreement that the Minnesota legislature had enacted the penalties for the two crimes without any intent of targeting a specific minority group, the judge contended that the absence of racial prejudice or negative intent in the law's enactment was less relevant in considering the constitutionality of the crack law than whether enactment affected blacks disproportionately and thus had the practical effect of discriminating against them. "There had better be a good reason for any law that has the practical effect of disproportionately punishing members of one racial group. If crack was significantly more deadly or harmful than cocaine that might be a good enough reason. But there just isn't enough evidence that they're different enough to justify the radical differences in penalties" (London 1991).

    The issue of racial disparities in sentencing for crack and powdered cocaine has become a hotly contested part of the national debate over mandatory federal sentences for drug offenses, where blacks were 90 percent of those convicted in Federal court crack offenses but only 30 percent of those convicted for cocaine. Studies show that the physiological and psychoactive effects of crack and powered cocaine are similar, and the independent U.S. Sentencing Commission recommended that Congress scrap laws that establish dramatically harsher sentences (by a ratio of 100 to 1) for possession of crack than for possession of cocaine. Nevertheless, in 1995 both the Clinton Administration and Congress refused to modify the disparate sentences given for possession of the two drugs, and in 1996 the Supreme Court rejected the argument that the dramatic racial differences in prosecution and penalties for crack possession reflected racial discrimination. However, the consequence of these decisions was to reinforce and maintain the dramatically disproportionate number of African Americans under the control of the criminal justice system (Morley 1995; Jones 1995; Greenhouse 1996; Wren 1996).

Institutional discrimination is central to two important recent interpretations of inequalities in American life that focus on opportunities in two institutions in American life—the economy and education. In a series of books—*The Declining Significance of Race* (1978a), *The Truly Disadvantaged* (1987), and *When Work Disappears* (1996), William Julius Wilson has identified several broad social structural factors that have dramatically transformed the economic opportunity structure for African Americans. He contends that the overall economic and social position of the inner-city poor has deteriorated in the past quarter century not only because of attitudinal discrimination but also because of impersonal structural economic changes—the shift from goods-producing to service-producing industries, increasing labor market segmentation, increased industrial technology, and the flight of industries from central cities—that have little to do with race. Earlier in the twentieth century, relatively uneducated and unskilled native and immigrant workers were able to find stable employment and income in manufacturing. Today, however, deindustrialization has created an economic "mismatch" between the available jobs and the qualifications of inner-city residents. On the one hand, manufacturing jobs, which in the past did not require highly technical skills, have either been mechanized or have moved from the inner cities to the suburbs, the sun belt, or overseas. Unskilled blacks in central cities are especially vulnerable to the relocation of high-paying manufacturing jobs. On the other hand, the jobs now being created in the cities demand highly technical credentials that most inner-city residents do not have. The economic opportunities of the African American urban poor, who lack the educational and occupational skills necessary for today's highly technological jobs, are therefore rapidly diminishing. The result is extremely high levels of unemployment.

These broad structural changes have triggered a process of "hyperghettoization" in which the urban poor are disproportionately concentrated and socially and economically isolated. As many stable working-class and middle-class residents with job qualifications have moved from inner-city neighborhoods, the stability of inner-city social institutions (churches, schools, newspapers, and recreational facilities) has been undermined, and the social fabric of neighborhoods and the community has deteriorated. As Wilson argues in Article 19 ("Work"), "A neighborhood in which people are poor but employed is different from a neighborhood in which people are poor and jobless."

Although the lack of educational and occupational skills among the African American urban poor reflects a historical legacy of attitudinal discrimination, institutional factors—the broad structural changes in the economy that were just mentioned—play a crucial role in sustaining black economic inequality. Even if all racial prejudice were eliminated, inner-city African Americans would still lack access to high-paying jobs that provide security and stability for both families and the black community (Wilson 1987; 1996).

Similar impersonal factors play a critical role in creating and sustaining dramatic racial disparities in educational opportunities. In his powerful book, *Savage Inequalities,* Jonathan Kozol (1991) has focused on the dramatic differences in the quality of public education in poor and in wealthy school districts in the United States and on the way in which these differences—these "savage inequalities"—affect educational opportunity. Focusing on the vast disparities in the quality of facilities, programs, and curricula that typically distinguish inner-city and suburban schools, Kozol contends that what is most glaringly apparent are the dramatic financial inequities among schools serving poor and affluent students, often in neighboring school districts; schools attended by poor students are invariably the most poorly funded, while those attended by students from affluent backgrounds have the highest per-pupil expenditures. Kozol reports that a study

> of 20 of the wealthiest and poorest districts of Long Island [New York], for example, matched by location and size of enrollment, found that the differences in per-pupil spending were not only large but had approximately doubled in a five-year period. Schools in Great Neck, in 1987, spent $11,265 for each pupil. In affluent Jericho and Manhasset the figures were, respectively, $11,325 and $11,370. In Oyster Bay the figure was $9,980. Compare this to Levittown, also on Long Island but a town of mostly working-class white families, where per-pupil spending dropped to $6,900. Then compare these numbers to the spending level in the town of Roosevelt, the poorest district in the county, where the schools are 99 percent non-white and where the fig-

ure dropped to $6,340. Finally, consider New York City, where in the same year, $5,590 was invested in each pupil—less than half of what was spent in Great Neck. The pattern is almost identical to that [in the Chicago and many other metropolitan areas] (Kozol 1991:120).

The principal source of these glaring financial inequities is the mechanism—local property taxes—that traditionally has been used to fund public schools. Reliance upon local property taxes to fund public schools, although perhaps initiated as public policy with no racial considerations in mind, has, given the history of racial residential segregation in American society, created dramatically different educational opportunities for white and for minority children. Recently these disparities have increased at precisely the same time that cities have undertaken extensive urban redevelopment programs; by offering tax abatements to businesses and corporations that locate in central city locations, the tax bases from which inner-city schools are funded lose an estimated $5 to $8 billion annually (Lewin 1997). Kozol contends that, because states require school attendance but allocate their resources inequitably, they "effectively require inequality. Compulsory inequity, perpetuated by state law, too frequently condemns our children to unequal lives" (Kozol 1991:56).

Similarly, in an analysis of school desegregation within and between American cities and their suburbs, David James (Article 21; 1989) has shown that the state, by creating political boundaries that separate school districts and by refusing to accept interdistrict desegregation, has been instrumental in creating school segregation, thereby reinforcing patterns of social inequality. Suburban rings surrounding major American cities tend to have multiple school districts, and black suburbanites tend to be concentrated in areas close to the central cities. Therefore, because the Supreme Court has ruled that racial segregation *within* school districts is unconstitutional but that segregation *between* districts is not, whites can avoid living in school districts with large proportions of black students. They are able to implement a form of attitudinal discrimination precisely because the structure of school districts (in many instances created without racial intent) provides such opportunities.

Institutional discrimination, although not intended to victimize racial groups directly, is thus more subtle, covert, complex, and less visible and blatant than attitudinal discrimination. Because it does not result from the motivations or intentions of specific individuals, but rather from policies that appear race-neutral, institutional discrimination is more impersonal than attitudinal discrimination, and its effects are more easily denied, ignored, overlooked, or dismissed as "natural," inevitable, or impossible to change. Nevertheless, institutional discrimination has the same discriminatory consequences for minority group members. In examining institutional discrimination, therefore, it is more important to consider the *effect* of a particular policy or practice on a minority group than it is to consider the *motivations* of the majority group.

ENDNOTES

1. Reflecting the dynamic, fluid, and socially defined nature of racial and ethnic categories, both the categories and the terms used to identify them frequently change. For example, over the last two hundred years, a variety of terms—colored, Negro, Afro-American, black—have been used to refer to Americans of African descent. Recently, many black leaders have urged adoption of the term *African American*. However, although that term has gained increasing acceptance among both black and white Americans, no

consensus on terminology has emerged. Therefore, we will use both *African American* and *black American* throughout this book. Similarly, there is no consensus today concerning the appropriate terminology for two other important racial and ethnic categories in the United States: American Indian, Native American, or Native peoples, on the one hand, or Hispanic or Latino, on the other. In each case we will use the terms interchangeably.

2. This situation of black numerical superiority and complete political exclusion was explicitly prohibited by the 14th Amendment of the Constitution, which includes a provision that required a reduction of Congressional representation for states that practiced such exclusion. "When the right to vote at any election for . . . President and Vice-President of the United States, Representatives in Congress, the executive and judicial officers of a State, or the members of the legislature thereof, is denied . . . or in any way abridged . . . , the basis of representation therein shall be reduced in the proportion which the number of such male citizens shall bear to the whole number of male citizens twenty-one years of age in such State" (*Constitution of the United States* 1996:520). Reflecting the *majority* power of whites in these two (and numerous other) states, this Constitutional provision was never implemented; no state's representation was ever thus reduced, despite the wholesale disfranchisement of African Americans for well over half a century.

ONE

Race, Caste, and Other Invidious Distinctions in Social Stratification

Gerald D. Berreman

A society is socially stratified when its members are divided into categories which are differentially powerful, esteemed, and rewarded. Such systems of collective social ranking vary widely in the ideologies which support them, in the distinctiveness, number and size of the ranked categories, in the criteria by which inclusion in the categories is conferred and changed, in the symbols by which such inclusion is displayed and recognized, in the degree to which there is consensus upon or even awareness of the ranking system, its rationale, and the particular ranks assigned, in the rigidity of rank, in the disparity in rewards of rank, and in the mechanisms employed to maintain or change the system.

For purposes of study, such systems have been analyzed variously depending upon the interests and motives of the analyst. One of the most frequently used bases for categorizing and comparing them has been whether people are accorded their statuses and privileges as a result of characteristics which are regarded as individually acquired, or as a result of characteristics which are regarded as innate and therefore shared by those of common birth. This dichotomy is often further simplified by application of the terms "achieved" versus "ascribed" status. Actually, what is meant is *non*-birth-ascribed status versus birth-ascribed status. The former is usually described as class stratification, referring to shared statuses identified by such features as income, education, and occupation, while the latter is frequently termed caste or racial stratification or, more recently, ethnic stratification, referring to statuses defined by shared ancestry or attributes of birth.

Regardless of its characteristics in a particular society, stratification has been described as being based upon three primary dimensions: class, status, and power, which are expressed respectively as wealth, prestige, and the ability to control the lives of people (oneself and others).[1] These dimensions can be brought readily to mind by thinking of the relative advantages and disadvantages which accrue in Western class systems to persons who occupy such occupational statuses as judge, garbage man, stenographer, airline pilot, factory worker, priest, farmer, agricultural laborer, physician, nurse, big businessman, beggar, etc. The distinction between class and birth-ascribed stratification can be made clear if one imagines . . . two Americans, for example, in each of the above-mentioned occupations, one of whom is white and one of whom is black. This quite literally changes the complexion of the matter. A similar contrast could be drawn if, in India, one were Brahmin and one untouchable; if in Japan one were Burakumin and one were not; if in Europe one were Jew and one were Gentile; or if, in almost any society, one were a man and one a woman. Obviously something significant has been added to the picture of stratification in these examples which is entirely missing in the first instance—something over which the individual generally has no control, which is determined at birth, which cannot be changed, which is shared by all those of like birth, which is crucial to social identity, and which vitally affects one's opportunities, rewards, and social roles. The new element is race (color), caste, ethnicity (religion, language, national origin), or sex. The differences in opportunities and behavior

Reprinted from *Race* (Volume XIII, no. 4, April 1972) by permission of the author and The Institute of Race Relations, London.

accorded people as a result of these criteria are described by such pejorative terms as racism, casteism, communalism (including especially ethnic and religious discrimination), and sexism. To be sure, the distinctions are manifest in class, status, and power, but they are of a different order than those considered in the first examples: they are distinctions independent of occupation, income, or other individually acquired characteristics. While the list includes a variety of criteria for birth-ascription and rank with somewhat different implications for those to whom they are applied, they share the crucial facts that: (1) the identity is regarded as being a consequence of birth or ancestry and hence immutable; (2) the identity confers upon its possessor a degree of societally defined and affirmed worth which is regarded as intrinsic to the individual; (3) this inherent worth is evaluated relative to that of all others in the society—those of different birth are inherently unequal and are accordingly adjudged superior or inferior, while those regarded as being of similar birth are innately equal. The crucial fact about birth-ascription for the individual and for society lies not so much in the source of status (birth), as in the fact that it cannot be repudiated, relinquished, or altered. Everyone is sentenced for life to a social cell shared by others of like birth, separated from and ranked relative to all other social cells. Despite cultural differences, therefore, birth-ascribed stratification has common characteristics of structure, function, and meaning, and has common consequences in the lives of those who experience it and in the social histories of the societies which harbor it.

The specific question motivating the present discussion is this: is social ranking by race absolutely distinctive, not significantly distinctive at all, or is race one criterion among others upon which significantly similar systems of social ranking may be based? While identifying the last of these as "correct" from my perspective, I shall insist that the answer depends entirely upon what one means by "race," and by "distinctive," and what one wishes to accomplish by the inquiry. No satisfactory answer can be expected without comparative, cross-cultural analysis encompassing a number of systems of social differentiation, social separation, and social ranking, based on a variety of criteria, embedded in a variety of cultural *milieux*, analyzed by reference to various models of

social organization, and tested against accounts of actual social experience. The attempt to do this leads to a number of issues central and tangential to the study of stratification and race, some of which have been overlooked or given short shrift in the scholarly literature, while others are well discussed in particular disciplinary, regional, or historical specialties without necessarily being familiar to students of other academic domains to whose work and thought they are nevertheless relevant.

There is not space here to present ethnographic and historical documentation for particular instances of birth-ascribed stratification. I have done so briefly in another paper, citing five societies on which there is fortunately excellent published material vividly exemplifying the kinds of social system I refer to in this paper, and their implications for those who comprise them: Rwanda, India, Swat, Japan, and the United States. I recommend those accounts to the reader.[2]

MODELS FOR ANALYSIS

In the course of scholarly debate concerning the nature and comparability of systems of collective social ranking, a number of models and concepts have been suggested, implied, or utilized. A framework can be provided for the present discussion by identifying some of these and analyzing whether and to what extent each is relevant and applicable to all or some systems of birth-ascribed social separation and inequality, with special attention to the five societies cited above.

Stratification

By definition, stratification is a common feature of systems of shared social inequality—of ranked social categories—whether birth-ascribed or not. Where membership in those categories is birth-ascribed, the ranking is based on traditional definitions of innate social equivalence and difference linked to a concept of differential intrinsic worth, rationalized by a myth of the origin, effect, and legitimacy of the system, perpetuated by differential power wielded by the high and the low, expressed in differential behaviors required and differential rewards accorded them, and experienced by them as differential access to goods, services, livelihood, respect, self-determination, peace of mind, pleasure, and other valued things including nourishment, shelter, health, independence, justice, security, and long life.

Louis Dumont, in *Homo Hierarchicus,* maintains that the entire sociological notion of stratification is misleading when applied to South Asia, for it is of European origin, alien and inapplicable to India. He holds that the term implies an equalitarian ideology wherein hierarchy is resented or denied, and that it therefore obscures the true nature of India's hierarchical society, based as it is on religious and ideological premises peculiar to Hinduism which justify it and result in its endorsement by all segments of Indian society. Stratification, he maintains, is thus a "sociocentric" concept which cannot cope with the unique phenomenon of Indian caste.[3] My response to this is twofold; first, the caste hierarchy based on the purity-pollution opposition, as Dumont insists, is well within any reasonable definition of stratification, for the latter refers to social structure and social relations rather than to their ideological bases; and second, Dumont's description of the functioning of, and ideological basis for, the caste hierarchy is idealized and similar to the one commonly purveyed by high caste beneficiaries of the system. Few low caste people would recognize it or endorse it. Yet their beliefs and understandings are as relevant as those of their social superiors to an understanding of the system. The low caste people with whom I have worked would find Dumont's characterization of "stratification" closer to their experience than his characterization of "hierarchy."[4]

Use of the stratification model focuses attention upon the ranking of two or more categories of people within a society, and upon the criteria and consequences of that ranking. Often, but not inevitably, those who use this concept place primary emphasis upon shared values and consensus, rather than power and conflict, as the bases for social ranking and its persistence. This emphasis is misleading, at best, when applied to systems of birth-ascribed ranking, as I shall show. It is obvious, however, that while many systems of stratification are not birth-ascribed, all systems of social stratification, and any theory of social stratification must encompass them.

Ethnic Stratification

Probably the most recent, neutral, and non-specific term for ascriptive ranking is "ethnic stratification." "An ethnic group consists of people who conceive of themselves as being alike by virtue of common ancestry, real or fictitious, and are so regarded by others,"[5] or it comprises "a distinct category of the population in a larger society whose culture is usually different from its own [and whose] members . . . are, or feel themselves, or are thought to be, bound together by common ties of race or nationality or culture."[6] Undoubtedly the systems under discussion fit these criteria. Use of the adjective "ethnic" to modify "stratification" places emphasis upon the mode of recruitment, encompassing a wide variety of bases for ascription, all of which are determined at birth and derive from putative common genetic make-up, common ancestry, or common early socialization and are therefore regarded as immutable. This commonality is held responsible for such characteristics as shared appearance, intelligence, personality, morality, capability, purity, honor, custom, speech, religion, and so forth. Usually it is held responsible for several of these. The ranked evaluation of these characteristics, together with the belief that they occur differentially from group to group and more or less uniformly within each group serves as the basis for ranking ethnic groups relative to one another.

Van den Berghe has held that "ethnic" should be distinguished from "race" or "caste" in that the former implies real, important, and often valued social and cultural differences (language, values, social organization), while the latter are artificial and invidious distinctions reflecting irrelevant (and sometimes non-existent) differences in physiognomy, or artificial differences in social role.[7] This is a useful point. In the recent sociological literature, however, "ethnic" has increasingly been used to refer to *all* social distinctions based on birth or ancestry, be they associated with race, language, or anything else. This is the usage adopted here. Moreover, as I shall elaborate in discussing pluralism below, race and caste entail the kinds of cultural distinctions cited by van den Berghe as diagnostic of ethnic diversity, for the social separation implied by those systems ensures social and cultural diversity. For example, van den Berghe's assertion that "nonwithstanding all the African mystique, Afro-Americans are in fact culturally Anglo-American,"[8] has been countered by ample evidence that the African origin, social separation, and collective oppression of blacks in

America *has* resulted in an identifiable Afro-American culture.[9]

All systems of ethnic stratification are thus based on ancestry, approximating a theory of birth-ascription, and if the definitions set forth by advocates of this term are accepted, most systems of birth-ascribed stratification can properly be designated ethnic stratification. Perhaps the only recurrent exception is sexual stratification, wherein inherent, birth-ascribed, and biologically determined characteristics which are *independent* of ancestry are the basis for institutionalized inequality. This instance, exceptional in several respects, will be discussed separately below, and hence will not be alluded to repeatedly in intervening discussions although most of what is said applies to it also.

Caste

A widely applied and frequently contested model for systems of birth-ascribed rank is that of "caste," deriving from the example of Hindu India where the *jati* (almost literally, "common ancestry") is the type-case. *Jati* in India refers to interdependent, hierarchically ranked, birth-ascribed groups. The ranking is manifest in public esteem accorded the members of the various groups, in the rewards available to them, in the power they wield, and in the nature and mode of their interaction with others. *Jatis* are regionally specific and culturally distinct, each is usually associated with a traditional occupation and they are usually (but not always) endogamous. They are grouped into more inclusive, pan-Indian ranked categories called *varna* which are frequently confused with the constituent *jatis* by those using the term "caste." The rationale which justifies the system is both religious and philosophical, relying upon the idea of ritual purity and pollution to explain group rank, and upon the notions of right conduct *(dharma)*, just deserts *(karma)*, and rebirth to explain the individual's fate within the system. As an explanation of caste inequalities this rationale is advocated by those whom the system benefits, but is widely doubted, differently interpreted, or regarded as inappropriately applied by those whom the system oppresses.

Many students of stratification believe that the term "caste" conveys an impression of consensus and tranquility that it does not obtain in systems of rigid social stratification outside of India. That notion, however, is no more applicable to, or derivable from Indian caste than any other instance of birth-ascribed stratification.[10]

If one concedes that caste can be defined cross-culturally (i.e., beyond Hindu India), then the systems under discussion here are describable as caste systems. That is, if one agrees that a caste system is one in which a society is made up of birth-ascribed groups which are hierarchically ordered, interdependent, and culturally distinct, and wherein the hierarchy entails differential evaluation, rewards, and association, then whether one uses the term "caste," or prefers "ethnic stratification," or some other term is simply a matter of lexical preference. If one requires of a caste system that it be based on consensus as to its rationale, its legitimacy, and the legitimacy of the relative rank of its constituent groups, then none of the examples mentioned here is a caste system. If one requires social tranquillity as a characteristic, then too, none of these is a caste system. If one allows that a caste system is held together by power and the ability of people within it to predict fairly accurately one another's behavior while disagreeing on almost anything or everything else, then all of these systems will qualify. If one requires a specifically Hindu rationale of purity and pollution and/or endogamy and/or strict and universal occupational specialization, then one restricts caste to India and to only certain regions and groups within India at that. If one requires for castes, as some do, a tightly organized corporate structure, then too one would exclude even in India some *jatis* and other groups commonly called "castes." (This, however, does seem to me to be the structural criterion which comes closest to differentiating Indian *jati* from other systems of birth-ascribed stratification, such as that of the United States. Corporateness evidently emerges as a response to oppression and as a mechanism for emancipation even where it has been previously minimal, e.g., in Japan, Rwanda, and the United States. Thus, the corporateness of Indian *jatis* may represent a late stage of development in caste systems rather than a fundamental difference in the Indian system.)

Jati in Hindu India and the equivalent but non-Hindu *quom* organization in Swat and Muslim India are each unique; yet both share the criteria by which I have defined caste, as do the tri-partite system of Rwanda and the essentially dual systems of Japan and the United States, and all share in addition (and in consequence, I believe) a wide variety of social and personal concomitants. Caste is a useful and widely used term because it is concise, well-known, and in fact (as contrasted to fantasy), the structural, functional, and existential analogy to Indian caste is valid for many other systems.

Race. Systems of "racial" stratification are those in which birth-ascribed status is associated with alleged physical differences among social categories, which are culturally defined as present and important. Often these differences are more imagined than real, sometimes they are entirely fictional and always a few physical traits are singled out for attention while most, including some which might differently divide the society if they were attended to, are ignored. Yet systems so described share the principle that ranking is based on putatively inborn, ancestrally derived, and significant physical characteristics.

Those who use this model for analysis generally base it upon the negative importance attached by Europeans to the darker skin color of those they have colonized, exterminated, or enslaved. A good many have argued that racially stratified societies are *sui generis;* that they are unique and hence not comparable to societies stratified on any other basis.[11] There is often a mystical quality to these arguments, as though race were an exalted, uniquely "real," valid, and important criterion for birth ascription, rendering it incomparable to other criteria. An element of inadvertent racism has in such instances infected the very study of race and stratification. In fact, as is by now widely recognized, there is no society in the world which ranks people on the basis of biological race, i.e., on the basis of anything a competent geneticist would call "race," which means on the basis of distinctive shared genetic makeup derived from a common gene pool. "Race," as a basis for social rank is always a *socially* defined phenomenon which at most only very imperfectly corresponds to genetically transmitted traits and then, of course, only to phenotypes rather than genotypes. Racists regard and treat people as alike or different because of their group membership defined in terms of socially significant ancestry, not because of their genetic makeup. It could not be otherwise, for people are rarely geneticists, yet they are frequently racists.

To state this point would seem to be superfluous if it were not for the fact that it is continually

ignored or contested by some influential scholars and politicians as well as the lay racists who abound in many societies. To cite but one well known recent example, Arthur Jensen, in his article on intelligence and scholastic achievement, maintains that there is a genetic difference in learning ability between blacks and whites in the United States.[12] Nowhere, however, does he offer evidence of how or to what extent his "Negro" and "White" populations are genetically distinct. All of those, and only those, defined in the conventional wisdom of American folk culture to be "Negro" are included by Jensen, regardless of their genetic makeup in the category whose members he claims are biologically handicapped in learning ability. Thus, large numbers of people are tabulated as "Negroes," a majority of whose ancestors were "white," and virtually all of Jensen's "Negroes" have significant but highly variable percentages of "white" ancestry. Although, also as a result of social definition, the "whites" do not have known "Negro" ancestry, the presumed genetic homogeneity of the "whites" is as undemonstrated and unexplored as that of the "Negroes." In short, there was no attempt to identify the genetic makeup or homogeneity of either group, the genetic distinctiveness of the two groups, or whether or how genetic makeup is associated with learning ability, or how learning ability is transmitted. This kind of reasoning is familiar and expectable in American racism, but not in a supposedly scientific treatise —a treatise whose author berates those who deplore his pseudo-science as themselves unscientific for failing to seriously consider his "evidence." The fallacy in Jensen's case is that he has selected for investigation two socially defined groupings in American society which are commonly regarded as innately different in social worth and which as a result are accorded widely and crucially divergent opportunities and life experiences. Upon finding that they perform differentially in the context of school and test performance, he attributes that fact to assumed but undemonstrated and uninvestigated biological differences. Thus, socially defined populations perform differently on socially defined tasks with socially acquired skills, and this is attributed by Jensen to biology. There are other defects in Jensen's research, but none more fundamental than this.[13] One is reminded of E. A. Ross's succinct assessment of over fifty years ago, that " 'race' is the cheap explanation tyros offer for any collective trait that they are too stupid or too lazy to trace to its origin in the physical environment, the social environment, or historical conditions."[14]

The point to be made here is that systems of "racial" stratification are social phenomena based on social rather than biological facts. To be sure, certain conspicuous characteristics which are genetically determined or influenced (skin color, hair form, facial conformation, stature, etc.) are widely used as convenient indicators by which ancestry and hence "racial" identity is recognized. This is the "color bar" which exists in many societies. But such indicators are never sufficient in themselves to indicate group membership and in some instances are wholly unreliable, for it is percentage rather than appearance or genetics which is the basis for these distinctions. One who does not display the overt characteristics of his "racial" group is still accorded its status if his relationship to the group is known or can be discovered. The specific rules for ascertaining racial identity differ from society to society. In America, if a person is known to have had a sociologically black ancestor, he is black regardless of how many of his ancestors were sociologically white (and even though he looks and acts white). In South Africa, most American blacks would be regarded as "colored" rather than "black." Traditionally, in a mixed marriage, one is a Jew only if ones mother is a Jew. In contemporary India, an Anglo-Indian has a male European ancestor in the paternal line; female and maternal European ancestry are irrelevant. In racially stratified societies, phenotypical traits are thus never more than clues to a person's social identity.

As Shibutani and Kwan have noted, "a color line is something existing in the presuppositions of men."[15] ". . . What is decisive about 'race relations' is not that people are genetically different but that they approach one another with dissimilar perspectives."[16] Van den Berghe makes a similar point: "Race, of course, has no intrinsic significance, except to a racist. To a social scientist, race acquires meaning only through its social definition in a given society."[17]

This is illustrated by the title of DeVos and Wagatsuma's book, *Japan's Invisible Race*, dealing with the hereditarily stigmatized and oppressed Burakumin. The Japanese believe that these people are physically and morally distinct, and their

segregation and oppression are explained on that basis when in fact they are not so at all. Instead they are recognizable only by family (ancestry), name, occupation, place of residence, life style, etc. The Burakumin thus comprise a "race" in the sociological sense of Western racism, but an "invisible" (i.e., not genetic or phenotypic) one. The authors subtitled the book, *Caste in Culture and Personality,* shifting the analogy from that of race (in the West) to that of caste (in India). The book could as well have been entitled: *Caste in Japan: Racial Stratification in Culture and Personality.*

The Japanese example brings up a point which needs to be made about the alleged uniqueness of "racial" stratification. *All* systems of birth-ascribed stratification seem to include a belief that the social distinctions are reflected in biological (i.e., "racial") differences. That is, caste and other ethnic differences are said to be revealed in physical makeup or appearance. Associated with these supposed natural and unalterable inherited physical characteristics are equally immutable traits of character, morality, intelligence, personality, and purity. This is the case in Japan, where no actual physical differences can be detected; it is true in India and Swat where physical stereotypes about castes abound but actual differences are minimal; it is true in Rwanda where the ranked groups are all black but are said to differ in stature and physiognomy as well as in culture; it is true in the United States where the physical differences are commonly and erroneously thought to be absolute. Cultural factors have to be relied upon in addition to whatever biological ones may be present, in order to make the important discriminations upon which ranked social interaction depends, and even then mistakes are frequently made. Throughout the world, people who look distinctive are likely to be regarded as socially different; people who are regarded as socially different are likely to be thought to look distinctive. They are also likely to be required to dress and act distinctively.

I suggest that, just as societies frequently dramatize the social differences among kin groups (e.g., sibs, clans, phratries) by giving to them totemic names and attributing to them characteristics of animals or plants, thereby identifying the social differences with biological species differences,[18] so also, societies with birth-ascribed status hierarchies dramatize and legitimize these crucial social differences by attributing to them innate biological, hence "racial," differences. As a result the concept of miscegenation arises, based on an ideology of innate difference contradicted by a persistent and recurrent perception of similarity by people of opposite sex across social boundaries.[19]

Thus, caste organization and ethnic stratification include racism; racial stratification is congruent with caste and ethnic stratification. Their ultimate coalescence is in the imputation of biological differences to explain and justify birth-ascribed social inequality. In this regard, sexual stratification can be seen to be a phenomenon of the same order.

This universality of racism in birth-ascribed stratification can be understood in the fact that physical traits not only dramatize social differentiation, but can also explain and justify it. The effect of such explanation is to make social inequality appear to be a natural necessity rather than a human choice and hence an artificial imposition. Social distinctions are man-made and learned; what man makes and learns he can unmake and unlearn. What God or biology has ordained is beyond man's control. The former may be defined as artificial, unjust, untenable, and remediable; the latter as inevitable or divinely sanctioned. This is important because birth-ascribed stratification is widely or universally resented by those whom it oppresses (at least as it affects them), and advocated by those it rewards. Both categories share the human capability of empathy, and it inspires envy and resentment in the one and fear or guilt in the other. Racism—the self-righteous rationalization in terms of biology—is a desperate and perhaps ultimately futile attempt to counteract those subversive emotions.

In sum, "race," as commonly used by social scientists, emphasizes common physical characteristics (as does "sex"); "caste" emphasizes common rank, occupational specialization, endogamy, and corporate organization; "ethnic stratification" emphasizes cultural distinctiveness. These are real differences in meaning, but the degree of empirical overlap in systems so described, and the commonalities in the existential worlds of those who live within them are so great as to render the distinctions among them largely arbitrary, and irrelevant, for many purposes. Individual cases differ, but as types of social stratification, they are similar. With equal facility and comparable effect, they utilize as evidence of social identity anything

which is passed on with the group: skin color, hair form, stature, physiognomy, language, dress, occupation, place of residence, genealogy, behavior patterns, religion. None is wholly reliable, all are difficult to dissimulate. In any case, strong sanctions can be brought to bear to minimize the temptation to "pass" among those who might be capable and tempted. As the case of India suggests and Japan confirms, social criteria can be as rigid as physical ones.

"Race" versus "Caste"

Considerable controversy has surrounded the terms "race" and "caste" when applied outside of the contexts in which they originated and to which they have been most widely applied: Western colonialism and Hindu India, respectively. This is understandable because there are important peculiarities in each of these situations, and to extend the terms beyond them requires that those peculiarities be subordinated to significant similarities. Systems of birth-ascribed inequality are sufficiently similar, however, to invite comparative study, and some general term is needed to refer to them. "Caste" has seemed to me more useful than "race," because it refers to social rather than allegedly biological distinctions, and it is the social distinctions which are universal in such systems. If it were a catchier term, "ethnic stratification" might replace both in the social scientific literature. Unfortunately it is not, so we must probably await a better term or tolerate continuing terminological dispute and confusion. In any case, it is the nature of birth-ascribed stratification—the ideas, behaviors, and experiences which comprise it, the effects it has on persons and societies and, quite frankly, the means by which it may be eliminated—in which I am interested. The words applied to it are of little importance. When I try to explain American race relations to Indians, I describe and analyze America as a caste stratified society, with attention to the similarities and differences in comparison with India. If I am trying to explain Indian caste stratification to Americans, I describe and analyze India as a racist society, with attention to the similarities and differences in comparison to the United States. I do this as a matter of translation from the social idiom of one society to the other. It is the most economic, vivid, and accurate way I know to convey these phenomena to people whose experience is limited to one system or the other. I do not think Indian caste *is* American race, or vice versa, but neither do I think that race stratification in America *is* race stratification in South Africa or that caste in India *is* caste in Swat, or that caste in the Punjab *is* caste in Kerala. Neither do I think racial stratification and racism are the same for blacks, Chicanos, and whites in America, or that caste stratification and casteism are the same for sweepers, blacksmiths, and Rajputs in Hindu India. There are features in all of these which are the same in important ways, and by focusing on these I think we can understand and explain and predict the experience of people in these diverse situations better than if we regard each of them as unique in every way.

Colonialism

The concept of colonialism has gained popularity in recent years for the analysis of racism and racial stratification in the West.[20] It therefore merits further discussion. This model focuses on the history of Western expansion and the exploitation of alien peoples, emphasizing notions of the superiority of the dominant, Western, white society whose members arrogated privilege to themselves through the exercise of power (usually technological, often military) to dominate, control, exploit, and oppress others. Racism has been an integral aspect of this process, for there usually have been differences in color between the colonizer and the colonized which were used to account for the alleged inferiority in ability, character, and mentality which in turn were used to justify colonial domination. Colonialism has been most often described as the result of overseas conquest, in which case the colonizing group has usually comprised a numerical minority. Less often colonialism has included conquest or expansion across national boundaries overland, but the results are the same, if the romance is less. These phenomena have recently come to be termed "external colonialism," in contrast to "internal colonialism," which refers to similar domination and exploitation, within a nation, of an indigenous, over-run, or imported minority. This distinction directs attention to the *locus* of colonial domination whereas the distinction between third-world and fourth-world colonies, cited above, directs attention to the *sources* of that domination.

While it has not been much easier to gain acceptance of the colonial model for analysis of American race relations than it has been to gain acceptance of the caste model, it is clear that here again, the problem is semantic rather than substantive. Some of those who argue persuasively the cross-cultural and multi-situational applicability of the colonial model deny such applicability for the caste model and in so doing use precisely the logic and data they deplore and regard as faulty when their intellectual adversaries deny applicability of "colonialism" outside of the classical overseas context.[21]

Colonialism, external and internal, is a process which has occurred repeatedly, in many contexts with many specific manifestations and many common results. It long antedates the recent period of European and American expansion. Caste stratification, racial stratification, ethnic stratification, and "pluralism" have been its recurrent products.[22] The point can be made with specific reference to caste in India. Rather than regarding colonialism as an antecedent condition which excludes traditional India from the category of racially or ethnically stratified societies, it can well be used as a basis for assigning India historical priority among such societies, in the contemporary world. That is, traditional India may represent the most fully evolved and complex post-colonial society in the world. It is easy to obtain explanations of caste from informants or books in India which refer directly to the presumed early domination of primitive indigenes by advanced invaders. There is little doubt that the present caste system had its origins some 3,000 to 3,500 years ago in a sociocultural confrontation that was essentially colonial. Low status was imposed on technologically disadvantaged indigenes by more sophisticated, militarily and administratively superior peoples who encroached or invaded from the north and west, arrogating to themselves high rank, privileges, and land. The large number of local and ethnically distinct groups on the subcontinent were fitted into a scheme of social hierarchy which was brought in or superimposed by the high status outsiders, culminating in the caste system we know today.[23] Social separation and social hierarchy based on ancestry became the essence of the system; colonial relations were its genesis. Even today, most tribal people—those who are geographically and economically marginal and culturally distinct—are incorporated into Hindu society, if at all, at the bottom of the hierarchy (except in those rare instances where they have maintained control over land or other important sources of income and power).

If one were to speculate on the course of evolution which ethnic stratification might take in the United States in the context of internal colonialism, of rigid separation, hierarchy, and discrimination which are part of it, and the demands for ethnic autonomy which arise in response to it, one possibility would be a caste system similar to, though less complex than that of India. The historical circumstances may be rather similar despite the separation of many hundreds of years, many thousands of miles and a chasm of cultural differences. Actually, development of the degree of social separation common in India seems at this point unlikely given the mass communications and mass education in the United States, its relative prosperity, and the rather widespread (but far from universal) commitment to at least the trappings of social equality. But surely if anything is to be learned from history and from comparison, the case of the Indian subcontinent should be of major interest to students of American race and ethnic relations, social stratification, and internal colonialism.

In sum, colonialism is as inextricable from caste and race as caste and race are from one another. There may be instances of colonialism where birth-ascription is or becomes irrelevant, but every instance of caste, race, and ethnic stratification includes, and relies for its perpetuation upon, the kind of ethnic domination and exploitation that defines colonialism.

Class

Closely associated with each of the models discussed here is that of social class. Class is a matter of acquired status rather than of birth-ascription, and is in this respect distinct from race, caste, and ethnic stratification, with different social consequences. In a class system, one is ranked in accord with his behavior and attributes (income, occupation, education, life style, etc.). In a birth-ascribed system, by contrast, one behaves and exhibits attributes in accord with his rank. In a class system, individual mobility is legitimate, albeit often difficult, while in ascribed stratification it is explicitly forbidden. Systems of acquired rank—class systems—prescribe the means to social mobility; systems of ascribed rank proscribe them. As

a consequence, a class system is a continuum; there are individuals who are intergrades, there are individuals in the process of movement, there are individuals who have experienced more than one rank. Miscegenation is not an issue because there are no ancestrally distinct groups to be inappropriately mixed. A birth-ascribed system is comprised of discrete ranks on the pattern of echelon organization, without legitimate mobility, without intergrades; the strata are named, publicly recognized, clearly bounded. Miscegenation is therefore a social issue. In a system of acquired ranks, the strata may be indistinct, imperfectly known, or even unknown to those within the system. In fact, there is considerable debate among students of stratification as to whether or not awareness of class is essential to a definition of class. Some hold that social classes are properly defined by analysts who use such criteria as income to designate categories which may be entirely unrecognized by those in the society.

In a class system individuals regard themselves as potentially able to change status legitimately within the system through fortune, misfortune, or individual and family efforts. In a birth-ascribed system, individuals know that legitimate status change is impossible—that only dissimulation, revolution, or an improbable change in publicly accorded social identity can alter one's rank and hence life-chances.

Despite these differences, class is in no way incompatible with birth-ascribed systems. In fact, in so far as it is a term of categories of people ranked by income, occupation, education, and life style, it co-occurs with them. Low castes, despised races, ethnic minorities, and colonized people comprise economically and occupationally depressed, exploited classes who are politically and socially oppressed; high castes, exalted races, privileged ethnic groups, and colonizers comprise economically and occupationally privileged, power-wielding, elite classes who live off the labor of others. In this respect, class differences pervade and reinforce systems of birth-ascribed stratification. Furthermore, it is not unusual to find significant class differentials within a caste, racial, or ethnic group or within a colonized or colonial group.[24] That is, class, in the conventional sense, often occurs conspicuously within such groups, and may also bridge their boundaries without obscuring them. But it is not possible to

analyze birth-ascribed stratification solely in terms
of class, for no amount of class mobility will exempt a person from the crucial implications of his
birth in such systems.

Those who have sought to identify the positions of European immigrants to America such as
the Poles, Italians, and Irish, with the position of
blacks, Native Americans, Chicanos, and Asians
have failed to discern the essential fact that racism
is the basis of American caste, and that it be-
stows upon those who experience it a unique social, political, and economic stigma which is not
bestowed by class or national origin. Second generation white Europeans can meet all of the criteria for acceptance into the American white
race-caste, for they are regarded as being only culturally different. A fifteenth generation American
black, or a fifteen-hundredth generation American
Indian cannot, for their differences are regarded
as innate, immutable, and crucial. Equalitarianism
has produced no "American dilemma" among
racists, as Myrdal believed, simply because it is an
equality for whites only, and its extension to other
groups has moved slowly, painfully, and with ve-
hement opposition, even where it has moved at all.

Systems of collective social rank, whether ascribed or acquired, are systems for retaining privilege among the powerful and power among the
privileged, reserving and maintaining vulnerability, oppression, and want for those upon whom it
can be imposed with minimal risk while retaining
their services and their deference. In this way they
are similar. In the principles of recruitment and
organization by which that similarity is effected
and in the individuals' prospects for mobility they
differ, and those differences have important consequences for individual life experience and social
processes in the societies which harbor them.

Pluralism
Pluralism is a model which has been applied to socially and culturally diverse societies since the
writings of Furnivall on South-East Asia.[25] Cultural pluralism obtains when "two or more different cultural traditions characterize the population
of a given society"; it is "a special form of differentiation based on institutional divergences."[26] Systems of birth-ascribed stratification are inevitably
systems of social and cultural pluralism because
they are accompanied by social separation. In a
caste system, "Because intensive and status-equal

interaction is limited to the caste, a common and
distinctive caste culture is assured. This is a function of the quality and density of communication
within the group, for culture is learned, shared
and transmitted."[27] The same is true for any system of racial or ethnic stratification. M.G. Smith
has noted, "It is perfectly clear that in any social
system based on intense cleavages and discontinuity between differentiated segments the community of values or social relations between these
sections will be correspondingly low. This is precisely the structural condition of the plural society."[28] And I have noted elsewhere that

> . . . castes are discrete social and cultural entities. . . .
> They are maintained by defining and maintaining
> boundaries between castes; they are threatened when
> boundaries are compromised. Even when interaction
> between castes is maximal and cultural differences are
> minimal, the ideal of mutual isolation and distinctive-
> ness is maintained and advertised among those who
> value the system. Similarly, even when mobility within,
> or subversion of the system is rampant, a myth of sta-
> bility is stolidly maintained among those who benefit
> from the system.[29]

Mutual isolation of social groups inevitably leads
to group-specific institutions (an important criterion for pluralism according to Furnivall), because members are excluded from participation
in the institutions of other groups.

Caste, race, and ethnic stratification, like all
plural systems, therefore, are systems of social
separation and cultural heterogeneity, maintained
by common or over-riding economic and political
institutions rather than by agreement or consensus regarding the stratification system and its rationale.[30] This does not deny consensus, it only
defines its nature:

> In caste systems, as in all plural systems, highly differ-
> entiated groups get along together despite widely differing
> subjective definitions of the situation because they agree
> on the objective facts of what is happening and what is
> likely to happen—on who has the power, and how,
> under what circumstances, and for what purposes it is
> likely to be exercised. They cease to get along when this
> crucial agreement changes or is challenged.[31]

The constituent social elements of plural societies need not be birth-ascribed, and they need not
be (and sometimes are not) ranked relative to one
another, although by Furnivall's definition, one element must be dominant. In fact, unranked plu-

ralism is the goal many ethnic minorities choose over either stratification or assimilation. But a system of birth-ascribed stratification is always culturally, socially, and hence institutionally heterogeneous, and thus pluralistic.

Hierarchy as Symbolic Interaction

I have elsewhere described the universality among social hierarchies of patterns of interaction which symbolize superiority and inferiority.[32] Social hierarchy, after all, exists only in the experiences, behaviors, and beliefs of those who comprise it. Interpersonal interaction becomes the vehicle for expression of hierarchy: for asserting, testing, validating or rejecting claims to status. Almost every interaction between members of ranked groups expresses rank claimed, perceived, or accorded. When the hierarchy is birth-ascribed, the membership of its component groups is ideally stable, well-known, and easily recognizable. In such systems people are perceived by those outside of their groups almost wholly in terms of their group identity rather than as individuals. They are regarded as sharing the characteristics which are conventionally attributed to the group and they share the obligations, responsibilities, privileges, and disabilities of their group. In intergroup relations, therefore, one individual is substitutable for another in his group, for all are alike and interchangeable. This is the setting for prejudice, discrimination, bigotry, chauvinism, and is an ideal situation for scapegoating. These attitudes and their behavioral consequences are designated and deplored by such terms as racism, casteism, communalism (referring to ethnic chauvinism of various sorts), and recently, sexism. They are characterized by domination, deprivation, oppression, exploitation, and denigration directed downward; obedience, acquiescence, service, deference, and honor demanded from above. They result in envy, resentment, dissimulation, and resistance arising from below, balanced from above by fear, guilt, and that combination of arrogant self-righteousness and rationalization which is found in all such systems. Maya Angelou has aptly characterized the result in American race relations as "the humorless puzzle of inequality and hate; the question of worth and values, of aggressive inferiority and aggressive arrogance"[33] which confronts and exacts its toll not only from black Americans, but from the denizens of all those jungles of inherited inequality I call caste systems. It is this quality of

interpersonal relations rather than any particular event or structural feature which struck me most vividly, forcefully, and surprisingly as similar in Alabama and India when I first experienced them for over a year each within a period of five years.[34] For me, this is the hallmark of oppressive, birth-ascribed stratification.

A specifically interactional definition of caste systems applies equally to all systems of birth-ascribed stratification: *"a system of birth-ascribed groups each of which comprises for its members the maximum limit of status-equal interaction, and between all of which interaction is consistently hierarchical."*[35] The cultural symbols of hierarchical interaction vary; the presence and importance of such symbols is universal and essential to racism, casteism, and their homologs.

Hierarchy as Ideology

Dumont has emphasized the point that Indian caste is unique in that it is based on an ideology of hierarchy defined in terms of ritual purity and pollution.[36] He regards other systems of hierarchical social separation as non-comparable because of the inevitable differences in the ideologies supporting them. In the comparative framework which I advocate, I maintain simply that the Hindu rationale is one of several ideologies (cf. those of Islamic Swat, of the South Indian Lingayats to whom purity is irrelevant, of Rwanda, of Japan, and the United States) which can and do underlie and justify systems of birth-ascribed social hierarchy. Each is unique to the culture in which it occurs; each is associated with remarkably similar social structures, social processes, and individual experiences. I believe that anyone who has experienced daily life in rural India and the rural American South, for example, will confirm the fact that there is something remarkably similar in the systems of social relations and attitudes. I believe that anyone who has experienced daily life in an urban slum, a public market, or a factory in India and the United States would come to the same conclusion. That similarity is generated by birth-ascribed stratification and it is not concealed by differential ideologies.[37]

Contrary to another of Dumont's assumptions (shared with Cox), there is nothing incompatible between an ideology which underwrites a hierarchy of groups and a notion of equality within each group. This combination, in fact, is found not only in the United States where it accounts for the above-mentioned absence of a real "American dilemma" in race relations, but also in each of the other systems described here. Members of each ranked group are *inherently unequal* to those of each other group and are by birth *potentially equal* to those of their own group. More importantly, the existence of an ideology of hierarchy does not mean that this ideology is conceived and interpreted identically by all within the system it is presumed to justify or even that it is shared by them. Acquiescence must not be mistaken for concurrence. Dumont's assumption to the contrary is the most glaring weakness in his analysis of Indian caste.[38]

Sexual Stratification

Finally, in my discussion of models for analysis, I turn to the controversial and sociologically puzzling matter of sex as a basis for social separation and inequality. The special problems which the sexual criterion poses for the student of stratification are both academic and substantive. The academic problems derive from the history of the study of stratification. Although the role of women in various non-Western societies has been discussed by anthropologists (including prominently Margaret Mead), and the position of women in European societies has been discussed by some social historians, the sexual dichotomy rarely appears in sociological works on stratification. That this criterion has been largely ignored or dismissed by stratification theorists is attributable to several factors, not the least of which is no doubt that members of the privileged sex have authored most of the work and to them such ranking has not been a problem and hence has not been apparent. Also, their culturally derived biases have been such that this kind of ranking was taken for granted as a manifestation of biological differences. "Many people who are very hip to the implications of the racial caste system . . . don't seem to be able to see the sexual caste system and if the question is raised they respond with: 'that's the way it's supposed to be. There are biological differences.' Or with other statements which recall a white segregationist confronted with integration."[39] The biological rationale—what Millett refers to as the "view of sex as a caste structure ratified by nature"[40]—recalls also the justification offered for all birth-ascribed dominance-exploitation relationships be they caste

in India, Burakumin status in Japan, sexual roles, or any other. In each instance the plea is that these are uniquely real, significant, unavoidable, and natural differences, and therefore they must be acted upon. Thus, in an interview about their book, *The Imperial Animal* which is said to claim that males have dominated human history because "the business of politics . . . is a business that requires skills and attitudes that are peculiarly male," anthropologists Robin Fox and Lionel Tiger were reported to have vehemently denied that their theory about the reasons for women's roles might be a sexist theory. "'These are the facts, don't accuse us of making up the species,'" Tiger said. And again, "'Because this is a racist country, people relate sexism to racism.' But these two reactions are actually different because while there are no important biological differences between races, there are very important differences between the sexes."[41] Whether the differences are real or not (and who would deny that males and females differ in important ways?), the sociological and humanistic question is whether the differences require or justify differential opportunities, privileges, responsibilities, and rewards or, put negatively, domination and exploitation.

Birth-ascribed stratification, be it sexual, racial, or otherwise, is always accompanied by explanations, occasionally ingenious but usually mundane and often ludicrous, as to why putative natural differences *do* require and justify social differences. Those explanations are widely doubted by those whose domination they are supposed to explain, and this includes increasing numbers of women.

The substantive issues which becloud the topic of sexual stratification have to do with the mode of recruitment, the socialization, membership, and structural arrangements of sexually ranked categories. First, there is the fact that while sex is determined at birth, it is not contingent upon ancestry, endogamy, or any other arrangement of marriage or family, and is not predictable. It is the only recurrent basis for birth-ascribed stratification that can be defensibly attributed solely to undeniably physical characteristics. Even here there are individual or categorical exceptions made for transvestites, hermaphrodites, homosexuals, etc., in some societies as in the case of *hijaras* in India.[42] The significance (as contrasted to the fact) of the diagnostic physical traits—of sexual differences—is, however, largely socially defined, so that their cultural expressions vary widely over time and space. Second, as a concomitant to the mode of recruitment, males and females have no distinct ethnic or regional histories. It must not be overlooked, however, that they do have distinct social histories in every society. Third, the universal coresidence of males and females within the household precludes the existence of lifelong, separate male and female societies as such, and usually assures a degree of mutual early socialization. But note that it does not preclude distinct male and female social institutions, distinct patterns of social interaction within and between these categories, or distinguishable male and female subcultures (in fact the latter are universal) including, for example, distinct male and female dialects.

Partly as a consequence of these factors, the nature and quality of segregation of the sexes has not been defined by sociologists as comparable to that of the other ascriptive social categories discussed here. Nevertheless, most of the characteristics of birth-ascribed separation and stratification (racial, caste, ethnic, colonial, class, and pluralistic characteristics), and virtually all of the psychological and social consequences of inborn, lifelong superiority-inferiority relations are to be found in the relationship of males and females in most societies. These stem from similar factors in early socialization and from stereotypes and prejudices enacted and enforced in differential roles and opportunity structures, rationalized by ideologies of differential intrinsic capabilities and worth, sustained and defended through the combination of power and vested interest that is common to all birth-ascribed inequality. I have elsewhere contrasted some of the consequences of these assumptions and behaviors in the United States and India as reflected in the political participation of women in the two nations, although this is dwarfed by Millett's more recent work on male domination, its sources, and manifestations in the West.[43]

If we agree with van den Berghe that "race can be treated as a special case of invidious status differentiation or a special criterion of stratification,"[44] I think we are bound to agree that sex is another.

CONSEQUENCES OF INHERITED INEQUALITY

Assuming that there are significant structural and interactional similarities among systems of birth-ascribed stratification, the question can still be legitimately asked, "so what?" Is this merely a more or less interesting observation—even a truism—or does it have some theoretical or practical significance? My answer would be that it has both, for such systems have common and predictable consequences in the individual lives of those who live them and in the cumulative events which comprise the ongoing histories of the societies which harbor them.

> Caste systems are living environments to those who comprise them. Yet there is a tendency among those who study and analyze them to intellectualize caste, and in the process to squeeze the life out of it. Caste is people, and especially people interacting in characteristic ways. Thus, in addition to being a structure, a caste system is a set of human relationships and it is a state of mind.[45]

Their "human implications" are justification enough for studying and comparing systems of birth-ascribed stratification. There are neither the data nor the space to discuss these implications fully here, but I will suggest the nature of the evidence briefly, identifying psychological and social consequences. I am well aware that many features of such systems are found in all sharply stratified societies. Some are characteristic of all relationships of superordination and subordination, of poverty and affluence, of differential power. Others are found in all societies made up of distinct sub-groups whether stratified or not. It is the unique combination of characteristics in the context of the ideal of utter rigidity and unmitigable inequality which makes systems of stratification by race, caste, ethnicity, and sex distinctive in their impact on people, individually and collectively.

Psychological Consequences
Beliefs and attitudes associated with rigid stratification can be suggested by such terms as paternalism and dependence, *noblesse oblige*, arrogance, envy, resentment, hatred, prejudice, rationalization, emulation, self-doubt, and self-hatred. Those who are oppressed often respond to such stratification by attempting to escape either the circumstances or the consequences of the system. The realities of power and dependence make more usual an accommodation to oppression which, however, is likely to be less passive than is often supposed, and is likely to be unequivocally revealed when the slightest change in the perceived

distribution of power occurs. Those who are privileged in the system seek to sustain and justify it, devoting much of their physical effort to the former and much of their psychic and verbal effort to the latter. When these systems are birth-ascribed, all of these features are exacerbated.

Kardiner and Ovesey conclude their classic, and by now outdated, study of American Negro personality, *Mark of Oppression*, with the statement: "The psycho-social expressions of the Negro personality that we have described are the *integrated* end products of the process of oppression."[46] Although it is appropriate to question their characterization of that personality in the light of subsequent events and research, there is no doubt that such oppression has recurrent psychological consequences for both the oppressor and the oppressed, as Robert Coles has demonstrated in *Children of Crisis* and subsequent works.[47]

Oppression does not befall everyone in a system of birth-ascribed inequality. Most notably, it does not befall those with power. What does befall all is the imposition by birth of unalterable membership in ranked, socially isolated, but interacting groups with rigidly defined and conspicuously different experiences, opportunities, public esteem and, inevitably, self-esteem. The black in America and in South Africa, the Burakumin of Japan, the Harijan of India, the barber or washerman of Swat, the Hutu or Twa of Rwanda, have all faced similar conditions as individuals and they have responded to them in similar ways. The same can be said for the privileged and dominant groups in each of these societies, for while painful consequences of subordination are readily apparent, the consequences of superordination are equally real and important. Thus, ethnic stratification leaves its characteristic and indelible imprint on all who experience it.

The consequences of birth-ascribed stratification are self-fulfilling and self-perpetuating, for although low status groups do not adopt views of themselves or their statuses which are consistent with the views held by their superiors, they are continually acting them out and cannot avoid internalizing some of them and the self-doubts they engender, just as high status groups internalize their superiority and self-righteousness. The oppression of others by the latter serves to justify and bolster their superiority complex and to rationalize for them the deprivation and exploitation of those they denigrate. "Once you denigrate someone in that way," say Kardiner and Ovesey, "the sense of guilt makes it imperative to degrade the subject further to justify the whole procedure."[48] Gallagher notes that in the southern United States,

> *By the attitudes of mingled fear, hostility, deprecation, discrimination, amused patronage, friendly domination, and rigid authoritarianism, the white caste generated opposite and complementary attitudes in the Negro caste. It is a touch of consummate irony that the dominant group should then argue that the characteristics which exhibit themselves in the submerged group are "natural" or "racial."*[49]

The products of oppression are thus used to justify oppression.

Change and Emancipation

The self-reinforcing degradation described above combines with greed and fear of status-loss or revolt to comprise a dynamic of oppression which, in birth-ascribed stratification, probably accounts for the widespread occurrence of pariah status or untouchability. Elites characteristically justify oppression by compounding it; they enhance their own rewards by denying them ever more stringently to social inferiors, and they strive to protect themselves from challenges to status and privilege from below by rigidifying the status boundaries, reinforcing the sanctions which enforce them, and increasing the monopoly on power which makes the sanctions effective. This assures increasing social separation and hierarchical distance between groups until such time as it generates rebellion, reform, or disintegration.

The fact that social order prevails most of the time in any given instance of inherited inequality does not mean that all of those in the system accept it or their places within it willingly, nor does it mean that the system is either stable or static. It most often means that power is held and exercised effectively by those in superordinate statuses, for the time being. Such systems are based on conformity more than consensus, and are maintained by sanctions more than agreement. Nevertheless, change is inherent, resistance and mobility-striving are universal, and effective challenges to such systems are probably ultimately inevitable because the response they elicit from those they oppress is subversive. The possibility of acting out the subversion depends largely upon the balance of power among the stratified groups and the definitions of the situation their members hold. The processes of change and patterns of conflict which lead to them are major areas of commonality in such systems.[50]

The history of every caste system, of every racially stratified system, of every instance of birth-ascribed oppression is a history of striving, conflict, and occasional revolt. That this is not generally acknowledged is largely a result of the fact that most of these actions occur in the context of overwhelming power and uncompromising enforcement by the hereditary elites and are therefore expressed in the form of day-to-day resentment and resistance handled so subtly and occurring so routinely that it goes unmarked.[51] Even conspicuous manifestations are likely to be quickly and brutally put down, confined to a particular locality or group, and knowledge of their occurrence suppressed by those against whom they have been directed. These phenomena often can only be discovered by consulting and winning the confidence of members of oppressed groups, and this is rarely done.

Only the most spectacular instances of resistance, and the few successful ones are likely to be well-known. Immediately to mind come such martyrs to the cause of emancipation of oppressed peoples as the Thracian slave Spartacus, who led a rebellion against Rome; the American slave rebellion leaders Gabriel and Nat Turner, the white abolitionist John Brown, and the contemporary leaders of black emancipation in America, Martin Luther King, Medgar Evers, and others (too many of them martyred) among their fellow leaders and supporters, black and white. No doubt there are many more, most of them unknown and unsung, in the history of all groups whose members society condemns by birth to oppression. In the folk history of every such group, and in the memory of every member, are instances of courageous or foolhardy people who have challenged or outwitted their oppressors, often at the cost of their own foreseeable and inevitable destruction.

Better-known and better-documented than the individuals who led and sometimes died for them, are the emancipation movements which have occurred in most such societies—movements such as those for black power and black separatism in the United States, anti-casteism and anti-touchability in India, Hutu emancipation in Rwanda and Burundi, Burakumin emancipation in Japan, and anti-

apartheid in South Africa. All have depended primarily upon concerted efforts to apply political, economic, or military power to achieve their ends. They have comprised direct challenges to the systems. Most have followed after the failure of attempts less militant, less likely to succeed, and hence less threatening to social elites—attempts towards assimilation or mobility within the systems such as those of status emulation.

Henry Adams characterized the slave society of Virginia in 1800 as "ill at ease."[52] This seems to be the chronic state of societies so organized—the privileged cannot relax their vigilance against the rebellious resentment of the deprived. That such rigid, oppressive systems do function and persist is a credit not to the consensus they engender any more than to the justice or rationality of the systems. Rather, it is a tribute to the effectiveness of the monopoly on power which the privileged are able to maintain. When in such systems deprived people get the vote, get jobs, get money, get legal redress, get guns, get powerful allies, get public support for their aspirations, they perceive a change in the power situation and an enhancement of the likelihood of successful change in their situation, and they are likely to attempt to break out of their oppressed status. These conditions do not generate the desire for change, for that is intrinsic; they merely make it seem worthwhile to attempt the change. Sometimes the triggering factor is not that the deprived believe conditions have changed so that success is more likely, but rather that conditions have led them to define the risk and consequences of failure (even its virtual certainty) as acceptable. Resultant changes are often drastic and traumatic of achievement, but they are sought by the oppressed and by enlightened people of all statuses precisely because of the heavy individual and societal costs of maintaining inherited inequality and because of its inherent inhumanity.

An important difference between the dynamics of inherited stratification and acquired stratification results from the fact that in the latter, power and privilege accompany achievable status, emulation is at least potentially effective, and mobility and assimilation are realistic goals. Therefore energies of status resentment may rationally be channeled toward mobility. Most immigrant groups in the United States, for example, have found this out as they have merged with the larger society after one or two generations of socialization. But in a system where inherited, unalterable group identity is the basis for rewards, emulation alone cannot achieve upward mobility, and assimilation is impossible so long as the system exists (in fact, prevention of assimilation is one of its main functions). Only efforts to destroy, alter, or circumvent the system make sense. In the United States, blacks, Chicanos, and Native Americans have found this out. Only in response to changes in the distribution of power is such inherited status likely to be re-evaluated and the distribution of rewards altered.

CONCLUSION

"Race" as the term is used in America, Europe, and South Africa, is not qualitatively different in its implications for human social life from caste, *varna,* or *jati* as applied in India, *quom* in Swat and Muslim India, the "invisible race" of Japan, the ethnic stratification of Rwanda and Burundi. Racism and casteism are indistinguishable in the annals of man's inhumanity to man, and sexism is closely allied to them as man's inhumanity to woman. All are invidious distinctions imposed unalterably at birth upon whole categories of people to justify the unequal social distribution of power, livelihood, security, privilege, esteem, freedom— in short, life chances. Where distinctions of this type are employed, they affect people and the events which people generate in surprisingly similar ways despite the different historical and cultural conditions in which they occur.

If I were asked, "What practical inference, if any, is to be drawn from the comparative study of inherited inequality—of ascriptive social ranking?" I would say it is this: There is no way to reform such institutions; the only solution is their dissolution. As Kardiner and Ovesey said long ago, *"there is only one way that the products of oppression can be dissolved, and that is to stop the oppression."*[53] To stop the oppression, one must eliminate the structure of inherited stratification upon which it rests. Generations of Burakumin, Hutu, blacks, untouchables, and their sympathizers have tried reform without notable success. Effective change has come only when the systems have been challenged directly.

The boiling discontent of birth-ascribed deprivation cannot be contained by pressing down the lid of oppression or by introducing token flexibility, or by preaching brotherly love. The only hope lies in restructuring society and redistributing its rewards so as to end the inequality. Such behavioral change must come first. From it may follow attitudinal changes as meaningful, status-equal interaction undermines racist, casteist, communalist, and sexist beliefs and attitudes, but oppressed people everywhere have made it clear that it is the end of oppression, not brotherly love, which they seek most urgently. To await the latter before achieving the former is futility; to achieve the former first does not guarantee achievement of the latter, but it increases the chances and makes life livable. In any case, the unranked pluralism which many minorities seek requires only equality, not love.

To those who fear this course on the grounds that it will be traumatic and dangerous, I would say that it is less so than the futile attempt to prevent change. Philip Mason spoke for all systems of inborn inequality when he called the Spartan oppression of the Helots in ancient Greece a trap from which there was no escape.

> It was the Helots who released the Spartans from such ignoble occupations as trade and agriculture. . . . But it was the Helots who made it necessary to live in an armed camp, constantly on the alert against revolt. . . . They had a wolf by the ears; they dared not let go. And it was of their own making; they had decided—at some stage and by what process one can only guess—that the Helots would remain separate and without rights forever.[54]

That way, I believe, lies ultimate disaster for any society. A thread of hope lies in the possibility that people can learn from comparison of the realities of inherited inequality across space, time, and culture, and can act to preclude the disaster that has befallen others by eliminating the system which guarantees it. It is a very thin thread.

ENDNOTES

1. Max Weber, *From Max Weber: Essays in Sociology,* H. H. Gerth and C. W. Mills, trans. and ed. (New York, Oxford University Press, 1946); W. G. Runciman, "Class, Status and Power?" in *Social Stratification,* J. A. Jackson, ed. (London, Cambridge University Press, 1968), pp. 25–61.
2. See for Rwanda: Jacques J. Maquet, *The Premise of Inequality in Ruanda* (London, Oxford University Press, 1961); for India: F. G. Bailey, "Closed Social Stratification in India," *European Journal of Sociology* (Vol. IV, 1963); Gerald D. Berreman, "Caste: The Concept," in

International Encyclopedia of the Social Sciences, D. Sills, ed. (New York, Macmillan and The Free Press, 1968), Vol. II, pp. 333–9; André Béteille, *Castes Old and New* (Bombay, Asia Publishing House, 1969); Louis Dumont, *Homo Hierarchicus* (London, Weidenfeld and Nicolson, 1970); J. H. Hutton, *Caste in India, Its Nature, Functions and Origins* (London, Cambridge University Press, 1946); Adrian C. Mayer, "Caste: The Indian Caste System," in D. Sills, ed., op. cit., pp. 339–44; M. N. Srinivas, *Caste in Modern India and Other Essays* (Bombay, Asia Publishing House, 1962), and *Social Change in Modern India* (Berkeley, University of California Press, 1966); for Swat: Fredrik Barth, "The System of Social Stratification in Swat, North Pakistan," in *Aspects of Caste in South India, Ceylon and North-West Pakistan,* E. Leach, ed. (London, Cambridge University Press, 1960), pp. 113–48; for Japan: George DeVos and Hiroshi Wagatsuma, eds. *Japan's Invisible Race: Caste in Culture and Personality* (Berkeley, University of California Press, 1966); Shigeaki Ninomiya, "An Inquiry Concerning the Origin, Development and Present Situation of the *Eta* in Relation to the History of Social Classes in Japan," *The Transactions of the Asiatic Society of Japan* (Second series, Vol. 10, 1933); cf. Herbert Passin, "Untouchability in the Far East," *Monumenta Nipponica* (Vol. 2, No. 3, 1955); for the United States: Allison Davis, B. Gardner, and M. R. Gardner, *Deep South: A Social Anthropological Study of Caste and Class* (Chicago, The University of Chicago Press, 1941); John Dollard, *Caste and Class in a Southern Town* (Garden City, New York, Doubleday, 1957); Gunnar Myrdal, *An American Dilemma: The Negro Problem in Modern Democracy* (New York, Harper, 1944); Alphonso Pinkney, *Black Americans* (Englewood Cliffs, New Jersey, Prentice-Hall, 1969); Peter I. Rose, ed., *Americans from Africa,* Vol. 1: *Slavery and its Aftermath* and Vol. II: *Old Memories, New Moods* (New York, Atherton Press, 1970). See also contrasts with South Africa: Pierre van den Berghe, *South Africa, a Study in Conflict* (Berkeley, University of California Press, 1967); Latin America: Marvin Harris, *Patterns of Race in the Americas* (New York, Walker, 1964); Julian Pitt-Rivers, "Race, Color and Class in Central America and the Andes," *Daedalus* (Spring, 1967); the Caribbean: M. G. Smith, *The Plural Society in the British West Indies* (Berkeley, University of California Press, 1965); G. D. Berreman, *Caste and Other Inequities* (New Delhi, Meerut, 1979).

3. Dumont, op. cit.

4. Gerald D. Berreman, "A Brahmanical View of Caste: Louis Dumont's *Homo Hierarchicus,*" *Contributions to Indian Sociology* (New Series, No. V, 1972).

5. Tamotsu Shibutani and Kian M. Kwan, *Ethnic Stratification: A Comparative Approach* (New York, Macmillan, 1965), p. 572.

6. H. S. Morris, "Ethnic Groups," in D. Sills, ed., op. cit., Vol. 5, p. 167.

7. Pierre van den Berghe, "The Benign Quota: Panacea or Pandora's Box," *The American Sociologist* (Vol. 6, Supplementary Issue, June 1971).

8. Ibid., p. 43.

9. Cf. Robert Blauner, "Black Culture: Myth or Reality?" in Rose, *Old Memories, New Moods,* pp. 417–43.

10. Gerald D. Berreman, "Caste in India and the United States," *The American Journal of Sociology* (Vol. LXVI, September, 1960); cf. Berreman, "A Brahmanical View of Caste . . . ," op. cit.

11. Oliver C. Cox, "Race and Caste: A Distinction," *The American Journal of Sociology* (Vol. L, March, 1945); cf. Oliver C. Cox, *Caste, Class and Race* (Garden City, New York, Doubleday, 1948).

12. Arthur R. Jensen, "How Much Can We Boost I.Q. and Scholastic Achievement?" *Harvard Educational Review* (Vol. 39, No. 1, Winter, 1969).

13. See the various articles comprising the "Discussion," of Jensen's article in *Harvard Educational Review* (Vol. 39, No. 2, Spring, 1969).

14. E. A. Ross, *Social Psychology* (New York, Macmillan, 1914), p. 3.

15. Shibutani and Kwan, op. cit., p. 37.

16. Ibid., p. 110.

17. Pierre van den Berghe, *Race and Racism* (New York, Wiley, 1967), p. 21.

18. Claude Lévi-Strauss, "The Bear and the Barber," *Journal of the Royal Anthropological Institute* (Vol. 93, Part 1, 1963).

19. Winthrop D. Jordan, *White over Black* (Baltimore, Penguin Books, 1969), pp. 137–8.

20. Robert Blauner, "International Colonialism and Ghetto Revolt," *Social Problems* (Vol. 16, No. 4, Spring 1969); Stokely Carmichael and Charles Hamilton, *Black Power* (New York, Random House, 1967); Frantz Fanon, *The Wretched of the Earth* (New York, Grove Press, 1966); O. Mannoni, *Prospero and Caliban: The Psychology of Colonization* (New York, Praeger, 1956); Albert Memmi, *The Colonizer and the Colonized* (Boston, Beacon Press, 1967).

21. Cf. Blauner, "Internal Colonialism . . . ," pp. 395–6.

22. Gerald D. Berreman, "Caste as Social Process," *Southwestern Journal of Anthropology* (Vol. 23, No. 4, Winter, 1967); Blauner, *Racial Oppression in America* (New York, Harper & Row, 1942); S. F. Nadel, "Caste and Government in Primitive Society," *Journal of the Anthropological Society of Bombay* (Vol. 8, 1954); J. S. Furnivall, *Colonial Policy and Practice: A Comparative Study of Burma and Netherlands India* (London, Cambridge University Press, 1948); M. G. Smith, *The Plural Society in the British West Indies* (Berkeley, University of California Press, 1965); James B. Watson, "Caste as a Form of Acculturation," *Southwestern Journal of Anthropology* (Vol. 19, No. 4, Winter 1963).

23. Cf. Irawati Karve, *Hindu Society: An Interpretation* (Poona, Deccan College Postgraduate and Research Institute, 1961).

24. Davis, Gardner, and Gardner, op. cit.; St. Clair Drake and Horace R. Cayton, *Black Metropolis* (New York, Harcourt, Brace, 1945); Dollard, op. cit.; Marina Wikramanayake, "Caste and Class among Free Afro-Americans in Ante-bellum South Carolina," paper delivered before the 70th Annual Meeting of the American Anthropological Association (New York, November 1971).

25. Furnivall, op. cit.; cf. Malcolm Cross, ed., *Special Issue on Race and Pluralism, Race* (Vol. XII, No. 4, April 1917).

26. M. G. Smith, op. cit., pp. 14, 83.

27. Gerald D. Berreman, "Stratification, Pluralism and Interaction: A Comparative Analysis of Caste," in *Caste and Race: Comparative Approaches,* A. deReuck and J. Knight, eds., p. 51.

28. M. G. Smith, op. cit., p. xi.

29. Berreman, "Stratification, Pluralism and Interaction . . . ," op. cit., p. 55.

30. Cf. Furnivall, op. cit.

31. Berreman, "Stratification, Pluralism and Interaction . . . ," op. cit., p. 55.

32. Ibid.; cf. McKim Marriott, "Interactional and Attributional Theories of Caste Ranking," *Man in India* (Vol. 39, 1959).

33. Maya Angelou, *I Know Why the Caged Bird Sings* (New York, Bantam Books, 1971), p. 168.

34. Cf. Berreman, "Caste in India and the United States," op. cit.

35. Berreman, "Stratification, Pluralism and Interaction . . . ," op. cit., p. 51.

36. Dumont, op. cit.

37. Cf. Berreman, "Caste in India and the United States," op. cit.; Berreman, "Caste in Cross-Cultural Perspective . . . ," op. cit.; Berreman, "Social Categories and Social Interaction in Urban India," *American Anthropologist* (Vol. 74, No. 3).

38. Cf. Berreman, "A Brahmanical View of Caste . . . ," op. cit.

39. Kate Millett, *Sexual Politics* (New York, Avon Books, 1971), p. 19.

40. Casey Hayden and Mary King, "Sex and Caste," *Liberation* (April, 1966), p. 35; cf. Millett, op. cit.

41. Fran Hawthorne, "Female Roles Examined by Rutgers Professors," *Daily Californian* (Berkeley, 6 October, 1971), p. 5. See also Millett, op. cit., p. 57, for a summary of the common psychological traits and adaptational mechanisms attributed to blacks and women in American society as reported in three recent sociological accounts.

42. Cf. G. Morris Carstairs, *The Twice-Born* (Bloomington, Indiana University Press, 1958), pp. 59–62 et passim; Morris E. Opler, "The Hijarā (Hermaphrodites) of India and Indian National Character: A Rejoinder," *American Anthropologist* (Vol. 62, No. 3, June, 1960).

43. Gerald D. Berreman, "Women's Roles and Politics: India and the United States," in *Readings in General Sociology,* R. W. O'Brien, C. C. Schrag, and W. T. Martin, eds. (4th Edition, Boston, Houghton Mifflin Co., 1969). First published, 1966. Cf. Millett, op. cit.

44. van den Berghe, *Race and Racism,* op. cit., p. 22.

45. Berreman, "Stratification, Pluralism and Interaction . . . ," op. cit., p. 58.

46. Abram Kardiner and Lionel Ovesey, *Mark of Oppression* (Cleveland, The World Publishing Co., 1962), p. 387.

47. Robert Coles, *Children of Crisis* (Boston, Atlantic–Little, Brown, 1964); Robert Coles and Jon Erikson, *The Middle Americans* (Boston, Little, Brown, 1971).

48. Kardiner and Ovesey, op. cit., p. 379.

49. B. G. Gallagher, *American Caste and the Negro College* (New York, Columbia University Press, 1938), p. 109.

50. Berreman, "Caste as Social Process," op. cit.

51. Raymond Bauer and Alice Bauer, "Day to Day Resistance to Slavery," *Journal of Negro History* (Vol. 27, October 1942); Douglas Scott, "The Negro and the Enlisted Man: An Analogy," *Harpers* (October 1962), pp. 20–21; cf. Berreman, "Caste in India and the United States," op. cit.

52. Henry Adams, *The United States in 1800* (Ithaca, New York, Cornell University Press, 1961), p. 98.

53. Kardiner and Ovesey, op. cit., p. 387.

54. Philip Mason, *Patterns of Dominance* (London, Oxford University Press for the Institute of Race Relations, 1970), p. 75.

T W O

Constructing Ethnicity
Creating and Recreating Ethnic Identity and Culture

Joane Nagel

INTRODUCTION

Contrary to expectations implicit in the image of the "melting pot" that ethnic distinctions could be eliminated in U.S. society, the resurgence of ethnic nationalism in the United States and around the world has prompted social scientists to rethink models of ethnicity rooted in assumptions about the inevitability of assimilation.[1] Instead, the resiliency of cultural, linguistic, and religious differences among populations has led to a search for a more accurate, less evolutionary means of understanding not only the resurgence of ancient differences among peoples, but also the actual emergence of historically new ethnic groups.[2] The result has been the development of a model of ethnicity that stresses the fluid, situational, volitional, and dynamic character of ethnic identification, organization, and action—a model that emphasizes the socially "constructed" aspects of ethnicity, i.e., the ways in which ethnic boundaries, identities, and cultures, are negotiated, defined, and produced through social interaction inside and outside ethnic communities.[3]

According to this constructionist view, the origin, content, and form of ethnicity reflect the creative choices of individuals and groups as they define themselves and others in ethnic ways. Through the actions and designations of ethnic groups, their antagonists, political authorities, and economic interest groups, ethnic boundaries are erected dividing some populations and unifying others (see Barth 1969; Moerman 1965, 1974).

Ethnicity is constructed out of the material of language, religion, culture, appearance, ancestry, or regionality. The location and meaning of particular ethnic boundaries are continuously negotiated, revised, and revitalized, both by ethnic group members themselves as well as by outside observers.

To assert that ethnicity is socially constructed is not to deny the historical basis of ethnic conflict and mobilization.[4] However, a constructionist view of ethnicity poses questions where an historical view begs them. For instance, to argue that the Arab-Israeli conflict is simply historical antagonism, built on centuries of distrust and contention, asserts a certain truth, but it answers no questions about regional or historical variations in the bases or extent of the conflict, or about the processes through which it might be ameliorated. In fact, scholars have asserted that both Israeli and Palestinian ethnic identities are themselves fairly recent constructions, arising out of the geopolitics of World War II and the Cold War, and researchers have documented the various competing meanings of the Arab-Israeli conflict in American political culture.[5]

Similarly, to view black-white antagonism in contemporary American society simply as based in history—albeit a powerful and divisive history—is to overlook the contemporary demographic, political, social, and economic processes that prop up this ethnic boundary, reconstructing it, and producing tension along its borders and within the two bounded ethnic groups.[6] For instance,

Lemann's (1991) study of the post–World War II demographic shift of African Americans from rural to urban areas and from the South to the North reveals a reconfiguration of the black-white ethnic boundary in northern and southern cities. This migration magnified urban ethnic segregation, stratified black society, increased interethnic tensions, promoted ethnic movements among both blacks and whites, and produced a black urban underclass. All of these changes reflect the dynamic, constructed character of black ethnicity in U.S. society.[7]

Since ethnicity is not simply an historical legacy of migration or conquest, but is constantly undergoing redefinition and reconstruction, our understanding of such ethnic processes as ethnic conflict, mobilization, resurgence, and change might profit from a reconsideration of some of the core concepts we use to think about ethnicity. This paper examines two of the basic building blocks of ethnicity: identity and culture. Identity and culture are fundamental to the central projects of ethnicity: the construction of boundaries and the production of meaning. In this paper, I attempt to answer several questions about the construction of identity and culture: What are the processes by which ethnic identity is created or destroyed, strengthened or weakened? To what extent is ethnic identity the result of internal processes, and to what extent is ethnicity externally defined and motivated? What are the processes that motivate ethnic boundary construction? What is the relationship between culture and ethnic identity? How is culture formed and transformed? What social purposes are served by the construction of culture? Rather than casting identity and culture as prior, fixed aspects of ethnic organization, here they are analyzed as emergent, problematic features of ethnicity. By specifying several mechanisms by which groups reinvent themselves—who they are and what their ethnicity means—I hope to clarify and organize the growing literature documenting the shifting, volitional, situational nature of ethnicity. Next I examine the construction of ethnic identity, followed by a discussion of the construction of culture.

CONSTRUCTING ETHNIC IDENTITY

Ethnic identity is most closely associated with the issue of boundaries. Ethnic boundaries determine who is a member and who is not and designate which ethnic categories are available for individual identification at a particular time and place. Debates over the placement of ethnic boundaries and the social worth of ethnic groups are central mechanisms in ethnic construction. Ethnicity is created and recreated as various groups and interests put forth competing visions of the ethnic composition of society and argue over which rewards or sanctions should be attached to which ethnicities.

Recent research has pointed to an interesting ethnic paradox in the United States. Despite many indications of weakening ethnic boundaries in the white American population (due to intermarriage, language loss, religious conversion or declining participation), a number of studies have shown a maintenance or increase in ethnic identification among whites (Alba 1990; Waters 1990; Kivisto 1989; Bakalian 1993; Kelly 1993, 1994). This contradictory dualism is partly due to what Gans terms "symbolic ethnicity," which is "characterized by a nostalgic allegiance to the culture of the immigrant generation, or that of the old country; a love for and pride in a tradition that can be felt without having to be incorporated in everyday behavior" (1979:205). Bakalian (1991) provides the example of Armenian-Americans:

> For American-born generations, Armenian identity is a preference and Armenianness is a state of mind. . . . One can say he or she is an Armenian without speaking Armenian, marrying an Armenian, doing business with Armenians, belonging to an Armenian church, joining Armenian voluntary associations, or participating in the events and activities sponsored by such organizations (Bakalian 1991:13).

This simultaneous decrease and increase in ethnicity raises the interesting question: How can people behave in ways which disregard ethnic boundaries while at the same time claim an ethnic identity? The answer is found by examining ethnic construction processes—in particular, the ways in which individuals and groups create and recreate their personal and collective histories, the membership boundaries of their group, and the content and meaning of their ethnicity.

Negotiating Ethnic Boundaries

While ethnicity is commonly viewed as biological in the United States (with its history of an obdurate ethnic boundary based on color), research has shown people's conception of themselves along ethnic lines, especially their ethnic identity, to be situational and changeable (see especially Waters 1990, Chapter Two). Barth (1969) first convincingly articulated the notion of ethnicity as mutable, arguing that ethnicity is the product of social ascriptions, a kind of labeling process engaged in by oneself and others. According to this perspective, one's ethnic identity is a composite of the view one has of oneself as well as the views held by others about one's ethnic identity. As the individual (or group) moves through daily life, ethnicity can change according to variations in the situations and audiences encountered.

Ethnic identity, then, is the result of a dialectical process involving internal and external opinions and processes, as well as the individual's self-identification and outsiders' ethnic designations—i.e., what *you* think your ethnicity is, versus what *they* think your ethnicity is. Since ethnicity changes situationally, the individual carries a portfolio of ethnic identities that are more or less salient in various situations and vis-à-vis various audiences. As audiences change, the socially-defined array of ethnic choices open to the individual changes. This produces a "layering" (McBeth 1989) of ethnic identities which combines with the ascriptive character of ethnicity to reveal the negotiated, problematic nature of ethnic identity. Ethnic boundaries, and thus identities, are constructed by both the individual and group as well as by outside agents and organizations.

Examples can be found in patterns of ethnic identification in many U.S. ethnic communities.[8] For instance, Cornell (1988) and McBeth (1989) discuss various levels of identity available to Native Americans: *subtribal* (clan, lineage, traditional), *tribal* (ethnographic or linguistic, reservation-based, official), *regional* (Oklahoma, California, Alaska, Plains), *supratribal* or *pan-Indian* (Native American, Indian, American Indian). Which of these identities a native individual employs in social interaction depends partly on where and with whom the interaction occurs. Thus, an American Indian might be a "mixed-blood" on the reservation, from "Pine Ridge" when speaking to someone from another reservation, a "Sioux" or "Lakota" when responding to the U.S. census, and "Native American" when interacting with non-Indians.

Pedraza (1992), Padilla (1985, 1986), and Gimenez, Lopez, and Munoz (1992) note a similar layering of Latino or Hispanic ethnic identity, again reflecting both internal and external defining processes. An individual of Cuban ancestry may be a Latino vis-à-vis non-Spanish-speaking ethnic groups, a Cuban-American vis-à-vis other Spanish-speaking groups, a Marielito vis-à-vis other Cubans, and white vis-à-vis African Americans.[9] The chosen ethnic identity is determined by the individual's perception of its meaning to different audiences, its salience in different social contexts, and its utility in different settings. For instance, intra-Cuban distinctions of class and immigration cohort may not be widely understood outside of the Cuban community since a Marielito is a "Cuban" or "Hispanic" to most Anglo-Americans. To a Cuban, however, immigration cohorts represent important political "vintages," distinguishing those whose lives have been shaped by decades of Cuban revolutionary social changes from those whose life experiences have been as exiles in the United States. Others' lack of appreciation for such ethnic differences tends to make certain ethnic identity choices useless and socially meaningless except in very specific situations. It underlines the importance of external validation of individual or group ethnic boundaries.

Espiritu (1992) also observes a layering of Asian-American identity. While the larger "Asian" pan-ethnic identity represents one level of identification, especially vis-à-vis non-Asians, national origin (e.g., Japanese, Chinese, Vietnamese) remains an important basis of identification and organization both vis-à-vis other Asians as well as in the larger society. Like Padilla (1985, 1986), Espiritu finds that individuals choose from an array of pan-ethnic and nationality-based identities, depending on the perceived strategic utility and symbolic appropriateness of the identities in different settings and audiences. She notes the larger Asian-American pan-ethnic boundary is often the basis for identification where large group size is perceived as an advantage in acquiring resources or political power. However she also observes that Asian-American pan-ethnicity tends to be transient, often giving way to smaller, culturally distinct nationality-based Asian ethnicities.

Waters (1991) describes similar situational levels of ethnic identification among African Americans. She reports that dark-skinned Caribbean immigrants acknowledge and emphasize color and ancestry similarities with African Americans at some times; at other times Caribbeans culturally distinguish themselves from native-born blacks. Keith and Herring (1991) discuss the skin tone distinctions that exist among African Americans, with the advantages and higher social status that accrue to those who are lighter skinned. This color consciousness appears to be embraced by blacks as well as whites, and thus demarcates an internal as well as external ethnic boundary.

White Americans also make ethnic distinctions in various settings, vis-à-vis various audiences. They sometimes emphasize one of their several European ancestries (Waters 1990; Alba 1990); they sometimes invoke Native American lineage (Beale 1957; Quinn 1990); they sometimes identify themselves as "white," or simply assert an "American" identity (Lieberson 1985). The calculations involved in white ethnic choices appear different from those of other ethnic groups, since resources targeted for minority populations are generally not available to whites, and may not directly motivate individuals to specify an ethnicity based on European ancestry or "white"-ness. In these cases, white ethnicity can take the form of a "reverse discrimination" countermovement or "backlash" against the perceived advantages of non-whites (Burstein 1991). In other cases, white ethnicity is more symbolic (Gans 1979), representing less a rational choice based on material interests than a personal option exercised for social, emotional, or spiritual reasons (Waters 1990; Fischer 1986).

External Forces Shaping Ethnic Boundaries
The notion that ethnicity is simply a personal choice runs the risk of emphasizing agency at the expense of structure. In fact, ethnic identity is *both* optional and mandatory, as individual choices are circumscribed by the ethnic categories available at a particular time and place. That is, while an individual can choose from among a set of ethnic identities, that set is generally limited to socially and politically defined ethnic categories with varying degrees of stigma or advantage attached to them. In some cases, the array of available ethnicities can be quite restricted and constraining.

For instance, white Americans have considerable latitude in choosing ethnic identities based on ancestry. Since many whites have mixed ances-

tries, they have the choice to select from among multiple ancestries, or to ignore ancestry in favor of an "American" or "unhyphenated white" ethnic identity (Lieberson 1985). Americans of African ancestry, on the other hand, are confronted with essentially one ethnic option—black. And while blacks may make intra-racial distinctions based on ancestry or skin tone, the power of race as a socially defining status in U.S. society makes these internal differences rather unimportant in inter-racial settings in comparison to the fundamental black/white color boundary.[10]

The differences between the ethnic options available to blacks and whites in the United States reveal the limits of individual choice and underline the importance of external ascriptions in restricting available ethnicities. Thus, the extent to which ethnicity can be freely constructed by individuals or groups is quite narrow when compulsory ethnic categories are imposed by others. Such limits on ethnic identification can be official or unofficial. In either case, externally enforced ethnic boundaries can be powerful determinants of both the content and meaning of particular ethnicities. For instance, Feagin's (1991, 1992) research on the day-to-day racism experienced by middle-class black Americans demonstrates the potency of *informal* social ascription. Despite the economic success of middle-class African Americans, their reports of hostility, suspicion, and humiliation in public and private interactions with non-blacks illustrate the power of informal meanings and stereotypes to shape interethnic relations (see also Whitaker 1993).

If informal ethnic meanings and transactions can shape the everyday experiences of minority groups, formal ethnic labels and policies are even more powerful sources of identity and social experience. Official ethnic categories and meanings are generally political. As the state has become the dominant institution in society, political policies regulating ethnicity increasingly shape ethnic boundaries and influence patterns of ethnic identification. There are several ways that ethnicity is "politically constructed," i.e., the ways in which ethnic boundaries, identities, cultures, are negotiated, defined, and produced by political policies and institutions (J. Nagel 1986): by immigration policies, by ethnically-linked resource policies, and by political access that is structured along ethnic lines.

Immigration and the Production of Ethnic Diversity. Governments routinely reshape their internal ethnic maps by their immigration policies. Immigration is a major engine of new ethnic group production as today's immigrant groups become tomorrow's ethnic groups (Hein 1994). Around the world, immigrant populations congregate in both urban and rural communities to form ethnic enclaves and neighborhoods, to fill labor market niches, sometimes providing needed labor, sometimes competing with native-born workers, to specialize in particular commodity markets, and as "middlemen."[11] Whether by accident or design, whether motivated by economics, politics, or kinship, immigrant groups are inevitably woven into the fabric of ethnic diversity in most of the world's states.

It is also through immigration that both domestic and foreign policies can reshape ethnic boundaries. The growing ethnic diversity and conflict in France and Britain are direct legacies of both their successes and failures at colonial empire-building. In many other European states, such as Sweden and Germany, economic rather than political policies, in particular the importation of guest workers to fill labor shortages, encouraged immigration. The result has been the creation of permanent ethnic minority populations. In the United States, various Cold War policies and conflicts (e.g., in Southeast Asia and Central America) resulted in immigration flows that make Asians and Latin Americans the two fastest growing minority populations in the United States (U.S. Census 1991). Political policies designed to house, employ, or otherwise regulate or assist immigrant populations can influence the composition, location, and class position of these new ethnic subpopulations.[12] Thus the politics of immigration are an important mechanism in the political construction of ethnicity.

Resource Competition and Ethnic Group Formation. Immigration is not the only area in which politics and ethnicity are interwoven. Official ethnic categories are routinely used by governments worldwide in census-taking (Horowitz 1985), and acknowledgment of the ethnic composition of populations is a regular feature of national constitutions (Maarseveen and van der Tang 1978; Rhoodie 1983). Such designations can serve to reinforce or reconstruct ethnic boundaries by providing incentives for ethnic group formation and mobilization or by designating particular ethnic subpopulations as targets for special treatment. The political recognition of a particular ethnic group can not only reshape the designated group's self-awareness and organization, but can also increase identification and mobilization among ethnic groups not officially recognized, and thus promote new ethnic group formation. This is especially likely when official designations are thought to advantage or disadvantage a group in some way.

For instance, in India, the provision of constitutionally guaranteed parliamentary representation and civil service posts for members of the "Scheduled Castes" or "Untouchables" contributed to the emergence of collective identity and the political mobilization of Untouchables from different language and regional backgrounds; one result was the formation of an Untouchable political party, the Republican Party (Nayar 1966; Rudolph and Rudolph 1967). This affirmative action program produced a backlash and a Hindu revival movement, mainly among upper caste Indians who judged Untouchables to have unfair political and economic advantages (Desai 1992). Such backlashes are common around the world. In Malaysia, constitutional provisions granting political advantages to majority Malays prompted numerous protests from non-Malays—mainly Chinese and Indians (Means 1976). In many of the new republics of the former Soviet Union, nationalist mobilizations are built as much on a backlash against Russia and local Russians (who comprise a significant part of the population in most republics) than on a strong historic pattern of national identity.[13] In the United States, white ethnic self-awareness was heightened as desegregation and affirmative action programs got under way in the 1960s and 1970s. The result was a white anti-busing movement, and a "legal countermobilization" and cultural backlash against affirmative action (Rubin 1972; Burstein 1991; Faludi 1991). American Indians have also been the targets of white backlashes, mainly against treaty-protected hunting and fishing rights in the Pacific Northwest and the northern Great Lakes region (Adams and La Course 1977; Wright 1977; Kuhlmann forthcoming).

Official ethnic categories and policies can also strengthen ethnic boundaries by serving as the basis for discrimination and repression, and thus reconstruct the meaning of particular ethnicities. Petonito (1991a, 1991b) outlines the construction of both "loyal American" and "disloyal Japanese" ethnic boundaries during World War II, a process which led to the internment of thousands of Japanese-Americans. Similarly, violence directed toward Iranians and Middle Easterners in the United States increased when American embassy staff were taken hostage during the Iranian revolution in 1980 and attacks against Iraqis and Arab-Americans escalated during the 1991 Gulf War (Applebome 1991). In the former case, official actions of the Carter administration, such as requiring Iranian nationals in the United States to report for photographing and fingerprinting, contributed to an elevation of ethnic awareness and tended to legitimate the harassment of Iranians. In the latter case, official U.S. military hostilities against Iraq "spread" into U.S. domestic politics, prompting attacks on Arab and Iraqi "targets" living in the United States.

Political policies and designations have enormous power to shape patterns of ethnic identification when politically controlled resources are distributed along ethnic lines. Roosens (1989) attempts to trace the rise of ethnicity and ethnic movements in the contemporary United States. He argues that the mobilization of ethnic groups in the United States has paralleled the development of the U.S. welfare state and its racial policies:

> There were few advantages in the United States . . . of the 1930s to define oneself visibly as a member of the Sicilian or Polish immigrant community. When one considers the current North American situation, however, one concludes that ethnic groups emerged so strongly because ethnicity brought people strategic advantages (Roosens 1989:14).

Padilla's (1985, 1986) description of the emergence of a Latino ethnicity among Mexicans and Puerto Ricans in Chicago in response to city programs focused on Hispanics, is consistent with Roosens's analysis. Another example is Espiritu's (1992) account of the emergence of Asian-American ethnic identity as a strategy to counter official policies thought to disadvantage smaller Asian nationality groups. Similarly, the white backlashes described above represent one response to exclusion from what are seen as ethnically-designated rights and resources.

The observation that ethnic boundaries shift, shaping and reshaping ethnic groups according to strategic calculations of interest, and that ethnicity and ethnic conflict arise out of resource competition, represent major themes in the study of ethnicity (see Banton 1983). Barth and his associates (1969) link ethnic boundaries to resource niches. Where separate niches are exploited by separate ethnic groups (e.g., herders versus horticulturalists), ethnic tranquility prevails; however, niche competition (e.g., for land or water) results in ethnic boundary instability due to conflict or displacement (see also Despres 1975). Examining labor markets, Bonacich (1972) and Olzak (1989, 1992) have shown how informal job competition among different ethnic groups can heighten ethnic antagonism and conflict, strengthening ethnic boundaries as ethnicity comes to be viewed as crucial to employment and economic success. Hannan argues that the pursuit of economic and political advantage underlies the shift in ethnic boundaries upward from smaller to larger identities in modern states.[14] Thus, in electoral systems, larger ethnic groups mean larger voting blocs; in industrial economies regulated by the political sector, and in welfare states, larger ethnic constituencies translate into greater influence (see also Lauwagie 1979 and B. Nagel 1986).

This research paints a picture of ethnicity as a rational choice (Hechter 1987a). According to this view, the construction of ethnic boundaries (group formation) or the adoption or presentation of a particular ethnic identity (individual ethnic identification), can be seen as part of a strategy to gain personal or collective political or economic advantage.[15] For instance, Katz (1976) reports the creation of racially restrictive craft unions by white settlers in South Africa in order to gain an edge in labor market competition and create class distance from competing black laborers. Such competitive strategies not only provide ethnic advantages, they stimulate ethnic identity and group formation. An example is "whiteness" which Roediger (1991:13–14) argues emerged as an American ethnicity due to the efforts of working class (especially Irish) whites who sought to distance themselves and their labor from blacks and blackness; by distinguishing their "free labor" from "slave labor," they redefined their work from "white slavery" to "free labor."

Political Access and Ethnic Group Formation. The organization of political access along ethnic lines can also promote ethnic identification and ethnic political mobilization. As Brass notes, "the state . . . is not simply an arena or an instrument of a particular class or ethnic group . . . the state is itself the greatest prize and resource, over which groups engage in a continuing struggle" (1985:29). Much ethnic conflict around the world arises out of competition among ethnic contenders to control territories and central governments. The civil war in the former republic of Yugoslavia is a clear example of ethnic political competition (Hodson, Sekutic, and Massey forthcoming).[16] The long-standing grievances of the various warring linguistic and religious groups there did not erupt into combat until the Soviet Union lifted the threat of intervention in the late 1980s and opened the door to the possibility of ethno-political competition. The result was an armed scramble for territory based on a fear of domination or exclusion by larger, more powerful ethnic groups.

In the United States, the construction of ethnic identity in response to ethnic rules for political access can be seen in the national debate over affirmative action, in the composition of judicial (judges, juries) and policy-making bodies (committees, boards), and in the enforcement of laws designed to end discrimination or protect minorities (see Gamson and Modigliani 1987). For example, the redistricting of U.S. congressional districts based on the 1990 census led to ethnic mobilization and litigation as African-American and Latino communities, among others, sought improved representation in the federal government (Feeney 1992). Similarly, concern based on the importance of ethnic population size for representation and resource allocation led Asian Americans to demand that the Census Bureau designate nine Asian nationality groups as separate "races" in the 1980 and 1990 census (Espiritu 1992; Lee 1993).[17]

Ethnic Authenticity and Ethnic Fraud

Politically-regulated ethnic resource distribution and political access have led to much discussion about just what constitutes legitimate membership in an ethnic group, and about which individuals and groups qualify as disadvantaged minorities. For instance, Hein (1991:1) outlines the debate concerning the extent to which Asian immigrants to the United States should be seen to be ethnic "minorities" with an "historical pattern of discrimination," and thus eligible for affirmative action remedies. In universities, concerned with admissions practices, financial aid allocation, and non-discriminatory employment and representation, the question of which ethnic groups fulfill affirmative action goals is often answered by committees charged with defining who is and is not an official minority group (see Simmons 1982).

Discussions about group eligibility are often translated into controversies surrounding individual need, individual ethnicity, and ethnic proof. The multi-ethnic ancestry of many Americans combines with ethnically-designated resources to make choosing an ethnicity sometimes a financial decision. In some instances, individuals respond to shifting ethnic incentive structures (Friedman and McAdam 1987, 1992) by asserting minority status or even changing their ethnicity. Ethnic switching (Barth 1969) to gain advantage can be contentious when resources are limited. In many cases, particularly those involving individuals of mixed ancestry, the designation of a resource-endowed ethnicity for public or official purposes can elicit suspicion and challenge. For instance, Snipp (1993) reports concern among Native American educators about "ethnic fraud" in the allocation of jobs and resources designated for American Indian students; this concern was reflected in the inclusion of ethnic fraud among the topics of discussion at a recent national conference on minority education.[18]

Indeed, questions of who is Indian or Latino or black[19] are often raised and often are difficult to resolve one way or the other. Even when ancestry can be proven, questions can arise about the cultural depth of the individual's ethnicity (Was he or she raised on a reservation or in the city? Does he or she speak Spanish?), or the individual's social class (Was he or she raised in the inner city or in the suburbs?). Solutions to questions of authenticity are often controversial and difficult to enforce. For instance, the federal government has attempted to set the standards of ethnic proof in the case of American Indian art. The Indian Arts and Crafts Act of 1990 requires that in order for artwork to be labeled as "Indian produced," the producer must be "certified as an Indian artisan by a [federally recognized] Indian tribe" (United

States Statutes at Large 1990:4663). By this legal definition, artists of Indian ancestry cannot produce Indian art unless they are enrolled in or certified by officially recognized tribes. The act has thus led a number of Indian artists to seek official tribal status (some have refused to do this) and has also served to exclude some recognized American Indian artists from galleries, museums, and exhibits (Jaimes 1992; *Kansas City Star* 1991).[20] Similar local restrictions on who can sell Indian art and where it can be sold have caused bitter divisions among American Indians and other minority communities in the Southwest (Evans-Pritchard 1987).[21]

In sum, the construction of ethnic boundaries through individual identification, ethnic group formation, informal ascriptions, and official ethnic policies illustrates the ways in which particular ethnic identities are created, emphasized, chosen, or discarded in societies. As the result of processes of negotiation and designation, ethnic boundaries wax and wane. Individual ethnic identification is strongly limited and influenced by external forces that shape the options, feasibility, and attractiveness of various ethnicities.

As we have seen above, research speaks fairly clearly and articulately about how ethnic boundaries are erected and torn down, and the incentives or disincentives for pursuing particular ethnic options. However, the literature is less articulate about the *meaning* of ethnicity to individuals and groups, about the forces that shape and influence the contents of that ethnicity, and about the purposes ethnic meanings serve. This requires a discussion of the construction of culture.

Culture and history are the substance of ethnicity. They are also the basic materials used to construct ethnic meaning. Culture and history are often intertwined in cultural construction activities. Both are part of the "toolkit"—as Swidler (1986) called it—used to create the meaning and interpretative systems seen to be unique to particular ethnic groups (see Tonkin, McDonald, and Chapman 1989). Culture is most closely associated with the issue of meaning. Culture dictates the appropriate and inappropriate content of a particular ethnicity and designates the language, religion, belief system, art, music, dress, traditions, and lifeways that constitute an authentic ethnicity. While the construction of ethnic boundaries is very much a saga of structure and external

forces shaping ethnic options, the construction of culture is more a tale of human agency and internal group processes of cultural preservation, renewal, and innovation. The next section explores the ways in which ethnic communities use culture and history to create common meanings, to build solidarity, and to launch social movements.

CONSTRUCTING CULTURE

In his now classic treatise on ethnicity, Fredrik Barth (1969) challenged anthropology to move away from its preoccupation with the content of culture, toward a more ecological and structural analysis of ethnicity:

> . . . *ethnic categories provide an organizational* vessel *that may be given varying amounts and forms of content in different socio-cultural systems. . . . The critical focus of investigation from this point of view becomes the ethnic* boundary *that defines the group, not the cultural stuff that it encloses* (Barth 1969:14–15 [emphasis mine]).

Barth's quarrel was not with the analysis of culture, per se, but with its primacy in anthropological thinking. In fact, by modernizing Barth's "vessel" imagery, we have a useful device for examining the construction of ethnic culture: the shopping cart. We can think of ethnic boundary construction as determining the *shape* of the shopping cart (size, number of wheels, composition, etc.); ethnic culture, then, is composed of the things we put into the cart—art, music, dress, religion, norms, beliefs, symbols, myths, customs. It is important that we discard the notion that culture is simply an historical legacy; culture is *not* a shopping cart that comes to us already loaded with a set of historical cultural goods. Rather we construct culture by picking and choosing items from the shelves of the past and the present. As Barth reminds us:

> . . . *when one traces the history of an ethnic group through time, one is* not *simultaneously . . . tracing the history of "a culture": the elements of the present culture of that group have not sprung from the particular set that constituted the group's culture at a previous time"* (Barth 1969:38).

In other words, cultures change; they are borrowed, blended, rediscovered, and reinterpreted. My use of the shopping cart metaphor extends

Swidler's (1986) cultural toolkit imagery. Swidler argues that we use the cultural tools in the toolkit in our everyday social labors; I argue that we not only use the tools in the toolkit, but that we also determine its contents—keeping some tools already in the kit, discarding others, adding new ones. However, if culture is best understood as more than mere remnants of the past, then how did it get to its present state—how did the cart get filled, and why? What does culture do?

Culture is constructed in much the same way as ethnic boundaries are built, by the actions of individuals and groups and their interactions with the larger society. Ethnic boundaries function to determine identity options, membership composition and size, and form of ethnic organization. Boundaries answer the question: Who are we? Culture provides the content and meaning of ethnicity; it animates and authenticates ethnic boundaries by providing a history, ideology, symbolic universe, and system of meaning. Culture answers the question: What are we? It is through the construction of culture that ethnic groups fill Barth's vessel—by reinventing the past and inventing the present.

CULTURAL CONSTRUCTION TECHNIQUES

Groups construct their cultures in many ways which involve mainly the *reconstruction* of historical culture, and the *construction* of new culture. Cultural reconstruction techniques include revivals and restorations of historical cultural practices and institutions; new cultural constructions include revisions of current culture and innovations—the creation of new cultural forms. Cultural construction and reconstruction are ongoing group tasks in which new and renovated cultural symbols, activities, and materials are continually being added to and removed from existing cultural repertoires.[22]

Cultural revivals and restorations occur when lost or forgotten cultural forms or practices are excavated and reintroduced, or when lapsed or occasional cultural forms or practices are refurbished and reintegrated into contemporary culture. For example, for many, immigrant and indigenous ethnic groups' native languages have fallen into disuse. Efforts to revitalize language and increase usage are often major cultural reconstruction projects. In Spain, both in Catalonia and the Basque region, declining use of the native tongues (Catalan and Euskera, respectively) due to immigration and/or Castilian Spanish domination, has spurred language education programs and linguistic renewal projects (Johnston 1991; Sullivan 1988). In the United States, the threatened loss of many Native American languages has produced similar language documentation and education programs, as well as the creation of cultural centers, tribal museums, and educational programs to preserve and revive tribal cultural traditions. Study and instruction in cultural history is often a central part of cultural reconstruction.

Cultural revisions and innovations occur when current cultural elements are changed or when new cultural forms or practices are created. As part of U.S. authorities' various historical efforts to destroy Native American cultures by annihilation or assimilation, many Indian communities and groups used cultural revision and innovation to insulate cultural practices when they were outlawed by authorities. Champagne (1989, 1990) reports that the Alaska Tlingits revised traditional potlatch practices, incorporating them into Russian Orthodox or Protestant ceremonies to conceal the forbidden exchanges. Prucha (1984) reports a form of cultural innovation to protect the use of peyote in American Indian religious rites. The creation of the Native American Church imbedded peyote use in a syncretic, new Indian-Christian religious institution, thus protecting practitioners under the First Amendment of the U.S. constitution. Such cultural camouflage in the form of religious syncretism is reported in many societies, particularly those penetrated by missionaries operating under governmental auspices.[23]

These various cultural construction techniques, and others that will be described below, serve two important collective ends which will be the focus of the remainder of this paper. They aid in the construction of community and they serve as mechanisms of collective mobilization. Cultural constructions assist in the construction of community when they act to define the boundaries of collective identity, establish membership criteria, generate a shared symbolic vocabulary, and define a common purpose. Cultural constructions promote collective mobilization when they serve as a basis for group solidarity, combine into symbolic systems for defining grievances and setting agendas for collective action, and provide a blueprint or repertoire of tactics.

The Cultural Construction of Community

In *Imagined Communities,* Benedict Anderson argues that there is no more evocative a symbol of modern nationalism than the tomb of the unknown soldier. The illustrative power of this icon lies in the fact that such tombs "are either deliberately empty or no one knows who lies inside them" (Anderson 1991:9)—thus, they are open to interpretation and waiting to be filled. The construction of culture supplies the contents for ethnic and national symbolic repositories. Hobsbawm (1983) refers to this symbolic work as "the invention of tradition"—i.e., the construction or reconstruction of rituals, practices, beliefs, customs, and other cultural apparatus. According to Hobsbawm, invented traditions serve three related purposes: a) to establish or symbolize social cohesion or group membership, b) to establish or legitimize institutions, status, and authority relations, or c) to socialize or inculcate beliefs, values, or behaviors (1983:9). By this analysis the invention of tradition is very much akin to what Cohen (1985) calls "the symbolic construction of community."

The construction of history and culture is a major task facing all ethnic groups, particularly those that are newly forming or resurgent. In constructing culture, the past is a resource used by groups in the collective quest for meaning and community (Cohen 1985:99). Trevor-Roper provides an example of the construction of a national culture:

> Today, whenever Scotchmen gather to celebrate their national identity, they assert it openly by certain distinctive national apparatus. They wear the kilt, woven in a tartan whose colour and pattern indicates their 'clan'; and if they indulge in music, their instrument is the bagpipe. This apparatus, to which they ascribe great antiquity, is in fact largely modern. . . . Indeed the whole concept of a distinct Highland culture and tradition is a retrospective invention. Before the later years of the seventeenth century, the Highlanders of Scotland did not form a distinct people. They were simply the overflow of Ireland (Trevor-Roper 1983:15).

Other scholars concur with Trevor-Roper's assertions about the constructed character of Scottish identity and culture (Chapman 1979; Prebble

1963). However, the fictive aspects of Scottish ethnicity in no way lessen the reality of Scottish nationalism in Great Britain, particularly during its heyday during the 1970s and early 1980s. During that time, Scottish and Welsh nationalism combined with the escalating violence in Northern Ireland to represent a major political and economic threat to the integrity of the United Kingdom.[24] Indeed, despite its invented origins, Scottish nationalism contributed to a major devolution of political authority to the British Celtic states (Mercer 1978; Davies 1989; Harvie 1977).

For newly forming ethnic and national groups, the construction of community solidarity and shared meanings out of real or putative common history and ancestry involves both cultural constructions and reconstructions. Smith refers to ethnic and national groups' "deep nostalgia for the past" that results in efforts to uncover or, if necessary, invent an earlier, ethnic "golden age" (1986:174). For instance, Karner (1991) describes the reconstruction of Finnish cultural history (folklore, music, songs) by Swedish-speaking Finnish intellectuals during the mobilization for Finnish independence. Similarly, Kelly (1993) discusses the efforts of Lithuanian-Americans to learn the Lithuanian language and to reproduce Lithuanian foods, songs, dances, and customs illustrating the process whereby people transform a common ancestry (whether by birth or by marriage) into a common ethnicity.[25] And in their homeland, Lithuanians themselves are embarked on a journey of national reconstruction, as decades of Russian influence are swept away in an effort to uncover real and historical Lithuanianness.

The importance of cultural construction for purposes of community building is not limited to the creation of national unity. Cultural construction is especially important to pan-ethnic groups, as they are often composed of subgroups with histories of conflict and animosity. For instance, Padilla (1985) discusses the challenges facing Mexican-Americans and Puerto Ricans in Chicago as they attempt to construct both Latino organizations and an identity underpinned by the assertion of common interests and shared culture—a commonality that is sometimes problematic. Espiritu (1992) also documents the tensions surrounding nationality and cultural differences in the evolution of an Asian-American pan-ethnicity.

One strategy used by polyethnic groups to overcome such differences and build a more unified pan-ethnic community is to blend together cultural material from many component group traditions. About half of the American Indian population lives in urban areas (U.S. Census Bureau 1989). Urban Indians have borrowed from various tribal cultures as well as from non-Indian urban culture to construct supratribal or "Indian" cultural forms such as the powwow, the Indian Center, Indian Christian churches, Indian bowling leagues and softball teams, and Indian popular music groups. In the urban setting, tribal differences and tensions can be submerged in these pan-Indian organizations and activities.[26]

Building a cultural basis for new ethnic and national communities is not the only goal prompting cultural reconstruction. Cultural construction is also a method for revitalizing ethnic boundaries and redefining the meaning of ethnicity in existing ethnic populations. The Christmas season celebration of Kwanzaa by African Americans is an example of the dynamic, creative nature of ethnic culture, and reveals the role scholars play in cultural construction. Created in the 1960s by Professor Maulana Karenga, Kwanzaa is a seven-day cultural holiday which combines African and African-American traditions (Copage 1991).[27] The reconstruction and study of cultural history is also a crucial part of the community construction process and again shows the importance of academic actors and institutions in cultural renewal. Examples can be found in the recent emergence of various ethnic studies programs (e.g., Latino, American Indian, African-American, Asian Studies) established in colleges and universities around the United States during the past three decades (Deloria 1986). Such programs are reflective of a renewed and legitimated interest in ethnicity and cultural diversity. These programs, as well as classes in oral history and ethnic culture, serve as important resources in cultural revivals and restorations.[28]

Cultural Construction and
Ethnic Mobilization

Cultural construction can also be placed in the service of ethnic mobilization. Cultural renewal and transformation are important aspects of ethnic movements. Cultural claims, icons, and imagery are used by activists in the mobilization process; cultural symbols and meanings are also produced and transformed as ethnic movements emerge and grow. While there is a large literature on the structural determinants of ethnic mobilization,[29] recent social movement research reflects increased interest in the nature of social movement culture and the interplay between culture and mobilization (see Morris and Mueller 1992). An examination of this literature offers insight into the relationship between culture and ethnic mobilization.

For instance, Snow and his associates argue that social movement organizers and activists use existing culture (rhetorical devices and various techniques of "frame alignment") to make movement goals and tactics seem reasonable, just, and feasible to participants, constituencies, and political officials (Snow et al. 1986; Snow and Benford 1988, 1992). For example, nuclear disarmament movement leaders responded to questions about the hopelessness of opposing a military-industrial complex bent on the production of nuclear weapons by drawing a parallel between the elimination of nuclear weapons and the abolition of slavery—namely, the success of abolitionism was achieved despite an equally daunting opposition (Snow et al. 1986). Thus, by drawing on available cultural themes, the discourse surrounding movement objectives and activism is more likely to recruit members, gain political currency, and achieve movement goals.

Gamson and his associates document the ideational shifts and strategies used by movements, policymakers, and opposition groups to shape debates, define issues, and to paint the most compelling portrait of each side's claims and objectives (Gamson 1988, 1992; Gamson and Modigliani 1987; Gamson and Lasch 1983). For instance, Gamson and Modigliani (1987) argue that the changing culture of affirmative action results from a struggle over the definition of equality, justice, and fairness, as various political actors frame the issues in competing ways, e.g., affirmative action as "remedial action" versus "reverse discrimination." The rhetorics, counter-rhetorics, and rhetorical shifts characterized in this research are common to all social movements, including ethnic movements. They reflect the use of cultural material and representations in a symbolic struggle over rights, resources, and the hearts and minds of constituents, neutral observers, and opponents alike.

The work of Snow and Gamson illustrates the use of existing culture by movement organizers and activists, and shows several forms of cultural reconstruction, where cultural symbols and themes are borrowed and sometimes repackaged to serve movement ends. There is another way in which cultural construction occurs in movements—where protest is a crucible of culture. For instance, Fantasia (1988) describes a "culture of solidarity" that arises out of activism. Cultures of solidarity refer to the emergence of a collective consciousness and shared meanings that result from engaging in collective action. Ethnic movements often challenge negative hegemonic ethnic images and institutions by redefining the meaning of ethnicity in appealing ways or by using cultural symbols to effectively dramatize grievances and demands.

Examples of the construction and reconstruction of history and culture in order to redefine the meaning of ethnicity can be found in the activities of many of the ethnic groups that mobilized during the civil rights era of the 1960s and 1970s in the United States. During these years, a renewed interest in African culture and history and the development of a culture of black pride—"Black is Beautiful"—accompanied African-American protest actions during the civil rights movement. The creation of new symbolic forms and the abandonment of old, discredited symbols and rhetoric reflected the efforts of African Americans to create internal solidarity and to challenge the prevailing negative definitions of black American ethnicity. For instance, the evolution of racial nomenclature for African Americans can be excavated by a retrospective examination of the names of organizations associated with or representing the interests of black Americans: the National Association for the Advancement of Colored People, the United Negro College Fund, the Black Panther Party, and the National Council of African-American Men, Inc. The fluidity of names for other American ethnic groups reflects similar shifts in constructed ethnic definitions and revised meanings associated with evolving collective identities: from Indians to American Indians to Native Americans; from Spanish-Surnamed to Hispanics to Latinos.[30] Such changes in ethnic nomenclature were an important part of the discourse of civil rights protest, as were changes in dress, new symbolic themes in art, literature, and music, and counterhegemonic challenges to prevailing standards of ethnic demeanor and interracial relations.[31]

The expropriation and subversion of negative hegemonic ethnic definitions and institutions is an important way that culture is used in ethnic mobilization around the world. British conceptions of "tribe" and "tribal" shaped many of their colonial policies, such as geographic administrative boundaries, education policies, and hiring practices. These tribal constructions were reshaped by Africans into the anti-colonial ethnic politics of a number of African states (Melson and Wolpe 1971; Young 1976). For instance, Wallerstein (1960) and Iliffe (1979) document the mobilization of various "tribal" unions and associations into nationalist movements for independence in many African countries. In India, similar subversion of colonial cultural constructions designed to facilitate British domination occurred. Cohn (1983) argues that the pomp and ceremony of the British Imperial Assemblage and the Imperial Durbars in nineteenth century India were expropriated by Indian elites, who indigenized and institutionalized this invented tradition, incorporating it into the symbolism and idiom of an independent Indian politics.[32]

This "turning on its head" of cultural symbols and institutions can be seen in the ways ethnic activists use culture in their protest strategies. The tactics used in ethnic movements rely on the presentation, and sometimes the reconstruction, of cultural symbols to demonstrate ethnic unity, to dramatize injustice, or to animate grievances or movement objectives. For instance, Zulaika (1988), Sullivan (1988), and Clark (1984) report the use of various cultural symbols and conventions by Basque nationalist groups, noting, for instance, the central symbolic importance of demands for Basque language rights, although fewer than half of the Basque population speaks the Basque language. The Red Power movement for American Indian rights during the 1960s and 1970s drew its membership from mainly urban Indians from a variety of tribal backgrounds. The movement created a unified pan-Indian cultural front by borrowing cultural forms from many native communities (e.g., the teepee, eagle feathers, the war dance, the drum). Red Power repertoires of contention—as Tilly (1986) called them—also employed a rhetorical and dramaturgical cultural style that reflected movement leaders' sensitivity to the place of the American Indian in American popular culture and history. The American Indian Movement (AIM) was especially skilled in the use of such symbolic dramaturgy, as illustrated in the following description of an AIM-sponsored counter-ceremony in 1976:

> Custer Battlefield, Mont. *Today, on the wind-buffeted hill . . . where George Armstrong Custer made his last stand, about 150 Indians from various tribes danced joyously around the monument to the Seventh Cavalry dead. Meanwhile, at the official National Parks Service ceremony about 100 yards away, an Army band played. . . . Just as the ceremony got underway, a caravan of Sioux, Cheyenne, and other Indians led by Russell Means, the American Indian Movement leader, strode to the speakers' platform to the pounding of a drum. Oscar Bear Runner, like Mr. Means, a veteran of the 1973 takeover of Wounded Knee, carried a sacred peace pipe (Lichtenstein 1976:II-1).*

The above example shows the interplay between pre-existing cultural forms and the new uses to which they are put in ethnic movements. What we see is the National Parks Service's efforts to commemorate the "official story" (Scott 1990), and the American Indian Movement's challenge to this hegemonic interpretation of history. Both groups employed the symbolic paraphernalia available to them, drawn from similar strands of American history and culture, but used in opposing ways. By recasting the material of the past in innovative ways, in the service of new political agendas, ethnic movements reforge their own culture and history and reinvent themselves.

CONCLUSION

At the beginning of this paper I posed a number of questions about ethnic boundaries and meaning, inquiring into the forces shaping ethnic identity and ethnic group formation, and the uses of history and culture by ethnic groups and movements. My answers have emphasized the interplay between ethnic group actions and the larger social structures with which they interact. Just as ethnic identity results both from the choices of individuals and from the ascriptions of others, ethnic boundaries and meaning are also constructed from within and from without, propped up by internal and external pressures. For ethnic groups,

questions of history, membership, and culture are the problematics solved by the construction process. Whether ethnic divisions are built upon visible biological differences among populations or rest upon invisible cultural and ideational distinctions, the boundaries around and the meanings attached to ethnic groups reflect pure social constructions.

Yet questions remain. What is driving groups to construct and reconstruct ethnic identity and culture? What is it about ethnicity that seems to appeal to individuals on so fundamental a level? From what social and psychological domains does the impulse toward ethnic identification originate? Why is ethnicity such a durable basis for group organization around the world? If ethnicity is in part a political construction, why do the goals of some ethnic activists favor equal rights, while others demand autonomy or independence? Other questions remain about the social meaning of ethnicity. How are particular meanings (values, stereotypes, beliefs) attached to different ethnic groups, and by whom? What are the implications of these different meanings for conceptions of social justice, intergroup relations, political policy? Concomitantly, how does ethnic stratification (material and ideational) arise? Can constructionist explanations of ethnicity account for persistent prejudice and discrimination, particularly where race or color are involved? To the extent that the constructionist model emphasizes change, how should we understand intractable racial and ethnic antagonism and stratification?

These questions comprise not only an agenda for future research, they are also warnings. While ethnic boundaries and the meanings attributed to them can be shown to be socially constructed, they must not, therefore, be underestimated as social forces. In fact, the constructionist model constitutes an argument for the durability, indeed the inevitability, of ethnicity in modern societies. As such, it represents a challenge to simple historical, biological, or cultural determinist models of human diversity.

ACKNOWLEDGMENTS
I wish to thank Richard Alba, Stephen Cornell, Jim Holstein, Carol A. B. Warren, and Norman Yetman for their helpful comments on an earlier version of this paper.

ENDNOTES

1. The failure of the American melting pot is a qualified one. As Alba and Logan (1991) point out, some groups, particularly whites, have "melted" quite well. Despite the maintenance of a kind of social or symbolic ethnicity among white groups, white ethnicity does not generally involve high levels of ethnic exclusiveness or ethnic group affiliation.

2. An ethnic group can be seen as "new" or "emergent" when ethnic identification, organization, and collective action is constructed around previously nonexistent identities, such as "Latino" or "Asian-American." An ethnic group can be seen as "resurgent" when ethnic identification, organization, or collective action is constructed around formerly quiescent historical identities, such as "Basque" or "Serbian" (see Yancey, Erickson, and Juliani 1976).

3. See Berger and Luckmann (1967) and Spector and Kitsuse (1977) for discussions of the social constructionist model; see Holstein and Miller (1993) for an assessment of the current state of social constructionism.

4. I define ethnic mobilization as the organization of groups along ethnic lines for collective action.

5. See Gerner (1991); Plascov (1981); Gamson (1982). Layne (1989) also describes the construction of a Jordanian national identity in the decades following World War I, and especially during King Hussein's rule beginning in 1953.

6. The use of the term "ethnic group" rather than "race" or "racial group" to describe African Americans is not intended to discount the unique importance of color or race as a basis for discrimination and disadvantage in U.S. society (and elsewhere). However, the arguments about ethnicity I put forth here are meant to apply to all racial and ethnic groups, whether distinguished by color, language, religion, or national ancestry.

7. See Wilson (1987); Burstein (1991); James (1989); Massey (1985); Massey and Denton (1993); Morris (1984).

8. The examples here are drawn from American groups, but the layering of identity is not unique to the United States. Similar levels of ethnic identification have been observed around the world. See Horowitz (1985), Young (1976), and Enloe (1973) for other examples.

9. The racial self-definition of the Hispanics represents an interesting example of the negotiated and constructed character of ethnicity. In 1980 and 1990, nearly half of respondents who identified themselves as "Hispanic" on an ancestry item, reported their race as "other," i.e., they did not choose any of the more than a dozen "races" offered in the Census or Current Population Survey questionnaires (e.g., black, white, American Indian, Japanese, Chinese, Filipino, Vietnamese, etc.). The Census Bureau recoded most of them as "white" (U.S. Bureau of the Census 1980, 1990).

10. Despite the practice of "hypodescent" (Harris 1964) or the "one drop rule" in the classification of African Americans as "black," Davis (1991) shows that throughout U.S. history, there has been considerable controversy and reconstruction of the *meaning* and *boundaries* associated with blackness.

11. See Cohen (1974); Bonacich (1972, 1973); Fernandez-Kelly (1987); Light and Bonacich (1988); Portes and Rumbaut (1990); Sassen (1988, 1991).

12. See Yetman (1983, 1991); Pedraza-Bailey (1985); Horowitz (1985); Light and Bonacich (1988); Whorton (1994).

13. This is more the case in the southern republics, such as Tadzhikistan or Uzbekistan, than in formerly independent republics such as in the Baltics—Latvia, Estonia, Lithuania—where national identities are more historically fixed (see Allworth 1989).

14. Examples are from the town-based Oyo or Ilorin to Yoruba linguistic, regional identity in Nigeria (Laitin 1985); from various regional or linguistic Untouchable groups into an organized national party in India (Nayar 1966); from Chicano or Puerto Rican to Latino or from Cherokee or Apache to Native American in the United States (Padilla 1986; Cornell 1988).

15. See also Hechter (1987b, 1992); Hechter and Friedman (1984); Hechter, Friedman, and Appelbaum (1982).

16. The distinction between "ethnic" and "national" groups is the subject of much definition and debate in the sciences. I use the terms synonymously, thus "ethnic" group includes religious, linguistic, cultural, and regional groups with claims to political rights, sovereignty, or autonomy. See Connor (1991), Hobsbawm (1990), Smith (1986), and Gellner (1983, 1987) for discussions of nationalism, ethno-nationalism, and ethnicity.

17. On the 1990 census form there were actually 10 Asian nationality groups designated as separate races. They were: Asian Indian, Chinese, Filipino, Guamanian, Hawaiian, Japanese, Korean, Samoan, Vietnamese, and Other Asian or Pacific Islander. Asian American groups were concerned that if the term "Asian" were used in the census race item (Item number 4: "What is this person's race"), that many Asian Americans would not mark the choice, and the result would be an undercount of the Asian-American population (Espiritu 1992).

18. In an October, 1993 conference sponsored by the American Council on Education in Houston (American Council on Education 1993), Jim Larimore (Assistant Dean and Director of the American Indian Program at Stanford University) and Rick Waters (Assistant Director of Admissions at University of Colorado, Boulder) presented a session, "American Indians Speak Out Against Ethnic Fraud in College Admissions." The session was designed to "identify the problem and its impact on the American Indian community . . . [and to] discuss effective institutional practices for document-

ing and monitoring tribal affiliations" (Larimore and Waters 1993).

19. An example is when individuals who are not of African-American ancestry, such as dark-skinned Asians or native-born Africans, are counted as "black" or "minority" for such purposes as demonstrating compliance with affirmative action hiring goals.

20. The entire Indian art authentication process has been criticized as having as its primary purpose, a way of guaranteeing the value of art for mainly non-Indian art owners and purchasers. My thanks to C. Matthew Snipp for bringing this to my attention.

21. The importance and meaning of official recognition as a basis for individual ethnicity, ethnic group formation, and ethnic mobilization is by no means unique to Native Americans or to the United States. Where a particular ethnicity is especially stigmatizing, ethnic conversions (or "passing") often occur. For example, Schermerhorn (1978) reports a common form of ethnic switching in India—religious conversion, when Hindu Untouchables convert to Islam in order to escape untouchability. Also in India, the British colonial preference for Sikh military recruits, led to many Sikh conversions in order to qualify (Nayar 1966). Lelyveld (1985) discusses the phenomenon of individuals officially changing their race under South African apartheid regulations (see also Adam and Moodley 1993). Official recognition or resources tied to particular ethnic groups can prompt not only individual, but also ethnic group formation and mobilization as well. Burstein (1991) documents a white ethnic legal counter-assault against the perceived ethnic advantages of American minority populations. In Canada, the passage of policies favoring the use of the French language in Quebec during the 1970s and 1980s led to ethnic organizational formation and protests among non-French-speaking Canadian ethnic groups, such as those of Italian and Portuguese descent, who feared disadvantage or exclusion under the new language policies (Murray 1977; Lupul 1983).

22. For a detailed discussion of cultural construction, see Nagel (1994).

23. For example, see Whiteman (1985); Salamone (1985); Sanneh (1989); and Taber (1991).

24. Given the location of Britain's North Sea oil holdings off Scotland's coast.

25. An interesting aspect of Lithuanian-American ethnic renewal is what Kelly calls the "ethnic pilgrimage," where Lithuanian-Americans visit Lithuania to learn firsthand about their ethnic roots and to participate in building the new independent state and nation (Kelly 1994).

26. See Hertzberg (1971); Weibel-Orlando (1991); Steele (1975); Whitehorse (1988); Clark (1988).

27. Tanzanian-born Maulana Karenga is professor and chair of Black Studies at the University of California at Long Beach.

28. The use of historical or anthropological research by ethnic groups engaged in reconstruction projects has its pitfalls. These center on the accuracy and objectivity of such academic work. Recent research "deconstructing" historical and contemporary ethnographies (Wagner 1975; Clifford 1988; Clifford and Marcus 1986; Geertz 1988) has been aimed at revealing the voices and viewpoints of researchers imbedded in "objective" reports of their subjects' social and cultural organization.

29. See Enloe (1973); Hechter (1975); Young (1976); Nagel and Olzak (1982); Brass (1985); Horowitz (1985); Olzak (1992); A. Smith (1992).

30. See Martin (1991), Stein (1989), and T. Smith (1992) for a discussion of shifting nomenclature among African Americans. My thanks to Norm Yetman for raising the issue of evolving nomenclature.

31. See Cleaver (1968); Carmichael and Hamilton (1967); Willhelm (1970); Lester (1968).

32. A less liberating but common cultural construction technique used in ethnic mobilization is the demonization or villification of opposition ethnic groups in civil wars, pogroms, and genocides (e.g., against Armenians in World War I Turkey, against Jews in World War II Germany, against Muslims in post-Soviet Yugoslavia).

THREE

Dominant Group Ethnic Identity in the United States
The Role of "Hidden" Ethnicity in Intergroup Relations

Ashley W. Doane, Jr.

The sociological understanding of intergroup relations and ethnic stratification in the United States has been limited by a lack of attention paid to issues of *dominant* group ethnic identity. Historically, the sociology of race and ethnic relations in the United States has tended to focus on minority or subordinate groups, with an emphasis on issues of identity and change, oppression and resistance. When attention has been devoted to the dominant group—especially during the past thirty years—it has concentrated on attitudes toward subordinate groups (Schuman, Steeh, and Bobo 1985; Firebaugh and Davis 1988; Klugel 1990) or on mechanisms of exploitation and control (Blauner 1972; Feagin and Feagin 1978; Omi and Winant 1986). What is missing is the examination of the characteristics of the dominant group itself, particularly the nature of dominant group ethnic identity. Nearly fifty years ago, Robert Bierstedt (1948, p. 700) commented on sociology's neglect of majorities. Similarly, Everett C. Hughes and Helen M. Hughes (1952, p. 158) decried the tendency to "study ethnic relations as if we had to know only one party to them." These observations remain valid today.

The core thesis of this article is that the ethnic identity (or sense of peoplehood) of dominant groups in the United States has assumed a unique nature as a result of dominant status; that is, being in a position of dominance shapes the nature of group ethnicity. This in turn generates sev-

eral subsidiary propositions. First, the study of dominant group ethnicity—and race and ethnic relations in the United States—has been influenced by the nature of dominant group ethnic identity. This leads to an examination—in the spirit of the sociology of knowledge—of the nature and causes of what could be termed the "underdevelopment" of the study of dominant group ethnic identity. Second, dominant group ethnicity has played a key role in intergroup relations, especially in terms of enabling the dominant group to maintain its position atop the ethnic hierarchy. The strategic use of dominant group identity and its role in the reproduction of group hegemony are a third focal issue, for the sociological significance of dominant group ethnicity stems from its use in intergroup resource competition. Finally, given that ethnicity is socially constructed and variable in nature, the ethnic identity of the dominant group has evolved and changed in the course of intergroup relations. The final section of this article examines the process through which dominant group ethnicity has evolved and considers the consequences of these changes for race and ethnic relations in the United States.

One conceptual issue that is crucial to this analysis involves what is meant by the notion of a *dominant* ethnic group. While work in the area of race and ethnic relations often makes reference to the dominant group (or, less frequently, the majority), definitions or discussions of dominance are rarely provided, thus leaving "dominant group" as a residual "nonminority" category. For purposes of this analysis, I define a dominant ethnic group as the ethnic group in a society that exercises power to create and maintain a pattern of economic, political, and institutional advantage, which in turn results in the unequal (disproportionately beneficial to the dominant group) distribution of resources. With respect to intergroup relations, a key element of dominance is the disproportionate ability to shape the sociocultural understandings of society, especially those involving group identity and intergroup interactions. Historically, the origins of dominance lie in processes such as conquest, colonialism, and labor migration—situations where intergroup contact, resource competition, and power differentials combine to produce a system of ethnic stratification (Noel 1968; Lieberson 1961; Shibutani and Kwan 1965; Bonacich and Cheng 1984; Barrera 1979). Thus, dominance is grounded in the existence of unequal power employed to derive material benefit.

At the same time, it is important to emphasize the relative nature of dominance. Without the existence of a rigid caste system, dominant ethnic group power is not absolute but is constrained by the ability of subordinate groups to resist or even veto dominant group actions (Willie 1996). Thus, dominant-subordinate relations are a dialectical process, with power levels and institutional arrangements evolving through intergroup struggle (Whitt 1979). Similarly, the existence of a system of ethnic stratification does not mean that all dominant group members enjoy higher social, economic, and political status; it merely means that dominant group members are overrepresented at higher levels and that dominant group membership constitutes an advantage (or at least the absence of ethnic and racial obstacles) in intergroup resource competition. As we will see below, this dynamic nature of ethnic dominance or stratification plays an important role in shaping group identity.

THE NATURE OF DOMINANT GROUP ETHNICITY

From a definitional standpoint, the significant elements of ethnicity are that it is a group affiliation based on a sense of peoplehood (i.e., belief in common ancestry, shared history, and joint destiny) and that it is expressed in relation to other such groups within a society (thus, identities such as Mexican American, Polish American, and Japanese American assume relevance in the context of race and ethnic relations in the United States). We can speak of ethnicity or ethnic identity as both a characteristic of individuals, in the sense of locating a place among others (Dashefsky 1972), and of groups, in the sense of a collective notion of place. Ethnicity is a reciprocal phenomenon—a "we-they" relationship where all persons are labeled and groups are differentiated via a culturally delineated but socially defined "boundary" (Barth 1969); that is, cultural markers are imbued with social significance as a means of distinguishing between ingroups and out-groups. Sociologically, ethnicity assumes salience in intergroup interactions—as groups compete for valued social, economic, and political resources (Despres 1975; Olzak 1992; Nagel 1996). Thus, ethnicity emerges and evolves through intergroup processes.

In addition, it is important to appreciate that ethnicity has a complex and variable nature (Cohen 1974, p. xiv). As many have observed, ethnicity is socially constructed; it can evolve over time and change according to circumstance (Lyman and Douglass 1973, p. 358; Cohen 1981; Keyes 1981; Okamura 1981; Nagel 1994; 1996). Given this variability, the *salience* or strength of identification becomes a key element of ethnicity (Alba 1990, p. 38). The awareness, salience, and assertion of ethnic affiliations may vary considerably among different groups and even among the members of a particular group (Banks and Gay 1978, p. 245; Obidinski 1978). If we view ethnicity as an independent variable that influences social behavior, then variations in the salience of ethnicity should produce changes in behavior. This leads to a core question: Does dominant group status in and of itself influence the salience and form of ethnic identity?

In the U.S. case, evidence suggests that the answer is yes, that the ethnic identity of the dominant group (in the United States, the boundaries of the dominant group have expanded from Anglo Americans to include, successively, Protestant European Americans and European Americans in general) is less intensely felt than that of subordinate ethnic groups. Tom W. Smith (1980) found that "old stock" Americans were the most likely of any group to be unable or unwilling to identify with an ethnic group, Stanley Lieberson (1985) describes the emergence of a significant group of "unhyphenated whites" primarily of northern or western European ancestry, while Richard D. Alba (1990, pp. 50–51), in a study of ethnicity among whites in the Albany area of New York, found that one-third of native-born whites were unable to identify themselves in ethnic terms and one-quarter of those who did provide an ethnic affiliation subsequently qualified or disavowed it. Although most white Americans can name a country in response to ancestry questions (Lieberson and Waters 1988; Hout and Goldstein 1994), there are several indicators that these identities have limited salience. Nearly half of Americans of European ancestry give more than one response to ancestry questions (Farley 1991). There is considerable variation and inconsistency in the reporting of ethnic identities for family members and even for individuals themselves (Lieberson and Waters 1986; 1988; 1993; Hout and Goldstein 1994). Ancestry responses for European Americans are also vulnerable to an "example effect," where responses fluctuate in accordance with sample answers provided by the U.S. Census Bureau (Waters 1994, pp. 7–8). These patterns of nonresponse and flux are strong indicators of a diminished sense of ethnicity.

I believe that the explanation both for the inability or unwillingness to identify oneself ethnically and for the seeming weakness of ethnic ties lies in the nature of dominant group status. Unlike members of subordinate groups—especially visibly distinct (i.e., "racially" distinct) groups—dominant group members are less likely to be reminded of social and cultural differences on a day-to-day basis, less likely to have their identity anchored in overtly ethnic institutions and social structures, and less likely to have experienced prejudice, discrimination, or disadvantage due to ethnicity or race. In general, dominant group ethnicity is less likely to be perceived as salient by group members, for advantages are often less evident than obstacles (McIntosh 1989; Frankenberg 1993, p. 49). For dominant group members, ethnicity plays little or no overt role in everyday life. Awareness of ancestry (e.g., to know that one has English, Irish, German, and/or Italian ancestors) is not necessarily the same as the sense of peoplehood involved in ethnic identification. The awareness of ancestry, or even the sporadic ethnic identification asserted on special occasions captured in Herbert Gans's (1979) "symbolic ethnicity" or Mary C. Waters's (1990) "optional" ethnicity, is relevant more as an individual trait than as a meaningful group affiliation.

Another way in which dominant group status affects group identity is when dominant group culture assumes normative status and group customs and practices are built into a "mainstream" culture that is not overtly linked to a particular ethnic group (Blackwell 1981). Both the form and content of educational institutions, the mass media, politics, and the judicial system—to give a few examples—generally reflect European American and especially English American standards (Feagin and Feagin 1996, pp. 81–92; Fischer 1989). Such a claim does not mean that other groups have failed to contribute to the American mainstream—indeed, the dominant group often overlooks ways in which it has been influenced by others (Yinger 1985, p. 155)—but rather that the dominant group has appropriated the mainstream. This normalization of dominant group culture is significant in that it enhances a sense of culturelessness and of being the "same as everybody else." Accordingly, where W. E. B. Du Bois ([1903] 1995) describes the "double consciousness" of subordinate groups—a need for minorities to learn the ways of the dominant group in addition to their own—we could speak of the "taken-for-grantedness" or nonconsciousness of a dominant group identity that serves as the social norm. This leads to an important point: The diminished or even completely absent sense of ethnicity does *not* mean that members of the dominant group have shed their ethnicity. Without the existence of a society where all people belong to the same ethnic group, there is no such thing as "non-ethnicity," even though it has been popular to view the dominant group in the United States as lacking any ethnic affiliation. Instead, what exists is a phenomenon best described as *hidden ethnicity*—the lack of awareness of an ethnic identity that is not normally asserted in intergroup interaction.

The notion of "hidden" ethnicity is essential to understanding the role of dominant group ethnicity in the United States. In some ways, this concept is similar to symbolic ethnicity (Gans 1979), optional ethnicity (Waters 1990), and the "privatization" of ethnicity (Alba 1990, p. 300); however, it is explicitly centered upon the dominant group as opposed to the emphasis of the other concepts on what are seen as vestiges of nondominant ethnic identities. In addition, where the notions of symbolic, optional, and private ethnicity focus upon the form, sporadic nature, or venue of ethnic identity, hidden ethnicity highlights issues of consciousness. Indeed, the introduction of hidden ethnicity suggests that ethnic identification can vary in a manner similar to class consciousness. In terms of ethnic self-awareness, hidden ethnicity captures the reality that, for dominant group members, ethnicity does not generally intrude upon day-to-day experience and that the privileges of group membership are taken for granted. Thus, ethnic identity is especially "hidden" for members of dominant groups; it is likely that subordinate group members may be more likely to consider the group affiliation of dominant group members. At the same time, it is important to underscore the variable nature of ethnic consciousness. While hidden ethnicity may capture the day-to-day masking of dominant group identity, group consciousness can change and identity can be asserted when dominant group interests are threatened by challenges from subordinate groups.

One factor that is crucial to understanding the attenuation of dominant group ethnicity in the United States is the historical role of racial ideologies in intergroup relations. As is true for ethnicity, race is a social construct that takes on explicit meanings in specific social and historical contexts. For example, the malleability of race is manifest in past attempts to draw "racial" distinctions between European peoples in the United States (Grant 1916) and in the changing racial categories used in the U.S. census (Lee 1993). Throughout U.S. history, "race" entailed attaching social and political significance to physiological traits in order to create more rigid intergroup boundaries, increase social distance, and provide a rationale for extreme forms of domination and oppression. Thus, "whiteness" was not generally presented as a sense of peoplehood but rather as an assertion of privilege vis-à-vis nonwhites, an assertion historically buttressed by pseudoscientific claims of white superiority and nonwhite inferiority. While race and ethnicity are analytically distinct (although often confused, cf. Jaret 1995, pp. 74–80) in that individuals have both racial and ethnic identities, they have been inextricably intertwined throughout the

course of intergroup relations in the United States. Indeed, ethnicity in the United States cannot be understood in any meaningful sense without anchoring it in issues of race. For purposes of this analysis, it is important to observe that the preeminence of the politics of race in intergroup relations has often undermined the assertion of dominant group ethnic identity, that ethnicity has been obscured by "whiteness." Parenthetically, as a dominant racial identity, "whiteness" has often exhibited many of the "hidden" aspects of dominant group ethnicity (Roediger 1994; Frankenberg 1993; Feagin and Vera 1995; Doane 1997). As Robert W. Terry (1981, p. 120) observed, *"to be white in America is not to have to think about it."*

Another important determinant of less salient dominant group ethnic identity is the relationship between the ethnic identity of the dominant group and the "national" identity of the larger society. Nationality, in contrast to ethnicity, can be defined as a group identity or sense of peoplehood linked to a defined territory and a political state. Thus, nationality is a more inclusive identity; a nation may contain many ethnic groups. Throughout U.S. history, the nature of the national identity—the notion of what it means to be an "American"—has been a contested issue subject to repeated redefinition (Gleason 1980; Takaki 1993). As Philip Gleason (1980) has observed, American national identity has vacillated between two competing visions. On the one hand, American nationality is essentially a political (as opposed to ethnic) identity grounded in such principles as democracy, equality, and manifest destiny. Membership was open beyond Anglo Americans to "all" who embraced these ideals—with the exception, reflecting the racist origins of U.S. society, of African Americans, Native Americans, and other people of color (Ringer and Lawless 1989). On the other hand, a second conceptualization of American has been even more exclusionary, reflecting nativist or "Anglo-Saxon" concerns with increasing ethnic differentiation during the period 1860–1924 (Horsman 1981; Higham 1963). From this perspective, Americanization meant "Anglo-conformity" (Gordon 1964). The struggles over definitions of American national identity persist in current debates over multiculturalism, linguistic supremacy, and more inclusive visions of society.

Political and cultural struggles over the nature of national identity have important implications for dominant group identity. To the extent that the dominant ethnic group has successfully cast the national identity as isomorphic with its own identity (i.e., American = Anglo American or European American), dominant group members have the prerogative of identifying with the nation as opposed to the ethnic group; that is, dominant group members are most likely to identify themselves as "just American" as opposed to using an ethnic label (Frankenberg 1993, p. 198). Even if the claim to the national identity is not accepted by subordinate groups, the process of claims making alone would tend to diminish the sense of ethnic identification among dominant group members. This dynamic creates ideal conditions for the emergence of what Michael Banton (1983, p. 64) has termed "minus-one" ethnicity, the sense that dominant group members are not ethnic. In such circumstances, the ethnic self-awareness of the dominant group is limited as a consequence of its real or claimed position at the cultural center and its influence on the institutions of the larger society (Enloe 1981).

In addition to being less salient, dominant group ethnicity assumes a different form as a result of group position at the top of the ethnic hierarchy. As is the case with subordinate groups, dominant group ethnicity serves as a unifying ideology in intergroup interactions. What is different, however, is the goal of dominant group ethnic assertion, which is the legitimation of dominance or the defense of group position in the face of real or perceived challenges by subordinate groups. As a legitimating or defensive ideology, dominant group ethnicity may entail claimed status as a "chosen people" (e.g., nineteenth-century notions of "manifest destiny") or the argument that past accomplishments such as the colonial and postimmigrant struggle to "build" America justify current advantages. Such an approach often involves the negation of subordinate group claims and the justification of exclusion through the use of ideologies of inherent superiority/inferiority (e.g., Anglo-Saxonism; see Horsman 1981) or through the selective interpretation of history (Loewen 1995). The key element here is that dominant group ethnic assertion tends to focus upon the defense of existing social structures and cultural norms (i.e., the "mainstream") and the negation of subordinate group claims. Consequently, there is less effort devoted to elevating group identity and

cultural practices—as opposed to the cultural or psychological decolonization practiced by subordinate groups—and lower group self-awareness.

If dominant group status shapes group identity, then it is also important to recognize that dominance is a variable in itself and that variations in the level of dominance should in turn affect the salience of group identity. The higher the level of power and influence—of dominant group hegemony—the more group identity is likely to be taken for granted. On the other hand, the historical pattern has been for the dominant Anglo American/European American group—or elements within the group—to assert its identity in response to perceived challenges to group hegemony stemming from social changes, migration, or subordinate group mobilization. Examples of such dominant group assertion include the Know-Nothing Party, the Ku Klux Klan, Anglo-Saxonism, the Americanization movement, the English-only movement, the various immigration restriction movements, and current white supremacist movements (Higham 1963; Gleason 1980; Horsman 1981). The core dynamic is that dominant group ethnic assertion is reactionary in nature; it is asserted as a political and ideological defense of group position within the system of ethnic stratification.

One final consideration in understanding dominant group ethnicity is that both the salience and assertion of group identity may exhibit intragroup variation. Dominant ethnic groups are not monolithic. Not all members of the dominant group will have similar levels of identification and not all will be involved in group mobilization. One element in explaining this variation involves the divergent material or class interests of classes or class "fractions" within the dominant group. These "eth-classes"—groupings determined by ethnic and class location, as distinguished from the multiethnic classes of society as a whole (Gordon 1964; Marger 1978; Doane 1996a)—may have different material interests and different levels of vulnerability to changes in the existing system of ethnic stratification (especially inroads by subordinate groups) and, hence, varying strategies of assertion or nonassertion in order to defend their dominant group privilege. For example, while the dominant group may be overrepresented among the elite (Alba and Moore 1982), the network of elite institutions (clubs, schools, etc.) described by such observers as C. Wright Mills (1956), E. Digby Baltzell (1964), and G. William Domhoff (1970) lack an overt ethnic nature (e.g., there is nothing overtly ethnic about the Chicago Club). Indeed, the general economic, political, and institutional power of the dominant group elite tends to preclude ethnic assertion; however, elites may attempt to use ethnic symbols to forge cross-class alliances with the dominant group working class in the face of challenges from subordinate groups (Breen 1973; Bloom 1987). Likewise, segments of the dominant group working class may feel vulnerable to wage competition or replacement by subordinate group members and use their dominant group status to limit competition. This has been manifest in labor support for restriction or exclusion of immigrants, pressure for colonial labor systems, and other forms of ethnic conflict (Bonacich 1972; Blauner 1972; Olzak 1986; 1989; Roediger 1991). At an extreme, the contradiction between lower class position and dominant ethnic status has provided fertile soil for reactionary/racist populism and a source of membership for racially and ethnically based hate groups.

UNDERDEVELOPMENT OF THE STUDY OF DOMINANT GROUP IDENTITY

Historically, the study of race and ethnic relations in the United States has tended to follow two lines of analysis with regard to dominant group ethnicity, both of which have contributed to an underdeveloped understanding of dominant group identity. In one approach, ethnicity has been viewed solely as an attribute of subordinate or "minority" groups, and ethnic group has become "synonymous with minority" (Connor 1978, p. 386). As the term "ethnic" moved into the lexicon of American sociology during the 1940s, we find definitions such as that of Leonard Bloom (1948, p. 171, emphasis added) who described ethnic groups as "groups which are *set off from the rest of the population* on the basis of racial criteria, religious identity, cultural attributes, or national or ancestral backgrounds." Likewise, W. Lloyd Warner and Leo Srole (1945, p. 28, emphasis added) employ ethnic to characterize "a member of a group with a *foreign* culture" even though such a person "may be either of foreign or of native birth." Thus, ethnic initially carried a connotation of immigrant/foreigner and nondominant

status. This practice has continued over the years (cf. Isajiw 1974; Burgess 1978; Obidinski 1978), with an expanded emphasis on the "minority" aspect of ethnicity (Gleason 1992). The popular term "white ethnic" implies white "non-ethnics," while assimilation has often been taken to involve the shedding of ethnicity amid absorption into the ethnically neutral "larger society." More recently, Gans (1992, p. 51) defined ethnic groups as groups that share some elements of a common past or present non-American culture. The outcome of this line of thought has been to create a condition of "minus-one" ethnicity (Banton 1983, p. 64), that is, where the dominant group—Anglo Americans/WASPs/"old stock" Americans—is viewed as not ethnic (cf. Abramson 1980, p. 150). This effectively privileges Anglo/European Americans by establishing them as a hidden center of intergroup relations.

In the second approach, the dominant group is recognized as an ethnic group but its characteristics are systematically ignored in favor of a focus on subordinate groups. For example, Nathan Glazer and Daniel Patrick Moynihan (1963, p. 8) in *Beyond the Melting Pot* include "old stock" or "White Anglo-Saxon Protestants" as one of the seven major ethnic groups in New York City; however, WASPs (and, tellingly, German Americans) are absent from their analysis. In general, little attention has been devoted to the nature of dominant group ethnic identity (Feagin and Feagin 1996, p. 72; Yetman 1991, p. 13). Widely used texts for courses in race and ethnic relations either omit the dominant group or make only isolated references to dominant group, majority, Anglo Americans, or WASPs, with limited or no discussion. When European-origin groups are discussed (e.g., Irish Americans, Italian Americans), texts emphasize the period prior to entry into the dominant group. Those works focusing on the dominant group (e.g., Berthoff 1953; Baltzell 1964; Anderson 1970; Erickson 1972; Fischer 1989) tend to be historical in nature and limited in scope. As is the case with the "minus-one" view of ethnicity, this approach leaves the dominant group as the hidden center of race and ethnic relations in the United States.

Why has American sociology downplayed dominant group ethnicity? In part, we can posit that this reflects the "hidden" or less overt nature of dominant group ethnicity outlined above, that dominant group ethnicity is generally overlooked because it is less visible. More significant, however, is another element of dominance—the ability to control the means of intellectual production and thus to shape the sociocultural understandings of society. While the relationship between sociology and the larger society is one of reciprocal influence, and the power of the dominant group is constrained by the power of subordinate groups, the evolution of the field of race and ethnic relations has been shaped by the political interests and general worldview of the dominant group. The result is a sociology of race and ethnic relations—and a social discourse on ethnicity—in which the nature of dominant group ethnicity is deemphasized or overlooked entirely.

In its late nineteenth- and early twentieth-century origins, mainstream American sociology was dominated by European American Protestants and oriented toward "social problems" and social reform (Coser 1978). Dominant group members were particularly concerned with the "problem" or "threat" posed by the influx of immigrants, the social "pathologies" associated with foreign status, and the policy debate over the exclusion or the "Americanization" of subordinate groups. These concerns were reflected in the social science research agenda during the first half of the twentieth century. Indeed, following an early flirtation with scientific racism (McKee 1993; Lyman 1991), the study of U.S. race and ethnic relations was dominated by the assimilationist paradigm, with its emphasis on studying the absorption of immigrant/minority groups into the mainstream (as defined by the dominant group) of American society (Gordon 1964; Abramson 1980; Hirschman 1983). As concern broadened to include the "dilemma"—to use Gunnar Myrdal's (1944) term —posed by the caste-like status of African Americans, assimilation theory expanded to suggest that they would also undergo assimilation (Myrdal 1944; Parsons 1966; Metzger 1971).

The emphasis on assimilation existed in a mutually reinforcing relationship with more general sociological perspectives on ethnicity and race. American sociology until the 1960s had an anti-ethnic bias in that it viewed ethnicity as a declining social phenomenon. As many observers have noted, the major theoretical paradigms in sociology —functionalism and Marxism/conflict theory— both predicted the ultimate disappearance of eth-

nicity (which was viewed as a non-rational, pre-capitalist identity) in modern industrial society (Doane 1996a). This characterization of ethnicity as an artifact from earlier social forms created a context that encouraged sociologists to study ethnic groups as culture groups (rather than as interest groups) and to focus upon the gemeinschaft-like social relations of immigrant enclaves. In contrast, the dominant group was viewed as more "advanced" (its culture was that of the more modern "mass society") and hence as less "ethnic" than immigrants from less-developed societies. Consequently, much of social science theorizing on the nature of ethnicity and group identities has been shaped by the "minus-one" approach to ethnicity, that is, it has been grounded in the analysis of subordinate groups while ignoring the other side of the ethnic equation.

Significantly, assimilation theory in American sociology resonated with the ideology of assimilation that dominated in nineteenth- and early twentieth-century social thought (Newman 1973, p. 51). As Gleason (1980; 1992) has documented, debates over the nature of assimilation—in both the Anglo-conformity and melting pot variants (cf. Gordon 1964)—in American social thought paralleled the evolution of the assimilationist paradigm in sociology. From J. Hector St. John de Crevecoeur ([1782] 1925) to Israel Zangwill (1906), assimilation (popularly depicted as the "melting pot") captured public discourse and emerged as the dominant group prescription for the shape of American society. Competing perspectives, such as cultural pluralism (Kallen 1924; Adamic 1938) with its emphasis on ethnic persistence, exerted little influence on social science research. Much to its detriment, sociological theory had become convoluted with dominant group ideology. The crucial point here is that the political agenda of the dominant group shaped sociological theory and research, leading to a focus on subordinate groups and a view of the dominant group as the invisible "mainstream."

In the 1960s, mainstream American sociology experienced a paradigmatic crisis (cf. Kuhn 1970) in the study of race and ethnic relations as a result of its failure to foresee the mass mobilization of African Americans (Hughes 1963; Lyman 1991; McKee 1993; Steinberg 1995). Indeed, even the relevance of assimilationist theory for European immigrants underwent serious challenge (Glazer and Moynihan 1963; Greeley 1974). As a result, the last three decades have seen an explosion of scholarship seeking to account for the persistence of ethnic and racial conflict, including internal colonialism (Blauner 1972), class theories (Bonacich 1972; 1980; Barrera 1979), competition theories (Olzak 1986; 1989; 1992), and social constructionism (Nagel 1994; 1996). Nevertheless, what is significant for this analysis is that these challenging paradigms (reflecting the increased political power of historically dominated peoples) have focused upon subordinate group victimization and resistance or dominant group mechanisms of oppression (Feagin and Feagin 1978; Feagin and Vera 1995). Dominant group ethnicity has continued to be overlooked, despite some promising work on whiteness (Roediger 1991; 1994; Frankenberg 1993) and on the evolution of ethnic identity (assimilation of non-Anglo Americans into the dominant group) among European Americans (Lieberson 1985; Lieberson and Waters 1988; Waters 1990; Alba 1990). Ethnic and racial politics and the "hidden" nature of dominant group identity continue to preclude examination of dominant group ethnicity by social scientists.

DOMINANT GROUP IDENTITY AND THE REPRODUCTION OF DOMINATION

Central to any system of dominance/stratification are the processes through which domination is reproduced and dominant groups maintain their advantages in the face of challenges from subordinate groups. As William M. Newman (1973, p. 140) has observed, "Socially dominant groups generally attempt to maintain or increase their position of dominance over other groups in society." Within the broader framework of ethnic stratification, there is the ideological terrain in which the ethnic and racial understandings of a society are contested and manipulated as groups strive to challenge or defend both the legitimacy of the existing order and their individual position within this order (on the process of "racial formation," see Omi and Winant 1986; on the "political construction of ethnicity," see Nagel 1986; 1994). This implies a strategic component to ethnic identity; that is, that group identity may be accentuated or masked in response to perceived costs and benefits in intergroup interactions (cf. Cohen 1974; Despres 1975, p. 199; Keyes 1981, pp. 14–16;

Worsley 1984, pp. 248–250). In this context, the nature of dominant group ethnicity—the hidden aspect of group identity and the claimed position at the cultural center—plays a key role in the persistence and reproduction of group hegemony.

One way in which dominant group ethnicity may facilitate the reproduction of ethnic dominance is that the sometimes hidden nature of dominant group identity, along with a disproportionate share of political power, enables dominant group interests to be deliberately confounded with those of the larger society. As Herbert Marcuse (1964) has argued, the normalization of power—its incorporation in the routine symbols and understandings of everyday life—creates a "one-dimensional" framework in which it becomes difficult to perceive, or to challenge, elements of the existing system of domination. In such a setting, the legitimacy of dominant group power becomes a given. This is particularly evident when, as in the case of the United States, the dominant group is able to appropriate—or at least play the major role in defining—the national identity. As a result, the state is portrayed as a neutral arbiter between groups, and state and institutional actions promoting the interests of the dominant group (e.g., immigration restriction, English-only legislation) are cast as representing the interests of the larger society, thus masking their ethnic content and increasing their legitimacy. Similarly, public officials present themselves not as members of the dominant group but as agents of the larger society (Ringer and Lawless 1989, p. 76). This issue is especially meaningful given the expanding role of the modern state. Indeed, as Michael Omi and Howard Winant (1986, pp. 76–78) point out, there are arguably few state institutions whose actions do not affect race and ethnic relations either directly (e.g., the Immigration and Naturalization Service, the Bureau of Indian Affairs) or indirectly (e.g., the Departments of Education or Health and Human Services). "Hidden" ethnic action also occurs beyond the realm of the state in institutional spheres (e.g., the economy, the media, and education), where seemingly neutral actions serve to reproduce the ethnic order and ethnic stratification. Indeed, the hidden nature of dominant group identity masks processes of institutional discrimination.

U.S. history is replete with examples of the confounding of dominant group and national interests. The use of state power for the systematic appropriation of Native American lands, the pattern of immigration restriction and quotas designed to exclude southern and eastern Europeans and people of color, and even the Reagan-Bush attack on affirmative action as antithetical to the values of a "color-blind" society all clearly served to advance the interests of the dominant group. Furthermore, as Cynthia Enloe (1981, pp. 132–133) and Omi and Winant (1986, pp. 110–113) have observed, the U.S. state has often played a key role in forging compromises, co-opting social movements, and demobilizing subordinate group challenges to ethnic hegemony (on the passage of civil rights legislation and the distribution of funding in response to African American mobilization and urban uprisings in the 1960s, see Piven and Cloward 1971; on Native American policy, see Nagel 1996). In each instance, the key element is that by concealing the ethnic nature of such initiatives, conflict is reduced and dominance legitimated, thereby making easier the work of domination.

A second outcome of the denial or deemphasis of dominant group ethnicity is the "delegitimation" of the ethnic identity of subordinate groups. If ethnicity is viewed as attachment to a "foreign" culture—an attribute not possessed by the dominant group—then the ethnic identity of subordinate groups becomes an undesirable quality that must be shed in order to claim full membership in society. In this context, Anglo-conformity/assimilation becomes a social prescription that is difficult to challenge. Alternatively, if dominant group ethnicity has become "symbolic" or "optional," then it becomes easier to frame ethnicity as a matter of individual ancestry and identity, a personal trait devoid of any group affiliation (cf. Gans 1979; Alba 1990, pp. 299–301; Waters 1990, pp. 150–158). Thus, the vision of American society becomes one in which ethnicity is reduced to ancestry, and all members must conform to an institutionalized (and hidden) dominant group ethnicity. In either case, subordinate groups who seek to retain their identity, to have their experiences and cultural understandings included in the larger "societal" culture (i.e., cultural pluralism or, in U.S. popular discourse, diversity or multiculturalism), or to make group claims for a reallocation of society's resources are viewed as divisive, "politically correct," seeking "special treatment," or encouraging the "Balkanization" of the United States. In this deethnicized context, claims of

"reverse" discrimination against the dominant group are given equal (or even greater) standing with claims of discrimination by members of subordinate groups. Thus, non-ethnicity and individualized ethnicity constitute the ideological underpinnings of the effort by the dominant group to maintain its position of advantage.

Finally, the masking of dominant group identity also encourages the use of racist ideologies to explain inequality. The hidden nature of dominant group ethnicity and the normalization of cultural, political, and economic dominance tend to obscure the advantages that accrue to dominant group members. This taken-for-granted aspect of dominant group privilege, when coupled with the removal of formal barriers to subordinate group advancement, leads to the denial of ethnicity or race as a meaningful social force amid the promotion of ideologies of individualism (Gans 1988; Khleif 1992). Such a worldview is compatible with the practice of explaining persistent ethnic and racial inequality as due to the "cultural deficiencies" (e.g., "culture of poverty" or "family values") of subordinate groups. From the vantage point of the dominant group, social problems are not the result of ethnic or racial barriers but rather the failure of individual subordinate group members to conform to "societal" (i.e., dominant group) norms. Consequently, the social discourse on problems of ethnic and racial inequality is shifted from barriers erected by the dominant group to the cultural characteristics of subordinate groups. This is reflected in such phenomena as the differing perceptions of African Americans and European Americans with regard to the opportunity structure (cf Klugel and Smith 1982; 1986; Klugel 1990). Politically, this serves to neutralize demands for a redistribution of resources and to legitimize policy initiatives (e.g., attacks on the welfare state and the retreat from affirmative action and school desegregation) that benefit the dominant group. In the post–civil rights movement era, this denial of group advantages has been an effective ideological weapon in the attempt to maintain group dominance.

THE EVOLUTION OF DOMINANT GROUP ETHNICITY

As a socially constructed identity, dominant group ethnicity is dynamic; it evolves as a result of intergroup interactions (cf. Yancey, Ericksen, and Juliani 1976). In the course of intergroup resource competition, the perceived advantages or disadvantages of masking or asserting identities and expanding or contracting group boundaries shape the evolution of group identity. Although dominant group status generally entails a disproportionate ability to set intergroup boundaries and to define the ethnic and racial order of the larger society, the ethnic understandings of a society are by no means a dominant group project. The creation and reproduction of the ethnic order of a society is a dialectical process that reflects both dominant group power and the ability of subordinate groups to resist dominant group initiatives and pursue their own political agendas (on "reciprocal goal definition," see Schermerhorn 1970, pp. 77–84; on the process of racial formation, see Omi and Winant 1986, pp. 68–69). Thus, the racial and ethnic order of a society is contested terrain, and the core elements of dominant group ethnicity (group identity, legitimacy of dominant status, and group ability to appropriate the national identity) are open to challenge, renegotiation, and redefinition.

This evolutionary process has been evident in the United States. Initially, a dominant group English or settler identity emerged through the fusion of regional identities and was asserted in opposition to Native Americans and non-English immigrants (Fischer 1989; Parillo 1994). Following independence, an Anglo-dominated "American" identity slowly emerged, as dominant group appropriation of the national identity was facilitated by slow immigration, the absorption of non-English colonial-era immigrants, and the exclusion from citizenship of African Americans and Native Americans. As will be detailed below, what has transpired since that time has been a slow expansion of the boundaries of the dominant group, as they have stretched to include progressively greater numbers of Americans of *European* ancestry. These changes reflect strategic adjustments by the dominant group to changing social conditions in the United States.

The process of evolution of dominant group identity was shaped by the specific social and historical context—the intergroup arena (Doane 1992)—in which groups met. Demographic factors such as changes in the number or relative size of groups, especially as a result of immigration, have continually reconfigured the ethnic composition of the United States. The process of capitalist development (industrialization and the evolution of relations of production, territorial expansion, and the movement of the United States into the core of the world economy) shaped both patterns of immigration and settlement and the course of intergroup relations (Bonacich 1984, Bodnar 1985). International and domestic political developments (e.g., wars, decolonization) also reshaped the intergroup arena. These events affected material interests, perceptions of interests, relative power levels, and patterns of immigration.

With respect to the evolution of dominant group ethnicity in the United States, the following observations seem particularly relevant. First, where it has occurred, the process of expansion of dominant group boundaries—the assimilation of other groups—has been slow, uneven, and in general considerably more complex than the processes described by Robert E. Park (1950), Marcus L. Hansen (1954), and Milton M. Gordon (1964). Periods of boundary reduction were interspersed with periods of Anglo-Saxon assertion (cf. Higham 1963; Gleason 1980; Horsman 1981), particularly when the dominant group perceived threats to its position due to immigration or subordinate group mobilization. This slow and uneven expansion also reflects the strategic use of ethnic enclaves and networks by immigrants, as well as the resistance to assimilation of non-Anglo European ethnic groups and the reluctance of the dominant group to accept persons of non-English ancestry into "full" membership in society.

The first stretching of dominant group boundaries involved the incorporation and assimilation of groups of northern and western European Protestant ancestry (on the "triple melting pot," see Kennedy 1952; Herberg 1960). From the standpoint of the dominant group, this reflected an adjustment to immigration from southern and eastern Europe and the expansion of racial politics. While this process resulted in the shedding of non-Anglo ethnic identities, it also effected the dilution of English American ethnicity and the emergence of a more general white Protestant/WASP/"old stock" American identity (Anderson 1970).

The second expansion of dominant group boundaries has involved, particularly since the 1960s, the progressive incorporation of groups of southern and eastern European origin. This assertion is more problematic given the ongoing and less complete nature of this process (on the greater relative salience of southern and eastern

European ethnic identities, see Alba 1990, pp. 59–70; on ethnic persistence among European Americans, see Greeley 1974), especially in ethnic enclaves, in the face of religious differences (e.g., Jewish Americans), and among more recent immigrants (e.g., Poles and Russians). Nevertheless, the general trend is toward the declining salience of these group identities as a whole (Alba 1985; Lieberson and Waters 1988; Waters 1990). This continued broadening of dominant group boundaries can be attributed to dominant group policies of assimilation (including immigration restriction), economic expansion that facilitated this absorption, and the declining utility of European ethnic identities in U.S. racial politics (on the "wages of whiteness," see Roediger 1991).

In interpreting current trends in the evolution of dominant group identity, I would agree with Alba (1990) that what is transpiring is the emergence of a European American ethnic group. This group is best characterized as possessing a generalized awareness of European ancestry (either single or multiple countries of origin) and an identity grounded in a postcolonial, postimmigrant "American" experience. Moreover, I believe that this process is further along than even many assimilationists (e.g., Lieberson, Waters) would suggest. As noted earlier, awareness of ancestry is not necessarily the same as the sense of peoplehood involved in ethnic identification, while "optional" ethnicity (Waters 1990) is not a meaningful group affiliation.

This emergence of a generalized (and often hidden) European American identity is grounded in the nature of U.S. race and ethnic relations, a context where the most significant intergroup interaction involves *macroethnic* or racial/ethnic divisions: African American, Asian American, European American, Latino American, Native American, and Arab American. These categories reflect a historical tendency toward the emergence of new, more inclusive identities (ethnogenesis) through the merger of smaller groups, a tendency that reflects both out-group (especially dominant group) labeling and the political strategies of the in-group (Giminez 1992; Calderon 1992). In the past, this involved the fusion (in the context of the U.S. experience) of identities, for example, the merging of Sicilian, Neapolitan, and Roman (among others) to form an Italian American identity (Lopreato 1970; Barton 1975). More recently, this process of

ethnic merging has included the emergence of Native American, Asian American, Arab American, West Indian, Latino/Hispanic, and other pan-ethnic identities (Nagel 1996; Espiritu 1992; Khleif 1989). Given the historical prevalence of racial politics in intergroup relations in the United States, the macroethnic divisions of the 1990s are *racially* based. Indeed, even seemingly nonracial (in terms of traditional usage) identities such as Latino/Hispanic or Arab American have been racialized; that is, they have become socially constructed groupings (based on presumed physiological similarity) that correspond to positions in the American racial hierarchy. Among other effects, this process of ethnic change has created a terminological dilemma for government agencies, social scientists, and the general public.

For the emerging European American ethnic group, this process means that the core of its identity is the distinction from non-European groups. Other more specific identities operate primarily as lower-level identities relevant within the confines of the macroethnic group. Thus, individuals may, depending upon the context, articulate identities on a variety of levels (Nagel 1996, p. 21). This means that while the English-Irish-Italian-German (etc.) divisions may at times be salient to European-Americans, they are generally irrelevant to Latinos, African Americans, and other non-European groups. Given the nature of dominant group identity, dominant group subethnic identities are generally less salient than the subethnic identities of subordinate groups (e.g., the Mexican, Puerto Rican, Cuban, etc., divisions within the Latino group). Indeed, one revealing example of out-group indifference to ethnic divisions within macroethnic categories is the increased use of Anglo to describe non-Hispanic whites, a phenomenon evident even in sociological journals (e.g., Martinez 1996; Santiago and Wilder 1991).

To recapitulate briefly, the above outline of the U.S. experience illustrates the evolution of dominant group identity via the expansion of boundaries and the absorption and inclusion of new groups. This has meant a change in group identity —a result that conforms to neither the melting pot nor the Anglo-conformity models (cf. Gordon 1964)—to a broader European (or perhaps white American) identity, albeit with a strong (and often hidden) Anglo influence. The dominant group has not entirely had its own way in shaping intergroup relations but instead has experienced a diffusion of identity in the course of intergroup interactions. The evolution of dominant group identity reflects both the ability of subordinate groups (of European ancestry) to gain entry into the upper echelons of the ethnic order and the willingness of the dominant group to relax ethnic boundaries and expand the mainstream of society. This latter phenomenon is at least in part a strategic retreat in the face of potential challenges from both European and non-European groups, especially in light of the declining proportion of European Americans in the U.S. population (Fischer 1989). This leads us to what is perhaps the most important point: While the original English-American dominant group has repeatedly had to expand its ranks and admit new members, the overall social, political, and economic dominance of a central group of white Protestant Americans/European Americans has persisted.

Following this outline of the evolution of U.S. dominant group identity to the present, it is germane to ask how this process might play itself out in the future. While social forecasting is always problematic, I suspect that the forces that reduced boundaries between European American groups (intermarriage, upward mobility, assimilative institutions, pressure from non-European groups) will effect the continuing consolidation of a European American (white American) identity. This process is not incompatible with the existence and persistence of increasingly symbolic identities linked to a specific country of ancestral origin— essentially the knowledge that one's ancestors hailed from a specific country (or countries), perhaps augmented by a few isolated traditions. Nevertheless, the more salient ethnic (or racial) division will continue to be the European/non-European dichotomy. As a dominant ethnicity, European American identity will continue to display tendencies toward taken-for-grantedness inasmuch as it will be less evident in day-to-day interaction. To this extent, it will remain a hidden ethnicity, with all of the attributes described earlier.

At the same time, I think that it is also plausible to expect some heightened dominant group ethnic assertion in the face of increasing racial and ethnic diversity (the projected decline in the proportion of European Americans to a bare majority of the U.S. population by the middle of the twenty-first century) and the ongoing post–civil rights movement challenges to dominant group hegemony (in-

cluding the claimed right to define who is "American"). This observation is particularly pertinent in the context of continued economic uncertainty and crisis amid the international challenge to U.S. hegemony in the world-economy. After all, it was the expansion of the American economy during the nineteenth and twentieth centuries that facilitated the broadening of dominant group boundaries by providing more resources (thus making subordinate group mobility relatively cost-free for the dominant group), a scenario unlikely to be repeated. To the extent that altering ethnic inequality becomes (or is perceived as) a zero-sum game, it would be reasonable to predict increased dominant group resistance to subordinate group mobilization. Such resistance could follow the patterns outlined above (masking the ethnic nature of state actions, asserting the need for a "color-blind" society, attacks on "political correctness" and multiculturalism, and pressure for immigration restriction), or it could take a more overtly ethnic tenor (emphasizing the "superiority" of "Western" culture, claiming the legitimacy, based on the postcolonial, postimmigrant saga, of European American hegemony, attacking "reverse discrimination," increasing the portrayal of Europeans/whites as victims, and increased ethnoviolence). Changing structural conditions will inevitably lead to changes in the ethnic understandings of American society, including the nature and role of dominant group ethnicity.

To the extent that subordinate group challenges make hidden ethnicity more difficult to sustain, one significant future issue will involve the emergence of an ethnic label for the dominant group. As has been the case with other groups (e.g., Native Americans, Hispanics/ Latinos), the choice of labels (influenced by both in-groups and out-groups) both reflects and shapes the racial and ethnic understandings of society. Historically, the taken-for-granted nature of dominant group ethnicity has combined with group appropriation of the national identity to make "unhyphenated American" an alternative group label; however, with the increasing contestation of the American label by subordinate groups, this may no longer be an option (cf. Horton 1995, p. 187). In addition, the inclusion of non-Protestants in the larger European American group may preclude continuation of the WASP label, while the European American label has experienced little usage outside of academic circles. Given this terminological vacuum, one possible outcome might be the transmutation of "white" from a racial category into an ethnic-like identity possessing an invented sense of peoplehood and common historical experience, what we might term the "ethnicization of race." This blurring of ethnicity and race—which may also happen with other macroethnic groups—may give rise to attempts to divorce whiteness from its historical legacy of oppression and privilege and to recast it as simply another identity (Gallagher 1994). Such a task would be facilitated by the "hidden" nature of current dominant group privilege and could be promoted by discourses emphasizing the existence of a "color-blind" meritocracy and/or the claimed victimization of whites (Doane 1996b). If successful, this strategy would enable whites/ European Americans to participate in the new politics of race and ethnicity without bearing the ideological burden of past injustices. In the same vein, the European American label, with its similarity to other group labels, could also be employed to avoid the legacy of whiteness and to foster claims of equality and the denial of privilege. While the outcome of this process is unclear, how the dominant group defines itself (and is defined by others) will play a key role in shaping intergroup relations in the twenty-first century.

Given the likelihood of increased intergroup conflict, I suspect that any further expansion of dominant group boundaries will be problematic, at least in the foreseeable future. Perhaps the emerging ethnic order in the United States (the macroethnic groupings African American, Asian American, European American, Latino American, and Native American) will constitute an end stage —or a long period of stasis—in the process of ethnic evolution, although it is possible to envision a slight shifting of dominant group boundaries to include Latinos of primarily European ancestry, Japanese Americans, and other groups characterized as "model minorities." One other possibility would be the emergence (ethnogenesis) of new "multiracial" identities (cf. Root 1992; Waters 1994; Zack 1995) if the progeny of the increasing number of interracial marriages deliberately assert a new identity and successfully promote new ethnic labels (e.g., in the U.S. census). This could in turn lead to a blurring of macroethnic/racial boundaries and the emergence of a new racial/ ethnic order, perhaps along the lines of the Caribbean/South American model (Harris 1964;

Davis 1991). Such a scenario, if it happens at all, is several generations away.

If this is indeed an end stage or a long pause in the evolution of ethnic identities in the United States, two types of outcomes are possible. In the best-case scenarios, American race and ethnic relations would move toward the multicultural model of diverse identities amid increasing social, political, and economic integration. In the worst case, we would see a descent into the maelstrom of increased intergroup antagonism and conflict. These future outcomes will be influenced by such factors as changing demographics, the evolving position of the United States in the global economy, and the nature of intergroup political and economic competition.

CONCLUSION

In this article, I have examined the core issues of a sociology of dominant group ethnicity in the United States. The central element in this framework is a conceptualization of dominant group ethnic identity as less salient as a consequence of being in a position of dominance. For dominant group members, ethnicity is optional—a matter of choice rather than a core identity—a situation that has sometimes led dominant group members (and many sociologists) to view the dominant group as "not ethnic." In contrast, I have argued that dominant group ethnicity is present (in the U.S. case, there is no such thing as non-ethnicity) but *hidden*— serving as the unacknowledged mainstream of American society. For the sociology of race and ethnic relations, this implies that it may be necessary to revisit, at least for the dominant group, the emphasis on self-awareness that exists in many definitions of ethnicity (e.g., Weber [1923] 1968, p. 389; Schermerhorn 1970, p. 12). Clearly, the study of race and ethnic relations has been limited by ignoring dominant group ethnicity.

At the same time, dominant group ethnicity has played a key role in intergroup relations. For individual dominant group members, hidden ethnicity has provided what Du Bois ([1935] 1956, pp. 700–701) referred to as a "public and psychological wage," an invisible benefit that is taken for granted. For the dominant group, the invisibility of its "hidden" ethnicity has served as a powerful weapon in the struggle to maintain its position. The nature of dominant group ethnicity has facilitated appropriation of the national ("American") identity and permitted state actions promoting the interests of the dominant group to be presented as neutral actions in the national interest. Of equal importance, the hidden nature of dominant group ethnicity has enabled the dominant group to formulate a set of ethnic and racial understandings—a discourse on ethnicity and race—that denies the legitimacy of subordinate group claims and, by obscuring advantages, allows the dominant group to blame subordinate groups for ethnic and racial inequality and to make claims of legitimacy for policies that perpetuate group advantages.

This hidden nature of dominant group ethnicity has important ties to American sociology and social thought. The underdevelopment of the study of dominant group ethnicity reflects both the less overt nature of dominant group ethnic identity and a political agenda that emphasizes the problems posed by subordinate groups and issues of assimilation. This downplaying of dominant group ethnicity is significant in that it maintains a mutually reinforcing relationship. To the extent that dominant group identity is less evident, it is understudied; to the extent that it is understudied, it remains less evident.

At the same time, the hidden aspect of dominant group ethnic identity does not mean that it is stagnant in nature. Dominant group identity may be asserted in a defensive manner in response to real or perceived threats to group hegemony. In the U.S. case, dominant group identity has evolved over time, as the group boundary has expanded—from English Americans to white Protestant Americans to European Americans—in response to changes in intergroup relations and the ethnic composition of the United States. This process has significant implications for the future of intergroup relations in the United States, as we can foresee both the increasing consolidation of a European American/white identity and the possible expanded assertion of this identity in an increasingly diverse society. Nevertheless, dominant group identity will probably remain less salient than that of subordinate groups, which means that it is increasingly essential to explore the nature of dominant group ethnicity.

While the framework presented here serves as a useful basis for understanding dominant group ethnicity, much remains to be done. At present, we have a limited empirical base for understanding dominant group identity. We need to move beyond studies of assimilation and persistence and instead to examine how dominant group members define and articulate their identity in intergroup interactions. This is particularly important in developing a microlevel understanding of how the hidden nature of dominant group ethnic identity perpetuates group privilege in routine interactions (on "everyday racism," see Essed 1991). On the macrolevel, it will be necessary to analyze how dominant group identity continues to be used to frame the ethnic and racial understandings of American society, as the dominant group responds to challenges from subordinate groups in an increasingly diverse society. Clearly, focusing on the role of dominant group ethnicity in intergroup interactions will be essential to understanding the future course of race and ethnic relations in the United States.

Although this analysis has been grounded in the case of race and ethnic relations in the United States, it could be argued that the unique aspects of the U.S. experience (its origins as a settler society, massive immigration, economic growth, slavery, and the racialization of society) limit the utility of this case in providing a more general understanding of the nature of dominant group ethnicity. Indeed, there is much to be gained from applying a global and comparative approach to the study of dominant group ethnic identity. How is ethnicity defined and expressed for dominant groups? Are there varying types of hidden ethnicity? What roles do various dominant group identities play in intergroup relations and the persistence of dominant group hegemony? For example, what are the roles of German or Tutsi identities? Does dominant group identity assume different forms in different circumstances? For example, we could compare the experiences of Afrikaners during apartheid in South Africa, a dominant group that constituted a small percentage of the population; the Sinhalese in Sri Lanka, a dominant group operating in a more bipolar context; and the Japanese in Japan, a dominant group that constitutes an overwhelming majority. Awareness and understanding of dominant group ethnicity may be a small piece in the larger social mosaic, but I believe that it is a critical component of the sociology of race and ethnic relations.

ACKNOWLEDGMENTS
Special thanks to Richard Alba, Bud B. Khleif, Lelia Lomba De Andrade, and the anonymous *TSQ* reviewers for their comments on previous drafts.

Historical Perspectives

2

The United States, which has been called a "nation of nations," is one of the most ethnically diverse societies in the modern world (Table 1). Despite an ideology—the "American Creed"—formally committed to human equality, racial and ethnic criteria have frequently determined social status in American society, and conflict for economic, social, and political preeminence among its numerous racial and ethnic groups has been one of the most salient features of the American experience. Figure 1 presents data on the distribution of major racial and ethnic groups in the United States. Presently, members of the largest racial and ethnic minorities (African Americans, Latinos, Asians, and American Indians comprise more than one-quarter (28.5 percent) of the population. This section provides a brief overview of the history of American ethnic relations. Because they are so numerous, it would be impossible to examine the experience of all American ethnic groups in this brief section (for a comprehensive survey, see the superb essays in the *Harvard Encyclopedia of American Ethnic Groups* [Thernstrom 1980] and the *Gale Encyclopedia of Multicultural Groups* [Galens, et al. 1995]). The articles included here provide conceptual and substantive continuity to the volume as a whole. This survey of several of the major ethnic and racial categories that collectively comprise the American people—what Hollinger (Article 4) terms the American "ethnoracial pentagon"—is organized in roughly the chronological order of their migration to North America. We begin by sketching some key features of the experience of the earliest inhabitants—American Indians—and conclude with a discussion of some of the most recent immigrants to the United States.

American Indians/Native Americans

The first Americans migrated from Asia between 12,000 to 40,000 years ago, slowly dispersing throughout North, Central, and South America. Although the length of time that they have inhabited the American continents is brief when compared with human societies elsewhere in the world, American Indian peoples developed a great diversity of cultures with widely different levels of technology, cultural complexity, and languages. The large and highly sophisticated Aztec, Inca, and Mayan civilizations contrast

TABLE 1   *Racial Populations in the United States, 1970–1998*

	NUMBER (THOUSANDS)				PERCENT OF THE POPULATION			
	1970	*1980*	*1990*	*1998*	*1970*	*1980*	*1990*	*1998*
Total	203,212	226,546	249,398	269,073	100.0	100.0	100.0	100.0
White	177,749	188,341	209,173	222,304	87.5	83.2	83.9	82.6
Black	22,580	26,488	30,598	34,200	11.1	11.7	12.3	12.7
American Indian, Eskimo, and Aleut	827	1,418	2,073	2,343	0.4	0.6	0.8	0.9
Asian and Pacific Islander	1,539	3,501	7,554	10,225	0.8	1.5	3.0	3.8
Chinese	435	806	1,645	*	0.2	0.4	0.7	*
Filipino	343	775	1,407	*	0.2	0.3	0.6	*
Japanese	591	701	848	*	0.3	0.3	0.3	*
Asian Indian	*	362	815	*	*	0.2	0.3	*
Korean	69	355	799	*	0.0	0.2	0.3	*
Vietnamese	*	262	615	*	*	0.1	0.2	*
Hispanic†	9,073	14,609	22,558	29,960	4.5	6.4	9.0	11.1
Mexican American	4,532	8,740	13,496	*	2.2	3.9	5.4	*
Puerto Rican	1,429	2,014	2,728	*	0.7	0.9	1.1	*
Cuban	544	803	1,044	*	0.3	0.4	0.4	*
Other Hispanic	2,566	3,051	5,086	*	1.2	1.3	2.0	*

Sources: U.S. Bureau of the Census, *U.S. Census of the Population: 1970,* vol. 1, Part I: *Characteristics of the Population,* Summary Section 2, Washington, D.C.: U.S. Government Printing Office, 1973; U.S. Bureau of the Census, *U.S. Census of the Population: 1970,* Subject Reports PC(2)-1G; *Japanese, Chinese, Filipinos,* Washington, D.C.: U.S. Government Printing Office, 1973; U.S. Bureau of the Census, *Census of the Population*: 1980, vol. 1: *Characteristics of the Population,* "Detailed Population Characteristics, Part I: U.S. Summary," PC80-1-D1-A, Washington, D.C.: U.S. Government Printing Office, 1984; U.S. Bureau of the Census, *Census and You,* Washington, D.C.: U.S. Government Printing Office, 1991. U.S. Bureau of the Census, Population Division, [online] "United States Population Estimates, by Age, Sex, Race, and Hispanic Origin," (1997). Available: http://www.census.gov/population/estimates/nation/intfile3-1.txt [1998, April 16].

*Not available.

†Hispanics are also included in "White," "Black," and "Other Hispanic."

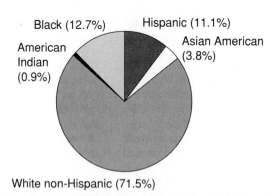

FIGURE 1   *Racial and Hispanic Population of the United States, 1998.*

Source: U.S. Bureau of the Census, [Online], "Resident Population of the United States: Estimates by Sex, Race, and Hispanic Origin, with Median Age," (1998). Available: http://www.census.gov/population/estimates/nation/intfile3-1.txt [1998, April 16].

sharply with the simpler societies of the Yavapai, Onondaga, and Kansa. As Cynthia Enloe has written, even "before the arrival of Europeans the American continent was already ethnically plural" (Enloe 1981:126). Today the U.S. government officially recognizes 554 Indian tribes and Alaska Native groups (U.S. Department of the Interior, 1997).

A bewildering diversity of native peoples was present when Europeans first invaded the Americas. Perhaps the best index of this extraordinary cultural diversity is the myriad number of languages found in the Americas; as Ruhlen (1987) has pointed out, the Americas were linguistically as diverse as the Eurasian land mass. Native American languages can be classed into about a dozen different stocks (each as distinct from the other as the Semitic from the Indo-European) and within each stock into languages as distinct as English from Russian. Despite a dramatic decline of native languages, about two-hundred distinct languages are still spoken among American Indian peoples in North America. Although Indians represent less than 1 percent of the American people, this number is equal to the number spoken among the other 99 percent of the population combined (Hodgkinson 1990:1). This cultural diversity persists among American Indians to the present day, despite the popular perception among outsiders that they are a single distinct ethnic group.

The European invasion of North America had a pervasive and enduring impact on American Indian peoples and cultures. Examination of the effects of Indian-white contact illustrates the process by which a system of ethnic stratification develops. As we noted in Part 1, *ethnic stratification* is a system of social ranking in which one ethnic group acquires greater power, privilege, and prestige than another (or others). An unequal relationship between two or more ethnic groups is not inevitable, however. In other words, some groups are not inherently dominant and others inherently subordinate; the establishment of a system of ethnic inequalities is the result of a historical process.

As mentioned in Part 1, Donald Noel (1968) has suggested that three conditions are necessary for a system of ethnic stratification to be created: *ethnocentrism, competition,* and differences in *power.* Noel applied these conditions to the development of the caste system of black-white relations in the United States, but let us here examine how these variables influenced patterns of Indian-white relations.

Ethnocentrism is the idealization of the attributes of the group to which an individual belongs. People of all societies tend to think of themselves as the chosen people or, at the very least, as those at the center of humanity. People of any society tend to think that their ways of doing things are correct, just, righteous, and virtuous—the way God intended. On the other hand, people tend to perceive the ways of other people as odd, incorrect, or immoral, and to reject or ridicule groups from which they differ. Ethnocentrism seems to be an inevitable outgrowth of the socialization process, during which cultural values and standards of right and wrong, beauty and ugliness, and so forth, are internalized.

Most European settlers regarded Native Americans as heathen savages, possessing cultures vastly inferior to their own. Indeed, among many Puritans of New England, Indians were regarded as agents of Satan, to be exterminated by gunfire or disease. The European invaders considered agriculture a superior economic activity and an index of their own cultural superiority. Therefore, they perceived the lands they entered to be "wilderness"—in their eyes, wild, unoccupied, and unused territory. Europeans also sought to Christianize the Indians and to eliminate their traditional religious practices. The ethnocentrism that underlay the missionary impulse is exemplified by the following speech by a Boston missionary to a group of Seneca Indians:

> There is but one religion, and but one way to serve God, and if you do not embrace the right way, you cannot be happy hereafter. You have never worshiped the Great Spirit in a manner acceptable to him; but have all your lives been in great errors and darkness. To endeavor to remove these errors, and open your eyes, so that you might see clearly, is my business with you. (quoted in Washburn 1964:210)

When two different ethnic groups come into initial contact, ethnocentrism is not restricted to one group. Rather, both sides respond with mutual ethnocentrism. Noel has noted this reciprocal process when he cites the reply of representatives of the Six (Indian) Nations to an offer by the Virginia Commission in 1744 to educate Indian youth at the College of William and Mary:

> Several of our young people were formerly brought up at Colleges of the Northern Provinces; they were instructed in all your sciences; but when they came back to us, they were bad runners, ignorant of every means of living in the woods, unable to bear either cold or hunger, knew neither how to build a cabin, take a deer, or kill an enemy, spoke our language imperfectly, were therefore neither fit for hunters, warriors, or counselors; they were totally good for nothing. We are, however, not the less obliged by your kind offer, though we decline accepting it; and to show our grateful Sense of it, if the Gentlemen of Virginia will send us a Dozen of their Sons we will take great care of their education, instruct them in all we know and make Men of them. (quoted in Noel 1968)

It is clear that the American Indian leaders felt their ways to be superior to those of the Virginians.

The second condition necessary for a system of ethnic stratification to develop is *competition;* that is, two or more individuals or groups must strive for a goal or objective that only one can achieve. From the beginning of Indian-European contacts, competition between the two groups centered around land. American Indian and white looked on land differently. The former emphasized the notion of *usufruct,* or user's rights. The land could be occupied, hunted, cultivated, and otherwise used as long as a group wished. Once it was abandoned, it became available for use by others. To most Indian peoples, land was not something that could be individually owned or bought or sold, as Europeans conceived of it. Many land transactions between Native Americans and Europeans were based on radically different conceptions of what rights were being conveyed.

A system of ethnic stratification ultimately rests on differences in *power.* Initial contacts between Indians and whites usually took place in a context of equality and were not necessarily destructive of Indian cultures and societies. In fact, many items of white technology—especially guns, knives, cloth, fishhooks, pots, and other tools—were eagerly sought. For instance, it was only after the introduction of the horse by Europeans that the Plains Indian cultures flourished (Washburn 1964:66–70). The posture of equality is reflected by the white recognition of American Indian peoples as independent powers—nations (like the Cherokee Nation and the Navajo Nation)—and by numerous diplomatic treaties, gifts, and even politically arranged marriages. (The marriage of Pocahontas and John Rolfe, for example, was primarily a political match to ensure the survival of early Virginia colonists.)

Initially, the desire of Europeans for land they could cultivate did not strain Indian-white relationships; but as the number of Europeans increased throughout the seventeenth, eighteenth, and nineteenth centuries, their demand for land became the primary source of conflict with American Indians. Moreover, cultivation soon reduced the supply of game and forced an Indian retreat. The advance of European settlement eventually overwhelmed even the most resolute Indian resistance. Armed with superior military technology and bolstered by increasing numbers, Europeans moved inexorably westward. As the whites expanded westward, American Indian peoples were frequently expelled from their traditional settlements to lands beyond the immediate frontier. Removal was frequently legitimated by an underlying Anglo-Saxon ethnocentrism, exemplified by President Theodore Roosevelt's assertion that "this great continent could not have been kept as nothing but a game preserve for squalid savages" (quoted in Lurie 1968:66).

As control of lands they had formerly occupied increasingly passed to whites, the status of American Indians came increasingly to resemble what C. Matthew Snipp (1986) has called "captive nations." The Native American land base, which initially had been over 2 billion acres, dwindled to 155 million acres in 1871 and to 54 million acres in 1997 (Dorris 1981; U.S. Department of the Interior 1997). Diseases carried by the Europeans, such as smallpox, scarlet fever, measles, and cholera, were fatal to large numbers of native peoples, who for centuries had been physically isolated from the Old World and had developed little or no resistance to these diseases. Epidemics ravaged American Indian peoples throughout American history, frequently killing more than half of a tribe. Washburn concludes that "unwittingly, disease was the white man's strongest ally in the New World" (1975:107). Moreover, substantial numbers of Indians died as a result of warfare with Europeans, policies of removal from ancestral lands, and deliberate extermination. The American Indian population, which had numbered between 5 and 6 million when Columbus reached the New World, dwindled to 237,000 by 1900 (Thornton 1987:32). American Indians experienced a decline not only in their numbers but also in the number of tribes or ethnic groups—from an estimated 1,000 at the time of initial European contact to 318 officially recognized tribes residing in the lower 48 states in 1992 (Nagel 1996:4, 14).[1]

The reservation system that developed most fully during the nineteenth century symbolized both the end of the era of Indian-white equality and the relegation of native peoples to a minority status. Most Indians had to obtain passes to leave the reservation, were denied the vote, and were forcefully prohibited from engaging in native religious and ceremonial practices. Traditional Indian cultures and patterns of authority were undermined as their economic resources eroded, their numbers plummeted, and the administration and control of the reservation were placed in the hands of white agents. Reservation peoples lost control over their fate. As a consequence, they came to resemble a "captive nation" characterized by white political domination.

In the last quarter of the nineteenth century, most white Americans agreed that Native Americans were a vanishing race and that forced assimilation—socialization to white culture—represented the most "humane" means of dealing with the dilemma of the American Indian's continued existence. Whites employed a strategy of destroying tribal governments, breaking up the reservations, and granting land to Indians on an individual basis. The federal government subsidized American Indian schools, many of which were controlled by white religious groups. In many instances, Indian children were forcibly taken from their families and enrolled in boarding schools, where they were compelled to adopt white styles of dress and were punished for speaking their own native languages (see Adams 1988). The underlying assumption of these policies was that Indians should be forced to give up their cultural heritages and to adopt the European values of rugged individualism, competition, and private enterprise. To ethnocentric whites, these values represented more "civilized" forms of behavior, in contrast to the "savage" practices of American Indians. In 1887 Carl Schurz, the German-born Secretary of the Interior, justified these practices: "The enjoyment and pride of individual ownership of property is one of the most effective civilizing agencies" (U.S. Commission on Civil Rights 1961:122). Theodore Roosevelt, reflecting the late nineteenth-century Social Darwinist theory that emphasized the "survival of the fittest," agreed: "This will bring the whites and Indians into close contact, and while, of course, in the ensuing struggle and competition many of the Indians will go to the wall, the survivors will come out American citizens" (Quoted in Washburn 1975:242).

Nevertheless, the striking feature of Native American Indian life in the twentieth century has been the ability of Indian cultures to endure. Despite intense pressures to assimilate into the mainstream of American society, American Indians have clung tenaciously to their cultural values, standards, and beliefs. Although plagued by the nation's poorest health standards, the American Indian population increased by 1990 to nearly 2 million, better than a 40 percent increase over 1980. Census Bureau estimates place the Native American population in 1998 at more than 2.3 million, nearly ten times the number a century ago. Moreover, Census Bureau projections estimate that by 2050 the American Indian population will reach 4.6 million (1.2 percent of the population) (Day 1993; Harris 1994b). This dramatic increase in the number of people identifying themselves as Native Americans reflects an Indian cultural and political renaissance during the past quarter century. During the 1960s and 1970s ethnic consciousness and political militancy, particularly among the younger and better educated, increased substantially. As a result, many people who once were ashamed of their Native American ancestry today acknowledge or assert it. In addition, some people may be motivated by special educational, medical, and economic benefits available to Indians through treaties with the federal government (Snipp 1997). Finally, the number of "wannabees"—whites for whom it is fashionable to proclaim Indian ancestry— may have increased (Nagel 1995, 1996).

As noted before, a substantial portion of American Indian lands were ceded to colonists and early settlers by treaties, first with the colonial British governments and later with the United States government. In signing these treaties, Indian peoples agreed to give up certain things (most frequently, land) in return for concessions and commitments to them by the United States government. Most treaties, which involved water, fishing, and territorial agreements, guaranteed that Indians would retain the treaty rights granted to them (including sovereignty over remaining lands) in perpetuity—"as long as the grass shall grow and the rivers shall run." Treaties therefore form the basis of the unique legal and political status of American Indians today. In contrast to other American racial and ethnic minorities, American Indian tribes "are due certain privileges, protections, and benefits of yielding some of their sovereignty to the United

States" (Dorris 1981:54). Among these commitments are the obligations of the federal government to protect Indian lands and to provide social, medical, and educational services. These legal responsibilities, however, are invariably affected by national, state, and local politics, in which Indian interests are usually of little concern. Recently efforts by the Congress and the President to balance the federal budget led to cutbacks in programs critical to many American Indians. For example, between 1995 and 1996, the Federal repair budget for Indian housing was cut by one-third, leaving many Indians ill-equipped to confront the harsh winters in northern states (Brooke 1996: A1).

Despite persistent and recurring efforts to undermine the reservation system, these treaties did permit Indians to preserve some of their dwindling lands. Although the lands held by American Indians today represent only a small portion of those originally guaranteed in treaties, they include vast and extremely valuable agricultural, water, timber, fishing, and energy resources. However, until recently Indians have seldom received significant income from these resources because they have been developed and exploited primarily by non-Indian interests. For example, Indian reservations have provided water for the extensive urban development of the Southwest and have received almost nothing in return. Similarly, mining and mineral development on Indian lands has often resulted in exploitative leases that provided only a small fraction of the value of the resources being used; for example, because of leases signed by the Bureau of Indian Affairs on their behalf, in 1981 the Navajo Nation received 15 to 38 cents a ton for coal that was sold by American suppliers to foreign buyers for $70 a ton (Snipp 1986). Development also had a devastating effect on the environment of many reservations, destroying habitat, polluting streams and rivers, and desecrating Indian spiritual sites (Robbins 1997:17).

Snipp contends that the increasing attempts to develop and exploit American Indian resources for external economic interests reflect a shift in policy toward Indian peoples from "captive nationhood" to *internal colonialism*. The former represented political domination but did not dramatically disrupt the economic lives of American Indian people. Internal colonialism, on the other hand, involves economic as well as political domination. As pressures for development of the scarce resources found on tribal lands continue, such internal colonialism is likely to become more pronounced.

As a result, Native Americans are today among the poorest and least educated groups in American society. In 1989 Indian median household income was less than two-thirds (64 percent) that of whites; nearly one-third (31 percent) of Native Americans lived below the poverty level. The problems of poverty are especially acute on Indian reservations—the lands to which native peoples have title and over which they exercise sovereignty. Among reservation Indians, from one-third to one-half of all families have incomes below the poverty level; on some reservations the unemployment rates exceed 80 percent. By 1990, two-thirds (66 percent) of all Indians twenty-five and older had completed high school, compared with four-fifths (80 percent) of whites. The percentage of Indians at that age category (9.3 percent) who had graduated from college was less than half the percentage of whites (21.5) (U.S. Bureau of the Census 1992b).

In response to the exploitation and depletion of their resources, Native Americans are increasingly challenging their political and economic domination by outsiders, and they are seeking to exert Indian control over reservation resources in order to address some of the severe economic problems confronting Indian peoples (Cornell 1988a). Indian activists have mounted legal challenges to ensure that the U.S. government honors the terms of treaties that it has made with Indian tribes. In one of the most celebrated legal cases involving Indian claims that the Federal Government had not fulfilled its treaty obligations, in 1975 a Federal District judge awarded half the annual salmon catch in Puget Sound to Indian tribes who had signed an 1855 treaty with the United States (Egan 1992). Similarly, in 1990 the Passamaquoddy Indians gained a $40 million settlement of their land claims against the state of Maine, and the Puyallup (Washington) tribe ceded 20,000 acres of land in Tacoma for a $162 million package (Associated Press: 1990). New York Seneca Indians threatened to reclaim the lands on the Allegheny reservation on which the town of Salamanca, New York, was built, under a ninety-nine year lease that expired in 1991. As part of the settlement, the annual lease payments of non-Indians living in Salamanca increased dramatically (*New York Times* June 11, 1990).

Indian activism has also been reflected in their efforts to develop organizations to advance Indian economic interests by resisting external exploitation of their resource base, including timber, water, and, especially, minerals. One of the most prominent of these has been the Council of Energy Resource Tribes (CERT), which was formed to promote Indian economic interests in the substantial coal, gas, oil, and uranium reserves that are found on Indian lands (Snipp 1986). Moreover, rather than lease their lands to drill for oil or gas or mine for coal, several tribes have formed their own high-technology mining ventures that enable them, rather than large energy companies, to retain the profits from these enterprises (Johnson 1994). As the powerful economic and political pressures intensify over increasingly scarce and valuable native resources, it seems inevitable that conflicts will increase in the future (Cornell 1988a; Erdrich and Dorris 1988).

In addition to exploiting their own energy resources, Indian peoples have embarked on a number of other forms of economic development, such as tourism among the White Mountain Apache and Havasupai tribes of Arizona and the Nez Percé in northeastern Oregon; the Wisconsin Oneida and the Mississippi Choctaw have invested in plants that manufacture products as diverse as auto parts and greeting cards (White 1990; Egan 1996).

Probably the most widely publicized enterprise that Indians have developed on reservations lands, however, is gambling. In 1987 the Supreme Court ruled that American Indian tribes had the authority to operate gambling enterprises on tribal lands and were exempt from most state gambling laws and regulations. The next year, Congress passed the Indian Gaming Regulatory Act (IGRA) of 1988, which established federal regulations for the overall conduct of Indian gaming. By 1997, 184 tribes had opened gambling facilities and another 32 had such facilities in the planning stages. A study by the U.S. General Accounting Office (1997) found that during the decade between 1985 and 1995, income from Indian gaming rose dramatically, increasing from $125 million to over $4.5 billion. By 1995 Indian gaming accounted for at least 10 percent of all revenues from legal gambling in the United States; revenues generated by Indian casinos throughout the country were comparable to those of Atlantic City casinos and were more than half the revenues of Nevada casinos.

However, whether gambling is the solution to the problems of Native American poverty is questionable. Many critics—Indian and non-Indian—have criticized the social and cultural consequences of gambling and its corrosive effects on traditional Indian values (Dao 1993). Moreover, reservations located in areas remote from major population centers encounter difficulties attracting patrons. The GAO study found that a few tribes (for example, the Pequot, a Connecticut tribe that operates Foxwoods, the nation's wealthiest casino) are doing very well; about half of all the Indian casino revenues were generated by just eight facilities that had incomes of over $100 million each. However, a majority of tribes had revenues of less than $15 million (U.S. General Accounting Office 1997), and their overall impact on tribal economic development was modest, at best. The Oglala Sioux of the Pine Ridge Reservation in South Dakota, for example, earned $1 million annually from their casinos—about $38 per capita (Kilborn 1997). Despite widely publicized examples of casino-generated wealth, the vast majority of American Indian people have yet to experience an economic renaissance.

European Americans

The migratory movement of European peoples from the seventeenth through the twentieth centuries has been the greatest in human history. Since the beginning of the seventeenth century, more than seventy million people have emigrated from Europe; about three-fourths of this number have come to the United States. The uprooting that millions of European immigrants experienced comprises one of the most dramatic sagas in American—indeed, world—history. This massive migration and its impact on American society, and the experience of European immigrants and their descendants have been widely described and debated among social historians and sociologists (Handlin 1951; Taylor 1971; Jones 1960, 1976; Seller 1977; Daniels, 1990; Dinnerstein, Nichols, and Reimers 1996; Dinnerstein and Reimers 1987; Bodnar 1985; Archdeacon 1983).

For nearly two centuries—from the beginning of the seventeenth to the beginning of the nineteenth century—the European population of America was overwhelmingly Protestant and British. The first European immigrants to settle permanently in what is now the United States were almost exclusively English. The first substantial English migration occurred between 1607 and 1660. The economic, legal, and political traditions that English settlers brought to America established an English foundation for American institutions, language, and culture. Although ethnic groups who later migrated contributed substantially to the distinctively American nature of political, economic, and social institutions, language and culture, they were also forced to adapt to the cultural and social systems that the English had established.

Although the English comprised the greatest proportion of the total colonial population, the middle colonies (New York, New Jersey, Pennsylvania, Delaware) contained substantial settlements of Germans, Dutch, Scotch-Irish, Scots, Swedes, and French Huguenots. Because the middle colonies contained the greatest variety of European cultures, they provided a context within which interethnic relations among European peoples in American society can first be observed. Here the ideal of America as a *melting pot,* in which diverse cultures come together to form a new people, was first formulated. In 1782 a Frenchman, Hector St. John de Crèvecoeur, wrote the following:

> *What then is the American, this new man. . . . Here in America individuals of all nations are melted into a new race of men, whose labours and posterity will one day cause great changes in the world. (Crèvecoeur 1782/1957:39)*

As we will consider more fully in Part 3, the idealistic notion of the melting pot has greatly influenced later conceptions of how the various cultures comprising the American people have adapted and interacted (for many people, how they *should* adapt and interact).

However, relations between ethnic groups in the middle colonies sometimes fell short of this ideal. Spurred by William Penn's promotional efforts during the late seventeenth and early eighteenth centuries, many Germans settled in Pennsylvania, where they formed prosperous farming communities. Because they insisted on maintaining their own language, churches, and culture, their presence generated some of the earliest recorded conflicts among European ethnic groups in America. In 1752 Benjamin Franklin expressed the widely held fears of the "Germanization" of Pennsylvania:

> *Why should the Palatine Boors [Germans] be suffered to swarm into our Settlements, and by herding together, establish their Language and Manners, to the Exclusion of ours? Why should Pennsylvania, founded by the English, become a Colony of Aliens, who will shortly be so numerous as to Germanize us instead of Anglifying them . . . ? (Cited in Dinnerstein and Reimers 1987:7)*

Thus, colonial attitudes toward immigrants were marked by considerable ambivalence. This same uncertainty still characterizes America's response to ethnic diversity. Throughout the American experience, immigrant groups have been regarded both positively and negatively. On the one hand, immigration has provided a steady source of labor that has fueled the country's economic development and expansion. Until the twentieth century, inducements in the form of land, jobs, and exemption from taxation were offered to encourage settlement and to assist American economic development. Americans have also celebrated the idea of America as a haven for the oppressed, as in Emma Lazarus's classic poem, "Give me your tired, your poor / your huddled masses yearning to breathe free . . . ," which is inscribed on the Statue of Liberty.

On the other hand, the concern expressed by Benjamin Franklin over the impact of ethnic diversity on the society's institutions has been a persistent one. Lazarus's poem further characterizes those "tired," "poor," "huddled masses" as "wretched refuse," and, in fact, many immigrant groups have been perceived as undesirable wretched refuse. In practice, Americans have been less charitable than their idealized accounts indicate. Americans have frequently rejected ethnic differences as alien and as a threat to American political, social, and cultural institutions. Some ethnic groups in particular have been rejected or excluded as un-American and incapable of assimilating. Thus, while the labor of immigrants was accepted, their cultural traditions usually were not.

In 1790 when the first United States census was taken, the population of the new American nation numbered nearly four million. It was overwhelmingly British in composition, with the English comprising 60 to 80 percent of the population, and with other people from the British Isles (Scots, Welsh, and Scotch-Irish) contributing substantially. Between 1830 and 1930, the United States population experienced dramatic growth and change. During this period, the nation changed from a small group of tenuously related state governments to the most politically and economically powerful nation on earth. The area of European settlement moved progressively westward at the same time that the country became the world's leading industrial nation.

Peoples of many lands contributed to this dramatic growth. During the century between 1830 and 1930, nearly 35 million immigrants entered the country, swelling its

total population to more than 123 million (see Figure 2). In contrast to the relative ethnic homogeneity of colonial immigration, the immigrants who arrived in the nineteenth and early twentieth centuries represented many different countries and
peoples, including German, Russian, Mexican, British, Polish, Japanese, Scandinavian,
Irish, Italian, Slavic, Greek, Chinese, and Portuguese. European immigration since
1790 has been divided into two broad categories: *"old" immigrants* from northern and
western Europe and *"new" immigrants* from southern and eastern Europe (see Figure 3).

The "Old" Immigration

Immigration to the United States increased dramatically throughout the nineteenth
century. In the peak year of the 1830s, slightly more than 70,000 immigrants entered.
By the 1850s, this annual figure had increased to 400,000; by the 1880s, to 650,000;
and by the first decade of the twentieth century, there were several years in which
more than one million immigrants were admitted.

Until the 1890s, immigration was drawn principally from countries of northern
and western Europe: Germany, Ireland, Great Britain (England, Scotland, and Wales),
and Scandinavia (Norway, Sweden, and Denmark). With the exception of the Roman
Catholic Irish, the old immigration was substantially Protestant. These groups, again

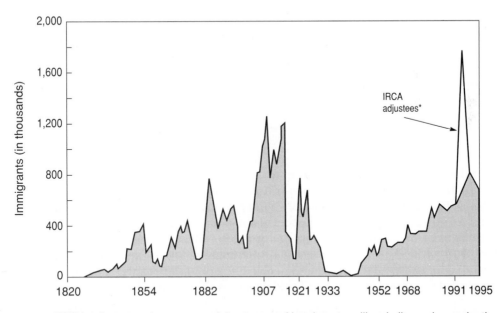

*IRCA adjustees refers to a special category of immigrants—illegal aliens who, under the
provisions of the Immigration and Control Act of 1986 (IRCA), were permitted to apply for
regular permanent resident status in the United States. By 1994 virtually all those eligible
for permanent residence had achieved that status.

FIGURE 2 *Immigration to the United States, 1821–1995*

Source: U.S. Immigration and Naturalization Service. *Statistical Yearbook of the Immigration and Naturalization Service, 1993.* Washington, D.C.: U.S. Government Printing Office, 1994. Data for 1994 and 1995
provided by Immigration and Naturalization Service internet home page, 1996.

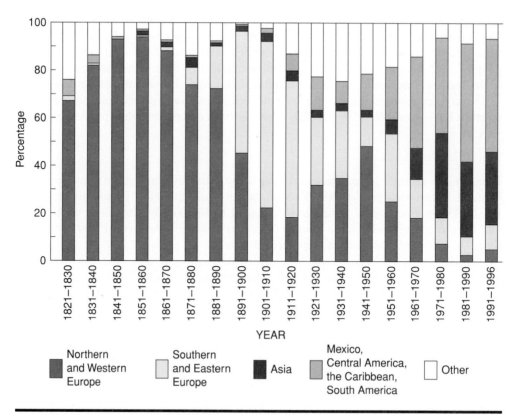

FIGURE 3 *Origins of U.S. Immigration by Region, 1821–1996*

Source: Statistical Yearbook of the Immigration and Naturalization Service,1988, pp. 11–12; Statistical Year-
book of Immigration and Naturalization Service, 1996, p. 28.

with the exception of the Irish, the first immigrant group to settle primarily in cities, were attracted by the opportunities of free or relatively cheap land, and therefore often settled in the rural areas of the country. There were several common factors in their countries of origin that led people to emigrate: drastic population increases, displacement of traditional handicraft industries by the Industrial Revolution, an upheaval in agriculture that transformed traditional agrarian land patterns, and the migration of substantial numbers of people from rural to urban areas. Above all, the promise of economic opportunity lured people to the United States.

The "New" Immigration

European immigration to the United States reached its peak between 1890 and the outbreak of World War I in 1914. During this period, the United States received more than 14 million immigrants. As dramatic as the numerical increase was the shift in the sources of immigration. Prior to the 1880s, immigrants had come almost exclusively from northern and western Europe. By the first decade of the twentieth century, however, more than 70 percent of all immigrants came from southern and eastern Europe.

This shift brought large numbers of immigrants from a great variety of countries—Greeks, Croatians, Italians, Russians (primarily Jews), Poles, Hungarians, Czechs, and Lithuanians. These groups were culturally different from those who had previously migrated to this country. Unlike the old immigration, which was heavily Protestant and followed agricultural pursuits, the new immigrants were overwhelmingly Roman Catholic or Jewish, and, although they may have originated in rural areas or small towns, were drawn primarily to the economic opportunities in the rapidly expanding cities. The changes in the ethnic composition of this immigration caused "native" whites to fear the impact of non-English cultures on American institutions.

The shift in immigration patterns coincided with the flowering of the ideology of "scientific" racism, which reached its height about the turn of the twentieth century. As noted in the introduction to Part 1, at this time scientific and lay opinion concurred in the idea of the inherent mental and moral inferiority of all those who were not of Anglo-Saxon or Teutonic ancestry. To the already existing conceptions of black, American Indian, and Asian inferiority was added the notion of the racial inferiority and the unassimilability of immigrant groups from southern and eastern Europe. Never before or since have racist ideologies been so pervasive and so intellectually respectable in the United States as they were at this time. Moreover, these racist ideologies, which have had an enduring impact on policies and practices in American society throughout the twentieth century, were given intellectual legitimation by the nation's social and intellectual elites—the "best and brightest."

Such beliefs in the racial and cultural inferiority of new immigrants provided foundation for American immigration policy from 1917 to 1965. The first general restrictive legislation, passed in 1917, was a literacy test, which was used precisely because it was believed to discriminate against "new" immigrants, limiting their numbers while still permitting substantial numbers of "old" immigrants to enter. In the 1920s, even more stringent restrictive measures were enacted, each one assuming the desirability of restricting immigration in order to include those from the countries of the "old" immigration. In 1921 and 1924 further legislation designed to curtail new immigration was enacted. Finally, in 1929, the National Origins Quota Act, which was based on the rationale of ensuring the maintenance of Anglo-Saxon "racial" purity, went into effect. The law limited total immigration to 150,000 annually and established numerical quotas for each nation. Derived by a complicated calculation, each nation's quota was supposed to be "in proportion to its [the nation's] contribution to the American population." The measure assigned the highest quotas to those nations of northern and western Europe whose "racial" stock was believed to be closest to that of the original settlers of the country and who were therefore considered more assimilable and more desirable. More than four-fifths of the total quota was allocated to countries of the "old" immigration. For instance, Great Britain had an admission quota exceeding 65,000, but Italy was allocated fewer than 6,000, Hungary fewer than 1,000, and Greece a mere 310. Reflecting the racist assumptions on which it was based, the law excluded most Asians and Africans completely. These blatantly racist immigration policies were retained virtually intact until 1965, when the Immigration Act, which we will describe more fully in Part 4, was enacted.

Despite fears that they were undesirable and unassimilable and that they represented a threat to American society, the descendants of new immigrants, today referred to as *white ethnics*, have achieved socioeconomic attainments comparable to descendants of the old immigrants (see also Model 1988). In Article 23, "The New Immigration and Ethnicity in the United States," Douglas Massey contends that "the remarkable amalgamation of European immigrants into the society and culture of the United States is a historical fact." By almost any measure, descendants of southern and eastern European immigrants (Italians, Jews, Poles, Greeks, Hungarians) have become culturally and structurally assimilated into American life to a degree that few would have predicted even as late as the end of World War II. Indeed, Milton Gordon (Article 12), in his classic discussion of the process of assimilation in American life, which was published in 1961, contended that, although the descendants of the "new" immigrants had become culturally assimilated into the mainstream of American life, they remained structurally unassimilated—that is, they were living, working, and marrying within their own separate worlds. However, a scant decade later, Andrew Greeley was able to celebrate what he termed the "ethnic miracle." Greeley contended that, despite their lowly socioeconomic status three generations earlier, "the ethnics have made it." By the early 1970s Jews had attained the highest income levels of all European ethnic groups in American society, and they were followed by Irish, German, Italian, and Polish Catholics, not by white Anglo-Saxon Protestants. Moreover, when parental educational levels were held constant, Catholic ethnics showed higher educational achievement than any other European groups except Jews. Writing nearly twenty years later, Richard Alba ("Assimilation's Quiet Tide," Article 15) has confirmed that the trends toward greater structural assimilation that Greeley identified have become even more pronounced. "Assimilation was, and is, a reality for the majority of the descendants of earlier waves of immigration from Europe. . . . Long-term processes . . . have whittled away at the social foundations for ethnic distinctions . . . [and produced] a rough parity of opportunities to attain such socioeconomic goods as educational credentials and prestigious jobs. . . ."

Despite their economic and educational achievements, many white ethnics still retain a sense of cultural identity with their ethnic and national roots (Waters 1990). But, as we noted in the introduction to Part 1, increasingly people of European descent, no matter what their ethnic or national origins, are subsumed within the broad category of "white," and their ethnic identity (as, for instance, Irish, Italian, English, Norwegian) increasingly has become what Gans has characterized as "symbolic"— that is, primarily of ritual or symbolic significance but of little consequence on a daily basis.

In 1990, three-fourths of the American people were identified by the U.S. census as non-Hispanic whites. However, primarily because of their lower fertility and immigration rates, the white population is projected to decline to less than two-thirds of the total population in 2020 and to about only one-half of the American people by 2050 (Day 1993). In Part 3 we will examine in greater depth some of the competing explanations for differences in adaptation among ethnic groups in American society. Moreover, because the experience of European American ethnic groups often serves as an implicit and unspoken background to current discussions of multiculturalism and the future of ethnic integration in American society, in Part 4 we will explore some of the implications and consequences of the "quiet tide" of assimilation of European ethnic groups to which Alba refers.

African Americans

From the earliest settlement to the present, the principal racial division in American society has been between white and black, between those of European ancestry and those whose ancestral origins can be traced to the African continent. From the arrival of the first African at Jamestown in 1619 to the present, the meanings attributed to the physical traits of black people have been more important than all other racial divisions in American society; no other minority group has experienced discrimination so intense, pervasive, and enduring as have African Americans. African Americans were enslaved for more than two centuries, and although more than a century has passed since slavery was legally abolished, the rationale for slavery that emphasized the racial and cultural differences between blacks and whites persists to this day.

By 1998 numbering more than 34 million—nearly 13 percent of the total American population—African Americans have been the largest racial minority in American society since the eighteenth century. Today their numbers total more than the entire population of Canada or of the Scandinavian countries of Sweden, Denmark, Norway, Finland, and Iceland combined. Only Nigeria, Ethiopia, and Zaire have larger black populations than the United States has. Moreover, the black population of the United States is expected to double in the first half of the twenty-first century, reaching 62 million, or about one-sixth of the American population, by 2050 (Day 1993).

In Article 7, "The Declining Significance of Race," William Julius Wilson distinguishes among three major periods or stages of black-white relations in American history: preindustrial, industrial, and modern industrial. Let us review briefly here the African American experience during the first two of these three periods. (We will examine the racial dynamics of the most recent period, the modern industrial stage, in Part 4.)

Slavery: The "Peculiar Institution"

During the preindustrial period, a plantation economy dominated and defined the lives of black people, the most important aspect of which was the institution of slavery. Slavery is a system of social relations in which some persons are involuntarily placed in perpetual servitude, are defined as property, and are denied rights generally given to other members of the society. Throughout human history, many societies have limited the freedom and rights of particular classes of people. Other systems of servile status, such as serfdom, debt bondage, and indentureship, have involved some degree of unfreedom and rightlessness. What distinguishes these statuses from slavery is therefore not absolute. "Slaves are [simply] the most deprived and oppressed class of serviles" (Noel 1972:5). This definition of slavery is useful because it provides a standard against which social systems can be compared. In other words, if slavery is conceived as being located at the far end of a continuum ranging from absolute rightlessness, on the one hand, to absolute autonomy on the other, one may examine each case of oppression in terms of its location between the extremes on this continuum.

Slavery was not an American invention. It existed in ancient civilizations, was widespread throughout the Middle Ages, and was practiced legally until 1962 on the Arabian peninsula; and it remains today, unofficially, in countries such as the Sudan and Mauritania. For example, in 1996, in response to a United Nations report of "an alarming increase . . . in cases of slavery, slave trade, and forced labor" and to subsequent denials of these charges by Sudanese officials and by Reverend Louis Farrakhan, head of the Nation of Islam, two *Baltimore Sun* reporters journeyed illegally to the Sudan, where they bought two Dinka boys for $500 each from an Arab trader and returned them to their families, from whom they had been kidnapped (Lewthwaite and Kane 1996). Similarly, although slavery was formally abolished in Mauritania in 1961, it remained so widespread that in 1980 the country's president once again proclaimed it illegal. However, because the law freeing slaves specified that masters should be compensated for the loss of their property, the practice has persisted virtually unchanged to this day. As a woman whose ancestors had for generations been held in similar bondage recently reported to a *New York Times* reporter, "God created me to be a slave, just as he created a camel to be a camel" (Burkett 1997:56).

Even though there was a surge of historical interest in the institution of American slavery, especially during the 1970s and 1980s (Elkins 1959; Davis 1966, 1975; Genovese 1974; Gutman 1976; Yetman 1970, 1984; Blassingame 1972; Rawick 1972; Fogel and Engerman 1974; Levine 1977; Parish 1989), there has been a relative dearth of attention to comparisons of the wide range of forms of unfreedom that have existed throughout human history and that persist today. As we suggested earlier, examining the institution of slavery in the United States raises questions not only of its similarities to and differences from other slave systems, but also about what constitutes unfreedom itself and, thus, about the more general question of the nature and effects of institutional regimentation and exploitation. The implications of an analysis of slavery in America could be used to examine the dynamics of other total institutions (Goffman 1961) and other dominant-subordinate relationships (serfdom, caste systems, debt bondage, racial or ethnic ghettos, and various aboriginal reservation systems) that have not yet been considered in these terms.

Thus slavery and slave trading were well established among European and African peoples by the late–fifteenth century, when Columbus's encounter with the Americas triggered a dramatic expansion of European exploration, expansion, and colonization. However, the slave trade from Africa to the Western Hemisphere from the mid-1400s to the 1800s resulted in a system of exploitation that dwarfed the forms of slavery developed in Africa. The introduction of national monarchies and the growing industrial and commercial revolutions in the sixteenth through the nineteenth centuries acted as catalysts for the development of Western slave systems, in which slave labor became an indispensable component of European expansion and settlement of the New World. Between twelve to fifteen million people were uprooted in a forced migration unparalleled in human history. By the mid–nineteenth century, the United States had become the world's leading slave power, but slave systems had penetrated societies throughout South and Central America and the Caribbean.

Despite a history of slavery that preceded European settlement of the New World and some similarities to other slave systems in the Americas, the slave system that emerged in the United States was the outcome of a process that developed primarily in this country. Earlier we used Noel's (1972) model of the development of ethnic stratification to describe the process whereby Indian-European equality at their initial contacts was eventually transformed into a system of vast inequalities between them. We return to Noel's model, which emphasizes three conditions—ethnocentrism, competition, and differences in power—to examine the manner in which the system of racial stratification emerged in what is now the United States.

Anglo-American attitudes toward Africans had their origins in late sixteenth-century Elizabethan England, an era during which England had begun to expand its power and domination throughout the world. World exploration and colonial expansion brought the English into increasing contact with African peoples. From the beginning, these contacts were marked by extreme ethnocentrism on the part of the English. Because Africans had vastly different customs, languages, religious practices, and skin color, they were viewed negatively by the English.

In the English mainland colonies in America, some blacks initially held the same legal status—indentured servant—as certain whites and Indians. Upon completion of a stipulated period of service (usually seven years), indentured servants were entitled to the rights of free persons. Although blacks initially possessed a similar legal status with white indentured servants, by the 1660s the slave status, with its assumption of lifetime hereditary service, had evolved, and whatever ambiguity of status had previously existed for African peoples had now vanished. Thereafter the status of slave became reserved almost exclusively for blacks, and whites came to think of blacks primarily as slaves.

Ethnocentrism alone would not have resulted in blacks' being placed in a slave status. As Cornell points out in his analysis of the development of the minority statuses of Indians and African Americans (Article 8, "Land, Labour, and Group Formation"), the English need for land and for labor, respectively, undergirded their relationships with these two different categories of peoples. Whereas the desire for land led to competition with native peoples, cheap and abundant labor was essential if the English were to develop a dynamic plantation economy in the New World. The English turned to the vast labor supply that was to be found on the African continent and to the trade in enforced labor that was already flourishing by the time the English began to establish their mainland colonies in the seventeenth century.

Slavery was, above all, a power relationship. Had the English not possessed greater power in the form of superior weaponry, naval technology, and products with which to induce some Africans to assist them in enslaving other blacks, the system could not have developed. In other words, if one group had not possessed superior power, it would have been impossible to create a system of social inequality based on race alone. The Africans who were imported to the British colonies were doubly disadvantaged. Of all the groups (such as other English, Irish, and American Indians) whom the English had employed in the role of indentured servants, Africans were culturally and physically most alien and thus the object of greatest ethnocentrism. Equally critical, however, was that Africans were also the most defenseless and powerless. Africans had been forcibly uprooted from their own land, separated from family, kin, and tribe, and transported to a new and strange continent where they were thrown together with other Africans from a great diversity of ethnic backgrounds. This diversity undermined the unity or social solidarity upon which they might have collectively drawn to resist.

By contrast, because American Indians retained their tribal organizations and posed a substantial political and military threat to the colonies, they were less vulnerable to white domination as slaves. Indian slaves were also much more difficult to retain because, being familiar with the terrain, they could escape relatively easily and be reunited with their own peoples. Finally, because trade with Indian nations was important to local economies, Native Americans possessed power to discourage wholesale enslavement of their people to a far greater degree than did blacks. "Though [they were] exploited, excluded, and sometimes decimated in [their] contacts with European civilization, Indians always maneuvered from a position of strength which Africans, devoid of tribal unity, unaccustomed to the environment, and relatively defenseless, never enjoyed" (Noel 1972:148). Blacks were enslaved primarily because they provided a labor supply crucial to an emerging American economy, were culturally and physically distinct from the English, and, most important, possessed few resources with which to resist the imposition of the slave status by whites.

Slavery and Caste

However, if one closely examines the dynamics of black-white relations throughout the American experience, it is problematic whether slavery alone was the most critical feature in defining the enduring social inequalities that have characterized the status of African Americans. Crucial to an understanding of the dynamics of black-white relations in the United States is a racial distinction; slaves in the United States were subjected to racial discrimination as well as legal servitude. The most distinctive feature of black-white relations in the United States was not slavery, per se, but that blacks—slave or free—occupied a lower *caste* status as well. American slaves had to contend with the sanctions and effects of *two* inferior statuses—slave and lower-caste member—that were mutually reinforcing. Unlike the situation in many other slave societies, manumission (granting of freedom) of slaves in the United States was extremely difficult, and blacks who were free could not anticipate participation in the society on an equal basis.

Although slavery represented the most extreme form of institutionalized inequality between black and white in America, Leon Litwack (1961) has pointed out that during the slavery era, the rights and privileges of free blacks also were severely circumscribed throughout the entire society; critical to the understanding of the dynamics of race relations in the United States is that even those African Americans who were free during the slavery era (more than one-tenth of the black population) did not have the same rights and privileges as whites and were not accepted into society on an equal basis. Oppression of African Americans was by no means restricted to the South or to slaveholders; throughout the North, too, the freedom, rights, and privileges of free blacks were severely curtailed. At no time did the words *free person* or *freedom* mean the same thing to blacks as to whites. In many states, barriers to voting were initiated for blacks at the same time that restrictions for whites were being liberalized or eliminated. Court testimony and the formation of legal contracts and lawsuits by African Americans were also forbidden in many states. Several states prohibited immigration; others required that blacks carry identification passes (as in South Africa under apartheid). Excluded from public schools, African Americans were generally denied the benefits of formal education. In addition to these officially imposed disabilities, blacks in most areas were subjected to ridicule, harassment, and occasional mob violence (Litwack 1961).

Thus, in contrast to slaves in many other societies, slaves in the United States were subject to *racial* as well as legal servitude. For example, although Brazilian slavery was racially based, the inferior status of the slave did not persist into freedom in

Brazil with anything near the tenacity that it did in the United States. "In Brazil the slave may have been feared, but the black man was not, whereas in the United States both the slave and the black man were feared. . . . In the United States, slavery was always a means of organizing dangerous blacks as well as a way of organizing labor" (Degler 1971:89). Brazilians did not assume that a black person was a slave or that he or she would identify with slaves, an attitude that was in striking contrast to the perception in the United States. Brazilians used free blacks extensively as overseers, slave catchers, and slave dealers, a situation that would have been unthinkable in the United States. Brazilians also did not develop an elaborate racial justification for or defense of slavery. In sum, in Brazil, in contrast to the United States, a person's *legal* status (whether slave or free), not his or her *racial* identity, determined his or her standing in Brazilian society. In the United States, an individual's racial identity, not his or her legal status, was crucial.[2]

Therefore, the relegation of blacks to a lower caste status is of crucial importance, for it not only defined the experiences of both blacks and whites in the United States for the more than two-hundred years of slavery but also provided the basis for a system of social inequality that persisted long after the "peculiar institution" had been legally abolished in 1865. The most enduring feature of black-white relations in the United States has been that of caste.

The Aftermath of Slavery

Immediately after the Civil War, a period of fluid race relations occurred. Bolstered by passage of the 13th Amendment, which abolished slavery; the 14th Amendment, which extended to former slaves the equal protection of the law; and the 15th Amendment, which guaranteed to them the right to vote, African Americans actively sought to realize the opportunities and responsibilities of their new status (Litwak 1979).

Nevertheless, the reality of caste persisted. Patterns of black-white relations formed under slavery did not automatically change after emancipation; race relations continued to be based on a rigid caste system. The roles of African Americans after their emancipation became well defined and tightly circumscribed. The new legal status conferred by emancipation and the Reconstruction Amendments did little to alter the patterns of social relations in the plantation South, or to promote the acquisition of new values, habits, and attitudes by either black or white. Former slaves were formally given liberty but not the means (that is, economic, political, educational, and social equality) to realize it. Through intimidation, violence, lynching, and terrorism, African Americans were kept in a subordinate status and subjected to systematic racial discrimination long after slavery had been legally abolished. Blacks remained largely unskilled and illiterate, most of them living lives of enforced dependence on the still-dominant whites. The result was a black peasantry dominated by an agricultural system that ensured dependence on the land and isolation from the main currents of American society.

Northern troops, which had occupied the South during the period of Reconstruction, were removed in 1877, and Southern whites then resorted to a wide range of devices to ensure the maintenance of white dominance. Blacks, who during Reconstruction had voted and held public office, were systematically disenfranchised by a variety of mechanisms: white primary elections from which African Americans were excluded; poll taxes (which were cumulative); "grandfather clauses," which restricted voting to those (and their descendants) who had been eligible to vote before the Civil War; and literacy requirements, which, because they were selectively enforced, restricted even the most educated and literate African Americans from exercising the constitutionally mandated right to vote. The effects of these efforts to disfranchise blacks were dramatic. For example, in 1896 over 130,000 blacks were registered to vote in Louisiana; by 1904 this number had dropped to 1,342 (Norton et al. 1982:459). Moreover, although the 14th Amendment, which was adopted in 1868, includes explicit provisions that states restricting black access to the franchise would have their Congressional representation reduced, those provisions were never enforced.

Moreover, to ensure that white dominance would be perpetuated, a series of laws designed to maintain a strict caste system of black subordination and white dominance was enacted throughout the South during the last decade of the nineteenth and the first two decades of the twentieth century. Southern state legislatures enacted an extraordinary variety of state and municipal ordinances requiring racial separation and exclusion of African Americans from the legal, political, economic, and educational opportunities available to most other Americans. Virtually every aspect of contact between whites and blacks was legally regulated. The pervasiveness of the segregated system was signaled by a profusion of "Whites Only" and "Colored" signs that governed working conditions, public accommodations, state institutions, recreation, resorts, cemeteries, and housing.

It is important to emphasize that the racially segregated system of the South, which became known as "Jim Crow," was not simply a "natural" result of "traditional" relationships between black and white; rather, it was consciously *created* by whites to impose and maintain their political and economic power. During the 1950s and 1960s conservative resistance to the enactment of civil rights legislation to outlaw racial discrimination frequently invoked the argument that such legislation was unnecessary and inappropriate, and would be ineffective because "laws can't change the mores." Most who used this argument conveniently failed to recognize that the Jim Crow system itself had been constructed by the myriad number of discriminatory laws that had been enacted around the turn of the twentieth century.

In 1896 in the famous *Plessy v. Ferguson* decision, the United States Supreme Court provided judicial legitimation for the Jim Crow system, contending that

> the object of [Fourteenth Amendment's "equal protection clause"] was undoubtedly to enforce the absolute equality of the two races before the law, but in the nature of things it could not have been intended to abolish distinctions based upon color, or to enforce social, as distinguished from political equality, or a commingling of the two races upon terms unsatisfactory to either. (quoted in Kluger 1975:74)

Therefore, the Court reasoned, racially separate facilities required by the state do not imply the superiority of one group and the inferiority of another. If blacks perceive the restrictions placed on them as implying a "badge of inferiority," it is solely because they interpret the restrictions that way. The result was that, so long as the facilities were equal, legal segregation could not be construed as discrimination and was therefore constitutional. The *Plessy* "separate-but-equal" doctrine would stand for more than half a century as the law of the land, during which time the barriers of caste in virtually all arenas of American life—especially throughout the South—would be strengthened.

However, the Jim Crow system of racial segregation and the racial caste system on which it was based not only was supported by "legal" means but also was ultimately maintained through the use of force, violence, and intimidation, including lynching and terrorism. Between 1879 and 1909, more than 2,400 blacks were lynched throughout the South, often in response to white perceptions that they had violated "acceptable" patterns of deference expressed in terms of address, demeanor, and social relationships (the "etiquette of race relations") (Norton et al. 1994:524).

As a result of these legal and extralegal sanctions, the subordinate and subservient status of African Americans in the South persisted long after slavery had been abolished. Writing in 1929, Charles S. Johnson, a pioneer African American sociologist, noted the continuity between the slave plantation and rural Macon County, Alabama, during the 1920s:

> There have been retained only slightly modified most of the features of the plantation under the institution of slavery. . . . The Negro population of this section of Macon County has its own social heritage which, in a relatively complete isolation has had little chance for modification from without or within. Patterns of life, social codes, as well as social attitudes were set in the economy of slavery. The political and economic revolution through which they have passed has affected only slightly the social relationships of the community or the mores upon which these relations have been based. The strength and apparent permanence of this early cultural set have made it virtually impossible for new generations to escape the influence of the patterns of work and general social behavior transmitted by their elders. (Johnson 1934:16)

Similar reports noted the persistence of the slave plantation in many areas of the rural south well into the 1930s.

The Great Migration: From Plantation to Ghetto

In response to these oppressive conditions, after the turn of the twentieth century African Americans began to leave the South, a movement that has been called the Great Migration. For nearly a half century after Emancipation, the overwhelming majority of blacks lived in the South; in 1860, 92 percent lived there, and by 1910, this percentage had declined only slightly—to 89 percent. Although blacks migrated from east to west *within* the South during the late nineteenth century, the most noteworthy movement of African Americans out of the South was the "Exoduster Movement" of blacks to Kansas in the late 1870s. As Table 2 indicates, although there was a steady increase in black out-migration from the South after 1870, it was not until the 1910s that substantial numbers began to leave. Except for the 1930s, when the nation was locked in the throes of the Great Depression, these numbers increased in every decade until the 1960s, with the greatest numbers occurring during and after World War II.

Moving primarily to Northern urban areas, African Americans congregated in urban ghettos, geographically defined residential areas to which minority groups are restricted. This migration out of the rural South and the transformation of African Americans from an essentially rural to a predominantly urban people has been one of the most momentous events in the African-American experience and one of the most important demographic shifts in American history. As noted before, in 1900 almost

TABLE 2   *Black Out-Migration from the South, 1870–1970 (in thousands)*

1870–80	71
1880–90	80
1890–00	174
1900–10	197
1910–20	525
1920–30	877
1930–40	398
1940–50	1,468
1950–60	1,473
1960–70	1,380

Source: Farley and Allen 1987:113.

90 percent of the black population lived in the South; by 1990 the percentage in the South had declined to only 53 percent. In 1900 blacks were primarily rural residents, with only 23 percent living in urban areas. By 1996 nearly nine-tenths (86 percent) of the African American population lived in urban areas, indicating that blacks have become a more urbanized population than whites. Although a substantial portion of the increase in the number of urbanized African Americans was in the North, many lived in southern cities, such as Atlanta, Birmingham, New Orleans, Miami, and Houston as well. Between 1900 and 1996, the percentage of the Southern black population residing in metropolitan areas increased from 17 percent to 77 percent. Table 3 shows the percentage that blacks comprised in the major American cities for the years 1920, 1950, 1970, 1980, and 1990.

TABLE 3   *African American Population as Percent of the Total Population of the Ten Largest U.S. Cities,* * 1920, 1950, 1970, 1980, and 1990*

	1920[†]	*1950*[†]	*1970*	*1980*	*1990*
New York	2.7%	9.8%	21.1%	25.2%	28.7%
Los Angeles	2.7	10.7	17.9	17.0	14.0
Chicago	4.1	14.1	32.7	39.8	39.1
Houston	24.6	21.1	25.7	27.6	28.1
Philadelphia	7.4	18.3	33.6	37.8	39.9
San Diego	1.2	4.5	7.6	8.9	9.4
Detroit	4.1	16.4	43.7	63.1	75.7
Dallas	15.1	13.2	24.9	29.4	29.5
Phoenix	3.7	6.0	4.8	4.8	5.2
San Antonio	8.9	6.7	7.6	7.3	7.0

Source: U.S. Census of 1920; U.S. Census of 1950; U.S. Bureau of the Census. *Negroes in the United States, 1920–1932,* Washington, D.C.: U.S. Government Printing Office, 1935; "Characteristics of the Population," *Statistical Abstract of the United States,* 1972, pp. 21–23; *Statistical Abstract of the United States,* 1984, pp. 28–30; U.S. Department of Commerce, *Statistical Abstract of the United States, 1996,* Washington, D.C.: U.S. Government Printing Office, 1996, pp. 44–46.

*These were the ten largest cities in the United States in 1990.

[†]Figures pertain to "nonwhite" population, of which over 90 percent was black.

The massive migration of African Americans out of the South transformed race relations in the United States. As Waldo Martin has written, "urbanization has nationalized the locus of African American life and culture" (Martin 1992:354).

Wilson has characterized the period from the late nineteenth century to the post–World War II era as the *industrial* period of race relations. His description of the transition from preindustrial to industrial parallels van den Berghe's distinction between *paternalistic* race relations, which were characteristic of a plantation economy, and *competitive* race relations, which are found in an urban, industrial setting. In the industrial setting, competition for jobs generated considerable racial antagonism, tension, and conflict. (For a superb analysis of this conflict, see Tuttle 1972, especially Chapter 4.)

The Great Migration of African Americans out of the South ultimately proved to be one of the most important factors underlying the Black Protest Movement that swept the nation during the late 1950s and 1960s. Although discrimination against African Americans in education, employment, housing, and the administration of justice also prevailed in the North, a greater range of opportunities for blacks was available in northern urban areas than in the South. Especially after World War II, increasing numbers of African Americans obtained college educations and found employment in skilled and white-collar occupations. These changes expanded the African American middle class, which provided the primary source of leadership for the Black Protest Movement. The educated and articulate African American middle class played an especially important role in providing legal challenges to the southern Jim Crow system, which culminated in the Supreme Court's 1954 *Brown vs. Board of Education* decision that segregated schools were inherently unequal and therefore unconstitutional. The *Brown* decision, which overturned the 1896 separate-but-equal doctrine, symbolized the beginning of an era in which the legal basis for the caste system would crumble. In Part 4, we will examine the changing status of African Americans during the post–World War II era, the period that Wilson has characterized as the *modern industrial* stage of American race relations.

Hispanic Americans/Latinos

Hispanic Americans constitute one of the largest and most rapidly growing ethnic categories in contemporary American society. During the 1980s the *Hispanic* or *Latino* population grew nearly five times faster than the rest of the population, and their rate of growth has declined only slightly during the 1990s. By 1998 the U.S. Census Bureau estimated the Hispanic population at nearly 30 million, or 11.1 percent of the total population. Recent projections suggest that the Latino population will surpass the African American population by 2010, and total nearly 90 million, or 22 percent of the population, by 2050 (Day 1993). This dramatic increase in the Hispanic population in the United States is the result of both higher Hispanic fertility rates and substantially increased rates of immigration from Latin America, especially from Mexico.

The recent growth of the Latino population has produced some dramatic changes in the ethnic composition of many American cities. By 1994 Hispanics outnumbered blacks in four of the nation's ten largest cities—Los Angeles, Houston, Phoenix, and San Antonio, as well as such other major cities as Miami, El Paso, Pittsburgh, and San

Francisco. And, given their higher growth rates, Hispanics are projected to exceed blacks in New York City in the very near future.

As we will see in Part 4, vast social inequalities, poverty, and political repression all influence migration pressures in Latin America. A crucial dimension contributing to these problems is demographic: the recent rapid population growth in both Central and South America. During the 1950s, the total population for all of Latin America was approximately the same as that of the United States—about 150 million. However, by 2025 it is expected to be 845 million, or about three times the projections of the U.S. population (Fallows 1983:45; Davis, Haub, and Willette 1983:39).

The overall economic status of Latinos, which until the 1990s had been consistently higher than that of African Americans, began a steady decline in the early 1980s, which by 1995 resulted in a median family income below that of African Americans. In 1979 Hispanic median family income stood at $29,180 (in 1995 dollars) —71 percent of white median family income; it has never since achieved this level, standing at $24,569 (or 58 percent of white income) in 1995 (see Table 4). More than one-quarter (27 percent) of Hispanic families lived in poverty. Reflecting the interrelated impact of class, gender, and ethnicity, more than half (53 percent) of poor Hispanic families were headed by women (compared with 30 percent of non-Hispanic white families in poverty) (U.S. Bureau of the Census 1996a; 1996b). Forty percent of all Hispanic children lived in poverty, and during the 1980s, childhood poverty increased more rapidly among Hispanics than among any other racial or ethnic category (U.S. Bureau of the Census 1996b). Finally, by 1993 the median net worth of Hispanic households had declined to one-tenth that of white households, approximately the same as that of African Americans (U.S. Bureau of the Census 1997).

Since 1970 the educational attainments of Hispanic Americans have improved substantially. The proportion of adult Hispanics with less than a fifth-grade education declined. The proportion who were high school graduates increased from less than one-third (32 percent) in 1970 to more than half (53 percent) in 1993; similarly, the proportion who were college graduates doubled, increasing from less than one-twentieth (4.5 percent) in 1970 to nearly one-tenth (9.4 percent) of the adult Hispanic population in 1992 (U.S. Bureau of the Census 1993; 1994). Nevertheless, Hispanics still lag considerably behind the educational attainments of non-Hispanic whites, Asian Americans, and African Americans. In 1995 only slightly more than half of 18- to 24-year-old Hispanics had graduated from high school, compared with seven-eighths (87 percent) of both blacks and non-Hispanic whites. Moreover, only 21 percent of 18- to 24-year old Latinos were enrolled in college, compared with 35 percent of non-Hispanic whites and 25 percent of African Americans (Carter and Wilson 1994; 1995).

The Latino political presence in American society has changed substantially in the past quarter century. Between 1972 and 1992 the Latino electorate increased by 162 percent—from 5.6 million to 14.7 million. Reflecting the impact of the 1965 Voting Rights Act and the rapidly increasing Hispanic population, in the past two decades Latinos have gained political strength; by 1995, 5,459 Hispanics held public office in the United States. Nevertheless, Hispanics still accounted for only about 1 percent of all elected public officials, far below the nearly 11 percent of the population that they represent (Brimhall-Vargas 1994).

One reason for the relatively small number of Latino elected officials figures is that although Latinos have been numerically the fastest-growing ethnic category in the United States in the past quarter century, Latino political *participation*—both as voters and as candidates for public office—has not increased proportionately. On the one hand, a substantial portion of the Hispanic population is recent immigrants, who are ineligible for citizenship until they have lived in the country for at least five years. Moreover, Latinos (Mexican Americans, in particular) are characterized by extremely low rates of naturalization. For example, in 1989, only 13 percent of Mexican immigrants who had arrived in the U.S. during the 1970s had become citizens, whereas 55 percent of Asians had. Moreover, the Hispanic population is very young, with a median age of twenty-six, compared with thirty-four for whites, twenty-eight for blacks, and thirty for Asians. Thus a substantial proportion of the Hispanic population is either not yet old enough to vote or among the extremely young voters, whose rates of political participation are typically the lowest. However, as their population ages and increasing numbers of immigrants achieve citizenship, "Latinos remain poised to wield the political power that has remained elusive thus far" (Coleman 1995:28). The increasing impact of Latino political strength was apparent during the 1996 presidential and congressional elections, in which Hispanic voters went to the polls in record numbers, where they overwhelmingly supported President Clinton and contributed to upset victories by several Hispanic congressional candidates.

However, to refer to Spanish-speaking people as a single ethnic category is misleading. The terms *Hispanic* or *Latino,* which are of recent origin, obscure the great diversity of historical, cultural, and geographic backgrounds among them. Although Latinos are more likely than the rest of the U.S. population to be Spanish-speaking, Catholic, and poor, they do not constitute a single ethnic category. The category of "Hispanics" includes representatives from more than twenty Latin American and Caribbean nations, as well as from Spain and Portugal. More than three-fourths of Hispanic Americans are of Mexican, Puerto Rican, or Cuban descent, but there are also substantial communities of people from the Dominican Republic, Colombia, Ecuador, El Salvador, Guatemala, Nicaragua, and several other Caribbean, Central American, and South American nations (U.S. Bureau of the Census 1993). These groups also differ in their socioeconomic status and in their regional distribution in the United States. We focus here on the three largest Hispanic groups: Mexicans, Puerto Ricans, and Cubans, which together make up more than three-fourths of the Hispanic population.

Mexican Americans

Mexican Americans, or Chicanos (from the Spanish *Mexicanos),* are the largest Hispanic group and (after African Americans) the second largest ethnic minority in American society. Today nearly 18 million people of Mexican ancestry live in the United States, about 90 percent of them in the five southwestern states of Texas, New Mexico, Arizona, Colorado, and California. Next to the North American Indians, with whom they share a common ancestry, they represent the oldest ethnic category in American society. The Mexican American people are the biological and cultural descendants of the Spanish military and religious conquest of the native peoples of northern Central America. From the early 1600s to the mid-1800s, Spain, and, later, Mexico, colonized and exerted political, economic, and cultural dominance over the region. By the turn of the nineteenth century, Mexican culture, a mixture of Spanish and American Indian influences, was well established throughout what is today the southwestern United States.

The process of contact between Mexicans and the Anglo immigrants who settled in Texas in increasing numbers during the early nineteenth century provides another opportunity to test Noel's model of the emergence of ethnic stratification. Initially Anglos and Mexicans coexisted, although each viewed the other warily and with antipathy and distrust that had grown out of two centuries of English and Spanish competition for world dominance. Mutual ethnocentrism between the two peoples occurred from the start, with Anglos regarding the darker-skinned Mexicans as "racially" and culturally inferior, and with Mexicans seeing in the growing encroachment of the Americans confirmation of their stereotypes of Yankee aggressiveness and greed. Anglos and Mexicans also differed in religion and class structure. To ensure the loyalty of early–nineteenth-century Anglo colonists, most of whom were Protestants, the Mexican government required that they become Roman Catholics as well as Mexican citizens. Even more offensive to the sensibilities of Anglo settlers, many of whom had emigrated from the American South and were slaveholders, was the Mexican prohibition of slavery. Although slavery was illegal, Mexican society was highly stratified, with a small, wealthy upper class and a large class of the very poor. Anglo-Americans, literate and middle-class in outlook, developed a perception of the Mexican people as indolent and lazy (McLemore 1973).

Despite these differences, Anglo and Mexican Texans initially coexisted, cooperated, and in the Texas Revolt of 1835–36 together fought a common enemy, the Mexican central government controlled by Santa Ana. Both Anglos and Mexicans died fighting Santa Ana in the Alamo. After Santa Ana's defeat, however, competition between Anglo and Mexican for land in the newly independent Texas Republic became increasingly intense. In 1845 the United States granted statehood to Texas, and a year later the United States and Mexico were engaged in a war that would result in the loss of over half of Mexico's previous territory. The 1848 Treaty of Guadalupe-Hidalgo, in which Mexico ceded to the United States most of the land of the present-day Southwest, signaled the triumph of Anglo power. Although the treaty guaranteed legal and property rights to Mexican citizens in the newly acquired territories, Mexican Americans soon became the object of persistent discrimination. Anglos, especially in Texas, established a system of caste relations, which ensured Chicano political, social, and economic subordination. By the eve of the Civil War, the American military conquest of Mexican lands in the Southwest had been completed. In the ensuing years those Mexicans who chose to remain in the annexed territories were largely dispossessed of both their land and the prominence they had occupied in Mexican society. By the turn of the twentieth century, Mexicans had been "relegated to a lower-class status, [in which] they were overwhelmingly dispossessed landless laborers, politically and economically impotent," which was justified by notions of racial inferiority (Estrada et al. 1981:109). For this reason, Alvarez (1973) has argued that the subjugation of this "creation generation" after the Mexican War was formative, in much the same sense that Bryce-Laporte (1969) has characterized slavery as "the contextual baseline of Black American experience."

The vast territory incorporated into the United States as a result of the 1848 Treaty of Guadalupe-Hidalgo was at the time extremely sparsely settled, with those identifying themselves as Mexican (as opposed to various American Indian identities) numbering only about 60,000. However, as American settlement increased throughout the last half of the nineteenth century, the Mexican presence dwindled and their political and economic influence declined.

Whereas the earliest Mexican American population became an American minority through the annexation of Mexican lands by the United States, the primary source of the majority of the Chicano population in the United States has been immigration, both legal and undocumented.

Although a substantial proportion of the contemporary Chicano population is derived from the migrant generation that followed that surge of European immigration into the United States during the early twentieth century, the situation of Mexican immigrants differed substantially from that of European immigrant groups because Mexican immigrants entered a society that had already adopted a clearly defined lower-caste role for them as a result of the mid–nineteenth-century conquest patterns of subordination.

This immigration, most of which has occurred during the twentieth century, has been instrumental in the economic development of the American Southwest. Mexican immigrants provided a readily available and exploitable source of cheap labor, especially for the expansion of the railroad industry, mining, and above all, agriculture (Estrada et al. 1981). Indeed, Mexican labor played an integral role in the dramatic expansion of agribusiness interests in the Southwest. During the first two decades of the twentieth century, many Mexicans fled to the United States from the upheavals of the Mexican Revolution. As European immigration to the United States was curtailed by the outbreak of World War I and the passage of the restrictive legislation of the 1920s, Mexican labor filled the growing demand for agricultural workers to replace those who had left for jobs in the nation's industrial sector. The defense employment boom generated by World War II produced a shift of the Chicano population away from rural areas and agricultural pursuits, while at the same time the bracero program, which ran from 1942 to 1965, ensured a continuing source of cheap agricultural labor from Mexico. As Massey (1986b; Massey et al. 1987) and Rouse (Article 26) have pointed out, the general migration of Mexicans to work in the United States earlier in the twentieth century and in the bracero program, in particular, played a major role in establishing the circular migration networks that sustain Mexican migration to the United States today.

Several indicators reveal that Mexican Americans lag considerably behind the mainstream of American society in socioeconomic status. Despite some evidence of improvement among younger generations, Mexican American educational attainment is less than that of both whites and African Americans. However, they tend to be found primarily in low-paying blue-collar and semiskilled occupations that have been especially hard hit by the decline of manufacturing and by the downsizing of economic sectors, such as military-related jobs, that have contributed to rising Hispanic unemployment during a period of economic growth (1992—1998) in which overall unemployment declined. As Table 4 indicates, in 1995 median family income for Mexican Americans was only 58 percent of white median family income; more than one-fourth (28 percent) of Mexican American families had incomes below the poverty level (U.S. Bureau of the Census 1995).

Although Chicanos still comprise a substantial proportion of the nation's migratory farmworkers, today they are overwhelmingly—more than 80 percent—urban residents, especially in the major urban areas of the Southwest. Indeed, today more people of Mexican descent live in Los Angeles than in any other city except Mexico City and Guadalajara. As their numbers and their concentration in urban areas has increased, Mexican Americans, like other Hispanic groups, have also become an increasingly

TABLE 4 *Median Family Income, 1995*

	Income in Dollars	*Percent of White Income*
All races	40,612	
White	42,646	
Black	25,970	61%
Hispanic	24,569	58
Mexican	23,485	55
Puerto Rican	22,121	52
Cuban	32,471	76
Central & South American	26,915	63
Other Hispanic*	26,826	63

Sources: U.S Bureau of the Census, "Money Income in the United States, 1995," *Current Population Reports,* P60–193, Washington, D.C.: U.S. Government Printing Office, 1996. U.S. Bureau of the Census, "The Hispanic Population of the United States: Current Population Survey, March 1996." [online] Available: http://www.census.gov/population/socdemo/hispanic/cps96/sumtab-4.txt [1998, March 12].

*Includes those who identified themselves as from Spain or as Hispanic, Spanish, Spanish American, Hispanic, or Latino.

salient force in American politics, especially because of their substantial presence in the electorally significant states of Texas and California.

The other major groups of Spanish-speaking people are relatively recent immigrant groups who have settled primarily in urban areas on the East coast since the end of World War II. Although the number of immigrants from countries throughout the Caribbean and Central and South America has increased markedly during this period, the two Caribbean islands of Puerto Rico and Cuba have been the primary sources of this influx of Spanish-speaking peoples. These two groups provide an interesting contrast in backgrounds and adaptations to American society.

Puerto Ricans

Puerto Ricans, who, unlike other immigrants, are American citizens, began migrating to the mainland primarily after World War II. Today nearly two-thirds of the more than 2 million Puerto Ricans on the mainland live in New York City, which has been the principal magnet for these immigrants. This migration to the mainland has been prompted primarily by economic pressures among the impoverished lower strata of Puerto Rican society.

Among Hispanic groups, Puerto Ricans have a unique relationship with the United States. The island of Puerto Rico was ceded to the United States in 1898 after the United States defeat of Spain in the Spanish-American War. Despite changes in the twentieth century, the status of Puerto Rico has in many respects continued to resemble that of a colonial dependency. Although Puerto Ricans were granted American citizenship in 1917, they have retained their language and cultural traditions, which are different from the dominant language and culture of the United States. Puerto Ricans' determination to maintain their cultural distinctiveness has been an important element in the continuing debate over whether the island should become an independent nation, become the fifty-first American state, or retain its present commonwealth status.

Numbering 2.3 million people on the mainland, Puerto Ricans are today the largest Hispanic group outside the Southwest. Puerto Rican residents began migrating to the United States early in the twentieth century, but it was not until the advent of relatively cheap commercial air travel after World War II that they began to arrive in substantial numbers, settling primarily in New York City. Today about 40 percent of all Puerto Ricans live on the mainland, and because of the ease of travel to and from the island and the personal networks that it has facilitated, it has been estimated that half of all island Puerto Ricans have at some time shared the mainland experience (Levine 1987:95). Although Puerto Ricans continue to reside primarily on the East coast, especially in New York City, increasing numbers have recently begun to settle in midwestern and far western cities such as Chicago, Cleveland, and Los Angeles.

The Puerto Rican migration to the mainland must be seen in the context of the economic and political relationship between the United States and Puerto Rico, which Levine (1987) has characterized as "imperial development." The migration was prompted primarily by extremely high unemployment in Puerto Rico, and it has fluctuated in response to economic opportunities in the United States. Given the historic underdevelopment of the Puerto Rican economy, Puerto Rican immigrants to the United States have been overwhelmingly unskilled and have experienced difficulties in an increasingly technological society. Concentrated in blue-collar semiskilled and unskilled occupations and subjected to racial discrimination, Puerto Ricans are, as Bean and Tienda (Article 10) point out, "the most socially and economically disadvantaged of Hispanic origin groups with poverty, labor force participation and unemployment rates and average earnings comparable to those of Native Americans and blacks." As Table 4 indicates, Puerto Rican median family income (in 1995, 52 percent of white median family income) is the lowest, and their poverty rate (36 percent) is among the highest among American ethnic groups.

Cuban Americans

Although Cuban immigrants to the United States have been recorded as early as the 1870s, the Cuban American community today is composed primarily of relatively recent political refugees. Approximately 750,000 Cubans have entered the United States since Fidel Castro's rise to power in 1959, and today they number more than one million. In contrast to most previous immigrations to the United States (with the notable exception of the Huguenots during the colonial period and those fleeing from Nazi Germany during the 1930s), the initial Cuban émigrés tended to be drawn mainly from the upper social and economic strata of Cuban society. Drawn disproportionately from well-educated middle-class and upper-class professional and business backgrounds, they brought skills (educational, occupational, business, and managerial), entrepreneurial values, and substantial amounts of financial capital that enabled them to prosper and achieve relatively rapid socioeconomic success. Assisted by federal government programs that facilitated their adjustment to American society, in the thirty years since their initial migration, Cubans have become the most affluent of all Hispanic groups and are an integral part of the economies of a number of American cities, especially Miami, Florida, which they have transformed into a major international business and commercial center with ties throughout Latin America. Nevertheless, in 1995 Cuban family income was still only three-fourths (76 percent) of non-Hispanic white income, and the Cuban poverty rate was 16 percent compared with the overall white rate of 11 percent (U.S. Bureau of the Census 1995).

The most recent influx of Cubans—those who left Cuba during the so-called Freedom Flotilla or Mariel Boatlift of 1980—numbered about 125,000. A substantial proportion of this recent migration was people of working-class and lower-class origins (Davis, Haub, and Willette 1983:23).

Asian Americans

Asians are an extremely diverse category, differing in linguistic, cultural, historical, national, and class backgrounds. Historically the Chinese, the Japanese, and, later, the Filipinos, have been the most prominent Asian groups; most Koreans, Asian Indians, Vietnamese, Cambodians, and Laotians are more recent arrivals. Compared with the many millions of Europeans who have migrated to the United States, Asian immigration has, until recently, been modest. At no time until the past two decades did the numbers of Asian immigrants ever approximate those from Europe. For example, Chinese immigration reached its peak during the decade from 1873 to 1882, when 161,000 Chinese entered the country (a period during which nearly half a million Irish and nearly a million German immigrants were received). Peak Japanese immigration occurred during the decade between 1900 and 1909, when 139,000 entered (at the same time that nearly 2 million immigrants from Italy and more than 1.5 million from what later became the Soviet Union were admitted). In contrast, between 1840 and 1920 there were thirty-one different years when the number of immigrants from a *single* European country alone exceeded 150,000. As Figure 3 on page 98 reveals, the total number of immigrants from Asia, in general, and Japan and China, in particular, have been insubstantial when considered in the context of American immigration as a whole. What is significant, however, is the response that the presence of Asian immigrants generated, and the subsequent adaptation of Asian peoples to discrimination in the United States, which we will discuss later.

However, partly as a result of changes in American immigration laws, which before 1965 had virtually excluded them, Asians are today *proportionately* the nation's fastest-growing racial category. Since 1970, Asians have constituted more than one-third (35 percent) of all legal immigrants, and the Asian population of the United States has increased by 648 percent, compared with increases by Hispanics of 219 percent, by American Indians of 179 percent, by African Americans of 50 percent, and by European Americans of 24 percent. By 1998 Asians numbered 10.2 million, which represented 3.8 percent of the American people. The rapid growth of the Asian American population is expected to continue during the twenty-first century, reaching over 40 million (or 10 percent of the population) by 2050 (Day 1993). Although almost all states have experienced substantial increases in Asian residents during the last quarter of the twentieth century, almost 40 percent of Asian Americans live in California, where they make up 10 percent of the state's population (Barringer 1991; U.S. Immigration and Naturalization Service 1997; U.S. Bureau of the Census online 1997).

Early Immigrants: Chinese and Japanese

The earliest modern Asian immigrants were the Chinese, who migrated to North America beginning in the 1840s. During the next four decades more than 200,000 Chinese immigrants, primarily unskilled laborers, arrived. Filling a need for labor created by the economic development of the West in the mid–nineteenth century (especially in mining and in building the transcontinental railroad), the Chinese were initially welcomed. As their numbers increased, however, the Chinese became perceived as an economic threat to native labor, and racist opposition to them mounted. As a consequence the Chinese were subjected to various forms of harassment, mob violence, and discriminatory legislation, including laws designed specifically to harass them. Finally, in response to anti-Chinese agitation in California, Congress passed the Chinese Exclusion Act of 1882, which was the first federal law to restrict immigration of a specific nationality to the United States. In contrast, more than forty years were to pass before substantial restrictions were placed on European immigration (Hsu 1971; Lyman 1974; Nee and Nee 1973).

The anti-Asian sentiment that pervaded the hysteria over Chinese immigration was revived when the Japanese immigrated in the early twentieth century. Although the Japanese represented an extremely small proportion of the population of both California and the nation as a whole, their presence generated intense nativist hostility. Like the Chinese before them, the Japanese were the object of legislation designed to harass and intimidate them. In 1906 the San Francisco Board of Education precipitated an international incident when it attempted to place all Japanese children, native and foreign-born, in a segregated "Oriental" school in Chinatown. Immediate protests from the Japanese ambassador ultimately led the school board to rescind its order; but the Board of Education's segregation efforts in reality were stymied only because President Theodore Roosevelt was able in 1907 to negotiate the so-called Gentleman's Agreement with Japan. Under this agreement, the American government agreed to end discrimination against Japanese living in the United States, and Japan pledged to grant visas to the United States only to family members of Japanese citizens residing there.

Even this accommodation failed to satisfy exclusionists, and in 1913 the California legislature enacted an alien land law barring the Japanese, who had become successful farmers, from owning agricultural land. As sentiment for the general restriction of immigration increased during the first three decades of the twentieth century, further limitations were placed on Asian immigration; in 1924 the Johnson-Reed Act prohibited completely all Asian immigration, and the provisions of this legislation remained virtually intact (with some minor adjustments during the 1940s and 1950s) until the antidiscriminatory Immigration Act of 1965 went into effect in the late 1960s.

This anti-Asian agitation, to which the early Chinese and Japanese immigrants especially were subjected, drew support from the same "scientific" sources that provided the intellectual respectability for racist thought described earlier. Ultimately, this fear of the "yellow peril" contributed to the forcible evacuation and relocation of nearly 120,000 Japanese Americans—more than two-thirds of them American citizens—by the federal government during World War II (Thomas and Nishimoto 1969; Grodzins 1966; Bosworth 1967; Kitano 1969; Daniels 1972, 1993). In Article 11, "Asian Pacific Americans," Don Mar and Marlene Kim contextualize Asian migration and adaptation to the United States in terms of broad structural changes in American society and the global economy.

Despite early antipathy toward the Chinese and Japanese, and the particular hostility toward the Japanese during World War II, both groups have made substantial improvements in socioeconomic status. Their achievements have contributed substantially to the overall socioeconomic status of Asian Americans. By 1990, 37 percent of the Asian population over age twenty-five had completed at least four years of college, which was nearly double the figure (22 percent) for non-Hispanic whites (U.S. Bureau of the Census 1992). So extraordinary have Asian educational attainments been that charges have been raised that many of the nation's most prestigious universities have placed limits on the numbers of Asian students they would admit (Mathews 1987).

As a consequence of their relatively high educational attainments, a disproportionate percentage of Japanese and Chinese are found in professional occupational categories. By the 1980s the income levels of American-born and immigrant Asians were not significantly different from those of whites who had comparable skills, and by 1990 actually slightly exceeded those of whites; in 1990 more than one-third (35 percent) of Asian American households had incomes of $50,000 or more, compared with 26 percent of non-Hispanic white households. By 1995 Asian median family income was 109 percent of white family income (compared with 61 percent for black and 58 percent for Hispanic families) (U.S. Bureau of the Census 1992; U.S. Bureau of the Census 1997 online). As we will explore more fully in Parts 3 and 4, these educational and economic attainments have contributed to the stereotype of Asian Americans as "model minorities."

The public perception of Asian educational and economic success, however, masks continued discrimination against them (Kuo 1995). Asians generally earn less than do non-Hispanic whites of the same age and educational characteristics, and studies have demonstrated that Asians gain 21 percent less than do non-Hispanic whites from each year of schooling. Moreover, the relatively high levels of Asian household income may reflect a greater number of family household members who work (O'Hare and Felt 1991). Finally, focusing on overall income and educational attainments obscures substantial differences among Asian groups. Although Japanese, Chinese, and Koreans have incomes above those of whites, Filipinos, Asian Indians, and Vietnamese earn less. Reflecting this fact, during the 1980s the poverty rate for Asians actually increased, and by 1995 it was 12.4 percent, nearly double the rate (6.4 percent) for non-Hispanic whites (U.S. Commission on Civil Rights 1988; U.S. Bureau of the Census 1996, vii).

*Later Immigrants: Filipinos, Koreans,
Indochinese, and Indians*

As the data in Figure 3 on page 98 indicate, the numbers of several Asian groups—especially Chinese, Filipinos, Koreans, Indochinese, and Asian Indians—have recently increased dramatically. With the exception of the Chinese, whose presence in the United States was firmly established in the nineteenth century, these groups have emerged primarily since passage of the 1965 Immigration Reform Act.

Like Puerto Rico, the Philippine Islands were acquired by the United States from Spain in 1898 after the Spanish-American War, and the country has been economically dependent on the United States throughout the twentieth century, even after it gained its political independence in 1946. Because the Philippines was considered a territory of the United States, Filipinos were not initially subject to the immigration restrictions placed on other Asian groups. As residents of a U.S. possession, Filipinos were not included in the provisions of the 1924 Johnson-Reed Act that excluded immigration from elsewhere in Asia. Thus, when other Asian immigration was halted, Filipino laborers replaced the Chinese and Japanese as agricultural workers in California and Hawaii, and they also worked in the Alaskan salmon fisheries. However, in 1935, in the midst of the Great Depression, Filipino immigration was restricted as well. An annual quota of 50 Filipinos was established, and it was "liberalized" to 100 in 1946, when the Philippines was granted full political independence. Thus Filipino immigration between 1935 and 1965, when the Immigration Act eliminated national quotas, was negligible.

In 1960 Filipinos numbered only 176,000, a substantial portion of whom lived in Hawaii. The great preponderance of Filipino immigration to the United States, therefore, has come since 1965. The 1970 census recorded 343,000 Filipinos. Their numbers more than doubled, to 775,000 during the 1970s and nearly doubled again during the 1980s, recording a total of 1.4 million in 1990 (see Table 1). However, because Filipinos, unlike other recent Asian immigrants, have not established identifiable ethnic communities, they have tended to be invisible, and their status as the second-largest Asian group in the United States today may therefore come as a surprise to many people. Like many other recent Asian immigrant groups, Filipino immigrants today have much higher educational levels than previous Filipino immigrants, and they have included high percentages of professional and technical workers, especially physicians and nurses. Despite these qualifications, Filipinos are much more likely than whites to work in occupations below their educational levels (Takaki 1989:434–436).

Koreans are also a relatively recent ethnic group in American society. Although a small number of Koreans, primarily agricultural laborers who migrated to Hawaii, were recorded in the census as early as 1910, as late as 1950 there were still fewer than 10,000 in the United States. A small portion of the increase since 1950 resulted from marriages of Koreans to members of the American armed forces stationed in Korea during and after the Korean War and from the adoption of Korean orphans.

However, most of the dramatic increase in Korean Americans—nearly 800,000 in 1990—has occurred since the 1965 Immigration Act went into effect in 1968. Reflecting their relatively recent arrival, in 1980 nearly seven in ten Koreans (69.3 percent) had arrived in the previous decade (Xenos et al. 1987:256). Reflecting the post–Korean War modernization of South Korea, Koreans, like most other recent Asian immigrants, have had high educational attainments—for example, in 1980 more than 93 percent of Koreans had completed high school (Xenos 1987:270). Moreover, Koreans are more likely than the white population to be found in the two most prestigious and best paid occupational categories: executive, administrative, and managerial positions and the professions (Xenos et al. 1987). In contrast to the invisibility of the Filipinos, Korean communities have recently become very visible in several American cities, most notably New York City and Los Angeles. One of the most distinctive features of these communities has been the prominence of Korean small business enterprises, a phenomenon that is discussed in Part 3. Utilizing ethnic resources such as the *kye,* or rotating credit association, and capital accumulated in Korea, they have been especially prominent as proprietors of greengroceries, fish retail businesses, and dry cleaning establishments (Kim 1981, 1988; Light and Bonacich 1988; Takaki 1989:436–445).

The migration of Asian Indians to the United States began as early as the 1880s, when Hawaii's sugar planters recruited Indian workers to supply their labor needs. During the last decade of the nineteenth and the first two decades of the twentieth century, small numbers of Indians—primarily male sojourners who worked in the railroad and lumber industries and in agriculture—immigrated to the U.S. mainland. Although these early immigrants were called "Hindus" by Americans, they included Muslims and Sikhs as well. Although Caucasian, they were included in the anti-Asian hysteria directed against the Chinese, Japanese, and Koreans and the subsequent legislation restricting Asian immigration. By the end of World War II, the Asian-Indian population numbered only 1,500 (Takaki 1989). Most Asian Indians in the United States today, therefore, are products of the second wave of Indian migration begun after 1968. The 1980 census found 362,000 Indians, and this number increased to 815,000 by 1990 (see Table 1). Unlike earlier Indian immigrants, who were unskilled, this second wave has overwhelmingly been comprised of highly educated professionals. For example, 1980 census data revealed that nearly 90 percent of all Asian Indians over the age of twenty-five had completed high school, and two-thirds had completed college, in contrast to two-thirds of the total U.S. population who had completed high school and only one-sixth who had completed college (Bouvier and Gardner 1986:22).

Peoples from Indochina, the country's most recent arrivals, represent a diversity of ethnic groups from Vietnam, Laos, and Cambodia. Most Indochinese have been refugees who have immigrated since the fall of Saigon in 1975. In 1990 they collectively totaled about 1 million, approximately two-thirds of whom are Vietnamese (Bouvier and Agresta 1987:292). It is anticipated that, because of the continuing social, political, and economic upheavals in southeast Asia, these numbers will continue to be reinforced in the near future. Many of the earliest Vietnamese immigrants were highly educated and possessed marketable technical skills. Later arrivals, including most Laotians, Cambodians, and Hmong have had fewer such resources and no established ethnic enclave to provide economic and social support. Consequently, their adjustment to American society has been much more difficult than that of many other recent Asian immigrants.

The recent increase of immigration from the Third World—especially from Latin America and Asia—has contributed substantially to some of the most dramatic changes in the ethnic composition of the United States in its history. Today more than one-quarter of all Americans are of Native American, African, Hispanic, or Asian descent. By the year 2020—approximately one generation from now—nearly one-third of the nation will be nonwhite (Quality Education for Minorities Project 1990). Any effort to comprehend both the short-term and long-term implications of these changes in the ethnic composition of American society must consider at least three basic factors: (1) recent changes in global political and economic structures; (2) structural changes in the American economy; and (3) the patterns of ethnic and racial relations that have previously been manifested in the American experience. In Parts 3 and 4 we will examine the nature of intergroup relations in, and ethnic adaptations to, American society. We will also speculate on how these recent trends may affect future patterns of race and ethnicity in the United States.

ENDNOTES
1. The total number of federally recognized Indian tribes and Alaska Native groups in 1997 was 554 (U.S. Department of the Interior, 1997).
2. Whether these historical differences have produced a racially more open society—a "racial democracy" —in contemporary Brazil, as much of the previous scholarship has assumed, has recently been questioned. See, for example, Skidmore 1993.

FOUR

Postethnic America

David A. Hollinger

If Alex Haley had carried out on his father's side the genealogical inquiry reported in *Roots,* he would have experienced his great moment of self-knowledge in Ireland, not Gambia. This observation was made by Ishmael Reed in the course of a symposium entitled, "Is Ethnicity Obsolete?"[1] Haley's choice of roots and Reed's comment on it together constitute an emblem for three points this essay addresses. The United States is endowed with a *non-ethnic* ideology of the nation. It is possessed by a predominantly *ethnic* history. It may be now squandering an opportunity to create for itself a *postethnic* future in which affiliation on the basis of shared descent would be voluntary rather than prescribed.

The national ideology is "non-ethnic" by virtue of the universalist commitment—proclaimed in the prevailing constitutional and political discourse—to provide the benefits of citizenship irrespective of any ascribed or asserted ancestral affiliations. This commitment lies behind our sense that Haley had a real choice, and one that was truly his to make: individual Americans are to be as free as possible from the consequences of social distinctions visited upon them by others. Yet the decision Haley made was driven by a history predominantly "ethnic" in the extent to which each American's individual destiny has been determined by ancestrally-derived distinctions flagged, at one time or another, by such labels as Negro, Jewish, Indian, Caucasian, Hispanic, Oriental, Italian, Chinese, Polish, white, black, Latino, Euro-American, Native American, Chicano, and African-American.[2] That any person now classified as "black" or "African-American" might see his or her own life as more the production of African roots—however small or large a percent-age of one's actual genealogy—than of European roots reflects this history.

Hence "Haley's Choice" comes close to being the "Hobson's Choice" of genealogy in America. Haley could choose to identify with Africa, accepting, in effect, the categories of the white oppressors who had determined that the tiniest fraction of African ancestry would confer one identity and erase another, or, Haley could choose to identify with Ireland, denying, in effect, his solidarity with the people who shared his social destiny, and appearing to wish he was white. The nature of this "choice" is illuminated by an experience reported by Reed, who shares Haley's combination of African and Irish ancestry and who has flirted with the other option in the structured dilemma I am calling "Haley's Choice": Reed mentioned his "Irish-American heritage" to a "Professor of Celtic Studies at Dartmouth," who "laughed."[3]

A "postethnic" America is one in which someone of Reed's color could comment casually about his Irish heritage without our finding it a joke. A postethnic America would offer Haley a choice more real than the one Hobson offered visitors to his livery. But the notion of postethnicity entails more than this. To clarify this ideal, and to explore its prospects in the context of the nation's non-ethnic ideology and its ethnic history, is the chief concern of this essay.[4]

Any such enterprise must begin by underscoring the inequalities that have dominated the historical record, and by recognizing that these inequalities now lend credibility to claims made on behalf of communities defined by descent. Not every citizen's fortune has been influenced to the same degree, or in the same direction, by Amer-

Reprinted from *Contention* 2:1 (Fall 1992) by permission of the author. Thanks to Nikki Keddie and *Contention.*

ica's notorious failure to act on its universalist aspirations. Being classified as Euro-American, white, or Caucasian has rarely been a basis for being denied adequate employment, housing, education, or protection from violence. One response to the patently unequal consequences of ethno-racial distinctions has been to invoke and sharpen the nation's official, Enlightenment-derived commitment to protect all its citizens from any negative consequences of ethno-racial distinctions. What this commitment means has been contested, of course, from the day a committee of the Second Continental Congress deleted from the Declaration of Independence Thomas Jefferson's denunciation of slavery right down to the most recent decisions of the Supreme Court concerning the limits of affirmative action. The commitment is plain enough, however, to make obvious the gap between the theory and the practice of American nationality.[5] Indeed, the magnitude and persistence of this gap have inspired a second, very different response: the applying of pressure from the gap's other side, its ethnic side.

This alternative strategy for closing the gap asks public authorities to facilitate and actively support affiliation on the basis of ancestry. By promoting the development of communities defined by descent, one might reasonably hope for more equal treatment of every descendant of every "tribe." After all, the results produced by the long-preferred method of gap-closing—the invoking and sharpening of the non-ethnic ideological tradition—remain disappointing even to most people who believe progress has been substantial. Hence the non-ethnic character of the ideological tradition can be construed as part of the problem, rather than part of the solution. That tradition treats as irrelevant to citizenship the very distinctions that, in this view, need to be asserted, reinforced, and celebrated.[6] This feeling that equality's interests demand for America a future even more ethnic than its past is reflected in much of what is said in the name of "multiculturalism."

Yet "multiculturalism" sometimes functions as a shibboleth behind which are concealed a range of initiatives often not in agreement about just how much ethno-racial particularism is wise. The debate over multiculturalism is often scripted as a two-sided confrontation, but it has generated a number of distinctions, refinements, and possibilities that get missed when participants character-

ize each other as separatists or as defenders of Eurocentric domination, and when they construct the issue as a choice between similarity or difference, wholeness or fragmentation, assimilation or dissimilation, monism or pluralism.[7] No doubt these terms describe fairly some participants in this debate, and some of the doctrines advanced, but not all. A convenient example of a perspective not encompassed by these familiar dichotomies is a recent essay by the historian Gary B. Nash.

Nash defends multiculturalism, which in the context of American historical studies he takes to be an emphasis on cultural diversity, an elimination of ethnocentrism, and the "integration of the histories of both genders and people of all classes and racial or ethnic groups."[8] Indeed, Nash is the author not only of scholarly works that manifest these ideals; he is, in addition, the principal author of the widely-discussed series of textbooks recently adopted by most public school districts in California, designed explicitly with these multicultural goals in mind.[9] Yet Nash is resoundingly critical of the Afrocentrism that is sometimes counted as a version of multiculturalism, and he mocks the ethnocentric reasoning by which our schools might be asked to design "Sinocentric," "Khmer-centric," and "Hispanocentric" curricula, and to ignore the needs of "mixed-race children in a society where . . . interracial marriage is at an all-time high." Nash defends the idea of "common ground" as routinely invoked by critics of multiculturalism. "If multiculturalism is to get beyond a promiscuous pluralism that gives everything equal weight and adopts complete moral relativism," says Nash in words that might have come from Diane Ravitch, Arthur M. Schlesinger, Jr., or even William Bennett, "it must reach some agreement on what is at the core of American culture."[10]

Moreover, Nash is forthright in telling us what we should take as that "core": the democratic values "clearly stated" in the nation's "founding documents." These old principles "are a precious heritage" endowing with the same rights all "individuals" of "whatever group attachments." Nash thus invokes the non-ethnic ideological tradition, identifies himself with one of this tradition's greatest defenders, Gunnar Myrdal, and points to that tradition's helpful role in "virtually every social and political struggle carried out by women, religious minorities, labor, and people of color." Scorning the varieties of particularism that encourage young people to identify only with antecedents of their own ethno-racial category, Nash insists that "Harriet Tubman and Ida B. Wells should inspire all students, not simply African-American females," and reminds us that W. E. B. Dubois once "wed" a color-neutral "Truth," and sought to "live above the veil" of color by learning from Aristotle and Shakespeare. Nash several times invokes "cosmopolitanism," a concept that matches his ideas more comfortably than does the more ambiguous "multiculturalism" with which he, like so many other opponents of an Anglo-Protestant curriculum and public culture, finds himself saddled.[11]

"Cosmopolitanism" should be sorted out from several other persuasions and counter-persuasions that sometimes get confused in the multiculturalism debates. Part of the confusion derives from the fact that virtually no one defends "monoculturalism," with the result that multiculturalism is deprived of an honest, natural opposite. "Eurocentrism" is often said to be the enemy, but this word is more an opprobrious epithet than a fair description of any but a few of the people who have expressed concerns about fragmentation and loss of pedagogic focus.[12] And many who do uphold European traditions insist that what makes these traditions worth defending is their decidedly multicultural character.[13] Hence the "opponents" of multiculturalism sometimes end up seeming to claim its banner for their own, apparently different programs.[14] Another alleged opposite of multiculturalism is "universalism," but here the highly problematic claim that a given, single culture is good enough for the entire globe is often conflated with more modest assertions that some truths and rights apply to every member of the species, and that all the world's peoples share a destiny sufficiently common to demand mutual engagement and cooperations.[15] These assertions can be consistent with multiculturalism unless the latter is understood—as it sometimes is—as a mere multiplicity of ethnocentrisms. Universalism's suspicion of enclosures is shared by "cosmopolitanism," which is defined by an additional element not essential to universalism itself: recognition, acceptance, and eager exploration of diversity. Cosmopolitanism urges each polity and each individual to absorb as much experience as it can while retaining its capacity to function as a unit. Although this ideal is attractive to many adherents of multi-

culturalism, the latter notion's amorphousness obscures a crucial distinction between cosmopolitanism and "pluralism."[16]

"Pluralism" differs from cosmopolitanism in the degree to which it endows with privilege particular groups, especially the communities that are well established at whatever time the ideal of pluralism is invoked. While cosmopolitanism is willing to put the future of every culture at risk through the critical, sympathetic scrutiny of other cultures, and is willing to contemplate the creation of new affiliations, pluralism is more concerned to protect and perpetuate particular, existing cultures.[17] In its extreme form, this conservative element in pluralism takes the form of a bargain: "You keep the acids of your modernity out of my culture, and I'll keep the acids of mine away from yours." If cosmopolitanism is casual about community-building and community-maintenance, and tends to seek voluntary affiliations of wide compass, pluralism promotes affiliations on the narrower grounds of shared history and is quicker to see reasons for drawing boundaries between communities. Cosmopolitanism is more oriented to the individual, whom it is likely to understand as a member of a number of different communities simultaneously, while pluralism is more oriented to the group, and is likely to identify each individual with reference to a single, primary community. Cosmopolitanism is more suspicious than is pluralism of the potential for conformist pressures within the communities celebrated by pluralists, while pluralism is more suspicious than is cosmopolitanism of the variousness and lack of apparent structure in the wider world celebrated by cosmopolitans. Arguments offered by universalists that certain interests are shared by many groups will get a longer hearing from cosmopolitans than from pluralists, who are more likely to see in such arguments the covert advancement of the interests of one, particular group. Pluralism and cosmopolitanism have often been united in the common cause of promoting "tolerance" and "diversity," and thus both are strong ideological tributaries feeding the multiculturalism of our own time. But a tension between pluralist and cosmopolitan tendencies runs throughout the multiculturalist debate, and is rarely acknowledged.

Cosmopolitanism is worth singling out because its renewal in the context of the debate over multiculturalism can yield what I want to call a "post-ethnic" perspective. The latter is more historically specific than cosmopolitanism. *Post*ethnicity reacts against the nation's invidiously ethnic history, builds upon the current generation's unprecedented appreciation of previously ignored cultures, and supports on the basis of revocable consent those affiliations by shared descent that were previously taken to be primordial. The great pluralist Horace Kallen thought he had made a knockdown argument for the primacy of ethno-racial identities when he observed that one thing no one can change is his or her grandfather, but a postethnic perspective challenges the right of one's grandfather or grandmother to determine primary identity. Let individuals affiliate or disaffiliate with others of shared or differing descent as they choose.[18] The postethnic ideal recognizes the need for affiliations that mediate between the individual and such gross entities as the state, the economy, and the species. If this need has been often slighted by universalists—for whom the species as a whole can be community enough—the reality of this need has led some pluralists to reify ethnoracial categories and to deny the contingent, contextual character of the process of affiliation. Part of the "post" in postethnicity is the latter's acceptance of the constructed character of "races" and "ethnic groups": a postethnic perspective is willing to "problematize"—as we say nowadays—identities that unreconstructed ethnocentrists preferred to take as given.[19]

The shifting, socially constructed character of ethno-racial groups is apparent in the recent amalgamation of what were once a host of distinctive "ethnic identities" into "Euro-American," now widely seen alongside Asian-American, African-American, Latina/o, and Native American as one of the five basic demographic blocs that constitute the bulk of American society. American multiculturalism accomplished in short order a task that centuries of British imperial power could not complete: the making of the Irish indistinguishable from the English.[20] Jewish identity, too, receded in significance when all Americans of predominantly "European" stock were grouped together.[21] It is tempting to see the new system of classification as a "quintuple melting pot," replacing Will Herberg's "triple melting pot" of Protestants, Catholics, and Jews, all of whom are now grouped together as "Euro-Americans."[22]

If the new American ethno-racial pentagon, or "quintuple melting pot," serves to erase dramatically much of the cultural diversity within the Euro-American bloc, the very drama of this transformation is salutary in two respects. First, this drama is a reminder of the contingent, contextual character of the entire process by which social identities are created, perpetuated, and altered. A New Hampshire resident of French-Canadian ethnicity may learn, by moving to Texas, that he or she is actually an "Anglo." Many European immigrants of the nineteenth century did not come to see themselves as significantly "Italian" or "German" until these identities were thrust upon them by the novel demographic conditions of the United States that rendered obsolete the local identities into which they had been acculturated in Sicily and Swabia. Distinctions between Protestants, Catholics, and Jews of European extraction were once taken as seriously as are the distinctions now made between Euro-Americans and Asian-Americans. Most ironically, those from Arab countries and Iran are not, by most indexes, called Asian-Americans, but "whites," or, by transfer, "Euro-American."

A second valuable consequence of the sudden transformation of a host of ethnic identities into "Euro-America" is the invitation this experience provides to recognize the comparable erasures of diversity that victimize people within the other four, pseudo-primal categories. The tribal and linguistic distinctions among Native Americans have long been lost on many non-Indian observers. The purchase one gets on Koreans, Cambodians, Chinese, Vietnamese, and Japanese by calling them all "Asian-Americans" (or, in the older usage, "Orientals") is obtained at the cost of diminishing the significance of the differences between these, and other, Americans of Asian extraction. The Hispanic, or Latina/o bloc has more linguistic cohesion than does the Asian-American or the Native American bloc, but it, too, can be broken down into subgroups defined, for example, by such points of origin as Puerto Rico, Cuba, Mexico, and El Salvador. The internal diversity of the African-American bloc may be the least striking, as measured by some indicators, but nothing illustrates more tellingly the selective suppression of diversity and the socially constructed character of these ethno-racial blocs than the historic denial, by generations of empowered whites, that they share with black Americans a substantial pool of genes. As Barbara Fields has put the point, we still have a convention "that considers a white woman capable of giving birth to a black child but denies that a black woman can give birth to a white child."[23] Hence, "Haley's Choice."

And it is choice, so highly valued by the post-ethnic perspective, that by its very limits within the new ethno-racial pentagon, defines it. A Cambodian-American does not have to remain so in the eyes of non-Asian-Americans, but only with great difficulty can he or she cease to be an Asian-American. So, too with Japanese-Americans or Chinese-Americans (and, as might be asked by the Euro-American auto worker from Detroit who clubbed to death the Chinese-American Vincent Chin, thinking him Japanese, "what's the difference, anyway?"). The same applies to the other blocks: Native Americans might care who is a Cherokee and who is a Kwakiutl, but outside that section of the pentagon, an Indian is an Indian. Some Euro-Americans might make a big deal of being Jewish, but from the viewpoint of many African-Americans—returning an old favor—it is the whiteness of the whole lot of them that counts. And so on.

The lines between the five unequally inhabited sides of the ethnoracial pentagon mark the limits of individual movement, as set by an implicit, informal concord among the most well-positioned of the people who practice identity politics in America today.[24] These several lines are not resistant in exactly the same degree to intermarriage and other types of border-crossing and category-mixing, but all are strong enough to function as "racial" as opposed to "ethnic" boundaries. Exactly where ethnicity ends and race begins has been much contested in our time, when zoologists and anthropologists have found so little scientific utility in the concept of race, and when humanists and social scientists have found so much evidence for the socially constructed character of ethnicity, of race, and even of gender. What is shown by the prominence of what I am calling the "ethno-racial pentagon," however, is that two kinds of lines are, in fact, being drawn, and widely accepted, at least for now: fainter lines distinguish the "ethnicities" found within each of the five blocs, while bolder, thicker lines render these five blocs themselves into "races," or race-equivalents.

Nowhere within the entire ethno-racial pentagon do individuals have more freedom to choose how much or how little emphasis to place on their "ethnicity"—speaking now about the identities conferred by the "faint" lines noted above—than within the Euro-American "race," or, as I would prefer to say, bloc. The ease with which Euro-Americans can affirm or ignore their ethnic identity as Italians, Norwegians, Irish, etc., has often been noted by sociologists, and was convincingly documented recently by Mary C. Waters in *Ethnic Options: Choosing Identities in America*. Many white, middle-class Americans of third- or fourth-generation immigrant descent get a great deal of satisfaction out of their ethnic affiliations, which, in the current cultural and political environment, cost them little.[25] Waters found that these "white ethnics" tended to shy away from aspects of communal life that imposed obligations and intruded on their privacy and individuality, but affirmed what Herbert Gans calls "symbolic ethnicity": a subjective "feeling" of identity, rather than the socially substantive ethnicity entailed by involvement in a concrete community with organizations, mutual commitments, and some elements of constraints.[26]

Although Waters found abundant evidence for the voluntary character of the ethnicity affirmed by middle class whites, she also encountered the persistence, among these manifestly voluntary ethnics, of the notion that ethnicity is a primordial, biological status. Waters's subjects' denial of the voluntary character of their own ethnic identities rendered them, in turn, insensitive to the involuntary character of the ethno-racial identities of non-whites: they see a formal "equivalence between the African-American and, say, Polish-American heritages," while often denying the depth and durability of the racism that has largely constructed and persistently bedeviled the former. Waters's book is intended, in part, to liberate whites from these blindnesses, which inhibit the extending to all Americans of the freedom now experienced by middle-class whites to affiliate and disaffiliate at will. When Waters argues for such a consummation—a time when "all Americans" are equally "free to exercise their 'ethnic option' "—she upholds the ideal I am calling postethnic.[27] In such a consummation, the vividly etched lines that define the ethno-racial pentagon would be fainter, more like the lines internal to each of the five segments. An "ethnic" America, on the other hand, would be what we have already had, only more so: the lines now vivid would be underscored, and the lines now faint would become more bold. Some programs expressed in the name of multiculturalism—those deriving more from "pluralism" than from "cosmopolitanism"—proceed in this contrary, "ethnic" direction.

It would be a mistake to ask the ideal of postethnicity to do more than serve as a distinctive frame within which can take place argument and contention over the nature of American nationality and over more specific issues in social policy. It is a frankly idealistic frame, embodying the hope that the United States can be more than an empire serving as a site for a variety of diasporas and of projects in colonization and conquest. The ideal is not a blueprint, nor a set of concrete programs. Its generality is not, however, a reason to doubt its utility. The notion of "multiculturalism" is considerably less specific, yet the work we have been asking this concept to do in our national discussion of ourselves testifies to our need for sweeping concepts. We cannot do without them. When we try, someone else's sweeping concept comes into the discourse and fills the relevant space.

Among the resources available to support the ideal of postethnicity is the tradition of cosmopolitanism as found in modern American intellectual history. "It is not because of diversity that we are in trouble," nor should our goal be to "cancel" or even to "conceal" our "differences" in the interests of "uniformity," wrote one figure in this tradition, the editor of a collection entitled *Unity and Difference in American Life.* "The problem is to get along with these differences," which should be welcomed in this "endlessly varied" universe filled with "all kinds of differences" displayed in many "groups" and many "communities."[28] The book is from 1947, and the voice is that of the Columbia University sociologist, Robert M. McIver. As a theorist of diversity, McIver is not superior to most of the participants in our multiculturalist debate, but his voice, if heard at today's symposia, would be conventionally harmonious on many points. Examples of the anti-provincial strain of cultural criticism cited more widely than McIver include the careers of Randolph Bourne, John Dewey, Walter Lippmann, Margaret Mead, Ruth Benedict, and Lionel Trilling, but the literature in which they are cited is a decidedly monographic one, informing little of the popular debate over multiculturalism.[29]

It would not do to insist that these intellectuals solved effectively the problems that we struggle with today,[30] nor would it do to deny that nearly all of us would find "provincial" and sexist the specific range of ideas they took up in a spirit of cosmopolitanism. Yet the vitality of a tradition of cosmopolitan aspiration among a substantial minority of Euro-American intellectuals is worth emphasizing at this multiculturalist moment, when the imperative to confront and renounce the racism and ethnocentrism within the Euro-American bloc threatens to erase from the history of that bloc the anti-racist and anti-ethnocentric voices raised from within it. If historical representation inevitably entails the selective silencing and perpetuating of specific voices from the inventory of the accessible past—as we are now reminded at every turn by our analysts of discourse as a form of power—it is in the interests of a potentially postethnic future to keep within our hearing the cosmopolitan voices that opposed some of the same evils now being fought, and that rendered the academic culture of the mid-century decades a terrain more contested than some of our current savants find it convenient to recall. Some multiculturalist programs for academic reform justify themselves by means of a slash-and-burn rendition of the intellectual and academic history of the United States (and sometimes of Europe), according to which even the relatively recent past partook of a virtually monolithic culture of Anglo-conformist domination that remained mystified and concealed until courageously exposed by the present generation of keynote speakers and deans of humanities. But the American academy's critical tradition offers contemporary egalitarians more aid than some of them have noticed; "not everybody," as the distinguished classicist Frank M. Snowden, Jr., has put the point cogently, "is a racist."[31]

Of racists there remain all too many, of course, but revulsion at racism is now sufficiently strong in our society to render the ideal of postethnicity worth discussing. Even the failure of the "Rodney King jurors" to convict the Los Angeles police officers of criminal assault should not distract us, as Orlando Patterson and Chris Winthrop have wisely cautioned, from recognizing long-term indicators that "the vestigially prejudiced majority may be changing."[32] In an age when community closure on the basis of shared descent is being sought in so many parts of the globe, the relatively open, contingent, negotiated character of American nationality renders the United States a world-historical project more conducive than are most nationalist endeavors to the development of postethnicity. Yet the idea of a postethnic America is a challenge to be met rather than a description of a reality already achieved. The latter misrepresentation is tempting when one contemplates the range and intensity of ethnic violence in Balkan Europe, the Caucasus, East Africa, India, and in many other locales throughout the world. But a misrepresentation it truly would be, and one comparable to a misrepresentation against which this essay warned at the start: the confusion of the nation's actual condition—its persistently ethnic history—with its non-ethnic ideology.

The democratic-egalitarian core of that old ideology remains vital to the vision of America I am calling postethnic. The potential of democratic-egalitarian ideals to serve as a common ground for persons of diverse descent will be diminished to the extent that these ideals become "ethnicized," which is the effect of defining them as "Eurocentric" in an era when people are encouraged in many quarters to line up their culture with their genes. The routes by which "democracy" and "equality" have travelled to reach the modern United States have been overwhelmingly Anglo-American and Western European, but that need not mean that Euro-Americans of today have a greater claim on these ideals than does anyone else. Americans within the other four ethno-racial blocs need not feel the slightest pressure to reserve their enthusiasm for democratic-egalitarian ideals until such time as evidence is produced that their own ancestral group experienced libertarian moments no less portentous than the Putney Debates of New Model Army.

The jealous particularisms that fear "common ground" as a field for covert Euro-American domination are not, however, what most immediately threatens progress toward a postethnic America. Critics of "the Balkanization of America" who focus their complaints on the educational and political programs of ethno-racial "separatists" would do well to concentrate, instead, on the rigidification of the class structure.

Economic opportunities have been vital to the process by which the once-bold lines dividing the various Euro-American ethnic groups from one another have become relatively faint, but today's poor and unskilled are offered fewer, smaller opportunities for advancement than were their comparably positioned predecessors. Persons outside

the Euro-American bloc who enter the American social system with strong skills and relatively high class position often flourish, even in the current political economy. Many of these individuals—as recent immigration from Korea, Taiwan, and Vietnam demonstrates especially well—respond very positively indeed to the public culture of the United States, and in their behavior approximate the classic pattern of a certain amount of "enclaving" and a certain amount of "assimilation." If all citizens of the United States had a reasonable hope of attaining the standard of living associated with "the middle class," the prospects for a postethnic America at this point in history—when so many energies are deployed against racism—would be encouraging. But the opportunity of the United States to create for itself a postethnic future may well be squandered through its own refusal to address the needs of its poor and unskilled citizens of all ethno-racial blocs.

ACKNOWLEDGMENTS

This essay has been influenced by the University of Michigan's Faculty Seminar on the Genealogy and Geography of Affiliation, Winter 1992. I wish to thank these colleagues for their vigorous discussions of the problem of "affiliation" in world-historical perspective. I owe special debts to Alexander Aleinikoff, Kenneth DeWoskin, Don Herzog, and Earl Lewis. I am also grateful for the many helpful comments by an audience responding to a draft of this essay presented to the Annual Meeting of the American Council of Learned Societies, Chicago, May 1, 1992.

ENDNOTES

1. Ishmael Reed, et al., "Is Ethnicity Obsolete?" in Werner Sollors, ed., *The Invention of Ethnicity* (New York: Oxford University Press, 1989), p. 227, commenting on Alex Haley, *Roots: The Saga of an American Family* (New York: Dell, 1976). Reed does not take the position that ethnicity *is* obsolete; on the contrary, he argues (229) that "ethnicity will never become obsolete" in the United States so long as "public attitudes" tend to type as "black" anyone with the slightest apparent African ancestry, and to associate with "Black America" many problems common to the society as a whole.
2. I confine this list to labels understood to be neutral or honorific. But the ethno-racial map of American society owes much to a dynamic of contempt, including the colloquial, hate-speech epithets that correspond to these socially accepted labels.

3. Reed, in Sollors, *Invention,* p. 229.

4. This essay elaborates on the argument of my "How Wide the Circle of the We? American Intellectuals and the Problem of the *Ethnos* Since World War Two," in Ronald G. Walters, ed., *Science and Social Reform in Modern America* (Baltimore: The Johns Hopkins University Press, 1993). There, I sketch the movement from species-centered to *ethnos*-centered discourse in American thought during the last several decades, and outline a "postethnic perspective" on epistemic, moral, and political communities. The concept of "postethnic" became known to me through the writings of Werner Sollors.

5. In speaking of American nationality, I do not mean that virtually everyone was a liberal egalitarian "in theory" and only choked when it came time to put the theory "into practice." The "theory" itself was often contested by people who preferred more narrowly communitarian and ethno-racially homogeneous visions of nationality. Regarding efforts to move the theory of American citizenship in "ethnic" directions, see Rogers M. Smith, "The 'American Creed' and American Identity: The Limits of Liberal Citizenship in the United States," *Western Political Quarterly* 41 (1988): 225–251.

6. The non-ethnic national ideology is sometimes said to suppress "difference" in the interest of "sameness," but this misses the real issues: What kind of difference? What kind of sameness? And for what purpose might a difference be suppressed? No one now says that ancestral differences should be considered in deciding which citizens vote, but our refusal to consider such differences is certainly an example of the suppression of difference.

7. Defenders of multiculturalism have complained with reason that critics have lumped together a range of distinctive ideas; but their next step is all too often to sweep all critics of multiculturalism into a single reactionary, establishmentarian group. A striking example of this is Evan Carton, "The Self Besieged: American Identity on Campus and in the Gulf," *Tikkun* 4 (July/August 1991):40–47, which characterizes as "Operation Campus Storm" criticisms of multiculturalism and attacks on "political correctness" published in *Time, Newsweek,* the *New Republic,* and *Atlantic.* Carton links these to "Operation Desert Storm" in the Gulf, and treats as a fair emblem for this George Will's praise for Lynne Cheney as our "secretary of domestic defense." For a sharply contrasting mode of response see Louis Menand, "Illiberalisms," *New Yorker* (May 20,1991): 101—107, in which Menand dares to acknowledge—amid a scorching and effective critique of Dinesh D'Souza's *Illiberal Education* (New York: Free Press, 1991)—that some of what is said in the name of multiculturalism is pretty silly, and implies that we should not shrink from saying so for fear of being linked with the Far Right.

8. Gary B. Nash, "The Great Multicultural Debate," *Contention,* I, 3 (Fall 1992): 11.

9. See the three books, for different grade levels, by Beverley J. Armento, Gary B. Nash, Christopher L. Salter, and Karen K. Wixson, all by Houghton-Mifflin (Boston, 1991): *From Sea to Shining Sea, America Will Be,* and *A More Perfect Union.* Based on a selective reading of these books, I believe they do fulfill the goals of multiculturalism as Nash defines it. These books devote extensive and sympathetic attention to a great variety of American ethno-racial groups, and interpret the major episodes in the history of British North America and the United States in terms that are refreshingly consistent with the anti-racist scholarship of professional historians during the past generation.

10. Nash, "Debate," 22, 24. Diane Ravitch, "In the Multicultural Trenches," *Contention,* I 3 (Fall 1992), distinguishes as sharply as does Nash between Afrocentrism and multiculturalism, and pleads for the recognition of commonalities amid easily distinguished cultural diversities. See also Ravitch, "Multiculturalism," *American Scholar* 59 (1990): 337–354, and Arthur M. Schlesinger, Jr., *The Disuniting of America: Reflections on a Multicultural Society* (New York: Norton, 1992). I do not mean to slight the differences between Nash, on the one hand, and Ravitch and Schlesinger, on the other. Nash is more deeply critical of the interpretations of American history and culture that prevailed before the multicultural enthusiasms of recent years, and more insistent that ways be found to articulate and appreciate the variety of cultural traditions that have gone into the making of the contemporary United States. Yet their writings confirm that some of multiculturalism's defenders and critics are backing into one another as they recoil from the ethnocentrism of either the European or the African variety.

11. Nash, "Debate," 23, 24, 25. Nash's intervention in the multicultural debate can be compared with that of another historian, Elizabeth Fox-Genovese, "Between Individualism and Fragmentation: American Culture and the New Literary Studies of Race and Gender," *American Quarterly* 42 (1990): 7–34. See also Bruce Robbins, "Othering in the Academy: Professionalism and Multiculturalism," *Social Research* 58 (1991): 354–372, which makes a vigorous and discerning defense of "cosmopolitanism," an "unfashionable term that needs defending" (358-359). Robbins also vindicates democratic values as the desired "common project" (372).

12. The term "Eurocentric" may be fair, however, as applied to Lewis S. Feuer, who identifies "disease and massacre" as the "principal offerings" of "Central African culture," and attacks multiculturalism as "a secession from Western Civilization" comparable to that carried out by the Christian anti-intellectual sects who burned the library in ancient Alexandria. See Feuer, "From Pluralism to Multiculturalism," *Society* 29 (1991): 19–22.

13. For an agitated example of this insistence, see Reed Way Dasenbrock, "The Multicultural West," *Dissent* (Fall 1991): 550–555. Dasenbrock does not, however, disparage the study of non-European cultures; he argues (553) that "Multiculturalism is simply the standard human condition," and that it applies to Europe and the United States as a matter of course, and endows both with much of the value they have.

14. Diane Ravitch comes out foursquare for multiculturalism in her contribution to *Contention,* cited above.

15. A vivid example of a universalist pronouncement in American discourse is the great courtroom speech of Eugene Victor Debs: "So long as there is a lower class, I am in it; so long as there is a criminal element, I am of it; so long as there is a soul in prison, I am not free." These proclamations of extensive fraternity contrast with all prescriptions to look after "one's own kind."

16. I have tried to distinguish "cosmopolitanism" from "pluralism" in my *In the American Province: Studies in the History and Historiography of Ideas* (Bloomington, Ind.: Indiana University Press, 1985), p. 57, using Randolph Bourne as an exemplar of the former and Horace Kallen as an exemplar of the latter.

17. There exists a rich literature on pluralism that has gone remarkably little used in the multiculturalism debate. Especially important is John Higham, "Ethnic Pluralism in Modern American Thought," in Higham's *Send These to Me: Immigrants in American Life* 2nd. ed. (Baltimore: The Johns Hopkins University Press, 1984), pp. 198–232. A helpful overview is Olivier Zunz, "The Genesis of American Pluralism," *Tocqueville Review* 9 (1988): 201–219. See also Werner Sollors, "A Critique of Pure Pluralism," in Sacvan Bercovitch, ed., *Reconstructing American Literary History* (Cambridge, Mass.: Harvard University Press, 1986), pp. 250–279, with its provocative interpretation of Horace Kallen, the most prominent theorist of "cultural pluralism" in the United States.

18. The partial reconfiguration of the discourse over "race" and "ethnicity" into the terms "descent" and "consent" has been a contribution of Werner Sollors, *Beyond Ethnicity* (New York: Oxford University Press, 1986).

19. A recognition that ethno-racial groups are constructed in contingent circumstances, and shift their boundaries according to context, is a major theme in recent scholarship. Alexander Nehamas summarizes the implications of this scholarship in a recent challenge to Richard Rorty, "when the very idea of one's *ethnos* is being put everywhere into question how can one be 'ethnocentric'?" See Nehamas, "A Touch of the Poet," *Raritan* 10 (1990): 113.

20. This point is made by the journalist Bob Callahan in a clever account of a decision by the California Arts Council concerning who was and was not a "minority"; see Callahan in Sollors, *Invention,* 232.

21. "So much for the distinctiveness that has enlivened our souls for three millennia," complains Arnold Eisen on behalf of Jews, "and, again recently, led to the destruction of our bodies." See Eisen, "University Truths," *Tikkun* 6 (1991): 55. But cf. Walter P. Zenner, "Jewishness in America: Ascription and Choice," in Richard D. Alba, ed., *Ethnicity and Race in the U.S.A.: Toward the Twenty-First Century* (New York: Routledge, 1988), pp. 117–133, which addresses the diminished distinctness of the Jewish population within the Euro-American bloc, regardless of what perspective may be brought to the issue by members of other blocs.

22. Will Herberg, *Protestant-Catholic-Jew: An Essay in American Religious Sociology* (Garden City, N.Y.: Doubleday, 1955).

23. Barbara J. Fields, "Ideology and Race in American History," in J. Morgan Kousser and James M. McPherson, eds., *Region, Race, and Reconstruction* (New York: Oxford University Press, 1982), p. 149.

24. Although this ethno-racial pentagon is now in vogue, it is not the only demographic map being advanced. One prominent competitor centers on "people of color," which implies a bi-polar construction. In this view, white and non-white are the two relevant categories, and all distinctions between the various "colored" peoples are less significant than their being non-white. The greater acceptance of the ethno-racial pentagon is indicated by the frequency with which one is asked to identify oneself in terms of this pentagon on application forms, on health-care questionnaires, and on other forms.

25. Mary C. Waters, *Ethnic Options: Choosing Identities in America* (Berkeley: University of California Press, 1990), p. 147. See also Richard D. Alba, "The Twilight of Ethnicity Among Americans of European Ancestry: The Case of the Italians," in Alba, ed., *Ethnicity and Race,* pp. 134–158.

26. Herbert Gans, "Symbolic Ethnicity in America," *Ethnic and Racial Studies* 2 (1979): 1–20, esp. 9.

27. Waters, *Ethnic Options,* 157–158, 167, 164.

28. R. M. McIver, "What We All Can Do," in McIver, ed., *Unity and Difference in American Life* (New York: Columbia University Press, 1947), pp. 152–153. This volume is an interesting document in the history of American discourse about unity and difference. See, for example, the essays by Lawrence K. Frank (33–40), E. Franklin Frazier (43–59), and Clyde R. Miller (107–118).

29. Examples of this literature include Terry A. Cooney, *The Rise of the New York Intellectuals: Partisan Review and Its Circle, 1934–1945* (Madison: University of Wisconsin Press, 1986); Thomas Bender, *New York Intellect* (New York: Knopf, 1987); Thomas Bender, "Lionel Trilling and American Culture," *American Quarterly* 42 (1990): 324–347; Richard Handler, "Boasian Anthropology and the Critique of American Culture," *American Quarterly* 42 (1990): 252–273; Leslie J. Vaughan, "Cosmopolitanism, Ethnicity, and American Identity: Randolph

Bourne's 'Trans-National America'," *Journal of American Studies* 25 (1991):443–459; and Susanne Klingenstein, *Jews in the American Academy, 1900–1940: The Dynamics of Intellectual Assimilation* (New Haven: Yale University Press, 1991).

30. One feature of this earlier discourse that seems significant in today's context is the struggle of Jewish intellectuals to work out an orientation toward Jewish identity consistent with their identity as Americans and as cosmopolitans.

31. As quoted by Molly Myerowitz Levine, "The Use and Abuse of *Black Athena,*" *American Historical Review* 98 (1992): 440.

32. Orlando Patterson and Chris Winthrop, "White Poor, Black Poor," *New York Times,* May 3, 1992, IV, 17.

F I V E

The First Americans
American Indians

C. Matthew Snipp

By the end of the nineteenth century, many observers predicted that American Indians were destined for extinction. Within a few generations, disease, warfare, famine, and outright genocide had reduced their numbers from millions to less than 250,000 in 1890. Once a self-governing, self-sufficient people, American Indians were forced to give up their homes and their land, and to subordinate themselves to an alien culture. The forced resettlement to reservation lands or the Indian Territory (now Oklahoma) frequently meant a life of destitution, hunger, and complete dependency on the federal government for material needs.

Today, American Indians are more numerous than they have been for several centuries. While still one of the most destitute groups in American society, tribes have more autonomy and are now more self-sufficient than at any time since the last century. In cities, modern pan-Indian organizations have been successful in making the presence of American Indians known to the larger community, and have mobilized to meet the needs of their people (Cornell 1988; Nagel 1986; Weibel-Orlando 1991). In many rural areas, American Indians and especially tribal governments have become increasingly more important and increasingly more visible by virtue of their growing political and economic power. The balance of this chapter is devoted to explaining their unique place in American society.

THE INCORPORATION OF AMERICAN INDIANS

The current political and economic status of American Indians is the result of the process by which they were incorporated into Euro-American society (Hall 1989). This amounts to a long history of efforts aimed at subordinating an otherwise self-governing and self-sufficient people that eventually culminated in widespread economic dependency. The role of the U.S. government in this process can be seen in the five major historical periods of federal Indian relations: removal, assimilation, the Indian New Deal, termination and relocation, and self-determination.

Removal

In the early nineteenth century, the population of the United States expanded rapidly at the same time that the federal government increased its political and military capabilities. The character of Indian-American relations changed after the War of 1812. The federal government increasingly pressured tribes settled east of the Appalachian Mountains to move west to the territory acquired in the Louisiana purchase.

Numerous treaties were negotiated by which the tribes relinquished most of their land and eventually were forced to move west.

Initially the federal government used bargaining and negotiation to accomplish removal, but many tribes resisted (Prucha 1984). However, the election of Andrew Jackson by a frontier constituency signaled the beginning of more forceful measures to accomplish removal. In 1830 Congress passed the Indian Removal Act, which mandated the eventual removal of the eastern tribes to points west of the Mississippi River, in an area which was to become the Indian Territory and is now the state of Oklahoma. Dozens of tribes were forcibly removed from the eastern half of the United States to the Indian Territory and newly created reservations in the west, a long process ridden with conflict and bloodshed.

As the nation expanded beyond the Mississippi River, tribes of the plains, southwest, and west coast were forcibly settled and quarantined on isolated reservations. This was accompanied by the so-called Indian Wars—a bloody chapter in the history of Indian-White relations (Prucha 1984; Utley 1984). This period in American history is especially remarkable because the U.S. government was responsible for what is unquestionably one of the largest forced migrations in history.

The actual process of removal spanned more than a half-century and affected nearly every tribe east of the Mississippi River. Removal often meant extreme hardships for American Indians, and in some cases this hardship reached legendary proportions. For example, the Cherokee removal has become known as the "Trail of Tears." In 1838, nearly 17,000 Cherokees were ordered to leave their homes and assemble in military stockades (Thornton 1987, p. 117). The march to the Indian Territory began in October and continued through the winter months. As many as 8,000 Cherokees died from cold weather and diseases such as influenza (Thornton 1987, p. 118).

According to William Hagan (1979), removal also caused the Creeks to suffer dearly as their society underwent a profound disintegration. The contractors who forcibly removed them from their homes refused to do anything for "the large number who had nothing but a cotton garment to protect them from the sleet storms and no shoes between them and the frozen ground of the last stages of their hegira. About half of the Creek nation did not survive the migration and the difficult early years in the West" (Hagan 1979, p. 77–81). In the West, a band of Nez Perce men, women, and children, under the leadership of Chief Joseph, resisted resettlement in 1877. Heavily outnumbered, they were pursued by cavalry troops from the Wallowa valley in eastern Oregon and finally captured in Montana near the Canadian border. Although the Nez Perce were eventually captured and moved to the Indian Territory, and later to Idaho, their resistance to resettlement has been described by one historian as "one of the great military movements in history" (Prucha 1984, p. 541).

Assimilation

Near the end of the nineteenth century, the goal of isolating American Indians on reservations and the Indian Territory was finally achieved. The Indian population also was near extinction. Their numbers had declined steadily throughout the nineteenth century leading most observers to predict their disappearance (Hoxie 1984). Reformers urged the federal government to adopt measures that would humanely ease American Indians into extinction. The federal government responded by creating boarding schools and the allotment acts—both were intended to "civilize" and assimilate American Indians into American society by Christianizing them, educating them, introducing them to private property, and making them into farmers. American Indian boarding schools sought to accomplish this task by indoctrinating Indian children with the belief that tribal culture was an inferior relic of the past and that Euro-American culture was vastly superior and preferable. Indian children were forbidden to wear their native attire, to eat their native foods, to speak their native language, or to practice their traditional religion. Instead, they were issued Euro-American clothes, and expected to speak English and become Christians. Indian children who did not relinquish their culture were punished by school authorities. The curriculum of these schools taught vocational arts along with "civilization" courses.

The impact of allotment policies is still evident today. The 1887 General Allotment Act (the Dawes Severalty Act) and subsequent legislation mandated that tribal lands were to be allotted to individual American Indians in fee simple title, and the surplus lands left over from allotment were to be sold on the open market. Indians who received allotted tribal lands also received citizenship, farm implements, and encouragement from Indian agents to adopt farming as a livelihood (Hoxie 1984, Prucha 1984).

For a variety of reasons, Indian lands were not completely liquidated by allotment, many Indians did not receive allotments, and relatively few changed their lifestyles to become farmers. Nonetheless, the allotment era was a disaster because a significant number of allotees eventually lost their land. Through tax foreclosures, real estate fraud, and their own need for cash, many American Indians lost what for most of them was their last remaining asset (Hoxie 1984).

Allotment took a heavy toll on Indian lands. It caused about 90 million acres of Indian land to be lost, approximately two-thirds of the land that had belonged to tribes in 1887 (O'Brien 1989). This created another problem that continues to vex many reservations: "checkerboarding." Reservations that were subjected to allotment are typically a crazy quilt composed of tribal lands, privately owned "fee" land, and trust land belonging to individual Indian families. Checkerboarding presents reservation officials with enormous administrative problems when trying to develop land use management plans, zoning ordinances, or economic development projects that require the construction of physical infrastructure such as roads or bridges.

The Indian New Deal

The Indian New Deal was short-lived but profoundly important. Implemented in the early 1930s along with the other New Deal programs of the Roosevelt administration, the Indian New Deal was important for at least three reasons. First, signaling the end of the disastrous allotment era as well as a new respect for American Indian tribal culture, the Indian New Deal repudiated allotment as a policy. Instead of continuing its futile efforts to detribalize American Indians, the federal government acknowledged that tribal culture was

worthy of respect. Much of this change was due to John Collier, a long-time Indian rights advocate appointed by Franklin Roosevelt to serve as Commissioner of Indian Affairs (Prucha 1984).

Like other New Deal policies, the Indian New Deal also offered some relief from the Great Depression and brought essential infrastructure development to many reservations, such as projects to control soil erosion and to build hydroelectric dams, roads, and other public facilities. These projects created jobs in New Deal programs such as the Civilian Conservation Corps and the Works Progress Administration.

An especially important and enduring legacy of the Indian New Deal was the passage of the Indian Reorganization Act (IRA) of 1934. Until then, Indian self-government had been forbidden by law. This act allowed tribal governments, for the first time in decades, to reconstitute themselves for the purpose of overseeing their own affairs on the reservation. Critics charge that this law imposed an alien form of government, representative democracy, on traditional tribal authority. On some reservations, this has been an on-going source of conflict (O'Brien 1989). Some reservations rejected the IRA for this reason, but now have tribal governments authorized under different legislation.

Termination and Relocation

After World War II, the federal government moved to terminate its long-standing relationship with Indian tribes by settling the tribes' outstanding legal claims, by terminating the special status of reservations, and by helping reservation Indians relocate to urban areas (Fixico 1986). The Indian Claims Commission was a special tribunal created in 1946 to hasten the settlement of legal claims that tribes had brought against the federal government. In fact, the Indian Claims Commission became bogged down with prolonged cases, and in 1978 the commission was dissolved by Congress. At that time, there were 133 claims still unresolved out of an original 617 that were first heard by the commission three decades earlier (Fixico 1986, p. 186). The unresolved claims that were still pending were transferred to the Federal Court of Claims.

Congress also moved to terminate the federal government's relationship with Indian tribes. House Concurrent Resolution (HCR) 108, passed in 1953, called for steps that eventually would abolish all reservations and abolish all special programs serving American Indians. It also established a priority list of reservations slated for immediate termination. However, this bill and subsequent attempts to abolish reservations were vigorously opposed by Indian advocacy groups such as the National Congress of American Indians. Only two reservations were actually terminated, the Klamath in Oregon and the Menominee in Wisconsin. The Menominee reservation regained its trust status in 1975 and the Klamath reservation was restored in 1986.

The Bureau of Indian Affairs (BIA) also encouraged reservation Indians to relocate and seek work in urban job markets. This was prompted partly by the desperate economic prospects on most reservations, and partly because of the federal government's desire to "get out of the Indian business." The BIA's relocation programs aided reservation Indians in moving to designated cities, such as Los Angeles and Chicago, where they also assisted them in finding housing and employment. Between 1952 and 1972, the BIA relocated more than 100,000 American Indians (Sorkin 1978). However, many Indians returned to their reservations (Fixico 1986). For some American Indians, the return to the reservation was only temporary; for example, during periods when seasonal employment such as construction work was hard to find.

Self-Determination

Many of the policies enacted during the termination and relocation era were steadfastly opposed by American Indian leaders and their supporters. As these programs became stalled, critics attacked them for being harmful, ineffective, or both. By the mid-1960s, these policies had very little serious support. Perhaps inspired by the gains of the Civil Rights movement, American Indian leaders and their supporters made "self-determination" the first priority on their political agendas. For these activists, self-determination meant that Indian people would have the autonomy to control their own affairs, free from the paternalism of the federal government.

The idea of self-determination was well received by members of Congress sympathetic to American Indians. It also was consistent with the "New Federalism" of the Nixon administration. Thus, the policies of termination and relocation

were repudiated in a process that culminated in 1975 with the passage of the American Indian Self-Determination and Education Assistance Act, a profound shift in federal Indian policy. For the first time since this nation's founding, American Indians were authorized to oversee the affairs of their own communities, free of federal intervention. In practice, the Self-Determination Act established measures that would allow tribal governments to assume a larger role in reservation administration of programs for welfare assistance, housing, job training, education, natural resource conservation, and the maintenance of reservation roads and bridges (Snipp and Summers 1991). Some reservations also have their own police forces and game wardens, and can issue licenses and levy taxes. The Onondaga tribe in upstate New York have taken their sovereignty one step further by issuing passports that are internationally recognized. Yet there is a great deal of variability in terms of how much autonomy tribes have over reservation affairs. Some tribes, especially those on large and well-organized reservations have nearly complete control over their reservations, while smaller reservations with limited resources often depend heavily on BIA services.

INDIAN COUNTRY

As their name suggests, reservations (along with tribal trust lands) represent the last remaining landholdings subject to the control of American Indians; these lands are known as "Indian Country." About one-half of all American Indians live in these places, and most are located west of the Mississippi River. Since their creation, reservations have been places marked by severe economic distress. In 1928, the Meriam Report first documented the economic hardships of reservation life, and since then, studies continue to show that little has changed (Snipp 1989). American Indian reservations were and continue to be among the poorest places in America.

Welfare dependency has been a fact of life in Indian country since tribes were first interned on reservations and forced to depend on military rations for survival. Since then, this dependency has become considerably more complex and manifest in federal programs, such as the "war on poverty" efforts or the projects sponsored by the

Comprehensive Employment and Training Acts (CETA) of the 1960s and 1970s. The abrupt termination of many of these programs in the conservative era of the 1980s reminded tribal leaders about the uncertainty of federal largesse and the need for achieving financial independence.

Instead of simply abandoning these destitute places, urban and reservation Indians alike view measures to revitalize and improve reservation life as essential. For reservation Indians, reservation projects that provide jobs and improve the quality of life make it possible to stay in the community, near not only family but also close to significant spiritual and cultural events, making it possible to follow traditional cultural practices. Reservations are also important because only on reservations are Indian communities allowed some measure of self-government. Furthermore, many urban Indians maintain close ties to family and friends on reservations, as reservations are places for cultural renewal. In some instances, they are places to return to when jobs and opportunities become available.

Indian Country has an unparalleled importance to American Indians because it represents the last remaining land base for Indian communities. For many American Indians, the land has spiritual as well as monetary value. As a result, efforts to develop tribal lands involve complex considerations such as how to profitably develop tribal lands without compromising cultural values. Nonetheless, reservation and trust lands represent a considerable resource that American Indians are beginning to develop for the benefit of their communities.

Natural Resources

There are 278 federally recognized American Indian reservations ranging in size from less than 100 acres to the largest reservation of 16 million acres—the Navajo—covering parts of Arizona, Utah, and New Mexico; an area about the size of West Virginia. These reservations account for most of the 56.2 million acres of Indian lands supervised by the federal government. The four major types of natural resources include agricultural land, timber, water, and mineral resources.

Since the late nineteenth century, the federal government has encouraged American Indians to adopt agriculture. Yet for most of the twentieth century, agriculture has been a declining industry in the American economy. Furthermore, the allotment policies actually caused declines in Indian agriculture (Carlson 1981). Not surprisingly, there is a long history of failed attempts to establish tribal farms and livestock herds. Some tribes suffered disastrous land losses during allotment. Other tribes, such as those in the Southwest had practiced agriculture for centuries, but they refused to adopt non-Indian technologies and their collective farm systems were also disrupted by allotment.

Since the late 1800s, non-Indians have been responsible for agricultural production on tribal lands. For example, when members of the Ute tribe in Utah refused to become farmers, Indian agents leased their lands to nearby Mormon farmers. This is typical of how agricultural land has been managed on most reservations. One study even found that non-Indians cultivated the most productive farmland while Indians were more likely to control less productive grazing land (Levitan and Johnston 1975).

The productivity of tribal land is a serious problem. Not surprisingly, reservations were established in places that have very little productive land. For example, the BIA classifies less than 1 percent of all reservation lands as highly productive and less than 5 percent of the giant Navajo reservation as highly productive farmland. For the average reservation, about one acre of productive agricultural land per resident (Summers n.d.).

Despite these problems, there are notable exceptions. For example, the Passamaquoddy tribe in Maine used funds from land claims settlements to acquire and develop a high-quality blueberry farm that supplies gourmet markets, premium hotels, and Ben and Jerry's Ice Cream. The Ak Chin reservation south of Phoenix has a large and profitable agribusiness with over 10,000 acres of cotton and alfalfa in production (White 1990).

Although agricultural production is not widespread on many reservations, timber production is more common. Timber is often cut and processed outside the reservation, but a growing number of reservations have built mills to produce finished lumber. One of the oldest of these mills was established on the Menominee reservation in Wisconsin.

Historically, the BIA has had primary responsibility for overseeing tribal forests and for the harvesting and sale of tribal timber. In 1989, 237 federal reservations possessed nearly 16 million acres of forestland with potentially harvestable timber. Perhaps more significant is that in 1989, 149 reservations held about 6 million acres in commercial forests, not an inconsequential resource as its total harvested value is estimated at $158 million.

In the last twenty years, the BIA has been subject to numerous complaints as well as congressional investigations regarding its management of tribal forests. These complaints alleged fraud and mismanagement, particularly "sweetheart" deals between BIA employees and lumber companies, improper accounting, and incompetent resource management (Richardson and Farrell 1983). As a result, tribes are now considerably more involved in the management of their timber; and some tribes have instituted specialized forestry programs.

Water resources are also very important to reservations. The *Winters* doctrine, stemming from a 1908 Supreme Court decision over tribal water rights, guarantees that tribes have prior claims on water destined for their reservation. In the arid western United States, this gives reservations a powerful claim on a scarce and vital resource. This is perhaps most important for reservation development, especially in water-intensive projects such as agriculture. However, developing water for lease or sale off the reservation is tangled in the complex legal web of water rights, and has not been extensively pursued. Nonetheless, it is possible for tribes with extensive water rights, such as the Navajo, to lease their water to the arid cities of the Southwest, just as large growers have found it more profitable to lease their water than to use it for farming. Water also can be used to produce revenue in other ways; for instance, the Salish-Kootenai in Montana sell hydroelectric power from a dam on their reservation. In addition to water, the minerals available on reservation lands run the gamut from gravel to zinc and copper to energy resources such as uranium, coal, petroleum, and natural gas. Needless to say, the immense potential wealth associated with energy resources has attracted the most attention. By some estimates, 40 percent of all uranium and 30 percent of the strippable coal west of the Mississippi is located on tribal lands (Jorgensen et al. 1978).

Despite the enormous real and potential value of these resources, those tribes possessing coal and petroleum are not significantly wealthier than other tribes (Snipp 1988). Some tribes, such as the northern Cheyenne in Montana, view mining as a violation of their sacred relationship with the land. This traditional belief is frequently a source of conflict among those tribal members who adhere to traditional beliefs and tribal members who wish to develop the resources. A more important reason is that for many years, the BIA failed to exercise proper oversight in the process of making leases. Bureau of Indian Affairs oversights caused millions of tons of coal to be sold at prices far below market value (Richardson and Farrell 1983; Snipp 1988).

Congressional inquiries and complaints by tribal leaders resulted in revamping BIA leasing procedures. The tribes also became more proactive in the negotiation of lease agreements, as with the creation of the Council of Energy Resource Tribes (CERT), which was formed in 1975 for the purpose of increasing tribal involvement in lease negotiations and for providing technical assistance to aide tribes in negotiations (Ambler 1990). Since then, many old leases have been renegotiated and tribal involvement has considerably improved the prices received for energy resources. However, more recently, a sluggish world market for coal and petroleum has dampened the earlier enthusiasm for exploiting these resources. The tribes have not had much direct involvement in mining the resources on their reservations. The capital required for mining operations vastly exceeds tribal resources. However, some tribes such as the Crow have investigated limited partnerships with energy companies, as well as imposing severance taxes on extracted resources.

Human Resources

Across the nation, education is a resource that is sorely lacking among American Indians. Indians lag far behind Whites by any measure of educational attainment. American Indian youth drop out at alarmingly high rates. In 1990, about 18 percent of American Indians ages sixteen to nineteen were not in school and had not completed high school, compared with 14 percent of Blacks and 10 percent of Whites. Surprisingly, among adults twenty-five years and older, American Indians are *more* likely to have graduated from high school than African Americans. This may be due to American Indians eventually completing their schooling with a GED instead of a regular high school diploma.

American Indians also seldom complete four or more years of college. In 1990, only about 9 percent of American Indians had completed four or more years of college, compared to 11 percent of African Americans and 22 percent of Whites. High drop-out rates and disrupted school experiences are undoubtedly major contributors to this problem. Moreover, American Indians are concentrated in two-year colleges aimed at vocational education. In 1984, for example, about 55 percent of American Indians in college were enrolled in two-year programs (Center for Education Statistics 1987, Table 2).

Although these statistics are for the nation as a whole, they are certainly indicative of reservation conditions. Education, training, and work experience are the best indicators of the human capital reserves belonging to reservations. The low levels of educational attainment bespeak the limited human resources for reservation development. The shortage of job opportunities in reservation communities further exacerbates the shortage of human capital as the best educated, most able-bodied workers have to leave the reservation for employment elsewhere.

Many tribes have decided to address this problem by establishing tribal colleges. The first tribal college was established in 1968 by the Navajo tribe. During the next twenty years, another twenty-three tribal colleges were established on reservations across the western United States. Most of them are small, two-year community college programs. A few such as Sinte Galeska College in South Dakota have a limited number of four-year programs. Almost all of these institutions depend heavily on federal funding and struggle to maintain the facilities and personnel adequate to meet accreditation standards. Because the students attending these schools have few economic resources, revenue from tuition or property taxes hardly exists.

Although relatively new, tribal colleges have the potential to play a key role for human resource development on reservations. The students attending these colleges are typically older and they frequently have very poor academic preparation; they are returning to upgrade their basic skills, obtain vocational training, or acquire a GED. The students who typically attend tribal colleges are not being diverted from educational opportunities elsewhere. They are students who would not be attending college under most circumstances, except that a tribal college gives them an opportunity to do so (Carnegie Foundation 1989). In 1989, an estimated 4,400 full-time students were enrolled at the twenty-four tribal colleges (Carnegie Foundation 1989). The advent of tribal colleges is a development of potentially profound importance. These institutions are training persons who in the past would have been labeled "hard-core unemployed." Their location also means they are able to coordinate program curriculum with projects designed to meet special needs on specific reservations.

TRIBAL DEVELOPMENT

The presence of economic poverty amid the abundance of resources found on some reservations is a long-standing paradox. This can be partly explained as a consequence of misguided policies such as allotment and bureaucratic mismanagement by the BIA. However, a complete answer is much more complex. More importantly, many tribes are actively trying to improve economic conditions in their communities in a variety of ways; some are based on conventional development strategies, others are unconventional in their approach.

Conventional Development Strategies

Since the 1950s, and even earlier in some areas, federal officials and tribal leaders adopted more or less "textbook" models for economic development. Like other rural communities, tribes have tried to attract industry by emphasizing a low-wage workforce, nonexistent taxes, or by building infrastructure such as roads or industrial parks. Unlike other rural communities, they also have tried to start up their own businesses in construction, light manufacturing, agriculture, and a hodgepodge of other activities. There also have been a variety of efforts to encourage entrepreneurship. Many of these efforts reached a peak under the Economic Development Administration (EDA) and the Small Business Administration (SBA). Federal cutbacks in the early 1980s significantly reduced these programs, although some continue to offer assistance. Currently, most conventional development strategies focus on tribal operations or individual entrepreneurs.

The activities of tribes in promoting economic development are divided between attracting industries from outside the reservation and their own business start-ups. Attracting industries owned by non-Indians is a strategy that has been a mixed success. Often the goal of attracting outside industries is job creation, making labor-intensive and often low-wage industries most appealing. Light manufacturing, such as electronics assembly plants, has been located on a number of reservations. However, this strategy is problematic for at least two reasons. One is that the jobs created by such firms are typically low-skill, low-wage jobs with few benefits. Management jobs are seldom filled by Indians. While these firms have the virtue of providing employment, they do not often yield a significantly improved standard of living. Making the welfare poor into the working poor can be considered an improvement, but it is a small one.

A second problem with such industries is that it pits reservation workers against workers in developing nations. Like other rural communities, a number of reservations have watched local industries join the exodus overseas to obtain cheap labor. However, some tribes have been able to resist this trend. According to Chief Philip Martin of the Mississippi Choctaw, his tribe has been successful with light manufacturing because they can offer superior workmanship to compensate for lower overseas labor costs.

Tribally owned businesses face other dilemmas. One crucial problem is deciding whether a tribal business will operate to maximize employment, or whether it will seek to become an efficient, highly competitive enterprise. In theory, there is no necessary conflict between these goals. But in practice, such a conflict often exists when decisions about layoffs or dismissing incompetent employees must be made.

The decision to choose between jobs or profits is often made more complicated by another problem—tribal politics. Like other communities, there are often disagreements among American Indians about the best course of action for tribal government. In connection with economic development, disputes may arise over the types of development, who is involved, and the disposition of jobs and revenues. Decisions that are politically astute may be disastrous for tribal enterprises. Some tribes have attempted to deal with this conflict by establishing business committees separate

from the tribal government. This is intended to distance business decisions from tribal politics, but too often it merely shifts political disputes from the arena of tribal government to the business committee. Cornell and Kalt (1990) argue that political development is a necessary antecedent to economic development. For tribal governments to successfully undertake complex economic development projects, they must be able to exercise a great deal of administrative expertise as well as have the political stability to carry out long-range plans. Cornell and Kalt (1990) echo others (for example, Vinje 1985) when they note that economic development projects must be consistent with tribal culture and lifestyles, and especially with the political culture of the tribe. Tribes accustomed to diffuse, highly decentralized decision-making processes will not accommodate economic development projects organized with a highly centralized management plan.

Unconventional Development Strategies
Unconventional development strategies are so named because they are development strategies based on the special legal and political status of American Indians—hence they are not options for economic development by non-Indians. This approach to economic development has become more common in the late 1970s and 1980s, possibly because there has been less federal support for conventional development projects. This approach has also been called the "legal road to economic development" (Olson 1988), and central to this strategy is the doctrine of tribal sovereignty.

Tribal sovereignty is a concept implicit in much of the preceding discussion because it is a central organizing principle in federal-Indian relations. The legal theory behind tribal sovereignty dates back to the founding of the United States and early decisions of the Supreme Court (Barsh and Henderson 1980). Briefly, tribal sovereignty means that by treaty and other agreements tribes have reserved certain legal rights of self-government. This provides tribal governments with a measure of self-rule subject to the authority of the federal government and exempt from most state and all local authority. With only a few exceptions, tribal governments have most of the same powers as state governments.

The so-called "legal road to economic development" exploits the powers of tribal sovereignty, treaty rights, and other legal agreements for the sake of developing a market niche for tribal enterprises. The ability to use tribal sovereignty for creating a market niche is crucial for having a successful enterprise. And indeed, there are a number of successful operations stemming from treaty rights, land claim settlements, and the use of tribal sovereignty to create a market niche.

Two of the best known developments stemming from treaty rights settlements are located in Maine and in the Puget Sound region of Washington State. In 1975, the Passamaquoddy and Penobscot tribes of Maine won a major court victory and a ruling that these tribes might be eligible to claim up to two-thirds of the state. After protracted negotiations, a federal task force concluded negotiations with these tribes with a settlement of $82 million. With this settlement, the tribes purchased lands, established investment portfolios, and initiated economic development projects. The Passamaquoddy invested a full third of their settlement in economic development projects such as a construction firm, cement factory, and blueberry farm. These projects were meant to produce income for tribal services and provide jobs for tribal members. Some of these projects have been more successful than others, but they have been sufficiently capitalized and well managed that they are counted as successes by the tribe (White 1990).

The state of Washington in the 1950s and 1960s was the site of protracted struggles over Indian fishing rights. These struggles culminated in the court case of *U.S. v. Washington,* also known as the Boldt Decision. In 1974, federal judge George Boldt rendered a verdict that treaties signed with the Puget Sound tribes entitled them to 50 percent of the salmon harvested in this region each year in perpetuity. This was a major victory for these tribes, who shortly afterwards initiated economic development projects based on fishing. The Lummi and the Quinault in particular have vertically integrated aquaculture programs with fish hatcheries and fish processing plants. These tribes play key roles in Puget Sound conservation efforts and have a major stake in improving fisheries production. Furthermore, these activities are also a major source of tribal employment and revenue.

Because tribal sovereignty gives tribal governments the right to legislate for themselves, another direction in the legal road to economic development has been for tribes to make available goods and services restricted by local and state laws. In the mid-1970s, retail tobacco shops with products exempt from local and state taxes began appearing on Indian land across the United States. These are typically small shops with only a few employees and are operated either by individuals or tribal governments. Little systematic data exists about these shops, but anecdotally they are usually profitable operations, although the revenue they produce is not spectacular. They are nonetheless controversial because state and local governments resent the loss of tax revenues and local merchants complain about unfair competition.

However, compared to gambling, the controversy and revenues generated by tobacco shops are negligible. In 1978, the Florida Seminole won in court the right to operate a high-stakes bingo hall on their reservation. This enterprise was enormously successful and produced revenues in the millions of dollars. The success of the Seminole was quickly noticed by other tribes, and within a few years reservations across the country were engaged in high-stakes bingo. By the mid-1980s, many tribes were testing the legal waters by offering other types of gambling explicitly outlawed outside their reservations. After a series of legal tangles and complaints by state governments and by tribal officials, Congress enacted the Indian Gaming Act of 1988.

The Indian Gaming Act set the ground rules for tribes desiring to have gambling on their reservation and created the Indian Gaming Commission to oversee reservation gambling. The law establishes different classes of gaming and permits reservation gambling if the games offered are not fundamentally different from the gambling permitted outside the reservation in activities such as state lotteries. This law represents a mixed victory for the tribes because while they do not have the unconditional right to offer gambling, it does institutionalize gambling and protects it from state and local interference.

The future of reservation gambling is unclear. It has been a huge success for some tribes, especially those close to large urban areas. On reservations in remote places, it has been less successful and has attracted mainly a reservation clientele instead of wealthier non-Indian players. Reservation gambling also has become more competitive between reservations and from outside the reservation as more states liberalize their restrictions on gambling. These developments may eventually shrink tribal revenues from gaming, but in the short run they have been an enormous cash resource for many tribes.

A handful of tribes have also passed legislation skirting state and local zoning and environmental protection laws. However, these measures have proved as controversial on the reservation as they have been outside the reservation. A proposal to place a nuclear waste facility on the Pine Ridge reservation produced a heated conflict, as did a proposal for toxic waste that was summarily rejected by the Mississippi Choctaw. The Mescalero Apache are currently considering a nuclear waste storage facility, but this is also becoming controversial on and off the reservation.

URBAN AMERICAN INDIANS

Tribal resources and tribal development efforts, despite their undeniable importance for reservations, are largely outside the interests of urban American Indians. This is because few, if any, urban Indians live on tribal lands, receive services from a tribal government, or participate in tribal politics. In 1990, about 51 percent of all American Indians were city dwellers. As a result, urban American Indians are a very important part of the American Indian population.

The Urbanization of American Indians

In small numbers, American Indians have lived among Euro-Americans in towns since the founding of colonial settlements (Szasz 1988). However, beginning in the late nineteenth century, American Indians slowly began to become more urbanized; this process gradually accelerated throughout the twentieth century. Several factors hastened their urbanization.

Intermarriage with non-Indians—historically at relatively high rates—certainly influenced their residential choices. Some of these mixed-race families stayed near tribal communities, but in other instances Indian spouses, especially wives may have followed their partners to cities. The ubiquitous racism and antimiscegenation laws in place in many areas of the country at the turn of the century probably limited such movement. However, the children of such marriages, being less identifiable as Indian, probably found it easier to "pass" into Euro-American society. By the early 1920s, there were sufficient numbers of urban Indians, including many of mixed ancestry, that pan-Indian

interest organizations began to appear; two such organizations were the Teepee Order and the Indian Association of America (Hertzberg 1971).

The federal government's actions also have hastened the urbanization of American Indians. The court decision of *Standing Bear v. Crook* in 1879 established that federal authorities did not have the absolute right to forcibly confine Indians to reservations. American Indians were thus free to leave their reservations, and reservations no longer could serve to isolate the Indian population from the American mainstream.

Efforts to force the assimilation of American Indians into Euro-American society also had a predictable impact on American Indian urbanization. The allotment acts and subsequent land losses meant that to survive some Indians had to take up wage labor. The need to find wage labor probably encouraged the drift toward cities. Moreover, the Indian boarding schools also encouraged "outings" in which Indian students were placed in middle-class Euro-American homes. This exposure also may have led to some migration toward cities.

However, a major impetus for urban migration was that of the first and second World Wars. As the United States entered World War I, American Indians became became part of the war effort, from producing food to buying war bonds. More significantly, approximately 8,000 to 10,000 American Indians served in the military (Prucha 1984, p. 771). Again, there is little documentation, but participation in the war gave these men exposure to mainstream urban America as well as the skills to cope with cultural expectations of white society—prerequisites for urban migration.

American Indians still remained concentrated in rural areas after World War I. In 1930, when over half of the United States population lived in urban locales, barely 10 percent of the Indian population lived in urban areas (Snipp 1989). However, World War II and events afterward were major forces affecting the urbanization of the American Indian population.

World War II involved an unprecedented number of American Indians in the military. Approximately 25,000 American Indians served in World War II, in combat as well as in technical support positions. For tribes with a strong warrior tradition, the rate of enlistment was high, and the volunteers enjoyed considerable status in their communities (Hagan 1979, p. 158). Nearly twice as many American Indians were involved in the war effort at home, working in defense plants and related activities (Hagan 1979, Prucha 1984). After the war, many did not return to their rural origins.

The experience of World War II exposed American Indians to urban American culture and to the industrial society outside their reservations; it provided many with new job skills and work experience, and it was an impetus for many to leave their communities while they fought or worked in wartime industries (Prucha 1984). Equally important, the GI Bill provided an unprecedented number of American Indians with the opportunity to attend college. Out of necessity, many of these graduates settled in cities to find employment. The GI Bill also trained a generation of Indian leaders, many of whom returned to their reservations or became active in urban Indian social issues (cf. Ambler 1990; Snipp 1989; Weibel-Orlando 1991).

Postwar federal policy also played a role in moving American Indians to cities. As part of its effort to abolish the reservation system, the federal government's relocation programs resettled thousands of American Indians in cities. In doing so, it established a vital link for patterns of chain migration between cities such as Los Angeles and western reservations. An entire generation of urban Indian migrants to Los Angeles can be directly or indirectly linked to the use of this city as a relocation center (Price 1968; Weibel-Orlando 1991).

Considerable disagreement exists about the costs and benefits of urbanization for American Indians. When it was first proposed, one of the principle justifications for urban relocation was that economic opportunities would be greater in urban areas (Fixico 1986). However, the economic benefits of urban relocation appear to be questionable. Some evidence suggests that urban relocation improved the economic circumstances of participants (Clinton et al. 1975, Sorkin 1978) while other studies are less sanguine (Gundlach and Roberts 1978; O'Brien 1990; Snipp and Sandefur 1988).

Coping with Urban Life

The large influx of American Indians to urban areas prompted numerous studies in the 1960s and early 1970s (Thornton et al. 1982) of how American Indians coped with the alien culture and lifestyle they found in cities. Cultural assimilation is a central theme in this literature; the stress of urban adaptation is another.

The experience of urban American Indians contradicted the assimilationist expectations. Unlike other urban immigrants, American Indians did not readily adopt Euro-American culture, rather tribal culture and ethnic identity persisted. One possible reason is that racial discrimination posed barriers that denied entry into the dominant culture (Ablon 1964, 1965, 1971; Chadwick and Strauss 1975; Chadwick and White 1973; Guillemin 1975; Roy 1962; Strauss and Chadwick 1979). American Indian resistance to assimilating Euro-American ways has caused social scientists to rethink their expectations of the anticipated dissolution of Indian culture toward the apparent persistence and vitality of cultural traditions in urban environments (Vogt 1957). One explanation for this persistence of tribal culture in cities is that they are able to find in ordinary urban landscapes the opportunity for cultural expression (Guillemin 1975). For example, the danger and physical demands of high steel construction work provide Mohawk men with opportunities to exhibit the bravery and risk-taking traditionally expected of them (Blumenfeld 1965).

In cities, social interaction and cultural expression take place in bars, pow-wows, Indian Centers, and churches (Weibel-Orlando 1991). Powwows are tribal events transported directly from reservation traditions. On reservations, powwows are held in ceremonial locations, while in cities they are most often sponsored by informal groups or pan-Indian organizations and held in gyms or public auditoriums. Similarly, urban Indian churches resemble reservation missions (Weibel-Orlando 1991), and bars and Indian Centers provide urban analogs to the tribal headquarters and nearby bars of reservation life (Weibel-Orlando 1991).

Also important in the persistence of Indian ethnicity in cities has been the emergence of pan-Indianism—a supratribal ideology that unites the interests of American Indians by virtue of their common heritage, independent of the varying social and political agendas of particular tribes such as the Sioux or the Navajo (Thomas 1965). In cities, pan-Indianism is particularly important as a unifying force because urban Indian populations come from a multitude of tribes. Since 1950, the spread of pan-Indianism has been extremely important as an organizational basis for urban Indian social life (Cornell 1988). With a few exceptions, community events and social gatherings for urban Indians are typically pan-Indian affairs—all tribes are welcome. Furthermore, the ideology of pan-Indianism itself has been an important resource for mobilizing political action locally (Nagel 1986; Weibel-Orlando 1991) as well as for building support for Indian issues across the nation (Cornell 1988). Pan-Indianism, therefore, has been a very positive result of urbanization.

However, a very negative result is that the transition to urban life may be partly responsible for problem drinking among urban Indians. While alcohol abuse and related health problems are a leading killer of American Indians on reservations and cities alike (Snipp 1989), the move to urban areas is for many American Indians an intensely alienating and anomic experience (Graves 1971). It removes them from the tight bonds of reservation life—traditions, family, friends—and places them in alien, disorienting city environments.

This difficult transition promotes heavy drinking and related problems such as incidents with police (Ablon 1965; Dozier 1966; Ferguson 1968; Graves 1971). Drinking among urban Indians may also differ from that of reservation Indians because urban Indian bars are an important venue for affirming ethnic identity within the community (Ablon 1965; Weibel-Orlando 1991). Furthermore, in cities where substantial status differences exist within the Indian community, shared drinking in a recognized Indian bar may serve as a leveling mechanism for building ethnic solidarity. In fact, shared drinking experiences among urban Indians may be "a way for one successful in the larger society to demonstrate to fellow Indians that he is still 'Indian' "(Thornton et al. 1982, p. 43). Local Indian leaders report that drinking in the local Indian bar is important for staying in touch with their constituents (Weibel-Orlando 1991). Of course, excessive alcohol consumption leads to encounters with police and to arrest rates that are considerably higher than for Blacks or Whites. American Indians are also disproportionately represented in prison populations; American Indians receive harsher treatment in the judicial system and do not effectively utilize resources such as legal assistance (Hagan 1976).

To many American Indians, many elements of city life fundamentally contradict the ethics of tribal culture and lifestyles. Many, if not most, are able to reconcile these conflicts. But there are many American Indians who struggle unsuccessfully with these dilemmas; they extract a toll manifest in substance abuse, mental disorder, family conflict, and involvement with the criminal justice system—personal "costs" of urban life.

CONCLUSION

Though small in number, American Indians have an enduring place in American society. Growing numbers of American Indians occupy reservation and other trust lands, and equally important has been the revitalization of tribal governments. Tribal governments now have a larger role in reservation affairs than ever in the past. Another significant development has been the urbanization of American Indians. Since 1950, the proportion of American Indians in cities has grown rapidly. These American Indians have in common with reservation Indians many of the same problems and disadvantages, but they also face other challenges unique to city life.

The challenges facing tribal governments are daunting. American Indians are among the poorest groups in the nation. Reservation Indians have substantial needs for improved housing, adequate health care, educational opportunities, and employment, as well as developing and maintaining reservation infrastructure. In the face of declining federal assistance, tribal governments are assuming an ever-larger burden. On a handful of reservations, tribal governments have assumed completely the tasks once performed by the BIA.

As tribes have taken greater responsibility for their communities, they also have struggled with the problems of raising revenues and providing economic opportunities for their people. Reservation land bases provide many reservations with resources for development. However, these resources are not always abundant, much less unlimited, and they have not always been well managed. It will be yet another challenge for tribes to explore ways of efficiently managing their existing resources. Legal challenges also face tribes seeking to exploit unconventional resources such as gambling revenues. Their success depends on many complicated legal and political contingencies.

Urban American Indians have few of the resources found on reservations, and they face other difficult problems. Preserving their culture and identity is an especially pressing concern. However, urban Indians have successfully adapted to city environments in ways that preserve valued customs and activities—powwows, for example, are an important event in all cities where there is a large Indian community. In addition, pan-Indianism has helped urban Indians set aside tribal differences and forge alliances for the betterment of urban Indian communities.

These alliances are essential, because unlike reservation Indians, urban American Indians do not have their own form of self-government. Tribal governments do not have jurisdiction over urban Indians. For this reason, urban Indians must depend on other strategies for ensuring that the needs of their community are met, especially for those new to city life. Coping with the transition to urban life poses a multitude of difficult challenges for many American Indians. Some succumb to these problems, especially the hardships of unemployment, economic deprivation, and related maladies such as substance abuse, crime, and violence. But most successfully overcome these difficulties, often with help from other members of the urban Indian community.

Perhaps the greatest strength of American Indians has been their ability to find creative ways for dealing with adversity, whether in cities or on reservations. In the past, this quality enabled them to survive centuries of oppression and persecution. Today this is reflected in the practice of cultural traditions that Indian people are proud to embrace. The resilience of American Indians is an abiding quality that will no doubt ensure that they will remain part of the ethnic mosaic of American society throughout the twenty-first century and beyond.

S I X

Inbetween Peoples
Race, Nationality, and the "New Immigrant" Working Class

James R. Barrett
David Roediger

By the Eastern European immigration the labor force has been cleft hori-
zontally into two great divisions. The upper stratum includes what is
known in mill parlance as the 'English-speaking' men; the lower contains
the 'Hunkies' or 'Ginnies.' Or, if you prefer, the former are the 'white men,'
the latter the 'foreigners.'

John Fitch, *The Steel Workers*

In 1980, Joseph Loguidice, an elderly Italian American from Chicago, sat down to give his life story to an interviewer. His first and most vivid childhood recollection was of a race riot that had occurred on the city's near north side. Wagons full of policemen with "peculiar hats" streamed into his neighborhood. But the "one thing that stood out in my mind," Loguidice remembered after six decades, was "a man running down the middle of the street hollering . . . 'I'm White, I'm White!'" After first taking him for an African American, Loguidice soon realized that the man was a white coal handler covered in dust. He was screaming for his life, fearing that "people would shoot him down." He had, Loguidice concluded, "got caught up in . . . this racial thing."

Joseph Loguidice's tale might be taken as a metaphor for the situation of millions of Eastern and Southern European immigrants who arrived in the United States between the end of the nineteenth century and the early 1920s. The fact that this episode made such a profound impression is in itself significant, suggesting both that this was a strange, new situation and that thinking about race became an important part of the consciousness of immigrants like Loguidice. We are concerned here in part with the development of racial awareness and attitudes, and an increasingly racialized worldview among new immigrant workers themselves. Most did not arrive with conventional United States attitudes regarding "racial" difference, let alone its significance and implications in the context of industrial America. Yet most, it seems, "got caught up in . . . this racial thing." How did this happen? If race was indeed socially constructed, then what was the raw material that went into the process?

We are also concerned with how these immigrant workers were viewed in racial terms by others—employers, the state, reformers, and other workers. Like the coal handler in Loguidice's story, their own ascribed racial identity was not always clear. A whole range of evidence—laws; court cases; formal racial ideology; social conventions; popular culture in the form of slang, songs, films, cartoons, ethnic jokes, and popular theater—suggests that the native born and older immigrants often placed these newer immigrants not only *above* African and Asian Americans, for example, but also *below* "white" people. Indeed, many of the older immigrants and particularly the Irish had themselves been perceived as "non-white" just a generation earlier. As labor historians, we are interested in the ways in which Polish, Italian, and other European artisans and peasants became American workers, but we are equally concerned with the process by which they became "white." Indeed, in the United States the two identities intertwined and this explains a great deal of the persistent divisions within the working-class population. How did immigrant workers wind up "inbetween"? . . .

We sometimes assume that such immigrants really were "white," in a way that they were not initially American. And, being white, largely poor, and self-consciously part of imagined communities with roots in Europe, they were therefore "ethnic." If social scientists referred to "national" groups as races (the "Italian race") and to Southern and East European pan-nationalities as races (Slavonic and Mediterranean "races"), they did so because they used race promiscuously to mean other things. If the classic work on American exceptionalism, Werner Sombart's 1906 *Why Is There No Socialism in The United States?* has a whole section on "racial" division with scarcely a mention of any group modern Americans would recognize as a racial minority, this is a matter of semantic confusion. If Robert Park centered his pioneering early twentieth-century sociological theory of assimilation on the "race relations cycle," with the initial expectation that it would apply to African Americans as well as European immigrants, he must not have sorted out the difference between race and ethnicity yet. Indeed, so certain are some modern scholars of the ability of "ethnicity" to explain immigrant experiences which contemporaries described largely in terms of race and nationality that a substantial literature seeks to describe even the African-American and native American experiences as "ethnic."

Racial identity was also clearly gendered in important ways, and historians are just beginning to understand this gendered quality of racial language, conventions, and identity. It is apparent even in the sorts of public spheres privileged here—citizenship, the state, the union, the workplace. But we are *most* apt to find the conjunctions between gender and race in places that are not probed here—at those points where more intimate relations intersected with the rule of law.

The taboo against interracial sex and marriage was one obvious boundary between low-status immigrant workers and people of color with whom they often came in contact. As Peggy Pascoe has noted, "although such marriages were infrequent throughout most of U.S. history, an enormous amount of time and energy was spent in trying to prevent them from taking place . . . the history of interracial marriage provides rich evidence of the formulation of race and gender and of the connections between the two." Yet we have little understanding of how this taboo was viewed by immigrant and African- or Asian-American workers. One obvious place to look is at laws governing interracial marriage and court cases aimed at enforcing such laws. Native-born women who became involved with immigrant men could lose their citizenship and, if the immigrant were categorized as non-white, they could be prosecuted for "race-mixup." "Race mixing" occurred in spite of all this, of course. Chinese men who lived under particularly oppressive conditions because of restrictions on the immigration of Chinese women, tended to develop relationships with either African Americans or Poles and other "new immigrant" women. We have not attempted to unravel this fascinating and complex problem or the racial identity of immigrant women here. Except where clearly indicated, we are describing situations where racial identity was informed and shaped by, often even conflated with, notions of manhood.

Thus, we make no brief for the consistency with which "race" was used, by experts or popularly, to describe the "new immigrant" Southern and East Europeans who dominated the ranks of those coming to the United States between 1895 and 1924 and who "remade" the American working class in that period. We regard such inconsistency as important evidence of the "inbetween" racial status of such immigrants. The story of Americanization is vital and compelling, but it took place in a nation also obsessed by race. For immigrant workers, the processes of "becoming white" and "becoming American" were intertwined at every turn. The "American standard of living," which labor organizers alternately and simultaneously accused new immigrants of undermining and encouraged them to defend via class organization, rested on "white men's wages."

Political debate turned on whether new immigrants were fit to join the American nation and on whether they were fit to join the "American race." Nor do we argue that Eastern and Southern European immigrants were in the same situation as non-whites. Stark differences between the racialized status of African Americans and the racial inbetween-ness of these immigrants meant that the latter *eventually* "became ethnic" and that their trajectory was predictable. But their history was sloppier than their trajectory. From day to day they were, to borrow from E. P. Thompson, "protonothing," reacting and acting in a highly racialized nation. . . .

INBETWEEN IN THE POPULAR MIND

America's racial vocabulary had no agency of its own, but rather reflected material conditions and power relations—the situations that workers faced on a daily basis in their workplaces and communities. Yet the words themselves were important. They were not only the means by which native born and elite people marked new immigrants as inferiors, but also the means by which immigrant workers came to locate themselves and those about them in the nation's racial hierarchy. In beginning to analyze the vocabulary of race, it makes little sense for historians to invest the words themselves with an agency that could be exercised only by real historical actors, or meanings that derived only from the particular historical contexts in which the language was developed and employed.

The word *guinea,* for example, had long referred to African slaves, particularly those from the continent's northwest coast, and to their descendants. But from the late 1890s, the term was increasingly applied to southern European migrants, first and especially to Sicilians and southern Italians who often came as contract laborers. At various times and places in the United States, guinea has been applied to mark Greeks, Jews, Portuguese, Puerto Ricans and perhaps any new immigrant.

Likewise, *hunky,* which began life, probably in the early twentieth century, as a corruption of "Hungarian," eventually became a pan-Slavic slur connected with perceived immigrant racial characteristics. By World War One the term was frequently used to describe any immigrant steel-worker, as in *mill hunky.* Opponents of the Great 1919 Steel Strike, including some native-born skilled workers, derided the struggle as a "hunky strike." Yet Josef Barton's work suggests that for Poles, Croats, Slovenians, and other immigrants who often worked together in difficult, dangerous situations, the term embraced a remarkable, if fragile, sense of prideful identity across ethnic lines. In *Out of this Furnace,* Thomas Bell's 1941 epic novel based on the lives of Slavic steelworkers, he observed that the word hunky bespoke "unconcealed racial prejudice" and a "denial of social and racial equality." Yet as these workers built the industrial unions of the late 1930s and took greater control over their own lives, the meaning of the term began to change. The pride with which second- and third-generation Slavic-American steelworkers, now women as well as men, wore the label in the early 1970s seemed to have far more to do with class than with ethnic identity. At about the same time the word *honky,* possibly a corruption of hunky, came into common use as Black nationalism reemerged as a major ideological force in the African-American community.

Words and phrases employed by social scientists to capture the inbetween identity of the new immigrants are a bit more descriptive, if a bit more cumbersome. As late as 1937, John Dollard wrote repeatedly of the immigrant working class as "our temporary Negroes." More precise, if less dramatic, is the designation "not-yet-white ethnics" offered by Barry Goldberg. The term not only reflects the popular perceptions and everyday experiences of such workers, but also conveys the dynamic quality of the process of racial formation.

The examples of Greeks and Italians particularly underscore the new "immigrants" ambiguous positions with regard to popular perceptions of race. When Greeks suffered as victims of an Omaha "race" riot in 1909 and when eleven Italians died at the hands of lynchers in Louisiana in 1891, their less-than-white racial status mattered alongside their nationalities. Indeed, as in the case of Loguidice's coal handler, their ambivalent racial status put their lives in jeopardy. As Gunther Peck shows in his fine study of copper miners in Bingham, Utah, the Greek and Italian immigrants were "nonwhite" before their tension-fraught cooperation with the Western Federation of Miners during a 1912 strike ensured that "the category of Caucasian worker changed and expanded." Indeed, the work of Dan Georgakas and Yvette Huginnie shows that Greeks and other Southern Europeans often "bivouacked" with other "nonwhite" workers in Western mining towns. Pocatello, Idaho, Jim-Crowed Greeks in the early twentieth century and in Arizona they were not welcomed by white workers in "white men's towns" or "white men's jobs." In Chicago during the Great Depression, a German-American wife expressed regret over marrying her "half-nigger," Greek-American husband. African-American slang in the 1920s in South Carolina counted those of mixed American Indian, African American and white heritage as *Greeks.* Greek Americans in the Midwest showed great anxieties about race, and were perceived not only as Puerto Rican, mulatto, Mexican or Arab, but also as non-white *because of* being Greek.

Italians, involved in a spectacular international diaspora in the early twentieth century, were racialized as the "Chinese of Europe" in many lands. But in the United States their racialization was pronounced and, as *guinea's* evolution suggests, more likely to connect Italians with Africans. During the debate at the Louisiana state constitutional convention of 1898, over how to disfranchise blacks, and over which whites might lose the vote, some acknowledged that the Italian's skin "happens to be white" even as they argued for his disfranchisement. But others held that "according to the spirit of our meaning when we speak of 'white man's government,' [the Italians] are as black as the blackest negro in existence." More than metaphor intruded on this judgment. At the turn of the century, a West Coast construction boss was asked, "You don't call the Italian a white man?" The negative reply assured the questioner that the Italian was "a dago." Recent studies of Italian and Greek Americans make a strong case that racial, not just ethnic, oppression long plagued "nonwhite" immigrants from Southern Europe.

The racialization of East Europeans was likewise striking. While racist jokes mocked the black servant who thought her child, fathered by a Chinese man, would be a Jew, racist folklore held that Jews, inside-out, were "niggers." In 1926 Serbo-Croatians ranked near the bottom of a list of forty "ethnic" groups whom "white American" respondents were asked to order according to the respondents' willingness to associate with members of each group. They placed just above Negroes, Filipinos, and Japanese. Just above them were Poles, who were near the middle of the list. One sociologist has recently written that "a good many groups on this color continuum [were] not considered white by a large number of Americans." The literal inbetween-ness of new immigrants on such a list suggests what popular speech affirms: The state of whiteness was approached gradually and controversially. The authority of the state itself both smoothed and complicated that approach.

WHITE CITIZENSHIP AND INBETWEEN AMERICANS: THE STATE OF RACE

The power of the national state gave recent immigrants both their firmest claims to whiteness and their strongest leverage for enforcing those claims. The courts consistently allowed "new immigrants," whose racial status was ambiguous in the larger culture, to be naturalized as "white" citizens and almost as consistently turned down non-European applicants as "nonwhite." Political reformers therefore discussed the fitness for citizenship of recent European immigrants from two distinct angles. They produced, through the beginning of World War One, a largely benign and hopeful discourse on how to Americanize (and win the votes of) those already here. But this period also saw a debate on fertility rates and immigration restriction which conjured up threats of "race suicide" if this flow of migrants were not checked and the fertility of the native-born increased. A figure like Theodore Roosevelt could stand as both the Horatio warning of the imminent swamping of the "old stock" racial elements in the United States and as the optimistic Americanizer to whom the play which originated the assimilationist image of the "melting pot" was dedicated.

Such anomalies rested not only on a political economy, which at times needed and at times shunned immigrant labor, but also on peculiarities of United States naturalization law. If the "state apparatus" both told new immigrants that they were and were not white, it was clearly the judiciary which produced the most affirmative responses. Thus United States law made citizenship racial as well as civil. Even when much of the citizenry doubted the racial status of European migrants, the courts almost always granted their whiteness in naturalization cases. Thus, the often racially based campaigns against Irish naturalization in the 1840s and 1850s and against Italian naturalization in the early twentieth century aimed to delay, not deny, citizenship. The lone case which appears exceptional in this regard is one in which United States naturalization attorneys in Minnesota attempted unsuccessfully to bar radical Finns from naturalization on the ethnological grounds that they were not "caucasian" and therefore not whites.

The legal equation of whiteness with fitness for citizenship significantly shaped the process by which race was made in the United States. If Southern and Eastern European immigrants remained "inbetween people" because of broad cultural perceptions, Asians were in case after case declared unambiguously non-white and therefore unfit for citizenship. This sustained pattern of denial of citizenship provides, as the sociologist Richard Williams argues, the best guide to who would be racialized in an ongoing way in the twentieth-century United States. It applies, of course, in the case of Native Americans. Migrants from Africa, though nominally an exception in that Congress in 1870 allowed their naturalization (with the full expectation that they would not be coming), of course experienced sweeping denials of civil status both in slavery and in Jim Crow. Nor were migrants from Mexico truly exceptional. Despite the naturalizability of such migrants by treaty and later court decisions, widespread denials of citizenship rights took place almost immediately—in one 1855 instance in California as a result of the "Greaser Bill"—as the Vagrancy Act was termed.

Likewise, the equation between legal whiteness and fitness for naturalizable citizenship helps to predict which groups would *not* be made nonwhite in an ongoing way. Not only did the Irish, whose whiteness was under sharp question in the 1840s and 1850s, and later the "new immigrants" gain the powerful symbolic argument that the law declared them white and fit, but they also had the power of significant numbers of votes, although naturalization rates for new immigrants were not always high. During Louisiana's disfranchising constitutional convention of 1898, for example, the bitter debate over Italian whiteness ended with a provision passed extending to new immigrants protections comparable, even superior, to those which the "grandfather clause" gave to native white voters. New Orleans' powerful Choctaw Club machine, already the beneficiary of

Italian votes, led the campaign for the plank When Thomas Hart Benton and Stephen Douglas argued against Anglo-Saxon superiority and for a pan-white "American race" in the 1850s, they did so before huge blocs of Irish voters. When Theodore Roosevelt extolled the "mixture of blood" making the American race, a "new ethnic type in this melting pot of the nations," he emphasized to new immigrant *voters* his conviction that each of their nationalities would enrich America by adding "its blood to the life of the nation." When Woodrow Wilson also tailored his thinking about racial desirability of the new European immigrants, he did so in the context of an electoral campaign in which the "foreign" vote counted heavily. In such a situation, Roosevelt's almost laughable proliferation of uses of the word *race* served him well, according to his various needs as reformer, imperialist, debunker and romanticizer of the history of the West, and political candidate. He sincerely undertook seemingly contradictory embraces of Darwin and of Lamarck's insistence on the hereditability of acquired characteristics, of melting pots and of race suicide, of an adoring belief in Anglo-Saxon and Teutonic superiority and in the grandeur of a "mixed" American race. Roosevelt, like the census bureau, thought in terms of the nation's biological "stock"—the term by now called forth images of Wall Street as well as the farm. That stock was directly threatened by low birth rates among the nation's "English-speaking race." But races could also progress over time and the very experience of mixing and of clashing with other races would bring out, and improve, the best of the "racestock." The "American race" could absorb and permanently improve the less desirable stock of "*all* white immigrants," perhaps in two generations, but only if its most desirable "English-speaking" racial elements were not swamped in an un-Americanized Slavic and Southern European culture and biology.

The neo-Lamarckianism which allowed Roosevelt to use such terms as "English-speaking race" ran through much of Progressive racial thinking, though it was sometimes underpinned by appeals to other authorities. We likely regard choosing between eating pasta or meat, between speaking English or Italian, between living in ill-ventilated or healthy housing, between taking off religious holidays or coming to work, between voting Republican or Socialist as decisions based on environment, opportunity and choice. But language loyalty, incidence of dying in epidemics, and radicalism often defined *race* for late nineteenth- and early twentieth-century thinkers, making distinctions between racial, religious and anti-radical varieties of nativism messy. For many, Americanization was not simply a cultural process but an index of racial change which could fail if the concentration of "lower" races kept the "alchemy" of racial transformation from occurring. From its very start, the campaign for immigration restriction directed against "new" Europeans carried a strong implication that even something as ineluctable as "moral tone" could be inherited. In deriding "ignorant, brutal Italians and Hungarian laborers" during the 1885 debate over the Contract Labor Law, its sponsor framed his environmentalist arguments in terms of color, holding that "the introduction into a community of any considerable number of persons of a lower moral tone will cause general moral deterioration as sure as night follows day." He added, "The intermarriage of a lower with a higher type certainly does not improve the latter any more than does the breeding of cattle by blooded and common stock improve the blooded stock generally." The restrictionist cause came to feature writings that saw mixing as always and everywhere disastrous. Madison Grant's *The Passing of the Great Race* (1916), a racist attack on recent immigrants which defended the purity of "Nordic" stock, the race of the "white man par excellence," against "Alpine," "Mediterranean" and Semitic invaders, is a classic example.

Professional Americanizers and national politicians appealing to immigrant constituencies for a time seemed able to marginalize those who racialized new immigrants. Corporate America generally gave firm support to relatively open immigration. Settlement house reformers and others taught and witnessed Americanization. The best of them, Jane Addams, for example, learned from immigrants as well and extolled not only assimilation but the virtues of ongoing cultural differences among immigrant groups. Even progressive politicians showed potential to rein in their own most racially charged tendencies. As a Southern academic, Woodrow Wilson wrote of the dire threat to "our Saxon habits of government" by "corruption of foreign blood" and characterized Italian and Polish immigrants as "sordid and hapless." But as a presidential candidate in 1912, he reassured immigrant leaders that "We are all Americans," of-

fered to rewrite sections on Polish Americans in his *History of the American People* and found Italian Americans "one of the most interesting and admirable elements in our American life."

Yet Progressive Era assimilationism, and even its flirtations with cultural pluralism, could not save new immigrants from racial attacks. If racial prejudice against new immigrants was far more provisional and nuanced than anti-Irish bias in the antebellum period, political leaders also defended *hunkies* and *guineas* far more provisionally. Meanwhile the Progressive project of imperialism and the Progressive non-project of capitulation to Jim Crow ensured that race thinking would retain and increase its potency. If corporate leaders backed immigration and funded Americanization projects, the corporate model emphasized standardization, efficiency and immediate results. This led many Progressives to support reforms that called immigrant political power and voting rights into question, at least in the short run. In the longer term, big business proved by the early 1920s an unreliable supporter of the melting pot. Worried about unemployment and about the possibility that new immigrants were proving "revolutionary and communistic races," they equivocated on the openness of immigration, turned Americanizing agencies into labor spy networks, and stopped funding for the corporate-sponsored umbrella group of professional Americanizers and conservative new immigrant leaders, the *Inter-Racial Council.*

Reformers, too, lost heart. Since mixing was never regarded as an unmitigated good but as a matter of proportion with a number of possible outcomes, the new immigrants' record was constantly under scrutiny. The failure of Americanization to deliver total loyalty during World War One and during the postwar "immigrant rebellion" within United States labor made that record one of failure. The "virility," "manhood" and "vigor" that reformers predicted race mixture would inject into the American stock had long coexisted with the emphasis on obedience and docility in Americanization curricula. At their most vigorous, in the 1919–1920 strike wave, new immigrants were most suspect. Nationalists, and many Progressive reformers among them, were, according to John Higham, sure that they had done "their best to bring the great mass of newcomers into the fold." The failure was not theirs, but a reflection of the "incorrigibly unassimilable nature of the material on which they had worked."

The triumph of immigration restriction in the 1920s was in large measure a triumph of *racism* against new immigrants. Congress and the Ku Klux Klan, the media and popular opinion all reinforced the inbetween, and even non-white, racial status of Eastern and Southern Europeans. Grant's *Passing of the Great Race* suddenly enjoyed a vogue which had eluded it in 1916. The best-selling United States magazine, *Saturday Evening Post,* praised Grant and sponsored Kenneth Roberts's massively mounted fears that continued immigration would produce "a hybrid race of people as worthless and futile as the good-for-nothing mongrels of Central America and Southeastern Europe." When the National Industrial Conference Board met in 1923, its director allowed that restriction was "essentially a race question." Congress was deluged with letters of concern for preservation of a "distinct American type" and of support for stopping the "swamping" of the Nordic race. In basing itself on the first fear and setting quotas pegged squarely on the (alleged) origins of the current population, the 1924 restriction act also addressed the second fear, since the United States population as a whole came from the northern and western parts of Europe to a vastly greater extent than had the immigrant population for the last three decades. At virtually the same time that the courts carefully drew a color line between European new immigrants and non-white others, the Congress and reformers reaffirmed the racial inbetween-ness of Southern and Eastern Europeans. . . .

"INBETWEEN" JOBS: CAPITAL, CLASS AND THE NEW IMMIGRANT

Joseph Loguidice's reminiscence of the temporarily "colored" coal hauler compresses and dramatizes a process that went on in far more workaday settings as well. Often while themselves begrimed by the nation's dirtiest jobs, new immigrants and their children quickly learned that "the worst thing one could be in this Promised Land was 'colored.'" But if the world of work taught the importance of being "not black," it also exposed new immigrants to frequent comparisons and close competition with African Americans. The results of such clashes in the labor market

did not instantly propel new immigrants into either the category or the consciousness of whiteness. Instead management created an economics of racial inbetween-ness which taught new immigrants the importance of racial hierarchy while leaving open their place in that hierarchy. At the same time the struggle for "inbetween jobs" further emphasized the importance of national and religious ties among immigrants by giving those ties an important economic dimension.

The bitterness of job competition between new immigrants and African Americans has rightly received emphasis in accounting for racial hostility, but that bitterness must be *historically* investigated. Before 1915, new immigrants competed with relatively small numbers of African Americans for northern urban jobs. The new immigrants tended to be more recent arrivals than the black workers, and they came in such great numbers that, demographically speaking, they competed far more often with each other than with African Americans. Moreover, given the much greater "human capital" of black workers in terms of literacy, education and English language skills, immigrants fared well in this competition. After 1915, the decline of immigration resulting from World War One and restrictive legislation in the 1920s combined with the Great Migration of Afro-Southerners to northern cities to create a situation in which a growing and newly arrived black working-class provided massive competition for a more settled but struggling immigrant population. Again, the results were not of a sort that would necessarily have brought bitter disappointment to those whom the economic historians term SCEs (Southern and Central Europeans). The Sicilian immigrant, for example, certainly was at times locked in competition with African Americans. But was that competition more bitter and meaningful than competition with, for example, northern Italian immigrants, "hunkies," or white native-born workers, all of whom were at times said to be *racially* different from Sicilians?

The ways in which capital structured workplaces and labor markets contributed to the idea that competition should be both cutthroat and racialized. New immigrants suffered wage discrimination when compared to the white native born. African Americans were paid less for the same jobs than the immigrants. In the early twentieth century, employers preferred a labor force divided by race and national origins. As the radical cartoonist Ernest Riebe understood at the time, and as the labor economists Richard Edwards, Michael Reich and David Gordon have recently reaffirmed, work gangs segregated by nationality as well as by race could be and were made to compete against each other in a strategy designed not only to undermine labor unity and depress wages in the long run but to spur competition and productivity every day.

On the other hand, management made broader hiring and promotion distinctions which brought pan-national and sometimes racial categories into play. In some workplaces and areas, the blast furnace was a "Mexican job"; in others, it was a pan-Slavic "hunky" job. "Only hunkies," a steel industry investigator was told, worked blast furnace jobs which were "too damn dirty and too damn hot for a white man." Management at the nation's best-studied early twentieth-century factory divided the employees into "white men" and "kikes." Such bizarre notions about the genetic *"fit"* between immigrants and certain types of work were buttressed by the "scientific" judgments of scholars like the sociologist E. A. Ross, who observed that Slavs were "immune to certain kinds of dirt . . . that would kill a white man." "Scientific" managers in steel and in other industries designed elaborate ethnic classification systems to guide their hiring. In 1915 the personnel manager at one Pittsburgh plant analyzed what he called the "racial adaptability" of thirty-six different ethnic groups to twenty-four different kinds of work and twelve sets of conditions and plotted them all on a chart. Lumber companies in Louisiana built what they called "the Quarters" for black workers and (separately) for Italians, using language very recently associated with African-American slavery. For white workers they built company housing and towns. The distinction between "white" native-born workers and "non-white" new immigrants, Mexicans and African Americans in parts of the West rested in large part on the presence of "white man's camps" or "white man's towns" in company housing in lumbering and mining. Native-born residents interviewed in the wake of a bitter 1915 strike by Polish oil refinery workers recognized only two classes of people in Bayonne, New Jersey: "foreigners" and "white men." In generalizing about early twentieth-century nativism, John Higham concludes: "In all sections native-born

and Northern European laborers called themselves 'white men' to distinguish themselves from Southern Europeans whom they worked beside." As late as World War Two, new immigrants and their children, lumped together as "racials," suffered employment discrimination in the defense industry.

There was also substantial management interest in the specific comparison of new immigrants with African Americans as workers. More concrete in the North and abstract in the South, these complex comparisons generally, but not always, favored the former group. African-Americans' supposed undependability "especially on Mondays," intolerance for cold, and incapacity of fast-paced work were all noted. But the comparisons were often nuanced. New immigrants, as Herbert Gutman long ago showed, were themselves counted as unreliable, "especially on Mondays." Some employers counted black workers as more apt and skillful "in certain occupations" and cleaner and happier than "the alien white races." An occasional blanket preference for African Americans over immigrants surfaced, as at Packard in Detroit in 1922. Moreover, comparisons carried a provisional quality, since ongoing competition was often desired. In 1905 the superintendent of Illinois Steel, threatening to fire all Slavic workers, reassured the immigrants that no "race hatred" [against Slavs!] motivated the proposed decision, which was instead driven by a factor that the workers could change: their tardiness in adopting the English language.

The fact that recent immigrants were relatively inexperienced *vis-à-vis* African-American workers in the North in 1900 and relatively experienced by 1930 makes it difficult for economic historians to measure the extent to which immigrant economic mobility in this period derived from employer discrimination. Clearly, timing and demographic change mattered alongside racism in a situation in which the immigrant SCEs came to occupy spaces on the job ladder between African Americans below and those who were fed into the economic historians' computers as NWNPs (native-born whites with native-born parents). Stanley Lieberson uses the image of a "queue" to help explain the role of discrimination against African Americans in leading to such results. In the line-up of workers ordered by employer preference, as in so much else, new immigrants were inbetween.

In a society in which workers did in fact show up in lines to seek jobs, the image of a queue is wonderfully apt. However, the Polish worker next to an African American on one side and an Italian American on the other as an NWNP manager hired unskilled labor did not know the statistics of current job competition, let alone what the results would be by the time of the 1930 census. Even if the Polish worker had known them, the patterns of mobility for his group would likely have differed as much from those of the Italian Americans as from those of the African Americans (who in some cities actually out-distanced Polish immigrants in intra-working-class mobility to better jobs from 1900 to 1930). Racialized struggles over jobs were fed by the general experience of brutal, group-based competition, and by the knowledge that black workers were especially vulnerable competitors who fared far less well in the labor market than any other native-born American group. The young Croatian immigrant Stephan Mesaros was so struck by the abuse of a black coworker that he asked a Serbian laborer for an explanation. "You'll soon learn something about this country," came the reply, "Negroes never get a fair chance." The exchange initiated a series of conversations which contributed to Mesaros becoming Steve Nelson, an influential radical organizer and an anti-racist. But for most immigrants, caught in a world of dog-eat-dog competition, the lesson would likely have been that African Americans were among the eaten.

If immigrants did not know the precise contours of the job queue, nor their prospects in it, they did have their own ideas about how to get on line, their own strategies about how to get ahead in it, and their own dreams for getting out of it. These tended to reinforce a sense of the advantage of being "not nonwhite" but to also emphasize specific national and religious identifications rather than generalized white identity. Because of the presence of a small employing (or subcontracting) class in their communities, new immigrants were far more likely than African Americans to work for one of "their own" as an immediate boss. In New York City, in 1910, for example, almost half of the sample of Jewish workers studied by Suzanne Model had Jewish supervisors, as did about one Italian immigrant in seven. Meanwhile, "the study sample unearthed only one industrial match between laborers and supervisors among Blacks."

In shrugging at being called *hunky,* Thomas Bell writes, Slovak immigrants took solace that they "had come to America to find work and save money, not to make friends with the Irish." But getting work and "making friends with" Irish-American foremen, skilled workers, union leaders and politicians were often very much connected, and the relationships were hardly smooth. Petty bosses could always rearrange the queue. But over the long run, a common Catholicism (and sometimes common political machine affiliations) gave new immigrant groups access to the fragile favor of Irish Americans in positions to influence hiring which African Americans could not achieve. Sometimes such favor was organized, as through the Knights of Columbus in Kansas City packing-houses. Over time, as second-generation marriages across national lines but within the Catholic religion became a pattern, kin joined religion in shaping hiring in ways largely excluding African Americans. . . .

Similarly, those many new immigrants (especially among the Greeks, Italians and Jews) who hoped to (and did) leave the working class by opening small businesses, set great store in saving, and often catered to a clientele composed mainly of their own group.

But immigrant saving itself proved highly racialized, as did immigrant small business in many instances. Within United States culture, African Americans symbolized prodigal lack of savings as the Chinese, Italians and Jews did fanatical obsession with saving. . . .

Moreover, in many cases Jewish and Italian merchants sold to African-American customers. Their "middleman minority" status revealingly identifies an inbetween position which, as aggrieved Southern "white" merchants complained, rested on a more humane attitude toward black customers and on such cultural affinities as an eagerness to participate in bargaining over prices. Chinese merchants have traditionally and Korean merchants more recently occupied a similar position. . . .

Other immigrants, especially Slovaks and Poles, banked on hard labor, homeownership and slow intergenerational mobility for success. They too navigated in very tricky racial cross-currents. Coming from areas in which the dignity of hard, physical labor was established, both in the countryside and in cities, they arrived in the United

States eager to work, even if in jobs which did not take advantage of their skills. They often found, however, that in the Taylorizing industries of the United States, hard work was more driven and alienating. It was, moreover, often typed and despised as "nigger work"—or as "dago work" or "hunky work" in settings in which such categories had been freighted with the prior meaning of "nigger work." The new immigrants' reputation for hard work and their unfamiliarity with English and with American culture generally tended to lead to their being hired as an almost abstract source of labor. *Hunky* was abbreviated to *hunk* and Slavic laborers in particular treated as mere pieces of work. This had its advantages, especially in comparison to black workers; Slavs could more often get hired in groups while skilled workers and petty bosses favored individual "good Negroes" with unskilled jobs, often requiring a familiarity and subservience from them not expected of new immigrants. But being seen as brute force also involved Eastern Europeans in particularly brutal social relations on the shopfloor

Hard work, especially when closely bossed, was likewise not a badge of manliness in the United States in the way that it had been in Eastern Europe. Racialized, it was also demasculinized, especially since its extremely low pay and sporadic nature ensured that new immigrant males could not be breadwinners for a family. The idea of becoming a "white man," unsullied by racially typed labor and capable of earning a family wage, was therefore extremely attractive in many ways, and the imperative of not letting one's job become "nigger work" was swiftly learned. Yet, no clear route ran from inbetweenness to white manhood. "White men's unions" often seemed the best path, but they also erected some of the most significant obstacles.

WHITE MEN'S UNIONS AND NEW IMMIGRANT TRIAL MEMBERS

While organized labor exercised little control over hiring outside of a few organized crafts during most of the years from 1895 until 1924 and beyond, its racialized opposition to new immigrants did reinforce their inbetweenness, both on the job and in politics. Yet the American Federation of Labor also provided an important venue in which "old immigrant" workers interacted with new im-

migrants, teaching important lessons in both whiteness and Americanization.

As an organization devoted to closing skilled trades to any new competition, the craft union's reflex was to oppose outsiders. In this sense, most of the AFL unions were "exclusionary by definition" and marshaled economic, and to a lesser extent political, arguments to exclude women, Chinese, Japanese, African Americans, the illiterate, the non-citizen, and the new immigrants from organized workplaces, and, whenever possible, from the shores of the United States. . . .

. . . A great deal of trade unions' racist opposition to the Chinese stressed the connection between their "slave-like" subservience and their status as coolie laborers, schooled and trapped in the Chinese social system and willing to settle for being "cheap men." Dietary practices (rice and rats rather than meat) symbolized Chinese failure to seek the "American standard of living." All of these are cultural, historical and environmental matters. Yet none of them prevented the craft unions from declaring the Chinese "race" unassimilable nor from supporting exclusionary legislation premised largely on racial grounds. The environmentalist possibility that over generations Asian "cheap men" might improve was simply irrelevant. By that time the Chinese race would have polluted America.

Much of anti-Chinese rhetoric was applied as well to Hungarians in the 1880s and was taken over in AFL anti–new immigration campaigns after 1890. Pasta, as Mink implies, joined rice as an "un-American" and racialized food. Far from abjuring arguments based on "stock," assimilability and homogeneity, the AFL's leaders supported literacy tests designed specifically "to reduce the numbers of Slavic and Mediterranean immigrants." They supported the nativist racism of the anti-labor Sen. Henry Cabot Lodge, hoped anti-Japanese agitation could be made to contribute to anti–new immigrant restrictions, emphasized "the incompatibility of the new immigrants with the very nature of American civilization," and both praised and reprinted works on "race suicide." They opposed entry of "the scum" from "the least civilized countries of Europe" and "the replacing of the independent and intelligent coal miners of Pennsylvania by the Huns and Slavs." They feared that an "American" miner in Pennsylvania could thrive only if he "Latinizes" his name. They explicitly asked, well before World War One: "How much more [new] immigration can this country absorb and retain its homogeneity?" (Those wanting to know the dire answer were advised to study the "racial history" of cities.)

Robert Asher is undoubtedly correct in arguing both that labor movement reaction to new immigrants was "qualitatively different from the response to Orientals" *and* that AFL rhetoric was "redolent of a belief in racial inferiority" of Southern and Eastern Europeans. Neither is likewise on the mark in speaking of "semi-racial" union arguments for restriction directed against new immigrants. Gompers' characterization of new immigrants as "beaten men of beaten races" perfectly captures the tension between fearing that Southern and Eastern Europe was dumping its "vomit" and "scum" in the United States and believing that Slavic and Mediterranean people were scummy. . . .

. . . Some craft unions excluded Italians, Jews and other new immigrants. Among laborers, organization often began on an ethnic basis, though such immigrant locals were often eventually integrated into a national union. Even among craftsmen, separate organizations emerged among Jewish carpenters and painters and other recent immigrants. The hod carriers union, according to Asher, "appears to have been created to protect the jobs of native construction workers against competing foreigners." The shoeworkers, pianomakers, barbers, hotel and restaurant workers and United Textile Workers likewise kept out new immigrants, whose lack of literacy, citizenship, English-language skills, apprenticeship opportunities and initiation fees also effectively barred them from many other craft locals. This "internal protectionism" apparently had lasting results. Lieberson's research through 1950 shows new immigrants and their children having far less access to craft jobs in unionized sectors than did whites of northwestern European origin.

Yet Southern and Eastern European immigrants had more access to unionized work than African Americans, and unions never supported outright bans on their migration, as they did with Asians. Organized labor's opposition to the Italians as the "white Chinese," or to recent immigrants generally as "white coolies" usually acknowledged and questioned whiteness at the same time, associating whites with non-whites while leaving open the possibility that contracted labor, and not race,

was at issue. A strong emphasis on the "brotherhood" of labor also complicated matters. Paeans to the "International Fraternity of Labor" ran in the *American Federationist* within fifteen pages of anti-immigrant hysteria such as A. A. Graham's "The un-Americanizing of America." Reports from Italian labor leaders and poems like "Brotherhood of Man" ran hard by fearful predictions of race suicide.

Moreover, the very things that the AFL warned about in its anti-immigrant campaigns encouraged the unions to make tactical decisions to enroll Southern and Eastern Europeans as members. Able to legally enter the country in large numbers, secure work, and become voters, *hunkies* and *guineas* had social power which could be used to attack the craft unionism of the AFL from the right or, as was often feared, from the left. To restrict immigration, however desirable from Gompers' point of view, did not answer what to do about the majority of the working class which was by 1910 already of immigrant origins. Nor did it speak to what to do about the many new immigrants already joining unions, in the AFL, in language and national federations or under socialist auspices. If these new immigrants were not going to undermine the AFL's appeals to corporate leaders as an effective moderating force within the working class, the American Federation of Labor would have to consider becoming the Americanizing Federation of Labor.

Most importantly, changes in machinery and Taylorizing relations of production made real the threat that crafts could be undermined by expedited training of unskilled and semi-skilled immigrant labor. While this threat gave force to labor's nativist calls for immigration restriction, it also strengthened initiatives toward a "new unionism" which crossed skill lines to organize recent immigrants. Prodded by independent, dual-unionist initiatives like those by Italian socialists and the United Hebrew Trades, by the example of existing industrial unions in its own ranks, and by the left-wing multi-national, multi-racial unionism of the Industrial Workers of the World, the AFL increasingly got into the business of organizing and Americanizing new immigrant workers in the early twentieth century. . . . Even so, especially in those where new immigrant women were the potential union members and skill dilution threatened mainly immigrant men, the Gompers' leadership at times refused either to incorporate dual unions or to initiate meaningful organizing efforts under AFL auspices.

Although self-interested, wary, and incomplete, the AFL's increasing opening to new immigrant workers initiated a process which much transformed "semi-racial" typing of recently arrived immigrants. Unions and their supporters at times treasured labor organization as the most meaningful agent of democratic "Americanization from the bottom up," what John R. Commons called "The only effective Americanizing force for the southeastern European." In struggles, native-born unionists came to observe not only the common humanity, but also the heroism of new immigrants. Never quite giving up on biological cultural explanations, labor leaders wondered which "race" made the best strikers, with some comparisons favoring the recent arrivals over Anglo-Saxons. Industrial Workers of the World leader Covington Hall's reports from Louisiana remind us that we know little about how unionists, and workers generally, conceived of race. Hall took seriously the idea of a "Latin race," including Italians, other Southern Europeans *and Mexicans,* all of whom put Southern whites to shame with their militancy. . . .

. . . Thus, the "new unionism" provided an economic logic for progressive unionists wishing to unite workers across ethnic and racial lines. With their own race less open to question, new immigrants were at times brought into class conscious coalitions, as whites and with African Americans. The great success of the packinghouse unions in forging such unity during World War One ended in a shining victory and vastly improved conditions. The diverse new immigrants and black workers at the victory celebration heard Chicago Federation of Labor leader John Fitzpatrick hail them as "black and white together under God's sunshine." If the Irish-American unionists had often been bearers of "race hatred" against both new immigrants and blacks, they and other old immigrants also could convey the lesson that class unity transcended race and semi-race.

But even at the height of openings toward new unionism and new immigrants, labor organizations taught very complex lessons regarding race. At times, overtures toward new immigrants coincided with renewed exclusion of nonwhite workers, underlining W. E. B. DuBois's point that the former were mobbed to make them join unions and the latter to keep them out. Western Federa-

tion of Miners (WFM) activists, whose episodic radicalism coexisted with nativism and a consistent anti-Chinese and anti-Mexican racism, gradually developed a will and a strategy to organize Greek immigrants, but they reaffirmed exclusion of Japanese mine workers and undermined impressive existing solidarities between Greeks and Japanese, who often worked similar jobs. The fear of immigrant "green hands," which the perceptive Lithuanian immigrant quoted above credited with first sparking the Butcher Workmen to organize recent immigrants in 1904 was also a fear of black hands, so that one historian has suggested that the desire to limit black employment generated the willingness to organize new immigrants.

In 1905, Gompers promised that "Caucasians are not going to let their standard of living be destroyed by negroes, Chinamen, Japs, or any others." Hearing this, new immigrant unionists might have reflected on what they as "caucasians" had to learn regarding their newfound superiority to non-whites. Or they might have fretted that *guineas* and *hunkies* would be classified along with "any others" undermining white standards. Either way, learning about race was an important part of new immigrants' labor education.

Teaching Americanism, the labor movement also taught whiteness. The scattered racist jokes in the labor and socialist press could not, of course, rival blackface entertainments or the "coon songs" in the Sunday comics in teaching new immigrants the racial ropes of the United States, but the movement did provide a large literature of popularized racist ethnology, editorial attacks on "nigger equality" and in Jack London, a major cultural figure who taught that it was possible and desirable to be "first of all a white man and only then a socialist."

But the influence of organized labor and the left on race thinking was far more focused on language than on literature, on picket lines than lines on a page. Unions which opened to new immigrants more readily than to "nonwhites" not only reinforced the "inbetween" position of Southern and Eastern Europeans but attempted to teach immigrants intricate and spurious associations of race, strikebreaking and lack of manly pride. Even as AFL exclusionism ensured that there would be black strikebreakers and black suspicion of unions, the language of labor equated scabbing with "turning nigger." The unions organized much of their critique around a notion of "slavish" behavior which could be employed against ex-slaves or against Slavs, but indicted the former more often than the latter. Warning all union men against "slave-like" behavior, unions familiarized new workers with the ways race and slavery had gone together to define a standard of unmanned servility. In objectively confusing situations, with scabs coming from the African-American, immigrant and native-born working classes (and with craft unions routinely breaking each others' strikes), Booker T. Washington identified one firm rule of thumb: "Strikers seem to consider it a much greater crime for a Negro who had been denied the opportunity to work at his trade to take the place of a striking employee than for a white man to do the same thing."

In such situations, whiteness had its definite appeals. But the left and labor movements could abruptly remind new immigrants that their whiteness was anything but secure. Jack London could turn from denunciations of the "yellow peril" or of African Americans to excoriations of "the dark-pigmented things" coming in from Europe. The 1912 Socialist party campaign book connected European immigration with "race annihilation" and the "possible degeneration of even the succeeding American type." The prominence of black strike-breakers in several of the most important mass strikes after World War One strengthened the grip of racism, perhaps even among recent immigrants, but the same years also brought renewed racial attacks on the immigrants themselves. In the wake of these failed strikes, the *American Federationist* featured disquisitions on "Americanism and Immigration" by John Quinn, the National Commander of the nativist and anti-labor American Legion. New immigrants had unarguably proven the most loyal unionists in the most important of the strikes, yet the AFL now supported exclusion based on "racial" quotas. Quinn brought together biology, environment and the racialized history of the United States, defending American stock against Italian "industrial slaves" particularly and the "indigestion of immigration" generally.

INBETWEEN AND INDIFFERENT: NEW IMMIGRANT RACIAL CONSCIOUSNESS

One Italian-American informant interviewed by a Louisiana scholar remembered the early twentieth century as a time when "he and his family had been badly mistreated by a French plantation owner near New Roads where he and his family were made to live among the Negroes and were treated in the same manner. At first he did not mind because he did not know any difference, but when he learned the position that the Negroes occupied in this country, he demanded that his family be moved to a different house and be given better treatment." In denouncing all theories of white supremacy, the Polish language Chicago-based newspaper *Dziennik Chicagoski* editorialized, "if the words 'superior race' are replaced by the words 'Anglo-Saxon' and instead of 'inferior races' such terms as Polish, Italian, Russian and Slavs in general—not to mention the Negro, the Chinese, and the Japanese—are applied, then we shall see the political side of the racial problems in the United States in stark nakedness." In the first instance, consciousness of an inbetween racial status leads to a desire for literal distance from non-whites. In the second, inbetweenness leads to a sense of grievances shared in common with non-whites.

In moving from the racial categorization of new immigrants to their own racial consciousness, it is important to realize that "Europeans were hardly likely to have found racist ideologies an astounding new encounter when they arrived in the U.S.," though the salience of whiteness as a social category in the United States was exceptional. "Civilized" Northern Italians derided those darker ones from Sicily and the *mezzogiorno* as "Turks" and "Africans" long before arriving in Brooklyn or Chicago. And once arrived, if they spoke of "little dark fellows," they were far more likely to be describing Southern Italians than African Americans. The strength of anti-Semitism, firmly ingrained in Poland and other parts of Eastern Europe, meant that many immigrants from these regions were accustomed to looking at a whole "race" of people as devious, degraded, and dangerous. In the United States, both Jews and Poles spoke of riots involving attacks on African Americans as "pogroms." In an era of imperialist expansion and sometimes strident nationalism, a preoccupation with race was characteristic not only of the United States but also of many European regions experiencing heavy emigration to the United States.

Both eager embraces of whiteness and, more rarely, flirtations with non-whiteness characterized these immigrants' racial identity. But to assume that new immigrants as a mass clearly saw their identity with non-whites or clearly fastened on their differences is to miss the confusion of inbetweenness. The discussion of whiteness was an uncomfortable terrain for many reasons and even in separating themselves from African Americans and Asian Americans, immigrants did not necessarily become white. Indeed, often they were curiously indifferent to whiteness.

Models that fix on one extreme or the other of immigrant racial consciousness—the quick choice of whiteness amidst brutal competition or the solidarity with non-white working people based on common oppression—capture parts of the new immigrant experience. At times Southern and Eastern Europeans were exceedingly apt, and not very critical, students of American racism. Greeks admitted to the Western Federation of Miners saw the advantage of their membership and did not rock the boat by demanding admission for the Japanese American mine workers with whom they had previously allied. Greek Americans sometimes battled for racial status fully within the terms of white supremacy, arguing that classical civilization had established them as "the highest type of the Caucasian race." In the company town of Pullman and adjacent neighborhoods, immigrants who sharply divided on national and religious lines coalesced impressively as whites in 1928 to keep out African-American residents. Recently arrived Jewish immigrants on New York City's Lower East Side resented reformers who encouraged them to make a common cause with the "schwartzes." In New Bedford, "white Portuguese" angrily reacted to perceived racial slights and sharply drew the color line against "black Portuguese" Cape Verdeans, especially when preference in jobs and housing hung in the balance. Polish workers may have developed their very self-image and honed their reputation in more or less conscious counterpoint to the stereotypical *niggerscab.* Theodore Radzialowski reasons that "Poles who had so little going for them (except their white skin—certainly no mean advantage but more important later than earlier in their American experience), may have grasped this image of themselves as honest, honorable, non-scabbing workers and stressed the image of the black scab in order to distinguish themselves from . . . the blacks with whom they shared the bottom of American society."

Many new immigrants learned to deploy and manipulate white supremacist images from the vaudeville stage and the screens of Hollywood films where they saw "their own kind" stepping out of conventional racial and gender roles through blackface and other forms of cross-dress. "Facing nativist pressure that would assign them to the dark side of the racial divide," Michael Rogin argues provocatively, immigrant entertainers like Al Jolson, Sophie Tucker and Rudolph Valentino, "Americanized themselves by crossing and recrossing the racial line."

At the same time, immigrants sometimes hesitated to embrace a white identity. Houston's Greek Americans developed, and retained, a language setting themselves apart from *i mavri* (the blacks), from *i aspri* (the whites) and from Mexican Americans. In New England, Greeks worked in coalitions with Armenians, whom the courts were worriedly accepting as white, and Syrians, whom the courts found non-white. The large Greek-American sponge fishing industry based in Tarpon Springs, Florida, fought the Ku Klux Klan and employed black workers on an equal, share-the-catch system. Nor did Tarpon Springs practice Jim Crow in public transportation. In Louisiana and Mississippi, southern Italians learned Jim Crow tardily, even when legally accepted as whites, so much so that native whites fretted and black Southerners "made unabashed distinctions between Dagoes and white folks," treating the former with a "friendly, first name familiarity." In constructing an anti-Nordic supremacist history series based on "gifts" of various peoples, the Knights of Columbus quickly and fully included African Americans. Italian and Italian-American radicals "consistently expressed horror at the barbaric treatment of blacks," in part because "Italians were also regarded as an inferior race." Denouncing not only lynchings but "the republic of lynchings" and branding the rulers of the United States as "savages of the blue eyes," *Il Proletario* asked: "What do they think they are as a race, these arrogant whites?" and ruthlessly wondered, "and how many kisses have their women asked for from the strong and virile black servants?" Italian radicals knew exactly how to go for the jugular vein in United States race relations. The Jewish press at times identified with both the suffering and the aspirations of African Americans. In 1912, Chicago's *Daily Jewish Courier* concluded

that "In this world . . . the Jew is treated as a
Negro and Negro as a Jew" and that the "lynching
of the Negroes in the South is similar to massacres
on Jews in Russia."

Examples could, and should, be piled higher
on both sides of the new immigrants' racial consciousness. But to see the matter largely in terms
of which stack is higher misses the extent to
which the exposed position of racial inbetween-
ness could generate both positions at once, and
sometimes a desire to avoid the issue of race entirely. The best frame of comparison for discussing
new immigrant racial consciousness is that of the
Irish Americans in the mid-nineteenth century. Especially when not broadly accepted as such, Irish
Americans insisted that politicians acknowledge
them as part of the dominant race. Changing the
political subject from Americanness and religion
to race whenever possible, they challenged anti-
Celtic Anglo-Saxonism by becoming leaders in the
cause of white supremacy. New immigrant leaders
never approximated that path. With a large segment of both parties willing to vouch for the possibility of speedy, orderly Americanization and
with neither party willing to vouch unequivocally
for their racial character, Southern and Eastern
Europeans generally tried to change the subject
from whiteness to nationality and loyalty to American ideals.

One factor in such a desire not to be drawn into
debates about whiteness was a strong national/cul-
tural identification as Jews, Italians, Poles and so
on. At times, the strongest tie might even be to a
specific Sicilian or Slovakian village, but the first
sustained contact between African Americans and
"new immigrants" occurred during World War
One when many of these immigrants were mes-
merized by the emergence of Poland and other
new states throughout eastern and southeastern
Europe. Perhaps this is why new immigrants in
Chicago and other riot-torn cities seem to have ab-
stained from early twentieth-century race riots, to
a far greater extent than theories connecting racial
violence and job competition at "the bottom" of society would predict. Important Polish spokespersons and newspapers emphasized that Chicago
riots were between the "whites" and "Negroes."
Polish immigrants had, and should have, no part
in them. What might be termed an *abstention from
whiteness* also characterized the practice of rank-
and-file East Europeans. Slavic immigrants played

little role in the racial violence which was spread
by Irish-American gangs.

Throughout the Chicago riot, so vital to the future of Slavic packinghouse workers and their
union, Polish-American coverage was sparse and
occurred only when editors "could tear their attention away from their fascination with the momentous events attending the birth of the new
Polish state." And even then, comparisons with
pogroms against Jews in Poland framed the discussion. That the defense of Poland was as important as analyzing the realities in Chicago emerges
starkly in the convoluted expression of sympathy
for riot victims in the organ of the progressive,
pro-labor Alliance of Polish Women, *Glos Polek:*

> The American Press has written at length about the al-
> leged pogroms of Jews in Poland for over two months.
> Now it is writing about pogroms against Blacks in
> America. It wrote about the Jews in words full of sor-
> row and sympathy, why does it not show the same today
> to Negroes being burnt and killed without mercy?

Both "becoming American" and "becoming
white" could imply coercive threats to European
national identities. The 1906 remarks of Luigi Vil-
liari, an Italian government official investigating
Sicilian sharecroppers in Louisiana, illustrate the
gravity and inter-relation of both processes. Vil-
liari found that "a majority of plantation owners
cannot comprehend that . . . Italians are white,"
and instead considered the Sicilian migrant "a
white-skinned negro who is a better worker than
the black-skinned negro." He patiently explained
the "commonly held distinction . . . between 'negroes,' 'Italians' and 'whites' (that is, Americans)."
In the South, he added, the "American will not engage in agricultural, manual labor, rather he leaves
it to the negroes. Seeing that the Italians will do
this work, naturally he concludes that Italians
lack dignity. The only way an Italian can emanci-
pate himself from this inferior state is to abandon
all sense of national pride and to identify completely with the Americans."

One hundred percent whiteness and one hundred percent Americanism carried overlapping
and confusing imperatives for new immigrants
in and out of the South, but in several ways the
former was even more uncomfortable terrain
than the latter. The pursuit of white identity, so
tied to competition for wage labor and to political
citizenship, greatly privileged male perceptions.

But identity formation, as Americanizers and immigrant leaders realized, rested in great part on the activities of immigrant mothers, who entered discussions of nationality and Americanization more easily than those of race. More cast in determinism, the discourse of race produced fewer openings to inject class demands, freedom and cultural pluralism than did the discourse of Americanism. The modest strength of herrenvolk democracy, weakened even in the South at a time when huge numbers of the white poor were disfranchised, paled in comparison to the opportunities to try to give progressive spin to the idea of a particularly freedom-loving "American race."

In a fascinating quantified sociological study of Poles in Buffalo in the mid-1920s, Niles Carpenter and Daniel Katz concluded that their interviewees had been "Americanized" without being "de-Polandized." Their data led to the conclusion that Polish immigrants displayed "an absence of strong feeling so far as the Negro is concerned," a pattern "certainly in contrast to the results which would be sure to follow the putting of similar questions to a typically American group." The authors therefore argued for "the inference that so-called race feeling in this country is much more a product of tensions and quasi-psychoses born of our own national experience than of any factors inherent in the relations of race to race." Their intriguing characterization of Buffalo's Polish community did not attempt to cast its racial views as "pro-Negro" but instead pointed out that "the bulk of its members express indifference towards him." Such indifference, noted also by other scholars, was the product not of unfamiliarity with, or distance from, the United States racial system, but of nationalism compounded by intense, harrowing and contradictory experiences inbetween whiteness and non-whiteness. Only after the racial threat of new immigration was defused by the racial restriction of the Johnson-Reed Act would new immigrants haltingly find a place in the ethnic wing of the white race.

This brief treatment of a particularly complicated issue necessarily leaves out a number of key episodes especially in the latter stages of the story. One is a resolution of sorts in the ambiguous status of inbetween immigrant workers which came in the late 1930s and the World War II era. In some settings these years brought not only a greater emphasis on cultural pluralism and a new, broader language of Americanism that embraced working-class ethnics, but also a momentary lull in racial conflict. With the creation of strong, interracial industrial unions, African-American local officials and shop stewards fought for civil rights at the same time they led white "ethnic" workers in important industrial struggles. Yet in other settings, sometimes even in the same cities, the war years and the period immediately following brought riots and hate strikes over the racial integration of workplaces and, particularly, neighborhoods. Most second-generation ethnics embraced their Americanness, but, as Gary Gerstle suggests, this "may well have intensified their prejudice against Blacks, for many conceived of Americanization in racial terms: becoming American meant becoming white."

During the 1970s a later generation of white ethnics rediscovered their ethnic identities in the midst of a severe backlash against civil rights legislation and new movements for African-American liberation. The relationship between this defensive mentality and more recent attacks on affirmative action programs and civil rights legislation underscores the contemporary importance in understanding how and why these once inbetween immigrant workers became white.

SEVEN

The Declining Significance of Race

William Julius Wilson

Race relations in the United States have undergone fundamental changes in recent years, so much so that now the life chances of individual blacks have more to do with their economic class position than with their day-to-day encounters with whites. In earlier years the systematic efforts of whites to suppress blacks were obvious to even the most insensitive observer. Blacks were denied access to valued and scarce resources through various ingenious schemes of racial exploitation, discrimination, and segregation, schemes that were reinforced by elaborate ideologies of racism.

But the situation has changed. However determinative such practices were in the previous efforts of the black population to achieve racial equality, and however significant they were in the creation of poverty-stricken ghettos and a vast underclass of black proletarians—that massive population at the very bottom of the social class ladder plagued by poor education and low-paying, unstable jobs—they do not provide a meaningful explanation of the life chances of black Americans today. The traditional patterns of interaction between blacks and whites, particularly in the labor market, have been fundamentally altered.

NEW AND TRADITIONAL BARRIERS

In the pre–Civil War period, and in the latter half of the nineteenth through the first half of the twentieth century, the continuous and explicit efforts of whites to construct racial barriers profoundly affected the lives of black Americans. Racial oppression was designed, overt, and easily documented. As the nation has entered the latter half of the twentieth century, however, many of the traditional barriers have crumbled under the weight of the political, social, and economic changes of the civil rights era. A new set of obstacles has emerged from basic structural shifts in the economy.

These obstacles are therefore impersonal, but may prove to be even more formidable for certain segments of the black population. Specifically, whereas the previous barriers were usually designed to control and restrict the entire black population, the new barriers create hardships essentially for the black underclass; whereas the old barriers were based explicitly on the racial motivations derived from intergroup contact, the new barriers have racial significance only in their consequences, not in their origins. In short, whereas the old barriers portrayed the pervasive features of racial oppression, the new barriers indicate an important and emerging form of class subordination.

It would be shortsighted to view the traditional forms of racial segregation and discrimination as having essentially disappeared in contemporary America; the presence of blacks is still firmly resisted in various institutions and social arrangements, for example, residential areas and private social clubs. However, in the economic sphere class has become more important than race in determining black access to privilege and power. It is clearly evident in this connection that many talented and educated blacks are now entering positions of prestige and influence at a rate comparable to or, in some situations, exceeding that of whites with equivalent qualifications. It is equally clear that the black underclass is in a hopeless state of economic stagnation, falling further and further behind the rest of society.

THREE STAGES OF AMERICAN RACE RELATIONS

American society has experienced three major stages of black-white contact, and each stage embodies a different form of racial stratification structured by the particular arrangement of both the economy and the polity. Stage one coincides with antebellum slavery and the early postbellum era and may be designated the period of *plantation economy and racial-caste oppression.* Stage two begins in the last quarter of the nineteenth century and ends at roughly the New Deal era, and may be identified as the period of *industrial expansion, class conflict, and racial oppression.* Finally, stage three is associated with the modern, industrial, post-World War II era which really began to crystallize during the 1960s and 1970s, and may be characterized as the period of *progressive transition from race inequalities to class inequalities.* The different periods can be identified as the preindustrial, industrial, and modern industrial stages of American race relations, respectively.

Although this abbreviated designation of the periods of American race relations seems to relate racial change to fundamental economic changes rather directly, it bears repeating that the different stages of race relations are structured by the unique arrangements and interaction of the economy and polity. More specifically, although there was an economic basis of structured racial inequality in the preindustrial and industrial periods of race relations, the polity more or less interacted with the economy either to reinforce patterns of racial stratification or to mediate various forms of racial conflict. Moreover, in the modern industrial period race relations have been shaped as much by important economic changes as by important political changes. Indeed, it would not be possible to understand fully the subtle and manifest changes in race relations in the modern industrial period without recognizing the dual and often reciprocal influence of structural changes in the economy and political changes in the state. Thus different systems of production and/or dif-

ferent arrangements of the polity have imposed different constraints on the way in which racial groups have interacted in the United States, constraints that have structured the relations between racial groups and that have produced dissimilar contexts not only for the manifestation of racial antagonisms, but also for racial group access to rewards and privileges.

In contrast to the modern industrial period in which fundamental economic and political changes have made the economic class position of blacks the determining factor in their prospects for occupational advancement, the preindustrial and industrial periods of black-white relations have one central feature in common: overt efforts of whites to solidify economic racial domination (ranging from the manipulation of black labor to the neutralization or elimination of black economic competition) through various forms of judicial, political, and social discrimination. Since racial problems during these two periods were principally related to group struggles over economic resources, they readily lend themselves to the economic class theories of racial antagonisms that associate racial antipathy with class conflict.

Although racial oppression, when viewed from the broad perspective of historical change in American society, was a salient and important feature during the preindustrial and industrial periods of race relations in the United States, the problems of subordination for certain segments of the black population and the experience of social advancement for others are more directly associated with economic class in the modern industrial period. Economic and political changes have gradually shaped a black class structure, making it increasingly difficult to speak of a single or uniform black experience. Although a small elite population of free, propertied blacks did in fact exist during the pre–Civil War period, the interaction between race and economic class only assumed real importance in the latter phases of the industrial period of race relations; and the significance of this relationship has grown as the nation has entered the modern industrial period.

Each of the major periods of American race relations has been shaped in different measure both by the systems of production and by the laws and policies of the state. However, the relationships between the economy and the state have varied in each period, and therefore the roles of both institutions in shaping race relations have differed over time.

ANTEBELLUM SOUTH

In the preindustrial period the slave-based plantation economy of the South allowed a relatively small, elite group of planters to develop enormous regional power. The hegemony of the southern ruling elite was based on a system of production that required little horizontal or vertical mobility and therefore could be managed very efficiently with a simple division of labor that virtually excluded free white labor. As long as free white workers were not central to the process of reproducing the labor supply in the southern plantation economy, slavery as a mode of production facilitated the slaveholder's concentration and consolidation of economic power. And the slaveholders successfully transferred their control of the economic system to the political and legal systems in order to protect their class interest in slavery. In effect, the polity in the South regulated and reinforced the system of racial caste oppression, depriving both blacks and nonslaveholding whites of any meaningful influence in the way that slavery was used in the economic life of the South.

In short, the economy provided the basis for the development of the system of slavery, and the polity reinforced and perpetuated that system. Furthermore, the economy enabled the slaveholders to develop a regional center of power, and the polity was used to legitimate that power. Since nonslaveholding whites were virtually powerless both economically and politically, they had very little effect on the developing patterns of race relations. The meaningful forms of black-white contact were between slaves and slaveholders, and southern race relations consequently assumed a paternalistic quality involving the elaboration and specification of duties, norms, rights, and obligations as they pertained to the use of slave labor and the system of indefinite servitude.

In short, the pattern of race relations in the antebellum South was shaped first and foremost by the system of production. The very nature of the social relations of production meant that the exclusive control of the planters would be derived from their position in the production process, which ultimately led to the creation of a juridicial system that reflected and protected their class interests, including their investment in slavery.

WORKERS' EMERGING POWER

However, in the nineteenth century antebellum North the form of racial oppression was anything but paternalistic. Here a more industrial system of production enabled white workers to become more organized and physically concentrated than their southern counterparts. Following the abolition of slavery in the North they used their superior resources to generate legal and informal practices of segregation that effectively prevented blacks from becoming serious economic competitors.

As the South gradually moved from a plantation to an industrial economy in the last quarter of the nineteenth century, landless whites were finally able to effect changes in the racial stratification system. Their efforts to eliminate black competition helped to produce an elaborate system of Jim Crow segregation. Poor whites were aided not only by their numbers but also by the development of political resources which accompanied their greater involvement in the South's economy.

Once again, however, the system of production was the major basis for this change in race relations, and once again the political system was used to reinforce patterns of race emanating from structural shifts in the economy. If the racial laws in the antebellum South protected the class interests of the planters and reflected their overwhelming power, the Jim Crow segregation laws of the late nineteenth century reflected the rising power of white laborers; and if the political power of the planters was grounded in the system of producing in a plantation economy, the emerging political power of the workers grew out of the new division of labor that accompanied industrialization.

CLASS AND RACE RELATIONS

Except for the brief period of fluid race relations in the North between 1870 and 1890 and in the South during the Reconstruction era, racial oppression is the single best term to characterize the black experience prior to the twentieth century. In the antebellum South both slaves and free blacks occupied what could be best described as a caste position, in the sense that realistic chances for occupational mobility simply did not exist. In the antebellum North a few free blacks were able to acquire some property and improve their socioeconomic position, and a few were even able to make use of educational opportunities. However, the overwhelming majority of free northern Negroes were trapped in menial positions and were victimized by lower-class white antagonism, including the racial hostilities of European immigrant ethnics (who successfully curbed black economic competition). In the postbellum South the system of Jim Crow segregation wiped out the small gains blacks had achieved during Reconstruction, and blacks were rapidly pushed out of the more skilled jobs they had held since slavery. Accordingly, there was very little black occupational differentiation in the South at the turn of the century.

Just as the shift from a plantation economy to an industrializing economy transformed the class and race relations in the postbellum South, so too did industrialization in the North change the context for race-class interaction and confrontation there. On the one hand, the conflicts associated with the increased black-white contacts in the early twentieth century North resembled the forms of antagonism that soured the relations between the races in the postbellum South. Racial conflicts between blacks and whites in both situations were closely tied to class conflicts among whites. On the other hand, there were some fundamental differences. The collapse of the paternalistic bond between blacks and the southern business elite cleared the path for the almost total subjugation of blacks in the South and resulted in what amounted to a united white racial movement that solidified the system of Jim Crow segregation.

However, a united white movement against blacks never really developed in the North. In the first quarter of the twentieth century, management attempted to undercut white labor by using blacks as strikebreakers and, in some situations, as permanent replacements for white workers who periodically demanded higher wages and more fringe benefits. Indeed, the determination of industrialists to ignore racial norms of exclusion and to hire black workers was one of the main reasons why the industrywide unions reversed their racial

policies and actively recruited black workers during the New Deal era. Prior to this period the overwhelming majority of unskilled and semiskilled blacks were nonunionized and were available as lower-paid labor or as strikebreakers. The more management used blacks to undercut white labor, the greater were the racial antagonisms between white and black labor.

Moreover, racial tension in the industrial sector often reinforced and sometimes produced racial tension in the social order. The growth of the black urban population created a housing shortage during the early twentieth century which frequently produced black "invasions" or ghetto "spillovers" into adjacent poor white neighborhoods. The racial tensions emanating from labor strife seemed to heighten the added pressures of racial competition for housing, neighborhoods, and recreational areas. Indeed, it was this combination of racial friction in both the economic sector and the social order that produced the bloody riots in East Saint Louis in 1917 and in Chicago and several other cities in 1919.

In addition to the fact that a united white movement against blacks never really developed in the North during the industrial period, it was also the case that the state's role in shaping race relations was much more autonomous, much less directly related to developments in the economic sector. Thus, in the brief period of fluid race relations in the North from 1870 to 1890, civil rights laws were passed barring discrimination in public places and in public institutions. This legislation did not have any real significance to the white masses at that time because, unlike in the pre–Civil War North and the post–Civil War South, white workers did not perceive blacks as major economic competitors. Blacks constituted only a small percentage of the total population in northern cities; they had not yet been used in any significant numbers as cheap labor in industry or as strikebreakers; and their earlier antebellum competitors in low-status jobs (the Irish and German immigrants) had improved their economic status in the trades and municipal employment.

POLITY AND RACIAL OPPRESSION

For all these reasons liberal whites and black professionals, urged on by the spirit of racial reform that had developed during the Civil War and Reconstruction, could pursue civil rights programs without firm resistance; for all these reasons racial developments on the political front were not directly related to the economic motivations and interests of workers and management. In the early twentieth century the independent effect of the political system was displayed in an entirely different way. The process of industrialization had significantly altered the pattern of racial interaction, giving rise to various manifestations of racial antagonism.

Although discrimination and lack of training prevented blacks from seeking higher-paying jobs, they did compete with lower-class whites for unskilled and semiskilled factory jobs, and they were used by management to undercut the white workers' union movement. Despite the growing importance of race in the dynamics of the labor market, the political system did not intervene either to mediate the racial conflicts or to reinforce the pattern of labor-market racial interaction generated by the system of production. This was the case despite the salience of a racial ideology system that justified and prescribed unequal treatment for Afro-Americans. (Industrialists will more likely challenge societal racial norms in situations where adherence to them results in economic losses.)

If nothing else, the absence of political influence on the labor market probably reflected the power struggles between management and workers. Thus legislation to protect the rights of black workers to compete openly for jobs would have conflicted with the interests of white workers, whereas legislation to deny black participation in any kind of industrial work would have conflicted with the interest of management. To repeat, unlike in the South, a united white movement resulting in the almost total segregation of the work force never really developed in the North.

But the state's lack of influence in the industrial sector of private industries did not mean that it had no significant impact on racial stratification in the early twentieth century North. The urban political machines, controlled in large measure by working-class ethnics who were often in direct competition with blacks in the private industrial sector, systematically gerrymandered black neighborhoods and excluded the urban black masses from meaningful political participation throughout the early twentieth century. Control by the white ethnics of the various urban political machines

was so complete that blacks were never really in a position to compete for the more important municipal political rewards, such as patronage jobs or government contracts and services. Thus the lack of racial competition for municipal political rewards did not provide the basis for racial tension and conflict in the urban political system. This political racial oppression had no direct connection with or influence on race relations in the private industrial sector.

In sum, whether one focuses on the way race relations were structured by the system of production or the polity or both, racial oppression (ranging from the exploitation of black labor by the business class to the elimination of black competition for economic, social, and political resources by the white masses) was a characteristic and important phenomenon in both the preindustrial and industrial periods of American race relations. Nonetheless, and despite the prevalance of various forms of racial oppression, the change from a preindustrial to an industrial system of production did enable blacks to increase their political and economic resources. The proliferation of jobs created by industrial expansion helped generate and sustain the continuous mass migration of blacks from the rural South to the cities of the North and West. As the black urban population grew and became more segregated, institutions and organizations in the black community also developed together with a business and professional class affiliated with these institutions. Still, it was not until after World War II (the modern industrial period) that the black class structure started to take on some of the characteristics of the white class structure.

CLASS AND BLACK LIFE CHANCES

Class has also become more important than race in determining black life chances in the modern industrial period. Moreover, the center of racial conflict has shifted from the industrial sector to the sociopolitical order. Although these changes can be related to the more fundamental changes in the system of production and in the laws and policies of the state, the relations between the economy and the polity in the modern industrial period have differed from those in previous periods. In the preindustrial and industrial periods the basis of structured racial inequality was primarily economic, and in most situations the state was merely an instrument to reinforce patterns of race relations that grew directly out of the social relations of production.

Except for the brief period of fluid race relations in the North from 1870 to 1890, the state was a major instrument of racial oppression. State intervention in the modern industrial period has been designed to promote racial equality, and the relationship between the polity and the economy has been much more reciprocal, so much so that it is difficult to determine which one has been more important in shaping race relations since World War II. It was the expansion of the economy that facilitated black movement from the rural areas to the industrial centers and that created job opportunities leading to greater occupational differentiation in the black community (in the sense that an increasing percentage of blacks moved into white-collar positions); and it was the intervention of the state (responding to the pressures of increased black political resources and to the racial protest movement) that removed many artificial discrimination barriers by municipal, state, and federal civil rights legislation, and that contributed to the more liberal racial policies of the nation's labor unions by protective union legislation. And these combined political and economic changes created a pattern of black occupational upgrading that resulted, for example, in a substantial drop in the percentage of black males in the low-paying service, unskilled laborer, and farm jobs.

However despite the greater occupational differentiation within the black community, there are now signs that the effect of some aspects of structural economic change has been the closer association between black occupational mobility and class affiliation. Access to the means of production is increasingly based on educational criteria (a situation which distinguishes the modern industrial from the earlier industrial system of production) and thus threatens to solidify the position of the black underclass. In other words, a consequence of the rapid growth of the corporate and government sectors has been the gradual creation of a segmented labor market that currently provides vastly different mobility opportunities for different segments of the black population.

On the one hand, poorly trained and educationally limited blacks of the inner city, including that growing number of black teenagers and young adults, see their job prospects increasingly restricted to the low-wage sector, their unemployment rates soaring to record levels (which remain high despite swings in the business cycle), their labor force participation rates declining, their movement out of poverty slowing, and their welfare roles increasing. On the other hand, talented and educated blacks are experiencing unprecedented job opportunities in the growing government and corporate sectors, opportunities that are at least comparable to those of whites with equivalent qualifications. The improved job situation for the more privileged blacks in the corporate and government sectors is related both to the expansion of salaried white-collar positions and to the pressures of state affirmative action programs.

In view of these developments, it would be difficult to argue that the plight of the black underclass is solely a consequence of racial oppression, that is, the explicit and overt efforts of whites to keep blacks subjugated, in the same way that it would be difficult to explain the rapid economic improvement of the more privileged blacks by arguing that the traditional forms of racial segregation and discrimination still characterize the labor market in American industries. The recent mobility patterns of blacks lend strong support to the view that economic class is clearly more important than race in predetermining job placement and occupational mobility. In the economic realm, then, the black experience has moved historically from economic racial oppression experienced by virtually all blacks to economic subordination for the black underclass. And as we begin the last quarter of the twentieth century, a deepening economic schism seems to be developing in the black community, with the black poor falling further and further behind middle- and upper-income blacks.

SHIFT OF RACIAL CONFLICT

If race is declining in significance in the economic sector, explanations of racial antagonism based on labor-market conflicts, such as those advanced by economic class theories of race, also have less significance in the period of modern industrial race relations. Neither the low-wage sector nor the corporate and government sectors provide the basis for the kind of interracial job competition and conflict that plagued the economic order in previous

periods. With the absorption of blacks into industrywide labor unions, protective union legislation,
and equal employment legislation, it is no longer
feasible for management to undercut white labor
by using black workers. The traditional racial
struggles for power and privilege have shifted
away from the economic sector and are now concentrated in the sociopolitical order. Although
poor blacks and poor whites are still the main actors in the present manifestations of racial strife,
the immediate source of the tension has more to
do with racial competition for public schools, municipal political systems, and residential areas
than with the competition for jobs.

To say that race is declining in significance,
therefore, is not only to argue that the life chances
of blacks have less to do with race than with economic class affiliation, but also to maintain that
racial conflict and competition in the economic
sector—the most important historical factors in
the subjugation of blacks—have been substantially
reduced. However, it would be argued that the
firm white resistance to public school desegregation, residential integration, and black control of
central cities all indicate the unyielding importance of race in the United States. The argument
could even be entertained that the impressive occupational gains of the black middle class are only
temporary, and that as soon as affirmative action
pressures are relieved, or as soon as the economy
experiences a prolonged recession, industries will
return to their old racial practices.

Both of these arguments are compelling if not
altogether persuasive. Taking the latter contention
first, there is little available evidence to suggest
that the economic gains of privileged blacks will
be reversed. Despite the fact that the recession of
the early 1970s decreased job prospects for all educated workers, the more educated blacks continued to experience a faster rate of job advancement
than their white counterparts. And although it is
always possible that an economic disaster could
produce racial competition for higher-paying jobs
and white efforts to exclude talented blacks, it
is difficult to entertain this idea as a real possibility in the face of the powerful political and social
movement against job discrimination. At this point
there is every reason to believe that talented and
educated blacks, like talented and educated whites,
will continue to enjoy the advantages and privileges of their class status.

My response to the first argument is not to
deny the current racial antagonism in the sociopolitical order, but to suggest that such antagonism has far less effect on individual or group
access to those opportunities and resources that
are centrally important for life survival than antagonism in the economic sector. The factors that
most severely affected black life chances in previous years were the racial oppression and antagonism in the economic sector. As race declined in
importance in the economic sector, the Negro
class structure became more differentiated and
black life chances became increasingly a consequence of class affiliation.

Furthermore, it is even difficult to identify the
form of racial contact in the sociopolitical order as
the source of the current manifestations of conflict between lower-income blacks and whites, because neither the degree of racial competition
between the have-nots, nor their structural relations in urban communities, nor their patterns of
interaction constitute the ultimate source of present racial antagonism. The ultimate basis for current racial tension is the deleterious effect of basic
structural changes in the modern American economy on black and white lower-income groups,
changes that include uneven economic growth,
increasing technology and automation, industry
relocation, and labor market segmentation.

FIGHTING CLASS SUBORDINATION

The situation of marginality and redundancy created by the modern industrial society deleteri-
ously affects all the poor, regardless of race.
Underclass whites, Hispano Americans, and
Native Americans all are victims, to a greater or
lesser degree, of class subordination under advanced capitalism. It is true that blacks are disproportionately represented in the underclass
population and that about one-third of the entire
black population is in the underclass. But the significance of these facts has more to do with the
historical consequences of racial oppression than
with the current effects of race.

Although the percentage of blacks below the
low-income level dropped steadily throughout the
1960s, one of the legacies of the racial oppression
in previous years is the continued disproportionate
black representation in the underclass. And since
1970 both poor whites and nonwhites have evi-

denced very little progress in their elevation from the ranks of the underclass. In the final analysis, therefore, the challenge of economic dislocation in modern industrial society calls for public policy programs to attack inequality on a broad class front, policy programs—in other words—that go beyond the limits of ethnic and racial discrimination by directly confronting the pervasive and destructive features of class subordination.

E I G H T

Land, Labour, and Group Formation
Blacks and Indians in the United States

Stephen Cornell

This article begins with a puzzle. Simply put: Why is it that a comprehensive 'racial' consciousness emerged early among Blacks in what is now the United States, but only relatively recently among Native Americans? The puzzle, in other words, has to do with explaining very different patterns of group formation in two subordinated North American populations.

Both first encountered Euro-Americans as members of diverse ethnic or national groups. The Africans who were forcibly brought to what is now the United States came not as 'blacks' or 'Africans' but as Mbundas or Ibos or Wolof and so on: as members of distinct and various ethnic populations. Native Americans likewise first dealt with Euro-Americans not as 'Indians' or 'Native Americans' but as members of hugely diverse nations. In neither case did a self-consciously solidary 'racial' population—as that term is conventionally understood—exist at the time of contact with Europeans or entry into what is now the United States. Quite the contrary: in each case a self-conscious, comprehensive group identity was constructed in the course of extended interaction with Euro-American society.

The pattern of that construction, however, was different in each case. A comprehensive group consciousness forms early among Blacks in North America. It is evident in aspects of slave culture and community, in freedmen's organizations, in the outburst of Black institution-building in the South during Reconstruction, and in a myriad of other ways.

But despite the even longer historical interactions between Indians and non-Indians, a similar consciousness appears much later among Native Americans. It is not until nearly the middle of the twentieth century that a comprehensive 'Indian' consciousness appears on a large scale as a widespread basis of collective identity and action.

Why should such different patterns of group formation occur in these two severely subordinated, early-contact populations?

ANALYSING DIFFERENTIAL OUTCOMES

This sort of question is scarcely foreign to the analysis of intergroup relations in the United States. A number of scholars have undertaken to explain the structured variety of those relations

Reprinted from Stephen Cornell, "Land, Labour, and Group Formation: Blacks and Indians in the United States," *Ethnic and Racial Studies*, Vol. 13, No. 3, July 1990 by permission of Routledge Ltd.

and their outcomes, and in particular the fact that those outcomes tend to take a limited number of forms. Among these attempts two seem particularly relevant to the question at hand, offering schematic tools for analysing different outcomes in the United States' racial and ethnic relations: Lieberson (1961) and Blauner (1972).

These are venerable works, and they remain stimulating places to look for ideas and explanations. Blauner's argument can be summarized quickly. He does not explicitly approach the subject of group formation, but he does wish to explain the different historical sociologies of the United States' racial and ethnic populations. He begins by wondering to what extent the analytical tools used to understand the experience of European migrants to the United States can be applied to the experience of so-called third world minorities in the US. He concludes that there are in fact two distinct processes by which minority populations are incorporated into a society: immigration and colonization. The first process is essentially voluntary; in the second, the minority is coerced. Immigrant minorities in the U.S. include most European groups; colonized minorities include African-Americans, many Latinos, Native Americans, and Asians.

The key to Blauner's argument, however, is not simply the mode of entry into the society. It is the different labour systems involved: free and unfree. This distinction is held to be the fundamental determinant of the different histories that characterize these groups subsequent to entry, with each labour system having distinctive effects on the groups involved. The tools traditionally used to analyse free migrants (and free labour systems), he argues, cannot account for the experiences of the unfree, i.e., of people of colour.

Obviously the primary concern in this model is not the differences among 'colonized' groups but the commonalities among them vis-à-vis 'immigrants'. Since it places both Blacks and Indians under the 'colonized' label, it cannot distinguish between these two cases. At the same time, its attention to labour systems is suggestive: Blacks were slaves whereas Indians, for the most part, were not.[1] Perhaps this fact can help to account for the different patterns of group formation in these cases. But a labour system analysis, on its own, cannot cope effectively with two facts. First, for most of the history of Indian-white interaction, Indian labour was, if not wholly ignored, at least not pursued on a large scale by the larger society. Barring a few other exceptions, only in the fur trade, in the earliest years of Indian-white relations, was Indian labour critical to those relations. Second, Indian labour-system involvement, while often enforced by economic circumstances that left few alternatives, was generally free in its form, more closely resembling the European immigrant than the Black case, yet Indian group formation follows a pattern different from both. In sum, neither the emphasis on mode of entry nor that on free versus unfree labour helps particularly with the question posed by this article.

Lieberson's argument is more elaborate. His aim is to account for different outcomes in intergroup relations, including nationalism, assimilation, and group extinction: group formation is at least implicitly a part of his subject. In a situation of intergroup contact and interaction, he argues, the problem for any group is to maintain political and economic conditions compatible with its own established social institutions or ways of doing things. Noting that ethnic contact typically involves at least one indigenous (or well-established) population and at least one migrant population, Lieberson suggests that the critical factor shaping the resolution of this problem has to do with which of these groups is superordinate and which subordinate in the early stages of contact. Where the migrating group is superior in technology and organization, it usually imposes its way of doing things on the indigenous population, often with drastic consequences such as intense conflict, steep indigenous population declines, and the collapse of indigenous institutions. Where the indigenous population is superior to the migrating group, on the other hand, conflict tends to be reduced or at least less dramatic. The indigenous population typically has substantial control over immigration and can limit numbers if it so desires, removing much of the threat to indigenous institutions, while many migrant populations retain the option of returning to the sending society. Migrants are introduced into the indigenous economy instead of forcibly reconstructing it to suit their needs or interests.

Lieberson's article, which is more subtle than so brief a summary can convey, has justly become a classic, but it turns out to be of limited help with the issue at hand. Certainly in the matter of conflict his scheme appears to work. Black-white conflict historically has been low, largely as a consequence of the very high degree of control that whites (the superordinate indigenous or well-established group) exercised over Black-white relations. Indian-white conflict historically has been high as Native Americans (the subordinate indigenous group) fiercely resisted European invasion.

The issue here, however, has to do not with the degree of intergroup conflict but with transformations in collective identity, and in particular with the apparent timing of the emergence of a racial consciousness in the Black and Indian cases. In the Black case, the indigenous population is superordinate: in the Indian case, the indigenous population is subordinate. But in neither case does assimilation occur; on the contrary, racial solidarity is the eventual outcome in both. Importantly, however, this racial solidarity comes at very different times: early among Blacks, late among Indians. While the difference in indigenous/migrant superordination helps to account for the variation in conflict in the two cases, it does not appear to account for these very different trajectories of group formation. Indeed, the suggestion in Lieberson's argument is that subordinate indigenous populations rapidly undergo significant institutional transformations leading to consolidation and a comprehensive racial consciousness. Certainly, Indian tribes underwent such transformations, but in many cases much of the indigenous institutional repertoire survived, while the anticipated racial consciousness took a very long time indeed to emerge. These facts cannot be explained using only the factors that Lieberson identifies. Other factors must be taken into account.

The approach taken here is broadly informed by what has come to be known as the 'resource competition' perspective. In broadest terms, the key suppositions of this perspective are that ethnic identification is substantially a response to economic and political interests—people emphasize ethnic boundaries when it is in their interest to do so—and that the salience of ethnic boundaries and ethnic conflict is largely a function of competition for scarce resources (e.g., Banton 1983; Despres 1975; Olzak and Nagel 1986).

Given its concern with collective action, the resource competition approach focuses squarely on group formation, or, in its own terms, on the dynamics of ethnic boundaries. It suggests that we look to the political and economic interests of various groups in order to understand the boundaries of group identification and the collective bases of

mobilization. But group formation is shaped not only by material interests; it is shaped as well by concrete organizational and conceptual possibilities and constraints. In the Indian and Black cases, at least, these factors, and in particular the organizational ones, are driven in part by the distinctive character of the specific resources that are at stake and the political systems developed to manage access to those resources. *What groups compete for* and *how they compete* turn out to be important determinants of group formation.

In other words, the key to the larger Indian/Black puzzle lies in foundational processes of economic and political incorporation,[2] processes which themselves responded to fundamental systemic needs. In the Black case the systemic need was for labour; in the Indian case it was for land.[3] These needs were pursued through specific, and different, systems of economic and political organization. These differing combinations of economic demand and political/economic organization to meet that demand led to quite different trajectories of group formation, setting the terms within which each group forged distinctive self-concepts and sought out different bases of collective action. The economic organization of slavery and the political organization of southern society sustained race as the primary principle of collective identity in Black-white relations, while the treaty-based tribal-federal relationship, itself derivative in part of the need for land, sustained political tribalism in Indian-white relations. The result in the Black case was that the need for labour, combined with the political and economic tools for its expropriation, ultimately undermined African ethnic identities and promoted a Black, racial consciousness. In the Indian case, the need for land, combined with the tools for *its* expropriation, ultimately preserved tribal identities and inhibited the emergence of a supratribal, Indian consciousness.

The remainder of this article offers an analytical overview of the process of group formation, and then examines these two cases more closely.

THE PROCESS OF GROUP FORMATION

Group formation is a process of boundary construction: the drawing of social boundaries sufficiently salient to organize self-consciously collective life and action (cf. Barth 1969). This process takes place at the point where structure and agency intersect. Boundaries, in other words—and therefore groups—are formed and transformed in the continuing interaction between the structure of opportunities available to persons in their encounters with successive social environments, and their own attempts to act upon or within that opportunity structure.

The process itself is set in motion by social change: the disruption of existing social ties and relationships and therefore boundaries. Disruption may result from long-term events such as migration, urbanization, economic or demographic transitions, or from shorter-term events such as warfare, epidemic, natural disaster, or political upheaval. Short or long, what these events initiate are new interactions between preexisting but disrupted populations on the one hand and new structures of opportunity (which are also structures of constraint) on the other. These interactions, in turn, typically either demand reconceptualization of the self, or require reorganization of the social arena into newly manageable categories, or stimulate new competition over scarce resources and thereby necessitate solidary group formation. So the critical event is confrontation between disrupted populations and new opportunity structures.

These structures of opportunity and constraint are constructed in various ways. Generally speaking, they emerge as products of two kinds of factors. The first is the actions of more powerful segments of the society that intentionally limit the opportunities enjoyed by incoming or transformed subject populations. An example would be the effort to exclude Chinese immigrants from certain sectors of the economy in late-nineteenth-century California (Saxton 1971), or simply the systematic discrimination against Blacks and other peoples of colour throughout U.S. history. The second is the consequences of ongoing societal developments—the decline of manufacturing, jobs in major cities, for example—that are essentially indifferent to those populations. But whatever their derivations, such structures typically include three elements.

First, they are structures of economic opportunity, sets of possible positions in the economic system which, combined with the human capital or other resources of newcomers, shape the potential pattern of individual or collective incorporation into that system (see, for example, Steinberg 1981;

Yancey, Erikson, and Juliani 1976). The critical features of such structures from the point of view of group formation have to do with boundedness, exhaustiveness, and density. That is, to the extent that those positions are available only to members of the subject population, to the extent that they exhaust the available set of opportunities for that population, and to the extent that they provide opportunities for personal interactions within the boundary thus described, they maximize the probabilities of group formation, leading to a consciousness of the group itself as distinct and in some way interconnected (cf. Oberschall 1973).

Second, they are structures of political opportunity. The organizational structures of states are typically discriminatory. Via the franchise, legal provisions, administrative organization and other, less formal constraints, they treat certain classes of interests or of persons differently from others, and thereby both construct group boundaries and shape opportunities for group action (Nagel 1986; Skocpol 1985). Thus, for example, administrative provisions in many European colonies specified both the rules and the collective bases of political participation, in effect constructing groups through the political process (Young 1976). In the contemporary United States affirmative-action programmes not only shape material opportunities for certain populations, but they also specify relevant boundaries of identification and action, and thereby help to create or sustain those boundaries, sometimes at the expense of others (see, for example, Padilla 1985). Less formally organized structures of power can have similar effects. To the extent that such structures reinforce intragroup ties and undermine intergroup ties, they promote group formation.

And third, the opportunity structure is also conceptual: it is a structure of available categories or bases of identification (see, for example, Dominguez 1986, and, more generally, Shibutani and Kwan 1965). This is clearly the case in formal political arrangements that specify group boundaries and entitlements, but conceptual opportunities can be less formally organized as well. To illustrate: recent black migrants to the city of Somerville, Massachusetts, from the Cape Verde islands typically came, in their own minds, as Cape Verdeans or Portuguese. On arrival, however, they had to deal with the local classification scheme, the categories that members of local communities use to organize the world around them. This scheme had a Portuguese 'slot'—Portuguese migrants and their descendants being common in eastern Massachusetts—but the Cape Verdeans, being black, did not seem to fit. There was no Cape Verdean 'slot' as their numbers were relatively few, but there was a 'slot' for Blacks, and that is how, eventually, the newcomers were categorized. By the second generation, reports Ito-Adler (1980), even Cape Verdeans were thinking of themselves as Black (see also Woldemikael 1989).

Italian migrants of several generations ago found themselves in a similar situation. Coming not as Italians but as Neapolitans or Sicilians or as carriers of even narrower village identities, they discovered that the classification scheme of the larger society was incapable of such fine distinctions. In the informal taxonomy of the society-at-large they were Italians, and this, among other things, encouraged the emergence of a more comprehensive Italian-American identity and group (Alba 1985).

Thus the opportunity set constructs not only the subordinate group's experience of the society through its construction of relationships. To varying degrees it also shapes, in a reflexive fashion and through the prevailing pattern of discourse, taxonomy, and policy, the group's experience of itself (see, for example, Gomez 1986).

Of course these three aspects of the opportunity or constraint system are interactive. Other things being equal, similarly subordinated populations will tend not to organize collectively if the prevailing classification scheme treats them as separate and distinct groups, but are more likely to so organize if they are treated conceptually as a single population.

At the same time, within the limits of the opportunity structure—and often against it—people also assert their own conceptions of who they are, of where the appropriate boundaries lie. Their logic is variable. It may simply reflect received categories, an attempt to carry learned boundaries and self-concepts across the disruptive divide, to maintain an already-existing sense of self that makes the world intelligible and provides an effective guide to action. This is often evident early in migration, forced or voluntary, before an analysis of the new social situation has had time to promote a reconceptualization of how the relevant world is organized.

Alternatively, assertion may reflect particular socio-economic or political interests. James Loewen has written, for example, of Chinese in Mississippi, descendants of workers brought there after the Civil War in an effort to replace portions of the Black plantation labour force. These migrants and their descendants found themselves in a social order still organized on a racial basis, in which there were only two categories, white and Black. Realizing the costs of being classified as Black, they struggled either to be classified as white, or to force the system to establish a third category, Chinese (Loewen 1971). Similarly, Chinese migrants to Jamaica organized on a Chinese basis because it was clear to them that their chances for economic success would be enhanced to the extent that they could maintain themselves as a distinct and solidary group (Patterson 1975).

Thus group formation, as Ito-Adler (1980) has pointed out, takes place as an interaction between assignment and assertion, or, in the terms of this article, between the structure of opportunities and constraints on the one hand and the assertions of agents—the entering or disrupted populations—on the other (cf. See and Wilson 1988). The outcome of that interaction, of course, is highly contingent, dependent on the resources each set of actors is able to bring to bear on the system as a whole.

To understand group formation, then, we need to ask three questions:

First, what kinds of group organization—what associations of human beings—does the structure of political and economic opportunity make possible and likely?

Second, what bases of identification and action—what self-concepts—does the dominant pattern of discourse—the conceptual opportunity structure—make available?

And third, what intentions and what conceptual and other resources do disrupted populations bring to their encounter with altered circumstance?

Answers to these questions can help solve the puzzle of Black and Indian group formation.

THE EMERGENCE OF A BLACK RACIAL CONSCIOUSNESS

Black American involvement with the society that is now the United States has a history longer than that of almost any other American minority population. The common discourse about that history is largely a discourse about "Black" or "African-American" history: along with the larger colloquial culture, it suggests the historical existence of a single people, a self-consciously solidary population that shares far more internally than it does with non-blacks. Current intellectual debates often underline this suggestion. Much of the discussion regarding contemporary black political economy wrestles uneasily with recent signs of division, with the possibility that a more or less solidary population may be fragmenting along class or other lines into multiple constituencies, some with growing circumstantial links to non-blacks (e.g., Petersen 1987; Wilson 1978; 1987).

Yet the Africans who came to North America came not, in their own minds, as Blacks or African-Americans, as members of some monolithic population, but as carriers of hugely diverse cultures and ethnic identities. This diversity was made inevitable by their geographic origins: from Senegambia to Angola on Africa's Atlantic coast, the area from which the bulk of slaves bound for the United States were shipped, is a distance of more than 3,000 miles. Inland from this coast lay a vast universe of peoples, languages, and lifeways. Other slaves came from still more distant parts of the continent (on the origins of American slaves, see Rawley 1981).

This immense diversity was by no means lost on slave-traders or slave-owners. Advertisements of new slave cargoes frequently referred to ethnic origins, while slave-owners often purchased slaves on the basis of national identities and the characteristics they supposedly indicated (Rawley 1981). While the trans-Atlantic crossing itself mixed slaves from different groups, regional and even national concentrations often survived. Up to and often through the Middle Passage, African-Americans formed not one but many peoples.

The crucible of slavery, however, transformed these populations. Several factors were prominent in this process, among them the market mechanisms of slavery, the concerns of slave-holders, the political and legal status of slaves, and the classificatory terms of the society at large. Because the market for slaves operated not as a market for groups of persons but as a market in individual human beings, it had the inevitable effect of systematically breaking down ethnic concentrations, over time dispersing members of a single group and producing, in any given location, a mixture of peoples. Certainly there were exceptions, areas where substantial, ethnically-linked African populations survived, but the overall effect was to undermine indigenous group structures.

Concerns for security reinforced such market effects. Fearing the insurrectionary potential of ethnic concentrations, slave-holders often tried to keep such concentrations small, mixing the origins of their human property. Newly-arrived slaves were mixed with old, African with West Indian; ethnic groups and language groups were systematically split apart (Huggins 1979).

At the same time, slavery brought Africans into a society in which the overwhelming organizing factor was race. More than anything else, race determined life chances and entitlements. Race and power were covariant, but not continuously. The dichotomies were sharply drawn: black and white, powerlessness and power. In such a situation ethnic distinctions carried from Africa had little relevance at the societal level; their organizational significance was miniscule next to the monstrous importance of colour.

Furthermore, the prevailing terms used to delineate collective identity in the society-at-large were also dichotomous. While slave-traders and some slave-owners may have maintained an awareness of subracial distinctions, the broader social discourse tended to ignore them, relying on negro, coloured, or black on the one hand, white on the other, and thus reinforcing in language the organizational foundation of the society (Jordan 1968; Omi and Winant 1986).

This combination of ethnic mixing and racial subordination had a number of critical effects. It led to the rapid emergence of pidgin and creole languages and, ultimately, to the spread of English within the Black population (Genovese 1976; Mintz 1971). Writing of the 'Afro-Americanization' of slaves, Nathan Huggins (1979, p. 62) states simply: 'Bridges of language were the first efforts to link them into one people.'

These processes also initiated and eventually accomplished the emergence of a broad community of common and distinctive culture. Building on African roots, slaves quickly began to construct institutions—not only language but kinship systems, religion, customary practice—designed to cope with the severely constraining circumstances of slavery, along with world-views and expressive culture which tied together persons of diverse origins (see, for example, Genovese 1976; Huggins 1979; Raboteau 1978; Rawick 1972; Stuckey 1987; Wood 1974). 'With some regional variation,' argues Thomas Webber (1978, p. 243), 'the preparation of food, the songs and stories, the language, and most important, the themes of quarter communities throughout the South were similar.' 'Slaves,' writes Lawrence Levine (1977, p. 80), 'created and maintained a world apart.'

And finally, these processes powerfully encouraged a racial consciousness, reminding African-Americans constantly of the disproportionate importance of what they shared, in comparison to what they did not. In his analysis of slave narratives, Paul Escott reports that

> the narratives make clear that masters and slaves lived in different worlds, indeed. The evil of enslavement and the strength of cultural differences set these two groups apart from each other and gave the slaves a fundamental sense of themselves as an oppressed racial group. (1979, p. 20)

He goes on to say (p. 65): 'For the great majority their common plight had generated a common outlook and a sense that blacks faced the same problems in relation to whites.'

Thus the organization of slavery undermined distinct African national or ethnic identities, while the organization of society promoted comprehensive racial ones. This is not to say that distinct African cultures did not survive in various forms, but only that the bases of individual and collective identity and action rapidly moved from ethnicity towards race. At the heart of that process lay the labour-based incorporation of Blacks into the larger society, combined with a strictly racial pattern of political stratification and a set of classificatory terms that organized the world by race. The result was to set in motion a distinctive trajectory of racial group formation.

It was not, of course, a momentary process. The culture of Black America in slavery, and the identity rooted in it, was built generationally, drawing on multiple sources and fashioned in the extended experience of subordination. While much of what we know of slave culture may come from the first half of the nineteenth century, when that culture was well advanced, the basic point remains: from early in their history in what is now the United States, Blacks found a common experience and a common cause, and the result

was a gradual but continuous process of group construction.

None of which is to say that this emergent community was infinitely solidary. Not only were there regional variations in culture and consciousness, but within plantation communities there were often significant divisions, while internal stratification, particularly in large plantation labour forces, was itself a source of conflict. What is more, the lack of comprehensive Black organizations in the South in the ante-bellum period—they were, of course, impossible under prevailing political conditions—make the nature and extent of a comprehensive and self-conscious Black 'group' difficult to delineate precisely.

That group becomes dramatically apparent, on the other hand, early in Reconstruction, in the immediate aftermath of slavery. With the political and legal constraints substantially removed, at least for a time, there is an outburst of Black organizational and political activity throughout the South, activity that makes clear the presence of a vital, comprehensive, and politicized racial consciousness (Franklin Litwack 1979). Furthermore, it is a consciousness that contests not so much the category as its content: at issue in these years is not the racial boundary but the value attached to it and the consequent denial of equality.

Of course the constraints of slavery were soon replaced with new controls, maintaining the basic pattern of group formation. In the second half of the nineteenth century and the first half of the twentieth, both national and local state policies and the *de facto* organization of local politics continued to emphasize the fundamental importance of Black/white distinctions. Both in the South, where the political rights established in the aftermath of the Civil War were systematically withdrawn in the last decades of the nineteenth century, and in the North, where migrant Blacks in the first half of this century found themselves denied full participation in the political institutions, in particular the urban political machines, that most closely controlled their fortunes (Katznelson 1976), the state stepped in to protect the powers and interests of non-blacks. The systematic exploitation of Black labour may not have played as central a role in these developments as it did in slavery—other issues were often at stake, and at times the object was as much to exclude Black labour from certain parts of the economy as to make use of it—but the trajectory of group formation set in place under slavery was sustained by patterns of political incorporation that drew as sharp a boundary around the Black population as the need for labour had done in centuries past.

In the last two decades, however, that boundary has begun to show signs of strain, not so much as a consequence of any decline in its importance for the society at large, but because of its apparent discontinuity with the experiences of some African-Americans. The success of the civil rights movement in more securely establishing political rights, the growth of structurally-founded economic divisions within the Black population, and the emergence of cultural differences accompanying those divisions have produced on what seems a far larger scale than before a divergent set of interests and self-concepts within that population. Widespread discrimination and a rigid conceptual apparatus continue to operate in the society at large, but their unifying effects are being challenged at some levels by gradually changing political and economic opportunity structures and altered Black perceptions (Collins 1983; Wilson 1978; 1987). As a consequence we may be seeing a change in the trajectory of Black group formation.

INDIANS: TRIBALISM AND SUPRATRIBALISM

How does this compare with the Indian case? Native Americans likewise have a lengthy history of involvement with Euro-American society, but the pattern of their involvement is very different. It is, in its own way, no less oppressive: Indian enslavement was common only in the earliest years and in limited areas, but the expropriation of Indian lands, taken as a whole, was an extraordinarily violent enterprise. But herein lies the point: only in the earliest stage of Indian-white relations was Indian labour critical to those relations or to the development of the larger society (Cornell 1988a). This fact has significant consequences for group formation among Native Americans.

Like Africans, Indians formed no monolithic population when they first came into contact with Euro-Americans. As Hazel Hertzberg (1971) has written, at the time of contact the Indian nations were culturally far more diverse than the European ones. Organizationally various, carriers of a multitude of languages and cultures, and of distinct and elaborate identities, they at first had little sense of the socio-cultural distances or the geographical origins that separated them as a general category from the Europeans. Indeed, Robert Thomas (1968) argues that early tribespeople looked at the first Europeans as simply another variety of stranger; more peculiar, perhaps, than most, and possessors of unusual powers, but primarily as part of a world of nations—Indian and white—very different from themselves.

They also lacked, in many cases, the kinds of rigid boundaries that we have come to associate with nationhood. While some of the groups today called tribes were at contact clearly defined corporate bodies, many, if not most, were not, but instead comprised shifting sets of allegiances and interactions among culturally-homogeneous but highly autonomous, kinship-linked collectivities (see Cornell 1988b).

Like Africans also, Indians in the early years were of interest to Euro-Americans primarily as workers. But it was a very different, and relatively short-lived, pattern of labour that was involved.

At the heart of Indian-white relations in the seventeenth and much of the eighteenth centuries lay not the quest for Indian lands so much as the quest for other resources that Indians controlled. Heading the list of those resources were animal hides and furs. For the better part of a century and a half, the fur trade was the centrepiece of Indian-white relations in the eastern United States, and it was substantially dependent on Indian labour. Only Indians had access to the large fur-bearing populations of animals; only Indians had the requisite hunting and processing skills; only Indians could provide the labour force necessary for large-scale fur production. It was Indian procurement and processing of furs that made possible a broad set of economic and political relationships between Europeans and the Indian nations (Jennings 1976).

But this was a kind of labour quite distinct from that in which, African-Americans were involved. Both the fur trade and the relationships that it supported were more or less freely entered into by Native Americans. They retained control of the production process, met Europeans not at the point of production but in the marketplace, with a finished product in hand, and used the trade to maximize their own political power. It was different in another, crucial way as well: it was temporary. With the passing of the fur trade, which

—with a few exceptions, most importantly in Canada and the northern plains—was over as an Indian enterprise by late in the eighteenth century, labour disappeared as a critical element in Indian-white relations.

From the late-eighteenth century on, it was not labour but land that lay at the heart of those relations (see Jacobson 1984). What was of interest to the larger society was not Indians themselves but Indian lands. For the next century the expropriation of those lands became the organizing enterprise in Indian-white relations. Indian labour was not wholly ignored—in parts of California, Nevada, and the southwest, for example, Indian workers played significant roles in local economies (Hurtado 1982; Jacobson 1984; Knight 1978; Phillips 1980; Spicer 1962)—but it was no longer the organizing principle of widespread formal or informal relations between Indians and whites.

The result was that Indians were seldom incorporated into larger economic structures as individual workers, but instead were removed *en masse* from lands desired by whites and relocated on less valuable lands remote from Euro-American society. Furthermore, this process was accomplished through a series of treaties signed between the United States and separately sovereign, if increasingly powerless, Indian nations. That is, the structure of political relations refined a trajectory of group formation already set in motion by the economic agenda. Politics supported economics: tribal lands were obtained through formal relations with tribal bodies. This reinforced emergent national (tribal) identities, many rooted in aboriginal experience, and discouraged the development of a comprehensive, supratribal consciousness.

Had Indians been important primarily as a labour force, these group concentrations, presumably, would have been broken up. Individuals would have moved into the larger economy in response to market forces or coercion, and a massive dispersion leading eventually either to an emergent Indian consciousness or to assimilation would have occurred. But land, not labour, was at issue. Thus the peculiar 'fit' between the economic needs of the larger society and the resources of Native Americans set in place a fundamentally different trajectory of group formation.

In the aftermath of the forced expropriation of Indian lands, reformist politics sustained this trajectory. The reservation system that emerged in the mid- to late-nineteenth century further promoted the same, preservative process, but towards different ends. Committed to the cultural transformation of Indians into whites, the federal government looked upon the reservations as both refuge and school, where older and unsalvageable tribespeople could be allowed to fade away, while the young were educated and prepared for participation in the larger society, all under the benevolently tutelary protection of the government (Hagan 1976; Trennert 1975).

But even as policy sought, quite explicitly, to destroy tribalism and to seed American individualism in its place, the organization of Indian affairs inadvertently undermined the enterprise. The reservation system itself tended to sustain tribal identities, and to sustain the landbased communities that a labour-oriented set of relations would almost certainly have destroyed.

To be sure, the terms or discourse necessary for a more comprehensive identity were available; the larger society tended to think not in tribal but in 'Indian' terms, while Indian policy, especially as time went on, came to be articulated more and more in Indian terms as well. Native Americans were not only aware of this more comprehensive, assigned identity but often used the term 'Indian' themselves. But the practical organization and administration of Indian affairs meant that an Indian identity had far less relevance to their daily lives than tribal identities did (Cornell 1988a). Despite a continuing conceptual scheme that emphasized Indianness as the identity of consequence, experience taught otherwise, and helped to sustain tribalism.

This pattern lasted well into the present century. As late as the early 1940s it is difficult to find a substantial number of Indians who organized and acted on the basis of an 'Indian' identity. Tribe remained both focal point and vehicle of Indian experience and aspiration.

It was not until World War II and the following decades, when large numbers of Indians began moving to American cities, that a large-scale, supratribal consciousness began to emerge as a widespread basis of action. This is not to say that a supratribal politics was absent before the mid-twentieth century. But it was a politics largely removed from the day-to-day life of the reservations and the experience of most tribespeople. In the 1950s and 1960s, however, in American cities, Indians not only began to form significant multi-tribal communities, but they moved into a political situation in which tribal identities had little relevance. The problems of urban areas were better approached on an Indian, as opposed to a tribal, basis. At the same time, as a consequence of the federal 'termination' policy of the 1950s, which threatened tribal survival, tribes themselves began to understand the necessity of co-operation. By the 1960s a supratribal politics, rooted in an emergent supratribal identity, was appearing on a large scale (Bahr 1972; Cornell 1988a). Ironically, however, that identity, shaped substantially by the Euro-American conception of 'Indians', became itself a resource turned to less comprehensive agendas as various tribes articulated their claims in 'Indian' terms and thus gained support well beyond their own boundaries.[4]

DISCUSSION

By way of summary: African peoples brought to the United States encountered an economic system that systematically broke down ethnic or subracial group identities and emphasized race as the primary boundary; a political system that coercively supported the comprehensive boundary organized by economy; and a conceptual scheme in the society at large that employed and reinforced the same. Economy, polity, and conception were unanimous in their implications and their effects.

Furthermore, and importantly, they constructed a Black experience that in turn reinforced the same trajectory of group formation. Black experience was, in fact, organized racially, and consequently Black assertions—as during early Reconstruction—were made on a racial basis as well. Much of the Black struggle has had to do not so much with altering the boundary as with changing its implications and consequences.

Indians likewise encountered a conceptual scheme that emphasized the racial boundary: what mattered to the society at large was not tribal but Indian identity. However, owing largely to the nature of the resource the larger society coveted and the power that Indian nations at contact possessed, the economic and political structures that governed their relations ultimately supported the ethnic or subracial identities by which Native Americans themselves organized their world.

Because of that distinctive organization, Indian assertions, with some important exceptions but virtually until the last three or four decades, have been for the most part tribal assertions. Much of the Indian agenda has been to persuade the larger society to recognize tribalism as something more than just the political residue of historical processes. Only when it made sense in the Indian experience—that is, in the last few decades—did Native Americans themselves begin to assert on a major scale the supratribal identity the larger society had long assigned to them.

Thus the patterns of group formation in the African-American and Indian cases turn out to be more complex than certain of our traditional analytical conceptions, such as Blauner's (1972) and Lieberson's (1961), allow. The nature of the resources at issue in group interaction, of the political tools employed to secure those resources, and of the prevailing societal conceptions of the groups involved, all contribute to distinctive trajectories of collective identification.

In this regard, three general points need to be made. First, the fundamental distinction around which these two trajectories of group formation diverge is economic. In the Black case we have a labour-oriented history of intergroup relations which, over time, undermines a pre-existing set of identities and provides the foundation for another, more comprehensive one. In the Indian case we have a land-oriented history of intergroup relations which, over time, sustains a pre-existing set of identities and inhibits the emergence of another, more comprehensive one.

On the other hand—and this is the second point—economy alone cannot carry the full burden of explanation. It may have been the labour markets of slavery and the concerns of slave-holders that undermined African identities, but it was the political organization of slavery and, in later years, institutionalized discrimination that enforced the more comprehensive boundary, leading Blacks to replace African ethnic identities with a comprehensive racial one. It was political factors also, combined with a classificatory tradition systematically reproduced in the institutions of daily life, that sustained the racial schematic long past slavery, so that Caribbean migrants and others—even Cape Verdeans today—are received as 'Blacks', and eventually become so (Bryce-Laporte 1972; Ito-Adler 1980; Waters 1988; Woldemikael 1989).

Similarly, it was the tribal-federal relationship, embedded in treaties that carry eminent legal standing in the courts of the United States and realized in the reservation system that remains to this day, that helped to sustain the original pattern of Indian group formation long after the quest for Indian lands had abated. It was this same relationship that encouraged Indians, when acting politically, to proceed in tribal terms, The different patterns of political incorporation, then, while linked as tools to the economic imperatives noted here, have their own distinctive effects.

These political effects continue today, often in new forms. Affirmative-action programmes replicate and reinforce group boundaries, while the needs of both administrators and claimants for government services shape collective identities. On the US Census race question, Indians are asked for a tribal identification, while Black immigrants to the United States must identify themselves as Black to be eligible for certain government programmes. In both cases also, the classificatory systems of the larger society set the terms on which much of intergroup interaction proceeds, offering to each group a particular logic of collective identity and action.

But there is still more to it. The land/labour distinction, resultant political relations, and interpenetrating conceptual schemas go a long way towards constructing groups. But what of the groups involved? Are they innocent in the formative process, merely products of circumstances beyond their control? Or do they, in some way, construct themselves?

Surely they do, and this is the third point. We tend too often to see group formation as essentially circumstantially determined. Circumstances do create groups, but not on their own. Rather, they shape and constrain a process whose ultimate outcomes are products not only of circumstance but of action as well. Indians had choices, larger ones than Blacks. During much of the last century and a half, Indians have been invited, indeed encouraged, to leave the tribal embrace and enter the larger society as free individuals. Some have chosen to do so. Far more have chosen not to. They, too, are the builders of groups. Furthermore, Indians might have chosen, much sooner than they did, to organize on a supratribal basis. Certainly, that identity was promoted vigorously enough by a society and a series of policy regimes

that often refused to recognize the profound differences that existed among Native American peoples. Yet a supratribal identity emerged on a large and productive scale not when it made sense to whites, which it did virtually from contact on, but when it made sense to Indians, which happened only recently.

African-Americans, too, asserted their own notions of who they were. Their alternatives were fewer, the shaping influence of circumstance more powerful. But even as the form of Black identity responded to the severe constraints they faced, the content of that identity—the subjective meanings that the racial boundary signified—challenged the negative implications of those constraints, and asserted a far more positive sense of peoplehood. Within a structure imposed from without, Blacks formed a community of their own, and one at odds with the dehumanizing message that circumstances, in and of themselves, conveyed.

Group formation, then, is both a multi-dimensional process, in which economic, political, and conceptual apparatuses interact, and a contested one, in which populations both discover who and what the larger world will allow them to be, and struggle to assert their own distinctive notions of who they are.

ENDNOTES

1. Indians were enslaved at various times in parts of America north of the Rio Grande, particularly in the southern colonies and in Spanish California. Overall, however, Indian slavery involved relatively few Indians, and was only occasionally a critical factor in regional economics.
2. By incorporation I refer to the pattern of political and economic relationships linking subordinate populations to larger societies, and to the process of constructing those relationships. For a different but complementary, and considerably more detailed and elaborate, conception, see Hall (1986; 1987).
3. Lieberson notes that Indian populations were not widely used for their labour power. But—understandably, given the intent of his paper—he does not take the next step of considering which Indian resources *were* at issue, and what the consequences were for indigenous processes of group formation.
4. In both the Indian and the Black cases, of course, there are problems in objectively identifying those populations whose subjective identities are at issue, and in disentangling the various identities they carry. These problems are beyond the scope of this article, but see, for example, Petersen (1987); Snipp (1986).

The Construction of the Ghetto

Douglas S. Massey
Nancy A. Denton

The problem of the 20th Century is the problem of the color line.

W. E. B. Du Bois

Surveying the harsh black-and-white landscape of contemporary urban America, it is hard to imagine a time when people of European and African origin were not highly segregated from one another. In an era when Watts, Harlem, and Roxbury are synonymous with black geographic and social isolation, it is easy to assume that U.S. cities have always been organized to achieve a physical separation of the races. The residential segregation of blacks and whites has been with us so long that it seems a natural part of the social order, a normal and unremarkable feature of America's urban landscape.

Yet it wasn't always so. There was a time, before 1900, when blacks and whites lived side by side in American cities. In the north, a small native black population was scattered widely throughout white neighborhoods. Even Chicago, Detroit, Cleveland, and Philadelphia—cities now well known for their large black ghettos—were not segregated then. In southern cities such as Charleston, New Orleans, and Savannah, black servants and laborers lived on alleys and side streets near the mansions of their white employers. In this lost urban world, blacks were more likely to share a neighborhood with whites than with other blacks.

In most cities, to be sure, certain neighborhoods could be identified as places where blacks lived; but before 1900 these areas were not predominantly black, and most blacks didn't live in them. No matter what other disadvantages urban blacks suffered in the aftermath of the Civil War, they were not residentially segregated from whites. The two racial groups moved in a common social world, spoke a common language, shared a common culture, and interacted personally on a regular basis. In the north, especially, leading African American citizens often enjoyed relations of considerable trust, respect, and friendship with whites of similar social standing.

Of course, most blacks did not live in northern cities, and didn't experience these benign conditions. In 1870, 80% of black Americans still lived in the rural south, where they were exploited by a sharecropping system that was created by white landowners to replace slavery; they were terrorized by physical violence and mired in an institutionalized cycle of ignorance and poverty. Over the next century, however, blacks in the rural south increasingly sought refuge and betterment in burgeoning cities of the south and north. By 1970, 80% of black Americans lived in urban areas, and nearly half were located outside the south.

This shift of blacks from south to north and from farm to city radically transformed the form, nature, and substance of African American life in the United States. As we shall see, the way in which blacks from the rural south were incorporated into the geographic structure of American cities in the years after 1900 proved to be decisive in determining the path of black so-

Reprinted by permission of the publisher from *American Apartheid* by Douglas S. Massey and Nancy A. Denton, Cambridge, Mass.: Harvard University Press, Copyright © 1993 by the President and Fellows of Harvard College. References have been omitted.

cial and economic development later in the twentieth century.

Southern blacks were not the only rural people migrating to American cities at the turn of the century. Between 1880 and 1920 millions of eastern and southern Europeans arrived as well, and after 1920 their place was taken by a growing number of Mexicans. For these groups, however, U.S. cities served as vehicles for integration, economic advancement, and, ultimately, assimilation into American life. For rural blacks, in contrast, cities became a trap—yet another mechanism of oppression and alienation. The urban ghetto, constructed during the first half of the twentieth century and successively reinforced thereafter, represents the key institutional arrangement ensuring the continued subordination of blacks in the United States.

The term "ghetto" means different things to different people. To some observers it simply means a black residential area; to others it connotes an area that is not only black but very poor and plagued by a host of social and economic problems. In order to distinguish clearly between race and class in discussing black residential patterns, our use of the term "ghetto" refers only to the racial make-up of a neighborhood; it is not intended to describe anything about a black neighborhood's class composition. For our purposes, a ghetto is a set of neighborhoods that are exclusively inhabited by members of one group, within which virtually all members of that group live. By this definition, no ethnic or racial group in the history of the United States, except one, has ever experienced ghettoization, even briefly. For urban blacks, the ghetto has been the paradigmatic residential configuration for at least eighty years.

The emergence of the black ghetto did not happen as a chance by-product of other socioeconomic processes. Rather, white Americans made a series of deliberate decisions to deny blacks access to urban housing markets and to reinforce their spatial segregation. Through its actions and inactions, white America built and maintained the residential structure of the ghetto. Sometimes the decisions were individual, at other times they were collective, and at still other times the powers and prerogatives of government were harnessed to maintain the residential color line; but at critical points between the end of the Civil War in 1865 and the passage of the Fair Housing Act in 1968, white America chose to strengthen the walls of the ghetto.

BEFORE THE GHETTO

At the close of the Civil War, American cities were just beginning to throw off the trappings of their pre-industrial past. Patterns of urban social and spatial organization still reflected the needs of commerce, trade, and small-scale manufacturing. Public transportation systems were crude or nonexistent, and production was largely organized and carried out by extended households or in small shops. People got around by walking, so there was little geographic differentiation between places of work and residence. Land use was not highly specialized, real estate prices were low, and socially distinctive residential areas had not yet emerged. In the absence of structural steel, electricity, and efficient mechanical systems, building densities were low and urban populations were distributed uniformly.

Such an urban spatial structure is not conducive to high levels of segregation by class, race, or ethnicity, and the small African American population that inhabited northern cities before 1900 occupied a niche in the urban geography little different from that of other groups. Before 1900, blacks were not particularly segregated from whites, and although they were overrepresented in the poorest housing and the meanest streets, their residential status did not differ markedly from that of others in the same economic circumstances.

If the disadvantaged residential condition of blacks in the nineteenth century can be attributed to racial prejudice and discrimination, it is to prejudice and discrimination in employment rather than in housing. Because blacks were systematically excluded from most skilled trades and nonmanual employment, they were consigned to a low economic status that translated directly into poor housing. Those few blacks who were able to overcome these obstacles and achieve success in some profession or trade were generally able to improve their housing conditions and acquire a residence befitting their status. Studies of black residential life in northern cities around the time of the Civil War reveal little systematic exclusion from white neighborhoods on the basis of skin color.

Indeed, before 1900 African Americans could be found in most neighborhoods of northern cities. Although blacks at times clustered on certain streets or blocks, they rarely comprised more than 30% of the residents of the immediate area; and these clusters typically were not spatially contiguous. Maps from the period reveal a widely dispersed spatial pattern, with black households being unevenly but widely scattered around the urban landscape. In no city of the nineteenth century is there anything resembling a black ghetto.

This view is verified by historical studies that report quantitative indices of racial segregation. The standard measure of segregation is the index of dissimilarity, which captures the degree to which blacks and whites are evenly spread among neighborhoods in a city. Evenness is defined with respect to the racial composition of the city as a whole. If a city is 10% black, then an even residential pattern requires that every neighborhood be 10% black and 90% white. Thus, if a neighborhood is 20% black, the excess 10% of blacks must move to a neighborhood where the black percentage is under 10% to shift the residential configuration toward evenness. The index of dissimilarity gives the percentage of blacks who would have to move to achieve an "even" residential pattern—one where every neighborhood replicates the racial composition of the city.

Several studies have computed dissimilarity indices for American cities circa 1860, and their findings are summarized in the first column of Table 1. These numbers measure the extent of black-white segregation across city "wards," which are large spatial units of 6,000 to 12,000 people that are frequently used to approximate neighborhoods in historical data. A simple rule of thumb in interpreting these indices is that values under 30 are low, those between 30 and 60 are moderate, and anything above 60 is high.

According to these criteria, black-white segregation in northern cities was quite moderate around 1860. The average index was 46, meaning that, on average, just under half of urban blacks would have to move to achieve an even, or "integrated," city. Wilmington, San Francisco, and St. Louis had especially modest indices of 26.1, 34.6, and 39.1, respectively. The only city that displayed a segregation index in the high range (barely) was Boston, with a value of 61.3. Boston's segregation, however, was much lower earlier in the century,

with an index of only 44.4 in 1830. Moreover, even though segregation was relatively high in 1860, by 1890 it had gone back to a moderate level of 51, and racial segregation did not reach 60 again until 1910.

Black-white segregation scores in the 30 to 60 range are not terribly different from those observed for European immigrant groups in the same period. Before 1880, immigrants to the United States came principally from Ireland and Germany. According to a variety of studies, the level of segregation between these two European groups and native whites ranged from 20 to 45 in northern cities in 1850 and 1860. Thus black segregation scores were only slightly greater than those typical of European immigrant groups in the same era.

Such modest levels of segregation, combined with small black populations, led to substantial contact between blacks and whites in northern cities. This conclusion accords with historical studies of black communities in nineteenth-century northern cities. In places such as Cleveland, Chicago, Detroit, and Milwaukee, the small black communities were dominated by an elite of educated professionals, business owners, and successful tradespeople, most of whom were northern-born or migrants from border states. Within the upper stratum, interracial contacts were frequent, cordial, and often intimate. Members of this elite were frequently of mixed racial origin and tended to be light-skinned. Although the black lower classes usually did not maintain such amicable interracial ties, they too interacted frequently with whites in their places of work and on the streets.

Typical of the northern black elite of the nineteenth century was John Jones, a mulatto who was the "undisputed leader of Chicago's Negro community until his death in 1879." After his arrival in the city in 1845, he established a tailoring shop and built a successful business making clothes for wealthy whites. Before the Civil War, he was prominent in the abolitionist movement, where he had extensive contact with liberal whites, and after the war he ran for the Cook County Board of Commissioners and was elected with widespread white support.

Other members of Chicago's nineteenth-century African American elite included physicians, dentists, journalists, attorneys, and clergymen, all of whom relied substantially on the white com-

TABLE 1 *Indices of Black-White Segregation (Dissimilarity) in Selected Northern and Southern Cities: Circa 1860–1870, 1910, and 1940*

	Free Blacks vs. Whites, circa 1860	Blacks vs. Native Whites, 1910	Nonwhites vs. Whites, 1940
Northern Cities			
Boston	61.3	64.1	86.3
Chicago	50.0	66.8	95.0
Cincinnati	47.9	47.3	90.6
Cleveland	49.0	69.0	92.0
Indianapolis	57.2	—	90.4
Milwaukee	59.6	66.7	92.9
New York	40.6	—	86.8
Philadelphia	47.1	46.0	88.8
St. Louis	39.1	54.3	92.6
San Francisco	34.6	—	82.9
Wilmington	26.1	—	83.0
Average	45.7	59.2	89.2
Southern Cities			
Augusta	—	58.8	86.9
Baltimore	22.1	—	90.1
Charleston	23.2	16.8	60.1
Jacksonville	—	39.4	94.3
Louisville	20.2	—	81.7
Mobile	29.8	—	86.6
Nashville	43.1	—	86.5
New Orleans	35.7	—	81.0
Average	29.0	38.3	81.0

Sources: For first column: Ira Berlin, *Slaves Without Masters: The Free Negro in the Antebellum South* (New York: Pantheon, 1974), pp. 250–65; except Cleveland, which is Kenneth L. Kusmer, *A Ghetto Takes Shape: Black Cleveland, 1870-1930* (Urbana: University of Illinois Press, 1976), p. 43; and Milwaukee, which is Joe William Trotter, Jr., *Black Milwaukee: The Making of an Industrial Proletariat, 1915-45* (Urbana: University of Illinois Press, 1985), p. 23. Segregation is by wards and indices for Cleveland and Milwaukee are for 1870.

For second column: Stanley Lieberson, *Ethnic Patterns in American Cities* (New York: Free Press, 1963), p. 122; except Milwaukee, which is Trotter, *Black Milwaukee,* p. 23; and Augusta, Charleston, and Jacksonville, which are Karl Taeuber and Alma Taeuber, *Negroes in Cities: Residential Segregation and Neighborhood Change* (Chicago: Aldine Publishing, 1965), pp. 49-53. Segregation is by wards and index for Augusta is for 1909.

For third column: Taeuber and Taeuber, *Negroes in Cities,* pp. 39–41. Segregation is by blocks.

munity for economic and political support; and all maintained close social and professional relationships with individual whites. Like Jones, they supported the ideal of integration and opposed the formation of separate black community insti-

tutions. Above all they stressed the importance of economic self-improvement for racial progress.

A similar picture of African American life emerges from other studies of nineteenth-century northern cities. In Cleveland, a light-skinned

African American, Charles W. Chestnut, pursued a highly visible career as a court stenographer, lawyer, and writer, sending his children to integrated schools and maintaining a close circle of white associates. He argued that blacks could best overcome their disabilities by adopting the culture and values of the white middle class. In Detroit, members of the black elite lived a similarly integrated existence and displayed their commitment to integration by attending predominantly white churches. In Milwaukee, the nineteenth-century black elite included a number of successful professionals who catered to white clients, including a lawyer, William T. Green; a dentist, Clifton A. Johnson; and a physician, Allen L. Herron.

A high degree of interracial contact in northern cities is confirmed by an analysis of the racial composition of the neighborhoods inhabited by nineteenth century blacks. Given racial breakdowns for ward populations, the percentage of blacks in the ward of the average black citizen can be computed. This average, known as the isolation index, measures the extent to which blacks live within neighborhoods that are predominantly black. A value of 100% indicates complete ghettoization and means that all black people live in totally black areas; a value under 50% means that blacks are more likely to have whites than blacks as neighbors.

Stanley Lieberson made this calculation for black Americans in seventeen northern cities between 1890 and 1930, and his results are reproduced in Table 2. We see from the first column that blacks in the north tended to live in predominantly white neighborhoods during the nineteenth century. The most "ghettoized" city in 1890 was Indianapolis, where the average black person lived in a neighborhood that was 13% black; in three-quarters of the cities, the percentage was under 10%. In other words, the typical black resident of a nineteenth-century northern city lived in a neighborhood that was close to 90% white. Even in cities that later developed large black ghettos, such as Chicago, Cleveland, Detroit, Los Angeles, Newark, and New York, blacks were more likely to come into contact with whites than with other blacks.

TABLE 2 *Indices of Black Isolation Within Wards of Selected Northern Cities, 1890–1930*

	ISOLATION INDICES BY YEAR				
	1890	*1900*	*1910*	*1920*	*1930*
Boston	8.5	6.4	11.3	15.2	19.2
Buffalo	1.0	4.4	5.7	10.2	24.2
Chicago	8.1	10.4	15.1	38.1	70.4
Cincinnati	9.4	10.1	13.2	26.9	44.6
Cleveland	4.7	7.5	7.9	23.9	51.0
Detroit	5.6	6.4	6.8	14.7	31.2
Indianapolis	12.9	15.1	18.5	23.4	26.1
Kansas City	12.7	13.2	21.7	23.7	31.6
Los Angeles	3.3	3.2	3.8	7.8	25.6
Milwaukee	1.4	2.4	1.9	4.1	16.4
Minneapolis	1.6	1.6	1.7	2.1	1.7
Newark	4.1	5.5	5.4	7.0	22.8
New York	3.6	5.0	6.7	20.5	41.8
Philadelphia	11.7	16.4	15.7	20.8	27.3
Pittsburgh	8.1	12.0	12.0	16.5	26.8
St. Louis	10.9	12.6	17.2	29.5	46.6
San Francisco	1.4	1.1	0.7	1.0	1.7
Average	6.7	7.8	9.7	16.8	29.9

Source: Stanley Lieberson, *A Piece of the Pie: Blacks and White Immigrants Since 1880* (Berkeley: University of California Press, 1980), pp. 266, 288. Isolation is measured by ward.

There is also little evidence of ghettoization among southern blacks prior to 1900. Indeed, segregation levels in the south tend to be lower than those in the north. Prior to the Emancipation Proclamation, urban slaves were intentionally dispersed by whites in order to prevent the formation of a cohesive African American society. Although this policy broke down in the years leading up to the Civil War—when free blacks and slaves who were "living out" gravitated toward black settlements on the urban periphery to escape white supervision—historical studies are consistent in reporting a great deal of racial integration in housing prior to 1900.

The bottom half of Table 1 presents black-white dissimilarity indices computed by several investigators to measure the extent of segregation between whites and free blacks in six southern cities circa 1860. Levels of racial segregation are considerably lower than those observed in the north. The average segregation score of 29 is some 17 points below the average for northern cities and, by the criteria set forth earlier, four of the six cities display indices in the low range (below 30). The most segregated southern city is Nashville, where 43% of free blacks would have had to leave their ward to achieve an even residential configuration.

No study has systematically examined the degree of black isolation within neighborhoods of southern cities in the nineteenth century, but published data on ward populations in Louisville in 1845 and Charleston in 1861 permit us to carry out this calculation ourselves. In Louisville, the average free black lived in a neighborhood that was only 14% black, whereas in Charleston the figure was 45%. The higher figure in the latter city is attributable to the fact that blacks comprised 44% of Charleston's 1861 population, not to higher segregation per se; with an even distribution of blacks and whites in Charleston, every neighborhood would still be 44% black owing to the number of blacks alone. In any event, free blacks in both cities were more likely to share a ward with whites than with other blacks.

Free blacks, of course, were a minority of all African Americans in the antebellum south; most were slaves. The data from Louisville and Charleston reveal, however, that slaves were even less segregated from whites than were free blacks: the slave-white dissimilarity index was 14.2 in Louisville in 1845 and 11.4 in Charleston in 1861. Thus whether one considers slaves or free blacks, there is little evidence of a distinctive black ghetto in southern cities in the nineteenth century. Throughout the south, African Americans were scattered widely among urban neighborhoods and were more likely to share neighborhoods with whites than with members of their own group.

In contrast to the situation in the north, however, residential integration in the postbellum south was not accompanied by a relatively open set of race relations among elites. As the Reconstruction Era drew to a close, black-white relations came to be governed by the increasingly harsh realities of the Jim Crow system, a set of laws and informal expectations that subordinated blacks to whites in all areas of social and economic life. The implementation of Jim Crow did not increase segregation, however, or reduce the frequency of black-white contact; it governed the terms under which integration occurred and strictly regulated the nature of interracial social contacts.

Neighborhoods in many southern cities evolved a residential structure characterized by broad avenues interspersed with small streets and alleys. Large homes on the avenues contained white families, who employed black servants and laborers who lived on the smaller streets. The relationship of master and slave was supplanted by one of master and servant, or a paternalistic relationship between boss and worker. Despite their economic and social subjugation, however, blacks in southern cities continued to have direct personal contacts with whites, albeit on very unequal terms. As in the north, the social worlds of the races overlapped.

CREATING THE GHETTO, 1900–1940

The era of integrated living and widespread interracial contact was rapidly effaced in American cities after 1900 because of two developments: the industrialization of America and the concomitant movement of blacks from farms to cities. The pace of change was most rapid in the north, not only because industrialization was quicker and more complete there, but also because the south's Jim Crow system provided an effective alternative to the ghetto in bringing about the subjugation of blacks. Moreover, the interspersed pattern of black and white settlement in southern cities carried with it a physical inertia that retarded the construction of the ghetto.

Industrialization in the north unleashed a set of social, economic, and technological changes that dramatically altered the urban environment in ways that promoted segregation between social groups. Before industrialization, production occurred primarily in the home or small shop, but by the turn of the century manufacturing had shifted decisively to large factories that employed hundreds of laborers. Individual plants clustered in extensive manufacturing districts together demanded thousands of workers. Dense clusters of tenements and row houses were constructed near these districts to house the burgeoning work force.

The new demand for labor could not be met by native white urbanites alone, so employers turned to migrants of diverse origins. Before World War I, the demand for unskilled labor was met primarily by rural immigrants from southern and eastern Europe. Their migration was guided and structured by social networks that connected them to relatives and friends who had arrived earlier. Drawing upon the ties of kinship and common community origin, the new migrants obtained jobs and housing in U.S. cities, and in this way members of specific ethnic groups were channeled to particular neighborhoods and factories.

At the same time, the need to oversee industrial production—and to administer the wealth it created—brought about a new managerial class composed primarily of native white Americans. As their affluence increased, the retail sector also expanded dramatically. Both administration and retail sales depended on face-to-face interaction, which put a premium on spatial proximity and high population densities. The invention of structural steel and mechanical elevators allowed cities to expand upward in skyscrapers, which were grouped into central business districts that brought thousands of people into regular daily contact. The development of efficient urban rail systems permitted the city to expand outward, creating new residential districts in suburban areas to house the newly affluent class of middle-class managers and service workers.

These developments brought about an unprecedented increase in urban social segregation. Not only was class segregation heightened; but the "new" immigrant groups—Jews, Poles, Italians, Czechs—experienced far more segregation from native whites than did the "old" immigrant groups of Irish and Germans. Whereas European

immigrant segregation, as measured by the index of dissimilarity, rarely exceeded 50 before 1870, after the turn of the century values in the range of 50 to 65 were common.

Southern blacks also formed part of the stream of migrants to American cities, but until 1890 the flow was relatively small; only 70,000 blacks left the south during the 1870s and 80,000 departed during the 1880s. In contrast, the number of European immigrants ran into the millions in both decades. Immigration, however, was cyclical and strongly affected by economic conditions abroad. When the demand for labor in European cities was strong, migration to the United States fell, and when European demand flagged, immigration to the United States rose.

This periodic ebb and flow of European immigration created serious structural problems for American employers, particularly when boom periods in Europe and America coincided. When this occurred, European immigrants moved to their own industrial cities and U.S. factories had difficulty attracting new workers. Periodic labor shortages caused northern employers to turn to domestic sources of labor, especially migrants from American rural areas and particularly those in the south. Thus black migration to northern cities oscillated inversely with the ebb and flow of European immigration.

But northern employers also found another reason to employ southern blacks, for by the turn of the century, they had discovered their utility as strikebreakers. Blacks were repeatedly employed in this capacity in northern labor disputes between 1890 and 1930: black strikebreakers were used seven times in New York between 1895 and 1916, and were employed in Cleveland in 1896, in Detroit in 1919, in Milwaukee in 1922, and in Chicago in 1904 and 1905. Poor rural blacks with little understanding of industrial conditions and no experience with unions were recruited in the south and transported directly to northern factories, often on special trains arranged by factory owners.

The association of blacks with strikebreaking was bound to earn them the enmity of white workers, but discrimination against blacks by labor unions cannot be attributed to this animosity alone. European groups had also been used as strikebreakers, but labor leaders overcame these attempts at union-busting by incorporating each new wave of immigrants into the labor movement. Unions never employed this strategy with southern blacks, however. From the start, African Americans suffered unusually severe discrimination from white unions simply because they were black.

Most of the skilled crafts unions within the American Federation of Labor, for example, excluded blacks until the 1930s; and the Congress of Industrial Organizations accepted blacks only grudgingly, typically within segregated Jim Crow locals that received poorer contracts and lower priorities in job assignments. Being denied access to the benefits of white unions, blacks had little to lose from crossing picket lines, thereby setting off a cycle of ongoing mutual hostility and distrust between black and white workers.

Black out-migration from the south grew steadily from the end of the nineteenth century into the first decades of the new century. During the 1890s, some 174,000 blacks left the south, and this number rose to 197,000 between 1900 and 1910. The event that transformed the stream into a flood, however, was the outbreak of World War I in 1914. The war both increased the demand for U.S. industrial production and cut off the flow of European immigrants, northern factories' traditional source of labor. In response, employers began a spirited recruitment of blacks from the rural south.

The arrival of the recruiters in the south coincided with that of the Mexican boll weevil, which had devastated Louisiana's cotton crops in 1906 before moving on to Mississippi in 1913 and Alabama in 1916. The collapse of southern agriculture was aggravated by a series of disastrous floods in 1915 and 1916 and low cotton prices up to 1914. In response, southern planters shifted production from cotton to food crops and livestock, both of which required fewer workers. Thus the demand for black tenant farmers and day laborers fell just when the need for unskilled workers in northern cities skyrocketed.

This coincidence of push and pull factors increased the level of black out-migration to new heights and greatly augmented the black populations of Chicago, Detroit, Cleveland, Philadelphia, and New York. Between 1910 and 1920, some 525,000 African Americans left their traditional homes in the south and took up life in the north, and during the 1920s the outflow reached

877,000. This migration gradually acquired a dynamic of its own, as established migrants found jobs and housing for their friends and relatives back home. At the same time, northern black newspapers such as the *Chicago Defender,* which were widely read in the south, exhorted southern blacks to escape their oppression and move northward. As a result of this dynamic, black out-migration from the south continued at a substantial rate even during the Great Depression.

Northern whites viewed this rising tide of black migration with increasing hostility and considerable alarm. Middle-class whites were repelled by what they saw as the uncouth manners, unclean habits, slothful appearance, and illicit behavior of poorly educated, poverty-stricken migrants who had only recently been sharecroppers, and a resurgence of white racist ideology during the 1920s provided a theoretical, "scientific" justification for these feelings. Working-class whites, for their part, feared economic competition from the newcomers; and being first- or second-generation immigrants who were themselves scorned by native whites, they reaffirmed their own "whiteness" by oppressing a people that was even lower in the racial hierarchy. Blacks in the early twentieth century frequently said that the first English word an immigrant learned was "nigger."

As the size of the urban black population rose steadily after 1900, white racial views hardened and the relatively fluid and open period of race relations in the north drew to a close, Northern newspapers increasingly used terms such as "nigger" and "darkey" in print and carried unflattering stories about black crimes and vice. After decades of relatively integrated education, white parents increasingly refused to enroll their children in schools that included blacks. Doors that had permitted extensive interracial contact among the elite suddenly slammed shut as black professionals lost white clients, associates, and friends.

The most dramatic harbinger of the new regime in race relations was the upsurge in racial violence. In city after northern city, a series of communal riots broke out between 1900 and 1920 in the wake of massive black migration. Race riots struck New York City in 1900; Evansville, Indiana, in 1903; Springfield, Illinois, in 1908; East St. Louis, Illinois, in 1917; and Chicago in 1919. In each case, individual blacks were attacked because of the color of their skin. Those living away from recognized "black" neighborhoods had their houses ransacked or burned. Those unlucky or unwise enough to be caught trespassing in "white" neighborhoods were beaten, shot, or lynched. Blacks on their way to work were pulled from trolleys and pummeled. Rampaging bands of whites roamed the streets for days, attacking blacks at will. Although most of the rioters were white, most of the arrests, and nearly all of the victims, were black.

As the tide of violence rose in northern cities, blacks were increasingly divided from whites by a hardening color line in employment, education, and especially housing. Whites became increasingly intolerant of black neighbors and fear of racial turnover and black "invasion" spread. Those blacks living away from recognized Negro areas were forced to move into expanding "black belts," "darkytowns," "Bronzevilles," or "Niggertowns." Well-educated, middle-class blacks of the old elite found themselves increasingly lumped together with poorly educated, impoverished immigrants from the rural south; and well-to-do African Americans were progressively less able to find housing commensurate with their social status. In white eyes, black people belonged in black neighborhoods no matter what their social or economic standing; the color line grew increasingly impermeable.

Thus levels of residential segregation between blacks and whites began a steady rise at the turn of the century that would last for sixty years. The indices shown in the second column of Table 1 reveal the extent of this increase. By 1910, the average level of racial segregation in seven northern cities was 59 (compared with 46 in 1860) and four cases fell clearly within the high range (with index scores above 60). The initial stages of ghetto formation are most clearly revealed in Chicago (where the index increased from 50 to 67), Cleveland (an increase from 49 to 69), Milwaukee (from 60 to 67), and St. Louis (from 39 to 54).

The progressive segregation of blacks continued in subsequent decades, and by World War II the foundations of the modern ghetto had been laid in virtually every northern city. The last column of Table 1 presents dissimilarity indices computed by Karl and Alma Taeuber for 1940. Some caution must be exercised in interpreting these figures, because they are based on block statistics rather than on ward data. Blocks are substantially

smaller than wards, and the degree of segregation that can be measured tends to increase as the geographic size of units falls: what may appear to be an "integrated" ward actually may be quite segregated on a block-by-block basis.

The shift from wards to blocks adds at least 10 points to the dissimilarity indices (and probably more), but even making a liberal allowance for this artifact of the "neighborhood" unit used, it is clear that the level of black-white segregation rose substantially after 1910. At the block level, the degree of black-white segregation in northern cities reached an average value of 89 by 1940, with indices varying narrowly in the range from 80 to 100; this implies a range of about 70 to 90 using ward data, with an average around 80. It is safe to surmise, therefore, that by 1940 at least 70% of northern black city dwellers would have had to move to achieve an even residential configuration in northern cities (compared with a figure of only 46% in 1860).

With a rapidly growing black population being accommodated by an ever-smaller number of neighborhoods and an increasingly uneven residential configuration, the only possible outcome was an increase in the spatial isolation of blacks. As can be seen in Table 2, levels of racial isolation in northern cities began to move sharply upward after 1900, and especially after 1910. By 1930, African Americans were well on their way to experiencing a uniquely high degree of spatial isolation in American cities. Chicago led the way: its isolation index increased from only 10% in 1900 to 70% thirty years later. As of 1930 the typical black Chicagoan lived in a neighborhood that was over two-thirds black. That the level of black racial isolation also rose in other cities indicated the growth of more incipient ghettos: from 8% to 51% in Cleveland, from 5% to 42% in New York, and from 13% to 47% in St. Louis.

The increasing ghettoization of blacks was not simply a result of their growing numbers. Stanley Lieberson has clearly demonstrated that the segregation of blacks in the urban north increased after 1900 not only because their share of the population grew but because the same racial composition led to more isolation than it had during earlier periods. As the new century wore on, areas of acceptable black residence became more and more narrowly circumscribed: the era of the ghetto had begun.

Migration and industrial development also segregated the "new" European immigrant groups, of course, but recent studies have made it clear that immigrant enclaves in the early twentieth century were in no way comparable to the black ghetto that formed in most northern cities by 1940. To be sure, certain neighborhoods could be identified as "Italian," "Polish," or "Jewish"; but these ethnic enclaves differed from black ghettos in three fundamental ways.

First, unlike black ghettos, immigrant enclaves were never homogeneous and always contained a wide variety of nationalities, even if they were publicly associated with a particular national origin group. In Chicago's "Magyar district" of 1901, for example, twenty-two different ethnic groups were present and only 37% of all family heads were Magyar (26% were Polish). Similarly, an 1893 color-coded block map of Chicago's West Side prepared by the U.S. Department of Labor showed the location of European ethnic groups using eighteen separate colors. The result was a huge rainbow in which no block contained a single color. The average number of colors per block was eight, and four out of five *lots* within blocks were mixed. In none of the "Little Italys" identified on the map was there an all-Italian block.

The myth of the immigrant ghetto was perpetuated by Ernest Burgess, a founder of the "Chicago School" of urban sociology. In 1933 he published a well-known map showing the spatial location of Chicago's various immigrant groups. On it, he identified specific German, Irish, Italian, Russian, Polish, Swedish, and Czech "ghettos." A closer examination of these data by Thomas Philpott, however, revealed that Burgess's immigrant "ghettos" were more fictive than real. The average number of nationalities per ghetto was twenty-two, ranging from twenty in ostensibly Italian and Czech neighborhoods to twenty-five in areas that were theoretically Irish, German, and Swedish. In none of these "ghettos" did the ghettoized group constitute even a bare majority of the population, with the sole exception of Poles, who comprised 54% of their enclave. In areas that Burgess identified as being part of the black ghetto, however, blacks comprised 82% of the population.

A second crucial distinction is that most European ethnics did not live in immigrant "ghettos," as ethnically diluted as they were. Burgess's Irish ghetto contained only 3% of Chicago's Irish population, and only 50% of the city's Italian lived in the "Little Italys" he identified. Only among Poles did a majority, 61%, live in neighborhoods that were identified as being part of the Polish enclave. In contrast, 93% of Chicago's black population lived within the black ghetto.

Thus even at the height of their segregation early in this century, European ethnic groups did not experience a particularly high degree of isolation from American society, even in 1910 at the end of the peak decade of European immigration. Among the 100 or so indices that Stanley Lieberson computed for seven European ethnic groups in seventeen cities in 1910, only seven cases had isolation indices above 25%, and all but two were under 40%. The highest recorded levels of spatial isolation were for Italians in Boston (44%), Buffalo (38%), and Milwaukee (56%), and for Russians (i.e., Jews) in New York (34%). In contrast, black isolation exceeded 25% in eleven of the seventeen cities Lieberson examined in 1930 (see Table 2); and what is startling about this fact is that black ghettos were still in their formative stages in 1930 and had not yet begun to approach their maximum isolation.

The last difference between immigrant enclaves and black ghettos is that whereas, ghettos became a permanent feature of black residential life, ethnic enclaves proved to be a fleeting, transitory stage in the process of immigrant assimilation. The degree of segregation and spatial isolation among European ethnic groups fell steadily after 1910, as native-born children of immigrants experienced less segregation than their parents and as spatial isolation decreased progressively with socioeconomic advancement. For European immigrants, enclaves were places of absorption, adaptation, and adjustment to American society. They served as springboards for broader mobility in society, whereas blacks were trapped behind an increasingly impermeable color line.

The emergence of severe racial segregation in the north was not primarily a reflection of black housing preferences or a natural outcome of migration processes. On the contrary, as the ghetto walls grew thicker and higher, well-to-do class blacks complained bitterly and loudly about their increasing confinement within crowded, dilapidated neighborhoods inhabited by people well below their social and economic statuses.

Although they fought the construction of the ghetto as best they could, the forces arrayed against them proved to be overwhelming.

Foremost among the tools that whites used to construct the ghetto was violence. The initial impetus for ghetto formation came from a wave of racial violence, already noted, that swept over northern cities in the period between 1900 and 1920. These disturbances were communal in nature, and victims were singled out strictly on the basis of skin color. As history has repeatedly shown, during periods of communal strife, the only safety is in numbers. Blacks living in integrated or predominantly white areas—or even simply traveling through white areas to their own homes—proved to be extremely vulnerable.

Blacks that survived these attacks were loath to return to their former dwellings where they feared (correctly) that they would be subject to further violence. Following the riots, there was an outflow of blacks from outlying neighborhoods into the emerging ghetto, as the old integrated elite resigned itself to the new realities of racial segregation. Blacks who had been contemplating a move to better housing in white areas before the riots thought better of the idea afterward.

Racial violence did not end when the riots ceased in 1920, however; it simply assumed new, more controlled forms. As the black settlement pattern imploded and scattered areas of black residence were eliminated or consolidated, a contiguous core of solidly black neighborhoods formed in most northern cities during the first decades of the century. By the time black immigration quickened during the 1920s, new arrivals had to be accommodated within a very compact and spatially restricted area that was not open to easy expansion.

After 1920 the pattern of racial strife shifted from one of generalized communal violence aimed at driving blacks out of white neighborhoods to a new pattern of targeted violence concentrated along the periphery of an expanding ghetto. As migration continued and housing within the ghetto became intolerable, and as health, sanitary, and social conditions deteriorated, middle-class black families were eventually driven across the color line into white neighborhoods adjacent to the ghetto. Their moves set off an escalating pattern of racial violence.

The pattern typically began with threatening letters, personal harassment, and warnings of dire consequences to follow. Sometimes whites, through their churches, realtors, or neighborhood organizations, would take up a collection and offer to buy the black homeowner out, hinting of less civilized inducements to follow if the offer was refused. If these entreaties failed to dislodge the resident, spontaneous mobs would often grow out of neighborhood meetings or barroom discussions, and a pack of agitated, angry whites would surround the house, hurling rocks and insults and at times storming the home and ransacking it. Periodic outbursts of mob violence would be interspersed with sporadic incidents of rock-throwing, gunshots, cross burnings, and physical attack.

If the escalating violence still failed to produce the desired result, the last step was dramatic and guaranteed to attract the attention, not only of the homeowner, but of the entire black community: bombing. During and after World War I, a wave of bombings followed the expansion of black residential areas in cities throughout the north. In Chicago, fifty-eight black homes were bombed between 1917 and 1921, one every twenty days; and one black real estate agent, Jesse Binga, had his home and office bombed seven times in one year. In Cleveland, a wealthy black doctor who constructed a new home in an exclusive white suburb had his house surrounded by a violent mob, and when this attack failed to dislodge him, the home was dynamited twice. Bombings were also reported to be a common means of combating the expansion of Detroit's ghetto.

The wave of violence and bombings crested during the 1920s, although the sporadic use of these techniques has continued up to the present. Violence, however, has its problems as a strategy for maintaining the residential color line. Although it was employed by whites of all classes at first, those in the middle and upper classes eventually realized its limitations. Not only did violent actions often destroy property within neighborhoods being "defended," but injuries or death could bring legal charges as well as unfavorable publicity that decreased an area's stability. After the 1920s, middle-class whites increasingly turned to more civilized and institutionalized methods to build the ghetto.

A typical organizational solution to the threat of black residential expansion was the formation of neighborhood "improvement associations." Although ostensibly chartered for the purpose of promoting neighborhood security and property values, their principal raison d'être was the prevention of black entry and the maintenance of the color line. On Chicago's South Side, for example, the Hyde Park Improvement and Protective Club and the Woodlawn Society were formed implicitly to rid their neighborhoods of unwanted black settlers and to prevent future black entry. In New York, whites banded together in Harlem's Property Owners' Improvement Corporation and Brooklyn's Gates Avenue Association, again for the same reasons. In other cities, similar organizations dedicated themselves to checking the expansion of black settlement along the ghetto's frontier.

These voluntary associations employed a variety of tools in their efforts to preserve the racial homogeneity of threatened neighborhoods. They lobbied city councils for zoning restrictions and for the closing of hotels and rooming houses that attracted blacks; they threatened boycotts of real estate agents who sold homes to blacks; they withdrew their patronage from white businesses that catered to black clients; they agitated for public investments in the neighborhood in order to increase property values and keep blacks out by economic means; they collected money to create funds to buy property from black settlers or to purchase homes that remained vacant for too long; they offered cash bonuses to black renters who agreed to leave the neighborhood. In the exclusive Chicago suburb of Wilmette, a committee of citizens went so far as to ask wealthy homeowners to lodge all maids, servants, and gardeners on premises, or else to fire all Negroes in their employ.

One of the most important functions of the neighborhood associations, however, was to implement restrictive covenants. These documents were contractual agreements among property owners stating that they would not permit a black to own, occupy, or lease their property. Those signing the covenant bound themselves and their heirs to exclude blacks from the covered area for a specified period of time. In the event of the covenant's violation, any party to the agreement could call upon the courts for enforcement and could sue the transgressor for damages. As typically employed, covenants took effect when some fixed percentage of property owners in a given area had signed, whereupon the remaining non-signatories were pressured to sign also. A typical

covenant lasted twenty years and required the assent of 75% of the property owners to become enforceable.

Prior to 1900, such covenants did not exist. Legal restrictions on the transfer of property to blacks took the form of deed restrictions, which covered single parcels and did not solve the problem of massive black entry into white neighborhoods. Deed restrictions also did not lend themselves to forceful collective action. After 1910, the use of restrictive covenants spread widely throughout the United States, and they were employed frequently and with considerable effectiveness to maintain the color line until 1948, when the U.S. Supreme Court declared them unenforceable.

Local real estate boards often took the lead in establishing restrictive covenants and arranging for their widespread use. In 1927, for example, the Chicago Real Estate Board devised a model covenant that neighborhood organizations could adapt for their own use; the board then organized a special drive to ensure its adoption by all of the "better" neighborhoods in the city. Although Chicago's local board may have been unusually active in defending the color line, these actions were consistent with official policies of the National Association of Real Estate Brokers, which in 1924 adopted an article in its code of ethics stating that "a Realtor should never be instrumental in introducing into a neighborhood . . . members of any race or nationality . . . whose presence will clearly be detrimental to property values in that neighborhood," a provision that remained in effect until 1950.

The maintenance of a rigid color line in housing through violence and institutionalized discrimination paradoxically also created the conditions for ghetto expansion. Rapid black migration into a confined residential area created an intense demand for housing within the ghetto, which led to a marked inflation of rents and home prices. The racially segmented market generated real estate values in black areas that far exceeded anything in white neighborhoods, and this simple economic fact created a great potential for profits along the color line, guaranteeing that some real estate agent would specialize in opening up new areas to black settlements.

White real estate boards, of course, attempted to forestall such actions by threatening agents who violated the color line with expulsion, but because black agents were excluded from real estate boards anyway, this threat had little effect on them. Furthermore, the potential profits were great enough that many whites were willing to face public opprobrium for the sake of the money to be earned. In the end, the real estate industry settled on a practical compromise of keeping "blacks from moving into white residential areas haphazardly and to see to it that they filled a block solidly before being allowed to move into the next one." Essentially this strategy represented a policy of containment and tactical retreat before an advancing color line. For some, it proved to be a very profitable compromise.

The methods that realtors used to open up neighborhoods to black entry and to reap profits during the transition came to be known as "blockbusting." The expansion of the ghetto generally followed the path of least resistance, slowing or stopping at natural boundaries such as rivers, railroad tracks, or major thoroughfares, and moving toward low status rather than high status areas. Blockbusting agents would select a promising area for racial turnover, most often an area adjacent to the ghetto that contained older housing, poorer families, aging households, and some apartment buildings. Agents would then quietly acquire a few homes or apartments in the area, and rent or sell them to carefully chosen black families.

The inevitable reaction of white violence and resistance was countered with deliberate attempts to increase white fears and spur black demand. Agents would go door to door warning white residents of the impending "invasion" and offer to purchase or rent homes on generous terms. They often selected ostentatiously lower-class blacks to be the first settlers in the neighborhood in order to heighten fears and encourage panic; at times, these "settlers" were actually confederates of the realtor. In neighborhoods of family homes, a realtor might divide up the first black-occupied house into small units, which were intentionally rented to poor southern arrivals, who were desperate for housing and willing to pay high rents for cramped rooms of low quality. While white panic was spreading, the realtors would advertise widely within the black community, pointing out the availability of good housing in a newly opened neighborhood, thereby augmenting black demand.

Given the intensity of black demand and the depths of white prejudice, the entry of a relatively small number of black settlers would quickly surpass the threshold of white tolerance and set off a round of racial turnover. No white renters or home buyers would enter the area under the cloud of a black invasion, and as the rate of white departures accelerated, each departing white family would be replaced with one or more black families. As the threat of violence subsided and whites gave up defending the neighborhood, black demand soared and agents reaped substantial profits, because the new entrants were willing to pay prices much higher than those previously paid by whites.

In neighborhoods of single-family homes, the initial black entrants tended to be middle- and upper-class families seeking to escape the deplorable conditions of the ghetto. Like other middle-class people, they sought more agreeable surroundings, higher-quality schools, lower crime rates, bigger houses, larger properties, and a "better class of people." Because white banks did not make loans to black applicants, realtors were able to augment their profits by acting as bankers as well as sales agents; and given the racially segmented credit market, they were able to charge interest rates and demand down payments well above those paid by whites.

The attempts of black middle-class families to escape the ghetto were continually undermined, however, by real estate agents seeking quick profits. Often they sold homes to black families who needed quality housing but were in no position to pay for it. As both seller and lender, the agent would collect a cash advance and several months of mortgage payments before the buyer defaulted; then the family was evicted and the house was resold to another family under similar terms. In this way, agents could "sell" a home several times in the course of a year, generating extra profits. Frequently agents bought homes in single-family neighborhoods, subdivided them into rooming houses, and then leased the resulting "kitchenette" apartments at high rents to poor families.

The prevalence of these quick-profit schemes meant that the ghetto constantly followed the black middle class as it sought to escape from the poverty, blight, and misery of the black slum. Following resegregation, neighborhoods fell into progressive neglect and disrepair as owners were shuffled in and out of homes, which sat vacant between sales. Nor could owners who were paying rents and mortgages beyond their means afford repairs and routine maintenance. In addition, the illegal subdivision of single-family homes brought the very poor into what were originally middle-class areas. Complaints to city inspectors by black homeowners usually went unheard, because real estate agents were typically careful to pay off local officials; many were only too happy to turn a blind eye to problems in the black community if there was money to be made.

During the 1920s and 1930s, therefore, black ghettos expanded behind a leading edge of middle-class pioneers who were subsequently swamped by an influx of poor families, which caused the progressive deterioration of the neighborhood. As the decline accelerated, affluent families were prompted to seek new quarters in adjacent white neighborhoods, beginning a new round of neighborhood transition and decay. This process, when repeated across neighborhoods, yielded a distinct class gradient in the ghetto, with the poorest families being concentrated toward the center in the worst, most crowded, and least desirable housing, and the middle and upper classes progressively increasing their share of the population as one moved from the core toward the periphery of the ghetto.

As the black ghetto became more dense and spatially concentrated, a struggle for power, influence, and ideological control emerged within the black community between the old elite and the "New Negroes" of the 1920s and 1930s. The latter were politicians and, to a lesser extent, business owners who benefited from the spatial concentration of black demand within a racially segmented market. In ideological terms, the struggle was symbolized by the debate between the adherents of W. E. B. Du Bois and the followers of Booker T. Washington. The former argued that blacks should fight white injustice and demand their rightful share of the fruits of American society; the latter advocated accommodating white racism while building an independent black economic base.

The rise of the ghetto, more than anything else, brought about the eclipse of the old elite of integrationist blacks who dominated African American affairs in northern cities before 1910. These professionals and tradespeople who catered to white clients and aspired to full membership in American society were supplanted by a class of politicians and entrepreneurs whose source of power and wealth lay in the black community itself. Rather than being caterers, barbers, doctors, and lawyers who served a white or racially mixed clientele, the new elite were politicians and business owners with a self-interested stake in the ghetto. With their ascendancy, the ideal of an integrated society and the fight against racial segregation went into a long remission.

These "New Negroes" included real estate tycoons, such as Chicago's Jesse Binga and New York's Philip A. Payton, men who specialized in opening up new areas for black settlement and made millions in the process. Publishing newspapers for a black audience brought wealth and influence to Robert S. Abbott, who built the *Chicago Defender* into the most important black newspaper in the country, and Dr. P. M. H. Savory, who published the *Amsterdam News* from the 1920s until his death in the 1965. With the concentration of black population, moreover, came the concentration of black votes and buying power, and a new generation of politicians and business owners came to the fore—people such as Oscar DePriest, who became Chicago's first black alderman and the first African American elected to Congress from the north, and New York's Madame C. J. Walker, who made a fortune with a line of black cosmetics and hair-straightening products. The interests of these new economic and political leaders were tied to the ghetto and its concerns rather than to issues growing out of an attempt to pursue an integrated life within the mainstream of American society.

Meanwhile, in the south, conditions for urban blacks were considerably less tolerant than in the north. The Jim Crow system of race relations was in its heyday during the early years of the twentieth century, but its paternalistic system of race relations guaranteed the subordination of blacks and paradoxically lessened the need for a rigid system of housing segregation. Among older southern cities, in particular, the traditional grid pattern of white avenues and black alleys kept segregation levels relatively low. Although direct evidence on the degree of racial segregation in southern cities is limited, the few available studies suggest that it was less severe in the early twentieth century than in the emerging ghettos of the north.

In 1910, the three southern cities for which there is data in Table 1 had an average black-white dissimilarity score of only 38, 21 points lower than the average in the north. In Charleston the level was particularly low at about 17; and although this value appears to represent an increase since the nineteenth century, it is an artifact of the exclusion of slaves from the earlier computation. When they are included in the 1860 calculation, the index falls to 11.5. Of the three cities shown in 1910, moreover, none displays an index in the range generally accepted as high.

Southern whites were not completely immune to threats posed by black urbanization. After 1910 black populations also began to rise in southern cities, for essentially the same reasons as in the north, and whites similarly became alarmed at the influx of black migrants. In the context of Jim Crow, however, the reaction of southern whites never reached the extremes of panic and fear experienced in the north. Rather, given the tradition of legally enforced segregation in other spheres, southern whites turned to the law to promote greater separation between the races in housing.

The movement toward legally enforced residential segregation began in 1910, when Baltimore's city council passed an ordinance establishing separate white and black neighborhoods in the city. Additional laws to establish legal segregation in housing were passed in Virginia between 1911 and 1913, when Ashland, Norfolk, Portsmouth, Richmond, and Roanoke all adopted ordinances emulating Baltimore's. By 1913, the movement had spread southward to Winston-Salem and Greenville, North Carolina, and it reached Atlanta, Georgia, in the same year. By 1916, Louisville, St. Louis, Oklahoma City, and New Orleans all had passed laws establishing separate black and white districts in their cities. As the movement gathered steam, some northern cities began to consider the possibility of adopting similar ordinances to resolve their racial difficulties.

In 1916, however, the National Association for the Advancement of Colored People filed suit in federal court to block the implementation of Louisville's segregation law, and one year later the U.S. Supreme Court declared it unconstitutional. The movement toward legally sanctioned housing segregation ended, and thereafter racial segregation in southern cities was accomplished

by the same means as in the north: through violence, collective antiblack action, racially restrictive covenants, and discriminatory real estate practices. Segregation, nonetheless, continued to develop at a slower pace than in northern cities owing to the slower pace of industrialization, the unique spatial organization of southern cities, and the greater social control of blacks afforded by Jim Crow.

The 1940 black-white segregation indices in Table 1 conceal the lower segregation in the south because they rely on block rather than ward data. Although the average score of 81 is eight points lower than in the north, it is still quite high. The use of blocks rather than wards interacts with a classic white avenue/black alley settlement pattern to produce a misleading picture of segregation in the south. When ward tabulations are used, the level of segregation in Charleston falls from 60 to 27 (compared with a ward-level index of only 17 in 1910) while that in Jacksonville drops from 94 to 47 (up from 39 thirty years before). Although the walls of the ghetto were rising in the south by 1940, they had not yet reached the height of those in the north, particularly in the older cities.

SHORING THE BULWARKS OF SEGREGATION, 1940–1970

The outlines and form of the modern black ghetto were in place in most northern cities by the outbreak of World War II. Events unleashed by the war would not change the frontiers of black settlement so much as fill in the gaps. Once World War II was over, a great boom ushered in a new economic order that again dramatically transformed the social and spatial organization of cities, creating sprawling decentralized metropolises where compact settlements once stood. This new urban political economy mixed the public and private sectors to an unprecedented degree, and the distinguishing feature of racial segregation in the postwar era is the direct role that government played not only in maintaining the color line but in strengthening the walls of the ghetto.

By 1930 the perimeters of black settlement were well established in most cities and the level of black-white residential dissimilarity had reached a stable and very high level. Blacks were nearly as unevenly distributed in American cities as they would ever be, but as late as 1930 a significant number of whites still lived within the circumscribed areas that had been ceded to black settlement. The Great Depression and World War II eliminated this residual white population and made northern ghettos the homogeneously black communities they are today.

The advent of the Depression brought widespread unemployment to blacks in the north. But if northern economic conditions were bad, they were worse in the south, and given the self-perpetuating dynamic inherent in mass migration, the movement from south to north continued: from 1930 to 1940, some 400,000 black migrants left the south for northern cities. When they arrived, they faced unusually bleak residential circumstances, for the Great Depression had virtually ended new residential construction after 1929. Although housing construction began to pick up by 1940, the entry of the United States into World War II once again brought homebuilding to a halt. During the 1930s and 1940s, therefore, black migrants entered an urban environment with an essentially fixed and very limited supply of housing.

At first, the newcomers took the place of whites departing from racially changing neighborhoods located near the fringe of the ghetto. Once these neighborhoods had become all black, however, further ghetto expansion proved to be difficult because, given the housing shortage, there was nowhere for whites on the other side of the color line to go. As whites in adjacent neighborhoods stood firm and blocked entry, the expansion of the ghetto slowed to a crawl, and new black arrivals were accommodated by subdividing housing within the ghetto's boundaries. Apartments were carved out of bedrooms, closets, garages, basements, and sheds. As population densities within the ghetto rose, black spatial isolation increased.

U.S. entry into the war brought full mobilization and a shortage of factory workers in the north. In response to the new demand for labor, black migration from south to north soared during the 1940s. The new migrants arrived in cities plagued by intense housing shortages and vacancy rates under 1%, even in white areas. Population densities within the ghetto increased to new, often incredible heights, a phenomenon that Otis and Beverly Duncan appropriately labeled "piling up." This stage in the process of ghetto formation in-

creased black isolation to new extremes, and from this time forward African Americans in large northern cities were effectively removed—socially and spatially—from the rest of American society.

World War II brought recovery from the economic malaise of the Great Depression, but four years of full employment combined with wartime consumer shortages produced a large surplus of savings and a tremendous pent-up demand for housing. Additional capital for home ownership was soon made available through new loan programs at the Federal Housing Administration and the Veterans Administration. The mix of surplus capital and frustrated demand ignited an unparalleled postwar boom in residential home construction.

As home construction skyrocketed during the late 1940s and 1950s, men and women began to marry and have babies at remarkable rates. After postponing marriage and childbearing during the hard times of the Depression and through the disruptions of war, American couples sought to make up for lost time: the baby boom was on. The growing families of the 1950s sought large houses on spacious lots in areas with good schools and plenty of room for supervised play, conditions that were most easily met by constructing new homes on inexpensive land located outside of central cities. The suburbanization of America proceeded at a rapid pace and the white middle class deserted inner cities in massive numbers. Only one-third of U.S. metropolitan residents were suburban residents in 1940, but by 1970 suburbanites constituted a majority within metropolitan America.

In making this transition from urban to suburban life, middle-class whites demanded and got massive federal investments in highway construction that permitted rapid movement to and from central cities by car. The surging demand for automobiles accelerated economic growth and contributed to the emergence of a new, decentralized spatial order. Whereas early industrialism was based on steam power, rail transportation, and rudimentary communications (e.g., the telegraph and surface mail), the new political economy grew up around electric power, automotive transport, and advanced telecommunications.

Industrial-era technology had encouraged spatial concentration in human activities. Factories were built compactly to conserve mechanical power and agglomerated to use common steam plants; rail lines moved large numbers of people along fixed routes to a single point, and crude communications put a premium on face-to-face interaction. In the new post-industrial order, however, the substitution of electricity for steam power eliminated the impetus for centralized manufacturing districts, and a growing reliance on truck transport made congested cities undesirable as centers of manufacturing and shipping. Widespread commuting by automobile extended residential development in all directions around the central city, not just along fixed rail lines. As workers and factories took advantage of the new technologies and moved to the suburbs, retail activities followed.

This period of rapid economic growth and growing spatial deconcentration was accompanied by relatively low levels of immigration; and with the expansion of educational opportunities and the rise in service employment, the children of earlier immigrants increasingly left the ranks of manual workers. Employers once again turned to black migrants from the rural south to fill the demand for labor in manufacturing, heavy industry, and low-wage services. Within the south, a wave of mechanization and capital investment spread through agriculture, which put a definitive end to the share-cropping system and constricted the demand for rural labor. As in earlier times, the coincidence of push and pull factors led to extensive black out-migration, with the net flow totaling 1.5 million during the 1950s and 1.4 million during the 1960s.

Despite this rapid transformation of American cities, however, one feature of urban geography remained unchanged: the black ghetto. The institutional practices and private behaviors that had combined to maintain the color line before the war remained to support it afterward, with one significant change. Although whites were still highly resistant to racial integration in housing, withdrawal to the suburbs provided a more attractive alternative to the defense of threatened neighborhoods and led to a prevalence of flight over fight among whites in racially changing areas. The combination of rapid white suburbanization and extensive black in-migration led to an unprecedented increase in the physical size of the ghetto during the 1950s and 1960s.

In the postwar years, therefore, the percentage of blacks within northern cities shifted rapidly

upward. Between 1950 and 1970, the percentage of blacks more than doubled in most large northern cities, going from 14% to 33% in Chicago, from 16% to 38% in Cleveland, from 16% to 44% in Detroit, and from 18% to 34% in Philadelphia. In the space of two decades Gary, Newark, and Washington were transformed from predominantly white to predominantly black cities; Gary was 53% black by 1970, and Newark and Washington were 54% and 71% black, respectively.

What is striking about these transformations is how effectively the color line was maintained despite the massive population shifts. The white strategy of ghetto containment and tactical retreat before an advancing color line, institutionalized during the 1920s, was continued after 1945; the only change was the rate at which the leading edge of the ghetto advanced. In a few short years, the population of vast areas of Chicago's south and west sides became virtually all black, as occurred on Cleveland's east side, Philadelphia's north and west sides, and in most of central city Newark, Detroit, Baltimore, and Washington, D.C. All the while, however, the residential segregation of blacks was maintained.

In cities receiving large numbers of black migrants, racial turnover was so regular and so pervasive that most neighborhoods could be classified by their stage in the transition process: all white, invasion, succession, consolidation, or all black. In six northern cities studied by Karl and Alma Taeuber, 90% of all neighborhoods inhabited by blacks in 1960 were either all black or clearly moving in that direction, a pattern that prevailed through 1970.

The persistence of segregation despite the massive redistribution of whites and blacks is confirmed by Table 3, which presents indices of residential dissimilarity calculated at the block level for thirty U.S. cities from 1940 through 1970. These measures show that racial segregation became a permanent structural feature of the spatial organization of American cities in the years after World War II. In the three decades after 1940, black-white segregation remained high and virtually constant, averaging over 85 at all times in all regions. Segregation levels in the north peaked in 1950, and then edged slightly downward by 1970, whereas southern cities peaked somewhat later, in 1960. Only one city,

TABLE 3 *Block-Level Indices of Nonwhite-White Segregation for Thirty Cities, 1940-1970*

	SEGREGATION INDICES BY YEAR			
	1940	*1950*	*1960*	*1970*
Northern Cities				
Boston	86.3	86.5	83.9	79.9
Buffalo	87.9	89.5	86.5	84.2
Chicago	95.0	92.1	92.6	88.8
Cincinnati	90.6	91.2	89.0	83.1
Cleveland	92.0	91.5	91.3	89.0
Columbus	87.1	88.9	85.3	84.1
Detroit	89.9	88.8	84.5	80.9
Gary	88.3	93.8	92.8	82.9
Indianapolis	90.4	91.4	91.6	88.3
Kansas City	88.0	91.3	90.8	88.0
Los Angeles	84.2	84.6	81.8	78.4
Milwaukee	92.9	91.6	88.1	83.7
Newark	77.4	76.9	71.6	74.9
New York	86.8	87.3	79.3	73.0
Philadelphia	88.0	89.0	87.1	83.2
Pittsburgh	82.0	84.0	84.6	83.9
St. Louis	92.6	92.9	90.5	89.3
San Francisco	82.9	79.8	69.3	55.5
Average	87.0	88.4	85.6	81.7
Southern Cities				
Atlanta	87.4	91.5	93.6	91.5
Baltimore	90.1	91.3	89.6	88.3
Birmingham	86.4	88.7	92.8	91.5
Dallas	80.2	88.4	94.6	92.7
Greensboro	93.1	93.5	93.3	91.4
Houston	84.5	91.5	93.7	90.0
Memphis	79.9	86.4	92.0	91.8
Miami	97.9	97.8	97.9	89.4
New Orleans	81.0	84.9	86.3	83.1
Norfolk	96.0	95.0	94.6	90.8
Tampa	90.2	92.5	94.5	90.7
Washington	81.0	80.1	79.7	77.7
Average	87.3	90.1	91.9	89.1

Source: Annemette Sørensen, Karl E. Taeuber, and Lesslie J. Hollingsworth, Jr., "Indexes of Racial Residential Segregation for 109 Cities in the United States, 1940 to 1970," *Sociological Focus* 8 (1975): 128–30.

San Francisco, experienced a significant long-term decline in the level of racial segregation. By 1970, at least 70% of blacks would have had to move to achieve an even residential configuration in most cities, and in many places the figure was closer to 90%.

Such consistently high levels of segregation imply that blacks and whites occupied separate and wholly distinct neighborhoods at each point between 1940 and 1970. Given the fact that northern cities received about 4.5 million black migrants during the period, the only possible outcome was a substantial increase in degree of black spatial isolation. Although no studies have computed decade-by-decade isolation indices for U.S. cities, census data allow us to carry out this task for 1970. Table 4 presents our results for thirty cities, along with Lieberson's 1930 isolation indices, which indicate long-term trends.

Among northern cities, the average level of black spatial isolation more than doubled between 1930 and 1970, going from 32% to nearly 74%. Whereas a typical northern black resident was likely to live in a neighborhood dominated by whites in 1930 (only Chicago and Cleveland were exceptions), by 1970 the situation had completely reversed. Now blacks in *all* northern cities were more likely to live with other African Americans than with whites, and in four cities the average black person lived in a neighborhood that was over 80% black (in Chicago, Cleveland, Gary, and St. Louis). Unless they worked in the larger mainstream economy, blacks in these cities were very unlikely to have any contact with whites.

Although we lack an earlier reference point to discern long-term trends in the south, black isolation was clearly an accomplished fact in southern cities by 1970 as well. The average level of black isolation within cities of the south was slightly higher than in the north (76% versus 74%), and the index exceeded 80% in six cases (Atlanta, Baltimore, Dallas, Memphis, Miami, and Washington, D.C.). In all cities, blacks were very unlikely to share a neighborhood with members of other racial groups. Indeed, the *lowest* isolation index was 58% (in Birmingham), so that blacks throughout the south tended to live in residential areas where the vast majority of residents were black. Patterns for 1970, therefore, represent a complete reversal of conditions during the late nineteenth

TABLE 4 *Indices of Black Isolation within Neighborhoods of Thirty Cities, 1930-1970*

NORTHERN CITIES

City	1930	1970
Boston	19.2	66.1
Buffalo	24.2	75.2
Chicago	70.4	89.2
Cincinnati	44.6	63.9
Cleveland	51.0	86.6
Columbus	—	65.2
Detroit	31.2	77.1
Gary	—	83.2
Indianapolis	26.1	65.5
Kansas City	31.6	75.6
Los Angeles	25.6	73.9
Milwaukee	16.4	74.5
New York	41.8	60.2
Newark	22.8	78.3
Philadelphia	27.3	75.6
Pittsburgh	26.8	70.8
St. Louis	46.6	85.1
San Francisco	1.7	56.1
Average	31.7	73.5

SOUTHERN CITIES

City	1970
Atlanta	88.0
Baltimore	84.8
Birmingham	57.9
Dallas	82.0
Greensboro	62.0
Houston	72.1
Memphis	82.9
Miami	81.5
New Orleans	75.6
Norfolk	79.8
Tampa	62.3
Washington	88.1
Average	76.4

Sources: Indices for 1930 are computed from ward-level data and come from Stanley Lieberson, *A Piece of the Pie: Blacks and White Immigrants since 1880* (Berkeley: University of California Press, 1980), pp. 266, 288. Indices for 1970 are computed from tract-level data and were calculated by the authors using U.S. Bureau of the Census, *Census of Population and Housing 1970: Fourth Court Summary Tapes, File A* (Washington, D.C.: U.S. Bureau of the Census, 1970).

century, when residential contact between southern blacks and whites was the rule.

Throughout the United States—in both southern and northern cities—the ghetto had become an enduring, permanent feature of the residential structure of black community life by 1940, and over the next thirty years the spatial isolation of African Americans only increased. The highest isolation index ever recorded for any ethnic group in any American city was 56% (for Milwaukee's Italians in 1910), but by 1970 the *lowest* level of spatial isolation observed for blacks anywhere, north or south, was 56% (in San Francisco).

The universal emergence of the black ghetto in American cities after 1940 rests on a foundation of long-standing white racial prejudice. Although attitudes cannot be studied directly before 1940, after this date opinion polls are available to confirm the depth of white prejudice against blacks in the area of housing. In 1942, for example, 84% of white Americans polled answered "yes" to the question "Do you think there should be separate sections in towns and cities for Negroes to live in?"; and in 1962, 61% of white respondents agreed that "white people have a right to keep blacks out of their neighborhoods if they want to, and blacks should respect that right." It was not until 1970 that even a bare majority of white respondents (53%) disagreed with the latter statement.

Throughout the period from 1940 to 1970, in other words, there was widespread support among whites for racial discrimination in housing and for the systematic exclusion of blacks from white neighborhoods. As a result, whites continued to resist any attempt at black entry through acts of harassment and violence, and once entry was achieved, the neighborhood was avoided by subsequent white homeseekers, thereby guaranteeing racial turnover and resegregation. The only difference from earlier times was that the racial turnover was quicker and the ghetto's physical expansion more rapid.

The institutionalization of discrimination within the real estate industry likewise continued in the postwar era. Although racially restrictive covenants were declared unenforceable by the U.S. Supreme Court in 1948, a comprehensive study of real estate policies in the 1950s by Rose Helper revealed a pervasive pattern of discrimination against blacks in most American cities. In her survey of real estate agents in Chicago, she found that 80% of realtors refused to sell blacks property in white neighborhoods, and 68% refused to rent them such property. Moreover, among those agents who did sell or rent to blacks, half said they would do so only under restrictive conditions, such as when a significant number of blacks had already entered the area. Another survey of Chicago's real estate agents carried out by Harvey Molotch in the mid-1960s found that only 29% of agents were willing to rent to blacks unconditionally (regardless of local market conditions or racial composition), and half of these open-minded agents were black.

Helper presented similar findings from studies of housing discrimination in other cities during the 1950s. One study carried out in suburban New York identified forty-six separate techniques used by white realtors to exclude blacks from neighborhoods, and Helper identified twenty-six different methods in her Chicago survey; most could be grouped in one of two basic categories: 56% used a flat refusal and 24% employed some kind of subterfuge (e.g., saying a unit was sold when it was not). When handling properties in black areas, 22% said they were more careful screening black applicants than whites, 14% said they required security deposits of blacks but not whites, and 25% said they charged higher rents to blacks.

In their personal views, the realtors studied by Helper appeared to share the prejudices of their white clients. Some 59% of her respondents rejected racial integration in principle, and 84% espoused an ideological stance that supported the exclusion of blacks from white neighborhoods. Some 65% said they believed that the entry of blacks was bad for neighborhoods; and among realtors who were members of Chicago's Real Estate Board, support for the exclusion of blacks was even stronger: 91% held views consistent with an exclusionary ideology.

In her interviews with realtors, Helper also uncovered considerable evidence of discrimination by banks and savings institutions in denying loans to black homeseekers. Among realtors offering information on the issue, 62% felt that few or very few banks were willing to make loans to blacks, and half of the agents confirmed that banks would not make loans to areas that were black, turning black, or threatened with the possibility of black entry.

There is, in summary, considerable evidence pointing to the persistence of prejudice against

blacks in the postwar period, and to the widespread translation of this sentiment into systematic, institutionalized racial discrimination within urban housing markets. These private beliefs and actions, however, were not the only forces shoring the walls of ghetto between 1940 and 1970. What was new about the postwar era was the extent to which the federal government became involved in perpetuating racial segregation.

Beginning in the 1930s, the federal government launched a series of programs designed to increase employment in the construction industry and make home ownership widely available to the American public. The Home Owners' Loan Corporation (HOLC) was the first of these programs, and it served as a model for later efforts. Passed in the depression year of 1933, it provided funds for refinancing urban mortgages in danger of default and granted low-interest loans to former owners who had lost their homes through foreclosure to enable them to regain their properties. The HOLC was the first government-sponsored program to introduce, on a mass scale, the use of long-term, self-amortizing mortgages with uniform payments.

Unfortunately for blacks, the HOLC also initiated and institutionalized the practice of "redlining." This discriminatory practice grew out of a ratings system HOLC developed to evaluate the risks associated with loans made to specific urban neighborhoods. Four categories of neighborhood quality were established, and lowest was coded with the color red; it and the next-lowest category virtually never received HOLC loans. The vast majority of mortgages went to the top two categories, the highest of which included areas that were "new, homogenous, and in demand in good times and bad" (to HOLC this meant areas inhabited by "American business and professional men"); the second category consisted of areas that had reached their peak, but were still desirable and could be expected to remain stable.

The HOLC's rating procedures thus systematically undervalued older central city neighborhoods that were racially or ethnically mixed. Jewish areas, for example, were generally placed in category two if their economic status was high enough, but if they were working class or located near a black settlement they would fall into the third category because they were "within such a low price or rent range as to attract an undesirable element." Black areas were invariably rated as fourth grade and "redlined." As Kenneth Jackson points out, the HOLC did not invent these standards of racial worth in real estate—they were already well established by the 1920s—it bureaucratized them and applied them on an exceptional scale. It lent the power, prestige, and support of the federal government to the systematic practice of racial discrimination in housing.

According to Jackson, HOLC underwriters were far more concerned about the location and movement of blacks than about any other demographic trend. He cites a confidential 1941 HOLC survey of real estate prospects in the St. Louis area that repeatedly mentions "the rapidly increasing Negro population" and the consequent "problem in the maintenance of real estate values." Every neighborhood analysis in the report includes maps of the density of black settlement. Black neighborhoods are always coded red; and even those with small black percentages were usually rated as "hazardous" and placed in the lowest category.

Through this discriminatory ratings system, HOLC mortgage funds were invariably channeled away from established black areas and were usually redirected away from neighborhoods that looked as though they *might* contain blacks in the future. But funds distributed through the HOLC program itself were modest, and the major role that the agency played lay in serving as a model for other credit institutions, both private and public.

During the 1930s and 1940s, private banks relied heavily on the HOLC system to make their own loan decisions, and the agency's "Residential Security Maps" were widely circulated throughout the lending industry. Banks adopted the HOLC's procedures (and prejudices) in constructing their own maps and ratings, thereby institutionalizing and disseminating the practice of redlining. Thus HOLC not only channeled federal funds away from black neighborhoods but was also responsible for a much larger and more significant disinvestment in black areas by private institutions.

By far the greatest effect of the HOLC rating system, however, came from its influence on the underwriting practices of the Federal Housing Administration (FHA) and the Veterans Administration (VA) during the 1940s and 1950s. The FHA loan program was created by the National Housing Act in 1937, and the VA program was authorized by the Servicemen's Readjustment Act of 1944. These loan programs together completely reshaped the residential housing market of the United States and pumped millions of dollars into the housing industry during the postwar era. Loans made by the FHA and the VA were a major impetus behind the rapid suburbanization of the United States after 1945.

The FHA program operated by guaranteeing the value of collateral for loans made by private banks. Before this program, mortgages generally were granted for no more than two-thirds of the appraised value of a home, so buyers needed to acquire at least 33% of the value of a property in order to make a down payment; frequently banks required half the assessed value of a home before making a loan. The FHA program, in contrast, guaranteed over 90% of the value of collateral so that down payments of 10% became the norm. The FHA also extended the repayment period to twenty-five or thirty years, resulting in low monthly payments, and insisted that all loans be fully amortized. The greater security afforded by FHA guarantees virtually eliminated the risk to banks, which lowered the interest rates they charged borrowers. When the VA program was established, it followed practices established by the earlier FHA program.

As the cost and ease of purchasing a house dropped, home ownership became a mass phenomenon for the first time in American history. Between 1934 and 1969 the percentage of families living in owner-occupied dwellings increased from 44% to 63%; and during the 1940s and 1950s, the marriage of FHA financing and new construction techniques made it cheaper to buy new suburban homes than to rent comparable older dwellings in the central city. As a result, the FHA and VA contributed significantly to the decline of the inner city by encouraging the selective out-migration of middle-class whites to the suburbs.

The bias in favor of the suburbs was evident in FHA practices and regulations, which favored the construction of single-family homes but discouraged the building of multi-family units. In addition, FHA loans for the remodeling of existing structures were small and had a short amortization period, making it easier and cheaper for a family to purchase a new home than to renovate an older one. But the most important factor encouraging white suburbanization and reinforcing the segregation of blacks was the FHA requirement for an "unbiased," professional appraisal of insured properties, which naturally included a rating of the neighborhood.

In rating the home, the FHA established minimum standards for lot size, setbacks, and separation from existing structures that essentially eliminated front eligibility many inner-city dwellings, notably row houses and attached dwellings. In evaluating neighborhoods, the agency followed the HOLC's earlier lead in racial matters; it too manifested an obsessive concern with the presence of what the 1939 FHA *Underwriting Manual* called "inharmonious racial or nationality groups." According to the manual, "if a neighborhood is to retain stability, it is necessary that properties shall continue to be occupied by the same social and racial classes."

Thus, in the late 1940s, the FHA recommended the use and application of racially restrictive covenants as a means of ensuring the security of neighborhoods, and it did not change this recommendation until 1950, two years after covenants were declared unenforceable and contrary to public policy by the Supreme Court. Like the HOLC, the FHA compiled maps and charts showing the location and movement of black families, and it frequently drew updated versions of the HOLC Residential Security Maps to determine the suitability of neighborhoods for FHA loans.

As a result of these policies, the vast majority of FHA and VA mortgages went to white middle-class suburbs, and very few were awarded to black neighborhoods in central cities. It is difficult to determine the full extent of the resulting disinvestment in black neighborhoods, however, because the FHA did not publish loan statistics below the county level, which is curious given the agency's obsessive concern with neighborhood data prior to making the loans. Kenneth Jackson has partially overcome this limitation by focusing on cases in which cities and counties are coterminous.

St. Louis County, for example, is a suburban area that surrounds the City of St. Louis, which has the status of a county in Missouri. From 1934 to 1960, the former received five times as many FHA mortgages as did the latter, and nearly six times as much loan money; per capita mortgage spending was 6.3 times greater. Jackson observed similar differentials in the dispersal of FHA mortgages between Washington, D.C., and its suburbs. Most startling was the case of New York City and

its suburbs. Per capita FHA lending in Nassau County, New York (i.e., suburban Long Island) was eleven times that in Kings County (Brooklyn) and sixty times that in Bronx County (the Bronx).

As the new post-industrial urban order developed, the disinvestment in central cities at the expense of suburbs increasingly meant the disinvestment in blacks as opposed to whites. Sometimes FHA procedures rendered whole cities ineligible for FHA-guaranteed loans simply because of a minority presence, thereby accelerating their decline. In 1966, for example, the FHA had no mortgages in either Paterson or Camden, New Jersey, both older cities where the non-Hispanic white population was declining during the 1950s (and actually became a minority in the 1970s). Given the importance of the FHA in the residential housing market, such blanket redlining sent strong signals to private lending institutions, which followed suit and avoided making loans within the affected areas. The lack of loan capital flowing into minority areas made it impossible for owners to sell their homes, leading to steep declines in property values and a pattern of disrepair, deterioration, vacancy, and abandonment.

Thus, by the late 1950s, many cities were locked into a spiral of declining that was directly encouraged and largely supported by federal housing policies. As poor blacks from the south entered cities in large numbers, middle-class whites fled to the suburbs to escape them and to insulate themselves from the social problems that accompanied the rising tide of poor. As the growing demand for city services—and particularly social services—drove up the cost of local government, politicians were forced to raise taxes, which further accelerated the flight of the white middle class, creating additional pressures for tax increases, and so on.

Nevertheless, most cities were not completely stripped of their middle and upper classes. Whites associated with a variety of elite institutions—universities, hospitals, libraries, foundations, businesses—were often tied physically to the city by large capital investments, spatially immobile facilities, and long-standing traditions. Faced with a steady decline in the physical stock of the city and the progressive encroachment of the black ghetto, these powerful interests turned to the federal government for relief.

They received it from Congress in the form of the housing acts of 1949 and 1954, which provided federal funds to local authorities to acquire slum properties, assemble them into large parcels, clear them of existing structures, and prepare them for "redevelopment." But in order to qualify for federal funding, local redevelopment authorities had to guarantee that an adequate supply of replacement housing would be made available to displaced families at rents within their means. To satisfy the latter provision, local planning agencies turned to public housing.

During the 1950s and 1960s, local elites manipulated housing and urban renewal legislation to carry out widespread slum clearance in growing black neighborhoods that threatened white business districts and elite institutions. Public housing was pressed into service to house black families displaced by the razing of neighborhoods undergoing renewal. Although liberal planners often tried to locate the projects away from ghetto areas, white politicians and citizens mobilized to block the construction of projects within their neighborhoods; white city councils and mayors usually obtained the right of veto over any proposed project site. As a result, projects were typically built on cleared land within or adjacent to existing black neighborhoods. In order to save money, maximize patronage jobs, and house within the ghetto as many blacks as possible, local authorities constructed multi-unit projects of extremely high density.

The razing of neighborhoods near threatened areas did check the spread of "urban blight," and "saved" many areas, but black critics complained that "urban renewal" simply meant "Negro removal," and the evidence largely bears them out. As black neighborhoods adjacent to threatened white areas were torn down and converted to other uses, thereby blocking the expansion of the ghetto in that direction, public housing for displaced residents had to be constructed elsewhere. Because for political reasons projects could only be built in ghetto areas, other black neighborhoods were razed and high-density units constructed there to accommodate the residents of both neighborhoods.

In the end, urban renewal almost always destroyed more housing than it replaced. Many poor blacks were permanently displaced into other crowded ghetto neighborhoods, which contributed to their instability and further decline. Moreover, delays between the time when neighborhoods were torn down and new projects were

erected displaced many others into the ghetto on a temporary basis. Thus urban renewal programs frequently only shifted the problems of blight, crime, and instability from areas adjacent to elite white neighborhoods to locations deeper inside the black ghetto.

Established black neighborhoods, however, could not absorb all the families displaced by urban renewal and public housing construction, and some were forced to seek entry within working-class white neighborhoods located at points along the ghetto's periphery. An important secondary effect of urban renewal was to accelerate racial turnover, expand the ghetto, and shift the threat of ghetto expansion from elite white districts to working-class white neighborhoods.

By 1970, after two decades of urban renewal, public housing projects in most large cities had become black reservations, highly segregated from the rest of society and characterized by extreme social isolation. The replacement of low-density slums with high-density towers of poor families also reduced the class diversity of the ghetto and brought about a geographic concentration of poverty that was previously unimaginable. This new segregation of blacks—in economic as well as social terms—was the direct result of an unprecedented collaboration between local and national government.

This unholy marriage came about when private actions to maintain the color line were overwhelmed by the massive population shifts of the 1950s and 1960s. The degree of racial segregation in public housing is directly and unambiguously linked to the differential growth of black and white urban populations in the postwar era: blacks are now most segregated in public housing precisely in the urban areas where their numbers were growing most rapidly compared with whites during the 1960s. Public housing, in the words of the historian Arnold Hirsch, represents a new, federally sponsored "second ghetto," one "solidly institutionalized and frozen in concrete," where "government took an active hand not merely in reinforcing prevailing patterns of segregation, but in lending them a permanence never seen before."

EPILOGUE: THE RIOTS
AND THEIR AFTERMATH

By the late 1960s, virtually all American cities with significant black populations had come to house large ghettos characterized by extreme segregation and spatial isolation. Whereas before 1940 no racial or ethnic group in American history had ever experienced an isolation index above 60%, by 1970 this level was normal for blacks in large American cities. By the end of the 1960s, in other words, the average black city dweller lived in a neighborhood where the vast majority of his or her neighbors were also black.

Not only was the segregation of European ethnic groups lower, it was also temporary. Whereas Europeans' isolation indices began to drop shortly after 1920, the spatial isolation characteristic of blacks had become a permanent feature of the residential structure of large American cities by 1940. This profound segregation reversed nineteenth-century patterns, where neighborhoods were racially integrated and the social worlds of blacks and whites overlapped. Under the residential configurations prevailing in 1970, meaningful contact between blacks and whites outside the work force would be extremely unlikely.

These conditions came about because of decisions taken by whites to deny blacks access to urban housing markets and to exclude them from white neighborhoods. Throughout the postwar era, whites displayed a high degree of prejudice against black neighbors, and this sentiment was repeatedly expressed in violence directed at blacks who attempted to leave the ghetto. Restrictive covenants and deed restrictions were employed by neighborhood "improvement" associations to exclude blacks from housing outside the ghetto, boycotts were organized to punish merchants or agents who sold to blacks, and social pressure was applied to realtors, property owners, and public officials who did not adhere to the principle of racial exclusion. Discrimination in the real estate industry was institutionalized from 1920 onward.

After 1940, the federal government was drawn into the defense of the residential color line. Federally sponsored mortgage programs systematically channeled funds away from minority neighborhoods, bringing about a wholesale disinvestment in black communities during the 1950s and 1960s. Meanwhile, local officials, using funds from the U.S. Department of Housing and Urban Development, carried out systematic slum clearance in ghetto neighborhoods adjacent to threatened white districts and then built large blocks of high-density public housing in other black neighborhoods to contain black

families displaced by this "renewal." The result was a new, more permanent, federally sponsored "second ghetto" in which blacks were isolated by class as well as by race.

The economic deprivation, social isolation, and psychological alienation produced by decades of segregation bore bitter fruit in a series of violent urban riots during the 1960s. The violence began in Birmingham, Alabama, in the summer of 1963, but the real bellwether was the Los Angeles riot of August 1965, which did $35 million worth of damage and left 4,000 injured and 34 dead. After sporadic violence in Chicago and Cleveland during the summer of 1966, a convulsive wave of mob violence erupted during July and August of 1967, when black ghettos in sixty U.S. cities exploded in a cataclysm of frustration and rage. The violence was particularly destructive in Detroit, Newark, and Milwaukee; Chicago's inferno followed Martin Luther King's assassination in April of 1968.

Unlike the communal race riots of the early 1900s, these disturbances arose from within the black community itself and were "commodity riots," directed at property rather than people. Outside of confrontations with police and guardsmen, there was little black-on-white or white-on-black violence. Attacks were confined largely to the ghetto and were directed at white property, institutions, or authority symbols. Looting became the characteristic act of the disturbances. White people were not singled out for assault, and black rioters did not attempt to leave the ghetto. The participants did not express a racial hatred of whites per se, but an anger with the conditions of racial oppression and economic deprivation that had been allowed to fester in the ghetto for sixty years.

In the wake of the violence and destruction, President Johnson appointed a national commission of elected officials and public figures chaired by Governor Otto Kerner of Illinois. The Kerner Commission issued its report in March 1968 and firmly concluded that the riots stemmed from the persistence of racial discrimination and a historical legacy of disadvantages in employment, education, and welfare; but one additional factor was clearly identified by the commissioners as underlying all other social and economic problems: segregation.

A point "fundamental to the Commission's recommendations" was that "federal housing programs must be given a new thrust aimed at overcoming the prevailing pattern of racial segregation. If this is not done, those programs will continue to concentrate the most impoverished and dependent segments of the population into central-city ghettos where there is already a critical gap between the needs of the population and the public resources to deal with them." To accomplish this aim, the commission recommended that the federal government "enact a comprehensive and enforceable open housing law to cover the sale or rental of all housing," and that it "reorient federal housing programs to place more low and moderate income housing outside of ghetto areas."

Within months of the commission's report, the nation seemed to be moving decisively toward the implementation of these recommendations. In April 1968 the Fair Housing Act was passed by Congress and signed into law by the President; it banned discrimination in the sale or rental of housing. The following year a federal judge in Chicago ruled favorably on a major lawsuit alleging discrimination in public housing and ordered the Chicago Housing Authority to take remedial action. Given these new tools in the fight against residential segregation, observers looked forward to the dismantling of the ghetto during the 1970s and to a reversal of historical trends toward segregation.

T E N

The Structuring of Hispanic Ethnicity
Theoretical and Historical Considerations

Frank D. Bean
Marta Tienda

Although common ancestral ties to Spain and/or Latin America, as well as frequent usage of the Spanish language, might seem to imply an underlying cultural similarity among peoples of Hispanic origin, the diverse settlement and immigration experiences of Mexicans, Puerto Ricans, Cubans, and other Hispanic groups have created distinct subpopulations with discernible demographic and economic characteristics. Persisting socioeconomic differences among these groups not only challenge the idea that the term "Hispanic" is appropriate as an ethnic label, they also suggest that a careful scrutiny of the historical commonalities and divergencies among these groups as they have settled in the United States is relevant to understanding their contemporary sociodemographic situations. This article attempts such a scrutiny.[1]

Our purpose is to lay the theoretical and historical groundwork for interpreting the extensive variation in demographic and socioeconomic characteristics of peoples of Spanish origin in 1980, as well as for understanding changes in these characteristics since 1960. A portion of this effort involves examining the concept of ethnicity, which Yinger defines as "a segment of a larger society whose members are thought, by themselves and/or others, to have a common origin and to share important segments of a common culture and who, in addition, participate in shared activities in which the common origin and culture are significant ingredients" (Yinger 1985). In an at-

From Frank D. Bean and Marta Tienda, *The Hispanic Population of the United States,* © 1987 Russell Sage Foundation, New York, New York. Reprinted by permission.

tempt to clarify the meaning of Hispanic ethnicity in contemporary United States society, we explore how each of the major Hispanic national origin groups has entered the country and how this has shaped their definitions of ethnicity. This task initially requires separating conceptually the structural elements of ethnicity from its cultural manifestations. To assist us in accomplishing this objective we draw upon historical comparisons among Mexicans, Puerto Ricans, and Cubans—the three largest Hispanic groups each of which has come from a single national origin—calling attention to the social and political factors affecting their migration to this country, their incorporation into the labor market, and their settlement patterns. Although our primary goal is to describe the demographic and social history of these Spanish origin groups, we also comment on the usefulness of the idea of Hispanic ethnicity and on the extent to which it constitutes a sociopolitical force shaping the contemporary pattern of ethnic stratification in the United States.

ON THE SOCIAL CONSTRUCTION OF ETHNICITY: THEORETICAL CONSIDERATIONS

In the context of the United States as a nation of immigrants, it is impossible to define ethnicity simply as a collection of ascriptive traits. While the importance of such traits as rallying points for people of similar cultural backgrounds cannot be denied, primordial ties—defined by Geertz as "the longing not to belong to any other group" (Geertz 1963:109)—are not sufficient to explain ethnic group solidarity. Ethnicity is also a social phenomenon. This is demonstrated by the fact that ethnic group boundaries are defined not only by socially produced rules of descent, but also can be changed by group members themselves. One becomes an ethnic by virtue of leaving the homeland and by virtue of one's social status vis-à-vis the dominant majority in the receiving society. Frequently a common sense of nationality emerges only after immigration. This was the case with many European immigrants and can be seen today in the emergence to a certain degree of a common sense of identification among Hispanics and Asian Americans who have come from previously distinct and often hostile national groups (Bonacich 1980; Yancey, Erickson, and Juliani 1976). But the

very fact that recent ethnic labels for Hispanics have been ever-changing—from Latins to Hispanics to Latinos—itself reflects the social tensions that render the concept of Hispanic ethnicity problematic and the political cohesion of the diverse groups questionable.

The complexities involved in interpreting ethnicity are aptly demonstrated in the case of the United States Hispanic population. Although their presence in the United States predates the emergence of the American nation, their political strength and national visibility, resulting in part from high fertility and the continued influx of new immigrants, presents a challenge for students of ethnic stratification. "Hispanic" as a label combines second-generation natives and their offspring, foreigners, and political refugees under one ethnic umbrella, but the adequacy of this and other singular labels is questionable on theoretical and historical grounds.

As the flow of immigrants from Latin America and the Spanish-speaking Caribbean into the United States continues to increase the size of the Hispanic population, a partially unified sense of nationality seems to be emerging among Hispanic origin groups. However, this sense of identification is fragile for political and demographic reasons. Not only do the short-term social goals of the various national origin groups differ, but the varying geographical distributions of the groups undermine the possibility of an overarching cohesion. Moreover, unlike the European immigrants of the nineteenth and early twentieth centuries, many Hispanics, perhaps because they are more recent immigrants, have not yet become fully integrated into the broader society. And, in contrast to the case of other white immigrants, use of the mother tongue has not disappeared among third- or later-generation Mexicans and Puerto Ricans reared in the United States. Today Hispanic enclaves and the Spanish language thrive in different regions of the country, although considerable linguistic acculturation can be observed among all Spanish-speaking national origin groups who have lived in the United States for longer than a generation. That these processes have not occurred at uniform rates among various national origin and cultural groups lends support to the view that ethnicity is socially produced.

A frequent depiction of the social and economic experiences of U.S. immigrants is that most groups have confronted similar opportunities in the host society. Without taking into account differences in the historical contexts of the migrations, differences in the ways the various groups have been received in the new society, and differences in the nature of the migration process itself, many observers often evaluate ethnic groups in terms of how they fare in "becoming American." "Americanization," however, is a multifaceted process which encompasses cultural, social, and psychological dimensions as well as those which are purely economic, yet the latter seem to weigh most heavily in assessments of which groups have and which have not become well integrated into the American mainstream. Those who do not succeed socially or economically—the unmeltable ethnics—undermine the idea that the "melting pot" is the dominant metaphor guiding our understanding of ethnic relations. Despite alternative interpretations that have surfaced to explain the social significance of ethnicity and the persistence of racial and ethnic stratification in contemporary U.S. society, the melting pot metaphor has yet to be replaced.

One perspective on the persistence of racial and ethnic stratification maintains that ethnic cohesion persists as the natural extension of primordial ties. This view gives rise to the notion that the disadvantaged, marginal position of certain ethnic and racial groups results from their cultural deficiencies, and that these disappear as individuals assimilate into the dominant culture. A contrasting theoretical perspective views ethnic divisions as mere reflections of class divisions. Several variants of the class interpretation of persisting ethnic differentiation exist, but the unifying theme is their focus on economic rather than cultural factors as determinants of ethnic inequality and their emphasis on structural instead of individual factors in the explanation of rates of assimilation. The great diversity in the ethnic experience in the United States challenges both of these perspectives and most that fall between them. Reducing ethnic stratification to a class phenomenon is reasonable only under the assumption that all members of an ethnic group are in the same class. Similarly, because ethnic identity and solidarity shift across groups and historical eras, it is equally inappropriate to deny the importance of social factors in molding ethnicity over time and place. Members of ethnic groups who combine high levels of economic success with strong ethnic identi-

fications present a troublesome inconsistency for theories that would see ethnicity and class as nearly perfectly overlapping categories (Hirschman 1983).

In acknowledging that ascriptive traits are far less salient determinants of ethnic group boundaries than socially constructed membership rules, we believe that ethnicity is predominantly a social phenomenon organized around outwardly visible physical and cultural differences between two or more groups. Moreover, the fact that ethnic boundaries can be changed by group members to make the collectivity more or less inclusive requires a dynamic conception of ethnicity and a view that is sensitive to the historical setting in which it occurs. Finally, whether an individual is a member of an ethnic group depends not only on outwardly visible ascriptive traits, but also on the person's identification with a particular ethnic group.

That ethnic boundaries are defined by a constellation of social forces, including the degree of ethnic and racial antagonism in the host society, calls attention to a third aspect of the social construction of ethnicity—that is, its interactive character. While the common sense of nationality which constitutes the minimum criterion for ethnic identification emerges only after immigration and the ensuing process of social comparison between the newcomers and the members of the majority group, the extent to which ethnic boundaries become clearly defined varies directly with the reception the group experiences in the host society at the time of immigration and for some time following. For many groups the elaboration of ethnicity is a direct reaction to manifestations of ethnic antagonism and hostility against newcomers who are perceived to be in direct competition for a limited pool of social and economic resources (Olzak 1980; Lieberson 1961). Whether immigrant groups are eventually successful in overcoming such hostility is a critical distinction between those who become disadvantaged and those who do not.

Ideas about the social construction of ethnicity are illustrated in the work of William Yancey and his associates which focuses on European immigrants and their experiences in becoming part of American society (Yancey, Erickson, and Juliani 1976). Although quite different in many ways, the comparison of the European and Latin American immigration experiences can fruitfully illustrate the importance of social and historical factors in structuring the dimensions and manifestations of ethnicity. Although the amalgamation experiences of the predominantly white European immigrants gave birth to the melting pot metaphor, it remains to be seen whether the relatively more recent experiences of Latin American and Asian immigrants will lead to a similar result. That many Hispanic immigrants and their descendants have yet to assimilate culturally or socially and occupy lower socioeconomic positions raises the possibility that a greater congruence of ethnic distinctiveness and socioeconomic position may characterize their experience. This issue needs to be further explored in both theoretical and empirical terms if we are to understand the experiences of Hispanic immigrant groups in the United States.

Starting with the idea that ethnicity is a variable, William Yancey and his associates identify several factors that contribute to the emergence of ethnicity among immigrant groups, including (1) the legal and political guidelines determining who can immigrate, (2) the need for and availability of wage labor, (3) the changing structure of industry, and (4) the ecological configuration of urban areas. Yancey and his collaborators argue that these structural variables played an important role in shaping the integration experiences of European immigrants. They claim—and we agree —that these supra-individual variables better explain the residential and occupational concentration of foreign-born groups than the traditional notion of cultural disposition or preference for certain types of work. Accordingly, we argue below that similar factors have operated for Hispanic groups.

Two factors—residential and occupational concentration—are especially crucial to the formation of ethnic group solidarity in that they produce common interests, lifestyles, and friendships. When the ethnic experience includes rejection, discrimination, and oppression, ethnic ties provide a ready system of support for groups that are readily distinguishable by race, national origin, and/or language. As we will see below, the migration and settlement patterns, and the ensuing labor market experiences of Hispanic origin groups, have had much more to do with contemporary expressions of socioeconomic differentiation among peoples of Spanish origin than have any tendencies to embrace aspects of a common Latin American or Spanish culture.

In order to distinguish between and compare the waves of immigration from Europe, about which Yancey and his colleagues wrote, and the historically later Hispanic flow, one must also draw attention to the timing of immigration and to the various modes of entry and integration of specific national origin groups. Time of immigration is crucial because of temporal changes in employment opportunities and changing demand for various skills as the economy has shifted from goods to service production. Europeans settled in large eastern and western cities during a period of industrial expansion (Cafferty, et al. 1985). In contrast, the early Hispanic influx, involving mostly Mexicans, began as a rural phenomenon (Tienda 1981). As a predominantly urban population after the 1950s, Hispanics have faced an economic system characterized by periods of restricted growth coupled with dramatic changes in the structure of production (Singelmann and Tienda 1985). Race and racial discrimination must also be considered as a force shaping the integration experiences of Hispanics, especially those of Puerto Rican origin, even though a racial classification of Hispanics is complicated by the fact that they are brown, black, and white. The changes in the political and legal rights of people of color in the United States should enhance opportunities in the world of work and schooling, but evidence of such outcomes is limited.

A critical question is why certain ethnic groups are singled out for segregation in the least desirable low-skill, low-paying jobs, while others are not. A related and perhaps more central question for understanding the persistence and nature of ethnic stratification is why some groups manage to experience mobility from low- to high-status jobs while others do not. Racism is an important element in this explanation, but it is a mistake to view the situation of white European immigrants as completely distinct from that of racial minorities. At the time of initial entry European immigrants served many of the same functions that racial and ethnic minority workers currently do and also were segregated residentially and occupationally by national origin (Lieberson 1980). The key issue is why Europeans made the transition from low-status occupational positions to the higher-status, better-paying jobs while blacks and Hispanics have not yet done so.

More than any other single comparison, these contrasting outcomes make a critical distinction between ethnic groups and minority groups. Minority groups and ethnic groups are not isomorphic, yet virtually all minorities are distinguishable by ethnic (and/or racial) traits. However, many ethnic groups are not minorities in the sense of being ethnically identifiable and economically disadvantaged. For example, Cubans and other Latin American immigrants are seldom identified as a minority group, but Mexicans and Puerto Ricans usually are. The reason, we maintain, has to do with their very different modes of incorporation and socioeconomic integration experiences.

Vincent has elaborated at some length the distinction between minorities and ethnics, and her interpretation is helpful for understanding the diverse experiences of Hispanics in the United States. A minority, according to Vincent, is a group whose members are treated unequally by a dominant group, usually through prejudice and discrimination. Ethnic groups, on the other hand, are collectivities sharing common cultural norms, values, identities, and behaviors, and who both recognize themselves and are recognized by others as being ethnic (Vincent 1974).

The extent to which ethnicity is a matter of individual choice depends on the group's access (or lack thereof) to the reward system of the dominant society. For members of lower socioeconomic strata opportunities to elaborate or conceal national origin are considerably more limited, if they exist at all. In this light the convergence of ethnic origin and economic disadvantage requires an investigation of the circumstances that translate ethnicity into a disadvantaged economic position for some and a symbolic identity with few if any socioeconomic consequences for others (Gans 1979). Such a pursuit might fruitfully uncover the areas of convergence and divergence among Hispanic origin groups and help to clarify the origins of the differential access to resources and social rewards that impart a different socioeconomic connotation to the phrase "Hispanic ethnicity" for Mexicans, Puerto Ricans, Cubans, and other Latin Americans.

THE EMERGENCE AND CONSOLIDATION OF "HISPANICITY"

To guide our interpretation of the historical circumstances that have shaped the integration of the diverse Hispanic origin groups into the U.S. society and economy, we first set forth the theoretical framework which outlines the processes underlying the emergence, consolidation, and reformulation of Hispanic ethnicity. For this outline we draw heavily on the work of Yancey and his associates (1976), adapting the particulars of their analysis of European ethnics to the experience of Hispanics. Subsequently we compile brief historical vignettes of the integration experiences of Mexican, Puerto Rican, and Cuban origin populations in an attempt to illustrate the diversity of experiences which help explain the extensive socioeconomic and demographic heterogeneity of the peoples of Spanish origin.

Figure 1 maps the major historical and social processes describing the emergence, transformation, and reformulation of ethnicity which help in interpreting the diverse integration experiences and socioeconomic standing of Hispanics. These processes are by nature interactive, and the ways in which the social and historical dimensions intersect are central to understanding the relegation of Hispanics to a minority group status, or their eventual adoption of a more symbolic ethnicity, one less intertwined with economic and social standing.

The Hispanic population emerged as an ethnic group historically through international migration and, to a lesser extent in the Mexican case, through conquest. The reasons for their entry into the United States, combined with the historical moment of that entry, affected both the composition of the Spanish-speaking groups according to national origin and their eventual geographical configuration and socioeconomic standing. Patterns of interethnic contact, once established, were determined by occupational and residential segregation and the changing climate of prejudice and xenophobic sentiment. Integration processes also changed in accordance with shifting economic conditions, the passing of generations, and legal prescriptions governing both immigration flows and labor practices.

Once consolidated, ethnic groups can reformulate their position vis-à-vis the dominant society in response to any number of circumstances. Hispanics having more "successful" integration experiences are more likely to have maintained a symbolic connection to their ethnic heritage, as manifested by the continued observance of holidays, the revival of ethnic foods, the practice of cultural rituals, and so on, while in the areas of oc-

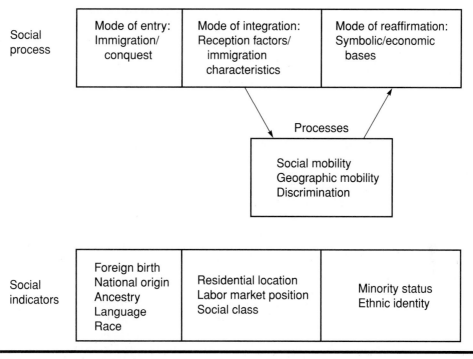

Social process

Mode of entry: Immigration/ conquest	Mode of integration: Reception factors/ immigration characteristics	Mode of reaffirmation: Symbolic/economic bases

Processes

Social mobility
Geographic mobility
Discrimination

Social indicators

Foreign birth National origin Ancestry Language Race	Residential location Labor market position Social class	Minority status Ethnic identity

FIGURE 1 *Structuring of Hispanic Ethnicity: A Conceptual Framework*

cupation, education, language, and residence they have increasingly modeled Anglos. The elaboration of these ethnic traits acquires a symbolic character which reinforces the validity of cultural pluralism as a perspective on ethnic stratification. In a stratified society it is possible for some members of a group to be socioeconomically successful while the group as a whole occupies a disadvantaged position vis-à-vis the dominant majority.

Alternatively, for Hispanics who have not gained access to new opportunities, and for whom isolation within minority occupational and residential enclaves and systematic discrimination have remained the rule, ethnicity becomes synonymous with minority status. For ethnic minorities the significance of ethnicity not only extends beyond the symbolic manifestations of cultural heritage, but it also is more than a simple reflection of economic relationships. The survival of distinct ethnic cultures, while structurally determined, attests to the reflexive nature of ethnicity as it offers refuge to its adherents against the very system that produces stratification and oppression.

Theoretical constructs such as those abstractly presented thus far need to be translated into concrete social experiences through the stories of real people. It is to these that our focus now shifts. In discussing the very different integration experiences of Mexicans, Puerto Ricans, and Cubans in the United States, the elements that translated Hispanic origin to a symbolic ethnicity for some and a minority status for others will become apparent. So, too, will the fluid character of Hispanic ethnicity as a social construct.

Mexicans

In comparison with other national and immigrant minorities, including Puerto Ricans, Cubans, and other Latin Americans, Chicanos[2] are distinguished because for some of the members of this group entry into the United States came about through conquest and subordination (Almaquer 1974; Murguia 1975). Historically and today residentially concentrated in the Southwest, the Mexican ancestry population is not only the largest of the Spanish-speaking nationalities, constituting roughly 60 percent of the total Hispanic population in 1980 . . . but also the most hetero-geneous in socioeconomic characteristics and generational composition (Tienda 1981; Bean, Stephen, and Optiz 1985). The social antecedents of this heterogeneity are rooted in the history of U.S. westward expansion, the geographic proximity and poverty of Mexico that has facilitated continued immigration, and the historical labor functions of Mexican workers in the U.S. economy. These factors, along with changes in immigration policies and the resurgence of Mexican ethnicity that accompanied the Chicano movement of the 1960s, were decisive in molding the contemporary socioeconomic position of people of Mexican origin.

By annexing the states of California, Arizona, New Mexico, Colorado, and Texas at the conclusion of the Mexican-American War, the Treaty of Guadalupe Hidalgo which ended the war also created the Mexican American population as a people. Beyond its political and military implications, the territorial annexation of the Southwest was socially significant in establishing the social destiny of the Mexican American population. Unlike other immigrant groups who voluntarily migrated to the United States and whose sense of peoplehood and ethnicity was shaped by the immigration process and subsequent reception in the new society, Mexicans residing on U.S. territory at that time had neither cause nor power to challenge the new Anglo rulers. Not only did a rapid and clear break with the parent country occur, together with ensuing socioeconomic and cultural subjugation, but the land itself that the indigenous population considered its own was often lost (Alvarez 1973).

Once conquered, the Southwest was opened for Anglo "settlement." This invitation resulted in an influx of thousands of non-Hispanic whites who took control of the land and brought about the eventual destruction or transformation of the indigenous social systems governing the lives of the original Mexican residents. The subsequent development of the area by Anglos depended on the abundant and cheap labor of foreigners in the three major economic sectors—agriculture, mining, and the railroad industry. As Cardoso has described, the construction of the railroads in the Southwest was very important in providing employment and determining settlement patterns (Cardoso 1980). Also, the expansion of commercial agriculture in the West contributed significantly to capital accumulation that made the economic transformation of the area possible. However, this economic growth came at the social expense of the Mexican people who were paid "Mexican wages" for Mexican work. While mechanization began to affect grain crops prior to World War II, fruits, vegetables, and cotton remained labor intensive into the 1960s and early 1970s. Their importance as a commercial crop for agricultural corporations rose steadily and required a large seasonal labor force. Because of the historical role of Chicanos in the development of U.S. agriculture, Chicano workers constituted up to 85 percent of common labor employed in the fields well into the twentieth century (Almaguer 1974).

As Chicanos lost their land, their social mobility became blocked, and this eventually led to a deterioration of their social position vis-à-vis Anglos. Racism was employed to pursue economic interests (all racial minorities in the area were subjected to similar treatment); although Mexicans are white, their brown skin and indigenous features encouraged racism and discrimination by the Anglo majority. That Mexicans were viewed as "non-white" is attested to by the fact that they were classified as a racial group in the 1930 census. The results of racial discrimination and subordination led to a set of conditions that both structured the lives of Chicanos and gave racial and ethnic prejudice a life of its own in the Southwest, but particularly in Texas.

Equally important to an understanding of Chicano ethnicity is the phenomenon of immigration which gained momentum after the Mexican Revolution of 1910 and propelled thousands north of the Rio Grande in search of refuge and employment. Initially the flow of workers over the United States–Mexico border was relatively slow. For the 30-year period following the annexation of the Southwest territory there was relatively little migratory movement over the newly established boundary between Mexico and the United States. In many ways the American Southwest operated as an isolated area that was culturally and economically removed from the rest of the country (Massey 1983). However, this situation changed dramatically after 1880. At that point immigration became the main vehicle by which the Mexican population grew and consolidated its regional and residential segregation in the

Southwest; its social and demographic significance cannot be overstated.

The increased flow of Mexican workers into the United States after 1880 coincided with the rapid economic development of the Southwest largely owing to the expansion of employment opportunities in commercial agriculture, mining, and railroad construction. Massive political upheavals in Mexico which culminated in a bloody revolution (1910–1917) further drove thousands of Mexicans to "El Norte" in search of employment opportunities and political refuge. Employers in the United States gladly hired Mexicans as cheap laborers, especially as labor shortages resulting from World War I diminished output and profit margins.

The history of Mexican immigration in the twentieth century is cyclical, with the doors open in times of labor shortages, followed by restrictive policies and even massive deportations during periods of economic recession (Acuña 1971; Samora 1971). Between 1880 and 1929, when Mexican workers began to enter the United States in significant numbers and the U.S. economy expanded, Mexican immigration policy was relatively unrestricted. Consequently, by the time of the Great Depression, the U.S. Census enumerated over 1 million persons of Mexican ancestry in the United States (Massey 1983). However, the flow of immigrants from Mexico ebbed considerably during the 1930s when widespread domestic unemployment contributed to a wave of anti-Mexican sentiment which culminated in a massive repatriation campaign that, unfortunately, affected native-born residents as well as the foreign-born. Although the Mexican origin population declined during the 1930s as a consequence of forced and voluntary emigration (Jaffe, Cullen, and Boswell 1980), by that time the Mexican origin population was firmly established in the Southwest and selected communities of the industrial Midwest.

World War II triggered another period of labor shortages, particularly in the agricultural industry which had not yet mechanized, and led to the establishment of the contract labor system between Mexico and the United States. Conceived as a temporary solution to the labor shortages in agriculture, the bracero program, which lasted from 1942 to 1964, revived the tradition of regular migration to the United States and reversed the emigration of Mexicans witnessed during the 1930s. Since the mid-1950s the volume of immigration from Mexico has continued to increase, and during the latter 1970s legal immigration reached levels not experienced since the 1920s. However, as the restrictions on who could enter limited the number of legal immigrants from Mexico, the volume of illegal entrants has also increased (Samora 1971; Massey 1981; Keely 1979).

The significance of the pre-1930 immigrant flow for the structuring of Chicano ethnicity was far-reaching. First, it increased the size of the Mexican origin population of the United States while consolidating its regional and residential segregation in the Southwest. Second, it reinforced the relegation of the Mexican origin people to a virtually unnegotiable—at least until the 1960s—low-status position in the social hierarchy. This legacy of social and economic disadvantage persists until the present day. Third, it channeled a significant share of the Mexican origin work force into the rural economy as a largely mobile, seasonal, and docile agricultural work force (Alvarez 1973; Tienda 1981). Like the rest of the U.S. population during the 1930s, 1940s, and 1950s, the Chicano population became an increasingly urban population during this period, especially as the mechanization of cotton production and that of several fruits and vegetables reduced the demand for agricultural labor.

The dimensions of immigration from Mexico to the United States in the twentieth century are so staggering that some have argued that the process has become self-sustaining via kinship ties and ethnic barrios which provide contacts and resources for incoming workers (Barrera 1979; Tienda 1980). This helps explain its apparently "irrational" continuation despite the stricter immigration policies and the shrinking job market of the 1970s and 1980s. The relationship between family networks and ongoing migration has several implications for Chicano ethnicity. Reliance of low-wage Chicano workers on assistance from their families is a form of subsidy to employers in that their wages do not have to cover all of their maintenance costs (Buroway 1976; Tienda 1980). Also, the influx of recent arrivals from the Mexican community juxtaposes the values of Mexican culture and those of Anglo culture as transmitted through the schools, mass media, industrial discipline, and so on, thus serving as a constant reminder of differences between the two (Saragoza

1983). If the numbers of immigrants created excess labor supply during much of the first half of the twentieth century, exerting downward pressure on wages and undermining efforts at union organization, it also resulted in resentment on the part of Anglo workers. This hostility, which combined with opposition from small farmers who were unable to compete with large enterprises employing cheap labor, isolated Chicanos from the Anglo working class and further cut them off from potential avenues of integration into the social and economic mainstream. The racism practiced by employers resulted in a set of conditions that both structured the lives of Chicanos and augmented racial and ethnic prejudice in the Southwest. The continuing entry of new immigrants maintains and renews this process.

The longer history of Mexicans in the United States makes them more generationally diverse than other Hispanic origin groups. After the hysteria of the repatriation of the 1930s subsided, a segment of the Mexican origin population—largely urban, upwardly mobile natives—developed a sense of cultural loyalty to the United States. Their receptivity to cultural assimilation was advanced by several factors, including the transition from an agricultural, nonmetropolitan, and foreign-born population to a blue-collar, metropolitan, and native-born group. Noticeable advances in education, income, and political efficacy engendered in this segment a false sense of social acceptance and security, one fueled by the belief of brighter prospects for their offspring (Tienda 1981). However, the Chicano movement of the late 1960s rekindled the pain of social rejection and accumulated disadvantages. Moreover, the critical absence of older role models with certified middle-class status bolstered the development of a new consciousness among the supporters of the Chicano movement. The more militant advocated separation and decolonization, whereas the resurgence of Mexican ethnicity among the less militant activists was articulated in demands for self-determination, equality, and a cultural self-redefinition as Chicanos rather than as Mexican Americans (Loomis 1974).

Despite the success of the Chicano movement of the mid-1960s in calling attention to the social injustices endured by earlier generations of Mexican and Mexican American workers, a decade later, the imprint of social inequality persists.

Today, although the historical legacy remains, dramatic changes have occurred in the residence patterns and the structure of opportunity open to Chicanos. Although Mexicans as a group are principally now an urban-based population, one clear vestige of the rural origins characteristic of part of the population is their current disproportionate representation in agriculture—not as farmers, but as seasonal and permanent laborers. That these vestiges should persist, despite gains from unionization efforts and legal sanctions against discriminatory practices, is a reminder of the strength of their influence in the past. However, urban residence has provided access to a wider range of employment opportunities and has gradually eroded the viability of the colonial labor system. Cultural manifestations of changes associated with the urbanization experience include the trend toward a language shift away from Spanish (Gardner 1977), the declining isolation of the barrio (Moore 1970), and indicators pointing to a greater degree of assimilation into Anglo society (Massey 1981). Mario Barrera concedes that the segmentation line separating Chicanos from the majority culture across all classes has been weakening since World War II (Barrera 1979). This indicates that class divisions could be more salient than ethnic ones as Chicanos become more integrated into the nonsubordinate part of the labor force, but the prospects of this occurring also depend on the process of immigration and the vitality of the U.S. economy. The historical record to date is mixed, providing signs of hope as well as signs of distress.

Puerto Ricans
Compared with Mexicans, Puerto Ricans have a much shorter history in the United States, and they make up a smaller share of all Hispanics than do Mexicans. In 1980 Puerto Ricans constituted approximately 14 percent of the Hispanic population living on the mainland. Designated a U.S. territory at the culmination of the Spanish-American war in 1898, Puerto Rico became a semi-autonomous Commonwealth in 1952. This status has obliterated economic boundaries and protective mechanisms that many Third World nations employ to defend local interests and has fostered the economic dependency of the island on the United States. The processes set in motion by the United States' domination of the island's economy have been intense since the island ac-

quired Commonwealth status, bringing on rapid economic changes, restructuring class relations, and introducing new value conflicts largely owing to an extensive migration process that continues to the present day (Mintz 1973). As time passes, the nature of the relationship between the island Commonwealth and the United States makes it even more difficult to define the island culturally or ethnically, for that which is Puerto Rican is partly North American as well.

While the island is self-governing in all domestic matters, the governance structure is bounded by the provisions of the federal constitution (Jaffe et al. 1980). Commonwealth status confers on the Puerto Rican population several privileges and obligations. Among the former are "common citizenship, common defense, common currency, and a common loyalty to the value of democracy" (National Puerto Rican Coalition 1985). That Puerto Rican island residents may not vote in U.S. presidential elections, are not represented in the U.S. Senate, and have a nonvoting Resident Commission in the House of Representatives attests to their second-class citizenship. Moreover, the privilege of citizenship which gives Puerto Ricans unrestricted entry to the United States mainland is a mixed blessing. With the benefit of national defense comes the requirement of military service. In exchange for unequal representation and voting privileges, the U.S. Congress has exempted Puerto Rican residents from federal income taxes and federal excise taxes.

Puerto Ricans have lived in the continental United States for more than a century, but the emergence of a visible Puerto Rican community is essentially a post–World War II phenomenon. Like most ethnic communities in the United States (with the notable exceptions of the Mexican and Native American populations), the Puerto Rican population on the mainland emerged through migration. Although there existed a small Puerto Rican community in New York before World War II, the major exodus from the island to the continental United States began in the 1940s and accelerated after 1950. Average migration rates from Puerto Rico to New York more than doubled during the 1950s, rising from an average annual flow of 18,700 persons between 1940 and 1950 to 41,200 between 1950 and 1960. The sharp decline in the average annual Puerto Rican conflux between 1960 and 1970 is even more impres-

sive, falling to less than 15,000 per year (Centro de Estudio's Puertorriqueños 1979). Presumably a circular migration flow, which is characteristic of Puerto Ricans, underlies these dramatic changes in the number of Puerto Rican migrants arriving on the mainland.

As a result of this massive migration process, the Puerto Rican population residing in the continental United States increased from roughly 70,000 in 1940 to over 300,000 in 1950 and 893,000 in 1960. With the drop in migration during the 1960s, the growth rate of the stateside Puerto Rican population also slowed. Even with moderate migrant inflows, the Puerto Rican population continued to increase, reaching 1.4 million in 1970 and 1.8 million in 1980 (Massey 1983). While the 56 and 29 percent increases in the size of the Puerto Rican population during the 1960s and 1970s, respectively, are impressive by most standards, they are strikingly low compared with the three- to four-fold increases experienced during the two prior decades.

These sharp demographic changes are largely the result of a decision to transform and develop Puerto Rico's plantation economy through a program of rapid industrialization. The apparent success of the infamous Operation Bootstrap (in effect from 1948 to 1965) hinged on several key factors, including unrestricted migration between the mainland and the island. Even with the help of the burgeoning Commonwealth bureaucracy (employing three workers in ten by 1976), the new industrial order could not absorb the available workers, whose numbers rose steadily, owing to population growth and to a severe employment decline in the plantation sector. Agricultural employment dropped from 50 to 10 percent of all jobs between 1940 and 1970. Migration to the mainland provided a temporary solution to the acute unemployment problem. So intense was the outflow of wage laborers that during the 1950s Puerto Rico provided the unusual spectacle of a booming economy with a shrinking labor force (Centro de Estudios Puertorriqueños 1979).

Other influences on the migration flows from Puerto Rico to the U.S. mainland included easy, inexpensive air travel;[3] the impact of mass communication on potential job-seekers; obligatory military service; and the absence of immigration restrictions—all of which were rooted in the special relationship between Puerto Rico and the

United States (Rodriguez 1979). One might expect, then, that the relatively easy access of Puerto Ricans to the United States and their legal status as U.S. citizens would facilitate their integration into U.S. society by giving them a comparative advantage in securing employment and living quarters. Oftentimes the opposite occurred. As we will see in subsequent chapters, Puerto Ricans were often relegated to the lowest levels of the labor market. They frequently experienced social deprivation and discrimination in both the housing and job markets, and they often fared as badly or worse economically than blacks who migrated to the North.

It is both striking and significant for an understanding of the contemporary socioeconomic position of Puerto Ricans that of the 400,000 foreign contract workers brought to the United States during World War II, few were Puerto Rican, despite a 100 percent increase in unemployment on the island and despite the fact that Puerto Ricans were legal U.S. citizens who were serving in the military. This unfortunate fact concurs with the view that Puerto Ricans were incorporated into the mainland society as a second-class citizenry, one whose social and economic welfare was never represented in the national immigration policies (via relocation assistance such as that received by Cubans or recent Southeast Asian refugees) or in the economic policies allegedly designed to improve the vitality of the island economy.

The persistent inability of many island migrants to secure steady employment on the mainland, coupled with the displacement of Puerto Rican workers from declining textile and garment industries in the Northeast during the decade of the 1970s, set in motion a return migration process whose scale and duration cannot be predicted. The worsening labor market position of Puerto Rican men and women during the 1970s makes more glaring their position vis-à-vis other Hispanics, and their marginal labor market position carries over to other indicators of social well-being. Of all Hispanic origin groups they have the lowest labor force participation rates, the highest unemployment levels, the highest incidence of poverty, and the lowest levels of education (Tienda 1984).

Despite the very different circumstances leading to the establishment of the Puerto Rican and Mexican communities in the United States, there are several parallels between them which are pertinent to an understanding of the contemporary

socioeconomic positioning of the two groups (Massey 1983). First, both migratory movements were fundamentally wage labor flows destined for unskilled blue collar jobs. Second, both groups were destined for regional labor markets, the industrial Northeast in the case of Puerto Ricans and the agricultural Southwest in the case of Mexicans. Third, like Mexicans in the Southwest, Puerto Ricans in the Northeast have been the victims of intense discrimination and prejudice, perhaps even greater than that experienced by Mexicans in Texas (U.S. Commission on Civil Rights 1976; Massey and Bitterman 1985).

Similarities between the Mexican and Puerto Rican experiences should not be overstated (Massey 1983). Unlike Mexicans, whose labor market integration began as a largely agricultural experience, Puerto Ricans have been almost exclusively urban-based and concentrated in the manufacturing and service sectors of New York City (Tienda 1984). Thus, more than most groups—immigrants and natives alike—Puerto Ricans have disproportionately entered industries whose operations are seasonal in nature and in the declining manufacturing sector of the city; the suburbanization of industry, coupled with inadequate mass transit, has further restricted opportunities for those tied to their central city neighborhoods. This situation seemed to worsen during the 1970s as the flight of industry from the Frostbelt to the lower-wage Sunbelt progressed. Finally, the fact that Puerto Ricans are citizens by birth differentiates their entry to the mainland society from that of Mexicans, particularly those who enter in an undocumented status. Theoretically, their citizenship could give them greater political leverage in lobbying for their interests in the future, but this has not happened. Such a prospect depends much on the effectiveness of the community leaders in setting and pursuing a social agenda to rectify past injustices (National Puerto Rican Coalition 1984).

In brief, circular migration and relegation to the lowest levels of the socioeconomic ladder are two important defining features of the ethnic structuring process for Puerto Ricans.[4] These two dimensions are interrelated in complex and fluid ways. The circular migration means that the island population and mainland community are two parts of a whole. It means that elements of both cultures thrive in both places, which requires a dual functional ability: Children must be able to switch school systems and must cope with competing value systems. It has resulted, as Frank Bonilla states, in "an unprecedented job of psychological and cultural reconstitution and construction that must rest on a very special political and economic infrastructure" (Bonilla 1974).

Despite the strong cultural and economic ties between Puerto Rico and the United States, the image of a single monolithic Puerto Rican community spanning the two locations is not entirely accurate. Members of the second generation raised in New York City have been dubbed "Nuyoricans," indicating their simultaneous separateness from Puerto Rico and their connection to it. Being caught between two value systems, especially with respect to race and ethnicity, is not only a feature of life on the mainland but also, given the U.S. domination over the island, plays an important role there as well, producing ideological divisions that transcend those of class hierarchy.

Thus, Puerto Rican ethnicity can be interpreted as structurally determined by their dependent status, a pattern of migration that places Puerto Ricans between two worlds, and extreme occupational segregation. All of these contribute to their marginality vis-à-vis the rest of society. Their reaction is found in the maintenance of strong ethnic communities, low intermarriage rates (Fitzpatrick and Gurak 1979), and the rejection of a quick transfer of cultural identity. Although in part a response to and protection against oppression, the persistence of ethnic distinctiveness, despite massive pressure toward a homogeneous consumer culture, can also be interpreted as a form of protest. The settings for most Puerto Ricans—the schools, the streets, the military, the prisons, and the sweatshops—are radicalizing contexts. That Puerto Rican ethnicity is reaffirmed here is "a sign of remarkable survival in the face of radical ambiguity" (Bonilla 1974).

Cubans

The experience of Cubans, who by 1980 constituted roughly 6 percent of all Hispanic origin persons in the United States, presents a case of quite different features and outcomes that both challenges and supports the theoretical assumptions made with respect to the Mexican and Puerto Rican experiences. That Cubans have been relatively successful socioeconomically relative to Puerto Ricans and Mexicans is of critical comparative value in distinguishing their incorporation experience from that of the other groups. Three

factors stand out. First, the early immigrants were primarily political rather than economic refugees. Second, during the early phase of the exodus from Cuba, individuals from professional, urban, and more highly educated sectors were greatly overrepresented. Third, their reception in this country, especially their early reception, was not the tacit acceptance by employers hungry for cheap labor but rather a public welcome by the federal government eager to harbor those seeking refuge from a Communist dictatorship.

Although the 1950 census enumerated roughly 34,000 persons of Cuban birth, the Cuban presence in the United States increased during the late 1950s and throughout the 1960s because of the exit of thousands seeking asylum from the Castro regime (Jaffe et al. 1980). So intense was the initial exodus from the tiny island located just 90 miles from Key West that the 1960 census enumerated over 79,000 Cuban-born persons, representing more than a two-fold increase in less than two years following the 1959 Cuban Revolution. The flow of refugees intensified throughout the 1960s so that by 1970 more than half a million Cuban origin persons resided in the United States, with nearly 80 percent born in Cuba (Massey 1983). By the time the Cuban government imposed restrictions on the exodus of Cubans seeking asylum in the United States during the early 1970s, Cuban communities were firmly established and highly visible in southern Florida and large northeastern cities.

Owing largely to the volume of the refugee flow, the Cuban stock population had increased 25-fold in a 30-year period, rising to approximately 831,000 by 1980 (U.S. Bureau of the Census 1981e). Following the Mariel incident of 1980, when over 125,000 Cuban refugees were admitted to the United States (Bach 1980; Bach et al. 1981), the Cuban population exceeded 1 million, but these individuals were not included in the 1980 enumeration because they entered several weeks after the census was taken. Given their relatively recent immigration history, Cubans also show relatively little generational diversity, with the clear majority being first-generation immigrants or offspring of foreign-born.

Until the Cuban refugees arrived, no other immigrant group in this hemisphere has been so advantaged in terms of socioeconomic background and host country reception. That individuals from the upper and middle classes were dominant among the early exiles (Portes et al. 1977) led some to characterize the Cuban exodus as "the greatest brain drain ever to occur, leaving the Cuban middle class virtually gutted" (Casal and Hernandez 1975). However, this popular portrayal overlooks the fact that Cuban émigrés arrived in several successive waves, with the latter ones greatly diversifying the exile population. That is, while the earliest waves consisted of elite wealthy Batistianos, upper-class landholders, and businessmen who were able to leave with their wealth and possessions, those who arrived after the Bay of Pigs invasion had their assets confiscated and were left only the barest necessities (Rogg 1974).

Successive waves were younger and less well educated, neither rich nor part of the pre-Castro establishment. Roughly 40 percent of the refugees who came during the airlift years between 1965 and 1973 were students, women, and children joining relatives already in the United States (Casal and Hernandez 1975). Thus, while the label of self-imposed political exiles is largely an accurate description of Cubans who left during the early 1960s, studies of later waves have found significant numbers resembling traditional immigrants whose decisions to leave were governed by economic factors (Bach 1980).

In marked contrast to the reception of Mexican and Puerto Rican immigrants, the arrival of the Cubans involved the United States in the largest refugee aid operation in its history to that point. Any portrayal of the reception extended to Cubans must take this as its point of departure. Like the Puerto Rican migrants, Cuban exiles were offered cheap air transportation and permission to enter the United States without visas, not as immigrants but as special entrants, pending the possibility that the Communist government would not last. Unlike Puerto Ricans, Cuban refugees were provided with some resettlement assistance. Included in the Cuban refugee resettlement program were provisions for job training, professional recertification, assistance in securing employment, reimbursement to public schools for costs incurred by the entrance of Spanish-speaking Cuban children, and funds for special research and teaching opportunities for Cuban scholars (Rogg 1974).

The Cuban influx into Miami, combined with restrictive state aid laws, caused Florida authorities to appeal to the federal government for help with their resettlement. President Eisenhower's emergency relief measures were followed by Kennedy's Cuban Refugee Program in providing extensive aid for relocation away from Miami. Of the 251,000 Cubans initially registered with the government's refugee program in 1967, 153,000 (or 60 percent) had been relocated away from Miami (Wilson and Portes 1980). However, this policy of dispersal proved largely futile, as by 1970 two Cubans in three were living in either the Miami or the New York urbanized areas (Massey 1978), and recent census data indicate that the gravitation toward Miami has continued. Massey estimated that about 56 percent of all Cubans lived in Miami in 1980, up from 40 percent in 1970 (Massey 1983).

Given that the early waves of Cubans were from advantaged socio-economic backgrounds and received modest help from the federal government in relocating themselves in the United States, their socioeconomic success would not be surprising were it not for the serious obstacles they initially faced. Not the least of these was their widespread downward occupational mobility vis-à-vis positions held in Cuba. A comparison of early occupational positions in the United States with last occupations held in Cuba showed that in Miami the percentage of unskilled laborers had doubled. Cubans who had been employed as professionals, managers, and technicians dropped from 48 percent in Cuba to 13 percent in the United States (Casal and Hernandez 1975).

In many ways Cubans found themselves in a situation similar to that of many other immigrants during the 1960s. They were residentially segregated, they were concentrated in blue collar "ethnic" jobs, they were lacking English language skills, and they were tied to their ethnic communities. In New York and Miami they formed strong ethnically enclosed communities of extended families and friends who relied on each other for support and financial assistance. Whether this implied an affirmation of cultural identity is unclear, but their common national origin and political orientations provided a ready basis for the elaboration and cementing of intragroup social relations. Initially, their "commitments to old values and to a 'return' goal, together with a strong identification with Cuba and their past lives, [were] the most potent forces working against the Cubans' integration into the United States" (Portes 1969).

Despite the initial handicaps they encountered, and the belief by many that their stay in the United

States would be temporary, Cubans were never restricted to a position of second-class workers in an ethnically split labor market, nor was their success patterned after the gradual integration patterns of earlier European immigrants. In addition to the warm welcome and massive aid received under the auspices of the Cuban Refugee Program, two factors help explain their very different integration experience. These are class background and the formation of an ethnic enclave economy in Miami (Wilson and Portes 1980; Portes and Bach 1980).

Unlike Puerto Ricans and Mexicans, Cubans did not enter the United States as predominantly subordinate workers. They were fleeing the real and perceived persecution and harassment of a new regime. The same individualism that led upper- and middle-class Cubans to reject Castro provided both the cultural link to the socioeconomic values of the United States and the basis for effective competition. Their strong individualism and an orientation toward the future often compensated the initial loss of occupational position. Moreover, the opportunities for economic and social integration that the Cuban Refugee Program offered were perhaps more valuable for their symbolic political message than for the cash and in-kind resettlement assistance provided the Spanish-speaking newcomers.

Once it became clear that an eventual return to Cuba would not be possible, middle-class Cubans aggressively sought to learn English and new skills necessary for the economic rewards that would eventually signal their social integration. In this undertaking, class background proved indispensable. Because of the downward mobility initially experienced by the Cuban exiles, and particularly the early arrivals, occupational position in Cuba was unrelated to first job acquired in the United States. However, last job in Cuba was found to be a principal factor affecting subsequent upward mobility, along with education and age on arrival (Rogg and Cooney 1980). Clearly, then, the current advantaged position of Cubans relative to other Hispanics is partly the result of the differential attitudes and resources derived from their class background (Portes 1969).

The emergence of the Cuban enclave economy (also class-related) is the second key factor in understanding the Cuban experience in the United States. Close to one third of all businesses in Mia-

mi are Cuban-owned while 75 percent of the work force in construction is Cuban and 40 percent of the industry is Cuban-owned (Bach 1980). Twenty percent of the Miami banks are controlled by Cubans, who account for 16 out of 62 bank presidents and 250 vice presidents (Wilson and Portes 1980). Other ethnic strongholds in the enclave economy include textiles, food, cigars, and trade with Latin America.

In Miami one can proceed from birth to death "Cuban style" (Bach 1980). For the refugee with fewer marketable skills, the enclave not only provides a home, but also can shelter workers from the harsh realities of the open competitive market. Its success depends on low wages paid to Cuban workers, ethnic preference in hiring, *and* the reciprocal obligation to help fellow ethnic members in their own financial ventures. The other crucial components are, of course, sufficient operating capital and entrepreneurial skills to initiate a successful enterprise, as well as an economic climate conducive to the flourishing of small-scale, private enterprises. The early Cuban exodus, with its upper-class bias and access to financial credit, was able to provide both elements. Later arrivals, however, became the working class for the "golden exiles" of the 1960s. As Bach concludes, "Thus there has been a total transplantation of the pre-revolutionary Cuban social structure to Miami, with all the, implications of unequal wealth, power and prestige" (Bach 1980).

The importance of the Cuban enclave economy together with similar structures in other ethnic groups (that is, the Japanese and the Koreans) requires that it be added to any theoretical explanations of the immigrant experience. Enclave workers, while ethnically segregated and often paid lower wages, cannot be considered a mere extension of the secondary sector in an ethnically split labor market. Wilson and Portes report that ethnic workers integrated in an enclave experience a pay-off to human capital investments similar to those workers in the primary sector, thus providing them with advantages usually unavailable to minorities employed in the peripheral industries of the economy (Wilson and Portes 1980). The nagging question is whether subsequent generations will follow suit in expanding or protecting the forms and functions of the enclave economy. Not enough time has passed to make this assessment, but recent survey data provide a unique opportunity to begin this evaluation (Portes and Bach 1985).

SUMMARY AND CONCLUSION

This article has outlined features of the Mexican, Puerto Rican, and Cuban immigration experiences. Although other Hispanic national origin groups are much smaller and thus are not discussed here, the Central and South American and other Hispanic cases are similarly diverse. Our purpose has been to demonstrate that each of the major Hispanic groups has been subjected to a distinctive set of experiences that have shaped their economic and cultural integration into American society and that have affected the development of Hispanic ethnicity. The Puerto Rican case provides the strongest support for an isomorphic link between ethnicity and lower socioeconomic status. That Cubans have not remained segregated in a secondary labor market, have been the most successful of all groups, and are demonstrating strong tendencies toward integration into the larger society provides evidence in the other direction. Their distinct status at entry and their more favorable economic resources are the most significant factors distinguishing Cuban refugees from Mexican and Puerto Rican and other Latin American immigrants. The greater diversity of the Mexican American experience, which results in part from this group's greater numerical size and longer history in the United States, makes an analysis of the development of ethnicity in the case of this group more ambiguous.

Indicators pointing to increasing assimilation of Chicanos must be weighed against the isolation, extreme poverty, and lack of control over life as it exists in the barrios. In contrast to Barrera's claim to class integration, can the small rising Chicano middle class play the role of native elite within a group whose initial entry into the United States came about by conquest (Almaguer 1974)? How is one to interpret ongoing intraethnic contact as it exists between social class groups (as Chicano businesses, for example, increasingly rely on a Chicano clientele) or as it is affected by continued immigration of lower-status Mexicans? For Chicanos it is difficult to envision a future when ethnic distinctions within social class divisions will fade away. The cloudiness of what Barrera has labeled "the current period of confusion

and redefinition" is maintained by the continuing influx of new immigrants.

For Mexicans and Puerto Ricans isolation in ethnic communities and other manifestations of ethnicity are structurally produced by their concentrations in minority labor markets and by the continued influx of immigrants who help to renew cultural traditions and subsequently elaborate them as a basis for social solidarity. In turn, ethnically based solidarity serves as a protection and source of resistance against oppression. For Cubans the cohesiveness of their ethnic community has been a key factor facilitating initial adjustment and success. Whether that success will ensure the survival of the ethnically enclosed community or lead to its decline remains to be seen. Initial evidence based on the most recent census suggests a decline as the first generation of native-born Cubans demonstrates an unusual ability to assimilate (Nelson and Tienda 1985).

In summary, although we have introduced many aspects of the immigration experiences of Hispanics, we wish to close our discussion by emphasizing four factors in particular as important in shaping the ethnicity of Hispanic groups in the United States, especially when viewed in comparison with the experience of European immigrants. First, a crucial difference between Europeans and Hispanics is that European immigration was concentrated in a 40-year period from 1880 to 1920, after which it virtually ceased, leaving the United States 60 years to "assimilate" these massive immigrant cohorts. By contrast, Hispanic immigration has been relatively strong since 1942 and will probably not abate in the near future, so the United States may not have a comparably long period within which to assimilate the recent cohorts. This may render assimilation more difficult and affect tendencies toward ethnic identification on the part of the Hispanic groups, depending on differences among them in their immigration histories, which we have discussed at length above. Second, the economic order which the immigrant groups encounter shapes and determines ethnicity. The industrial regime prevailing between 1880 and 1920 tended to concentrate immigrants spatially and occupationally, while the post-industrial economy of the 1970s and 1980s acts to disperse immigrants both socially and spatially. Third, European immigrants were all white, while Hispanics are a mixture of blacks, Amerindians, and whites. This factor is especially important for groups with a large black admixture, like Puerto Ricans and, increasingly, Cubans. Fourth, an ethnic group is *created* by the entry of an immigrant group into American society, and its initial configuration depends on the characteristics of both the group and the society at the point of contact. Ethnicity is subsequently shaped by the social and economic experiences of the group in a changing society. Key elements in creating ethnicity include the ensuing immigration history of the group itself, changes in the economic organization of society, and prevailing patterns of racial and ethnic prejudice.

ENDNOTES

1. Parts of this article originally appeared in Nelson and Tienda (1985).

2. We use the terms "Mexican American" and "Chicano" interchangeably to refer to populations of Mexican origin and descent, irrespective of generational status. However, the terms differ in their sociopolitical connotation. The term "Chicano" rather than "Mexican American" appears to be more closely associated with the rising level of ethnic consciousness and the movement for equitable treatment. The term "Chicano" eulogizes the Mestizo (Spanish and Indian) heritages and a legacy of exploitation.

3. Jaffe, et al. (1980) notes that following the end of World War II the conversion of surplus military aircraft to commercial use considerably lowered the cost of travel between the island and the mainland.

4. The U.S. Commission on Civil Rights' *Puerto Ricans in the United States* reported that in 1969–70 alone 129,000 persons returned to Puerto Rico. By 1972 14 percent of the island's population consisted of return migrants, according to Lopez (1974).

E L E V E N

Asian Pacific Americans
Historical Trends

Don Mar
Marlene Kim

The history of most Americans—especially minorities and immigrants—has been subject to legal and political restrictions as well as by economic forces. Nowhere is this more apparent than among Asian Pacific Americans. Their fortunes, livelihoods, and lifestyles have been shaped by immigration laws curtailing their arrival, laws proscribing where they could live and what livelihoods they could pursue, and labor shortages or surpluses that have either beckoned to them or refused their passage to America. This article provides an overview of how the state of the economy and formal and informal sanctions shaped the lives of Asian Pacific Americans. Rather than provide an exhaustive analysis, we summarize how political and economic constraints shaped Asian Americans' experiences in the economy. As a result, there are some topics that will have limited coverage due to considerations of brevity. For example, there is relatively little discussion of "push" factors that led Asians to escape from their home countries.

We discuss these factors during three time periods: the period covering 1850 to World War II, from World War II to 1965, and the post-1965 period. The first period focuses on the stories of early immigrants and the severe restrictions they faced during a period of major conflict between labor and capital. The second period discusses the decline of some of these restrictions and the entrance of large numbers of American-born Asians into a mature industrial economy with the U.S. as the world economic leader. The final period discusses the consequences of having new immigrant workers enter the U.S. during the relative decline and restructuring of the U.S. economy. This article closes with a discussion of future labor market prospects for Asian Pacific Americans.

THE EARLY IMMIGRANT EXPERIENCE: PRE-WORLD WAR II

From 1850 to World War II, Asians were subject to the whims of a rapidly developing industrialized economy. Massive changes swept the U.S. economy: production evolved from the traditional craft method of production to factory production with labor specialization and wage labor predominant (Gordon, Edwards, and Reich 1982; Braverman 1974); small, regionally diverse markets were connected by transportation innovations allowing the growth of large, nationally integrated markets (Davis et al., 1972), mechanization and specialization in agriculture created larger farms with single cash crops (Hughes and Cain 1994); increased labor productivity created pressure for U.S. expansion into world markets (Williams 1969).

U.S. race relations also underwent a dramatic change in the late 19th century. The end of slavery ushered in a new set of racial institutions such as Jim Crow, laws segregating workers based on race, and laws demarcating the place of nonwhites in society. These new racial restrictions arose in the midst of societal conflict largely between capital and labor during American industrialization (Reich 1981) that severely circumscribed the labor market opportunities of early Asian immigrants.

Against this tumultuous background, Chinese immigrants were hired to build the industrial and agricultural infrastructures on the West Coast during the 19th century. Although the initial arrival of Chinese in the 1850s was the result of the Gold Rush in the Sierra Nevada, the Foreign Miners' Tax in 1853 discouraged Chinese from continuing

in mining (Chan 1991:28), scattering them into a host of occupations. Chinese workers, recruited by the Central Pacific Railroad, were responsible for constructing the western half of the first transcontinental railroad that was essential for integrating U.S. markets and providing a passageway to Pacific markets. The Chinese also built the spur lines that fed the transcontinental railroad and constructed the dikes and levees that allowed the Sacramento river delta to be reclaimed as farmland (Melendy 1984:51). They became urban businessmen, specializing in laundries, dry goods, and restaurants and established themselves in small-scale manufacturing industries such as textiles and woolens, boot and shoe making, and cigar making in the urban areas. By the 1880s, over 100,000 Chinese resided in the United States, mainly in the West and primarily composed of prime-age working men.

Formal and informal restrictions placed on Asians during this time period were prevalent and severe. Legal restrictions on occupations, citizenship, and immigration severely limited Asian American opportunities in the economy. Formal and informal sanctions against the Chinese began as early as the 1850s (Daniels 1988:29–76). Informal sanctions included anti-Chinese marches, formation of anti-coolie clubs, demonstrations, and violence. Daniels (1988) and Saxton (1971) discuss the role of labor supporting and developing the anti-Chinese movement. Although several individuals in the labor movement often spoke out against Chinese discrimination, elements of the labor movement often supported the ant-Chinese movement. Ong (1981) argues that the conflict between labor and capital in the latter part of the 19th century led to the exclusion of Chinese workers from the high-paying, dynamic sectors of the economy. Formal social and occupational sanctions raised against the Chinese were numerous. Social sanctions included the inadmissibility of Chinese testimony in courts and anti-miscegenation laws. The California Foreign Miners' Tax (1850) and the 14 San Francisco Laundry Ordinances (1873–1884) were all targeted to exclude Chinese from certain occupations. In general, many of these formal sanctions were restrictions instituted at the local and state levels.

The conflict between labor and capital during industrialization ultimately resulted in national legislation to end Chinese immigration to the United States (Ong and Liu 1994). The 1882 Immigration Act, which was renewed in subsequent decades, effectively ended Chinese immigration to the United States. The results of these formal and informal sanctions were to exclude new Chinese immigration and to circumscribe economic opportunities for Chinese residing in the United States. In fact, by the end of the 19th century, the restrictions against the Chinese were so onerous that many left the U.S., decreasing the population of Chinese in the mainland United States from approximately 100,000 in 1880 to 80,000 by 1900.

The chronic shortage of labor in the West made it difficult for West Coast agriculture to expand at the end of the 19th century. West Coast agriculture in wheat and other specialty crops became increasingly important to the national economy during the latter part of the 19th century. During the 1890s, Japanese laborers were recruited to fill these agricultural jobs. By the early 20th century, many Japanese made the transition from agricultural worker to tenant farmer (O'Brien and Fugita 1991). Given the relatively small size of Japanese farms, farmers grew labor intensive, high value added, specialty crops such as berries, celery, onions, and sugar beets.

Japanese immigration to the United States differed markedly from the earlier Chinese immigration due to a greater number of female immigrants. The higher number of women allowed more family formation among the Japanese compared to the Chinese. Family labor was critical in providing labor for Japanese enterprises, primarily the family farm and, to a lesser degree, in family retailing businesses in the early part of the 20th century. By the 1920s and 1930s, Japanese women had also extended their employment outside ethnic enterprises into urban service occupations (Glenn 1986).

The Japanese, like the Chinese, faced both informal and formal sanctions. By the early 1900s, numerous groups and individuals such as the Asiatic Exclusion League (Daniels 1988:118) were calling for an end to Japanese immigration. In an attempt to curtail Japanese, and to a lesser degree Chinese, expansion into small farms, various land acts were passed to prevent Japanese farmers from owning land. In California (1913) and Wash-

ington (1921), state alien land acts were enacted, banning land ownership by foreign nationals. Although the passage of these acts did discourage some Japanese from entering farming, the overall impact was minimal as the Japanese found numerous means to circumvent the law. Japanese exclusion became national policy with the passage of the 1924 Immigration Act, which set a numerical quota on immigration based on the number of each nationality's population in the U.S. as of 1880. As there were few Japanese residing in the United States in 1880, the Act effectively ended Japanese immigration to the U.S.

Like the Chinese, the Japanese began to diversify into small businesses, particularly hotels, grocery stores, and restaurants. However, the Japanese remained predominantly involved in agriculture throughout most of the pre-war period. As a result, the Japanese were not as urbanized as the Chinese during the 1920s and 1930s. The numbers of Japanese Americans continued to increase after the 1924 Immigration Act due to the birth of the Nisei (the second generation). By 1940, the population of Japanese in the United States was approximately 127,000, while the Chinese population numbered 77,500.

The shortage of agricultural labor in the West Coast also contributed to the arrival of Filipinos into the United States. American colonization of the Philippines allowed large numbers of Filipinos to circumvent the 1924 Immigration Act as migrant farm workers harvesting sugar beets, lettuce, asparagus, and fruits (Melendy 1984). Unlike the earlier Chinese and Japanese immigrants, the Filipinos did not move into ethnic enterprises or farm ownership. Falling agricultural prices, combined with informal sanctions, limited employment opportunities and wages for Filipino workers during the 1920s and 1930s. With the granting of commonwealth status to the Philippines in 1935, Filipino immigration was limited to 50 persons per year. By the end of the 1930s, the population of Filipinos numbered approximately 100,000 with the majority consisting of single men employed primarily in agriculture.

Asians provided agricultural labor not only for California but also Hawaii. The "Great Mahele" of 1848 allowed Hawaiian lands to be bought and sold by private individuals, creating large land holdings with no adequate labor force to work the land (Kent 1983). The native Hawaiians were decimated by contact with Western civilization and proved to be an inadequate labor force for plantation owners (Takaki 1983). Chinese farm workers initially formed the backbone of the plantation labor force during most of the 19th century. However, by the end of the 19th century, sugar planters began recruiting laborers from Japan in large numbers. By 1902, Japanese laborers made up 73 percent of the plantation workforce. The passage of the Gentleman's Agreement in 1907 curtailed further immigration of Japanese into Hawaii. Planters then recruited workers from the Philippines, as well as the rest of the world, beginning large-scale immigration of Filipinos into Hawaii such that by 1920, Filipinos accounted for almost 30 percent of the agricultural labor force.

By the end of the Depression, the Japanese and Filipinos were largely employed in agriculture, whereas the Chinese had become predominantly urban workers. In 1940, over 20 percent of Japanese males on the mainland were employed as farm managers or farm owners. In addition, one in four Japanese workers was employed as an agricultural worker. Almost half the Filipino workers in the mainland U.S. were employed in agriculture. However, unlike the Japanese, Filipinos were rarely owners of the farms they worked. The Chinese were heavily urbanized by 1940 and were largely employed as operatives in the garment industry and food service sector. A large number of Chinese were also self-employed as small shopkeepers in the retail, restaurant, and service industries (see Table 1).

TABLE 1 *Occupational Distribution of Chinese, Japanese, and Filipinos Compared to All U.S. Workers, 1940*

Occupation	All U.S.	Chinese	Japanese	Filipino
Men				
Professional and technical	6%	2%	4%	1%
Managerial, official, and proprietor	10	21	13	—
Sales and clerical	13	10	9	2
Craft	15	1	3	2
Operative	18	22	7	6
Service	6	31	7	22
Private household	—	6	5	6
Farmers and farm managers	15	1	21	5
Farm laborer	8	3	27	49
Laborer	9	2	6	7
Not reported	1	1	1	1
Women				
Professional and technical	13%	8%	3%	
Managerial, official, and proprietor	4	9	5	
Sales and clerical	28	26	20	
Craft	1	—	—	
Operative	18	26	9	
Service	11	19	11	
Private household	18	10	19	
Farmers and farm managers	1	—	2	
Farm laborer	3	1	28	
Laborer	1	1	2	
Not reported	2	1	—	

Source: U.S. Bureau of Census, 1940, 1% Public Use Microdata Sample.

THE FIRST AMERICAN-BORN GENERATION: THE POST-WAR PERIOD UNTIL 1965

World War II brought several changes to the American economy. By the end of World War II, the U.S. economy had completed the transition from a relatively small industrial economy to the preeminent urban industrial economy. High-paying semi-skilled jobs abounded in the manufacturing sector with the dominance of U.S. manufacturing in the world economy. The infrastructure development and housing boom of the post-war period also generated construction jobs throughout the national economy. The increasing U.S. military role around the world provided high-wage jobs in the defense industry. Finally, the expanding role of both the local and federal government generated relatively high-paying white collar jobs (Duboff 1989). As a result, labor markets were relatively tight during this period with unemployment averaging between 4 to 7 percent.

Race relations improved considerably during this period, as is usual during boom periods. With plentiful jobs, legal restrictions based on race became less acceptable, although informal sanctions remained. As evidence of this change, Roosevelt ended employment discrimination in the federal government with the signing of Executive Order 8802 in 1941. By the 1950s, the Civil Rights Movement had begun formal challenges to the pattern of racial segregation in schools, politics, and society in general that had been instituted since slavery. The easing of tensions between organized labor and management in the post-war period also meant that race was less likely to emerge as a political issue. Moreover, the emergence of the United States as a leader in the world economy meant that the U.S. could no longer formally pursue racial segregation as a state policy in order to remain credible as a world leader to the non-European nations (Ong and Liu 1993).

As a result of the changes in race relations and the strength of the U.S. economy, Asian Pacific American workers, particularly the U.S.-born, were able to expand their occupational choices in the post-war period. Income differences between Asian Pacific Americans and non-Hispanic whites narrowed. These same factors affected all racial minorities in the United States, as African Americans were also able to narrow the differential in incomes (Smith and Welch 1989).

The war had an immediate and severe economic impact on Japanese Americans via the internment. The internment hastened the end of a concentration in the ethnic niches of agriculture and small businesses. Although these niches still provided employment in 1950, occupational diversification of Japanese Americans occurred in the wake of the internment. Two additional reasons account for the increasing occupational diversification of Japanese Americans in the post-war period. First, more of the Nisei (the second generation) came of age after the war and were finally able to use their American educations as overt racial discrimination lessened. Second, the post-war job expansion created opportunities in engineering, medical, and white collar sales and clerical occupations for both men and women (see Table 2).

Although the post-war expansion allowed Japanese Americans access to a broader range of occupations, they were not able to fully participate in all areas of the labor market. For example, higher-paying blue collar manufacturing jobs and construction jobs were generally not available. Moreover, earnings for Japanese continued to lag behind whites. Daniels (1988) cites a 1965 California Fair Employment Practices Commission report which found that Japanese males received only $43 for every $51 made by white males.

The second generation Chinese Americans also moved away from the traditional pre-war occupations, although at a slower pace. Without the shock of the internment, a greater number of Chinese ethnic businesses survived through the war with less disruption. The survival of these ethnic enterprises meant the continuation of employment in restaurant services and in low-paying garment work for the aging immigrants. However, substantial numbers of American-born men and women increased their employment in professional and technical occupations, again concentrating in engineering and medical fields. Like the Japanese, Chinese Americans were denied access to higher-paying manufacturing and craft jobs. And like the Japanese, Chinese American earnings lagged behind that of whites in 1960.

As few Filipinas immigrated prior to the war, there was not a significant number of American-born Filipino workers entering the post-war labor market. Some immigrant Filipino workers did leave farm work as a result of the economic

TABLE 2 *Occupational Distribution of Chinese, Japanese, and Filipinos Compared to All U.S. Workers, 1960*

Occupation	All U.S.	Chinese	Japanese	Filipino
Men				
Professional and technical	10%	18%	14%	8%
Managerial, official, and proprietor	11	16	10	2
Sales and clerical	14	4	15	6
Craft	20	7	17	10
Operative	20	16	10	16
Service	6	23	6	22
Private household	—	1	1	1
Farmers and farm managers	6	1	11	11
Farm laborer	3	—	8	22
Laborer	7	2	9	11
Not reported	5	7	—	—
Women				
Professional and technical	13%	17%	11%	16%
Managerial, official, and proprietor	4	6	3	1
Sales and clerical	38	38	36	33
Craft	1	1	1	2
Operative	15	21	20	19
Service	13	9	13	18
Private household	8	2	8	3
Farmers and farm managers	1	—	2	—
Farm laborer	1	—	5	8
Laborer	1	—	—	—
Not reported	6	6	—	—

Source: U.S. Bureau of Census, 1960, 1% Public Use Microdata Sample.

expansion, but most remained in low-paying service or manufacturing occupations. These included jobs in restaurants and food processing. Still, by 1960, almost a third of Filipino workers were employed in agriculture compared to just 9 percent of the overall U.S. population.

Japanese and Chinese American women entered the labor force in larger numbers during the post-war period. Although the post-war period is marked by the increasing labor force participation of all U.S. women, Chinese and Japanese women entered the labor force in even greater numbers. In 1940, approximately 32 percent of all Japanese American women between the ages of 14 and 65 were in the labor force. By 1960, the percentage of Japanese American women had increased to 47 percent. For Chinese American women, the comparable figures are 24 percent and 42 percent. By

comparison, only 34 percent of all U.S. women were in the labor force.

By the end of this second period, the segregation of Asian Americans in the labor market had diminished. Legal restrictions against Asian Pacific Americans were falling due to the relatively affluent times and the growing Civil Rights Movement. American-born Chinese and Japanese were able to find employment within the growing professional and technical occupations. However, the American-born did not fully benefit from the growth of high-paying craft and manufacturing jobs as these jobs were still not available. Although the differential in earnings had narrowed, Asian American earnings still lagged behind white incomes. The immigrant Japanese, Chinese, and Filipinos largely remained employed in the occupational niches from the first period, although there was some diversification into low-paying service occupations.

NEW IMMIGRANTS AND CIVIL RIGHTS: THE POST-1965 PERIOD

The passage of the 1965 Immigration Act marked a turning point in U.S. immigration policy by ending the 1924 National Origins Act that had effectively curtailed Asian immigration to the U.S. for the preceding decades. The 1965 Act established new quotas of 20,000 immigrants per year and provisions for non-quota immigrants, and instituted a preference system for immigrants which determined who could emigrate to the United States. These preference categories emphasized family reunification and immigrants with special job skills. The 1965 Immigration Act, plus the subsequent refugee acts in 1975 and 1980, allowed for renewed large-scale immigration of Filipinos, Koreans, Chinese, and Southeast Asians to the United States. In the period from 1971 to 1990, approximately 855,500 Filipinos, 610,800 Koreans, 576,100 Chinese, and 581,100 Vietnamese entered the United States (U.S. Bureau of the Census, *Statistical Abstract of the United States,* 1992).

These new immigrants entered a U.S. labor market that, while still growing, encountered difficulties by the end of the 1960s. The post-war dominance of the U.S. economy in the world economy had eroded, adversely affecting the domestic labor market. For example, unemployment increased from an annual average of 4.8 percent in the 1960s to 7.3 percent in the 1980s. Real wage growth also decreased dramatically, falling from an annual average increase of 1.7 percent in the decade from 1955 to 1965 to an annual decrease of –0.1 percent during the 1975 to 1985 decade.

Structural change in occupations altered the labor market in this period with the number of high-paying manufacturing jobs decreasing and the number of lower-paying service jobs increasing (see, for example, Eitzen and Zinn 1989). The U.S. share of total world manufacturing declined from 29 percent in 1953 to 13 percent in 1976. U.S. productivity slowed considerably with productivity increasing by only 12 percent from 1967 to 1978, compared to Japan's 95 percent increase and West Germany's 55 percent increase, making U.S. products less competitive in world markets. These factors meant a continual weakening of the

manufacturing sector in the United States that had provided the bulk of high-paying semi-skilled jobs in the post-war expansion.

Race relations in the United States were transformed during this period. The Civil Rights Movement worked to end *de jure* segregation in the United States, as well as *de facto* segregation. Not only did the Civil Rights Movement ask for the end of state supported racial segregation, it made claims to the state to remedy the entire history of racial discrimination. Affirmative action programs, political redistricting, community action and urban renewal programs were instituted in response to these new demands for state remedies. Instead of a homogeneous American society, the "politics of difference" moved to redefine the meaning of race in American society (Omi and Winant 1983).

Recent Filipino immigration to the United States was largely influenced by U.S. immigration laws which gave preference to immigrants with professional and technical skills (Pido 1986). As a result, recent Filipino immigrants have higher levels of education then previous Filipino immigrants. Over one in five Filipinas have professional occupations, primarily in the health care field. Filipino men are also heavily employed in professional and technical occupations (Pido 1986). However, not all Filipinos are employed in higher paying occupations. Due to the family reunification preferences, many Filipinos follow the purely economic immigrants. Many of these immigrants are concentrated in low-paying service occupations (see Table 3).

Immigration laws have also shaped the pattern of Korean immigration. Although there is controversy over the degree to which the professional preference category selected Korean immigrants with higher skill levels (Barringer and Cho 1989), we find significant numbers of Koreans in the higher-paying professional occupations in 1980 and today, particularly among men. Like the Filipinos, large number of recent Korean immigrants are also employed as low-paid service and garment workers.

Korean immigrants demonstrate a significant amount of self-employment in ethnic enterprises. Many of these ethnic enterprises are the result of limited job alternatives available for high-skill immigrants. In 1982, there were over 31,000 Korean businesses with combined sales of $2.7 billion dollars (U.S. Bureau of the Census, *Survey of*

TABLE 3   *Occupational Distribution, Selected Asian Americans Compared to All U.S. Workers, 1990*

Occupation	All	Chinese	Japanese	Filipino	Koreans	Vietnamese
Men						
Managerial	13%	15%	20%	10%	15%	5%
Professional	12	24	20	12	16	13
Technical and sales	15	18	17	15	29	18
Administrative support	7	8	9	16	6	8
Service	10	19	9	16	10	12
Fish and forest	4	< 1	4	2	1	2
Production and craft	19	8	12	12	12	19
Operators	20	9	8	15	12	22
Women						
Managerial	11%	15%	14%	10%	9%	7%
Professional	17	17	19	20	11	9
Technical and sales	16	17	16	16	25	17
Administrative support	28	21	28	25	14	18
Service	17	14	14	17	20	19
Fish and forest	1	< 1	1	1	< 1	< 1
Production and craft	2	3	3	3	6	10
Operators	8	13	5	7	14	20

Source: U.S. Bureau of Census, *Asian and Pacific Islanders in the United States 1990*, CP-3-5, August 1993.

Minority-Owned Business Enterprises, 1986). The majority of these firms were small retail establishments, restaurants, or providers of personal services.

The impact of these ethnic enterprises on Asian immigrant earnings, particularly among Chinese, Koreans, and Vietnamese, is often debated. For example, Portes and Bach (1985) and Zhou and Logan (1991) argue that ethnic enterprises reduce unemployment among new immigrants as well as provide a path of economic mobility for immigrant entrepreneurs. Sanders and Nee (1985) and Mar (1991) argue that ethnic enterprises do provide jobs for immigrant workers, but at extremely low wages with little mobility via future self-employment for workers in the ethnic economy.

Recent Chinese immigration resembles the Korean pattern with large percentages of both highly-skilled and relatively low-skilled immigrants (see Table 3). Ethnic enterprises have also increased among the Chinese with almost 52,000 firms and receipts of six billion dollars in 1982. Again, like the Koreans, large numbers of recent Chinese immigrants are concentrated in lower paying service and manufacturing jobs.

The general involuntary nature of Vietnamese immigration to the United States has severely affected their labor market experience. Borjas (1990) argues that involuntary immigrants are usually significantly worse off in the labor market due to lack of preparation, savings, and other factors. Vietnamese occupations are largely concentrated in the lower paying service and manufacturing occupations. The Vietnamese have also made significant entries into ethnic enterprises, although these businesses are generally smaller in scale and concentrated in food and personal services.

In contrast to earlier immigration patterns of predominantly males, recent immigration includes equal numbers of women. Due to lower spousal earnings, the majority of recent immigrant women have entered the labor force. In 1980, for married immigrant women between the ages of 25 and 64 years of age, 61 percent of Korean women, 65 percent of Chinese women, and 83 percent of Filipino women were in the labor force (Duleep and Sanders 1993).

Although American-born Asians have made substantial progress in earnings, the degree of economic parity achieved by Asian Americans is still controversial. Numerous studies demonstrate that earnings problems still exist for most American-born Asians. Studies by Duleep and Sanders (1992) and Cabezas and Kawaguchi (1988) argue that due to regional location, different rates of returns to education, and different occupations of employment, even Japanese and Chinese Americans have not achieved earnings parity with non-Hispanic whites. Moreover, these studies argue that Asian Americans have particular difficulties in obtaining managerial and executive positions. Other studies (Hirschman and Wong 1984; Chiswick 1983) argue that American-born Japanese and Chinese have achieved parity with non-Hispanic whites. However, most studies show that post-1965 immigrants are still experiencing earnings discrimination in the labor market. Finally, many of the recent immigrant groups have a high incidence of poverty. Ong and Hee (1994)

. . . find that 46 percent of Southeast Asian, 25 percent of Vietnamese, 15 percent of Korean, and 14 percent of Chinese households fell below the poverty line in 1990.

The passage of the 1965 Immigration Act was clearly a watershed for Asian Pacific American labor in the United States. Immigration vastly increased the numbers of Asians as well as allowing immigrants from other Asian countries into the U.S. These immigrant workers joined the American-born in a labor market undergoing a sweeping transformation due to structural change and the decline of the U.S. in the world economy. In addition, the Civil Rights Movement entered a new phase, seeking remedies from the government for past injustices. This change in race relations completed the removal of the legal restrictions to Asian Pacific workers in the labor market.

Patterns of Ethnic Integration in America

3

The dominant conceptual framework in the analysis of American ethnic and racial relations has been an assimilation model. One of the earliest and most influential statements of the assimilation model was embodied in the classic "race relations cycle" advanced by sociologist Robert E. Park in 1926:

> In the relations of races there is a cycle of events which tends everywhere to repeat itself. The race relations cycle, which takes the form . . . of contacts, competition, accommodation, and eventual assimilation, is apparently progressive and irreversible. Customs regulations, immigration restrictions, and racial barriers may slacken the tempo of the movement; may perhaps halt it altogether for a time, but cannot change its direction, cannot, at any rate, reverse it. (Park 1950:150)

According to the assimilation model of intergroup contact, interethnic relations inevitably go through successive stages of competition, conflict, accommodation, and assimilation. In Article 13 ("Revisiting Assimilation") Russell Kazal documents the widespread and enduring impact of the assimilation model.

In Part 2 we focused especially on the first phase of Park's race relations cycle: the *origins* of ethnic stratification that are characterized by contact and competition. However, the succeeding stages in Park's cycle are more problematic. For example, Lieberson (1961) contends that the Park race relations cycle is inadequate because it fails to recognize that differences in power relations in the original contact situations produce different stratification outcomes. Lieberson distinguishes between two different situations of ethnic stratification: one in which the migrating group is the dominant ethnic group (immigrant superordination) and one in which the group residing in the region at the time of contact is dominant (indigenous superordination). In migrant superordination, the economic, political, and cultural institutions of the subjugated indigenous population are undermined. However, because the subordinate indigenous group seeks to maintain its traditional institutions, conflict with the dominant group can persist over long periods of time. This situation, exemplified by Indian-white relations in the United States, is classic colonialism, in which the subordinate group strenuously resists assimilation. When the migrating group is subordinate, on the other hand, its decision to enter another society is more likely to be voluntary, and it is much more likely to accept assimilation into the dominant society, as exemplified by the experience of most European immigrants to America. In Article 18 ("Minority Status and Literacy in Comparative Perspective"), John Ogbu explores the implications of these differences in explaining varying ethnic responses to educational achievement.

Most discussions of assimilation in the United States have focused on the adaptation of immigrant groups that have voluntarily entered American society. The experience of African Americans, whose ancestors were involuntarily imported from Africa, does not fall into either contact situation—migrant or indigenous subordination. Wilson (1973) maintains that slave transfers constitute a third major contact situation, the one in which the power and coercion of the dominant group is greatest. In contrast to colonization, in which the indigenous group, although subordinate, is able to maintain elements of its own cultures, slave transfers involve the forcible and involuntary uprooting of people from families and traditional cultures, which places them in a much greater dependent relationship with the dominant group (Wilson 1973:19–20). The extent to which differences between migrant superordination, indigenous superordination, and slave transfers have affected the nature of intergroup relations has been the subject of considerable controversy among social scientists, especially as they have sought to compare the patterns of integration among different ethnic groups and to develop explanations for the differences that exist.

An important assumption of the assimilation model has been that, as American society became more modernized, ethnic and racial distinctions would become insignificant, diminish, or eventually disappear. According to this conception, the forces of modernity—democratic and egalitarian political norms and institutions, industrialization, urbanization, and bureaucratization—place increasing emphasis on rationality, impersonality, status by achievement, physical and social mobility, and equal opportunity. Traditional social systems, in which social position is based on ascriptive racial and ethnic origins rather than on individual merit, become increasingly burdensome (and even expensive) to maintain. Thus, the Southern caste system, in which selection was based on the irrational ascriptive criterion of race, was perceived by advocates of an assimilation model to be a vestige of a premodern, agrarian society that ultimately and inevitably would be undermined as the modernization process transformed the society by emphasizing a selection process based on merit, credentials, and skills.

This position was nowhere more clearly articulated than in Gunnar Murdal's *An American Dilemma,* probably the most important book ever written on the subject of American race relations. Published in 1944, *An American Dilemma* became an instant classic and exerted a profound influence on white America by drawing attention to the dynamics of race in American society in a way that had not been accomplished since the formal abolition of slavery. Myrdal's title reflected his basic thesis: the American creed of "liberty, equality, justice, and fair opportunity" was violated by the subordinate status to which African Americans had been relegated. Myrdal felt that the contradiction between white America's deeply felt professions of equality and brotherhood, on the one hand, and its treatment of African American people, on the other, presented an "embarrassing" dilemma that made for "moral uneasiness" in the hearts and minds of white Americans. He also optimistically thought that the primary thrust of American institutions was in a direction that would ultimately undermine the last vestiges of the racial caste system.

The assumption that the forces of modernization will progressively weaken the ties of race and ethnicity has been questioned, however (see, for example, Nagel's discussion in Article 2). In his classic essay, "Industrialization and Race Relations," Herbert Blumer (1965) noted that the projected effects of industrialization are not, in reality, inevitable. An emphasis on rationality may not make job opportunities available to the best qualified individuals irrespective of race; rather, the goal of efficiency and social harmony may impel managers *rationally* to discriminate because to hire minority applicants might disrupt the efficient and harmonious functioning of the enterprise. "*Rational* operation of industrial enterprises which are introduced into a racially ordered society may call for a deferential respect for the canons and sensitivities of that racial order" (Blumer 1965:233). In other words, modernization and industrialization do not necessarily change the order of majority-minority relations; rather, these processes adapt and conform to existing systems of racial etiquette. Blumer contended that changes in race relations in the workplace are brought about not by an inherent dynamic of the modernization process but by forces outside the world of work.

The Assimilation Model as Ideology

Assimilation involves efforts to integrate or incorporate a group into the mainstream of a society. The objective of assimilation is a homogeneous society. In general, the assimilation model of racial and ethnic contact assumes that the unique and distinctive characteristics of a minority will be erased and that the minority's culture, social institutions, and identity will be replaced by those of the dominant group.

Critics of the assimilation model have charged that it reflects a "liberal" view of the manner in which racial and ethnic diversity should be resolved. That is, an assimilationist perspective has frequently served an ideological function of specifying how racial and ethnic groups *should* relate to each other, instead of assessing the process whereby they *do* interact. In many circumstances, assimilationist analyses have served to legitimize the basic ideology of American society as a land of opportunity. Metzger (1971) has argued that, in general, the assimilationist perspective assumes that

> The incorporation of America's ethnic and racial groups into the mainstream culture is virtually inevitable. . . . Successful assimilation, moreover, has been viewed as synonymous with equality of opportunity and upward mobility for the members of minority groups. "Opportunity," in this system, is the opportunity to discard one's ethnicity and to partake fully in the "American Way of Life." In this sense, assimilation is viewed as the embodiment of the democratic ethos. (Metzger 1971:628–629)

Myrdal's monumental *An American Dilemma* reflected this general liberal notion of how racial and ethnic groups should come together in American society. The basic framework within which Myrdal conceptualized American race relations is perhaps most clearly reflected in his examination of the nature of African American culture

and community life. To the extent to which African American culture diverged from
dominant white culture patterns, Myrdal considered it a "distorted development, or
a pathological condition, of the general American culture." Therefore, the primary
thrust of black efforts toward institutional change in American society should be toward acquiring the characteristics of the dominant group. "It is to the advantage of
American Negroes as individuals and as a group," wrote Myrdal, "to become assimilated into American culture, to acquire the traits held in esteem by the dominant
white Americans."

     One of the implications of such a model is that frequently the sources of ethnic
conflict are perceived to reside not within the structure of society or within the dominant group but within the "pathological" or "maladjusted" behavior of the minority
group. In such circumstances, resolution of ethnic conflict involves a minority group
adapting to the standards of the majority. As we will note more fully in the introduction to Part 4, the Black Protest Movement of the late 1960s and early 1970s was in
many respects a reaction against such an assimilationist stance.

Majority Policies Toward Racial
and Ethnic Minorities

The nature of the assimilation process and the extent to which various racial and ethnic groups should be permitted or permit themselves to be integrated, incorporated,
or absorbed into American society have been the source of considerable controversy.
In his now classic analysis, *Assimilation in American Life* (1964), Milton Gordon (Article 12) distinguished among three ideologies—Anglo-conformity, the melting pot, and
cultural pluralism—that have been used to explain the dynamics of intergroup relations in American life.

Anglo-Conformity/Transmuting Pot

The principal assimilationist model in the American experience has emphasized conformity by minority groups to dominant group standards—the desirability and necessity of maintaining English social institutions, language, and cultural patterns. Termed
Anglo-conformity, this model assumes that ethnic minorities should give up their distinctive cultural characteristics and adopt those of the dominant group. It can be expressed by the formula $A + B + C = A$, in which A is the dominant group and B and
C represent ethnic minority groups that must conform to the values and life styles of
the dominant group; they must "disappear" if they wish to achieve positions of power
and prestige in the society (Newman 1973:53).

     Not only does a policy of Anglo-conformity seek a homogeneous society orga-
nized around the idealized cultural standards, social institutions, and language of the
dominant group, but it also assumes the inferiority of the cultures of other ethnic
groups. Many first- and second-generation Americans retain vivid and painful recol-
lections of the ridicule of their cultural ways and the pressures for them to become
"Americanized." Many tried to rid themselves of their traditional beliefs and practices.
A daughter of Slovenian immigrant parents recalled her childhood:

*In the 9th grade, a boy said to me, "You talk funny." I wondered what he meant. I listened to
my friends, and I did not think they "talked funny." Then, that great American experiment, the
public high school, opened my ears. I heard the English language spoken as I had never heard
it spoken. . . . I began to hear that I did indeed pronounce my words differently, and so did my
friends. I practiced [English] in secret, in the bathroom, of course, until I could pronounce properly the difficult "th" sound, which seemed the most distinctive and, therefore, the most necessary to conquer. How superior I felt when I had mastered this sound. . . . Alas, however, I
refused to speak Slovenian. (Prosen 1976:2–3)*

Such a conception of how a minority group should relate to the majority is not
unique to the United States. Consider, for example, the statement of an Australian Minister for Immigration concerning the objective of his country's immigration policy:

*It is cardinal with us that Australia, though attracting many different people, should remain a
substantially homogeneous society, that there is no place in it for enclaves or minorities, that all
whom we admit to reside permanently should be equal here and capable themselves of becoming substantially Australians after a few years of residence, with their children in the next generation wholly so. (Opperman 1966)*

For this model to be applicable to majority-minority relations in societies other than
the United States, the culture-specific term *Anglo-conformity* must be replaced by the
more general term *transmuting pot* (Cole and Cole 1954).

The Melting Pot

Like Anglo-conformity, the objective of a *melting pot* policy is a society without ethnic
differences. More tolerant than a policy of Anglo-conformity, the melting pot ideal
sees ethnic differences as being lost in the creation of a new society and a new people
—a synthesis unique and distinct from any of the different groups that formed it. Unlike Anglo-conformity, none of the contributing groups is considered to be superior;
each is considered to have contributed the best of its cultural heritage to the creation
of something new. The melting pot ideal can be expressed by the formula $A + B + C
= D$, in which A, B, and C represent the different contributing groups and D is the
product of their synthesis (Newman 1973:631). As Ralph Waldo Emerson expressed it
in the mid–nineteenth century:

*As in the old burning of the Temple at Corinth, by the melting and intermixture of silver and gold
and other metals a new compound more precious than any, called Corinthian brass, was formed,
so in this continent—asylum of all nations—the energy of Irish, Germans, Swedes, Poles, and
Cossacks and all the European tribes—of the Africans and of the Polynesians—will construct a
new race, a new religion, a new state, a new literature. (Quoted in Gordon 1964:117)*

The melting pot conception has been perhaps the most widely idealized popular
conception of how ethnic groups have been integrated into American society. As
both Gordon and Kazal point out, the melting pot notion has pervaded American intellectual life and popular culture. It was a prominent feature of Frederick Jackson
Turner's 1893 frontier thesis, which for generations provided the most definitive and

compelling interpretation of what was most distinctive about American society. According to Turner, "in the crucible of the frontier the immigrants were Americanized, liberated, and fused into a mixed race" (Turner 1894/1966:12).

Pluralism

Pluralism, on the other hand, rejects the inevitability of cultural assimilation. As the term has been applied to American society, pluralism refers to a system in which groups with different cultural practices can coexist and be preserved but simultaneously embrace common values and beliefs and participate in common economic, political, and social institutions. According to this notion, which is embedded in assumptions of American multiculturalism, the strength and vitality of American society is derived from the many different ethnic groups that have made it a "nation of nations." Each group should be permitted to retain its unique qualities while affirming its allegiance to the larger society. It can be expressed by the equation $A + B + C = A + B + C$, in which A, B, and C are each ethnic groups that maintain their distinctiveness over time (Newman 1973).

Pluralism is more tolerant of diversity than either Anglo-conformity or the melting pot, for it implies recognition of cultural equality among ethnic groups, not the superiority of one group. It accepts and encourages—even celebrates—cultural differences but generally assumes that different ethnic groups will coexist within a common political and economic framework. For example, religion in American society has historically been characterized by denominational pluralism, so that today more than 1,200 different religious organizations coexist. Members of most religious groups retain their doctrinal and ritualistic distinctiveness while simultaneously participating in the political and economic life of the country.

However, the American conception of pluralism is a much narrower conception of ethnic coexistence than is implied in the use of the term in many other societies. In the American conception of pluralism, diverse ethnic groups maintain some elements of cultural distinctiveness but accept core elements of the dominant culture and seek participation in the mainstream economic and political institutions. However, in addition to possessing cultural heterogeneity, most genuinely "plural" societies are characterized by "mutually incompatible institutional systems—social structures, value and belief systems, and systems of action" (Horowitz 1985:136) akin to what we will define later as separatism.

The three types that Gordon delineated can be placed on a continuum ranging from lesser to greater minority-group integrity and autonomy. Each type merges imperceptibly with the adjacent type. For example, Anglo-conformity is much closer to the melting pot than it is to pluralism. Moreover, the range of possible alternatives can be logically extended. Examination of the history of racial and ethnic contact in the United States and throughout the world makes it apparent that Anglo-conformity (the transmuting pot), the melting pot, and pluralism do not exhaust the theoretical possibilities or the historical examples of the consequences of intergroup contact. A policy of genocide, at one extreme, permits less minority autonomy, obviously, than does a policy based on the transmuting pot model. At the other extreme, *separatism,* or complete autonomy for the minority group, comprises a more expansive ideology than pluralism. When all of these ideologies are placed on a continuum, the result looks like

Figure 1. Let us review the alternative possible dominant policies toward racial and ethnic minorities suggested by this continuum.

Genocide/Extermination

The most repressive and destructive dominant-group policy toward a minority group is *extermination* or *genocide,* which denies the minority's very right to live. The objective of a policy of extermination is to eliminate or substantially reduce the minority group. The post–World War II International Genocide Convention, which was convened in response to the atrocities committed by the Nazi regime between 1933 and 1945, developed the following definition of genocide:

> . . . *any of the following acts committed with intent to destroy, in whole or in part, a national, ethnic, racial, or religious group as such: (a) killing members of the group; (b) causing serious bodily or mental harm to members of the group; (c) deliberately inflicting on the group conditions of life calculated to bring about its physical destruction in whole or in part; (d) imposing measures intended to prevent births within the group; (e) forcibly transferring children of the group to another group. (O'Brien 1968:516)*

Although efforts to exterminate minorities are not confined to the modern era, some of the most notorious instances of genocide have occurred in the twentieth century. In 1915 1.5 million Armenians were massacred by the Turks. As noted in Part 1, in the small African country of Burundi, members of the Hutu minority have been periodically systematically murdered by the dominant Tutsi people; in 1972 more than 100,000 were killed, and the wholesale slaughter of the Hutu population was renewed in clashes that erupted with increasing frequency between 1988 and 1995. In 1994 the tables were turned in the neighboring country of Rwanda, where an estimated 750,000 Tutsi were systematically annihilated in just a few months and over 1 million refugees fled to neighboring countries (such as Zaire [now the Congo], where this ethnic strife still smolders).

During the 1970s approximately one million Cambodians—30 percent of the population—were killed or died from hunger, disease, and overwork as a result of conditions created by the American bombing that devastated the country and by atrocities committed by the Khmer Rouge. The country's ethnic and religious minorities, especially the Muslim Chams, were special targets for extermination by the Pol Pot regime (Kiljunen 1985; Kiernan 1988). During their 1975 invasion of East Timor, Indonesians indiscriminately wiped out entire villages, killing over a hundred thousand in a population of less than one million. Moreover, the Indonesian destruction of East Timorese

	Exclusion/ Expulsion		Transmuting Pot		Pluralism	
Genocide/ Extermination		Oppression		Melting Pot		Separatism

FIGURE 1 *Types of Dominant Group Policies Toward Racial and Ethnic Minorities*

farms and villages led to famine, starvation, and disease, as a consequence of which "half a generation of Timorese children has been rendered mentally retarded" (Sidell 1981:50).

A clearly articulated policy of genocide was most systematically implemented under the Nazi extermination program, in which Hitler's objective was the extinction of several million Jews and other "non-Aryan" groups (such as Gypsies). Between 1935 and 1945 more than six million people perished as a consequence of this policy.

In American society, a policy of genocide was one of the several policies pursued by dominant whites in their effort to wrest control of the country's vast lands from the American Indians. The slogan "the only good Indian is a dead Indian" was common among frontier whites, who consistently encountered Indian resistance to their continued encroachment on Indian lands. As noted in Part 2, by the turn of the twentieth century, the American Indian population of the United States had been brought to the point of virtual extinction by a combination of European diseases, disintegration of tribal cultures, and an aggressive military policy by the federal government.

Because genocide violates the sanctity of human life, an ideology of *racism* is often developed to justify it. Racism involves a belief in the inherent superiority of one racial group and the inherent inferiority of others. Its primary function is to provide a set of ideas and beliefs that can be used to explain, rationalize, and justify a system of racial domination. By denying that a racial minority has human qualities or by depicting it as subhuman or destructive of human values and life, the minority's extermination is made morally justifiable and acceptable. For example, in 1876 an Australian writer defended efforts to annihilate the native people of New Zealand (Maoris), Australia, and Tasmania: "When exterminating the inferior Australian and Maori races . . . the world is better for it. . . . [By] protecting the propagation of the imprudent, the diseased, the defective, the criminal . . . we tend to destroy the human race" (quoted in Hartwig 1972:16).

Expulsion and Exclusion

Extermination clearly represents the most extreme dominant-group method for dealing with the existence of minorities and the potential for interethnic conflict in a multicultural society. The objective of extermination is to reduce or eliminate contact between majority and minority and to create an ethnically (or racially) homogeneous society. A similar rationale underlies the process of *expulsion,* that is, the ejection of a minority group from areas controlled by the dominant group. Minorities are told, in essence, not "You have no right to live" (as in a policy of genocide), but rather "Because you differ from us so greatly, you have no right to live *among us.*"

Expulsion can be of two types: *direct* and *indirect* (Simpson and Yinger 1985: 19–20), which are often interrelated. *Direct expulsion* occurs when minorities are forcibly ejected by the dominant group, often through military or other governmental force. A policy of direct expulsion was at no time more pronounced in American history than during the nineteenth century, when thousands of American Indians were removed from the East to areas beyond the Mississippi River. During World War II, 120,000 Japanese Americans, two-thirds of them United States citizens, were forcibly removed from their homes and placed in detention camps in remote areas of the country.

Indirect expulsion occurs when harassment, discrimination, and persecution of a minority become so intense that members "voluntarily" choose to emigrate. Harassment and persecution of minorities, particularly religious minorities, have led many groups to seek refuge in the United States. Persecuted Protestant sects were among the earliest European immigrants to the American colonies, and the tradition of America as an asylum for the oppressed has continued to be a prominent feature of American ideals. The most dramatic emigration in modern Jewish history occurred in the late nineteenth and early twentieth centuries when millions (more than one-third of all Eastern European Jews) fled czarist Russia. Recently the persecution of Jews has revived in Russia and other former Soviet-bloc countries in Eastern Europe, forcing Jews by the thousand to seek refuge in other countries.

Several noted instances of expulsion have occurred throughout the world in the past two decades. In 1989 more than 310,000 Bulgarians of Turkish descent (of a Bulgarian Turkish community estimated at between 900,000 and 1.5 million), whose ancestors had lived in Bulgaria for generations, fled to Turkey, forming one of Europe's largest refugee populations since World War II. Some Turks were forcibly expelled by Bulgarian authorities, while others were subjected to forced assimilation and repression of their Muslim faith, were forced to take Slavic names, and were beaten and abused for speaking Turkish in public (Haberman 1989:1). On two separate occasions—in 1983 and 1985—the government of Nigeria resorted to mass expulsion. In 1983 Nigeria expelled about 2 million immigrants from the neighboring countries of Ghana, Cameroon, Benin, Chad, and Niger. In 1985 another 700,000 people were forced to leave (*The Economist* 1985). In Israel, Meir Kahane, a U.S.-born rabbi, gained considerable political support for his proposal to resolve Arab-Jewish tensions in that country by forcibly removing all Arabs from Israel and its occupied territories and making Israel into an exclusively Jewish state (Friedman 1985:1).

However, the most dramatic recent example of expulsion has occurred in the former nation of Yugoslavia, which since its dissolution in 1991 has been the scene of brutal ethnic violence that has driven more than 2.3 million people from their homes and villages. Formerly one of the Yugoslav republics, Bosnia and Herzegovina was the home of three ethnic groups—Slavic Muslims (44 percent), Serbs (31 percent), and Croats (17 percent). After Bosnia declared its independence in 1992, Serbian militiamen embarked on a campaign to create ethnically homogeneous enclaves by forcibly removing and displacing non-Serbs, especially Muslims. The Serbian campaign took many forms: arson, rape, and terror against civilian populations; executions; imprisonment and torture in concentration camps and prisons; removal and confinement to ghetto areas for non-Serbs; and forcible deportation. Moreover, non-Serbs were intimidated by the Serbian reign of terror into signing "voluntary" letters giving up their property and possessions in return for being "permitted" to leave Bosnia alive (Human Rights Watch 1992). The terms that the Serbs used to describe their objectives—"ethnic cleansing" and "ethnic purification"—epitomize the quest for ethnic homogeneity and exclusivity that underlies a policy of expulsion.

Essential to an expulsionist policy is the desire to achieve or retain ethnic or racial homogeneity. This end may occur not only when an ethnic group is expelled from the society but also when a host society refuses to admit another group because that group is perceived as a threat to the society's basic social institutions. Policies that refuse to admit ethnically or racially different groups can be termed *exclusion*. As noted in

Part 2, between 1917 and 1965 American immigration policy was based on the assumption that immigrants from southern and eastern Europe and Asia represented a threat to the biological, social, and political fabric of American society and therefore should be substantially or completely restricted. This assumption was embodied in the 1924 immigration legislation, which established numerical quotas for each nation. More than four-fifths of the quotas were assigned to those nations of northern and western Europe whose ethnic characteristics were perceived to be most similar to those of the "original" European settlers of the country. Although Great Britain had an admissions quota exceeding 65,000, Italy was allocated less than 6,000, and Hungary less than 1,000. Asians were almost completely excluded. As we will note more fully in Part 4, this policy remained virtually intact until its repeal in 1965.

Oppression

Oppression involves exploitation of a minority group by excluding it from equal participation in a society (Turner, Singleton, and Musick 1984:1–2). Oppression "depends on exclusiveness rather than exclusion" (Bonacich 1972:555). Positions of higher prestige, power, and income are reserved exclusively for dominant group members. Unlike extermination, expulsion, or exclusion, a system of oppression accepts the existence of minorities but subjugates them and confines them to inferior social positions. The majority group uses its power to maintain its access to scarce and valued resources in a system of social inequality.

Slavery, in which the slave's labor was a valuable resource exploited by the slave owner, was an example of oppression in American society. As we noted in the introduction to Part 2, even after slavery was legally abolished, the Jim Crow system of racial segregation that ensued was organized to exploit blacks for the benefit of the dominant whites. After taking a tour of the South at the turn of the twentieth century, a prominent journalist remarked on the exploitative nature of black-white relations:

> One of the most significant things I saw in the South—and I saw it everywhere—was the way in which the white people were torn between their feelings of race prejudice and their downright economic needs. Hating and fearing the Negro as a race (though often loving individual Negroes) they yet want him to work for them; they can't get along without him. In one impulse a community will rise to mob Negroes or to drive them out of the country because of Negro crime or Negro vagrancy or because the Negro is becoming educated, acquiring property, and "getting out of his place," and in the next impulse laws are passed or other remarkable measures taken to keep him at work—because this South can't get along without him. (Baker 1964:81)

A classic contemporary example of oppression was the South African system of apartheid, or "separate development," which functioned to maintain the privileged position of whites, who enjoyed one of the highest standards of living in the world but who represent only 15 percent of the country's population. On the other hand, South African blacks, who comprise more than two-thirds (69 percent) of the population, were excluded from genuine participation in the nation's political system and were legally confined to rural reserves, or "homelands," that represented only 13 percent of the land. However, black labor provided a cheap labor supply for South African mines, farms, manufacturing, and domestic help that was—and is—essential to the South African economy and the system of white privilege that persists. Therefore, the entire system of state controls restricting black political power, residence, and education was designed to perpetuate the system of white privilege (Cohen 1986).

Separatism

At the other end of the continuum from genocide is *separatism,* which is the most tolerant and expansive of the several majority group policies or practices that we have considered. Like pluralism, *separatism* implies social and cultural equality among ethnic groups, not the superiority of one. Both pluralism and separatism accept and encourage—even celebrate—cultural diversity. Separatism differs from pluralism in that the former includes some form of geographic and social separation.

In the American experience, pluralism and separatism have seldom been advocated by the majority; the primary advocates of each stance have been minority spokespersons, whose desire to maintain their distinct ethnic identity and organizational structure has led such groups to proscribe contact with the broader society and culture. The basic difference between policies of separatism and exclusion is that under separatism, the minority chooses to place itself apart culturally, socially, and physically, whereas under exclusion, the separation is dictated by the majority group. Under separatism the majority does not require separation of ethnic and racial groups; it simply permits it.

Throughout the American experience many ethnic groups have tried to avoid pressures of forced assimilation with the dominant society by embracing a form of ethnic pluralism as the most appropriate means of adjusting to American society. The adjustment of the immigrant Irish typifies a pluralist response that is characteristic of many other ethnic groups. Although the objects of discrimination by Protestant Americans, the Irish avoided much of the hostility directed toward them by creating a society within a society, a separate institutional system centered around the Roman Catholic church. The institutional system that developed around the church—its schools, hospitals, orphanages, asylums, homes for the aged, charitable and athletic organizations, and informal groups—integrated the Irish community and served to maintain Irish American solidarity and identity (Yetman 1975).

Separatism, on the other hand, involves minimal interaction by a minority group with the majority. The impulse for separatism frequently has been created by considerable conflict with the majority group and a desire to avoid a recurrence of discrimination or subjugation. For example, this impulse was an important factor contributing to the creation of the state of Israel. A separate nation was also the objective of the pre–Civil War colonization movement that aimed to return American slaves to Africa and of the African American Back-to-Africa campaign of Marcus Garvey during the 1920s.

The idea of separate ethnic areas or states has been advocated by spokespersons of a number of different ethnic groups in the United States—by African Americans, American Indians, and German Americans, among others. Religious groups such as the Amish, the Hutterites, and the Doukhobors have sought to protect their identity from the influences of the larger society by remaining not only culturally but also socially— and, often, geographically—separate from the rest of the society. Thus, in addition to seeking to retain their cultural distinctiveness, such groups refrain from extensive participation in the economic, political, and social life of the broader society in order to maintain their own subsocieties. For example, having endured great persecution for their beliefs during the mid–nineteenth century, members of the Church of Jesus Christ of Latter Day Saints (the Mormons) sought to isolate themselves from the corrupting influences of the larger society, an impulse reflected in a favorite Mormon hymn,

> *We'll find a place which God for us prepared*
> *Far away in the West*
> *Where none shall come to hurt or make afraid*
> *There the Saints will be blessed.*

The transmuting pot, the melting pot, and pluralism are all assimilation ideologies that imply the integration of majority and minority groups in some manner, whereas expulsion, exclusion, oppression, and separatism imply some form of minority group separation. The crucial distinction between separation ideologies is whether the separation of the minority group is achieved voluntarily or involuntarily, and whether the minority is relatively autonomous or relatively powerless. Thus, *exclusion* refers to separation by the decision of the majority group, whereas *separatism* means that the minority group has decided to place itself apart and is not prevented from doing so by the dominant group.

The case of American Indians demonstrates that these policies are not mutually exclusive; one or more of them may be embraced simultaneously or in different historical periods. In the early years of the republic, United States policy moved from genocide to expulsion and exclusion (the reservation system). Since the late nineteenth century, the ideology of Anglo-conformity has been predominant, with exclusion an acceptable alternative. For example, the purpose of governmental actions such as the Indian Allotment Act of 1887 was to force Indians to assimilate culturally. Even though many Indians would have welcomed separatism, their confinement to reservations has more closely resembled exclusion, because the reservations have been substantially controlled by the federal government and other extensions of white society (for example, missionaries, traders, and external economic interests).

Neither Anglo-conformity nor exclusion permits American Indians to exercise free choice. To assimilate or adopt the European-derived norms, values, and cultural standards of the larger society means to cease being an American Indian culturally. On the other hand, to be restricted to the reservation is to have life choices and chances severely circumscribed by powerful external forces. In spite of these exigencies, there seems little likelihood that the stubbornly purposeful maintenance of Indian traditions, values, and aloofness from the rest of the society will be surrendered. As Snipp points out in Article 5, even in urban areas, where increasing numbers have migrated since World War II, American Indians are resisting assimilation, forming their own ongoing communities, and increasingly asserting their rights to sovereignty and self-determination.

Dimensions of Assimilation

In his classic article, "Assimilation in America" (Article 12), which was published in 1961, Milton M. Gordon recognizes that each of the three theories—Anglo-conformity, melting pot, and cultural pluralism—on which his analysis focuses are primarily ideologies: that is, prescriptive models of how the process of intergroup relations in American society *should* proceed. He contends, therefore, that such idealized conceptions are of limited utility in analyzing precisely how diverse ethnic groups in American society have interacted.

Gordon argues that in order to assess accurately how extensively different ethnic groups have intermingled, it is essential to recognize that assimilation is not a single phenomenon but involves several related but analytically distinct processes. The three most important of these processes are cultural assimilation, structural assimilation, and marital assimilation, each of which may take place in varying degrees (Gordon 1964:71).

Popular discussions of assimilation usually are concerned with *cultural assimilation,* or what Gordon terms *behavioral assimilation* or *acculturation*—that is, the acquisition of the *cultural* characteristics of the dominant group, including its values, beliefs, language, and behaviors. However, Gordon contends that cultural assimilation is not sufficient to ensure *structural*—or social—assimilation. Writing during the early 1960s, he perceived that, although many ethnic groups—primarily the "white ethnic" descendants of European "new" immigrants—had become fully acculturated to the dominant American culture and had lost most traces of their ancestral cultures, they still had not been able to achieve full *social* participation in American society. Therefore, he concludes that sharing the same language, norms, behaviors, and cultural characteristics does not ensure access to informal social organizations, clubs, cliques, and friendship groups. Even sharing membership in secondary groups such as schools, jobs, and community and political organizations does not necessarily provide access to primary-group associations for those who have been culturally assimilated.

Because it is possible for a group to become culturally assimilated but to remain socially excluded, isolated, or segregated, it is important to distinguish cultural assimilation from *structural assimilation,* which involves social interaction among individuals of different ethnic and racial backgrounds. Two types of structural assimilation can be distinguished: secondary and primary. *Secondary structural assimilation* is the ethnic or racial integration of settings characterized by impersonal secondary relationships: jobs, schools, political organizations, neighborhoods, and public recreation. However, even sharing participation in such secondary groups does not necessarily involve primary-group associations—relationships that are warm, intimate, and personal. *Primary structural assimilation* is the ethnic integration of primary relationships, such as those found in religious communities, social clubs, informal social organizations, close friendships, and family relationships. Finally, the third subprocess, which is closely related to and, Gordon maintains, follows from primary structural assimilation, is *marital assimilation* —amalgamation or intermarriage among different ethnic or racial groups.

These distinctions enable us to compare and contrast the relative degree of integration or separation of different ethnic groups in American society in a relatively systematic fashion. Considerable research has been directed toward developing empirical indicators with which to measure assimilation: among the indicators are years of schooling, income levels, occupational characteristics, segregation indices, and rates of intermarriage.

One of the important issues in assessing Park's original model of the assimilation process, however, is whether rates of assimilation are changing over time. In other words, are there differences between the first generation (the immigrants themselves), the second generation (the American-born offspring of immigrants), the third genera-tion (the grandchildren of immigrants), and subsequent generations?

There have been two basic interpretations of the effect of generational differ-ences on ethnicity. *Straight-line theory,* most closely identified with Herbert Gans (see Article 22, "Symbolic Ethnicity"), predicts increasing assimilation with each suc-ceeding generation. According to this model, English would be more likely to be spoken in the home, occupational characteristics would be higher, and there would be higher rates of intermarriage among the second generation than among the first, and, moreover, these trends toward assimilation would increase with each succeed-ing generation.

A contrasting model of the assimilation process was proposed by the historian Marcus Lee Hansen. Hansen contended that whereas children of immigrants seek to shed evidence of their foreignness as fully as possible and to "become American," the immigrants' grandchildren—the third generation–seek to rediscover their roots and retain their ethnic distinctiveness. He formulated the notion of the *third generation re-turn:* "What the son wishes to forget, the grandson wishes to remember" (Hansen 1938:9). This model, which has become known as *Hansen's Law,* suggests that increas-ing assimilation with each succeeding generation is not inevitable. Instead, there can be variations among generations in rates of assimilation; the third generation, in par-ticular, may identify more closely with their grandparents' ethnic backgrounds than did their parents, producing a cultural or ethnic revival.

In one of the most celebrated interpretations of American religious life, Will Her-berg (1955) employed a variant of Hansen's Law to account for changing patterns of re-ligiosity in America. Herberg argued that because American religious communities have been so strongly linked to ethnicity, Hansen's model could be extended to explain patterns of religious practice among American ethnic groups. According to Herberg, re-ligiosity was high among the first generation, but because it was perceived as some-thing "foreign" and thus something to escape, it declined among the second generation. For the third generation, however, affiliation with and participation in one of the three broad American religious traditions—Protestantism, Catholicism, and Judaism—provided a socially acceptable way in which to maintain ethnic identity in modern so-ciety. Therefore, Herberg argued, members of the third generation would tend to have higher rates of religious participation than their second-generation parents.

Herberg's bold and imaginative interpretation stimulated considerable contro-versy. In one important study, Abramson (1975) showed that empirical data did not support the three-generations hypothesis as a general interpretation of the process of immigrant adjustment. Analyzing data on the religious beliefs and behavior of ten re-ligioethnic groups, Abramson found great variation in generational patterns of reli-giosity. In general there was little support for the hypothesized decline-and-rise pattern; only one of the ten religioethnic groups in his study (Eastern European Cath-olics) conformed to the pattern. Although more groups manifested a consistent de-cline in religiosity over three generations, there was a sufficient number of alternative patterns (for example, an increase in religiosity in the second generation) to preclude unequivocal support for a straight-line interpretation. Abramson's study reveals that although ethnicity is still a salient factor affecting religious behavior, the diversity of experiences among American ethnic groups (such as the differences among Irish, Pol-ish, and Italian Catholics) has been substantial.

Scholars have challenged the assimilation model on a variety of grounds, especially Park's view that assimilation is a linear process leading ultimately from cultural to marital assimilation and to the disappearance of ethnic identity. However, as Nagel argued in "Constructing Ethnicity" (Article 2), ethnicity remains a viable and vital force in modern societies precisely because it is functional and provides a source of emotional support and social solidarity in an increasingly fragmented and anonymous society. Thus Portes and Bach (1985), in their study comparing the adaptations of Cuban and Mexican immigrants to the United States, conclude that these immigrants' cultural and socioeconomic adaptation to American society, rather than being impeded, is facilitated by the maintenance of ethnic identity and close ethnic ties:

> *Those immigrants more able to relate effectively to various aspects of life in America are often those who most strongly adhere to personal relationships within their own communities. Awareness of barriers and, at times, outright hostility confronting them on the outside has its counterpart in the reaffirmation of primary relations within protected ethnic circles. . . . Rather than abandoning personal relationships within their own groups, immigrants who have moved farthest into the outside world seem to rely more heavily on such bonds. Ethnic resilience, not assimilation, is the theoretical perspective more congruent with this interpretation. This resilience is not, however, a force leading to collective withdrawal, but rather a moral resource, an integral part of the process of establishing and defining a place in a new society. (Portes and Bach 1985:333)*

In other words, maintaining ethnic primary group supports may actually enhance cultural and secondary structural assimilation.

Assimilation, therefore, is not a unidimensional or unilinear phenomenon, leading ultimately to an ethnically homogeneous society. Recognizing the multidimensional nature of assimilation, Gordon deplored the tendency to use the term in an inclusive way, and he argued that it was essential to identify its several forms. As we noted before, he argued that although extensive cultural assimilation had taken place in American life through the 1950s, there was only limited evidence of structural assimilation. For Gordon, a more accurate description of the realities of ethnic relations in American life at that time was *structural pluralism,* in which racial, ethnic, and, in particular, religious categories "retained their separate sociological structures."

To what extent has assimilation proceeded nearly forty years after Gordon published his classic essay? It is impossible to review in its entirety all of the voluminous research on the several dimensions of assimilation here, but we will examine several salient issues suggested by this literature. We will focus especially on the three key areas of socioeconomic status—income levels, occupational status, and educational attainment—as well as spatial assimilation and patterns of intermarriage.

Socioeconomic Assimilation

By almost any measure, descendants of southern and eastern European immigrants (Italians, Jews, Poles, Greeks, Hungarians) have become structurally assimilated into American life to a degree that few would have predicted at the end of World War II. During the 1950s one of the most striking findings in the social science literature dealing with assimilation was the rapid socioeconomic mobility of Jews, who, like most other "new" immigrant groups entering the United States between 1890 and 1915, had arrived virtually penniless (Strodtbeck 1958). By the 1960s, despite the relatively brief time in which they had resided in the United States, Jews had come to exceed all other ethnic groups (including the once-dominant white Anglo-Saxon Protestants) on the most common measures of socioeconomic status: median family income, educational attainment, and occupational prestige. The extremely rapid rise in the socioeconomic status of Jews historically contrasted sharply with that of other "new" immigrant groups (primarily southern and eastern European Catholics) who, with Jews, had entered American society in the massive wave of immigration near the turn of the twentieth century.

By the early 1970s, however, Andrew Greeley, the prolific sociologist and novelist, was able to celebrate what he characterized as the "ethnic miracle." Using extensive national social-survey data compiled between 1945 and 1970, Greeley contended that despite their lowly socioeconomic status three generations earlier, "the ethnics have made it." By 1970 the income levels of Irish, German, Italian, and Polish Catholics were exceeded only by that of Jews, not by white Anglo-Saxon Protestants, who in many accounts were still defined as the "establishment," or the "core" group to which all other ethnic groups compared themselves. In overall educational achievement, Polish, Italian, and Slavic Catholics still lagged somewhat behind the national white average, but when parental educational levels were held constant, Catholic ethnics showed higher educational levels than any other ethnic group except Jews. Indeed, Irish Catholics, once among the most despised and unfavorably stereotyped of all European ethnic groups, had by 1970 become "the richest, best educated, and most prestigious occupationally of any gentile religioethnic group." Thus, Greeley concluded, "In a very short space of time, the length of one generation, more or less, the American dream has come true" for European Catholic ethnic groups (Greeley 1976).

Neidert and Farley (1985) reported similar, although not identical, findings in their analysis of differences in socioeconomic status in a 1979 national survey of American ethnic groups. Their data showed that occupational returns for educational attainment tend generally to increase with each succeeding generation, thus providing strong support for a straight-line theory of assimilation. They also found that although ethnic differences exist in educational attainment, occupational prestige, and per capita income among non-English European ethnic groups, they were not at a disadvantage compared with those of English ancestry.

Several subsequent studies have reinforced these general findings. Generalizing from a comprehensive review of the voluminous literature on the economic attainments of American ethnic and racial groups, Model concluded that "members of most pre-1924 immigrant backgrounds fare at least as well as do other white Americans" (Model 1988:366). Similarly, Alba (Article 15) contends that "assimilation was, and is, a reality for the majority of the descendants of earlier waves of immigration from Europe." Basing his analysis on 1990 census data, Alba concluded that "long-term processes . . . have whittled away at the social foundations for ethnic distinctions [among European ancestry groups and] have brought about a rough parity of opportunities to attain such socioeconomic goods as educational credentials and prestigious jobs. . . . [T]he disadvantages that once were quite evident [among European ethnic] groups have largely faded and their socioeconomic attainments increasingly resemble, if not even surpass, those of the average white American."

However, as we have noted in the introduction to Part 2 and as Waters and Eschbach point out in Article 14, these patterns of educational and economic attainment are not repeated among all of the other categories in the American ethno-racial pentagon. Asian Americans, especially Chinese and Japanese, have been the object of considerable discrimination throughout their history in the United States. Indeed, so unfavorable were the perceptions of Asians by whites that, unlike any European ethnic groups, they were virtually excluded from immigrating to the United States for more than half a century. Moreover, in one of the most notorious instances of racism in American history, American citizens of Japanese descent were subjected to the humiliation of incarceration in detention camps during World War II.

As Waters and Eschbach point out in Article 14, numerous researchers have reported striking patterns of educational and economic social mobility among Asian Americans. As a result, during the past quarter century, there has been a notable change in perceptions of Asian Americans; the unfavorable stereotypes that were widely embraced by white Americans before, during, and immediately after World War II have metamorphosed into the controversial characterization of them as "model minorities," who, despite discrimination, have demonstrated remarkable patterns of educational, occupational, and financial success (Mazumdar 1996). Today the educational levels of Japanese, Chinese, Asian Indians, and Filipinos—immigrant as well as native-born—equal or exceed those of whites. These high levels of educational attainment are particularly pronounced among the younger segments of the population. Moreover, Asians are overrepresented in higher-status occupations, especially the professions. Although income levels among those of comparable occupational backgrounds tend to be lower than those of whites overall, income levels for native-born Japanese, Chinese, and Filipino males are about the same as for white males. Nevertheless, Hirschman and Wong (1986) caution against generalizing from these selected indices of secondary structural assimilation to other dimensions of assimilation. They conclude that Asian Americans tend to remain greatly underrepresented in many sectors of the dominant economy, society, and polity. Moreover, Hurh and Kim (1989) have shown that Asians with comparable educational attainments, occupational prestige, and hours worked per week earn less than their white counterparts. Thus, images of Asian American "success" obscure both the relatively heavier investments required for Asians to achieve such income levels and the discrimination to which they are still subject. It is because of images of Asian success that they encounter discrimination as a consequence of their minority status: Asians tend to be excluded from governmental programs designed to address such discrimination.

Hurh and Kim suggest that the widespread perception of the success image of Asian Americans has an additional consequence. If the situation of Asian Americans appears favorable, it is only in reference to the greater disadvantages of other minorities —African Americans, Hispanics, and American Indians. Indeed, the "model minority" stereotype of Asians serves to reinforce negative stereotypes of these other minorities and to blame them for the social, economic, and political conditions under which they find themselves.

However, as we noted in Part 2 and will discuss more fully in Part 4, the patterns of educational, occupational, and financial achievement found among European and Asian ethnic groups are not duplicated among Hispanics and African Americans. Bean and Tienda (1987) and Davis, Haub, and Willette (1983) have demonstrated that substantial gaps separate Hispanics from the Anglo population on these dimensions. Davis, Haub, and Willette anticipate that because there is evidence of increasing Hispanic educational attainments with each succeeding generation, the gap between Hispanics and Anglos in levels of educational achievement should narrow in the future. On the other hand, the historic concentration of Hispanics in lower-paid, less-skilled occupations has persisted, and the overall economic status of Hispanics, which until the 1990s had been consistently higher than for African Americans, began a steady decline in the early 1980s that by 1995 resulted in a median family income below that of African Americans. In 1979 Hispanic median family income stood at $29,180 (in 1995 dollars)—71 percent of white median family income; it has never since achieved this level, declining to $24,569 (or 58 percent of white income) in 1995. Today more than one-quarter of Hispanic families lives in poverty. Reflecting the interrelated impact of class, gender, and ethnicity, as well as their relatively recent arrival in American society, more than half (53 percent) of poor Hispanic families were headed by women (compared with 30 percent of non-Hispanic families in poverty) (U.S. Bureau of the Census 1996a; 1996b). Forty percent of all Hispanic children lived in poverty, and during the 1980s childhood poverty increased more rapidly among Hispanics than among any other racial or ethnic category (U.S. Bureau of the Census 1996b). Finally, the median net worth of Hispanic households was approximately one-eighth the net worth of white households (U.S. Bureau of the Census 1997). However, among Hispanic groups there are obvious disparities, most prominently those between Cubans, whose early migration, especially, was comprised substantially of middle-class and professional people, and Puerto Ricans, who were much more likely to have had lower levels of educational attainment and fewer occupational skills than Cubans.

As we will note more fully in Part 4, similar patterns have characterized African American socioeconomic status. During the 1970s, the African American community in general experienced gains in educational attainment and political participation. Paralleling the decline in income among Hispanics, though, the overall financial condition of black families deteriorated. However, Wilson (Article 7; 1987) contends that such generalizations obscure the increasing economic divergence within the African American community. Wilson contends that in the past two decades, blacks have had occupational opportunities unprecedented in the African American experience in America. On the other hand, the economic distress of the African American underclass, in particular, of female-headed families, has grown increasingly acute.

Spatial Assimilation

Each of the dimensions previously mentioned—years of schooling, occupational distribution, and income levels—in itself reveals little about the extent of social assimilation, integration, or incorporation of different ethnic groups in a society. In a genuinely plural society with unranked parallel social structures, for example, it is hypothetically possible for two or more ethnic groups to manifest high educational attainment, occupational status, and income levels without substantial physical interaction.

Patterns of residential integration have been one of the most frequently examined indices of assimilation. Massey and Mullan (1984) have referred to it as *spatial assim-*

ilation and defined it as the process whereby a group attains residential propinquity with members of a host society. Numerous scholars (such as Hershberg et al. 1979; Lieberson 1963, 1980; Marson and Van Valey 1979; Pettigrew 1979; Roof 1979; Taeuber 1990; Massey and Denton 1993; Farley and Frey 1994) have shown that there is a close interrelationship between housing and jobs, educational opportunities, and income. Indeed, Pettigrew (1979:122) has characterized racial residential segregation as the "structural linchpin" of American race relations, and Massey and Denton (Article 9) have underscored the critical role that it has played in the concentration of black poverty. Therefore, an ethnic group's spatial location is a crucial variable affecting its overall socioeconomic position. Residential location affects life chances in a wide variety of ways, including "cost and quality of housing, health and sanitary conditions, exposure to crime and violence, quality of services (the most important of which is education), and access to economic opportunity, as well as a host of less tangible factors ranging from the character of one's children's playmates to the kinds of role models they emulate" (Massey and Mullan 1984:838).

In *A Piece of the Pie: Black and White Immigrants since 1880* (1980), Stanley Lieberson undertook an exhaustive comparative analysis of the experiences of African Americans and "new" European immigrants in twentieth-century America. His examination of the patterns of residential segregation of African Americans and various "new" immigrant groups revealed several important features. First, at the beginning of the period of massive immigration from southern and eastern Europe (the last decade of the nineteenth century), blacks living in northern cities were less spatially segregated than the new southern and eastern European groups (e.g., Jews, Poles, Italians) who were beginning to arrive in substantial numbers. Second, the residential segregation of African Americans increased during the twentieth century, a process that correspondingly cut them off and isolated them from participation in most of the activities of the larger community. The position of blacks in northern cities deteriorated from the turn of the twentieth century onward. Moreover, the patterns of residential segregation of African Americans and southern European immigrant groups moved in opposite directions: at the same time that the rates of spatial assimilation for African Americans were declining, rates were increasing for southern and eastern European immigrants. Thus the deterioration of African Americans' position in northern urban areas occurred at precisely the time that the position of immigrant whites was beginning to improve.

As we noted in Part 2, the massive migration of African Americans out of the South to the North and from rural areas to the nation's cities has been one of the most important demographic shifts in American history. Today, African Americans are much more likely to live in metropolitan areas than are whites. Moreover, the percentage of metropolitan blacks who reside in central cities is more than double that of whites, creating the urban racial polarization that is one of the basic racial demographic facts of American life today (Pettigrew 1979:122; see Massey and Denton, Article 9, for a superb analysis of the historical development of American racial residential patterns).

The patterns of residential segregation experienced by African Americans in the twentieth century are not comparable to the immigrant neighborhoods or enclaves in which "new" immigrant groups congregated around the turn of the century. First, as Massey and Denton point out, although they were spatially isolated, at no time were immigrant neighborhoods as homogeneous or their spatial isolation as pronounced as in black neighborhoods today. In other words, the spatial isolation of white ethnics was never so extreme as that of African Americans during the last half century. From their examination of the experience of African Americans and ethnic groups in Philadelphia, Hershberg and his colleagues (1979) report that

> The typical Irish immigrant in 1880 and the typical Italian immigrant in 1930 . . . shared a similar aspect of their residential experience. When the hypothetical immigrant in each era walked through his neighborhood, what kind of people might he have met? The Irishman in 1880 lived with 15 percent other Irish immigrants, 34 percent Irish stock, 26 percent all foreign-born persons and 68 percent all foreign stock. The typical Italian immigrant in 1930 had an almost identical experience. He lived with 14 percent other Italian immigrants, 38 percent Italian stock, 23 percent all foreign born persons and 57 percent all foreign stock. In striking contrast, the typical black in 1970 lived in a census tract in which 73 percent of the population was black. (Hershberg et al. 1979: 74–75)

Thus the residential enclaves or neighborhoods of European immigrants were never so homogeneous as those of African Americans. The residential experience of European immigrants also differed from that of African Americans in that most European ethnics were not concentrated primarily in immigrant ghettos. Finally, as previously noted, patterns of European ethnic residential segregation were not enduring or permanent, but began to break down relatively quickly, whereas the characteristic feature of racial residential segregation since 1940 has been its persistence (Sorensen, Taeuber, and Hollingsworth 1975; Taueber 1983, 1990). As Massey and Denton (Article 9) point out, "for European immigrants, enclaves were places of absorption, adaptation, and adjustment to American society. They served as springboards for broader mobility in society, whereas blacks were trapped behind an increasingly impermeable color line."

One prominent measure that sociologists have developed to determine the extent of residential segregation or spatial isolation is the segregation index or *index of dissimilarity*. With this measure a score of 100 represents complete racial segregation, in which every city block is exclusively black or exclusively white; conversely, a score of zero represents a housing pattern in which members of different racial and ethnic groups are evenly distributed and each city block has the same percentage of blacks and whites as the city's overall population.

Taeuber (1990) analyzed trends in the index of dissimilarity between whites and nonwhites from 1940 to 1988 for 109 large cities. The average segregation index was 85 in 1940, 87 in 1950, 86 in 1960, 82 in 1970, 75 in 1980, and 76 in 1988 (Taeuber 1990:144–145). However, the segregation index was even higher for the twenty-eight cities that had an African American population of more than 100,000 in 1980. Already highly segregated by 1940, the patterns of racial residential isolation remained relatively stationary during the 1950s and 1960s. By 1970 the average segregation index for the twenty-eight American cities with African American populations of more than 100,000 was 87; by 1980 the index for these cities had declined to 81, although in some (such as Chicago and Cleveland) the index remained above 90 (Taeuber 1983). During the 1970s and 1980s, racial residential segregation declined modestly for the country as a whole. It persisted most dramatically in large industrial cities of the Northeast and Midwest (for example, Detroit, Chicago, Cleveland, Milwaukee, Newark, and Philadelphia still had segregation indices of over 80 in 1990). Indeed, Denton (1994) contends that those cities that were "hypersegregated" (that is, highly segregated on at least four of five different statistical measures) in 1980 remained equally—and in some instances more—hypersegrated in 1990. However, Farley and Frey (1994) point out that for most metropolitan areas—especially those in the South and West with substantial new housing construction and those centered around university communities or military bases—segregation indices declined during the 1990s (Farley and Frey 1994; Farley 1997).

These data document the highly segregated residential patterns that have characterized American cities during the modern industrial period. Despite declines in the previous two decades, by 1990 the general pattern of spatial isolation for African Americans was still more pronounced than for any other racial or ethnic group in American history. Moreover, the declines in residential segregation that did occur were so modest as to make problematic whether substantial increases in spatial assimilation for African Americans are likely in the near future.

As Massey and Denton point out in Article 9 ("The Construction of the Ghetto"), the black ghetto did not simply occur "naturally" but developed primarily in response to deliberate actions rooted in white prejudices throughout the twentieth century. Many different discriminatory mechanisms have been used to create the pattern of residential "apartheid" that today characterizes the housing patterns of black and white in American society: laws excluding blacks from "white" neighborhoods; violence, terrorism, and intimidation; the creation of neighborhood "improvement" associations designed principally to keep out black residents; *restrictive covenants* on real estate deeds specifying that properties would not be sold, leased, or rented to "undesirable" racial or ethnic groups; real estate "codes of ethics" and federal government (FHA and VA) policies specifying that "if a neighborhood is to retain stability, it is necessary that properties shall continue to be occupied by the same social and racial classes"; *racial steering*—the practice by realtors of showing white and black clients homes or apartments primarily in neighborhoods with residents similar to the client; and *redlining*—the deliberate decision by banks, other home lending institutions, and insurance companies to refuse loans or insurance to people trying to buy homes or insurance in lower-income minority neighborhoods.

A major source of housing discrimination involves home loans. A study that analyzed over 10 million applications for home loans from every savings and loan association in the country between 1983 and 1988 showed that applications from blacks were rejected more than twice as often as were applications from whites. Moreover, the applications of high-income blacks were rejected more often than were those of low-income whites. In 1991 a comprehensive Federal Reserve Board study of mortgage lending showed that even within the same income groups, whites were nearly twice as likely as blacks (and one-and-a-half times as likely as Hispanics) to get loans. Similarly, a 1993 study of five Midwestern cities found that insurance agents were five times more likely to refuse to sell insurance to inner-city homeowners than they were to residents of high-income areas. Studies such as these have led to increasing scrutiny of banking and insurance industry practices and, in some cases, legal settlements in which mortgage-lending and insurance companies have agreed to extend their activities more fully to lower-income neighborhoods (Dedman 1989; *Federal Reserve Bulletin* 1991; *USA Today* 1991; Kerr 1993; Passell 1996; Lewis 1997).

Although some of the mechanisms (e.g., restrictive covenants) through which residential racial segregation is perpetuated are no longer used as widely as in the past, the existence of racial housing discrimination has been extensively documented in what are called "fair housing audit studies." Like the bias studies described in Part 1, fair housing audits involve sending equally qualified individuals (auditors) who differ only in their racial or ethnic identity to investigate the availability of sale or rental housing. During the 1970s and 1980s more than 70 such studies were undertaken throughout the country and overwhelmingly documented widespread discrimination in virtually all phases of the process of seeking housing—from initial contacts with realtors to financing. The most comprehensive study, involving over 3,800 audits in 25 different metropolitan areas, found that

> between 5 and 10 percent of the time, all information about available housing units was withheld from black and Hispanic customers; that black and Hispanic home buyers and black renters were informed about 25 percent fewer housing units than comparable whites; and that whites were significantly more likely than blacks or Hispanics to receive follow-up calls from the housing agent or to hear positive comments about an available house, apartment, or apartment complex. (Yinger 1995)

The barriers that minority applicants encounter from real estate brokers in locating housing are repeated as minority auditors seek to obtain financing and insurance. "The evidence for discrimination against blacks and Hispanics [provided by the fair housing audits] in the loan approval process is strong, recent, and compelling. . . . After accounting for the applicant, property, and loan characteristics that lenders say they consider, minority applicants are turned down at a rate that is over 50 percent higher than the rate for comparable whites" (Yinger 1995:85).

Even if these practices had not been employed, federal government policies would have ensured that the suburban population that expanded dramatically after World War II would be overwhelmingly white and that African Americans would be relegated primarily to the inner cities. Most important was the decision—perfectly consistent with a capitalist economy—to permit private enterprise to meet the great demand for housing that had developed during the Depression and World War II. As a result, suburban housing was built almost exclusively for those who could afford to pay, while people unable to meet financing requirements were forced to accept housing vacated by those moving to the suburbs. On the other hand, low-cost, government-subsidized housing, which attracted a primarily black clientele, was constructed mostly in center cities rather than in the suburbs (Grier and Grier 1965). Therefore, organized neighborhood resistance to proposals for low-income and moderate-income housing is often a veiled form of attitudinal discrimination that serves to reinforce the patterns of residential segregation.

In their historical analysis of the development of residential racial segregation and economic opportunity in Philadelphia, Hershberg and his associates (1979) note the crucial importance of residential proximity to jobs in American history. For many whites, occupational opportunities have been the primary factor in determining where to live. Blacks, on the other hand, have been circumscribed by racial exclusion. In the nineteenth century, when they resided in close proximity to occupational opportunities, African Americans were arbitrarily excluded from jobs. Today, when employment discrimination has declined, they are excluded by physical distance. Pettigrew assesses the implications of the continuing spatial isolation of African Americans:

> *This massive metropolitan pattern of housing segregation has now become the principal barrier to progress in other realms. Indeed, the residential segregation of blacks and whites has emerged as a functional equivalent for the explicit state segregation laws of the past in that it effectively acts to limit the life chances and choices of black people generally. (Pettigrew 1979:124)*

Today, despite federal fair-housing legislation, a Supreme Court decision that declared housing discrimination illegal, generally more favorable racial attitudes by whites toward African Americans, and a substantial growth of the black middle class, residential segregation still persists on a massive scale in the United States.

Is the residential segregation of African Americans a result of racial discrimination, or is it a reflection of the generally lower overall class position of blacks? Taeuber and Taeuber (1965) have shown that the residential segregation of African Americans is not primarily a result of black income levels, which, they maintain, can account for only a small portion of residential segregation. High-income whites and high-income blacks do not live in the same neighborhoods, nor do low-income whites and low-income blacks; Massey and Denton conclude that in the debate over race versus class, when residence is considered, "race clearly predominates" (Massey and Denton 1993). Nevertheless, if, as Wilson argues, class factors have increasingly come to affect the life chances of American racial and ethnic minorities—not merely African Americans, but Hispanics and American Indians, as well—then these other minorities should experience comparable forms of residential segregation.

However, critics dispute the arguments that the effects of structural economic changes are equally devastating to other contemporary racial and ethnic minorities such as Hispanics and American Indians. Rather, they argue, because race remains an important determinant of opportunity in American life, other minorities, even those from comparable class locations, have been and will be able to experience spatial assimilation more easily than African Americans.

Massey and Mullan (1984) found substantial differences in the changes that occurred during the 1960s in the residential patterns of Hispanics and African Americans: "A barrio-centered residential pattern simply does not typify the experience of Hispanics in the same way that a ghetto-centered pattern typifies that of blacks" (Massey and Mullan 1984:870). African Americans who moved into previously white neighborhoods found that their presence led to white flight, but Hispanics did not:

> *Residential succession (an exodus of current residents) is likely to follow the entry of Hispanics into an Anglo area when the incoming Hispanics are poorly educated and foreign, with low occupational statuses and incomes, and when the tract is near an established black or Hispanic area. In contrast, residential succession follows black entry into an Anglo area no matter what the objective social characteristics of the incoming blacks. . . . Because the Anglo response to Hispanic invasion is not universally one of avoidance and flight, Hispanics are much better able than blacks to translate social into residential mobility. . . .*
>
> *[Moreover,] the social status required of blacks before they are not threatening to Anglos appears to be significantly higher than that required of Hispanics. In other words, a black lawyer or doctor may be able to move into a mixed neighborhood with other professionals, but a black*

plumber or bricklayer cannot buy into a working-class Anglo neighborhood. What is required for black spatial assimilation is a quantum leap in social status. (Massey and Mullan 1984: 851–852, 854, 856)

Massey and Mullan conclude that "Anglos avoid blacks on the basis of race, not class," whereas the converse was more likely to be true for Hispanics.

As previously noted, the processes of suburbanization and residential segregation have been intimately interwoven. As Americans—including racial and ethnic minorities—experience upward socioeconomic mobility, they try to move to better neighborhoods, which in the post–World War II era has frequently meant the suburbs. However, the range of residential opportunities available to African Americans has been much more limited than those for whites—or even for Hispanics or Asians. Although affluent Hispanics and Asians have been able to translate improved socioeconomic status into suburban spatial assimilation, blacks have largely been restricted to equally segregated black suburbs immediately adjacent to central cities. Massey and Mullan (1984) and Massey and Denton (1987) found that throughout the 1960s and 1970s, Asians and Hispanics (except for Puerto Ricans, who are more likely than other Hispanics to be identified as black) were not confronted with the same residential barriers encountered by blacks. As a consequence, "middle-class blacks live[d] in much poorer neighborhoods than [did] middle-class whites, Hispanics, or Asians" (Massey and Denton 1993:144).

During the 1980s, however, the residential patterns of African Americans, Latinos, and Asians converged somewhat. As we have seen, black segregation indices in many American cities and for the country as a whole declined between 1980 and 1990—from a mean segregation for 232 metropolitan areas of 69 in 1980 to 64 in 1990. On the other hand, while Latinos and Asians were significantly less segregated than blacks in 1980 (with overall indices of 42 and 41, respectively), each experienced slight overall increases in segregation by 1990. Frey and Farley (1996) found that during the 1980s "segregation between Latinos and non-Latinos increased in more than half (52%) [of the metropolitan areas] and between Asians and non-Asians in almost three-quarters (74%). In contrast, segregation between blacks and nonblacks rose in only 12% of the areas. In 1990, Latinos and Asians were far less segregated than blacks (with average segregation scores of 43, 43, and 64, respectively). Yet these averages for the former two groups increased over the 1980s while the score for blacks fell" (Frey and Farley 1996:36–37).

Unlike Wilson, who contends that economic class factors will in the future affect similar life chances for African Americans and Hispanics, Massey and Mullan (1984) contend that because blacks are unable to translate economic mobility into spatial assimilation in the same manner as Hispanics, "the discrepant patterns of black and Hispanic spatial assimilation portend very different futures for these groups." Because residential integration has strong effects on other patterns of social interaction such as friendships, marriage, and schooling, African Americans are likely to remain socially and spatially isolated in the United States. They therefore dispute the notion that Hispanics can be seen as an underclass in the same way as blacks: "Unlike blacks, [Hispanics] are able to translate social mobility into residential mobility. Hispanics are simply not trapped in the barrio in the same way that blacks are trapped in the ghetto" (Massey and Mullan 1984:870).

However, the growing concentration of Hispanic and Asian communities in proximity to black neighborhoods in many metropolitan areas suggests an increased "potential for greater mixed-race neighborhood living" (Frey and Farley 1996:49) and that
in the future segregation *within* metropolitan areas may be less dramatic than what
Frey (1996) has termed the "demographic balkanization" of the United States—the
concentration of African Americans, Latinos, and Asians in certain metropolitan areas
and regions and the white population in others.

Marital Assimilation

Gordon maintains that once structural assimilation has occurred, other dimensions of
assimilation—most importantly, intermarriage, or what he terms marital *assimilation*
or *amalgamation*—will follow. Marital assimilation, he claims, represents the final outcome of the assimilation process, in which "the minority group ultimately loses its
ethnic identity in the larger host or core society" (Gordon 1964:80).

The extent to which marital assimilation has occurred among different ethnic
groups has been the subject of considerable research. One of the most celebrated interpretations of intermarriage patterns among white Americans was the "triple melting
pot" thesis, which saw intermarriage increasing across ethnic lines but remaining
within the three religious communities of Protestants, Catholics, and Jews (Kennedy
1944, 1952). Although this interpretation was integral to Herberg's discussion (1955) of
general patterns of ethnic identity discussed before, subsequent analyses have raised
many questions concerning its validity (Peach 1981; Hirschman 1983). Richard Alba's
analysis of ethnic marriage patterns among American Catholics (1981) demonstrated
increasing rates of religious intermarriage, which in turn "point to a decline in the
salience of religious boundaries for a good part of the Catholic group." This general inference about the waning significance of religious boundaries could be extended to
Protestants, with whom Catholics most frequently intermarry, as well. In other words,
religious affiliation is declining in salience as a factor influencing mate selection.

Moreover, recent analyses suggest that white ethnic groups generally have experienced substantial marital assimilation, especially among third and fourth generations
and those from higher occupational categories. In national studies of assimilation
among American Catholics, Alba (1976, 1981) and Alba and Kessler (1979) found that
as early as 1963, marriage outside ethnic groups was extensive. Rates of intermarriage
were most pronounced among the third generation and among the youngest adult
members of each ethnic group. Similarly, in a study of ethnic consciousness in Provi-
dence, Rhode Island, Goering found that among the Irish and Italians, only 15 percent
of the first generation had married outside their own ethnic group, whereas 63 percent
of the third generation had done so (Goering 1971:382n). Later, utilizing the 1979 population survey on ancestry, Alba and Golden (1986) found high rates of intermarriage
among Europeans but, except for Native Americans, relatively low rates between Europeans and non-Europeans, especially blacks. Intermarriage rates were higher for
"old" immigrant European ancestry groups (British, Irish, German, and Scandinavian)
than for "new" immigrant ancestory groups (Italian, Polish, Russian, and Slavic). However, in "Assimilation's Quiet Tide" (Article 15), Alba contends that 1990 census data
point to dramatic increases in intermarriage among "new" immigrant ancestry groups
as well. These data show that "more than half . . . of whites have spouses whose ethnic

backgrounds do not overlap their own at all . . . [and] only one-fifth have spouses with similar ethnic backgrounds" and that these trends are especially pronounced among Italians and Poles.

Further dramatic evidence of this trend toward increased marital assimilation is shown in the rates of intermarriage for American Jews. Jewish rates of intermarriage vary by city. For example, in New York City less than one-sixth (14 percent of men and 12 percent of women) of Jews married non-Jewish spouses whereas in Denver more than half of spouses married were born as gentiles (Cohen 1988:27). The national rate of Jewish intermarriage with non-Jews has been most pronounced in the last generation. Basing their conclusions on a 1990 survey of American Jews—the most comprehensive ever undertaken—a study by the Council of Jewish Federations reported that 91 percent of Jews who married before 1965 had married non-Jews, but that this percentage had declined substantially in each succeeding decade. Of those Jews who married after 1985, less than half (48 percent) married other Jews. Moreover, the authors found that of those Jews who had married non-Jews, only slightly more than one-fourth (28 percent) of their children were being raised as Jews (Council of Jewish Federations 1991:13–16). This trend toward increasing rates of religious intermarriage has raised concerns among many Jews that the future of the American Jewish community may be threatened (Glazer 1987; Cohen 1988; Goldberg 1997).

Although interethnic and interfaith marriages among whites have been increasingly common through the twentieth century, interracial marriages have been—and continue to be—relatively rare in American society. As Table 1 indicates, in 1970 less than one percent (0.7%) of all marriages were across racial lines, while in 1995 that figure had increased substantially—more than doubling between 1980 and 1995—but still represented only 2.5 percent of all marriages.

Among racial categories, marital assimilation has been most pronounced among Asians. As early as 1973, Tinker (1973) found that more than half of the marriages by Japanese were to non-Japanese. Montero (1981), basing his analysis on 1970 census data, found that, except for American Indians, the rates of intermarriage for Asians were higher than for any other racial category. Levine (1989) has reported that 60 percent of the Sansei (third-generation Japanese Americans) have Caucasian spouses. Similarly, Wong (1989) documented a major increase in intermarriage among Chinese Americans during the past half century. Whereas Chinese American marriages were basically endogamous up to the 1930s, by 1980 over 30 percent of Chinese marriages were to non-Chinese, primarily whites. Extending this analysis to 1990, Qian (1997) examined data and found that only 39 percent of Asian men and 34 percent of Asian women between the ages of 20 and 29 had married other Asians.

However, the patterns of extensive intermarriage for European ethnic groups, Asians, and American Indians are not duplicated among Hispanics and especially African Americans, although recent data indicate substantial increases in intermarriages for these two categories (Qian 1997). The percentages of Hispanics marrying other Hispanics declined between 1980 and 1990; by 1990 the marriages of nearly identical proportions of 20- to 29-year-old Hispanic men and women (64% and 63%, respectively) were endogamous. Although the number of African American intermarriages also increased between 1980 and 1990, African Americans were the racial minority most likely to be endogamous; in 1990 better than 90 percent of 20- to 29-year-old African American men and women were married to other African Americans.

TABLE 1   *Married Couples of Same or Mixed Races and Origins, 1970 to 1995*

Race and Origin of Spouses	1970*	1980	1990	1995
Married Couples, total	44,598	49,714	53,256	54,937
RACE				
Same-race couples	43,922	48,264	50,889	51,733
White/white	40,578	44,910	47,202	48,030
Black/black	3,344	3,354	3,687	3,703
Interracial couples	310	651	964	1,392
Black/white	65	167	211	328
Black husband/white wife	41	122	150	206
White husband/black wife	24	45	61	122
White/other race[†]	233	450	720	988
Black/other race[†]	12	34	33	76
All other couples[†]	366	799	1,401	1,811
HISPANIC ORIGIN				
Hispanic/Hispanic	1,368	1,906	3,085	3,857
Hispanic/other origin (not Hispanic)	584	891	1,193	1,434
All other couples (not of Hispanic origin)	42,645	46,917	48,979	49,646

Source: U.S. Bureau of the Census. *Statistical Abstract of the United States: 1995.* (Washington, D.C.: Government Printing Office, 1996), p. 57.

*As of April and based on Census of Population

[†]Excluding white and black

In thousands. As of March, except as noted. Persons 15 years old and over. Persons of Hispanic origin may be of any race. Except as noted, based on Current Population Survey.

Thus, black-white marriages are the least frequent of all interracial marriage patterns. Although there was a five-fold increase in the number of black-white marriages between 1970 and 1995, such unions still represented only 0.59 percent of all marriages in the United States. In general, intermarriage rates among different racial and ethnic categories are influenced by such factors as cultural similarities, generational status, residential dispersion, and socioeconomic status.

Why Assimilation Rates Vary

Analyses of race and ethnicity in American life have frequently reflected social and political controversies within the broader society. As we noted in Part 1, the research agenda in the field of racial and ethnic relations—the issues considered and the questions posed—frequently has been drawn from social policy concerns, not from sociological theory alone.

   One of the most striking changes in the research agenda in the field of racial and ethnic relations over the past two decades has been a shift to a broadly comparative perspective. Some scholars have taken a cross-cultural perspective, examining the dynamics of race and ethnicity throughout the world (for example, Burgess 1978; Francis 1976; Glazer and Moynihan 1975; Gordon 1978; Hechter 1975; Henry 1976; Horowitz 1985; Olzak and Nagel 1986; Rose 1976).

However, the black protest activity of the 1950s and 1960s, which sought to eliminate the chasm historically separating African Americans from the American mainstream, contributed substantially to a resurgence of interest in ethnicity that focused on other ethnic groups in American society as well. Since the late 1970s, research dealing with ethnicity in American society has proliferated (for example, Dinnerstein and Reimers 1983, 1987; Greeley 1976; Kinton 1977; Lieberson 1980; Mindel and Habenstein 1976; Patterson 1977; Seller 1977; Sowell 1978, 1980, 1981; Steinberg 1981). This shift from a focus almost exclusively on black-white relations to an examination of the role of ethnicity in American life was stimulated in part by the conflicts that emerged from African Americans' claims for equal participation and opportunity. As Steinberg has pointed out, "That the ethnic resurgence involved more than nostalgia became clear as racial minorities and white ethnics became polarized on a series of issues relating to schools, housing, local government and control over federal programs" (Steinberg 1981:50).

The resentment fueled by these conflicts with African Americans was reflected in the question frequently posed by white ethnics: "If we made it, why can't they?" If Greeley's characterization of the "ethnic miracle" is correct—if Jews, Poles, Italians, and the Irish today have "made it," how have they been able to do so while other groups have not? How do we account for the "extraordinary success story" of Catholics and Jews, who had to overcome poverty, discrimination, illiteracy, and chronic overcrowding in America's urban ghettos?

Explanations for differences in socioeconomic status—levels of income, educational attainment, and occupational prestige—among American ethnic groups that formerly were debated informally and privately in bull sessions, dinner parties, and cocktail parties, have increasingly become the focus of formal inquiry by social scientists, whose interpretations have become part of that public discourse. During the past decade, especially, there have been numerous comparative studies of American ethnic groups: advancing explanations for the differences in achievement levels among American ethnic groups has become a major preoccupation of specialists in the field.

Several explanations for the differences among American ethnic groups have been advanced. Although there are considerable differences among them, they can be divided into two broad categories: those that emphasize qualities and characteristics internal to an ethnic group, and those that emphasize the influence of factors external to an ethnic group—forces over which members of the group have little or no control.

Internal Explanations

Internal explanations of social inequality attribute racial and ethnic inequalities to each group's perceived abilities, attributes, and characteristics. An internal model explains an ethnic group's adaptation, adjustment, achievement, or assimilation as the result primarily of the traits, qualities, or characteristics that the group brings with it—the group's own "personality," if you will. The emphasis in this argument is on the "inheritance" or transmission of behavioral traits and characteristics and on their continuity across generations. Dominant groups have achieved their status because they possess desirable qualities; on the other hand, the economic, political, and social status of subordinate groups is attributed to their own deficiencies. Therefore, in this view, racial and ethnic groups are responsible for their own fate—for their own success or lack of it.

Biology

The most simplistic of the internal explanations is a biological or genetic argument. One of the oldest internal explanations is that American ethnic or racial groups have different *biological* endowments—innately different mental, emotional, and moral characteristics—that are genetically transmitted from generation to generation. Such biological explanations flourished during the late nineteenth and early twentieth centuries, when differences between the political, social, and economic institutions of Anglo-Saxon and non–Anglo-Saxon peoples were attributed to biologically transmitted—that is, "racial"—traits. Thus Senator Henry Cabot Lodge, in an 1896 Senate speech condemning continued unrestricted immigration by peoples from southern and eastern Europe, argued that the Anglo-Saxon capacity for democracy was instinctual:

> The men of each race possess an indestructible stock of ideas, traditions, sentiments, modes of thought, an unconscious inheritance from their ancestors, upon which argument has no effect. What makes a race are their mental and, above all, their moral characteristics, the slow growth and accumulation of centuries of toil and conflict. These are the qualities which determine the social efficiency as a people, which make one race rise and another fall. (Lodge 1896:2819)

Lodge, and most other intellectuals of the day, believed that the "old" immigrants from northern and western Europe (the British, Germans, and Scandinavians) were descended from common ancestors who were "historically free, energetic, and progressive," whereas Slavic, Latin, and Asiatic races were historically downtrodden, atavistic, and stagnant" (Quoted in Solomon 1956:111).

Given these assumptions, which were supposed to be scientifically valid, unrestricted immigration meant the introduction of millions of unassimilable people who lacked the "superior" instincts of northern and western Europeans. The absence of these instincts, Lodge believed, would ultimately bring about the "decline of human civilization." Much of the "scientific" research concerning racial inequality in the last half of the nineteenth and first half of the twentieth centuries involved examination of physical differences and differences in intelligence test performances among American racial and ethnic groups. Frequently, inferences from such studies were cited as evidence of the biological inferiority of non–Anglo-Saxon groups and then used to justify their subordinate status. As a consequence, during this period the ideology of racism gained respectability. As we noted in Part 1, *racism* refers to the belief that the members of one group are biologically superior, whereas other groups are inherently inferior and "incapable of ever achieving intellectual and moral equality" with them (Noel 1972:157).

For more than a century, the ideology of racism has been shaped and justified by "science." Early in the twentieth century, studies of cranial capacity—brain sizes and structures—became fashionable. Assuming that brain size and intelligence are related, scientists established a racial hierarchy of intelligence, with northern Europeans highest and Africans lowest. Recalculation of the data in many of these studies has shown that the procedures that were used to establish this hierarchy were not accurate and simply reflected the scientists' prejudices; these procedures amounted to "advocacy masquerading as objectivity" (Gould 1981). Although the studies were far from scientific, they were used to "prove" the biological superiority of northern and western Europeans and to justify social policies of racial domination.

Early in the twentieth century, intelligence testing replaced anatomic studies as a way of "scientifically" measuring and validating the "natural superiority" of socially dominant groups. Since then, intelligence tests have been widely administered, have played a crucial role in reinforcing the belief that racial, ethnic, and class inequalities result from innate qualities, and have had a widespread impact on public policy. For example, the poor performances of southern and eastern European immigrants (in which 80 percent of Hungarians, 79 percent of Italians, and 87 percent of Russians scored in the "feeble-minded" category) were frequently cited in the congressional debates that resulted in the discriminatory immigration quotas established during the 1920s. Moreover, racial differences in intelligence test results for years provided the justification for racial segregation, the vastly unequal school systems for blacks and whites, and the near-exclusion of blacks from higher education (Gould 1981; Weinberg 1983).

By the mid–twentieth century, as criticisms of these tests and their uses mounted, the notion of racial differences in intelligence found little support in the scientific community. After the Supreme Court's 1954 *Brown* decision, however, the issue of racial differences in intelligence was revived and became a prominent argument in the Southern campaign of "massive resistance" to school desegregation.

The alleged genetic component in racial differences in intelligence test performance became the subject of international debate in 1969 with the publication of an article by Arthur R. Jensen in the *Harvard Educational Review.* Jensen distinguished between two types of learning: *associative* (involving memory and rote learning) and *conceptual* (involving problem solving and the use of abstractions). He contended that although all children possess associative learning abilities, poor and minority children are deficient in conceptual learning abilities, and that these differences are "genetically conditioned" (Jensen 1969). Jensen's article was greeted by an avalanche of criticism from psychologists, sociologists, and geneticists who attacked his methods, logic, evidence, and, above all, the implication that differences in intelligence test scores should influence social and educational policy (Richardson and Spears 1972).

A quarter century later, *The Bell Curve,* a book by Richard Hernnstein and Charles Murray (1994), once again raised the claim that certain groups in American society— especially African Americans—are intellectually inferior because they generally have lower scores on standardized intelligence tests. Equally important, Hernnstein and Murray claim that the stratification system of the United States directly reflects the differential intelligence of individuals and groups and that intelligence is primarily inherited or genetic. The authors argue that intelligence ("a person's capacity for complex mental work") describes a real attribute of humans that is "substantially" (60 percent) inherited and remains stable over a person's lifetime. Moreover, they assert that intelligence "can be measured with accuracy and fairness by any number of standardized mental tests, [which] . . . are not biased against socioeconomic, ethnic, and racial groups." Numerical intelligence test (IQ) scores thus accurately reflect individual and group intelligence levels.

Examining a voluminous amount of data, Herrnstein and Murray maintain that in American society today, measured intelligence (IQ) is positively correlated with success as measured by educational and occupational attainment and overall socio-economic status, and that IQ is negatively correlated with poverty, unemployment, single-parent families, and criminality. They conclude that the class structure of contemporary American society reflects the distribution of intelligence; the upper classes comprise members of the "cognitive elite," whereas the less intelligent are overrepresented in the lower classes. Moreover, they contend that races differ in intelligence and that the lower IQ test performance of blacks and Latinos indicate that they are less intelligent than whites and Asians. Finally, they find that many modern social problems—poverty, unemployment, poor parenting, single-parent families, welfare dependency, and crime—result from low intelligence and, that, as a consequence, social and educational programs (e.g., Head Start) designed to improve and remedy such conditions are ineffective (Herrnstein and Murray 1994).

The response to Herrnstein and Murray's book was similar to that to Jensen's argument: critics vigorously challenged their basic assumptions, procedures and methods, evidence, interpretations, and conclusions. They argue that, despite the wealth of data Hernnstein and Murray cite in their massive (845-page) book, the authors ignore, omit, misrepresent, or use selectively evidence that contradicts their basic argument. *The Bell Curve,* according to one reviewer, is "clearly the most incendiary piece of social science to appear in the last decade or more" (Fraser 1995:1).

First, critics challenge Herrnstein and Murray's assumption that intelligence is a single, primarily inherited, trait that can be accurately measured by IQ tests; rather, they argue that intelligence involves multiple and distinctly different attributes —language skills, mathematical skills, musical ability, interpersonal skills, artistic ability, and spatial relations abilities, for example—that cannot be reduced to a single overall measure. Moreover, they reject the magnitude of Herrnstein and Murray's estimates of the genetic heritability of intelligence, which are based on inferences drawn from studies of pairs of biological relatives (i.e., different IQ correlations between identical twins, fraternal twins, siblings, and first cousins). Such studies measure not only inheritance but also the effects of environmental factors, which Hernnstein and Murray minimize. "The more similar a pair is biologically, then the more similar they are as well in their environments"—even among twins separated early in life and raised in different environments (Taylor 1995:156). Thus, performance on IQ tests depends not simply on an individual's innate "intelligence," but on what a person has previously learned (Hanson 1995:24).

Critics also contest Herrnstein and Murray's contention that because intelligence is substantially genetic, it changes little in the lives of individuals or the histories of racial and ethnic groups. Contrary to Herrnstein and Murray's objections that programs such as Head Start have failed to enhance educational performance, the American Psychological Association asserted that "there is a wealth of research evidence showing that early educational interventions are effective in raising performance and achievement levels for disadvantaged groups." Similarly, after recalculating data used by Hernnstein and Murray, Hauser and Nisbitt independently showed that improvements in black test scores between 1969 and 1990 undermine notions of the immutability of intelligence over time. Similarly, conservative economist Thomas Sowell has noted that the test performances of numerous American ethnic groups (Jews, Italians, Poles) have improved dramatically over the course of the twentieth century (Hauser 1995; Nisbitt 1995; Sowell 1995).

The reliability of IQ tests themselves has been questioned. Taylor rejects Herrnstein and Murray's assertion that such tests are free of cultural bias and argues that the authors selectively ignored evidence of such cultural bias in some of the studies that they themselves cite (Taylor 1995). Moreover, studies by psychologist Claude Steele suggest that, given the pervasiveness of stereotypes of black intellectual inferiority, black and white students respond differently to testing situations. When confronted with situations—including standardized tests, such as the SAT or ACT—in which they perceive that their academic performance will reflect upon or be interpreted in racial terms, African Americans are subject to what Steele terms "stereotype vulnerability." He contends that situations in which blacks risk conforming to negative stereotypes of their intellectual abilities introduce subtle psychological stresses that can undermine performance; when black students are presented with identical tests under conditions not defined as measuring their intellectual abilities, they perform as well as white students (Steele and Aronson 1995; Watters 1995; Steele 1997).

Wolfe (1995) challenges the notion that IQ predicts later career success, contending that there is no evidence that IQ test performance is related to job performance or to income attainments. Finally, assertions of intelligence differences between racial groups ignores the arbitrary, socially constructed nature of such categories. In American society the categories of "white," "black," and "Asian" are not real "biological" entities but rather consist of people with a wide range of biological characteristics. In order for inferences to be drawn about racial characteristics, it would necessary to have distinct, "pure" biological pools, which, given the extraordinary ethnic diversity of the American people, obviously is not the case in the United States.

Herrnstein and Murray conclude *The Bell Curve* with a discussion of the public policy implications of their findings. Critics charge that their social policy discussion reveals the real objective of *The Bell Curve:* to advance and provide justification for the authors' conservative political agenda; although Herrnstein and Murray cloak their argument in the mantle of "science," their real objective is to attack a number of public policies, including welfare, affirmative action, and immigration. Recognizing that the controversy over race and intelligence is primarily political, the Genetics Society of America addressed the issue with the following statement: "In our views, there is no convincing evidence as to whether there is or is not an appreciable genetic difference in intelligence between races. . . . Whether or not there are significant genetic inequalities in no way alters our ideal of political equality, nor justifies racism or discrimination in any form" (Quoted in Weinberg 1983:74).

As we pointed out in Part 1, the conceptions of "race" entertained by Henry Cabot Lodge, which, in one form or another, were shared by virtually all American social scientists at the turn of the twentieth century, are radically different from prevailing scientific notions today. As the intense critique of Jensen's and of Herrnstein and Murray's work indicates, biological explanations for racial and ethnic inequalities enjoy little legitimacy among contemporary social scientists. The important conceptual distinction between biological explanations and those embraced today resides in the understanding of the *process* by which behavioral traits and characteristics are transmitted. Traits that once were considered to be "instinctual," innate, and biologically inherited are today conceived to be learned—a product not of the genes but of socialization. Ethnic group traits and characteristics are considered by most social scientists to be derived not from biological but from cultural and social factors.

Culture

The most prominent contemporary internal explanation attributes an ethnic group's position in a society's stratification system to its *cultural* characteristics: the values, attitudes, beliefs, store of knowledge, customs, and habits learned in the family and the community. Almost by definition, ethnic groups are perceived to differ in their distinctive cultural inventory. Those groups that have succeeded have done so because they possess the values and cultural traits that make for success in American society—such as high achievement motivation, industriousness, perseverance, future orientation, ability to postpone immediate gratification for later rewards, and so forth. Groups that have internalized such values succeed, whereas those lacking them are doomed to failure. Those who have succeeded have done so because of the traits that their cultural tradition bequeathed them. On the other hand, a group's low socioeconomic status can be attributed to the fact that its cultural inventory did not include the requisite values, attitudes, and personal qualities. An underlying assumption of a cultural interpretation, therefore, is that "American society provides ample opportunity for class mobility and it is [the minority's] cultural institutions—'home and family and community'—that are problematic" (Steinberg 1981:119). Whether an ethnic group succeeds or fails, it is perceived as being responsible for its own fate—what William Ryan (1971) has called a "blaming the victim" ideology. By implication, those who have been less successful than others can ensure their entrance into the mainstream of American society by becoming more fully culturally assimilated, by adopting the cultural values of the dominant group.

Hershberg and his associates (1979) have identified two variants of the cultural argument: the "bootstraps" and the "last of the immigrants" explanations. The *bootstraps* explanation for the socioeconomic success of white ethnics and Asians is that they were able to overcome the disabilities with which they were confronted because through hard work, industriousness, perseverance, self-reliance, and thrift, they exploited as fully as possible the economic opportunity that America afforded. They pulled themselves up by their own bootstraps without governmental assistance. Andrew Greeley, whose empirical research on the socioeconomic attainments of European ancestry groups established that by the early 1970s, the "white ethnic" descendants of "new immigrants" had reached parity with and, indeed, in some instances had surpassed "old" immigrants, subscribes to a cultural explanation in his analysis of the post–World War II socioeconomic achievements of Catholic and Jewish Americans. Their achievements, he writes, were the consequence of "something in the culture of the immigrants themselves." Greeley contends that when "new" immigrants began their struggle for upward mobility in the first two decades of the twentieth century,

> There were no quotas, no affirmative action, no elaborate system of social services and, heaven knows, no ethnic militancy. There was no talk of reparations, no sense of guilt, no feeling of compassion for these immigrants. . . . Hard work, saving, sacrifice—such is a tentative explanation of the "ethnic miracle." (Greeley 1976:21, 31)

However, a cultural argument has been nowhere more clearly and effectively articulated than by Thomas Sowell, an economist who has written widely concerning American ethnic groups (Sowell 1978, 1980, 1981). Sowell contends that the variations in rates of socioeconomic status and achievement among American ethnic groups can best be explained by examining a group's cultural inheritance. "Whether in an ethnic context or among peoples and nations in general, much depends on the whole constellation of values, attitudes, skills, and contacts that many call a culture and that economists call 'human capital.'" That is, different rates of achievement among American ethnic groups are a result of differences in the cultural inventories that have been transmitted to them from previous generations. The different values, attitudes and moral disciplines that comprise each group's cultural inheritance, which "can be more important than biological inheritance," therefore provide the crucial ingredients that account for success or failure in American society. On the one hand, ethnic groups "that arrived in America financially destitute have rapidly risen to affluence, when their cultures stressed the values and behavior required in an industrial and commercial economy." On the other hand, "groups today plagued by absenteeism, tardiness, and a need for constant supervision at work or in school are typically descendants of people with the same habits a century or more ago" (Sowell 1981:282, 284).

An emphasis on education has often been cited as an explanation for the extremely high levels of achievement among Jews. For example, in a widely noted cultural explanation of differences in ethnic group achievement levels, Fred Strodtbeck (1958) argued that Jewish goals, values, and cultural norms were more compatible with the dominant values of American society than were those of other ethnic groups. In particular, the value of education, learning, and scholarly inquiry was long expressed in the intellectual tradition of orthodox Jewish culture. Jewish immigrants placed high prestige on education and educational attainments: the scholar was venerated and accorded respect. As Abraham Cahan wrote in his classic novel of Jewish immigrant life, *The Rise of David Levinsky,* "The ghetto rang with a clamor for knowledge. . . . To save up some money and prepare for college seemed to be the most natural thing to do" (Cahan 1966:156). By contrast, most Catholic "new" immigrants came from peasant backgrounds where formal education and learning were alien and remote. Southern Italian immigrants, who in many respects were typical of Catholic "new" immigrants, came from a society in which formal education clashed with traditional values. For them, education and learning were regarded as a threat to the integrity and strength of the family. Unlike Jews, Italian parents saw little value in education and did not encourage their children toward educational attainments (Strodtbeck 1958; Vecoli 1964).

A cultural explanation is frequently invoked to explain the economic and educational attainments of Asian Americans, who have frequently been characterized as "model minorities." As *Time* magazine recently proclaimed, "Asians have become exemplary immigrants . . . [who] have produced a veritable galaxy of stellar performers in the U.S., from the arts and sciences to business and finance. Like immigrating Jews of earlier generations, they have parlayed cultural emphases on education and hard work into brilliant attainments. . . . There is something in the Asian family that promotes success" (Walsh 1993:55). By contrast, the disadvantaged socioeconomic positions of African Americans, Latino Americans, and American Indians today are portrayed simply as a consequence of *their* cultural characteristics, which are perceived to be incompatible with a modern industrial society. By implication, groups that have been less successful can enter the American mainstream by changing their value system—by getting rid of the values that have kept them back and becoming more fully culturally assimilated, by simply adopting the cultural values of the dominant group.

The other, sometimes complementary, explanation is the *last-of-the-immigrants* argument. Whereas a bootstraps argument emphasizes the cultural characteristics of minorities who have attained socioeconomic mobility, a last-of-the-immigrants model focuses on the social system, or opportunity structure, within which they achieved their successes. According to this argument, ethnic socioeconomic success is only a matter of time, and those ethnic groups who have most recently migrated to the nation's cities (Chicanos, Puerto Ricans, American Indians, and, in particular, African Americans) must not be impatient with their present position at the bottom of the economic ladder. In several generations they will inevitably repeat the experience of European ethnic groups and climb into the American economic, educational, and political mainstream. Thomas Sowell, for example, contends that today's patterns of white flight from the central cities to the haven of suburbia are merely repeating the process of ethnic succession that has long been a characteristic feature of America's ethnically diverse cities; ethnic groups who arrive first move when their territory is invaded by a new and "inferior" ethnic group (Sowell 1981:277–278). Similarly, a recent *Time* magazine feature on the ethnic diversity of Lowell, Massachusetts, stressed the progression of immigrant groups—rural Yankees, Irish, French Canadian, Greek, Cambodian, and Lebanese—who have inhabited an area of the city known as the Acre. The city's Greek mayor, who grew up in the neighborhood, described the process of social mobility: "The Acre is the bottom of the social ladder. . . . The last group that comes in is always on the bottom rung. But you can climb that ladder. You just have to prove your worth to the group ahead of you to be accepted" (Blackman 1993:54).

Social Class

The traditional cultural explanation for the rapid mobility of Jewish immigrants (as contrasted to Catholic "new" immigrants) stressed the high value placed on education, learning, and scholarly achievement among immigrant Jews. However, Stephen Steinberg rejects the interpretation that Jewish *values* are the explanation for their success. Instead, he focuses on the impact of the different social-class backgrounds of entering immigrants. In *The Ethnic Myth* (1981/1989), he points out that although Jewish and Catholic "new" immigrants entered the United States with about the same meager amounts of money, their occupational backgrounds were not identical. Immigrant Jews came overwhelmingly from towns and cities of eastern Europe, where they had had extensive experience with manufacturing and commerce. More than two-thirds of Jewish immigrants were skilled workers, professionals, or merchants, as opposed to only one-sixth of southern Italians and one-sixteenth of Polish immigrants. More than two-thirds of Italian and three-fourths of Polish immigrants were unskilled laborers or farmers, in contrast to about one-seventh of entering Jews. The skills the Jews brought with them to the United States were needed by an expanding American economy and enabled them to enter at a higher-status level than most unskilled immigrants. These occupational backgrounds and experiences of immigrant Jews enabled their children—the second generation—to acquire relatively easily the middle-class skills that were a prerequisite for entrance into the professions—in particular, academic pursuits.

Jewish and Catholic "new" immigrants differed on another important characteristic: literacy. About one-fourth of all Jews entering the United States between 1899 and 1910 were unable to read and write, whereas more than half (54 percent) of southern Italians and one-third (35 percent) of Poles were illiterate. Similarly, because many Italians and Poles immigrated to the United States as temporary workers and did not intend to settle permanently in this country, they were much less likely to learn to speak English than were Jews, most of whom were fleeing religious persecution in eastern Europe and did not intend to return there. This stronger commitment to settlement in the United States increased the process of cultural assimilation for Jews. Italians and Poles, whose frames of reference remained in the old country, were much more likely to resist assimilation to American culture, a factor that greatly limited the occupational mobility of the second generation.

Steinberg shows how these background factors affected the occupational mobility of Jews and Catholics within the academic profession. Because professionals, especially academics, tend to be drawn from professional, managerial, and small-business backgrounds, individuals whose parents had such characteristics were favored in their access to such pursuits. Hence, the social class characteristics of Jewish and Catholic "new" immigrants were important influences on their patterns of occupational mobility. It was not simply that Jews embraced cultural values that extolled education and revered learning. It was rather "that cultural factors have little independent effect on educational outcomes, but are influential only as they interact with class factors. Thus, to whatever extent a reverence for learning was part of the religious and cultural heritage of Asians and Jews, it was activated and given existential significance by their social class circumstances" (Steinberg 1981:132).

The implication of Steinberg's analysis is that the social class characteristics of different American ethnic groups have played a crucial role in influencing the socioeconomic status of their descendants. As Portes and Bach have argued in their comparison of Mexican and Cuban immigrants to the United States, "the class composition of the different immigrant flows . . . played a decisive role in determining their modes of incorporation and subsequent economic destiny in the United States" (Portes and Bach 1985:48).

Culture and Social Class: A Synthesis

The prominence of small business enterprises among immigrants is one of the most widely documented and debated phenomena in recent ethnic group literature (Cheng and Bonacich 1984; Bonacich and Light 1988; Kim 1981; Waldinger 1987). In Article 16, "Immigrant and Ethnic Enterprise in North America," Ivan Light notes that since 1880, the foreign-born have been overrepresented in commercial small businesses, and he asks why immigrants should have higher rates of self-employment than native-born minorities. Light has sought to develop a synthesis of the role of cultural and class factors that more adequately explains this disproportion and, by implication, variations in ethnic socioeconomic status as well.

Light argues that immigrants may utilize either *ethnic resources* or *class resources* in developing business enterprises. The traditional "ethnic only," or what Light terms the "orthodox" cultural, argument of Greeley and Sowell is that a "tradition of enterprise" is part of the cultural inventory that certain immigrant groups (such as Jews or Japanese) bring with them from their countries of origin. In this "orthodox" cultural explanation of entrepreneurship, a version of Weber's Protestant Ethic, immigrant cultural endowments are transferred relatively intact and unmodified from the old country to the new. On the other hand, a "class only" argument, represented here by Steinberg, explains immigrant socioeconomic success as a function of immigrants' class position—most importantly, the human capital (educational and technical skills) that immigrants bring with them as a result of their class position.

Light suggests a more complex and dynamic model. He contends that it is not merely the cultural baggage or endowments that are crucial in determining the mode of economic incorporation into a new society; instead, cultural attributes are but *one* aspect of ethnic resources that can be drawn upon to promote entrepreneurship. The experience or process of migration and alien status themselves elicit certain distinctive responses from immigrants that contribute to the establishment of entrepreneurship; alien status releases "latent facilitators" that provide entrepreneurial resources independent of immigrants' cultural endowments. Among these factors are relative satisfaction—that many immigrants from low-wage countries are frequently willing to accept economic conditions that Americans are not; reactive solidarity—that ethnic minority status promotes ethnic solidarity, networks, and mutual aid organizations such as rotating credit associations; and that many immigrants come as sojourners, who, wishing to amass money as quickly as possible, consume little and save much. Through each of these mechanisms, the resources with which to establish small businesses are created.

Class resources, on the other hand, may be either cultural or material. The former include bourgeois values and attitudes that are, as Steinberg stressed, a function of class position, not of an entire culture. Material resources include property and money to invest. Light contends that, whereas ethnic resources were most important in establishing immigrant entrepreneurship in the past as the class backgrounds of contemporary immigrants (Koreans, Hong Kong Chinese, Cubans, Iranians) have shifted, class resources in the form of money, human capital, and bourgeois cultural values have increasingly played a prominent role. Therefore, Light argues, traditional cultural and class explanations are inadequate; entrepreneurial activity will be most pronounced when class resources are combined with ethnic resources; comprehending the dynamics of immigrant entrepreneurship today must take account of both factors.

The Enclave Economy Model

The emphasis on ethnic solidarity that is a crucial dimension of Light's ethnic enterprise model is also central to the immigrant enclave model, which emphasizes the social mobility opportunities that an immigrant enclave affords. As previously mentioned, in a dual or segmented labor market model, minorities and women are likely to be relegated to low-wage, dead-end jobs in the "peripheral" or "secondary" labor market, which provides few opportunities for promotion. Because immigrant workers are likely to be incorporated into the secondary sector of the economy, their prospects for mobility and, hence, assimilation into the receiving society are likely to be limited. Given the preference for skills in recent American immigration policy, a substantial portion of immigrants to the United States in the past three decades has been highly skilled and educated professionals and managers. For example, the 1980 census revealed that nearly half (45.6 percent) of all African immigrants and more than two-thirds (69.9 percent) of all Asian Indian immigrants had completed college (Bouvier and Gardner 1986:22). These highly skilled workers are much more likely to be incorporated into the "core" or "primary" sector of the economy than those who are less skilled. Thus, as Waters and Eschbach (Article 14) and Light (Article 16) point out, differences in the levels of class and ethnic resources with which immigrant groups enter American society can have a substantial impact on their incorporation into it.

On the other hand, Waters and Eschbach, summarizing the work of Portes and his associates (Wilson and Portes 1980; Portes and Bach 1985; Portes and Rumbaut 1996), emphasize that the social and economic contexts that immigrants encounter when they arrive are also critical to their incorporation into American society. Immigrant socio-economic mobility is not simply a function of the immigrants' skill levels or of whether they enter the primary or secondary sector of the economy. Rather, they emphasize that the immigrant community is itself a major factor influencing the range of opportunities available to individual immigrants and, as a consequence, their adaptation to a new society. They have developed the concept of an *enclave economy,* which focuses on the manner in which several immigrant groups have been incorporated into the American economy. A critical element of the enclave model is the presence of coethnics with sufficient capital to provide employment opportunities for newly arrived immigrants. In an enclave economy, immigrant workers are not trapped in the secondary sector of a segmented labor market. Although immigrants are forced to work hard for low wages, their opportunities for upward mobility are not blocked, as is the case for most workers in the secondary labor market. Workers in an immigrant enclave "can be empirically distinguished from workers in both the primary and secondary labor market. Enclave workers will share with those in the primary sector a significant economic return to past human capital investments. Such a return will be absent among those in the 'open' secondary labor market" (Wilson and Portes 1980:302). In other words, the human capital resources (education and skills) brought from the home country will result in greater economic returns for individuals located in an ethnic enclave economy than for those in the outside labor market; an individual entering an enclave economy will ultimately fare better economically than someone with exactly the same level of skills who does not have the advantages of incorporation into an enclave.

The enclave model has been subjected to considerable criticism. For example, Sanders and Nee (1987) found that an enclave economy did not provide overall economic benefits to its participants. Immigrants living outside the enclave had higher socioeconomic status than those living in it. Moreover, they found that immigrant workers in the enclave economy received lower wages than workers in the outside economy. They questioned how truly effective employment in an enclave economy is in facilitating a worker's movement into self-employment. Responding to recent criticisms of the enclave model, Portes and Leif Jensen (1989) refined the notion to refer to a situation in which individuals both live in a community composed predominantly of coethnics and work in enterprises owned by coethnics. In an analysis of the Cuban enclave economy in Miami, they found that self-employed entrepreneurs earned significantly higher incomes if they were located within the enclave. In other words, Cuban entrepreneurship had a positive effect on earnings when it occurred within the enclave economy. Self-employment produced significantly higher increases in earnings among Cubans employed in the enclave when compared with those employed outside the enclave. Moreover, employment in Cuban firms did not reduce the earnings of fellow Cubans. Indeed, for women it actually increased them. Thus Portes and Jensen reject the thesis that small ethnic businesses are economically successful because they exploit their coethnics—the pattern in which entrepreneurship is economically advantageous for employers but comes at the expense of their coethnic employees. They found "no indication of a pattern of overall disadvantage or lower human capital returns among employees in enclave firms" (Portes and Jensen 1989:943).

External Explanations

Most American ethnic groups that have achieved prominence in American life have had to overcome obstacles, hardships, and barriers of some sort, and from an internal perspective their success is a result of their own efforts—they relied on their own resources and are therefore responsible for, and are the architects of, their own fate. Many people will point to the substantial obstacles that they and their ancestors overcame, the barriers that they confronted, and will argue, "We made it, why can't they?" Most internal explanations of social inequality tend to ignore or minimize the impact of external factors that may, on the one hand, limit group opportunities or, on the other, enhance them. An internal explanation therefore assumes that American society provides a relatively constant and level playing field for all racial and ethnic groups—that the structure of opportunity is basically the same for all.

On the other hand, throughout the American experience, different racial and ethnic groups have encountered dramatically different opportunity structures. In contrast to internal explanations of social inequality, *external explanations* emphasize the impact of factors external to the group over which they have no control—both the available opportunities and the constraints, disabilities, limitations, obstacles, and barriers to which a group is subjected. For example, in Article 23, Massey emphasizes two critical conditions that facilitated the dramatic socioeconomic attainments of "white ethnics": the period of unparalleled prosperity and economic opportunity following World War II and the hiatus that characterized immigration from Europe between 1930 and the post–World War II era, both of which contributed to opportunities for structural mobility that will not necessarily be available in the future for immigrant groups that have recently entered American society.

By contrast, some groups (for example, African Americans) have been confronted with substantial barriers that have circumscribed the resources and opportunities available to them and have precluded their full and equal participation in society. As noted in Part 2, there is a range of possible dominant-group policies that, to a greater or lesser degree, limit the options available to a minority group. These range from extermination to discrimination in many different forms.

A cultural explanation tends to minimize or dismiss the role of external factors, especially in contemporary American society. Sowell, for example, contends that the intergroup animosities and discrimination that existed in American society in the past have lessened in intensity and "in some respects disappeared" (Sowell 1981:7). Such a perspective presupposes that social structure is blind to group differences and does not play a significant role in affecting patterns of ethnic group achievement. Put another way, it assumes that the social structure is neutral when it comes to racial and ethnic factors, and that individuals from all ethnic backgrounds have relatively equal opportunities to succeed.

Moreover, a cultural interpretation assumes that external barriers are insignificant in affecting group outcomes because the opportunities of all American ethnic groups have at one time or another been circumscribed in some way. In a variant of the last-of-the-immigrants model, Sowell has contended that all American ethnic groups "have been discriminated against to one degree or another. Yet some of the most successful —such as the Orientals—have experienced worse discrimination than most, and the extraordinary success of Jews has been achieved in the face of centuries of anti-Semitism" (Sowell 1981:6).

Finally, a cultural model assumes that the distinctive traits and capacities that characterize a group will manifest themselves in spite of harsh and restrictive treatment by other groups. Thus, Sowell argues that the characteristics of "working harder and more relentlessly" will overcome even the most pronounced adversity (Sowell 1981:283).

Each of these assumptions has been vigorously challenged by critics who contend that the structural barriers confronting Chicanos, Puerto Ricans, American Indians, and, in particular, African Americans have been more severe and repressive than those encountered by "new" immigrants or even by Asians.

The most apparent external barrier distinguishing the experience of African Americans has been the disability of race, which has subjected blacks, in both the South and the North, to discrimination far more severe than that experienced by any European ethnic groups. For example, Lieberson's analysis (1980) demonstrates that prejudice and discrimination against African Americans in Northern cities intensified rather than diminished during the first few decades of the twentieth century. At the same time that spatial isolation declined for "new" immigrants, it increased markedly for African Americans. Moreover, the discrimination that African Americans encountered in education and employment was never so consistently a feature of the experience of "new" immigrant groups. Hershberg's analysis of Philadelphia (1979), showed that historically the occupational opportunity structure for African Americans had never been as open as that for *white* immigrants and that, because of levels of residential segregation never encountered by any European ancestry groups, blacks have been excluded from recent occupational opportunities.

The experience of Asians, in particular the Japanese and the Chinese, frequently is cited to support the claim that being nonwhite is not an insurmountable barrier to achievement in American society. In other words, Asian success casts considerable doubt on the notion that nonwhite racial status is inherently a liability to achievement. Indeed, as Waters and Eschbach (Article 14) point out, Asians are frequently cited as "model minorities" because they have been able to succeed despite extremely virulent forms of discrimination. They have been able to do so, Sowell writes, because of their cultural traits of "effort, thrift, dependability and foresight, [which] built businesses out of 'menial tasks' and turned sweat into capital" (Sowell 1981:7).

However, Asians were not forced to endure the historical experience of slavery and the discriminatory barriers that persisted on a pervasive scale after its legal elimination. Moreover, unlike the African American circumstance, the number of Asians in the United States was never so large as to represent a real threat to the existing white population. Even in California, the state in which Asians have been most highly concentrated, the highest-ever proportion of Japanese in the state's population was 2.1 percent, and the Chinese proportion was even smaller (Peterson 1971:30). When these extremely small numbers of Asians appeared to increase even slightly, the perceived threat they represented was reduced by changes in American immigration laws that effectively limited the Asian population to a tiny proportion of the total (Lieberson 1980:368). Moreover, Nee and Wong (1985:20) suggest that the number of African Americans who migrated to the West during and after World War II exceeded the small Asian population. Their increased presence, and the greater prejudice toward them on the part of white Americans, lessened the impact of anti-Asian discrimination and thus facilitated Asian American socioeconomic mobility.

Anthropologist John Ogbu (1978, 1988, 1990) contends that to focus solely on the cultural characteristics of various minority groups ignores the extent to which their different cultures have themselves been "shaped by the initial terms of their incorporation into American society and their subsequent treatment by white Americans" (Ogbu 1990:149). In Article 18, "Minority Status and Literacy in Comparative Perspective," Ogbu distinguishes between what he broadly terms *immigrant* or *voluntary* minorities, on the one hand, and *castelike* or *involuntary* minorities, on the other, and he argues that there have been qualitative differences in the experiences of these two categories. However much their immigration was compelled by conditions in their homelands over which they had no control, voluntary minorities have chosen to live in the United States, and they generally enter optimistically, with expectations that their lives will be improved. Consequently, they are much more likely to interpret the prejudice and discrimination they encounter in the host society as temporary, a consequence of their foreign origins, and something that they can overcome. In general, they are much more likely to accept the institutional structure (including the school system) uncritically and to encourage their children to work within it.

Most Asian Americans would be included in the category of voluntary minorities, and the academic achievements of Asian Americans generally could be cited as evidence of the manner in which Asian groups generally have accepted the existing culture and social institutions. For example, recently Caplan et al. (1992) have argued that the academic achievement of Vietnamese boat people has occurred because they perceive the language and cultural conflicts that they encounter in school and the wider society as hurdles that *can* be overcome, and they trust school officials and accept school rules and the formally prescribed practices for achieving academic success.

The historical and contemporary experiences of involuntary minorities, on the other hand, provide no such optimism that their minority status is likely to be temporary or that striving within existing institutions will, in fact, have the promised payoff. In contrast to voluntary minorities, involuntary minorities have been subjected to systematic, long-range economic subordination that has affected their perceptions of the nation's social, economic, political, and educational opportunity structures. Thus Ogbu contends that black academic performance is greatly affected by African American perceptions that academic achievement will not be rewarded because of the discriminatory job ceiling that African Americans historically have encountered. In other words, Ogbu argues that the absence of high educational aspirations, high achievement motivation, and a future orientation on the part of some minority-group members is a response to external circumstances, to their realistic perception that their opportunities in the work world are extremely restricted and circumscribed. Lower school performance is merely a symptom of the broader and more central societal problem of caste. Minority educational achievement will be improved only when there is a dramatic societal commitment to end discrimination in jobs and housing, and more fully to include American minorities in the decision-making process in institutions throughout the whole of American society. "The only lasting solution to the problem of academic retardation," he writes, "is the elimination of caste barriers" (Ogbu 1978:357).

However, their exclusion from societal opportunity structures not only has affected the aspirations of involuntary minorities but also has had an impact on the group's cultural characteristics and the ways in which they perceive and respond to members of the dominant group and the social institutions (such as schools) that they control. A prominent response among involuntary minorities is *cultural inversion,* or the development of an oppositional culture—the tendency to reject certain forms of behavior, events, symbols, and meanings as inappropriate because they are characteristics of the dominant group and, conversely, to accept other forms of behavior, symbols, norms, and values, precisely because they are not (Ogbu 1990:148). Thus, because in the United States the school and its representatives symbolize the dominant culture, the cultures of involuntary minorities tend to disparage academic achievement, and those who are academically successful are subject to ridicule and ostracism from their peers. "Those minority students who adopt the attitudes and behaviors conducive to school success, who use standard English and behave according to standard school practices, are accused by their peers of 'acting white' or, in the case of black students, of being Uncle Toms." (Ogbu 1990:160–161)

Ogbu's interpretation of the disparities in levels of academic attainment among American ethnic and racial groups does not deny the importance of the cultural predispositions with which each group encounters the nation's social institutions; Ogbu's model clearly involves *both* cultural and structural dimensions. Cultural differences *are* important in accounting for these differences—certain voluntary minorities possess values that strongly support, encourage, and reward academic achievement, whereas among involuntary minorities, the behaviors necessary for success within the dominant educational institutions are disparaged. However, for Ogbu what is important are the sources of these differences in cultural perspectives toward formal education. He distinguishes between *primary* and *secondary* cultural differences. The former refer to cultural characteristics of groups before contact, while the latter occur in response to contact with other groups. This distinction is especially important because it recognizes that the cultural inventory of involuntary minorities is not simply inherited from the past or is inherent in a group's "essence." Rather, the cultural values with which groups perceive and respond to social institutions, including schools, are adaptive mechanisms that are shaped and molded by a group's historical experiences.

An external perspective places primary emphasis on a society's opportunity structure and interprets a minority's cultural characteristics as dependent variables. Although Ogbu's model involves a synthesis of cultural and structural variables in accounting for the different socioeconomic positions occupied by different ethnic groups, it emphasizes the structural constraints within which the cultural inventory of involuntary minorities was developed. From an external perspective, therefore, it is the opportunity structure, not biological or cultural characteristics, that accounts for racial and ethnic inequalities. Consequently, it is the opportunity structure, not minority cultures, that must first be changed to reduce inequalities in American life.

As noted in Part 1, the structure of opportunity may be circumscribed by what we have termed attitudinal discrimination, which is motivated by prejudices against racial or ethnic minorities. For example, as noted there, although there is evidence of a decline in attitudinal discrimination in the past quarter century, as Feagin points out in Article 20, it still remains a potent force in a wide range of settings in American life. However, an external model of racial and ethnic inequality also focuses on the impersonal, objective economic circumstances that confront caste minorities today, and compares them with those that ethnic groups—in particular "new" immigrants—encountered in the past.

Therefore, the assumptions of an internal explanation of inequality have been challenged by people who contend that the barriers confronting Chicanos, Puerto Ricans, American Indians, and, in particular, African Americans, have been qualitatively different from those encountered by European immigrants or even by Asians. External explanations focus on the broad social, economic, and political contexts confronting different ethnic groups and especially on the role of prejudice and discrimination in creating and maintaining racial and ethnic inequality.

Institutional Discrimination

As we noted in the Introduction to Part 1, the structure of opportunity may be limited by attitudinal discrimination, which is motivated by prejudices against racial and ethnic minorities. *Institutional discrimination,* by contrast, refers to rules, policies, practices, and laws that appear to be race-neutral (or gender-neutral) but still have a discriminatory effect on minorities. In its origins, unlike attitudinal discrimination, institutional discrimination may not have been intentional or a consequence of prejudice, but it still has an adverse impact on a minority group. In other words, even if all racial prejudice were suddenly and miraculously eliminated from the hearts and minds of Americans, it is unlikely that racial inequalities would disappear, primarily because racial discrimination and inequalities are perpetuated by the way in which economic and political institutions are structured and organized in American society.

William Julius Wilson has been among the foremost critics of a cultural perspective. As noted in Part 2, in *The Declining Significance of Race* (1978), Wilson divided the history of American race relations into three periods or stages—the preindustrial, industrial, and modern industrial, each reflecting changes in the nation's economic structure. Wilson acknowledged that in contemporary American society—the modern industrial period—attitudinal discrimination is still pervasive in many areas, such as housing, education, and municipal politics, and serves as a barrier to black participation in society's mainstream. However, he contended that in the economic sphere, institutional, not attitudinal, discrimination has become the primary source of continuing black inequalities. In the economic life of African Americans, "class has become more important than race in determining black access to privilege and power." (See Article 7, "The Declining Significance of Race," in Part 2.)

Wilson's thesis is based on the contention that during the modern industrial era, African American economic status has been influenced by substantial structural economic changes "such as the shift from goods-producing to service-producing industries, the increasing segmentation of the labor market, the growing use of industrial technology, and the relocation of industries out of the central city" that, in themselves, have little to do with race (Wilson 1981a:38).

As a result of changes in the economic structure and political culture of American life, the structure of the African American community has been altered. On the one hand, "educated blacks are experiencing unprecedented job opportunities in the growing government and corporate sectors, opportunities that are at least comparable to those of whites with equivalent qualifications." This advance has come about as a result of the expansion of salaried, white-collar positions and of changes in the role of government. Before the modern industrial era, the state merely reinforced patterns of race relations established in the economic sector. Recently, in response to the civil rights movement, the government has stood in formal opposition to discriminatory barriers. Indeed, with the enactment of affirmative action programs in the 1960s, government undertook the initiative in combating discrimination.

On the other hand, the social conditions of the African American underclass have deteriorated in the last quarter of a century. In *The Truly Disadvantaged* (1987) and his most recent book, *When Work Disappears* (1996), Wilson focuses on the crisis of the underclass in the inner city, where the broad economic changes mentioned before have caused extremely high levels of unemployment. Earlier in the twentieth century, relatively uneducated and unskilled native and immigrant workers were able to find stable employment and income in manufacturing. Today, however, the process of deindustrialization has created an economic "mismatch" between the kinds of jobs available and the qualifications of inner-city residents lacking highly sophisticated educational and technical skills. On the one hand, manufacturing jobs that do not require advanced skills have moved from inner cities to the suburbs, to the Sun Belt, or overseas. On the other hand, the jobs created in the cities demand highly technical credentials for which most inner-city residents are unqualified. Thus many inner-city residents find themselves without prospects for work. Moreover, as many stable working-class and middle-class residents with job qualifications have moved from the inner cities into better residential neighborhoods, the stability of neighborhood social institutions (such as churches, schools, newspapers, and recreational facilities) has been undermined, and the social fabric of community life has deteriorated. The underclass has become increasingly isolated, socially and economically. "Today's ghetto residents face a closed opportunity structure." In Article 19, "Work," Wilson describes the impact of institutional and structural changes in triggering a process of "hyperghettoization" or concentration of the very poor.

Wilson's argument has been subjected to considerable—often intense—criticism. One of the most frequent is that, in stressing the nonracial structural sources of the urban underclass, he ignores or underestimates the role of race. One of the most prominent examples of this perspective is Joe R. Feagin's "The Continuing Significance of Race" (Article 20), which represents a direct response to Wilson's contention that middle-class blacks—those whose education and skills provide them access to middle-class occupational opportunities—are no longer vulnerable to discrimination in employment and public accommodations. Drawing from in-depth interviews with a wide range of middle-class blacks, Feagin concludes that even African Americans who have achieved success and status continue to experience discrimination on a regular basis. Indeed, racial discrimination continues to be a pervasive and enduring feature of their lives, and, most important, its effects are cumulative: "Blacks confront not just isolated incidents [of discrimination] . . . but a lifelong series of such incidents."

Massey and Denton (Article 9; 1993) differ with Wilson's emphasis on the impersonal effects of deindustrialization on concentrating urban poverty in the ghettos of America's major cities. Race, they contend, has been and continues to be a fundamental cleavage in American society. The pervasive racial segregation of African Americans in most American metropolitan areas—what they refer to as "American apartheid"—is a consequence of both historic and contemporary patterns of racial discrimination in the sale and rental of housing, and it has led almost inevitably to the concentrated poverty and associated social dislocations that characterize many African American urban neighborhoods. While industrial restructuring and an exodus of middle-class blacks have contributed to the increasing concentration of urban poverty, the residential segregation of Africans Americans was *the* critical factor. Especially since the onset of the Great Migration out of the South early in the twentieth century, African Americans have been more highly residentially segregated regardless of their socioeconomic characteristics than any other racial or ethnic group in American history, so they have been more vulnerable to the cumulative impact of economic dislocations. As a consequence, as David R. James (Article 21) puts it, "Racial segregation in general and the racial ghetto in particular are race-making situations that perpetuate the color line in America."

Other critics have argued that Wilson's analysis tends to obscure continuing attitudinal discrimination in the economic sphere; not only is the contemporary underclass a consequence of historical patterns of racial discrimination, but also such discrimination continues today to affect black economic opportunities and life chances. For example, Steinberg has challenged Wilson's use of the "mismatch" explanation for black exclusion from the expanding service sector of the economy. The "mismatch" hypothesis, he contends, "seriously underestimates the color line in the world of work" (Steinberg 1989:289). It overlooks the large number of jobs that do not require extensive education, training, and skills, and it ignores the virtual exclusion of African Americans from certain segments of the labor market.

On the other hand, the mismatch hypothesis ignores the extent to which recent immigrants have taken many relatively unskilled jobs. Newcomers to America's major cities today are increasingly likely to be immigrants, not native-born whites or blacks. Waldinger (Article 27) contends that, far from declining, lower-level jobs in the postindustrial city have increased but have been filled by recent imimgrants from abroad rather than by African Americans. Waldinger argues that the shift to a postindustrial economy has resulted in a new ethnic division of labor; however, recent ethnic occupational restructuring cannot be reduced to a question simply of whether immigrants take jobs away from native-born workers (especially from the most prominent previous migrants to the nation's major cities—African Americans). Rather, Waldinger contends that it is necessary to focus on the complex and subtle processes through which different ethnic groups have come to fill and sustain the specific occupational niches that provide mobility ladders in this new ethnic division of labor.

Waldinger's critique of the mismatch hypothesis raises a critical question: If economic restructuring has left economic opportunities in the inner cities so bleak, why have immigrant groups flocked to them—contributing to an "urban renaissance"—in the past two decades? In Part 4 we will consider more fully the increasingly multiracial (not simply biracial) nature of American cities in the global, postindustrial economy, as well as the implications of these changes in ethnic composition for the future of racial and ethnic relations in American life.

Assimilation in America
Theory and Reality

Milton M. Gordon

Three ideologies or conceptual models have competed for attention on the American scene as explanations of the way in which a nation, in the beginning largely white, Anglo-Saxon, and Protestant, has absorbed over 41 million immigrants and their descendants from variegated sources and welded them into the contemporary American people. These ideologies are Anglo-conformity, the melting pot, and cultural pluralism. They have served at various times, and often simultaneously, as explanations of what has happened—descriptive models—and of what should happen—goal models. Not infrequently they have been used in such a fashion that it is difficult to tell which of these two usages the writer has had in mind. In fact, one of the more remarkable omissions in the history of American intellectual thought is the relative lack of close analytical attention given to the theory of immigrant adjustment in the United States by its social scientists.

The result has been that this field of discussion —an overridingly important one since it has significant implications for the more familiar problems of prejudice, discrimination, and majority-minority group relations generally—has been largely preempted by laymen, representatives of belles lettres, philosophers, and apologists of various persuasions. Even from these sources the amount of attention devoted to ideologies of assimilation is hardly extensive. Consequently, the work of improving intergroup relations in America is carried out by dedicated professional agencies and individuals who deal as best they can with day-to-day problems of discriminatory behavior, but who for the most part are unable to relate their efforts to an adequate conceptual apparatus. Such an apparatus would, at one and the same time, accurately describe the present structure of American society with respect to its ethnic groups (I shall use the term "ethnic group" to refer to any racial, religious, or national-origins collectivity), and allow for a considered formulation of its assimilation or integration goals for the foreseeable future. One is reminded of Alice's distraught question in her travels in Wonderland. "Would you tell me, please, which way I ought to go from here?" "That depends a good deal," replied the Cat with irrefutable logic, "on where you want to get to."

The story of America's immigration can be quickly told for our present purposes. The white American population at the time of the Revolution was largely English and Protestant in origin, but had already absorbed substantial groups of Germans and Scotch-Irish and smaller contingents of Frenchmen, Dutchmen, Swedes, Swiss, South Irish, Poles, and a handful of migrants from other European nations. Catholics were represented in modest numbers, particularly in the middle colonies, and a small number of Jews were residents of the incipient nation. With the exception of the Quakers and a few missionaries, the colonists had generally treated the Indians and their cultures with contempt and hostility, driving them from the coastal plains and making the western frontier a bloody battleground where eternal vigilance was the price of survival.

Although the Negro at that time made up nearly one-fifth of the total population, his predominantly slave status, together with racial and

Reprinted by permission from *Daedalus,* Journal of the American Academy of Arts and Sciences, Boston, Massachusetts, Volume 90, Number 2 (Spring 1961), pp. 263–285.

cultural prejudice, barred him from serious consideration as an assimilable element of the society. And while many groups of European origin started out as determined ethnic enclaves, eventually, most historians believe, considerable ethnic intermixture within the white population took place. "People of different blood" [sic]—write two American historians about the colonial period, "English, Irish, German, Huguenot, Dutch, Swedish—mingled and intermarried with little thought of any difference."[1] In such a society, its people predominantly English, its white immigrants of other ethnic origins either English-speaking or derived largely from countries of northern and western Europe whose cultural divergences from the English were not great, and its dominant white population excluding by fiat the claims and considerations of welfare of the non-Caucasian minorities, the problem of assimilation understandably did not loom unduly large or complex.

The unfolding events of the next century and a half with increasing momentum dispelled the complacency which rested upon the relative simplicity of colonial and immediate post-Revolutionary conditions. The large-scale immigration to America of the famine-fleeing Irish, the Germans, and later the Scandinavians (along with additional Englishmen and other peoples of northern and western Europe) in the middle of the nineteenth century (the so-called "old immigration"), the emancipation of the Negro slaves and the problems created by post–Civil War reconstruction, the placing of the conquered Indian with his broken culture on government reservations, the arrival of the Oriental, first attracted by the discovery of gold and other opportunities in the West, and finally, beginning in the last quarter of the nineteenth century and continuing to the early 1920s, the swelling to proportions hitherto unimagined of the tide of immigration from the peasantries and "pales" of southern and eastern Europe—the Italians, Jews, and Slavs of the so-called "new immigration," fleeing the persecutions and industrial dislocations of the day—all these events constitute the background against which we may consider the rise of the theories of assimilation mentioned above. After a necessarily foreshortened description of each of these theories and their historical emergence, we shall suggest analytical distinctions designed to aid

in clarifying the nature of the assimilation process, and then conclude by focusing on the American scene.

ANGLO-CONFORMITY

"Anglo-conformity"[2] is a broad term used to cover a variety of viewpoints about assimilation and immigration; they all assume the desirability of maintaining English institutions (as modified by the American Revolution), the English language, and English-oriented cultural patterns as dominant and standard in American life. However, bound up with this assumption are related attitudes. These may range from discredited notions about race and "Nordic" and "Aryan" racial superiority, together with the nativist political programs and exclusionist immigration policies which such notions entail, through an intermediate position of favoring immigration from northern and western Europe on amorphous, unreflective grounds ("They are more like us"), to a lack of opposition to any source of immigration, as long as these immigrants and their descendants duly adopt the standard Anglo-Saxon cultural patterns. There is by no means any necessary equation between Anglo-conformity and racist attitudes.

It is quite likely that "Anglo-conformity" in its more moderate aspects, however explicit its formulation, has been the most prevalent ideology of assimilation goals in America throughout the nation's history. As far back as colonial times, Benjamin Franklin recorded concern about the clannishness of the Germans in Pennsylvania, their slowness in learning English, and the establishment of their own native-language press.[3] Others of the founding fathers had similar reservations about large-scale immigration from Europe. In the context of their times they were unable to foresee the role such immigration was to play in creating the later greatness of the nation. They were not all men of unthinking prejudices. The disestablishment of religion and the separation of church and state (so that no religious group—whether New England Congregationalists, Virginian Anglicans, or even all Protestants combined—could call upon the federal government for special favors or support, and so that man's religious conscience should be free) were cardinal points of the new national policy they fostered. "The Government of the United States," George Washington had written to the Jewish congregation of Newport during his first term as president, "gives to bigotry no sanction, to persecution no assistance."

Political differences with ancestral England had just been written in blood; but there is no reason to suppose that these men looked upon their fledgling country as an impartial melting pot for the merging of the various cultures of Europe, or as a new "nation of nations," or as anything but a society in which, with important political modifications, Anglo-Saxon speech and institutional forms would be standard. Indeed, their newly won victory for democracy and republicanism made them especially anxious that these still precarious fruits of revolution should not be threatened by a large influx of European peoples whose life experiences had accustomed them to the bonds of despotic monarchy. Thus, although they explicitly conceived of the new United States of America as a haven for those unfortunates of Europe who were persecuted and oppressed, they had characteristic reservations about the effects of too free a policy. "My opinion, with respect to immigration," Washington wrote to John Adams in 1794, "is that except of useful mechanics and some particular descriptions of men or professions, there is no need of encouragement, while the policy or advantage of its taking place in a body (I mean the settling of them in a body) may be much questioned; for, by so doing, they retain the language, habits and principles (good or bad) which they bring with them."[4] Thomas Jefferson, whose views on race and attitudes towards slavery were notably liberal and advanced for his time, had similar doubts concerning the effects of mass immigration on American institutions, while conceding that immigrants, "if they come of themselves . . . are entitled to all the rights of citizenship."[5]

The attitudes of Americans toward foreign immigration in the first three-quarters of the nineteenth century may correctly be described as ambiguous. On the one hand, immigrants were much desired, so as to swell the population and importance of states and territories, to man the farms of expanding prairie settlement, to work the mines, build the railroads and canals, and take their place in expanding industry. This was a period in which no federal legislation of any consequence prevented the entry of aliens, and such state legislation as existed attempted to bar on an individual basis only those who were likely to become a burden on the community, such as convicts and paupers. On the other hand, the arrival in an overwhelmingly Protestant society of large numbers of poverty-stricken Irish Catholics, who settled in groups in the slums of Eastern cities, roused dormant fears of "Popery" and Rome. Another source of anxiety was the substantial influx of Germans, who made their way to the cities and farms of the mid-West and whose different language, separate communal life, and freer ideas on temperance and sabbath observance brought them into conflict with the Anglo-Saxon bearers of the Puritan and Evangelical traditions. Fear of foreign "radicals" and suspicion of the economic demands of the occasionally aroused workingmen added fuel to the nativist fires. In their extreme form these fears resulted in the Native-American movement of the 1830s and 1840s and the "American" or "Know-Nothing" party of the 1850s, with their anti-Catholic campaigns and their demands for restrictive laws on naturalization procedures and for keeping the foreign-born out of political office. While these movements scored local political successes and their turbulences so rent the national social fabric that the patches are not yet entirely invisible, they failed to influence national legislative policy on immigration and immigrants; and their fulminations inevitably provoked the expected reactions from thoughtful observers.

The flood of newcomers to the westward expanding nation grew larger, reaching over one and two-thirds million between 1841 and 1850 and over two and one-half million in the decade before the Civil War. Throughout the entire period, quite apart from the excesses of the Know-Nothings, the predominant (though not exclusive) conception of what the ideal immigrant adjustment should be was probably summed up in a letter written in 1818 by John Quincy Adams, then Secretary of State in answer to the inquiries of the Baron von Fürstenwaerther. If not the earliest, it is certainly the most elegant version of the sentiment, "If they don't like it here, they can go back where they came from." Adams declared:[6]

They [immigrants to America] come to life of independence, but to a life of labor—and, if they cannot accommodate themselves to the character, moral, political and physical, of this country with all its compensating balances of good and evil, the Atlantic is always open to them to return to the land of their nativity and their fathers. To one thing they must make up their minds, or they will be disappointed in every expectation of happiness as Americans. They must cast off the European skin, never to resume it. They must look forward to their posterity rather than backward to their ancestors; they must be sure that whatever their own feelings may be, those of their children will cling to the prejudices of this country.

The events that followed the Civil War created their own ambiguities in attitude toward the immigrant. A nation undergoing wholesale industrial expansion and not yet finished with the march of westward settlement could make good use of the never faltering waves of newcomers. But sporadic bursts of labor unrest, attributed to foreign radicals, the growth of Catholic institutions and the rise of Catholics to municipal political power, and the continuing association of immigrant settlement with urban slums revived familiar fears. The first federal selective law restricting immigration was passed in 1882, and Chinese immigration was cut off in the same year. The most significant development of all, barely recognized at first, was the change in the source of European migrants. Beginning in the 1880s, the countries of southern and eastern Europe began to be represented in substantial numbers for the first time, and in the next decade immigrants from these sources became numerically dominant. Now the notes of a new, or at least hitherto unemphasized, chord from the nativist lyre began to sound—the ugly chord, or discord, of racism. Previously vague and romantic notions of Anglo-Saxon peoplehood, combined with general ethnocentrism, rudimentary wisps of genetics, selected tidbits of evolutionary theory, and naive assumptions from an early and crude imported anthropology produced the doctrine that the English, Germans, and others of the "old immigration" constituted a superior race of tall, blonde, blue-eyed "Nordics" or "Aryans," whereas the peoples of eastern and southern Europe made up the darker Alpines or Mediterraneans—both "inferior" breeds whose presence in America threatened, either by intermixture or supplementation, the traditional American stock and culture. The obvious corollary to this doctrine was to exclude the allegedly inferior breeds; but if the new type of immigrant could not be excluded, then everything must be done to instill Anglo-Saxon virtues

in these benighted creatures. Thus, one educator writing in 1909 could state:[7]

These southern and eastern Europeans are of a very different type from the north Europeans who preceded them. Illiterate, docile, lacking in self-reliance and initiative, and not possessing the Anglo-Teutonic conceptions of law, order, and government, their coming has served to dilute tremendously our national stock, and to corrupt our civic life. . . . Everywhere these people tend to settle in groups or settlements, and to set up here their national manners, customs, and observances. Our task is to break up these groups or settlements, to assimilate and amalgamate these people as a part of our American race, and to implant in their children, so far as can be done, the Anglo-Saxon conception of righteousness, law and order, and popular government, and to awaken in them a reverence for our democratic institutions and for those things in our national life which we as a people hold to be of abiding worth.

Anglo-conformity received its fullest expression in the so-called Americanization which gripped the nation during World War I. While "Americanization" in its various stages had more than one emphasis, it was essentially a consciously articulated movement to strip the immigrant of his native culture and attachments and make him over into an American along Anglo-Saxon lines—all this to be accomplished with great rapidity. To use an image of a later day, it was an attempt at "pressure-cooking assimilation." It had prewar antecedents, but it was during the height of the world conflict that federal agencies, state governments, municipalities, and a host of private organizations joined in the effort to persuade the immigrant to learn English, take out naturalization papers, buy war bonds, forget his former origins and culture, and give himself over to patriotic hysteria.

After the war and the "Red scare" which followed, the excesses of the Americanization movement subsided. In its place, however, came the restriction of immigration through federal law. Foiled at first by presidential vetoes, and later by the failure of the 1917 literacy test to halt the immigrant tide, the proponents of restriction finally put through in the early 1920s a series of acts culminating in the well-known national-origins formula for immigrant quotas which went into effect in 1929. Whatever the merits of a quantitative limit on the number of immigrants to be admitted to the United States, the provisions of the formula, which discriminated sharply against the countries of southern and eastern Europe, in effect institutionalized the assumptions of the rightful dominance of Anglo-Saxon patterns in the land. Reaffirmed with only slight modifications in the McCarran-Walter Act of 1952, these laws, then, stand as a legal monument to the creed of Anglo-conformity and a telling reminder that this ideological system still has numerous and powerful adherents on the American scene.

THE MELTING POT

While Anglo-conformity in various guises has probably been the most prevalent ideology of assimilation in the American historical experience, a competing viewpoint with more generous and idealistic overtones has had its adherents and exponents from the eighteenth century onward. Conditions in the virgin continent, it was clear, were modifying the institutions which the English colonists brought with them from the mother country. Arrivals from non-English homelands such as Germany, Sweden, and France were similarly exposed to this fresh environment. Was it not possible, then, to think of the evolving American society not as a slightly modified England but rather as a totally new blend, culturally and biologically, in which the stocks and folkways of Europe, figuratively speaking, were indiscriminately mixed in the political pot of the emerging nation and fused by the fires of American influence and interaction into a distinctly new type?

Such, at any rate, was the conception of the new society which motivated that eighteenth-century French-born writer and agriculturalist, J. Hector St. John de Crèvecoeur, who, after many years of American residence, published his reflections and observations in *Letters from an American Farmer*.[8] Who, he asks, is the American?

He is either an European, or the descendant of an European, hence that strange mixture of blood, which you will find in no other country. I could point out to you a family whose grandfather was an Englishman, whose wife was Dutch, whose son married a French woman, and whose present four sons have now four wives of different nations. He is an American, who leaving behind him all his ancient prejudices and manners, receives new ones from the new mode of life he has embraced, the new government he obeys, and the new rank he holds. He becomes an American by being received in the broad lap of our great Alma Mater. Here individu-

als of all nations are melted into a new race of men, whose labours and posterity will one day cause great changes in the world.

Some observers have interpreted the open-door policy on immigration of the first three-quarters of the nineteenth century as reflecting an underlying faith in the effectiveness of the American melting pot, in the belief "that all could be absorbed and that all could contribute to an emerging national character."[9] No doubt many who observed with dismay the nativist agitation of the times felt as did Ralph Waldo Emerson that such conformity-demanding and immigrant-hating forces represented a perversion of the best American ideals. In 1845, Emerson wrote in his Journal:[10]

I hate the narrowness of the Native American Party. It is the dog in the manger. It is precisely opposite to all the dictates of love and magnanimity, and therefore, of course, opposite to true wisdom. . . . Man is the most composite of all creatures. . . . Well, as in the old burning of the Temple at Corinth, by the melting and intermixture of silver and gold and other metals a new compound more precious than any, called Corinthian-brass, was formed: so in this continent,—asylum of all nations,—the energy of Irish, Germans, Swedes, Poles, and Cossacks, and all the European tribes,—of the Africans, and the Polynesians,—will construct a new race, a new religion, a new state, a new literature, which will be as vigorous as the new Europe which came out of the smelting-pot of the Dark Ages, or that which earlier emerged from the Pelasgic and Etruscan barbarism. La Nature aime les croisements.

Eventually, the melting-pot hypothesis found its way into historical scholarship and interpretation. While many American historians of the late nineteenth century, some fresh from graduate study at German universities, tended to adopt the view that American institutions derived in essence from Anglo-Saxon (and ultimately Teutonic) sources, others were not so sure.[11] One of these was Frederick Jackson Turner, a young historian from Wisconsin, not long emerged from his graduate training at Johns Hopkins. Turner presented a paper to the American Historical Association meeting in Chicago in 1893. Called "The Significance of the Frontier in American History," this paper proved to be one of the most influential essays in the history of American scholarship, and its point of view, supported by Turner's subsequent writings and his teaching, pervaded the field of American historical interpretation for at least a generation. Turner's thesis was that the dominant influence in the shaping of American institutions and American democracy was not this nation's European heritage in any of its forms, nor the forces emanating from the eastern seaboard cities, but rather the experiences created by a moving and variegated western frontier. Among the many effects attributed to the frontier environment and the challenges it presented was that it acted as a solvent for the national heritages and the separatist tendencies of the many nationality groups which had joined the trek westward, including the Germans and Scotch-Irish of the eighteenth century and the Scandinavians and Germans of the nineteenth. "The frontier," asserted Turner, "promoted the formation of a composite nationality for the American people. . . . In the crucible of the frontier the immigrants were Americanized, liberated, and fused into a mixed race, English in neither nationality nor characteristics. The process has gone on from the early days to our own." And later, in an essay on the role of the Mississippi Valley, he refers to "the tide of foreign immigration which has risen so steadily that it has made a composite American people whose amalgamation is destined to produce a new national stock."[12]

Thus far, the proponents of the melting pot idea had dealt largely with the diversity produced by the sizeable immigration from the countries of northern and western Europe alone—the "old immigration," consisting of peoples with cultures and physical appearance not greatly different from those of the Anglo-Saxon stock. Emerson, it is true, had impartially included Africans, Polynesians, and Cossacks in his conception of the mixture; but it was only in the last two decades of the nineteenth century that a large-scale influx of peoples from the countries of southern and eastern Europe imperatively posed the question of whether these uprooted newcomers who were crowding into the large cities of the nation and industrial sector of the economy could also be successfully "melted." Would the "urban melting pot" work as well as the "frontier melting pot" of an essentially rural society was alleged to have done?

It remained for an English-Jewish writer with strong social convictions, moved by his observation of the role of the United States as a haven for the poor and oppressed of Europe, to give utterance to the broader view of the American melting pot in a way which attracted public attention. In 1908, Israel Zangwill's drama, *The Melting Pot,* was produced in this country and became a popular success. It is a play dominated by the dream of its protagonist, a young Russian-Jewish immigrant to America, a composer, whose goal is the completion of a vast "American" symphony which will express his deeply felt conception of his adopted country as a divinely appointed crucible in which all the ethnic division of mankind will divest themselves of their ancient animosities and differences and become fused into one group, signifying the brotherhood of man. In the process he falls in love with a beautiful and cultured Gentile girl. The play ends with the performance of the symphony and, after numerous vicissitudes and traditional family opposition from both sides, with the approaching marriage of David Quixano and his beloved. During the course of these developments, David, in the rhetoric of the time, delivers himself of such sentiments as these:[13]

> America is God's crucible, the great Melting Pot where all the races of Europe are melting and reforming! Here you stand, good folk, think I, when I see them at Ellis Island, here you stand in your fifty groups, with your fifty languages and histories, and your fifty blood hatreds and rivalries. But you won't be long like that, brother, for these are the fires of God you've come to—these are the fires of God. A fig for your feuds and vendettas! Germans and Frenchman, Irishmen and Englishmen, Jews and Russians—into the Crucible with you all! God is making the American.

Here we have a conception of a melting pot which admits of no exceptions or qualifications with regard to the ethnic stocks which will fuse in the great crucible. Englishmen, Germans, Frenchmen, Slavs, Greeks, Syrians, Jews, Gentiles, even the black and yellow races, were specifically mentioned in Zangwill's rhapsodic enumeration. And this pot patently was to boil in the great cities of America.

Thus around the turn of the century the melting-pot idea became embedded in the ideals of the age as one response to the immigrant receiving experience of the nation. Soon to be challenged by a new philosophy of group adjustment (to be discussed below) and always competing with the more pervasive adherence to Anglo-conformity, the melting-pot image, however, continued to draw a portion of the attention consciously directed toward this aspect of the

American scene in the first half of the twentieth century. In the mid-1940s a sociologist who had carried out an investigation of intermarriage trends in New Haven, Connecticut, described a revised conception of the melting process in that city and suggested a basic modification of the theory of that process. In New Haven, Ruby Jo Reeves Kennedy[14] reported from a study of intermarriages from 1870 to 1940 that there was a distinct tendency for the British-Americans, Germans, and Scandinavians to marry among themselves—that is, within a Protestant "pool"; for the Irish, Italians, and Poles to marry among themselves—a Catholic "pool"; and for the Jews to marry other Jews. In other words, intermarriage was taking place across lines of nationality background, but there was a strong tendency for it to stay confined within one or the other of the three major religious groups, Protestants, Catholics, and Jews. Thus, declared Mrs. Kennedy, the picture in New Haven resembled a "triple melting pot" based on religious division, rather than a "single melting pot." Her study indicated, she stated, that "while strict endogamy is loosening, religious endogamy is persisting and the future cleavages will be along religious lines rather than along nationality lines as in the past. If this is the case, then the traditional 'single-melting-pot' idea must be abandoned, and a new conception, which we term the 'triple-melting-pot' theory of American assimilation, will take its place as the true expression of what is happening to the various nationality groups in the United States."[15] The triple melting-pot thesis was later taken up by the theologian Will Herberg, and formed an important sociological frame of reference for his analysis of religious trends in American society, *Protestant-Catholic-Jew.*[16] But the triple melting-pot hypothesis patently takes us into the realm of a society pluralistically conceived. We turn now to the rise of an ideology which attempts to justify such a conception.

CULTURAL PLURALISM

Probably all the non-English immigrants who came to American shores in any significant numbers from colonial times onward—settling either in the forbidding wilderness, the lonely prairie, or in some accessible urban slum—created ethnic enclaves and looked forward to the preservation of at least some of their native cultural patterns. Such a development, natural as breathing, was supported by the later accretion of friends, relatives, and countrymen seeking out oases of familiarity in a strange land, by the desire of the settlers to rebuild (necessarily in miniature) a society in which they could communicate in the familiar tongue and maintain familiar institutions, and, finally, by the necessity to band together for mutual aid and mutual protection against the uncertainties of a strange and frequently hostile environment. This was as true of the "old" immigrants as of the "new." In fact, some of the liberal intellectuals who fled to America from an inhospitable political climate in Germany in the 1830s, 1840s, and 1850s looked forward to the creation of an all-German state within the union, or, even more hopefully, to the eventual formation of a separate German nation, as soon as the expected dissolution of the union under the impact of the slavery controversy should have taken place.[17] Oscar Handlin, writing of the sons of Erin in mid-nineteenth-century Boston, recent refugees from famine and economic degradation in their homeland, points out: "Unable to participate in the normal associational affairs of the community, the Irish felt obliged to erect a society within a society, to act together in their own way. In every contact therefore the group, acting apart from other sections of the community, became intensely aware of its peculiar and exclusive identity."[18] Thus cultural pluralism was a fact in American society before it became a theory—a theory with explicit relevance for the nation as a whole, and articulated and discussed in the English-speaking circles of American intellectual life.

Eventually, the cultural enclaves of the Germans (and the later arriving Scandinavians) were to decline in scope and significance as succeeding generations of their native-born attended public schools, left the farms and villages to strike out as individuals for the Americanizing city, and generally became subject to the influences of a standardizing industrial civilization, The German-American community, too, was struck a powerful blow by the accumulated passions generated by World War I—a blow from which it never fully recovered. The Irish were to be the dominant and pervasive element in the gradual emergence of a pan-Catholic group in America, but these developments would reveal themselves only in the twentieth century. In the meantime, in the last two decades of the nineteenth, the influx of immigrants from southern and eastern Europe had begun. These groups were all the more sociologically visible because the closing of the frontier, the occupational demands of an expanding industrial economy, and their own poverty made it inevitable that they would remain in the urban areas of the nation. In the swirling fires of controversy and the steadier flame of experience created by these new events, the ideology of cultural pluralism as a philosophy for the nation was forged.

The first manifestations of an ideological counterattack against draconic Americanization came not from the beleaguered newcomers (who were, after all, more concerned with survival than with theories of adjustment), but from those idealistic members of the middle class who, in the decade or so before the turn of the century, had followed the example of their English predecessors and "settled" in the slums to "learn to sup sorrow with the poor."[19] Immediately, these workers in the "settlement houses" were forced to come to grips with the realities of immigrant life and adjustment. Not all reacted in the same way, but on the whole the settlements developed an approach to the immigrant which was sympathetic to his native cultural heritage and to his newly created ethnic institutions.[20] For one thing, their workers, necessarily in intimate contact with the lives of these often pathetic and bewildered newcomers and their daily problems, could see how unfortunate were the effects of those forces which impelled rapid Americanization in their impact on the immigrants' children, who not infrequently became alienated from their parents and the restraining influence of family authority. Were not their parents ignorant and uneducated "Hunkies," "Sheenies," or "Dagoes," as that limited portion of the American environment in which they moved defined the matter? Ethnic "self-hatred" with its debilitating psychological consequences, family disorganization, and juvenile delinquency, were not unusual results of this state of affairs. Furthermore, the immigrants themselves were adversely affected by the incessant attacks on their cultures, their language, their institutions, their very conception of themselves. How were they to maintain their self-respect when all that they knew, felt, and dreamed, beyond their sheer capacity for manual labor—in other words, all that they *were*—was

despised or scoffed at in America? And—unkindest cut of all—their own children had begun to adopt the contemptuous attitude of the "Americans." Jane Addams relates in a moving chapter of her *Twenty Years at Hull House* how, after coming to have some conception of the extent and depth of these problems, she created at the settlement a "Labor Museum," in which the immigrant women of the various nationalities crowded together in the slums of Chicago could illustrate their native methods of spinning and weaving, and in which the relation of these earlier techniques to contemporary factory methods could be graphically shown. For the first time these peasant women were made to feel by some part of their American environment that they possessed valuable and interesting skills—that they too had something to offer—and for the first time, the daughters of these women who, after a long day's work at their dank "needletrade" sweatshops, came to Hull House to observe, began to appreciate the fact that their mothers, too, had a "culture," that this culture possessed its own merit, and that it was related to their own contemporary lives. How aptly Jane Addams concludes her chapter with the hope that "our American citizenship might be built without disturbing these foundations which were laid of old time."[21]

This appreciative view of the immigrant's cultural heritage and of its distinctive usefulness both to himself and his adopted country received additional sustenance from another source: those intellectual currents of the day which, however overborne by their currently more powerful opposites, emphasized liberalism, internationalism, and tolerance. From time to time an occasional educator or publicist protested the demands of the "Americanizers," arguing that the immigrant, too, had an ancient and honorable culture, and that this culture had much to offer an America whose character and destiny were still in the process of formation, an America which must serve as an example of the harmonious cooperation of various heritages to a world inflamed by nationalism and war. In 1916 John Dewey, Norman Hapgood, and the young literary critic Randolph Bourne published articles or addresses elaborating various aspects of this theme.

The classic statement of the cultural pluralist position, however, had been made over a year before. Early in 1915 there appeared in the pages of

The Nation two articles under the title "Democracy *versus* the Melting-Pot." Their author was Horace Kallen, a Harvard-educated philosopher with a concern for the application of philosophy to societal affairs, and, as an American Jew, himself derivative of an ethnic background which was subject to the contemporary pressures for dissolution implicit in the "Americanization," or Anglo-conformity, and the melting-pot theories. In these articles Kallen vigorously rejected the usefulness of these theories as models of what was actually transpiring in American life or as ideals for the future. Rather he was impressed by the way in which the various ethnic groups in America were coincident with particular areas and regions, and with the tendency for each group to preserve its own language, religion, communal institutions, and ancestral culture. All the while, he pointed out, the immigrant has been learning to speak English as the language of general communication, and has participated in the over-all economic and political life of the nation. These developments in which "the United States are in the process of becoming a federal state not merely as a union of geographical and administrative unities, but also as a cooperation of cultural diversities, as a federation or commonwealth of national cultures,"[22] the author argued, far from constituting a violation of historic American political principles, as the "Americanizers" claimed, actually represented the inevitable consequences of democratic ideals, since individuals are implicated in groups, and since democracy for the individual must by extension also mean democracy for his group.

The processes just described, however, as Kallen develops his argument, are far from having been thoroughly realized. They are menaced by "Americanization" programs, assumptions of Anglo-Saxon superiority, and misguided attempts to promote "racial" amalgamation. Thus America stands at a kind of cultural crossroads. It can attempt to impose by force an artificial, Anglo-Saxon oriented uniformity on its peoples, or it can consciously allow and encourage its ethnic groups to develop democratically, each emphasizing its particular cultural heritage. If the latter course is followed, as Kallen puts it at the close of his essay, then,[23]

The outlines of a possible great and truly democratic commonwealth become discernible. Its form would be that of the federal republic: its substance a democracy

of nationalities, cooperating voluntarily and autonomously through common institutions in the enterprise of self-realization through the perfection of men according to their kind. The common language of the commonwealth, the language of its great tradition, would be English, but each nationality would have for its emotional and involuntary life its own peculiar dialect or speech, its own individual and inevitable esthetic and intellectual forms. The political and economic life of the commonwealth is a single unit and serves as the foundation and background for the realization of the distinctive individuality of each nation that composes it and of the pooling of these in a harmony above them all. Thus "American civilization" may come to mean the perfection of the cooperative harmonies of "European civilization"—the waste, the squalor and the distress of Europe being eliminated—a multiplicity in a unity, an orchestration of mankind.

Within the next decade Kallen published more essays dealing with the theme of American multiple-group life, later collected in a volume.[24] In the introductory note to this book he used for the first time the term "cultural pluralism" to refer to his position. These essays reflect both his increasingly sharp rejection of the onslaughts on the immigrant and his culture which the coming of World War I and its attendant fears, the "Red scare," the projection of themes of racial superiority, the continued exploitation of the newcomers, and the rise of the Ku Klux Klan all served to increase in intensity, and also his emphasis on cultural pluralism as the democratic antidote to these ills. He has since published other essays elaborating or annotating the theme of cultural pluralism. Thus, for at least forty-five years, most of them spent teaching at the New School for Social Research, Kallen has been acknowledged as the originator and leading philosophical exponent of the idea of cultural pluralism.

In the late 1930s and early 1940s the late Louis Adamic, the Yugoslav immigrant who had become an American writer, took up the theme of America's multicultural heritage and the role of these groups in forging the country's national character. Borrowing Walt Whitman's phrase, he described America as "a nation of nations," and while his ultimate goal was closer to the melting-pot idea than to cultural pluralism, he saw the immediate task as that of making America conscious of what it owed to all its ethnic groups, not just to the Anglo-Saxons. The children and grandchildren of immigrants of non-English origins, he was convinced, must be taught to be proud of the cultural heritage of their ancestral ethnic group and of its role in building the American nation; otherwise, they would not lose their sense of ethnic inferiority and the feeling of rootlessness he claimed to find in them.

Thus in the twentieth century, particularly since World War II, "cultural pluralism" has become a concept which has worked its way into the vocabulary and imagery of specialists in intergroup relations and leaders of ethnic communal groups. In view of this new pluralistic emphasis, some writers now prefer to speak of the "integration" of immigrants rather than of their "assimilation."[25] However, with a few exceptions,[26] no close analytical attention has been given either by social scientists or practitioners of intergroup relations to the meaning of cultural pluralism, its nature and relevance for a modern industrialized society, and its implications for problems of prejudice and discriminations—a point to which we referred at the outset of this discussion.

CONCLUSIONS

In the remaining pages I can make only a few analytical comments which I shall apply in context to the American scene, historical and current. My view of the American situation will not be documented here, but may be considered as a series of hypotheses in which I shall attempt to outline the American assimilation process.

First of all, it must be realized that "assimilation" is a blanket term which in reality covers a multitude of subprocesses. The most crucial distinction is one often ignored—the distinction between what I have elsewhere called "behavioral assimilation" and "structural assimilation."[27] The first refers to the absorption of the cultural behavior patterns of the "host" society. (At the same time, there is frequently some modification of the cultural patterns of the immigrant-receiving country, as well.) There is a special term for this process of cultural modification or "behavioral assimilation" —namely, "acculturation." "Structural assimilation," on the other hand, refers to the entrance of the immigrants and their descendants into the social cliques, organizations, institutional activities, and general civic life of the receiving society. If this process takes place on a large enough scale, then a high frequency of intermarriage must result. A

further distinction must be made between, on the one hand, those activities of the general civic life which involve earning a living, carrying out political responsibilities, and engaging in the instrumental affairs of the larger community, and, on the other hand, activities which create personal friendship patterns, frequent home intervisiting, communal worship, and communal recreation. The first type usually develops so-called "secondary relationships," which tend to be relatively impersonal and segmental; the latter type leads to "primary relationships," which are warm, intimate, and personal.

With these various distinctions in mind, we may then proceed.

Built on the base of the original immigrant "colony" but frequently extending into the life of successive generations, the characteristic ethnic group experience is this: within the ethnic group there develops a network of organizations and informal social relationships which permits and encourages the members of the ethnic group to remain within the confines of the group for all of their primary relationships and some of their secondary relationships throughout all the stages of the life cycle. From the cradle in the sectarian hospital to the child's play group, the social clique in high school, the fraternity and religious center in college, the dating group within which he searches for a spouse, the marriage partner, the neighborhood of his residence, the church affiliation and the church clubs, the men's and the women's social and service organizations, the adult clique of "marrieds," the vacation resort, and then, as the age cycle nears completion, the rest home for the elderly and, finally, the sectarian cemetery—in all these activities and relationships which are close to the core of personality and selfhood—the member of the ethnic group may if he wishes follow a path which never takes him across the boundaries of his ethnic structural network.

The picture is made more complex by the existence of social class divisions which cut across ethnic group lines just as they do those of the white Protestant population in America. As each ethnic group which has been here for the requisite time has developed second, third, or in some cases, succeeding generations, it has produced a college-educated group which composes an upper middle class (and sometimes upper class, as well) segment of the larger groups. Such class divisions

tend to restrict primary group relations even further, for although the ethnic-group member feels
a general sense of identification with all the bearers of his ethnic heritage, he feels comfortable in
intimate social relations only with those who also
share his own class background or attainment.

In short, my point is that, while *behavioral assimilation* or acculturation has taken place in
America to a considerable degree, *structural assimilation,* with some important exceptions has not
been extensive.[28] The exceptions are of two types.
The first brings us back to the "triple-melting-pot"
thesis of Ruby Jo Reeves Kennedy and Will Herberg. The "nationality" ethnic groups have tended
to merge within each of the three major religious
groups. This has been particularly true of the
Protestant and Jewish communities. Those descendants of the "old" immigration of the nineteenth century, who were Protestant (many of the
Germans and all the Scandinavians), have in considerable part gradually merged into the white
Protestant "subsociety." Jews of Sephardic, German, and Eastern-European origins have similarly
tended to come together in their communal life.
The process of absorbing the various Catholic nationalities, such as the Italians, Poles and French
Canadians, into an American Catholic community
hitherto dominated by the Irish has begun, although I do not believe that it is by any means
close to completion. Racial and quasi-racial groups
such as the Negroes, Indians, Mexican-Americans,
and Puerto Ricans still retain their separate sociological structures. The outcome of all this in contemporary American life is thus pluralism—but it
is more than "triple" and it is more accurately described as *structural pluralism* than as cultural pluralism, although some of the latter also remains.

My second exception refers to the social structures which implicate intellectuals. There is no
space to develop the issue here, but I would argue
that there is a social world or subsociety of the
intellectuals in America in which true structural
intermixture among persons of various ethnic
backgrounds, including the religious, has markedly
taken place.

My final point deals with the reasons for these
developments. If structural assimilation has been
retarded in America by religious and racial lines,
we must ask why. The answer lies in the attitudes
of both the majority and the minority groups and
in the way these attitudes have interacted. A saying

of the current day is, "It takes two to tango." To
apply the analogy, there is no good reason to
believe that white Protestant America has ever extended a firm and cordial invitation to its minorities to dance. Furthermore, the attitudes of the
minority-group members themselves on the matter have been divided and ambiguous. Particularly
for the minority religious groups, there is a certain
logic in ethnic communality, since there is a commitment to the perpetuation of the religious ideology and since structural intermixture leads to
intermarriage and the possible loss to the group of
the intermarried family. Let us, then, examine the
situation serially for various types of minorities.

With regard to the immigrant, in his characteristic numbers and socio-economic background,
structural assimilation was out of the question.
He did not want it, and he had a positive need for
the comfort of his own communal institutions.
The native American, moreover, whatever the
implications of his public pronouncements, had
no intention of opening up his primary group
life to entrance by these hordes of alien newcomers. The situation was a functionally complementary standoff.

The second generation found a much more
complex situation. Many believed they heard the
siren call of welcome to the social cliques, clubs,
and institutions of white Protestant America.
After all, it was simply a matter of learning American ways, was it not? Had they not grown up as
Americans, and were they not culturally different
from their parents, the "greenhorns"? Or perhaps
an especially eager one reasoned (like the Jewish
protagonist of Myron Kaufmann's novel, *Remember Me to God,* aspiring to membership in the
prestigious club system of Harvard undergraduate social life) "If only I can go the last few steps
in Ivy League manners and behavior, they will
surely recognize that I am one of them and take
me in." But, alas, Brooks Brothers suit notwithstanding, the doors of the fraternity house, the city
men's club, and the country club were slammed
in the face of the immigrant's offspring. That invitation was not really there in the first place; or,
to the extent it was, in Joshua Fishman's phrase, it
was a " 'look me over but don't touch me' invitation to the American minority group child."[29] And
so the rebuffed one returned to the homelier but
dependable comfort of the communal institutions
of his ancestral group. There he found his fellows

of the same generation who had never stirred from the home fires. Some of these had been too timid to stray; others were ethnic ideologists committed to the group's survival; still others had never really believed in the authenticity of the siren call or were simply too passive to do more than go along the familiar way. All could not join in the task that was well within the realm of the sociologically possible—the build-up of social institutions and organizations within the ethnic enclave, manned increasingly by members of the second generation and suitably separated by social class.

Those who had for a time ventured out gingerly or confidently, as the case might be, had been lured by the vision of an "American" social structure that was somehow larger than all subgroups and was ethnically neutral. Were they, too, not Americans? But they found to their dismay that at the primary group level a neutral American social structure was a mirage. What at a distance seemed to be a quasi-public edifice flying only the all-inclusive flag of American nationality turned out on closer inspection to be the clubhouse of a particular ethnic group—the white Anglo-Saxon Protestants, its operation shot through with the premises and expectations of its parental ethnicity. In these terms, the desirability of whatever invitation was grudgingly extended to those of other ethnic backgrounds could only become a considerably attenuated one.

With the racial minorities, there was not even the pretense of an invitation. Negroes, to take the most salient example, have for the most part been determinedly barred from the cliques, social clubs, and churches of white America. Consequently, with due allowance for internal class differences, they have constructed their own network of organizations and institutions, their own "social world." There are now many vested interests served by the preservation of this separate communal life, and doubtless many Negroes are psychologically comfortable in it, even though at the same time they keenly desire that discrimination in such areas as employment, education, housing, and public accommodations be eliminated. However, the ideological attachment of Negroes to their communal separation is not conspicuous. Their sense of identification with ancestral African national cultures is virtually nonexistent, although Pan-Africanism engages the interest of some intel-

lectuals and although "black nationalist" and "black racist" fringe groups have recently made an appearance at the other end of the communal spectrum. As for their religion, they are either Protestant or Catholic (overwhelmingly the former). Thus, there are no "logical" ideological reasons for their separate communality; dual social structures are created solely by the dynamics of prejudice and discrimination, rather than being reinforced by the ideological commitments of the minority itself.

Structural assimilation, then, has turned out to be the rock on which the ships of Anglo-conformity and the melting pot have foundered. To understand that behavioral assimilation (or acculturation) without massive structural intermingling in primary relationships has been the dominant motif in the American experience of creating and developing a nation out of diverse peoples is to comprehend the most essential sociological fact of that experience. It is against the background of "structural pluralism" that strategies of strengthening intergroup harmony, reducing ethnic discrimination and prejudice, and maintaining the rights of both those who stay within and those who venture beyond their ethnic boundaries must be thoughtfully devised.

ENDNOTES

1. Allen Nevins and Henry Steele Commager, *America: The Story of a Free People* (Boston, Little, Brown, 1942), p. 58.
2. The phrase is the Coles'. See Stewart G. Cole and Mildred Wiese Cole, *Minorities and the American Promise* (New York, Harper & Brothers, 1954), ch. 6.
3. Maurice R. Davie, *World Immigration* (New York, Macmillan, 1936), p. 36, and (cited therein) "Letter of Benjamin Franklin to Peter Collinson, 9th May, 1753, on the condition and character of the Germans in Pennsylvania," in *The World of Benjamin Franklin, with Notes and Life of the Author,* by Jared Sparks (Boston, 1828), vol. 7, pp. 71–73.
4. *The Writings of George Washington,* collected by W. C. Ford (New York, G.P. Putman's Sons, 1889), vol. 12, p. 489.
5. Thomas Jefferson, "Notes on Virginia, Query 8"; in *The Writings of Thomas Jefferson,* ed. A. E. Bergh (Washington, The Thomas Jefferson Memorial Association, 1907), vol. 2, p. 121.
6. *Niles Weekly Register,* vol. 18, 29 April 1820, pp. 157–158; see also Marcus L. Hansen, *The Atlantic Migration, 1607-1860,* pp. 96–97.

7. Ellwood P. Cubberly, *Changing Conceptions of Education* (Boston, Houghton, 1909), pp. 15–16.

8. J. Hector St. John de Crèvecoeur, *Letters from an American Farmer* (New York, Albert and Charles Boni, 1925; reprinted from the 1st edn., London, 1782), pp. 54–55.

9. Oscar Handlin, ed., *Immigration as a Factor in American History* (Englewood, Prentice-Hall, 1959), p. 146.

10. Quoted by Stuart P. Sherman in his Introduction to *Essays and Poems of Emerson* (New York, Harcourt Brace, 1921), p. xxxiv.

11. See Edward N. Saveth, *American Historians and European Immigrants, 1875–1925* (New York, Columbia University Press, 1948).

12. Frederick Jackson Turner, *The Frontier in American History* (New York, Henry Holt, 1920), pp. 22–23, 190.

13. Israel Zangwill, *The Melting Pot* (New York, Macmiuan, 1909), p. 37.

14. Ruby Jo Reeves Kennedy, "Single or Triple Melting-Pot? Intermarriage Trends in New Haven, 1870–1940," *American Journal of Sociology,* 1944, 49:331–339. See also her "Single or Triple Melting-Pot? Intermarriage in New Haven, 1870–1950," *ibid.,* 1952, 58:56–59.

15. Kennedy, "Single or Triple Melting-Pot? . . . 1870–1940," p. 332 (author's italics omitted).

16. Will Herberg, *Protestant-Catholic-Jew* (Garden City, Doubleday, 1955).

17. Nathan Glazer, "Ethnic Groups in America: From National Culture to Ideology," in Morroe Berger, Theodore Abel, and Charles H. Page, eds., *Freedom and Control in Modern Society* (New York, D. Van Nostrand, 1954), p. 161; Marcus Lee Hansen, *The Immigrant in American History* (Cambridge, Harvard University Press, 1940), pp. 129–140; John A. Hawgood, *The Tragedy of German-America* (New York, Putnam's, 1940), *passim.*

18. Oscar Handlin, *Boston's Immigrants* (Cambridge, Harvard University Press, 1959, rev. edn.), p. 176.

19. From a letter (1883) by Samuel A. Barnett; quoted in Arthur C. Holden, *The Settlement Idea* (New York, Macmillan, 1922), p. 12.

20. Jane Addams, *Twenty Years at Hull House* (New York, Macmillan, 1914), pp. 231–258; Arthur C. Holden, *op. cit.,* pp. 109–131, 182–189; John Higham, *Strangers in the Land* (New Brunswick, Rutgers University Press, 1955), p. 236.

21. Jane Addams, *op. cit.,* p. 258.

22. Horace M. Kallen, "Democracy *versus* the Melting-Pot," *The Nation,* 18 and 25 February 1915; reprinted in his *Culture and Democracy in the United States,* New York, Boni and Liveright, 1924; the quotation is on p. 116.

23. Kallen, *Culture and Democracy . . . ,* p. 124.

24. *Op. cit.*

25. See W. D. Borrie *et al., The Cultural Integration of Immigrants* (a survey based on the papers and proceedings of the UNESCO Conference in Havana, April 1956), Paris, UNESCO, 1959; and William S. Bernard, "The Integration of Immigrants in the United States" (mimeographed), one of the papers for this conference.

26. See particularly Milton M. Gordon, "Social Structure and Goals in Group Relations"; and Nathan Glazer, "Ethnic Groups in America: From National Culture to Ideology," both articles in Berger, Abel, and Page, *op. cit.;* S. N. Eisenstadt, *The Absorption of Immigrants* (London, Routledge and Kegan Paul, 1954) and W. D. Borrie *et al., op. cit.*

27. Milton M. Gordon, "Social Structure and Goals in Groups Relations," p. 151.

28. See Erich Rosenthal, "Acculturation without Assimilation?" *American Journal of Sociology,* 1960, 66:275–288.

29. Joshua A. Fishman, "Childhood Indoctrination for Minority-Group Membership and the Quest for Minority-Group Biculturism in America," in Oscar Handlin, ed., *Group Life in America* (Cambridge, Harvard University Press, forthcoming).

Revisiting Assimilation
The Rise, Fall, and Reappraisal of a Concept in American Ethnic History

Russell A. Kazal

On what terms have immigrants and their descendants come to live in the United States? For years, popular and scholarly discussion of this question revolved around the notion of "assimilation." The word, sometimes used interchangeably with "Americanization," implied that immigrants, especially European ones, would acquire what were defined as American ways. In an era of multiculturalism, however, "assimilation" has taken on an almost archaic ring. When diversity is a watchword, nothing seems so wrongheaded as identifying an American norm, let alone bringing all Americans into line with it. Assimilation in the sense of recasting newcomers in a uniform American mold remains out of fashion with historians and the general public alike.

But the scholarly concept of assimilation was never quite that simple. Over this century, discerning how immigrants assimilated to American society, sociologists and historians found, required a more nuanced portrait of that society. To know how newcomers came to fit in, one had to understand what it was they were fitting into. This developing understanding of assimilation, which reached its high-water mark in the early 1960s, came to see the process as occurring within a society made up of groups clustered around an Anglo-American core. Scholars disagreed on the type and degree of assimilation bringing immigrant ethnic groups together, or closer to the core. But, they agreed, such processes were at work.

When the notion of an Anglo-American core collapsed amid the turmoil of the 1960s, assimilation lost its allure, and students of European immigration retreated to a focus on one of the building blocks of the earlier accounts: the ethnic group. Social historians, in particular, tended to stress the persistence of such groups and, correspondingly, to neglect, deny, or minimize assimilation's role in eroding them. In narrowing their focus, these scholars also tended to lose sight of the larger society within which both ethnic groups and assimilatory processes fit. Historian David Gerber's comment that much of social history "concentrated on groups in isolation from one another, . . . or in conflict" had special resonance for immigration studies: "It was easy to get the notion . . . that our history is the story of vaguely related groups which inhabit the same space, fail to communicate, and often get in one another's way."[1]

The concept of an unchanging, monolithic, Anglo-American cultural core is dead. Shorn of that Anglo-conformist assumption, however, assimilation in recent years has drawn renewed scholarly interest. Since the early 1980s, historians in three distinct subspecialties have returned to looking at relations among European ethnic groups within a larger American society and, in turn, to processes of homogenization that have brought groups, or their members, together on common ground. The first group of historians, a

Russell Kazal, "Revisiting Assimilation: The Rise, Fall, and Reappraisal of a Concept in American Ethnic History," *American Historical Review.* Vol. 100, No. 2 (April 1995), pp. 437–471. Reprinted by Permission of the American Historical Association.

circle of scholars of ethnicity, has proposed ways of understanding American society as one with room both for a multitude of ethnicities and for processes affecting them—including assimilation between groups. The second group, made up of labor historians exploring the rise of twentieth-century industrial unionism, in effect has described a kind of assimilation: the formation of a more unified working class out of an ethnically divided work force. Scholars of racial identity—the third group—have begun to trace another kind of trans-ethnic homogenization: the development of a common feeling of "whiteness" among European ethnics during this century and the last. Historians in all three specialties have explored Americanization, examining how newcomers have come to define themselves as "American." Here, something resembling an American "core" ideology has re-emerged—but an ideology subject to change and contestation.

This article examines how historians have revisited assimilation—in fact, if not always in name—and places that reappraisal in the context of the history of assimilation as an idea. For by tracing assimilation's historiographical trajectory, we can better understand how recent work takes up issues that surrounded the concept before scholars largely abandoned it in the 1960s. The massiveness of the relevant literature requires that the essay focus on European newcomers and their descendants in the nineteenth and twentieth centuries but not that it ignore questions of race. Indeed, they are among the most interesting questions being asked by the reappraisers.

In seeking to trace how others have defined assimilation and Americanization, an author should offer his own definitions of those terms. I conceive of assimilation as referring to processes that result in greater homogeneity within a society.[2] Such processes may operate at different levels: among individuals, between groups—whether defined in ethnic, racial, or religious terms—or between groups and a dominant group in the society. They may operate within different arenas, with groups, for example, drawn together in terms of culture, or intermarriage, or shared political institutions, or shared elements of identity, such as class consciousness. And they may operate to varying degrees within and across different arenas.[3]

This understanding of assimilation becomes more concrete when we consider the experience of European immigrants and their descendants in the United States. Here, the unit of analysis is commonly understood to be the immigrant ethnic group, whether defined as an interest group, a primordially rooted collectivity, or one sharing a sense of peoplehood, to note a few such definitions.[4] Such groups, differentiated by presumed national origin and religion, may themselves be seen as emerging from assimilatory processes of "ethnicization" that merged provincial Old World identities into "nationalities" in the New World.[5] Yet scholars most often have presumed the objects of "assimilation" to be already-formed ethnic groups and their members.[6] Given this background, I find it most useful to define assimilation in the immigrant context as referring to processes that generate homogeneity *beyond* the ethnic-group level. Such processes bring different immigrant ethnic groups, or their members, together in any number of arenas, creating common ground among them, or between them and a socially dominant group.[7] Thus understanding assimilation requires understanding how ethnic groups relate to one another within the larger society.[8]

Such processes of assimilation can occur in any society. "Americanization" is more limited; it implies that one becomes "American," in some sense, by adopting something that sets one off from non-Americans. Assimilation in America amounts to Americanization if it results in the acquisition of a distinct "American" culture, behavior, or set of values. The reality of such an overall American culture or ideology is hotly disputed. While leaving open whether it exists, I can offer a minimum definition of Americanization as that particular variant of assimilation by which newcomers or their descendants come to identify themselves as "American," however they understand that identity.[9] This version of Americanization can also be considered a form of American nationalism, in which immigrants join the "imagined community," in Benedict Anderson's sense, of Americans.[10]

This article lays out the history of the concept of assimilation beginning in the early twentieth century with the University of Chicago sociologists who formulated such approaches to assimilation as the "race relations cycle" and the disorganization-reorganization axis. Oscar Handlin later carried some of their ideas—and contradictions—into historical writing. His *Boston's Immigrants* showed that city's Irish adjusting to their new home as a group functioning within a pluralistic system, while, in *The Uprooted,* he offered a somewhat contradictory portrayal of Americanization as in part a journey toward individualism.

Then I will explore how scholars from the late 1930s to the early 1960s elaborated a more supple understanding of assimilation. Marcus Lee Hansen signaled a move away from seeing assimilation as a one-way ticket to modernity, suggesting that ethnicity might reemerge among the descendants of immigrants, while Ruby Jo Reeves Kennedy helped to anchor assimilation more firmly in a pluralist setting by depicting American society as homogenizing the children of newcomers into separate communities of Protestants, Catholics, and Jews. Will Herberg used these ideas to argue that three religious melting pots were transmuting their third-generation congregants toward "an idealized 'Anglo-Saxon' model." Milton Gordon discerned a trend toward "structural pluralism," in which the three religious communities, racial minorities, and some ethnic remnants kept separate social networks yet increasingly were adopting Anglo-American cultural patterns.[11] In complicating the notion of assimilation, these scholars progressively qualified it, effectively clearing the way for its downfall. The collapse became visible in *Beyond the Melting Pot* (1963), an analysis of ethnicity in New York City by Nathan Glazer and Daniel Patrick Moynihan. They also saw ethnic groups submerged in religious melting pots—in New York's future. But the future, they suggested, was a long way off. This declaration's historiographical equivalent appeared a year later in Rudolph Vecoli's critique of *The Uprooted.* The peasants Vecoli studied, far from being transformed by immigration, used their heritage to adjust to America.

Such affirmations of ethnic persistence presaged the 1960s rise of identity politics and a turn away from assimilation, a turn that is the subject of the article's third section. The "New Social History" of the 1960s, 1970s, and early 1980s, particularly its cultural vein, tended to ignore or minimize assimilation. Historians such as Herbert Gutman, John Bodnar, and Paul Buhle instead stressed the strength of separate immigrant, or immigrant working-class, cultures.

Finally, I will explore how, since the early 1980s, historians have edged back toward questions of assimilation. Philip Gleason and John Higham, who stayed with the concept through the 1970s, foreshadowed elements of the new work with analyses of American identity that noted its changing and, at times, fragmented nature. More recently, scholars such as Kathleen Neils Conzen and David Gerber, who make ethnic groups their primary topic of study, have suggested viewing American society as a pluralism of constantly interacting and changing ethnicities. While rejecting the idea of "a hegemonic Anglo-American core culture,"[12] this model still provides room for the waning of particular ethnicities and the acquisition of "American" identities. Labor historians have taken a kind of assimilation seriously in pondering how an ethnically diverse working class gained enough cohesion in the twentieth century to unionize. For Lizabeth Cohen, the key lies in the creation of an "integrated working-class culture"; for James R. Barrett and Gary Gerstle, a major factor is the use ethnic workers made of "Americanist" language to draw themselves together.[13] Another kind of assimilation, the acceptance of European ethnics as "white," is implied by the work of David Roediger, Arnold Hirsch, and others probing the construction of racial identity. The trans-ethnic class consciousness explored by the labor historians seems at odds with the ethnic pluralism depicted by Conzen, Gerber, and others. Work on the rise of the "white" ethnic suggests that those approaches may not recognize sufficiently, the role of race in marking boundaries in American life. I would invite these three groups of historians, who have separately revisited assimilation, to take the next step in understanding that process by conversing with one another.[14]

By the 1920s, American thinking on assimilation could be characterized broadly in terms of three main stances Americans took toward immigrants. Milton Gordon, writing more than thirty years ago, described these three "central ideological tendencies" as "Anglo-conformity," "the melting pot," and "cultural pluralism." Ideas of Anglo-conformity "demanded the complete renunciation of the immigrant's ancestral culture in favor of the behavior and values of the Anglo-Saxon core group." Melting pot concepts foresaw "a biological merger of the Anglo-Saxon peoples with other immigrant groups and a blending of their respective cultures into a new indigenous American type." Theories of "cultural pluralism" advocated retaining "the communal life and significant portions of the culture of the later immigrant groups" within a common political framework. Although Gordon classed cultural pluralism as a kind of assimilation, many have seen it as an alternative, with the melting pot and Anglo-conformity standing for assimilation as such. The Anglo-conformist and melting pot stances predominated in colonial America and the nineteenth-century United States.[15] Cultural pluralism developed primarily in the twentieth century, elaborated by such intellectuals as Horace Kallen, who proposed an American "democracy of nationalities."[16] Americans have invoked these concepts as descriptions of past or present social reality, as predictions of the future, and as declarations of what they wanted that future to look like.[17]

Against this backdrop of assimilationist thought, sociologists at the University of Chicago developed, in the first four decades of this century, the most influential scholarly theories of how immigrants adjusted to American life. Yet their work remained curiously imprecise in respect to the three stances outlined above. As Stow Persons argues, while the Chicago scholars examined the assimilation of immigrants in America, they did not specify the nature of the society—melting pot, Anglo-centered, or pluralistic—to which immigrants were presumed to assimilate. The contribution of William Isaac Thomas, Robert Ezra Park, and other members of the Chicago School lay instead in several concepts bearing on immigrant adjustment: migration as a process of disorganization and reorganization, the "race relations cycle," symbiosis, and ecological succession. The first three, as Persons outlines in *Ethnic Studies at Chicago* (1987), had their roots in German sociology. German "conflict" theorists saw social order as originating in racial conquest; their ideas and those of Georg Simmel would reemerge at Chicago in the form of a focus on conflict, relationships of subordination, and relations among ethnic groups. Simmel's work and Ferdinand Toennies' theory of *Gemeinschaft* and *Gesellschaft* also formed the basis for a view of human development as a journey from a rural, face-to-face community to an urban, impersonal, and individualistic world.[18]

The theme of emigration as a process by which Old World peasants urbanized in the New World emerged most strongly in W. I. Thomas's and Florian Znaniecki's study *The Polish Peasant in Europe*

and America (1918–20). It portrayed peasants in transit from relatively self-sufficient communities regulated by the "half-conscious" social rules of primary, or face-to-face, groups such as the family, to a social order—typified by the city—of greater individualization and individual self-control, based more in "rational co-operation."[19] This transition occurred along an axis of "disorganization" and "reorganization." In Poland, peasant communities had undergone "disorganization" as contacts with outsiders, migration to cities, and upward mobility eroded "the influence of existing social rules of behavior" on individual primary-group members.[20] The authors focused in particular on the peasant family. Traditionally, this institution included not just the "marriage-group" of husband, wife, and children but also blood relatives and in-laws to a certain degree: a "family group" knit together by a web of obligation, assistance, and control. Disorganization spelled the isolation of the marriage-group and an individualization whereby one counted socially more as oneself than as a family member.[21] A corresponding loss of familial controls encouraged personal "demoralization" in the form of desertion, murder, and juvenile delinquency. In the United States, Polish immigrants facing familial and communal disorganization supplemented what remained of their old primary-group organization with "reflective social activity," in the form of the mutual benefit society and the parish. Thus the journey to America involved not only a shift from "spontaneous" primary-group life to conscious social organization but also "the formation of a new Polish-American society."[22]

The development of this ethnic group in itself counted as a kind of "assimilation," in that the group as a whole was "slowly evolving from Polonism to Americanism," with members "continually acquiring more American attitudes."[23] Yet, ultimately, the very success of such societies in preparing immigrants for American conditions led to their demise, as Thomas wrote in *Old World Traits Transplanted* (1921). These groups were "constantly graduating their members into general American life," making group collapse and members' "[a]ssimilation . . . as inevitable as it is desirable."[24] This type of assimilation both involved a harmonizing of immigrant and "American" "attitudes and values" and implied, as Persons argues, "the emancipation of individuals from the uniformities of ethnic group experience."[25]

The "race relations cycle," which comprehended European as well as non-European ethnic groups, was a modified version of the "fundamental social process . . . of interaction" described by Robert Park and Ernest Burgess in their textbook *Introduction to the Science of Sociology* (1921).[26] Interaction, in its "four typical forms" of competition, conflict, accommodation, and assimilation, brought individuals together into community. Through those processes, the community assumed "the form of a society."[27] One form grew out of another in a discernible progression. In one possible path, for example, contact between individuals or groups would lead to conflict (in which competition became conscious), which in turn created new social situations requiring adjustment through accommodation. The resulting social equilibrium still contained antagonisms, which could only be wholly dissolved through assimilation.[28] Park and Burgess defined assimilation as "a process of interpenetration and fusion in which persons and groups acquire the memories, sentiments, and attitudes of other persons or groups, and, by sharing their experience and history, are incorporated with them in a common cultural life."[29]

When Park later recast the interaction process as the race relations cycle, he all but decreed the ultimate inevitability of immigrant assimilation. Writing in 1926 on Asian immigration to the West Coast, he depicted this cycle of "contacts, competition, accommodation and eventual assimilation" as "apparently progressive and irreversible."[30] But, eventually, Park seemed to back away from a view of assimilation as preordained. In 1937, he conceded that the cycle could also end in a system of castes or one that included a permanent racial minority.[31] After 1930, he paid increasing attention to the idea of a symbiotic relationship between racial and ethnic groups as a state short of assimilation. In such a relationship, members of "different races and divergent cultures" lived within the same local economy and "in physical contiguity, but in more or less complete moral isolation" from one another.[32]

The concept of ecological succession served to unite elements of the race relations cycle, symbiosis, the disorganization-reorganization axis, and individual assimilation into one spatial framework. Burgess sketched out the idea in the early 1920s. He saw city growth as organized in terms of concentric zones. Traveling away from a central business district, one passed through a deteriorating "zone in transition," holding "immigrant colonies"; a "zone of workingmen's homes," an area of second, and generally second-generation, immigrant settlement; a "residential zone" of middle-class housing; and finally a suburban "commuters' zone." Each zone tended to extend its area by invading its outer neighbor in a process of "succession."[33] Chicago scholars such as Louis Wirth and Paul Frederick Cressey used this model to give assimilation a spatial dimension. In 1938, Cressey described "[i]mmigrant stocks" as following "a regular sequence of settlement" in Chicago that took them from a transitional-zone colony to a series of new districts. As it moved, a group grew less concentrated physically, less united culturally, and more accepting of "American standards of living." The final stage saw a "gradual dispersion through cosmopolitan residential districts," which marked "the disintegration of the group and the absorption of the individuals into the general American population."[34]

The Chicago theorists, as suggested above, did not clearly define the target society to which immigrants assimilated. As Persons points out, Park and Burgess saw assimilation as a process by which groups shared attitudes and forged a common culture—implying a view of American society as a cultural melting pot. But they simultaneously defined assimilation as "the process by which the culture of . . . a country is transmitted to an adopted citizen,"[35] a potentially Anglo-conformist definition. Thomas succumbed to the same fuzziness when he described assimilation both as the "harmonizing" of immigrant and American cultures and as the individual's journey from the ethnic group to the larger society.[36] Park's later emphasis on symbiosis implied he might be open as well to the idea of ethnic groups persisting in a pluralist order, as did his definition in 1930 of "social assimilation" as "political," a process by which an "adopted citizen" acquired "the generally accepted social customs and political ideas and loyalties of a community or country." Yet Park explicitly rejected Kallen's brand of cultural pluralism. In Persons' words, the Chicago sociologists examined how ethnic groups lost their ethnicity by merging with the majority, without examining "the ultimate nature of that majority" and hence assimilation's "cultural content."[37] This presented a problematic legacy to scholars of assimilation, one that would come into full view in the work of Oscar Handlin.

Handlin emerged as a central figure in the school of immigration history that developed in the 1920s, 1930s, and 1940s. His reputation rested on *Boston's Immigrants, 1790–1865: A Study in Acculturation* (1941), a case study, and his synthesis, *The Uprooted* (1951). Both contained a healthy dose of Chicago-style sociology.[38] Together, they displayed that sociology's contradictions, for they offered sometimes diametrically opposed accounts of assimilation.

Boston's Immigrants focused on the adjustment of newcomers, especially the Irish, to life in that nineteenth-century city. "Adjustment" was the book's key word: Handlin traced it in the physical, economic, and cultural realms. The narrative followed a route somewhat similar to the race relations cycle in depicting the Irish as refugees driven to America by economic change and famine who came into cultural conflict with native Bostonians and found a measure of accommodation on the basis of cooperation, "if not . . . social equality."[39] Yet this accommodation stopped short of assimilation. Much like Thomas and Znaniecki's Polish-American immigrants, the Irish in Boston had formed an ethnic group. But unlike such groups as the Germans, the Irish did not melt into what Handlin painted as an Anglo-dominated majority, at least within the nineteenth century. Rather, they assumed a subordinate position in symbiosis with native residents and a constellation of better-assimilated immigrants.[40]

Boston's Immigrants went beyond Chicago ethnic studies by demonstrating that the persistence of the Irish ethnic group was due in part to Boston's "social *milieu*," especially its constricted economy. Flight from Ireland left these peasants bereft of training or capital in a city with little industry. Without opportunities, most were forced into "an unemployed resourceless proletariat" that found a permanent place only when entrepreneurs exploited their labor to bring industrialism to Boston. The resulting poverty encouraged "intemperance, crime, and prostitution"; Handlin did not find a breakdown of the family caused by individualization behind these ills.[41]

If the key word of *Boston's Immigrants* was "adjustment," that of *The Uprooted* was "alienation." *The Uprooted* retained a concern for the environ-

ment that immigrants entered, but it added a heavy overlay of disorganization-reorganization theory. The result was some ambiguity as to what constituted Americanization, a term Handlin preferred over "assimilation."[42]

For the Handlin of *The Uprooted*, "the history of immigration is a history of alienation and its consequences." In terms reminiscent of Thomas and Znaniecki, he told of how "the old equilibrium" that had sustained the peasant village and its system of family, marriage, and land fell apart, forcing its inhabitants to leave. Convinced that village ways no longer worked, the peasant began to act as an individual, starting with the journey to America. Once there, the factory cut "him" off from the soil that had "given meaning to his being." In his ghetto home, "the disorganizing pressure of the environment" bred pauperism and gambling; the individual had "grown uncertain as to his own proper role." As with Thomas and Znaniecki, "[r]eorganization would involve first the creation of new means of social action within which the man alone could locate himself." He read an ethnic newspaper or joined a mutual aid association. Such actions, on the one hand, were "steps in his Americanization." On the other, they "added up to . . . [an ethnic] society whole and coherent within the larger American society."[43]

Handlin offered a view of Americanization similar to the account in *The Polish Peasant* of an emerging Polish-American society. The creation of an ethnic group counted as Americanization, since "[b]ecoming an American meant . . . not the simple conformity to a previous pattern, but the adjustment to the needs of a new situation." At the same time, the very individualism that migration induced and that undermined ethnic institutions was in itself the essence of America. Immigrants "were on the way toward being Americans almost before they stepped off the boat, because their own experience of displacement had already introduced them to what was essential in the situation of Americans." Such upheaval was also "in some degree the experience of all modern men." This second kind of Americanization resembled the assimilation Thomas and Znaniecki saw in the individual's flight from the ethnic group. Yet Handlin also argued that whether immigrants belonged in America hinged on the views of others, including many "Anglo-Saxon" citizens who considered ethnics to be outsiders.[44]

Unfortunately, these versions of Americaniza-tion tended to conflict with each other and did not entirely jibe with *Boston's Immigrants. The Uprooted,* in essence, implied three definitions of Americanization: adjustment to the new country via ethnic group formation, individualization (which was also modernization) and acceptance by "old-stock" Americans. The first two defini-tions might be reconciled by seeing individual-ism as following group formation, yet Handlin had peasants becoming individuals with the crossing. Handlin did not use the word "Ameri-canization" when asking whether immigrants belonged in America; but if one takes acceptance as the third definition, it robs the first two of use-fulness. Individualization had little to do with the symbiotic "acculturation" described in *Boston's Immigrants,* although Handlin may simply have changed his mind in the decade between the two books. Handlin's concepts of Americanization were inconsistent with each other in ways that echoed the inconsistencies of Chicago theory. Here, as in the work of Thomas and Park, vistas of inevitable individualism, where newcomers faded into an ill-defined America, clashed with views that allowed for symbiosis within a plural-ist order. The latter approach, that of *Boston's Immigrants,* would prove more compelling to sub-sequent scholars.

The concept of assimilation reached its apogee in the 1950s and early 1960s, undergoing an elab-oration that, in some ways, proved its undoing. Sociologists and other scholars moved beyond Handlin's approaches to "Americanization," look-ing past the first two generations of newcomers to see patterns that had eluded him and the Chicago School. The patterns, identified by Marcus Lee Hansen and Ruby Jo Reeves Kennedy and ana-lyzed in greater detail by Will Herberg and Milton Gordon, suggested that ethnic consciousness, or a proxy, could reemerge after an assimilatory inter-lude and that assimilation might mute ethnicity without producing uniformity. In the short term, this work seemed to strengthen a view of Ameri-can society as tending toward Anglo-conformity. But the twists it built into that tendency ultimately weakened the Anglo-conformist argument. This became evident in the work of Nathan Glazer and Daniel Patrick Moynihan, work echoed in histori-cal writing by Rudolph Vecoli.

The call to move away from seeing assimilation as a one-way process was sounded by Hansen in his 1937 address, "The Problem of the Third Gen-eration Immigrant." He introduced what he called "the principle of third generation interest." While the children of immigrants attempted to dispense with foreign ways, the next generation harbored a different impulse, expressed in the phrase, "what the son wishes to forget the grandson wishes to re-member." Accepted as an American, the grandson, proud of his achievements, wondered about his hardy forefathers and began to delve into the his-tory of his ethnic group.[45] Hansen did not see this ethnic consciousness—or, in his words, a common interest in "the heritage of blood"—as enduring. America would prove a melting pot in the long run, since it was "the ultimate fate of any national group to be amalgamated into the composite American race." Nevertheless, he had contributed the suggestion that ethnicity, in a cultural sense might reappear as well as disappear.[46]

Within a decade, Kennedy sought to revise the melting pot idea itself. In a 1944 article, "Single or Triple Melting-Pot?" she argued that Ameri-can ethnic groups appeared to be fusing along religious lines, rather than into one homoge-neous mass. Kennedy studied marriage trends in New Haven between 1870 and 1940 and found that while the in-marriage rate among each of seven ethnic groups had fallen, those marrying "out" tended to pick spouses of their own reli-gion. Roman Catholics—Irish, Italians, and Poles —intermarried mostly among themselves, as did New Haven's Protestants, listed as British-Amer-icans, Germans, and Scandinavians. The city's Jews, too, married within their religion. Kennedy saw these trends as indicating that "assimilation through intermarriage is occurring along three vertical lines—Jewish, Catholic, and Protestant— and not . . . indiscriminately." Hence "future cleavages will be along religious lines rather than along nationality lines," suggesting a "'triple-melting-pot' theory of American assimilation."[47]

Will Herberg merged Kennedy's insights with Hansen's in his reflections on secularism in Amer-ica, published in 1956 as *Protestant-Catholic-Jew.* Herberg sought to explain how contemporary Americans could display increasing religiosity and still live in "a framework of reality and value re-mote from the religious belief, simultaneously professed." He argued that immigrants had always assimilated culturally to an "'Anglo-Saxon' proto-type" but had never been expected to change their religion. Immigration restriction in the 1920s set the stage for a gradual decline in ethnic-group consciousness and the third generation's rise for "the great bulk of the immigrant community." That generation, following Hansen's principle, sought a sense of ancestral identity and found a permissible version in "the old ethnic religion." Once religion became "the primary context of self-identification and social location," religious association itself changed, falling into Kennedy's "fundamental tripartite division." "Men were Catholics, Protestants, or Jews, categories based less on theological than on social distinctions."[48]

Although Herberg saw the religious community becoming "the over-all medium" for expressing ethnic concerns, he also held that each confessional melting pot was casting the same product, a "'new man' . . . along the same 'American' ideal type," that is, the Anglo-Saxon model. Influencing the three religions was the "'common faith' of American society," a "spiritual structure" of ideals and values that Herberg dubbed "the American Way of Life." This underlying faith, "the symbol by which Americans define themselves and establish their unity," took in beliefs in democracy, free enterprise, and a social equalitarianism entwined with high mobility. From the American Way's standpoint, Protestantism, Catholicism, and Judaism were three "expressions of an over-all American religion, standing for essentially the same 'moral ideals' and 'spiritual values.'" In that the three faiths all promoted the American Way,[49] it would seem that Herberg believed they were assimilating their congregants to the Anglo-American model.

Herberg tended to ignore questions of class, and while he noted that the black church "as a segregated division of American Protestantism constitutes an anomaly of considerable importance" in his argument, he failed to account for the anomaly.[50] Both matters were taken up by Milton Gordon in *Assimilation in American Life* (1964). This work laid out a model of American society that, for all its resemblance to Herberg's, was much more sophisticated. Gordon began by defining assimilation systematically. He imagined a hypothetical case of total assimilation, then broke the process down into seven steps, which furnished definitions of different kinds of assimilation. The

most important were cultural assimilation, involving a change of cultural patterns to those of the host society; structural assimilation, the "[l]arge-scale entrance into cliques, clubs, and institutions of [the] host society," on the level of primary interaction; and marital assimilation, or large-scale intermarriage. Structural assimilation was the key variant. The social interaction involved in it would lead inevitably to marital assimilation, which would bring all the other kinds of assimilation in tow.[51]

Cultural assimilation could take place without leading to structural assimilation, however, and this was what was happening in the United States. Gordon portrayed America as a national society holding a series of internally organized "subsocieties," each with a corresponding "subculture." Subsocieties based on ethnicity intersected with those based on social class to create "ethclass" subsocieties. The "core subsociety" was made up of white, middle-class Protestants, with their English-derived "core subculture." For the most part, the children of European immigrants had assimilated culturally to this group. Blacks were right behind, followed by Indians and Latin-American minorities. But Anglo-conformity had not happened structurally, except for early non-English immigrants. Racial, religious, and, to a lesser extent, ethnic groups had retained their own organizational networks, which tended to keep "primary group contacts" of their members "within the ethnic enclave." Lack of structural assimilation to Anglo-America stalled the remaining five kinds of assimilation.[52]

Structurally, then, American society consisted of "a number of 'pots,'" including Kennedy's three religious containers, which were "melting down the white nationality background communities" within them. Other pots held "racial groups which are not allowed to melt structurally" and "substantial remnants" of immigrants, along with some of their children. Given the success of cultural Anglo-conformity, what one saw in American society was "structural pluralism accompanied by an ever-decreasing degree of cultural pluralism."[53]

Assimilation in American Life remains one of the most carefully thought-out treatises on the subject. Of the selections reviewed so far, it gives the clearest picture of the society to which ethnic Americans were thought to assimilate, one structured in terms of subgroups. Indeed, the work capped a line of scholarship, stretching back to *Boston's Immigrants,* that strove to clarify the pluralist framework within which assimilatory processes operated. In this sense, it represented the peak of postwar writing on assimilation.[54] All the same, Gordon must have found the decade after the volume's publication unnerving. The rebellions of the 1960s in many ways represented a frontal assault on the white, middle-class Protestant cultural patterns he saw at assimilation's core. He might have caught a premonition of that upheaval in two works that appeared almost simultaneously with his: Nathan Glazer and Daniel Patrick Moynihan's *Beyond the Melting Pot* —published in 1963 just before Gordon's work— and Rudolph J. Vecoli's 1964 critique of Handlin and *The Uprooted.*

Beyond the Melting Pot was as much the end of one line of scholarship as the beginning of another. The book shared some basic themes with the work advanced by Kennedy, Herberg, and Gordon. Glazer and Moynihan concluded their study of New York City's ethnic groups with a portrait of a future in which religion and race determined "the major groups into which American society is evolving as the specifically national aspect of ethnicity declines." Those groups, not surprisingly, were Catholics, Jews, white Protestants, and blacks.[55]

Where the authors broke with Kennedy and Herberg, and clashed with Gordon, was in their insistence that the future would not arrive anytime soon. "Perhaps the meaning of ethnic labels will yet be erased in America," they declared, but as of 1963, "it has not yet worked out this way in New York." America not only created but "continually recreated" ethnic groups, even after the third generation and the loss of distinctive customs and language.[56] These groups—not simply Catholic New Yorkers, for example, but Irish and Italian and Puerto Rican New Yorkers—were sustained through mechanisms of common economic interest, family ties, fellow feeling, and ethnic organizational life. But the authors' most intriguing arguments concerned Gordon's "core subsociety": the "Anglo-Saxon center." First, they held, the "center" had acquired the status of an ethnic group, leaving little to assimilate to, at least in New York. Second, they questioned the ability of the "center" to assimilate more than "its ethnic cousins," such as the Dutch. Something about American society—

its "group-forming characteristics"—ensured that it "could not, or did not, assimilate the immigrant groups fully or in equal degree."[57]

In everything but its last few pages, *Beyond the Melting Pot* represented a full-blown attack, not only on the erosion of ethnicity but also on the idea of an Anglo-Saxon center that assimilated effectively. Yet, while the book dispensed with Herberg and Gordon's Anglo-conformist assumptions, Herberg had helped to pave the way for it, and Gordon offered it a degree of implicit support. As those authors and Kennedy elaborated their versions of assimilation, they offered progressively more fragmented pictures of American society. Kennedy split that society into three melting pots; Herberg, despite his depiction of Anglo-conformity, implied that a persistent ethnic consciousness underlay those pots; Gordon added yet more pots, limited Anglo-conformity to the cultural sphere, and implied that America was still a land of structural pluralism. All Glazer and Moynihan did, in a sense, was to take a vision of society that reached fullest expression in Gordon's work, insist it had not yet arrived, and imply that it might never do so.

Beyond the Melting Pot was followed, one year later, by its historiographical equivalent. Rudolph Vecoli's "*Contadini* in Chicago: A Critique of *The Uprooted*" attacked Handlin's classic in great part by arguing for the persistence of immigrants' Old Country ways. Examining southern Italians in their homeland, Vecoli found that Handlin's "idealized peasant village" did not exist in late nineteenth-century Italy and that the *contadini* in their hill towns were "pursuing family and self-interest" as economic individualists. These peasants customarily arrived in Chicago not as alienated newcomers but "as a group from a particular town," and they reconstructed those native towns in the city. Their aid societies were not American creations but transplanted versions of Italian institutions that did little to create Italian-American solidarity. And their Old World customs survived in festivals and the practice of magic. "The social character of the south Italian peasant did not undergo a sea change," Vecoli wrote, "and the very nature of their adjustments to American society was dictated by their 'Old World traits.'"[58]

Glazer, Moynihan, and Vecoli were aiming at different targets. The first two authors cast doubt on two decades' worth of theorizing about the submergence of ethnic groups in religious ones. Vecoli's parting shot was meant to criticize a reliance on Chicago concepts: Handlin had been misled by the rigidity "of a sociological theory."[59] But all three insurgents made the same overall point: their professions had underestimated the staying power of ethnicity, whether expressed in the re-creation of ethnic groups or the persistence of Old World cultures. Assimilation, they seemed to say, was an overrated concept. Historians would do them the favor of taking them seriously; over the next two decades, assimilation as a topic faded from view.

When Olivier Zunz surveyed writing on ethnicity in 1985, he was struck by the "remarkable" neglect of assimilation by "the current generation of social historians."[60] That neglect had much to do with the political and cultural upheaval of the 1960s. The decade's stresses undermined key assumptions behind assimilation theory as it had developed over the previous twenty years. The Vietnam War and the domestic turmoil it helped to spark discredited "the Anglo-American establishment" and belief in the virtue of a uniform American Way of Life. The flowering of black separatism hastened the rise of movements that emphasized group identities, such as feminism and gay liberation. As Vecoli noted in 1985, "Black Pride" as a movement "legitimated the affirmation" of such identities, including, ultimately, white ethnic ones; an "ethnic revival" emerged in the early 1970s.[61] This eruption of cultural pluralism made a mockery of arguments such as Gordon's that saw cultural pluralism in decline.

The rise of the "New Social History" in many ways echoed these developments; together, they drowned out assimilation as a topic. As Zunz suggested, the postwar tendency to see American history as more about consensus than conflict had encouraged the study of processes, such as assimilation, that facilitated social unity. The lack of consensus manifested in the 1960s helped to shatter the "consensus school," weakening the rationale for examining assimilation. Social history shifted focus from social unity to social justice, as scholars pursued mobility studies and history "from the bottom up." Mobility, of course, was often invoked as an assimilative mechanism, and historians did carry out much research on immi-

grants, addressing them as actors and examining ethnicity's nature.[62] But, with some exceptions,[63] this work avoided the kind of generalizing about the structure of American society that Handlin, Kennedy, Herberg, and Gordon had engaged in, including their explorations of relations between ethnic groups and homogenizing processes above the ethnic-group level.[64] What eventually emerged was a pluralistic view of an America "fragmented into an endless number of autonomous communities." At the same time, labor and urban historians whose studies of class required looking at ethnic groups treated ethnicity as a "secondary attribute."[65]

The New Social History had quantitative practitioners and those more culturally oriented. One could argue that cultural approaches, with their focus on an actor's state of mind, might prove more amenable than statistical ones to the study of certain kinds of assimilation. Statistical indexes of assimilation exist, to be sure. But cultural analysis may be better at dealing with assimilation defined in terms of the acceptance of immigrants or shared values. Yet even historians who looked at working-class and immigrant culture tended to ignore, deny, or minimize assimilation. Three works by Herbert Gutman, John Bodnar, and Paul Buhle exemplify this trend.

In the title essay of *Work, Culture, and Society in Industrializing America* (1976), Gutman argued that first-generation factory workers both before 1843 and after 1893 had brought similarly pre-modern work habits with them. Those habits caused manufacturers in the two periods similar headaches, although the workers bearing them were predominantly native-born in the first period and immigrants in the second and came from "quite different premodern cultures." This suggested that both sets of workers had undergone the same kind of transition to industrial life, which yielded "common modes of thought and patterns of behavior," including recurring "[c]haracteristic European forms of 'pre-modern' . . . protest." But each group took the journey at a different time; thus their experiences were disconnected. "It was not possible for the grandchildren of the Lowell mill girls to understand that their Massachusetts literary ancestors shared a great deal with their contemporaries, the peasant Slavs in the Pennsylvania steel mills and coal fields."[66] These later immigrants themselves hardly constituted a monolithic group, as Gutman suggested in noting that "Slavic and Italian immigrants carried with them to industrial America subcultures quite different from that of village Jews." Gutman also traced the persistence of artisan work habits into the late nineteenth century to immigrants who retained their culture long after arrival. These newcomers inhabited "ethnic subcultures that varied greatly among particular groups," where "tenacious traditions" flourished.[67]

The essay was striking for what it failed to discuss. Where Handlin might have interpreted the transition to industrial work habits as evidence of Americanization—and Gutman did make several references to that word—the question of "becoming American" hardly arose in "Work, Culture, and Society," for Gutman was concerned not with the journey to "Americanness" as such but with the transition to an industrial proletariat. Evidence of this lay in the fact that those who already were old-stock "Americans" made the same transition. The resulting working class, however, even its immigrant component, remained divided among "diverse ethnic working-class subcultures," as Gutman noted of the mid-to-late nineteenth century.[68] Because he wished to show that immigrants had preserved Old Country ways (if only to plague American factory managers), he had to stress group persistence. Any assimilation past the first generation was not addressed, since his dynamic focused precisely on the series of first generations that had entered the factories.

Somewhat similarly, John Bodnar interpreted the immigrant experience in the century after 1830 as a confrontation with the "new economic order" of capitalism. His synthesis of immigration history, The Transplanted, though published in 1985, brought together the myriad case studies of the previous twenty years. The book aimed to refute Handlin's portrayal of immigrants as uprooted individuals and supersede Vecoli's view of newcomers organizing their lives around imported traditions.[69] To Bodnar, what gave their experience coherence was their struggle to sustain the institution of the family-household. Their homeland livelihoods threatened by manufactured goods and commercial agriculture, immigrants came to the United States, often temporarily, to salvage their economic prospects. The family, the Old World center of economic and social life, aided their adjustment to urban capitalism in the New. Members found jobs through kinship ties

and pooled resources in order to survive. They also forged a "culture of everyday life" that drew on folk thought and other "ethnic traditions," as well as such "present realities" as work, to explain their place in a world of family, job, and neighborhood. Most working-class immigrants inhabited this culture, while some better-off newcomers moved toward a new one of "acquisitiveness and personal gain" that Bodnar identified as middle class.[70]

On its face, Bodnar's work could be seen as reflecting a concern with a kind of assimilation, that is, immigrants' adjustment to capitalism in "capitalist America."[71] Yet a closer reading shows The Transplanted tends to minimize, deny, or neglect assimilation and Americanization—whether one accepts the book's, or this article's, definitions of those terms.

When Bodnar used the terms "Americanization" and "assimilation," he appeared to distinguish them from the larger process of immigrant adjustment and to deny that they had happened for the majority of immigrants and their children. The book tended to portray "Americanization" as a project middle-class immigrants and educational reformers directed at other, largely working-class, ethnics. When this project took the form of extended schooling, immigrant workers were "invariably resistant."[72] Similarly, Bodnar seemed to equate assimilation with a journey away from the culture of everyday life and into an acquisitive middle class that represented mainstream America. He argued that most immigrants and their children did not make that transition. Thus he faulted a version of "assimilation" that depicted ethnic communities as way stations where newcomers "acquired the necessary values and behavioral patterns to move inevitably into middle-class American society." He doubted that the mass of immigrants had taken this path toward "the lofty plateaus of the American mainstream," since the majority, and most of their children, remained at the lower end of the work force.[73] Bodnar similarly discounted "the possibility of rapid and widespread cultural attachment of newcomers to the thought and institutions of capitalist America." Most immigrants, who "ultimately would acquiesce" in urban capitalism, did so "on terms somewhat of their own making," including the culture of everyday life. This separated them from those who forsook that culture for "the single-minded culture of power, wealth, and personal gain" associated with the middle class—the culture, presumably, of "capitalist America."[74]

This conflation of mainstream and middle class points to the book's larger conflation of capitalism with "America." Bodnar titled one chapter "America on Immigrant Terms" but ended it stating that immigrants came to terms with "the new order of urban capitalism." Since America had no monopoly on urban capitalism, equating the two left nothing distinctly "American" toward which to assimilate. Americanization in this larger sense could not be his theme, nor was it in the minimal sense of ethnic peoples identifying themselves as "American." The potential to Americanize existed, since Bodnar hinted at one point that the "affirmation of a desire to become an American" was part of the culture of everyday life. Immigrants forging that culture could pick and choose among ideologies, and one of the choices, presumably, might be American nationalism. But Bodnar essentially left this point unaddressed. He noted in an aside that immigrants "were always very sensitive" to charges of being unpatriotic, but he nowhere explored the implications of that remark.[75]

The Transplanted also neglected assimilation, that is, homogenization above the ethnic-group level, for all but the small set of middle-class strivers who pursued mainstream capitalist ways.[76] Bodnar's effort to reach beyond a group-by-group analysis led him to focus below the ethnic-group level, to an everyday immigrant experience rooted in the family-household and the networks of kin and friends that tied it to the worlds of work, neighborhood, and worship. From this vantage point, Bodnar could survey the class tensions that divided ethnic communities.[77] Yet the narrative implied that ethnic-group boundaries mattered greatly. Immigrants lived in heavily working-class "urban-ethnic enclaves"; they tended not to marry out of the ethnic group, even in the second generation; they clustered by ethnicity in particular lines of work; ethnic as well as skill-level differences helped to frustrate labor solidarity; immigrant workers "quickly adopted" middle-class celebrations of ethnicity; and the culture of everyday life was informed by traditions that varied from group to group.[78]

In describing such ethnic divisions while focusing below the ethnic-group level, Bodnar neglected to address how these groups interacted

—with some exceptions, as in his brief discussion of Catholic education and his observation that the quest for household stability could help 1930s unions "temporarily transcend ethnic and skill differentials."[79] Nor did he discuss how ethnic groups related, as a set of groups, to mainstream America. This selectivity gave the impression of an America populated by a collection of ethnic groups that confronted capitalism *separately,* each within its own boundaries. That left little room for explorations of assimilation between ethnic groups, while the "culture of everyday life" marked a fairly deep divide between Americans of longer standing and the immigrant working class. Bodnar described how immigrants adjusted to capitalism, but his approach discouraged looking at how they might have assimilated to each other or to other workers, or come to see themselves as "American."

The potential liabilities of such a stance could be seen in Paul Buhle's essay, "Jews and American Communism: The Cultural Question" (1980). Buhle argued that the American Left, particularly the interwar Communist Party, paid heavily for rejecting ethnic pluralism. Communists steeped in Yiddish culture had been eager to use this resource and had met with a promising reception from Yiddish-speaking workers. But the party discouraged ethnic organizing, which crippled the cultural work that was its "main attraction . . . to working class neighborhoods." Buhle undercut his argument by noting in an aside that "the assimilation process continued in an unrevolutionary America."[80] If workers were moving closer to the "American" mainstream, how could their attraction to a Yiddish-infused Communism be expected to persist? Did such assimilation mean the Yiddish activists had been wrong? To answer such questions required a closer look at "assimilation."

Gutman, Bodnar, and Buhle rightly stressed the degree to which the America they studied had held a host of ethnic enclaves that did not immediately dissolve into a larger American society. But in refusing to take "assimilation" or "Americanization" seriously, they begged important questions. What was the fate of these enclaves past the first two generations? What was the nature of the wider society in which the enclaves nestled, and what held it together? Was this America a pluralism solely of fragmentation, or could one speak of kinds of homogenization over time, whether labeled assimilation, the rise of class consciousness, or the growth of racial identity? In the 1980s, historians began to see the shortcomings in the dismissal of assimilation and initiated a cautious reappraisal of the concept.

Historians once again took up the topic of assimilation, but they did not simply resurrect the concept as postwar scholars understood it. Too many assumptions about American society had changed to permit such a straightforward return; above all, few believed any longer in the unchanging cultural hegemony of an Anglo-Saxon "core." Rather, what emerged, fitfully in the early 1980s but with gathering strength by the decade's end, was a renewed interest in certain questions basic to the postwar assimilation studies. Historians who focused on immigrant groups began to ask how ethnic enclaves fit together and hence returned to a concern with the larger American social order and interaction among ethnic groups that would have been familiar to Gordon or Herberg. Labor historians examining class consciousness among ethnic workers started to look into homogenization along class lines, much as Kennedy had studied the homogenization of ethnic groups along the lines of religion. A growing interest in the question of racial identity among Americans of European origin led some scholars to explore Americanization as a process of claiming "whiteness," which suggested homogenization along color lines within a racially structured pluralism. Each foray marked a return to an interest both in assimilatory processes and in how European immigrants and their descendants came to see themselves as "Americans."

For a few historians, of course, those topics had never disappeared, even in the 1970s. John Higham and Philip Gleason, in particular, responded to that decade's ethnic politics by asking what held American society together.[81] Like Herberg, both stressed the unifying role of a common ideology, one that defined what it meant to be "American." In addressing American identity, Higham and Gleason touched on Americanization; but they endowed that identity with notes of change and contestation largely absent from Herberg's "American Way."

They also followed on a bevy of scholars in various fields—including postwar "consensus historians"[82]—who had described American identity in terms of adherence to a set of universalistic principles. As Gleason argued, World War II, and the ideological challenge of the Third Reich, fueled a "reaffirmation of American ideology as the basis of national identity."[83] This revival, which drew strength as well from the Cold War,[84] lasted into the 1960s.[85] Herberg's "American Way of Life" was one of several phrases invoked during these years to describe an American ideology encompassing beliefs in democracy, liberty, and equality, from Gunnar Myrdal's "American Creed" to Horace Kallen's "American Idea."[86]

Gleason's own definition of American identity drew on Hans Kohn's evocation in 1957 of the United States as "the embodiment of an idea"; still valid was Kohn's, "central insight that American nationality rests on a structure of ideas about freedom, equality, and self-government," an ideology both universalistic and practical. This endorsement of Kohn, a student of American nationalism, was telling, for it pointed up an equation of American identity with American nationality—terms that Gleason used interchangeably.[87] To Americanize, in the sense of feeling oneself to have become "American," could be seen as subscribing to a form of American nationalism.

In 1980, Gleason argued for the continued existence of an American identity—a "sense of peoplehood shared by all Americans"—based on commitment to such "universalist ideals." He followed that identity's career from the eighteenth century, tracing the changing salience of ethnicity in the debate over "what it means to be an American."[88] Despite its partly British roots, and the British-derived majority's "latent predisposition toward an ethnically defined concept of nationality," American identity was seen in the early republic "in abstract ideological terms much more than in ethnic terms" (although it did not extend to Indians or African Americans). This made becoming "American" an act of self-will, open to all of European background and accomplished by adopting the ideology. Cultural differences rooted in ethnicity became more salient with nineteenth-century immigration, as first anti-Catholic nativism and then a racialist "Anglo-Saxon version of American nationality" emerged.[89] Concern with ethnicity ebbed with immigration restriction in the 1920s. While the resurgent American ideology discussed above incorporated tolerance for ethnic diversity as a corollary value, it did not allow for a diversity "that divided Americans against each other in any serious way."[90] The mid-1960s saw a shift back toward a greater stress on ethnic difference, along with a weakening of the national ideology through a "passionate critique" growing out of the racial crisis and the Vietnam War—a critique Gleason found overdrawn.[91]

Higham, writing in 1981, examined how, in the late nineteenth century, white Americans began to see European assimilation as a "problem." He explored contradictions between the theory and reality of assimilation, particularly the capacity of white Americans for holding an abstract faith in the assimilation of remote peoples while feeling repulsion toward outsiders close at hand. This contrast stemmed in part from a combination of localism and the national ideology, which viewed the United States as "an open and free society resting on universal, self-evident principles . . . dedicated to the separation of church and state and the elimination of all barriers to mobility and opportunity, a society of individuals rather than groups." The lack of a centralized state hindered "Anglo-Americans" from defining an exclusive identity. Decentralization also allowed ethnic groups, to some extent, to keep their distance. An ideological definition of America offered a "single canopy of beliefs" that made comprehensible this "otherwise loose-knit society."[92] The universalist ideology itself was, however, "profoundly split," in that America's white, Protestant majority entertained it while also viewing the country as its possession. When localism began to wane at the century's end, Americans became less willing to live with this division. The resulting Progressive impulse toward consistency eventually erupted in a nativism and anti-black racism that sought to ensure white Protestant hegemony. Yet Progressivism's "humanistic side" also asserted itself. The conflict between these two forces widened the rift in American ideology, mobilizing minorities and sparking pluralist thought.[93]

Both Higham and Gleason saw a return to assimilation, with Higham detecting among historians and sociologists by the late 1970s "a renewed appreciation of assimilation" as a powerful and desirable force.[94] Indeed, Americanization, understood as assimilation achieved through the adoption of an "American" identity, was a prominent theme for a number of the scholars discussed below. Yet they, even more than Gleason and Higham, tended to treat that identity as contested terrain, fought over by ethnics with their own definitions of Americanism.

Immigration historians revisited assimilation and Americanization by way of a renewed interest in the nature of American pluralism, that is, in the social order as an order of ethnic groups. Their pluralism amounted to more than a collection of tenacious ethnic communities. It had room for relations *between* ethnicities, for ethnicities dwindling into the world of native white Protestants, for immigrants who saw no contradiction in claiming both homeland and "American" identities, for ethnics who shaped the changing meaning of "American," and, in some cases, for a dash of American ideological glue to hold the order together.

Paradoxically enough, this interest in social orders stemmed in part from these historians' encounter with theories of deconstruction. Scholars who had spent the previous decade examining ethnicity realized it was a category like any other and deserved to be dissected. Werner Sollors asked whether ethnicity itself was an invention. In the ensuing debate, historians such as Kathleen Neils Conzen and David Gerber staked out a position that saw ethnic group formation as a continuing process within a larger pluralism.

In the title essay of the collection *The Invention of Ethnicity* (1989), Sollors suggested that "ethnicity" could be viewed as one among many "widely shared, though intensely debated, collective fictions that are continually reinvented." Noting how postmodern theorists saw language itself as constituting the terms on which reality is socially constructed, he argued that historians should examine "the ability of ethnicity to present (or invent) itself as a 'natural' and timeless category." Sollors conceived of ethnicity as emerging from the workings of a larger system within which what was "ethnic" was defined by that which was "not-ethnic."[95]

Sollors' essay prompted a response from five historians. Conzen, Gerber, Vecoli, Ewa Morawska, and George E. Pozzetta wrote in 1992 that they agreed with Sollors in viewing ethnicity as "a cultural construction accomplished over historical time." But they did not see it as a collective fiction; ethnic consciousness was "grounded in real life context and social experience." Ethnicity was "a process of construction or invention which incorporates, adapts, and amplifies preexisting communal solidarities, cultural attributes, and historical memories." This process involved negotiation between a given immigrant group, other such groups, and "the dominant ethnoculture, in this case, the Anglo American." Thinking about ethnicity in this way had the virtue of forcing a focus on the relationships among these groups.[96]

The authors argued that antebellum Americans invented the category of "nationality"—that is, ethnicity—as a part of their own "self-conscious project of inventing a national identity." The category of ethnicity gave native-born Americans a way to define themselves as "Americans." They also used it to define newcomers as immigrant ethnic groups, but those newcomers already had been constructing their own sense of peoplehood in Ireland and Germany. Out of these processes came "a new pluralistic social order" that involved all Americans in "a continual renegotiation of identities."[97]

American pluralism so defined could encompass a number of processes aside from ethnic persistence. Ethnicities could disappear. The Scottish and English of antebellum Buffalo, for example, who lived among native white Protestants, sponsored saint's day banquets—a new ethnic tradition emerging "in the life of weak groups, which were faltering even as they were being invented." Likewise, ethnics could acquire a double identity that included an "American" self-definition. East Europeans who had identified with homeland localities developed, in turn-of-the-century America, "a translocal, national identity as Poles, Ukrainians," and so forth. The symbols of an Old Country "fatherland" aided this process. By the 1930s, however, "America" had emerged as a parallel ideological fatherland. Ethnic celebrations "rallied under two sets of national emblems: Old Country and American," symbolizing, as with one slogan that "proclaimed *Polacy-Amerykanie* (Poles-American), the immigrants' double identity."[98]

The American identities so acquired were neither unchanging nor uninfluenced by immigrants. "[M]uch of ethnic cultures was incorporated into changing definitions of what was American and what it meant to be an American. Without corresponding to either the Anglo-conformity or Melting Pot models of assimilation, the interaction of mainstream ethnoculture and sidestream ethnoculture wrought major changes in both." The authors believed that this element of change overcame the mainstream's "Anglo-Saxon" aspects. "Rather than positing a hegemonic Anglo-American core culture," their conception held "the notion that what is distinctively American has been itself a product of this synergistic encounter of multiple peoples and cultures."[99]

This view of American society was reflected in other work by Gerber and Conzen, with Gerber stressing the development of ethnic groups within a pluralist order and Conzen focusing on the syncretic aspects of ethnic interaction. Gerber's study of antebellum Buffalo, *The Making of an American Pluralism* (1989), viewed the American city as "a hothouse environment" for the creation of a kind of social system that absorbed groups "pluralistically—as groups." He saw these groups, including native-born Americans as well as Germans and the Irish, as in the process of formation. Electoral politics both integrated ethnic groups into the political system and encouraged their development. The resulting pluralist order was enormously stable, containing conflict generated by immigration and capitalist development through "appeals to common interests in opportunity" and coalition politics that "brought together diverse and competing groups." Gerber acknowledged Handlin as a model, and, much like the Handlin of *Boston's Immigrants,* he stepped back to see "society whole" and found a symbiotic order. Within Gerber's pluralism, one could also make out a hint of Americanization—in the "rhetoric of opportunity" that helped to seal an inter-ethnic Republican coalition before the Civil War.[100]

Conzen, writing of late nineteenth-century Stearns County, Minnesota, found indications of what she termed "pluralisms of place." The county's German majority had neither "assimilated into Yankee society" nor kept itself "as an ethnic world apart." Rather, it had Germanized the local mainstream. The county's "local culture of thrift and non-ostentation, for example,. . . [was] initially molded in a German ethnic matrix, but quickly overflowed its bounds to define the county's values." Conzen called this process "the localization of an immigrant culture." By following "the immigrant story into the second generation and beyond," historians might find a pluralism that included many ethnically diverse yet locally dominant cultures. Further, those local cultures might also be found to have an influence on the larger public culture of America and thus indicate "the immigrant role in the shaping of values central to the nation itself."[101] Here, Conzen addressed a form of ethnic interaction that, on the local level, implied a kind of assimilation—one of Yankees to ethnic ways—and, on the national level, suggested both the existence of "American" values and their susceptibility to immigrant influence.

Perhaps the most ambitious pluralist model, and the one most obviously wedded to the concept of a unifying American ideology, came from political scientist Lawrence Fuchs. His book *The American Kaleidoscope* (1990) fused Americanization with ethnicization. Fuchs argued that European immigrants long had undergone "ethnic-Americanization," whereby ancestral loyalties were adapted to American circumstances, "even as immigrants and their children embrace[d] American political ideals" and institutions. A "voluntary pluralism" allowed individuals to "choose to be ethnic" and simultaneously claim an American identity by subscribing to "a unifying civic culture" based on a founding myth keyed to ideals of self-government, political equality, toleration of "private" matters, and economic opportunity. Before the 1960s, Americans of European origin had denied entry to voluntary pluralism to those of Indian, African, Asian, and Mexican ancestry by maintaining other, coercive pluralisms of a tribal, caste, and "sojourner" nature.[102] But with the recent dismantlement or erosion of such systems, these groups also began to "ethnic-Americanize." Increasingly, they rewarded the civic culture with loyalty, while that culture added ethnic diversity to its values. Fuchs discussed ethnic conflict and warned that, without efforts to combat poverty, the poorest Americans of color would remain "substantially outside of the civic culture." Overall, however, his portrait of contemporary, pluralistic America seemed remarkably sanguine.[103]

The writings of Conzen, Gerber, and Fuchs tended to work against conceptions of Anglo-conformity and stress those of pluralism—but not the disconnected variety of the New Social History.[104] These authors sketched variations on a group-based American social system, returning to Gordon's systematizing spirit, though with different results. And their pluralisms, like his, had room for processes of homogenization above the ethnic-group level.

In truth, the distance between discussing pluralistic social orders and explicitly reappraising the concept of assimilation was not all that great,

as Morawska demonstrated in a 1994 article, "In Defense of the Assimilation Model." She argued that elements of the "classical" model, defined as a Gordon-like series of stages running from acculturation to social integration to identification, could be used to describe the experience of particular ethnics at particular times and places. Morawska pointed to examples of integration into "the dominant group, the Anglo-Protestant middle class"; of the near disappearance of collective ethnic identity among Jews in small towns; and of the disappearance of individuals' ethnic identity. This approach was compatible with Conzen's pluralism, which allowed for different processes of immigrant adjustment—"even complete assimilation"—in different places. Morawska proposed renovating assimilation theory, not as "a universally applicable proposition" but as a historical one, as "one of a number of possible explanatory frameworks in which the immigrants' adaptation to the host (American) society can be accounted for."[105]

Labor historians in the 1980s were less interested in charting a profusion of ethnicities than in explaining class formation and consciousness. The twentieth century labor movement itself posed an obvious problem. During World War I, unions enjoyed short-term success organizing among workers from diverse ethnic backgrounds. In the 1930s, the industrial union movement enlisted massive numbers of immigrants and their children. How had people so ethnically divided come to a collective sense of themselves as workers? To ask this question, as James R. Barrett, Lizabeth Cohen, and Gary Gerstle did, was to confront working-class formation as a kind of inter-ethnic assimilation.[106] For Barrett and Gerstle, that process also involved Americanization—the acquisition by ethnic workers of an identity they saw as "American."

The road to these studies was prepared in part by Roy Rosenzweig and Olivier Zunz. Both discerned a shift from a late nineteenth-century urban landscape defined by ethnic enclaves to an early twentieth-century one organized to a greater degree by class. Between 1880 and 1900, Zunz argued in *The Changing Face of Inequality* (1982), Detroit was made up "largely of cross-class ethnic communities," with larger groups, such as the Germans, dominating particular neighborhoods. The bonds between an ethnic group's working and middle-class members in a given neighborhood were strengthened, and working-class solidarity thwarted, by the experience of social mobility within the ethnic community.[107] By 1920, however, as native white control over large-scale industry translated into control over the city's opportunity structure, such cross-class communities yielded to neighborhoods dominated by working-class members of a particular ethnic group. Newer immigrants, such as Poles, gathered in ethnic mill towns; older ones, such as the Irish, tended to live among native whites of the same social level.[108]

If Zunz saw working-class communities still separated by ethnicity in the 1920s, Rosenzweig found Worcester workers drawing away from their enclaves and closer to each other and the American "mainstream." This was evident in their changing patterns of leisure between 1870 and 1920, he argued in *Eight Hours for What We Will* (1983). Ethnic July 4th celebrations began to encounter competition from amusement parks, where the mix of patrons aided "the creation of a multiethnic working-class culture." The movie theaters of the 1920s challenged "the intense localism of the saloon," providing an arena for ethnic groups to mingle. Working-class viewers became "less suspicious of other workers" from different backgrounds and "attracted by the material promise of American life" on the screen. Such cultural shifts had deeper causes. But the friendships made, expectations raised, and "American" self-perceptions encouraged at the movies may have eased the way to union activism in the 1930s and 1940s.[109] Rosenzweig's "working-class culture" and his concluding discussion of workers' "new perception of themselves as 'Americans'" foreshadowed the work of Barrett, Cohen, and Gerstle.

While these accounts tended to stress the impact of outside forces on ethnic communities,[110] more recent studies have paid greater attention to worker agency, as in Barrett's "Americanization from the Bottom Up" (1992). Working-class ethnics, he argued, had done much to Americanize each other. Barrett sought to understand "how working-class formation took place in the midst of great ethnic, cultural, and racial diversity and change" between 1880 and 1930. In essence, he defined Americanization as class formation. Americanization "from the bottom up" was "the gradual acculturation of immigrants and their socialization in working-class environments and contexts." This process, "of necessity interethnic," could take the

form of labor unions bringing immigrant workers together around common grievances. Organizers also used a rhetoric of "Americanism" that stressed civil liberties and tried to appropriate democratic vocabulary and symbols from wartime propaganda. While reminiscent of Gleason's American ideology, this Americanism was, nonetheless, "a contested ideal." The union version championing free speech and collective demands for rights likely differed from the employer variant. From such union campaigns, from fellow workers, and their own heritage, immigrants drew the elements for the multiple identities they fashioned.[111]

"Assimilation" as a term did not figure prominently in Cohen's 1990 study of industrial unionism in interwar Chicago, *Making a New Deal*. If defined as the creation of a trans-ethnic common ground, however, that process could hardly have received a more intriguing treatment. The book described how workers badly divided along racial and ethnic lines in the 1920s forged a common working-class culture in the 1930s. Their lives in the 1920s had been circumscribed by ethnicity and marked by political apathy and a reliance on ethnic communities and employers for welfare services. The 1930s, in contrast, saw workers supporting a Democratic administration, successfully organizing unions, looking to both government and unions for a social safety net, and holding a set of national affiliations, from radio fan to CIO unionist. Cohen ascribed this shift in part to the Depression, which ended most employers' welfare capitalist schemes and weakened ethnic institutions, forcing workers to look elsewhere for aid. They succeeded in uniting in large part because the rise of mass culture gave them "more in common culturally from which to forge alliances." The CIO also sought to create a union-centered "culture of unity" that would transcend racial, ethnic, and neighborhood lines. Workers were becoming "more like each other," and thus "more like other Americans," but the upshot was more "an integrated working-class culture than a classless American one." Ethnic identity did not vanish in this transition; rather, people recombined their multiple identities, and their "self-images as ethnic and working class became more compatible."[112]

Gerstle's book *Working-Class Americanism* (1989) similarly described how workers from different ethnic groups managed in the 1930s to organize a union and "fashion a class identity for themselves." Americanization campaigns and economic troubles in 1920s Woonsocket, Rhode Island, opened up the "insular ethnic worlds" of the city's French Canadians and Franco-Belgians, setting the conditions for that identity. But a key factor in its creation was their elaboration of a "language of Americanism" that used concepts and symbols from democratic ideals to American heroes to articulate labor's demands. This language fostered an "American identity" among ethnic workers—though one with different meanings for different groups—and "worked remarkably well in giving ideological and linguistic unity" to a divided working class. Its very malleability, however, meant control of it was tenuous. Ultimately, the state's "efforts to reappropriate Americanism in the 1940s . . . undermined working-class efforts to make capital-labor relations the true test of the nation's democratic character."[113]

Gerstle came the closest of all the labor historians to describing something like an American "core" culture or ideology, although he did not identify it as such. This core potentially lies in the language of Americanism itself, particularly its "democratic," "nationalist," and "traditionalist" dimensions.[114] One wonders what effect these dimensions may have had on workers' Americanism. To the extent that Americanism stemmed from "Americanization" campaigns, the reader might see in it traces of a kind of "old stock" cultural hegemony.[115] The language's hegemonic aspect seems most apparent in the fact that workers ultimately lost control of it to the state.

In tracing the rise of trans-ethnic class consciousness in twentieth-century America, the labor historians discussed here evinced a concern with processes of homogenization that harkened back to the assimilation studies of the 1940s and 1950s. One could argue that they revived the postwar conviction that ethnic groups were assimilating along certain lines, but they made those lines ones of class rather than confession. A portrayal of class homogenization as Americanization, however, reminds us of how exclusive a sense of "becoming American" could be, for that homogenization tended to stop at the color line.

The question of whether Americanization meant becoming part of a *white* working class points to another body of work bearing on assimilation: the burgeoning literature on the construction of "whiteness." The work of David Roediger,

Arnold Hirsch, and, more recently, Gerstle raised the issue of whether European immigrants and their children became American by being redefined as "white." The question admits of two readings. First, did European ethnic workers, in acquiring "American" identities, become specifically *white* Americans, "joining a relatively homogeneous "white" population rather than becoming Americans "in general"? Second, to what extent, in that population's eyes, has being American required being "white"?

The first reading runs against understandings of pluralism that stress the continual reconfiguration of separate European ethnicities. Some recent sociological research, however, finds a decline in ethnic differences among Americans of European origin. Richard Alba's study *Ethnic Identity* (1990) saw a growing "social integration among persons with European ancestry," evidenced especially by a rise in intermarriage among non-Hispanic whites across both ethnic and religious lines, a trend dating at least to the late 1940s. The persistence of ethnic labels among whites suggested the emergence of a "European-American" ethnic group alongside an "old-stock" "unhyphenated American identity." Here, identifying oneself as "Italian," for instance, meant claiming membership in the European-American group and a common past seen in terms of immigration, mobility, and sacrifice. The book suggested that as differences among European Americans faded, those between them, African Americans, and the largest Hispanic groups stood out even more.[116] One might see in this a trend toward a racially defined pluralism, with separate melting pots for European Americans and African Americans.

Alba's argument was not far from that of scholars who saw European ethnics claiming a specifically white identity. This might involve immigrants drawing together on the common ground of whiteness—in a European-American pot, perhaps—or asserting white identity in the belief that only whites counted as American.[117] As both formulations described a kind of transethnic, racial homogenization, work on "white ethnicity" necessarily addressed assimilation.

That work, by scholars such as Roediger, Hirsch, and Gerstle, has begun to sketch a chronology of how particular European immigrant groups claimed whiteness. Roediger's book *The Wages of Whiteness* (1991) tackled the subject in regard to Irish immigrants, noting that before the Civil War, "it was by no means clear that the Irish were white." They claimed that status in part as a basis for equal citizenship with native-born Americans and a weapon in the struggle against blacks *and* native whites for jobs. Roediger more recently noted that immigrants "often were moved to equate whiteness with Americanism in order to turn arguments over immigration from the question of who was foreign to the question of who was white." But he also saw Irish-American whiteness in psychological terms, as a way for a population subjected to a new work discipline to deal with its anxieties and longings by projecting them onto blacks.[118]

The "New Immigrants" of the late nineteenth and early twentieth centuries appear to have recapitulated this progression from "not-yet-white ethnic" to white.[119] Higham long ago described the turn-of-the-century rise of a racialized nativism aimed at Jews, Italians, and Slavs. Nationwide, by 1910, workers of northwest European origin "called themselves 'white men' to distinguish themselves from the southern Europeans whom they worked beside."[120] How rapidly New Immigrants came to claim whiteness is not yet clear.[121] But Gerstle and Hirsch pointed to the 1940s as the crucial moment. World War II, which sparked a revival of American ideology, likewise, Gerstle argued, brought to popular consciousness a version of "cultural pluralism" that decreed "the absolute equality of all people regardless of their racial or cultural character." This ideology became a mainstay of the government's mobilization effort. For European ethnic workers, this semi-official celebration of diversity marked "the historic moment when they felt fully accepted as Americans." Yet, Gerstle suggested, their "embrace of America may well have intensified their prejudice against blacks, for many conceived of Americanization in racial terms: becoming American meant becoming white." And white status did not elevate unless it could be compared to a denigrated blackness. Hence European ethnic workers who saw discrimination against them lose force during the war frequently wished to reinforce the boundary between white and black. They did so partly through hate strikes and race riots aimed at barring African Americans from their neighborhoods. Hirsch, in his 1983 study of race and housing in Chicago, *Making the Second Ghetto,* argued that such attacks

by mixed mobs of Irish, East European, and southern European ethnics were made in part in defense of their new-found whiteness. For these rioters, who championed "white" rather than "ethnic" rights, whiteness represented "their badge of rank and status in their adopted home."[122]

In the past fifteen years, historians have revisited assimilation without fully resurrecting it, and with good reason. Before the mid-1960s, the concept often presupposed a rather static, Anglo-Saxon "core" American society to which one was presumed to assimilate. The individualization models offered by Chicago sociologists potentially shared this feature with the Anglo-conformity models of Herberg and Gordon. The collapse of the core in the 1960s allowed later historians room to develop more inclusive conceptions of American society. Those conceptions are reflected in three distinct ways of understanding the assimilation of European ethnics. Labor historians see a twentieth-century homogenization along class lines that may represent the emergence of an American working class and, to some scholars, a corresponding "American" identity. Historians of racial identity discern a merging of immigrants and their descendants into a common whiteness, perhaps also spelling their emergence as "Americans." But these accounts of assimilation do not necessarily dovetail, and they present a problem for historians of immigrant groups who see ethnicities constantly recreated within a larger American pluralism. How can one reconcile these visions? Should we take a leaf from the immigration scholars and see the 1930s and 1940s as an example of the variability of ethnic identity, with labor struggles submerging an attribute that came roaring back in the 1960s and 1970s? Or have Gerber and Conzen, in focusing on the nineteenth century, missed two profound, twentieth-century transformations? If so, how do these transformations—working-class homogenization and the rise of the "white ethnic"—fit with one another? My own provisional answer would be to see the emergence in the twentieth century of a pluralism following racial lines, one in which class formation took place in separate melting pots. More important, however, I would urge these three sets of historians to pursue an answer together, taking the next step in reappraising assimilation by talking with one another.

ENDNOTES

1. David A. Gerber, *The Making of an American Pluralism: Buffalo, New York, 1825–60* (Urbana, Ill., 1989), xii.

2. This is the definition given by Harold J. Abramson, "Assimilation and Pluralism," in *Harvard Encyclopedia of American Ethnic Groups,* Stephan Thernstrom, ed. (Cambridge, Mass., 1980), 150.

3. I draw here on Milton M. Gordon's typology of varieties and degrees of assimilation; Gordon, *Assimilation in American Life: The Role of Race, Religion, and National Origins* (New York, 1964), 69–71.

4. A recent analysis of ethnicity in immigration history discussed below briefly reviews the dominant conceptions, including that of ethnicity as "primordial," growing out of the work of Clifford Geertz and Harold Isaacs, and that of ethnic groups as interest groups, proposed by Daniel Patrick Moynihan and Nathan Glazer and also discussed below; Kathleen Neils Conzen, David A. Gerber, Ewa Morawska, George E. Pozzetta, and Rudolph J. Vecoli, "The Invention of Ethnicity: A Perspective from the U.S.A.," *Journal of American Ethnic History,* 12 (Fall 1992): 4. The definition of an ethnic group as "a group with a shared feeling of peoplehood," keyed to a perception of a common ancestry and future, is from Gordon, *Assimilation,* 24, 29.

5. For a recent discussion of ethnicization, see Conzen, *et al.,* "Invention of Ethnicity," 9, 11–16, *passim.* John Higham sees this process of ethnic group formation as a "very successful, intermediate level of assimilation"; Higham, "Integrating America: The Problem of Assimilation in the Nineteenth Century," *Journal of American Ethnic History,* I (Fall 1981): 9.

6. For example, the classical conceptualization of assimilation, as Ewa Morawska describes it, foresaw "the progressive weakening and ultimate disappearance of the primordial traits and bonds of ethnicity as succeeding generations adopt the general society's unitary system of cultural values and become absorbed into economic, social, and political networks that are blind to ethnicity"; Morawska, "The Sociology and Historiography of Immigration," in *Immigration Reconsidered: History, Sociology, and Politics,* Virginia Yans-McLaughlin, ed. (New York, 1990), 189.

7. Some scholars would see such homogenizations as potentially creating new "ethnicities" in America, as with the "ethnogenesis" of the Appalachians. Such conceptions appear to rely on broader definitions of ethnicity that place less stress on a shared sense of far-reaching ancestry and more on a sense of common, and perhaps recent, historical origin; see Abramson, "Assimilation and Pluralism," 150–51. Potentially, this type of "ethnicity" could be taken to include most white ethnics understood as European Americans, as Richard D. Alba suggests, or even all Americans, sharing a national identity that, as Philip Gleason argues, "is *not* different in kind" from immigrant ethnic identity; Alba, *Ethnic*

Identity: The Transformation of White America (New Haven, Conn., 1990); Gleason, "American Identity and Americanization," in Thernstrom, *Harvard Encyclopedia of American Ethnic Groups,* 55 (italics in original). However, when discussing immigrant assimilation, I find such expansive conceptions of ethnicity less analytically useful than a more restrictive one of "ethnic group" as referring to groups with a shared sense of peoplehood tied, in some fashion, to specific Old World ancestries.

8. That is to say, for any given conception of assimilation, one needs to know the setting: whether society is seen as a constellation of separate ethnic groups, or of groups clustered around a dominant "core" group, or of groups "melting" into larger categories of, for instance, class or race, or even a larger whole. The setting allows one to see the direction and degree of homogenization beyond the ethnic group level—to what, and how far, an individual or a group is assimilating.

9. This definition of "Americanization" may include, but is much broader than, the use of the term to refer to coercive programs of forced assimilation aimed by nativists and, eventually, manufacturers at immigrants from the turn of the century through the early 1920s; on the latter use, see Gleason, "American Identity and Americanization," 39–41. Americanization as an acquired sense of identity with the "American" people bears some resemblance to Gordon's "identificational assimilation"; *Assimilation,* 70–71.

10. Benedict Anderson, *Imagined Communities: Reflections on the Origin and Spread of Nationalism,* rev. edn. (London, 1991). The convergence suggested here between American nationalism and the adoption of an American identity can be seen, for example, in Gleason's use of "American identity" and "American nationality" interchangeably; "American Identity and Americanization," 31.

11. Will Herberg, *Protestant-Catholic-Jew: An Essay in American Religious Sociology* (Garden City, N.Y., 1956), 34; Gordon, *Assimilation,* 159, 130.

12. Gleason, "American Identity and Americanization"; Higham, "Integrating America"; Conzen, *el al.,* "Invention of Ethnicity," 32.

13. Lizabeth Cohen, *Making a New Deal: Industrial Workers in Chicago, 1919–1939* (Cambridge, 1990), 357; James R. Barrett, "Americanization from the Bottom Up: Immigration and the Remaking of the Working Class in the United States, 1880–1930," *Journal of American History,* 79 (December 1992): 996–1020; Gary Gerstle, *Working-Class Americanism: The Politics of Labor in a Textile City, 1914–1960* (Cambridge, 1989).

14. David R. Roediger, "Whiteness and Ethnicity in the History of 'White Ethnics' in the United States," in Roediger, *Towards the Abolition of Whiteness: Essays on Race, Politics, and Working Class History* (London, 1994), 181–98; Roediger, *The Wages of Whiteness: Race and the*

Making of the American Working Class (London, 1991); Arnold R. Hirsch, *Making the Second Ghetto: Race and Housing in Chicago, 1940–1960* (Cambridge, 1983). My accounting of these three groups of historians as "reappraisers" of assimilation is by no means meant to be exhaustive. Similar trends may be at work among historians who focus on dimensions of experience other than those of class and race, such as gender, sexuality, and religion, to name a few potential arenas for forging transethnic common ground. This article's invitation to dialogue is meant to extend not simply to the three groups I have identified but to all historians who find themselves taking up such questions of assimilation.

15. Gordon, *Assimilation,* 85, 86. Gleason notes that the term "assimilation" itself came into general use around 1900; Philip Gleason, "The Odd Couple: Pluralism and Assimilation," in Gleason, *Speaking of Diversity: Language and Ethnicity in Twentieth-Century America* (Baltimore, Md., 1992), 49.

16. Gordon, *Assimilation,* 86, 137, 140–57. Gordon noted attempts at pluralist models by some nineteenth-century ethnic leaders; 135 n. Kathleen Neils Conzen has explored such efforts among German-American intellectuals, including some who "took the complete step to a principled defense of permanent ethnic diversity"; see Conzen, "German-Americans and the Invention of Ethnicity," in *America and the Germans: An Assessment of a Three-Hundred-Year History,* Frank Trommler and Joseph McVeigh, eds., 2 vols. (Philadelphia, Pa., 1985), 1: 141. Horace M. Kallen, "Democracy *versus* the Melting Pot," in *The Nation,* February 18 and 25, 1915; reprinted in Horace M. Kallen, *Culture and Democracy in the United States: Studies in the Group Psychology of the American Peoples* (1924; rpt. edn., New York, 1970), 124; Kallen's quotation is cited in Gordon, *Assimilation,* 142.

17. Gordon, *Assimilation,* 84.

18. Stow Persons, *Ethnic Studies at Chicago, 1905–45* (Urbana, Ill., 1987), 33–36. I first came to the Chicago sociologists' work on assimilation through Persons' insightful study, and I draw on him in my discussion of disorganization, the race relations cycle, and symbiosis. I have come to differ with him on some points in my readings of particular works, however, as is evident in the footnotes below.

19. William I. Thomas and Florian Znaniecki, *The Polish Peasant in Europe and America: Monograph of an Immigrant Group,* 5 vols. (Boston, 1918–20), 4: x, vii, viii; 1: 2, 87–90, 72. Martin Bulmer provides a detailed account of the circumstances surrounding the writing of *The Polish Peasant* in *The Chicago School of Sociology: Institutionalization, Diversity, and the Rise of Sociological Research* (Chicago, 1984), chap. 4.

20. Thomas and Znaniecki, *Polish Peasant,* 4: x–xi, 13, 178, 74; 1: 98–99, 104–05; 4: 2 (quotation originally in italics).

21. Thomas and Znaniecki, *Polish Peasant,* 1: 87, 89–96, 102, 98.

22. Thomas and Znaniecki, *Polish Peasant,* 5: 165–71, xiii, 35–48, 41, 40, xi (quotation originally in italics).

23. Thomas and Znaniecki, *Polish Peasant,* 5: xi, xvi. My reading of *The Polish Peasant* in this and the preceding paragraph generally concurs with that of Persons, *Ethnic Studies,* 46–53. But I find Thomas and Znaniecki somewhat more willing to see the formation of a Polish-American ethnic group as a type of assimilation; compare Persons, 51, 53.

24. Robert E. Park and Herbert A. Miller [orig. author, William I. Thomas], *Old World Traits Transplanted* (New York, 1921), 308. Thomas's authorship of, at the least, the early manuscript of *Old World Traits* has been established; the names of Park and Miller replaced that of Thomas as author of the published book as a result of the sexual scandal that forced Thomas's departure from the Chicago faculty in 1918. Persons, *Ethnic Studies,* 54, 54 n, 45–46.

25. Thomas, *Old World Traits,* 265, 294, 296–97; Persons, *Ethnic Studies,* 54.

26. Robert E. Park and Ernest W. Burgess, *Introduction to the Science of Sociology,* 2d edn. (Chicago, 1924), 280; Persons, *Ethnic Studies,* 60, 62. Persons describes the stages of the interaction process, calling it the "interaction cycle," and uses the term "ethnic cycle" for the race relations cycle. However, he notes that Park did not distinguish between "race" and what more recent scholars refer to as European "ethnicity," and that Park tended to identify race with nationality. Persons, 60–62, 82. While Park and Burgess could use the term "ethnic groups," they also cast the "struggles of the minor nationalities for self-determination" as "a phase of racial conflict." *Introduction,* 645, 646. Park elsewhere termed the Jews in Europe a "racial minority" and East European "nationalities" "fragments of the great Slavic race." Robert E. Park, "The Race Relations Cycle in Hawaii," and "Racial Assimilation in Secondary Groups," in Park, *Race and Culture* (New York, 1950), 194, 217.

27. Park and Burgess, *Introduction,* 785, 341; Persons, *Ethnic Studies,* 60.

28. Park and Burgess, *Introduction,* 507, 575, 509, 664–65. The example here represents one path interaction could take, given the definitions laid down by Park and Burgess. The interaction process as described in the book did not necessarily follow these stages in as clear-cut a fashion as this example implies. Nor did interaction seem to have a required ending in assimilation, although the authors called that stage interaction's "final perfect product." Park and Burgess stated, for example, that contact "inevitably initiates conflict, accommodation, *or* assimilation" (italics mine). Further, competition among individuals or groups might not involve contact, but it became "conscious and personal" in conflict. The stage of conflict, on the other hand,

seemed certain to lead at least to that of accommodation; conflict, the authors declared, "invariably issues
in a new accommodation." *Introduction,* 736, 507, 574,
575, 665. Persons' account of the interaction process,
including his terming it the "interaction cycle," seems
to me to imply a more clear-cut succession of stages
than Park and Burgess suggested; compare Persons,
Ethnic Studies, 60–62.

29. Park and Burgess, *Introduction,* 735; Persons, *Ethnic
Studies,* 62.

30. Robert E. Park, "Our Racial Frontier on the Pacific," in Park, *Race and Culture,* 150, see also 151; Persons, *Ethnic Studies,* 68–69. Persons terms this article
"the first full and explicit application of the interaction
cycle theory to problems of race relations"; 68.

31. Persons, *Ethnic Studies,* 88; Park, "Race Relations
Cycle in Hawaii," 194–95.

32. Persons, *Ethnic Studies,* 87; Robert E. Park, "Reflections on Communication and Culture," in Park, *Race
and Culture,* 48–49. Park stated that symbiosis of this
kind, in fact, had been to an extent "the situation of
every immigrant people" that had sought a place in the
economy of an established society while trying to maintain its own "cultural tradition." Still, he argued in the
same article that "[i]nevitably," the immigrant would
try to flee such isolation, and his consequent struggle
for status would involve a kind of "acculturation that
sounds very much like assimilation. "Reflections on
Communication and Culture," 49, 50, 48.

33. Ernest W. Burgess, "The Growth of the City: An Introduction to a Research Project," in Robert E. Park,
Ernest W. Burgess, and Roderick D. McKenzie, *The City*
(Chicago, 1925), 50–51, 56. This discussion draws on
Olivier Zunz's account of the evolution of the concept
of succession in *The Changing Face of Inequality: Urbanization, Industrial Development and Immigrants in Detroit, 1880–1920* (Chicago, 1982), 42–45. Zunz, who
cites Burgess, Louis Wirth, and Paul Frederick Cressey,
notes here that Burgess first defined this model of population succession. Thomas, however, earlier hinted at
a type of succession involving immigrant Jews and
Poles; Thomas, *Old World Traits,* 203–04, 212.

34. Louis Wirth, *The Ghetto* (Chicago, 1928); Paul Frederick Cressey, "Population Succession in Chicago:
1898–1930," *American Journal of Sociology,* 44 (July
1938): 61.

35. Persons, *Ethnic Studies,* 84; Park and Burgess, *Introduction,* 735, 734. Persons argues that *Introduction* "im-
plicity rejected the expectation of Anglo-Americans
that their cultural traits should predominate," at least
with children of mixed marriages; Persons, 62; see *Introduction,* 737–38.

36. Thomas, *Old World Traits,* 265–71, 296–97, 303–08;
Persons, *Ethnic Studies,* 57, 54.

37. Park, "Reflections on Communication and Culture," 49; Park, "Race Relations Cycle in Hawaii," 194;

Robert E. Park, "Assimilation, Social," in *Encyclopaedia
of the Social Sciences,* Edwin R. A. Seligman and Alvin
Johnson, eds., 15 vols. (New York, 1930-35), 2: 281,
283: Robert E. Park, "Culture and Cultural Trends," in
Park, *Race and Culture,* 30–31; Persons, *Ethnic Studies,*
87, 89, 146.

38. Maldwyn A. Jones notes that in *Boston's Immigrants,* Handlin "took as his model the community studies produced by sociologists in the 1920's and 1930's,"
including those of Park and his students, as well as the
"Middletown" studies of Muncie, Indiana, carried out
by Robert S. Lynd and Helen M. Lynd. Jones also finds
that *The Uprooted* "clearly owed a good deal" to *The Polish Peasant;* Jones, "Oscar Handlin," in *Pastmasters:
Some Essays on American Historians,* Marcus Cunliffe
and Robin W. Winks, eds. (New York, 1969), 245, 260.
Thomas and Znaniecki's book was one of a handful of
works Handlin cited by name in the acknowledgments
of *The Uprooted;* Oscar Handlin, *The Uprooted: The Epic
Story of the Great Migrations That Made the American
People* (Boston, 1951), 309.

39. Oscar Handlin, *Boston's Immigrants, 1790–1865: A
Study in Acculturation* (Cambridge, Mass., 1941), 221.

40. Handlin, *Boston's Immigrants,* 140, 221. "[T]hough
the Irish acquired a secure place in the community,"
Handlin noted, "they remained distinct as a group."
The "economic and physical adjustment" of the Germans, in contrast, "was relatively simple, so that within
a short time they shared the ideas of the natives." While
all immigrants had an awareness of ethnic group identity, group consciousness among non-Irish newcomers
waned over time. Handlin, *Boston's Immigrants,* 221,
140, 156, 213. On assimilationist tendencies among
non-Irish immigrant groups, see also 128, 150–53,
162–63, 166, 168–69, 182.

41. Handlin, *Boston's Immigrants,* vii, 60, 24, 12, 9–10,
60, 124.

42. See, for example, his uses of "Americanization" and
"assimilation"; Handlin, *Uprooted,* 185, 274.

43. Handlin, *Uprooted,* 4, 24, 9, 12, 61–62, 38, 79, 162,
169, 185.

44. Handlin, *Uprooted,* 186, 200, 305, 263–64, 274–75.

45. Marcus Lee Hansen, "The Problem of the Third
Generation Immigrant," Address to the Augustana Historical Society, Rock Island, Illinois, May 15, 1937;
reprinted as Augustana College Library Occasional
Paper, no. 16, with introductions by Peter Kivisto and
Oscar Handlin (Rock Island, Ill., 1987), 15, 13–14,
16–17.

46. Hansen, "Problem of the Third Generation," 19,
21, 24; Kivisto, introduction to Hansen, "Problem of
the Third Generation," 7.

47. Ruby Jo Reeves Kennedy, "Single or Triple Melting-
Pot? Intermarriage Trends in New Haven, 1870-1940,"
American Journal of Sociology, 49 (January 1944): 331,
332, 339. Kennedy bolstered this article with a follow-

up study, "Single or Triple Melting-Pot? Intermarriage in New Haven, 1870–1950," *American Journal of Sociology,* 58 (July 1952): 56–59. She has had her critics; see, for example, Ceri Peach, "Which Triple Melting Pot? A Re-examination of Ethnic Intermarriage in New Haven, 1900–1950," *Ethnic and Racial Studies,* 3 (January 1980): 1–16.

48. Herberg, *Protestant-Catholic-Jew,* 14, 35, 40, 42, 43–45.

49. Herberg, *Protestant-Catholic-Jew,* 47–48, 50, 94–96, 88, 91–92, 101, 96.

50. Herberg, *Protestant-Catholic-Jew,* 129. One should note that, far from celebrating the American Way of Life, Herberg worried in his last chapter that the three historic faiths had been vitiated by their relation to it, resulting in a religiousness "without serious commitment, without real inner conviction, without genuine existential decision." Herberg, 285, 276.

51. Gordon, *Assimilation,* 68–70, 71, 81, 80.

52. Gordon, *Assimilation,* 37, 38, 47, 51, 72–74, 105–09, 126–29, 110, 114.

53. Gordon, *Assimilation,* 130, 262.

54. I see Herberg and Gordon as scholars of assimilation because they made that phenomenon their subject, even as they placed it in a framework of pluralism. John Higham portrays them as offering pluralist positions at a time when other scholars saw an inevitable assimilation of ethnic minorities into an American mainstream. Higham, "Ethnic Pluralism in Modern American Thought," in Higham, *Send These to Me: Immigrants in Urban America,* rev. edn. (Baltimore, Md., 1984), 226–27. Philip Gleason, in contrast, views Herberg as regarding "assimilationist forces as much stronger in American society" than those preserving cultural diversity. Gleason's portrayal of Gordon is closer to Higham's: Gordon's book implied "that pluralism was a much deeper and more meaningful reality in American society than assimilation," and it was "generally regarded as having discredited the 'assimilationist myth.'" Gleason makes these observations in the context of a larger argument that cultural pluralism, from the late 1930s through the 1960s, "resembled assimilation much more closely" than before or after that period. Gleason, "Odd Couple," 70, 74, 49, 56, 60.

55. Nathan Glazer and Daniel Patrick Moynihan, *Beyond the Melting Pot: The Negro, Puerto Ricans, Jews, Italians, and Irish of New York City* (Cambridge, Mass., 1963), 314.

56. Glazer and Moynihan, *Beyond the Melting Pot,* 12, 17.

57. Glazer and Moynihan, *Beyond the Melting Pot,* 17–19, 20, 291, 14.

58. Rudolph J. Vecoli, "*Contadini* in Chicago: A Critique of *The Uprooted," Journal of American History,* 51 (December 1964): 404, 407–08, 412–13, 415–17.

59. Vecoli, "*Contadini* in Chicago," 417.

60. Olivier Zunz, "American History and the Changing Meaning of Assimilation," *Journal of American Ethnic History,* 4 (Spring 1985): 53.

61. Rudolph J. Vecoli, "Return to the Melting Pot: Ethnicity in the United States in the Eighties," *Journal of American Ethnic History,* 5 (Fall 1985): 11, 12.

62. Zunz, "Changing Meaning of Assimilation," 53–54, 55–57.

63. As discussed below, even in the 1970s, John Higham and Philip Gleason continued to explore that type of assimilation—that is, Americanization—involved in the adoption of an overarching American identity. Among social historians, Josef J. Barton, *Peasants and Strangers: Italians, Rumanians, and Slovaks in an American City, 1890–1950* (Cambridge, Mass., 1975), examined intermarriage among second-generation ethnics in Cleveland, in a style reminiscent of Kennedy's studies, while Ronald H. Bayor, *Neighbors in Conflict: The Irish, Germans, Jews, and Italians of New York City, 1929–1941* (Baltimore, Md., 1978), looked at inter-ethnic relations, although his study had to do more with conflict than common ground. In addition, students of groups for which assimilation had proved a pressing concern may have found the topic one they could not help but address. Ewa Morawska points out that a consistent focus of the literature on Jewish immigrants has been the nature of the host society into which those newcomers integrated. Personal communication, January 19, 1995. A 1975 survey of American ethnic history that explored assimilation at length was co-authored by Leonard Dinnerstein, who, perhaps not coincidentally, has written extensively on the Jewish experience in America. Leonard Dinnerstein and David M. Reimers, *Ethnic Americans: A History of Immigration and Assimilation* (New York, 1975). Scholars of the German-American experience dealt with a group whose ethnicity had undergone a "thorough submergence" that, as Conzen noted in 1983, did not fit historians' "models of pluralistic ethnic maintenance." Kathleen Neils Conzen, "Patterns of German-American History," in *Germans in America: Retrospect and Prospect; Tricentennial Lectures Delivered at the German Society of Pennsylvania in 1983,* Randall M. Miller, ed. (Philadelphia, Pa., 1984), 15. (I am indebted to James M. Bergquist for this reference.) Conzen herself addressed German-American assimilation in the 1970s, as did Frederick C. Luebke and La Vern J. Rippley; see Kathleen Neils Conzen, "Immigrants, Immigrant Neighborhoods, and Ethnic Identity: Historical Issues," *Journal of American History,* 66 (December 1979): 603–15; Frederick C. Luebke, *Bonds of Loyalty: German-Americans and World War I* (De Kalb, Ill., 1974); and La Vern J. Rippley, *The German-Americans* (Boston, 1976).

64. Historians of social mobility such as Stephan Thernstrom did discuss assimilation and did not shrink from generalizing about American society. But the study

of social mobility did not necessarily yield information about cultural or structural assimilation, in Gordon's terms, or about the relations among ethnic groups in the larger social order. Thernstrom, *The Other Bostonians: Poverty and Progress in the American Metropolis, 1880–1970* (Cambridge, Mass., 1973), for example, appeared to measure assimilation in terms of how the mobility patterns of an immigrant group and its children compared to those of native-born whites of native parentage, or to all Bostonians. That the occupational gap between European ethnics and Yankees had narrowed by the mid-twentieth century certainly indicated a kind of assimilation. But this fact did not tell one whether ethnics and Yankees were drawing closer in terms of sharing institutions or intermarrying. Indeed, Thernstrom's conclusion that differences in achievement between Catholics and Jews were rooted partly in distinctive immigrant "habits and attitudes that were slow to disappear and that influenced the occupational trajectories of the two groups long into the future" sounded remarkably like Gutman's anti-assimilationist argument for the persistence of immigrant cultures. See Thernstrom, 143, 175.

65. Zunz, "Changing Meaning of Assimilation," 57, 58–61.

66. Herbert G. Gutman, "Work, Culture, and Society in Industrializing America, 1815–1919," chap. in *Work, Culture, and Society in Industrializing America: Essays in American Working Class and Social History* (New York, 1976), 19, 22–26, 18, 74–75, 55.

67. Gutman, "Work, Culture, and Society," 24, 41.

68. Gutman, "Work, Culture, and Society," 49.

69. John Bodnar, *The Transplanted: A History of Immigrants in Urban America* (1985; Bloomington, Ind., 1987), xvi.

70. Bodnar, *Transplanted*, 72, 54–55, 23–30, 56, 38, 83, 72, 210, 209, 212, 213.

71. Bodnar, *Transplanted*, 184.

72. Bodnar, *Transplanted*, 143, 128, 190, 143, 193. For the implication that Americanization was a middle-class initiative, see also 118, 140–41, 204, 214. Interestingly, Bodnar did note at one point that turn-of-the-century Chicago butchers made "unionization . . . a process of Americanization," and cited James Barrett's dissertation; at another point, he referred to Irish-American nationalism as "a step in the assimilation of immigrant laborers into American working-class traditions"; Bodnar, 101, 101 n, 111. But Bodnar did not develop these ideas, which Barrett would use later in helping to renew discussions of assimilation.

73. Bodnar, *Transplanted*, 118, 169, 183, 170, 174.

74. Bodnar, *Transplanted*, 184, 205, 208–11, 213. Bodnar offered a more succinct version of this argument in a comment on Zunz's 1985 review essay, while acknowledging as correct Zunz's point that assimilation "has been largely ignored in recent historical scholarship"; John Bodnar, "Comment," *Journal of American Ethnic History*, 4 (Spring 1985): 75–76, 73. Bodnar took a similar approach to assimilation in his study of Steelton, Pennsylvania, *Immigration and Industrialization: Ethnicity in an American Mill Town, 1870–1940* (Pittsburgh, Pa., 1977). Although this book did look to some extent at relations among ethnic groups, it portrayed cooperation across ethnic lines primarily as occurring within the "old stock" middle class and upper class, which had "minimized" internal ethnic differences to preserve class position and dominate the town. Newer immigrants, excluded from power and skilled jobs, constructed separate ethnic communities. Bodnar did briefly discuss the advent of the CIO in the late 1930s as a vehicle of inter-ethnic cooperation and an "emerging, working-class consciousness." Yet second-generation immigrants, who backed the union, appeared "unwilling to weaken their own ethnic ties," and Bodnar did little to explore the nature of their rising class consciousness (other than to ascribe it to a search for job security) or its assimilatory implications. *Immigration and Industrialization*, 144–55, 137, and *passim*.

75. Bodnar, *Transplanted*, 205, 209, xx, 112. The hint, if it was such, was worded ambiguously, as part of a string of negatives: the culture of everyday life "was not a simple extension of [the immigrants'] past, an embracement of the new order of capitalism, or simply an affirmation of a desire to become an American"; *Transplanted*, 209. Bodnar more recently has turned to the topic of American identity; see John Bodnar, *Remaking America: Public Memory, Commemoration, and Patriotism in the Twentieth Century* (Princeton, N.J., 1992).

76. Bodnar, *Transplanted*, 208.

77. Bodnar, *Transplanted*, xvii, 207, 71, 178, 148, 119–20.

78. Bodnar, *Transplanted*, 215, 76, 61–70, 93–96, 139, 209–10. Bodnar noted too that churches riven by class and ideological tensions also saw ethnic divisions and that ethnic intermediaries linked immigrant voters to urban machines; *Transplanted*, 150–55, 202–04.

79. Bodnar, *Transplanted*, 194–95, 115.

80. Paul Buhle, "Jews and American Communism: The Cultural Question," *Radical History Review* 23 (Spring 1980): 29, 20–21, 28.

81. Higham, writing in the early 1970s, noted a need to rediscover "what values can bind together a more and more kaleidoscopic culture." John Higham, "Another American Dilemma," in Higham, *Send These to Me*, 248.

82. For perceptive overviews of "consensus history," see Peter Novick, *That Noble Dream: The "Objectivity Question" and the American Historical Profession* (Cambridge, 1988), chap. 11; and John Higham's own *History: Professional Scholarship in America*, rev. edn. (Baltimore, Md., 1989), 212–32.

83. Gleason, "American Identity and Americanization," 48, 47.

84. Higham notes the influence of "the totalitarian challenge to democracy" on ethnic studies in the 1940s and 1950s; Higham, "Ethnic Pluralism," 221. The theme of ideological confrontation with the Soviet Union was particularly strong, for example, in Hans Kohn's 1957 interpretation of American ideology. Kohn urged a "union of the West" under American leadership which would constitute a "return to common roots." "In this return, American nationalism fulfills itself in the broader community of its North Atlantic origins." Not surprisingly, Kohn lauded NATO as a vehicle through which "the nations on the two shores of the North Atlantic" had started to realize their commonality; Hans Kohn, *American Nationalism: An Interpretative Essay* (New York, 1957), 223, 228, 221.

85. Gleason, "American Identity and Americanization," 47. Higham, however, sees the "ideological fervor of American intellectuals" as having waned over the 1950s. "Ethnic Pluralism," 225.

86. Gleason, "American Identity and Americanization," 51, 50; Gunnar Myrdal, with the assistance of Richard Sterner and Arnold Rose, *An American Dilemma: The Negro Problem and Modern Democracy,* 2 vols. (New York, 1944); Horace Kallen, *Cultural Pluralism and the American Idea: An Essay in Social Philosophy,* with comments by Stanley H. Chapman, *et al.* (Philadelphia, Pa., 1956). The "cultural pluralism" Kallen championed in the 1950s was quite different from that he advocated when he introduced the term in the 1920s, as Gleason argues; "American Identity and Americanization," 50, 43; "Odd Couple," 57–58.

87. Kohn, *American Nationalism,* 13; Gleason, "American Identity and Americanization," 32, 31.

88. Gleason, "American Identity and Americanization," 55, 56, 31.

89. Gleason, "American Identity and Americanization," 56, 32–34, 36, 39.

90. Gleason, "American Identity and Americanization," 47, 48, 50. World War II generated a need for national unity, Gleason noted elsewhere, but this was sought "on the common ground of ideological consensus"; tolerance for diversity was "a key element in the democratic ideology behind which all were supposed to rally." Hence the demand for unity was "usually couched in the language of pluralism and diversity instead of . . . assimilation or Americanization." This was the context within which the idea of "cultural pluralism" dwelled during and after the war. Gleason, "Odd Couple," 58, 59; see also 60, 62–63, 67.

91. Gleason, "American Identity and Americanization," 52, 55–57.

92. Higham, "Integrating America," 7, 9–13, 15, 13–14.

93. Higham, "Integrating America," 15, 19, 20–22. Higham more recently posited that the ideology's egalitarian principles, in the form of "American universalism," helped to fuel twentieth-century movements for equality, before losing force amid the rise of ethnic separatism in the 1960s. John Higham, "Multiculturalism and Universalism: A History and Critique," *American Quarterly,* 45 (June 1993): 196–97, 200–01, 205–06. Higham's analysis of multiculturalism drew dissenting comments in the same issue from several scholars, including Gary Gerstle, "The Limits of American Universalism," 230–36, and Nancy A. Hewitt, "A Response to John Higham," 237–42.

94. Higham, "Introduction," *Send These to Me,* xii. For Gleason, the return manifested itself as an affirmation of assimilation "understood as a social policy" promoting the identification of Americans of all backgrounds with "the traditional values of democratic universalism." Gleason, "Odd Couple," 82.

95. Werner Sollors, "Introduction: The Invention of Ethnicity," in *The Invention of Ethnicity,* Werner Sollors, ed. (New York, 1989), xi, x, xiv, xv.

96. Conzen, *et al.,* "Invention of Ethnicity," 4–5.

97. Conzen, *et al.,* "Invention of Ethnicity," 6, 9.

98. Conzen, *et al.,* "Invention of Ethnicity," 5, 19, 22, 23, 25–26.

99. Conzen, *et al.,* "Invention of Ethnicity," 6, 32.

100. Gerber, *Making of an American Pluralism,* 119, xii, xv, xiv, 325–26, 412, xiii, 405.

101. Kathleen Neils Conzen, "Mainstreams and Side Channels: The Localization of Immigrant Cultures," *Journal of American Ethnic History,* 11 (Fall 1991): 13, 6, 15, 7.

102. Lawrence H. Fuchs, *The American Kaleidoscope: Race, Ethnicity, and the Civic Culture* (Hanover, N.H., 1990), 20, 5, 482, 492, 77–79, 149.

103. Fuchs, *American Kaleidoscope,* 109, 149, 187, 203, 224, 236, 269–71, 492, 363, 371, 372–80, 493. Fuchs' optimism marked a sharp contrast to the forebodings of other American historians who saw American identity in ideological terms. His faith in the integrative potential of voluntary pluralism was such that he appeared to interpret the Black Power movement—which Higham saw as weakening American Universalism—as a necessary stage in the "ethnic-Americanization" of African Americans; Higham, "Multiculturalism," 205, 206; Fuchs, 184, 187. Such equanimity stood out in comparison to the worried tone of Higham's critique and, especially, to the anxiety shown in Arthur Schlesinger, Jr.'s attack on multiculturalism, *The Disuniting of America* (New York, 1992). Schlesinger, who asserted his belief in a "national creed" that had made Americans into "one people," denounced an anti-assimilationist "cult of ethnicity" and worried that "when a vocal and visible minority pledges primary allegiance to their groups, whether ethnic, sexual, religious, or, in rare cases (communist, fascist), political, it presents a threat to the brittle bonds of national identity that hold this diverse and fractious society together." *Disuniting of America,* 13, 130, 112, 113.

104. While Gleason gave the ideals that cemented American identity partially English roots, Fuchs seemed reluctant to follow suit for his founding myth. He did so, if at all, indirectly, in offhandedly citing Jefferson's observation that American principles were "based on 'a composition of the freest principles of the English Constitution, with others derived from natural right and natural reason.'" The myth had also changed since Jefferson's day, incorporating diversity as a value. Voluntary pluralism itself was a "new invention of Americans," launched "principally" in colonial Pennsylvania; Fuchs, *American Kaleidoscope*, 12, 5.

105. Ewa Morawska, "In Defense of the Assimilation Model," *Journal of American Ethnic History*, 13 (Winter 1994): 76, 77, 78–81, 81–82, 82–84; Conzen, "Mainstreams and Side Channels," 7. One should note that Morawska, like Higham, saw an at least partial trend back to assimilation in sociological and historical work on ethnicity. Scholars abandoned "the classical assimilation model of linear progression toward a common American amalgamate" because "it turned out to be much too simplistic," she wrote in 1990. The focus shifted first "toward stressing 'resilient ethnicity' in opposition to assimilation" and then toward "emphasizing ethnic resilience but acknowledging its coexistence with parallel assimilation processes." Morawska, "Sociology and Historiography of Immigration," 212–13.

106. On World War I–era union drives among ethnics, see Barrett, "Americanization from the Bottom Up," 1015, 1018. Peter Friedlander anticipated this work to some degree in his analysis of unionization in one Michigan plant, *The Emergence of a UAW Local, 1936–1939: A Study in Class and Culture* (Pittsburgh, Pa., 1975). Especially when generalizing to the world outside the plant, however, he stressed the persistence of ethnocultural subcultures, arguing that the large-scale entry of Poles and native white Protestants into the United Automobile Workers was reflected in a conservative political shift within the union. Friedlander, 93, 111–31, and *passim*.

107. Zunz, *Changing Face of Inequality*, 139, 55, 87, 194, 219–20, 224.

108. Zunz, *Changing Face of Inequality*, 4–5, 401, 327, 357–59. Zunz's portrayal of a shift from cross-class ethnic enclaves to working-class ones was at odds with accounts of nineteenth-century urbanization offered by some other historians, as he noted; Zunz, 41–42, 178. Scholars studying Philadelphia, for example, argued that industry "was more important than ethnicity in organizing the city's residential patterns" between 1850 and 1880, with workers having "more in common residentially with coindustrial workers than with those of common cultural background"; Theodore Hershberg, *et al.*, "A Tale of Three Cities: Blacks, Immigrants, and Opportunity in Philadelphia, 1850–1880, 1930, 1970," in *Philadelphia: Work, Space, Family, and Group Experience*

in the Nineteenth Century; Theodore Hershberg, ed. (New York, 1981), 469. Zunz and Hershberg debated the Philadelphia findings in Zunz's "Comment" on *Philadelphia* and Hershberg's "Response," *Journal of Urban History*, 8 (August 1982): 463–71, 472–84.

109. Zunz, *Changing Face of Inequality*, 402; Roy Rosenzweig, *Eight Hours for What We Will: Workers and Leisure in an Industrial City*, 1870–1920 (Cambridge, 1983), 5, 181–82, 219–20, 227, 215, 228.

110. Rosenzweig did emphasize the degree to which ethnic workers put their own stamp on commercial leisure; see *Eight Hours*, 199–201.

111. Barrett, "Americanization from the Bottom Up," 997–98, 1000, 1008, 1010–11, 1009, 1014, 997, 1011–12, 1017.

112. Cohen, *Making a New Deal*, 362, 364–65, 333, 356–57, 6–7.

113. Gerstle, *Working-Class Americanism*, 1, 4, 8, 190, 195, 331.

114. Gerstle, *Working-Class Americanism*, 9–12. The "democratic" dimension, which focused on ideals, bore some relation to Higham's American Universalism, although its broader terms took in tensions between individual and equal rights, and free enterprise and industrial democracy. The "nationalist" aspect required admiration of such (Anglo-) American heroes as the Pilgrims and the Founding Fathers. The "traditionalist" dimension hearkened back to a mythic rural past of hardy, pious, and virtuous folk, when all Americans "were white, Anglo-Saxon, and Protestant." Gerstle noted that working-class Catholics could not embrace the "traditionalist" aspect, with its nativist overtones, until after World War II had rendered Protestant nativism untenable.

115. Thomas Childers makes a similar point in tracing "pre-industrial" mentalities in the politics of Weimar Germany, not to vestigial pre-capitalist elites but to the language middle-class Germans used "to define themselves socially for political action." That language made occupation central to one's self-definition, and it tended to describe occupations in terms of "estates" rather than classes. Childers, "The Social Language of Politics in Germany: The Sociology of Political Discourse in the Weimar Republic," *AHR*, 95 (April 1990): 357.

116. Alba, *Ethnic Identity*, 291, 11–12, 14, 312, 314–15, 3, 9–13.

117. David Roediger hints at such a distinction in "Whiteness and Ethnicity," 184, 187–90. That Americans of European background have historically equated Americanness exclusively with whiteness has been observed by black commentators from Malcolm X to Toni Morrison. See, for example, Malcolm X's statement, "Everything that came out of Europe, every blue-eyed thing, is already an American . . . being born here in America doesn't make you an American," cited in Fuchs, *American Kaleidoscope*, 175. Reflecting on what

she termed the "Africanist presence" in American literature, Morrison argued that "[i]t is no accident and no mistake that immigrant populations (and much immigrant literature) understood their 'Americanness' as an opposition to the resident black population . . . Deep within the word 'American' is its association with race . . . American means white, and Africanist people struggle to make the term applicable to themselves with ethnicity and hyphen after hyphen after hyphen." Morrison, *Playing in the Dark: Whiteness and the Literary Imagination* (Cambridge, Mass., 1990), 47.

118. Roediger, *Wages of Whiteness*, 134, 136, 143–44, 149–50, 150–56; Roediger, "Whiteness and Ethnicity," 189.

119. The phrase is John Bukowczyk's, cited in Roediger, "Whiteness and Ethnicity," 184.

120. John Higham, *Strangers in the Land: Patterns of American Nativism, 1860–1925*, 2d edn. (New York, 1981), 156, 172, 173. Roediger, "Whiteness and Ethnicity," 184–85, gives further examples of the casting of southern and eastern European immigrants as nonwhite.

121. Roediger, "Whiteness and Ethnicity," 185, saw a pressing need for studies of how and why particular immigrant groups chose whiteness. Alexander Saxton, *The Rise and Fall of the White Republic: Class Politics and Mass Culture in Nineteenth-Century America* (London, 1990), 298, depicted late nineteenth-century European immigrants in the American West as drawn to a strain of white egalitarianism that cast whiteness as a symbol of producer solidarity against those who manipulated racially subordinate populations at white producers' expense. Similarly, Barrett's article, which covered the period between 1880 and 1930, suggested that Irish workers "Americanizing" East European laborers may have passed along their own anti-black and anti-Asian attitudes; Barrett, "Americanization from the Bottom Up," 1001–02. However, at certain times and places, such as World War I-era Chicago and turn-of-the-century Louisiana, one could find New Immigrants who did not consider themselves "white"; Roediger, "Whiteness and Ethnicity," 186–87.

122. Gerstle, *Working-Class Americanism* 289, 290; Gary Gerstle, "The Working Class Goes to War," *Mid-America*, 75 (October 1993): 313, 318; Hirsch, *Making the Second Ghetto*, 80–81, 186, 187. One wonders whether the war against Japan, as well as that against Germany, played a role in redefining whiteness. While World War II is often seen as a fight against racism, John W. Dower has argued that, to many on both sides, the conflict in the Pacific itself amounted to a race war. In American propaganda and the press, the war frequently pitted GIs against Japanese variously depicted as monkeys, primitives, children, and madmen—stereotypes previously deployed against blacks, Indians, and Chinese immigrants and recycled for the war effort; Dower, *War without Mercy: Race and Power in the Pacific War* (New York, 1986), 4, 10, and *passim*. It is possible the war also allowed and encouraged European ethnics across the United States to see themselves, and be seen, as part of a nation of whites defending itself against a "yellow" menace.

FOURTEEN

Immigration and Ethnic and Racial Inequality in the United States

Mary C. Waters
Karl Eschbach

The half century since the close of World War II has seen numerous changes to the face of racial and ethnic inequality in the United States, while the problem of inequality has endured. When Myrdal published *An American Dilemma* (1944), the segregationism tolerated by Plessy v. Ferguson was the law of the land, and caste-like barriers separated blacks from whites. Myrdal's chief task was to comprehend the vicious circle that perpetuated these rigid distinctions between the races. By contrast, when Warner & Srole (1945) described the ethnic structure of a representative American city, they described the patterned relationships among its various European national descent groups. The variable these authors used to explain the unequal standing of these groups was the relative lapse of time since each group had migrated to the United States—time for initial distinctions among European descent populations to be erased through homogenization of the social positions of members of different groups.

In the intervening five decades, ascriptive inequality has been transformed by several interrelated events. The economic growth of the postwar decades formed the backdrop for a period of both legal and substantive changes in racial and ethnic inequality in the United States. The formal disabilities of Jim Crow separatism were dismantled by court decisions and by legislative action. Differences between blacks and whites on education and income narrowed. These changes, together with rising general levels of prosperity, created for the first time a substantial black middle class. At the same time, the open opportunity structure created by the expanding economy eased the incorporation of the children and grandchildren of members of the waves of migrants who had flooded to the United States from Europe before and during the early decades of the century.

Yet the story of changing inequality is not a Pollyanna-ish tale. At the close of the twentieth century, group differences have changed shape rather than disappeared. The background of these changes is the changed economic position of the United States. The rapid pace of economic growth in the immediate postwar period could not be sustained after the 1960s, stalling further progress toward racial equality. The export of manufacturing employment has put particular pressure on workers at the lower end of the education distribution where members of racial minority groups are overrepresented. An era of diminished expectations has thrown into relief the continuing relevance of race to economic opportunity.

The new global order has changed the racial and ethnic map of the United States one further way. Immigration has had a very large impact on American society since the 1960s, and most especially it has increased the diversity of the nonwhite population of the United States. In 1990 7.9% of the US population was foreign born. The 19.8 million foreign-born people in the United States is the largest number in US history. The sources of immigration flows have also shifted as a consequence of changes in immigration law and in the international pattern of migration flows. In 1990, 25.2% of the foreign-born population was Asian, 42.5% Latin American, 22% European, and

10.3% from other countries. The decade of the 1980s produced a large number of immigrants; 44% of the total 1990 foreign-born population arrived in that decade (Bureau of Census 1993).

In this paper, we review recent literature assessing the impact of three factors—economic restructuring, racial discrimination, and immigration—on the current patterns of racial inequality in the United States. Because of the enormous impact of immigration on the composition of America's nonwhite populations, we stress the importance of combining analyses of the economy and of racial and ethnic discrimination, along with the new evidence we have about immigrant absorption and change.

RACIAL AND ETHNIC CATEGORIES

Scholars who study ethnicity are in general agreement that racial and ethnic categories are social constructions rather than natural entities that are simply "out there" in the world. This constructed character of ethnic groups has several implications for research. One is that the categories the analyst uses are bound to be arbitrary. For example, Office of Management and Budget (OMB) Directive 15 specifies whites, blacks, Hispanics, Native Americans, Asians, and Pacific Islanders as racial and ethnic categories for purposes of enforcement of civil rights legislation. In fact, this is an arbitrary classification scheme which may owe its high level of recognition to Directive 15 itself. Each aggregation includes subpopulations that are themselves diverse, both in the social and cultural organization of sending countries and in the average experiences of group members in the United States. For example the term "Asian" covers the experiences of so-called "model minorities" like the Japanese and Koreans who have high socioeconomic standing in the United States, as well as Southeast Asian populations that have experienced more difficulties.

There are no easy methodological solutions to this problem of classification, except for the recognition of the arbitrariness of any set of ethnic categories. We concentrate on the OMB minority groups in this paper—paying close attention to the distinct subpopulations that make up each aggregation. We do not survey the important literature on white ethnic group inequality because of space limitations. (For a good overview, see Alba

1990, Lieberson 1980, Lieberson & Waters 1988, Hirschman 1983.)

For most racial and ethnic populations in the United States, classification problems also arise because of the progress of amalgamation and assimilation. The significant exception remains African Americans. Because of the rigidity of the boundary between blacks and whites, few definitional problems arise: rates of intermarriage between blacks and others have historically been low. Even with recent increases, in 1983–86, only 5% of African American males had marriages involving white spouses, and 2% of African American females had white spouses (Kalmijn 1993). Further, the common use in the United States of the rule of hypodescent (the one-drop rule) to classify persons of remote black African descent as African American reduces ambiguity about the boundaries of this population (Davis 1991).

At the other extreme, white ancestry groups have experienced extremely high rates of intermarriage with one another, so that many members of the conventional European national descent populations are of mixed ethnic descent. Scholars have debated whether the patterns of intermarriage and ambiguity about identity among white ethnics mean that assimilation theory accurately portrays the fate of the European descent ethnicities (Greeley 1974, Gans 1979, Alba 1990).

Intermarriage may be especially important in the future evolution of ethnic categories that are neither European nor African. As we discuss in this review, current conditions of incorporation may sustain the structural segregation and the social significance of ethnic descent for these other groups that on average are much greater than for European Americans, but much less than for African Americans.

American Indians, for example, remain the most disadvantaged of major American ethnic categories on census measures of poverty and educational attainment. The persistence of the social significance of a Native American ethnic category 500 years after Columbus's voyage is evidence that ethnic distinctions may in some cases be durable. Yet one of the mechanisms that has sustained the distinctiveness of American Indian communities has been the spinoff of many migrants from these communities into the general American population. Because of the subsequent amalgamation and assimilation of many of these off-reservation migrants and their descendants, far more of the descendants of the inhabitants of North America self-identify as whites rather than as American Indians (Snipp 1989, Eschbach 1995). Thus the assimilation process walks hand in hand with the maintenance of ethnic boundaries.

New immigrant populations from Asia and Latin America may well experience processes of incorporation into the United States that will create considerable confusion about who is a member of a given ethnic population. Data from 1990 showed that because of intermarriage "about one quarter of the 2 million children with at least one Asian parent, and of the 5.4 million with at least one Hispanic parent live in inter-racial households with a white parent or step parent" (Harrison & Bennett 1995:40). These percentages will be likely to increase in subsequent generations of descendants. Available evidence suggests that Americans do not consistently use the rule of hypodescent to classify persons of part-Hispanic or part-Asian descent with the 'minority' component of their descent (Davis 1991); ethnic self-identification is inconsistent in these mixed descent populations (Harrison & Bennett 1995).

These facts suggest the need for considerable caution in making comparisons of different racial and ethnic populations. At any given cross section, different immigrant-ethnic populations will be at different stages of incorporation into the United States population and will be different in the degree to which they are composed of ethnically mixed stock. Differences in the process of amalgamation and subsequently in the formation of ethnic identity may form an important component of the explanation of the size and socioeconomic composition of different groups (Hout & Goldstein 1994). The social scientific analyst of patterns of ethnic inequality is ill-advised to overlook the transitory quality of the most basic ethnic categories.

BASIC DATA ON INEQUALITY

With this caveat in mind, Table 1 provides information, based on data from the 1990 census, on median family income, labor force participation, and poverty rates for the major minority groups and whites in the United States. These data show the continuing inequality among American minor-

ity groups, when compared with whites. Of the major racial/ethnic minorities in the United States, only Asians have a higher median family income than do whites, with an income of $41,583, compared to $37,630 for non-Hispanic whites. American Indians have the lowest median income with $21,750, followed closely by blacks and Hispanics. Data on unemployment follow this general pattern, with blacks and American Indians the worst off, followed by Hispanics. Asians have unemployment rates comparable to whites. Poverty rates also follow this general pattern, with blacks showing a poverty rate for individuals that is three times the rate for whites.

Measurement Issues

These simple rankings mask a more complex picture. The most important variables used to decompose these overall patterns are subethnic groups, gender, and family and household composition. Panethnic groupings such as black, Hispanic, and Asian mask very important differences among subgroups, which we explore further in this review.

There are also important gender differences in relative success of members of these groups—in general, women from minority groups look better in comparison to white women than do minority men compared with white men. So too, family structure is an important variable affecting the levels of success or poverty that a group experiences. For instance, while rates of unemployment and income are much less favorable for blacks and Puerto Ricans than for whites, some of those differences lessen when only husband-wife families are compared across the groups; but because blacks and Puerto Ricans have more families headed by single females, they have lower overall income and success rates. Asians tend to have households with more workers in them than whites; thus when household and family incomes are compared, Asians look better off than when per capita income is compared.

Because of the differences in overall demographics of the groups, as well as differences in the levels of education and other human capital that groups have because of differential migration or the legacy of past inequality and discrimination, sociologists and economists interested in understanding the causes and consequences of racial/

TABLE 1   *Selected Socioeconomic Indicators for Groups in the United States, 1990*

Ethnic Racial Groups	Median Family Income, 1989	Percentage Persons in Poverty	Labor Force Participation* (%)
White not Hispanic	$37,630	10.0	65.0
Black	22,430	29.5	63.0
American Indian[†]	21,750	30.9	66.1
Hispanic	25,064	25.3	67.5
Mexican	24,119	26.3	68.3
Puerto Rican	21,941	31.7	60.4
Cuban	32,417	14.6	65.0
Asian	41,583	14.0	67.4
Japanese	51,550	7.0	64.5
Chinese	41,316	14.0	65.9
Filipino	46,698	6.4	75.4
Korean	33,909	13.7	63.3
Asian Indian	49,309	9.7	72.3
Vietnamese	30,550	25.7	64.5
Cambodian	18,126	42.6	46.5
Hmong	14,327	63.6	29.3
Laotian	23,101	34.7	58.0

Source: U.S. Census of Population, 1990. Social and Economic Characteristics CP-2-1, Washington, DC. U.S. Government Printing Office, 1993.

*Persons 16 years and over in labor force.

[†]Includes Eskimos and Aleuts.

ethnic inequality also look at the net returns to human capital for different groups. Using statistical controls, they ask whether a given person with the same background characteristics, such as level of education, region of residence, gender, marital characteristics, has the same earnings as a statistically equivalent person from a different ethnic/racial group. The differences in these returns of earnings for human capital characteristics are variously interpreted as proof of some sort of market inequality or, often, as evidence of discrimination.

In addition to measuring income differences, an important difference across groups involves labor force participation, as well as unemployment. Researchers who focus only on earnings or income differences across groups miss differences in overall socioeconomic outcomes that come about because laborers are discouraged in the labor market or are unable to participate. Thus comparing income and earnings between groups

will miss some of the causes of black poverty, given that black men have a labor force participation rate 8% lower than that of whites, and their participation is appreciably lower than that of all other groups except for American Indians. The labor force participation rate includes in the denominator individuals who are actively employed, who have a job but are not currently at work, and those who are looking for work. It can be affected by different cultural norms and values regarding women working outside the home, the age structure of a population, the overall health and disability prevalence across a population, and other factors not necessarily measuring "willingness to work." However, as a gross indicator, it tells us something about attachment to the labor force and the discouragement of workers.

In addition, monetary inequality is not the only measure of the lack of equality of outcomes in our society. There are other ways to measure inequality among racial and ethnic groups that we do not have the space to review here, including health and demographic measures such as infant mortality rates, life expectancy, morbidity, and disability. Ethnic and racial groups also differ in rates of home ownership, residential segregation, overall wealth, exposure to crime and toxic pollutants, and in access to power in the upper reaches of our society. In this article we concentrate on income inequality, recognizing that this does not tell a complete story.

THE SITUATION OF BLACK AMERICANS

How has this current pattern of inequality emerged? The story is somewhat different for the different ethnic categories, because of the varying histories of the groups. For black Americans, the removal of formal legal segregation in the 1960s, along with the rising economic prosperity in that decade, brought rises in weekly or hourly earnings and increased education and returns to education. However, these promising trends have been coupled with changes in family structure that have led to the deterioration of household income for women and children in single-parent families. Growing rates of black male joblessness mean that rising earnings are distributed over a narrowing portion of the potential labor force. Recent developments raise no particular optimism that the wage gains that occurred into the 1970s will quickly eradicate group differences. Economic restructuring in the context of global competition helps to create structural barriers to improvement of the situation of persons with the least education and fewest skills to offer to employers. In addition, evidence suggests that racial discrimination remains an obdurate problem for African Americans regardless of social and economic class.

In 1940, 92% of blacks were poor; by the early 1970s the black poverty rate had declined to 31% (Farley 1993). The relative black/white odds of being in poverty fell from more than 6:1 in 1930 to less than 4:1 in 1985 (Jaynes & Williams 1989). Smith & Welch (1989) estimated that the annual earnings in constant 1987 dollars for a full year, full-time black male worker, inferred from weekly earnings, rose from just under $5000 in 1940 to more the $20,000 in 1980, and that black male wages rose from 43% to 73% of white male wages in this same period. The ratio for actual annual earnings, given differences in

labor supply, in 1980, however, was somewhat less at 62% (Farley & Allen 1987).

Economic growth was a primary engine for improving the economic status of both blacks and whites from the end of the depression through the early 1970s (Jaynes & Williams 1989, Smith & Welch 1989, Farley 1993). Decompositions of changes in black-white differences show that the lion's share of the explanation for the narrowing of the wage gap for males is attributable to the narrowing in the education gap between blacks and whites, and to declines in the racial disparity in earnings as returns to schooling (Smith & Welch 1989, Farley & Allen 1987). Concentration in the south also had a smaller depressive effect on black earnings in 1980 than in 1940, because of redistribution of the black population from the south, but even more because of declining regional wage disparities and racial disparities within the south (Smith & Welch 1989). White and black distribution to occupations also became more similar across this period. Jaynes & Williams (1989) reported that from 1950 to 1982, because of shifts in the American occupational structure, the percentage of white men in professional or managerial positions increased from 20% to 32%, and for black men from 6% to 20%.

The story about transformations affecting women is different. In 1940, black women had higher rates of labor force participation and employment than did white women. Using census data Farley (1993) estimates that, based on 1940 employment rates, black women have been employed for 14.5 of their 40 years between ages 25 and 64, compared to just 8.8 years for white women. Increases of labor force participation by both black and white women led to increases in years in employment for both groups thereafter. By 1991, Bureau of Labor Statistics data showed that white women's years in employment during these ages would be 24.4 years, compared to 23.7 years for black women. By 1980, earnings ratios had closed for women in most education categories; for women with college degrees the earnings of black women exceeded those for white women (Farley 1993). However preliminary analysis of CPS data for the years 1969 to 1987 by M. Corcoran and S. Parrott (unpublished paper) found that white women's wages grew more rapidly than black women's wages after 1977. Corcoran & Parrott suggest that as the labor force participation of white women increases, advantages of black women deriving from unmeasured differences in labor force attachment may disappear, unmasking a racial wage gap among women.

The economic gap between blacks and whites seems unlikely to close soon because the American economy seems to have stalled well short of the mark that would allow full equality. The impact of economic restructuring is particularly acute for those at the bottom of the education and skill distribution where blacks are overrepresented. Many scholars point to declines of middle level jobs (Harrison & Bluestone 1988), the redistribution of manufacturing jobs away from the central cities where many jobless blacks live (Sassen 1988), and the rise of earnings inequality among workers of all races (Danziger & Gottschalk 1993) as causes for pessimism about the prospect for rapid future narrowing of the racial gap.

One manifestation of these changes may be that gains in earnings have been offset by a growing racial disparity in joblessness (unemployment and non-participation in the civilian labor force) between black and white men (Moss & Tilly 1991). In part, this increased joblessness reflects the substitution by young black men of "good" activities such as military service and education for work (Mare & Winship 1984, Smith & Welch 1989). Yet there is a trend toward relatively high rates of joblessness and nonparticipation in the labor force for African American males even at older ages (Smith & Welch 1989, Jencks 1991). Changes in the social fabric of some African-American communities, partly a consequence of the narrow opportunity structure for many African Americans, help to perpetuate structural barriers to improvement in the well-being of African Americans. Growing rates of female headship in African-American families have increased racial disparity in incomes and may create difficulties in the socialization of the next generation.

Female headship has been increasing for both black and white families, but especially for blacks. In 1940, 20% of black families with children under 18 were headed by women; by 1990 this figure had increased to 52%. For white families over the same period, families headed by women increased from 8% to 17% (Farley 1993). Because female headship is associated with high rates of poverty, this increase in female headship for blacks has expanded somewhat the disparity in

poverty rates for white and black families. Farley estimates that if the 1960 distribution of family type had held in 1980, black poverty rates would then have been 26% rather than the observed 33%. Bane (1986) estimated that in 1983 differences in household composition accounted for 44% of the difference in overall poverty rates between blacks and whites. However, Bane also cautioned that such decompositions could partially be artifacts of selection into household type, and particular caution was advised in the interpretation of trend data.

One important line of research associated with William Julius Wilson (1987) has focused in particular on the effects of these changes on African Americans who live in areas of concentrated poverty in the central city core of metropolitan areas. On the employment side these subpopulations suffer from a lack of education and skills and a mismatch between their urban location and the relocation of employment opportunities outside of cities (Kasarda 1985, Wilson 1987). On the social side, Wilson suggests that neighborhood concentrations of the most disadvantaged black populations have propagated destructive attitudes and behaviors that perpetuate the disadvantage, such as high rates of teenage childbearing, female family headship, drug use, illegal market activity, and detachment from the labor force.

A large research literature attempts to model the impact of these "neighborhood" effects—net of personal characteristics—on destructive behaviors and poor social and economic outcomes. These studies have shown inconsistent and generally relatively minor effects (Brooks-Gunn et al 1993, Crane 1991). (For a good overview see Jencks & Mayer 1990.)

While the emphasis in much of the literature on the social and economic impacts of economic restructuring on the most disadvantaged blacks has considerable justification, Jencks (1991, 1992) reminds us that the population that suffers from the full range of problems associated with the concept of the urban underclass is relatively narrowly circumscribed.

Despite the gains that have been made by some middle class and working class blacks in recent decades, there is a strong body of evidence that discrimination remains an important part of the explanation of black-white inequality. Farley & Allen (1987) show that for a black male there is still an earnings disadvantage at all levels of economic attainment. From studies testing the reaction of employers to job applicants of different races, Kirschenman & Neckerman (1991) find strong evidence of direct racial discrimination at the point of hiring by white employers. Feagin & Sikes (1994) show that the experience of racial hostility is routine for African Americans across social classes. These studies suggest that the fact that a particularly heavy share of the burden of current economic changes is borne by poor African Americans is not simply an artifact of the uncompetitive labor market position of many black workers; the civil rights revolution has by no means eradicated racial discrimination in American social and economic life.

AMERICAN INDIANS, HISPANICS, AND ASIANS

Questions sometimes arise about the prevalence and importance of discrimination to the employment and earnings of Hispanics or Latinos, Asians, as well as Native North Americans. Peoples in these categories are often categorized together with Americans of African descent as peoples of color, or racial minorities, though this attribution is particularly ambiguous for many Latino and Indian Americans given the large volume of intermixing between European and indigenous American peoples. What are the patterns of earnings inequality compared to the white population, and what costs does ascriptive discrimination impose, given the historical importance of color consciousness in the United States?

Studies of the labor market experiences of Hispanics as a whole, and of the different subgroups, find that while Hispanics are disadvantaged in the labor market compared to whites, only Puerto Ricans are as severely disadvantaged as blacks and American Indians. Although, overall, Asians have a higher median family income than do American whites ($41,583 vs. $37,630) in 1990, there is a great deal of variation among the subgroups. They range from the severely distressed Hmong population with a median family income of $14,327, a poverty rate of 63.6%, and a labor force participation rate of 29.3% to the successful Japanese with a median family income of $51,550 and a poverty rate of only 7%. The longer established Chinese, Japanese, Filipino, and Asian Indians are doing well—better than the white non-Hispanic average.

However, the Southeast Asian refugees from Laos, Cambodia, and Vietnam are not achieving as well.

What explains this pattern of variation? Multivariate earnings models suggest some evidence of wage and employment discrimination against Hispanics, Native Americans, and Asians, but that it is a less important factor than in the case of blacks. For many Asian groups, of course, there is no pattern of net disadvantage to explain, though this result is compatible with the finding of discrimination in returns to education and other human capital attributes. For many Latino groups, problems in the United States reflect in part the attributes of the migrant pool. At a migrant's destination, his/her poor human capital characteristics interact with the effects of American economic restructuring to perpetuate disadvantages. For Asians and Latinos, the characteristics of immigrants and their absorption into the country are an integral part of the story. The regional concentrations and different modes of incorporation of the different subgroups as well as their differing times of arrival and social class backgrounds also help to explain variations in outcomes (Portes & Truelove 1987, Nelson & Tienda 1985, Bean & Tienda 1987). We turn now to an examination of these groups in detail.

American Indians

The poorest of all the groups in the United States is also the group least influenced by immigration. In 1990, the Census counted 1.96 million American Indians and Alaskan Natives, which makes this the smallest of the four conventional minority categories in the United States. It was also among the poorest—a condition that has been noted by researchers historically (Meriam 1928, Brophy & Aberle 1966, Levitan & Hetrick 1971). This poverty has been associated with the underdevelopment of many reservation communities because of their geographical isolation, lack of resources, and political domination by federal authorities (Cornell & Kalt 1990, Snipp 1986, Trosper 1994, White 1983).

Earnings models for Indians confirm sharp wage disparities between Native Americans and white Americans. These are primarily attributable to large differences in human capital. Scholars disagree about whether the data show discrimination effects (Gwartney & Long 1978, Trosper 1974, Sandefur & Scott 1983).

One difficult theoretical and policy question about Indian reservation communities concerns the impact of residence on reservations on earnings disadvantages. Standard migration models would anticipate labor outflows exceeding those observed from these resource-poor rural enclaves. For other ethnic populations concentrations of disadvantaged group members such as those found on reservations might be considered evidence for the existence of imposed barriers to exit; for Indian tribes these are taken as an expected consequence of sovereignty. However, using data from the question as to place of residence five years ago on the 1980 census, Snipp & Sandefur (1988) could not find consistent earnings returns to migration from reservation areas.

Hispanics

In 1990, persons of Mexican origin formed the largest Hispanic group, numbering nearly 13.5 million persons. Puerto Ricans were the second largest with 2.7 million living on the mainland. There were slightly more than 1 million persons of Cuban origin. There were 5.1 million persons in the composite "Other Hispanic" category, including mostly Central and South Americans and other Caribbean people. Dominicans were the largest group within this category with over 500,000 people.

The outstanding theme characterizing the heterogeneity of Latinos is that Puerto Ricans do exceptionally badly in terms of employment and income, and Cubans do exceptionally well. Puerto Ricans are legally US citizens; they are concentrated in the industrialized northeast and work in industrial jobs. They have the highest proportion of persons living in poverty, show increasing withdrawal from formal labor markets, and have the highest rates of any Latino group of welfare dependency and family disruption (Morales & Bonilla 1993).

Mexicans have high labor force participation rates, but partly because of their lower overall educational attainment, they work for very low wages. Some of them are illegal immigrants, thought to be a docile and pliable work force, and so preferred by employers.

Many of the Cubans are political refugees, and a large number of them are concentrated in the city of Miami where they have created an enclave economy that provides employment opportunities for other Cubans, even those who speak little English or who are new arrivals (Portes & Bach 1985).

DeFrietas (1985, 1991) shows that unemployment and earnings differentials between Hispanics and non-Hispanics depend mostly on differences in worker characteristics. Both Reimers (1985) and Abowd & Killingsworth (1985) conclude that unequal educational attainment is the major determinant of the observed wage gap. The evidence on educational attainment shows Latinos doing poorly relative to other groups. Comparing college completion rates, Morales & Bonilla (1993:12) note that between 1980 and 1990 the white population increased college enrollment from 31% to 39%, African Americans from 28% to 33%, while Latinos remained level at 29%. However, Harrison & Bennett (1995) argue that the popular press reports of a crisis in education for Hispanics are overblown. They argue that "native born Hispanics are almost as likely to complete high school as blacks and American Indians; the very low percentage of Hispanic immigrants with high school diplomas reduces the completion rates of the group as a whole."

Standard multivariate studies of economic attainment of Hispanic men and women do show evidence of discrimination. Stolzenberg (1990) found, using the 1976 Survey of Income and Education (SIE), that Hispanics who speak English well and who have completed high school have returns to schooling about equal to white non-Hispanics. However, he did find that less educated Hispanics do have less return to their education than do statistically comparable non-Hispanic men. DeFrietas (1991) used 1980 census data on income in 1979 and found a gap of 10% or more between Hispanics and non-Hispanics after controlling for age, education, English language ability, nativity, and State/Metro residence. The Urban Institute found additional evidence of discrimination against Hispanic job applicants in an audit study of employers in Chicago and San Diego (Kenney & Wissoker 1994).

According to Morales & Bonilla (1993) changes in the American economy in the last few decades have hit Latinos particularly hard because of their low educational attainment and their labor market positions. Earnings for Latino men, controlled for inflation, actually dropped in the period between 1978 and 1987; in constant dollars they earned an average $49 per year less in 1987 than in 1978. Morales & Bonilla attribute part of this decline to the erosion of the minimum wage and the fact that 23.8% of Latino men were minimum wage workers.

Carnoy et al (1993), using 1980 census and Current Population Survey data from 1982, 1985, and 1987, found a decline in Latino relative incomes for both males and females in the 1980s. They argue that the relatively favorable trends in convergence between Latino and white earnings in the 1960s and 1970s were due to educational increases and a shift in employment from agriculture to manufacturing. They attribute the recent declines to increased numbers of immigrants with low education and English ability and the concentration of Latinos in low-paid service jobs and to the decline of higher-paid manufacturing jobs. Harrison & Bennett (1995) used a 1990 census data to find that some Hispanic men continue to earn less than comparably educated white men. Hispanic men with less than an associate degree earned only 76% of what white males with equivalent education earned.

The recent trends for women Hispanics as with other women minorities are better than the trends for men. Harrison & Bennett (1995) found that among all education levels, except among selected cohorts either without high school diplomas or with associate degrees, Hispanic and non-Hispanic white women have achieved parity in earnings. More detailed analyses should be done with 1990 census data for specific Hispanic groups because studies done with earlier data show strong differences by national origin. Reimers (1985), using 1976 SIE data, found that Central and South American men received wage offers 36% below those for white non-Hispanic men; the differential was 18% for Puerto Rican men, 12% for Other Hispanics, and 6% for Mexicans. Cubans, by contrast, showed a 6% advantage over white non-Hispanics with a similar background.

Scholars have paid particular attention to the puzzle of high poverty rates and declining labor force participation among Puerto Ricans, despite the "advantage" of US citizenship. The concentration of Puerto Ricans in declining manufacturing jobs, and the possibility of more virulent discrimination against Puerto Ricans of darker complexions are possible explanations, along with the availability of means tested transfer payments, the growth of households headed by women, and the growth of circular migration (Bean & Tienda 1987, Tienda et al 1992).

Because in 1990 35.8% of Hispanics were foreign born, the question of how the new immigrants are affecting the overall standing of Hispanics as a whole and of the different subgroups is an extremely important one. Factors such as changing migration streams, the proportion of workers who are undocumented, and particular economic strategies of the foreign-born affect the overall profile of the different groups.

In the 1980s the group "Other Hispanic" grew at a fast pace through immigration. This growth also contributed greatly to the heterogeneity of the Hispanic population. Many Central Americans from countries like El Salvador, Guatemala, and Nicaragua as well as Caribbean immigrants from the Dominican Republic tend to have limited educations, high poverty rates, and low median family incomes. South American immigrants from countries like Colombia, Peru, and Bolivia have much higher educational attainment, lower poverty rates, and higher incomes.

Undocumented workers, who are disproportionately Latin American, differ from legal immigrants in ways that also reinforce the low income profile of the group. Borjas & Tienda (1993:712) examined the employment experiences and wages of undocumented workers who applied for and received legalization under the 1986 IRCA amnesty program. They found that the legalized immigrants had higher rates of labor force participation than did the foreign-born population as a whole, exceeding those rates by 5% for men and 17% for women. Undocumented workers earned lower wages than legal immigrants—they earned 30% less than their legal counterparts from the same regional origins.

Asians

Asian Americans are the fastest growing minority group in the country. The Asian American population doubled in size in the 1980s and now totals 6.9 million, an increase from 1.5% to 2.9% of the total US population. This growth was due in great part to immigration. Of Asian Americans 66% were foreign born in 1990, and 28% of all Asian Americans entered the United States between 1980 and 1990. Southeast Asians from Vietnam, Laos, and Cambodia had the highest percentages of foreign-born, around 79%. Japanese had the lowest at 32.4% (Bureau of Census 1993).

Those people classified as Asian in the census and other sources come from a number of different countries with different cultures, languages, and histories. Within national origin groups there are also differences in social class background, timing of arrival, and labor market opportunities (Yamanaka & McClelland 1994:82).

Part of the explanation of Asian socioeconomic achievement lies in their greater-than-average educational attainment. The lower incomes and higher poverty of Southeast Asians are largely attributable to the much lower average educational attainment of members of these groups. While 23.3% of the total US male population had a college degree or higher, 48.7% of Asian Indian men, 41.6% of Filipino men, and 35% of Chinese men were college graduates; among Cambodians, Hmong, and Laotians, only 3% of men had a college degree or higher. Harrison & Bennett (1995) report that Asians were about two-thirds more likely to have completed college than whites.

This high educational attainment is partly a result of Asian immigration selectivity. Many Asians enter under highly selective immigration criteria. Harrison & Bennett report that native-born Asians are still substantially more likely to complete college (32%) than are whites and other groups, but the differential is smaller than for foreign-born Asians.

Though the relatively high education and earnings of many Asian groups mean that these groups do not suffer the same magnitude of disadvantages as many other groups, there is some evidence that returns to education are lower for Asian Americans than for whites, though this pattern may be changing (Hirschman & Wong 1984, Wong 1986). Asian men and women needed more education to receive the same income as whites. This can be attributed to discrimination in the higher end of the occupational structure (the glass ceiling effect) or to other unobservable human capital differences in things like quality of schooling or English language skills.

Hirschman & Wong (1984:584) analyzed 1960 and 1970 census data and 1976 SIE data for Japanese, Chinese, and Filipinos, as well as for other non-Asian groups. They found a marked decline in the direct negative effect of ethnicity on earnings (except among Chinese). They speculate that perhaps Chinese Americans do worse than others because the enclave of Chinatown serves as a funnel that directs Chinese Americans into low paying jobs. (This hypothesis is revisited when we review the more recent debate about the effects of ethnic enclaves on returns to education.) However, Hirschman & Wong found that there still were costs associated with Asian ethnicity—when adjusted for background variables, all groups except the Japanese had incomes somewhat less than comparable whites. Japanese men actually earned more than comparable white men in 1976. In a similar study, Wong & Hirschman (1983) found that Asian women had higher incomes overall than whites because they had higher amounts of education, lived in higher income areas, and were younger overall than whites.

In a multivariate study of income by education and by occupation, Barringer et al (1993:265) found that when other factors were controlled, "whites earned more than Asian Americans in almost all occupational categories except in the professions, where Asian Americans had much higher incomes, but even there they bested whites only among the self employed." They conclude that Asian Americans are highly educated and convert that education into high status occupations, but nevertheless they are paid less than whites for the same or comparable positions (Barringer et al 1993:266).

Recent evidence from the 1990 census shows that Asian returns to education are approaching those of non-Hispanic whites at upper levels of education. Compared to other minorities, Asians are approaching parity in their ability to convert their educational status into income and occupational standing, at 92% and 97% of comparable whites for the annual and hourly earnings of Asians with graduate degrees (Harrison & Bennett 1995). However, these analyses were not broken down by specific national origin groups.

Much of the literature on Asian Americans concerns the question of whether Asians' success makes them a "model minority" whose high education and income are due to cultural factors and hard work, which allow them to rise above adversity (Kitano 1976). The academic achievement of Asian American children, and the more stable family structure of Asian Americans, compared to other groups in America, are cited as examples of the ways their overall cultural values lead to success. Researchers critical of the success model of understanding Asian Americans stress:

1. The heterogeneity of the Asian population, the economic distress of Southeast Asian refugees, and the existence of unskilled workers employed in the low end of the split labor market (Poston 1988, 1994, Hein 1993, Lee 1989). These authors stress that there are dangers in viewing all Asians as successful, because the extreme poverty of Southeast Asians and the poverty of low skilled members of other groups will then not receive the public policy interventions that are needed.

2. The extra effort and household strategies Asian Americans are forced to use to overcome continuing discrimination, and the costs of that effort (Caplan et al 1989, Kibria 1994, Rumbaut 1989, Yamanaka & McClelland 1994, Huth & Kwang 1989, Espenshade & Ye 1994). These researchers stress the fact that many Asians avoid extreme poverty or welfare dependence through hard work and long hours that take physical and psychic tolls on individuals and families. Also families survive by dispatching many workers into the economy and by combining wage labor, government transfers, and other creative strategies to get by.

3. The specific problems faced by Asian entrepreneurs (Min 1990). These include long hours and combining many family workers in one households as well as facing the physical dangers of crime in shops in inner city neighborhoods, and the racial tensions, boycotts, and even riots such as those faced by Korean shop owners in black neighborhoods.

While all of these criticisms of the blind equation of Asian Americans with socioeconomic success are valid, the fact remains that many Asian Americans are doing as well, or better than, whites. Southeast Asians are not doing well overall—however, these refugees came with little formal education and little preparation for their move to the United States. The question of what will happen to their children—the second generation—is a very important one for this debate. Caplan et al. (1989, 1991) cite the educational success of the children of the boat people as a hopeful sign that there will be a great deal of economic mobility. In fact they cite the educational success of children of boat people as "truly startling and extraordinary" (although their study did not include the severely distressed Cambodians and Hmong). If the children of the Southeast Asian boat people do show enormous socioeconomic mobility and high educational attainment in the future, this will indeed call forth the model minority descriptions, and it will be up to analysts to revisit the debate.

NEW IMMIGRANTS AND NATIVE MINORITIES

Perhaps the most perplexing question about the current pattern of racial and ethnic inequality in the United States is how—given the economic restructuring and loss of manufacturing jobs that have occurred—some new immigrants manage to do well in the labor force compared to native minorities? Portes & Zhou (1992:498) describe this as the "peculiar American paradox of rising labor market marginalization of native-born blacks and Puerto Ricans, along with growing numbers and employment of third world immigrants" (see also Sassen 1988). This is related to the important policy question of whether the foreign-born take jobs from native minorities. Another question that motivates research in this area is why some immigrants seem to do better than others—how to explain the relative success of Cubans or East Indians compared to Puerto Ricans or Vietnamese?

The classic economic approach to understanding the incorporation of immigrants has been to measure individual level data on human capital endowments such as education, language ability, and the like, and then assess the returns of wages and earnings to those human capital characteristics. The standard model (such as in Chiswick 1979) finds that the longer immigrants are present in the United States labor force, the more their initial earnings disadvantage is overcome. Chiswick found that the crossover point when the foreign-born equal or surpass the native-born is 15 years.

The current debate about immigrants and their human capital skills revolves around the argument of Borjas (1990, 1991) that the average skill levels or "quality" of immigrants has declined over time. This is important for understanding the assimilation process of immigrants because of the frequently used assumption that convergence between foreign-born and native-born wages and earnings equals assimilation. If it is assimilation, recent immigrants would be expected to catch up to or cross over the earlier immigrants and natives. However, if recent immigrants are of lower overall quality than earlier immigrants, then the progress seen in cross-sectional data is illusory, and more recent immigrants would be expected to have lower earnings than natives permanently.

Borjas' conclusions have been criticized on a number of points, including a failure to take into account emigration by the less successful foreign-born, (Jasso & Rosenzweig 1990) and the confusion of "immigrant quality" with national origin differences and differences in contexts of reception and modes of incorporation. As Tienda (1983b) points out, the standard human capital approach, with its emphasis on individual differences, does not explain why, after extensive controls for various determinants of earnings, there persist differences in the rate at which foreign workers of differing national origins reach income parity with the native-born population. For instance Poston (1994) in an analysis of economic attainment among foreign-born men, finds that men from European origins do much better than those from other regions of the world. He also finds that refugees-turned-immigrants from places such as El Salvador, Guatemala, Haiti, Honduras, Laos, Nicaragua, Panama, and Vietnam are not doing as well as economic immigrants from other countries in terms of their economic attainment.

Tienda (1983b) and Portes & Rumbaut (1990) argue for an analysis based on looking at the mode of incorporation or context of reception that different national origin groups face. The very evaluation of worker characteristics by employers is often not done on an individual basis but is affected by things like the degree of ethnic concentration of particular groups, and the degree of prejudice toward those groups present in American culture. The national origin differences Borjas finds in returns to human capital may be due to some unobservable individual characteristic that is a measure of "quality", or it may be due to some group level characteristics, such as the effects of ethnic networks on economic incorporation, or discrimination in the form of hiring queues, lesser pay for equal work, or some other sort of differ-

ential reaction on the part of American society based on something other than individual characteristics. Lieberson (1980) showed that greater concentrations of particular ethnic groups in a particular labor market increased the chances for competition and discrimination against those groups (see also Tienda & Wilson 1992). Later cohorts by definition face greater concentrations of their group as they join earlier migrants from their ethnic groups.

An approach that emphasizes the social as well as the economic context of the reception of immigrants includes an analysis of community level variables that condition the kinds of achievement individuals experience (Portes & Zhou 1992). An example of this approach is the discussion of the ethnic enclave as a pathway for mobility for immigrants.

The Enclave Debate

When immigrants enter a new society they often face barriers to full inclusion in the economic activities of the host society. Besides through outright discrimination, this occurs, for example, because of the absence of network ties necessary to gain access to or to succeed in certain kinds of activities, because of barriers to entry to professional or internal labor markets that have the effect of excluding those with foreign credentials, because the skills of immigrants are concentrated in specific occupations, and because these skills may not be well matched to the needs of the employers in the host society.

An immigrant group's economic standing depends in part on the way in which it overcomes these barriers to become incorporated into the economy. Often entrepreneurism has been an avenue. A consistent finding in the examination of immigrant earnings and employment is the overrepresentation of immigrants in entrepreneurial activities, and a positive relationship between self-employment and income (Portes & Zhou 1992: 495). The involvement of immigrants in small business has been investigated by a number of scholars including Light (1972), Bonacich (1973), Light & Bonacich (1988), Waldinger (1986, 1989), and Waldinger et al (1990). The ethnic enclave (first defined by Wilson & Portes 1980 and Portes & Bach 1985) is a particularly important avenue of mobility for Cuban Americans. The enclave is defined as a concentration of ethnic firms in physical space—generally a metropolitan area—that employ a significant proportion of workers from the same minority" (Portes & Jensen 1992:418).

Portes and his associates have argued that the enclave allows immigrants to find employment that brings better returns to their human capital than would be found in the secondary labor market outside of the enclave, and that it is therefore beneficial for workers as well as employers. They cite the Cuban enclave in Miami as an example of the use of an enclave as an unorthodox mobility path that in part explains the relative success of Cubans compared to other Hispanics. This view of the ethnic enclave has direct implications for long-held assumptions about assimilation. The argument is that people who stay within the ethnic enclave do better than those who leave it for employment, which is of course in direct contradiction to an assimilation model that would posit greater success for those leaving the ethnic concentration.

The enclave hypothesis has engendered a great deal of debate. While Portes & Jensen (1987, 1989) see the enclave as offering opportunities for economic mobility, Sanders & Nee (1987, 1992) see it as an ethnic mobility trap. These authors conducted an analysis of census data on Cubans in Miami and Chinese in California and concluded that while employers may be better off in the enclave economy, workers were not better off and may be exploited by their co-ethnic employers.

One difficulty with the debate about the impact of enclaves is that limitations of the census data that have formed the basis of many of the studies make it difficult to operationalize theoretical concepts directly. Different researchers have also used different definitions of the enclave, defining it by place of work (Portes & Jensen 1989, 1992) or place of residence (Sanders & Nee 1987, 1992). Zhou & Logan (1991) operationalized the enclave in three different ways, as place of residence, place of work, and place of industry. Using place of residence as the definition of the Chinese enclave in New York, they found positive returns for human capital for workers both inside and outside the enclave. Zhou & Logan also raise the possibility that some enclave economies provide better opportunities than others and that there may be gender differences in the operation of enclave effects.

Logan et al. (1994) point out that the ethnic enclave is a relatively rare phenomenon, characterizing the Cubans in Miami, Los Angeles, and Jersey City; Mexicans in Los Angeles and Houston; Chinese in New York, San Francisco, and Los Angeles; Koreans in Los Angeles; and Japanese in Los Angeles, San Francisco, San Jose, Anaheim, and Honolulu. Many other cities have large numbers of minorities without a spatial overrepresentation of an ethnic group corresponding to an ethnic enclave. This uneven pattern of enclave development across different cities and different ethnic groups is an intriguing one, worthy of further research investigating the mechanisms by which enclaves become established.

Research about the structuring and impact of ethnic enclaves constitutes an important part of the agenda for the study of the incorporation of immigrant ethnic groups. While we do not agree with Waldinger (1993) that the term ethnic enclave should be abandoned because of the difficulty of definition and measurement, we do believe that many of the central questions about its operation are dependent not on further analyses of census data, but on gathering new data with direct measurements of theoretically relevant variables of the sort gathered by Portes & Bach (1985).

Implications of Immigration
for Native Minorities

Another important set of questions about immigrants concerns their impact on native minorities. Immigrants have higher rates of entrepreneurship and labor force participation than do blacks and Puerto Ricans in the nation's cities, and lower rates of unemployment. Do immigrants take jobs from native minorities? Jackson (1983) cites the possibilities for increased interethnic tensions if immigrants succeed and leave America's longtime resident minorities behind. Some of the popular media suggested the stress caused by competition for jobs was one reason behind ethnic tensions that surfaced in the 1992 Los Angeles uprising (Muller 1993:197).

Despite these expectations, at the aggregate level, econometric studies show that immigrants do not compete with native workers and do not decrease their wages or employment levels (Borjas & Tienda 1987, Borjas 1990, LaLonde & Topel 1991). Muller (1993:181) argues that middle class blacks in gateway cities such as New York, Chicago, and Los Angeles experience upward mobility into professional and managerial sectors at rates higher than they do in cities without immigrants.

However, certain industry case studies and local area studies have found substitution and competition (Waldinger 1986, Bailey 1987, Waters 1994).

Various explanations have been advanced to account for the finding that immigrants do not take jobs from native minorities. The bimodal distribution of skills among immigrants means that some immigrants arrive with high education and skills. These immigrants do not compete with those members of native minorities who are overrepresented at the lower end of the skill distribution, and they may even begin businesses that then create jobs for native workers. Simon (1989) also argued that consumption by immigrants stimulates the economy, because immigrants upon arrival begin consuming before they are employed, thus increasing demands for goods and services even if they do not find employment. However, the effect is likely negligible at best.

Waldinger's (1994) work on immigrants and natives in New York City shows that the establishment of ethnic networks and the decline in the population of native whites leads to the establishment of ethnic niches in employment and job vacancies that defuse immigrant native competition.

One important line of research studies the effect of unskilled immigrants on the employment of unskilled natives. Many reason that illegal immigrants accept lower wages and worse working conditions because of their need to work and avoid detection by immigration authorities, and because conditions of employment considered substandard in the United States exceed those available at the margin in many countries of origin.

In the economics literature, a standard approach to the study of the effect of immigrants on native workers is to treat different analyses of cities within the United States as distinct labor markets and to compare labor market outcomes across cities with higher and lower immigrant densities. Using this approach, Butcher & Card (1991) examine whether the declines in the 1980s of the real earnings of the least skilled workers in the US economy were related to immigration. They found that while the rise in wage inequality in the 1980s was bigger in cities with relatively bigger immigrant inflows, immigration was more associated with growth in wages at the high end for workers than in decline of wages at the low end.

Muller (1993) finds a negative correlation between blacks' income and the percentage of immigrants and between black youth unemployment and immigration. He concludes that either immigrants create economic growth, which in turn improves job prospects for blacks, or that Mexicans and Asians as well as blacks are all attracted to urban areas where employment opportunities are growing.

One possibility is that unskilled native workers migrate out of cities where immigrant workers are arriving. Filer (1990) analyzed population movements between 1975 and 1980 and found that intercity migration decisions of natives were sensitive to immigrant growth, and that immigrant arrivals are almost completely offset by native outflows. However, Butcher & Card (1991) find the opposite in their analysis of native migration and immigrants in the 1980s. These authors conclude that there is a positive link between immigrant inflows and net native in-migration.

Although these aggregate comparisons across cities do not show effects on unskilled native minorities of a rise in immigration, this does not mean that there are not substitution effects in particular occupations, industries, or work sites. Many black Americans believe that they are losing jobs to immigrant workers (Waters 1994). In a survey of hiring practices among Chicago area employers, Kirschenman & Neckerman (1991) found strong employer preferences in hiring decisions for immigrants over inner city blacks (see also Muller 1993:179). Substitution of immigrants for blacks in unskilled work sites might take place in ways that are difficult to measure directly. For instance large numbers of immigrants available to do contract work or working in small enterprises might affect the ability of cities and industries to hire nonunion contractors to do work previously done by unionized workers. Blacks who had been employed in unionized public work sectors could suffer as a result (Muller 1993).

These aggregate studies based on correlations between presence of immigrants and black employment and earnings in specific cities do not make clear whether blacks might have done better had immigrants not been present, and had there been economic growth. Employers may have been forced to raise wages for low skilled jobs, which might have made them more attractive to native workers.

Given the stagnation of movement toward closing the wage gap between blacks and whites, the fact that many immigrant groups do better than native populations, and the historical tendency of native labor to look warily on immigrant competition, questions about the role of immigrants on disadvantaged native minorities seem likely to generate continuing interest. One important area for research in the future is reconciling the perception by many unskilled minority workers that immigrants take jobs from them with the econometric findings that substitution is not occurring.

The Second Generation

Because new immigrants are predominantly nonwhite, the success of some new immigrants relative to native minorities leads to an intriguing question about the future of the children and grandchildren of the immigrants. Will they follow some of the more hopeful patterns of success and mobility that seem to characterize their parents? Or will they experience downward social mobility as they join America's native nonwhite minority in disproportionate poverty, low skilled work, and unemployment? While there have been no wide-scale studies of the second generation of the post-1965 immigrants, recent years have produced a number of case studies and a few thoughtful and important hypotheses about the experiences of the second generation.

Gans (1990) suggests that in contrast to the children of European immigrants early in this century, the second generation of post-1965 immigrants may well experience socioeconomic decline relative to their parents because of the much changed opportunity structure in the American economy. He outlines several scenarios of possible socioeconomic and social integration of this new second generation. He hypothesizes that some of the children of the immigrants might "Americanize" by adopting the negative attitudes of many American youths toward the low-level, low-pay jobs to which they, like their parents, appear to be confined. On the other hand, some may remain tied to their parents' ethnic community and values; by rejecting the negative attitudes toward school, opportunity, hard work, and the "American dream" that some among the native poor have adopted, these children may end up doing better. If this is true, the ironic result may well find "the people who have secured an economically viable ethnic niche acculturating less than did the European 2nd and 3rd generations" (Gans 1990:189), and those without such a niche may become American

but experience downward social mobility and reclassification as "undeserving members of the so-called underclass" (Gans 1990:183).

Portes & Zhou (1993) make a similar argument. They argue that the mode of incorporation of the first generation creates differential opportunities and cultural and social capital in the form of ethnic jobs, networks, and values that create differential pulls on the allegiances of the second generation.

For immigrant groups who face extreme discrimination in the United States and who are close in proximity to American minorities who have faced a great deal of discrimination, "reactive ethnicity" emerges in the first generation. For groups who come with strong ethnic networks, access to capital, and with fewer ties to minorities in the United States, "linear ethnicity" develops. Groups with linear ethnicity may resist acculturation in the United States and end up providing better opportunities for the second generation through the "social capital" created through ethnic ties. The second generation of those with reactive ethnicity, by contrast, are likely to develop the "adversarial stance" toward the dominant white society that American minorities such as poor blacks and Hispanics hold. They conclude: "Children of nonwhite immigrants may not even have the opportunity of gaining access to middle class white society, no matter how acculturated they become. Joining those native circles to which they do have access may prove a ticket to permanent subordination and disadvantage" (Portes & Zhou 1993: 96). These hypotheses rest on notions of network ties, community resources, and social capital that require in-depth study among both native minority groups and the second generation. Because the census no longer asks a question about birthplace of parents (last asked in the 1970 census) the second generation disappears statistically into the native minority population. This is a serious problem in assessing overall trends of assimilation and success for the post-1965 immigrant cohort, as well as in measuring negative or positive impacts of immigrants on native-born minorities. Determining which of the scenarios outlined by these analysts actually will occur will be dependent on careful ethnographic research in these communities, on gathering detailed and expensive survey data, and on reinstituting the census question on parental birthplace.

CONCLUSION

The research literature on ethnic inequality reviewed here shows that progress in narrowing the gap between minorities and whites and among white ethnics was made when the economy was expanding through the mid-1970s. After that, for many groups, the progress slowed, stopped, or reversed. The restructuring of the American economy in the last few decades has hit many unskilled minority workers hard. In addition, the evidence indicates that direct discrimination is still an important factor for all minority subgroups except very highly educated Asians. The large numbers of immigrants entering the United States in recent decades have had mixed success, but there are some intriguing ways in which im-

migrants seem to have achieved mobility in spite of hard economic times and nonwhite status.

In addition to the questions and data needs described in the above discussions of the second generation and of the ethnic enclave, we see some additional important avenues for further research. These include the unraveling of the separate and interactive effects of gender and race/ethnicity, an analysis of the involvement of immigrants in affirmative action programs, and the effects any such involvement may have on native minorities. In addition a sustained look is needed at the question of what continues to cause direct labor market discrimination by employers in favor of whites and immigrants over blacks in hiring decisions.

ACKNOWLEDGMENTS
We are grateful to Sarah Song for research assistance, and to Lynne Farnum and Victoria Kent for secretarial assistance.

F I F T E E N

Assimilation's Quiet Tide

Richard D. Alba

Assimilation has become America's dirty little secret. Although once the subject of avid discussion and debate, the idea has fallen into disrepute, replaced by the slogans of multiculturalism. At best, assimilation is considered of dubious relevance for contemporary minorities, who are believed to want to remain outside the fabled "melting pot" and to be, in any event, not wholly acceptable to white America.

However, assimilation was, and is, a reality for the majority of the descendants of earlier waves of immigration from Europe. Of course, it does

have its varieties and degrees. Among Americans descended from the immigrants of the nineteenth and early twentieth centuries, assimilation is better viewed as a direction, rather than an accomplished end state.

Assimilation need not imply the obliteration of all traces of ethnic origins, nor require that every member of a group be assimilated to the same degree. That ethnic communities continue to exist in many cities and that many individuals identify with their ethnic ancestry do not indicate that assimilation is a myth. What, then, does assimilation

Reprinted with permission of the author and *The Public Interest*, Number 119, Spring 1995, pp. 3–18. ©
1995 by National Affairs, Inc.

mean when applied to American ethnic groups derived from European immigration?

It refers, above all, to long-term processes that
have whittled away at the social foundations for
ethnic distinctions. These processes have brought
about a rough parity of opportunities to attain
such socioeconomic goods as educational credentials and prestigious jobs, loosened the ties between ethnicity and specific economic niches,
diminished cultural differences that serve to signal ethnic membership to others and to sustain
ethnic solidarity, shifted residence away from
central-city ethnic neighborhoods to ethnically intermixed suburbs, and, finally, fostered relatively
easy social intermixing across ethnic lines, resulting ultimately in high rates of ethnic intermarriage and ethnically mixed ancestry.

The assimilation associated with these outcomes should not be viewed as imposed upon
resistant individuals seeking to protect their cultural identities—a common image of assimilation in recent, largely negative, discourse—nor as
self-consciously embraced by individuals seeking
to disappear into the mainstream (though, in
both instances, there may be some who fit the
description).

Rather, it is, in general, the perhaps unintended, cumulative byproduct of choices made by
individuals seeking to take advantage of opportunities to improve their social situations. For many
white ethnics, these opportunities opened especially in the period following World War II, due to
more favorable attitudes towards groups such as
Jews and Italians, the expansion of higher education and middle-class and upper-middle-class
employment, and the mushrooming growth of
housing in suburban communities.

The decision to make use of these opportunities sometimes has greater impact on the following generations than on the one responsible for
them. When socially mobile families forsake the
old neighborhood, where the stamp of ethnic
ways on everyday life could be taken for granted,
for a suburb, it is the children who grow up in a
multi-ethnic, or even non-ethnic, environment.

WHAT'S IN A NAME

The rising tide of assimilation is illustrated by
data from the most recent U.S. census (1990). A
first sign is given by responses to the ancestry

question, which appeared for the first time in the
1980 census. From the 1980 to the 1990 census,
there were surprising changes in the way ancestries were reported. In contrast to the racial- and
Hispanic-origin data collected by the census, the
distributions of responses across European-
ancestry categories underwent sharp alterations,
which appear to correlate strongly with the specific ancestry examples offered on the census ques-
tionnaire. These ancestry examples were listed
immediately below the question, and their influence on the resulting responses implies that many
whites are suggestible when it comes to the way
they describe their ancestry.

For instance, in 1980, "English" was among the
first examples given, and 49.6 million Americans
claimed English ancestry; in 1990, it was omitted
from the list of examples, and the number who
identified themselves as of English ancestry fell to
32.7 million, a decline of one-third. Similarly, in
1990, German and Italian were the first two
ancestry examples given; though both were also
listed in 1980, their positions were not as prominent. Both ancestry groups increased in number
by about 20 percent between the two censuses,
an increase substantially larger than that for
European-ancestry categories in general. Such
shifts suggest that ethnic ancestry is not a firmly
anchored self-concept for many Americans, and
alert us to the need to take ancestry data with a
dose of caution, for the "Germans" and "Italians"
of 1990 have changed in unknown ways from the
"Germans" and "Italians" of 1980.

INCREASING SOCIOECONOMIC PARITY

Historically, one of the most important moorings
of ethnicity has been the concentration of different ethnic groups in specific socioeconomic strata.
This brings the members of an ethnic group together by circumstances other than ethnicity and
gives them common material and other interests
arising from their shared situations. As Nathan
Glazer and Daniel Patrick Moynihan explained
in their seminal book, *Beyond the Melting Pot*, "to
name an occupational group or a class is very
much the same thing as naming an ethnic group."

However, in recent years, there has been a
growing and impressive convergence in the average socioeconomic opportunities for members of
white ethnic groups. Convergence here means

that the disadvantages that were once quite evident for some groups of mainly peasant origins in Europe, such as the Italians, have largely faded, and their socioeconomic attainments increasingly resemble, if not even surpass, those of the average white American.

This phenomenon is quite demonstrable for education (a convenient indicator because its level is, for the great majority, fixed by the age of 25), but it is hardly limited to this sphere. Table 1 [a and b] presents the educational attainments of younger and older cohorts for the major European-ancestry categories. The data compiled in the table are

limited to "non-Hispanic whites" (a population overwhelmingly of European ancestry) and to individuals born in the United States, thus avoiding any confounding with the characteristics of immigrants themselves. Though the data cannot tell us about the quality of education received, the evidence of convergence is strong.

To evaluate changes, two comparison groups are presented: one contains all non-Hispanic whites and the other individuals whose ancestry is solely from the British Isles (exclusive of the Republic of Ireland). The latter is commonly viewed as one of America's privileged ethnic

TABLE 1a   *Educational Attainment by Ethnic Ancestry—Men*

	COHORT BORN 1956–1965		COHORT BORN 1916–1925	
	Percentage Attended College	*Percentage Completed Bachelor's Degree*	*Percentage Attended College*	*Percentage Completed Bachelor's Degree*
All non-Hispanic white	55.9	25.5	34.6	16.2
Solely British	66.3	31.8	46.6	23.5
German	57.6	25.9	35.2	16.0
Irish	59.4	26.5	33.8	15.4
French	52.6	21.9	32.4	14.4
Italian	61.9	30.2	25.8	12.1
Polish	61.4	32.9	29.2	14.2
All southern and eastern European	64.4	33.8	32.2	16.0

Source: 1-in-1000 Public Use Microdata Sample of the 1990 Census.

TABLE 1b   *Educational Attainment by Ethnic Ancestry—Women*

	COHORT BORN 1956–1965		COHORT BORN 1916–1925	
	Percentage Attended College	*Percentage Completed Bachelor's Degree*	*Percentage Attended College*	*Percentage Completed Bachelor's Degree*
All non-Hispanic white	57.7	24.6	25.1	8.7
Solely British	66.3	31.5	38.1	15.7
German	60.7	24.8	25.8	9.2
Irish	60.4	25.0	24.0	7.7
French	56.2	20.3	26.5	9.9
Italian	61.2	27.8	16.5	4.9
Polish	62.2	29.4	14.4	3.8
All southern and eastern European	64.1	31.8	19.3	6.1

Source: 1-in-1000 Public Use Microdata Sample of the 1990 Census.

groups. The other groups presented are the largest non-British groups, divided between the early-arriving groups from northern and western Europe (Germans, Irish, French, in order of size), and the later-arriving groups from southern and eastern Europe (Italians, Poles, and a separate category containing all individuals with ancestry from southern and/or eastern Europe).

In the case of each ancestry category, individuals are included in the tabulations regardless of whether their ancestry is solely or partly from the category. Limiting tabulations to individuals with ancestry exclusively from one category would, in effect, eliminate one of the important mechanisms of assimilation—growing up in an ethnically mixed family.

The groups from southern and eastern Europe are often regarded as the acid test of assimilation because of the relative recency of their arrival and the prominence of their ethnicity in American cities. For the men of these groups who were born between 1916 and 1925, moderate disadvantages are evident when they are compared to the average non-Hispanic white or to men of German, Irish, and French ancestries; the disadvantage appears more substantial when compared to men of exclusively British ancestry. For instance, only a quarter to a third of Italian and Polish men attended college, compared to almost half of the British men. About one in eight Italians and Poles completed bachelor's degrees, compared to nearly one in four British men.

In the cohort born between 1956 and 1965 (whose education was largely complete by the time of the 1990 census), the southern and eastern Europeans have just about pulled even with the British men and are ahead of the average white and the men of other northern- and western-European origins. The figures for southern and eastern Europeans in general and for Poles may be affected by the extraordinary accomplishments of Jewish men (who are nevertheless minorities of these categories), but the same argument cannot be made in the case of the Italians.

The process of convergence is also quite striking among women. For predominantly rural immigrant groups, like the Italians and Poles, the education of daughters was of secondary importance compared to the education of sons. In the older cohort, British women had rates of college attendance and graduation more than twice those of their Italian and Polish contemporaries. This disparity has been largely eradicated in the younger cohort: Italian and Polish women are slightly behind British women in college attendance and graduation but tied with, if not slightly ahead of, the average non-Hispanic white woman as well as those of German, Irish, and French ancestries. The younger women in the general southern- and eastern-European category have above-average educational attainments that are similar to those of British women; this parity represents a marked improvement over their situation in the older cohort.

DECLINE OF EUROPEAN MOTHER TONGUES

Declines in overt cultural differences are a second component of assimilatory change. In census data, these are measurable in terms of the languages spoken in the home. Communication in a mother tongue marks a social boundary, which includes those who share the same ethnic origin and can speak its language and excludes all others. In addition, many aspects of ethnic culture that are embedded in a mother tongue are diminished or lost as exposure and fluency wane.

All available evidence reveals a powerful pattern of conversion to English monolingualism within three generations, from which only a small minority of any group escapes (a pattern first established by the sociologist Calvin Veltman). Consequently, the use in the home of European mother tongues (other than Spanish), and even exposure to them, have dropped off quite precipitously among those with southern- and eastern-European ancestries. Many older members of these groups spoke these languages in the immigrant homes and communities where they grew up. Data collected by the Census Bureau's Current Population Survey in the late 1970s show that three-quarters of southern- and eastern-European ethnics born in the United States before 1930 grew up in homes where a language other than English was spoken.

The situation for younger members of these and other groups, as depicted in the 1990 census, is presented in Table 2 (which omits the English-speaking ethnic categories). The younger cohort contains individuals who were between the ages

TABLE 2 *Language at Home by Ethnic Ancestry*

	COHORT BORN 1976–1985	COHORT BORN 1916–1925
	Percentage Speak Other than English	*Percentage Speak Other than English*
All non-Hispanic white	3.5	6.1
German	2.2	2.9
French	3.3	13.4
Italian	4.0	19.4
Polish	3.5	24.2
All southern and eastern European	5.1	19.8

Source: 1-in-1000 Public Use Microdata Sample of the 1990 Census.

of five and fourteen in 1990 (the census does not record the language of children under the age of five). In general, 95 percent or more of the children in each ethnic category speak only English at home. There are scarcely differences to be noted among the categories, except perhaps for the slightly higher percentage of German children who speak English only.

Speaking a mother tongue at home is more common among the older members of these groups. Germans are still an exception, testifying to the deep impact of wartime hostility on the survival of German culture in the United States. For the Italians, Poles, and other southern and eastern Europeans, about 20 percent of their older members continue to speak a mother tongue, presumably on a daily basis. The figure is nearly as high for the French. Of course, still higher percentages spoke mother tongues during their childhoods. A major transition in language is evidently underway.

Qualifiers, however, should not be overlooked here. Perhaps fluency in a language is not required for it to serve an ethnic purpose; the use of words and phrases from a mother tongue, interspersed in English conversation, can signal an ethnic loyalty to others. This sort of knowledge cannot be measured from census data, but it does seem plausible that, where languages cease to be everyday means of communication, knowledge of words and phrases will drop off, too. Also, it is impossible to measure from census data the number of individuals who acquire a mother tongue through schooling or other formal instruction. Yet, given the generally sorry record of Americans' mastery of foreign languages, one would not

want to depend too much on this source for cultural support.

THE DECLINING ETHNIC NEIGHBORHOOD

Educational and occupational mobility and language acculturation, combined with the potent catalyst of competition with racial and new immigrant minorities over urban turf, have spurred residential changes. These have brought many white ethnics out of inner-city ethnic neighborhoods and into suburban settings, where ethnic residential concentrations tend to be diluted, if they exist at all. As a result of the continued visibility of surviving ethnic neighborhoods, some of which have become meccas for those seeking an "authentic" ethnic experience, the magnitude and implications of residential shifts are less appreciated than they should be.

In depicting residential shifts, I will switch from the trends in aggregate national census samples to the changes in a single but special geographic context, the Greater New York metropolitan region. This broad swath of cities and suburbs, covering 23 densely settled counties stretching from the Hudson Valley and Long Island in New York to the New Jersey shore, was home to 17 million people in 1990. Examining residential patterns in a single region avoids the risk of decontextualizing residential situations and losing sight of their location in relation to ethnic communities. No doubt due to the New York region's historic role as a gateway for immigrants, white ethnic communities continue to play a visible role in its ethnic geography. If such communities are important anywhere, they are sure to be so here.

Three large groups—Germans, Irish, and Italians—are used to trace residential patterns. Each has between two and three million members in the region, according to both 1980 and 1990 census data, and has figured in significant ways in the region's ethnic neighborhoods in the past. However, based on their histories and the results of past investigations (such as *Beyond the Melting Pot*), the Germans could be expected to be the least residentially distinctive (i.e., with the fewest ethnic areas), while the Italians should be the most.

In fact, all of these groups are now found mainly in the suburban parts of the region, where ethnic residential concentrations are demonstrably thinner (though not nonexistent). By 1980, the Germans and Irish were already disproportionately located in suburbs: roughly three-quarters of both were outside central cities, compared to two-thirds of all non-Hispanic whites (but just one-quarter of Hispanics and nonwhites). Moreover, in suburbia, the residential distributions of the Germans and Irish are barely distinguishable from that of other non-Hispanic whites. In other words, these groups are residentially intermixed.

The Italians present a different, but more dynamic, picture. In 1980, they were slightly less likely to be found in suburbs than the average white (64 percent versus 66 percent), but during the 1980s their numbers in large cities fell while rising in the suburbs. By 1990, 70 percent resided in suburbs. While they were still not as suburbanized as the Germans and Irish, they were more so than the average non-Hispanic white. For the Italians, too, suburban residence means a greater probability of living in an ethnically diverse community.

ETHNIC EXODUS

This picture gains further credibility when it is taken to the level of specific ethnic neighborhoods. To accomplish this, John Logan, Kyle Crowder, and I have identified the region's ethnic neighborhoods in 1980 and 1990 census data as clusters of census tracts where any of the three groups has an above-average concentration (operationally defined as 35 percent or more of the population).

For the Germans and Irish, these neighborhoods are, generally speaking, few and small; only

tiny fractions of each group could be considered to reside in them (just 4 percent of the Irish in 1990, for instance). For the Italians, however, there are a number of these neighborhoods, some of which are quite large and most of which take on familiar outlines, identifiable with well-known Italian areas (such as Brooklyn's Bensonhurst). Nevertheless, it is still the case that just a minority of the group—a quarter in both 1980 and 1990—resides in Italian neighborhoods.

The Italian neighborhoods, moreover, underwent substantial changes during the 1980s. The outflow of Italians from the region's large cities especially drained inner-city ethnic neighborhoods. Bensonhurst was the largest contiguous Italian area in 1980, home to nearly 150,000 persons of Italian ancestry. By 1990, it had shrunk in its Italian population to less than 100,000, while also diminishing in spatial extent. Most other inner-city Italian neighborhoods also lost population, though not on such a dramatic scale. In effect, this outflow removed Italians from their most ethnic neighborhoods.

The suburban areas with growing numbers of Italians are very different in character. In the first place, the great majority of suburban Italians reside outside of anything resembling an ethnic neighborhood. Moreover, population growth bypassed inner-suburban ethnic neighborhoods, such as the Italian areas of Yonkers, and insofar as growth was funneled into outer-suburban areas of Italian concentration, these are not very ethnic, as measured for example by the number of residents who are intermarried.

In sum, even in the New York region, the ethnic mosaic *par excellence,* trends favor the further residential assimilation of white ethnic groups. The Irish, long a prominent ethnic group in the region, are already residentially intermixed. The Italians, some of whose ethnic communities are still conspicuous, reside mostly in non-ethnic areas, and their continuing suburbanization is eroding the most ethnic Italian neighborhoods.

THE INTERMARRIAGE MELTING POT

Intermarriage is usually regarded, with justification, as the litmus test of assimilation. This remains true even if marriage can no longer be taken for granted as a lifetime commitment. A high rate of intermarriage signals that individuals of putatively different ethnic backgrounds no longer perceive social and cultural differences significant enough to create a barrier to a long-term union. In this sense, intermarriage could be said to test the salience, and even the existence, of a social boundary between ethnic categories. Moreover, intermarriage carries obvious and profound implications for the familial and, more broadly, the social contexts in which the next generation will be raised. Its significance in this respect is not much diminished by a high rate of divorce because the children of divorces usually carry on close relationships with both sides of their families.

Among whites, intermarriage has advanced to the point where a substantial majority of marriages involve some degree of ethnic intermixing. In 1990 census data, more than half (56 percent) of whites have spouses whose ethnic backgrounds do not overlap with their own at all (included in this count are spouses whose ethnic ancestries are described as just "American" or in some other non-ethnic way). Only one-fifth have spouses with identical ethnic backgrounds. The remainder, not quite one-quarter, have spouses whose ancestries overlap their own in some respect but differ in some other. Of necessity, one or both partners in these marriages have mixed ancestry (as when, for instance, a German-Irish groom takes an Irish-Italian bride).

Intermarriage has had an especially deep impact on the groups from southern and eastern Europe. This is partly because their smaller size (in

comparison, say, with the German ancestry group) makes them more vulnerable to what is called "out-marriage." It may also be due to their concentration in regions of the nation where ethnic diversity is greater among whites (the Northeast compared to the South, for instance), increasing the likelihood that they will have close relationships with individuals of diverse backgrounds.

Intermarriage patterns are displayed in Table 3 for the seven largest ancestry categories of whites. It shows that, among those aged 25 to 34 in 1990, a majority of each category had married unambiguously outside of it, with out-marriage being more common among the smaller ethnic groups.

For the large, long-established categories (English, Germans, and Irish), marriages to individuals whose ancestry is partly from the group figure prominently in the pattern and help explain why the incidence of unambiguous out-marriage is not greater. Perhaps some of these marriages, where there is an ethnic ingredient in common, deserve to be viewed as in-group marriages. However, in the majority of cases, both spouses have ethnically mixed ancestry and share only one ethnic element in common. Thus, they should probably be viewed as akin to intermarriages, even if not so in the strictest sense.

Intermarriage has attained, by any standard, very high levels among the Italians and Poles, the two groups in the table from southern and eastern Europe. Close to three-quarters of the younger Italians have spouses without Italian ancestry; for

TABLE 3 *Marriage Patterns of Major Ancestry Groups*

Ancestry Groups (in order of size)	COHORT BORN 1956–1965 SPOUSE'S ANCESTRY			COHORT BORN 1916–1925 SPOUSE'S ANCESTRY		
	Percentage Entirely from Group	*Percentage Partly from Group*	*Percentage Not from Group*	*Percentage Entirely from Group*	*Percentage Partly from Group*	*Percentage Not from Group*
German	22.6	25.6	51.8	26.3	21.3	52.4
Irish	12.7	22.4	64.9	20.1	21.0	58.9
English	17.7	20.4	61.9	24.0	24.7	51.2
Italian	15.0	11.7	73.3	49.2	2.4	48.3
French	12.1	10.0	77.9	13.2	13.0	73.9
Scots/Scots-Irish	7.0	10.8	82.1	11.9	12.8	75.4
Polish	7.6	8.3	84.1	36.0	3.9	60.1

Source: 1-in-1000 Public Use Microdata Sample of the 1990 Census.

Poles, the equivalent figure is higher still. However, marriages involving spouses who both have some ancestry from these groups is higher than it would be if marriage were "random" with respect to ancestry, and there is some sign that the increase in intermarriage may be leveling off. A likely forecast is that intermarriage will continue at high levels but that a significant minority of each of these groups will continue to look within for marriage partners.

The rising tide of intermarriage is sweeping over religious barriers as well. This is demonstrated most tellingly by the surge of intermarriage among Jews since the 1960s. Data from the 1990 National Jewish Population Survey reveal that 57 percent of Jews marrying since 1985 have married partners raised in other religions. Just two decades earlier, the figure had been only 11 percent. The consequences of Jewish-Gentile intermarriage are still debatable, at least in principle, because of the possibilities of the non-Jewish spouse converting or of the children being raised as Jewish. However, the data suggest that neither possibility characterizes a majority of intermarried couples. Besides, even if these possibilities were the rule, they do not diminish the import of the fact that religious origins are playing a lesser role in the choice of a spouse than they once did.

An obvious consequence of intermarriage is ethnically mixed ancestry, which holds potentially profound implications for ethnic groups. Though the mere fact of mixed ancestry is certainly no bar to ethnic feelings and loyalties, it is likely to reduce their intensity, especially because most individuals with mixed ancestry are raised with limited exposure to ethnic cultures in their most robust form.

MARRIAGE ACROSS RACIAL LINES

What is unfolding among whites through intermarriage resembles, then, the proverbial melting pot, but with mainly European ingredients to this point. It is still the case that just a small proportion of marriages by whites (2 percent) are contracted with Hispanics or with nonwhites. The vast majority of their intermarriages, in other words, involve individuals of European ancestries only (the most notable exception being the nontrivial fraction of whites who claim some American-Indian ancestry, typically mixed with European).

Lower rates of racial intermarriage are partly a result of residential segregation, which particularly affects blacks and new immigrant groups, and partly a consequence of the reluctance of many whites, the largest pool of potential marriage partners, to accept a nonwhite or Hispanic spouse. No doubt, there is also a greater desire on the part of many minority-group members to find husbands and wives from their own groups. For the new immigrant groups, from the Caribbean, Latin America, and Asia, the overall intermarriage rate is also driven down by their concentration in the first and second generations, where intermarriage tends to be lower in general.

The extreme case is that of African Americans ("non-Hispanic blacks" in census terminology). According to 1990 census data, just 4 percent of African Americans have married outside their group. However, this figure hides an important and long-standing gender discrepancy: intermarriage is considerably more prevalent among black men than among black women (6 percent versus 2 percent). For both sexes, most intermarriage takes place with non-Hispanic white partners.

Hispanics on the whole exhibit considerably higher, but still modest, levels of intermarriage, even in the second generation. Seventy percent of U.S.-born Hispanics are married to other Hispanics, mostly to individuals of the same national origin. In the Hispanic case, there is no gender gap in intermarriage. Its frequency does, however, vary considerably by specific group, and the total for Hispanics overall is influenced especially by the high rate of endogamy on the part of the largest Hispanic group, Mexican Americans.

Intermarriage is only a bit more common among U.S.-born Asians overall, two-thirds of whom marry other Asians. As with Hispanics, this total disguises substantial variation by specific national origin and is heavily affected by a high level of endogamy in one group, Japanese Americans, who form the largest contingent among U.S.-born Asian adults.

American Indians bracket the intermarriage spectrum at the high end. More than half have married outside the American-Indian population; the great majority of their intermarriages are to non-Hispanic whites. However, since American Indians represent less than 1 percent of the national population, their intermarriage tendency does not have a great influence on the total pattern.

The predominantly European cast to the contemporary melting of ethnic lines through intermarriage may be changing, at least to some degree. One indication is the higher-than-average frequency of marriage to Hispanics or nonwhites on the part of younger non-Hispanic whites. Among those in the 25 to 34 age group, close to 4 percent have married minority-group members; though still low in absolute terms, this figure represents a measurable increase over past levels.

Rising intermarriage with racial minorities is having its most dramatic effects among African Americans, as the demographer Matthijs Kalmijn first documented (in the September 1993 issue of the journal *Social Forces*) with an analysis of marriages for the two-decade period following the Supreme Court's 1967 invalidation of the last anti-miscegenation law. In 1990 census data, 10 percent of 25- to 34-year-old black men have intermarried, most with white women. This figure, while obviously not high, nevertheless represents a stunning upward shift from the historical level. The change has not been as striking for black women, but the level of intermarriage has risen among younger black women to nearly 4 percent.

Intermarriage involving members of groups from new immigration is virtually certain to increase in the near future, as the ranks of their second- and third-generation adults swell. Yet, whether marriage across social boundaries defined by non-European ancestries will attain the acceptability—indeed the unremarkableness—that intermarriage appears to have attained in the case of European ancestries remains to be seen.

ASSIMILATION'S CONTINUING RELEVANCE

The assimilation trends tracked by the census can, to be sure, appear somewhat crude, lacking the nuanced *chiaroscuro* of personal experience where ethnicity may still be present. Nevertheless, taken together, these trends convincingly show that the social bases for ethnic distinctiveness are eroding among Americans of European ancestry. Indeed, the erosion would continue even if the trends were to come to a halt. As older, currently more ethnic generations are replaced by their children and grandchildren, who are less ethnic on average, the groups as a whole become less ethnic.

Decline, however, does not mean disappearance, certainly not in the foreseeable future. The overall picture is mixed, with the proportions of the different elements—i.e., "assimilated" versus "ethnic," to portray them in their extremes—shifting in the assimilated direction.

A larger question, and an unanswerable one for the moment, concerns the relevance of the European-American experience of assimilation for non-European minorities. Even if one narrows the question by accepting that assimilation is probably most relevant for immigrant groups, as opposed to those whose entry to American society was coerced by enslavement or conquest, the conditions of contemporary immigration are sufficiently different from those prevalent in the past that generalizations based on earlier experience are open to doubt.

Currently, we lack good theories and hard-and-fast empirical knowledge about the genesis of European-American assimilation. To what extent does it reflect persisting forces in American society—the lure of opportunities in the mainstream economy, for instance, or the permeability of ethnic boundaries in a society populated largely by immigration? To what extent is it the product of historically unique events and conditions, such as the period of economic expansion following World War II or the virtual shutdown of immigration after 1930, which prevented the renewal of ethnic communities through continuing immigration? To what extent is it restricted to those with European ancestry and white skin? Without answers to these questions, we will have to wait to observe the trajectories of new immigrant groups to assess the ultimate relevance of assimilation for them. Yet, one has to suspect that assimilation is far from a spent force.

Immigrant and Ethnic Enterprise in North America

Ivan Light

In the decade 1820–30, 80 percent of free white Americans owned their own means of livelihood (Corey, 1966:113). This decade was the highwater mark of self-employment in America, and subsequent trends have shown an almost uninterrupted decline. Generations of sociologists have declared that business self-employment in the modern United States has become an economic anachronism which is in the process of disappearance (Light, 1979:31). Following Marx on this point, they have observed that the progressive concentration of capital reduced the once numerous class of free entrepreneurs that existed in the last century. Indeed, three decades ago C. W. Mills (1951) already showed the steady decline of agricultural and non-agricultural self-employment in the United States between 1870 and 1950:

> A larger number of small businesses are competing for a smaller share of the market. The stratum of urban entrepreneurs has been narrowing, and within it concentration has been going on. Small business becomes smaller, big business becomes bigger (Mills 1951:24).

After Mills wrote this evaluation the decline of self-employment in the American labor force unambiguously continued until 1973. In that year a slim majority of American farmers continued to be self-employed, but less than 7 percent of non-farm workers were self-employed (Ray, 1975). Given these trends, government and business analysts agreed that the probability of self-employment had become poorer than in the past and its rewards correspondingly more meager (Cingolani, 1973:8–10; Special Task Force, 1973: 21). In this economic context, social scientists generally concluded that small business self-employment was incompatible with capitalist economic concentration and could be expected to slide into oblivion for this reason (Bottomore, 1966:50; O'Connor, 1973:29–30; Horvat, 1982: 11–15; Auster and Aldrich, 1984).

However, on the cultural side, sociologists had to explain the atavistic persistence of entrepreneurial values and ambitions in the American labor force (Chinoy, 1952; Walker and Guest, 1952) as well as the extent of self-employment among the wage-earning population (Lipset and Bendix, 1959:102–3, 177–81). Given the USA's *laissez-faire* traditions (Meyer, 1953) it was easy to understand entrepreneurial ambitions and frustrated aspirations as cultural residuals of an economically bygone era (Vidich and Bensman, 1960:305–6). Thus Riesman (1950) juxtaposed the "inner-directed" old-fashioned individualism of yesteryear's entrepreneurs with the glad-handed "other-direction" of corporate executives, finding in this contrast a shift in the modal personality from the former to the latter. In a similar exercise, Miller and Swanson (1958:123) found that achievement imagery in the American middle class had shifted away from self-employment toward bureaucratic careers in corporate hierarchies. Bell's (1976:84) analysis of the "cultural contradictions of capitalism" identified the Puritan tradition as a self-destructive rationality whose adolescent heirs had discarded the disciplines of planning and work in favor of "voluptuary hedonism."

Entrepreneurship's protracted decline provided a neat illustration of cultural lag, the belated adjustment of superstructure to changes in

Reprinted from "Immigrant and Ethnic Enterprise in North America" by Ivan Light, *Ethnic and Racial Studies* 7:2 (April 1984) by permission of Routledge & Kegan Paul PLC.

production relations (Aronowitz, 1973:257). A small business economy needed entrepreneurial motivations in its labor force. When the economic basis of small business deteriorated, socialization lagged behind, continuing to produce entrepreneurial ambitions and values in lifelong wage workers (Lynd and Lynd, 1937:70). The temporary result was a glut of disappointed aspirants for small business self-employment, a situation of imbalance between supply and demand (O'Connor, 1973:29–30). Ultimately, the market's surplus of aspiring entrepreneurs reached back into the socialization system, causing reallocation of motivational resources away from this overpopulated occupation in diminishing demand. As salaried workers corrected their aspirations for realistic prospects, the social origins of American small business owners declined (Newcomer, 1961:490; Meyer, 1947:347: Mills, 1966). By 1952 the "creed of the individual enterpriser" had become "a working class preoccupation" (Lipset and Bendix, 1966:462).

ETHNIC AND IMMIGRANT ENTERPRISE IN AMERICA

Taken very generally, cultural lag still offers a satisfactory explanation of what happened to entrepreneurial individualism in twentieth-century America. However, the cultural lag orthodoxy encounters two serious objections, one empirical, the other conceptual. First, as Giddens (1973: 177–8) has observed, the *rate* of decline in self-employment was never so rapid as Marxists had expected even though the direction of change was mostly negative. Moreover, in the specific period 1972–9, "the number of self-employed Americans rose by more than 1.1 million, reversing decades of steady decreases" (Fain, 1980:3). This stabilization suggests that a plateau in self-employed population firmly supports an ideology of entrepreneurship among a minority (see Table 1). This conclusion is particularly appealing since Boissevain (1984) has reported that in 1978 "Common Market countries registered a net increase in the number of entrepreneurs and family workers" thus reversing their postwar trend of decline.

Second, cultural lag orthodoxy depends upon a simplifying, inaccurate assumption of homogeneity in economy and labor force. A homogeneous economy means uniformity in industrial conditions among the various sectors as well as a uniform rate of capitalist concentration in each. Labor force homogeneity means all workers are identical in values, attitudes, skills, employment access, and return on human capital. Both assumptions are unrealistic. The USA economy actually consists of a plurality of sectors which differ in respect to industrial conditions, capitalist concentration, and rates of change. O'Connor's (1973)

TABLE 1 *Self-Employed and Unpaid Family Workers in the United States, 1948–79 (Number in Thousands)*

	1948	1958	1968	1972	1979
Non-agricultural industries					
Total employed	51,975	56,863	72,900	78,929	94,605
Self-employed	6,109	6,102	5,102	5,332	6,652
Percent of total	11.8	10.7	7.0	6.8	7.0
Unpaid family workers	385	588	485	517	455
Percent of total	0.7	1.0	0.7	0.7	0.5
Agriculture					
Total employed	6,309	4,645	3,266	3,005	2,993
Self-employed	4,664	3,081	1,985	1,789	1,580
Percent of total	73.9	66.3	60.8	59.5	52.8
Unpaid family workers	1,318	941	550	467	304
Percent of total	20.9	20.3	16.8	15.5	10.1

Source: T. Scott Fain, "Self-Employed Americans: Their Number Has Increased," *Monthly Labor Review* 103 (1980): Table 1, p. 4.

distinctions between competitive, monopoly and state sectors need attention, and this tripartite division could easily be augmented in the interest of exactitude (reviewed in Kallenberg and Sorenson, 1979). Additionally, the USA labor force consists of unequally situated groups which differ in cultural heritages. At the very least, one must distinguish the immigrant, the nonwhite, and the native white labor force sectors. Workers in these sectors experience differential returns on human capital, rates of under- and unemployment, welfare and legislative support, and career opportunities.

Given variation in the economy and labor force, uneven resolution of cultural lag follows. On the one hand, some business sectors retain contrary-to-trend compatibility with entrepreneurial activities. On the other, some working populations retain atavistic aspirations for business self-employment. In point of fact, immigrant and nonwhite workers cluster heavily in the economy's competitive sector within which, by definition, a small business milieu persists (Waldinger, 1982:1–2; Zenner, 1982:474; Auster and Aldrich, 1984). Thus, on structural grounds alone, there is reason to predict that old-fashioned entrepreneurial ideology should remain among immigrant and minority sector workers long after native white workers have resigned themselves to salaried and wage employment in the monopoly and state sectors.

This situation is not really novel. In actual fact, the foreign-born have been overrepresented in American small business since 1880 and probably earlier (Light, 1980:33; Higgs, 1977:92). Two explanations seem plausible. The first is disadvantage in the labor market. Such disadvantage causes foreigners to concentrate in small business because they suffer under- and unemployment as a result of poor English, unvalidated educational credentials, discrimination, and so forth (Reitz, 1980:191). Anyone who is disadvantaged in the labor force derives from this unfortunate situation a special incentive to consider self-employment, and the greater his disadvantage, the greater his incentive. The unemployed apple vendors of the Great Depression epitomize the resourcefulness of workers who, unable to find wage-earning jobs, turn to any and every pitiful self-employment from economic desperation.

However, labor markets' disadvantage cannot be the whole explanation of this phenomenon, be-cause some immigrant and ethnic minority groups have higher rates of urban self-employment ("entrepreneurship") than do others (Goldscheider and Kobrin, 1980:262–75; Boissevain, 1984; Jenkins, 1984). Given equal disadvantage why do some foreign groups have higher rates than others, and why should the foreign-born in general have higher rates of business self-employment than disadvantaged native minorities, especially blacks (Handlin, 1959:74)? Native blacks are more disadvantaged than native whites, yet the blacks' rates of business self-employment have been and remain lower than the native whites' rates and much lower than the foreign-born rates despite presumptively higher disadvantage of the blacks (Light, 1972, 1979; Wright et al., 1982:724).

ORTHODOX AND REACTIVE CULTURAL CONTEXTS

The orthodox answer to this issue has fastened upon transplanted cultural endowments of various ethnic minority groups. Derived from Max Weber, this model of entrepreneurship has claimed that individuals introject cultural values in the course of primary socialization. When a group's values and motivations encourage business enterprise, cultural minorities produce socialized adults who prosper in business. The prototype is Weber's (1958a) Protestant sectarians who espoused the values of diligence in a calling, thrift, profit, and individualism. These values and attendant motivations caused adult sectarians to prosper in business. With appropriate adjustments, this model might account for the anomalous and persistent overrepresentation of selected cultural minorities in self-employment. American examples include Jews, Chinese, Japanese, Greeks, Macedonians, West Indians, Dominicans, Gypsies, Iraqi Christians, Lebanese, Koreans, and Arabs.[1] In all such cases, cultural theory has explained business overrepresentation and/or success in terms of intact, unmodified cultural heritages. A fine example is the migration of Gypsy fortunetellers. Before debarkation in New York City, the Gypsies already knew how to tell fortunes, and their cultural baggage included ready-to-use skills (crystal balls, tarot cards, palmistry) other groups simply lacked. Gypsy practice of these skills in the United States only involved the utilization of a cultural tradition for the specific purpose of self-employment (Sway, 1983).

This view has merit, but research in ethnic enterprise has disclosed its inadequacy. In reality, immigration and alien status release latent facilitators which promote entrepreneurship independently of cultural endowments (Turner and Bonacich, 1980:145, 148). Three facilitators are especially important. The first is psychological satisfaction arising from immigration to a high-wage country from a low-wage country. Immigrants in the United States have recurrently proven willing to accept low money returns, long hours of labor, job-related danger, and domestic penury in order to maintain business self-employment. Relative to their countries of origin, even adverse conditions look good to immigrants and until fully adapted to the American standard of living, immigrants obtain satisfaction from squalid proprietorships that would not attract native-white wage earners. This is *relative satisfaction.*

A second, much-documented reaction is enhanced social solidarity attendant upon cultural minority status. Chain migrations create immigrant communities with extraordinarily well-developed social networks. Numerous studies have shown that these social networks create resources upon which immigrant co-ethnics can draw for business purposes (Light, 1972; Bonacich, 1973, 1975b; Bonacich and Modell, 1980; Wilson and Portes, 1980). "The cornerstone of an ethnic subeconomy is the communal solidarity of a minority group" (Hraba, 1979:374). Insofar as reactive solidarity encourages immigrant entrepreneurship, a situation has brought out a collective response which is not cultural in the orthodox sense (Young, 1971). A concrete example is the influence of immigrant *Landsmannschaften* upon business enterprise. Immigrant *Landsmänner* belong to a primary group which did not exist as such in their country of origin. Thus, among Japanese of Los Angeles *Hiroshimakenjin* formed a solidaristic subgroup within the metropolitan population—all the brothers hailed from Hiroshima. On the other hand, contemporaneous residents of Hiroshima did not share the sense of local solidarity so the immigrants had obviously created a solidarity abroad that did not exist in Hiroshima, their city of origin (Modell, 1977: 99–117). This is a *reactive* solidarity which required alien status to liberate, and as such is quite

different from the practice of fortunetelling by immigrant Gypsies.

The third endowment is sojourning (Siu, 1952). Sojourning arises when immigrants intend to repatriate, and derive from this intention a desire to amass as much money as possible as quickly as possible. As Bonacich (1973) has shown, sojourning implies a battery of entrepreneurial motivations which give middlemen minorities an advantage in business competition over nonsojourners. Admittedly, the cultural status of sojourning is uncertain, and the phenomenon arguably arises liturgically as well as situationally (Light, 1979:33–4). Nonetheless, sojourning is a frequent (but not invariant) accompaniment to international immigration, and its presence provides an economic edge to the foreign born in small business enterprise (Zenner, 1982:458; Portes, Clark and Lopez, 1981–2:18).

Light's (1980:34–6) distinction between reactive and orthodox cultural contexts of entrepreneurship is a new one necessitated by the rapidly growing literature on this topic, but anticipated by earlier writers (Young, 1971). Orthodox and reactive contexts in Light's rubric correspond closely to what Turner and Bonacich (1980:145, 148) elsewhere identified as cultural and situational variables. In both cases, authors responded to the tendency of ethnic business researchers to "talk past" real issues on the one hand or, on the other, to engage in "unnecessary and wasteful polemics" about pseudo-issues (Turner and Bonacich, 1980: 145, 147). Authorities agree that, however named, the conceptual distinctions identified do not necessitate an empirical repugnance because different variables can contribute to the entrepreneurship of the same ethnic groups. Old-fashioned cultural analysis (Belshaw, 1955) stressed only orthodox etiologies, thus creating the erroneous implication that only culturally intact transmission affected entrepreneurship (Freedman, 1959). Conversely, Bonacich's (1973) model of "middleman minorities" ignored orthodox contributions, focusing only upon reactivities. In Light's (1972) treatment of prewar blacks and Asians in the USA the overrepresentation of Asians in business proprietorships is credited to reactions arising from relative satisfaction and immigrant solidarity *as well as* to rotating credit associations, culturally transmitted institutions fitting the orthodox model (see also Woodrum).

Orthodox, reactive, or mixed entrepreneurship arises when only-orthodox, only-reactive or mixed orthodox and reactive components of entrepreneurship figure in an empirical analysis. On the face of the available evidence, some groups belong in one, other groups in another category. The crucial evidence arises from two comparisons. On the one hand, the foreign-born in general have been overrepresented in American small business since at least 1880 and are still overrepresented. On the other hand some foreign-born groups have higher rates of business self-employment than do others. For example, Jews have been and remain extraordinarily entrepreneurial whereas Irish have been lower than the foreign-born average (Goldscheider and Kobrin, 1980). The general overrepresentation of the foreign-born betokens a situationally-induced responsiveness to self-employment. This responsiveness is *prima facie* evidence for a reactive model. On the other hand, the higher than average rates of selected foreign-born groups suggest unique cultural endowments. Unique endowments imply cultural heritages transmitted intact, the orthodox cultural model. The best fit of theory and evidence occurs when theory acknowledges the additive possibilities of orthodox and reactive components. On this view, the foreign-born in general experience the reactive entrepreneurship arising from their alien situation, but middleman minorities (Jews, Chinese, Greeks, etc.) add to this reaction their culturally intact heritages of sojourning entrepreneurship (Bonacich and Modell, 1980:Ch. 2). As a result, rates of entrepreneurship are higher among middleman minorities than among the foreign-born in general, and higher among the foreign-born than among the native-born whites.

ETHNIC AND CLASS RESOURCES

Efforts to explain ethnic and immigrant entrepreneurship invariably turn up batteries of special causes. That is, the immigrants developed higher than average rates of entrepreneurship because they drew upon special resources which native groups lacked. In Barth's (1962) terminology these facilities constitute entrepreneurial "assets" but the term resources is more general and does not lend itself to confusion with financial assets (Light, 1980:35). *Ethnic resources* are any and all

features of the whole group which coethnic business owners can utilize in business or from which their business benefits (Reitz, 1982; Wallman, 1979:ix; 1979:10). Thus, ethnic resources include orthodox cultural endowments, relative satisfaction, reactive solidarities, sojourning orientation, and these four encompass all types of ethnic resources empirically described in the existing literature (cf. Turner and Bonacich, 1980:152). As such, ethnic resources should be distinguished from class resources. *Class resources* are cultural and material. On the material side, class resources are private property in the means of production and distribution, human capital, and money to invest. On the cultural side, class resources are bourgeois values, attitudes, knowledge and skills transmitted intergenerationally in the course of primary socialization (DiMaggio, 1982:190–1). An established bourgeoisie equips its youth with appropriate class resources and, having them, the youth are well endowed to prosper in a market economy. Class resources exist, and sociological theory has amply and basically acknowledged their importance. An analytical dispute has arisen, however, when studies of ethnic entrepreneurship have sought to distinguish ethnic resources from class resources. The mainstream view ignored ethnic resources, assuming that only class resources do or even can exist. On this view, an ethnic bourgeoisie is just a bourgeoisie rather than a bourgeoisie which has unique access to ethnic resources.

In principle, class and ethnic resources might occur singly or in combination. This compatibility yields four basic etiologies: class-only, ethnic-only, class-ethnic mixed, and no resources. A class-only etiology explains ethnic minority or immigrant entrepreneurship strictly on the basis of class origins, property, money, and human capital. Class-only explanation is Type 1 in Table 2. Ethnic-only analysis omits the above, focusing explanation wholly upon ethnic resources such as cultural heritages, reactive solidarities, sojourning, and relative satisfaction. Ethnic-only explanation is Type 2 in Table 2. Mixed analysis combines elements of ethnic and class analysis to suit empirical cases of entrepreneurship. Mixed explanation is Type 3 in Table 2. Since class-only analysis is most compatible with a macro-theory of the economy, the mixed and ethnic-only analytic pos-

TABLE 2 *Ethnic and Class Resources of Entrepreneurship*

| | RESOURCE BASIS | | | |
| | Ethnic | | Class | |
	Orthodox	Reactive	Material	Cultural
1. Class-only	O	O	X	X
2. Ethnic-only	X	X	O	O
3. Mixed	X	X	X	X
4. Mixed: class predominant	x	x	X	X
5. Mixed: ethnic predominant	X	X	x	x
6. No resources	O	O	O	O

O = none

x = some

X = much

sibilities signal a newly discovered frontier of theoretical controversy. If the latter types exist, class macro-theory needs adjustment to take into account complexities currently ignored.

The North American literature contains no examples of class-only or ethnic-only resource-mobilizing entrepreneurial subgroups. All the empirical cases are mixed. The evidence thus reduces the theoretical polarities to ideal types. Admittedly some cases of ethnic minority or immigrant entrepreneurship weigh more heavily on one side or the other of this class/ethnic balance. Especially in the past, immigrant entrepreneurship seems to have depended more heavily upon ethnic resources than it currently does. Turn-of-the-century Chinese and Japanese immigrants in California are the best-documented illustrations. Disadvantaged in the general labor market, they turned in extraordinary proportion to self-employment, apparently mobilizing ethnic resources very effectively to this end (Light, 1972; Modell, 1977; Bonacich and Modell, 1980). Post-1970 Asian immigrants in North America continue to mobilize ethnic resources to support business ownership, but the balance has shifted toward money, human capital, and bourgeois culture. Thus, all cases of Asian entrepreneurship have been mixed, but in the last half-century the balance has appreciably swung from ethnic toward class resources (Thompson, 1979).

In contemporary American and Canadian society, immigrant entrepreneurship still combines ethnic and class resources, thus creating an empirical problem of sorting out each contributor and assessing its contribution. Thorny as is this measurement problem the empirical dualism is clear especially in the important cases of political refugees from the Third World. To a substantial extent, Korean, Vietnamese, Taiwanese, Hong Kong, Cuban, and Iranian immigrants now in the United States derived from property-owning upper classes in their countries of origin.[2] Fearing or experiencing sociopolitical turmoil in their homelands, these refugees entered the United States with only capital, money to invest, and bourgeois cultural values. Accordingly, it is no surprise that their involvement in small business has been extensive, their success in it remarkable, and their achievement much celebrated in popular media (Ramirez, 1980). On a class-only model the small business success of these refugees reflects only the class resources they brought with them, and any group of wealthy refugees would have created as many small businesses. Ethnicity conferred nothing: this is the null hypothesis.

Class resources indisputably help, but empirical research suggests that a class-only explanation is inadequate. An immigrant bourgeoisie utilizes ethnic resources in supplementation of class resources. The two best-studied examples are Cubans in Miami, and Koreans in Los Angeles.[3] Wilson and Portes (1980; Portes, 1981; Wilson and Martin, 1982) found that about one-third of Cubans in Miami were employed in Cuban-owned business and another fragment were self-employed. For the Cubans returns on human capital were more favorable among the self-employed than among those employed for wages in the competitive sector. Indeed, returns on human capital were equivalent to those in the primary sector. Explaining this success, Wilson and Portes (1980: 315) conclude:

> Immigrant entrepreneurs make use of language and cultural barriers and of ethnic affinities to gain privileged access to markets and sources of labor. . . . The necessary counterpart to these ethnic ties of solidarity is the principle of ethnic preference in hiring and of support of other immigrants in their economic ventures.

Since these resources would be unavailable in Cuba, the Cuban immigrant bourgeoisie acquires access to ethnic resources in Miami where they are members of a cultural minority. To a substantial extent, these reactive resources permit the Cubans to thrive in small business and even to outperform the native whites in this sphere despite the material advantages of the latter.

Bonacich, Light and Wong (1977; see also Light, 1980; Bonacich and Jung, 1982) have looked into the entrepreneurial success of 60,000 Koreans in Los Angeles. In 1980, approximately 40 percent of employed Korean men headed small firms (Yu, 1982:54).[4] An additional 40 percent of Koreans worked in these firms so only about 20 percent of the Korean immigrants found employment in non-Korean-owned firms or government agencies. Admittedly, the Korean immigrants were highly educated: on one account nearly 70 percent of men had college degrees compared with only 15 percent of Los Angeles County residents in general. Additionally, the Koreans brought with them sums of capital rarely less than $25,000 and sometimes millions. On the other hand, these class resources supplemented ethnic resources; they did not exclude them. As among the Cubans in Miami, Koreans in Los Angeles made effective business use of language and cultural barriers distinguishing coethnics from the general population, reactive social solidarity, nepotistic hiring, and formal and informal mutual support networks. Additionally, Koreans made some use of rotating credit associations,[5] nationalistic appeals for labor peace, vertical and horizontal integration of firms, informal and formal restraints of trade,[6] and political connections with City Hall developed by leading

Korean business organizations. In all these respects, Korean entrepreneurship drew upon ethnic resources, not merely upon class resources.

COLLECTIVIST AND INDIVIDUALIST STYLES OF ENTREPRENEURSHIP

Textbook treatments of entrepreneurship have long begun with the economistic assumption that small business owners are individualists. Indeed, the term "entrepreneurial individualism" remains in general currency as a reflection of this persisting assumption. Underlying the microeconomic theory of the firm are the class resources of the bourgeoisie which provide facilities for individual business owners. In Schumpeter's famous image, these entrepreneurs behave like spectators in a crowded stadium during a rainstorm. Feeling rain, each spectator independently decides to raise his umbrella, and decides to put it away when the sun once again comes out. In this analogy, the material resource is the umbrella, and the cultural resource is the trained wisdom to utilize it properly. But each entrepreneur thinks and acts independently albeit in utilization of class-linked resources.

Accepting Schumpeter's (1934:81, n.1, 2) class-only model of entrepreneurship,[7] sociology has, however, parted company with neoclassical economics on the issue of consciousness. Insofar as a resource-transmitting bourgeoisie develops self-consciousness, this consciousness becomes a class resource capable of affecting the economic success of members. Thus, elitist studies of the American upper class have long claimed that debutante cotillions, preparatory schools, swank vacation resorts, exclusive suburbs, and stuffy downtown clubs reflect and forge upper-class consciousness (Useem, 1980:53–8). Group consciousness enhances the chances of individual bourgeois to monopolize access to material and status rewards. For instance, clubs provide a private place to concoct business and political deals or to arrange marriages. Admittedly the importance of bourgeois group consciousness has not been so systematically examined in its economic as in its political ramifications. However, class-only theories of the bourgeoisie have acknowledged the development of an entrepreneurial collectivism which enhances the competitive chances of the individual members of the bourgeoisie. Evaluating two generations of social research on the American business elite, Useem (1980:58) finds "internal cohesion" strikingly in evidence. "Unity is far more extensively developed at the top than anywhere else in the class structure."

A similar evolution has characterized sociological studies of ethnic business (Jenkins, 1984). Classical sociologists called attention to cultural endowments which governed the style of business ownership, and explained in historical context the transition from merchant to bourgeois. The prototype was, of course, Weber's (1958a) Protestant sectarians whose economic style reflected religio-cultural values. Their disciplined lifestyle caused them to prosper in business, but they were expected to do so as noncooperating individuals standing or falling on individual merits. Of course, there is no denying that under some cultural or situational conditions, small business owners can be individualistic nor that introjected values of hard work, thrift, and economic rationality encourage business survival and success.[8] Bechofer et al.'s (1974) study of Scottish business owners in Edinburgh depicts individualistic business conduct. Jarvenpa and Zenner (1979) reported the same individualism among Scots in the Canadian fur trade. On the other hand, even Weber overstated the extent of individualism among Protestant sectarians and, aware of this error, was more careful (1958b) in some writings. Historical research among Puritan business owners in seventeenth-century New England has not disclosed the expected individualism. On the contrary, Bailyn (1955), Hall (1977), and Griffen and Griffen (1977: 150) concluded that observantly Calvinist business owners in New England were active participants in commercial networks knit together on the basis of extended kinship and friendship, these networks actually linking ports of origin in the British Isles and New England cities.

In the same sense, cultural treatments of middlemen minorities in North America began with the assumption that cultural subgroups acted out their values in enterprising individualism based upon hard work, thrift, rationality, and self-denial (Auster and Aldrich, 1984). In this model, immigrant entrepreneurs drew upon a cultural tradition, then fanned out into the economy in individualistic search for profitable opportunities. Equipped with cultural resources, coethnics knew how to make the most out of such business opportunities as they encountered—but each did so as an isolated individual.

There is, of course, no question that ethnic values and motivations do affect individual behavior. However, ethnic research has shown there exists a largely ignored dimension of collective action which goes beyond individualistic value or motivational effects, important as those are (Leff, 1979). This is the dimension of entrepreneurial collectivism in the ethnic minority (Young, 1971: 140–1; Cummings et al., 1980b). Collective styles of entrepreneurship depend upon group resources in which business owners only participate insofar as they maintain active, adult participation in community life (Herman, 1979:84). For example, a rotating credit association requires cooperators to establish a reputation for trustworthiness in the ethnic community, and this reputation depends in turn upon active involvement (Light, 1972:Ch. 2). Similarly, an immigrant or ethnic informational network confers benefits upon business owners, but to obtain these benefits an owner needs to belong to the network. Isolates cannot share network information so this ethnic resource only benefits participants in ethnic community networks. Finally, trade guilds may regulate and control internal competition, but the benefits of collusion in restraint of trade accrue to members. Isolates suffer the consequences of collusion by others.

In principle, class and ethnic resources both confer potentialities for individualist or collectivistic styles of business management. As before, however, all empirical cases in the literature have been mixed. For instance, Koreans in Los Angeles have utilized both class and ethnic resources, and these resources have here supported individualistic and there collectivistic entrepreneurship. Taken together, Korean entrepreneurship in Los Angeles is a pastiche of ethnic and class resources and individualist and collectivist styles. On the other hand, the balance of individualism and collectivism in immigrant entrepreneurship appears to have shifted in three generations. Chinese and Japanese immigrants in California at the turn of the century utilized entrepreneurial strategies which were more collectivistic than those currently utilized by Chinese immigrants in Toronto (Clian and Clieung, 1982. In the same manner, Polish, Finnish, Irish, Mormon, and Jewish entrepreneurship appears to have undergone a shift in this century away from an immigrant-generation dependence upon collective resources toward a native-born generation dependence upon individual resources.[9]

Two related changes explain this shifting balance. On the one hand, the competitive sector has become smaller in size and the price of admission higher in response to capitalist concentration. Ethnic collectivism may be less adequate than in the past. On the other hand, upward social mobility has conferred class resources upon native-born ethnics whose progenitors did not have them. Specifically, native-born descendants of immigrant business owners enter the business sector with money, education, and skills their forebears lacked. Possessing class resources, immigrant and ethnic minority entrepreneurs become more individualistic in style. Thus, impoverished immigrants needed to combine their small amounts of capital in rotating credit associations in order to assemble a sum large enough to finance small business. Dependent upon kinsmen and landsmen for initial capital, immigrant business owners could not thereafter operate their businesses as if they were isolated individualists. With personal money to invest, the descendants of these immigrants and contemporary "new" immigrants no longer need to borrow from kin and friends (Kim, 1977). Therefore, they establish their business enterprises without rotating credit associations, and operate them in a more individualistic manner.[10] Similarly, poor immigrants did not understand inventories or balance sheets so they turned to kin and friends for advice in business management. Equipped with MBAs, their descendants and North America's new immigrants possess the business skills they need as class resources. Therefore, they do not need to turn for management advice to informal, ethnically linked agencies, and they are free to operate their business enterprises as if they were isolated individuals. In this manner, access to class resources may obviate collectivism in ethnic enterprise—but not exclude it altogether. In Toronto, Thompson (1979) reports, a bipolar business class has actually emerged as a result of these processes. On the one side are the old-fashioned, ethnic-dependent Mom and Pop store owners; on the other, Hong Kong millionaires operating investment corporations. "The new stratum of entrepreneurial elites differs in both origin and lifestyle from the traditional merchant elites who for years controlled the [Chinese] ethnic community" (Thompson, 1979:311).

In principle, ethnic and immigrant small business ought to run out of solidarity to exploit because cultural assimilation and higher education undercut the ascriptive solidarities from which immigrant-generation business owners derived the resources to power their business network (Turner and Bonacich, 1980:157). Much evidence suggests that over generations ethnic resources do decay for this reason (Bonacich and Modell, 1980:Chs. 6, 9; Borhek, 1970; Goldscheider and Kobrin, 1980; Montero, 1981). "Over the long run," Reitz (1980:231) observes, "there is a progressive trend toward abandonment of ethnic group ties for all groups in which long-term experience can be measured." However, the rate of deterioration has been much slower than sociologists once expected (Witensky and Lawrence, 1979). The indisputable profitability of ethnic capitalism is an apparent cause of this retardation. Especially relative to equally qualified members of the same ethnic group in the general labor market, owners of ethnic sector business enterprises earn high incomes in business. Big profits make ethnic business attractive (Wilson and Portes, 1980:314; Sway, 1983; Reitz, 1982; Bonacich and Modell, 1981:257). Ethnic business owners identify with their ethnic community and participate actively in it. They provide the leadership for ethnic institutions. Ethnic attachments also persist more strongly among wage workers whose workplace is a co-ethnic firm whose language is that of the homeland, not English (Bonacich and Modell, 1980; Reitz, 1980; Woodrum, Rhodes and Feagin, 1980:1240–52). These two classes often account for between 40 and 80 percent of the total ethnic population. Ethnic-owned businesses "help prop up other institutions which recruit and maintain ethnic membership" (Reitz, 1980:223). Ethnicity supports the ethnic economy, and the ethnic economy supports ethnic perpetuation (Bonacich and Modell, 1981:257).

NO RESOURCES ENTREPRENEURSHIP

The preceding analysis offers a satisfactory account of why equally disadvantaged ethnic and immigrant minorities display unequal rates of entrepreneurship; survival and success depend upon group resources. Groups with more resources outperform groups with less; and groups with class resources are individualistic whereas groups with ethnic resources are collectivistic. On this view, entrepreneurship is highest when disadvantaged immigrant minorities are well endowed with class and ethnic resources; endowment with one or the other is intermediate; and negligible endowment in both class and ethnic resources implies correspondingly low rates of entrepreneurship.

Behind this conclusion lies the assumption that immigrant minorities' rate of business ownership is a fair measure of their entrepreneurship. The rate of business ownership has been operationally defined as self-employed per 1000 in the urban labor force.[11] A major objection to this definition, it is increasingly clear, arises from the inadequacy of published statistics (Karsh, 1977; Light, 1979: 39–40; US Small Business, 1980). "The Census has a completely nonsociological way of defining 'self employment' " (Wright et al., 1982:712n). US statistics routinely exclude petty traders without fixed business premises, no-employee firms, illegally operated firms in legitimate industries, and firms producing unlawful goods or services. Since minorities and immigrants bulk very large in such firms, their exclusion from official tabulations results in undercounts of minority-owned business enterprise as well as theoretical misperception of the whole phenomenon of ethnic entrepreneurship. No one knows how many untabulated firms exist nor what is their distribution among various sectors of the labor force.

The case of native-born Americans is instructive because blacks are disadvantaged but native-born. All statistical and ethnographic sources have uniformly reported that rates of business self-employment among urban blacks have been and remain lower than among even native-white, let alone the foreign-born (Light, 1972, 1979, 1980). At the same time, ethnographic sources have stressed the importance of "hustling" as an economic activity among underclass urban blacks (Valentine, 1978; Glasgow, 1980:9, 90; Light, 1977b). Hustling involves piecing together a livelihood by operating a variety of legal, semilegal, and sometimes illegal business activities. Legal enterprises of urban blacks include street corner and door-to-door peddling of trinkets, objets d'art, junk, salvage, and fire-damaged merchandise. Unlawfully conducted legal enterprises include unlicensed taxicabs, unlicensed pharmacies, unlicensed medical services,

welfare cheating, tax-evading labor services and so forth. Illegal enterprise includes gambling administration, pimping, prostitution, narcotics vending, and other victimless crimes (Light 1977a, 1977b). Predatory crimes include armed robbery, burglary, shop-lifting, and all similar activities. All these self-employed activities are entrepreneurial in that they involve risk and uncertain return (Harbison, 1956:365). Although comprehensive statistics are lacking, there seems little doubt that urban blacks are as overrepresented in marginal legal and unlawfully operated self-employment as crime statistics indicate they are in illegal enterprise and predatory crime. Taken together, this package suggests much higher than average self-employment among economically marginal blacks in unmeasured business at the same time that official statistics reveal much lower than average self-employment in measured business.

Given the presumptively high rates of black self-employment in these undocumented industries, it is improper to conclude that native blacks are less entrepreneurial than other economically disadvantaged immigrants and ethnic minorities. It rather appears that native-born blacks have elaborated an alternative, heavily illegal, highly individualistic style of coping with protracted economic marginality. Compared to the foreign-born in general, and middleman minorities in particular, native-born blacks are low in ethnic resources of entrepreneurship, but share economic disadvantage (Wong, 1977; Light, 1972:Chs. 2, 6–8; Venable, 1972:30). Compared to native whites, native blacks are high in economic disadvantage, low in class resources of entrepreneurship, but similar in respect to ethnic resources of entrepreneurship. Table 3 documents these contrasts. Low on ethnic resources of entrepreneurship but high in economic disadvantage, native-born blacks were compelled to depend upon class resources in which they have been underendowed for centuries. As an overall result, marginal black enterprises have not broken into the circle of legal, officially enumerated small business enterprises. Their problem has been nonpromotion of their very large class of petty but invisible enterprises such a visible minority enjoy upward social mobility within the legitimate, competitive sector (Glasgow, 1980:189). It is in the assistance of upward mobility that ethnic and class resources make themselves appreciably manifest (Gelfand,

TABLE 3 *Profiles of Entrepreneurship*

	COMPARISON GROUPS			
	Middleman Minorities	Foreign- Born	Native Blacks	Native Whites
Rotating credit associations	+			
Precapitalist commercial background	+			
Landsmannschaften	+	+		
Extended kinship	+	+		
Relative satisfaction	+	+		
Sojourning	+			
Unpaid family labor	+	+		
Labor force disadvantage	+	+	+	
Ineligible for public welfare	+	+		
Language barrier	+	+		
Special consumer demands	+	+		

1981:185, 190). Given labor force disadvantage, chronic unemployment or both, any ethnic or immigrant minority resorts to self-employment, but only resources make possible the promotion of marginal enterprises into small businesses whose longterm profitability brings along the social mobility of proprietors, their kin, and their heirs (Wilson and Martin, 1982:155–7).

SUMMARY AND CONCLUSION

Uneven development has created economic enclaves within which small business can still be profitable. Success in small business requires, however, a combination of class and ethnic resources with some evidence indicating the former have increased their importance in the last generation. Nonetheless, ethnic resources persist, and immigrant and ethnic minority groups are overrepresented in small business in large part because their access to ethnic resources permits them to outcompete native workers. In this comparative respect native whites and blacks are similar but the native blacks lack class resources and additionally suffer labor market disadvantage which gives them a motive to seek self-employment income. Underclass blacks do find this income in the form of hustling, but hustling has by and large failed to create firms that are large and legal enough to achieve visibility in government statistics.

Ethnic resources of entrepreneurship often depend upon premodern values and solidarities. So long as these survive in the ethnic community, co-ethnic business owners are able to utilize them in business, achieving advantage over fully proletarianized, native-born workers among whom blacks are conspicuous. In theory, ethnic capitalism and cultural assimilation should first undercut and then demolish precapitalist solidarities, thus eliminating an ethnic group's competitive edge in small business. In the perspective of history, this self-destruction probably occurs. However, its rate should not be exaggerated. Ethnic enterprises still earn handsome financial returns, and these substantial rewards prop up the ethnicity upon which owners depend for resources. Profitability brakes the rates of deterioration of ethnic solidarity, supports the persistence of ethnic-owned firms in the competitive sector, and perpetuates the whole competitive sector.

ENDNOTES

An earlier version of this paper was presented at the 10th World Congress of the International Sociological Association, Mexico City, August 19, 1982.

1. See Gelfand, 1981; Chs. 4, 5; Goldscheider and Koibrin, 1980; Light, 1972:Ch. 5; Light and Wong, 1975; Wong, 1977; Sasseh-Koob, 1981:30–1; Modell, 1977; Bonacich and Modell, 1981; Lovell-Troy, 1980, 1981: Chock, 1981; Sway, 1983; Sengstock, 1967; Bonacich, Light and Wong, 1977; Blackstone, 1981; Herman,

1979:90; Zenner, 1982; Waldinger, 1982; Yu, 1982; Bonacich and Jung, 1982.

2. "Most of the refugees are ethnic Chinese, most of whom were shopkeepers or businessmen who had little future under a communist system." "Bleak Outlook for Vietnam refugees," *East/West* (San Francisco), June 20, 1979:1. See also: McMillan, 1982; Rogg, 1971:480; Chan and Cheung, 1982; Thompson, 1979; Wilson and Portes, 1980.

3. But two recent studies have produced important new documentation. In New York City's garment industry, Waldinger (1982) reported extensive and critically important utilization of ethnic networks among Dominican entrepreneurs. In Los Angeles's taxi industry, Russell (1982) documented the mutual assistance common among Soviet Jews seeking to break into the occupation.

4. A similar situation apparently exists in New York City, site of the second largest Korean settlement in the United States. See Illsoo Kim, 1981:110; see also "Faced with prejudice and language difficulties, New York Koreans turn to private business," *Koreatown* (Los Angeles), December 14, 1981:8–9.

5. "$400,000 *kye* broke," *Joong-ang Daily News* (Los Angeles: in Korean), February 20, 1979; Kim, 1981:210–11.

6. "Markets agree to cut down on competition," *Korea Times English Section* (Los Angeles), November 23, 1981:1. "KCCI asks bizmen for more cooperation," *Korea Times English Section,* February 6, 1980; "Fifteen Korean chambers unite," *Koreatown,* November 17, 1980; "Prosperity of shops leads community development," *Korea Times English Section,* November 22, 1976.

7. Schumpeter's (1934) views are endorsed in Beveridge and Oberschall, 1979:207, 225, 229; criticized in Jones and Sakong, 1980:211; reviewed in Hagen, 1968:221–7.

8. "When individuals go into business they must be prepared to lower standards of living and make personal sacrifices until their firms begin to prosper," Cingolani, 1973.

9. See Chap. 4–10 in Cummings (ed.), 1980.

10. In the wake of extremely high interest rates, white Californians began to utilize the *Pandero,* a Brazilian rotating credit association, for purposes of home purchase. In this situation, a class-based, individualistic style reverted to old-fashioned collectivism as class resources became inadequate because of high interest rates. See DeWolfe, 1982.

11. Gerry and Birkbeck (1981) and Portes (1981) argue that marginal self-employed of the Third World are "thinly disguised wage workers" because of their indirect economic dependencies upon big firms. However, Aldrich and Weiss (1981) have shown that a linear relationship exists between employment size and business owners' incomes, and linearity persists in the USA when non-employer firms are introduced. "Owners without employees are simply the 'poorest of the poor' among small capitalists. This group . . . should be assigned to the owner class in future research."

The New Second Generation
Segmented Assimilation and Its Variants

Alejandro Portes
Min Zhou

My name is Herb
and I'm not poor;
I'm the Herbie that you're looking for,
like Pepsi,
a new generation
of Haitian determination—
I'm the Herbie that you're looking for.

A beat tapped with bare hands, a few dance steps, and the Haitian kid was rapping. His song, titled "Straight Out of Haiti," was being performed at Edison High, a school that sits astride Little Haiti and Liberty City, the largest black area of Miami. The lyrics captured well the distinct outlook of his immigrant community. The panorama of Little Haiti contrasts sharply with the bleak inner city. In Miami's Little Haiti, the storefronts leap out at the passersby. Bright blues, reds, and oranges vibrate to Haitian merengue blaring from sidewalk speakers.[1] Yet, behind the gay Caribbean exteriors, a struggle goes on that will define the future of this community. As we will see later on, it involves the second generation—children like Herbie—subject to conflicting pressure from parents and peers and to pervasive outside discrimination.

Growing up in an immigrant family has always been difficult, as individuals are torn by conflicting social and cultural demands while they face the challenge of entry into an unfamiliar and frequently hostile world. And yet the difficulties are not always the same. The process of growing up American oscillates between smooth acceptance and traumatic confrontation depending on the characteristics that immigrants and their children bring along and the social context that receives them. In this article, we explore some of these factors and their bearing on the process of social adaptation of the immigrant second generation. We propose a conceptual framework for understanding this process and illustrate it with selected ethnographic material and survey data from a recent survey of children of immigrants.

Research on the new immigration—that which arose after the passage of the 1965 Immigration Act—has been focused almost exclusively on the first generation, that is, on adult men and women coming to the United States in search of work or to escape political persecution. Little noticed until recently is the fact that the foreign-born inflow has been rapidly evolving from single adult individuals to entire family groups, including infant children and those born to immigrants in the United States. By 1980, 10 percent of dependent children in households counted by the census were second-generation immigrants.[2] In the late 1980s, another study put the number of students in kindergarten

Alejandro Portes and Min Zhou, "The New Second Generation: Segmented Assimilation and Its Variants," *Annals of the American Academy of Political Science.* (Volume 530) pp. 74–96, copyright © 1993 by Sage Publications. Reprinted by Permission of Sage Publications, Inc.

through twelfth grade in American schools who spoke a language other than English at home at 3 to 5 million.[3]

The great deal of research and theorizing on post-1965 immigration offers only tentative guidance on the prospects and paths of adaptation of the second generation because the outlook of this group can be very different from that of their immigrant parents. For example, it is generally accepted among immigration theorists that entry-level menial jobs are performed without hesitation by newly arrived immigrants but are commonly shunned by their U.S.-reared offspring. This disjuncture gives rise to a race between the social and economic progress of first-generation immigrants and the material conditions and career prospects that their American children grow to expect.[4]

Nor does the existing literature on second-generation adaptation, based as it is on the experience of descendants of pre–World War I immigrants, offer much guidance for the understanding of contemporary events. The last sociological study of children of immigrants was Irving Child's *Italian or American? The Second Generation in Conflict,* published fifty years ago.[5] Conditions at the time were quite different from those confronting settled immigrant groups today.

Two such differences deserve special mention. First, descendants of European immigrants who confronted the dilemmas of conflicting cultures were uniformly white. Even if of a somewhat darker hue than the natives, their skin color reduced a major barrier to entry into the American mainstream. For this reason, the process of assimilation depended largely on individual decisions to leave the immigrant culture behind and embrace American ways. Such an advantage obviously does not exist for the black, Asian, and mestizo children of today's immigrants.

Second, the structure of economic opportunities has also changed. Fifty years ago, the United States was the premier industrial power in the world, and its diversified industrial labor requirements offered to the second generation the opportunity to move up gradually through better-paid occupations while remaining part of the working class. Such opportunities have increasingly disappeared in recent years following a rapid process of national deindustrialization and global industrial restructuring. This process has left entrants to the American labor force confronting a widening gap between the minimally paid menial jobs that immigrants commonly accept and the high-tech and professional occupations requiring college degrees that native elites occupy.[6] The gradual disappearance of intermediate opportunities also bears directly on the race between first-generation economic progress and second-generation expectations, noted previously.

THE NEW AMERICANS AT A GLANCE

Before examining this process in detail, it is important to learn a little more about today's second generation. In 1990, the foreign-born population of the United States reached an estimated 21.2 million. In absolute terms, this is the highest number in the history of the nation, although relative to the native-born population, the figure is lower than that at the turn of the century. A century ago, in 1890, immigrants represented 14.8 percent of the total population, almost double today's figure of 8.6 percent. The foreign-stock population, composed of immigrants and their descendants, is, however, much higher. In 1990, roughly 46 million, or 18.5 percent of the total U.S. population, were estimated to be of foreign stock. This yields a net second-generation total of 24.8 million, or 10.9 percent of the American population.[7]

As an estimate of the new second generation, this figure is inflated by the presence of offspring of older immigrants. A team of demographers at the Urban Institute have estimated the contribution of post-1960 immigration, including immigrants and their children, to the total 1990 U.S. population. According to their estimate, if immigration had been cut off in 1960, the total population in 1990 would have been 223.4 million and not the 248.7 actually counted. Hence post-1960 immigration contributed approximately 25.3 million. Subtracting estimates of net immigration for 1960–90 provided by the same researchers, the new second generation, formed by children of post-1960 immigrants, represents 7.7 million, or 3.4 percent of the native-born population. This is a lower-bound estimate based on a demographic model and not on an actual count. It excludes children born to mixed foreign-native couples who are also normally counted as part of the second generation.[8]

More important, however, is the prospect for growth in future years. Given the record increase of immigration since 1960, the second generation as a whole is expected to grow rapidly, surpassing its former peak of roughly 28 million in 1940 sometime during this decade. As noted previously, however, the racial and ethnic composition of the component of the second generation attributable to post-1960 immigration is quite different from that which peaked just before World War II. Over 85 percent of children of immigrants in 1940 were born to Europeans, or, in current terminology, non-Hispanic whites. By contrast, approximately 77 percent of post-1960 immigrants are non-Europeans. Of the post-1960 immigrants, 22.4 percent are classified as Asians, 7.6 as blacks, and 47 percent as Hispanics. The latter group, which originates in Mexico and other Latin American countries, poses a problem in terms of phenotypical classification since Hispanics can be of any race.[9]

According to the 1990 census, 51.7 percent of the 22.3 million Hispanics counted were white, 3.4 percent black, and 42.7 percent of another race. The latter figure, possibly corresponding to the category of mixed race, or mestizos, was slightly larger among Mexicans, who constitute 60.4 percent of the total Hispanic population. Applying these figures with some adjustments to the post-1960 immigrant flow, it is reasonable to assume that approximately half of Hispanic immigrants would be classified as nonwhite. This phenotypical category would hence comprise a majority, roughly 54 percent, of the total inflow.[10]

Individual data from the 1990 census have not been released as of this writing. In an effort to learn more about the new second generation, Leif Jensen conducted an analysis of the one-in-a-thousand version of the Public Use Microdata Sample A (PUMS) from the 1980 census. He identified 3425 children living in households with at least one foreign-born parent and who themselves were either native-born or had immigrated to the United States at a young age.[11] The number represented 5.1 percent of native-born native-parentage children identified in the sample, a figure that is close to the estimated contribution of post-1960 immigration to the 1980 U.S. population, 5.8 percent.

The ethnic classification of Jensen's sample of new second-generation children in 1980 also cor-

responds closely with that of post-1965 immigrants reported previously. In Jensen's sample, 17.9 percent were classified as Asians, 6.8 percent as blacks, and 45.5 percent as Hispanics. The data do not provide a racial breakdown of Hispanics, but they do contain information on their national origin. Sixty-five percent of the 1564 post-1965 Hispanic children were of Mexican origin; 7.5 percent of Cuban origin; and the remaining 27.5 percent were from all other Latin American nationalities. Table 1 presents selected sociodemographic characteristics of this sample and compares them with those of native-born children of native parentage.

Not surprisingly, second-generation youths are far more likely to be bilingual than their native-parentage counterparts. Less than half of the children of immigrants speak English only, and two-thirds speak a language other than English at home in contrast with the overwhelming English exclusivity among native-parentage youth. However, linguistic assimilation is evident in the fact that only 12 percent of the second generation reports speaking English poorly. Households with immigrant parents are far more likely to be urban and to be found in central cities. Their geographic distribution by state also differs significantly from native-headed households. Just six states account for 71 percent of immigrant households while the same states contain only 33 percent of the natives. Not surprisingly, immigrant parents tend to have more modest socioeconomic characteristics, as indicated by their lower family income, higher poverty rates, and lower education of the family head. However, they are about twice less likely to head single-parent households than are natives. Greater family cohesiveness may have something to do with second-generation educational outcomes. Figures in Table 1 indicate that children of immigrants are as likely to attend private schools, as unlikely to be dropouts, and as likely to graduate from high school as native-parentage youth.[12]

These comparisons are, of course, based on averages that conceal great diversity within each universe. Among second-generation youths in particular, preliminary field research indicates wide differences in educational, linguistic, and social psychological outcomes. None is more important than the forms that an inexorable process of cultural assimilation takes among different immigrant nationalities and its effects on their

TABLE 1   *Selected Characteristics of Post-1965 Second-Generation Youths and Native Youths of Native Parentage, 1980 (Percentage unless noted)*

Children's Characteristics	Post-1965 Immigrant Parent (N = 3,425)	Native-Born Parents (N = 67,193)
Female	46.8	47.4
Mean age	7.5 years	11.9 years
Race or Ethnicity		
White	27.4	78.9
Black	6.8	14.4
Hispanic	45.7	5.4
Mexican	29.7	3.3
Cuban	3.5	0.0
Other	12.5	2.1
Asian	19.5	0.5
Chinese	4.3	0.1
Filipino	5.1	0.1
Korean	2.6	0.0
Vietnamese	1.4	0.0
Other	6.1	0.3
English Ability		
Speaks English only	47.7	95.5
Very well	26.5	2.7
Well	13.8	1.3
Not well or not at all	12.0	0.5
Language Spoken at Home		
English	33.6	94.9
Other	66.4	5.1
Household Type		
Couple	89.7	79.0
Single male head	1.5	2.7
Single female head	8.8	18.3
Area of Residence		
Central city	39.6	17.4
Non-central-city metropolitan area	48.4	49.8
Mixed	6.5	11.7
Nonmetropolitan	5.5	21.1
State of Residence*		
California	32.4	8.1
New York	12.8	7.2
Texas	9.9	6.1
Illinois	5.7	5.2
Florida	5.0	3.5
New Jersey	4.9	3.1
Mean family income	$19,502	$23,414
Poverty rate	20.8	13.8
Mean education of family head	10.9 years	12.2 years
Mean education, self[†]	11.5 years	12.0 years

(continued)

TABLE 1 *(continued)*

Children's Characteristics	Post-1965 Immigrant Parent (N = 3,425)	Native-Born Parents (N = 67,193)
High school dropout[†]	22.8	22.9
School Type		
Public	83.4	86.6
Private	16.6	13.4

Note: The youths in this sample reside in households with at least one parent present. This table is based on U.S. Census Public Use Microdata Sample A as reported in Leif Jensen, *Children of the New Immigration: A Comparative Analysis of Today's Second Generation,* paper commissioned by the Children of Immigrants Research Project, Department of Sociology, Johns Hopkins University, reprinted as Institute for Policy Research and Evaluation Working Paper no. 1990–32 (University Park: Pennsylvania State University, Aug. 1990), tabs. 1–8.

*The six states with the largest concentrations of post-1965 immigrant parents.

[†]Restricted to those aged 20 or more and not enrolled in school.

youths. We explore these differences and provide a theoretical explanation of their causes in the next sections.

ASSIMILATION AS A PROBLEM

The Haitian immigrant community of Miami is composed of some 75,000 legal and clandestine immigrants, many of whom sold everything they owned in order to buy passage to America. First-generation Haitians are strongly oriented toward preserving a strong national identity, which they associate both with community solidarity and with social networks promoting individual success.[13] In trying to instill national pride and an achievement orientation in their children, they clash, however, with the youngsters' everyday experiences in school. Little Haiti is adjacent to Liberty City, the main black inner-city area of Miami, and Haitian adolescents attend predominantly inner-city schools. Native-born youths stereotype Haitians as too docile and too subservient to whites and they make fun of French and Creole and of the Haitians' accent. As a result, second-generation Haitian children find themselves torn between conflicting ideas and values: to remain Haitian they would have to face social ostracism and continuing attacks in school; to become American—black American in this case—they would have to forgo their parents' dreams of making it in America on the basis of ethnic solidarity and preservation of traditional values.[14]

An adversarial stance toward the white mainstream is common among inner-city minority youths who, while attacking the newcomers' ways, instill in them a consciousness of American-style discrimination. A common message is the devaluation of education as a vehicle for advancement of all black youths, a message that directly contradicts the immigrant parents' expectations. Academically outstanding Haitian American students, "Herbie" among them, have consciously attempted to retain their ethnic identity by cloaking it in black American cultural forms, such as rap music. Many others, however, have followed the path of least effort and become thoroughly assimilated. Assimilation in this instance is not into mainstream culture but into the values and norms of the inner city. In the process, the resources of solidarity and mutual support within the immigrant community are dissipated.

An emerging paradox in the study of today's second generation is the peculiar forms that assimilation has adopted for its members. As the Haitian example illustrates, adopting the outlooks and cultural ways of the native-born does not represent, as in the past, the first step toward social and economic mobility but may lead to the exact opposite. At the other end, immigrant youths who remain firmly ensconced in their respective ethnic communities may, by virtue of this fact, have a better chance for educational and economic mobility through use of the material and social capital that their communities make available.[15]

This situation stands the cultural blueprint for advancement of immigrant groups in American society on its head. As presented in innumerable academic and journalistic writings, the expectation is that the foreign-born and their offspring will first acculturate and then seek entry and acceptance among the native-born as a prerequisite for their social and economic advancement. Otherwise, they remain confined to the ranks of the ethnic lower and lower-middle classes.[16] This portrayal of the requirements for mobility, so deeply embedded in the national consciousness, stands contradicted today by a growing number of empirical experiences.

A closer look at these experiences indicates, however, that the expected consequences of assimilation have not entirely reversed signs, but that the process has become segmented. In other words, the question is into what sector of American society a particular immigrant group assimilates. Instead of a relatively uniform mainstream whose mores and prejudices dictate a common path of integration, we observe today several distinct forms of adaptation. One of them replicates the time-honored portrayal of growing acculturation and parallel integration into the white middle-class; a second leads straight in the opposite direction to permanent poverty and assimilation into the underclass; still a third associates rapid economic advancement with deliberate preservation of the immigrant community's values and tight solidarity. This pattern of segmented assimilation immediately raises the question of what makes some immigrant groups become susceptible to the downward route and what resources allow others to avoid this course. In the ultimate analysis, the same general process helps explain both outcomes. We advance next our hypotheses as to how this process takes place and how the contrasting outcomes of assimilation can be explained. This explanation is then illustrated with recent empirical material in the final section.

VULNERABILITY AND RESOURCES

Along with individual and family variables, the context that immigrants find upon arrival in their new country plays a decisive role in the course that their offspring's lives will follow. This context includes such broad variables as political relations between sending and receiving countries and the state of the economy in the latter and such specific ones as the size and structure of pre-existing coethnic communities. The concept of modes of incorporation provides a useful theoretical tool to understand this diversity. As devel-

oped in prior publications, modes of incorporation consist of the complex formed by the policies of the host government; the values and prejudices of the receiving society; and the characteristics of the coethnic community. These factors can be arranged in a tree of contextual situations, illustrated by Figure 1. This figure provides a first approximation to our problem.[17]

To explain second-generation outcomes and their segmented character, however, we need to go into greater detail into the meaning of these various modes of incorporation from the standpoint of immigrant youths. There are three features of the social contexts encountered by today's newcomers that create vulnerability to downward assimilation. The first is color, the second is location, and the third is the absence of mobility ladders. As noted previously, the majority of contemporary immigrants are nonwhite. Although this feature may appear at first glance as an individual characteristic, in reality it is a trait belonging to the host society. Prejudice is not intrinsic to a particular skin color or racial type, and, indeed, many immigrants never experienced it in their native lands. It is by virtue of moving into a new social environment, marked by different values and prejudices, that physical features become redefined as a handicap.

The concentration of immigrant households in cities and particularly in central cities, as documented previously, gives rise to a second source of vulnerability because it puts new arrivals in close contact with concentrations of native-born minorities. This leads to the identification of the condition of both groups—immigrants and the native poor—as the same in the eyes of the majority. More important, it exposes second-generation children to the adversarial sub-culture developed by marginalized native youths to cope with their own difficult situation.[18] This process of socialization may take place even when first-generation parents are moving ahead economically and, hence, their children have no objective reasons for embracing a counter-cultural message. If successful, the process can effectively block parental plans for intergenerational mobility.

The third contextual source of vulnerability has to do with changes in the host economy that have led to the evaporation of occupational ladders for intergenerational mobility. As noted previously, new immigrants may form the backbone of what remains of labor-intensive manufacturing

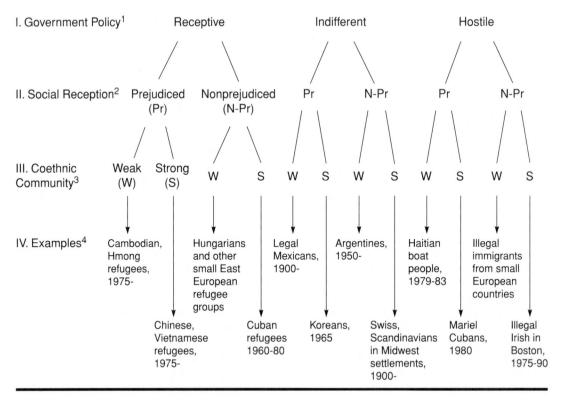

FIGURE 1 *Modes of Incorporation: A Typology*

Source: Adapted from Alejandro Portes and Rubén G. Rumbaut, *Immigrant America: A Portrait* (Berkeley: University of California Press, 1990), p. 91. Copyright © 1990 by The Regents of the University of California.

1. Receptive policy is defined as legal entry with resettlement assistance, indifferent as legal entry without resettlement assistance, hostile as active opposition to a group's entry or permanence in the country.

2. Prejudiced reception is defined as that accorded to nonphenotypically white groups; nonprejudiced is that accorded to European and European-origin whites.

3. Weak coethnic communities are either small in numbers or composed primarily of manual workers; strong communities feature sizable numerical concentrations and a diversified occupational structure including entrepreneurs and professionals

4. Examples include immigrant groups arriving from the start of the century to the present. Dates of migration are approximate. Groups reflect broadly but not perfectly the characteristics of each ideal type.

in the cities as well as in their growing personal services sector, but these are niches that seldom offer channels for upward mobility. The new hourglass economy, created by economic restructuring, means that children of immigrants must cross a narrow bottleneck to occupations requiring advanced training if their careers are to keep pace with their U.S.-acquired aspirations. This race against a narrowing middle demands that immigrant parents accumulate sufficient resources to allow their children to effect the passage and to

simultaneously prove to them the viability of aspirations for upward mobility Otherwise, assimilation may not be into mainstream values and expectations but into the adversarial stance of impoverished groups confined to the bottom of the new economic hourglass.

The picture is painted in such stark terms here for the sake of clarity, although in reality things have not yet become so polarized. Middle-level occupations requiring relatively modest educational achievements have not completely vanished. By

1980, skilled blue-collar jobs—classified by the U.S. census as "precision production, craft, and repair occupations"—had declined by 1.1 percent relative to a decade earlier but still represented 13 percent of the experienced civilian labor force, or 13.6 million workers. Mostly clerical administrative support occupations added another 16.9 percent, or 17.5 million jobs. In 1980, occupations requiring a college degree had increased by 6 percent in comparison with 1970, but they still employed less than a fifth—18.2 percent—of the American labor force.[19] Even in the largest cities, occupations requiring only a high school diploma were common by the late 1980s. In New York City, for example, persons with 12 years or less of schooling held just over one half of the jobs in 1987. Clerical, service, and skilled blue-collar jobs not requiring a college degree represented 46 percent.[20] Despite these figures, there is little doubt that the trend toward occupational segmentation has increasingly reduced opportunities for incremental upward mobility through well-paid blue-collar positions. The trend forces immigrants today to bridge in only one generation the gap between entry-level jobs and professional positions that earlier groups took two or three generations to travel.

Different modes of incorporation also make available, however, three types of resources to confront the challenges of contemporary assimilation. First, certain groups, notably political refugees, are eligible for a variety of government programs including educational loans for their children. The Cuban Loan Program, implemented by the Kennedy administration in connection with its plan to resettle Cuban refugees away from South Florida, gave many impoverished first- and second-generation Cuban youths a chance to attend college. The high proportion of professionals and executives among Cuban American workers today, a figure on a par with that for native white workers, can be traced, at least in part, to the success of that program.[21] Passage of the 1980 Refugee Act gave to subsequent groups of refugees, in particular Southeast Asians and Eastern Europeans, access to a similarly generous benefits package.[22]

Second, certain foreign groups have been exempted from the traditional prejudice endured by most immigrants, thereby facilitating a smoother process of adaptation. Some political refugees, such as the early waves of exiles from Castro's

Cuba, Hungarians and Czechs escaping the invasions of their respective countries, and Soviet Jews escaping religious persecution, provide examples. In other cases, it is the cultural and phenotypical affinity of newcomers to ample segments of the host population that ensures a welcome reception. The Irish coming to Boston during the 1980s are a case in point. Although many were illegal aliens, they came into an environment where generations of Irish Americans had established a secure foothold. Public sympathy effectively neutralized governmental hostility in this case, culminating in a change of the immigration law directly benefiting the newcomers.[23]

Third, and most important, are the resources made available through networks in the coethnic community. Immigrants who join well-established and diversified ethnic groups have access from the start to a range of moral and material resources well beyond those available through official assistance programs. Educational help for second-generation youths may include not only access to college grants and loans but also the existence of a private school system geared to the immigrant community's values. Attendance at these private ethnic schools insulates children from contact with native minority youths, while reinforcing the authority of parental views and plans.

In addition, the economic diversification of several immigrant communities creates niches of opportunity that members of the second generation can occupy, often without a need for an advanced education. Small-business apprenticeships, access to skilled building trades, and well-paid jobs in local government bureaucracies are some of the ethnic niches documented in the recent literature.[24] In 1987, average sales per firm of the smaller Chinese, East Indian, Korean, and Cuban enterprises exceeded $100,000 per year and they jointly employed over 200,000 workers. These figures omit medium-sized and large ethnic firms, whose sales and work forces are much larger.[25] Fieldwork in these communities indicates that up to half of recently arrived immigrants are employed by coethnic firms and that self-employment offers a prime avenue for mobility to second-generation youths.[26] Such community-mediated opportunities provide a solution to the race between material resources and second-generation aspirations not available through competition in the open labor market. Through creation of a capitalism of their own, some immigrant groups have thus been able to circumvent outside discrimination and the threat of vanishing mobility ladders.

In contrast to these favorable conditions are those foreign minorities who either lack a community already in place or whose coethnics are too poor to render assistance. The condition of Haitians in South Florida, cited earlier, provides an illustration of one of the most handicapped modes of incorporation encountered by contemporary immigrants, combining official hostility and widespread social prejudice with the absence of a strong receiving community.[27] From the standpoint of second-generation outcomes, the existence of a large but downtrodden coethnic community may be even less desirable than no community at all. This is because newly arrived youths enter into ready contact with the reactive subculture developed by earlier generations. Its influence is all the more powerful because it comes from individuals of the same national origin, "people like us" who can more effectively define the proper stance and attitudes of the newcomers. To the extent that they do so, the first-generation model of upward mobility through school achievement and attainment of professional occupations will be blocked.

THREE EXAMPLES

Mexicans and Mexican Americans

Field High School (the name is fictitious) is located in a small coastal community of central California whose economy has long been tied to agricultural production and immigrant farm labor. About 57 percent of the student population is of Mexican descent. An intensive ethnographic study of the class of 1985 at Field High began with school records that showed that the majority of U.S.-born Spanish-surname students who had entered the school in 1981 had dropped out by their senior year. However, only 35 percent of the Spanish-surname students who had been originally classified by the school as limited English proficient (LEP) had dropped out. The figure was even lower than the corresponding one for native white students, 40 percent. LEP status is commonly assigned to recently arrived Mexican immigrants.[28]

Intensive ethnographic fieldwork at the school identified several distinct categories in which the Mexican-origin population could be classified. Recent Mexican immigrants were at one extreme. They dressed differently and unstylishly. They claimed an identity as Mexican and considered Mexico their permanent home. The most academically successful of this group were those most proficient in Spanish, reflecting their prior levels of education in Mexico. Almost all were described by teachers and staff as courteous, serious about their schoolwork, respectful, and eager to please as well as naive and unsophisticated. They were commonly classified as LEP.

The next category comprised Mexican-oriented students. They spoke Spanish at home and were generally classified as fluent English proficient (FEP). They had strong bicultural ties with both Mexico and the United States, reflecting the fact that most were born in Mexico but had lived in the United States for more than five years. They were proud of their Mexican heritage but saw themselves as different from the first group, the *recién llegados* (recently arrived), as well as from the native-born Chicanos and Cholos, who were derided as people who had lost their Mexican roots. Students from this group were active in soccer and the Sociedad Bilingue and in celebrations of May 5th, the anniversary of the Mexican defeat of French occupying forces. Virtually all of the Mexican-descent students who graduated in the top 10 percent of their class in 1981 were identified as members of this group.

Chicanos were by far the largest Mexican-descent group at Field High. They were mostly U.S.-born second- and third-generation students whose primary loyalty was to their in-group, seen as locked in conflict with white society. Chicanos referred derisively to successful Mexican students as "schoolboys" and "schoolgirls" or as "wanna-bes." According to M. G. Matute-Bianchi,

To be a Chicano meant in practice to hang out by the science wing . . . not eating lunch in the quad where all the "gringos" and "schoolboys" hang out . . . cutting classes by faking a call slip so you can be with your friends at the 7–11 . . . sitting in the back of classes and not participating . . . not carrying your books to class . . . not taking the difficult classes . . . doing the minimum to get by.[29]

Chicanos merge imperceptibly into the last category, the Cholos, who were commonly seen as "low riders" and gang members. They were also native-born Mexican Americans, easily identifiable by their deliberate manner of dress, walk, speech, and other cultural symbols. Chicanos and Cholos were generally regarded by teachers as "irresponsible," "disrespectful," "mistrusting," "sullen," "apathetic," and "less motivated," and their poor school performance was attributed to these traits.[30] According to Matute-Bianchi, Chicanos and Cholos were faced with what they saw as a forced-choice dilemma between doing well in school or being a Chicano. To act white was regarded as disloyalty to one's group.

The situation of these last two groups exemplifies losing the race between first-generation achievements and later generations' expectations. Seeing their parents and grandparents confined to humble menial jobs and increasingly aware of discrimination against them by the white mainstream, U.S.-born children of earlier Mexican immigrants readily join a reactive subculture as a means of protecting their sense of self-worth. Participation in this subculture then leads to serious barriers to their chances of upward mobility because school achievement is defined as antithetical to ethnic solidarity. Like Haitian students at Edison High, newly arrived Mexican students are at risk of being socialized into the same reactive stance, with the aggravating factor that it is other Mexicans, not native-born strangers, who convey the message. The principal protection of *mexicanos* against this type of assimilation lies in their strong identification with home-country language and values, which brings them closer to their parents' cultural stance.

Punjabi Sikhs in California

Valleyside (a fictitious name) is a northern California community where the primary economic activity is orchard farming. Farm laborers in this area come often from India; they are mainly rural Sikhs from the Punjab. By the early 1980s, second-generation Punjabi students already accounted for 11 percent of the student body at Valleyside High. Their parents were no longer only farm laborers, since about a third had become orchard owners themselves and another third worked in factories in the nearby San Francisco area. An ethnographic study of Valleyside High School in 1980–82 revealed a very difficult process of assimilation for Punjabi Sikh students. According to its author, M. A. Gibson, Valleyside is "redneck country," and

white residents are extremely hostile to immigrants who look different and speak a different language: "Punjabi teenagers are told they stink . . . told to go back to India . . . physically abused by majority students who spit at them, refuse to sit by them in class or in buses, throw food at them or worse."[31]

Despite these attacks and some evidence of discrimination by school staff, Punjabi students performed better academically than majority Anglo students. About 90 percent of the immigrant youths completed high school, compared to 70–75 percent of native whites. Punjabi boys surpassed the average grade point average, were more likely to take advanced science and math classes, and expressed aspirations for careers in science and engineering. Girls, on the other hand, tended to enroll in business classes, but they paid less attention to immediate career plans, reflecting parental wishes that they should marry first. This gender difference is indicative of the continuing strong influence exercised by the immigrant community over its second generation. According to Gibson, Punjabi parents pressured their children against too much contact with white peers who may "dishonor" the immigrants' families, and defined "becoming Americanized" as forgetting one's roots and adopting the most disparaged traits of the majority, such as leaving home at age 18, making decisions without parental consent, dating, and dancing. At the same time, parents urged children to abide by school rules, ignore racist remarks and avoid fights, and learn useful skills, including full proficiency in English.[32]

The overall success of this strategy of selective assimilation to American society is remarkable because Punjabi immigrants were generally poor on their arrival in the United States and confronted widespread discrimination from whites without the benefit of either governmental assistance or a well-established coethnic community. In terms of our typology of vulnerability and resources, the Punjabi Sikh second generation was very much at risk except for two crucial factors. First, immigrant parents did not settle in the inner city or in close proximity to any native-born minority whose offspring could provide an alternative model of adaptation to white-majority discrimination. In particular, the absence of a downtrodden Indian American community composed of children of previous immigrants allowed first-generation parents to influence decisively the outlook of their offspring, including their ways of fighting white prejudice. There was no equivalent of a Cholo-like reactive subculture to offer an alternative blueprint of the stance that "people like us" should take.

Second, Punjabi immigrants managed to make considerable economic progress, as attested by the number who had become farm owners, while maintaining a tightly knit ethnic community. The material and social capital created by this first-generation community compensated for the absence of an older coethnic group and had decisive effects on second-generation outlooks. Punjabi teenagers were shown that their parents' ways paid off economically, and this fact, plus their community's cohesiveness, endowed them with a source of pride to counteract outside discrimination. Through this strategy of selective assimilation, Punjabi Sikhs appeared to be winning the race against the inevitable acculturation of their children to American-style aspirations.

Caribbean Youths in South Florida

Miami is arguably the American city that has been most thoroughly transformed by post-1960 immigration. The Cuban Revolution had much to do with this transformation, as it sent the entire Cuban upper class out of the country, followed by thousands of refugees of more modest backgrounds. Over time, Cubans created a highly diversified and prosperous ethnic community that provided resources for the adaptation process of its second generation. Reflecting this situation are average Cuban family incomes that, by 1989, approximated those of the native-born population; the existence in 1987 of more than 30,000 Cuban-owned small businesses that formed the core of the Miami ethnic enclave; and the parallel rise of a private school system oriented toward the values and political outlook of this community.[33] In terms of the typology of vulnerability and resources, well-sheltered Cuban American teenagers lack any extensive exposure to outside discrimination, they have little contact with youths from disadvantaged minorities, and the development of an enclave creates economic opportunities beyond the narrowing industrial and tourist sectors on which most other immigrant groups in the area depend. Across town, Haitian American teenagers face exactly the opposite set of conditions, as has been shown.

Among the other immigrant groups that form Miami's ethnic mosaic, two deserve mention because they represent intermediate situations between those of the Cubans and Haitians. One comprises Nicaraguans escaping the Sandinista regime during the 1980s. They were not as welcomed in the United States as were the Cuban exiles, nor were they able to develop a large and diversified community. Yet they shared with Cubans their language and culture, as well as a militant anti-Communist discourse. This common political outlook led the Cuban American community to extend its resources in support of their Nicaraguan brethren, smoothing their process of adaptation.[34] For second-generation Nicaraguans, this means that the preexisting ethnic community that provides a model for their own assimilation is not a downtrodden group but rather one that has managed to establish a firm and positive presence in the city's economy and politics.

The second group comprises West Indians coming from Jamaica, Trinidad, and other English-speaking Caribbean republics. They generally arrive in Miami as legal immigrants, and many bring along professional and business credentials as well as the advantage of fluency in English. These individual advantages are discounted, however, by a context of reception in which these mostly black immigrants are put in the same category as native-born blacks and discriminated against accordingly. The recency of West Indian migration and its small size have prevented the development of a diversified ethnic community in South Florida. Hence new arrivals experience the full force of white discrimination without the protection of a large coethnic group and with constant exposure to the situation and attitudes of the inner-city population. Despite considerable individual resources, these disadvantages put the West Indian second generation at risk of bypassing white or even native black middle-class models to assimilate into the culture of the underclass.

A recently completed survey of eighth- and ninth-graders in the Dade County (Miami) and Broward County (Ft. Lauderdale) schools includes sizable samples of Cuban, Haitian, Nicaraguan, and West Indian second-generation children. The study defined "second generation" as youths born in the United States who have at least one foreign-born parent or those born abroad who have lived in the United States for at least five years. All eligible students in the selected schools were included. The survey included both inner-city and suburban public schools, as well as private schools and those where particular foreign-origin groups were known to concentrate. The sample was evenly divided between boys and girls, and the students ranged in age between 12 and 17.[35]

Table 2 presents the responses of second-generation students from these nationalities to a battery of attitudinal and self-identification questions. The large Cuban-origin sample is divided between those attending public and private school. Large socioeconomic differences between the four groups are highlighted in the first panel of Table 2. Cuban children in private schools have the best-educated parents and those with the highest-status occupations. Haitians in public schools have parents who rank lowest on both dimensions. Nicaraguans and West Indians occupy intermediate positions, with parents whose average education is often higher than that of the parents of public school Cubans but whose occupational levels are roughly the same. Reflecting these differences, over half of private school Cuban respondents define their families as upper middle class or higher, while only a third of Haitians and Nicaraguans do so.[36]

The next panel of the table presents differences in ethnic self-identification. Less than one-fifth of these second-generation students identify themselves as nonhyphenated Americans. The proportion is highest among higher-status Cubans, but even among this group almost two-thirds see themselves as Cuban or Cuban American, a proportion close to their peers in public schools. Very few Cubans opt for the self-designation "Hispanic." Nicaraguan students, on the other hand, use this label almost as commonly as that of "Nicaraguan" itself. None of the Latin groups identify themselves as "black." Among Haitians and West Indians, however, roughly one-tenth already assume an identity as black American. Haitian self-identifications are similar to Nicaraguan in being less attached to the country of origin and in using pan-national labels more often than either Cubans or West Indians do. In total, about half of the Haitian children identified themselves as something other than "Haitian."[37]

Aspirations are very high in the entire sample, as indicated in the next panel of Table 2. Although significant differences in expectations of completing college do exist, at least four-fifths of every group expects to achieve this level of education. Similarly, roughly 70 percent of students from every nationality aspire to professional or business careers. These consistently high aspirations contrast with the reported wide differences in parental socioeconomic backgrounds and the differential effects of discrimination. The next panel of the table addresses the latter point, documenting the awareness that these teenagers have about the realities of American society. The two mostly black groups report discrimination against themselves twice to three times more frequently than do Cubans. Majorities of both Haitian and West Indian youths reported having been discriminated against, and about 20 percent said that discrimination was by their teachers. In contrast, only 5 percent of Cubans in private school report such incidents. Nicaraguans occupy an intermediate position, with half reporting discrimination against themselves and 13 percent pointing to their teachers as the source.

Congruent with these personal experiences, Haitian and West Indian teenagers are more likely to agree that there is racial discrimination in economic opportunities in the United States and to disagree that non-whites have equal opportunities. Interestingly, they are joined in these negative evaluations by private school Cubans. This result may reflect the greater information and class awareness of the latter group relative to their less privileged Latin counterparts. However, all Cuban students part company with the rest of the sample in their positive evaluation of the United States. Roughly three-fourths of second-generation Cubans endorse the view that "the United States is the best country in the world"; only half of Nicaraguans do so and the two mostly black groups take a distinctly less enthusiastic stance. These significant differences illustrate the contrasting levels of identification with their country and their local community by children of nationalities affected more or less by outside discrimination.

Introducing controls for native versus foreign birth of respondents attenuates these differences somewhat, but the overall pattern remains. Results of this survey illustrate the race between generalized career aspirations and the widely different vulnerabilities and resources created by first-generation modes of incorporation. Aspirations are very high for all groups, regardless of

TABLE 2 *Second-Generation Eighth- and Ninth-Grade Students by National Origin, South Florida Schools, 1992 (Percentage unless noted)*

	Cubans in Private School (N = 172)	Cubans in Public School (N = 968)	Hatians (N = 136)	Nicaraguans (N = 319)	West Indians (N = 191)	Total (N = 1,786)	p <	V^2 or Eta
Socioeconomic Characteristics								
Father college graduate	50.0	21.4	11.0	38.6	18.8	26.1	.001	.27
Mother college graduate	39.0	17.5	11.0	28.2	26.2	21.9	.001	.15
Father occupation, mean prestige scores*	52.6	44.2	37.6	43.7	43.6	44.5	.001	.22
Mother occupation, mean prestige scores*	51.1	45.1	39.7	40.1	44.8	44.3	.001	.23
Family wealthy or upper-middle class†	57.0	42.7	37.5	35.4	49.2	43.1	.001	.10
Self-identification								
American	33.1	19.9	16.2	10.0	16.2	18.8	.001	.64
Black American	—	—	12.5	—	9.9	2.2	.001	.64
Hispanic American	3.5	7.6	1.5	39.5	0.5	11.7	.001	.64
Cuban‡	61.6	67.5	—	0.3	—	42.6	.001	.64
Haitian‡	—	—	53.7	—	3.1	4.4	.001	.64
Nicaraguan‡	—	0.6	—	44.8	—	8.3	.001	.64
Other nationality§	1.8	4.4	16.2	5.3	70.2	12.2	.001	.64
Aspirations								
College education or higher‖	97.1	82.6	86.7	79.0	84.8	83.9	.001	.11
Professional or business occupation	72.1	70.0	75.0	69.9	71.2	70.6	n.s.	.06
Perceptions of Discrimination								
Has ever been discriminated against	29.1	38.2	67.6	50.8	64.4	44.6	.001	.23
Discriminated against by teachers	5.2	12.5	16.2	13.5	23.6	13.4	.001	.13
Attitudes toward U.S. Society								
There is racial discrimination in economic opportunities	91.3	79.2	84.6	81.5	89.5	82.3	.001	.11
Nonwhites have equal opportunities	30.8	53.6	44.9	52.4	41.9	49.3	.001	.14
The United States is the best country in the world	79.7	68.9	36.0	49.8	35.1	60.4	.001	.30
Friends								
Many or most friends have foreign-born parents	93.6	73.1	46.3	75.2	43.5	70.2	.001	.22
Friends' parents are								
Cuban	89.5	58.7	2.9	11.3	4.2	43.1	.001	.44
Haitian	—	1.2	30.1	1.3	12.6	4.5	.001	.44
Nicaraguan	7.6	24.8	2.9	69.0	2.1	26.9	.001	.44
West Indian	—	6.2	46.3	7.2	62.8	14.9	.001	.44
Other	2.9	9.1	17.7	11.2	18.3	10.6	.001	.44

Source: Alejandro Portes and Lisandro Perez, Children of Immigrants: The Adaptation Process of the Second Generation (project conducted at the Department of Sociology, Johns Hopkins University, in progress).

*Employed parents only; Treiman international prestige scale scores.

†Respondent's class self-classification.

‡Includes hyphenated self-identifications of the same nationality, for example, Nicaraguan American.

§West Indian self-identifications not classified individually by country.

‖Respondents' statements of the level of education that they realistically expect to attain.

origin; however, parental socioeconomic back-grounds, resources of the coethnic community—as exemplified by the existence of a private school system—and experiences of discrimination are very different. They influence decisively the out-look of second-generation youths, even at a young age, and are likely to have strong effects on the course of their future assimilation. Illustrating these differences is the enthusiasm with which children of advantaged immigrants embrace their parents' adopted country and the much less sanguine views of those whose situation is more difficult.

CONCLUSION

The last panel of Table 2 highlights another in-triguing fact about today's second generation. The best-positioned group—private-school Cubans—is the one least likely to step out of the ethnic circle in their interpersonal relationships, while the group in the most disadvantaged position—Haitians—is most likely to do so. Overall, the three Latin groups overwhelmingly select friends who are also children of immigrants, mostly from the same nationality. Less than half of the Hai-tians and West Indians do so, indicating much greater contact with native-parentage youths. Other Haitian American teenagers are not even the majority of foreign-parentage friends among our Haitian respondents.

Fifty years ago, the dilemma of Italian Ameri-can youngsters studied by Irving Child consisted of assimilating into the American mainstream, sacrificing in the process their parents' cultural heritage in contrast to taking refuge in the ethnic community from the challenges of the outside world. In the contemporary context of segmented assimilation, the options have become less clear. Children of nonwhite immigrants may not even have the opportunity of gaining access to middle-class white society, no matter how acculturated they become. Joining those native circles to which they do have access may prove a ticket to perma-nent subordination and disadvantage. Remaining securely ensconced in their coethnic community, under these circumstances, may be not a symp-tom of escapism but the best strategy for capitaliz-ing on otherwise unavailable material and moral resources. As the experiences of Punjabi Sikh and Cuban American students suggest, a strategy of

paced, selective assimilation may prove the best course for immigrant minorities. But the extent to which this strategy is possible also depends on the history of each group and its specific profile of vul-nerabilities and resources. The present analysis represents a preliminary step toward understand-ing these realities.

ENDNOTES

1. Alejandro Portes and Alex Stepick, *City on the Edge: The Transformation of Miami* (Berkeley: University of California Press, 1993), chap. 8.
2. Defined as native-born children with at least one foreign-born parent or children born abroad who came to the United States before age 12. See Leif Jensen, *Children of the New Immigration: A Comparative Analysis of Today's Second Generation,* paper commissioned by the Children of Immigrants Research Project, Department of Sociology, Johns Hopkins University, reprinted as In-stitute for Policy Research and Evaluation Working Paper no. 1990-32 (University Park: Pennsylvania State University, Aug. 1990).
3. Joan N. First and John W. Carrera, *New Voices: Im-migrant Students in U.S. Public Schools* (Boston: National Coalition of Advocates for Students, 1988).
4. Michael Piore, *Birds of Passage* (New York: Cam-bridge University Press, 1979); Herbert Gans, "Second-Generation Decline: Scenarios for the Economic and Ethnic Futures of the Post-1965 American Immigrants," *Ethnic and Racial Studies* 15:173–92 (Apr. 1992).
5. Irving L. Child, *Italian or American? The Second Gen-eration in Conflict* (New Haven, CT: Yale University Press, 1943).
6. See, for example, Saskia Sassen, "Changing Compo-sition and Labor Market Location of Hispanic Immi-grants in New York City, 1960–1980," in *Hispanics in the U.S. Economy,* ed. George J. Borjas and Marta Tienda (New York: Academic Press, 1985), pp. 299–322.
7. Jeffrey S. Passel and Barry Edmonston, "Immigra-tion and Race: Recent Trends in Immigration to the United States" (Paper no. PRIP-UI-22, Urban Institute, May 1992), tab. 2.
8. The new immigration is defined as that which started after the 1965 Immigration Act. Inclusion of 1960–65 im-migrants in the totals just mentioned leads to only a slight overcount due to the relatively low numbers arriv-ing before passage of the act. See ibid., tab. 9.
9. Ibid.
10. U.S. Department of Commerce, Bureau of the Cen-sus, *Race by Hispanic Origin, 1990 Census of Population and Housing,* special tabulation prepared by the Ethnic and Hispanic Branch (Washington, DC: U.S. Depart-ment of Commerce, 1992).
11. In most cases, before age 12. See Jensen, *Children of the New Immigration.*

12. Because of data limitations, comparisons of years of education completed and high school dropouts are limited to persons aged 20 or older still living with their parents. These results may not be representative of the respective universes of adult individuals. See ibid.

13. See Alex Stepick, "Haitian Refugees in the U.S." (Report no. 52, Minority Rights Group, London, 1982); Alex Stepick and Alejandro Portes, "Flight into Despair: A Profile of Recent Haitian Refugees in South Florida," *International Migration Review,* 20:329–50 (Summer 1986).

14. This account is based on fieldwork in Miami conducted in preparation for a survey of immigrant youths in public schools. The survey and preliminary results are described in the final section of this article.

15. On the issue of social capital, see James S. Coleman, "Social Capital in the Creation of Human Capital," *American Journal of Sociology,* supplement, 94:S95–121 (1988); Alejandro Portes and Min Zhou, "Gaining the Upper Hand: Economic Mobility among Immigrant and Domestic Minorities," *Ethnic and Racial Studies,* 15:491–522 (Oct. 1992). On ethnic entrepreneurship, see Ivan H. Light, *Ethnic Enterprise in America: Business and Welfare among Chinese, Japanese, and Blacks* (Berkeley: University of California Press, 1972); Kenneth Wilson and W. Allen Martin, "Ethnic Enclaves: A Comparison of the Cuban and Black Economies in Miami," *American Journal of Sociology,* 88:135–60 (1982).

16. See W. Lloyd Warner and Leo Srole, *The Social Systems of American Ethnic Groups* (New Haven, CT: Yale University Press, 1945); Thomas Sowell, *Ethnic America: A History* (New York: Basic Books, 1981).

17. See Alejandro Portes and Rubén G. Rumbaut, *Immigrant America: A Portrait* (Berkeley: University of California Press, 1990), chap. 3.

18. See Mercer L. Sullivan, *"Getting Paid": Youth, Crime, and Work in the Inner City* (Ithaca, NY: Cornell University Press, 1989), chaps. 1, 5.

19. U.S., Department of Commerce, Bureau of the Census, *Census of Population and Housing, 1980: Public Use Microdata Samples A (MRDF)* (Washington, DC: Department of Commerce, 1983).

20. Thomas Bailey and Roger Waldinger, "Primary, Secondary, and Enclave Labor Markets: A Training System Approach," *American Sociological Review,* 56:432–45 (1991).

21. Professionals and executives represented 25.9 percent of Cuban-origin males aged 16 years and over in 1989; the figure for the total adult male population was 26 percent. See Jesus M. García and Patricia A. Montgomery, *The Hispanic Population of the United States: March 1990,* Current Population Reports, ser. P-20, no. 449 (Washington, DC: Department of Commerce, 1991).

22. Portes and Rumbaut, *Immigrant America,* pp. 23–25; Robert L. Bach et al., "The Economic Adjustment of Southeast Asian Refugees in the United States," in *World Refugee Survey, 1983* (Geneva: United Nations High Commission for Refugees, 1984), pp. 51–55.

23. The 1990 Immigration Act contains tailor-made provisions to facilitate the legalization of Irish immigrants. Those taking advantage of the provisions are popularly dubbed "Kennedy Irish" in honor of the Massachusetts Senator who coauthored the act. On the 1990 act, see Michael Fix and Jeffrey S. Passel, "The Door Remains Open: Recent Immigration to the United States and a Preliminary Analysis of the Immigration Act of 1990" (Working paper, Urban Institute and RAND Corporation, 1991). On the Irish in Boston, see Karen Tumulty, "When Irish Eyes Are Hiding . . . ," *Los Angeles Times,* 29 Jan. 1989.

24. Bailey and Waldinger, "Primary, Secondary, and Enclave Labor Markets"; Min Zhou, *New York's Chinatown: The Socioeconomic Potential of an Urban Enclave* (Philadelphia: Temple University Press, 1992); Wilson and Martin, "Ethnic Enclaves"; Suzanne Model, "The Ethnic Economy: Cubans and Chinese Reconsidered" (Manuscript, University of Massachusetts at Amherst, 1990).

25. U.S., Department of Commerce, Bureau of the Census, *Survey of Minority-Owned Business Enterprises, 1987,* MB-2 and MB-3 (Washington, DC: Department of Commerce, 1991).

26. Alejandro Portes and Alex Stepick, "Unwelcome Immigrants: The Labor Market Experiences of 1980 (Mariel) Cuban and Haitian Refugees in South Florida," *American Sociological Review,* 50:493–514 (Aug. 1985); Zhou, *New York's Chinatown;* Luis E. Guarnizo, "One Country in Two: Dominican-Owned Firms in New York and the Dominican Republic" (Ph.D. diss. Johns Hopkins University, 1992); Bailey and Waldinger, "Primary, Secondary, and Enclave Labor Markets."

27. Stepick, "Haitian Refugees in the U.S."; Jake C. Miller, *The Plight of Haitian Refugees* (New York: Praeger, 1984).

28. M. G. Matute-Bianchi, "Ethnic Identities and Patterns of School Success and Failure among Mexican-Descent and Japanese-American Students in a California High School," *American Journal of Education,* 95:233–55 (Nov. 1986). This study is summarized in Rubén G. Rumbaut, "Immigrant Students in California Public Schools: A Summary of Current Knowledge" (Report no. 11, Center for Research on Effective Schooling for Disadvantaged Children, Johns Hopkins University, Aug. 1990).

29. Matute-Bianchi, "Ethnic Identities and Patterns," p. 253.

30. Rumbaut, "Immigrant Students," p. 25.

31. M. A. Gibson, *Accommodation without Assimilation: Sikh Immigrants in an American High School* (Ithaca, NY: Cornell University Press, 1989), p. 268.

32. Gibson, *Accommodation without Assimilation.* The study is summarized in Rumbaut, "Immigrant Students," pp. 22–23.

33. García and Montgomery, *Hispanic Population;* U.S., Department of Commerce, Bureau of the Census, *Survey of Minority-Owned Business Enterprises,* MB-2.
34. Portes and Stepick, *City on the Edge,* chap. 7.
35. Alejandro Portes and Lisandro Perez, Children of Immigrants: The Adaptation Process of the Second Generation (Project conducted at the Department of Sociology, Johns Hopkins University, in progress).
36. Because of the large sample size, .001 is used as the criterion of statistical significance in these tabulations.

Cramér's V^2 is used as the principal measure of strength of association. In comparison with other coefficients, it has the advantage of a constant range between 0 and 1. Higher values indicate stronger association. Eta is similarly defined but is used only for the continuous parental occupational status variables.
37. West Indian self-identification was not coded separately and hence is classified under "Other nationality" in Table 2.

E I G H T E E N

Minority Status and Literacy in Comparative Perspective

John U. Ogbu

In many contemporary plural societies racial and ethnic minorities lag behind members of the dominant groups in acquisition of literacy and numeracy, that is, in school performance. It is well known that in the United States many minorities do not perform as well as the dominant white Americans. Similar gaps in school performance between minorities and the dominant groups are also found in Britain, Japan, and New Zealand, to mention only a few (Ogbu 1978). At the same time, however, some other minorities perform as well as the dominant groups or even surpass them (Bullivant 1987; Taylor and Hegarty 1985; Ogbu 1978). In this essay I seek to explain why certain minority groups do not do particularly well in school while certain other minority groups do relatively better.

Most studies of minority schooling in the United States focus on what goes on inside the school, inside the home, or in the biology of the individual child. To take the last first, proponents of differential mental ability theory claim that children do well academically in school because they possess certain mental abilities defined as IQ, the amount and type of which can be determined by IQ tests. When such tests are administered, minority children score lower than their white peers; minorities do not do as well either on those parts of the test believed to indicate potential for school success. Some attribute these lower IQ test scores to inadequate genetic endowment (Jensen 1969). Others find the cause in inadequate home environment and early childhood experience (Ramey and Gallagher 1975; White et al. 1973). Both groups agree, however, that minority children's school failure is caused by an inadequate IQ or mental ability.

To raise minority children's IQ through preschool programs, compensatory education programs for older children and training of minority parents to raise children as white middle-class parents do have become common. Though minority children who participate in such programs may score higher on IQ tests while they are in the programs, later tests generally show that such higher scores tend to "fade out" after these children leave the programs or while they are in the middle years of elementary school (Goldberg 1971; Ramey and Campbell 1987).

If some insist that lower-class children generally do less well in school because they lack ability as measured by IQ tests, others stress the failure of their families to prepare them for school adjustment and academic success. Using socioeconomic status as a measure of class membership, most black youths are generally classified as belonging to the lower class; their school-adjustment problems and lower academic performance are attributed to this lower-class status (Coleman 1966).[1]

Such correlation studies fail, however, to explain why black students do not perform as well as their white peers of similar social class background. In a study of black and white candidates who took the Scholastic Aptitude Tests in 1980–1981, candidates from black families with annual average incomes of $50,000 or more had median verbal scores of about the same level as candidates from white families with average annual incomes of $13,000 to $18,000. Black candidates from homes with average annual incomes of $50,000 or more had median math scores slightly below the median math scores of white candidates from homes with average annual incomes of $6,000 or less (Slade 1981). Why? Other studies show similar results.

While there is a clear pattern for white students, with their academic performance tending to rise as their parents' education (and socioeconomic status) goes up, there is no such clear pattern for blacks. In a study of the performance of eighth-grade students in California on the California Assessment Program Survey of Basic Skills, it was found (a) that the gap between black students whose parents were highly educated and those whose parents had little formal education was only about half as great as the gap between such groups among white students; (b) that black students whose parents had advanced degrees scored, on the average, below white students whose parents had completed only high school education; and (c) that black students whose parents had completed only some college education consistently outperformed other black students whose

parents had actually completed college (Haycock and Navarro 1988).

The issue is clearly not whether minority children from middle-class backgrounds do better than minority children from lower-class or underclass backgrounds. The issue is whether minority children do as well as their white counterparts. They do not (Fordham and Ogbu 1986; Oliver, Rodriguez, and Mickelson 1985).

Anthropologists, less concerned about the effects of social class differences on minority education, have concentrated on the effects of cultural differences, broadly defined, in the belief that the problem is caused by cultural differences and cultural conflicts. Where children receive their education in a learning environment different from the one familiar to them at home, they have difficulty acquiring the content and style of learning presupposed by the curriculum and the teaching methods (Phillips 1976). Cultural conflicts occur when non-Western children attend Western-type schools and also when immigrant children, minority children, and lower-class children attend schools controlled by middle-class members of the dominant group in an urban industrial society like the United States (LaBelle 1976).

The conflict may be in language and communication, cognition, cognitive style, social interaction, values, or teaching and learning techniques. For example, it has been claimed that Puerto Rican children living on the mainland experience learning difficulties because they do not interpret eye contacts as their white middle-class teachers do (Byers and Byers 1972). The Oglala Sioux Indian children's learning difficulties seem also to stem from cultural miscommunication with white teachers. The Indians, it is said, resist the teachers' attempts to reach them because they are not used to a situation in which adults control child-adult communications (Dumont 1972).Warm Springs Indian children in Oregon fail to learn under white teachers because they require the use of rules of speech in the classroom different from those with which the children are familiar in their community (Phillips 1983). Similar situations exist among black children (Boykin 1986; Shade 1982).

While I agree that cultural differences and cultural conflicts cause real difficulties for non-Western children in Western-type schools and for minority children in the U.S. public schools (Gay and Cole 1967; Lancey 1983; Musgrove 1953; La-

Belle 1976), studies suggest that the persistent disproportionate school failure rates of blacks and similar minorities are not caused simply by conflicts in cognitive, communication, social interaction, teaching, and learning styles. In any case, such theories fail to explain why certain minorities cross cultural boundaries, why others seem to have greater difficulties in crossing them. All three theories fail to take account of the incentive motivation in a minority's pursuit of education.

In our attempt to understand the school performance of minority children, the field is dominated by what may be called "improvement research," or "applied research," studies designed to search for "what works" or "does not work" in minority education. These studies focus on the microsetting events of classroom, school, or home and sometimes on the biographies of minority children. Such events are rarely analyzed in the context of the minority group's history or its structural position in society. My view is that what goes on inside the classroom and school is greatly affected by the minority group's perceptions of and responses to schooling, and that is related to its historical and structural experience in the larger society.[2]

In my research on minority education I have found it useful to classify specific groups as autonomous minorities, immigrant or voluntary minorities, and castelike or involuntary minorities.[3]

Autonomous minorities, represented in the United States by Jews and Mormons, for example, are found also in most developing nations in Africa and Asia. While these minorities may be victims of prejudice or pillory, stratification does not define their position. Their separate existence is rarely based on a special economic, ritual, or political role; they generally employ a cultural frame of reference which encourages success.

Immigrant or *voluntary minorities* are those who have more or less chosen to move to the United States or to some other society, in the belief that this change will lead to an improvement in their economic well-being or to greater political freedom. These expectations influence the way they perceive and respond to white Americans and to institutions controlled by whites. The Chinese in Stockton, Califorinia, and the Punjabi in Valleyside, California, are representative examples (Gibson 1988; Ogbu 1974).[4]

Castelike or *involuntary minorities* are people initially brought into the United States through slavery, conquest, or colonization. Resenting the loss of their former freedom and perceiving the social, political, and economic barriers against them as part of an undeserved oppression, American Indians, black Americans, Mexican Americans, and native Hawaiians are characteristic American examples.[5] Similar minorities exist in Japan—the Buraku outcastes and the Koreans—and in New Zealand—the Maoris (Ogbu 1978).

By comparing the historical, structural, and psychological factors influencing school-adjustment problems of immigrants (i.e., voluntary minorities) with those of nonimmigrants (i.e., involuntary minorities) one can show why the latter are plagued by persistent poor academic performance while the former are not.

The cultural and language differences of various minorities vis-à-vis white American culture and language are not qualitatively the same. Such differences can be a significant factor in school adjustment, in the academic performance of a specific minority group. One must distinguish between primary and secondary cultural differences (Ogbu 1982). *Primary cultural differences* are those that existed before two specific populations came into continuous contact. For example, before Punjabis emigrated from the Punjab to California, they spoke Punjabi, often wore turbans, accepted arranged marriages, and practiced the Sikh, Hindu, or Muslim religion. They also had their distinctive child-rearing practices. In California these immigrants maintained these beliefs and practices to some degree (Gibson 1988). . . .

. . . Primary cultural differences are found among many immigrant minorities. Immigrant minority children confront problems because of such primary cultural differences. The problems may range from interpersonal relations with teachers and other students, to academic work. Under favorable conditions, immigrant children are generally able to overcome such problems in the course of time.

Secondary cultural and *language differences* are those which arise after two populations have come into contact, or after members of one population have begun to participate in an institution controlled by members of another. Secondary cultural and language differences develop as a response to such contact, often involving the domination of one group by another.

In the beginning, the minorities and the dominant group will usually show primary cultural and language differences. In the course of time, a new type of cultural and language difference may emerge, reflecting the way the minorities are treated by the dominant group and the way they have come to perceive, interpret, and respond to that treatment. For example, when slavery was common, white Americans used legal and extralegal means to discourage black Americans from acquiring literacy and the associated behaviors and benefits. After the abolition of slavery, whites created barriers in employment and in other areas of life, effectively denying blacks certain social and economic benefits, but also the incentives associated with the education whites made available to them. Such barriers extended to places of residence, public accommodations, and political and legal rights. Blacks, like other involuntary minorities, developed new or "secondary" cultural ways of coping, perceiving, and feeling in relating to whites and to the public schools controlled by whites.

Most descriptions of cultural differences between involuntary minorities and white Americans emphasize differences in the style of cognition (Ramirez and Castenada 1974; Shade 1982), communication (Gumperz 1981; Kochman 1982; Philips 1976), interaction (Au 1981; Philips 1976), and learning (Erickson and Mohartt 1982). In contrast, descriptions of primary cultural differences emphasize differences in the content of cognition, communication, and so on. A further distinguishing feature of a secondary cultural system is *cultural inversion*, the tendency for members of one population, in this case a minority group, to regard certain forms of behavior, events, symbols, and meanings as inappropriate, precisely because they are characteristic of members of another population, for example, white Americans. These minorities may claim other forms of behavior, events, symbols, and meanings as more appropriate precisely because they are not characteristic of members of the dominant group.

Involuntary minorities use cultural inversion to repudiate negative stereotypes or derogatory images attributed to them by members of the dominant group. Cultural inversion is also used as a strategy to manipulate whites, to get even with whites, or, as one observer says in the case of black Americans, "to turn the table against whites"

(Gay and Cole 1967; Gibson 1988). Because secondary cultural differences are developed in opposition to and in response to perceived unjustified treatment by the dominant group, such cultural differences are intimately tied to the minorities' sense of group identify.

Because researchers, policymakers, and educators in the field of minority education tend to idealize educational pursuit, they forget that schooling in the United States has generally been structured on the commonsense notion of training in marketable skills, credentialing for labor-force entry, remuneration, advancement. Thus, whatever other functions schooling may serve, the most important function, as perceived by most Americans, is economic; children go to school to secure the credentials for employment, remuneration, and advancement (Warner, Havighurst, and Loeb 1944; Ogbu 1974).

Schools, however, do not succeed uniformly in credentialing members of society by content or method of teaching. The labor-force experience of members of a given group, and their perceptions of and responses to schooling as a consequence of their overall status in U.S. society, are significant factors (Ogbu 1986; Ogbu and Matute-Bianchi 1986).[6]

In a plural society like the United States, the various segments of the society—the dominant whites and the minority groups—tend to have specific cultural models, understandings of their status, of how American society works and their place in that working order. The cultural model of white Americans, like that of a specific minority group, is never right or wrong, better or worse. As Bohannon puts it, "The folk systems [i.e., cultural models] are *never* right nor wrong. They exist to guide behavior, to interpret behavior and events" (Bohannon 1957:5).

The cultural models of minorities are shaped by the initial terms of their incorporation in American society, and their subsequent treatment by white Americans. The formative influence that differentiates the cultural model of immigrants from that of nonimmigrants or involuntary minorities is the initial term of incorporation—voluntary incorporation in the case of the immigrants, involuntary incorporation in the case of nonimmigrants.

What does it mean to be a minority in the United States? Voluntary and involuntary minorities answer this question differently. Immigrants generally regard themselves as "foreigners," "strangers" who came to America with expectation of certain economic, political, and social benefits. While anticipating that such benefits might come at some cost—involving discrimination and other hardships—the immigrants did not measure their success or failure primarily by the standards of other white Americans, but by the standards of their homelands. Such minorities, at least during the first generation, did not internalize the effects of such discrimination, of cultural and intellectual denigration. Their effects were not ingrained in their culture. Even when they were restricted to menial labor, they did not consider themselves to be occupying the lowest rung of the American status system, and partly because they did not fully understand that system, and partly because they did not consider themselves as belonging to it, they saw their situation as temporary.

For involuntary minorities, there were no expectations of economic, political, and social benefits. Resenting their initial incorporation by force, regarding their past as a "golden age," and seeing their future as grim in the absence of collective struggle (Shack 1970–1971), they understood that the American system was based on social class and minority conditions. Resenting exclusion from a status system available to whites, based on achieved criteria, they felt the power of white domination in almost every domain. While refusing to accept white denigration, the common white belief that they were biologically, culturally, and intellectually inferior to whites, their own thoughts and behaviors were not entirely free from the influence of such denigration and belief. Involuntary minorities tended to develop other explanations for their persistent menial status; they used these explanations to rationalize their responses.

Both voluntary and involuntary minorities face discrimination in various spheres of American life. Discriminated against in employment, usually through job ceilings, minorities are often relegated to menial jobs and low wages. Also, political barriers may exist, exacerbated by social and residential segregation. Their children, often channeled into inferior, segregated schools, discover as adults that they are denied employment and wages commensurate with their school credentials (Ogbu 1983; Blair 1972; Gibson 1988).

Immigrant and involuntary minorities suffer, in addition, expressive or symbolic discrimination. White Americans tend to denigrate such minorities, culturally and intellectually, stereotyping them, characterizing them by specific undesirable traits. Minorities are used as scapegoats, often subjected to violent treatment in times of economic and political crisis (Wallace 1970–1971). They are denied assimilation, admission into mainstream American society.

Immigrant and involuntary minorities, while resenting such treatment, perceive and interpret it differently, and appear to work out different collective solutions to their common collective problems. (In the case of blacks the problem is made more complicated by race and color.)

The coping responses are of three types: instrumental, relational, and expressive. *Instrumental responses* include: (1) a dual-status frame of comparison, a comparison that minorities make of their status and opportunities in the United States with the status and opportunities of their peers "back home," in the case of immigrants, or with the status and opportunities of white Americans, especially in the case of the nonimmigrants; (2) a folk theory or folk theories of "making it" in America; (3) collective efforts to change those rules of "getting ahead" that do not work well for minorities; (4) alternative survival strategies, developed by minorities to compensate for barriers encountered in the opportunity structure; and (5) role models. *Relational responses* have to do with the degree of trust that the minorities have for white Americans and the institutions they control. *Expressive, or symbolic, responses* reflect the minority-group members' sense of group identity, their cultural frames of reference, and their ideal ways of behaving.

On the instrumental side, immigrants appear to interpret the economic, political, and social barriers set against them as a more or less temporary problem that they can (and will) overcome with time through hard work and/or education.

Immigrants will often compare their situation in the United States with what they have known or what their peers are experiencing "back home." When making such comparisons, they find encouraging evidence to believe that they will enjoy greater opportunities in the United States for themselves or for their children. Even if they are permitted only marginal jobs, they see themselves as better off than they would be in their home-lands. They believe the United States to be a land of opportunity where success comes with hard work. They rationalize discrimination in employment and other things by attributing this to their status as "foreigners," to the fact that they do not speak the English language well, that they lack "an American education." Given these perceptions, immigrant minorities tend to adopt what they understand to be the folk theory of getting ahead among white Americans; they try to behave accordingly. Among such immigrants, schooling, knowledge, and individual effort emerge as the primary avenues for getting ahead. Contrast this with the situation that obtains in their countries of origin, where advancement occurs through a network of friends, nepotism, or *"por appellido"* (because of one's last name, in the case of a Latino immigrant), and not necessarily because of one's effort, knowledge, or educational credentials (Suarez-Orozco 1989).

Voluntary minorities also develop survival or alternative strategies to cope with their problems. The survival strategies include the option of returning to their former homelands or emigrating to yet another place. They recognize also the possibility of exploiting economic resources not desired by white Americans and involuntary minorities.

In the relational domain, voluntary minorities have a greater degree of trust for white Americans, for the societal institutions controlled by whites, than do involuntary minorities. Such immigrants acquiesce and rationalize the prejudice and discrimination against them by saying, in effect, that they are "strangers in a foreign land [and] have no choice but to tolerate prejudice and discrimination" (Gibson 1988). In relating to the public schools, they rationalize their accommodation by saying that they came to America to give their children the opportunity to secure an American education. Indeed, they find their relationship with the public schools to be "better" than what they knew in their homelands, and speak favorably of conditions where their children are given free textbooks and other supplies (Suarez-Orozco 1989).

In the expressive or symbolic domain, the immigrants' response to cultural and language differences is also influenced by expectations. The immigrants, such as the Punjabis, for example, interpret certain of the cultural and language differences as barriers to be overcome. Never imagining

that this requires them to abandon their own minority culture and language, they selectively learn the language and cultural features of the mainstream. There is no perceived threat to cultural or language identity. As for social or collective identity, voluntary minorities bring with them a keen sense of who they were before they emigrated. They perceive their social identities as different from rather than as opposed to the identity of white Americans. They appear to retain this social identity, at least during the first generation, all the time they are learning the English language and adapting other aspects of mainstream American culture.

The instrumental responses of involuntary minorities are different. They do not interpret the economic, social, and political barriers against them as temporary. Their reference group is different. Because they do not have a "homeland" to compare with the situation in the United States, they do not find solace in their menial jobs and low wages. Recognizing that they belong to a subordinate, indeed a disparaged, minority, they compare their situation with that of their white American peers. The prejudice against them seems permanent, indeed institutionalized.

In their folk theory of "making it," involuntary minorities often wish they could advance through education and ability as white Americans do, but know they cannot. They come to realize that it requires more than education and effort to overcome the barriers set up against them. Consequently, they develop a folk theory of getting ahead which differs from that of white Americans; it emphasizes collective effort as providing the best chances for overcoming barriers in those areas controlled by white Americans.[7]

Since involuntary minorities do not believe that the societal rules for self-advancement work for them, they try to change the rules. They may, for example, seek to alter the criteria for school credentialing, for employment. One strategy effectively used by black Americans is to change the rules through "collective struggle," one of several survival strategies developed to eliminate, lower, or circumvent specific barriers in securing desirable jobs and in advancing in other ways. Collective struggle includes what white Americans regard as legitimate "civil rights activities"; for the minorities, these include rioting and other forms of collective action that promise to increase the opportunities or the pool of resources available to them.

Patron-client relationships, or "Uncle Tomming" ("Tio Tacoing," etc.), is another survival strategy, more common in the past. Other survival strategies include opting for certain activities—sports, entertainment, hustling, pimping, and, nowadays, drug dealing.

In the relational domain, involuntary minorities distrust white Americans and their institutions. White Americans have a record that merits such mistrust. The public schools, for example, cannot be relied on to provide minority children with "the right education." Involuntary minorities find no justification for the prejudice and discrimination they find in school and society, which appears to be institutionalized, and enduring.

On the expressive side, involuntary minorities are characterized by secondary cultural systems, in which cultural differences arise or are reinterpreted after the groups have become involuntary minorities. They develop certain beliefs and practices, including particular ways of communicating or speaking, as coping mechanisms in conditions of subordination. These may be new creations or simply reinterpretations of old ones. The secondary cultural system, on the whole, constitutes a new cultural frame of reference, an ideal way of believing and acting which affirms one as a bona fide member of a group. Involuntary minorities perceive their cultural frames of reference not merely as different from but as opposed to the cultural frames of reference of their white "oppressors." The cultural and language differences emerging under these conditions serve as boundary-making mechanisms. Involuntary minorities do not interpret language and cultural differences encountered in school or society as barriers to overcome; they interpret such differences as symbols of their identity. Their culture provides a frame of reference that gives them a sense of collective or social identity, a sense of self-worth.

Involuntary minorities develop a new sense of peoplehood or social identity after their forced incorporation into American society, because of the ways they interpret the discrimination they are obliged to endure. In some instances, involuntary minorities may develop a new sense of peoplehood because of their forced integration into mainstream society (Castile and Kushner 1981; DeVos 1984; DeVos and Wagatsuma 1966; Spicer

1966, 1971). Many appear to believe that they cannot expect to be treated as white Americans, whatever their ability, training or education; whatever their place of origin, residence, economic status, or physical appearance (Green 1981). These involuntary minorities know that they cannot escape from their birth-ascribed membership in subordinate and disparaged groups by "passing" or returning to their "homelands" (Ogbu 1984; DeVos 1984). They do not see their social identity as different from that of their white "oppressors," but as opposed to the social identity of white Americans. This oppositional identity, combined with their oppositional or ambivalent cultural frames of reference, make cross-cultural learning, the "crossing of cultural boundaries," very problematic. Crossing cultural boundaries, behaving in a manner regarded as falling under the white American cultural frames of reference, is threatening to their minority identity and security, but also to their solidarity. Individuals seeking to behave like whites are discouraged by peer group pressures and by "affective dissonance" (DeVos 1984).

Factors affecting minority children's acquisition of literacy and numeracy came from "the system" and from "the minority community." In American folk terminology, "the system" is made up of the public schools, of the powers-that-be in the wider society. Before 1960, the United States, like other urban industrial societies, did not provide equal educational opportunity for minorities (Ogbu 1978). Even today, minorities do not enjoy equal educational opportunity, partly because vestiges of past discriminatory educational policies and practices survive. However, in some instances, significant improvements have been made to equalize the education provided minorities with that of the dominant group.

Denial of equal educational opportunity shows up in the denial of equal access to desirable jobs, to positions in adult life that require good education, where education clearly pays off. Generations of black Americans were regularly denied equal employment opportunity through a job ceiling (Ogbu 1978). Blacks with school credentials comparable to those of their white peers were not hired for similar jobs, were not paid equal wages, were not permitted to advance on the basis of education and ability. By denying minorities the opportunity to enter the labor force, by denying them equal rewards,

American society discouraged whole generations, especially involuntary minorities (blacks and Indians, for example), from investing time and effort in education to maximize their educational accomplishments. The experience may have discouraged such minorities from developing a strong tradition of striving for academic achievement.

Minorities were also denied equal access to good education. Before 1960, blacks were channeled into inferior schools by formal statutes in the South, and by informal practices in the North. Such schools, characterized by inadequately trained and overworked teachers, a different and inferior curriculum, inadequate funding, insufficient facilities and services, were conspicuous in the South, where black school terms were shorter than those of white schools. Although formal aspects of unequal educational opportunity have been abolished by law, recent desegregation cases continue to reveal that minority and majority education in the United States remain unequal. Inferior education guarantees that blacks and other minorities will not qualify as whites do for desirable jobs and other positions in adult life that require good education. More importantly, minority children receiving inferior education cannot learn as much or test as well as white children do who have access to better education.

Minority children receive inferior education also through what occurs inside the schools, inside individual classrooms. Among the mechanisms discovered to affect minority education adversely, none is more important than teachers' low expectations. So, also, too many minority children are treated as having educational "handicaps." A disproportionate number are channeled into "special education," a pseudonym for inferior education. Problems that arise from cultural and language differences are inadequately attended to. The failure of school personnel to understand the cultural behaviors of minority children often results in conflicts that affect the children's capacity to adjust and learn. While minority children have an obligation to understand and relate to the culture and language of the schools, this is a two-way thoroughfare.

As is obvious from what has already been said, complex and interlocking forces affect the social adjustment and academic performance of minority children. These forces are not limited to those of the wider society, of the schools and class-

rooms already described. They also derive from minority communities themselves. These, again, are different for voluntary and involuntary minorities. Among voluntary minorities, the interaction of community forces with societal and school factors does not necessarily discourage the striving for academic success. Among involuntary minorities, this interaction appears to discourage such striving.

Immigrant parents tend to stress education for their children and generally take steps to ensure that their children behave in a manner conducive to school success. For their part, the children, whether they are Chinese, Central or South American Latinos, Cubans, Koreans, Punjabi Indians, or West Indians, appear to share their parents' attitudes toward American education. They take their schoolwork seriously, and persevere. Immigrant minority parents do not care to have their children look upon them as role models; they expect their children to be different, to succeed according to the American mainstream system of status mobility. Nor do the children care to resemble their parents, who are often doing menial work (Gibson 1987, 1988; Suarez-Orozco 1989).

Symbolic responses work also to promote a striving for school success among voluntary minorities. Their nonoppositional group identity and their nonoppositional cultural frames of reference facilitate their children's ability to cross cultural and language boundaries in school. Such immigrants learn to distinguish what they need to know in order to achieve their goals for immigration—including learning the English language and adjusting to the standard practices of school and workplace—from other aspects of mainstream American culture which might threaten their minority language, culture, or identity. These children do not go to school to be taught their native languages or cultures. Rather, they expect to learn the English language, are anxious to do so, along with the standard practices of the school. This does not imply that certain of these children do not experience language and cultural difficulties; it is simply that they and their parents, together with their communities, perceive the language and cultural conflicts to be problems that have to be overcome, with appropriate help from the schools.

The *relational responses* of the immigrants serve also to enhance their school success. The immigrants' acquiescing and trusting relationship with teachers and other school personnel promotes such success. These immigrants consider schools in the United States to be better than those of their homelands; they think of the schools they left behind, not of the schools as they exist in the white suburbs of North America. The immigrants see themselves as being better treated by the public school personnel in their new homes than in their original homelands (Suarez-Orozco 1989). Even where they experience prejudice and discrimination, which they resent, they rationalize such treatment so as not to be discouraged from striving for school success (Gibson 1988). Ethnographic studies suggest that immigrant minority parents teach their children to trust school officials and to accept, internalize, and follow school rules and standard practices for academic success, and that the children more or less do follow these instructions.

The instrumental responses of involuntary minorities are not equally encouraging for school success. Comparing themselves unfavorably with white Americans, these minorities tend to conclude that they are worse off, whatever their education or ability. The role of education, the worth of a school credential is uncertain.

While the folk theory of involuntary minorities emphasizes the importance of education in getting ahead, such verbal endorsement is not generally accompanied by the appropriate and necessary effort partly because historically involuntary minorities have never been given the chance to get the sorts of jobs and wages available to whites of comparable education. These minorities have never had a "back home" situation with which to compare their new situation. Inevitably, they come to see their treatment as part of institutionalized discrimination, never entirely eliminated by securing an education (Ogbu 1982). Such minorities, never developing "effort optimism" toward academic work (Shack 1970–1971), have had no incentive to fashion a strong tradition of cultural know-how, emphasizing hard work and perseverance in academic tasks.

Given this circumstance, such minority parents have tended to teach their children contradictory things about getting ahead through schooling. In my own ethnographic research among blacks and Mexican Americans in Stockton, California, I have observed parents telling their children to get a good education, encouraging them verbally to do

well in school, while the actual texture of their own lives, with their low-level jobs, underemployment, and unemployment have provided a different kind of message, contradicting all their verbal exhortations. Unavoidably, such minority parents discuss their problems with "the system," with their relatives, friends, and neighbors in the presence of their children. The result, inevitably, is that such children become increasingly disillusioned about their ability to succeed in adult life through the mainstream strategy of schooling.

The folk theory of involuntary minorities stresses other means of getting ahead, survival strategies both within and beyond the mainstream. Such strategies tend to generate attitudes and behaviors in students that are not conducive to good classroom teaching or learning. Sometimes they convey contradictory messages about schooling itself. For example, when survival strategies are used, such as the collective struggle among black Americans to succeed in increasing the pool of jobs and other resources, they may indeed encourage certain minority youths to work hard in school. They may also lead such youths to blame "the system," even to rationalize their lack of serious school effort.

Clientship, or Uncle Tomming (Tio Tacoing), does not create role models for school success through good study habits and hard work. Instead, clientship teaches minority children manipulative attitudes and trains them in the knowledge and skills used by their parents to deal with white people and white institutions. As the children become familiar with other survival strategies, including hustling and pimping as well as drug dealing, their attitudes toward schooling are adversely affected. For example, in the norms that support such survival strategies, like hustling, the work ethic is reversed by the insistence that one ought to be able to make it without working, especially without "doing the white man's thing," which includes doing schoolwork. Furthermore, for students who are engaged in hustling, social interactions in the classroom are seen as opportunities to exploit, opportunities to gain prestige by putting others down.

Because survival strategies can become serious competitors with schooling as ways of getting ahead, leading young people to channel their time and efforts into nonacademic activities, particularly as minority children become older, more aware of how certain adults in their communities "make it" without mainstream school credentials and employment, this shift is dangerous (Bouie 1981; Ogbu 1974). There is evidence, for example, that among young black Americans, many see sports and entertainment, rather than education, as the way to get ahead. Their perceptions are reinforced by the realities they observe in the community, in society at large, as represented by the media. Blacks, for example, are overrepresented in such lucrative sports as baseball, basketball, and football. The average annual salary in the National Basketball Association is over $300,000; in the National Football League, it is over $90,000. Many of the superstars who earn between $1 million and $2 million a year are black; many have had little education. While the number of such highly paid athletes is low, the media make them, together with black entertainers, more visible than black lawyers, doctors, engineers, or scientists. There is preliminary evidence to suggest that black parents, imagining that such activities will lead to careers in professional sports, encourage their children's athletic activities (Wong 1987).

To summarize, while such children, like their parents, may verbally express interest in doing well in school, in obtaining school credentials for future employment in the mainstream economy, they do not necessarily match their wishes and aspirations with effort. Black and Mexican-American students in Stockton, California, for example, correctly explained that Chinese, Japanese, and white students are more academically successful because they expend more time and effort in their schoolwork, both at school and at home. The lack of serious academic attitudes, of substantial effort, appears to increase as these students grow older, become more aware of their own social reality, and accept the prevailing beliefs that as members of disparaged minority groups they have limited opportunities to get good jobs, even with a superior education. They increasingly divert their time and effort from schoolwork into nonacademic activities.

The symbolic or expressive responses of involuntary minorities contribute greatly to their school-adjustment and performance problems. Because they appear to interpret cultural and language differences as markers or symbols of group identity to be maintained, not as barriers to be overcome, they do not appear to make a clear distinction, as immigrants do, between what they

have to learn or do to enhance their school success (such as learning and using standard English and standard behavior practices) and what they must do to maintain a cultural frame of reference distinct from that of their "oppressors."

Involuntary minorities perceive or interpret learning certain aspects of white American culture, behaving according to white American cultural standards, as detrimental to their own cultures, languages, and identities. The equating of standard English and standard school practices with white American culture and white identity often results in conscious or unconscious opposition, showing itself in ambivalence toward learning. Those minority students who adopt the attitudes and behaviors conducive to school success, who use standard English and behave according to standard school practices, are accused by their peers of "acting white" or, in the case of black students, of being Uncle Toms (Petroni 1970; Fordham and Ogbu 1986). They are said to be disloyal to the cause of their groups; they risk being isolated from their peers.

Furthermore, as one authority has noted, even in the absence of peer pressures, such minority students appear to avoid adopting serious academic attitudes, persevering in their academic tasks (DeVos 1984). They have internalized their groups' interpretations of such attitudes and behaviors; also, they are uncertain, even if they succeed in learning to "act white," whether they will be accepted by whites. Minorities are afraid to lose the support of their own groups.

The dilemma of such students, is one observer has pointed out, is that they are compelled to choose between academic success and maintaining their minority identity and cultural frame of reference, a choice that does not arise for the children of immigrants (Petroni 1970). Those who wish to achieve academic success are compelled to adopt strategies that will shield them from peer criticism and ostracism.

Involuntary minorities tend to compare their schools with white schools, especially schools in the white suburbs; they usually end up with the negative judgment that they are being provided with an inferior education for which there is no justification. Since they mistrust the public schools and the whites who control them, the minorities are generally skeptical that the schools can educate their children well. This skepticism of parents, together with that of other members of the minority communities, is communicated to the children through family and community discussions, but also in public debates over minority education in general and debates on particular issues, such as school desegregation.

Another factor discouraging academic effort is that such minorities—parents as well as students—tend to question the schools' rules for behavior and their standard practices, the perception being that they represent the imposition of a white cultural frame of reference which does not necessarily meet their real educational needs.

The problems are only exacerbated by the tendency of schools to approach the educational issues defensively. In these circumstances, parents would have great difficulty teaching their children to accept and follow standard school rules of behavior, this being, true particularly of the older ones (Ogbu 1974, 1984, 1987, 1988).

I have described what appears to be the dominant patterns of academic orientation and adaptation for two types of minorities. Within each type, obviously, there are several culturally patterned strategies that enhance school success. However, in each, the degree of support—especially peer support—for the individual utilizing certain strategies to enhance school success is markedly different. Among immigrant minority youths, the collective orientation appears to be toward making good grades; social pressures from the community, family, and peer groups support this. Individuals threatened with criticism and peer isolation are those who do not achieve academically (Yu 1987). Partly to avoid ridicule, criticism, and isolation, which may extend to their families, immigrant minority youths tend to use strategies that are commonly known in the community to enhance their chances of success in school (Ogbu 1987).

Among involuntary minorities the situation is different, as are the responses of individual youths. Here, while making good grades is given lip service, there is less community and family pressure to achieve that goal. There is, for example, no stigma that attaches to youths who do not make good grades. As for peer groups, their collective orientation is almost precisely the opposite of what it is among immigrants; the orientation of involuntary minorities militates against academic success. Peer pressures among these students discourage the use of strategies to enhance individual success in school. Those subjected to peer criticism and isolation are those perceived to be behaving as if they wished to succeed academically, and those who actually do succeed. Under these circumstances, those who want to succeed academically often consciously choose from a variety of secondary strategies to enable themselves to succeed, and shield themselves from peer pressures and other forces. These secondary strategies go beyond the conventional strategies of correct academic attitudes, hard work, perseverance. They are strategies that allow such minority youths to practice a more conventional strategy.

Employing black Americans as an example, to indicate certain of the secondary strategies used, ethnographic studies suggest that one secondary strategy that promotes school success is assimilation, the emulation of whites. Black youths who choose this strategy seek to dissociate themselves from their black peers, from black cultural identity. They appear to prefer white norms and values, clearly in conflict with those of blacks. They reason that in order to succeed they must repudiate their black peers, black identity, and black cultural frames of reference (Fordham 1988).Such minority youths are often academically successful; the price paid is peer criticism and isolation.

Camouflage is another secondary strategy used by black youths. Some consciously choose gender-appropriate specific strategies to camouflage their real academic attitudes and efforts (Fordham 1985). These students adopt camouflaging techniques to escape adverse peer influences on their schoolwork. One technique is to become heavily involved in athletic or other team-oriented activities. This appears to reassure others that they are not simply pursuing their own interests and trying to get ahead of others.

Another camouflage technique is to assume the role of comedian or jester (Ogbu 1985a, 1985b). By acting foolishly, the black youth satisfies the peer expectation that he or she is not very serious about school. The jester, however, takes schoolwork seriously when he is away from his peers and often does well in school. Jesters conceal their school achievement and never brag about their school success. Some who are good at camouflaging, and are indeed academically successful, are regarded by their peers as being "naturally smart." Academically successful black males are the ones who very often play the role of class clown.

Some black youths adopt what may be regarded as the immigrants' strategy of accommodation without assimilation (Gibson 1988). While not rejecting their minority or black identity and cultural frames of reference, they elect to play by the rules of the system. Their stance appears to be "When in Rome, do as the Romans do."

Other secondary strategies include the security of mentors, attending private schools to get away from black peers, becoming involved in church activities where there are support groups for academic striving, getting a bully to protect oneself from one's peers in exchange for helping the bully with his homework, participating in mainstreaming or intervention programs.

Some black youths obviously become more or less imprisoned in peer orientation and activity that are hostile to academic striving. These youths not only equate school learning with "acting white," but make no attempt to "act white." They refuse to learn, to conform to school rules of behavior and standard practices; these are defined as being within the white American cultural frame of reference (Fordham and Ogbu 1986; Ogbu 1989).

To promote a greater degree of school success among the less academically successful minorities, it is essential to recognize and remove certain obstacles from the larger society, but also from within the schools. The obstacles within the minority communities need also to be acknowledged, which manifest themselves in specific perceptions and strategies of schooling.

ACKNOWLEDGMENTS

The preparation of this essay was made possible by grants to Minority Education Project from the Carnegie Corporation, Exxon Educational Foundation, W. T. Grant Foundation, John D. and Catherine T. MacArthur Foundation, Rockefeller Foundation, Russell Sage Foundation, and California State Department of Education. The data presented, the statements made, and the views expressed are solely the responsibility of the author.

ENDNOTES

1. I want to emphasize the fact that this essay is about minority groups, not about lower-class minorities. The problem of lower school performance is not limited to lower-class members of minority groups. The cases described in this section should make that clear in the case of black Americans: middle-class black children perform less well than middle-class white children; and lower-class black children perform less well than lower-class white children. The question is, Why do blacks as a minority group perform less well than whites and less well than some other minorities?

2. Commenting on an earlier draft of this essay, some colleagues said that it lacked "any real historical dimension." For example, in the case of black Americans the essay failed to note that after the Reconstruction in the nineteenth century, blacks in the South had achieved a higher rate of literacy than poor whites in some cities in Scotland, Italy, and elsewhere in Europe. This kind of information is interesting but not necessary for the theme of the essay.

The task of the essay is to explain differences in the school performance of different types of minorities as well as differences between the minorities and the dominant group of their society. The historical dimension relevant to this task includes the following: (a) an account of the history of the incorporation of the minority groups into their respective societies; (b) an account of how the minorities were subsequently treated by the dominant group, including their treatment in education; and (c) an account of the responses of the minorities to their treatment, including their responses in the field of education. The central point of the essay is that all these historical events impact on minorities' perceptions of and responses to schooling and should help to account for the variability in minority school performance.

3. Internal or external forces may cause a minority group to change from one type to another (see my book, *Minority Education and Caste: The American System in Cross-Cultural Perspective* [New York: Academic Press, 1978]). On the other hand, there are minorities that do not seem to change and seem to maintain the same status for centuries. These have been called "persistent peoples" or "cultural enclaves" (see G. P. Castile and G. Kushner, eds., *Persistent Peoples: Cultural Enclaves in Perspective* [Tucson: University of Arizona Press, 1981]).

4. I classify a minority group as "voluntary" if its members have chosen to come to the United States and have not been forced by the United States to become part of the country through conquest, slavery, or colonization. The fact that some immigrants were "forced" to leave their homeland by war, famine, political upheaval, and the like is not relevant to my typology. What matters is that members of the minority group do not *perceive their presence as forced on them* by white Americans.

5. There are differences among the groups included in the category of involuntary minorities, both in the way

they were incorporated and in the way they were subsequently treated by the dominant groups.

Some people will question the inclusion of Mexican Americans as well as Puerto Ricans among involuntary minorities and the exclusion of West Indians from the category. Mexican Americans are classified as an involuntary minority group because they were initially incorporated by conquest: the "Anglos" conquered and annexed the Mexican territory where the Chicanos were living in the Southwest, acts that were completed by the Treaty of Guadalupe Hildago in 1848. (See R. Acuna, *Occupied America: The Chicano's Struggle Toward Liberation* [San Francisco: Canfield Press, 1981]; C. Knowlton, "Neglected Chapters in Mexican American History," in G. Taylor, ed., *Mexican Americans Tomorrow: Educational and Economic Perspectives* [Albuquerque: New Mexico University Press, 1975]; and my article with M. E. Matute-Bianchi, "Understanding Sociocultural Factors: Knowledge, Identity, and School Adjustment," in *Beyond Language: Social and Cultural Factors in Schooling Language Minority Students* [Sacramento: Bilingual Education Office, State Department of Education, 1986].) Other Mexicans who later immigrated both legally and illegally were usually defined and treated by the Anglos in terms of the status of the conquered group. And the immigrants were often forced to live and work among members of the conquered group, with whom they developed and shared the same sense of peoplehood or group identity in the course of time. (See my book *Minority Education and Caste.*)

Puerto Ricans are classified as an involuntary minority because they are more or less "a colonized people." The United States conquered or colonized Cuba, the Philippines, and Puerto Rico in 1898. Both Cuba and the Philippines have since then achieved independence, so that

Cubans and Filipinos coming to the United States come more or less as immigrants or refugees. The status of Puerto Rico is, however, ambiguous—it is neither a state within the U.S. polity nor an independent nation in the real sense. To many Puerto Ricans, their "country" is still a U.S. colony. (See my book *Minority Education and Caste.*)

6. It seems strange to be asked, as I have been sometimes, why involuntary minorities like black Americans want to succeed like the dominant group, whites. American society qua society preaches equality and equal opportunity through education, presumably for everyone. Involuntary minorities are expected to "buy into" this ideology and mode of social mobility; they are expected to strive to succeed like whites through education. The trouble is that for generations the minorities were denied equal rewards given to whites for their educational accomplishments: equal employment opportunities, wages, advancement, and the like, commensurate with their education and ability. In this essay, it is suggested that such discriminatory treatment must have some adverse effects on the incentive motivation of the minorities to pursue education or school credentials.

7. In any given minority group there are likely to be competing "folk theories" of making it or at least some variants of the dominant theory. Thus, among black Americans some people emphasize making it through education; others emphasize making it through alternative strategies. However, even among those who emphasize using education as a way of achieving success, there is also the understanding that their minority status is a factor to be taken into account. Public statements by candidates for public office about the "traditional American way" of making it cannot be taken at face value, however.

Work

William Julius Wilson

The disappearance of work in the ghetto cannot be ignored, isolated or played down. Employment in America is up. The economy has churned out tens of millions of new jobs in the last two decades. In that same period, joblessness among inner-city blacks has reached catastrophic proportions. Yet in this Presidential election year, the disappearance of work in the ghetto is not on either the Democratic or the Republican agenda. There is harsh talk about work instead of welfare but no talk of where to find it.

The current employment woes in the inner city continue to be narrowly defined in terms of race or lack of individual initiative. It is argued that jobs are widely available, that the extent of inner-city poverty is exaggerated. Optimistic policy analysts—and many African-Americans— would prefer that more attention be devoted to the successes and struggles of the black working class and the expanding black middle class. This is understandable. These two groups, many of whom have recently escaped from the ghetto, represent a majority of the African-American population. But ghetto joblessness still afflicts a substantial—and increasing—minority: it's a problem that won't go away on its own. If it is not addressed, it will have lasting and harmful consequences for the quality of life in the cities and, eventually, for the lives of all Americans. Solutions will have to be found— and those solutions are at hand.

For the first time in the 20th century, a significant majority of adults in many inner-city neighborhoods are not working in a typical week. Inner cities have always featured high levels of poverty, but the current levels of joblessness in some neighborhoods are unprecedented. For example, in the famous black-belt neighborhood of Wash-

ington Park on Chicago's South Side, a majority of adults had jobs in 1950; by 1990, only 1 in 3 worked in a typical week. High neighborhood joblessness has a far more devastating effect than high neighborhood poverty. A neighborhood in which people are poor but employed is different from a neighborhood in which people are poor and jobless. Many of today's problems in the inner-city neighborhoods—crime, family dissolution, welfare—are fundamentally a consequence of the disappearance of work.

What causes the disappearance of work? There are several factors, including changes in the distribution and location of jobs, and in the level of training and education required to obtain employment. Nor should we overlook the legacy of historic racial segregation. However, the public debate around this question is not productive because it seeks to assign blame rather than recognizing and dealing with the complex realities that have led to economic distress for many Americans. Explanations and proposed solutions to the problem are often ideologically driven.

Conservatives tend to stress the importance of values, attitudes, habits and styles. In this view, group differences are reflected in the culture. The truth is, cultural factors do play a role; but other, more important variables also have to be taken into account. Although race is clearly a significant variable in the social outcomes of inner-city blacks, it's not the *only* factor. The emphasis on racial differences has obscured the fact that African-Americans, whites and other ethnic groups have many common values, aspirations and hopes.

An elderly woman who has lived in one inner-city neighborhood on the South Side of Chicago for more than 40 years reflects:

I've been here since March 11, 1953. When I moved in, the neighborhood was intact. It was intact with homes, beautiful homes, mini-mansions, with stores, Laundromats, with Chinese cleaners. We had drugstores. We had hotels. We had doctors over on 39th Street. We had doctors' offices in the neighborhood. We had the middle class and upper middle class. It has gone from affluent to where it is today. And I would like to see it come back, that we can have some of the things we had. Since I came in young, and I'm a senior citizen now, I would like to see some of the things come back so I can enjoy them like we did when we first came in.

In the neighborhood of Woodlawn, on the South Side of Chicago, there were more than 800 commercial and industrial establishments in 1950. Today, it is estimated that only about 100 are left. In the words of Loïc Wacquant, a member of one of the research teams that worked with me over the last eight years:

The once-lively streets—residents remember a time, not so long ago, when crowds were so dense at rush hour that one had to elbow one's way to the train station—now have the appearance of an empty, bombed-out war zone. The commercial strip has been reduced to a long tunnel of charred stores, vacant lots littered with broken glass and garbage, and dilapidated buildings left to rot in the shadow of the elevated train line. At the corner of 63d Street and Cottage Grove Avenue, the handful of remaining establishments that struggle to survive are huddled behind wrought-iron bars. . . . The only enterprises that seem to be thriving are liquor stores and currency exchanges, those 'banks of the poor' where one can cash checks, pay bills and buy money orders for a fee.

The state of the inner-city public schools was another major concern expressed by our urban-poverty study respondents. The complaints ranged from overcrowded conditions to unqualified and uncaring teachers. Sharply voicing her views on these subjects, a 25-year-old married mother of two children from a South Side census tract that just recently became poor stated: "My daughter ain't going to school here. She was going to a nursery school where I paid and of course they took the time and spent it with her, because they was getting the money. But the public schools, no! They are overcrowded and the teachers don't care."

A resident of Woodlawn who had left the neighborhood as a child described how she felt upon her return about the changes that had occurred:

I was really appalled. When I walked down 63d Street when I was younger, everything you wanted was there. But now, coming back as an adult with my child, those resources are just gone, completely. . . . And housing, everybody has moved, there are vacant lots everywhere.

Neighborhoods plagued by high levels of joblessness are more likely to experience low levels of social organization: the two go hand in hand. High rates of joblessness trigger other neighborhood problems that undermine social organization, ranging from crime, gang violence and drug trafficking to family breakups. And as these controls weaken, the social processes that regulate behavior change.

Industrial restructuring has further accelerated the deterioration of many inner-city neighborhoods. Consider the fate of the West Side black community of North Lawndale in Chicago: since 1960, nearly half of its housing stock has disappeared; the remaining units are mostly run-down or dilapidated. Two large factories anchored the economy of this neighborhood in its good days—the Hawthorne plant of Western Electric, which employed more than 43,000 workers, and an International Harvester plant with 14,000 workers. But conditions rapidly changed. Harvester closed its doors in the late 1960's. Sears moved most of its offices to the Loop in downtown Chicago in 1973. The Hawthorne plant gradually phased out its operations and finally shut down in 1984.

"Jobs were plentiful in the past," attested a 29-year-old unemployed black man who lives in one of the poorest neighborhoods on the South Side. "You could walk out of the house and get a job. Maybe not what you want, but you could get a job. Now, you can't find anything. A lot of people in this neighborhood, they want to work but they can't get work. A few, but a very few, they just don't want to work."

The more rapid the neighborhood deterioration, the greater the institutional disinvestment. In the 1960's and 1970's, neighborhoods plagued by heavy abandonment were frequently redlined (identified as areas that should not receive or be recommended for mortgage loans or insurance); this paralyzed the housing market, lowered property values and encouraged landlord abandonment.

As the neighborhood disintegrates, those who are able to leave depart in increasing numbers;

among these are many working- and middle-class families. The lower population density in turn creates additional problems. Abandoned buildings increase and often serve as havens for crack use and other illegal enterprises that give criminals —mostly young blacks who are unemployed— footholds in the community. Precipitous declines in density also make it even more difficult to sustain or develop a sense of community. The feeling of safety in numbers is completely lacking in such neighborhoods.

Problems in the new poverty or high jobless neighborhoods have also created racial antagonism among some of the high-income groups in the city. The high joblessness in ghetto neighborhoods has sapped the vitality of local businesses and other institutions and has led to fewer and shabbier movie theaters, bowling alleys, restaurants, public parks and playgrounds and other recreational facilities. When residents of inner-city neighborhoods venture out to other areas of the city in search of entertainment, they come into brief contact with citizens of markedly different racial or class backgrounds. Sharp differences in cultural style often lead to clashes.

Some behavior on the part of residents from socially isolated ghetto neighborhoods—for instance, the tendency to enjoy a movie in a communal spirit by carrying on a running conversation with friends and relatives or reacting in an unrestrained manner to what they see on the screen—is considered offensive by other groups, particularly black and white members of the middle class. Expressions of disapproval, either overt or with subtle hostile glances, tend to trigger belligerent responses from the ghetto residents, who then purposely intensify the behavior that is the source of irritation. The white and even the black middle-class moviegoers then exercise their option and exit, expressing resentment and experiencing intensified feelings of racial or class antagonism as they depart.

The areas surrendered in such a manner become the domain of the inner-city residents. Upscale businesses are replaced by fast-food chains and other local businesses that cater to the new clientele. White and black middle-class citizens complain bitterly about how certain areas of the central city have changed—and thus become "off-limits"—following the influx of ghetto residents.

The negative consequences are clear: where jobs are scarce, many people eventually lose their feeling of connectedness to work in the formal economy; they no longer expect work to be a regular, and regulating, force in their lives. In the case of young people, they may grow up in an environment that lacks the idea of work as a central experience of adult life—they have little or no labor-force attachment. These circumstances also increase the likelihood that the residents will rely on illegitimate sources of income, thereby further weakening their attachment to the legitimate labor market.

A 25-year-old West Side father of two who works two jobs to make ends meet condemned the attitude toward work of some inner-city black males:

> They try to find easier routes and had been conditioned over a period of time to just be lazy, so to speak. Motivation nonexistent, you know, and the society that they're affiliated with really don't advocate hard work and struggle to meet your goals such as education and stuff like that. And they see who's around them and they follow that same pattern, you know. . . . They don't see nobody getting up early in the morning, going to work or going to school all the time. The guys they be with don't do that . . . because that's the crowd that you choose—well, that's been presented to you by your neighborhood.

Work is not simply a way to make a living and support one's family. It also constitutes a framework for daily behavior because it imposes discipline. Regular employment determines where you are going to be and when you are going to be there. In the absence of regular employment, life, including family life, becomes less coherent. Persistent unemployment and irregular employment hinder rational planning in daily life, the necessary condition of adaptation to an industrial economy.

It's a myth that people who don't work don't want to work. One mother in a new poverty neighborhood on the South Side explained her decision to remain on welfare even though she would like to get a job:

> I was working and then I had two kids. And I'm struggling. I was making, like, close to $7 an hour. . . . I had to pay a baby-sitter. Then I had to deal with my kids when I got home. And I couldn't even afford medical in-

surance. . . . I was so scared, when my kids were sick or something, because I have been turned away from a hospital because I did not have a medical card. I don't like being on public aid and stuff right now. But what do I do with my kids when the kids get sick?

Working mothers with comparable incomes face, in many cases, even greater difficulty. Why? Simply because many low-wage jobs do not provide health-care benefits, and most working mothers have to pay for transportation and spend more for child care. Working mothers also have to spend more for housing because it is more difficult for them to qualify for housing subsidies. It is not surprising, therefore, that many welfare-reliant mothers choose not to enter the formal labor market. It would not be in their best economic interest to do so. Given the economic realities, it is also not surprising that many who are working in these low-wage jobs decide to rely on or return to welfare, even though it's not a desirable alternative for many of the black single mothers. As one 27-year-old welfare mother of three children from an impoverished West Side neighborhood put it: "I want to work. I do not work but I want to work. I don't want to just be on public aid."

As the disappearance of work has become a characteristic feature of the inner-city ghetto, so too has the disappearance of the traditional married-couple family. Only one-quarter of the black families whose children live with them in inner-city neighborhoods in Chicago are husband-wife families today, compared with three-quarters of the inner-city Mexican families, more than one-half of the white families and nearly one-half of the Puerto Rican families. And in census tracts with poverty rates of at least 40 percent, only 16.5 percent of the black families with children in the household are husband-wife families.

There are many factors involved in the precipitous decline in marriage rates and the sharp rise in single-parent families. The explanation most often heard in the public debate associates the increase of out-of-wedlock births and single-parent families with welfare. Indeed, it is widely assumed among the general public and reflected in the recent welfare reform that a direct connection exists between the level of welfare benefits and the likelihood that a young woman will bear a child outside marriage.

However, there is little evidence to support the claim that Aid to Families With Dependent Children plays a significant role in promoting out-of-wedlock births. Research examining the association between the generosity of welfare benefits and out-of-wedlock childbearing and teen-age pregnancy indicates that benefit levels have no significant effect on the likelihood that African-American girls and women will have children outside marriage. Likewise, welfare rates have either no significant effect or only a small effect on the odds that whites will have children outside marriage. The rate of out-of-wedlock teen-age childbearing has nearly doubled since 1975—during years when the value of A.F.D.C., food stamps and Medicaid fell, after adjusting for inflation. And the smallest increases in the number of out-of-wedlock births have not occurred in states that have had the largest declines in the inflation-adjusted value of A.F.D.C. benefits. Indeed, while the real value of cash welfare benefits has plummeted over the past 20 years, out-of-wedlock childbearing has increased, and postpartum marriages (marriages following the birth of a couple's child) have decreased as well.

It's instructive to consider the social differences between inner-city blacks and other groups, especially Mexicans. Mexicans come to the United States with a clear conception of a traditional family unit that features men as breadwinners. Although extramarital affairs by men are tolerated, unmarried pregnant women are "a source of opprobrium, anguish or great concern" as Richard P. Taub, a member of one of our research teams, put it. Pressure is applied by the kin of both parents to enter into marriage.

The family norms and behavior in inner-city black neighborhoods stand in sharp contrast. The relationships between inner-city black men and women, whether in a marital or nonmarital situation, are often fractious and antagonistic. Inner-city black women routinely say that black men are hopeless as either husbands or fathers and that more of their time is spent on the streets than at home.

The men in the inner city generally feel that it is much better for all parties to remain in a non-marital relationship until the relationship dissolves rather than to get married and then have to get a divorce. A 25-year-old unmarried West

Side resident, the father of one child expressed this view:

> Well, most black men feel now, why get married when you got six to seven women to one guy, really. You know, because there's more women out here mostly than men. Because most dudes around here are killing each other like fools over drugs or all this other stuff.

The fact that blacks reside in neighborhoods and are engaged in social networks and households that are less conducive to employment than those of other ethnic and racial groups in the inner city clearly has a negative effect on their search for work. In the eyes of employers in metropolitan Chicago, these differences render inner-city blacks less desirable as workers, and therefore many are reluctant to hire them. The white chairman of a car transport company, when asked if there were differences in the work ethic of whites, blacks and Hispanics, responded with great certainty:

> Definitely! I don't think, I know: I've seen it over a period of 30 years. Basically, the Oriental is much more aggressive and intelligent and studious than the Hispanic. The Hispanics, except Cubans of course, they have the work ethnic [sic]. The Hispanics are mañana, mañana, mañana—tomorrow, tomorrow, tomorrow." As for native-born blacks, they were deemed "the laziest of the bunch."

If some employers view the work ethic of inner-city poor blacks as problematic, many also express concerns about their honesty, cultural attitudes and dependability—traits that are frequently associated with the neighborhoods in which they live. A white suburban retail drugstore manager expressed his reluctance to hire someone from a poor inner-city neighborhood. "You'd be afraid they're going to steal from you," he stated. "They grow up that way. They grow up dishonest and I guess you'd feel like, geez, how are they going to be honest here?"

In addition to qualms about the work ethic, character, family influences, cultural predispositions and the neighborhood milieu of ghetto residents, the employers frequently mentioned concerns about applicants' language skills and educational training. They "just don't have the language skills," stated a suburban employer. The president of an inner-city advertising agency highlighted the problem of spelling:

> I needed a temporary a couple months ago, and they sent me a black man. And I dictated a letter to him. He took shorthand which was good. Something like "Dear Mr. So-and-So, I am writing to ask about how your business is doing." And then he typed the letter, and I read the letter, and it's "I am writing to ax about your business." Now you hear about them speaking a different language and all that, and they say "ax" for "ask." Well, I don't care about that, but I didn't say "ax," I said "ask."

Many inner-city residents have a strong sense of the negative attitudes that employers tend to have toward them. A 33-year-old employed janitor from a poor South Side neighborhood had this observation: "I went to a couple jobs where a couple of the receptionists told me in confidence: 'You know what they do with these applications from blacks as soon as the day is over?' They say, 'We rip them and throw them in the garbage.' " In addition to concerns about being rejected because of race, the fears that some inner-city residents have of being denied employment simply because of their inner-city address or neighborhood are not unfounded. A welfare mother who lives in a large public housing project put it this way:

> Honestly, I believe they look at the address and the— your attitudes, your address, your surround—you know, your environment has a lot to do with your employment status. The people with the best addresses have the best chances. I feel so, I feel so.

It is instructive to study the fate of the disadvantaged in Europe. There, too, poverty and joblessness are on the increase; but individual deficiencies and behavior are not put forward as the culprits. Furthermore, welfare programs that benefit wide segments of the population like child care, children's allowances (an annual benefit per child), housing subsidies, education, medical care and unemployment insurance have been firmly institutionalized in many Western European democracies. Efforts to cut back on these programs in the face of growing joblessness have met firm resistance from working- and middle-class citizens.

My own belief is that the growing assault on welfare mothers is part of a larger reaction to the mounting problems in our nation's inner cities. When many people think of welfare they think of young, unmarried black mothers having babies. This image persists even though roughly equal numbers of black and white families received A.F.D.C. in 1994, and there were also a good many Hispanics on the welfare rolls. Nevertheless, the rise of black A.F.D.C. recipients was said to be symptomatic of such larger problems as the decline in family values and the dissolution of the family. In an article published in Esquire, Pete Hamill wrote:

> The heart of the matter is the continued existence and expansion of what has come to be called the Underclass. . . . trapped in cycles of welfare dependency, drugs, alcohol, crime, illiteracy and disease, living in anarchic and murderous isolation in some of the richest cities on the earth. As a reporter, I've covered their miseries for more than a quarter of a century. . . . And in the last decade, I've watched this group of American citizens harden and condense, moving even further away from the basic requirements of a human life: work, family, safety, the law.
> One has the urge to shout, "Enough is enough!"

What can be done? I believe that steps must be taken to galvanize Americans from all walks of life who are concerned about human suffering and the public policy direction in which we are now moving. We need to generate a public-private partnership to fight social inequality. The following policy frameworks provide a basis for further discussion and debate. Given the current political climate, these proposals might be dismissed as unrealistic. Nor am I suggesting that we can or should simply import the social policies of the Japanese, the Germans or other Western Europeans. The question is how we Americans can address the problems of social inequality, including record levels of joblessness in the inner city, that threaten the very fabric of our society.

CREATE STANDARDS FOR SCHOOLS

Ray Marshall, former Secretary of Labor, points out that Japan and Germany have developed policies designed to increase the number of workers with "higher-order thinking skills." These policies require young people to meet high performance standards before they can graduate from secondary schools, and they hold each school responsible for meeting these standards.

Students who meet high standards are not only prepared for work but they are also ready for technical training and other kinds of post-secondary education. Currently, there are no mandatory academic standards for secondary schools in the United States. Accordingly, students who are not in college-preparatory courses have severely limited options with respect to pursuing work after high school. A commitment to a system of performance standards for every public school in the United States would be an important first step in addressing the huge gap in educational performance between the schools in advantaged and disadvantaged neighborhoods.

A system of at least local performance standards should include the kind of support that would enable schools in disadvantaged neighborhoods to meet the standards that are set. State governments, with Federal support, not only would have to create equity in local school financing (through loans and scholarships to attract more high-quality teachers, increased support for teacher training and reforms in teacher certification) but would also have to insure that highly qualified teachers are more equitably distributed in local school districts.

Targeting education would be part of a national effort to raise the performance standards of all public schools in the United States to a desirable level, including schools in the inner city. The support of the private sector should be enlisted in this national effort. Corporations, local businesses, civic clubs, community centers and churches should be encouraged to work with the schools to improve computer-competency training.

IMPROVE CHILD CARE

The French system of child welfare stands in sharp contrast to the American system. In France, children are supported by three interrelated government programs, as noted by Barbara R. Bergmann, a professor of economics at American University: child care, income support and medical care. The child-care program includes establishments for infant care, high-quality nursery schools (écoles maternelles) and paid leave for parents of newborns. The income-support program includes child-support enforcement (so that the absent parent continues to contribute financially to his or her child's welfare), children's allowances and welfare payments for low-income single mothers. Finally, medical care is provided through a universal system of national health care financed by social security, a preventive-care system for children and a group of public-health nurses who specialize in child welfare.

ESTABLISH CITY-SUBURBAN PARTNERSHIPS

If the other industrial democracies offer lessons for a long-term solution to the jobs problem involving relationships between employment, education and family-support systems, they also offer another lesson: the importance of city-suburban integration and cooperation. None of the other industrialized democracies have allowed their city centers to deteriorate as has the United States.

It will be difficult to address growing racial tensions in American cities unless we tackle the problems of shrinking revenue and inadequate social services and the gradual disappearance of work in certain neighborhoods. The city has become a less desirable place in which to live, and the economic and social gap between the cities and suburbs is growing. The groups left behind compete, often along racial lines, for declining resources, including the remaining decent schools, housing and neighborhoods. The rise of the new urban poverty neighborhoods has worsened these problems. Their high rates of joblessness and social disorganization have created problems that often spill over into other parts of the city. All of these factors aggravate race relations and elevate racial tensions.

Ideally, we would restore the Federal contribution to city revenues that existed in 1980 and sharply increase the employment base. Regardless of changes in Federal urban policy, however, the fiscal crisis in the cities would be significantly eased if the employment base could be substantially increased. Indeed, the social dislocations caused by the steady disappearance of work have led to a wide range of urban social problems, including racial tensions. Increased employment would help stabilize the new poverty neighborhoods, halt the precipitous decline in density and ultimately enhance the quality of race relations in urban areas.

Reforms put forward to achieve the objective of city-suburban cooperation range from proposals to create metropolitan governments to proposals for metropolitan tax-base sharing (currently in effect in Minneapolis-St. Paul), collaborative metropolitan planning and the creation of regional authorities to develop solutions to common problems if communities fail to reach agreement. Among the problems shared by many metropolises is a weak public transit system. A commitment to address this problem through a form of city-suburban collaboration would benefit residents of both the city and the suburbs.

The mismatch between residence and the location of jobs is a problem for some workers in America because, unlike the system in Europe, public transportation is weak and expensive. It's a particular problem for inner-city blacks because they have less access to private automobiles and, unlike Mexicans, do not have a network system that supports organized car pools. Accordingly, they depend heavily on public transportation and therefore have difficulty getting to the suburbs, where jobs are more plentiful. Until public transit systems are improved in metropolitan areas, the creation of privately subsidized car-pool and van-pool networks to carry inner-city residents to the areas of employment, especially suburban areas, would be a relatively inexpensive way to increase work opportunities.

The creation of for-profit information and placement centers in various parts of the inner city not only could significantly improve awareness of the availability of employment in the metropolitan area but could also serve to refer workers to employers. These centers would recruit or accept inner-city workers and try to place them in jobs. One of their main purposes would be to make persons who have been persistently unemployed or out of the labor force "job ready."

REINTRODUCE THE WPA

The final proposal under consideration here was advanced by the perceptive journalist Mickey Kaus of The New Republic, who has long been concerned about the growth in the number of welfare recipients. Kaus's proposal is modeled on the Works Progress Administration (W.P.A.), the large public-works program initiated in 1935 by President Franklin D. Roosevelt. The public-works jobs that Roosevelt had in mind included highway construction, slum clearance, housing construction and rural electrification. As Kaus points out: "In its eight-year existence, according to official records, the W.P.A. built or improved 651,000 miles of roads, 953 airports, 124,000 bridges and viaducts, 1,178,000 culverts, 8,000 parks, 18,000 playgrounds and athletic fields and 2,000 swimming pools. It constructed 40,000 buildings (including 8,000 schools) and repaired 85,000 more. Much of New York City—including La Guardia Airport, F.D.R. Drive, plus hundreds of parks and libraries —was built by the W.P.A."

A neo-W.P.A. program of employment, for every American citizen over 18 who wants it, would provide useful public jobs at wages slightly below the minimum wage. Like the work relief under Roosevelt's W.P.A., it would not carry the stigma of a cash dole. People would be earning their money. Although some workers in the W.P.A.-style jobs "could be promoted to higher-paying public service positions," says Kaus, most of them would advance occupationally by moving to the private sector. "If you have to work anyway," he says, "why do it for $4 an hour?"

Under Kaus's proposal, after a certain date, able-bodied recipients on welfare would no longer receive cash payments. However, unlike the welfare-reform bill that Clinton has agreed to sign, Kaus's plan would make public jobs available to those who move off welfare. Also, Kaus argues that to allow poor mothers to work, government-financed day care must be provided for their children if needed. But this service has to be integrated into the larger system of child care for other families in the United States to avoid creating a "day-care ghetto" for low-income children.

A W.P.A.-style jobs program will not be cheap. In the short run, it is considerably cheaper to give people cash welfare than it is to create public jobs. Including the costs of supervisors and materials, each subminimum-wage W.P.A.-style job would cost an estimated $12,000, more than the public cost of staying on welfare. That would represent $12 billion for every 1 million jobs created.

The solutions I have outlined were developed with the idea of providing a policy framework that could be easily adopted by a reform coalition. A broad range of groups would support the long-term solutions—the development of a system of national performance standards in public schools, family policies to reinforce the learning system in the schools, a national system of school-to-work transition and the promotion of city-suburban integration and cooperation. The short-term solutions, which range from job information and

placement centers to the creation of W.P.A.-style jobs, are more relevant to low-income people, but they are the kinds of opportunity-enhancing programs that Americans of all racial and class backgrounds tend to support.

Although my policy framework is designed to appeal to broad segments of the population, I firmly believe that if adopted, it would alleviate a good deal of the economic and social distress currently plaguing the inner cities. The immediate problem of the disappearance of work in many inner-city neighborhoods would be confronted. The employment base in these neighborhoods would be increased immediately by the newly created jobs, and income levels would rise because of the expansion of the earned-income tax credit. Programs like universal health care and day care would increase the attractiveness of low-wage jobs and "make work pay."

Increasing the employment base would have an enormous positive impact on the social organization of ghetto neighborhoods. As more people became employed, crime and drug use would subside; families would be strengthened and welfare receipt would decline significantly; ghetto-related culture and behavior, no longer sustained and nourished by persistent joblessness, would gradually fade. As more people became employed and gained work experience, they would have a better chance of finding jobs in the private sector when they became available. The attitudes of employers toward inner-city workers would change, partly because the employers would be dealing with job applicants who had steady work experience and would furnish references from their previous supervisors.

This is not to suggest that all the jobless individuals from the inner-city ghetto would take advantage of these employment opportunities. Some have responded to persistent joblessness by abusing alcohol and drugs, and these handicaps will affect their overall job performance, including showing up for work on time or on a consistent basis. But such people represent only a small proportion of inner-city workers. Most of them are ready, willing, able and anxious to hold a steady job.

The long-term solutions that I have advanced would reduce the likelihood that a new generation of jobless workers will be produced from the youngsters now in school and preschool. We must break the cycle of joblessness and improve the youngsters' preparation for the new labor market in the global economy.

My framework for long-term and immediate solutions is based on the notion that the problems of jobless ghettos cannot be separated from those of the rest of the nation. Although these solutions have wide-ranging application and would alleviate the economic distress of many Americans, their impact on jobless ghettos would be profound. Their most important contribution would be their effect on the children of the ghetto, who would be able to anticipate a future of economic mobility and harbor the hopes and aspirations that for so many of their fellow citizens help define the American way of life.

T W E N T Y

The Continuing Significance of Race
Antiblack Discrimination in Public Places

Joe R. Feagin

Title II of the 1964 Civil Rights Act stipulates that "all persons shall be entitled to the full and equal enjoyment of the goods, services, facilities, privileges, advantages, and accommodations of any place of public accommodation . . . without discrimination or segregation on the ground of race, color, religion, or national origin." The public places emphasized in the act are restaurants, hotels, and motels, although racial discrimination occurs in many other public places. Those black Americans who would make the greatest use of these public accommodations and certain other public places would be middle-class, i.e., those with the requisite resources.

White public opinion and many scholars have accented the great progress against traditional discrimination recently made by the black middle class. A National Research Council report on black Americans noted that by the mid-1970s many Americans "believed that . . . the Civil Rights Act of 1964 had led to broad-scale elimi-

nation of discrimination against blacks in public accommodations" (Jaynes and Williams 1989, p. 84). In interviews with whites in the late 1970s and early 1980s, Blauner (1989, p. 197) found that all but one viewed the 1970s as an era of great racial progress for American race relations. With some exceptions (see Willie 1983; Collins 1983; Landry 1987), much recent analysis of middle-class blacks by social scientists has emphasized the massive progress made since 1964 in areas where there had been substantial barriers, including public accommodations. Racial discrimination as a continuing and major problem for middle-class blacks has been downplayed as analysts have turned to the various problems of the "underclass." For example, Wilson (1978, pp. 110–1) has argued that the growth of the black middle class since the 1960s is the result of improving economic conditions and of government civil rights laws, which virtually eliminated overt discrimination in the workplace and public accom-

Reprinted from *American Sociological Review,* 56:101–116 (February 1991), by permission of the American Sociological Association.

modations. According to Wilson, the major problem of the 1964 Civil Rights Act is its failure to meet the problems of the black underclass (Wilson 1987, pp. 146–7).

Here I treat these assertions as problematic. Do middle-class black Americans still face hostile treatment in public accommodations and other public places? If so, what form does this discrimination take? Who are the perpetrators of this discrimination? What is the impact of the discrimination on its middle-class vice? How do middle-class blacks cope with such discrimination?

ASPECTS OF DISCRIMINATION

Discrimination can be defined in social-contextual terms as "actions or practices carried out by members of dominant racial or ethnic groups that have a differential and negative impact on members of subordinate racial and ethnic groups" (Feagin and Eckberg 1980. pp. 1–2). This differential treatment ranges from the blatant to the subtle (Feagin and Feagin 1986). Here I focus primarily on blatant discrimination by white Americans targeting middle-class blacks. Historically, discrimination against blacks has been one of the most serious forms of racial/ethnic discrimination in the United States and one of the most difficult to overcome, in part because of the institutionalized character of color coding. I focus on three important aspects of discrimination: (1) the variation in sites of discrimination; (2) the range of discriminatory actions; and (3) the range of responses by blacks to discrimination.

Sites of Discrimination

There is a spatial dimension to discrimination. The probability of experiencing racial hostility varies from the most private to the most public sites. If a black person is in a relatively protected site, such as with friends at home, the probability of experiencing hostility and discrimination is low. The probability increases as one moves from friendship settings to such outside sites as the workplace, where a black person typically has contacts with both acquaintances and strangers, providing an interactive context with greater potential for discrimination.

In most workplaces, middle-class status and its organizational resources provide some protection against certain categories of discrimination. This protection probably weakens as a black person moves from those work and school settings where he or she is well-known into public accommodations such as large stores and city restaurants where contacts are mainly with white strangers. On public streets blacks have the greatest public exposure to strangers and the least protection against overt discriminatory behavior, including violence. A key feature of these more public settings is that they often involve contacts with white strangers who react primarily on the basis of one ascribed characteristic. The study of the micro-life of interaction between strangers in public was pioneered by Goffman (1963; 1971) and his students, but few of their analyses have treated hostile discriminatory interaction in public places. A rare exception is the research by Gardner (1980; see also Gardner 1988), who documented the character and danger of passing remarks by men directed against women in unprotected public places. Gardner writes of women (and blacks) as "open persons," i.e, particularly vulnerable targets for harassment that violates the rules of public courtesy.

The Range of Discriminatory Actions

In his classic study, *The Nature of Prejudice,* Allport (1958, pp. 14–5) noted that prejudice can be expressed in a series of progressively more serious actions, ranging from antilocution to avoidance, exclusion, physical attack, and extermination. Allport's work suggests a continuum of actions from avoidance, to exclusion or rejection, to attack. In his travels in the South in the 1950s a white journalist who changed his skin color to black encountered discrimination in each of these categories (Griffin 1961). In my data, discrimination against middle-class blacks still ranges across this continuum: (1) avoidance actions, such as a white couple crossing the street when a black male approaches; (2) rejection actions, such as poor service in public accommodations; (3) verbal attacks, such as shouting racial epithets in the street; (4) physical threats and harassment by white police officers; and (5) physical threats and attacks by other whites, such as attacks by white supremacists in the street. Changing relations between blacks and whites in recent decades have expanded the repertoire of discrimination to include more subtle forms and to encompass discrimination in arenas from which blacks were formerly excluded, such as formerly all-white public accommodations.

Black Responses to Discrimination

Prior to societal desegregation in the 1960s much traditional discrimination, especially in the South, took the form of an asymmetrical "deference ritual" in which blacks were typically expected to respond to discriminating whites with great deference. According to Goffman (1956, p. 477) a deference ritual "functions as a symbolic means by which appreciation is regularly conveyed to a recipient." Such rituals can be seen in the obsequious words and gestures—the etiquette of race relations—that many blacks, including middle-class blacks, were forced to utilize to survive the rigors of segregation (Doyle 1937). However, not all responses in this period were deferential. From the late 1800s to the 1950s, numerous lynchings and other violence targeted blacks whose behavior was defined as too aggressive (Raper 1933). Blauner's (1989) respondents reported acquaintances reacting aggressively to discrimination prior to the 1960s.

Deference rituals can still be found today between some lower-income blacks and their white employers. In her northeastern study Rollins (1985, p. 157) found black maids regularly deferring to white employers. Today, most discriminatory interaction no longer involves much asymmetrical deference, at least for middle-class blacks. Even where whites expect substantial deference, most middle-class blacks do not oblige. For middle-class blacks contemporary discrimination has evolved beyond the asymmetrical deference rituals and "No Negroes served" type of exclusion to patterns of black-contested discrimination. Discussing race and gender discrimination in Great Britain, Brittan and Maynard (1984) have suggested that today "the terms of oppression are not only dictated by history, culture, and the sexual and social division of labor. They are also profoundly shaped at the site of the oppression, and by the way in which oppressors and oppressed continuously have to renegotiate, reconstruct, and re-establish their relative positions in respect to benefits and power" (p. 7). Similarly, white mistreatment of black Americans today frequently encounters new coping strategies by blacks in the ongoing process of reconstructing patterns of racial interaction.

Middle-class strategies for coping with discrimination range from careful assessment to withdrawal, resigned acceptance, verbal confrontation, or physical confrontation. Later action might include a court suit. Assessing the situation is a first step. Some white observers have suggested that many middle-class blacks are paranoid about white discrimination and rush too quickly to charges of racism (Wieseltier 1989, June 5; for male views of female "paranoia" see Gardner 1988). But the daily reality may be just the opposite, as middle-class black Americans often evaluate a situation carefully before judging it discriminatory and taking additional action. This careful evaluation, based on past experiences (real or vicarious), not only prevents jumping to conclusions, but also reflects the hope that white behavior is not based on race, because an act not based on race is easier to endure. After evaluation one strategy is to leave the site of discrimination rather than to create a disturbance. Another is to ignore the discrimination and continue with the interaction, a "blocking" strategy similar to that Gardner (1980, p. 345) reported for women dealing with street remarks. In many situations resigned acceptance is the only realistic response. More confrontational responses to white actions include verbal reprimands and sarcasm, physical counterattacks, and filing lawsuits. Several strategies may be tried in any given discriminatory situation. In crafting these strategies middle-class blacks, in comparison with less privileged blacks, may draw on middle-class resources to fight discrimination.

THE RESEARCH STUDY

To examine discrimination, I draw primarily on 37 in-depth interviews from a larger study of 135 middle-class black Americans in Boston, Buffalo, Baltimore, Washington, D.C., Detroit, Houston, Dallas, Austin, San Antonio, Marshall, Las Vegas, and Los Angeles. The interviewing was done in 1988–1990; black interviewers were used. I began with respondents known as members of the black middle class to knowledgeable consultants in key cities. Snowball sampling from these multiple starting points was used to maximize diversity.

The questions in the research instrument were primarily designed to elicit detailed information on the general situations of the respondents and on the barriers encountered and managed in employment, education, and housing. There were no specific questions in the interview schedule on public accommodations or other public-place discrimination; the discussions of that discrimination were volunteered in answer to general questions about barriers to personal goals and coping strategies or in digressions in answers to specific questions on employment, education, and housing. These volunteered responses signal the importance of such events. While I report below mainly on the responses of the 37 respondents who detailed specific incidents of public discrimination, in interpreting the character and meaning of modern discrimination I also draw on some discussions in the larger sample of 135 interviews and in five supplementary and follow-up interviews of middle-class blacks conducted by the author and two black consultants.

"Middle class" was defined broadly as those holding a white-collar job (including those in professional, managerial, and clerical jobs), college students preparing for white-collar jobs, and owners of successful businesses. This definition is consistent with recent analyses of the black middle class (Landry 1987). The subsample of 37 middle-class blacks reporting public discrimination is fairly representative of the demographic character of the larger sample. The subsample's occupational distribution is broadly similar to the larger sample and includes nine corporate managers and executives, nine health care or other professionals, eight government officials, four college students, three journalists or broadcasters, two clerical or sales workers, one entrepreneur, and one retired person. The subsample is somewhat younger than the overall sample, with 35 percent under age 35 vs. 25 percent in the larger sample, 52 percent in the 35–50 bracket vs. 57 percent, and 11 percent over 50 years of age vs. 18 percent. The subsample is broadly comparable to the larger sample in income: 14 had incomes under $36,000, seven in the $36,000–55,000 range, and 16 in the $56,000 or more range. All respondents had at least a high school degree, and more than 90 percent had some college work. The subsample has a somewhat lower percentage of people with graduate

work: 39 percent vs. 50 percent for the larger sample. Both samples have roughly equal proportions of men and women, and more than sixty percent of both samples reported residing in cities in the South or Southwest—37 percent of the overall sample and 34 percent of the subsample resided in the North or West.

DESCRIPTIVE PATTERNS

Among the 37 people in the subsample reporting specific instances of public-place discrimination, 24 reported 25 incidents involving public accommodations discrimination, and 15 reported 27 incidents involving street discrimination. Some incidents included more than one important discriminatory action: the 52 incidents consisted of 62 distinguishable actions. The distribution of these 62 actions by broad type is shown in Table 1.

Although all types of mistreatment are reported, there is a strong relationship between type of discrimination and site, with rejection/poor-service discrimination being most common in public accommodations and verbal or physical threat discrimination by white citizens or police officers most likely in the street.

The reactions of these middle-class blacks reflect the site and type of discrimination. The important steps taken beyond careful assessments of the situation are shown in Table 2. (A dual response is recorded for one accommodations incident.)

The most common black responses to racial hostility in the street are withdrawal or a verbal reply. In many avoidance situations (e.g., a white couple crossing a street to avoid walking past a black college student) or attack situations (e.g., whites throwing beer cans from a passing car), a verbal response is difficult because of the danger or the fleeting character of the hostility. A black victim often withdraws, endures this treatment with resigned acceptance, or replies with a quick verbal retort. In the case of police harassment, the response is limited by the danger, and resigned acceptance or mild verbal protests are likely responses. Rejection (poor service) in public accommodations provides an opportunity to fight back verbally—the most common responses to public accommodations discrimination are verbal counterattacks or resigned acceptance. Some black

TABLE 1   *Percentage Distribution of Discriminatory Actions by Type and Site: Middle-Class Blacks in Selected Cities, 1988–1990*

	SITE OF DISCRIMINATORY ACTION	
Type of Discriminatory Action	Public Accommodations	Street
Avoidance	3	7
Rejection/poor service	79	4
Verbal epithets	12	25
Police threats/harassment	3	46
Other threats/harassment	3	18
Total	100	100
Number of actions	34	28

victims correct whites quietly, while others respond aggressively and lecture the assailant about the discrimination or threaten court action. A few retaliate physically. Examining materials in these 37 interviews and those in the larger sample, we will see that the depth and complexity of contemporary black middle-class responses to white discrimination accents the changing character of white-black interaction and the necessity of continual negotiation of the terms of that interaction.

RESPONSES TO DISCRIMINATION: PUBLIC ACCOMMODATIONS

Two Fundamental Strategies: Verbal Confrontation and Withdrawal

In the following account, a black news director at a major television station shows the interwoven character of discriminatory action and black response. The discrimination took the form of

poor restaurant service, and the responses included both suggested withdrawal and verbal counterattack.

He [her boyfriend] was waiting to be seated. . . . He said, "You go to the bathroom and I'll get the table. . . ." He was standing there when I came back; he continued to stand there. The restaurant was almost empty. There were waiters, waitresses, and no one seated. And when I got back to him, he was ready to leave, and said, "Let's go." I said, "What happened to our table?" He wasn't seated. So I said, "No, we're not leaving, please." And he said, "No, I'm leaving." So we went outside, and we talked about it. And what I said to him was, you have to be aware of the possibilities that this is not the first time that this has happened at this restaurant or at other restaurants, but this is the first time it has happened to a black news director here or someone who could make an issue of it, or someone who is prepared to make an issue of it.

So we went back inside after I talked him into it and, to make a long story short, I had the manager come. I made most of the people who were there [while con-

TABLE 2   *Percentage Distribution of Primary Responses to Discriminatory Incidents by Type and Site: Middle-Class Blacks in Selected Cities, 1988–1990*

	SITE OF DISCRIMINATORY ACTION	
Response to Discriminatory Incident	Public Accommodations	Street
Withdrawal/exit	4	22
Resigned acceptance	23	7
Verbal response	69	59
Physical counterattack	4	7
Response unclear	—	4
Total	100	99
Number of responses	26	27

ducting myself professionally the whole time) aware that I was incensed at being treated this way. . . . I said, "Why do you think we weren't seated?" And the manager said, "Well, I don't really know." And I said, "Guess." He said, "Well I don't know, because you're black?" I said, "Bingo. Now isn't it funny that you didn't guess that I didn't have any money (and I opened up my purse) and I said, "because I certainly have money. And isn't it odd that you didn't guess that it's because I couldn't pay for it because I've got two American Express cards and a Master Card right here. I think it's just funny that you would have assumed that it's because I'm black." . . . And then I took out my card and gave it to him and said, "If this happens again, or if I hear of this happening again, I will bring the full wrath of an entire news department down on this restaurant." And he just kind of looked at me. "Not [just] because I am personally offended. I am. But because you have no right to do what you did, and as a people we have lived a long time with having our rights abridged. . . ." There were probably three or four sets of diners in the restaurant and maybe five waiters/waitresses. They watched him standing there waiting to be seated. His reaction to it was that he wanted to leave. I understood why he would have reacted that way, because he felt that he was in no condition to be civil. He was ready to take the place apart and . . . sometimes it's appropriate to behave that way. We hadn't gone the first step before going on to the next step. He didn't feel that he could comfortably and calmly take the first step, and I did. So I just asked him to please get back in the restaurant with me, and then you don't have to say a word, and let me handle it from there. It took some convincing, but I had to appeal to his sense of, this is not just you, this is not just for you. We are finally in a position as black people where there are some of us who can genuinely get their attention. And if they don't want to do this because it's right for them to do it, then they'd better do it because they're afraid to do otherwise. If it's fear, then fine, instill the fear.

This example provides insight into the character of modern discrimination. The discrimination was not the "No Negroes" exclusion of the recent past, but rejection in the form of poor service by restaurant personnel. The black response indicates the change in black-white interaction since the 1950s and 1960s, for discrimination is handled with vigorous confrontation rather than deference. The aggressive black response and the white backtracking underscore Brittan and Maynard's (1984, p. 7) point that black-white interaction today is being renegotiated. It is possible that the white personnel defined the couple as "poor blacks" because of their jeans, although the jeans were fashionable and white patrons wear jeans. In comments not

quoted here the news director rejects such an explanation. She forcefully articulates a theory of rights—a response that signals the critical impact of civil rights laws on the thinking of middle-class blacks. The news director articulates the American dream: she has worked hard, earned the money and credit cards, developed the appropriate middle-class behavior, and thus has under the law a *right* to be served. There is defensiveness in her actions too, for she feels a need to legitimate her status by showing her purse and credit cards. One important factor that enabled her to take such assertive action was her power to bring a TV news team to the restaurant. This power marks a change from a few decades ago when very few black Americans had the social or economic resources to fight back successfully.

This example underscores the complexity of the interaction in such situations, with two levels of negotiation evident. The negotiation between the respondent and her boyfriend on withdrawal vs. confrontation highlights the process of negotiating responses to discrimination and the difficulty in crafting such responses. Not only is there a process of dickering with whites within the discriminatory scene but also a negotiation between the blacks involved.

The confrontation strategy can be taken beyond immediate verbal confrontation to a more public confrontation. The president of a financial institution in a Middle Atlantic city brought unfavorable publicity to a restaurant with a pattern of poor service to blacks:

I took the staff here to a restaurant that had recently opened in the prestigious section of the city, and we waited while other people got waited on. And decided that after about a half hour that these people don't want to wait on us. I happened to have been in the same restaurant a couple of evenings earlier, and it took them about forty-five minutes before they came to wait on me and my guest. So, on the second incident, I said, this is not an isolated incident, this is a pattern, because I had spoken with some other people who had not been warmly received in the restaurant. So, I wrote a letter to the owners. I researched and found out who the owners were, wrote a letter to the owners and sent copies to the city papers. That's my way of expressing myself, and letting the world know. You have to let people, other than you and the owner, know. You have to let others know you're expressing your dismay at the discrimination, or the barrier that's presented to you. I met with the owners. Of course, they wanted to meet with their attorneys with me, because they wanted to sue me. I told them they're welcome to do so, I don't have a thing, but fine they can do it. It just happens that I knew their white attorney. And he more or less vouched that if I had some concern that it must have been legitimate in some form. When the principals came in—one of the people who didn't wait on me was one of the owners, who happened to be waiting on everybody else—we resolved the issue by them inviting me to come again. And if I was fairly treated, or if I would come on several occasions and if I was fairly treated I would write a statement of retraction. I told them I would not write a retraction, I would write a statement with regard to how I was treated. Which I ultimately did. And I still go there today, and they speak to me, and I think the pattern is changed to a great degree.

This example also demonstrates the resources available to many middle-class black Americans. As a bank executive with connections in the white community, including the legal community, this respondent used his resources not only to bring discrimination to public attention but also to pressure a major change in behavior. He had the means to proceed beyond the local management to both the restaurant owners and the local newspapers. The detailed account provides additional insight into the black-white bargaining process. At first the white managers and owners, probably accustomed to acquiescence or withdrawal, vigorously resisted ending the blatant discrimination. But the verbal and other resources available to the respondent forced them to capitulate and participate in a negotiation process. The cost to the victor was substantial. As in the first incident, we see the time-consuming and energy-consuming nature of grappling with poor-service discrimination. Compared to whites entering the same places, black Americans face an extra burden when going into public accommodations putatively made hospitable by three decades of civil rights law protection.

The confrontation response is generally so costly in terms of time and energy that acquiescence or withdrawal are common options. An example of the exit response was provided by a utility company executive in an east coast city:

I can remember one time my husband had picked up our son . . . from camp; and he'd stopped at a little store in the neighborhood near the camp. It was hot, and he was going to buy him a snowball. And the pro-

prietor of the store—this was a very old, white neighborhood, and it was just a little sundry store. But the proprietor said he had the little window where people could come up and order things. Well, my husband and son had gone into the store. And he told them, "Well, I can't give it to you here, but if you go outside to the window, I'll give it to you." And there were other [white] people in the store who'd been served [inside]. So, they just left and didn't buy anything.

Here the act seems a throwback to the South of the 1950s, where blacks were required to use the back or side of a store. This differential treatment in an older white neighborhood is also suggestive of the territorial character of racial relations in many cities. The black response to degradation here was not to confront the white person or to acquiesce abjectly, but rather to reject the poor service and leave. Unlike the previous examples, the impact on the white proprietor was negligible because there was no forced negotiation. This site differed from the two previous examples in that the service was probably not of long-term importance to the black family passing through the area. In the previous sites the possibility of returning to the restaurants, for business or pleasure, may have contributed to the choice of a confrontational response. The importance of the service is a likely variable affecting black responses to discrimination in public accommodations.

Discrimination in public accommodations can occur in many different settings. A school board member in a northern city commented on her experiences in retail stores:

[I have faced] harassment in stores, being followed around, being questioned about what are you going to purchase here. . . . I was in an elite department store just this past Saturday and felt that I was being observed while I was window shopping. I in fact actually ended up purchasing something, but felt the entire time I was there—I was in blue jeans and sneakers, that's how I dress on a Saturday—I felt that I was being watched in the store as I was walking through the store, what business did I have there, what was I going to purchase, that kind of thing. . . . There are a few of those white people that won't put change in your hand, touch your skin—that doesn't need to go on. [Do you tell them that?] Oh, I do, I do. That is just so obvious. I usually [speak to them] if they're rude in the manner in which they deal with people. [What do they say about that?] Oh, stuff like, "Oh, excuse me." And some are really unconscious about it, say "Excuse me," and put the change

in your hand, that's happened. But I've watched other people be rude, and I've been told to mind my own business. . . . [But you still do it?] Oh, sure, because for the most part I think that people do have to learn to think for themselves, and demand respect for themselves. . . . I find my best weapon of defense is to educate them, whether it's in the store, in a line at the bank, any situation, I teach them. And you take them by surprise because you tell them and show them what they should be doing, and what they should be saying and how they should be thinking. And they look at you because they don't know how to process you. They can't process it because you've just shown them how they should be living, and the fact that they are cheating themselves, really, because the racism is from fear. The racism is from lack of education.

This excessive surveillance of blacks' shopping was reported by several respondents in our study and in recent newspaper accounts (see Jaynes and Williams 1989, p. 140). Several white stereotypes seem to underlie the rejection discrimination in this instance—blacks are seen as shoplifters, as unclean, as disreputable poor. The excessive policing of black shoppers and the discourtesy of clerks illustrate the extra burden of being black in public places. No matter how affluent and influential, a black person cannot escape the stigma of being black, even while relaxing or shopping. There is the recurring strain of having to craft strategies for a broad range of discriminatory situations. Tailoring her confrontation to fit the particular discrimination, this respondent interrupted the normal flow of the interaction to call the whites to intersubjective account and make a one-way experience into a two-way experience. Forced into new situations, offending whites frequently do not know how "to process" such an aggressive response. Again we see how middle-class blacks can force a reconstruction of traditional responses by whites to blacks. The intensity of her discussion suggests that the attempt to "educate" whites comes with a heavy personal cost, for it is stressful to "psych" oneself up for such incidents.

The problem of burdensome visibility and the inescapable racial stereotyping by whites was underscored in the reply of a physician in an east coast city to a question about whether she had encountered barriers:

Yes. All the time. I hate it when you go places and [white] people . . . think that we work in housekeeping.

Or they naturally assume that we came from a very poor background. . . . A lot of white people think that blacks are just here to serve them, and [that] we have not risen above the servant position.

Here the discriminatory treatment comes from the white traveller staying in a hotel. This incident exemplifies the omnipresence of the stigma of being black—a well-dressed physician staying in an expensive hotel cannot escape. Here and elsewhere in the interview her anger suggests a confrontational response to such situations.

Middle-class black parents often attempt to protect their children from racial hostility in public places, but they cannot always be successful. A manager at an electronics firm in the Southwest gave an account of his daughter's first encounter with a racial epithet. After describing racist graffiti on a neighborhood fence in the elite white suburb where he lives, he described an incident at a swimming pool:

I'm talking over two hundred kids in this pool: not one black. I don't think you can go anywhere in the world during the summertime and not find some black kids in the swimming pool. . . . Now what's the worst thing that can happen to a ten-year-old girl in a swimming pool with all white kids? What's the worst thing that could happen? It happened. This little white guy called her a "nigger." Then called her a "motherfucker" and told her to "get out of the god-damn pool." . . . And what initiated that, they had these little inner tubes, they had about fifteen of them, and the pool owns them. So you just use them if they are vacant. So there was a tube setting up on the bank, she got it, jumped in and started playing in it. . . . And this little white guy decided he wanted it. But, he's supposed to get it, right? And he meant to get it, and she wouldn't give it to him, so out came all these racial slurs. So my action was first with the little boy. "You know you're not supposed to do that. Apologize right now. Okay, good. Now, Mr. Lifeguard, I want him out of this pool, and you're going to have to do better. You're going to have to do better, but he has to leave out of this pool and let his parents know, okay?"

Taking his daughter back the next day, he observed from behind a fence to make certain the lifeguard protected her. For many decades black adults and children were excluded from public pools in the South and Southwest, and many pools were closed during the early desegregation period. These accommodations have special significance for middle-class black Americans, and this may be one reason the father's reaction was so decisive. Perhaps the major reason for his swift action was because this was the first time that his daughter had been the victim of racial slurs. She was the victim of cutting racist epithets that for this black father, as doubtless for most black Americans, connote segregated institutions and violence against blacks. Children also face hostility in public accommodations and may never shake this kind of experience. At a rather early point, many black parents find it necessary to teach their children how to handle discriminatory incidents.

The verbal responses of middle-class blacks to stigmatization can take more subtle forms. An 80-year-old retired schoolteacher in a southern city recounted her response to a recent experience at a drapery shop:

> The last time I had some draperies done and asked about them at the drapery shop a young man at that shop—when they called [to him], he asked, and I heard him—he said, "The job for that nigger woman." And I said to the person who was serving me, "Oh my goodness, I feel so sorry for that young man. I didn't know people were still using that sort of language and saying those sorts of things." And that's the way I deal with it. I don't know what you call that. Is that sarcasm? Sarcasm is pretty good. . . . Well I've done that several times. This being 1989 . . . I'm surprised that I find it in this day and time.

One white clerk translated the schoolteacher's color in a hostile way while the other apparently listened. Suggested here is the way many whites are content to watch overt racist behavior without intervening. The retired teacher's response contrasts with the more confrontational reactions of the previous examples, for she used what might be called "strategic indirection." With composure she directed a pointedly sarcastic remark to the clerk serving her. Mockery is a more subtle tactic blacks can use to contend with antilocution, and this tactic may be more common among older blacks. Later in her interview this angry woman characterizes such recurring racial incidents as the "little murders" that daily have made her life difficult.

Careful Situation Assessments

We have seen in the previous incidents some tendency for blacks to assess discriminatory incidents before they act. Among several respondents who discussed discrimination at retail stores, the manager of a career development organization in the Southwest indicated that a clear assessment of a situation usually precedes confrontations and is part of a repertoire of concatenated responses:

> If you're in a store—and let's say the person behind the counter is white—and you walk up to the counter, and a white person walks up to the counter, and you know you were there before the white customer, the person behind the counter knows you were there first, and it never fails, they always go, "Who's next." Ok. And what I've done, if they go ahead and serve the white person first, then I will immediately say, "Excuse me, I was here first, and we both know I was here first." . . . If they get away with it once, they're going to get away with it more than once, and then it's going to become something else. And you have to, you want to make sure that folks know that you're not being naive, that you really see through what's happening. Or if it's a job opportunity or something like that, too, [we should do the] same thing. You first try to get a clear assessment of what's really going on and sift through that information, and then . . . go from there.

The executive's coping process typically begins with a sifting of information before deciding on further action. She usually opts for immediate action so that whites face the reality of their actions in a decisive way. Like the account of the school board member who noted that whites would sometimes not put money directly in her hand, this account illustrates another aspect of discrimination in public accommodations: For many whites racial hostility is imbedded in everyday actions, and there is a deep, perhaps subconscious, recoil response to black color and persona.

The complex process of evaluation and response is described by a college dean, who commented generally on hotel and restaurant discrimination encountered as he travels across the United States:

> When you're in a restaurant and . . . you notice that blacks get seated near the kitchen. You notice that if it's a hotel, your room is near the elevator, or your room is always way down in a corner somewhere. You find that you are getting the undesirable rooms. And you come there early in the day and you don't see very many cars on the lot and they'll tell you that this is all we've got. Or you get the room that's got a bad television set. You know that you're being discriminated against. And of course you have to act accordingly. You have to tell them, "Okay, the room is fine, [but] this television set has got to go. Bring me another television set." So in my personal experience, I simply cannot sit and let them get away with it [discrimination] and not

let them know that I know that that's what they are doing. . . .

When I face discrimination, first I take a long look at myself and try to determine whether or not I am seeing what I think I'm seeing in 1989, and if it's something that I have an option [about]. In other words, if I'm at a store making a purchase, I'll simply walk away from it. If it's at a restaurant where I'm not getting good service, I first of all let the people know that I'm not getting good service, then I [may] walk away from it. But the thing that I have to do is to let people know that I know that I'm being singled out for a separate treatment. And then I might react in any number of ways—depending on where I am and how badly I want whatever it is that I'm there for.

This commentary adds another dimension to our understanding of public discrimination, its cumulative aspect. Blacks confront not just isolated incidents—such as a bad room in a luxury hotel once every few years—but a lifelong series of such incidents. Here again the omnipresence of careful assessments is underscored. The dean's interview highlights a major difficulty in being black—one must be constantly prepared to assess accurately and then decide on the appropriate response. This long-look approach may indicate that some middle-class blacks are so sensitive to white charges of hypersensitivity and paranoia that they err in the opposite direction and fail to see discrimination when it occurs. In addition, as one black graduate student at a leading white university in the Southeast put it: "I think that sometimes timely and appropriate responses to racially motivated acts and comments are lost due to the processing of the input." The "long look" can result in missed opportunities to respond to discrimination.

Using Middle-Class Resources for Protection
One advantage that middle-class blacks have over poorer blacks is the use of the resources of middle-class occupations. A professor at a major white university commented on the varying protection her middle-class status gives her at certain sites:

If I'm in those areas that are fairly protected, within gatherings of my own group, other African Americans, or if I'm in the university where my status as a professor mediates against the way I might be perceived, mediates against the hostile perception, then it's fairly comfortable. . . . When I divide my life into encounters with the outside world, and of course that's ninety percent of my life, it's fairly consistently unpleasant at those sites where there's nothing that mediates between

my race and what I have to do. For example, if I'm in a grocery store, if I'm in my car, which is a 1970 Chevrolet, a real old ugly car, all those things—being in a grocery store in casual clothes, or being in the car—sort of advertises something that doesn't have anything to do with my status as far as people I run into are concerned.

Because I'm a large black woman, and I don't wear whatever class status I have, or whatever professional status [I have] in my appearance when I'm in the grocery store, I'm part of the mass of large black women shopping. For most whites, and even for some blacks, that translates into negative status. That means that they are free to treat me the way they treat most poor black people, because they can't tell by looking at me that I differ from that.

This professor notes the variation in discrimination in the sites through which she travels, from the most private to the most public. At home with friends she faces no problems, and at the university her professorial status gives her some protection from discrimination. The increase in unpleasant encounters as she moves into public accommodations sites such as grocery stores is attributed to the absence of mediating factors such as clear symbols of middle-class status—displaying the middle-class symbols may provide some protection against discrimination in public places.

An east coast news anchorperson reported a common middle-class experience of good service from retailers over the phone:

And if I was seeking out a service, like renting a car, or buying something, I could get a wonderful, enthusiastic reaction to what I was doing. I would work that up to such a point that this person would probably shower me with roses once they got to see me. And then when I would show up, and they're surprised to see that I'm black, I sort of remind them in conversation how welcome my service was, to put the embarrassment on them, and I go through with my dealings. In fact, once my sister criticized me for putting [what] she calls my "white-on-white voice" on to get a rental car. But I needed a rental car and I knew that I could get it. I knew if I could get this guy to think that he was talking to some blonde, rather than, you know, so, but that's what he has to deal with. I don't have to deal with that, I want to get the car.

Being middle-class often means that you, as many blacks say, "sound white" over the phone. Over the phone middle-class blacks find they get fair treatment because the white person assumes the caller is white, while they receive poorer (or no) service in person. Race is the only added variable in such interpersonal contact situations. Moreover, some middle-class blacks intentionally use this phone-voice resource to secure their needs.

RESPONSES TO DISCRIMINATION: THE STREET

Reacting to White Strangers

As we move away from public accommodations settings to the usually less protected street sites, racial hostility can become more fleeting and severer, and thus black responses are often restricted. The most serious form of street discrimination is violence. Often the reasonable black response to street discrimination is withdrawal, resigned acceptance, or a quick verbal retort. The difficulty of responding to violence is seen in this report by a man working for a media surveying firm in a southern industrial city:

> I was parked in front of this guy's house. . . . This guy puts his hands on the window and says, "Get out of the car, nigger." . . . So, I got out, and I thought, "Oh, this is what's going to happen here." And I'm talking fast. And they're, "What are you doing here?" And I'm, "This is who I am. I work with these people. This is the man we want to put in the survey." And I pointed to the house. And the guy said, "Well you have an out-of-state license tag, right?" "Yea." And he said. "If something happened to you, your people at home wouldn't know for a long time, would they?" . . . I said, "Look, I deal with a company that deals with television. [If] something happens to me, it's going to be a national thing. . . . So, they grab me by the lapel of my coat, and put me in front of my car. They put the blade on my zipper. And now I'm thinking about this guy that's in the truck [behind me], because now I'm thinking that I'm going to have to run somewhere. Where am I going to run? Go to the police? [laughs] So, after a while they bash up my headlight: And I drove [away].

Stigmatized and physically attacked solely because of his color, this man faced verbal hostility and threats of death with courage. Cautiously drawing on his middle-class resources, he told the attackers his death would bring television crews to the town. This resource utilization is similar to that of the news director in the restaurant incident. Beyond this verbal threat his response had to be one of caution. For most whites threatened on the street, the police are a sought-after source of protection, but for black men this is often not the case.

At the other end of the street continuum is nonverbal harassment such as the "hate stare" that so traumatized Griffin (1961). In her research on street remarks, Gardner (1980) considered women and blacks particularly vulnerable targets for harassment. For the segregation years Henley (1978) has documented the ways in which many blacks regularly deferred to whites in public-place communications. Today obsequious deference is no longer a common response to harassment. A middle-class student with dark skin reported that on her way to university classes she had stopped at a bakery in a white residential area where very few blacks live or shop. A white couple in front of the store stared intently and hatefully at her as she crossed the sidewalk and entered and left the bakery. She reported that she had experienced this hate stare many times. The incident angered her for some days thereafter, in part because she had been unable to respond more actively to it.

In between the hate stare and violence are many other hostile actions. Most happen so fast that withdrawal, resigned acceptance, or an immediate verbal retort are the reasonable responses. The female professor quoted earlier described the fleeting character of harassment:

> I was driving. This has [happened] so many times, but one night it was especially repugnant. I think it had to, with my son being in the car. It was about 9:30 at night, and as I've said, my car is old and very ugly, and I have been told by people shouting at intersections that it's the kind of car that people think of as a low-rider car, so they associate it with Mexican Americans, especially poor Mexican Americans. Well, we were sitting at an intersection waiting to make a turn, and a group of middle-class looking white boys drives up in a nice car. And they start shouting things at us in a real fake-sounding Mexican American accent, and I realized that they thought we were Mexican Americans. And I turned to look at them, and they started making obscene gestures and laughing at the car. And then one of them realized that I was black, and said, "Oh, it's just a nigger." And [they] drove away.

This incident illustrates the seldom-noted problem of "cross discrimination"—a black person may suffer from discrimination aimed at other people of color by whites unable to distinguish. The white hostility was guided by certain signals—an old car and dark skin—of minority-group status. The nighttime setting, by assuring anonymity, facilitated the hurling of racist epithets and heightened the negative impact on this woman, who found the harassment especially dangerous and repulsive because she was with her son. She drove away without replying. Later in the interview she notes angrily that in such incidents her ascribed characteristic of "blackness" takes precedence over her achieved middle-class characteristics and that the grouped thinking of racism obscures anything about her that is individual and unique.

For young middle-class blacks street harassment can generate shock and disbelief, as in the case of this college student who recounted a street encounter near her university in the Southwest:

I don't remember in high school being called a "nigger" before, and I can remember here being called a "nigger." [When was this?] In my freshman year, at a university student parade. There was a group of us, standing there, not knowing that this was not an event that a lot of black people went to! [laughs] You know, our dorm was going, and this was something we were going to go to because we were students too! And we were standing out there and [there were] a group of white fraternity boys—I remember the southern flag—and a group of us, five or six of us, and they went past by us, before the parade had actually gotten underway. And one of them pointed and said, "Look at that bunch of niggers!" I remember thinking, "Surely he's not talking to us!" We didn't even use the word "nigger" in my house. . . . [How did you feel?] I think I wanted to cry. And my friends they were from a southwestern city—they were ready to curse them, and I was just standing there with my mouth open. I think I wanted to cry. I could not believe it, because you get here and you think you're in an educated environment and you're dealing with educated people. And all of this backward country stuff . . . you think that kind of stuff is not going on, but it is.

The respondent's first coping response was to think the assailants were not speaking to her and her friends. Again we see the tendency for middle-class blacks to assess situations carefully and to give whites the benefit of the doubt. Her subsequent response was tearful acquiescence, but her friends were ready to react in a more aggressive way. The discriminators may have moved on before a considered response was possible. This episode points up the impact of destructive racial coding on young people and hints at the difficulty black parents face in socializing children for coping with white hostility. When I discussed these street incidents involving younger blacks with two older black respondents, one a southern civil rights activist and the other an Ivy League professor, both noted the problem created for some middle-class black children by their well-intentioned parents trying to shelter them from racism.

It seems likely that for middle-class blacks the street is the site of recurring encounters with various types of white malevolence. A vivid example of the cumulative character and impact of this discrimination was given by another black student at a white university, who recounted his experiences walking home at night from a campus job to his apartment in a predominantly white residential area:

So, even if you wanted to, it's difficult just to live a life where you don't come into conflict with others. Because every day you walk the streets, it's not even like once a week, once a month. It's every day you walk the streets. Every day that you live as a black person you're reminded how you're perceived in society. You walk the streets at night; white people cross the streets. I've seen white couples and individuals dart in front of cars to not be on the same side of the street. Just the other day, I was walking down the street, and this white female with a child, I saw her pass a young white male about 20 yards ahead. When she saw me, she quickly dragged the child and herself across the busy street. What is so funny is that this area has had an unknown white rapist in the area for about four years. [When I pass] white men tighten their grip on their women. I've seen people turn around and seem like they're going to take blows from me. The police constantly make circles around me as I walk home, you know, for blocks. I'll walk, and they'll turn a block. And they'll come around me just to make sure, to find out where I'm going. So, every day you realize [you're black]. Even though you're not doing anything wrong; you're just existing. You're just a person. But you're a black person perceived in an unblack world. (This quote includes a clarification sentence from a follow-up interview.)

In a subsequent comment this respondent mentioned that he also endured white men hurling beer cans and epithets at him as he walked home. Again the cumulation of incidents is evident. Everyday street travel for young black middle-class males does not mean one isolated incident every few years.

Unable to "see" his middle-class symbols of college dress and books, white couples (as well as individuals) have crossed the street in front of cars to avoid walking near this modest-build black student, in a predominantly white neighborhood. Couples moving into defensive postures are doubtless reacting to the stigma of "black maleness." The student perceives such avoidance as racist, however, not because he is paranoid, but because he has previously encountered numerous examples of whites taking such defensive measures. Many whites view typical "street" criminals as black or minority males and probably see young black males as potentially dangerous (Graber 1980, p. 55). This would seem to be the motivation for some hostile treatment black males experience in public places. Some scholars have discussed white perceptions of black males as threatening and the justifiability of that perception (Warr forthcoming), but to my knowledge there has been no discussion in the literature of the negative impact of such perceptions on black males. This student reports that being treated as a pariah (in his words, a "criminal and a rapist") has caused him severe psychological problems. When I discussed this student's experiences with a prominent black journalist in a northeastern city, he reported that whites sometimes stop talking—and white women grab their purses—on downtown office-building elevators when he enters. These two men had somewhat different responses to such discrimination, one relatively passive and the other aggressive. In a follow-up interview the student reported that he rarely responded aggressively to the street encounters, apart from the occasional quick curse, because they happened too quickly. Echoing the black graduate student's comments about processing input and missed opportunities, he added: "I was basically analyzing and thinking too much about the incident." However, the journalist reacts more assertively: he described how he turns to whites in elevators and informs them, often with a smile, that they can continue talking or that he is not interested in their purses.

On occasion, black middle-class responses to street hostility from white strangers are even more aggressive. A woman who now runs her own successful business in a southwestern city described a car incident in front of a grocery store:

We had a new car . . . and we stopped at 7-11 [store]. We were going to go out that night, and we were taking my son to a babysitter. . . . And we pulled up, and my husband was inside at the time. And this person, this Anglo couple, drove up, and they hit our car. It was a brand new car. So my husband came out. And the first thing they told us was that we got our car on welfare. Here we are able-bodied. He was a corporate executive. I had a decent job, it was a professional job, but it wasn't paying anything. But they looked at the car we were driving, and they made the assumption that we got it from welfare. I completely snapped; I physically

abused that lady. I did. And I was trying to keep my husband from arguing with her husband until the police could come. . . . And when the police came they interrogated them; they didn't arrest us, because there was an off-duty cop who had seen the whole incident and said she provoked it.

Here we see how some whites perceive blacks, including middle-class blacks, in interracial situations. The verbal attack by the whites was laced with the stereotype about blacks as welfare chiselers. This brought forth an angry response from the black couple, which probably came as a surprise to the whites. This is another example of Brittan and Maynard's (1984, p. 7) point that discriminatory interaction is shaped today by the way in which oppressors and oppressed mediate their relative positions. Note too the role of the off-duty police officer. The respondent does not say whether the officer was white or black, but this detail suggests that certain contexts of discrimination have changed—in the past a (white) police officer would have sided with the whites. This respondent also underscores her and her husband's occupational achievements, highlighting her view that she has attained the American middle-class ideal. She is incensed that her obvious middle-class symbols did not protect her from verbal abuse.

The importance of middle-class resources in street encounters was dramatized in the comments of a parole officer in a major West Coast city. He recounted how he dealt with a racial epithet:

I've been called "nigger" before, out in the streets when I was doing my job, and the individual went to jail. . . . [Ok, if he didn't call you a "nigger," would he have still gone to jail?] Probably not. . . . [Was the person white?] Yes, he was. And he had a partner with him, and his partner didn't say anything, and his partner jaywalked with him. However, since he uttered the racial slur, I stopped him and quizzed him about the laws. And jaywalking's against the law, so he went to jail.

On occasion, middle-class blacks have the ability to respond not only aggressively but authoritatively to street discrimination. This unusual response to an epithet was possible because the black man, unknown to his assailant, had police authority. This incident also illustrates a point made in the policing literature about the street-level discretion of police officers (Perry and Sornoff 1973). Jaywalking is normally a winked-at violation, as in the case of the assailant's companion. Yet this respondent was able to exercise his discretionary authority to punish a racial epithet.

Responses to Discrimination by White Police Officers

Most middle-class blacks do not have such governmental authority as their personal protection. In fact, white police officers are a major problem. Encounters with the police can be life-threatening and thus limit the range of responses. A television commentator recounted two cases of police harassment when he was working for a survey firm in the mid-1980s. In one of the incidents, which took place in a southern metropolis, he was stopped by several white officers:

"What are you doing here?" I tell them what I'm doing here. . . . And so me spread on top of my car. [What had you done?] Because I was in the neighborhood. I left this note on these peoples' house: "Here's who I am. You weren't here, and I will come back in thirty minutes." [Why were they searching you?] They don't know. To me, they're searching, I remember at that particular moment when this all was going down, there was a lot of reports about police crime on civilians. . . . It took four cops to shake me down, two police cars, so they had me up there spread out. I had a friend of mine with me who was making the call with me, because we were going to have dinner together, and he was black, and they had me up, and they had him outside. . . . They said, "Well, let's check you out." . . . And I'm talking to myself, and I'm not thinking about being at attention, with my arms spread on my Ford [a company car], and I'm sitting there talking to myself, "Man, this is crazy, this is crazy."

[How are you feeling inside?] Scared, I mean real scared. [What did you think was going to happen to you?] I was going to go to jail. . . . Just because they picked me. Why would they stop me? It's like, if they can stop me, why wouldn't I go to jail, and I could sit in there for ten days before the judge sees me. I'm thinking all this crazy stuff. . . . Again, I'm talking to myself. And the guy takes his stick. And he doesn't whack me hard, but he does it with enough authority to let me know they mean business. "I told you stand still; now put your arms back out." And I've got this suit on, and the car's wet. And my friend's hysterical. He's outside the car. And they're checking him out. And he's like, "Man, just be cool, man." And he had tears in his eyes. And I'm like, oh, man, this is a nightmare. This is not supposed to happen to me. This is not my style! And so finally, this other cop comes up and says, "What have we got here Charlie?" "Oh, we've got a guy here. He's

running through the neighborhood, and he doesn't want to do what we tell him. We might have to run him in." [You're "running through" the neighborhood?] Yeah, exactly, in a suit in the rain?! After they got through doing their thing and harassing me, I just said, "Man this has been a hell of a week."

And I had tears in my eyes, but it wasn't tears of upset. It was tears of anger; it was tears of wanting to lash back. . . . What I thought to myself was, man, blacks have it real hard down here. I don't care if they're a broadcaster; I don't care if they're a businessman or a banker. . . . They don't have it any easier than the persons on skid row who get harassed by the police on a Friday or Saturday night.

It seems likely that most black men—including middle-class black men—see white police officers as a major source of danger and death (See *Newsweek* 1980, June 2, pp. 32–34; Louis Harris and Associates 1989; Roddy 1990, August 26). Scattered evidence suggests that by the time they are in their twenties, most black males, regardless of socioeconomic status, have been stopped by the police because "blackness" is considered a sign of possible criminality by police officers (Moss 1990; Roddy 1990, August 26). This treatment probably marks a dramatic contrast with the experiences of young white middle-class males. In the incident above the respondent and a friend experienced severe police maltreatment—detention for a lengthy period, threat of arrest, and the reality of physical violence. The coping response of the respondent was resigned acceptance somewhat similar to the deference rituals highlighted by Goffman. The middle-class suits and obvious corporate credentials (for example, survey questionnaires and company car) did not protect the two black men. The final comment suggests a disappointment that middle-class status brought no reprieve from police stigmatization and harassment.

Black women can also be the targets of police harassment. A professor at a major white university in the Southwest describes her encounters with the police:

When the cops pull me over because my car is old and ugly, they assume I've just robbed a convenience store. Or that's the excuse they give: "This car looks like a car used to rob a 7-11 [store]." And I've been pulled over six or seven times since I've been in this city—and I've been here two years now. Then I do what most black folks do. I try not to make any sudden moves so I'm not accidentally shot. Then I give them my identification. And I

show them my university I.D. so they won't think that
I'm someone that constitutes a threat, however they de-
fine it, so that I don't get arrested.

She adds:

[One problem with] being black in America is that you
have to spend so much time thinking about stuff that
most white people just don't even have to think about. I
worry when I get pulled over by a cop. I worry because
the person that I live with is a black male, and I have a
teen-aged son. I worry what some white cop is going to
think when he walks over to our car, because he's hold-
ing on to a gun. And I'm very aware of how many black
folks accidentally get shot by cops. I worry when I walk
into a store, that someone's going to think I'm in there
shoplifting. And I have to worry about that because I'm
not free to ignore it. And so, that thing that's supposed
to be guaranteed to all Americans, the freedom to just
be yourself is a fallacious idea. And I get resentful that
I have to think about things that a lot of people, even my
very close white friends whose politics are similar to
mine, simply don't have to worry about.

This commentary about a number of encounters
underscores the pyramiding character of discrimination. This prominent scholar has faced excessive surveillance by white police officers, who
presumably view blacks as likely criminals. As in
the previous example, there is great fear of white
officers, but her response is somewhat different:
She draws on her middle-class resources for protection; she cautiously interposes her middle-
class status by pulling out a university I.D. card.
In the verbal exchange her articulateness as a professor probably helps protect her. This assertive
use of middle-class credentials in dealing with
police marks a difference from the old asymmetrical deference rituals, in which highlighting
middle-class status would be considered arrogant
by white officers and increase the danger. Note,
too, the explicit theory of rights that she, like
many other middle-class blacks, holds as part of
her American dream.

CONCLUSION

I have examined the sites of discrimination, the
types of discriminatory acts, and the responses of
the victims and have found the color stigma still
to be very important in the public lives of affluent
black Americans. The sites of racial discrimination range from relatively protected home sites, to
less protected workplace and educational sites, to
the even less protected public places. The 1964
Civil Rights Act guarantees that black Americans are "entitled to the full and equal enjoyment of the goods, services, facilities, privileges,
advantages, and accommodations" in public accommodations. Yet the interviews indicate that
deprivation of full enjoyment of public facilities is
not a relic of the past; deprivation and discrimination in public accommodations persist. Middle-
class black Americans remain vulnerable targets
in public places. Prejudice-generated aggression
in public places is, of course, not limited to black
men and women—gay men and white women are
also targets of street harassment (Benokraitis and
Feagin 1986). Nonetheless, black women and
men face an unusually broad range of discrimination on the street and in public accommodations.

The interviews highlight two significant aspects of the additive discrimination faced by
black Americans in public places and elsewhere:
(1) the cumulative character of an *individual's* experiences with discrimination; and (2) the *group's*
accumulated historical experiences as perceived
by the individual. A retired psychology professor
who has worked in the Midwest and Southwest
commented on the pyramiding of incidents:

I don't think white people, generally, understand the full
meaning of racist discriminatory behaviors directed to-
ward Americans of African descent. They seem to see
each act of discrimination or any act of violence as an
"isolated" event. As a result, most white Americans can-
not understand the strong reaction manifested by blacks
when such events occur. They feel that blacks tend to
"over-react." They forget that in most cases, we live lives
of quiet desperation generated by a litany of daily large
and small events that whether or not by design, remind
us of our "place" in American society.

Particular instances of discrimination may seem
minor to outside white observers when considered in isolation. But when blatant acts of avoidance, verbal harassment, and physical attack
combine with subtle and covert slights, and these
accumulate over months, years, and lifetimes, the
impact on a black person is far more than the sum
of the individual instances.

The historical context of contemporary discrimination was described by the retired psychologist, who argued that average white Americans

. . . ignore the personal context of the stimulus. That is,
they deny the historical impact that a negative act may

have on an individual. "Nigger" to a white may simply be an epithet that should be ignored. To most blacks, the term brings into sharp and current focus all kinds of acts of racism—murder, rape, torture, denial of constitutional rights, insults, limited opportunity structure, economic problems, unequal justice under the law and a myriad of . . . other racist and discriminatory acts that occur daily in the lives of most *Americans of African descent—including professional blacks.*

Particular acts, even antilocution that might seem minor to white observers, are freighted not only with one's past experience of discrimination but also with centuries of racial discrimination directed at the entire group, vicarious oppression that still includes racially translated violence and denial of access to the American dream. Antiblack discrimination is a matter of racial-power inequality institutionalized in a variety of economic and social institutions over a long period of time. The microlevel events of public accommodations and public streets are not just rare and isolated encounters by individuals; they are recurring events reflecting an invasion of the microworld by the macroworld of historical racial subordination.

The cumulative impact of racial discrimination accounts for the special way that blacks have of looking at and evaluating interracial incidents. One respondent, a clerical employee at an adoption agency, described the "second eye" she uses:

I think that it causes you to have to look at things from two different perspectives. You have to decide whether things that are done or slights that are made are made because you are black or they are made because the person is just rude, or unconcerned and uncaring. So it's kind of a situation where you're always kind of looking to see with a second eye or a second antenna just what's going on.

The language of "second eye" suggests that blacks look at white-black interaction through a lens colored by personal and group experience with cross-institutional and cross-generational discrimination. This sensitivity is not new, but is a current adaptation transcending, yet reminiscent of, the black sensitivity to the etiquette of racial relations in the old South (Doyle 1937). What many whites see as black "paranoia" (e.g., Wieseltier

1989, June 5) is simply a realistic sensitivity to white-black interaction created and constantly reinforced by the two types of cumulative discrimination cited above.

Blacks must be constantly aware of the repertoire of possible responses to chronic and burdensome discrimination. One older respondent spoke of having to put on her "shield" just before she leaves the house each morning. When quizzed, she said that for more than six decades, as she leaves her home, she has tried to be prepared for insults and discrimination in public places, even if nothing happens that day. This extraordinary burden of discrimination, evident in most of the 135 interviews in the larger sample, was eloquently described by the female professor who resented having to worry about life-threatening incidents that her "very close white friends . . . simply don't have to worry about." Another respondent was articulate on this point:

. . . if you can think of the mind as having one hundred ergs of energy, and the average man uses fifty percent of his energy dealing with the everyday problems of the world—just general kinds of things—then he has fifty percent more to do creative kinds of things that he wants to do. Now that's a white person. Now a black person also has one hundred ergs; he uses fifty percent the same way a white man does, dealing with what the white man has [to deal with], so he has fifty percent left. But he uses twenty-five percent fighting being black, [with] all the problems being black and what it means. Which means he really only has twenty-five percent to do what the white man has fifty percent to do, and he's expected to do just as much as the white man with that twenty-five percent. . . . So, that's kind of what happens. You just don't have as much energy left to do as much as you know you really could if you were free, [if] your mind were free.

The individual cost of coping with racial discrimination is great, and, as he says, you cannot accomplish as much as you could if you retained the energy wasted on discrimination. This is perhaps the most tragic cost of persisting discrimination in the United States. In spite of decades of civil rights legislation, black Americans have yet to attain the full promise of the American dream.

The Racial Ghetto as a Race-Making Situation
The Effects of Residential Segregation on Racial Inequalities and Racial Identity

David R. James

W. E. B. Du Bois declared in 1903 that "The problem of the twentieth century is the problem of the color-line,—the relation of the darker to the lighter races of men in Asia and Africa, in America and the islands of the sea."[1] Race problems persist in the United States and in other nations around the world but usually in different forms from those that confronted Du Bois. At the beginning of this century, racial privileges and disadvantages were routinely imposed and enforced as state policy in the United States and other countries and colonial regimes. Today, state-enforced racial discrimination is almost universally condemned by nations and international organizations.[2] States seldom impose racially discriminatory policies today, but they also seldom prevent many forms of racial discrimination by other societal actors or redress injuries that result from them.

For example, direct, state-enforced residential segregation in the United States was outlawed by the Supreme Court in 1917 (as recounted by Douglas S. Massey and Nancy A. Denton 1993:41–42), and the mechanisms that create and maintain residential segregation in the United States could no longer be imposed through state policies expressly designed for that purpose. By contrast, the policy of apartheid in South Africa deliberately and relentlessly segregated neighborhoods on the basis of race. Employing a more complicated race-classification scheme than the two race categories

used in the United States, separate urban areas were assigned to whites, coloureds, and Asians, whereas native African language speaking peoples were denied citizenship and were vulnerable to deportation to distant "homelands" within the territorial boundaries of South Africa.[3] Between 1960 and 1980, the South African government forcibly relocated over 4 million nonwhites to racially segregated areas on the peripheries of major cities because they were living in areas designated for whites only.[4] As a result, large proportions of South Africa's nonwhite populations are now concentrated in squalid townships and depressed neighborhoods where poverty, illiteracy, physical violence, and crime are endemic. Although South Africa abolished the most egregious apartheid policies during the early 1990s, apartheid's legacy complicates South Africa's attempt to make a peaceful transition to democracy.

The color line in the United States is less complicated than South Africa's multiple color lines, but the spatial distribution of people by race and class in America's cities bears a striking resemblance to that of South Africa. Poor African Americans are disproportionately concentrated in high-poverty neighborhoods plagued by poor infrastructure, inferior schools, large numbers of single-parent families, and high exposures to crime and physical violence.[5] In their provocatively titled *American Apartheid: Segregation and*

David R. James, "The Racial Ghetto as a Race-Making Situation: The Effects of Residential Segregation on Racial Inequalities and Racial Identity," *Law and Social Inquiry.* Vol. 19, No. 2, Spring 1994. The University of Chicago Press. © 1994 American Bar Foundation.

the Making of the Underclass, Massey and Denton call attention to the similarity of the patterns in South Africa and the United States.[6] Because apartheid was a deliberate policy of the South African state, few Americans have difficulty understanding the immediate links between South African state policies and the terrible living conditions and diminished life chances facing nonwhites in that country. By contrast, many Americans are unaware of the past and present links between state policies and the creation and maintenance of predominantly black, high-poverty urban neighborhoods in the United States. Perhaps this ignorance stems from the fact that the policies with the largest effects on creating and maintaining ghettos were seemingly directed toward other purposes and were justified on nonracial criteria. Lacking the constitutional and political bases to implement explicit policies of racial containment, U.S. "ghetto-building" practices were the indirect or even unintended effects of other policies focused on other problems and were less effective and efficient than South African apartheid policies in enforcing segregation.[7] Furthermore, racial segregation in U.S. cities has changed little since the Civil Rights revolution of the 1960s, and the concentration of poor blacks in high-poverty neighborhoods has recently increased. Is it possible that state policies are implicated in these trends?

Massey and Denton provide extensive evidence of how U.S. federal, state, and local governmental policies contributed to residential segregation (at 17–59). White hostility and prejudice toward blacks also contributed to the process, but public policies provided the institutional context within which the actions of individuals and institutional actors such as banks and real estate agencies combined to limit the residential mobility of African Americans. Confined to the mean conditions typical of high-poverty areas, large concentrations of poor African Americans have become the most visible component of what is now called the "underclass." Massey and Denton provide the best available summary of the behavioral consequences of the links between public policies, white prejudice, and residential segregation (at 83–114, 148–85).

Massey and Denton's most valuable contribution (at 115–46),[8] however, is to provide a compelling explanation for the proximate mechanisms

that concentrate poor African Americans in high-poverty areas. The following four conditions will *produce* high concentrations of poor African Americans in high-poverty areas and *disperse* poor whites into neighborhoods where poverty is less concentrated. The four conditions are (1) a higher poverty rate for blacks than whites, (2) more whites than blacks living in the metropolitan area,[9] (3) neighborhoods segregated by class, and (4) neighborhoods segregated by race.

These four conditions are met in all major metropolitan areas in the United States. The poverty rate for blacks is usually twice as high as the white rate.[10] The African American proportion in U.S. metropolitan areas is typically less than 30% of the population.[11] Cities are segregated by class because poor people cannot afford housing in wealthy neighborhoods and wealthy people typically avoid neighborhoods where poor people are concentrated. And, of course, U.S. metropolitan areas are highly segregated by race (at 60–82).[12] That these four conditions exist in U.S. metropolitan areas has been well known for a long time. What was not appreciated by most observers (including me) is that these four conditions *combine to create* unusually high concentrations of poor African Americans in high-poverty areas inhabited almost exclusively by African Americans. Massey and Denton deduce that these four conditions create much higher poverty concentrations for poor blacks than for poor whites. Consequently, their explanation is a theorem rather than a theory. It is not a speculation about causes that must be empirically verified; it is deduced from the premises and is correct if the premises are correct. Unfortunately, many readers either misunderstand the explanation or underestimate its significance.[13] Because the explanation has important policy and theoretical implications and because the link between the four conditions and their consequences is not obvious, I will elaborate it in the next section.

Massey's and Denton's theorem does not explain why black poverty rates are higher than white rates; it accepts the higher black rates as an initial condition. Nor does the theorem explain why racial segregation levels are so high; the high levels of race and class segregation are also taken as a given. The theorem does not depend on increases in racial or class segregation to explain changes in the concentration of poor people. Race and class segregation of neighborhoods changed little over the past three decades (at 60–82). Disproportionately high concentrations of poor black people occur because race and class segregation limit the opportunities of poor blacks to live in low-poverty areas more than they limit the opportunities of poor whites. The asymmetry of segregation's effects on blacks and whites stems directly from whites' lower poverty rates and larger population sizes in metropolitan areas. Furthermore, when economic conditions deteriorate and poverty rates increase, black poverty is increasingly concentrated because the existing high levels of class and race segregation disproportionately constrain poor blacks to live in high-poverty areas.

Massey and Denton argue that racial segregation is the most important force driving the concentration of black poverty, but other studies identify other mechanisms. For example, William Julius Wilson argues that recent trends in black poverty concentrations stem from the exodus of the African American middle class from high-poverty areas.[14] Jargowsky and Bane point out that downward economic mobility during economic declines can also concentrate poverty.[15] The debate over the merits of the different explanations does not turn on whether the mechanisms identified by competing explanations actually exist. All probably operate simultaneously. From a public policy point of view, the key question is which mechanism has the strongest impact on the concentration of poor blacks in high-poverty areas. Designing public policies that can effectively dismantle the ghetto depends on answering this question. The equation that shapes Massey's and Denton's policy recommendations is simple: To dismantle the racial ghetto, one must eliminate segregated housing. Their recommendations (at 217–36) are reviewed elsewhere.[16] I will not contribute to the policy debate, but I will review some recent evidence on the relative strength of the three explanations that should inform the policy debate. The new evidence suggests that, as Massey and Denton claim, segregation is the strongest force concentrating black poverty.

What are the causes of racially segregated housing? Based on inferences from their own analyses and their reading of a large literature, Massey and Denton argue that housing segregation stems primarily from the racially motivated

actions of white people (at 148–216). White people discriminate against blacks through their control of key institutions such as financial organizations, real estate firms, insurance companies, and governmental institutions. White people avoid blacks by choosing to live in white majority neighborhoods. African Americans who move into majority-white neighborhoods often encounter hostility and harassment from white inhabitants. Of course, some of the separation between whites and blacks is due to blacks choosing to live in majority-black neighborhoods, but the choice is constrained by blacks' knowledge of the risks involved in living in white areas.

Massey and Denton treat the racial attitudes and prejudices of white people as permanent forces supporting racially segregative practices in the United States. All research projects must start somewhere. Nevertheless, treating white racial attitudes and prejudices as unidirectional causal forces paints an incomplete picture of the links between racial attitudes and racial segregation. If white prejudice and discrimination are important causes of poverty concentration among African Americans *and* concentrations of African American poverty stimulate white prejudice, then urban America has produced a modern version of what Myrdal called the "vicious circle."[17]

Massey and Denton examine the first half of the loop. Although many scholars study trends in white racial attitude and prejudices, few try to identify the social circumstances that validate and legitimate racism, which is the second part of the loop, the feedback component of Myrdal's circle of causation. Nevertheless, a small but growing body of evidence suggests that racial segregation does reinforce racial attitudes and prejudices.[18] Social situations create the circumstances, the structures of inequality, in which particular notions of race can be sustained. Widely held racial prejudices provide individuals with commonsense explanations of why everyday circumstances are as they are. Racial identities are influenced by prejudices and other racial attitudes, but neither racial prejudice nor racial identities are independent of social circumstances. Social circumstances, especially stable structures of inequality, condition and nurture racial identities and prejudices by subjecting them to daily validation.

Slave plantations shaped racial identities and attitudes before the American Civil War. Labor-intensive agricultural practices together with disfranchisement and state-enforced racial segregation shaped racial identities and attitudes in the South during the late 19th and early 20th centuries. Today, racially segregated neighborhoods are the most important social situations maintaining racial identities and racial prejudices. The concentration of poor African Americans in high-poverty neighborhoods is not only an effect of racial prejudice and discrimination. It is a powerful referent in the minds of whites that defines how blacks are different from whites. The racially motivated actions of whites condition the racial identities of blacks by confining them to racially segregated neighborhoods and blocking the assimilation strategies of those who seek social relationships with whites. Thus, the "dark ghetto" is a race-making situation.[19]

In the next section, I discuss Massey's and Denton's theorem in more detail and compare its explanatory power to that of its competitors in light of new evidence. Then, I examine the proposition that the concentration of African American poverty, together with the social dysfunctions and problems that attend such circumstances, is a significant cause of racial prejudice and racial identities in the United States. I conclude with a short summary and some speculations about the possibilities for implementing policies that can eliminate racial discrimination in housing and dismantle the racial ghettos in U.S. cities.

HOW BLACK POVERTY IS CONCENTRATED BY RACE AND CLASS SEGREGATION

Massey's and Denton's theory is a simple proposition. Given that whites have lower poverty rates and greater numbers than blacks (conditions 1 and 2 above), race and class segregation of neighborhoods will disproportionately concentrate poor blacks in high-poverty neighborhoods. Race and class segregation concentrate white poverty too, but because the white population is larger than the black population and has lower poverty rates, white poverty is less (often much less) concentrated than black poverty.

Massey and Denton's proof of the proposition consists of an illustration of how racial differences in population proportions and poverty rates logically constrain the numbers of people of each race and poverty status who can inhabit different neighborhoods under different conditions of race and class segregation. They call their illustration of the logical constraints on neighborhood compositions a "simulation" (at 118–25), which may have led some readers to think that the numerical patterns revealed in the neighborhoods of their hypothetical city could somehow be avoided in a real city. In fact, the logical constraints are equally effective in real cities as well as hypothetical ones because the constraints are analogous to "balance-sheet identities."[20]

The illustration of the logical constraints on neighborhood compositions provided in the book is an abridged version of the one presented in Massey's *American Journal of Sociology* article. Rather than reproducing Massey's calculations (which are well explained in the article, less so in the book), I will illustrate the nature of the constraints using a hypothetical city that is much simpler than the one he examines.

Consider a hypothetical city with a population of 1,000 people and a poverty rate of 10%. If the city is not segregated by class, the 100 poor people will be equally distributed across all neighborhoods of the city and poor people will live in neighborhoods that are 10% poor. Suppose, however, that the city is segregated by class so that half the population (500 people) lives in neighborhoods that poor people cannot afford. The 100 poor people will then live among the 400 remaining nonpoor people who choose to live in the poorer neighborhoods. The poverty rate in the poor neighborhoods will now be 100/500 or 20%. Hence, class segregation concentrates poor people in neighborhoods with poverty rates that are higher than the overall poverty rate for the city.

Now suppose that the city is racially integrated and contains 200 black people (20%) and 800 whites. If blacks have a poverty rate of 20% and whites have a 10% rate, there are 40 poor blacks and 80 poor whites in the city. Hence, most of the poor are white, although the black poverty rate is higher, a typical situation in most U.S. cities. The overall poverty rate in our hypothetical city is now 12% (80 + 40)/1,000.

If the city is segregated by class as before, 500 people live in nonpoor areas and 500 live in poor areas. If the city is racially integrated, half the 200 blacks and half the 800 whites live in each area; that is, 100 blacks and 400 whites live in the nonpoor section of town and the same number of each race in the poor areas. In each area, 20% of the people are black (100/500). All poor people must live on the poor side of the tracks because the poor cannot afford to live in nonpoor areas. On the poor side of town, 40 of the 100 blacks will be poor and 80 of the 400 whites will be poor because the poor cannot afford to live in nonpoor areas. The poverty rate in poor neighborhoods is now 24% (80 + 40)/500. Class segregation concentrates poverty as before, and because the city is integrated, poor whites and poor blacks live in neighborhoods with identical poverty rates.

But suppose that the city is segregated by class as before and completely segregated by race. If nonpoor blacks avoid poor blacks in the same proportions that nonpoor whites avoid poor whites, 100 nonpoor blacks would live in racially segregated, nonpoor neighborhoods. The remaining 60 nonpoor blacks would live with the 40 poor blacks, which creates a poverty rate of 40% (40/100) in that poor, black neighborhood. This all-black neighborhood with a 40% poverty rate would be classified as an underclass neighborhood by most observers. Race and class segregation produce underclass neighborhoods.

By contrast, the 80 poor white people in the city live in neighborhoods with the 320 whites who choose to live in poorer neighborhoods. Hence, poor whites live in areas that have poverty rates of 20% (80/400). Racial segregation combines with class segregation to create racially asymmetric patterns of poverty concentrations. The poverty rates in neighborhoods inhabited by poor blacks is 40%, twice as high as the rates for poor whites.

The residential patterns in my hypothetical city are much simpler than those that exist in real cities, but the logical constraints illustrated here cannot be avoided in real life. Massey's and Denton's illustration (at 118–25), which better approximates residential patterns in typical U.S. cities, produces more realistic distributions of poverty by race and class, but they are similar to the results described here. While no city has residential race and class distributions as simple as the ones constructed by me or by Massey and Denton, the same demographic accounting procedures could in principle be applied to all cities. There is no way that class and racial segregation can *not* concentrate poverty by race given the currently existing

racial differences in population sizes and poverty rates in U.S. metropolitan areas. To borrow a phrase from Thomas Schelling, who identified a number of logical constraints applicable to circumstances such as these, "The simple mathematics of ratios and mixtures tells us something about what outcomes are logically possible."[21] In this case, racial segregation combines with class segregation to create underclass neighborhoods.

Massey's and Denton's "simulation" demonstrates the imperative ecological link between residential segregation and the concentration of African American poverty, but there are competing theories to explain the same patterns. William Julius Wilson, a colleague of Massey's at the University of Chicago and one of the first to call attention to the recent increases in the numbers of poor African Americans who live in high-poverty areas, argues that increases in underclass concentrations stem from the out-migration of the black middle class from high-poverty areas[22] because racial barriers to residential mobility were largely eliminated by the 1970s. He analyzed the migration streams of poor and nonpoor blacks in eight communities in Chicago between 1970 and 1980 and concluded that "the significant increase in the poverty concentration in these overwhelmingly black communities is related to the large out-migration of nonpoor blacks."[23]

Jargowsky and Bane provide a complementary argument.[24] People who are near the poverty line could be driven into poverty if economic conditions worsen. Because the near-poor tend to live in poorer areas, downward economic mobility during economic declines would concentrate larger numbers of poor people in high-poverty areas. Jargowsky and Bane find that the concentration of poverty varied greatly from city to city, increasing in large northern cities and declining in a number of southern cities. They conclude: "In cities where ghetto poverty increased, many census tracts that were not ghettos in 1970 became ghettos by 1980. The process was driven by a combination of increases in the poverty rate and differential out-migration of the poor and nonpoor."[25] Thus, Jargowsky and Bane find partial support for Wilson's "class migration" thesis but add that downward economic mobility also concentrates poverty. They did not attempt to assess the relative strength of the two mechanisms.[26]

None of these three explanations for the concentration of poverty precludes the operation of the others, and all three processes probably operate simultaneously. Which is strongest? All the studies completed by Massey and others before the publication of *American Apartheid* relied on inference to evaluate the relative importance of competing theories because no previously available data set permitted a direct assessment of effects.[27] A recent study by Massey and Gross takes advantage of a newly available data set[28] to provide the first direct appraisal of the relative strengths of the three explanations. They calculate the probability of migration and the probability of social mobility as a function of the economic class of individuals and the economic characteristics of individuals' census tracts of residence. These direct estimates of annual geographic and social mobility transition probabilities were then applied to "typical" census tracts in a hypothetical city to assess the relative power of each mechanism. Starting with tract characteristics typical of Chicago in 1980, neighborhood populations were projected ahead for five years. When all mechanisms were operating simultaneously, the neighborhood population of a typical poor black person reached a 30.1% poverty rate in five years.

The effects of eliminating black out-migration was then assessed by setting the probability of out-migration to zero. Eliminating out-migration but allowing social downward mobility and segregation to continue produced a poverty rate of 29.2% in the neighborhood of a typical black person instead of the 30.1% when all processes were operating. Hence, the "class migration" mechanism had a small effect on the concentration of poverty. Permitting residential mobility but eliminating black downward social mobility produced a poverty rate of 29.3% in a typical poor black neighborhood. Downward social mobility had about the same effect as the out-migration of the black middle class.

On the other hand, if blacks have the same neighborhood destination probabilities as whites, which is one way to eliminate racial segregation, the poverty rate in poor black neighborhoods reaches only 21.1% after five years, about ten percentage points lower than when all three processes are operating simultaneously. Consequently, residential segregation appears to be about ten times more powerful in concentrating black poverty than either of the other two mechanisms.

This estimate may exaggerate the effect of discriminatory barriers to residential mobility because some level of segregation is undoubtedly due to the preferences of African Americans. There is little evidence to suggest, however, that voluntary segregation on the part of African Americans is the most important cause of residential segregation. Attitude surveys conducted since 1970 consistently show that African Americans prefer neighborhoods that are racially integrated with approximately equal numbers of whites and blacks whereas whites typically prefer neighborhoods that are at least 80% white (at 85–96). Massey and Denton survey a large literature that demonstrates that the discriminatory mechanisms were many. Urban renewal programs, discrimination by real estate and lending institutions, white suburbanization to avoid neighborhood integration, widespread acts of harassment and violence by the white inhabitants of neighborhoods undergoing racial transition, and federal public housing policies all had strong segregative effects.

Massey and Kanaiaupuni provide some new evidence not summarized in *American Apartheid* on just one of those factors.[29] Locating a public housing project in a 90% black Chicago tract since 1950 raised the poverty rate in 1980 to 51.3% compared to a 31.4% rate in similar tracts located 1 mile from the nearest public housing project. Placing public housing in a tract that was 90% white raised the poverty rate from 17% to 37% by 1980. Of course, public housing projects in Chicago and other cities were disproportionately located in predominately black neighborhoods.[30]

Although uncertainty remains as to why black poverty rates exceed those of whites,[31] Massey's argument explaining racial differences in the concentration of poverty still holds regardless of the forces that create racial differences in poverty rates. Jencks and Mayer provide an independent summary of the studies that examine the links between residential segregation and access to jobs.[32] Their review of the evidence suggests that nothing is known about how the demand for black workers is affected by segregation.[33] They also argue that job proximity has no effect on African American adult male unemployment but does influence black teenage unemployment rates.[34] Furthermore, central-city jobs, which are the ones available to most urban blacks, appear to produce lower returns than suburban jobs. The studies evaluated by Jencks and Mayer indicate that by 1980 blacks who were employed in the suburbs earned more than those with identical education levels who lived in central cities.[35] Hence, segregated areas appear to be economically isolated. Furthermore, audit studies continue to demonstrate that discrimination limits African American access to housing, insurance, financial loans, and jobs.[36]

Residential segregation also plays a role in creating large racial inequalities in the financial resources available to public school systems. The provision of elementary and secondary education in most metropolitan areas is fragmented into a matrix of local school districts, each with different capacities to raise funds from local sources. Thus, the political boundaries between school districts buffer wealthy suburban districts from desegregative actions that would equalize pupil assignments by race and reduce financial inequities among districts.[37] Property-rich districts routinely hire more and better teachers and provide more resources for students than are available in poor districts like those that serve the African American underclass. Hence, racial differences in education and in the inventory of employable skills, a spatial mismatch between place of residence and available jobs, as well as discriminatory barriers to the employment of African Americans all play a role in producing higher poverty rates for blacks than whites.

Massey and Denton argue that barriers to residential mobility are at the same time barriers to social and economic mobility, and I find their evaluation of the evidence on this point convincing. Racial segregation and class segregation of neighborhoods concentrate social dysfunctions and pathologies as they concentrate poverty. Violent crime, high rates of single parent families living on welfare, drug abuse, higher dropout rates from school all abound in high-poverty neighborhoods. The link between social pathology and the concentration of poverty applies to whites as well as blacks. For example, whites who live in high-poverty areas exhibit the same patterns of violent crime as do blacks and for similar reasons.[38] Because African Americans experience higher rates of poverty concentration than do whites, they also experience higher levels of the social pathologies that accompany poverty.

HOW THE RACIAL GHETTO SHAPES RACIAL IDENTITIES AND ATTITUDES

Racial attitudes and prejudices are widely held ideas of differences between groups. In order for white people to be prejudiced against blacks, whites must identify with the group that is socially designated as "white" and recognize differences between "white" and those socially designated as "black." To pick a specific example, Massey and Denton (at 95) quote a 1990 study that found that 62% of nonblack respondents thought that blacks were lazier than nonblacks, which is a negative stereotype of blacks that has a long history.[39] Antiblack stereotypes such as this one express an identification with whites and a prejudice against blacks. Hence, reinforcement of racial prejudice simultaneously reenforces racial identities among members of different racial groups.[40]

The reinforcement of racial identities solidifies the boundaries between groups and makes existing societal rules for classifying people into racial groups appear natural and immutable. The race classification rule in the United States places people in the category called "black" if they have any known African black ancestors.[41] Consequently, children of a white parent and a black parent are classified as black. This peculiar social construction of racial identities, the so-called one-drop or hypo-descent rule, is accepted by most whites and African Americans in the United States but applies nowhere else in the world. F. James Davis points out that existing (or previously existing) societies use at least seven different race classification rules to classify the children of interracial couples.[42] For example, the mixed-race group may be assigned a status that is inferior or superior to either of the parents' races depending on the society.[43] Other societies assign mixed-race people to an intermediate status. In all seven cases but one, the racially mixed group is considered to be a member of a racial group that is distinct from the race of either parent.[44] The United States is the exception. The United States is the only society that assigns the same racial status to the mixed-race group and the lower-status racial group.[45] The child of a white parent and a parent with some African ancestry (no matter how remote) is assigned the same status as the nonwhite parent. Paradoxically, this rule applies only when one parent has some African ancestry. The child of an American Indian and a black is black, but a child of an American Indian and a white is part Indian and part white.[46]

Of course, race classifications are often incorrectly assigned to individuals because the phenotypical clues that people use to classify others are imperfect guides. For example, a person with some African ancestry may appear "white" and may be treated as "white" until the person's "black" racial status is clarified. The important issue for American race relations is not whether some people are incorrectly classified; many mistakes are made. The crucial constraint on racial identities and attitudes in the United States is that no matter how people are classified, they must be either black or white. "Black" and "white" are the only race categories that are broadly accepted in this country.

The one-drop rule, which defines who is black in the United States, originated in the relationship of domination and subordination that existed on American slave plantations before the Civil War and on tenant plantations after the Civil War. Edgar Thompson called the plantation a "race-making situation" because the idea of race helped planters control the plantation labor force.[47] Race classification and the theory of white supremacy that defined the relative status of the two races explained why whites dominated blacks economically, socially, and politically.[48] The idea of race legitimated the subordination of blacks on which labor-intensive plantation agriculture depended.

But the boundaries between racial groups are not permanently fixed; they must be constantly reinforced and revalidated in peoples' everyday lives or they will change over time.[49] In most societies, subordinate racial groups resist the imposition of inferior status by dominant races.[50] Early in this century, immigrants from southern, central, and eastern Europe were considered to be members of separate races; their descendants are now classified as white.[51]

Whereas the racial and ethnic identities of the descendants of European immigrant groups have been substantially dissolved, the white/black race dichotomy persists. Yet, the system of plantation authority relations that once was closely linked to race relations and race classifications in the United States has disappeared. What are the current social circumstances that validate racial identities and racial attitudes among whites and blacks? Some recent studies suggest that racial segregation and, especially, the predominantly black underclass ghettos in the centers of large cities are the most important race-making situations.

Elijah Anderson's study of the social interactions among black and white inhabitants of two adjacent urban communities in Philadelphia provides evidence of the power of the black ghetto to shape racial identities.[52] The first community is inhabited almost exclusively by African Americans with low to extremely poor incomes, an area that would be classified as an underclass neighborhood by most current definitions. The second community is a racially mixed, middle- to upper-middle-class gentrifying neighborhood that became increasingly white between 1975 and 1989, the period of the study. Each community has a dominant culture appropriate to its economic and social circumstances.

The culture that emerged in the underclass neighborhood is adapted to the conditions that exist there: "drugs, crime, illiteracy, poverty, and a high proportion of female-headed families on welfare, as well as one of the highest infant mortality rates in the country."[53] Young black males suffer high unemployment rates; the few jobs that are available are low-paying positions in service occupations or fast-food restaurants. The paucity of employment opportunities makes the high incomes available from drug trafficking and other criminal activities appear attractive. "For many young men the drug economy is an employment agency superimposed on the existing gang network" (Anderson, *Streetwise* at 244). Most young black males are civil and law-abiding, but those who assume the aggressive, loud-talking, profane, tough, posture of the streets provide the stereotype that stigmatizes them all.[54]

Because older members of the black community cannot provide reliable employment advice and are often unemployed themselves, youths rebuke their counsel to get a good education, a good job, and support their family. Instead, young black males treat women as sex objects, engage in sex to enhance their social status among their male peers, and father babies that they don't intend to (and often cannot) financially support. Teenage black females hope to find love and marriage, but the dream typically ends once they become pregnant. With little income other than that available from welfare or drugs, young mothers often cannot (and may not know how to) provide adequate care for their children. Rather than forming stable families that nurture children, groups of young mothers form "baby clubs" to replace the absent structure of family support, and young fathers remain attached to male peer groups that denigrate women and devalue the assumption of parental responsibilities (Anderson, *Streetwise* at 123–26).

The emergent culture that Anderson describes is not just a "culture of poverty" characterized by truncated ambitions, feelings of hopelessness, an inability to defer gratification, and other values that impede economic advancement.[55] The new "street" culture is an oppositional culture that rejects the possibility of participating in the wider, predominantly white, society. A "code of the streets" has emerged that regulates interactions among young black males and demands the defense of one's self-respect and honor even if that defense requires physical violence and the risk of death (Anderson, "Code" at 81 ff.). The absence of jobs and the flight of industry from the neighborhood are attributed to white racism. The view that better skills and education would prepare them for higher-paying jobs is replaced with claims that "You have to know someone" (*id.* at 111).[56] Young black males know and often exploit the knowledge that their behavior, loud talk, loud radios blaring rap music, swaggering gait, and aggressive posture intimidate and frighten white people when they encounter them on the streets and other public places (*id.* at 206).[57] The police are seen as an occupying army rather than as allies in times of need. Police authority is interpreted as an extension of white power, even though some police officers are black. Economic differences between middle-class and underclass neighborhoods are often given racial interpretations by black inhabitants of the underclass areas. Thus, perceptions of political and economic inequalities by black inhabitants of underclass neighborhoods reinforce racial identification and provide popular explanations for why racial inequalities exist.

The culture of the middle-class community studied by Anderson is typical of many American middle-class neighborhoods. Inhabitants tend to

be liberal on social issues and have middle-class values that embody a respect for property rights, a desire for good schools, and a tolerance for those who are considered to be less fortunate (*id.* at 237). Lower-class blacks tend to label this culture "white," but it includes both blacks and whites who share middle-class values. And both white and black members of the community are deeply concerned with the problems posed by the inhabitants of the nearby, predominantly black ghetto. Avoiding the potential danger posed by young black males is the chief concern of many of both races who use public spaces. Whites, however, are less likely to be "streetwise." They have greater difficulty in assessing the danger posed by beggars, drug addicts, and anonymous black youths they encounter on the streets than do their middle-class black neighbors. Unable to decode the behaviors and appearances of harmless blacks that signify their harmlessness, whites rely on race distinctions as keys to avoid danger.

> The public awareness is color-coded: white skin denotes civility, law-abidingness, and trustworthiness, while black skin is strongly associated with poverty, crime, incivility, and distrust. Thus, an unknown black male is readily deferred to. . . . This simplistic racial interpretation of crime creates a "we/they" dichotomy between whites and blacks. (Id. at 188)

Whites blame blacks for neighborhood crimes when no evidence on the race of the criminal is available. Fear sweeps through the neighborhood, especially among whites, when violent crimes occur (*id.* at 233–34). Rumors of the dangers that threaten inhabitants in the streets and in their homes quickly spread. A violent assault, a mugging, a murder, a rape, or even racial harassment may motivate white inhabitants to abandon the neighborhood in favor of a safe, suburban residence (*id.* at 155).

Middle-class whites and blacks are wary of young black males and take action to avoid them, especially at night, but whites are less able to distinguish which blacks are dangerous.

> When [young black males from the ghetto neighborhood] walking through the [middle-class mixed-race neighborhood] intimidate residents either verbally or physically, many middle-class people—whites in particular—become afraid of black males in general. They may have second thoughts about "open" and to some degree friendly displays they may previously have made toward

blacks in public. Blacks and whites thus become increasingly estranged. In fact there is a vicious circle of suspicion and distrust between the two groups and an overwhelming tendency for public relations between them to remain superficial and guarded. (Id. at 182)

Thus, race becomes the master status that defines how blacks perceive whites and are in turn perceived by whites.

Racial segregation also affects the race identification of middle-class African Americans because middle-class status does not protect blacks from the discriminatory acts of whites. A recent study plus numerous newspaper reports demonstrate that middle-class blacks still encounter discrimination in public accommodations and in public places.[58] Verbal assaults on the streets, police harassment, poor service, or refusals of service occur with regular frequency. Virtually all middle-class blacks have experienced racial incidents that place them in opposition to whites and reinforce their identities as blacks. The cumulative effect of the personal experience of discrimination and the recollection of descriptions of similar incidents experienced by others sometimes results in exaggerated responses to incidents that many whites would consider minor.[59] Middle-class blacks who live in white neighborhoods are burdened with the necessity of preparing daily to bear insults and other discriminatory acts from whites, a burden that whites are spared during their typical everyday routines.[60]

Not surprisingly, affluent blacks who can afford to live anywhere often choose to live in black-majority neighborhoods rather than run the constant risk of racial harassment in white-majority neighborhoods. Prince George's County, Maryland, has become the largest, affluent black-majority community in the United States in part because affluent blacks choose to live there.[61] A black senior railroad contract administrator explains, "I don't want to come home and always have my guard up."[62] A black urban planner in Washington, D.C., who attended the University of Connecticut at Storrs in 1970, chose to live in Prince George's for similar reasons:

I think that integration of black folks in the 60's was one of the biggest cons in the world. I was called a nigger the first week there [at Storrs] and held by the police until this white girl told them I hadn't attacked her. You want to call me a separatist, so be it. I think of myself

as a pragmatist. Why should I beg some cracker to integrate me into his society when he doesn't want to? Why keep beating my head up against a wall, especially when I've been there.[63]

Thus, major and minor acts of discrimination serve to reinforce the racial identity of middle-class blacks and sustain the experientially based we/they racial dichotomy identified by Anderson.

Even though most whites do not live near predominantly black neighborhoods, they appear to be keenly aware of where black neighborhoods are located and take steps to avoid those areas. Massey and Denton estimated the probabilities that metropolitan neighborhoods would lose white inhabitants between 1970 and 1980 as a function of the distance from areas with significant proportions of African Americans. Metropolitan neighborhoods have a 92% chance of white population declines if they are located within 5 miles of a neighborhood that is 30 to 40% black (controlling for other factors).[64] The probability of net white out-migration drops as the distance to the nearest black neighborhood increases: .77 at 5 to 10 miles, .54 at 10 to 25 miles, and a .46 probability of white population decline if the distance to the nearest 30% to 40% black neighborhood is more than 25 miles away.[65] Neighborhoods with lower black proportions produce lower probabilities of white population decline, but the basic patterns are the same.[66] Proximity to areas of high black concentrations appears to strongly repel whites, which is consistent with the notion that they serve as a powerful referent for the racial fears of whites.

All systems of prejudice and racial attitudes are shaped by the social conditions that give them daily validity. Racial attitudes and prejudices that are poor guides to everyday behaviors tend to be modified or abandoned over time. The social interactions on southern plantations between masters and slaves, and later between white landlords and black sharecroppers and tenant farmers, provided daily validation of existing racial attitudes and prejudices.[67] Racial attitudes and racial etiquette guided the behavior of both whites and blacks. Whites personally enforced the deference of blacks, which enhanced the self-esteem of whites and, not completely incidentally, contributed to the profitability of labor-intensive plantation agriculture. Blacks acquiesced to the indignities of the prevailing racial etiquette to avoid white violence and to obtain support and resources from white employers and benefactors. Thus, the plantation was a race-making situation.

Today, the racial ghetto sustains and nourishes the racial identifications, fears, and attitudes of blacks and whites. And as was the case in the plantation South, racial identifications and attitudes, however amplified by myth and false information, provide reasonable (although imperfect) guidelines for daily action. The lives and property of affluent whites are threatened by the aggressive, predatory actions of young black males who have internalized the oppositional culture of the ghetto. Information about the dangers of the ghetto is communicated daily to the white population through the popular media. The messages have some truth value. White people are usually safer in their property and person if they avoid black ghettos. Similarly, middle-class blacks who live in affluent black neighborhoods are more insulated from white hostility and discrimination than they would be in majority white areas.

The racial ghetto also sustains and nourishes the racial attitudes and identities of members of the black oppositional culture who live in the ghetto. Images of white affluence appear unfair when compared to the poverty that surrounds them. Physical assaults on whites in this context is justified as both retributive and redistributive justice. Robbery and muggings punish whites for their complicity in benefiting from living in a racist society and redistribute resources that are inequitably distributed among racial groups. Whites' fear of young black males, combined with whites' reluctance to fight back, makes them easy marks and the preferred targets of robbers and muggers.[68] Successful participation in the oppositional culture enhances the self-esteem, the manhood, and racial identity of young black males and wins them the approval of their peers.[69] Anderson argues that the vicious circle identified by Myrdal is still in operation:

A vicious circle has thus been formed. The hopelessness and alienation many young inner-city black men and women feel, largely as a result of endemic joblessness and persistent racism, fuels the violence they engage in. This violence serves to confirm the negative feelings many whites and some middle-class blacks harbor toward the ghetto poor, further legitimating the oppositional culture and the code of the streets in the eyes of many poor young blacks.[70]

Thus, racial identities and prejudices are revalidated daily as reliable guides for appropriate conduct for whites and blacks in America regardless of their class standing. Racial segregation in general and the racial ghetto in particular are race-making situations that perpetuate the color line in America.

SPECULATION CONCERNING THE POSSIBILITIES FOR CHANGE

Jargowsky and Bane define an underclass ghetto to be a census tract with a poverty rate greater than 40%.[71] They report that 27 million people were poor in 1980 (12.4% of the population). Of these, 16.5 million were non-Hispanic whites. Only 2.45 million poor people lived in ghettos in 1980; about 1.59 million of these were African Americans (65%). Nearly one third of the ghetto poor lived in New York, Chicago, and Philadelphia. Ten large cities accounted for 49% of the ghetto poor. Poor blacks were disproportionately concentrated in highly visible ghettos in the nation's largest cities. Poor whites were dispersed into areas of lower poverty concentrations.

Massey and Denton provide a compelling analysis of the causes that created and currently maintain the high concentrations of poverty in African American underclass communities. Given the four initial conditions, Massey and Denton's theorem is deductively correct. The relative sizes and poverty rates of racial groups, coupled with the class and race segregation of neighborhoods, will *inevitably* produce the spatial patterns of poverty by race observed in U.S. cities.

Race and class segregation of neighborhoods together constitute a powerful engine that concentrates poor black people in high-poverty, predominantly black neighborhoods. Race and class segregation also concentrates poor whites, but at much lower levels because poor whites have more opportunities to escape areas of high-poverty concentrations. The out-migration of the black middle class and downward mobility of the near-poor exacerbate the process, but the engines of race and class segregation are sufficiently powerful to produce the African American underclass ghettos that currently exist in U.S. cities.

American Apartheid implicates racial prejudice and discrimination as the most important forces maintaining racially segregated housing in U.S.

cities, but it does not seriously examine the possibility that racial segregation is a determinant of racial attitudes and prejudices. Some evidence reviewed here suggests that racial prejudice and fear may be both a cause and an effect of the high concentrations of poor African Americans in high-poverty areas. Reciprocal links between white prejudices and fears and the concentration of black poverty complicates the already difficult tasks of formulating and implementing effective public policies to dismantle the ghetto and eliminate housing discrimination.

As dismal as the prospects appear based on this analysis, there are some small indications of racial change, of a softening of the socially constructed rules of racial classification and identification. For example, the intermarriage rate between whites and blacks has increased dramatically since the 1960s.[72] Only about 4% of nonsouthern black men married white women in 1968; more than 10% married whites in 1986. The corresponding rates for nonsouthern black women marrying whites are 1.2% in 1968 and 3.7% in 1986. The increases for southern black men and women were lower than for nonsoutherners, but substantial given the almost negligible rates of intermarriage (less than 0.25%) in 1968. By 1986, 4.2% of southern black men and 1.7% of black women married whites. Compared with the historical rate of about 1% that applied before 1960, these intermarriage rates are large. Because whites greatly outnumber blacks in the United States, the intermarriage rate for whites with blacks is correspondingly lower than the rate for blacks marrying whites; for example, if all blacks married whites, the white intermarriage rate would be between 12% and 15%.

The greatest changes appear to be occurring in smaller cities with lower black concentrations. The highest intermarriage rates for blacks occurs in areas with smaller black populations that provide fewer opportunities for blacks to marry other blacks and greater opportunities for blacks to meet and marry whites. As the relative size of the black population increases, black rates of intermarriage with whites declines. In fact, higher black proportions in the South accounts for almost all the difference between southern and nonsouthern black intermarriage rates. By 1990, the number of interracial marriages increased to over 1 million from 310,000 in 1970.[73] The pattern of black/white intermarriage appears to be linked to the pattern of racial segregation of neighborhoods across cities. The greatest declines in residential segregation occurred in smaller cities with smaller black proportions which are the locations of the highest black/white intermarriage rates.[74]

Increasing rates of intermarriage reflect a blurring of the color line. And as the number of interracial marriages increases, greater numbers express dissatisfaction with the racial identifications assigned to their children by the one-drop rule. An indication of this dissatisfaction is the small but growing circulation of new magazines founded in the past five years to address the needs of interracial couples.[75] These magazines appear to be responding to a demand for a "biracial" or "multiracial" race classification to describe the children of interracial couples. Some individuals now self-identify as biracial or multiracial and resist external pressures to classify them as white or black.[76] At least 60 interracial support groups have been formed in cities across the country.[77]

As racial identity becomes more a function of personal choice than mandatory social assignment,[78] the discriminatory practices that enforce racial segregation will become less effective. The high levels of segregation between blacks and whites in the United States would not be possible if the one-drop rule were an unreliable guide for the segregative practices of individuals. If blacks no longer accept the one-drop rule and whites become less sure of who is black, the high levels of racial segregation in U.S. cities will decline and with it the high concentrations of poor people in racially distinctive neighborhoods. But the social forces producing pressures on the social construction of race in America are feeble engines of racial change at present. The changes identified here are too weak and too slow to have significant effects on the race-making situations in the major metropolitan areas of the country for the foreseeable future.

Nevertheless, policymakers should not consider the problems of dismantling the ghetto and eliminating the effects of discriminatory segregative pressures as too difficult to solve. The growing pressure for intermediate racial categories (neither black nor white but both) is evidence that race polarization can be reduced. The strength of the feedback loop between white prejudices and fears and the concentration of poverty can also be diminished. Recent survey research utilizing innovative designs indicate that the racial attitudes of white people are less strongly held than had previously been thought.[79] White people can often be induced to change their minds after expressing their opinion on a racial matter if presented with an effective counterargument. On affirmative action issues, however, whites are very unwilling to change their minds. State-enforced preferential treatment of blacks appears to be widely and strongly opposed by whites, not because whites are opposed to assisting blacks, but because the assistance is perceived as unfair.[80] According to this study, effective political leadership should be able to form effective political coalitions to fight racially discriminatory behaviors because racial discrimination is also widely viewed as unfair. Both whites and blacks stand to gain from the dismantling of the racial ghetto. The conundrum is that dismantling the ghetto requires interracial coalitions, whereas the existence of the ghetto reinforces racial beliefs and attitudes, making interracial coalitions difficult.

ENDNOTES

1. *The Souls of Black Folk* 23 (New York: Fawcett Publications, 1961).

2. The world's most notorious remaining example of state-enforced discrimination was officially eliminated with the inauguration of Nelson Mandela as President of South Africa's new nonracial democracy on 10 May 1994. U.S. Department of State, *Country Reports on Human Rights Practices for 1993* (Washington: GPO, 1994); David R. James, "Slavery and Involuntary Servitude," in E. G. Borgatta & M. L. Borgatta, eds., *Encyclopedia of Sociology* (New York: Macmillan, 1992).

3. Coloureds are people of mixed race. Asians are predominately descendants of indentured servants imported from India.

4. Laureen Platzky & Cheryl Walker, *The Surplus People* (Johannesburg: Ravan Press, 1985); Anthony Lemon, ed., *Homes Apart: South Africa's Segregated Cities* (Bloomington: Indiana University Press, 1991) ("Lemon, *Homes Apart*").

5. Whereas poverty is concentrated on a racial basis in both systems, the spatial patterns are different. Poor nonwhite populations tend to be concentrated in high-poverty neighborhoods in the central cities of major metropolitan areas in the United States. By contrast, South African segregation policies typically located coloured and Indian group areas and the African townships on the periphery of the "apartheid city." See Anthony Lemon, "The Apartheid City," *in id.*, *Homes Apart* 1–25.

6. See at 15–16 for an explicit analogy between the United States and South Africa.

7. The implementation of the New Deal farm programs and succeeding farm policies that drastically reduced the acres devoted to cotton and tobacco in the South is the best example of a policy with unintended ghetto-building consequences. The northward migration of 4 million southern blacks between 1940 and 1970 provided the people necessary for the dramatic postwar expansion of the ghettos in northern cities. Out-migration from the South was closely linked to the implementation of crop reduction programs that, in turn, led to the demise of labor-intensive agricultural practices employing large numbers of blacks. See Karl E. Taeuber & Alma F. Taeuber, "The Black Population in the United States," *in* M. M. Smythe, ed., *The Black American Reference Book* 159–206 (Englewood-Cliffs, N.J.: Prentice Hall, 1976); David R. James, "Local State Structure and the Transformation of Southern Agriculture," in A. E. Havens, ed., *Studies in the Transformation of U.S. Agriculture* 158–78 (Boulder, Col.: Westview Press, 1986); Warren Whatley, "Labor for the Picking: The New Deal in the South," 43 *J. Econ. Hist.* 913 (1983).

8. I attribute this contribution to Massey and Denton, although the first and most complete demonstration of how these four conditions combine to concentrate African American poverty appeared in Douglas S. Massey. "American Apartheid: Segregation and the Making of the Underclass," 96 *Am. J. Soc.* 329 (1990).

9. Blacks outnumber whites in the central cities of a number of metropolitan areas, but the entire metropolitan area is the appropriate ecological unit to examine here because the segregation of housing markets is a metropolitan process. Because work places can be far removed from home places, the concentration of blacks in central cities is part of the process that disperses whites into the suburbs.

10. See, e.g., Douglas S. Massey & Mitchell L. Eggers, "The Ecology of Inequality: Minorities and the Concentration of Poverty," 95 *Am. J. Soc.* 1153 (1990).

11. Only 16 of the 275 metropolitan areas defined by the Census in 1980 had black percentages in excess of 30%. All 16 cities were in the South. Jackson, Miss., had the highest black percentage (40.28%). U.S. Bureau of the Census, *State and Metropolitan Area Data Book, 1986* (Washington: GPO, 1986).

12. See also Karl E. Taeuber & Alma F. Taeuber, *Negroes in Cities* (Chicago: Aldine, 1965); Reynolds Farley & Walter R. Allen, *The Color Line and the Quality of Life in America* (New York: Oxford University Press, 1989).

13. I have not been able to find a review of *American Apartheid* that recognized the importance of Massey and Denton's theorem. Most concentrate on the book's policy recommendations and documentation of discrimination in housing. See, e.g., Nathan Glazer, "A Tale of Two Cities," *New Republic* 2 Aug. 1993, pp. 39–41; Andrew Billingsley, "Separate and Unequal," *Book World*, 4 July 1993, p. 5; Wilber C. Rich, "Ameri-

can Apartheid," 108 *Pol. Sci. Q.* 574 (1993); Roberto M. Fernandez, "American Apartheid," 22 *Contemp. Soc.* 364 (1993); Andrew Hacker, *N.Y. Rev. Books,* 7 Oct. 1993, pp. 21 ff.

14. William Julius Wilson, *The Truly Disadvantaged: The Inner City, the Underclass, and Public Policy* (Chicago: University of Chicago Press, 1987) ("Wilson, *Truly Disadvantaged*").

15. Paul A. Jargowsky & Mary Jo Bane, "Ghetto Poverty in the United States, 1970–1980" ("Jargowsky & Bane, 'Ghetto Poverty'"), in Christopher Jencks & Paul E. Peterson, eds., *The Urban Underclass* 235 (Washington: Brookings Institution, 1991) ("Jencks & Peterson, *Urban Underclass*").

16. Michael H. Schill, "Race, the Underclass and Public Policy: Massey and Denton's *American Apartheid,* 19 *Law & Soc. Inquiry* (1994).

17. Gunnar Myrdal, *An American Dilemma* 75 (New York: Harper & Bros., 1944) ("Myrdal, *American Dilemma*"). "White prejudice and discrimination keep the Negro low in standards of living, health, education, manners and morals. This, in its turn, gives support to white prejudice. White prejudice and Negro standards thus mutually 'cause' each other."

18. Massey and Denton mention the possibility that segregation affects racial attitudes, but this reverse causal link does not play a central role in their analysis (e.g., at 94–96, 236); see also Massey, 96 *Am. J. Soc.* at 353 (cited in note 8).

19. "Although the plight of the Negro in the ghetto and the chance of his escape from his predicament depend on his own strength, they depend also upon the willingness of the white to accept that strength. Negroes alone cannot abolish the ghetto. It will never be ended as long as the white society believes that it needs it." Kenneth B. Clark, *Dark Ghetto: Dilemmas of Social Power* 224 (New York: Harper & Row, 1965). The term "race-making situation" is borrowed from Edgar T. Thompson, "The Plantation as a Race-making Situation," in E. T. Thompson, *Plantation Societies, Race Relations and the South* 115–17 (Durham, N.C.: Duke University Press, 1975) ("Thompson, "Plantation"").

20. Thomas C. Schelling, *Micromotives and Macrobehavior* (Toronto: Norton, 1978). Schelling's book examines a variety of social processes that are constrained by population compositions and other similar factors. His comments on racial segregation and the possibilities for integration are pertinent (at 141):

Counting blacks and whites in a residential block or on a baseball team will not tell how they get along. But it tells something, especially if numbers and ratios matter to the people who are moving in or out of the block or being recruited to the team. With quantitative analysis there are a few logical constraints, analogous to the balance-sheet identities in

economics. (Being logical constraints, they contain no news unless one just never thought of them before.) The simplest constraint on dichotomous mixing is that, within a given set of boundaries, not both groups can enjoy numerical superiority.

21. *Id.* at 142.

22. Wilson, *Truly Disadvantaged.*

23. *Id.* at 50.

24. Jargowsky & Bane, "Ghetto Poverty" (cited in note 15). See also Mark A. Hughes, "Formation of the Impacted Ghetto: Evidence from Large Metropolitan Areas: 1970–1980," 11 *Urban Geography* 265 (1990).

25. *Id.* at 269.

26. Wilson also recognizes that downward mobility contributes to the concentration of poverty but attributes greater significance to middle-class out-migration; see, e.g., Wilson, *Truly Disadvantaged* 50 (cited in note 14). Note that economic declines would increase downward social mobility of blacks and whites, but blacks would be affected disproportionately because of higher proportions of near-poor blacks.

27. See, e.g., Wilson, *Truly Disadvantaged;* Jargowsky & Bane, "Ghetto Poverty" (cited in note 15); Massey & Denton, *American Apartheid;* Massey & Eggers, 95 *Am. J. Soc.* (cited in note 10); Hughes, 11 *Urban Geography;* Reynolds Farley, "Residential Segregation of Social and Economic Groups among Blacks, 1970–80," *in* Jencks & Peterson, *Urban Underclass* 274–98 (cited in note 15).

28. The Panel Study of Income Dynamics (PSID) is a large, longitudinal study that surveyed the members of the same sample households each year since 1968. Recently, PSID data were augmented with census tract identifying codes that permit linking the economic and social characteristics of individuals to the characteristics of the census tracts in which they reside. For details, see Douglas S. Massey & Andrew B. Gross, "Migration, Segregation, and the Spatial Concentration of Poverty" (presented at Population Association of America annual meeting, 1 April 1993).

29. Douglas S. Massey & Shawn M. Kanaiaupuni, "Public Housing and the Concentration of Poverty," 74 *Soc. Sci. Q.* 107 (1993).

30. Arnold Hirsch, *Making the Second Ghetto: Race and Housing in Chicago 1940–1960* (New York: Cambridge University Press, 1983).

31. E.g., see Christopher Jencks, *Rethinking Social Policy, Race, Poverty, and the Underclass* (New York: Harper/Collins, 1992); Christopher Jencks & Susan E. Mayer, "The Social Consequences of Growing Up in a Poor Neighborhood," in L. E. Lynn, Jr., & M. G. H. McGeary, eds., *Inner-City Poverty in the United States* 111 (Washington: National Academy Press, 1990) ("Lynn & McGeary, *Inner-City Poverty*"); Fernandez, 22 *Contemp. Soc.* (cited in note 13).

32. Christopher Jencks & Susan E. Mayer, "Residential Segregation, Job Proximity, and Black Job Opportunities," *in* Lynn & McGeary, *Inner-City Poverty* 187 ("Jencks & Mayer, 'Residential Segregation' ").

33. *Id.* at 196; John Kasarda, "City Jobs and Residential Segregation," 4 *Econ. Dev. Q.* 313 (1990), finds that residential segregation does diminish access to suburban jobs for blacks who live in cities.

34. Jencks & Mayer, "Residential Segregation" at 198.

35. *Id.* at 213.

36. Michael Fix & Raymond J. Struyk, eds., *Clear and Convincing Evidence: Measurement of Discrimination in America* (Washington: Urban Institute Press, 1992).

37. David R. James, "City Limits on Racial Equality: The Effects of City-Suburb Boundaries on Public-School Desegregation, 1968–1976," 54 *Am. Soc. Rev.* 963 (1989); Jonathan Kozol, *Savage Inequalities: Children in America's Schools* (New York: Harper, 1991); William L. Taylor & Dianne M. Piche, "A Report on Shortchanging Children: The Impact of Fiscal Inequity on the Education of Students at Risk" (prepared for the Committee on Education and Labor, U.S. House of Representatives, Serial No. 101-U) (Washington: GPO, 1990).

38. Robert J. Sampson, "Urban Black Violence: The Effects of Male Joblessness and Family Disruption," 93 *Am. J. Soc.* 348 (1987).

39. The percentage reported here is for the adult non-black population. Studies of the attitudes of college students show that the percentages who hold the "lazy blacks" stereotype declines from 75% in 1932 to 18% in 1982. Leonard Gordon, "College Student Stereotype of Blacks and Jews on Two Campuses," 70 *Sociology & Soc. Res.* 200–201 (1986). See also Howard Schuman et al., *Racial Attitudes in America* (Cambridge, Mass.: Harvard University Press, 1985).

40. William L. Yancey, Eugene P. Ericksen, & Richard N. Juliani, "Emergent Ethnicity: A Review and Reformulation," 41 *Am. Soc. Rev.* 391 (1976); Harry C. Triandis, "The Future of Pluralism Revisited," in P. A. Katz & D. A. Taylor, eds., *Eliminating Racism* 31–50 (New York: Plenum, 1988); Lawrence Bobo, "Group Conflict, Prejudice, and the Paradox of Contemporary Racial Attitudes," in *id.* at 85–114.

41. The ambiguity introduced by defining a people as black if they have any known African black ancestors is unavoidable. Logical consistency is not required in race definitions; wide social acceptance of the rule is sufficient justification. A popular textbook of the 1950s stated that the social definition of race takes precedence over legal and biological definitions and then described the U.S. definition as follows:

> According to this (social) definition, which holds throughout the United States, anyone is a Negro who has any known trace of Negro ancestry, regardless of how far back one must go to find it.

"One drop of Negro blood makes one a Negro" is the popular way of expressing the idea. The Census takes recognition of the American practice in its instructions to enumerators: "A person of mixed white and Negro blood should be returned as a Negro, no matter how small the percentage of Negro blood."

Brewton Berry, *Race and Ethnic Relations* 30 (Boston: Houghton Mifflin, 1958). Berry points out that the race definition used in the United States is not applied in other countries (at 31). The U.S. Census adopted the practice of accepting respondents' self-definition of their race in 1960.

42. *Who Is Black? One Nation's Definition* (University Park: Penn State University Press, 1991) ("Davis, *Who Is Black?*").

43. For example, Vietnam assigns mixed-race persons to the most despised status. Mexico classifies the descendants of Spaniards and American Indians as the superior racial status. See *id.*

44. According to Davis (*id.* at 82–122), the other four race definitions are (1) an intermediate status (e.g., coloureds in South Africa), (2) a highly variable status depending more on social class than on color (e.g., Jamaica, Puerto Rico, Brazil), (3) a variable status independent of racial traits (e.g., Hawaii), and (4) the status of an assimilated minority (e.g., the United States for the children of whites and either American Indians, Japanese Americans, or one of the other racially distinctive minorities except blacks).

45. *Id.* at 82.

46. Davis (*id.* at 12) states that individuals whose ancestry is one-quarter American Indian or less are not defined as Indian unless they want to be. For an example of an American Indian tribe seeking to enforce the one-drop rule, see Timothy Egan, "A Cultural Gap May Swallow a Child," *N.Y. Times,* 12 Oct. 1993, p. A8. In this case, the Oglala Sioux asked an Idaho court to remove a four-year-old boy from his white adoptive parents and return him to the tribe. The child's father, an Oglala Sioux, abandoned the child's white mother, who relinquished all parental rights in the adoption proceedings soon after birth. The basis of the suit is the federal Indian Child Welfare Act (passed in 1978), which gives Indian tribes special preference in adopting children of Indian parentage.

47. Thompson, "Plantation" (cited in note 19).

48. David R. James, "The Transformation of the Southern Racial State: Class and Race Determinants of Local-State Structures in the South," 53 *Am. Soc. Rev.* 191 (1988).

49. Several competing race definitions existed at different times in the United States. Davis, *Who Is Black?* 30–66; see also Joel Williamson, *New People: Miscegenation and Mulattoes in the United States* (New York: Free Press, 1980), who argues that the one-drop rule fi-

nally became almost universally accepted during the 1920s as a complicated result of the imposition of Jim Crow segregation in the South, black resistance to Jim Crow, and the development of a new American black culture in the cities (symbolized by the "Harlem Renaissance") which reinforced black identity and pride.

50. The Civil Rights Movement of the 1960s and the Afro-Centrism Movement today are recent examples of social movements that resisted blacks' confinement to a subordinate status. As part of their resistance, both movements have been successful in nourishing and solidifying the racial identities of blacks. Michael Omi & Howard Winant, *Racial Formation in the United States from the 1960s to the 1980s* (New York: Routledge & Kegan Paul, 1986).

51. Stanley Lieberson, *A Piece of the Pie* 5 (Berkeley: University of California Press, 1980). See also Richard D. Alba, *Ethnic Identity: The Transformation of White America* (New Haven, Conn.: Yale University Press, 1990), and Mary C. Waters, *Ethnic Options: Choosing Ethnic Identities in America* (Berkeley: University of California Press, 1990).

52. Elijah Anderson, *Streetwise: Race, Class, and Change in an Urban Community* (Chicago: University of Chicago Press, 1990) ("Anderson, *Streetwise*"). See also Elijah Anderson, "The Code of the Streets," *Atlantic Monthly,* May 1994, at 81–94 ("Anderson, 'Code' ").

53. *Id.* at 239. Neither Anderson nor I argue that the culture that has developed in black underclass communities today was completely determined by social and economic conditions. Arguing that the oppositional culture that emerged in underclass communities is an adaptive response to the social and economic conditions in those areas does not imply that the emergence of that culture was inevitable nor that similar conditions would produce similar cultures elsewhere. Social and economic conditions place limits on the possibilities of cultural change, but many different cultures may be consistent with a particular set of conditions.

54. Anderson, "Code."

55. See Massey & Denton at 5–7 for a brief review of the literature on the culture of poverty.

56. See also Jay MacLeod, *Ain't No Makin' It: Leveled Aspirations in a Low-Income Neighborhood* (Boulder, Col.: Westview, 1987).

57. See also Richard Majors & Janet M. Billson, *Cool Pose: The Dilemmas of Black Manhood in America* (Lexington, Mass.: Lexington Books, 1992).

58. Joe R. Feagin, "The Continuing Significance of Race: Antiblack Discrimination in Public Places," 56 *Am. Soc. Rev.* 101 (1991). For newspaper accounts, see, e.g., John Blake, "Miscast 'Monsters' of the Streets," *Chicago Tribune,* 15 Sept. 1987, sec. 2, p. 1; Isabel Wilkerson, "Campus Blacks Feel Racism's Nuances," *N.Y. Times,* 17 April 1988, p. 1; Brent Staples, "How a Young Black Scholar Learned the Language of Fear," *N.Y.*

Times Mag., 6 Feb. 1994, pp. 22 ff.; David J. Dent, "The New Black Suburbs," *N.Y. Times Mag.,* 14 June 1992, pp. 18 ff.

59. For example, angry, loud complaints about an unthinking racial insult or slur may appear exaggerated to the white person who committed the offense. The black victim tends to view the incident as the most recent example of a consistent pattern of abuse and discrimination. The white offender tends to view the insult as an isolated incident. Hence, the black victim's response is in part due to the cumulative effect of past discrimination. The white offender, on the other hand, does not feel responsible for the prior acts of others and therefore feels that the magnitude of the victim's angry response is not merited by the magnitude of the offense. See Feagin, 56 *Am. Soc. Rev.,* for other examples.

60. *Id.* at 115.

61. Dent, *N.Y. Times Mag.* In 1980, Prince George's County's population of 729,268 was 50.7% blacks. Over half of the census tracts in the county were more than 70% black. Over 37% of the black population had household incomes greater than $50,000. Only 25% of the total U.S. black population had incomes that high. About 9% of black households in Prince George's had incomes below $15,000 compared to the 37% of black households nationwide.

62. *Id.* at 20.

63. *Id.* at 20–21.

64. *American Apartheid* at 78–81. Similar patterns apply in the suburbs. Massey and Denton's probability calculations included controls for the presence of other racial groups in the neighborhood, the distance from Hispanic areas, rates of white and minority population growth, job creation rates, housing quality factors, and region.

65. A .46 probability of white population decline is just below the 50/50 point at which the chances of white decline and increase are equal; equivalently, there is a 54% chance of an increase in the white population.

66. By contrast, the neighborhood choices of blacks follow a pattern that is insensitive to the location of areas of high black concentrations: the probability of black population gain remains constant at about .56 to .58 up to a distance of 25 miles from city neighborhoods that are 30%–40% black. Massey and Denton argue that this pattern is consistent with decreased housing discrimination against blacks because the "old patterns of discrimination" should have produced high probabilities of black gain near black neighborhoods and smaller probabilities of black gain as distance from black areas increased (at 80). In fact, proximity to tracts with high or low black population proportions had little influence on the chances of black population increase.

67. Myrdal, *American Dilemma* (cited in note 17); Charles S. Johnson, *Backgrounds to Patterns of Negro Segregation* (New York: Thomas Y. Crowell, 1943).

68. Anderson, *Streetwise* at 163–89 (cited in note 50). Anderson may be right about the preference of young black muggers for white middle-class targets, but the opportunities to act on this preference are small compared to the opportunities to assault other blacks. Consequently, most black assailants attack black victims. For example, about half of the murders committed in 1990 were committed by blacks, a proportion much higher than one might expect given that blacks make up about 13% of the population. About 11% of the victims of black assailants were white. By contrast, about 6% or 7% of the victims of white murderers were black. See Andrew Hacker, *Two Nations: Black and White, Separate, Hostile, Unequal* 183 (New York: Charles Scribner's, 1992).

69. Anderson "Code" at 89.

70. *Id.* at 84.

71. Paul L. Jargowsky and Mary Jo Bane, "Ghetto Poverty: Basic Questions," in Lynn & McGeary, *Inner-City Poverty* 16–67 (cited in note 32).

72. Matthijs Kalmijn, "Trends in Black/White Intermarriage," 72 *Soc. Forces* 119 (1993).

73. U.S. Census data reported in Arthur M. Schlesinger, Jr., *The Disuniting of America* 133 (New York: Norton, 1992). Most interracial marriages were between blacks and whites.

74. Massey & Denton, "Trends in the Residential Segregation of Blacks, Hispanics, and Asians: 1970–1980," 52 *Am. Soc. Rev.* 802 (1987).

75. See, e.g., *Interrace: The Source for Interracial Living* (Atlanta, Ga.), founded in 1989; *New People: The Authority on Interracial News and Views* (Oak Park, Mich.), founded in 1990; *Biracial Child,* founded in 1993 by the publishers of *Interrace.*

76. See, e.g., *Just Black? Multi-racial Identity,* a film produced by F. W. Twine and J. F. Warren (1992), Filmakers Library, Inc., 124 E. 40th Street, New York, N.Y. P. 924;

Naomi Zack, *Race and Mixed Race* (Philadelphia: Temple University Press, 1993); Paul R. Spickard, *Mixed Blood: Intermarriage and Ethnic Identity in Twentieth-Century America* (Madison: University of Wisconsin Press, 1989).

77. See *New People* 4 (Nov./Dec. 1993), p. 25, for a list of interracial support groups complete with addresses and telephone numbers.

78. Although whites usually consider blacks to be members of a homogenous culture, increasing ethnic diversity among blacks stemming from recent voluntary migrations of blacks from Haiti, Africa, and Latin America creates additional pressure among blacks to resist the one-drop rule in America. American blacks increasingly differentiate themselves on the basis of ethnicity and national origins. See Roy Simón Bryce-Laporte, "Voluntary Immigration and Continuing Encounters between Blacks," 530 *Annals Am. Acad. Pol. & Soc. Sci.* 28 (1993).

79. Paul M. Sniderman & Thomas Piazza, *The Scar of Race* (Cambridge, Mass: Belknap Press, 1993). Typical surveys of racial attitudes ask respondents how much they support or oppose racial equality on a variety of social and political issues. Responses to such questions are treated as accurate indicators of the *fixed* attitudes of the respondent. Sniderman and Piazza recognized that people hold opinions with varying levels of conviction and designed an experiment to test how strongly racial opinions were held. After a respondent expressed support (or opposition) to racial equality on a particular issue, the respondent was presented with a strong argument contradicting their stated position. They then were asked whether they had changed their minds on the issue. The survey's innovative design made it possible to assess the probability that white Americans would change their mind on a racial issue and identify the reasons that they changed if they did.

80. *Id.* at 177.

TWENTY-TWO

Symbolic Ethnicity
The Future of Ethnic Groups and Cultures in America

Herbert J. Gans

INTRODUCTION

One of the more notable recent changes in America has been the renewed interest in ethnicity, which some observers of the American scene have described as ethnic revival. This paper argues that there has been no revival, and that acculturation and assimilation continue to take place. Among third and fourth generation "ethnics" (the grand and great-grandchildren of Europeans who came to America during the "new immigration"), a new kind of ethnic involvement may be occurring, which emphasizes concern with identity, with the feeling of being Jewish or Italian, etc. Since ethnic identity needs are neither intense nor frequent in this generation, however, ethnics do not need either ethnic cultures or organizations; instead, they resort to the use of ethnic symbols. As a result, ethnicity may be turning into symbolic ethnicity, an ethnicity of last resort, which could, nevertheless, persist for generations.

Identity cannot exist apart from a group, and symbols are themselves a part of culture, but ethnic identity and symbolic ethnicity require very different ethnic cultures and organizations than existed among earlier generations. Moreover, the symbols third generation ethnics use to express their identity are more visible than the ethnic cultures and organizations of the first and second generation ethnics. What appears to be an ethnic revival may therefore only be a more visible form of long-standing phenomena, or of a new stage of acculturation and assimilation. Symbolic ethnic-

ity may also have wider ramifications, however, for David Riesman has suggested that "being American has some of the same episodic qualities as being ethnic."[1]

ACCULTURATION AND ASSIMILATION[2]

The dominant sociological approach to ethnicity has long taken the form of what Neil Sandberg aptly calls straight-line theory, in which acculturation and assimilation are viewed as secular trends that culminate in the eventual absorption of the ethnic group into the larger culture and general population.[3] Straight-line theory in turn is based on melting pot theory, for it implies the disappearance of the ethnic groups into a single host society. Even so, it does not accept the values of the melting pot theorists, since its conceptualizers could have, but did not, use terms like cultural and social liberation from immigrant ways of life.

In recent years, straight-line theory has been questioned on many grounds. For one thing, many observers have properly noted that even if America might have been a melting pot early in the 20th century, the massive immigration from Europe and elsewhere has since then influenced the dominant groups, summarily labelled White Anglo-Saxon Protestant (WASP), and has also decimated their cultural, if not their political and financial power, so that today America is a mosaic, as Andrew Greeley has put it, of subgroups and subcultures.[4] Still, this criticism does not necessarily deny the validity of straight-line theory,

Reprinted from "Symbolic Ethnicity: The Future of Ethnic Groups and Cultures in America" by Herbert J. Gans, *Ethnic and Racial Studies* 2:1 (January 1979) by permission of Routledge & Kegan Paul Ltd., publishers.

since ethnics can also be absorbed into a pluralistic set of subcultures and subgroups, differentiated by age, income, education, occupation, religion, region, and the like.

A second criticism of straight-line theory has centered on its treatment of all ethnic groups as essentially similar, and its failure, specifically, to distinguish between religious groups like the Jews and nationality groups like the Italians, Poles, etc. Jews, for example, are a "peoplehood" with a religious and cultural tradition of thousands of years, but without an "old country" to which they owe allegiance or nostalgia, while Italians, Poles and other participants in the "new immigration" came from parts of Europe which in some cases did not even become nations until after the immigrants had arrived in America.

That there are differences between the Jews and the other "new" immigrants cannot be questioned, but at the same time, the empirical evidence also suggests that acculturation and assimilation affected them quite similarly. (Indeed, one major difference may have been that Jews were already urbanized and thus entered the American social structure at a somewhat higher level than the other new immigrants, who were mostly landless laborers and poor peasants.) Nonetheless, straight-line theory can be faulted for virtually ignoring that immigrants arrived here with two kinds of ethnic cultures, sacred and secular; that they were Jews from Eastern—and Western—Europe, and Catholics from Italy, Poland and elsewhere. (Sacred cultures are, however, themselves affected by national and regional considerations; for example, Italian Catholicism differed in some respects from German or Polish, as did Eastern European Judaism from Western.)

While acculturation and assimilation have affected both sacred and secular cultures, they have affected the latter more than the former, for acculturation has particularly eroded the secular cultures which Jews and Catholics brought from Europe. Their religions have also changed in America, and religious observance has decreased, more so among Jews than among Catholics, although Catholic observance has begun to fall off greatly in recent years. Consequently, the similar American experience of Catholic and Jewish ethnics suggests that the comparative analysis of straight-line theory is justified, as long as the analysis compares both sacred and secular cultures.

Two further critiques virtually reject straight-line theory altogether. In an insightful recent paper, William Yancey and his colleagues have argued that contemporary ethnicity bears little relation to the ancestral European heritage, but exists because it is functional for meeting present "exigencies of survival and the structure of opportunity," particularly for working class Americans.[5] Their argument does not invalidate straght-line theory but corrects it by suggesting that acculturation and assimilation, current ethnic organizations and cultures, as well as new forms of ethnicity, must be understood as responses to current needs rather than only as departures from past traditions.

The other critique takes the reverse position; it points to the persistence of the European heritage, argues that the extent of acculturation and assimilation has been overestimated, and questions the rapid decline and eventual extinction of ethnicity posited by some straight-line theorists. These critics call attention to studies which indicate that ethnic cultures and organizations are still functioning, that exogamous marriage remains a practice of numerical minorities, that ethnic differences in various behavior patterns and attitudes can be identified, that ethnic groups continue to act as political interest groups, and that ethnic pride remains strong.[6]

The social phenomena which these observers identify obviously exist; the question is only how they are to be interpreted. Straight-line theory postulates a process, and cross-sectional studies do not preempt the possibility of a continuing trend. Also, like Yancey, et al., some of the critics are looking primarily at poorer ethnics, who have been less touched by acculturation and assimilation than middle class ethnics, and who have in some cases used ethnicity and ethnic organization as a psychological and political defense against the injustices which they suffer in an unequal society.[7] In fact, much of the contemporary behavior described as ethnic strikes me as working class behavior, which differs only slightly among various ethnic groups, and then largely because of variations in the structure of opportunities open to people in America, and in the peasant traditions their ancestors brought over from the old country, which were themselves responses to European opportunity structures. In other words, ethnicity is largely a working-class style.[8]

Much the same observations apply to ethnic political activity. Urban political life, particularly among working class people, has always been structured by and through ethnicity, and while ethnic political activity may have increased in the last decade, it has taken place around working class issues rather than ethnic ones. During the 1960s, urban working class Catholic ethnics began to politicize themselves in response to black militancy, the expansion of black ghettos, and governmental integration policies which they perceived as publicly legitimated black invasions of ethnic neighborhoods, but which threatened them more as working class homeowners who could not afford to move to the suburbs. Similarly, working and lower-middle class Catholic ethnics banded together in the suburbs to fight against higher public school taxes, since they could not afford to pay them while they were also having to pay for parochial schools. Even so, these political activities have been *pan-ethnic,* rather than ethnic, since they often involved coalitions of ethnic groups which once considered each other enemies but were now united by common economic and other interests. The extent to which these pan-ethnic coalitions reflect class rather than ethnic interests is illustrated by the 1968 election campaign of New York City's Mario Proccaccino against John Lindsay. Although an Italian, he ran as a "candidate of the little people" against what he called the "limousine liberals."

The fact that pan-ethnic coalitions have developed most readily in conflicts over racial issues also suggests that in politics, ethnicity can sometimes serve as a convenient euphemism for anti-black endeavors, or for political activities that have negative consequences for blacks. While attitude polls indicate that ethnics are often more tolerant racially than other Americans, working class urban ethnics are also more likely to be threatened, as home-owners and job holders, by black demands, and may favor specific anti-black policies not because they are "racists," but because their own class interests force them to oppose black demands.

In addition, part of what appears as an increase in ethnic political activity is actually an increase in the visibility of ethnic politics. When the pan-ethnic coalitions began to copy the political methods of the civil rights and anti-war movements, their protests became newsworthy and were disseminated all over the country by the mass media. At about the same time, the economic and geographic mobility of Catholic ethnic groups enabled non-Irish Catholic politicians to win important state and national electoral posts for the first time, and their victories were defined as ethnic triumphs, even though they did not rely on ethnic constituents alone, and were not elected on the basis of ethnic issues.

The final, equally direct, criticism of straight-line theory has questioned the continued relevance of the theory, either because of the phenomenon of third-generation return, or because of the emergence of ethnic revivals. Thus, Marcus Hansen argued that acculturation and assimilation were temporary processes, because the third generation could afford to remember an ancestral culture which the traumatic Americanization forced the immigrant and second generations to forget.[9] Hansen's hypothesis can be questioned on several grounds, however. His data, the founding of Swedish and other historical associations in the Midwest, provided slender evidence of a widespread third generation return, particularly among non-academic ethnics. In addition, his theory is static, for Hansen never indicated what would happen in the fourth generation, or what processes were involved in the return that would enable it to survive into the future.[10]

The notion of an ethnic revival has so far been propounded mostly by journalists and essayists, who have supplied impressionistic accounts or case studies of the emergence of new ethnic organizations and the revitalization of old ones.[11] Since third and fourth generation ethnics who are presumably participating in the revival are scattered all over suburbia, there has so far been little systematic research among this population, so that the validity of the revival notion has not yet been properly tested.

The evidence I have seen does not convince me that a revival is taking place. Instead, recent changes can be explained in two ways, neither of which conflicts with straight-line theory: (1) Today's ethnics have become more visible as a result of upward mobility; and (2) they are adopting the new form of ethnic behavior and affiliation I call symbolic ethnicity.

THE VISIBILITY OF ETHNICITY

The recent upward social, and centrifugal geographic mobility of ethnics, particularly Catholics, has finally enabled them to enter the middle and upper middle classes, where they have been noticed by the national mass media, which monitor primarily these strata. In the process they have also become more noticeable to other Americans. The newly visible may not participate more in ethnic groups and cultures than before, but their new visibility makes it appear as if ethnicity had been revived.

I noted earlier the arrival of non-Irish Catholic politicians on the national scene. An equally visible phenomenon has been the entry of Catholic ethnic intellectuals into the academy, and its flourishing print culture. To be sure, the scholars are publishing more energetically than their predecessors, who had to rely on small and poverty-stricken ethnic publishing houses, but they are essentially doing what ethnic scholars have always done, only more visibly. Perhaps their energy has also been spurred in part by the need, as academics, to publish so that they do not perish, as well as by their desire to counteract the antiethnic prejudices and the entrenched vestiges of the melting pot ideal which still prevail in the more prestigious universities. In some cases, they are also fighting a political battle, because their writings often defend conservative political positions against what they perceive—I think wrongly—as the powerful liberal or radical academic majority. Paradoxically, a good deal of their writing has been nostalgic, celebrating the immigrant culture and its Gemeinschaft at the same time that young Catholic ethnics are going to college partly in order to escape the restrictive pressures of that Gemeinschaft. (Incidentally, an interesting study could be made of the extent to which writers from different ethnic groups, both of fiction and non-fiction, are pursuing nostalgic, contemporary or future-oriented approaches to ethnicity, comparing different ethnic groups, by time of arrival and position in the society today, on this basis.)

What has happened in the academy has also happened in literature and show business. For example, although popular comedy has long been a predominantly Eastern European Jewish occupation, the first generation of Jewish comic stars had to suppress their ethnicity and even had to change their names, much as did the first generation of academic stars in the prestigious universities. Unlike Jack Benny, Eddie Cantor, George Burns, George Jesel and others, the comics of today do not need to hide their origins, and beginning perhaps with Lenny Bruce and Sam Levinson, comics like Buddy Hackett, Robert Klein, Don Rickles and Joan Rivers have used explicitly Jewish material in entertaining the predominantly non-Jewish mass media audience.

Undoubtedly, some of the academics, writers and entertainers have undergone a kind of third generation return in this process. Some have reembraced their ethnicity solely to spur their careers, but others have experienced a personal conversion. Even so, an empirical study would probably show that in most cases, their ethnic attitudes have not changed; either they have acted more publicly and thus visibly than they did in the past, or in responding to a hospitable cultural climate, they have openly followed ethnic impulses which they had previously suppressed.

ETHNICITY IN THE THIRD GENERATION

The second explanation for the changes that have been taking place among third generation ethnics will take up most of the rest of this paper; it deals with what is happening among the less visible population, the large mass of predominantly middle class third and fourth generation ethnics, who have not been studied enough either by journalists or social scientists.[12]

In the absence of systematic research, it is even difficult to discern what has actually been happening, but several observers have described the same ethnic behavior in different words. Michael Novak has coined the phrase "voluntary ethnicity"; Samuel Eisenstadt has talked about "Jewish diversity"; Allan Silver about "individualism as a valid mode of Jewishness," and Geoffrey Bock about "public Jewishness."[13] What these observers agree on is that today's young ethnics are finding new ways of being ethnics, which I shall later label symbolic ethnicity.

For the third generation, the secular ethnic cultures which the immigrants brought with them are now only an ancestral memory, or an exotic tradition to be savored once in a while in a museum or at an ethnic festival. The same is true of the "Americanization cultures," the immigrant experience and adjustment in America, which William Kornblum suggests may have been more important in the lives of the first two generations than the ethnic cultures themselves. The old ethnic cultures serve no useful function for third generation ethnics who lack direct and indirect ties to the old country, and neither need nor have much knowledge about it. Similarly, the Americanization cultures have little meaning for people who grew up without the familial conflict over European and American ways that beset their fathers and mothers: the second generation which fought with and was often ashamed of immigrant parents. Assimilation is still continuing, for it has always progressed more slowly than acculturation. If one distinguishes between primary and secondary assimilation, that is, out of ethnic primary and secondary groups, the third generation is now beginning to move into non-ethnic primary groups.[14] Although researchers are still debating just how much intermarriage is taking place, it is rising in the third generation for both Catholic ethnic groups and Jews, and friendship choices appear to follow the same pattern.[15]

The departure out of secondary groups has already proceeded much further. Most third generation ethnics have little reason, or occasion, to depend on, or even interact with, other ethnics in important secondary group activities. Ethnic occupational specialization, segregation, and self-segregation are fast disappearing, with some notable exceptions in the large cities. Since the third generation probably works, like other Americans, largely for corporate employers, past occupational ties between ethnics are no longer relevant. Insofar as they live largely in the suburbs, third generation ethnics get together with their fellow homeowners for political and civic activities, and are not likely to encounter ethnic political organizations, balanced tickets, or even politicians who pursue ethnic constituencies.

Except in suburbs where old discrimination and segregation patterns still survive, social life takes place without ethnic clustering, and Catholics are not likely to find ethnic subgroups in the Church. Third generation Jews, on the other hand, particularly those who live in older upper-middle class suburbs where segregation continues, if politely, still probably continue to restrict much of their social life to other Jews, although they have long ago forgotten the secular divisions between German (and other Western) and Eastern European Jews, and among the latter, the division between "Litwaks" and "Galizianer." The religious distinction between German Reform Judaism, and

Eastern European Conservatism has also virtually disappeared, for the second generation that moved to the suburbs after World War II already chose its denomination on status grounds rather than national origin.[16] In fact, the Kennedy-Herberg prediction that eventually American religious life would take the form of a triple melting-pot has not come to pass, if only because people, especially in the suburbs, use denominations within the major religions for status differentiation.

Nevertheless, while ethnic ties continue to wane for the third generation, people of this generation continue to *perceive* themselves as ethnics, whether they define ethnicity in sacred or secular terms. Jews continue to remain Jews because the sacred and secular elements of their culture are strongly intertwined, but the Catholic ethnics also retain the secular or national identity, even though it is separate from their religion.[17]

My hypothesis is that in this generation, people are less and less interested in their ethnic cultures and organizations—both sacred and secular—and are instead more concerned with maintaining their ethnic identity, with the feeling of being Jewish, or Italian, or Polish, and with finding ways of feeling and expressing that identity in suitable ways. By identity, I mean here simply the socio-psychological elements that accompany role behavior, and the ethnic role is today less of an ascriptive than a voluntary role that people assume alongside other roles. To be sure, ethnics are still identified as such by others, particularly on the basis of name, but the behavioral expectations that once went with identification by others have declined sharply, so that ethnics have some choice about when and how to play ethnic roles. Moreover, as ethnic cultures and organizations decline further, fewer ethnic roles are prescribed, thus increasing the degree to which people have freedom of role definition.

Ethnic identity can be expressed either in action or feeling, or combinations of these, and the kinds of situations in which it is expressed are nearly limitless. Third generation ethnics can join an ethnic organization, or take part in formal or informal organizations composed largely of fellow-ethnics; but they can also find their identity by "affiliating" with an abstract collectivity which does not exist as an interacting group. That collectivity, moreover, can be mythic or real, contemporary or historical. On the one hand, Jews can express their identity as synagogue members, or as participants in a consciousness-raising group consisting mostly of Jewish women. On the other hand, they can also identify with the Jewish people as a long-suffering collectivity which has been credited with inventing monotheism. If they are non-religious, they can identify with Jewish liberal or socialist political cultures, or with a population which has produced many prominent intellectuals and artists in the last 100 years. Similar choices are open to Catholic ethnics. In the third generation, Italians can identify through membership in Italian groups, or by strong feelings for various themes in Italian, or Neapolitan or Sicilian culture, and much the same possibilities exist for Catholics whose ancestors came over from other countries.

Needless to say, ethnic identity is not a new, or third generation phenomenon, for ethnics have always had an ethnic identity, but in the past it was largely taken for granted, since it was anchored to groups and roles, and was rarely a matter of choice. When people lived in an ethnic neighborhood, worked with fellow ethnics, and voted for ethnic politicians, there was little need to be concerned with identity except during conflict with other ethnic groups. Also, the everyday roles people played were often defined for them by others as ethnic. Being a drygoods merchant was often a Jewish role; restaurant owners were assumed to be Greek; and bartenders, Irish.

The third generation has grown up without assigned roles or groups that anchor ethnicity, so that identity can no longer be taken for granted. People can of course give up their identity, but if they continue to feel it, they must make it more explicit than it was in the past, and must even look for ways of expressing it. This has two important consequences for ethnic behavior. First, given the degree to which the third generation has acculturated and assimilated, most people look for easy and intermittent ways of expressing their identity, for ways that do not conflict with other ways of life. As a result, they refrain from ethnic behavior that requires an arduous or timeconsuming commitment, either to a culture that must be practiced constantly, or to organizations that demand active membership. Second, because people's concern is with identity, rather than with cultural practices or group relationships, they are free to look for ways of expressing that identity which suit them

best, thus opening up the possibility of voluntary, diverse or individualistic ethnicity. Any mode of expressing ethnic identity is valid as long as it enhances the feeling of being ethnic, and any cultural pattern or organization which nourishes that feeling is therefore relevant, providing only that enough people make the same choice when identity expression is a group enterprise.

In other words, as the functions of ethnic cultures and groups diminish and identity becomes the primary way of being ethnic, ethnicity takes on an expressive rather than instrumental function in people's lives, becoming more of a leisure-time activity and losing its relevance, say, to earning a living or regulating family life. Expressive behavior can take many forms, but it often involves the use of symbols—and symbols as signs rather than as myths.[18] Ethnic symbols are frequently individual cultural practices which are taken from the older ethnic culture; they are "abstracted" from that culture and pulled out of its original moorings, so to speak, to become stand-ins for it. And if a label is useful to describe the third generation's pursuit of identity, I would propose the term symbolic ethnicity.

SYMBOLIC ETHNICITY

Symbolic ethnicity can be expressed in a myriad of ways, but above all, I suspect, it is characterized by a nostalgic allegiance to the culture of the immigrant generation, or that of the old country; a love for and a pride in a tradition that can be felt without having to be incorporated in everyday behavior. The feelings can be directed at a generalized tradition, or at specific ones: a desire for the cohesive extended immigrant family, or for the obedience of children to parental authority, or the unambiguous orthodoxy of immigrant religion, or the old-fashioned despotic benevolence of the machine politician. People may even sincerely desire to "return" to these imagined pasts, which are conveniently cleansed of the complexities that accompanied them in the real past, but while they may soon realize that they cannot go back, they may not surrender the wish. Or else they displace that wish on churches, schools, and the mass media, asking them to recreate a tradition, or rather, to create a symbolic tradition, even while their familial, occupational, religious and political lives are pragmatic responses to the imperatives of their roles and positions in local and national hierarchical social structures.

All of the cultural patterns which are transformed into symbols are themselves guided by a common pragmatic imperative: they must be visible and clear in meaning to large numbers of third generation ethnics, and they must be easily expressed and felt, without requiring undue interference in other aspects of life. For example, Jews have abstracted rites de passage and individual holidays out of the traditional religion and given them greater importance, such as the bar mitzvah and bas mitzvah (the parallel ceremony for 13 year old girls that was actually invented in America). Similarly, Chanukah, a minor holiday in the religious calendar, has become a major one in popular practice, partly since it lends itself to impressing Jewish identity on the children. Rites de passage and holidays are ceremonial; and thus symbolic to begin with; equally important, they do not take much time, do not upset the everyday routine, and also become an occasion for family reunions to reassemble family members who are rarely seen on a regular basis. Catholic ethnics pay special attention to saints' days celebrating saints affiliated with their ethnic group, or attend ethnic festivals which take place in the area of first settlement, or in ethnic churches.

Consumer goods, notably food, are another ready source for ethnic symbols, and in the last decades, the food industry has developed a large variety of easily cooked ethnic foods, as well as other edibles which need no cooking, for example, chocolate matzohs which are sold as gifts at Passover. The response to symbolic ethnicity may even be spreading into the mass media, for films and television programs with ethnic characters are on the increase. The characters are not very ethnic in their behavior, and may only have ethnic names—for example, Lt. Colombo, Fonzi, or Rhoda Goldstein—but in that respect, they are not very different from the ethnic audiences who watch them.

Symbolic ethnicity also takes political forms, through identification or involvement with national politicians and international issues which are sufficiently remote to become symbols. As politicians from non-Irish ethnic backgrounds achieve high state or national office, they become identity symbols for members of their group, supplying feelings of pride over their success. That such politicians do not represent ethnic constituencies, and thus do not become involved in ethnic political disputes only enhances their symbolic function; unlike local ethnic politicians, who are still elected for instrumental bread-and-butter reasons, and thus become embroiled in conflicts that detract from their being symbols of ethnic pride.

Symbolic ethnicity can be practiced as well through politically and geographically even more distant phenomena, such as nationalist movements in the old country. Jews are not interested in their old countries, except to struggle against the maltreatment of Jews in Eastern Europe, but they have sent large amounts of money to Israel, and political pressure to Washington, since the establishment of the State. While their major concern has undoubtedly been to stave off Israel's destruction, they might also have felt that their own identity would be affected by such a disaster. Even if the survival of Israel is guaranteed in the future, however, it is possible that as allegiances toward organized local Jewish communities in America weaken, Israel becomes a substitute community to satisfy identity needs. Similar mechanisms may be at work among other ethnic groups who have recently taken an interest in their ancestral countries, for example the Welsh and Armenians, and among those groups whose old countries are involved in internal conflict, for example the Irish, and Greeks and Turks during the Cyprus war of 1973.

Old countries are particularly useful as identity symbols because they are far away and cannot make arduous demands on American ethnics; even sending large amounts of money is ultimately an easy way to help unless the donors are making major economic sacrifices. Moreover, American ethnics can identify with their perception of the old country or homeland, transforming it into a symbol which leaves out its domestic or foreign problems that could become sources of conflict for Americans. For example, most American Jews who support Israel pay little attention to its purely domestic policies; they are concerned with its preservation as a state and a Jewish homeland, and see the country mainly as a Zionist symbol.

The symbolic functions of old countries are facilitated further when interest in them is historical; when ethnics develop an interest in their old countries as they were during or before the time of the ancestral departure. Marcus Hansen's notion of third-generation return was actually based on the emergence of interest in Swedish history, which suggests that the third generation return may itself only be another variety of symbolic ethnicity. Third generations can obviously attend to the past with less emotional risk than first and second generation people who are still trying to escape it, but even so, an interest in ethnic history is a return only chronologically.

Conversely, a new symbol may be appearing among Jews: the Holocaust, which has become a historic example of ethnic group destruction that can now serve as a warning sign for possible future threats. The interest of American Jews in the Holocaust has increased considerably since the end of World War II; when I studied the Jews of Park Forest in 1949–50, it was almost never mentioned, and its memory played no part whatsoever in the creation of a Jewish community there. The lack of attention to the Holocaust at that time may, as Nathan Glazer suggests, reflect the fact that American Jews were busy with creating new Jewish communities in the suburbs.[19] It is also possible that people ignored the Holocaust then because the literature detailing its horrors had not yet been written, although since many second generation American Jews had relatives who died in the Nazi camps, it seems more likely that people repressed thinking about it until it had become a more historical and therefore a less immediately traumatic event. As a result, the Holocaust may now be serving as a new symbol for the threat of group destruction, which is required, on the one hand, by the fact that rising intermarriage rates and the continued decline of interest and participation in Jewish religion are producing real fears about the disappearance of American Jewry altogether; and on the other hand, by the concurrent fact that American anti-semitism is no longer the serious threat to group destruction that it was for first and second generation Jews. Somewhat the same process appears to be taking place among some young Armenians who are now reviving the history of the Turkish massacre of Armenians some sixty years later, at a time when acculturation and assimilation are beginning to make inroads into the Armenian community in America.

I suggested previously that ethnicity per se had become more visible, but many of the symbols used by the third generation are also visible to the rest of America, not only because the middle class people who use them are more visible than their poorer ancestors, but because the national media are more adept at communicating symbols than the ethnic cultures and organizations or earlier generations. The visibility of symbolic ethnicity provides further support for the existence of an ethnic revival, but what appears to be a revival is probably the emergence of a new form of acculturation and assimilation that is taking place under the gaze of the rest of society.

Incidentally, even though the mass media play a major role in enhancing the visibility of ethnicity, and in communicating ethnic symbols, they do not play this role because they are themselves ethnic institutions. True, the mass media, like other entertainment industries, continue to be dominated by Jews (although less so than in the past), but for reasons connected with anti-semitism, or the fear of it, they have generally leaned over backwards to keep Jewish characters and Jewish fare out of their offerings, at least until recently. Even now, a quantitative analysis of major ethnic characters in comedy, drama and other entertainment genres would surely show that Catholic ethnics outnumber Jewish ones. Perhaps the Jews who write or produce so much of the media fare are especially sensitive to ethnic themes and symbols; my own hypothesis, however, is that they are, in this case as in others, simply responding to new cultural tendencies, if only because they must continually innovate. In fact, the arrival of ethnic characters followed the emergence and heightened visibility of ethnic politics in the late 1960s, and the men and women who write the entertainment fare probably took inspiration from news stories they saw on television or read in the papers.

I noted earlier that identity cannot exist apart from a group and that symbols are themselves part of a culture, and in that sense, symbolic ethnicity can be viewed as an indicator of the persistence of ethnic groups and cultures. Symbolic ethnicity, however, does not require functioning groups or networks; feelings of identity can be developed by allegiances to symbolic groups that never meet, or to collectivities that meet only occasionally, and exist as groups only for the handful of officers that keep them going. By the same token, symbolic ethnicity does not need a practiced culture, even if the symbols are borrowed from it. To be sure, symbolic culture is as much culture as practiced culture, but the latter persists only to supply symbols to the former. Indeed, practiced culture may need to persist, for some, because people do not borrow their symbols from extinct cultures that survive only in museums. And insofar as the borrowed materials come from the practiced culture of the immigrant generation, they make it appear as if an ethnic revival were taking place.

Then, too, it should be noted that even symbolic ethnicity may be relevant for only some of the descendants of the immigrants. As intermarriage continues, the number of people with parents from the same secular ethnic group will continue to decline, and by the time the fourth generation of the old immigration reaches adulthood, such people may be a minority. Most Catholic ethnics will be hybrid, and will have difficulty developing an ethnic identity. For example, how would the son of an Italian mother and Irish father who has married a woman of Polish-German ancestry determine his ethnicity, and what would he and his wife tell their children? Even if they were willing, would they be able to do so; and in that case to decide their children's ethnicity, how would they rank or synthesize their diverse backgrounds? These questions are empirical, and urgently need to be studied, but I would suggest that there are only three possibilities. Either the parents choose the single ethnic identity they find most satisfying, or they become what I earlier called pan-ethnics, or they cope with diversity by ignoring it, and raise their children as non-ethnic.

THE EMERGENCE OF SYMBOLIC ETHNICITY

The preceding observations have suggested that symbolic ethnicity is a new phenomenon that comes into being in the third generation, but it is probably of earlier vintage and may have already begun to emerge among the immigrants themselves. After all, many of the participants in the new immigration were oppressed economically, politically and culturally in their old countries, and could not have had much affection even for the village and regions they were leaving. Consequently, it is entirely possible that they began to jettison the old culture and to stay away from ethnic organizations other than churches and unions the moment they came to America, saving only their primary groups, their ties to relatives still left in Europe, and their identity. In small town America, where immigrants were a numerically unimportant minority, the pressure for immediate acculturation and assimilation was much greater than in the cities, but even in the latter, the seeds for symbolic ethnicity may have been sown earlier than previously thought.

Conversely, despite all the pressures toward Americanization and the prejudice and discrimination experienced by the immigrants, they were never faced with conditions that required or encouraged them to give up their ethnicity entirely. Of course, some of the earliest Jewish arrivals to America had become Quakers and Episcopalians before the end of the nineteenth century, but the economic conditions that persuaded the Jamaican Chinese in Kingston to become Creole, and the social isolation that forced Italians in Sydney, Australia, to abolish the traditional familial male-female role segregation shortly after arriving, have never been part of the American experience.[20]

Some conditions for the emergence of symbolic ethnicity were present from the beginning, for American ethnics have always been characterized by freedom of ethnic expression, which stimulated both ethnic diversity, and the right to find one's own way of being ethnic that are crucial to symbolic ethnicity. Although sacred and secular ethnic organizations which insisted that only one mode of being ethnic was legitimate have always existed in America, they have not been able to enforce their norms, in part because they have always had to compete with other ethnic organizations. Even in ethnic neighborhoods where conformity was expected and social control was pervasive, people had some freedom of choice about ethnic cultural practices. For example, the second generation Boston Italians I studied had to conform to many family and peer group norms, but they were free to ignore ethnic secondary groups, and to drop or alter Italian cultural practices according to their own preference.

Ethnic diversity within the group was probably encouraged by the absence of a state religion, and national and local heads of ethnic communities. For example, American Jewry never had a chief rabbi, or even chief Orthodox, Conservative and Reform rabbis, and the European practice of local Jewish communities electing or appointing local laymen as presidents was not carried across the ocean.[21] Catholic ethnics had to obey the cardinal or bishop heading their diocese, of course, but in those communities where the diocese insisted on an Irish church, the other ethnic groups, notably the Italians, kept their distance from the church, and only in parochial schools was there any attempt to root out secular ethnic patterns. The absence of strong unifying institutions thus created the opportunity for diversity and freedom from the beginning, and undoubtedly facilitated the departure from ethnic cultures and organizations.

Among the Jews, symbolic ethnicity may have been fostered early by self-selection among Jewish emigrants. As Liebman points out, the massive Eastern European immigration to America did not include the rabbis and scholars who practiced what he called an elite religion in the old countries; as a result, the immigrants established what he calls a folk religion in America instead, with indigenous rabbis who were elected or appointed by individual congregations, and were more permissive in allowing, or too weak to prevent, deviations from religious orthodoxy, even of the milder folk variety.[22] Indeed, the development of a folk religion may have encouraged religious and secular diversity among Jews from the very beginning.

Still, perhaps the most important factor in the development of symbolic ethnicity was probably the awareness, which I think many second generation people had already reached, that neither the practice of ethnic culture nor participation in ethnic organizations was essential to being and feeling ethnic. For Jews, living in a Jewish neighborhood or working with Jews every day was enough to maintain Jewish identity. When younger second generation Jews moved to suburbia in large numbers after World War II, many wound up in communities in which they were a small numerical minority, but they quickly established an informal Jewish community of neighborly relations, and then built synagogues and community centers to formalize and supplement the informal community. At the time, many observers interpreted the feverish building as a religious revival, but for most Jews, the synagogue was a symbol that could serve as a means of expressing identity without requiring more than occasional participation in its activities.[23] Thus, my

observations among the second generation Jews of Park Forest and other suburbs led me to think as far back as the mid 1950s that among Jews, at least, the shift to symbolic ethnicity was already under way.[24]

THE FUTURE OF ETHNICITY

The emergence of symbolic ethnicity naturally raises the question of its persistence into the fifth and sixth generations. Although the Catholic and Jewish religions are certain to endure, it appears that as religion becomes less important to people, they, too will be eroded by acculturation and assimilation. Even now, synagogues see most of their worshipers no more than once or twice a year, and presumably, the same trend will appear, perhaps more slowly, among Catholics and Protestants as well.

Whether the secular aspects of ethnicity can survive beyond the fourth generation is somewhat less certain. One possibility is that symbolic ethnicity will itself decline as acculturation and assimilation continue, and then disappear as erstwhile ethnics forget their secular ethnic identity to blend into one or another subcultural melting pot. The other possibility is that symbolic ethnicity is a steady-state phenomenon that can persist into the fifth and sixth generations.

Obviously, this question can only be guessed at, but my hypothesis is that symbolic ethnicity may persist. The continued existence of Germans, Scandinavians, and Irish after five or more generations in America suggests that in the larger cities and suburbs, at least, they have remained ethnic because they have long practiced symbolic ethnicity.[25] Consequently, there is good reason to believe that the same process will also take place among ethnics of the new immigration.

Ethnic behavior, attitudes, and even identity are, however, determined not only by what goes on among the ethnics, but also by developments in the larger society, and especially by how that society will treat ethnics in the future; what costs it will levy and what benefits it will award to them as ethnics. At present, the costs of being and feeling ethnic are slight. The changes which the immigrants and their descendants wrought in America now make it unnecessary for ethnics to surrender their ethnicity to gain upward mobility, and today ethnics are admitted virtually everywhere, provided they meet economic and status requirements, except at the very highest levels of the economic, political, and cultural hierarchies. Moreover, since World War II, the ethnics have been able to shoulder blacks and other racial minorities with the deviant and scapegoat functions they performed in an earlier America, so that ethnic prejudice and "institutional ethnism" are no longer significant, except again at the very top of the societal hierarchies.

To be sure, some ethnic scapegoating persists at other levels of these hierarchies; American Catholics are still blamed for the policies of the Vatican, Italo-Americans are criticized for the Mafia, and urban ethnics generally have been portrayed as racists by a sometime coalition of white and black Protestant, Jewish, and other upper-middle class cosmopolitans. But none of these phenomena, however repugnant, strike me as serious enough to persuade many to hide their ethnicity. More important but less often noticed, white working class men, and perhaps others, still use ethnic stereotypes to trade insults, but this practice serves functions other than the maintenance of prejudice or inequality.

At the same time, the larger society also seems to offer some benefits for being ethnic. Americans increasingly perceive themselves as undergoing cultural homogenization, and whether or not this perception is justified, they are constantly looking for new ways to establish their differences from each other. Meanwhile, the social, cultural and political turbulence of the last decade, and the concurrent delegitimation of many American institutions have also cast doubt on some of the other ways by which people identify themselves and differentiate themselves from each other. Ethnicity, now that it is respectable and no longer a major cause of conflict, seems therefore to be ideally suited to serve as a distinguishing characteristic. Moreover, in a mobile society, people who move around and therefore find themselves living in communities of strangers, tend to look for commonalties that make strangers into neighbors, and shared ethnicity may provide mobile people with at least an initial excuse to get together. Finally, as long as the European immigration into America continues, people will still be perceived, classified, and ranked at least in part by ethnic origin. Consequently, external forces exist to complement internal identity needs, and

unless there is a drastic change in the allocation of costs and benefits with respect to ethnicity, it seems likely that the larger society will also encourage the persistence of symbolic ethnicity.

Needless to say, it is always possible that future economic and political conditions in American society will create a demand for new scapegoats, and if ethnics are forced into this role, so that ethnicity once more levies social costs, present tendencies will be interrupted. Under such conditions, some ethnics will try to assimilate faster and pass out of all ethnic roles, while others will revitalize the ethnic group socially and culturally if only for self-protection. Still, the chance that Catholic ethnics will be scapegoated more than today seems very slight. A serious economic crisis could, however, result in a resurgence of anti-semitism, in part because of the affluence of many American Jews, in part because of their visibly influential role in some occupations, notably mass communications.

If present societal trends continue, however, symbolic ethnicity should become the dominant way of being ethnic by the time the fourth generation of the new immigration matures into adulthood, and this in turn will have consequences for the structure of American ethnic groups. For one thing, as secondary and primary assimilation continue, and ethnic networks weaken and unravel, it may be more accurate to speak of ethnic aggregates rather than groups. More important, since symbolic ethnicity does not depend on ethnic cultures and organizations, their future decline and disappearance must be expected, particularly those cultural patterns which interfere with other aspects of life, and those organizations which require active membership.

Few such patterns and organizations are left in any case, and leaders of the remaining organizations have long been complaining bitterly over what they perceive as the cultural and organizational apathy of ethnics. They also criticize the resort to symbolic ethnicity, identifying it as an effortless way of being ethnic which further threatens their own persistence. Even so, attacking people as apathetic or lazy, or calling on them to revive the practices and loyalties of the past have never been effective for engendering support, and reflect instead the desperation of organizations which cannot offer new incentives that would enable them to recruit members.

Some cultural patterns and organizations will survive. Patterns which lend themselves to transformation into symbols and easy practice, such as annual holidays, should persist. So will organizations which create and distribute symbols, or "ethnic goods" such as foodstuffs or written materials, but need few or no members and can function with small staffs and low overheads. In all likelihood, most ethnic organizations will eventually realize that in order to survive, they must deal mainly in symbols, using them to generate enough support to fund other activities as well.

The demand for current ethnic symbols may require the maintenance of at least some old cultural practices, possibly in museums, and through the work of ethnic scholars who keep old practices alive by studying them. It is even possible that the organizations which attempt to maintain the old cultures will support themselves in part by supplying ethnic nostalgia, and some ethnics may aid such organizations if only to assuage their guilt at having given up ancestral practices.

Still, the history of religion and nationalism, as well as events of recent years, should remind us that the social process sometimes moves in dialectical ways, and that acculturative and assimilative actions by a majority occasionally generate revivalistic reactions by a minority. As a result, even ethnic aggregates in which the vast majority maintains its identity in symbolic ways will probably always bring forth small pockets of neotraditionalism—of rebel converts to sacred and secular ways of the past. They may not influence the behavior of the majority, but they are almost always highly visible, and will thus continue to play a role in the ethnicity of the future.

SYMBOLIC ETHNICITY
AND STRAIGHT-LINE THEORY

The third and fourth generation's concern with ethnic identity and its expression through symbols seem to me to fit straight-line theory, for symbolic ethnicity cannot be considered as evidence either of a third generation return or a revival. Instead, it constitutes only another point in the secular trend that is drawn, implicitly, in straight-line theory, although it could also be a point at which the declining secular trend begins to level off and perhaps straightens out.

In reality, of course, the straight-line has never been quite straight, for even if it accurately graphs the dominant ethnic experience, it ignores the ethnic groups who still continue to make tiny small bumps and waves in the line. Among these are various urban and rural ethnic enclaves, notably among the poor; the new European immigrants who help to keep these enclaves from disappearing; the groups which successfully insulate themselves from the rest of American society in deliberately-enclosed enclaves; and the rebel converts to sacred and secular ways of the past who will presumably continue to appear.

Finally, even if I am right to predict that symbolic ethnicity can persist into the fifth and sixth generations, I would be foolish to suggest that it is a permanent phenomenon. Although all Americans, save the Indians, came here as immigrants and are thus in one sense ethnics, people who arrived in the seventeenth and eighteenth centuries, and before the mid-nineteenth century "old" immigration, are, except in some rural enclaves, no longer ethnics even if they know where their emigrant ancestors came from.

The history of groups whose ancestors arrived here seven or more generations ago suggests that eventually, the ethnics of the new immigration will be like them; they may retain American forms of the religions which their ancestors brought to America, but their secular cultures will be only a dim memory, and their identity will bear only the minutest trace, if that, of their national origin. Ultimately, then, the secular trend of straight-line theory will hit very close to zero, and the basic postulates of the theory will turn out to have been accurate—unless of course by then America, and the ways it makes Americans, has altered drastically in some now unpredictable manner.

ENDNOTES

1. Personal communication. Incidentally, David Riesman is now credited with having invented the term ethnicity as it is currently used. (Hereafter, I shall omit personal communication footnotes, but most of the individuals named in the text supplied ideas or data through personal communication.)
2. For reasons of brevity, I employ these terms rather than Gordon's more detailed concepts. Milton Gordon, *Assimilation in American Life,* New York, Oxford University Press, 1964, Chapter 3.

3. Neil C. Sandberg, *Ethnic Identity and Assimilation: The Polish-American Community,* New York, Praeger, 1974. The primary empirical application of straight-line theory is probably still W. Lloyd Warner and Leo Srole, *The Social Systems of American Ethnic Groups,* New Haven, Yale University Press, 1945.

4. See e.g., Andrew Greeley, *Ethnicity in the United States,* New York, Wiley, 1974, Chapter 1.

5. W. Yancey, E. Ericksen and R. Juliani, "Emergent Ethnicity: A Review and Reformulation," *American Sociological Review,* Vol. 41, June 1976, pp. 391–403, quote at p. 400.

6. The major works include Greeley, op. cit.; Harold J. Abramson, *Ethnic Diversity in Catholic America,* New York, Wiley, 1973; and Nathan Glazer and Daniel P. Moynihan, *Beyond the Melting Pot,* Cambridge, MIT Press, 2nd ed., 1970.

7. Class differences in the degree of acculturation and assimilation were first noted by Warner and Srole, op. cit.; for some recent data among Poles, see Sandberg, op. cit.

8. Herbert J. Gans, *The Urban Villagers,* New York, Free Press, 1962, chap. 11. See also Dennis Wrong, "How Important is Social Class," in Irving Howe, ed., *The World of the Blue Collar Worker,* New York, Quadrangle, 1972, pp. 297–309: William Kornblum, *Blue Collar Community,* Chicago, University of Chicago,Press, 1974; and Stephen Steinberg, *The Academic Melting Pot,* New Brunswick, Transaction Books, 1977.

9. Marcus L. Hansen, *The Problems of the Third Generation Immigrant,* Rock Island, Ill., Augustana Historical Society, 1938; and the "Third Generation in America," *Commentary,* Vol. 14, November 1952, pp. 492–500.

10. See also Harold J. Abramson, "The Religioethnic Factor and the American Experience: Another Look at the Three-Generations Hypothesis," *Ethnicity,* Vol. 2, June 1975, pp. 163–177.

11. One of the most influential works has been Michael Novak, *The Rise of the Unmeltable Ethnics,* New York, Macmillan, 1971.

12. Perhaps the first, and now not sufficiently remembered, study of third-generation Jews was Judith Kramer and Seymour Leventman, *The Children of the Gilded Ghetto,* New Haven, Yale University Press, 1961.

13. Geoffrey Bock, "The Jewish Schooling of American Jews," unpublished Ph.D. Dissertation, Graduate School of Education, Harvard University, 1976.

14. The notion of primary assimilation extends Gordon's concept of marital assimilation to include movement out of the extended family, friendship circles and other peer groups. In describing marital assimilation, Gordon did, however, mention the primary group as well. Gordon, op. cit., p. 80.

15. The major debate at present is between Abramson and Alba, the former viewing the amount of intermarriage among Catholic ethnics as low, and the latter as high. See Abramson, "Ethnic Diversity in Catholic America," op. cit.; and Richard Alba, "Social Assimilation of American Catholic National-Origin Groups," *American Sociological Review,* Vol. 41, December 1976, pp. 1030–1046.

16. See e.g., Marshall Sklare and Joseph Greenblum, *Jewish Identity on the Suburban Frontier,* New York, Basic Books, 1967; Herbert J. Gans, "The Origin and Growth of a Jewish Community in the Suburbs: A Study of the Jews of Park Forest," in Marshall Sklare, ed., *The Jews: Social Pattern of an American Group,* New York, Free Press, 1958, pp. 205–248, and Herbert J. Gans, *The Levittowners,* New York, Pantheon, 1967, pp. 73–80. These findings may not apply to communities with significant numbers of German Jews with Reform leanings. There are few Orthodox Jews in the suburbs, except in those surrounding New York.

17. Sandberg, op. cit. and James Crispino, *The Assimilation of Ethnic Groups. The Italian Case,* New York, Center for Migration Studies, 1979.

18. My use of the word symbol here follows Lloyd Warner's concept of symbolic behavior. See W. Lloyd Warner, *American Life: Dream and Reality,* Chicago, University of Chicago Press, 1953, Chapter 1.

19. See Nathan Glazer, *American Judaism,* Chicago, University of Chicago Press, 2nd ed. 1972, pp. 114–115.

20. On the Jamaica Chinese, see Orlando Patterson, *Ethnic Chauvinism,* New York, Stein and Day, 1977, Chapter 5; on the Sydney Italians, see Rina Huber, *From Pasta to Pavlova,* St. Lucia, University of Queensland Press, 1977, Part 3.

21. For a study of one unsuccessful attempt to establish a community presidency, see Arthur A. Goren, *New York Jews and the Quest for Community,* New York, Columbia University Press, 1970.

22. Charles S. Liebman, *The Ambivalent American Jew,* Philadelphia, Jewish Publication Society of America, 1973, Chapter 3. Liebman notes that the few elite rabbis who did come to America quickly sensed they were in alien territory and returned to Eastern Europe. The survivors of the Holocaust who came to America after World War II were too few and too late to do more than influence the remaining Jewish orthodox organizations.

23. Gans, "The Origin of a Jewish Community in the Suburbs," op. cit.

24. See Herbert J. Gans, "American Jewry: Present and Future," *Commentary,* Vol. 21, May 1956, pp. 422–430, which includes a discussion of "symbolic Judaism."

25. Unfortunately, too little attention has been devoted by sociologists to ethnicity among descendants of the old immigration.

Race and Ethnicity in the United States at Century's End

4

In a grandiloquent essay published in February 1941—ten months before the Japanese attack on Pearl Harbor—Henry Luce, head of the Time-Life publishing empire, provided one of the most provocative, enduring, and widely quoted characterizations of American society in the twentieth century: "The twentieth century is the American Century." Luce celebrated the rise of the United States to a position of economic, political, cultural, and military dominance in world affairs, but he also idealistically perceived America as the "sanctuary of the ideals of civilization" and called upon Americans to "spread throughout the world . . . the ideals of Freedom and Justice . . . [with] joy and gladness and vigor and enthusiasm" (Luce 1941:65).

However, as we near the end of the "American Century," the prescient words of W. E. B. DuBois, uttered at the beginning of the century, provide a different, but equally appropriate, epitaph: "The problem of the twentieth century is the problem of the color line—the relation of the darker to the lighter races of men in Asia and Africa, in America, and the islands of the sea" (DuBois 1903/1986:372). In the materials considered throughout this book, we have noted the changes that have occurred in the dynamics of race and ethnicity in American life throughout its history. Although the dynamics of the "problem of the color line" have changed dramatically throughout the course of the twentieth century, it remains perhaps the critical issue in defining the American people during that century. As Thomas and Mary Edsall have written, "When the official subject is presidential politics, taxes, welfare, crime, rights, or values . . . , the real subject is race" (Edsall and Edsall 1991:53).

In the last quarter century especially, the racial and ethnic composition of the United States has been altered significantly. Today the United States is characterized by a greater diversity of peoples and cultures than ever before. In 1960 African Americans, Asians, Hispanics, and American Indians represented less than one-sixth (15.2 percent) of the American population; by 1998 that figure had increased to more than one-fourth (28.5 percent), the highest proportion of non-Europeans in the country since it became an independent nation in the late eighteenth century. The increases were especially pronounced among the Asian and Hispanic populations, which grew by 825 percent and 325 percent, respectively, between 1960 and 1990. Census Bureau projections estimate that, if current trends in birth and immigration rates continue, by the middle of the twenty-first century, Hispanics and Asians together will comprise one-third (32 percent) of the total population and non-Hispanic whites will represent only a slight majority (53 percent) (Day 1993). As a consequence of these trends, *Time* magazine (1993) recently pronounced the United States "the world's first multicultural society," and Edward Luttwak has derisively talked of the "third-worldization of America" (Luttwak 1992).

Therefore, it is probable that issues of race and ethnicity, rather than diminishing in intensity, will assume even greater significance in American society in the twenty-first century. By the year 2000, one-third of all school-age children will be either African American, Hispanic, Asian, or American Indian (American Council on Education 1988). Furthermore, in some states (such as California), the majority of working-age adults will be members of these minorities (California Assembly Office of Research 1986). Therefore, in the very near future, "minority" peoples will affect the nation's prosperity more substantially than ever before in American history. All Americans, especially those who will be economically dependent on the productivity of the working-age population, will be directly affected by the manner in which racial and ethnic inequalities in American life are addressed.

This section will focus on several recent trends in American majority-minority relations: the impact of recent demographic changes, including the changing nature of immigration to the United States; the implications of the surge of interest in ethnicity and ethnic pluralism among European Americans; and the changing status of African Americans.

Demographic Changes in the Last Quarter of the Twentieth Century

In order to comprehend the dynamics of racial and ethnic relations during the past quarter century (and to anticipate the future), it is useful to examine briefly some of the demographic changes that have occurred during that time. See Table 1 in Part 2 (p. 88) for the basic data for several broad racial and ethnic categories.

As indicated in Part 2, African Americans, the nation's largest racial minority, today total more than 34 million, or more than the entire population of Canada or of Sweden, Denmark, Norway, Finland, and Iceland combined. As in 1990, African Americans continue to live overwhelmingly in urban areas, especially in the nation's largest cities. Today New York City has a black population of more than two million, more than any other city in the world (except Kinshasa, Democratic Republic of the Congo [formerly Zaire]) and more than any state (besides New York state) in the country. Chicago has more African Americans than Mississippi or South Carolina; and Philadelphia has about the same number as Arkansas and Kentucky combined. Throughout the 1980s and 1990s, blacks continued to be more likely than whites to live in urban areas, especially in central cities. However, during this period, for the first time in this century, the proportion of blacks living in the South increased, growing from 52 percent in 1980 to 55 percent in 1994 (Bennett 1995:35).

Since 1970, the Hispanic population has more than tripled, increasing from 9 million in 1970 to nearly 30 million in 1998. This increase is greater both proportionately and numerically than that of the African American population, which grew by 13 percent. In 1996 California had the greatest number of Hispanics—about ten million, or about 37 percent of the nation's total. Texas and New York together accounted for a nearly comparable number, thus bringing the Hispanic populations in these three states alone to nearly two-thirds (65 percent) of the Hispanics in the country overall. The Los Angeles metropolitan area contained the largest number of Hispanics (6.3 million), more than double the number in the metropolitan area with the next largest number—New York, with slightly over 3 million (National Association of Hispanic Publications 1995). Nevertheless, reflecting New York's historic role as the nation's— indeed the world's—most ethnically diverse city, in 1990 over 60 percent of its population was either Hispanic, African American, Asian American, or American Indian, and more than one-quarter (27 percent) of households of European ancestry were headed by immigrants (Halbfinger 1997).

Among the most striking demographic changes in the composition of the American people since 1970 has been the growth of the Asian population, which increased more than sixfold between 1970 and 1998. Like the dramatic growth among Hispanics, the increase in the Asian population has resulted primarily from substantial increases in immigration from Asian nations since the late 1960s. We will consider these increases more fully below. During the 1980s, the overall Asian population increased by 70 percent, with the most dramatic increases occurring among Koreans, Filipinos, Chinese, and Indochinese. By 1980 Chinese and Filipinos had both surpassed in number the Japanese, who until 1980 had been the largest Asian national group. Regionally, Asians were concentrated in the West, especially in California, which had more Chinese, Japanese, Filipinos, Koreans, and Vietnamese than any other state.

Contemporary Immigration and the Changing Face of America

When Henry Luce annointed the twentieth century as "The American Century" in 1941, he certainly was not thinking about the racial and ethnic diversity of the American people—indeed, he appears to have been oblivious to it. Thus, it is more than a little ironic that the two largest and most ethnically diverse waves of immigration in American history—or in the history of *any* nation, for that matter—took place at the beginning and at the end of The American Century, thus reflecting how crucial the notion of multiculturalism is to the very definition of what it means to be American.

In "The New Immigration and Ethnicity in the United States" (Article 23) Douglas Massey has divided The American Century into three distinct, albeit arbitrary, periods that roughly coincide with significant changes in American immigration policy. In Part 2 we considered the impact of the first of these periods—the era of massive European immigration that ended with restrictionist legislation enacted in the

1920s. During that era, Massey points out, the United States "became less black, more white, and more firmly European in culture and outlook." In this section we will examine the impact on American society and culture of the other two periods—the hiatus in immigration between 1930 and 1970, and the resumption of large-scale, primarily non-European immigration since 1970, both of which, in different ways, have affected patterns of racial and ethnic relations in contemporary American life.

The impact of the recent period has been most immediately visible; patterns of immigration into the United States have been radically transformed. This new immigrant wave promises to produce even more dramatic and far-reaching changes in the ethnic composition of the United States than the massive influx of southern and eastern European immigrants in the late nineteenth and early twentieth centuries. First, since the late 1960s, the number of immigrants to the United States has increased substantially. During the 1990s the number of immigrants admitted has averaged over one million annually, compared with 282,000 in the decade before 1965. In 1991 alone, more than 1.8 million immigrants were admitted, the greatest annual number in American history. Moreover, experts estimate that there is an annual net increase of about 275,000 illegal immigrants (Espenshade 1995; Martin and Midgley 1994).

The changes in the national origins of today's immigrants are as dramatic as their increasing numbers. Until the late 1960s immigration to the United States was overwhelmingly European, ranging from a high of 96 percent of all immigrants for the decade 1891–1900 to 53 percent for the decade 1950–1960. Today, as a result of changes in U.S. immigration laws, only a small percentage of immigrants come from Europe (see Table 1).

Today the predominant sources of immigration are Third World nations in Central and South America, the Caribbean, and Asia. As Table 2 indicates, in 1995 only *one* of the ten leading countries—Ukraine—from which the United States received immigrants was European; there were more immigrants from Ghana than from France, more from Bangladesh than from Ireland, more from Guatemala than from Italy, more from Bolivia than from Sweden, more from Ethiopia than from Germany, and more from Korea than from the United Kingdom (U.S. Immigration and Naturalization Service 1997:23, 52–53). The impact of these trends has been to create a genuinely multiracial, multicultural society—what Wattenberg has characterized as the "first universal nation" (Wattenberg 1991).

TABLE 1 *Immigrants from Europe as Percent of Total*

Years	Percentage
1941–1950	60%
1951–1960	53
1961–1970	34
1971–1980	18
1981–1990	10
1991–1996	14

Source: U.S. Immigration and Naturalization Service. *Statistical Yearbook of the Immigration and Naturalization Service 1995.* Washington, D.C.: U.S. Government Printing Service, 1997.

TABLE 2   *Immigrants Admitted to the United States from Top Ten Countries of Birth, 1995*

Country	Number
Mexico	89,932
Philippines	50,984
Vietnam	42,752
Dominican Republic	38,512
China	35,463
India	34,748
Cuba	17,937
Ukraine	17,432
Jamaica	16,398
Korea	16,047

Source: U.S. Immigration and Naturalization Service. *Statistical Yearbook of the Immigration and Naturalization Service, 1995.* U.S. Government Printing Office: Washington, D.C., 1997, p. 23.

When Americans think of immigrants, they often have an image of "huddled masses" who are poor, unskilled, and uneducated. Such a perception does not accurately characterize the recent wave of immigration, which is extremely complex in its composition. Changes in U.S. immigration laws since 1965 have affected the occupational and educational composition of the present immigrant population. Today the range of immigrants' occupations much more closely resembles that of the native population at the turn of the twentieth century.

On the one hand, whereas a substantial proportion of immigrants to the United States during the first two decades of the twentieth century were unskilled blue-collar workers, post–1965 immigration laws have established preferences for immigrants with skills needed in the United States. Physicians, nurses, scientists, architects, artists, entertainers, engineers, and others with highly technical skills have contributed to a "brain drain," first from Europe and later from Third World nations, and to the profile of contemporary immigrants as relatively highly educated and technically skilled. For example, the overall educational level of the foreign-born in the United States is similar to that of the native-born. The proportions of foreign-born and native who have completed college are virtually identical: in 1996, 23.6 percent of native-born U.S. adults aged twenty-five and over were college graduates, compared with 23.5 percent of foreign-born persons (Hansen and Faber 1997:4). Immigrants from Africa and Asia are especially well educated; in 1990, almost half (47 percent) of African and more than one-third (38) percent of Asian immigrants had completed college (Portes and Rumbaut 1996:61).

On the other hand, because the overwhelming majority of recent immigrants entered the United States under preferences for family reunification, a substantial proportion are also unskilled, poor, and relatively uneducated. Indeed, although immigrants are disproportionately represented among the nation's most highly educated people, they are also more likely than native-born Americans to be among the most poorly educated: in 1996 the proportion of the foreign-born who had not graduated from high school was double the proportion of natives (36 percent compared with 18 percent) (Hansen and Faber 1997). Immigrants are also more likely than natives to be poor and to be recipients of public assistance (Hansen and Faber 1997; Portes and Rumbaut 1996:78). Moreover, Borjas has argued that over the past two decades, overall immigrant skill levels have actually declined (Borjas 1994).

The preferences for immigrants with skills has meant that, unlike the situation for most of American history prior to 1965, it has become almost impossible for unskilled workers to enter the United States legally unless they can claim a close family relationship or a refugee status. As a consequence, less skilled workers, as well as skilled immigrants, such as students and tourists who overstay their visas, have increasingly resorted to entering the country illegally. In each year during the 1990s, more than a million illegal immigrants—from over one hundred countries—were apprehended, the vast majority from Latin America, especially Mexico (U.S. Immigration and Naturalization Service 1997:161–167). Although, as noted earlier, the annual net increase of illegal immigrants permanently living in the United States is lower than that from legal immigration, estimates of the total number of undocumented aliens range around 5 million (U.S. Immigration and Naturalization Service 1997:183; Espenshade 1995:201).

In a recent book, *Alien Nation,* Peter Brimelow, himself an immigrant to the United States, characterized American immigration policy—primarily the historic changes wrought by the 1965 Immigration Act—as a "disaster." Recent immigration, he wrote, has been "so huge and so systematically different from anything that had gone on before as to transform—and ultimately, perhaps even to destroy—the . . . American nation" (Brimelow 1995). Fears of an immigrant invasion that will destroy America have been voiced frequently throughout American history, especially during periods of heavy immigration and economic stagnation, often by previous immigrants or their immediate descendants.

Such sentiments have emerged again during the past quarter century. Until 1964, with the end of the Bracero Program, which enabled Mexican agricultural workers to enter the United States as temporary workers under legal contracts that provided a source of cheap labor for agricultural interests in the Southwest, illegal immigration was relatively low and was confined primarily to the rural Southwest. However, beginning in the late 1960s, the number of illegal immigrants apprehended increased dramatically, from 110,000 in 1965 to 250,000 in 1970 to 1.8 million in 1986 (U.S. Bureau of the Census 1997:164). Although Mexicans comprised the largest category of undocumented aliens, beginning in the 1960s, these illegal aliens were drawn increasingly from nations throughout the Caribbean, Latin America, and Asia as well. The growth of a large, urban illegal population dominated immigration politics during the 1970s and early 1980s. This rise in the apprehensions of illegal aliens, reinforced by sensational media coverage, contributed to growing fears that the United States was being threatened by a "silent invasion" of foreigners whose presence threatened to undermine the quality of American life. As the number of apprehensions increased, so did political pressures for the United States to curtail their numbers.

Responding to these pressures, in 1986 Congress enacted the Immigration Reform and Control Act (IRCA), which was concerned primarily with illegal immigration, but left legal immigration substantially intact. Enactment of IRCA represented a compromise among a disparate group of political interests, as well as the culmination of years of intense debate over the perceived threat of illegal immigration to American institutions. The term *control* in the bill's title was appropriate, for IRCA was designed to enable the United States once again to "take control of its borders."

IRCA prohibited the employment of illegal immigrants and required that employers verify—through documents such as Social Security cards, birth certificates, drivers' licenses, and passports—that new employees were either U.S. citizens or aliens legally authorized to work. Because *all* new employees are required to verify their citizenship or immigration status under the law, it has directly affected more Americans than any other piece of immigration legislation in American history. To enforce its provisions, IRCA established fines and jail terms for employers who knowingly hired illegal aliens. However, employers were not responsible for verifying the authenticity of the documents, but only to have in good faith determined that they were valid.

During the lengthy debate over IRCA between 1982 and 1986, one of the most frequent objections to employer sanctions was that citizens or resident aliens, especially Hispanics, who "appeared foreign" to employers would encounter discrimination. Consequently, strong antidiscrimination provisions were included in the bill; however, President Ronald Reagan's statements on signing the bill that in essence discouraged individuals from filing discrimination claims, diminished the force of these provisions.

On the other hand, IRCA provided amnesty—a grant of permanent legal residence—for illegal aliens who could prove that they had lived continuously in the United States since before 1982. It also included provisions for an agricultural guest-worker program that was intended to relieve shortages of agricultural—primarily migrant—labor.

The most controversial provision of IRCA was the offer of amnesty—legal status —to illegal aliens who had lived in the United State continuously since before January 1, 1982. Three million applications were filed, and those who did so had to undertake several additional steps to obtain permanent residency; in addition to proving that they had lived in the United States continuously since before 1982, they had to have no serious police record, prove financial responsibility, and demonstrate a knowledge of English and of American history. The impact of the IRCA on the volume of American immigration became apparent in 1989, when nearly half-a-million resident aliens were amnestied. By 1991 the number granted amnesty through the IRCA provisions exceeded one million, making the total number of immigrants admitted in that year—1.8 million—the highest for any year in American history.

Four years later, in 1990, Congress once again amended American immigration policy, increasing the numbers of immigrants admitted annually from 500,000 to 700,000. It also eliminated most of the social and political restrictions (against Communists and homosexuals, for example) adopted during the McCarthy era of the 1950s. Finally, while it retained the priority on the reunification of immediate family members, it substantially increased opportunities for highly skilled workers—scientists, artists, athletes, inventors, and professionals—as well as entrepreneurs willing to invest in businesses in the United States.

As was the case early in the twentieth century, the increasing number and variety of immigrants have created a sense of alarm among many native-born Americans that these immigrants will have a negative impact on American society, dramatically increasing population growth, draining economic resources, taking jobs from American citizens, and transforming (and for some undermining) American culture and social institutions. Immigration restrictionist sentiments have historically increased during and been aggravated by periods of economic recession and anxiety, and this relationship has recently been apparent in California, where immigrants account for nearly one-quarter (24.8 percent) of the population. In 1994, during a recession greatly influenced by substantial reductions in military spending, Californians overwhelmingly supported Proposition 187, a ballot referendum that denies state-supported health and educational services to illegal immigrants and their children.

The success of California's Proposition 187 galvanized restrictionist advocates throughout the country to demand that the United States "take control of its borders." In response, the Clinton Administration has devoted more money and political attention to immigration than any other recent administration has; it increased the Border Patrol budget, and Border Patrol agents substantially expanded enforcement of existing immigration law, particularly in their efforts to reduce border crossings of undocumented aliens from Mexico (Schmitt 1996:A1). In addition, in 1996 Congress passed new legislation directed primarily at illegal immigration, by increasing the number of Border Patrol agents, providing much more sophisticated technology with which to apprehend illegal immigrants, and authorizing enhanced barriers along the Southwest border. The law also called for new efforts to reduce the employment of unauthorized workers by establishing more effective means of verifying worker eligibility, and it substantially curtailed opportunities for people to claim asylum or refugee status. Finally, the law placed substantial restrictions on benefits for noncitizens (such as denying them Social Security or requiring foreign students attending American high schools to pay tuition). When coupled with the 1996 Welfare Reform Bill, which permitted states to deny welfare and Medicaid to *legal* immigrants, the effects were especially disastrous for elderly and disabled people. Because many legal immigrants stood to lose welfare benefits that they had worked years to establish, one of the consequences of these policies has been a dramatic increase in applications from legal immigrants for citizenship (Dugger 1997:A1).

One of the most bitterly contested and long-standing issues in the debate over immigration deals with the impact of immigrants on the domestic economy: do immigrants contribute to economic growth and income, or are they a drain on the country's economic resources generally and on native employment and earnings in particular? Among the voluminous studies on the economic impact of immigration, it is possible to find support for practically any position. However, the most recent report on the subject, a comprehensive five-hundred-page study released by the National Academy of Sciences, concluded that immigrants contribute substantial overall benefits—as much as $10 billion yearly—to the U.S. economy. However, the economic impact of immigration was not uniform; its effects were felt differently at the federal, state, and local levels. Because a substantial portion of the taxes that immigrants pay go to the federal government, immigration provided a boost to the national economy. But because state and local governments have fewer tax resources and are more likely to bear the costs (health, education, and so forth) of immigrants, they have "a negative fiscal impact at the state and local level" (Smith and Edmonston, 1997). Moreover, because immigrants are geographically concentrated in a small number of states, these costs and benefits are not felt uniformly throughout the United States; in several states, such as California, where immigrants are geographically concentrated, the tax burden to the state may be greater than the benefit from the jobs that immigrants create and the state taxes that they pay. In addition, the study found that although the overall impact of immigrants was positive, some categories of native (and earlier immigrant) workers—primarily low-skilled—were hurt by competition from immigrant labor (Smith and Edmonston 1997; Pear 1997:1; McDonnell 1997).

In addition to skilled immigrants and those being reunited with their families, since 1965 the number of immigrants entering the United States claiming refugee and asylum status has increased dramatically. Determining who can enter the country as a refugee is essentially a political judgment that is made by the federal government. Given that under the government's definition, there are an estimated 18.5 million political and economic refugees in the world today, the moral and political pressures to admit refugees are considerable. Although refugees from more than one hundred different nations have been admitted, official government policy has given special treatment to those fleeing Communism, and the vast majority of refugees to enter the United States during the 1970s and 1980s were from Cuba and Vietnam. By 1988 nearly one million Cubans and more than 500,000 Vietnamese had been admitted—both groups coming from nations where American-supported governments had been supplanted by Communist regimes. But the refugee quotas established under the 1965 law and its subsequent revisions proved inadequate to respond either to the global refugee pressures or to the specific pressures represented by groups such as the Cubans and the Vietnamese. In some instances, such as the Vietnamese, special laws were passed to enable the president to respond to emergency situations. In others, such as the case of the Cuban "Freedom Flotilla" in 1980, the political power of the Cuban American community and the propaganda value of thousands fleeing Fidel Castro's regime permitted a de facto circumvention of the law.

However, as indicated by the cases of the Haitians and the Salvadoreans, whose plight was less widely publicized, the admission of refugees for political reasons did not apply to non-Communist regimes, even those that were equally oppressive. Thus in 1984 the Reagan administration planned to offer legal status and citizenship opportunities to more than 100,000 Cubans who entered the United States during the Freedom Flotilla but failed to extend the same privileges to 7,200 Haitian refugees who had fled their nation in small boats at approximately the same time (Pear 1984:1). There was no similar groundswell of support for those fleeing government-sponsored terror in El Salvador, nor for the Haitians seeking to escape the nation's poverty and its political repression.

Sources of Migration Pressures

The growing influx of immigration to the United States in the past quarter century has been affected not only by American immigration laws, but more significantly by broader changes in the global economy. It has become increasingly apparent that American racial and ethnic relations and the adaptation of different ethnic groups to American society must be conceptualized from within the framework of a rapidly changing global economy and of the modes of incorporation of different nations and regions within it. As Saskia Sassen (Article 24), Roger Rouse (Article 26), and numerous other writers (e.g., Massey [1981a], Portes [1979], Piore [1979]) suggest, the dynamics of American immigration reflect the emergence of a broader international pattern of migration between low- and high-income countries that started in the 1960s. This pattern has contributed to the rise in legal immigration to the United States, but it has had a particular impact on illegal immigration, especially from Mexico and the Caribbean.

Conceptualizing the dynamics of contemporary immigration to the United States within a framework of globalization raises questions about the appropriateness of comparisons with previous migration waves. Traditionally, historians and social scientists have used a dualistic, "push-pull" model to explain immigration to the United States (Archdeacon 1983; Bodnar 1985; Handlin 1951; Jones 1960; Taylor 1971; Seller 1977; Dinnerstein and Reimers 1987). They have identified numerous "push" factors, such as population increases, economic deprivation, and religious and political repression, that impel people to leave their homelands. They have also identified "pull" factors, such as economic opportunity and abundance, and freedom of religious and political expression, that have lured immigrants to the United States.

A widespread assumption concerning the newest immigrant wave is that, as in the past, migration pressures—the push factors—are internal to those countries. In the past, the United States has been perceived to influence these migration pressures only to the extent that it offers a beacon of hope for emigrants to escape lives of economic impoverishment or political repression. Thus, the push factors that have impelled people to emigrate have been the consequence of policies, practices, and social arrangements that the United States has been relatively powerless to control or influence.

This traditional push-pull model is inadequate to explain forces stimulating immigration today. Pull factors, though greatly influenced by the pervasiveness of the mass media in even the remotest corners of the world, remain *qualitatively* the same as ever: the United States remains the epitome of economic abundance, affluence, and opportunity in the minds of people around the world. However, starting after World War II, the push factors that were producing immigration no longer lay largely outside U.S. influence. In the last half of the twentieth century, the United States has emerged as the world's dominant economic, political, and military power. This transformation has not only reshaped international relations but has also expanded U.S. influence on the internal affairs of many of the world's states. The major difference between immigration today and in the past, then, is the economic and political impact of the United States in those countries that have been among the major sources of immigration; that is, American policies and practices—economic, social, cultural, and political—have created or contributed to the conditions that have led to the uprooting of people in many societies, a number of whom have immigrated to the United States as a result. In other words, the increased numbers of immigrants entering the United States are an indirect—and sometimes direct—consequence of American policies and practices. Thus, as Saskia Sassen points out in "America's Immigration 'Problem' " (Article 24), the economic, political, social, and cultural impacts of immigration that many Americans define as "problems," are in many respects self-induced—a consequence of America's own policies and practices in the global economy. "By focusing narrowly on immigrants and the immigration process itself, U.S. policy makers ignored the broader international forces, many of them generated or at least encouraged by the United States, that have helped give rise to migration flows."

Accordingly, Sassen focuses on the operation of broad transnational, macrostructural factors in the global economy that affect migration. She contends that direct

American foreign investment in production for export is the critical factor linking the United States and emigrant-exporting nations today. She seeks to explain why foreign investment, which has produced rapid economic growth—and thus presumably diminishing emigration pressures—in fact contributes to high emigration levels. She focuses on the impact of foreign investment on the economic and occupational structure of developing countries, which typically involves the disruption of traditional social patterns, especially of work structures and the roles of women, who are heavily recruited into jobs in new industrial zones. The entry of women workers increases labor pools, contributing to male unemployment. Moreover, given high turnover in the export production labor market, many workers are left unemployed. Thus foreign investment not only undermines the traditional work structure and creates a pool of potential emigrants; it also promotes emigration through economic, cultural, and ideological linkages—that is, the westernization of taste and mentality—with the United States.

However, Sassen contends that, while the penetration of foreign investment into developing countries may have been instrumental in *initiating* migration to the United States, its *continuation* at record levels is a consequence of the structural transformation of the American economy in the last two decades. Thus the shift from manufacturing to service occupations has had a profound effect not only on native workers, but upon opportunities for immigrant laborers as well. Because the manufacturing sector is being transformed and dramatically diminished, job prospects for foreign workers are becoming primarily low-wage and relatively unskilled. They are also found primarily in the nation's largest cities, to which a disproportionate share of recent immigrants have been drawn. Moreover, immigrants are also widely used in the low-wage end of the service sector, many of them working in occupations (e.g., hotel workers, child-care providers, and so forth) that "service the lifestyles and consumption requirements of the growing high-income professional and managerial class."

While Sassen adopts a general model of the relationship between American policies and practices and recent increases in immigration, Alejandro Portes has applied a similar explanation to the continuing influx of Mexican workers to the United States. Portes (1979) has argued that, paradoxically, it is Third World economic *development*, not underdevelopment, that has contributed significantly to the growing pressures for emigration. The American model of economic development, with its emphasis on consumerism and consumption, and American economic forces have transformed the social structures of many developing societies. Simultaneously unemployment, underemployment, and income inequalities preclude access by the majority of the population of developing countries to these consumer goods. "In the eyes of the Mexican worker," Portes writes, "the United States stands as the place where the benefits of an advanced economy, promised but not delivered by the present national development strategy, can be turned into reality." Thus, ironically, the very forces generated by the American economic system and exported extensively to the economic life of Third World societies, have been instrumental in attracting the massive influx of immigrants to the United States.

However, both Sassen and Portes focus primarily on broad macrostructural dimensions—the migration pressures—that induce people to migrate from one country to another. On the other hand, although writers such as Massey (1987) and Roger Rouse (Article 26) recognize the formative role of macro factors in initiating Mexican migration to the United States, they also emphasize the critical role that micro

factors—migrant social networks—play in sustaining it. The origins of Mexican migration to the United States are located in the imbalance between Mexican and American economic and social structures and policies, but once the process of migration has
begun, it becomes self-perpetuating and is maintained through networks of individuals that sustain and expand the process itself.

Massey and his colleagues (1987) emphasize the *social* dimensions of the process
of Mexican migration to the United States. They document the critical importance of
social networks involving relatives, friends, and *paisonos* (community members) that
link sending communities in Mexico with work sites in the United States. The roots
of temporary and undocumented immigration from Mexico were firmly established
earlier in the twentieth century, in response to American policies that encouraged migration. Most apparent was the bracero program, which was designed to alleviate
labor shortages during World War II, but also provided a legal basis for the traditional
patterns of Mexican migration. As a result of these patterns as well as the social networks in which they are enmeshed, temporary migration from Mexico to the United
States has become institutionalized and "is now an integral part of economic strategies
in households throughout [western Mexico] and has become a common event in the
family life cycle" (Massey 1987:103).

Thus, it is not simply population pressures, under- or unemployment in Mexico,
or even the general lure of economic opportunity in the United States that contributes
to the continuation of undocumented migration. Rather, out-migration is directed to
the United States because of the social networks that American policies and practices
were instrumental in establishing. As a consequence, Mexican immigration today has
now become a firmly established and self-sustaining process.

The pressures of undocumented Mexican migration to the United States has also
been influenced by American involvement in the economic development of Mexican
border communities, which was organized to fill the void created when the bracero
program was unilaterally canceled in 1964 (Sklair 1989). Integral to the development
strategies developed in northern Mexico was the *maquiladora,* assembly plants built
on the Mexican side of the U.S.-Mexican border by American corporations. Here
American-made parts are assembled into consumer goods (e.g., televisions, refrigera-
tors, clothing, toys) by Mexican workers and returned virtually duty-free. For years
Mexican *maquila* workers received wages that ranged from one-fifth to one-seventh of
those paid to American industrial workers, and recent devaluations of the Mexican
peso have reduced those figures to as little as one-fifteenth of their American counterparts (Cockcroft 1986:110). Critics of the *maquiladoras* point out that, no matter how
contented workers may be in their *maquila* jobs, these factories serve as a magnet to
encourage migration to Mexican border cities (Kopinak 1996; Uchitelle 1993; Ruiz and
Tiano 1987). By 1974, one-third of the people on the Mexican side of the border were
migrants, but only 3 percent were employed in *maquiladoras* (Cockcroft 1986:109).
Therefore, as the population of Mexican border cities increased after the introduction
of the *maquiladoras,* so did unemployment and underemployment rates, which, in
turn, contributed to the flow of illegal immigrants to the United States. Therefore,
rather than easing the pressures of illegal migration to the United States by providing
jobs in Mexico, the presence of the *maquilas* has actually increased them.

Two implications can be drawn from this interpretation. First, given the thrust of
the modernization process and the impact of American political and economic power

throughout the world, the United States will continue to attract immigrants—legal and illegal—from Third World sources. This continuation of immigration for the foreseeable future will likely reinforce and recreate the ethnic diversity that has characterized American society almost from its founding. Second, although migration pressures are manifested in different ways in different countries, they frequently derive their impetus from American economic and political power abroad. Thus, comprehension of the dynamics of American immigration today cannot begin at America's borders. Rather, it must also examine the impact of the American presence in sending countries.

So the dynamics of American immigration today must be conceptualized more broadly as an integral component and consequence of a modern global economy that is characterized by dramatic inequalities between societies. Given the interdependent nature of a global economy characterized by inequalities between rich and poor countries, it is probable that, even as internal political opposition to immigration increases within the United States, the global presence of the United States and other Western nations throughout the world will continue to generate emigration pressures from less-developed countries, thus reinforcing the clamor at America's gates.

The Coalescing of "White" America

The "new immigrant wave" became a significant phenomenon just when ethnicity and the celebration of America's ethnic diversity became more fashionable than ever before. The main theme of the "ethnic revival" of the 1970s was the rediscovery and reassertion of the importance and value of cultural pluralism and a simultaneous rejection of Anglo-conformity and the melting pot, which envision an ideal society as culturally homogeneous rather than culturally diverse. African Americans, Chicanos, Puerto Ricans, American Indians, and Asians each asserted their cultural distinctiveness and rejected what they perceived as efforts to impose on them the culture of the white middle class.

Each of these assertions of cultural identity and distinctiveness can be seen as an effort at ethnic mobilization—"the process by which a group organizes along ethnic lines in pursuit of collective political ends" (Nagel and Olzak 1982:127). In Article 2, "Constructing Ethnicity," Joane Nagel provides an explanation for the emergence of recent tribal, pantribal, and pan-Indian movements. She sees such movements as responses to external stimuli—in particular, to policies of the American federal government that control resources available to Indians.

However, a critical impetus for the ethnic revival came from the descendants of southern and eastern European peoples, whose metamorphosis from "inbetween" peoples (see Barrett and Roediger, Article 6) to "white ethnics" reflected both their social mobility in the post–World War II era and their progressive incorporation into the category of "white." Michael Novak, grandson of Slovakian immigrants and author of *The Rise of the Unmeltable Ethnics* (1971), was one of the foremost proponents of the new ethnicity. He identified two basic elements in the movement: a sensitivity to and appreciation of the importance of ethnic pluralism; and a self-conscious examination of one's own cultural heritage (Novak 1971:17). Another prominent spokesman, Andrew Greeley, the Irish-American sociologist, priest, and novelist, noted several ways in which this ethnic "consciousness raising" was expressed: increased interest in the literary, intellectual, and artistic culture of one's ethnic background; visits to one's ancestral homeland; and increased use of one's ancestral language (Greeley 1975:149–151).

The case for a broadly based ethnic revival was supported by considerable impressionistic evidence. In 1969, for the first time, the Census Bureau asked Americans about their ethnic backgrounds. Those interviewed were given seven choices from which to select: German, English, Irish, Spanish, Polish, Italian, and Russian (and "mixed" or "other"). Thirty-eight percent of the respondents (equivalent to 75 million Americans) placed themselves in one of the seven categories. Three years later, when the Census Bureau conducted a similar survey, Americans appeared much more conscious of, or willing to indicate, their affiliation with an ethnic group. This time nearly 50 percent (equivalent to 102 million) identified with a specific national group. Moreover, during the late 1960s and early 1970s, numerous ethnic groups developed organizations, such as the Italian-American Civil Rights League, that were designed to combat negative perceptions of their group. Such self-consciously ethnic organizations also mobilized to obtain financial resources from the federal government and private foundations in order to fund activities to rekindle or awaken ethnic consciousness. In 1972 the Ethnic Heritage Studies Act gave federal government sanction to the ethnic revival by providing financial assistance to promote ethnic studies. The Act gave, in the words of one of its sponsors, "official recognition to ethnicity as a positive constructive force in our society today" (quoted in Polenberg 1980:246).

The notion of an ethnic revival was also reflected in increased academic attention to ethnicity. History, literature, and sociology courses that had focused almost exclusively on African Americans during the 1960s broadened their scope to include other ethnic groups in the 1970s. Indeed, student enrollments declined in black studies courses, and there were instances in which ethnic courses supplanted race courses completely. The increasing salience of ethnicity was also symbolized by the founding of several journals devoted to its analysis: *Ethnicity* (1974), *Journal of Ethnic Studies* (1974), *Ethnic and Racial Studies* (1978), *MELUS (Multiethnic Literature in the United States;* 1975), and the *Journal of American Ethnic History* (1981). Finally, one of the most salient indices of the rediscovery of ethnicity was the publication in 1980 of the *Harvard Encyclopedia of American Ethnic Groups,* the most comprehensive resource available on the subject today (Thernstrom 1980). Publication of the *Encyclopedia* under the aegis of the nation's most prestigious university press reflects the primacy that ethnicity has been accorded over the last three decades.

What are the reasons for this resurgence of ethnicity? Foremost was the impact that the Black Protest Movement had on the self-definition of other ethnic groups, in particular white ethnics. On the one hand, the emphasis on black pride and on understanding African American culture, stimulated by the civil rights movement of the late 1950s and 1960s, led many white ethnics to consider their own heritages more closely. Moreover, the "roots phenomenon" emerged among white ethnics that both reflected and was stimulated by the celebrated television saga "Roots," which was based on Alex Haley's attempt to trace and construct his ancestral origins in Africa.

More critical, however, were the structural contexts within which the "white ethnic" revival occurred. In Article 23 Massey points out that the economic "ethnic miracle" that European immigrants and their descendants experienced in the post–World War II era resulted from the confluence of several unique factors. First, the post-1920s hiatus in immigration from Europe effectively curtailed the infusion of "old country" cultural patterns into immigrant communities. "The cutting off of immigration from Europe eliminated the supply of raw materials for the grist mill of ethnicity in the United States, ensuring that whatever ethnic identities existed would be predominantly a consequence of events and processes occurring within the U.S." Second, the assimilation of second- and third-generation, "new" immigrant European Americans was greatly facilitated by the extraordinary post–World War II economic boom, which produced a period of economic prosperity unparalleled in American history. During the quarter of a century between 1948 and 1973, real median family income doubled. As a consequence, "first- and second-generation immigrants from southern and eastern Europe rode this wave of prosperity to achieve full economic parity with northern and western Europeans by 1980."

This economic prosperity greatly facilitated the adaptation of white ethnic groups to American society. Richard Alba (Article 15 and 1990) has shown how the experience of ethnicity among southern and eastern Europeans is affected by age and cohort. Older cohorts were far more likely to have been raised in homes in which a language other than English was spoken, to have had both parents from the same ethnic background, and not to have attended college. Members of younger cohorts, on the other hand, were much more likely to have grown up in homes in which only English was spoken, to have had ethnically mixed ancestry, and to have attended college. Moreover, members of younger cohorts were much more likely to have married spouses from different ethnic and religious backgrounds and to have switched religious affiliations than were members of the older cohorts. By the 1970s the fourth generation of the southern and eastern European immigrants was entering adulthood. As the distance from their ancestral roots increased, their identification with them weakened. The decline of the ancestral language, the dispersion of ethnic neighborhoods, the decreasing participation in and identification with the traditional religious community primarily among Catholics, especially those under thirty years of age, and the increased rates of ethnic and religious intermarriage contributed to the dwindling of a meaningful "white ethnic" identity.

Thus, white ethnics' economic, educational, and occupational mobility, as well as their geographical dispersion to ethnically undifferentiated suburbs and patterns of increased intermarriage, indicate that they have moved into the "white" mainstream, where their identification with their ethnic origins has become increasingly remote.

Moreover, there is considerable evidence that ethnicity as a source of social cohesion is decreasing, especially among the third and fourth generations. In Article 22, "Symbolic Ethnicity," Herbert Gans disputes the notion of an enduring ethnic revival, arguing that both cultural and social assimilation continue to take place in American society. Ethnicity is no longer rooted in group membership or cultural patterns but instead has become symbolic, a matter of choice, an ethnicity of "last resort." In his study of an Italian-American community in Boston in the 1960s, Gans did not find a sense of ethnic identity to be increasing. Instead, he found a straight-line decline in ethnicity over three generations. That is, ethnicity was less significant in each succeeding generation (Gans 1962). Similarly, a study by Sandberg showed a constant decline in ethnic consciousness, identification, and cohesion among Polish-Americans in Los Angeles; by the fourth generation, ethnicity had ceased to play an important role in their lives (Sandberg 1974). Finally, these findings are reinforced by increased rates of ethnic and religious intermarriage, which were discussed in Part 3.

Thus, paradoxically, at precisely the moment that white ethnics have become the most fully assimilated into American society, culturally and socially, their interest in and identification with their ethnic roots has also become the most pronounced. In *The Ethnic Myth* Stephen Steinberg argued that ". . . the impulse to recapture the ethnic past is a belated realization that ethnicity is rapidly diminishing as a significant factor in American life" (Steinberg 1981:73).

Although neither is especially sympathetic to the notion of an ethnic revival, both Irving Howe (1977) and Herbert Gans (Article 22, "Symbolic Ethnicity") suggest another source of the surge of interest in things ethnic. In an interpretation reminiscent of Herberg's (1955) explanation of the surge of religiosity a generation earlier, they find that ethnicity provides a fashionable, socially acceptable source of personal identity in an increasingly homogenized America. In Howe's words,

> We are all aware that our ties with the European past grow increasingly feeble. Yet we feel uneasy before the prospect of becoming "just Americans." We feel uneasy before the prospect of becoming as indistinguishable from one another as our motel rooms are, or as flavorless and mass-produced as the bread many of us eat. (Howe 1977:18)

Thus, although there appears to be widespread interest today among many European Americans in retrieving or maintaining a sense of ethnic identity (what Gans called *symbolic ethnicity*), precisely how deep and enduring such identities are remains problematic (for a similar interpretation, see Hirschman 1983).

Finally, Stanley Lieberson (1985) has suggested that a substantial number of white Americans have no sense of ethnic group identity other than a general notion that they are "American." The European origins of these "unhyphenated whites," as Lieberson dubs them, are either so remote or so mixed that they are able to define themselves only as "American." Lieberson's interpretation, which is reinforced by those of Doane, Alba, Gans, and Massey, suggests that increasingly ethnic identities of peoples of European descent have coalesced into an inclusive "white" category, which has emerged in response to the increasing national (as opposed to Southern regional) presence of a racial "other"—African Americans—against which to define themselves.

The Racial "Other": African Americans and the Changing Nature of Race in America

Near the end of World War II, Gunnar Myrdal, a Swedish economist and later a Nobel Prize winner, published *An American Dilemma* (1944), a massive two-volume study of American race relations that he had conducted with the financial support of the Carnegie Corporation. The book examined in greater depth than any previous study the subordinate political, economic, and social status of African Americans and the prospects for change of that status. The book's title reflected Myrdal's basic premise that American race relations were essentially a moral problem in the hearts and minds of Americans—that the caste status that constrained African Americans in virtually every aspect of their lives represented a violation of what he called the "American creed" of equality and brotherhood. The book became an immediate classic, influencing an entire generation of academics, students, clergy, and social workers, and providing the intellectual backdrop for the attack upon segregation during the 1950s and 1960s. The influence extended to the Supreme Court, which cited it in the historic 1954 *Brown* v. *Board of Education of Topeka* decision.

The pace of change in American race relations in the years following publication of *An American Dilemma* was more rapid than even Myrdal had anticipated. During the next two decades, resolution of the glaring contradiction between American ideals and African Americans' second-class citizenship became the nation's most prominent domestic political issue. Reflecting this focus, in 1965, in an introduction written for a series of essays entitled "The Negro American" in the scholarly journal *Daedalus,* President Lyndon Johnson wrote, "Nothing is of greater significance to the welfare and vitality of this nation than the movement to secure equal rights for Negro Americans" (*Daedalus* 1965:743). Johnson's crucial role in achieving passage of the landmark 1964 Civil Rights Act and the 1965 Voting Rights Act and his War on Poverty program are ample evidence that his support was not merely rhetorical.

Johnson wrote these words at the zenith of personal and national attention to the status of African Americans. However, reflecting the unrest created by their continued exclusion from mainstream American life, a wave of urban uprisings by blacks swept American cities during the mid-1960s. These uprisings claimed a toll of over one hundred lives and millions of dollars in property damage. President Johnson responded by appointing a blue-ribbon commission to investigate the causes of the civil disorders and to recommend ways in which the conditions that triggered them might be addressed. In 1968 the National Commission on Civil Disorders (popularly known as the Kerner Commission, after its chair, Illinois Governor Otto Kerner) attributed the primary responsibility for the outbreaks to "white racism" and warned that American society was moving toward "two societies, one black, one white—separate and unequal." It concluded that "there can be no higher claim on the Nation's conscience" than to eliminate "deepening racial division" by a "compassionate, massive, and sustained" commitment of resources and energy (National Advisory Commission on Civil Disorders 1968).

Johnson, by that time preoccupied with the escalation of the war in Vietnam, ignored the commission's recommendations, just as his successor, Richard Nixon, disputed its basic conclusions. Subsequently, despite several significant private and governmental efforts to implement programs to achieve racial equality, the status of African Americans no longer occupied the prominence in the American consciousness that it had done in 1965. By 1981 the editors of an issue of *Daedalus* devoted to American racial minorities would write, "It is a measure of the distance we have traveled in sixteen years that is almost unthinkable to imagine any white politician today making such a statement as Johnson's in 1965, giving such primacy to the issue of racial equality" (*Daedalus* 1981:vi).

Three decades after the Kerner Commission sounded its alarm that the nation was being divided into two societies, whether and to what extent the gap that separates black and white America has been narrowed has become the focus of intense national debate. Some observers, such as Abigail and Stephan Thernstrom (1997), have emphasized the substantial progress that African Americans have made. On the other hand, a 1998 report coauthored by Fred Harris, a former senator from Oklahoma and member of the original Kerner Commission, challenged such optimistic views, contending that "the rich are getting richer, the poor are getting poorer, and minorities are suffering disproportionately" (Eisenhower Foundation, 1998). In the section below, we will examine some of the continuities and changes in the status of African Americans since the 1960s.

There can be little doubt that the rise of black militancy was one of the most momentous developments of the turbulent 1960s. Each year during that decade, the scale of racial conflict and violence escalated. In retrospect, the beginnings appear relatively subdued. In 1960 the most dramatic events involved drugstore sit-ins in Greensboro, North Carolina, a tactic that quickly spread throughout the South. In the following years, the pace and intensity of protest increased dramatically. Civil disorders engulfed cities throughout the country, with great loss of property and lives. In the heated climate of those years, four of the most important figures in the movement for African American equality were the victims of assassins' bullets. Two of them, Malcolm X and Martin Luther King, Jr., were black; the other two, John F. Kennedy and Robert Kennedy, were white.

Between 1960 and 1970, the goals and means of the Black Protest Movement underwent substantial changes. As is characteristic of much social change, yesterday's radicalism became today's moderation. Many ideologies and tactics that came to be defined as moderate would have appeared unthinkably radical to concerned individuals—black and white—a decade earlier. Joseph C. Hough, Jr., has characterized this change as the "stretching of the extremism spectrum":

> About 1953 I had my first conversation with [a friend in the South] about race relations, and he and I agreed that while the Negro deserved a better chance in America, we must be careful to oppose two kinds of extremists—the NAACP and the Ku Klux Klan. In 1955, we had another conversation and again we agreed that Negroes ought to be able to attend desegregated public schools, but that we should oppose two kinds of extremes—White Citizens Councils and Martin Luther King. In 1966, this same friend said to me, "If we could get the good whites and the good Negroes to support Martin Luther King, perhaps we could put the brakes on these SNCC and CORE people and also put a stop to this ridiculous revival of the Ku Klux Klan. (Hough 1968:224–225)

By the late 1960s, the forms and direction of African American protest had shifted from the moderate civil rights movement to a more militant black power movement. The civil rights movement of the 1950s and early 1960s had been based essentially on an order model of society; the primary goal had been integration into the mainstream of the dominant society, and the primary means were nonviolent. As Skolnick (1969) has pointed out, the civil rights movement "operated for the most part on the implicit premise that racism was a localized malignancy within a relatively healthy political and social order; it was a move to force American morality and American institutions to root out the last vestiges of the 'disease' " (Skolnick 1969:31).

The fundamental ideological thrust of the black power movement, on the other hand, derived from a conflict model of societal functioning. In response to the intransigence and unresponsiveness of white America, articulate African American spokespersons increasingly questioned the capacity of traditional goals and means to ensure the dignity and autonomy of black people in a white society. After the Kerner Commission's report was published in 1968, militancy among African Americans, particularly among the young, increased even further. Perhaps the most important shift in attitudes among African Americans was the growing recognition that the racial problems were national and could not be confined to the South; that nonviolence was merely a *tactic* in a power struggle and in many instances was useless to obtain black equality and autonomy; and that racism was rooted in the society's institutions. Consequently, the primary efforts of the black power movement were to obtain a more equitable distribution of power in the many institutional spheres of American life and to search for new ideological forms, or cultural alternatives to those of white America.

For African Americans, however, the 1960s was a decade of progress: during this period, blacks experienced their greatest gains since their emancipation in 1865. These gains were brought about by the unprecedented efforts of federal, state, and local governments and private organizations to remove inequalities and redress injustices that had for years relegated African Americans to second-class citizenship.

Most visible and dramatic were the legal changes made by the federal government. For the first time in American history, the three branches of the federal government acted in concert on behalf of African Americans. The Supreme Court, whose *Brown* v. *Board of Education* decision had outlawed segregated schools in 1954, substantially extended the implications of the *Brown* decision, and symbolized the beginning of a new era for blacks. It outlawed state laws prohibiting racial intermarriage and racial discrimination in the rental and sale of private and public property. Moreover, the Court decisively rejected efforts by local school districts to evade its desegregation rulings, and it unanimously supported school busing as one means of achieving that goal. President Lyndon Johnson, a Southerner, provided the most unequivocal moral and political support of African American aspirations of any president in American history. Through his leadership, the Congress enacted legislation that outlawed discrimination in public accommodations, employment, housing, voting, and education. In addition, his Great Society economic programs provided federal funds to enhance occupational and educational opportunities for blacks.

By the end of the 1960s, African Americans, particularly the better educated and more highly skilled, had made substantial gains, both economically and educationally. One of the best indices of these changes was black median family income, which in 1959 was only half of that for whites. By 1964 black family income had risen to 54 percent of white income, and by 1969, reflecting the economic expansion and prosperity that characterized the decade, as well as national efforts to reduce black inequalities, it had risen to 61 percent. Thus, although problems remained acute for poorly educated and unskilled African Americans, the efforts of the 1960s had clearly produced some impressive advances.

However, the civil rights movement, which during the 1960s had generally displayed consensus concerning both goals and tactics despite internal differences, was now in disarray. Part of the reason was the movement's very success in achieving impressive legislative and judicial victories in the 1960s. The disarray also reflected the fact that for many African Americans, the optimism of the early 1960s had been shattered by the failure of these legislative changes to institute meaningful changes in their lives. It became increasingly apparent that the abolition of legal barriers to public accommodations and suburban housing, for example, did not address the essential problems of a substantial portion of the African American population. The erosion of the fragile consensus among African Americans was symbolized by the outbreaks of the civil disorders of the late 1960s, which did little to allay conscious and unconscious white anxieties concerning African American demands for substantial changes in the status quo. As many whites grew weary of what they perceived as government support for lawlessness and became tired of the constant media attention to blacks, the conservative mood of the country increased, contributing to the 1968 election of Richard Nixon to the presidency.

By the early 1970s, the impetus and fervor of the black power movement was spent. The frequency of mass social unrest dramatically declined during the decade. American involvement in Indochina formally ended, and the civil disorders that rent many American cities during the 1960s did not recur on an equally massive scale. The sense of concern for social justice that had inspired many white Americans was replaced by an indifference, even an aversion, to the problems of racial minority groups in the country. Indeed, the activism of the so-called concerned generation of the 1960s was replaced by a stance of "benign neglect." Compared with the progress achieved during the 1960s and throughout the 1970s, 1980s, and early 1990s, the rate of African American advance slowed appreciably; at worst, it was a time of retrogression and retrenchment.

Many of the most dramatic advances for African Americans since the 1960s have been in the political arena. The tactics of public confrontations, boycotts, and demonstrations, which in the late 1950s and early 1960s had been successful in effecting social change, were supplanted in the 1970s by more traditional political activity. "Politics is the civil-rights movement of the 1970s," said Maynard Jackson, the black mayor of Atlanta (Sitkoff 1981:229). Such a stance was possible because of the increase in African American political strength brought about by the Voting Rights Act of 1965, which provided federal protection for black efforts to register and vote in states throughout the South. The percentage of Southern blacks registered to vote increased from 35 percent in 1964 to 65 percent in 1969. In Alabama, the increase was from 19 to 61 percent; in Mississippi, from 7 to 67 percent; and in Georgia, from 27 to 60 percent (Polenberg 1980:192).

The increases in African American voters throughout the South substantially increased their political representation. In 1964 of all the nearly half-million elected officials in the entire country (ranging from local school-board member to President of the United States), only 103 blacks held elected offices. By 1970 this number of elected officials had increased to 1,400, and by 1994 stood at more than 8,400, more than two-thirds of them in the South. Moreover, the number of African American mayors increased from *none* in 1964 to more than 416 in 1996. Since 1964, African Americans have been elected mayor in each of the nation's five largest cities—New York, Los Angeles, Chicago, Houston, and Philadelphia; in 1998 Baltimore, Seattle, St. Louis, Kansas City, Detroit, Atlanta, Denver, San Francisco, and Washington, D.C., all had black mayors. Finally, by 1998 the Congressional Black Caucus, composed of Democratic African American members of the House of Representatives, claimed a membership of 38 out of the 435 seats.

Because of their strategic location in the major metropolitan areas of key industrial states, the combined voting strength of African Americans could swing close elections. This power was demonstrated first in 1960, when John F. Kennedy's narrow victory over Richard Nixon was due to the substantial margin that he obtained from black voters in the industrial Northeast and Midwest. It was even more noteworthy in the 1976 election, when over 90 percent of more than six-and-one-half million black voters voted for Jimmy Carter, who owed his victory margin in most of the Southern as well as several Northern states—and thus his election as a whole—directly to the overwhelming support of African American voters. Finally, the increasing significance of African American political power was made abundantly clear by Jesse Jackson's presidential campaigns in 1988 and 1991. His candidacy not only electrified the black community (and was instrumental in registering thousands of new black voters), but he gained the support of a substantial number of white voters as well.

Despite these highly visible changes, by 1994 African Americans remained less than 2 percent of all elected officials in the country, a percentage not even closely approximating their nearly 13 percent of the total population. In the South, where blacks comprise more than 20 percent of the population, only 3 percent of the elected officials were black. Moreover, in many instances the political power that black elected officials have today is limited by the fact that they are politically isolated. Finally, given the exodus of white middle-class residents and businesses to the suburbs, African Americans often find they have gained political power without the financial resources with which to provide the jobs and services (educational, medical, police and fire protection) that their constituents most urgently need.

During the 1950s, 1960s, and early 1970s, African Americans achieved substantial gains in education. In 1957 the proportion of whites aged 25–29 who had completed high school (63.3 percent) was double the proportion of blacks (31.6 percent), but by 1976 the proportions of each racial group who were high-school graduates were nearly the same (U.S. Bureau of the Census 1988a:75–76). In the late 1960s and early 1970s a steadily increasing percent of blacks began attending college, so that by 1976 the percentage of black high-school graduates enrolled in college was virtually equal to that of whites, a dramatic change when compared to the college attendance rates of blacks as late as the mid-1960s (Jones 1981).

However, between 1976 and 1985, the educational gains of the 1960s and early 1970s eroded, threatening to reverse the movement toward educational equality. The college participation rate for black high-school graduates declined dramatically, while the white participation rate remained virtually unchanged. Moreover, black college completion rates declined, as did the proportion of black students enrolled at four-year colleges and in graduate and professional schools (Carter and Wilson 1997).

However, from the mid-1980s through the 1990s, African American educational attainments have steadily improved; by 1995 the rates of high-school completion for 25–29-year-old blacks was similar (87 percent) to whites. Moreover, the college participation rates for both whites and blacks increased; the rates for both races stood at all-time highs in 1995. The white participation rate increased from 29 percent in 1985 to 34 percent in 1994, while the increase for blacks—from 20 to 27 percent—was slightly larger. After declining from 1976 to 1985, it took until 1992 for the percentage of bachelor's degrees earned by African Americans to return to the 1976 level of 6.4 percent. By 1994 the percentage of bachelor's degrees awarded to blacks stood at 7.2 percent—an all-time high (Carter and Wilson 1997).

Similarly, there was a dramatic decline in the number and percentage of graduate and professional degrees awarded to African Americans between 1976 and the mid-1980s. In 1976 blacks were awarded 6.6 percent of the nation's master's degrees, but by 1989 this figure had declined to 4.6 percent. During the 1990s, however, the percentage of master's degrees awarded to African Americans steadily increased, to 5.7 percent in 1994—still well below the 1976 figure. The number of doctoral degrees awarded to African Americans declined from 1,445 in 1980 to 771 in 1987, but it has steadily risen since then, reaching 1,287 in 1995. The greatest gains occurred in the category of professional degrees; whereas in 1976 African Americans were awarded 2,694 professional degrees, or 4.3 percent of the total, in 1994 they were awarded 4,444, or 5.9 percent of the total (Carter and Wilson 1997).

However, the somewhat dramatic educational gains during the late 1980s and early 1990s by minority students generally, and by African American students in particular, have recently slowed. The most disquieting feature of these declines is that they occurred *before* legal challenges to affirmative action programs in states such as California and Texas reduced the number of African American and Hispanic undergraduate and post-graduate students even further. After a Federal court decision that eliminated the affirmative action admissions program at the University of Texas Law School, the number of black and Mexican American students admitted dropped precipitously; five black and eighteen Mexican American students were admitted to the Law School in 1997 in contrast to sixty-five blacks and seventy Mexican Americans the previous year (Carter and Wilson 1997; Applebome 1997a:A9). Similarly, in 1998, undergraduate admissions of American Indians, African Americans and Latinos at the University of California, Berkeley, and the University of California, Los Angeles, dropped precipitously—by 45 percent at Berkeley and by 36 percent at UCLA—after the universities implemented policies based on the requirements of the 1996 California Proposition 209, which banned the use of race as a factor in considering admissions to California public colleges and universities (Bronner 1998).

However, these statistics obscure substantial qualitative differences in African American educational achievement. During the early 1990s, as a consequence of court decisions that made it easier for school districts to abandon desegregation plans that the courts had previously mandated, the nation's schools were resegregating at a faster rate than at any time since the Supreme Court's 1954 *Brown* v. *Board of Education* decision—that is, the isolation of black and Hispanic students in schools that are predominantly minority and poor was more pronounced than at any time since the 1950s, recreating the pattern of "separate and *un*equal" that the Supreme Court had ruled against in 1954 (Orfield et al. 1997; Applebome 1997b:A8). Since the 1970s, black students in the South have been more likely to attend racially integrated elementary and secondary schools than are black students in other regions of the country. However, the desegregation achieved during the 1960s and 1970s in the South has substantially eroded during the late 1980s and 1990s, coming much more closely to resemble the patterns of educational racial isolation that characterize other regions of the country. Because of the patterns of residential segregation in most American cities, two-thirds of black children attend schools that are composed predominantly of minority children. Whereas black children in rural areas, small and medium-sized towns, and suburbs are most likely to attend racially integrated schools, educational racial isolation is most acute in the central city school districts of the nation's largest cities. In 1994–1995, the ten largest central city school districts accounted for 18 percent of all black students (and 23 percent of Latino students), but only 2 percent of white students. "About a fifth of black and Latino students depend on districts that do not matter to 98 percent of white families" (Orfield et al. 1997:23). Most important, racially segregated schools tend also to be segregated by poverty. In other words, minority children—blacks and Hispanics in particular—are much more likely than whites to be disadvantaged because they attend schools with high poverty concentrations. Thus, although there have been significant educational advances for African Americans during the past two decades, the question as to whether these gains are enduring and can be translated into higher economic status remains problematic.

Thus the trends in both the political and educational areas indicate qualified improvements for African Americans. However, no such progress has taken place in the economic sphere, perhaps the most important institutional category. The economic gains of the 1960s were eroded by inflation, two recessions, and substantial reductions in federal, state, and local governmental commitments to racial progress. The economic recovery championed by the Reagan and Bush administrations during the 1980s did little to enhance the economic status of African Americans, which, until 1994, showed little improvement since the early 1970s. Although many blacks have experienced socioeconomic mobility, African Americans remain underrepresented in high-status professional, technical, and managerial positions, and overrepresented in service occupations, traditionally recognized as low-status jobs in American society (Farley and Allen 1987). During the 1970s, 1980s, and early 1990s, the income gap separating blacks and whites widened. Black median family income, which rose substantially during the 1960s—from 50 percent of white median family income in 1959 to 61 percent in 1970—began to decline in the mid-1970s and remained virtually stagnant (between 55 and 58 percent of white income) throughout the 1980s and the early 1990s. Finally, in 1995, black median family income rose to match the 61 percent it had achieved a quarter of a century earlier, but it declined once again in 1996 (see Figure 1).

However, measures of *income* inequality alone do not adequately measure the disparities between blacks and whites in economic status; indeed, the focus of many analyses of racial inequality on income understates the substantial economic black-white inequality. To obtain a more accurate picture of the racial distribution of economic resources, it is necessary to examine disparities in the distribution of wealth. *Income* refers to the economic resources that people receive during a specified period of time (usually a year), but *wealth* includes savings, investments, homes, and property; that is, wealth represents accumulated assets or stored-up purchasing power.

Most studies of the distribution of wealth in American society have relied on measures of *net worth*, which refers to the difference between a household's assets and its liabilities. In 1993 the median net worth of white households ($45,740) was more than ten times the median net worth of black households ($4,418). Or, to put it another way, in 1993 black median family income was 54.8 percent of white income, but the median net worth of black families was only 9.6 percent of white families (U.S. Bureau of the Census 1997a).

However, the net worth of many Americans who have accumulated some wealth is held almost exclusively in the equity that they have in their homes and automobiles. Oliver and Shapiro (1989a; 1989b; 1995) have therefore argued that the most accurate measures of the concentration of wealth in the United States should exclude equity in homes and vehicles, because these assets can seldom be converted to other purposes (such as financing a college education, establishing or expanding a business,

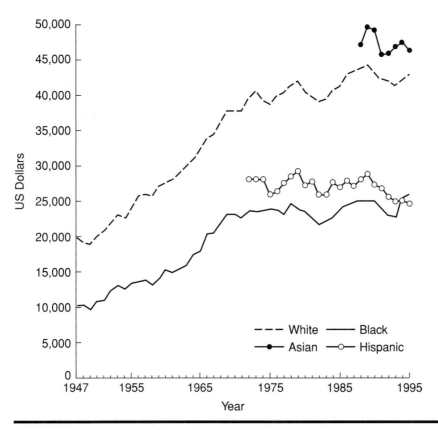

FIGURE 1 *Median Family Income, 1947–1995 (in 1995 dollars)*

or paying for emergency medical expenses). They suggest that a more appropriate measure of wealth is *net financial assets,* which refers to household wealth after the equity in homes and vehicles has been deducted. If this measure (rather than net worth) is used, figures on the overall wealth of American households and inequalities in the distribution of wealth in American society change dramatically; net financial assets tend to be much more heavily concentrated among the very wealthy. "Whereas the top 20 percent of American households earn over 43 percent of all income, the same 20 percent holds 67 percent of net worth and nearly 90 percent of net financial assets" (Oliver and Shapiro 1989a).

The disparities in net financial assets between black and white are even more pronounced than those for net worth. Oliver and Shapiro have shown that in 1988, white households had a median net worth of $43,800, but median net financial assets of only $6,999 (Oliver and Shapiro 1995:86). Black households, on the other hand, had a median net worth of $3,700, but *no* median net financial assets at all. Oliver and Shapiro conclude that blacks are therefore much more disadvantaged than whites when measures of wealth—especially net financial assets—rather than income, are used.

With the exception of three years during the 1970s, the annual black unemployment rate has been at least double that for whites since 1954, and during the

1980s, the gap between white and black unemployment rates actually increased. In 1997 black unemployment stood at nearly 10 percent of the black labor force, standing at nearly 2½ times the rate for whites (U.S. Bureau of the Census 1998). Unemployment was most acute for black teenagers. Despite declines in unemployment among all categories of workers since 1983, nearly one-fourth (22.6 percent) of black teenagers were unemployed in 1997, a figure also 2½ times higher than that for white teenagers (9.6 percent). Moreover, the National Urban League, whose research division annually surveys African American households, contends that the official unemployment rate substantially underrepresents real unemployment because it does not include discouraged workers who have dropped out of the labor force entirely. They also note that the unemployment data just cited are national averages, so they obscure the variations among different cities; the Urban League estimates that in some cities, the jobless rate for black teenagers during the 1980s may have risen to as high as 80 percent. Thus the overall economic status of African Americans appears to have made only limited gains at best during the economic boom of the 1990s.

However, William Julius Wilson (Articles 7 and 19; 1987; 1996b) has contended that this deterioration in economic status has not been felt uniformly throughout the black community. During the 1970s, middle-class blacks made impressive economic advances. The number of blacks in professional and managerial positions increased to 2½ times what it had been in 1965. Indeed, between 1975 and 1980, the largest gains in black employment were in higher-status occupations. During this period, the number of African Americans employed increased by 1.3 million, over half of them in managerial, professional, and craft jobs (Hill 1981:22). Moreover, Wilson notes that prior to 1960, the ratio of black to white income actually decreased as educational attainment increased, but that this pattern has now been reversed: the higher the black educational level, the more closely incomes approximate those of comparably educated whites.

Nevertheless, Wilson argues that because of macrostructural changes in the American economy, a growing division has emerged among African Americans between the middle class and a steadily increasing underclass—the nation's most impoverished social category, many of whom live in persistent poverty. Found predominantly in the nation's inner cities, the underclass is characterized by high rates of unemployment, out-of-wedlock births, female-headed families, welfare dependence, homelessness, and serious crime. Although those included in the underclass include some whites and, increasingly, Hispanics, its existence is most pronounced and most visible in the black ghettos of northern cities in the United States.

The nature and causes of the growing underclass have been the subject of considerable controversy. In an insightful analysis of the underclass phenomenon in the 1980s, Maxine Baca Zinn (1989) distinguishes between two broad ideologies or models—the cultural deficiency and the macrostructural—that correspond roughly to the "internal" and "external" explanations of ethnic group attainment developed in the Introduction to Part 3. These models, she argues, have been used both by social scientists and by laypeople to explain the underclass phenomenon. The cultural deficiency model emphasizes shortcomings either in the minority's culture or family system or in a welfare system believed to encourage personal traits that prevent people from pulling themselves out of poverty. The cultural deficiency model locates the explanation for the underclass in the cultural or psychological characteristics of each specific class level.

A macrostructural explanation of the underclass, on the other hand, focuses on the decline of opportunity structures. As noted in Part 3, William Julius Wilson has been one of the most prominent and articulate spokespersons for this perspective. In *The Truly Disadvantaged* (1987) and *When Work Disappears* (1996), Wilson argued that the growth of the urban underclass has resulted from major structural changes in the American economy that have caused extremely high levels of inner-city unemployment. As Wilson writes in "Work," (Article 19), "The disappearance of jobs . . . [is a critical factor in explaining] the catastrophic descent of America's ghettos into ever-deeper poverty and misery."

Earlier in the twentieth century, relatively uneducated and unskilled native and immigrant workers were able to find stable employment and income in the manufacturing sector of the economy. In the past quarter century, however, the process of deindustrialization has contributed to an economic mismatch between the available jobs and the qualifications of inner-city residents. On the one hand, most of the nation's major manufacturing centers in the industrial states of the North and Midwest have experienced dramatic declines in manufacturing—such jobs, which in the past did not require highly technical skills, have moved from the inner cities to the suburbs, the sun belt, or overseas, or have been eliminated by the introduction of more efficient technologies. On the other hand, the jobs being created in the cities demand highly technical credentials that most inner-city residents do not have. Because the African American urban poor lack the educational and occupational skills necessary for today's highly technological jobs, economic opportunities for them are rapidly diminishing. The result is disastrously high levels of unemployment.

These broad structural changes have triggered a process of "hyperghettoization," in which the urban poor are disproportionately concentrated and socially and economically isolated. As many stable working- and middle-class residents with job qualifications have moved from the inner-city neighborhoods, the stability of inner-city social institutions (churches, schools, newspapers, recreational facilities, and small businesses) has been undermined, and the social fabric of community life has deteriorated. Those remaining in such neighborhoods, increasingly the "most marginal and oppressed of the black community," have become increasingly socially isolated. "A neighborhood in which people are poor but employed," Wilson writes, "is different from a neighborhood in which people are poor and jobless" (Article 19).

Whereas Wilson's analyses have focused primarily on the black underclass, other writers (Zinn 1989; Moore and Pinderhughes 1993) argue that similar macrostructural conditions have affected Hispanics, especially Puerto Ricans and Mexicans. Increases in Hispanic poverty have been most pronounced in those regions (such as the Northeast and Midwest) in which broad structural changes in the economy have occurred. "The association between national economic shifts and high rates of social dislocation among Hispanics provides further evidence for the structural argument that economic conditions rather than culture create distinctive forms of racial poverty" (Zinn 1989).

Therefore, the major thrust of Wilson's argument is that, although both the African American and Hispanic underclass reflect a legacy of racial discrimination, class factors have become critical in sustaining the underclass today. Lacking the necessary training and job skills for positions in the modern economy, members of the underclass are instead the victims of broad economic and technological changes in American society. Even if all racial prejudice and discrimination were eliminated, African American and Hispanic members of the underclass would still lack the necessary qualifications with which to participate in the mainstream of the economy and would continue to be found primarily in the low-paying, unskilled sector where unemployment is extremely high. In the economic sphere, institutional, not attitudinal, discrimination has become critical to sustaining African American and Hispanic inequalities.

Thus the economic problems confronting African Americans are those of institutional discrimination. The thrust of Wilson's thesis is that major attention must be directed not only to the removal of racial barriers (which he acknowledges still confront African Americans in education, politics, and especially in housing) but also to the very structure of the American economy and its inability to provide opportunity for the substantial segment of its population. The challenge for American society in the next decade, therefore, is not only to ensure that the barriers of racial discrimination are dismantled, but also to make certain that class barriers now precluding minority access to economic opportunities are eliminated.

Wilson's emphasis on the structural factors contributing to black inequalities, especially his model of the effects of deindustrialization and joblessness on the creation and perpetuation of the ghetto underclass, has elicited numerous critiques. One of the most penetrating is Roger Waldinger's analysis of the changing occupational dynamics in New York City (Article 27). Waldinger argues that the shift to a post-industrial global economy has transformed the ethnic division of labor in America's major urban centers. His analysis focuses on the economic and social changes that have accompanied the decline of manufacturing and the rise of a service-oriented economy in New York City, the nation's largest and historically most ethnically diverse city. Waldinger disputes the "mismatch" hypothesis upon which much of Wilson's analysis lies. Instead, he argues that the substantial decline since 1950 in jobs previously held by whites actually provided opportunities for ethnic occupational realignment—for nonwhites to replace whites in the city's labor force. However, what was distinctive about the manner in which nonwhites succeeded whites was the salience of distinct economic niches in which different ethnic groups were concentrated. For example, blacks tended to concentrate in public-sector jobs while immigrants were more likely to be found in a wide range of small, ethnically distinct businesses. Waldinger argues that ethnic-network recruiting tends to exclude nonethnics and thus to reinforce the ethnic identification of specific occupations. The tendency for ethnic enterprises to hire coethnics has an especially significant impact on native-born blacks, who are thus excluded from occupational opportunities controlled by immigrants, as well as those dominated by native-born whites. Thus he concludes that "native blacks are the big losers in the new ethnic division of labor."

Moreover, Zinn (1989) has challenged Wilson's assumptions about gender roles in explaining the emergence and persistence of black poverty and, especially, the dramatic increase in female-headed families among African Americans and Hispanics in the past quarter century. Wilson argues that the absence of stable job opportunities in the nation's major industrial areas has undermined the conception, much more widely embraced by Hispanic immigrants, of a "traditional family unit that features men as breadwinners." Zinn contends that both the cultural deficiency and the macrostructural models have similar underlying conceptions about gender and gender roles. Both models "assume that the traditional family is a key solution for eliminating racial poverty. . . . Both models rest on normative definitions of women's and men's roles . . . and traditional concepts of the family and women's and men's roles within it." Both, therefore, tend to ignore the role of gender in explaining poverty.

Zinn's critique raises important questions concerning the ways in which racial and ethnic phenomena are affected by gender. Until recently, there has been a tendency in the literature of racial and ethnic relations in the United States to generalize about these phenomena without considering gender. However, scholars have increasingly focused on the manner in which gender intersects with race and ethnicity.

For example, as Waters and Eschbach (Article 14) point out, the historical experiences of African Americans created patterns of both male and female labor-force participation different from those of European Americans. Because black men historically have confronted substantial occupational barriers to which white men have not been subject, until recently African American women have been much more likely to work outside the home than European American women. Consequently, "labor and earnings of African American women have made a much greater relative contribution to the economic survival of the African American family" (Geschwender and Carroll-Seguin 1990:289). Moreover, labor-force participation rates for European American women are highest among working-class families and decline as the husband's income increases. However, because the incomes of African American men are lower than those of European American men, more than one income is necessary for a black family to achieve comparable income levels. Therefore, the rate of labor-force participation for African American women increases as their husband's income increases. Geschwender and Carroll-Seguin conclude that whatever economic improvements two-parent African American families have made since the 1960s have occurred because African American wives "have been far more likely to work, and to work full-time. . . . Thus, the earnings of African American wives constituted a much greater percentage of family income than was the case among European Americans" (1990:298). On the other hand, Waters and Eschbach indicate that as women's presence in the labor force has grown over the past quarter century, the proportion of white women has come to exceed that of black women, and the earnings disparity between white and black women is much narrower than it is among black and white men.

Similarly, in a superb review essay, Pedraza (1991) has examined the role of women in migration processes, highlighting issues of gender that until recently have been ignored. Proposing a "gendered understanding of the social processes of migration," she contends that gender must not simply be considered as a variable, but as a central organizing principle in comprehending the dynamics of immigration and immigrant adaptation. As she notes, gender factors are central to the decision to migrate; women tend to migrate to create or reunite families, thus facilitating the networks that sustain migration chains. As a consequence, women are a central link between macro and micro factors in the migration process. Thus there are substantial gender differences in the way in which immigrants are incorporated into the receiving society. Finally, because women in most countries of origin are limited in the social roles available to them, immigration—if not more liberating for women—is at least different for women than for men; Pedraza suggests that, as a consequence, they are more reluctant to return to their homelands and are more likely to sponsor the immigration of female relatives. In "Gendered Immigration" (Article 25) Pierrette Hondagneu-Sotelo provides a textured and nuanced case study of many of these generalizations, emphasizing not only the way in which gender influences the migration process, but also how the migration process reconstructs gender relations themselves.

Multicultural America and the Future of Race and Ethnicity

At the 1963 March on Washington, Martin Luther King, Jr., delivered one of the most memorable speeches ever uttered by an American. In this address he spoke of his dream for the future:

> *I say to you today, my friends [that] even though we face difficulties of today and tomorrow, I still have a dream. It is a dream deeply rooted in the American dream. I have a dream that one day this nation will rise up and live out the true meaning of its creed that "all men are created equal." I have a dream . . . [of] that day when all God's children, black men and white men, Jews and Gentiles, Protestants and Catholics, will be able to join hands and sing in the words of that old Negro spiritual, "Free at last! Free at last! Thank God almighty, we are free at last."* (quoted in Oates 1982:255)

Within two years of his historic address, two of the most far-reaching pieces of federal legislation to help African Americans realize this dream—the 1964 Civil Rights Act and the 1965 Voting Rights Act—were enacted. Moreover, as noted before, the predominant thrust of public policy during the late 1960s was to undermine and deny the legitimacy of the forces of ethnic and racial particularism—to eliminate the formal barriers that had previously relegated certain racial and ethnic groups to second-class citizenship. These efforts were suffused with an optimism that racial and ethnic criteria would cease to be salient issues in American life, and that the dream of racial and ethnic equality of which King had so eloquently spoken would be realized.

Today, thirty-five years after King's historic address, despite the repudiation of racist ideologies and substantial changes in many facets of society, race and ethnicity remain prominent features of American life. Civil rights legislation and well-intentioned commitments on the part of many whites have not eliminated controversies over racial and ethnic matters. For example, social programs such as affirmative action, busing, and bilingual education, all of which were implemented in order to remedy the effects of past discrimination and to achieve greater equity among racial and ethnic groups, have been denounced by scholars and politicians who contend that they contravene the very goals of equality for which they were enacted. Indeed, far from withering away, debates concerning what constitutes a racially and ethnically just society, and what are the appropriate mechanisms with which to achieve it, show little sign of diminishing in intensity.

Most important, however, is that these debates creatively and dramatically be translated into public policies that imaginatively address the racial and ethnic inequalities in American life documented throughout this book. The urgency with which this goal should be considered is reflected in numerous reports, speeches, and appeals, but never more so than in one report, *One-Third of a Nation.* Prepared by a commission cochaired by former presidents Jimmy Carter and Gerald Ford, the report warned that the future prosperity of the United States was jeopardized by the nation's failures to address the problems confronted by its racial and ethnic minorities.

> *America is moving backward—not forward—in its efforts to achieve the full participation of minority citizens in the life and prosperity of the nation. . . . In education, employment, income, health, longevity, and other basic measures of individual and social well-being, gaps persist— and in some cases are widening—between members of minority groups and the majority population. . . . If we allow these disparities to continue, the United States inevitably will suffer a compromised quality of life and a lower standard of living. . . . In brief, we will find ourselves unable to fulfill the promise of the American dream. (American Council on Education 1988:1)*

A decade later, a private bipartisan commission appointed by the Milton S. Eisenhower Foundation to assess changes in American race relations since the 1968 Kerner Commission report reached a similar conclusion: despite a substantial expansion of the African American middle class in the succeeding thirty years, the threat of "two societies—one black, one white, separate and unequal" has persisted. Today American society is characterized by a "millenium breach"—increasing social inequality —that has dramatically and disproportionately affected African Americans and Hispanics (Eisenhower Foundation 1998). The ability of the United States to respond to the challenges of these growing inequalities will, in large measure, determine the nation's future prosperity and its stature in the estimation of the world during the twenty-first century.

TWENTY-THREE

The New Immigration and Ethnicity in the United States

Douglas S. Massey

As anyone who walks the streets of America's largest cities knows, there has been a profound transformation of immigration to the United States. Not only are there more immigrants, but increasingly they speak languages and bear cultures that are quite different from those brought by European immigrants in the past. The rapidity of the change and the scale of the movement have led to much consternation about what the "new immigration" means for American society.

Some worry about the economic effects of immigration, although quantitative analyses generally show that immigrants do not compete with native workers and do not have strong effects on US wage rates and employment levels (Borjas and Tienda 1987; Borjas 1990; Borjas and Freeman 1992). Others worry about the social welfare burden caused by immigrants, but studies again suggest that, with the exception of some refugee groups, immigrants do not drain public resources (see Blau 1984; Simon 1984; Borjas 1994; but Rothman and Espenshade 1992 show that local fiscal effects may be significant). Observers also express fears of linguistic fragmentation, but research indicates that immigrants generally shift into English as time passes and that their children move decisively into English if they grow up in the United States (Grenier 1984; Stevens 1985; Veltman 1988).

Despite this reassuring evidence, however, considerable disquiet remains about the new immigration and its consequences (see Espenshade and Calhoun 1993). Indeed, an immigrant backlash appears to be gathering force. English-only amendments have passed in several locales; federal immigration law has grown steadily more re-strictive and punitive; and politicians, led by Governor Pete Wilson of California, have discovered the political advantages that may be gained by blaming immigrants for current social and economic problems. Given the apparent animus toward immigrants and the imperviousness of public perceptions to the influence of objective research findings, one suspects that deeper forces are at work in the American psyche.

This consternation may have less to do with ascertainable facts about immigration than with unarticulated fears that immigrants will somehow create a very different society and culture in the United States. Whatever objective research says about the prospects for individual assimilation, the ethnic and racial composition of the United States is clearly changing, and with it the sociocultural world created by prior European immigrants and their descendants. According to demographic projections, Americans of European descent will become a minority in the United States sometime during the next century (Edmonston and Passel 1991), and this projected shift has already occurred in some urban areas, notably Los Angeles and Miami. In other metropolitan areas, such as New York, Chicago, Houston, and San Diego, the transformation is well underway.

This demographic reality suggests the real nature of the anti-immigrant reaction among non-Hispanic whites: a fear of cultural change and a deep-seated worry that European Americans will be displaced from their dominant position in American life. Most social scientists have been reluctant to address this issue, or even to acknowledge it (nonacademics, however, are not so

Reprinted with the permission of the Population Council, from *Population and Development Review,* Volume 21, Number 3, September 1995, pp. 631–652.

reticent—see Lamm and Imhoff 1985; Brimelow 1995). As a result, analyses by academic researchers have focused rather narrowly on facts and empirical issues: how many undocumented migrants are there, do they displace native workers, do they drive down wage rates, do they use more in services than they pay in taxes?

Answers to these questions do not get at the heart of the matter, however. What the public really wants to know (at least, I suspect, the native white public) is whether or not the new immigrants will assimilate into the Euro-American society of the United States, and how that society and its culture might change as a result of this incorporation. While social scientists have analyzed the state of the trees, the public has worried about the future of the forest, and no amount of empirical research has quieted these anxieties. In this article, I assess the prospects for the assimilation of the new immigrant groups and judge their likely effects on the society, culture, and language of the United States.

I begin by placing the new immigration in historical perspective and pointing out the distinctive features that set it apart from earlier immigrations. I then appraise the structural context for the incorporation of today's immigrants and argue that because of fundamental differences, their assimilation is unlikely to be as rapid or complete as that achieved by European immigrants in the past. I conclude by discussing how the nature of ethnicity is likely to change as a result of a new immigration that is linguistically concentrated, geographically clustered, and temporally continuous into an American society that is increasingly stratified and unequal.

THE NEW IMMIGRATION
IN HISTORICAL PERSPECTIVE

The history of US immigration during the twentieth century can be divided roughly into three phases: a *classic era* of mass European immigration stretching from about 1901 to 1930; a *long hiatus* of limited movement from 1931 to 1970; and a *new regime* of large-scale, non-European immigration that began around 1970 and continues to the present. The cutpoints 1930 and 1970 are to some extent arbitrary, of course, but they correspond roughly to major shifts in US immigration policy. The 1924 National Origins Act, which imposed strict country quotas, took full effect in

1929; and the 1965 amendments to the Immigration and Nationality Act, which repealed those quotas, took effect in 1968 (see Jasso and Rosenzweig 1990: 26–97).

Information on the size and composition of immigrant flows during the three periods is presented in Table 1. Actual counts of immigrants by region and decade (the data from which the table was largely derived) are presented in the Data Appendix [to this article]. In both tables, the figures refer to legal immigrants enumerated upon entry; they do not include undocumented migrants (see Massey and Singer 1995 for recent annual estimates), nor do they adjust for return migration, which studies have shown to be significant in both the classic era (Wyman 1993) and the new regime (Warren and Kraly 1985; Jasso and Rosenzweig 1990).

The classic years 1901–30 are actually part of a sustained 50-year period of mass immigration that began sometime around 1880. During this period some 28 million immigrants entered the United States and, except for two years at the end of World War I, the yearly total never fell below 200,000, and in most years it exceeded 400,000. The largest flows occurred in the first decades of the twentieth century. From 1901 to 1930 almost 19 million people arrived on American shores, yielding an annual average of 621,000 immigrants (see Table 1). The peak occurred in 1907 when some 1.3 million immigrants arrived. Until recently, these numbers were unequalled in American history.

The vast majority of these people came from Europe. Although the composition shifted from Northern and Western Europe to Southern and Eastern Europe as industrialization spread across the American continent (see Massey 1988; Morawska 1990), the composition throughout the first three decades of the century remained overwhelmingly European, averaging 80 percent for the entire period. As a result, the United States became less black, more white, and more firmly European in culture and outlook.

This period of mass immigration gave rise to some of the nation's enduring myths: about the struggle of immigrants to overcome poverty, about the achievement of economic mobility through individual effort, about the importance of group solidarity in the face of ethnic prejudice and discrimination, and about the inevitability of assimilation into the melting pot of American life. In the

TABLE 1 *Patterns of Immigration to the United States in Three Period of the Twentieth Century*

	Classic Era 1901–30	Long Hiatus 1931–70	New Regime 1971–93
Whole Period			
Region of origin (percent)			
Europe	79.6	46.2	13.0
Americas	16.2	43.6	49.6
Asia	3.7	8.6	34.5
Other	0.5	1.6	2.9
Total	100.0	100.0	100.0
Total immigration (thousands)	18,638	7,400	15,536
Annual average (thousands)	621	185	675
Peak year	1907	1968	1991
Peak immigration (thousands)	1,285	454	1,827
First Ten Years			
Region of origin (percent)			
Europe	91.6	65.9	17.8
Americas	4.1	30.3	44.1
Asia	3.7	3.2	35.3
Other	0.6	0.6	2.8
Total	100.0	100.0	100.0
Total immigration (thousands)	8,795	528	4,493
Annual average (thousands)	880	53	449
Last Ten Years			
Region of origin (percent)			
Europe	60.0	33.8	10.2
Americas	36.9	51.7	54.0
Asia	2.7	12.9	32.7
Other	0.4	1.6	3.1
Total	100.0	100.0	100.0
Total immigration (thousands)	4,107	3,322	9,293
Annual average (thousands)	411	332	929

words of an influential social scientist at midcentury, the first decades of the century offer "The Epic Story of the Great Migrations that Made the American People" (Handlin 1951). Although a reaction against the melting pot myth later arose in the second and third generations, this was largely a symbolic opposition by people who had watched their parents and grandparents suffer under "Northern European" dominance, but who by the 1960s had largely penetrated arenas of power, prestige, and influence and wanted to let the world know about it (see Glazer and Moynihan 1970; Greely 1971; Novak 1971).

The classic era of mass immigration was followed by a 40-year hiatus during which immi-gration levels fell to very low levels and the predominance of European immigrants came to an end. From 1931 to 1970, average annual immigration fell to 185,000 and the share arriving from the Americas increased substantially, eventually equalling that from Europe. Over the entire hiatus period, 44 percent of immigrants came from the Americas, compared with 46 percent from Europe and 9 percent from Asia (the last region, according to the Immigration and Naturalization Service, includes the Middle East, which has contributed a small number of immigrants over the years, compared with such countries as China, Korea, the Philippines, and Japan). By the last decade of the hiatus, 52 percent of all immigrants were from the

Americas and only 34 percent came from Europe; the peak year of immigration occurred in 1968, when 454,000 people were admitted for permanent residence.

As I have already noted, the dividing points of 1930 and 1970 are somewhat arbitrary and were chosen partly for convenience, since decennial years are easy to remember and correspond to the decennial tabulations favored by demographers. Evidence of the coming hiatus was already apparent in the last decade of the classic era, when immigration levels were a third below their 1901–30 average (411,000 rather than 621,000) and about half the average that prevailed in the first decade of the century (880,000). Moreover, by the end of the classic era, immigrants' origins were already shifting toward the Americas. Whereas 92 percent of all immigrants in the first decade of the century were European, by the 1920s the percentage had dropped to 60 percent. Although it was not recognized for many years, the era of massive European immigration was already beginning to wind down.

The termination of mass immigration around 1930 is attributable to many factors. The one that scholars most often credit is the passage of restrictive immigration legislation. In response to a public backlash against immigrants, Congress passed two new "quota laws," in 1921 and 1924, that were designed to limit the number of immigrants and shift their origins from Southern and Eastern Europe back to Northern and Western Europe (where they belonged, at least in the view of the nativist voters of the time—see Higham 1963 and Hutchinson 1981).

Although the national origins quotas, combined with earlier bans on Asian immigration enacted in 1882 and 1917, did play a role in reducing the number of immigrants, I believe their influence has been overstated. For one thing, the new quotas did not apply at all to immigrants from the Western Hemisphere, leaving the door wide open for mass entry from Latin America, particularly Mexico. Indeed, beginning in the decade of the 1910s, employers in Northern industrial cities of the United States began to recruit extensively in Mexico, and immigration from that country mushroomed from 50,000 in the first decade of the century, to 220,000 in the second, to 460,000 in the third (see Cardoso 1980). Were it not for other factors, the change in immigration law would, at most, have shifted the na-

tional origins of immigrants more decisively toward the Americas in the 1930s, but it would not have halted immigration per se.

More than any change in legislation, however, the outbreak of World War I in 1914 brought a sudden and decisive halt to the flow of immigrants from Europe. During the first half of the decade, the outflow proceeded apace: 926,000 European immigrants arrived in the United States in 1910, 765,000 in 1911, and just over 1 million came in both 1913 and 1914. During the first full year of the war, however, immigration dropped to 198,000 and it fell every year thereafter to reach a low point of 31,000 in 1918. As a result, during the 1910s total immigration was halved compared with the prior decade (Ferenczi 1929).

During the 1920s, European immigration began to revive, despite the restrictive immigration quotas. Some 412,000 immigrants arrived from Germany during 1921–30, 455,000 came from Italy, 227,000 from Poland, and 102,000 from Czechoslovakia. These entries supplemented large numbers arriving from European countries that were not limited by the new quotas: 211,000 from Ireland, 340,000 from Britain, and 166,000 from Norway and Sweden combined. One country, however, is notably absent from European immigrant flows of the 1920s: Russia, or as it was now known, the Soviet Union (US Immigration and Naturalization Service 1994: 27).

Prior to World War I, immigration from Russia had been massive: 1.6 million Russian immigrants entered the United States during the first decade of the century, and 921,000 managed to get in during the subsequent decade despite the outbreak of war in 1914. The great majority of these people were Jews escaping the rampant anti-Semitism and pogroms of Czarist Russia (see Nugent 1992: 83–94); but with the Bolshevik Revolution of 1917 and the consolidation of the world's first communist state, the Russian Pale was abruptly disconnected from the capitalist West and emigration was suppressed by a new state security apparatus. As a result, immigration from Russia fell to a total of only 62,000 in the 1920s and to just 1,400 during the 1930s. The flow of Russian immigrants did not exceed 2,500 again until the 1970s (US Immigration and Naturalization Service 1994: 27–28).

Just as immigration from non-Russian Europe was gaining ground during the 1920s, another cataclysmic event virtually halted all international migration: the Great Depression. From a total of 241,000 immigrants in 1930, the flow dropped to 23,000 three years later. With mass unemployment in the United States, the demand for immigrant workers evaporated and during the 1930s total immigration fell below 1 million for the first time since the 1830s. Only 528,000 immigrants entered the United States from 1931 to 1940, yielding an annual average of only 53,000.

Before the Great Depression had ended, World War II broke out to add another barrier to international movement. During the war years the flow of immigrants to the United States fell once again. From a depression-era peak of 83,000 in 1939, the number of immigrants fell to only 24,000 in 1943; and during six years of warfare, the number of immigrants averaged only 40,000 per year, lower even than during the depression years of 1930–39 (US Immigration and Naturalization Service 1994: 27–28).

With the termination of hostilities in 1945, immigration from Europe finally resumed; but by 1945 the face of Europe had changed dramatically. The Cold War had begun and the boundary line marking the area of communist dominance had shifted westward. In addition to the Soviet Union, Eastern Europe was now cut off from the capitalist economy of the West. Countries such as Czechoslovakia, Hungary, Romania, and Yugoslavia, which had sent large numbers of immigrants before the depression, contributed few after 1945. Although 228,000 Polish immigrants came to the United States during the 1920s, only 10,000 entered during the 1950s.

Just as the avenues for emigration from Eastern Europe were blocked, the countries of Western Europe began to seek workers to rebuild their war-shattered economies. The wave of investment and economic growth triggered by the Marshall Plan created a strong demand for labor that, by the 1950s, began to exceed domestic supplies of most countries (Kindleberger 1967). As the postwar economy expanded and the pace of growth quickened, Germany, France, Britain, Belgium, and the Netherlands not only stopped sending migrants abroad, they all became countries of immigration themselves, attracting large numbers of immigrants from Southern Europe and then, as these sources dried up, from the Balkans, Turkey, North Africa, and Asia (see

Stalker 1994). The era of mass European migration to the United States was finally and decisively over.

Although immigrants were no longer available in large numbers from Europe, the postwar boom in the United States nonetheless created a strong demand for labor there. With Eastern Europe cut off and Western Europe itself a magnet for immigration, this new demand was met by Latin Americans, whose entry was unregulated under the quotas of the 1920s. The number of Mexican immigrants rose from 61,000 in the 1940s to 300,000 in the 1950s and 454,000 during the 1960s. This expansion of immigration was not limited to Mexico. During the last decade of the hiatus period, some 200,000 Cubans entered the United States, along with 100,000 Dominicans and 70,000 Colombians. A new era of non-European immigration was clearly on the rise (US Immigration and Naturalization Service 1994: 27–28).

It has become conventional to date the emergence of the new regime in US immigration from the passage of the 1965 amendments to the Immigration and Nationality Act, which were phased in and implemented fully in 1968. In keeping with the spirit of the times, this legislation abolished the discriminatory national-origins quotas and ended the ban on Asian entry. It put each nation in the Eastern Hemisphere on an equal footing by establishing a uniform limit of 20,000 entrants per country; it set an over-all hemispheric cap of 170,000 immigrants; and it established a "preference system" of family and occupational categories to allocate visas under these limits. The amendments exempted immediate relatives of US citizens from the numerical caps, however, and nations in the Western Hemisphere were subject only to a hemispheric cap of 120,000 immigrants, not a 20,000-per-country limit.

Although this legislation contributed to the creation of the new immigration regime, it was neither the sole nor the most important cause of the increase in numbers or the shift in origins. As with the national-origins quotas, I believe scholars have generally overstated the role of the 1965 amendments in bringing about the new immigration. The Immigration and Nationality Act was in no way responsible for the drop in European immigration, for example, since this trend was clearly visible before 1965 and followed from other conditions described above.

Nor did the 1965 Act increase the level of immigration from Latin America. On the contrary, by placing the first-ever cap on immigration from the Western Hemisphere, the legislation actually made it more difficult for Latin Americans to enter the United States. Since 1965, additional amendments have further restricted entry from nations in the Western Hemisphere, placing them under the 20,000-per-country limit, abolishing the separate hemispheric caps, eliminating the right of minor children to sponsor the immigration of parents, and repealing the "Texas Proviso" that exempted employers from prosecution for hiring undocumented migrants. Rather than promoting the shift toward Latin American origins, then, the 1965 Act and its successor amendments actually inhibited the transformation. The shift in origins occurred in spite of the legislation, not because of it.

The one effect that the 1965 Act did have was to remove the ban on Asian entry and thereby unleash an unprecedented and entirely unexpected flow of immigrants from Korea, Taiwan, China, the Philippines, and other Asian countries (see Glazer 1985). At the time, the legislation was seen as a way of redressing past wrongs that had been visited upon Eastern and Southern Europeans and of mollifying the resentment of their children and grandchildren, who had risen to wield powerful political influence in the Democratic Party, which dominated the US Congress. Rather than opening the United States to immigration from, say, Italy and Poland, however, as legislators such as Peter Rodino and Dan Rostenkowski had intended, its principal effect was to initiate large-scale immigration from Asia.

As Table 1 shows, the percentage of Asians rose from under 10 percent of immigrants during the classic and hiatus eras, to around 35 percent under the new regime that began after 1970. Whereas only 35,000 Chinese, 35,000 Indians, and 34,000 Koreans were admitted as immigrants during the 1960s, by the 1980s these numbers had become 347,000, 251,000, and 334,000, respectively (US Immigration and Naturalization Service 1994: 27–28). As a result of this sharp and sudden increase in Asian immigration, the percentage of Asians in the US population began rising for the first time in more than a century.

Yet by themselves the 1965 amendments cannot explain the remarkable surge in Asian immigration. Another key factor was the loss of the Vietnam War and the subsequent collapse of the US-backed governments in Indochina. With the fall of Saigon in 1975, the United States faced new demands for entry by thousands of military officers, government officials, and US employees fearful of reprisals from the new communist authorities. As economic and political conditions in Vietnam deteriorated during the late 1970s and early 1980s, larger numbers of soldiers, minor officials, and merchants took to the seas in desperate attempts to escape.

For both political and humanitarian reasons, the United States had little choice but to accept these people outside the numerical limits established under the 1965 Act. Although only 335 Vietnamese entered the United States during the 1950s and 4,300 arrived during the 1960s, 172,000 were admitted during the 1970s and 281,000 arrived during the 1980s. In addition to the Vietnamese, the US misadventure in Indochina led to the entry of many thousands of Cambodian, Laotian, and Hmong refugees, an influx that collectively totaled 300,000 by 1990. In all, about a third of Asian immigrants since 1970 can be traced to the failed intervention of the United States in Indochina (US Immigration and Naturalization Service 1994: 28).

For different reasons, therefore, immigration from Asia and Latin America has surged over the past two decades. According to official statistics, the total annual flow of immigrants averaged 675,000 during the period 1971–93, an influx that in absolute terms exceeds the 621,000 observed during the classic era from 1901 to 1930. Unlike the entrants during the earlier period, these 15.5 million new immigrants were overwhelmingly non-European: about half came from Latin America and over a third originated in Asia; 13 percent were from Europe. The peak year was 1991, when 1.8 million persons were admitted for permanent residence in the United States.

As large as the annual flow of 675,000 immigrants is, both absolutely and relative to earlier periods in US history, it nonetheless constitutes an underestimate of the true level of immigration, for it does not capture the full extent of undocumented migration to the United States, a category that became increasingly important during the 1970s and 1980s. Although the figures summarized in Table 1 include 3.3 million former undocumented migrants who legalized their status under the 1986 Immigration Reform and Control Act (IRCA), they do not include other illegal migrants who failed to qualify for the amnesty program or who entered after 1986.

Woodrow-Lafield (1993) estimates that about 3.3 million additional undocumented immigrants lived in the United States as of 1990, bringing the total number of immigrants for the period 1971–93 to around 854,000 per year. This figure still understates the true size of the inflow, however, because her estimate does not include immigrants who entered illegally and subsequently died, or those who subsequently emigrated. Full incorporation of all undocumented migrants into the figures of Table 1 would boost the relative share of Latin Americans even more, given the predominance of Mexicans in this population. Among undocumented migrants counted in the 1980 census, estimates suggest that 55 percent were Mexican (Warren and Passel 1987), and of those legalized under IRCA, 75 percent were from Mexico (US Immigration and Naturalization Service 1991).

Whatever allowance one makes for undocumented migration, it is clear that around 1970 the United States embarked on a new regime of immigration that marks a clear break with the past. The new immigration is composed of immigrants from Asia and Latin America, a large share of whom are undocumented and who are arriving in substantially larger numbers compared with earlier periods of high immigration. Although the 1965 amendments to the Immigration and Nationality Act played some role in creating this new regime, ultimately the effect of US immigration policy has been secondary. The dramatic change reflects more powerful forces operating in the United States and elsewhere in the world.

THE NEW IMMIGRATION AND THE FUTURE OF ETHNICITY

No matter what one's opinion of the melting pot ideology, the remarkable amalgamation of European immigrants into the society and culture of the United States is a historical fact. The disparate groups that entered the country in great numbers between 1880 and 1930—Italians, Poles, Czechs, Hungarians, Lithuanians, and Russian Jews—were not only quite different from prior waves of immigrants from Northern and Western Europe, they were also quite different from one another in terms of language, literacy, culture, and economic background. After several generations of US residence, however, the differences are largely gone and the various groups have to a great extent merged together to form one large, amorphous class of mixed European ancestry.

By 1980, most people reporting ancestry in Southern or Eastern Europe were in their third or fourth generation of US residence, and as a result of extensive intermarriage in earlier generations, they were increasingly of mixed origins. Over half of those reporting Polish, Russian, Czech, or Hungarian ancestry in the 1980 census were of mixed parentage; and the rate of intermarriage was 60 percent for women of Italian and Russian origin, 70 percent for Polish women, 83 percent for Czech women, and 88 percent for Hungarian women. For all women, the odds of intermarriage rose sharply as one moved from older to younger cohorts, and intergroup differences with respect to income, education, and occupation had all but disappeared (Lieberson and Waters 1988).

As a result of rapid growth in the population of mixed European ancestry, white Americans are gradually losing contact with their immigrant origins. Research by Alba (1990) shows that such people do not regularly cook or consume ethnic foods; they report experiencing little or no ethnic prejudice or discrimination; they are largely uninvolved and uninterested in ethnic politics; they are unlikely to be members of any ethnic social or political organization; and they tend not to live in ethnic neighborhoods.

Although most white Americans identify themselves ethnically, the labels are growing increasingly complex and the percentage who call themselves "American" or "nothing at all" is rising (Lieberson and Waters 1988; Alba 1990). In the late twentieth-century social world of European Americans, where intermarriage is pervasive, mixed ancestries are common, economic differences are trivial, and residential mixing is the norm, ethnicity has become symbolic (Gans 1979), a choice made from a range of "ethnic options" that are loosely tied to ancestry (Waters 1990).

Compared with the ascriptive ethnicity of the past, the descendants of European immigrants are moving into the "twilight of ethnicity" (Alba 1981), and rather than signaling a lack of assimilation, the use of ethnic labels proves how far assimilation has come. The amalgamation of European ethnic groups has proceeded to such an extent that expressions of ethnic identity are no longer perceived as threats to national unity. On the contrary, the use of ethnic labels has become a way of identifying oneself as American (Alba 1990).

It is natural to view the process of European assimilation as a model for the incorporation of Asians and Latin Americans into US society. Present fears of ethnic fragmentation are assuaged by noting that similar fears were expressed about the immigration of Italians, Poles, and Jews. Nativist worries are allayed by showing that today's immigrants appear to be assimilating much as in the past. According to available evidence, income and occupational status rise with time spent in the United States; patterns of fertility, language, and residence come to resemble those of natives as socioeconomic status and generations increase; and intermarriage becomes increasingly common with each succeeding generation and increment in income and education (Massey 1981; Jasso and Rosenzweig 1990).

Focusing on individual patterns of assimilation, however, ignores the structural context within which the assimilation occurs. By focusing on microlevel analyses of immigrant attainment, we forget that the remarkable absorption of European immigrants in the past was facilitated, and to a large extent enabled, by historical conditions that no longer prevail. Compared with the great European immigrations, the new immigration differs in several crucial respects that significantly alter the prospects for assimilation and, hence, the meaning of ethnicity for the next century.

The first unique historical feature of European immigration is that it was followed by a long hiatus when few additional Europeans arrived. Although nearly 15 million European immigrants entered the United States in the three decades between 1901 and 1930, for the next 60 years the flow fell to the functional equivalent of zero. Compared with an annual average of 495,000 European immigrants from 1901 to 1930, only 85,000 arrived each year from 1931 through 1970, and most of these were not Poles, Italians, or Russian Jews, the big groups before 1930. Although overall immigration revived after 1970, the flow from Europe remained small at around 88,000 per year.

Thus, after the entry of large numbers of Europeans for some 50 years, the influx suddenly stopped and for the next 60 years—roughly three generations—it was reduced to a trickle. The cutting off of immigration from Europe eliminated the supply of raw materials for the grist mill of ethnicity in the United States, ensuring that whatever ethnic identities existed would be predominantly a consequence of events and processes operating within the United States.

Without a fresh supply of immigrants each year, the generational composition of people labeled "Italians," "Poles," and "Czechs" inexorably shifted: first, foreigners gave way to the native-born, then first-generation natives yielded to the children of natives, and more recently the children of natives have given way to the grandchildren of natives. Over time, successive generations dominated the populations of European ethnic groups and came to determine their character. With each generational transition, ethnic identities and the meaning of ethnicity itself shifted until finally most groups moved into the "twilight of ethnicity."

This pattern of assimilation was undoubtedly greatly facilitated by the long hiatus in European immigration. In essence, it gave the United States a "breathing space" within which slow-moving social and economic processes leading to assimilation could operate. The hiatus shaped and constrained the meaning of ethnicity by limiting the generational complexity underlying each group's ethnic identity: the ending of European immigration in 1930 meant that for all practical purposes, ethnic groups would never include more than three generations at any point in time.

In addition to generational change, the other engine of immigrant assimilation is social mobility, and a second historical feature of European immigration is that it was followed by a sustained economic expansion that offered unusual opportunities for socioeconomic advancement. From 1940 through 1973, incomes rose, productivity increased, unemployment fell, income inequality diminished, poverty rates declined, rates of college attendance grew, and housing improved as the US standard of living seemed to rise effortlessly each year (Galbraith 1963; Levy 1987, 1995). First- and second-generation immigrants from Southern and Eastern Europe rode this wave of prosperity to achieve full economic parity with Northern and Western Europeans by 1980.

Thus, two structural conditions—the long hiatus in immigration and the economic boom that accompanied it—are primarily responsible for the remarkable assimilation of European immigrants into the United States. Were either of these factors lacking, the story of immigrant arrival, adaptation, and ultimate absorption would have had a very different conclusion than movement into the twilight of ethnicity or the emergence of symbolic ethnicity. On the other hand, neither of these two structural conditions is likely to hold for the new immigrants from Asia and Latin America, and the patterns and outcomes of assimilation are likely to be quite different as a result.

Rather than having the opportunity of a 60-year "breathing space" within which to absorb and accommodate large cohorts of immigrants, the United States will more likely become a country of perpetual immigration. Unlike the European ethnic groups of the past, today's Latin Americans and Asians can expect to have their numbers continuously augmented by a steady supply of fresh arrivals from abroad. Rather than being a one-time historical phenomenon, immigration has become a permanent structural feature of the postindustrial society of the United States.

Although the relative influence of the different causes is a matter of debate (Massey et al. 1993), international migration clearly stems from a complex interplay of forces operating at several levels (Massey et al. 1994). Wage differentials between poor and affluent countries provide incentives for individuals to migrate to reap higher lifetime earnings at the destination (Todaro 1976; Todaro and Maruszko 1987). Households send migrants to work in foreign labor markets as a means of self-insuring against risk and overcoming capital constraints created by market failures at home (Stark 1991). A demand for immigrants arises in postindustrial societies because market segmentation creates a class of jobs with low pay, little status, and few mobility prospects that native workers will not accept (Piore 1979); and the penetration of market forces into developing societies itself creates a mobile population disposed to international movement (Sassen 1988). The effect is amplified by rapid population growth in the developing world.

Once begun, migratory flows acquire a momentum that is resistant to management or regulation (Massey 1990a). Networks of social ties develop to link migrants in destination areas to friends and relatives in sending regions (Massey et al. 1994). Branch communities eventually form in the receiving society, giving rise to enclave economies that act as magnets for additional immigration (Portes and Bach 1985; Portes and Manning 1986; Logan, Alba, and McNulty 1994). Large-scale emigration causes other social and economic changes within both sending and receiving societies that lead to its cumulative causation over time (Massey 1990b).

Thus, current knowledge about the forces behind international migration suggests that movement to the United States will grow, not decline. None of the conditions known to play a role in initiating international migratory flows—wage differentials, market failures, labor market segmentation, globalization of the economy—is likely to end any time soon. Moreover, the forces that perpetuate international movement—network formation, cumulative causation—help to ensure that these flows will continue into the foreseeable future.

To a great extent, these forces are beyond the immediate reach of US policy, particularly immigration policy. Despite the passage of more-restrictive immigration laws and the enactment of increasingly punitive policies, illegal migration from Mexico (and elsewhere) has continued to grow and shows no signs of diminishing (Donato, Durand, and Massey 1992; Massey and Singer 1995). Although politicians call for even stronger measures (Lamm and Imhoff 1985), the forces producing and perpetuating immigration appear to be of such a magnitude that the new regime of US immigration may continue indefinitely.

The belief that immigration flows can be controlled through legislation stems from a misreading of US history. Although the cessation of European immigration in 1930 is widely attributed to the implementation of restrictive quotas in the early 1920s, I argue that the cutoff actually occurred because of a unique sequence of cataclysmic events: World War I, the Bolshevik Revolution, the Great Depression, and World War II. A similar string of destructive and bloody events might arise to extinguish the powerful migratory flows that have become well established through-out Latin America and Asia, but for the sake of the world we should hope they do not.

In all likelihood, therefore, the United States has already become a country of perpetual immigration, one characterized by the continuous arrival of large cohorts of immigrants from particular regions. This fact will inevitably create a very different structure of ethnicity compared with that prevailing among European immigrant groups in the past. Changes in the size of populations from Latin America and Asia will be brought about not only through assimilative processes such as generational succession and intermarriage, but also through the countervailing process of net immigration. In contrast to European ethnics, the ranks of Latin American and Asian ethnics will be augmented continuously with new arrivals from abroad.

Rather than creating relatively homogenous populations spanning at most three generations, the new regime will therefore produce heterogeneous ethnic populations characterized by considerable generational complexity. Processes of social and economic assimilation acting upon earlier arrivals and their children, when combined with the perpetual arrival of new immigrants, will lead to the fragmentation of ethnicity along the lines of class, generation, and ancestry. Rather than a slow, steady, and relatively coherent progression of ethnicity toward twilight, it will increasingly stretch from dawn to dusk.

Moreover, because the social and economic forces that produce assimilation operate slowly, while those promoting immigration work quickly, the rate at which ethnic culture is augmented by new arrivals from abroad will tend to exceed the rate at which new ethnic culture is created through generational succession, social mobility, and intermarriage in the United States. As a result, the character of ethnicity will be determined relatively more by immigrants and relatively less by later generations, shifting the balance of ethnic identity toward the language, culture, and ways of life of the sending society.

The future state of ethnicity in the United States is now seen most clearly in the Mexican American population. Upon the annexation of northern Mexico into the United States in 1848, fewer than 50,000 Mexicans became US citizens (Jaffe, Cullen, and Boswell 1980). Virtually all Mexican Americans today are descendants of immigrants who arrived in the 100 years between 1890 and the present. During this time, the United States experienced continuous immigration from Mexico except for a brief, ten-year span during the 1930s, thereby establishing a pattern that will probably characterize other streams of immigration in the future (Hoffman 1974; Cardoso 1980; Massey et al. 1987).

Owing to the long history of immigration from Mexico, Mexican Americans are distributed across a variety of generations, socioeconomic classes, legal statuses, ancestries, languages, and, ultimately, identities (Bean and Tienda 1987). Rather than the relatively coherent identity that characterized European ethnic groups, Mexican identity is rife with internal divisions, conflicts, contradictions, and tensions (Browning and de la Garza 1986; Nelson and Tienda 1985). The fragmented state of ethnicity is reflected in the fact that the US Bureau of the Census must use three separate identifiers in its Spanish Origin question—Mexican, Mexican American, and Chicano—each of which corresponds to a particular conception of Mexican identity (García 1981).

Not only will continuous immigration create a new, complex, and fragmented kind of ethnicity, but the new immigrants and their descendants are likely to encounter a very different economy from the one experienced by the European immigrants and their children. Rather than rising prosperity and occupational mobility, current economic trends point in the opposite direction. In the United States since 1973, wages have stagnated and income inequality has grown (Phillips 1990; Levy 1995); the long decline in poverty rates ended (Smith 1988); and mobility in the occupational structure has decreased (Hout 1988). Moreover, just at the point when public schools used by immigrants have fallen into neglect, the importance of education in the US stratification system has increased (Hout 1988; DiPrete and Grusky 1990; Levy 1995), particularly for Hispanics (Stolzenberg 1990).

Thus, not only will the United States lack the opportunity of an extended period within which to absorb and integrate an unprecedented number of new immigrants, but one of the basic engines of past assimilation may be missing: a robust economy that produces avenues of upward mobility for people with limited education. Continuous immigration will strengthen the relative influence of first-generation arrivals in creating ethnic culture, while the rigidification of the US stratification system will slow the rate of socioeconomic advancement among the second and third generations, making them look more like the first. Both of these structural conditions will increase the relative weight of the sending country's language and culture in defining ethnic identity.

The new immigration also differs from European immigration in other respects likely to influence the creation and maintenance of ethnicity in the United States. Although the flow of immigrants from 1971 to 1993 is actually smaller relative to the size of the US population than the flow during the classic era, it is more concentrated in terms of national origins and language. As Table 2 shows, the rate of legal immigration (3.0 per thousand population) is presently less than half that observed during the classic era (6.3 per thousand); and even making an allowance for undocumented migration (raising the total annual flow to 830,000) does not erase the differential (it increases the rate only to 3.8 per thousand population). But whereas the largest nationality of the classic era (Italians) represented only 19 percent

of the total flow of immigrants, the largest group under the new regime (Mexicans) constitutes 24 percent of the flow. Moreover, whereas the language most often spoken by immigrants in the classic era (Italian) was confined to immigrants from one country, the most important language among the new immigrants (Spanish) is spoken by migrants from a dozen countries who together constitute 38 percent of all arrivals.

Thus, although European immigrants were relatively larger in number, they were scattered across more national-origin groups and languages, thereby reducing their salience for native white Americans and limiting the possibilities for linguistic segmentation in the United States. For European immigrants during the classic era, the only practical lingua franca was English; but since nearly 40 percent of the new immigrants speak the same language, Spanish becomes viable as a second language of daily life, creating the possibility of a bilingual society.

The new immigrants are not only more concentrated linguistically, they are also more clustered geographically. In 1910 the five most important immigrant-receiving states of the United States—New York, Pennsylvania, Illinois, Massachusetts, and New Jersey—took in 54 percent of the total flow, whereas the five most important urban

TABLE 2 *Indicators of the Relative Size and Concentration of Immigration to the United States in Two Periods of the Twentieth Century*

	Classic Era 1901–30	New Regime 1971–93
Rate of immigration (per 1,000 population)	6.3	3.0
Rate of immigration (including undocumented migrants)	6.3	3.8
Share of largest national group (percent)	19.4	23.6
Share of largest linguistic group (percent)	19.4	38.4
Share of the five most important destination states, 1910 and 1990 (percent)*	54.0	78.2
Share of the five most important urban destinations, 1910 and 1990 (percent)†	35.6	47.9

Sources: US Immigration and Naturalization Service 1991, 1993: Tables 2, 17, and 18; US Bureau of the Census 1913: Tables 15 and 16.

*In 1910 the five most important destination states were New York, Pennsylvania, Illinois, Massachusetts, and New Jersey; in 1990 they were California, New York, Texas, Illinois, and Florida.

†In 1910 the five most important urban destinations were New York, Chicago, Philadelphia, Cleveland, and Boston; in 1990 they were Los Angeles, New York, Chicago, Anaheim-Santa Ana, and Houston.

destinations (New York, Chicago, Philadelphia, Cleveland, and Boston) received 36 percent of the flow. By 1990, in contrast, the five most important immigrant-receiving states—California, New York, Texas, Illinois, and Florida—absorbed 78 percent of the flow, and the five most important urban areas (Los Angeles, New York, Chicago, Anaheim–Santa Ana, and Houston) received nearly half of all entering immigrants. The metropolitan areas receiving these immigrants—notably New York, Chicago, and Los Angeles—were the most important centers of communication and mass media in the country, guaranteeing that the new immigration would be a visible presence not only in the cosmopolitan centers of the East and West coasts, but in the country at large.

The increasing concentration of Spanish-speaking immigrants in a few metropolitan areas will inevitably change the process of assimilation itself. Through the new immigration, large communities of Spanish speakers will emerge in many US urban areas, lowering the economic and social costs of not speaking English while raising the benefits of speaking Spanish. As a result, the new immigrants from Latin America are less likely to learn English than were their European counterparts at the turn of the century (Jasso and Rosenzweig 1990). The emergence of immigrant enclaves—a process already well advanced in many areas—also reduces the incentives and opportunities to learn other cultural habits and behavioral attributes of Euro-American society.

CONCLUSION

The new immigration to the United States from Asia and Latin America that has become increasingly prominent since 1970 has several features that distinguish it from the older European immigration of the early twentieth century. First, the new immigration is part of an ongoing flow that can be expected to be sustained indefinitely, making the United States a country of continuous immigration rather than a nation of periodic entry. Second, the new immigrants will likely enter a highly stratified society characterized by high income inequality and growing labor market segmentation that will provide fewer opportunities for upward mobility. Third, national origins and geographic destinations of the new immigrants are highly concentrated, creating large foreign-language and cultural communities in many areas of the United States.

That these distinctive conditions will prevail in the coming decades and beyond is, of course, conjectural—other scenarios are also possible. I would argue, however, that the conditions I described are the most likely outcome of existing and well-established trends. If so, the experience of European immigrants provides a poor model for the assimilation and incorporation of new immigrants from Asia and Latin America. Rather than relatively homogenous ethnic groups moving steadily toward assimilation with the American majority, the new immigration will create complex ethnic groups fragmented along the lines of generation, class, ancestry, and, ultimately, identity. Rather than ethnic populations moving toward the twilight of ethnic identity, ethnicity itself will be stretched out across the generations to reach from dawn to dusk.

The uninterrupted flow of immigrants from Latin America will also increase the prevalence and influence of the Spanish language and Latin culture in the United States. Large Spanish-speaking communities have already emerged in the gateway cities of New York, Los Angeles, Houston, and Chicago, and Latinos have become the majority in Miami, San Antonio, and in most cities along the Mexico–US border. The combination of continuous immigration and high regional and linguistic concentration will produce more such communities and will move the United States toward bilingualism and biculturalism. Assimilation will become more of a two-way street, with Euro-Americans learning Spanish and consuming Latin cultural products as well as Latins learning English and consuming Anglo-American products. Increasingly the economic benefits and prospects for mobility will accrue to those able to speak both languages and move in two cultural worlds.

Since these trends will occur in an increasingly rigid and stratified society, growing antagonisms along class and ethnic lines can be expected, both within and between groups. Given the salience of race in American life, the acceleration of black immigration from Africa and the Caribbean, and the history of racial conflict and hostility in the United States, the relationship between native blacks and the new immigrants is likely to be particularly conflict-ridden (see Portes and Stepick 1993; Portes and Zhou 1993).

Although these trends are now most apparent with respect to Latin Americans, especially Mexicans, the potential for immigration and ethnic transformation is probably greater in Asia, where migration to the United States has just begun. The potential for Chinese immigration alone is enormous. Already the Chinese make up 7 percent of all legal immigrants, not counting the ethnic Chinese from various Southeast Asian countries, and Chinatowns have arisen and expanded in many US cities. Since theory and empirical evidence suggest that large-scale emigration is created by economic development and market penetration (Massey 1988; Hatton and Williamson 1992), China's move-

ment toward markets and rapid economic growth may contain the seeds of an enormous migration.

Even a small rate of emigration, when applied to a country with more than a billion people, would produce a flow of immigrants that would dwarf levels of migration now observed from Mexico. Social networks linking China and the United States are now being formed and in the future will serve as the basis for mass entry. Immigration from China and other populous, rapidly developing nations in Asia has an unrecognized potential to transform America's ethnic composition and to further alter the meaning and conception of ethnicity in the United States.

DATA APPENDIX   *Immigrants to the United States from Major World Regions: Numbers by Decade 1901–90 and for 1991–93 (thousands)*

	REGION OF ORIGIN				
Years	*Europe*	*Americas*	*Asia*	*Other*	*Total*
1901–10	8,056	362	324	53	8,795
1911–20	4,322	1,144	247	23	5,736
1921–30	2,463	1,517	112	15	4,107
1931–40	348	160	17	3	528
1941–50	621	356	37	21	1,035
1951–60	1,326	997	153	39	2,515
1961–70	1,123	1,716	428	55	3,322
1971–80	800	1,983	1,588	122	4,493
1981–90	762	3,615	2,738	223	7,338
1991–93	466	2,104	1,032	103	3,705
1901–93	20,287	13,954	6,676	657	41,574

Source: US Immigration and Naturalization Service 1994: Table 2.

America's Immigration "Problem"

Saskia Sassen

Immigration has traditionally aroused strong passions in the United States. Although Americans like to profess pride in their history as "a nation of immigrants," each group of arrivals, once established, has fought to keep newcomers out. Over the past two centuries, each new wave of immigrants has encountered strenuous opposition from earlier arrivals, who have insisted that the country was already filled to capacity. (The single exception to this was the South's eagerness to import ever more slaves.) Similar efforts to shut out newcomers persist today. But those who would close the door to immigration are mistaken on two counts: not only do they underestimate the country's capacity to absorb more people, but they also fail to appreciate the political and economic forces that give rise to immigration in the first place.

U.S. policymakers and the public alike believe the causes of immigration are self-evident: people who migrate to the United States are driven to do so by poverty, economic stagnation, and overpopulation in their home countries. Since immigration is thought to result from unfavorable socioeconomic conditions in other countries, it is assumed to be unrelated to U.S. economic needs or broader international economic conditions. In this context, the decision on whether to take in immigrants comes to be seen primarily as a humanitarian matter; we admit immigrants by choice and out of generosity, not because we have any economic motive or political responsibility to do so. An effective immigration policy, by this reasoning, is one that selectively admits immigrants for such purposes as family reunification and refugee resettlement, while perhaps seeking to deter migration by promoting direct foreign investment, foreign aid, and democracy in the migrant-sending countries.

Although there are nuances of position, liberals and conservatives alike accept the prevailing wisdom on the causes of immigration and the best ways to regulate it. The only disagreement, in fact, is over how strictly we should limit immigration. Conservatives generally maintain that if immigration is not severely restricted, we will soon be overrun by impoverished masses from the Third World, although the demand for cheap agricultural labor at times tempers this position. Liberals tend to be more charitable, arguing that the United States, as the richest country in the world, can afford to be generous in offering a haven to the poor and oppressed. Advocates of a less restrictive policy also note the positive effects of immigration, such as the growth of cultural diversity and a renewed spirit of entrepreneurship.

Not surprisingly, U.S. immigration laws have reflected the dominant assumptions about the proper objectives of immigration policy. The last two major immigration reforms, passed in 1965 and 1986, have sought to control immigration through measures aimed at regulating who may enter legally and preventing illegal immigrants from crossing our borders. At the same time, the U.S. government has attempted to promote economic growth in the migrant-sending countries by encouraging direct foreign investment and export-oriented international development assistance, in the belief that rising economic opportunities in the developing world will deter emigration. Yet U.S. policies, no matter how carefully devised, have consistently failed to limit or regulate immigration in the intended way.

The 1965 amendment to the Immigration and Naturalization Act was meant to open up the United States to more immigration, but to do so in

"America's Immigration Problem" is reprinted from *World Policy Journal,* Volume VI, No. 4, Fall 1989 by permission.

a way that would allow the government to control entries and reduce illegal immigration. It sought to eliminate the bias against non-Europeans that was built into earlier immigration law and to regulate the influx of immigrants by setting up a series of preference categories within a rather elaborate system of general quotas.[1] Under this system, preference was given to immediate relatives of U.S. citizens and, to a lesser extent, to immigrants possessing skills in short supply in the United States, such as nurses and nannies.

The 1965 law brought about major changes in immigration patterns, but not necessarily the intended ones. The emphasis on family reunification should have ensured that the bulk of new immigrants would come from countries that had already sent large numbers of immigrants to the United States—that is, primarily from Europe. But the dramatic rise in immigration after 1965 was primarily the result of an entirely new wave of migrations from the Caribbean Basin and South and Southeast Asia. The failure of U.S. policy was particularly evident in the rapid rise in the number of undocumented immigrants entering the country. Not only did the level of Mexican undocumented immigration increase sharply, but a whole series of new undocumented flows were initiated, mostly from the same countries that provided the new legal immigration.

The outcry over rising illegal immigration led to a series of congressional proposals that culminated in the 1986 Immigration Reform and Control Act. This law was intended to rationalize immigration policy and, in particular, to address the problem of illegal immigration. It features a limited regularization program that enables undocumented aliens to legalize their status if they can prove continuous residence in the United States since before January 1, 1982, among other eligibility criteria. A second provision of the law seeks to reduce the employment opportunities of undocumented workers through sanctions against employers who knowingly hire them. The third element is an extended guest-worker program designed to ensure a continuing abundant supply of low-wage workers for agriculture.

So far, the law's overall effectiveness has been limited. While some 1.8 million immigrants applied to regularize their status[2] (a fairly significant number, though less than expected), there is growing evidence that the employer sanctions program

is resulting in discrimination against minority workers who are in fact U.S. citizens, as well as various abuses against undocumented workers. Meanwhile, illegal immigration has apparently continued to rise. Congressional efforts to correct the law's shortcomings have already begun. In a relatively promising departure from earlier immigration policy, the Senate recently approved a bill that seeks to give higher priority to applicants who satisfy labor needs in the United States.[3] Though the 54,000-per-year limit placed on such immigrants would still be small, the proposed law would set an important precedent by acknowledging that immigrants, while only about 7 percent of the U.S. labor force, have accounted for 22 percent of the growth in the work force since 1970, and by responding to U.S. Department of Labor forecasts of impending labor shortages in a variety of occupations.

Yet even a modified version of the 1986 law has little chance of successfully regulating immigration for one simple reason: like earlier laws, it is based on a faulty understanding of the causes of immigration. By focusing narrowly on immigrants and on the immigration process itself, U.S. policymakers have ignored the broader international forces, many of them generated or at least encouraged by the United States, that have helped give rise to migration flows.

In the 1960s and 1970s, the United States played a crucial role in the development of today's global economic system. It was a key exporter of capital, promoted the development of export-manufacturing enclaves in many Third World countries, and passed legislation aimed at opening its own and other countries' economies to the flow of capital, goods, services, and information. The emergence of a global economy—and the central military, political, and economic role played by the United States in this process—contributed both to the creation abroad of pools of potential emigrants and to the formation of linkages between industrialized and developing countries that subsequently were to serve as bridges for international migration. Paradoxically, the very measures commonly thought to deter immigration—foreign investment and the promotion of export-oriented growth in developing countries—seem to have had precisely the opposite effect. The clearest proof of this is the fact that several of the newly industrializing countries with the highest growth rates in the world are simultaneously becoming the most important suppliers of immigrants to the United States.

At the same time, the transformation of the occupational and income structure of the United States—itself in large part a result of the globalization of production—has expanded the supply of low-wage jobs. The decline of manufacturing and the growth of the service sector have increased the proportion of temporary and part-time jobs, reduced advancement opportunities within firms, and weakened various types of job protection. This "casualization" of the labor market has facilitated the absorption of rising numbers of immigrants during the 1970s and 1980s—a growing Third World immigrant workforce in what is supposedly one of the leading post-industrial economies.[4] Until we better understand the powerful political and economic forces that drive these international migration flows, and our own role in creating them, U.S. immigration policies will continue to be misguided and frustratingly ineffective. . . .

THE INADEQUACY
OF CLASSICAL EXPLANATIONS

The main features of the new immigration—in particular, the growing prominence of certain Asian and Caribbean Basin countries as sources of immigrants and the rapid rise in the proportion of female immigrants—cannot be adequately explained under the prevailing assumptions of why migration occurs. Even a cursory review of emigration patterns reveals that there is no systematic relationship between emigration and what conventional wisdom holds to be the principal causes of emigration—namely overpopulation, poverty, and economic stagnation.

Population pressures certainly signal the possibility of increased emigration. Yet such pressures —whether measured by population growth or population density—are not in themselves particularly helpful in predicting which countries will have major outflows of emigrants, since some countries with rapidly growing populations experience little emigration (many Central African countries fall into this category), while other countries with much lower population growth rates (such as South Korea), or relatively low density (such as the Dominican Republic), are major sources of migrants.

Nor does poverty in itself seem to be a very reliable explanatory variable. Not all countries with severe poverty experience extensive emigration, and not all migrant-sending countries are poor, as the cases of South Korea and Taiwan illustrate. The utility of poverty in explaining migration is further called into question by the fact that large-scale migration flows from most Asian and Caribbean Basin countries started only in the 1960s, despite the fact that many of these countries had long suffered from poverty.

The presumed relationship between economic stagnation and emigration is similarly problematic. It is commonly assumed that the lack of economic opportunities in less developed countries, as measured by slow growth of gross national product (GNP), plays a key role in inducing individuals to emigrate. But the overall increase in emigration levels took place at a time when most countries of origin were enjoying rather rapid economic growth. Annual GNP growth rates during the 1970s ranged from 5 to 9 percent for most of the leading migrant-sending countries. In fact, most of the key emigration countries were growing faster than other countries that did not experience large-scale emigration. South Korea is the most obvious example. With a GNP growth rate that was among the highest in the world during the 1970s, it was also one of the countries with the fastest growing level of migration to the United States.

This is not to say that overpopulation, poverty, and economic stagnation do not create pressures for migration; by their very logic, they do. But it is clear that the common identification of emigration with these conditions is overly simplistic. The evidence suggests that these conditions are not sufficient by themselves to produce large new migration flows. Other intervening factors need to be taken into account—factors that work to transform these conditions into a migration-inducing situation.

Take, for example, the cases of Haiti and the Dominican Republic. At first glance, the high levels of emigration from these countries would seem to offer support for the argument that overpopulation, poverty, and economic stagnation cause migration. Yet one is struck by the fact that these conditions were present in both countries long before the massive outflow of emigrants began. What, then, accounted for the sudden upsurge?

In the case of the Dominican Republic, the answer seems to lie in the linkages with the United States that were formed during the occupation of Santo Domingo by U.S. marines in 1965 in response to the election victory of the left-wing presidential candidate Juan Bosch. The occupation not only resulted in the growth of political and economic ties with the United States but also produced a stream of middle-class political refugees who emigrated to the occupying country. The settlement of Dominican refugees in the United States in turn created personal and family linkages between the two countries. U.S.-Dominican ties were subsequently further consolidated through U.S. investment in Dominican agriculture and manufacturing for export. Migration to the United States began to increase soon thereafter, rising from a total of 4,500 for the period from 1955 to 1959 to 58,000 between 1965 and 1969. Thus, the new developments that appear to have coincided with the initiation of large scale emigration were the establishment of close military and personal ties with the United States and the introduction of U.S. direct foreign investment.

Haiti, on the other hand, was not subjected to direct U.S. military intervention, but the establishment of linkages with the United States and the introduction of direct foreign investment seem to have played a similarly important role in producing emigration. Although Haiti has long been desperately poor, massive migration to the United States began only in the early 1970s. In this case, the key new development or intervening process appears to have been the adoption of an export-oriented economic growth policy by President Jean-Claude Duvalier in 1972. Haiti's economy was opened to foreign investment in export manufacturing and the large-scale development of commercial agriculture, with the United States serving as the key partner in this new strategy. The necessary labor supply for these new modes of production was obtained through the massive displacement of small landholders and subsistence farmers. This upheaval in Haiti's traditional occupational structure, in conjunction with growing government repression and the emergence of close political and economic links with the United States, coincided with the onset of a major migration flow to the United States.

In both cases, then, the establishment of political, military, and economic linkages with the United States seems to have been instrumental in creating conditions that allowed the emergence of large-scale emigration.[5] Such linkages also played a key role in the migration of Southeast Asians to the United States. In the period following the Korean War, the United States actively sought to promote economic development in Southeast Asia as a way of stabilizing the region politically. In addition, U.S. troops were stationed in Korea, the Philippines, and Indochina. Together, U.S. business and military interests created a vast array of linkages with those Asian countries that were later to experience large migration flows to the United States. The massive increase in foreign investment during the same period, particularly in South Korea, Taiwan, and the Philippines, reinforced these trends.

In other words, in most of the countries experiencing large migration flows to the United States, it is possible to identify a set of conditions and linkages with the United States that, together with overpopulation, poverty, or unemployment, induce emigration. While the nature and extent of these linkages vary from country to country, a common pattern of expanding U.S. political and economic involvement with emigrant-sending countries emerges.

A key element in this pattern is the presence of direct foreign investment in production for export. U.S. investment in the less developed countries quintupled between 1965 and 1980, with much of it going to a few key countries in the Caribbean Basin and Southeast Asia and a large proportion channeled into the development of export-oriented production, especially the manufacturing of consumer goods such as toys, apparel, textiles, and footwear. Industries producing for export are generally highly labor intensive (this is, of course, a primary rationale for locating factories in low-wage countries). The labor-intensive nature of these industries is one reason why several of the Asian and Caribbean Basin countries that have been major recipients of direct foreign investment have experienced rapid employment growth, especially in the manufacturing sector.

According to traditional understandings of why migrations occur, this combination of economic trends should have helped to deter emigration, or at least to keep it at relatively low levels. The deterrent effect should have been particularly strong in countries with high levels of export-oriented investment, since such investment creates more employment—managerial and clerical as well as production jobs—than other forms of investment. Yet it is precisely such countries, most notably the newly industrializing countries of Southeast Asia, that have been the leading sources of new immigrants. How, then, does foreign investment, especially foreign investment in export industries, explain this seeming contradiction? In particular, how is it that foreign investment can produce both rapid economic growth and high emigration levels in a single country?

THE INTERNATIONALIZATION OF PRODUCTION

To understand why large-scale migrations have originated in countries with high levels of job creation due to foreign investment in production for export, it is necessary to examine the impact of such investment on the economic and labor structure of developing countries.

Perhaps the single most important effect of foreign investment in export production is the uprooting of people from traditional modes of existence. It has long been recognized that the development of commercial agriculture tends to displace subsistence farmers, creating a supply of rural wage laborers and giving rise to mass migrations to cities. In recent years, the large-scale development of export-oriented manufacturing in Southeast Asia and the Caribbean Basin has come to have a similar effect (though through different mechanisms); it has uprooted people and created an urban reserve of wage laborers. In both export agriculture and export industry, the disruption of traditional work structures as a result of the introduction of modern modes of production has played a key role in transforming people into migrant workers and, potentially, into emigrants.

In export manufacturing, the catalyst for the disruption of traditional work structures is the massive recruitment of young women into jobs in the new industrial zones. Most of the manufacturing in these zones is of the sort that employs a high proportion of female workers in industrialized countries as well: electronics assembly and the manufacture of textiles, apparel, and toys. The exodus of young women to the industrial zones typically begins when factory representatives recruit young women directly in their villages and rural

schools; eventually, the establishment of continuous migration streams reduces or eliminates the need for direct recruitment.[6] The most obvious reason for the intensive recruitment of women is the firms' desire to reduce labor costs, but there are other considerations as well: young women in patriarchal societies are seen by foreign employers as obedient and disciplined workers, willing to do tedious, high-precision work and to submit themselves to work conditions that would not be tolerated in the highly developed countries.

This mobilization of large numbers of women into waged labor has a highly disruptive effect on traditional, often unwaged, work patterns. In rural areas, women fulfill important functions in the production of goods for family consumption or for sale in local markets. Village economies and rural households depend on a variety of economic activities traditionally performed by women, ranging from food preparation to cloth weaving, basket making, and various other types of crafts.[7] All these activities are undermined by the departure of young women for the new industrial zones.

One of the most serious—and ironic—consequences of the feminization of the new proletariat has been to increase the pool of wage laborers and thus contribute to male unemployment. Not only does competition from the increased supply of female workers make it more difficult for men to find work in the new industrial zones, but the massive departure of young women also reduces the opportunities for men to make a living in many rural areas, where women are key partners in the struggle for survival. Moreover, in some of the poorer and less developed regions and countries, export-led production employing primarily women has come to replace more diversified forms of economic growth that are oriented to the internal market and typically employ men as well. The impressive employment growth figures recorded by most of the main emigration countries in recent years have obscured the reality that export-led growth can lead to unemployment for some groups even as it creates jobs for others.[8]

For men and women alike, the disruption of traditional ways of earning a living and the ascendance of export-led development make entry into wage labor increasingly a one-way proposition. With traditional economic opportunities in the rural areas shrinking, it becomes difficult, if not impossible, for workers to return home if they are laid off or unsuccessful in the job search. This is a particularly serious problem for female workers in the new industrial zones, who are often fired after just a short period of employment. After three to five years of assembling components under microscopes, these workers typically suffer from headaches and deteriorating eyesight. In order to keep wage levels low and replace workers whose health begins to fail, firms continually fire their older workers and hire younger, healthier, and more compliant cohorts of women.[9] Moreover, in the late 1970s and early 1980s, many companies began to move their plants out of older export manufacturing zones, where tax concessions from local governments had been exhausted, and into "new" countries such as Sri Lanka, where labor was even cheaper. All these trends have contributed to the formation of a pool of potential migrants in developing countries such as the Philippines, South Korea, Taiwan, and the countries of the Caribbean Basin. People uprooted from their traditional ways of life, then left unemployed and unemployable as export firms hire younger workers or move production to other countries, may see few options but emigration, especially if an export-led growth strategy has weakened the country's domestic market–oriented economy.

But the role played by foreign investment in allowing the emergence of large-scale emigration flows does not end there. In addition to eroding traditional work structures and creating a pool of potential migrants, foreign investment in production for export contributes to the development of economic, cultural, and ideological linkages with the industrialized countries. These linkages tend to promote the notion of emigration both directly and indirectly. Workers actually employed in the export sector—whether managers, secretaries, or assemblers—may experience the greatest degree of westernization and be most closely connected to the country supplying the foreign capital; they are, after all, using their labor power to produce goods and services for people and firms in developed countries. For these workers, already oriented toward Western practices and modes of thought in their daily experience on the job, the distance between a job in the offshore plant or office and a comparable job in the industrialized country itself is subjectively reduced. It is not hard to see how such individuals might come to regard emigration as a serious option.

In addition to the direct impact on workers in the export sector, the linkages created by direct foreign investment also have a generalized westernizing effect on the less developed country and its people. This "ideological" effect in promoting emigration should not be underestimated; it makes emigration an option not just for those individuals employed in the export sector but for the wider population as well. Thus, a much larger number of people than those directly or indirectly employed by foreign-owned plants and offices become candidates for emigration. In fact, the workers actually employed in foreign plants, offices, and plantations may not be the ones most likely to make use of these linkages and emigrate.

While foreign investment, along with other political, military, and cultural links, helps to explain how migration becomes an option for large numbers of individuals in some developing countries, it does not fully explain why the United States has been overwhelmingly the main destination for migrants.[10] After all, Japan, West Germany, the Netherlands, and Great Britain all have substantial direct foreign investment in developing countries. The evidence seems to suggest that, given the complex and indirect relationship between foreign investment and migration, the national origin of the foreign capital that enters a country may matter less than the type of production it goes into (i.e. labor-intensive export production) and the other linkages that recipient countries may have already established with capital-sending countries. Thus, high levels of Japanese foreign investment in export production in the 1970s may well have ultimately promoted migration to the United States, since the United States had a greater number of other linkages with developing countries at the time and was presumably seen as a more hospitable country for immigration.

It is in this context that the 1965 liberalization of U.S. immigration law and the unfading image of the United States as a land of opportunity acquire significance. The conviction among prospective emigrants that the United States offers unlimited opportunities and plentiful employment prospects, at least relative to other countries, has had the effect of making "emigration" almost identical with "emigration to the United States." This has tended to create a self-reinforcing migration pattern to the United States. As new bridges for migrants are created by foreign investment (in conjunction with political and military activity) and strengthened by the existence of economic opportunities in the United States, the resulting new migrations create additional bridges or linkages between the United States and migrant-sending countries. These, in turn, serve to facilitate future emigration to the United States, regardless of the origin of the foreign investment that created the conditions for emigration in the first place.

Although the United States remains the most important destination for migrants, the recent experience of Japan may offer a glimpse of what the future holds. As Japan has become the leading global economic power and the major foreign investor in Southeast Asia in the 1980s, a familiar combination of migration-facilitating processes appears to have been set in motion: the creation of linkages that eventually come to serve as bridges for potential emigrants, and the emergence of emigration to Japan as something that would-be emigrants see as a real option.

Though fragmentary, the evidence clearly points to a rapid increase over the past few years in the number of foreigners working illegally in Japan. Typically, these workers enter the country on tourist visas and overstay their officially permitted time. (The new Hispanic immigration to New York City began in the same way.) By mid-1988, there were an estimated 200,000 illegal workers in Japan performing manual labor ranging from construction to restaurant work. Almost all of these illegal immigrants are Asians, with the largest national contingents coming from Taiwan, South Korea, Bangladesh, the Philippines, Thailand, and Pakistan—all countries where Japan now has substantial direct foreign investment, including investments in offshore assembly plants.[11] Japan, a country that has always taken pride in its homogeneity and kept its doors closed to immigrants, was clearly unprepared for this development. Thus, while the United States is likely to remain a primary destination for migrants for the foreseeable future, the rise of other global economic powers is likely to mean the rise of new and unexpected migration flows as well.

THE NEW LABOR DEMAND
IN THE UNITED STATES

At first glance, both the heavy influx of immigrants into the United States over the past two decades and their clustering in urban areas would appear to defy economic logic. Why would an increasing number of immigrants come to this country at a time of high overall unemployment and sharp losses of manufacturing and goods-handling jobs? And why would they settle predominantly in the largest U.S. cities, when many of these were in severe decline as centers of light manufacturing and other industries that traditionally employed immigrants? The liberalization of immigration legislation after 1965 and the prior existence of immigrant communities in major urban centers no doubt played some role in attracting immigrants from the older, primarily European, emigration countries. But the most important reason for the continuation of large inflows among the new migrant groups has been the rapid expansion of the supply of low-wage jobs in the United States and the casualization of the labor market associated with the new growth industries, particularly in the major cities.

Thus, any analysis of the new immigration is incomplete without an examination of the changes in labor demand in the United States. In fact, one might argue that while the internationalization of the economy has contributed to the *initiation* of labor migrations to the United States, their *continuation* at high and ever-increasing levels is directly related to the economic restructuring in the United States. This restructuring also helps to explain the concentration of most of the new immigrants in large cities.[12]

The increase in low-wage jobs in the United States is in part a result of the same international economic processes that have channeled investment and manufacturing jobs to low-wage countries. As industrial production has moved overseas, the traditional U.S. manufacturing base has eroded and been partly replaced by a downgraded manufacturing sector, which is characterized by a growing supply of poorly paid, semi-skilled or unskilled production jobs. At the same time, the rapid growth of the service sector has created vast numbers of low-wage jobs (in addition to the better-publicized increase in highly paid investment banking and management consulting jobs). Both of these new growth sectors are largely concentrated in major cities such as New York and Los Angeles. Such cities have seen their economic importance further enhanced as they have become centers for the management and servicing of the global economy; as Detroit has lost jobs to overseas factories, New York and Los Angeles have gained jobs managing and servicing the global network of factories.

These trends have brought about a growing polarization in the U.S. occupational structure since the late 1970s. Along with a sharp decline in the number of middle-income blue- and white-collar jobs, there has been a modest increase in the number of high-wage professional and managerial jobs and a vast expansion in the supply of low-wage jobs. Between 1963 and 1973, nine out of 10 new jobs created were in the middle-earnings group, while the number of high-paid jobs was shrinking. Since 1973, by contrast, only one in two new jobs has been in the middle-income category. If one takes into consideration the increase in the number of seasonal and part-time workers, then the growing inequality within the labor force becomes even more pronounced. The proportion of part-time jobs increased from 15 percent in 1955 to 22 percent in 1977.[13] By 1986, part-time workers made up fully a third of the labor force; about 80 percent of these 50 million workers earn less than $11,000 a year.[14]

These changes have been reflected in a decline in average wages and an increasing polarization of income distribution. Inflation-adjusted average weekly wages, which rose steadily during the postwar period and peaked in 1973, stagnated during the rest of the 1970s and fell in the 1980s. This decline was accompanied by an increase in the degree of inequality in the distribution of earnings, a trend that first emerged in the 1970s and accelerated in the 1980s.[15] A report released recently by the staff of the House Ways and Means Committee found that from 1979 to 1987, the bottom fifth of the population experienced a decline of 8 percent in its personal income, while the top fifth saw its income increase by 16 percent.[16]

As mentioned above, one important generator of new low-wage jobs has been the downgraded manufacturing sector. This sector of the U.S. economy was created by the convergence of three trends: the social reorganization of the work process, notably the growing practice of subcontracting out production and service work and the expansion of sweatshops and industrial homework (all of which have the effect of isolating workers and preventing them from joining together to defend their interests); the technological transformation of the work process, which has downgraded the skill levels required for a variety of jobs by incorporating skills into machines and

computers; and the rapid growth of high-technology industries that employ large numbers of low-wage production workers. Somewhat surprisingly, the downgrading of the skill and wage levels of industrial production jobs has taken place across a broad spectrum of industries—from the most backward to the most modern. Thus, while the garment and electronics industries would at first glance appear to have little in common, both have produced large numbers of dead-end, low-wage jobs requiring few skills. Both industries have made use of unconventional production processes such as sweatshops and industrial homework. Moreover, both have contributed to the disenfranchisement of workers, as is evident from the decline in union membership in areas of rapid high, technology growth such as Los Angeles and Orange counties in California.[17]

More important than the downgraded manufacturing sector as a source of new low-wage jobs, however, is the growth of the service sector.[18] Unlike traditional manufacturing, which is characterized by a preponderance of middle-income jobs, the majority of service jobs tend to be either extremely well paid or very poorly paid, with relatively few jobs in the middle-income range. The growth industries of the 1980s—finance, insurance, real estate, retail trade, and business services—feature large proportions of low-wage jobs, weak unions, if any, and a high proportion of part-time and female workers. Sales clerks, waitresses, secretaries, and janitors are among the growth occupations. The Bureau of Labor Statistics has reported declines in real earnings in these industries since the 1970s.[19]

In addition to employing low-wage workers directly, the expanded service sector also creates low-wage jobs indirectly, through the demand for workers to service the lifestyles and consumption requirements of the growing high-income professional and managerial class. The concentration of these high-income workers in major cities has facilitated rapid residential and commercial gentrification, which in turn has created a need for legions of low-wage service workers—residential building attendants, restaurant workers, preparers of specialty and gourmet foods, dog walkers, errand runners, apartment cleaners, childcare providers, and so on. The fact that many of these jobs are "off the books" has meant the rapid expansion of an informal economy in several major U.S. cities. For a variety of reasons, immigrants are more likely than U.S. citizens to gravitate toward these jobs: these jobs are poorly paid, offer little employment security, generally require few skills and little knowledge of English, and frequently involve undesirable evening or weekend shifts. In addition, the expansion of the informal economy facilitates the entry of undocumented immigrants into these jobs.[20]

Whether in the service sector or the downgraded manufacturing sector, the new low-paying jobs attract large numbers of immigrants. Significantly, even immigrants who are highly educated and skilled when they arrive in the United States tend to gravitate toward the low-wage sectors of the economy. The growing absorption of educated immigrants is partly linked to the growth of clerical and technical jobs in the service sector and the increased casualization of the labor market for these jobs.[21]

Thus, while the redeployment of manufacturing to less developed countries has helped promote emigration from these countries, the concentration of servicing and management functions in major U.S. cities has created conditions for the absorption of the immigrant influx in New York, Los Angeles, Miami, and Houston. The same set of processes that has promoted emigration from several rapidly industrializing countries has simultaneously promoted immigration into the United States.

The fact that it is the major growth sectors such as high technology and services, rather than the declining sectors of the U.S. economy, that are the primary generators of low-wage jobs suggests that the supply of such jobs will probably continue to expand for the foreseeable future. As long as it does so, the influx of immigrant workers to fill these jobs is likely to continue as well.

TOWARD A WORKABLE IMMIGRATION POLICY

The Achilles' heel of U.S. immigration policy has been its insistence on viewing immigration as an autonomous process unrelated to other international processes. It should be clear by now that powerful international forces are at work behind the outflow of emigrants from the developing world and the influx of immigrants into the United States. Yet U.S. officials and the public at large persist in viewing immigration as a problem whose roots lie in the inadequacy of socioeconomic conditions in the Third World, rather than as a by-product of U.S. involvement in the global economy. As a result, they fail to recognize that the proposals dominating the debate on immigration policy—sanctions on employers, deportation of illegal immigrants, stepped-up border patrols—are unlikely to stem the flow.

The 1986 immigration law, ostensibly designed to rationalize immigration policy, has not only failed to slow immigration but threatens to do harm both to our own society and to the immigrants themselves. The employer sanctions program will consolidate a supply of powerless, low-wage workers by further restricting the job opportunities of undocumented immigrants who do not qualify for regularization. The combination of such sanctions and a regularization program that excludes a large number of undocumented workers will contribute to the formation of an immigrant underclass that is legally as well as economically disadvantaged. The expanded guest-worker program is likely to hamper the efforts of domestic agricultural workers to improve their own wages and work conditions. Moreover, this guest-worker program may bring about the development of new linkages with the countries sending agricultural workers, thereby having the unintended effect of facilitating new illegal migration outside the bounds of the program.

A workable U.S. immigration policy would be based on the recognition that the United States, as a major industrial power and supplier of foreign investment, bears a certain amount of responsibility for the existence of international labor migrations. The past policies of the United States toward war refugees might serve as a model for a refashioned immigration policy. Few people would argue that flows of refugees from Indochina were the result of overpopulation or economic stagnation, even though the region may in fact have suffered from these problems. Instead, it is widely recognized that U.S. military activities were to some degree responsible for creating the refugee flows. When the United States granted Indochinese refugees special rights to settle here, it was acknowledging this responsibility, at least indirectly. A similar acknowledgment is due in the case of labor migrations.

When drafting laws in most areas of foreign relations, lawmakers generally make an effort to weigh the differing degrees of responsibility of various actors and take into account such complex phenomena as the globalization of production and international flows of capital and information. Why, then, is it not possible to factor in similar considerations in the designing of immigration policy? To be sure, international migration poses special problems in this regard, since the relationship of immigration to other international processes is not readily apparent or easily understood. But the overly simplistic approach most policymakers have adopted until now has greatly hindered the fashioning of a fair and effective immigration policy. The precise features of such a policy will have to be elaborated through further study and debate. But one thing is clear: U.S. immigration policy will continue to be counterproductive as long as it places the responsibility for the formation of international migrations exclusively on the shoulders of the immigrants themselves.

ENDNOTES

1. Earlier agreements barred Chinese labor immigration (1882), restricted Japanese immigration (1907), and culminated in the 1924 National Origins Act. This act was the first general immigration law in that it brought together the growing number of restrictions and controls that had been established over a period of time: the creation of classes of inadmissible aliens, deportation laws, literacy requirements, etc. The 1965 immigration law ended these restrictions. In this sense it was part of a much broader legislative effort to end various forms of discrimination in the United States, such as discrimination against minorities and women.

2. About 1.8 million aliens applied under the main legalization program; in addition, 1.2 million applied under special legalization programs for agriculture. While the majority applying under the main program are expected to obtain temporary resident status, it is now becoming evident that a growing proportion may not be complying with the second requirement of the procedure, that of applying for permanent residence.

3. Several clauses are attached to the bill, ranging from a doubling of Hong Kong's special visa allowance to the granting of 4,800 visas each year to millionaires prepared to employ at least 10 U.S. workers. The bill also expands two existing worker preferences: professionals who are outstanding artists and individuals in occupations that cannot be filled by U.S. workers.

4. Detailed documentation of these issues can be found in the book on which this article is based. See Saskia Sassen, *The Mobility of Labor and Capital: A Study*

in International Investment and Labor Flow (New York: Cambridge University Press, 1988).

5. See also *Labor Migration Under Capitalism: The Puerto Rican Experience*, a study by the history task force of the Centro de Estudios Puertorriqueños (New York: Monthly Review Press, 1979); Alejandro Portes and John Walton, *Labor, Class and the International System* (New York: Academic Press, 1981).

6. See, for example, Norma Diamond, "Women and Industry in Taiwan," *Modern China*, Vol. 5, No. 3 (July 1979), pp. 317–340. In her research in Taiwan, one of the most developed of the Asian countries, Diamond found that women were actively sought out by factory representatives who went to the rural sectors to recruit them. About 75 percent of the female industrial workforce in Taiwan is between 15 and 24 years of age. See also Helen I. Safa, "Runaway Shops and Female Employment: The Search for Cheap Labor," *Signs*, Vol. 7, No. 2 (Winter 1981), pp. 418–433.

7. See E. Boserup, *Women's Role in Economic Development* (New York: St. Martin's Press, 1970); also E. Boulding, *Women: The Fifth World*, Foreign Policy Association Headline Series No. 248 (Washington, DC: February 1980).

8. In a detailed examination of the employment impact of export-led industrialization, the United Nations Industrial Development Organization (UNIDO) found that, in general, this type of development eliminates more jobs than it creates because of its disruptive effect on the national manufacturing sector, especially in the less developed countries of the Caribbean and Southeast Asia. *World Industry Since 1960: Progress and Prospects* (Vienna: UNIDO, 1979).

9. See June Nash and Maria Patricia Fernandez Kelly, *Women and Men in the International Division of Labor* (Albany, NY: SUNY Press, 1983). See also the film, *The Global Assembly Line*, by Lorraine Gray.

10. Though inadequate, the available evidence on global international migration compiled by the United Nations (*Demographic Yearbook*, 1985; *World Population Prospects*, 1987) shows that the United States receives about 19 percent of global emigration (permanent settlement—excludes unofficial refugee flows between countries). It receives 27 percent of total Asian emigration, but 81.5 percent of all Korean emigration and almost 100 percent of emigration from the Philippines. It receives 70 percent of Caribbean emigration, but almost 100 percent of emigration from the Dominican Republic and Jamaica and 62 percent from Haiti. And it receives 19.5 percent of all emigration from Central America, but 52 percent of emigration from El Salvador, the country with the greatest U.S. involvement in that region.

11. Saskia Sassen, *The Global City: New York London Tokyo* (Princeton, NJ: Princeton University Press, forthcoming). I spent many hours speaking with illegal

immigrants in Tokyo in an attempt to learn how they decided to migrate to Japan, given its reputation as a closed society. It is impossible to do justice to their answers here, but the main points were as follows: first, they were individuals who had in one way or another become mobilized into migrant labor; second, Japan's growing presence in their countries, together with the availability of information about Japan as a result, had indeed created linkages and made Japan emerge in their minds as an option for emigration. The interesting question here is, to what extent are we witnessing the emergence of alternative "lands of opportunity" to the United States?

12. See *ibid.* for a discussion of how such tendencies toward casualization are also operating in major cities in Japan. This is an important process facilitating the labor market incorporation of new illegal immigration to Japan.

13. Paul Blumberg, *Inequality in an Age of Decline* (New York: Oxford University Press, 1980), pp. 67 and 79; W. V. Deutermann, Jr. and S. C. Brown, "Voluntary Part-Time Workers: A Growing Part of the Labor Force," *Monthly Labor Review*, No. 101 (June 1978).

14. Bennett Harrison and Barry Bluestone, *The Great U-Turn* (New York: Basic Books, 1988). Even the U.S. government, in an effort to cut labor costs, has increasingly encouraged the use of part-time and temporary workers in its own hiring. The result has been a growing trend toward subcontracting out such services as food preparation, building maintenance, warehousing, and data processing. U.S. Congressional Budget Office, *Contract Out: Potential for Reducing Federal Costs* (Washington, DC: U.S. Government Printing Office, June 1987).

15. It should be noted that notwithstanding an increase in multiple-earner families and an increase in transfer payments, family income distribution in the United States has also become more unequal. Blumberg found that family income adjusted for inflation increased by 33 percent from 1948 to 1958 and by 42 percent from 1958 to 1968, but grew by only 9 percent from 1968 to 1978. Median family income kept growing throughout the postwar period but stagnated after 1973. Blumberg (fn. 17).

16. Linda Bell and Richard Freeman, "The Facts About Rising Industrial Wage Dispersion in the U.S.," *Proceedings* (Industrial Relations Research Association, May 1987); Organization for Economic Cooperation and Development, OECD *Employment Outlook* (Paris: OECD, 1985), pp. 90–91. Several analysts maintain that the increase in inequality in the earnings distribution is a function of demographic shifts, notably the growing participation of women in the labor force and the large number of young workers of the "baby boom" generation. Both of these categories of workers traditionally earn less than white adult males. See Robert Z. Lawrence, "Sectoral Shifts and the Size of the Middle

Class," *Brookings Review*, Fall 1984. However, when Harrison and Bluestone (fn. 18) analyzed the data while controlling for various demographic factors as well as the shift to a service economy (another category with a prevalence of low-wage jobs), they found that these demographic variables did not adequately account for the increased inequality in the earnings distribution. Rather, they found that *within* each group, e.g., white women, young workers, white adult men, and so on, there has been an increase in earnings inequality. They also found that the growth of the service sector accounted for one-fifth of the increase in inequality, but that most of the rest of the growth in inequality occurred *within* industries. (See their appendix table A.2 for analysis of 18 demographic, sectoral, and regional factors.) The authors explain the increased inequality in the earnings distribution in terms of the restructuring of wages and work hours (Chapters 2 and 3).

17. See various articles on this topic in Nash and Fernandez Kelly (fn. 13).

18. The decline of mass production as the central force in national growth and the shift to services as the leading economic sector have contributed to the demise of a broader set of social and economic arrangements. In the postwar period, the economy functioned according to a dynamic that transmitted the benefits accruing to the core manufacturing industries to more peripheral sectors of the economy. The benefits of price and market stability and increases in productivity were transferred to a secondary set of firms, which included suppliers and subcontractors as well as less directly related industries. Although there were still firms and workers that did not benefit from this "shadow effect," their number was probably small in the postwar period. By the early 1980s, the shadow effect and the wage-setting power of leading industries had eroded significantly. The importance of this combination of processes for the expansion of the middle class and the overall rise in wages can be seen in the comparison of data for the postwar period with the income trends of the past two decades. See Barbara Ehrenreich, *Fear of Falling* (New York: Pantheon, 1989) on the meaning of this process for the middle class in the 1980s.

19. See Robert G. Sheets, Stephen Nord, and John J. Phelps, *The Impact of Service Industries on Underemployment in Metropolitan Economies* (Lexington, MA: D.C. Heath and Co., 1987). An overall measure of the weight of low-wage jobs in service industries can be found in this study, which is the most detailed analysis of the impact of service growth on the creation of low-wage jobs in major metropolitan areas. Using census data, the authors found that from 1970 to 1980, certain service industries had a significant effect on the growth of what they define as underemployment, that is, employment paying below poverty-level wages in the 100 largest metropolitan areas. The highest relative contri-

bution resulted from what the authors call "corporate services" (finance, insurance, real estate, business services, legal services, membership organizations, and professional services) such that a 1 percent increase in employment in these services was found to result in a 0.37 percent increase in full-time, year-round low-wage jobs; while a 1 percent increase in distributive services results in a 0.32 percent increase in such jobs. The retail industry had the highest effect on the creation of *part-time,* year-round, low-wage jobs, such that a 1 per-

cent increase in retail was found to result in a 0.88 percent increase in such jobs.
20. Sassen (fn. 15).
21. For example, according to the Immigration and Naturalization Service, 25 percent of both male and female immigrants entering between 1985 and 1987 reported managerial and professional occupations, and about 48 percent reported being operators (a broad category of jobs ranging from assembly line workers to elevator operators), laborers, or farmworkers.

TWENTY-FIVE

Gendered Immigration

Pierrette Hondagneu-Sotelo

GENDER ORGANIZES MIGRATION

Macrostructural rearrangements go a long way toward explaining the increasing numbers of Mexican women and entire families who migrate and settle in the United States without legal authorization. Since the late 1960s, the United States has generated many low-wage jobs centered in urban areas, constituting a feature of the global economic restructuring process that Sassen-Koob (1982) calls "peripheralization at the core." Small competitive firms in services and manufacturing, as well upper-income professionals and managers, increasingly rely on the labor provided by Mexican immigrants. Although many commentators have recognized these developments, they have not always observed that a significant number of the U.S. informal-sector occupations that grew during the 1970s and 1980s—paid domestic work, child care, garment and electronic assembly—recruited primarily female immigrant workers. An objective labor demand for immigrant women, one that is solicitous of workers with particular

configurations of class, gender, ethnicity, and legal status, partially explains the increased participation of Mexican women in undocumented immigration and settlement. In Mexico, the ongoing economic crisis intensified and encouraged northbound migration from sectors of Mexican society previously not drawn to the U.S. These same economic pressures also propelled more women into a Mexican labor market that could not produce a sufficient number of jobs. As economic problems deepened, permanent immigration emerged as an increasingly viable response for Mexican women as well as men.

But macrostructural factors alone do not explain how people respond to these new opportunities and pressures. Theories based on structural transformations cannot explain who migrates, when migration occurs, or how people organize migration. And while structural explanations can help account for the changing sex composition of the immigrant population, they cannot account for the distinctively gendered way that immigration and settlement occur. As I stated at the outset, political and economic trans-formations may set the stage for migration, but they do not write the script.

Taking the household as a unit of analysis offers a more grounded approach for developing an explanation of the recent changes in Mexican immigration, as this approach recognizes that social actors live in particular social contexts, not in a vacuum outlined only by huge structures. Yet, immigration is not the outcome of households strategizing or adapting to macrostructural economic pressures, but of the exercise of multiple interests and hierarchies of power that come to life within households.[1] Migration is not calculated at the household level in terms of costs and benefits that will accrue to household members. People make migration decisions in a context of uncertainty and imperfect knowledge about economic opportunities—even if they have a specific job waiting for them up north—and similarly, they can only speculate about the subsequent behavior of those who are assisting them. Resources are not always equally shared and automatically pooled within the household or family unit, and this is especially true of that crucial resource for immigration: social networks.

This study suggests that a more fruitful approach requires looking inside the household and inside the social networks to see how gender relations shape migration experiences. Although people live in households, the cultural meanings, ideologies, emotions, and beliefs they experience as most salient are embedded in family relations. Gender relations in families and social networks determine how the opportunities and constraints imposed by macrostructural factors translate into different migration patterns. Although patriarchal systems and ideals influence the migration process, patriarchal gender relations are fluid and exerted heterogeneously in different contexts.

Strictly defined patriarchal relations of family authority and male-dominated networks promote family stage migration. The implicit rules of patriarchal family authority constrain women's actions, but enable married men to act independently and relatively promptly when they are invited to accompany a friend or relative on the journey north. Yet it would be erroneous to see patriarchal privilege as necessarily strengthening class privilege under capitalism. For Mexican undocumented immigrant men, the contrary occurs.

Patriarchy allows men to depart, but it also mandates that men serve as good financial providers for their families, which they attempt to do by migrating and assuming jobs that are typically low-paying, physically arduous, and without opportunities for upward mobility. Thus, male migrant labor is produced by patriarchy for the benefit of U.S. capital.

Exclusively male networks favor the migration of men. But in the process of migration, patriarchy in the family sphere is realigned, as the women, out of necessity, act autonomously and assertively in managing household affairs. This new sense of social power—and later, for another cohort of migrant wives, additional access to women's networks—enable the wives to go north. Until the late 1960s, the married women I interviewed struggled to convince their husbands to help them migrate, although a minority of women were (and still are) coerced into migration by their husbands. By the 1970s and 1980s a substantial number of immigrant women had established themselves in the Oakview barrio. New immigrant women circumvented reliance on male-dominated networks by appealing to the assistance of immigrant women already established in the United States. And as more women migrated and settled in the U.S., women's social-network ties emerged and widened.

Women and men involved in family stage migration do not enter the process equally. Yet given the diverse historical and social contexts in which migration occurs, women in the same culture and in similar circumstances encounter different types of patriarchal obstacles and hence improvise different responses to migration. The women's contrasting migration trajectories are related to the establishment of a permanent immigrant settlement community, an accomplishment that reflects political and economic transformations. The legacy of the bracero program, passage of the 1965 amendments to the Immigration and Nationality Act, economic restructuring in Mexico, and the diversification of labor demand for Mexican immigrants in the U.S. encouraged the development of settlements such as the Oakview barrio. As more women and entire families settled in these urban communities, they helped to facilitate the migration of their friends and families. The women's variegated responses to family stage migration illustrate some of the ways in which gender interacts with macro-level political and economic transformations to produce particular immigration outcomes.

While others have noted that the range of immigrant social networks expands with the entry of each new migrant into the migration process, and that the networks subsequently embody more social capital (Massey et al., 1987; Mines, 1981), it is important to add that the networks themselves do not automatically become equally accessible to women and men. Immigrant social networks are highly contested social resources, and they are not always shared, even in the same family. Single women's networks are undeniably effective, but this study also reveals strong network ties developing among married women, a factor that cannot be underestimated in explaining the increase in the migration of both women and entire families.

The scenarios that emerged from this study also draw attention to several overlooked features of Mexican immigration. Contrary to what is posited by the household model, the men in this study often engaged in very little calculation about migrating. Many of them did not consult about their migration decisions with their spouses or families, nor did they invest considerable time in strategizing or planning their northward sojourn. Most of the men reported that they decided to migrate rather abruptly, when presented with an invitation or opportunity that had to be acted upon quickly. While they may have discussed and pondered this alternative earlier, they did not necessarily plan their move in advance. For many of these men, the social-network contact was all that was necessary to precipitate their departure. The wives of these men, precisely because they faced obstacles of patriarchal authority, reported investing time and energy in calculating and strategizing their immigration plans. Moreover, the women's motives for immigration arose over time. Interests are fluid, and decisions and actions are embedded in specific contexts. The unitary-household model cannot explain these changes because it does not recognize gender and generational power relations between women and men sharing the same household. Women praying for the Border Patrol to capture their husbands, and families in which spouses rely on different network resources and on separate income funds to cover their migration costs, call into question assumptions about unified household migration strategies.

Nuclear families who migrated together were characterized by a less rigid form of family patriarchy than were the families who migrated in stages. These families were characterized by shared decision making between spouses, and also by access to social networks composed of the wives' kin. Unlike the pattern of family stage migration, in these families the men did not enjoy uncontested, unilateral power, and the women participated in decision making about migration. These women were well positioned to act assertively in the migration process because of their income-earning work and their experience in sharing family authority.

Class affected this form of migration in two ways. First, the relatively more class-privileged backgrounds of some of these families appear to have allowed for more egalitarian practices of authority. This is because the families in this study who had achieved some semblance of a middle-class life-style in Mexico had done so only by relying on women's labor, often in a family business. This reliance legitimized the women's participation in decisions about migration. Negotiations about migration in these families were not necessarily harmonious, as they were characterized by some degree of bargaining, persuasion, and sometimes ultimatums, but they provide a sharp contrast to family stage migration, where unilateral decision making characterized the men's initial departure.

Another reason that women in these families played a primary role in migration decisions is that usually their kin provided the important social-network assistance for migration. In several cases, the women had accumulated direct migration experience when they were unmarried. Women's immigrant kin and, in a few instances, women's prior migration experience served as important social leverage for women, allowing for this pattern of family migration to emerge. These women avoided the "stay-at-home" scenario partially because they had access to decisive resources.

Class privileges also affected family unit migration in yet another way, as it afforded these families the financial ability to pick up and move the entire family at once. International migration is an expensive proposition, one that is generally not available to the poorest of the poor. Families that owned homes, small businesses, or apartment buildings were able to liquidate property, apply for loans based on their equity, or derive income from rent, and these financial resources funded migration costs for entire families.

Contrary to what much of the literature proposes, the immigrants in this case study who came to the United States while single were not "sent" or elected to migrate by their families or households. While many of these women and men did send money to their families in Mexico, at least during the initial part of their stays, their families' collective needs did not prompt their migration. In fact, patriarchal rules of authority often worked against the migration of sons and daughters, but this produced mixed results.

It is well known that throughout many areas of Mexico, young men are seeped in a culture of northbound migration. Sustained by vibrant transnational social networks and by the glories of return migrants, popular folklore defines a journey northward as a rite of passage. For many a young man, moreover, a journey northward signifies an important patriarchal rite of passage, as it reflects a young man's defiance of his father's authority and a step toward his own independence. These young men are departing not as family emissaries, but as independent seekers. Cohesive, patriarchally organized families may try to dissuade their sons from going north, but they are not always successful due to the strong social networks and the peer culture of migration that encourage this behavior, and due to patriarchal rules that see young men's autonomous actions as legitimate.

By contrast, the women in this study who migrated while single were either free of, or able to manipulate, familial patriarchal constraints. Most of these women came from relatively weakly bound families, characterized by lack of economic support and the absence of strong patriarchal rules of authority. When highly motivated women did encounter their fathers' resistance, they eventually negotiated their right to go north, suggesting the malleability of patriarchal power. For single women, the assistance of other women is often the key to migration. In the Oakview barrio, exclusively female social-network ties emerged in the 1970s and strengthened during the 1980s, a factor that cannot be discounted in explaining the increase in female migration to the community. This confirms survey materials collected in Mexico that suggest the formation of single women's immigrant networks in the 1970s.

This analysis of single and married women's networks underlines not only how the social capital embedded within social networks encourages migration by providing financial resources or job contacts, but more importantly, how these networks may allow women to circumvent or contest domestic patriarchal authority. This aspect of immigrant social networks, to the best of my knowledge, has not previously been acknowledged. The ramifications of this are significant for future increases in migration when we consider the broader realm of changing gender relations in Mexico and elsewhere.

Network ties dominated by men continue to operate and sometimes include the female kin of male participants, but new, women-centered networks have gained momentum. The ongoing economic crisis and contested gender hierarchies in Mexico, as well as occupational segregation by gender, have fed these new networks, giving further impetus to immigration of women and entire families.

While this study considers how generational dynamics operate within gender relations, a shortcoming of the study is that I did not examine children and adolescents as actors in the migration process. While a substantial body of literature examines immigrant children's educational needs and progress, no systematic research has examined how children actively influence their parents' decisions about migration, return migration, and settlement. Including children and adolescents in a research agenda may alter long-established beliefs about immigration.[2]

Labor migration is a process shaped in multiple ways by dynamic gender relations. One can, in short, conclude that migration is gendered. Women and men do not share the same experiences with migration, and their gender relations—patterns of separation, conflict, and cooperation—produce distinct migration patterns. Decision making about migration that occurs in families and the dynamics within the social networks are key in distinguishing migration routes and how immigrants are incorporated into the new society.

The onslaught of capitalism is often equated with the fortification of patriarchy. Yet in this study, both single and married Mexican women are contesting patriarchal dictates in the process of U.S.-bound migration, and men, as fathers, husbands, and brothers, are responding in various ways. Just as women often comply with their own subordination in patriarchal institutions, so conversely do men participate, albeit sometimes unwittingly, in the dismantling of patriarchy. Migration and settlement introduce new challenges and pressures for change in both women's and men's behavior.

IMMIGRATION RECONSTRUCTS GENDER RELATIONS

What are the implications for gender relations among Mexican immigrants who settle in the United States? Patriarchal relations do not automatically disintegrate or break down once immigrants adapt to new ways of life in the United States, yet neither does patriarchy remain preserved intact. People construct their lives out of cultural resources within a social structural context, but through the process of migration and resettlement, cultural ideals and guidelines for appropriate behavior change.

Patriarchal gender relations undergo continual renegotiation as women and men rebuild their families in the United States. Gender is reconstructed in different ways, guided by the limits imposed by particular contexts and patterns of migration, but family and community relations exhibit a general shift in the direction of gender egalitarianism. This was indicated in the study by shifts in women's and men's spatial mobility, patterns of family authority, and, in some instances, by transformations in the gendered division of household labor. These changes do not occur in ways that conform to any formulaic linear stages. They happen unevenly, and often result in contradictory combinations of everyday practices.

While they have been amply studied, immigrant men have not been examined in the immigration literature as men—i.e., as gendered persons. An exception is the work of anthropologist Roger Rouse (1990), who argues that Mexican immigrant men, especially those who are undocumented, experience limited spatial mobility in their daily lives, which compromises some of their patriarchal privileges. The public spaces open to the men in the Oakview barrio were indeed limited to certain street corners, and a few neighbor-

hood bars, pool halls, and doughnut shops. Although the men tried to create new spaces where they could recapture a public sense of self, the goal was not so readily achieved. As undocumented immigrants, these men remained apprehensive of harassment by the Immigration and Naturalization Service or the police, their jobs typically afforded little in the way of autonomy or mobility, and, as poor men who worked long hours at jobs as gardeners, dishwashers, or day laborers, they had very little discretionary income to afford leisure activities. While Mexican immigrant men may exhibit bravado and machismo, these behaviors are best understood as personally and collectively constructed performances of masculine gender display, and so should be distinguished from structurally constituted positions of power. Their displays are indicators of marginalized and subordinated masculinities (Hondagneu-Sotelo and Messner, 1994).

While cultural rules that segregate women in the domestic sphere are no longer as strictly enforced in rural and urban Mexico as they once were, a number of the women in this study had been, to some extent, secluded from public life in Mexico. After arrival in the U.S., some of these women stayed cloistered in their homes, usually due to fear of their new foreign surroundings and potential INS apprehension, but these practices changed quickly. In the U.S. nearly all of these immigrant women were employed. Many of the women in this study worked as paid domestic workers in private households, but job transportation typically required a combination of taking buses and walking substantial distances —practices that placed them outside of traditional normative expectations and squarely "in the street." The women also accompanied their children to school and medical visits, they shopped and visited friends, and they attended afternoon and evening meetings for informal associations and organizations, often unaccompanied by men and unrestricted by rules relegating them to the home or market.

Transformations in patterns of family authority occurred following immigration. Some of the men had acted as the undisputed patriarchs in all family decision-making processes in Mexico, but in the United States, these processes became more egalitarian. This trend toward more egalitarian patterns of shared authority occurred because many Mexican immigrant women became more autonomous and assertive through their immigration and settlement experiences. Egalitarianism was also promoted by the relative increase in women's and the decrease in men's economic contributions to the family. As the balance of relative resources and contributions shifted, the women assumed more active roles in key decision-making processes. Where the family might live, how to budget finances, where to go for legal advice—these are all decisions in which the women commonly participated. Similar shifts occurred with the older children, who were now often reluctant to subordinate their earnings and their autonomy to a patriarchal family hierarchy.

The household division of labor is another arena that in some cases reflected Mexican immigrant men's diminished status. An orthodox household division of labor proved to be quite resilient, as most families continued to organize their daily household chores along fairly traditional, patriarchal norms. But in the families that had experienced family stage migration and where the men had lived for many years in "bachelor communities," the men took responsibility for some of the housework. These changes of course are modest if we judge them by feminist ideals of egalitarianism, but they are significant when compared with the patriarchal family organization that was normative before immigration. And they are a striking departure from stereotypical views of Mexican immigrant families.

Changes in Mexican immigrant families' gender relations do not result from any "modernizing" Anglo influence or acculturation process. Most Mexican immigrants live their lives in the United States encapsulated in relatively segregated jobs and well-defined immigrant communities. Yet limited contact with Anglo society doesn't mean that past practices and beliefs are sustained intact. Nor is the trend toward greater egalitarianism among Mexican immigrant families elicited by feminist ideology. The immigrant women in this case study were not immersed in any self-conscious feminist movement, but still they have achieved goals, however modest, consonant with feminism. Immigrants are not unique in this respect. Research by Rosanna Hertz (1986) on high-income, dual-career couples —people who lie at the opposite end of the occupational hierarchy—also testifies to the absence of feminist ideology in fomenting more egalitarian conjugal relations. Hertz found that high-income, professional couples generate new family forms in order to accommodate employer demands and realize individual desires for career success, and that in turn, these new spousal relations foster more egalitarian ideologies.

Key to the movement toward greater equality within immigrant families was the change in the women's and men's relative positions of power and status in the larger social structure of power. As we have seen, Mexican immigrant men's public status in the U.S. is very low, due to racism, insecure and low-paying jobs, and (often) illegal status. For those families that underwent long periods of spousal separation, the women often engaged in formal- or informal-sector paid labor for the first time, developed more economic skills and autonomy, and assumed control over conducting household affairs with other societal institutions. In the U.S., nearly all of the women sought employment, so women made significant economic contributions to the family. And in the instances of family stage migration, these transformations in gender relations began once the men departed but before the women left Mexico. All of these factors tend to erode men's patriarchal authority in the family and empower women either to directly challenge that authority, or at least to negotiate "patriarchal bargains" (Kandiyoti, 1988) that are more palatable to themselves and their children.

While it would be premature to proclaim the demise of patriarchy and the triumph of gender egalitarianism in Mexican immigrant families, there is a significant trend in that direction. Immigration and settlement processes temper the expression of family patriarchy, eliciting a general trend toward greater egalitarianism. Women still have less power than men do in families, but they generally enjoy more autonomy, resources, and leverage than they previously did in Mexico. Empirical study thus contradicts the stereotypical image of dominant macho males and submissive females in Mexican immigrant families. While patriarchal authority is not entirely undermined, immigration diminishes the legitimacy of men's unchallenged domination in families.

In spite of, or perhaps because of, these new gender arrangements in families, the issue of settlement remains highly politicized: men generally indicated a desire to return to Mexico, while women most often expressed intentions of staying in the United States. While these stated preferences bear little on what people actually do, these statements are significant in that they suggest the diminished power that patriarchy exerts in the United States. For many men, the dream of the ultimate return to Mexico seems to provide social and psychological relief from the indignity of restricted control in both public and private spheres. Through the process of migration and resettlement, men lose monopolistic control over family resources, decisions, and privileges, and women gain social power and newfound autonomy within families. The gendered orientations to settlement reflect these losses and gains, and they echo the findings of Sherri Grasmuck and Patricia R. Pessar (1991) in their study of Dominican immigrants, many of them from the middle class, in New York City.

In the case of Mexican immigrant families, it is not feminist ideology but structural rearrangements that promote social change in spousal relations. This observation may lead to strategic reconsiderations for the feminist movement in the United States. Most immigrant women in this study did not identify as feminists or with any feminist organization. For many of these women, forms of oppression which derive from their class, ethnic, and legal status were experienced as more decisive than gender oppression. Immigrant women in this study reported that being poor, "illegal," overworked, nervous about meeting bills, and unable to obtain satisfactory medical assistance for their children were far more troublesome than gender inequality. Their responses reflect the findings of a needs-assessment survey conducted in San Francisco in 1990, where 345 Latina undocumented immigrant women identified housing assistance, employment training, and medical care as their most pressing needs (Hogeland and Rosen, 1990). While none of the immigrant women identified "gender subordination" as a primary problem, rearrangements induced by migration do result in the diminution of familial patriarchy, and these transformations may enable immigrant women to better confront problems derived from class, racial/ethnic, and legal-status subordination. Their endeavors may prompt more receptiveness to feminist ideology and organizations in the future.

Latina immigrant women, however, are not silently waiting to be organized; they are already organizing to address problems specific to their class, gender, ethnic, and citizenship status. In the Oakview barrio, undocumented women mobilized their kin, friends, and neighbors to push for school reform for their children and to ensure that community members received access to legal permanent-resident status available through IRCA, and informally, they exchanged information that bettered their occupational mobility as paid domestic workers. Larger institutional efforts are also under way.

In October 1991, the first national conference on immigrant and refugee women drew more than three hundred women, most of them Latina and Asian immigrants representing myriad organizations and agencies.[3] For three days, women convened panels on issues as diverse as domestic violence, alternative employment strategies, labor rights, leadership-training models, and health care. Although these organizations are not prevalent in every immigrant community, Latina immigrant women do participate in a range of advocacy groups—in domestic workers' cooperatives, church groups, street vendors' associations, anti–domestic-violence agencies, voter-registration drives, housing projects, and child-care cooperatives. Latina immigrant women enroll in special programs to develop self-esteem and learn political-leadership skills at the Dolores Mission Women's Cooperative and Leadership Training Program in Los Angeles, and at Mujeres Unidas y Activas (United and Active Women), a Latina immigrant and refugee women's organization in San Francisco's Mission district. At the Mujeres Unidas en Acción (Women United in Action) organization in Boston, Latina women learn English and participate in community politics (Young and Padilla, 1990). In Los Angeles, Latina immigrant women have mobilized on behalf of their rights as street vendors (Sirola, 1992), have joined Mexican American women to protest against the proposed placement of a state prison and a toxic-waste incinerator in a low-income residential neighborhood (Pardo, 1990), have joined together with men in union drives (Delgado, 1993), and have demanded that local businesses contribute to the fight against drugs and violent crime by providing jobs for gang youth (Amado, 1990). The diverse methods and organizing issues that Latina

immigrant women have used reflect both the exclusion of immigrants, Latinas, and impoverished
women from traditional avenues of political mobilization and electoral politics, and the vitality
that comes from using interpersonal relationships. In fact, Hardy-Fanta (1993) argues that
Latina women have been especially effective in
political organizing precisely because of their
strong interpersonal relationships and skills,
which allow them to mobilize others, and thus
serve as "connectors."

While these women's activism often derives
from their traditional responsibilities for their
children, families, and community, their activist
practices—marching in the streets, raising their
voices, and confronting authority—certainly break
with tradition. Other Latinas and poor, working
women are also challenging and expanding traditional forms of political expression. A range of unorthodox, creative political activities and motives
have been documented among Mexican women
in Guadalajara, Mexican American women in Los
Angeles, and Puerto Rican women and other Latinas in the northeastern U.S. (Logan, 1984; Pardo,
1990; Naples, 1991; Hardy-Fanta, 1993). While
women's motives for becoming political actors
and neighborhood community activists may be
rooted in their traditional identities as mothers,
their actions provide a rich source of support for
fundamental change in multiple arenas. And because of the range of embedded networks of kin
and friends, Mexican immigrant women are well
situated to become effective political actors.

HOW WOMEN CONSOLIDATE SETTLEMENT

Mexican undocumented immigrants must leap
over a veritable obstacle course to establish themselves in the United States. Daily encounters with
language difficulties, racism, poverty, vulnerability at the workplace and harassment in public
areas due to the lack of legal status, the problems
associated with missing loved ones "back home"
and becoming accustomed to new social circles in
a foreign environment—all of these factors may
conspire to encourage sojourner, not settler, migration. Yet in spite of these challenges, millions
of Mexican undocumented immigrants have incorporated themselves into U.S. society. In this
study, I placed women at the forefront of analysis
in order to understand this process.

My ethnographic materials suggest that immigrant women advance settlement along three
structural dimensions that constitute and define
it. These are the construction of community-
wide social ties; employment in relatively stable,
year-round jobs; and the utilization of private
and public institutional forms of assistance, including credit.

Immigrant women need to earn income in
order for their families to achieve permanent settlement in the U.S., and in Oakview most of the
long-staying immigrant women work as paid domestic workers, an informal-sector occupation
characterized by variable schedules and tenuous
security. Their employment was generally arranged according to terms that sociologist Mary
Romero (1988a) calls "job work," where a domestic worker maintains several employers and cleans
a particular house on a weekly or biweekly basis
in exchange for a flat rate of pay. While they are
not as severely underpaid or as deeply enmeshed
in paternalistic employer relations as are live-in
domestic workers (a job more typical for newly arrived immigrant women), the job-work situation
exacerbates the privatized nature of domestic
work, and it also confronts domestic workers with
having to secure multiple employers. The women
in this study dealt with these challenges by sharing information through informal networks of
support. Cross-gender links are also initially helpful in securing jobs. What appears to be an extreme atomization of the occupation is in fact
mitigated by a work culture transmitted through
many social interactions. In the process, the jobs
in private households become a stable source of
employment, which strengthens the conditions
for permanent family settlement.

Historically, paid domestic work has been a key
institution through which rural-urban migrant
and international immigrant women become integrated into a new society. Since domestic work is
generally viewed as a second-class job, studies
have typically investigated the extent of upward
mobility, both individual and intergenerational,
out of domestic work, concluding that the work either constitutes an "occupational bridge" or serves
as an "occupational ghetto" (Broom and Smith,
1963; Katzman, 1981; McBride, 1976; Glenn,
1986). The findings from this study suggest that
there is mobility within the occupation itself, and
that networks partially govern this mobility. A do-

mestic worker's position within the occupation is not static but subject to change, and may improve as she gains experience, learns to utilize the informational resources embedded in social networks, and establishes a set number of *casas* (houses) to clean. While the occupation remains largely unregulated by formal bureaucratic agencies, the domestic workers themselves create an informal but intensive social system of regulation.

The domestic workers' networks, however, also have a downside, and they are particularly constraining for newly arrived immigrant women who are trying to break into domestic work. These women generally face two alternatives: taking a live-in position, or working as a subcontracted helper to another domestic worker, usually a well-established immigrant woman. Both circumstances leave the women vulnerable to exceedingly low pay and trapped in an exploitative relationship, yet subcontracting can serve as a springboard to obtaining their own jobs. In this manner, paid domestic work can be conceptualized as a career, with the networks governing both entry into the occupation and internal occupational mobility. As one advances in the career, the network system becomes more advantageous and settlement is fortified.

What implications does immigrant women's concentration in domestic work hold for other sectors of society? Research by Hertz (1986) and by Hochschild (1989) indicates that the greater household equality enjoyed by class-privileged couples often relies on the exploitation of poor minority women, many of whom are immigrant women. Women in class-privileged couples purchase their way out of some aspects of gender subordination, which allows them to pursue conjugal relations that are, as the title of Hertz's book suggests, "more equal than others." The number of Mexican undocumented immigrant women working as domestic cleaning women in the U.S. will, in all likelihood, increase in coming years. As immigrant networks expand, bringing Mexican undocumented immigrant women to diverse points of destination in the U.S., we may see a more widespread use of immigrant women as paid domestic workers in diverse regions of the country, and we may see them employed by families less class privileged than those that employ them at the current time. Research conducted in San Francisco already indicates that seniors living on fixed incomes, dual-

earner working parents, and single mothers are no longer unusual employers of Latina immigrant domestic workers (Salzinger, 1991).

In addition to employment, immigrant women stabilize settlement by utilizing various institutional resources. The fact that some immigrants use public forms of support can be integrated into a conceptual framework for understanding Mexican immigrant settlement, a topic which is already controversial. This does not imply that all undocumented settled immigrants rely on public and private forms of assistance. Rather, the conceptual scheme highlights the fact that in settlement, the resources for daily maintenance and survival originate only in the U.S. While sojourner migrants often rely on the family "back home" as a refuge and a source of financial support during hard times, settlers do not always have access to these ties. Long-staying immigrants cannot always rely on kin in Mexico, and, coupled with undocumented immigrants' vulnerable economic status and low earning power, this results in the need to seek supplemental sources of support which include credit, charity, and sometimes modest uses of public assistance, which is mostly available for U.S.-citizen children. This raises questions for further research regarding generational privileges and resources in immigrant families.

As undocumented immigrant families stay in the U.S. for prolonged periods of time, their livelihood may depend, in part, on their ability to seek institutional forms of assistance that stretch scarce resources. In turn, the availability of publicly funded social services, private forms of credit, and installment purchase plans may serve to anchor immigrants in the U.S. Through the utilization of public and private forms of assistance, including private credit, immigrants become further integrated into the U.S. economy and society. Immigrant women actively seek out these resources.

In the case of northwestern Europe, Freeman (1986) has argued that the availability of social services and support provided by both public and private agencies helps to transform temporary migrants into permanent-settler immigrants. According to Freeman, the shift from temporary solo sojourner migration to permanent settlement of immigrant families signals a transition from immigrants constituting a fiscal bonus to a net drain on state welfare programs. An exception, Freeman notes, is when there is a predominance of young adults in the immigrant population (1986). Research supports this conclusion in the case of Mexican immigration to the United States. Demographic projections rendered by Hayes-Bautista et al. (1988) indicate that young Mexican and other Latino immigrants, including their children, will constitute a substantial portion of the U.S. labor force in coming years, and it is these future workers who will shoulder the burden of Social Security payments for the aging baby-boomer population. In this scenario, Mexican immigrants are an overall bonus—indeed a key—to social welfare, in spite of their temporary needs. In the case of Mexican immigrants and their children, public investment now will have a tremendous positive impact in the next century. The Oakview study suggests that women are the key people to reach with respect to delivery of social services in the immigrant community.

Women play a vital role in the efforts to build community among Mexican undocumented immigrants. An appreciation of men as the community pioneers, as the first migrant sojourners and settlers, must be complemented by a recognition of women as community builders. Women create important linkages with bureaucratic institutions, such as schools, medical offices, and other public and private organizations, and they also weave webs of interpersonal social ties among themselves and their families. These social webs hold immigrant settlement in place.

Many observers have posited a strong symbiosis between Chicanos and Mexican immigrants, as various waves of Mexican immigration provide cultural replenishment for U.S.-born Mexican Americans or Chicanos, renewing language, and religious and culinary traditions. Certainly the settlement of Mexican immigrants fortifies Spanish-language media and prompts the opening of ethnic markets, yet during eighteen months of fieldwork in the Oakview barrio, I observed minimal interaction between Mexican undocumented immigrants and Chicanos. The interactions that I did witness generally consisted of immigrants' brief, bureaucratic or service transactions with Chicano clerks, shopkeepers, teachers, nurses, or social workers. Although the second-generation children of immigrants, who experienced childhood and adolescence in the U.S., sometimes came to identify with and gain acceptance in Chicano culture, this was not true of their parents and kin, who came to the U.S. after adolescence.[4] None of the study participants thought of themselves as Chicano, and they did not seem to be directly replenishing Chicano culture.

Research conducted in two Texas cities—Austin and San Antonio—by Rodríguez and Nuñez (1986) sheds light on this issue, as their comparative study of these cities suggests that the relative and absolute size of the undocumented immigrant concentration affects this relation. In instances of relatively small undocumented immigrant concentrations, there are few resources within the undocumented population, so undocumented immigrants are more likely to go outside their group for economic and social resources. This pattern was borne out in the Oakview community during the early stages of male settlement, when many of the undocumented immigrant men relied on assistance from Chicanos and Euro-Latins—the Spanish, Portuguese, and Italian shopkeepers.

When the immigrant community has grown and matured, newly arrived immigrants depend on established Mexican immigrant friends and family, not on Chicanos. Moreover, as Rodríguez and Nuñez point out, social, economic, and cultural differences also mitigate against the establishment of personal relationships between the two groups. In Texas, the proximity to Mexico helps undocumented immigrants maintain their cultural identity. In the Oakview barrio, the encapsulation of the undocumented immigrant community accomplishes this.

How does gender affect these processes? Using the woman-centered model of settlement that I have proposed highlights not only the role of women in ameliorating the hardships of settlement, but also the manner in which a demographically diverse immigrant community is better able to access and share diverse resources. As more women and families settle, the immigrant community becomes more self-reliant. This is largely due to women's abilities to mobilize various resources, and also to the cross-generational and neighborhood ties that emanate from varied family members.

A significant number of Mexican undocumented immigrants participate in civic groups or secondary associations, belying the notion, which is deeply rooted in sociology, of conflict between primary groups and secondary organizations among immigrants. I found not only organizational participation among immigrants—even those lacking legal status—but also a symbiotic relationship between primary groups and the more formalized political and community organizations. Ties among family and friends feed the vitality of formal associations and organizations. Importantly, women's social ties among kin and friends bind many of the secondary associations together.

Undocumented immigrant women's participation in self-help groups, instructional classes, parents' organizations, and in church and neighborhood groups solidifies settlement in two ways. First, these activities are aimed at improving the material conditions of life in the United States for both the participants and their families. As such, these activities represent an investment of time and effort toward the end of permanent settlement. Second, in the process of participation, immigrants widen their circles of *conocidos* (acquaintances), construct social solidarity, and gain a sense of belonging which furthers the project of social integration.

Women play a fundamental role in consolidating settlement. Through their efforts in establishing stable forms of employment for themselves, seeking institutional modes of support for themselves and their families, and creating community ties, women forge linkages between their families and institutions and people in the U.S. As such, immigrant women concretize long-term family settlement.

Through settlement, women improve their own position in their families. The income which they earn in their jobs, the public and private resources which they tap for family use, and the social and community ties which they build further strengthen women's position in families. Immigrant women solidify the likelihood of permanent family settlement as they enhance their own status in their families.

The case of Mexican immigrant settlement in the United States parallels the trajectory followed by Algerian, Italian, and Turkish immigrant workers in Western Europe. These migrations began with primarily male migrant workers, unaccompanied by women and families. Institutionalized state mechanisms—the bracero program in the U.S. and the "guest worker" programs in Western Europe—recruited male migrant workers, and thus fostered men's temporary migrant sojourns while explicitly discouraging immigrant family reunifi-

cation and permanent immigrant settlement. These programs operated under the assumption that migrant workers would fill a seemingly temporary labor shortage, but as many commentators have noted, the programs responded to and eventually constituted structural features of U.S. and European labor markets.

One crucial factor distinguishing immigrant integration in Western Europe from that in the United States is the role played by the immigrants' home countries. Countries such as Italy, Turkey, and Yugoslavia sponsor immigrant organizations in Western Europe which address immigrants' legal, social, educational, and cultural needs.[5] Due to these efforts, Western European immigrant communities resemble immigrant exclaves more than enclaves, as the organizations strengthen immigrants' ties to social and political institutions in their home countries (Heisler, 1986). These institutional ties reinforce the ideology, indeed the plausibility, of return migration, leading to the indeterminacy of settlement.

The Mexican government has traditionally not sponsored such popular organizations for Mexican immigrants in the United States. Hometown organizations and soccer clubs, and more informal transnational social-network ties, certainly connect Mexican immigrants to Mexico, but these institutions do not appear to have the same impact as the more official organizations do in Western Europe. While in Europe a myriad of government programs and agencies fosters the indeterminacy of settlement, the Mexican government has not instituted similar organizations for Mexican immigrants in the United States. This may be changing as the electoral challenges faced by the PRI (Partido Revolucionario Institucionalizado), the ruling political party in Mexico, have prompted the Mexican government to take an active role in providing services to and defending the rights of Mexican citizens in the United States. Since 1988, the Mexican consuls have taken a more aggressive role, for example, in defending Mexican immigrants who are targets of violent hate crimes, in supporting regional and hometown clubs, and in promoting literacy programs and bilingual education for Mexican residents in the U.S. (Gutiérrez, 1993). These relatively modest efforts, however, still pale in comparison with the cumulative daily activities of immigrants that anchor settlement.

The permanent incorporation of new immigrants clearly signals the creation of new types of multiethnic and multiracial societies. Recognition that permanent immigrant settlement is well under way brings up both old and new questions regarding citizenship, nationhood, and membership, and an important area of future analysis lies in establishing how gender both conditions and intervenes in these processes.

The phenomenon of undocumented immigrants who are homeowners, taxpayers, school attendees, and small-business owners presents a challenge to the traditional dichotomous fashion in which we think about citizenship and "illegal aliens." The phrase "illegal alien" denotes not only unlawful, criminal activities but also marginal involvement in societal institutions. Long-term-staying, undocumented immigrants who are integrated into social and economic life in the U.S., who have developed strong, sometimes irreversible ties to their new home areas, cannot be equated with newcomer undocumented migrant workers, although both would technically fall into the same legal-status category. Given the current political and historical context, the critical category now is not citizenship, but membership. Questions of membership concern persons already well integrated into the economic, social, and cultural life in the territory, but excluded from the rights and obligations of citizenship and legal permanent-resident status. Like settlement, membership is not a neat category, but develops over time as immigrants establish ties while living and working in a particular country (Brubaker, 1989).

Long-staying undocumented immigrants are developing new social identities that are increasingly rooted in their migration and settlement experiences. As undocumented immigrant women and men mobilize to obtain fair labor conditions, to secure voting rights in school-board and other local elections, or to demand crime-free neighborhoods, their voices are not always well received. At times, the demands for enfranchisement and community empowerment have been met with blatant hostility.

The revival of xenophobia in Western Europe and the United States in the 1980s and the early 1990s targeted the unanticipated but seemingly permanent stay of undocumented immigrant workers and their families. Contemporary allegations that immigrants compete with citizens for jobs and depress wage levels, that immigrants are culturally unassimilable, and that immigrants threaten to become a permanent underclass, a drain on society's resources, are all directed at long-staying immigrants. Not incidentally, these allegations focus on the structural features of settlement, namely, nonseasonal employment, cohesive communities, and the use of institutional resources, both public and private. Contemporary nativists distort these features in their efforts to mobilize support against the permanent integration of Mexican immigrants.

Both the bracero program and Europe's "guest worker" programs provide stunning examples of immigration policy gone awry. Social policies designed to engineer particular outcomes often fail, pointing to the vitality of human agency and social dynamics—including gender relations—at the family and community levels. This serves as an important reminder to those who would dismiss as inconsequential for social outcomes or explanations the gendered activities in families and communities. Legislative measures may provide pressures and opportunities for migration and return migration, but the way people respond to these pressures is not so easily predicted.

ENDNOTES

1. Others who have made this observation suggest retaining a more modified use of the term "household" (e.g., Grasmuck and Pessar, 1991; Rouse, 1987). In a study of Mexican immigration, Roger Rouse (1987) suggests that we use the term "household projects" so as not to privilege collective over individual goals. In a study of young women's employment in Java, Diane Wolf suggests the term "household practices" as a reference to all household members' activities, decisions, and interactions. While the term "household practices" avoids many of the problems with the household-strategies model, it holds little explanatory power for the study of immigration. As Wolf (1992:263) wisely notes, "The most compelling view of the household comes from *unbundling* these relations, interactions, and activities. We should concern ourselves not only with the results of individual or household-level action, but also with the *process* involved in reaching that decision or action."

2. This observation is inspired by Barrie Thorne's (1993) research and perspective of children as actors in their own right.

3. The national conference on immigrant and refugee women, titled "Dreams Lost, Dreams Found: Women Organizing for Justice," was held in Berkeley, California, October 5–7, 1991, and was sponsored by the Fam-

ily Violence Prevention Fund and the Coalition for Immigrant and Refugee Rights and Services, a San Francisco Bay–area coalition that includes over eighty-five organizations.

4. Mexican-born youth and U.S.-born youth of Mexican descent do not always socialize together. In a study conducted in East Los Angeles, where recent immigration has "Mexicanized" Chicano neighborhoods, Moore and Vigil (1993) report that the White Fence gang prides itself on recruiting only U.S.-born Chicanos.

5. According to Heisler (1986),the governments of these immigrant-sending countries maintain immigrants' connections to political and social institutions in their home society. Embassies and consulates engage staffs of legal experts, social workers, and teachers who operate special schools in the language of origin for immigrants in Western Europe. Religious organizations, trade unions, and political parties from the immigrants' countries of origin also maintain representation.

T W E N T Y - S I X

Mexican Migration and the Social Space of Postmodernism

Roger Rouse

In a hidden sweatshop in downtown Los Angeles, Asian and Latino migrants produce automobile parts for a factory in Detroit. As the parts leave the production line, they are stamped "Made in Brazil."[1] In a small village in the heart of Mexico, a young woman at her father's wake wears a black T-shirt sent to her by a brother in the United States. The shirt bears a legend that some of the mourners understand but she does not. It reads, "Let's Have Fun Tonight!" And on the Tijuana–San Diego border, Guillermo Gómez-Peña, a writer originally from Mexico City, reflects on the time he has spent in what he calls "the gap between two worlds": "Today, eight years after my departure, when they ask me for my nationality or ethnic identity, I cannot answer with a single word, for my 'identity' now possesses multiple repertoires: I am Mexican but I am also Chicano and Latin American. On the border they call me 'chilango' or 'mexiquillo'; in the capital, 'pocho' or 'norteño,' and in Spain 'sudaca.' . . . My companion Emily is Anglo-Italian

but she speaks Spanish with an Argentinian accent. Together we wander through the ruined Babel that is our American postmodernity."[2]

1

We live in a confusing world, a world of crisscrossed economics, intersecting systems of meaning, and fragmented identities. Suddenly, the comforting modern imagery of nation-states and national languages, of coherent communities and consistent subjectivities, of dominant centers and distant margins no longer seems adequate. Certainly, in my own discipline of anthropology, there is a growing sense that our conventional means of representing both the worlds of those we study and the worlds that we ourselves inhabit have been strained beyond their limits by the changes that are taking place around us. Indeed, the very notion that ethnographers and their subjects exist in readily separable domains is increasingly being called into question.[3] But the problem is not confined to a single discipline, nor even to the academy at large. As Fredric Jameson has observed, the gradual unfolding of the global shift from colonialism and classic forms of dependency to a new transnational capitalism has meant that, during the last 20 years, we have all moved irrevocably into a new kind of social space, one which our modern sensibilities leave us unable to comprehend. With appropriate dramatic flair, he calls this new terrain "postmodern hyperspace."[4]

Jameson suggests that, in order to locate ourselves in this new space, we must make two moves. First, to understand why the crisis in spatial representation exists, we must identify as clearly as possible the broad politico-economic changes that have undermined the verisimilitude of existing images, and second, to understand where we are and where we can go from here, we must develop new images, new coordinates, a series of new and more effective maps. Jameson seeks to construct these alternative images through a critical reading of aesthetic forms such as novels, buildings, paintings, and films. But his focus seems unduly narrow. Given the ubiquity of the changes he describes and the profundity of their influence, the raw materials for a new cartography ought to be equally discoverable in the details of people's daily lives. And, from a radical perspective, the most significant materials surely lie in the circumstances and experiences of those working-class groups whose members have been most severely affected by the changing character of capitalist exploitation.

In this article, I will develop these ideas by drawing on my work with rural Mexicans involved in migration to and from the United States. After outlining the images conventionally used to map the social terrain they inhabit, I will first build on their experiences to suggest new images better suited to charting their current circumstances and then indicate how these images may, in fact, be increasingly useful to us all as we try to map social landscapes found throughout Mexico and the United States.

2

Two socio-spatial images have dominated the modern discourse of the social sciences concerning the people of rural Mexico. I claim neither novelty nor insight for recognizing their influ-

ence. By underlining their importance and delineating their attendant assumptions, however, I hope to make it easier to understand both the nature of their limitations and the significance of the alternatives I shall propose.

The first image is one to which I shall attach the label "community."[6] The abstract expression of an idealized nation-state, it has been used concretely at numerous different levels, from the peasant village to the nation itself. It combines two main ideas.[7] First, it identifies a discriminable population with a single, bounded space—a territory or place. In so doing, it assumes that the social relationships in which community members participate will be much more intense within this space than beyond. It also assumes that members will treat the place of the community as the principal environment to which they adjust their actions and, correspondingly, that they will monitor local events much more closely than developments further afield. Second, the image implies a certain commonality and coherence, generally expressed either in the functionalist dream of an entity whose institutional parts fit together neatly to form an integrated whole or in the structural-functionalist vision of a shared way of life that exists not only in a multiplicity of similar actions but, more profoundly, in a single and internally consistent set of rules, values, or beliefs. From the perspective that these two ideas establish, the heterogeneities and complexities of the worlds we actually encounter are normally understood in terms of either superficial interactions between distinct communities or transitional moments in the movement from one form of integrity and order to another.

The second image is one that I shall label "center/periphery."[8] The abstract expression of an idealized imperial system, it too has been realized concretely at many different levels, from the rural town to the entire world system. This image involves three main ideas. First, it suggests that differences are organized concentrically around a dominant core. Thus, power and wealth are greatest at the center and diminish gradually as one moves outwards through a series of surrounding zones, and different locations are associated with different ways of life according to the zone in which they are found. Second, the image implies a process of change in which the center exercises a privileged capacity to shape outcomes, whether it is extending its influence to the margins or molding people from the periphery who enter its terrain. And third, it suggests that fields ordered in this way are autonomous: each peripheral site is oriented to a single center and each center is independent of all others at the same level.

In many ways, these images are opposed. Formally, the idea of community tends to privilege homogeneity and stasis while the idea of center/periphery privileges variation and change. And, in practice, they have frequently been used against one another, community being the principal sociospatial image invoked by modernization theory and center/periphery, of course, serving as a crucial counterimage for dependency theory and the world systems approach. But their opposition should not be exaggerated. In many works they have been used in tandem and, in fact, the key tension between modernization theory and its critics lies less in frictions over spatial imagery than in disagreements about the intentions of the center and the nature of its influence.[9] Indeed, even when the two images have been in conflict, they have supported one another negatively, each being treated as the only viable alternative to the other. Opposed, combined, or alternating, they have long dominated work on rural Mexico with the casual authority of the commonsensical.

Migration has always had the potential to challenge established spatial images. It highlights the social nature of space as something created and reproduced through collective human agency and, in so doing, reminds us that, within the limits imposed by power, existing spatial arrangements are always susceptible to change. In practice, however, academics dealing with Mexican migration have rarely used it as the basis for a critical reappraisal of existing images. Instead, with a few notable exceptions, they have simply adapted the existing repertoire to make it fit the peculiarities of a mobile population. This is particularly apparent in the way they have used frameworks derived from the image of community to understand the experiences of the migrants themselves.

First, because migration is self-evidently a movement between places, it has commonly been treated as a movement from one set of social relationships to another. Thus, numerous studies have sought to gauge the changes that migrants have undergone by comparing the systems of family organization, kinship, and friendship dominant in their places of origin with those they have developed in the places to which they have moved.[10]

Second, as a movement between places, migration has also commonly been treated as a shift from one significant environment to another. Within a bipolar framework variously organized around oppositions between the rural and the urban, the traditional and the modern, and Mexico and the United States, many studies have examined how migrants take practices and attitudes adjusted to their original "niche" or setting and adapt them to the new locale in which they find themselves.[11]

And third, as a move between communities identified with distinct ways of life, migration has normally been seen as a process in which the migrants and their descendants experience a more or less gradual shift from one ordered arrangement to another, either fully converting to the dominant way of life or forging their own form of accommodation in an ordered synthesis of old and new. Such a perspective does recognize that contradictions can arise when people combine attitudes and practices associated with the place to which they have moved with others linked to their place of origin, but it has generally dealt with these in ways that sustain the primacy of order, treating them either as incongruities in form that disappear when viewed in terms of function or as temporary features peculiar to transitional situations. In the latter case, it has been particularly common to locate the contradictions within a widely used model of generational succession according to which the migrants themselves retain much of what they learned while growing up, they and their children balance traditional attitudes and practices maintained in intimate arenas such as the home and the ethnic neighborhood with others more appropriate to participation in the wider society, and a consistent sociocultural orientation appears only in the third generation.[12]

These ways of construing migration have faced a qualified challenge from accounts that treat it principally as a circular process in which people remain oriented to the places from which they have come. Under such circumstances, the patterns of social and cultural adjustment are clearly different.[13] But it is important to stress that the basic socio-spatial assumptions remain the same. As in accounts that emphasize a unidirectional shift, migrants are held to move between distinct, spatially demarcated communities and, in the long run, to be capable of maintaining an involvement in only one of them.

3

In recent years, however, this mobilization of modern socio-spatial images has become increasingly unable to contain the postmodern complexities that it confronts. Symptomatic of the unfolding shift to transnational capitalism, migration between rural Mexico and the United States since the Second World War, and especially since the mid-1960s, has been obliging us ever more insistently to develop an alternative cartography of social space. I can elaborate this argument most effectively by drawing on the case that I know best, the United States–bound migration that has been taking place since the early 1940s from the rural *municipio* of Aguililla in the southwest corner of the state of Michoacán.[14]

At first sight, Aguililla seems to be an isolated community dedicated to small-scale farming and manifestly part of the Mexican periphery. The *municipio* is located in the mountains that form the southern limit of the west-central region; its administrative center, also known as Aguililla, lies at the end of a poor dirt road, one of those points where the national transport system finally exhausts itself; the land has been used principally for the subsistence-oriented production of basic foodstuffs and the raising of livestock; and trade with the interior has been limited. It is the kind of place onto which urban dwellers find it easy to project their fantasies of difference and danger.

But appearances can be deceptive. Aguililla's growing involvement in transnational migration has profoundly changed both its economic orientation and its socio-spatial relationships. By the early 1980s, when I carried out fieldwork in the *municipio,* it had come to operate largely as a nursery and nursing home for wage-laborers in the United States. Almost every family had members who were or had been abroad; the local economy depended heavily on the influx of dollars; and many of the area's small farming operations continued only because they were sustained by migrant remittances. Concomitantly, the *municipio* has become part of a transnational network of settlements and, in so doing, has significantly modi-

fied its status as a marginal site within a purely national hierarchy of places. Over the years, migrants have established several outposts in the United States, by far the largest being the one they have formed amidst a rapidly growing Latino neighborhood in Redwood City, an urban area on the northern edge of California's famous Silicon Valley. There they now work principally in the service sector, as janitors, dishwashers, gardeners, hotel workers, house cleaners, and child minders—proletarian servants in the paragon of "postindustrial" society. Some Aguilillans have settled in Redwood City for long periods, but few abandon the *municipio* forever. Most people stay in the United States relatively briefly, almost all of those who stay longer continue to keep in touch with the people and places they have left behind, and even those who have been away for many years quite often return.

This pattern of migration must be understood as symptomatic of the way in which broad politico-economic developments involved in the unfolding of transnational capitalism have refracted themselves through the specificities of local circumstance. For many years, Aguilillans have placed a heavy emphasis on the capacity to create and maintain small-scale, family-run operations, ideally based in land, and, in relation to this goal, the broad developments have exerted contradictory pressures.

In the *municipio,* the nationwide diversion of capital to industry and commercial agriculture that has taken place since the 1940s has left the local economy without needed infrastructure, while the concentration of what government spending there has been in health and education has encouraged population growth and the broadening of people's horizons. As a result, it has become impossible for most Aguilillans to approach the realization of their goals solely through access to local resources. At the same time, however, the lack of large-scale land acquisitions in the *municipio* by commercially oriented owners, the periodic provision of small amounts of government aid to the area's farmers, and the entrepreneurial opportunities provided by the influx of dollars have all impeded full proletarianization. This, in turn, has meant that the old goals have not been abandoned and that migration has been seen principally as a way of raising outside funds to finance their local realization.[15]

Meanwhile, in the United States, the growing polarization of the labor market has created a mounting demand for Mexican workers to fill the bottom layers in agriculture, deskilled assembly, and, above all, services. Yet various factors have discouraged most Mexicans from staying permanently. In the case of Aguilillans, their cultural emphasis on creating and maintaining independent operations has led them to have deep-seated reservations about many aspects of life in the United States, prominent among them the obligation of proletarian workers to submit to the constant regulation of supervisors and the clock. In addition, the disappearance of many middle-level jobs and the attendant change in the shape of the labor market—from pyramid to hourglass—have made it increasingly difficult for people to see chances of upward mobility for themselves or, perhaps more significantly, for their children. And finally, the economy's steady downturn since the mid-1960s has markedly increased both the hostility and the legal restrictions that many of the migrants face.[16]

Influenced by these contradictory developments, Aguilillans have forged socio-spatial arrangements that seriously challenge the dominant ways of reading migration. First, it has become inadequate to see Aguilillan migration as a movement between distinct communities, understood as the loci of distinct sets of social relationships. Today, Aguilillans find that their most important kin and friends are as likely to be living hundreds or thousands of miles away as immediately around them. More significantly, they are often able to maintain these spatially extended relationships as actively and effectively as the ties that link them to their neighbors. In this regard, growing access to the telephone has been particularly significant, allowing people not just to keep in touch periodically but to contribute to decision-making and participate in familial events even from a considerable distance.

Indeed, through the continuous circulation of people, money, goods, and information, the various settlements have become so closely woven together that, in an important sense, they have come to constitute a single community spread across a variety of sites, something I refer to as a "transnational migrant circuit." Although the Aguilillan case undoubtedly has its local peculiarities, there is evidence that such arrangements are becoming increasingly important in the organization of Mexican migration to and from the United States.[17] Just as capitalists have responded to the new forms of economic internationalism by establishing transnational corporations, so workers have responded by creating transnational circuits.[18]

At the same time, as a result of these developments, it has become equally inadequate to see Aguilillan migration as a movement between distinct environments. Today, it is the circuit as a whole rather than any one locale that constitutes the principal setting in relation to which Aguilillans orchestrate their lives.[19] Those living in Aguililla, for example, are as much affected by events in Redwood City as by developments in the *municipio* itself, and the same is true in reverse. Consequently, people monitor what is happening in the other parts of the circuit as closely as they monitor what is going on immediately around them. Indeed, it is only by recognizing the transnational framework within which Aguilillans are operating that we can properly appreciate the logic of their actions. Thus, people in the United States may spend large amounts of time and money trying to obtain papers without ever seeking citizenship because it is as Mexican citizens with the right to "permanent residence" that they will be best equipped to move back and forth between the two countries. And they may send their children back to Mexico to complete their educations or to visit during school vacations at least in part because they want to endow them with the bilingual and bicultural skills necessary to operate effectively on both sides of the border.

Finally, it is mistaken to see Aguilillan experiences in terms of an inexorable move towards a new form of sociocultural order. Although transnational migration has brought distant worlds into immediate juxtaposition, their proximity has produced neither homogenization nor synthesis. Instead, Aguilillans have become involved in the chronic maintenance of two quite distinct ways of life. More importantly, the resulting contradictions have not come simply from the persistence of past forms amid contemporary adjustments or from involvement in distinct lifeworlds within the United States. Rather, they reflect the fact that Aguilillans see their current lives and future possibilities as involving simultaneous engagements in places associated with markedly different forms of experience. Moreover, the way in which at least some people are preparing their children to operate within a dichotomized setting spanning national borders suggests that current contradictions will not be resolved through a simple process of generational succession.

The different ways of life that Aguilillans balance can be understood partly by reference to spatially demarcated national or local cultures, but they should also be understood in terms of class. In numerous combinations, Aguilillans have come to link proletarian labor with a sustained attachment to the creation of small-scale, family-based operations; and even though these ways of making a living may be reconcilable economically, in cultural terms they are fundamentally distinct, involving quite different attitudes and practices concerning the use of time and space, the conduct of social relationships, and the orchestration of appearances.[20] Indeed, one of the main considerations preserving the polarized relationship between Aguililla and Redwood City has been the fact that the latter has offered Aguilillans so few opportunities to create independent operations while the former, partly through the continued influx of remittances, has remained a place in which such opportunities are still available.

Obliged to live within a transnational space and to make a living by combining quite different forms of class experience, Aguilillans have become skilled exponents of a cultural bifocality that defies reduction to a singular order. Indeed, in many respects, Aguilillans have come to inhabit a kind of border zone, especially if we follow Américo Paredes in recognizing that a border is "not simply a line on a map but, more fundamentally, . . . a sensitized area where two cultures or two political systems come face to face."[21] Socioeconomically, the relationship between Aguililla and Redwood City is strikingly similar to the relationship along the international border between twinned cities such as Ciudad Juárez and El Paso or Matamoros and Brownsville. They are mutually implicated in numerous ways, but the line between them never disappears. And culturally, life within the circuit corresponds closely to the situation that Gómez-Peña describes for the border linking Tijuana and San Diego: "In my fractured reality, but reality nonetheless, live two histories, languages, cosmogonies, artistic traditions, and political systems dramatically opposed—the border is the continuous confrontation of two or more ref-

erential codes."[22] For many years, the United States–Mexican border seemed like a peculiar space, a narrow strip quite different from what lay at the heart of the two countries. But this is no longer the case. Ties such as those between Aguililla and Redwood City, places two thousand miles apart, prompt us to ask how wide this border has become and how peculiar we should consider its characteristics.

4

Socio-spatial frames derived from the image of the community no longer serve to represent the local terrain that Aguilillans inhabit. It seems that images such as those of the circuit and the border zone may be more appropriate. But these claims do not apply solely to small-scale settlements. Partly as a result of the migration that Aguilillans exemplify, they are becoming increasingly relevant to social landscapes found throughout Mexico and the United States.

It is scarcely a revelation to suggest that Mexico's dependent status renders problematical any assumption of functional integration or the presence of a singular sociocultural order. However, the shift to transnational capitalism has both intensified and changed the nature of national disarticulation, particularly during the last 20 years. Foreign capital plays a more significant role in Mexico than ever before, and, more critically, thanks to the rising use of offshore plants that carry out only a part of the production process and the growing ease with which these plants can be transferred to other underdeveloped countries, the ties linking foreign capital to the rest of Mexican society are becoming progressively weaker. Moreover, as the massive flight of domestic capital during the last few years illustrates only too well, the Mexican bourgeoisie is also orchestrating its actions increasingly within a transnational framework. At the same time, the growing institutionalization of migration to the United States through the medium of transnational circuits means that more of the Mexican population is oriented to developments outside the country and that this orientation is becoming steadily more pronounced. And finally, because of the expansion of a television system that carries numerous U.S. programs, the mounting of satellite dishes that tune directly into U.S. broadcasts, and the increasing exposure to U.S. ways of life through migration, foreign cultural influences are becoming rapidly more pervasive. The black T-shirt with its English exhortation, defying any attempt to read the wake as the textual expression of a coherent local culture, is emblematic of a process pervading rural Mexico.

What is perhaps more striking is that a similar kind of disarticulation is beginning to appear in the United States, particularly in its major cities. The United States economy, long dominated by domestic capital, is now increasingly influenced by transnationally orchestrated foreign investment, especially from Britain, Canada, Germany, the Netherlands, and Japan.[23] As regards labor, although immigrant workers have been an important factor for many years, they are today arriving under circumstances that distance them much more fully from the rest of society. In particular, the declining availability of those middle-level jobs that once encouraged hope of upward mobility, the increased scapegoating and legal restrictions that have accompanied economic decline since the mid-1960s, and the related development of transnational circuits are all serving to subvert the older possibilities of assimilation to a single national order. And partly as a result, ways of life commonly identified with the Third World are becoming increasingly apparent in a country often treated as the apogee of First World advancement. Extreme poverty, residential overcrowding and homelessness, underground economies, new forms of domestic service, and sweatshops exist side by side with yuppie affluence, futuristic office blocks, and all the other accoutrements of high-tech postindustrialism.

Los Angeles is by no means typical, but the situation that had developed there by the mid-1980s offers a suggestive outline of emerging possibilities. In the downtown area, 75% of the buildings were owned wholly or in part by foreign capital, and as much as 90% of new multistory construction was being financed by investment from abroad.[24] In the larger conurbation, 40% of the population belonged to ethnic "minorities," many of them migrants from Asia and Latin America (estimates suggest that the figure will approach 60% by the year 2010).[25] And throughout the region, the growing contrasts between rich and poor and their increasingly apparent juxtaposition were prompting journalists to speculate about the "Brazilianization" of the City.[26] The hidden sweatshop in the heart of the metropolis, defying any attempt to claim a comfortable distance between Third World and First, calls attention to a trend that is gradually if unevenly affecting the whole of the country.[27]

Thus, in the United States as well as in Mexico, the *place* of the putative community—whether regional or national—is becoming little more than a *site* in which transnationally organized circuits of capital, labor, and communications intersect with one another and with local ways of life. In these circumstances, it becomes increasingly difficult to delimit a singular national identity and a continuous history, and the claims of politicians to speak authoritatively on behalf of this imagined community and its purported interests become increasingly hollow. But it is not just the image of the community which is compromised. The image of center and periphery is also coming under increasing strain. United States capital increasingly intersects with capital from other core countries not only in peripheral areas such as Mexico but also in the United States itself. The growing influence of foreign investment means that, in both countries, people must accommodate themselves to a capital that is increasingly heteroglot and culturally diverse. And the concentric distribution of differences in power, wealth, and ways of life is breaking down, in large part because the United States no longer works as effectively to transform those who enter its terrain. Alongside the more familiar tale of capitalist penetration in the periphery, we are beginning to witness what Renato Rosaldo has called "the implosion of the Third World into the first" ("Ideology" 85), or what Saskia Sassen-Koob calls "peripheralization at the core."

One of the results of these developments is that we are seeing a proliferation of border zones. The international border is widening and, at the same, time, miniature borders are erupting throughout the two countries. In Mexico, the provisions granting special tariff dispensations to offshore production have stretched and distended the border for capital, especially now that the offshore plants, first established in the northern part of the country, are steadily moving southwards. At the same time, in the United States, the provisions regarding employer sanctions in the new immigration law have exploded the border for labor and relocated it in a multitude of fragments at the entrance to every workplace, while the recent amnesty has encouraged transnationally oriented migrants to extend their presence throughout the country. Moreover, the most readily dramatized juxtapositions of citizens and migrants are no longer confined to major urban sites such as downtown Los Angeles. They are also beginning to appear on the margins of suburbia as members of the native middle classes, scared by the real and imagined violence of these inner-city border zones, are developing residential enclaves in rural areas long inhabited by migrant farm workers.

Conditions in northern San Diego County illustrate the last of these trends in a particularly vivid way. Here, against the background of a burgeoning military-industrial economy, rapidly expanding middle-class suburbs have recently encroached on areas long filled with the ramshackle encampments of Latino migrants. In the words of the *Los Angeles Times,* the result has been a world where "squalid, plywood-and-cardboard hooches sit in the shadow of million-dollar mansions, where the BMW and Volvo sets rub elbows at the supermarket with dusty migrants fresh from the fields." Put more pithily by an academic familiar with the area, "What you have . . . is the first of the First World intermixing with the last of the Third World. It's Nicaragua versus Disneyland." Or, as one local suburban resident observed, "It's like we're living in the Third World here. It doesn't seem to me that this is part of the American Dream."[28]

But these collisions and complaints are not the only markers of a newly emerging border zone. One man in a local trailer park, offended by migrants taking water from his spigot, put barbed wire on the chain-link fence behind his trailer, installed a set of floodlights, and armed himself with a 12-gauge shotgun (see Bailey 1988). Other residents have hunted migrants with paint-pellet guns and run them down with trucks. And, in November 1988, a local youth went one step further, shooting and killing two Latinos after confronting them near the camps. Asked to explain his actions, he said simply that he hated Mexicans (see Davidson 1990; Mydans 1990). This is Nicaragua versus Disneyland, then, not simply as Latino versus Anglo or Third World versus First but as the savage implosion of frontline violence within the sanitized dreamworlds of middle-class escape.

5

The forces shaping Aguilillans' lives are thus coming to affect everyone who inhabits the terrain encompassed by Mexico and the United States. Throughout this fractured territory, transnationalism, contradictions in development, and increasingly polarized economies are stretching images of community beyond their limits, bringing different ways of life into vivid, often violent juxtaposition, and encouraging the chronic reproduction of their incongruities. The impact of these changes clearly varies with the circumstances of the people they affect, but their reach is increasingly broad.

Under such circumstances, images such as the circuit and the border zone may help us understand not only the specificities of Aguilillan experience but social landscapes increasingly familiar to us all. If this is true, it adds weight to the idea that, in our attempts to orient ourselves amidst the complexities of postmodern hyperspace, we should look not only to art and literature but also to the lives of those "ordinary" people who inscribe their transient texts in the minutiae of daily experience. And this, in turn, suggests a pleasing irony with which to conclude, for it implies that, as in the case of Aguilillans and others like them, people long identified with an unworkable past may in fact be those from whom we have most to learn as we try to chart our way through the confusions of the present towards a future we can better understand and thus more readily transform.

ENDNOTES

The first version of this paper was written in early 1988 while I was a visiting research fellow at the Center for U.S.-Mexican Studies, University of California, San Diego. It draws on fieldwork carried out between 1982 and 1984 under a doctoral fellowship from the Inter-American Foundation. I am grateful to both organizations for their support. Many of the ideas contained in the paper were developed in a study group on postmodernism organized with colleagues from the center. My principal thanks—for comments, criticisms, and immensely pleasant company—go to the group's members: Josefina Alcazar, Alberto Aziz, Roger Bartra, Luin Goldring, Lidia Pico, Claudia Schatán, and Francisco Valdés. I have also benefited from Khachig Tololyan's sensitive reading of the text.

1. See Lockwood and Leinberger 1988:35. The assertion of a false point of origin is apparently used so that

the manufacturers can participate in foreign delivery contracts. See Soja 1989:217.

2. "Hoy, ocho años de mi partida, cuando me preguntan por mi nacionalidad o identidad étnica, no puedo responder con una palabra, pues mi 'identidad' ya posee repertorios múltiples: soy mexicano pero también soy chicano y latinoamericano. En la frontera me dicen 'chilango' o 'mexiquillo;' en la capital 'pocho' o 'norteño' y en España 'sudaca.' . . . Mi compañera Emilia es angloitaliana pero habla español con acento argentino; y juntos caminamos entre los escombros de la torre de Babel de nuestra posmodernidad americana." Gómez-Peña (my translation).

3. See, for example, Clifford 1986:22; and Rosaldo 1989:217.

4. Jameson 1984:83. Like Jameson, I find it useful to follow Ernest Mandel in arguing for the emergence since the Second World War of a new phase in monopoly capitalism, but I prefer to label this phase "transnational" rather than "late" partly to avoid the implication of imminent transcendence and, more positively, to emphasize the crucial role played by the constant movement of capital, labor, and information across national borders.

5. See Davis 1985; and Lipsitz 1986–87:161.

6. It is important to stress that I am concerned not with the various meanings of this particular term but instead with the image itself. The term serves merely as a convenient marker.

7. See Williams 1976:65–66.

8. Williams 1976:65–66.

9. The combination of these images is readily apparent in the classic works on rural social organization by Robert Redfield (1966) and Eric Wolf (1955), both of whom draw heavily on Mexican materials, and can also be seen in Immanuel Wallerstein's (1979) tendency to use nation-states as the constituent units of his world system, at least in the core.

10. This approach has been used in two related but different kinds of study. In work focusing on migration itself—especially on migration within Mexico—changes have commonly been gauged by comparing the forms of organization found in the points of destination with arrangements revealed by detailed research in the specific communities from which the migrants have come. See, for example, Butterworth 1962; Kemper 1977; and Lewis 1952. In work on communities known to contain a significant number of migrants and descendants of migrants—and especially in work on Mexican and Chicano communities in the United States—it has been more common to compare forms of organization found in these communities with arrangements discovered secondhand through reading literature on the general areas or types of society from which the migrants have come. See, for example, Achor 1978; Horowitz 1983; Humphrey 1944; Madsen 1964; Rubel 1966; and Thurston 1974.

11. See, for example, Achor 1978; Madsen 1964; Rubel 1966; Lomnitz 1977; and Ugalde 1974.

12. This approach has been manifest most commonly in work on migration to the United States, where the dominant tendency has been to challenge assumptions about full assimilation with analyses that stress the more or less gradual emergence of ethnic subcultures. See, for example, Achor 1978; Horowitz 1983; Madsen 1964; and Rubel 1966.

13. See, for example, Piore 1979.

14. A more detailed account of the *municipio* and the history of its involvement in migration can be found in Rouse 1989. A *municipio* is a relatively small administrative unit occupying the rung immediately below the level of the state. In 1980, for example, the *municipio* of Aguililla, covering an area of roughly 630 square miles, was one of 113 such entities with the state of Michoacán. The term is difficult to gloss with any precision, however. "Municipality" is misleading because of its urban associations, while a gloss such as "county" runs the risk of suggesting something too large and too powerful. Given these difficulties, I use the term in its untranslated form.

15. For a fuller understanding of the broad processes affecting rural Mexico over the last 40 years, see Cockcroft 1983; Hewitt de Alcantara 1976.

16. For a fuller understanding of the changing character of the United States economy, particularly since the 1960s, see Sassen 1988; and Davis 1986:181–230.

17. Such evidence can be found most readily in a series of studies that have appeared during the last decade charting the emergence of what are generally described as "binational migrant networks." See, for example, Baca and Bryan 1983; Kearney 1986; Massey et al. 1987; and Mines 1981.

18. I use the term "transnational" in preference to "binational" partly to evoke as directly as possible the association between migrant forms of organization and transnational corporations. ("Transnational" is gradually replacing the more popular adjective "multinational," at least in academic discourse.) I also prefer it to "binational" because it allows for the possibility that a circuit might include sites in more than two countries. Specifically in the case of Aguilillans, there are indications that this may be coming about as migrants from particular places in Central America arrive in the Redwood City area and gradually attach themselves to the Aguilillan circuit. One of the advantages of such an attachment is that, if they need to leave the United States, they can go to Aguililla and call on social ties established there instead of having to make the longer, more expensive, and often more dangerous journey back to their own country. I use the term "circuit" in preference to "network" because it more effectively evokes the circulation of people, money, goods, and information, the pseudo-institutional nature of the arrangement

(over purely individual ties), and the qualified importance of place (over purely social linkages). A fine
analysis, sensitive to many of these issues, can be found
in Kearney and Nagengast 1989.

19. For an account of the ways in which places linked
by migration can come to form a single "field of activity," see Roberts 1974:esp. 208–9.

20. These ideas are developed more fully in Rouse
1989a, 1989b.

21. Paredes 1978:68. See also Rosaldo 1989:esp.
196–217.

22. "En mi realidad fracturada, pero realidad al fin, co-
habitan dos historias, lenguajes, cosmogonías, tradi-
ciones artísticas y sistemas politicos drásticamente
opuestos (la frontera es el enfrentamiento continuo de
dos o más códigos referenciales)." Gómez-Peña 3 (my
translation). I do not mean to suggest by quoting
Gómez-Peña that he and Aguilillans experience their
particular border zones in exactly the same way.

Clearly, peoples experiences vary significantly according to their positions in local frameworks of power and
as a function of the routes they have followed in reaching such positions.

23. See Sassen 1988:esp. 171–85.

24. Davis 1987:71–72; and Soja 1989:221.

25. Lockwood and Leinberger 1988:41. According to
Soja (1989:215), more than two million Third World migrants settled in the Los Angeles area between the mid-
1960s and the mid-1980s.

26. See Richman and Schwarz 1987 (quoted in Davis
1987:77).

27. For a fuller picture of the changing political economy of Los Angeles, see Davis 1985, 1987; Sassen
1988:126–70; and Soja 1989:190–248. For reflections on
these trends in other parts of the United States, see
Franco 1985; and Koptiuch 1989.

28. All three quotations come from Bailey and Reza
1988.

T W E N T Y - S E V E N

The New Urban Reality

Roger Waldinger

New York's brush with fiscal insolvency in the
mid-1970s signaled the end for the old industrial
cities of the United States. Its revival in the 1980s
heralded the emergence of the nation's largest
cities as world service centers. The smokestack
cities of the industrial heartland unfortunately
have no replacement for their run-of-the-mill
production activities, steadily eroding under the
twin impact of computerization and foreign competition. But in the largest urban agglomerations
—Chicago, Los Angeles, Philadelphia, and, especially, New York—the advent of a postindustrial
economy has triggered a new phase of growth. The
key activities of the new economy—information
processing, the coordination of large organiza-

tions, and the management of volatile financial
markets—are overwhelmingly urban-based. And
their dynamism has yanked these largest cities out
of the economic torpor into which they had sunk.

The new urban vitality notwithstanding, cities
remain deeply troubled—perhaps more so than
before. The paradox of urban plenty is that com-
paratively few of the city's residents have been
able to enjoy the fruits of growth. The number of
poor people living in central cities has not fallen
but risen, and dramatically so. Instead of arrest-
ing social dislocation, the economic turnaround
has exacerbated the urban social problems identified thirty years ago. Though right and left differ
on social policy responses, both camps agree that

a sizable segment of the poor has been lopped off into an "urban underclass"—persistently poor and with no connection to legitimate ways of making a living.

Demography is the subtext to the contemporary tale of urban woe. "Back to the city" has been the catchword of the new urban professionals—today's huddled masses, piled up in neighborhoods in and around the downtown business centers. But the influx of this much maligned gentry never matched the attention it received in the press. The tide of people flowing cityward remains what it has been for the past forty years: America's big cities attract mainly nonwhites. First came blacks, displaced from the technological backwaters of the agrarian South. Then came a wave of immigrants from the labor-surplus areas of the developing world: today's urban newcomers are arriving in numbers that rival the great migrations of a century ago.

Thus the city of services is also a "majority minority" city. But how does this population base fit into the urban economy of today?

The received academic wisdom maintains that there is no fit at all. The industrial city grew because it possessed labor, and what it demanded of its labor was willing hands and strong muscles—not diplomas or technical expertise. But in the city of information processing and the transaction of high-level business deals, these qualities count no more. The equation between the city's economic function and its population base has no place for the unlettered, no matter how willing. The decline of the industrial city has left minorities high and dry.

But a dissenting interpretation, now sufficiently repeated to have become a conventional wisdom, tells a different tale. Modern urban development simultaneously generates high-level professional and managerial jobs and a proliferation of low-skilled, low-income "service" jobs. The polarized metropolis leaves minorities far from useless; instead, they serve as the new drawers of water and hewers of wood. In this version, it is not the poor who depend on the rich for their beneficence or for jobs and income to trickle down. Rather, the rich need the poor—to provide low-cost services, to maintain the city's underbelly, and to prop up what remains of the depressed manufacturing sector.

In this article I argue that both stories—however intuitively appealing they may be separately or together—have it wrong. Neither metaphor, of polarization or of dislocation, captures the impact of the postindustrial urban transformation. At root, both depict faceless, impersonal structures inexorably performing their actions on an inert urban mass. Not subjected to analysis, the structures are instead taken for granted, abstracted from any historical context, and divorced from the specific interests and forces that might have given them shape. Conflict and politics do not enter into these accounts of the making of the postindustrial economic world. Passing over dominant groups and their interests, these rival stories treat the new polyglot working and middle classes as an undifferentiated mass, helplessly playing out the scripts written for them by history.

But no *deus ex machina* determines which people get jobs, how they do so, and whether they then move ahead. The mechanisms of matching and mobility are social arrangements, shaped by the historical contexts in which they have grown up and subject to change—not simply as a result of pressures from the impersonal forces of the world economy, but in response to the actions of contending parties in specific societies and places. This book places the people and groups that have made, maintained, and changed the structures of today's postindustrial urban economy at the very center of the discussion.

My interpretation of the new urban reality will be developed in a single, sustained argument in the pages that follow. In briefest compass, the argument reads like this: The story of ethnics in America's cities is a collective search for mobility, in which the succession of one migrant wave after another alternatively stabilizes and disrupts the labor queue. In a market economy, employers allocate jobs to the most desirable workers they can recruit; but each market economy bears the imprint of the social structure in which it is embedded. In a race-conscious society like the United States, employers rank entire groups of people in terms of their ethnic and racial characteristics. All things being equal, members of the core cultural group stand at the top, followed by others.

The instability of America's capitalist economy subjects the labor queue's ordering to change. Growth pulls the topmost group up the totem pole; lower-ranking groups then seize the chance to move up the pecking order; in their wake, they leave behind vacancies at the bottom, which employers fill by recruiting workers from outside the economy—namely, migrants. The structure of the labor queue goes unchallenged as long as these newest arrivals are content to work in the bottom-level jobs for which they were initially recruited. But the economic orientations of the newcomers inevitably change, and when they do, complementarity is likely to be replaced by competition —which fans continuing ethnic strife over access to good jobs.

Competition between newcomers and insiders takes the form of conflict over the ethnic niche. Although migrants start at the bottom, they enter the economy under the auspices of friends or kin, which means that they begin with connections. Networks funnel the newcomers into specialized economic activities: as newcomers flow into the workplaces where earlier settlers have already gotten established, ethnic concentrations, or niches, gradually develop. The path up from the bottom involves finding a good niche and dominating it—which means that good jobs are reserved for insiders, leaving the next wave of outsiders excluded. Thus, the search by an earlier migrant group for labor market shelters eventuates in barriers that the next round of arrivals must confront.

Of course, economic life in America's cities is not all conflict. In some cases, the queue process simply pulls insider groups up the totem pole, leading them to abandon niches that a new group of outsiders can take over. In other instances, conditions in the niche undergo relative deterioration, in which case the barriers to outsiders get relaxed. These conditions ensure that ethnics in the labor market are sometimes noncompeting, segmented groups. But the scarcity of good jobs relative to the surplus of job seekers guarantees that competition never disappears.

Thus, the structures that African-Americans and new immigrants confront result from America's serial incorporation of outsider groups and from those groups' attempts to create protective economic shelters. The continuous recourse to migration as a source of low-level labor, so characteristic of the United States, has made ethnicity the crucial and enduring mechanism that sorts groups of categorically different workers into an identifiably distinct set of jobs. For this reason, the ethnic division of labor stands as the central division of labor in the cities of twentieth-century America; the fates of new immigrants and African Americans are bound up in its making and re-making.

New York City is the prism through which I develop this argument in full. As America's first postindustrial place, New York is a critical case for any explanation of urban change and its impact. I mean "first" in the sense of arriving at postindustrialism before its urban rivals and in the sense of having moved further toward the advanced service economy than any other principal urban center. New York also exemplifies the new melting pot—heated to full boil. New York is not only a minority majority city. It is also the Mecca for the newest immigrants, just as it has been throughout the history of the United States. Nowhere else does one find quite so complex an ethnic mosaic. Consequently, no other city provides as good a platform for studying how ethnic group resources and strategies interact with structural changes to shape ethnic group fates.

This book recounts the transformation of New York's ethnic division of labor since midcentury, a story I tell in two parts. One details how the very instability of the labor queue and the ethnic division of labor it engenders create opportunities for outsiders and newcomers. The second shows how these pieces of the pie have been divided up.

The conventional wisdom attributes urban disaster to the loss of white city residents. In fact, the outflow of white New Yorkers is what has given newcomers their chance. During economic downturns, whites fled the city faster than the rate of decline. And when the economy reheated, the outward seepage of whites slowed down but never stopped.

Over the years, the disproportionately declining white presence produced a ladder effect, creating empty spaces for newcomers up and down —though mainly down—the economic totem pole. Reflecting the influence of *prior* migration histories, the impact of white population decline rippled through New York's diversified economic complex in an uneven way. With the exception of those in construction and a few other skilled trades, New York's white ethnic proletariat disappeared after 1970, though a myriad of blue-collar jobs remained. Consequently, ethnic succession generated opportunities both in declining industries, where the rate of white outflows often outpaced the rate of job erosion, and in growth industries, where whites poured out of bottom-level positions even as demand for low-skilled workers increased. New York's small-business sector experienced the same round of musical chairs: newcomers moved in as white ethnics abandoned petty retailing, garment contracting, and other less remunerative business lines. A similar sequence of events occurred in many parts of the public sector, especially after 1975, when whites left municipal service for better opportunities elsewhere.

Since succession provides the backdrop for the economic stories of new immigrant and African-American New Yorkers, the central question concerns who got which jobs and why. In the 1970s and 1980s, black New Yorkers built up and consolidated the niche they had earlier established in government work. Public sector employment offered numerous advantages, including easier access to jobs and an employer that provided better, more equitable treatment. But convergence on government employment had the corollary effect of heightening the skill thresholds of the chief black economic base. To be sure, connections helped in gaining access to municipal jobs; and my case studies show that black civil servants networked as much as anyone else. However, civil service positions held promise only to those members of the community with the skills, experience, and credentials that government required—qualities not shared by the many African-American New Yorkers who have found themselves at economic risk.

Of course, work in the bowels of New York's economy could have been a possibility. Yet the data and the case studies demonstrate a steady erosion of African-Americans' *share* of the large number of remaining, low-skilled jobs—even as the *number* of low-level jobs held by minorities, native and immigrant, steadily grew. The African-American concentrations of old, from the most menial occupations in domestic service to later clusters like garment or hotel work, largely faded away. And African-Americans simultaneously failed to make headway in those low-skilled sectors where competition with whites had previously kept them locked out.

The immigrants, by contrast, responded to ethnic succession in ways that expanded their economic base. Initially, the match between their aspirations and broader labor market dynamics created openings that the newcomers could fill.

On the one hand, the immigrants' social origins predisposed them to embrace jobs that native New Yorkers would no longer accept; meager as they appeared to New Yorkers, the paychecks in the city's garment, restaurant, or retail sectors looked good in comparison to the going rate in Santo Domingo, Hong Kong, or Kingston. On the other hand, the city's factory sector was suffering a hemorrhage of older, native workers that outpaced the leakage of jobs, leading employers to take on new hands.

The initial portals into New York's economy channeled the newcomers into bottom-level jobs. The links between the workplace and the immigrant community helped convert these positions into platforms for upward movement. Immigrants were simply tied to others who would help them, right from the start. The connections among newcomers and settlers provided an informal structure to immigrant economic life; that structure, in turn, furnished explicit and implicit signposts of economic information and mechanisms of support that helped ethnics acquire skills and move ahead through business and other means.

In the end, new immigrant and African-American New Yorkers shaped their own fates by creating distinctive ethnic economic niches. But history had much to do with where each group could find a place. Looking over their shoulders toward conditions in the societies from which they have just departed, migrants move into industrial economies at the very bottom, taking up the jobs that natives will no longer do. While today's immigrants follow this traditional pattern, African-Americans, by contrast, are the migrants of a generation ago. The earlier pattern of rejections and successes shapes their searches of today, foreclosing options that immigrants, with their very different experiences and orientations, will pursue. Unlike the immigrants, African-Americans aspire to the rewards and positions enjoyed by whites. But the niches that African-Americans have carved out require skills that the least-educated members of that community simply don't have; African-American networks no longer provide connections to these more accessible jobs; and relative to the newcomers, employers find unskilled African-Americans to be much less satisfactory recruits. As for better-skilled African-Americans, they often compete with whites on unequal terrain, since past and present discrimination in housing and schools makes African-American workers less well prepared than whites. In this way, the mismatch between the aspirations of the *partly* disadvantaged and the requirements of the jobs to which they aspire provides the spark for persistent economic racial conflict between blacks and whites.

By contrast, immigrants have moved into noncompeting positions, taking over jobs that whites have deserted in their move up the occupational pecking order. Once the immigrants gain a lock on low-level jobs, ethnic connections funnel a steady stream of newcomers, excluding black New Yorkers who are not members of the same ethnic club.

Thus, the advent of a majority minority economy marks the emergence of a new division of labor, in which the various groups of new New Yorkers play distinct economic roles. Niche creation by African-Americans and immigrants has evolved into a mutually exclusive carving up of the pie: in carving out a place in the ethnic division of labor, the two groups effectively open or foreclose opportunities for each other. As in the past, control over good jobs and desired resources is subject to contest. Thus, the various components of New York's polyglot working and middle classes follow the example of their predecessors, continuing in, and reinvigorating, the pattern of interethnic economic competition that long characterized the city's white ethnic groups.

A SKILLS MISMATCH?

The mismatch thesis occupies the place of honor in the literature on urban poverty. The city was once a place where low-skilled newcomers could get a job and slowly start the climb up the occupational ladder. The advent of the postindustrial economy, argue mismatch proponents, undermined the city's historic role as staging ground of upward mobility.

The mismatch hypothesis first emerged as part of the structural unemployment controversy of the late 1950s and early 1960s. Analysts concerned by a then sluggish economy and fearful of an impending technological revolution fingered skill inadequacies as the source of employment dislocation. Whether the effects of the 1964 tax cut disproved the structural unemployment thesis, as some Keynesians argued, or not, the low unemployment rate of the late 1960s eclipsed the controversy as well as the fears of technological displacement. At the same time, the public policy agenda changed, with worries about the fate of blue-collar workers eclipsed by the preoccupation with race. In this context, the mismatch discussion took a new twist and began to focus on the problems of black workers.

More than two decades after this reformulation, the basics of the mismatch argument remain unchanged. It still emphasizes manufacturing's decline but now connects this shift to sinking black economic fortunes. As Frank Levy noted in his volume on income inequality in the 1980 Census Monograph series:

> Between 1950 and 1960 New York . . . had sustained its population through high birthrates and significant in-migration from rural areas. Many of the in-migrants were black, and over the decade the proportion of blacks in the city's population rose from 10 to 15 percent. The in-migrants were coming in search of higher incomes, and in these early postwar years the cities could accommodate them. Cities had both cheap housing, and most important, manufacturing jobs . . . Because of these jobs, cities could still serve as a place for rural migrants to get a start.

But what was true in the late 1950s rapidly changed. Developments in technology and communications, argued John Kasarda, decimated the "traditional goods-processing industries that once constituted the economic backbone of cities, and provided entry-level employment for lesser-skilled African-Americans." In return for the eroding factory sector, cities gained a new economy dominated by "knowledge-intensive white-collar service industries that typically required education beyond high school and therefore precluded most poorly employed inner city minorities from obtaining employment." Thus, on the demand side, the "very jobs that in the past attracted and socially upgraded waves of disadvantaged persons . . . were disappearing"; on the supply side, the number of "minority residents who lack the education for employment in the new information-processing industries [was] increasing." In part, the burgeoning ranks of low-skilled workers reflected the advent of African-American baby boomers; in part, it resulted from the renewal of mass immigration and the arrival of poorly schooled newcomers. But whatever the precise source of demographic change, it boded ill for urban America and its future.

And so, over the past thirty years demand and supply factors fell out of sync; in Kasarda's words, the "conflicting residential and employment base changes . . . placed the demographics and economics of our cities on a collision course." As we approach the year 2000, these woes take on a particularly aggravated form since the unfolding economic landscape will offer far fewer low-skilled opportunities than ever before. In the words of the scenario spinners at the Hudson Institute, "very few new jobs will be created for those who cannot read, follow directions, and use mathematics." Fast-track growth is predicted for jobs that require much higher education, although the bulk of employment will remain in less demanding positions like those filled by cooks, secretaries, and cashiers. But even these lower-level "workers will be expected to read and understand directions, add and subtract, and be able to speak and think clearly."

Put demand and supply trends together and you have an "impending U.S. jobs 'disaster.' " With the entire work force straining to keep up with enhanced job requirements, those minority workers who start out behind are unlikely to make up the gap. The Hudson Institute offers the following dim forecast:

> Given the historic patterns of behavior by employers, it is . . . reasonable to expect that they will bid up the wages of the relatively smaller numbers of white labor force entrants, seek to substitute capital for labor in many service occupations, and/or move job sites to the faster growing, more youthful parts of the country, or perhaps the world. Blacks, and particularly black men, are those most likely to be put at risk if such strategies dominate.

That the mismatch hypothesis has survived a quarter-century of intellectual twists and turns is testimony to its intuitive appeal, as well as the impact of repetition and the prestige of its proponents. But the mismatch hypothesis offers a particular, if not to say curious, interpretation of minority employment problems. A close look at those particularities highlights its deficiencies.

First, the mismatch hypothesis has a definite political twist. It blames not discriminating whites but rather the loss of central city manufacturing jobs and the failures of the educational system. To be sure, mismatch proponents do not deny that discrimination persists, though they claim its main effect results from the continuing legacy of bad deeds done in the past. They assert, moreover, that the significance of discrimination, like that of race, is on the decline. Twenty-five years ago the Kerner Commission argued that "racial discrimination is undoubtedly the *second* major reason why the Negro has been unable to escape from poverty." The contemporary literature is rarely so explicit in its causal ordering, but the failure of the literature on mismatch to more than mention discrimination speaks volumes.

If discrimination has lost its force, what explains the peculiar industrial and occupational distribution of blacks? Blacks, as I shall note, . . . are concentrated in a handful of sectors, not dispersed throughout the economy. The puzzle, from the skills mismatch point of view, is that the African-American economic niches do not happen to coincide with the principal clusters of low-skilled jobs. Take the case of construction. Construction workers learn their skills on the job, as in the past; educational levels are very low, relative to the urban average; and these are jobs that men are particularly likely to seek. But construction is an industry from which blacks continue to be excluded. Nationwide, the proportion of blacks employed in the industry is well below parity. And construction is just a special case of skilled blue-collar work: here is a domain, relatively low educational levels notwithstanding, in which blacks have much less than a fair share.

While mismatch proponents have no doubt about the source of the problem, they are not so consistent about the population at risk. In its early formulations, the theory centered on black migrants from the South. But black migrants were not the most seriously troubled. Indeed, a number of studies using the 1970 census showed that even controlling for age and education, black migrants from the South living in northern cities had higher incomes, lower incidence of poverty, lower unemployment, and less frequent reliance on welfare than northern-born blacks.

Two decades after the great black migration north, one no longer hears about the specific disabilities of black newcomers. Instead, cities are home to a new cohort of arrivals, this time immigrants from overseas. This latest batch of newcomers fits awkwardly with the basic framework, but mismatch proponents do what they can with this inconvenient fact. As of now, the population mismatched with the urban economy has become an undifferentiated aggregate of everyone not classified by the government as white.

This approach simply will not do: the mismatch hypothesis stands at odds with the immigrant phenomenon itself. If indeed urban employers are hiring none but the highly educated, then why have the leading postindustrial centers also emerged as the principal settlements of the new immigrant population? The key problem, first highlighted by the comparisons among northern- and southern-born blacks, is that labor market outcomes vary in ways that are not explicable in terms of differences in schooling and educational skills. In the largest U.S. cities, the employment of immigrant Hispanics has grown while the employment of native blacks has declined. Yet schooling levels among immigrant Hispanics are most out of sync with those of the rest of the labor force and way below African-Americans', whose educational standing has steadily improved.

A closer look at the employment patterns of immigrants raises even more questions about the basic mismatch assumption. Immigrants were far more dependent on manufacturing than were African-Americans in 1970—a time when the central city goods production base was almost intact. If the decline of manufacturing is to blame for the employment problems of African-Americans, then why has the economic base of immigrants not blown apart? And since no one argues that educational requirements are a barrier to African-American employment in manufacturing, why were immigrants and not African-Americans able to make substantial gains in factory jobs?

This line of questioning leads to another observation: manufacturing was not particularly important for the economic fate of blacks. Black New Yorkers were already underrepresented in manufacturing as of 1970, and in the years since then they have shifted even further away from goods production jobs. In fact, the move out of manufacturing is consistent with the overall evolution of African-American employment, which . . . has changed in ways that reduce exposure to the job loss resulting from industrial decline. Consequently, the concentrations established by 1980 should have left African-Americans well positioned to experience the changes of the 1980s. That African-American economic opportunities have *not* substantially widened suggests that there

is more to the game than being in the right industrial place at the right time.

As I noted earlier, the mismatch equation really has two sides: the supposedly fast-changing requirements of jobs and the slowly evolving schooling levels of blacks. Everyone "knows" that urban jobs demand more and more education; hence, mismatch proponents have not lingered overly long on establishing this fact. What everyone knows, however turns out to not quite be the case. Skill requirements have indeed gone up, but only to a modest degree. Consequently, people with modest levels of schooling have continued to fill a surprising number of jobs. In 1990, for example, persons with twelve years or less of schooling held close to half (44 percent) of all New York City jobs. In general, the tendency toward skill deepening has also slowed substantially since 1960. Ever since then, however, the job picture for blacks has become increasingly grim.

If mismatch proponents move quickly over the question of changing educational requirements, they never stop to examine their assumption about the schooling levels among blacks. Anyone familiar with the educational history of blacks will find irony in the argument that economic problems have been aggravated because schooling performance has gotten *worse*. The historical record, entirely obscured in contemporary debates, attests to tremendous progress against extraordinary obstacles: prohibitions against teaching reading and writing during slavery; not just separate, but woefully underfunded schools in the postbellum South; and the highly segregated, overcrowded systems that greeted the migrants when they came north. As bad as urban schools may be today, the educational environment of African-American schoolchildren never had any good old days.

The crucial issue, therefore, involves the pace and extent of change. Have disparities between blacks and whites in educational attainment narrowed or increased? More important, have blacks kept up with the educational requirements of urban employers—whose work force, as I have noted, is hardly lily white?

Nationwide, over the past twenty years African-Americans have made substantial, if still incomplete, strides toward catching up with whites. At least two indicators provide strong evidence of a diminishing gap. School enrollment rates among college-aged youth tell us about trends among those likely to acquire the up-to-date skills that employers supposedly want; on this count, the increase from 1970 to 1990 among blacks aged 18–24 was substantial and considerably greater than that among comparably aged whites. By contrast, high school dropout rates help identify the size of the population most likely to be hurt by heightened job requirements; here too, as Christopher Jencks has noted, with the dropout rate among blacks falling since 1970, the story is more encouraging among blacks than among whites.

Thus, the skills mismatch rests on a series of widely accepted "facts" that closer examination reveals to be untrue. Blacks never made it into the factory sector in such numbers that manufacturing's later decline would be a disaster. And the schooling story is far more complicated than the simplistic mismatch contentions, with plenty of evidence that blacks are less behind than they were ten, not to speak of twenty, years ago.

A DUAL CITY?

Inaccurate in depicting blacks, the mismatch theory also has nothing to say about the new immigrants who have flocked to the largest post-industrial cities. The puzzle is why the new immigrants converged on the largest urban centers at precisely the time when so many of the traditional routes of immigrant economic mobility have presumably been blocked.

The best-known answer to this question contends that the growth of producer services—finance, insurance, engineering, law, management consulting—has polarized the cities of high finance. The shift to producer services does indeed breed new jobs requiring high levels of education, as the mismatch hypothesis asserts. But critics of the American economy maintain that the growth of services also involves a process of economic restructuring. Service growth at the top simultaneously generates jobs for chambermaids and waiters, investment bankers and lawyers, while positions in between these extremes are slowly but steadily reduced. Restructuring also results in a deployment of new labor force groups, attracting immigrants from overseas to fill the expanded bottom-level jobs.

The coming of the hourglass economy thus creates the demand for immigrant labor. But the relationship between cities and immigrants works both ways: the arrival of the immigrants helps explain why the past two decades have seen an "urban renaissance." On the one hand, the influx of foreign-born workers has given the comatose manufacturing sector a new lease on life. Immigrants, so the story goes, have been a more pliable labor force, and so factory employers have not been obliged to keep wages at parity with national norms. In contrast to nationals, immigrant workers can also be deployed in more flexible ways, thereby giving urban manufacturers the scope to customize production and place greater reliance on subcontracting. As yet another plus, urban manufacturers can also draw on a large, vulnerable population of illegal immigrants. Their presence has given new meaning to the word exploitation, making "the new immigrant sweatshop . . . [a] major U.S. central city employment growth sector in the past decade."

Immigration has also propelled the service economy along. According to Saskia Sassen, who has researched New York:

> Immigration can be seen as a significant labor supplier for the vast infrastructure of low-wage jobs underlying specialized services, and the high-income life-styles of its employees. Messenger services, French hand laundries, restaurants, gourmet food stores, repair and domestic services—these are just a few examples of the vast array of low-wage jobs needed for the operation of the specialized service sector and its employees. Immigrants represent a desirable labor supply because they are relatively cheap, reliable, willing to work on odd shifts, and safe.

The immigrant presence also facilitates the continued expansion of the labor supply for newly created professional and managerial jobs. As Bennett Harrison and Barry Bluestone argue, "the provision of . . . services to the office workers becomes *the* major economic activity for the rest of the city." In their view, "the high cost of living in cities containing corporate headquarters requires that professional households include more than one wage earner in order to sustain a middleclass life style. This, in turn, forces this new aristocracy to consume more and more of the services that workers in an earlier generation would have produced for themselves." By furnishing the "large cohort of restaurant workers, laundry workers, dog walkers, residential construction workers, and the like," immigrants lower the costs of keeping a high-skilled labor force in place. Were it not for the foreign-born, the advanced service sectors in New York or Los Angeles would have to pay their highly skilled workers even more and thus lose out in the broader competitive game.

The contrast between restructuring and mismatch hypotheses shows that the virtues of one are the vices of the other. The restructuring hypothesis offers a plausible explanation of the immigrant arrival to the postindustrial city. Because proponents of the restructuring hypothesis do not even mention the economic problems of blacks, however, they beg the question of why all the new low-level jobs went to immigrants and not blacks. Amazingly enough, at a time when the specter of displaced, unemployed blacks looms so large in the mismatch hypothesis, the restructuring hypothesis has returned blacks to their old place as "invisible men."

Clearly any adequate account of the urban postindustrial change has to explain the new ethnic division of labor. But the restructuring hypothesis is not weak on this count alone; it also falls short on strictly factual grounds.

Consider the key contention about the changing *structure* of jobs and skills. Evidence that polarization is under way comes from Bureau of Labor Statistics projections of the absolute *number* of new jobs created between now and the turn of the century. Much has been made of the large number of jobs in low-skilled occupations that are expected to be added to the economy by the turn of the century. Of the ten occupations that will require the largest number of new workers, two —registered nurses and primary school teachers— necessitate college degrees. All of the others— janitors, cashiers, truck drivers, and the like —involve skills that can be picked up on the job with little, if any, schoolroom knowledge. But this pattern is largely an artifact of the occupational classification system itself. Low-skilled jobs tend to be less differentiated than higher-skilled jobs; one finds many highly discrete occupational categories at the top of the job hierarchy, in comparison to the situation at the bottom, where a relatively small group of categories lump together large groups of workers. Consequently, regrouping the occupational data presents a different picture of the trajectory of change. Once one reorganizes the occupations into broad categories (executive, administrative, managerial; professional; and so

forth), it turns out that the occupations that grew at above-average rates between 1975 and 1990 were the broad occupational groups with above-average educational levels. Projections indicate that those same occupational categories are likely to grow fastest between 1990 and 2005, whereas jobs with generally low educational levels, while remaining quite numerous, will continue to decline.

The figures just presented cover the U.S. economy as a whole. But what about the major urban centers? Occupational polarization mischaracterizes the job trajectory in New York. Although the number of jobs eroded during the bad days of the 1970s, some occupations did grow: professionals increased by 16.5 percent, managers were up 27 percent, and service workers gained an additional 5.8 percent. Meanwhile, all of the blue-collar occupations shrank. The growing tilt toward services explains part of this story, but only part. Within every sector—whether manufacturing or transport, retail or business services—the mix of occupations underwent considerable change, yielding a trend toward occupational upgrading, not polarization. The proportion of workers employed in all blue-collar occupations (craft, operative, laborer, and service) substantially declined in every sector except professional service. Good times in the 1980s breathed life back into some previously declining occupations, but the overall shape of change remained the same. Employment in professional, managerial, and sales jobs grew by about a third in each area in the course of the decade; together, the three occupations accounted for 95 percent of all the new jobs added during the 1980s.

Thus, despite tales of the growth in the number of janitors and fast-food workers, data on occupational change and projected occupational growth for the country as a whole and for New York fail to provide any support for the notion that low-skilled jobs are proliferating. Given this trend, how can the arrival of new immigrants be explained?

An immigrant-absorbing and generally growing service sector would be a possibility, but here again the polarization view leads us further off the track. Surprisingly, the traditional immigrant employing industries have continued as the shock absorbers for the latest immigrant inflow. Manufacturing and retail remain overwhelmingly the chief immigrant concentrations. As for the service side, there is only one sector in which the foreign-born are greatly overrepresented—that old immigrant standby, personal services. Those sectors comprising the "new" urban economy—finance, insurance, real estate, business services, professional services—rank below the average in their reliance on immigrant labor. Moreover, the trends since 1970 provide little evidence that the advanced service industries are becoming more immigrant-dependent.

Thus, the polarization hypothesis has the story about changing urban economies wrong. It also fails to account for the other side of the equation—immigrants. Though much is made of the exploitability of a large, illegal immigrant labor pool, this point cannot be pushed too far. The illegal immigration numbers game has now been played out: we know that the guesstimates from the early days widely inflated the size of the undocumented population. The number of illegal immigrants—about 3.5 million as of the late 1980s—is greatly overshadowed by the number of new legal immigrant residents and citizens. Similarly, the view that illegal immigrants are significantly more vulnerable than their legal counterparts can no longer be sustained. A decade and a half of research on illegal aliens has shown that their economic, demographic, and human capital characteristics differ little from those of legal immigrants of similar ethnic backgrounds. According to a 1989 U.S. Department of Labor report, "in many instances, illegal status does not lead to significantly lower earnings, nor does it appear to impede mobility substantially." In other words, there are fewer illegal immigrants than conventional accounts once suggested, and they are doing better—or not quite as badly—as one might have thought. Compared to Los Angeles, the destination overwhelmingly favored by illegal immigrants, New York has exercised a modest attraction for unauthorized migration—which makes it still more doubtful that the influx of an especially vulnerable labor force explains New York's rebound from economic collapse.

THE ETHNIC DIVISION
OF LABOR TRANSFORMED

If the prevailing accounts of the impact of the postindustrial urban economy do not hold up, what alternative might there be? The answer is an explanation that provides a single consistent story for African-Americans *and* for immigrants. I begin with a model of how jobs are allocated among ethnic groups.

The Ethnic Queue

The simplest model assumes that in a race-conscious society like ours, entire groups of people are *ordered* in terms of desirability for preferred jobs, with skill-relevant characteristics serving as additional weights. At each level of relevant skill, members of the core cultural group stand at the top of the ranking, followed by others. Under these conditions, job growth at the top of the hierarchy principally benefits the topmost ranked group; as members of this group ascend the totem pole and fill these new positions, jobs lower down the ladder open up for everyone else. Conversely, should the overall economy, or even particular sectors, turn down, the average position of the core cultural group will drop, pushing all others still further down.

Access to jobs also depends on the shape of the queue—that is, the relative sizes of groups. For our purposes, the critical development occurs when the relative size of the core cultural group declines—either as a result of an economic expansion that absorbs the existing labor force or as a consequence of out-migration. Changes in the shape of the queue trigger upward movement for those with positions lower down. But these shifts also create shortages in low-paying, low-status jobs where former incumbents have seized the chance to move toward better-paying, more prestigious positions. With employers limited in their ability to raise wages or substitute capital for labor, groups external to the labor market—migrants, whether native or foreign—move into the economy, entering the queue at the very bottom.

Whereas employers rank groups of workers in terms of their desirability, groups of workers rank jobs in terms of the relevant resources that jobs can provide. Rankings are also subject to change: erosion in a job's relative pay, prestige, or security may trigger its abandonment by members of the core cultural group, which in turn creates opportunities for lower-down groups, whose opportunities are more constricted. Of greater importance to us are the changes that occur in the rankings of migrants and their children. Differences in origin between natives and migrants yield disparate rankings, with migrants accepting jobs that natives will reject. Since preferences evolve with exposure to prevailing wage and status norms, differences between migrant and native rankings diminish over time; the children of the migrants are likely to operate with the same ranking system as natives.

This model of the ethnic queue moves us beyond mismatch and polarization hypotheses. First, it helps us identify the sources of opportunity within an otherwise unfavorable economic environment. Second, it allows us to link the process of serial migrant labor movements into the urban economy to a cycle of complementary and competitive relationships between old-timer and newcomer groups, and thus to place the changing ethnic division of labor in historical perspective.

Opportunity and the Ethnic Queue

Because changes in the shape of the queue will reallocate jobs among ethnic groups, the crucial factor involves the pacing of demographic relative to economic shifts. Although urban economies shifted steadily from goods to services throughout the postwar period, their demography changed at an even more rapid pace. Whites, who compose the preferred group, have been a steadily diminishing component of the population base. In cases of economic decline, as in New York in the 1970s, the white outflow greatly exceeded the erosion of jobs. And when economic growth turned New York around, as it did during the 1980s, the size of the white population did not keep pace with the increase in jobs.

Moreover, New York's economy has always been distinguished by its reliance on migrants, whether foreign or native, to fill low-level jobs. Industries in the "secondary sector," like retailing or restaurants, have traditionally been havens of employment for immigrants and their children. But that tradition has bred a chronic dependence on outside sources of new recruits, because workers' preferences have evolved with exposure to prevailing economic norms. Whereas migrants accept jobs that natives reject, the migrants' children share the natives' ranking system. Thus, as the second and later generations of European immigrants have entered the labor market, they have dropped out of the effective labor supply feeding into the secondary sector. This process of cycling through industries and sectors has bred an additional demand for replacement labor—beyond that generated by compositional changes alone.

This model provides an adequate prediction of how changes in the number and characteristics of white workers will affect the gross opportunities for new immigrants and for African-Americans. It does not tell us how the jobs vacated by departing whites will be allocated among the contending, successor groups. Here, the queuing metaphor leads us awry, with its suggestion that both jobs and groups are ranked in a stable, orderly way, with top-ranked groups moving into higher-ranked jobs, and so on down the line.

This image of orderly succession stands at variance from reality because ethnic ties serve as a basic mechanism for sorting workers among jobs. Groups are funneled into special places in the labor market—which I shall call niches—and then maintain those specializations, albeit at varying rates of persistence, over time. Thus, when ethnic succession occurs, it upsets an already established ethnic division of labor. And the fundamental *structuring* role of ethnicity means that compositional shifts simply create the circumstances under which the ethnic order in the labor market can be transformed. How the ethnic division of labor arises and changes are the issues to which I turn below.

The Making of the Immigrant Niche

We can think about the making of an immigrant niche as a two-stage process. First comes a phase of specialization in which placements are affected by skill, linguistic factors, or predispositions. Historians have argued that in the early to mid-nineteenth century migrants had far greater opportunities to transfer a skill directly into urban American economies than at any time since. And yet premigration skills still affect the match between newcomers and employers. Greeks from the province of Kastoria, where a traditional apprenticeship in fur making is common, tend to enter the fur industry; Israelis move into diamonds, a traditional Jewish business centered in New York, Tel Aviv, and Brussels; Indians from Gujarat, previously traders, become small store owners; and West Indians, many of whom have had exposure to mechanical crafts in oil fields, sugar refineries, or shipyards, find work in construction.

Language facility may similarly be a barrier to, or a facilitator of, specialization. English-language ability has steered immigrants from the anglophone Caribbean into health care, where the importance of interpersonal communication has been an impediment to immigrants that are not native speakers. By contrast, Koreans arrive with professional degrees, but, because they are poor

English speakers and lack appropriate credentials or licenses, turn to retailing.

Groups may also be predisposed toward certain types of work; the fact that migrants are people in a stage of transition has an especially important influence on the types of jobs they pick up. Not yet certain whether they will settle down for good or return home, still evaluating conditions in terms of lower-quality employment back home, immigrants are likely to be favorably disposed toward low-level, low-status jobs. And that favorable evaluation extends even to jobs in declining industries where the prospects for long-term employment are poor.

Whatever the precise mix of factors that determine the initial placements, occupational closure quickly sets in; this process represents the second stage. Networks of information and support are bounded by ethnic ties. Newcomers move and settle down under the auspices of friends, kin, and "friends of friends." When looking for work the new arrivals may prefer an environment in which at least some faces are familiar; they may feel uncomfortable with, or be ineligible for, the institutionalized means of labor market support; and they are likely to find that personal contacts prove the most efficient way of finding a place to work. Thus, later arrivals pile up in those fields where the first settlers established an early beachhead.

More important, the predilections of immigrants match the preferences of employers, who try to reproduce the characteristics of the workers they already have. Recruiting among the relatives and friends of incumbents is the cheapest way of finding help; it greatly increases the quantity and quality of information about the relevant characteristics of a prospective recruit; and since it brings new workers into an environment where they are surrounded by people who know them, network hiring provides an additional mechanism for maintaining control. Over time, hiring opportunities can become detached from the open market, being rationed instead to insiders' referrals as part of a quid pro quo between incumbents and employers.

From Immigrant to Ethnic Niche

What happens after the initial immigrant niche is put in place? The answer depends, in part, on the nature of the niche itself. If the niche provides re-

warding employment or mechanisms for expanding a group's economic base, specializations are likely to persist. Niches often vary by industry, with different industries holding out distinctive pathways for getting ahead. In a small-business industry, like retailing or construction, one succeeds by starting out on one's own. By contrast, where large organizations prevail, one moves up by getting more schooling, picking up a certification, acquiring seniority, or some combination of the three. Whatever the particulars of the employment context, acquiring industry-relevant contacts, information, and know-how can take place on the job in an almost costless way. By the same token, moving beyond the ethnic niche imposes considerable costs.

The structure of rewards among economic specializations varies, as does the potential for niche expansion. As already noted, time often changes the match between a group and its original niche. Immigrants, looking back at the conditions they left behind, are willing to start out at the bottom of the pecking ladder; their children, however, want a good deal more, looking askance at those very same jobs. The advent of the second generation, therefore, is a momentous event, though not so much, as some social scientists have suggested, because the second generation accepts the cultural patterns of natives. Far more important are the aspirations of the second generation, which in contrast to their parents' now extend to the economic goals and standards of natives. Moreover, job predispositions are rarely abstract preferences; rather, they are informed by understandings about the probability that movement down one economic branch or the other will lead to failure or success. If group A experienced discrimination in industry B, and has reason to think that some level of discrimination there will persist, job seekers from group A have good reason to look for work in other fields. This same assessment of opportunities and constraints might create a preference for those types of work where exclusionary barriers exercise the least effect.

Thus, members of the second generation may move on to different jobs. Do they shift as a group? Or do they scatter, moving outward as they filter upward from the ethnic niche, as the conventional thinking suggests? The argument for the latter view rests on its assumptions about why the first generation concentrated in the first place. To the extent that concentration is explained by lack of skills and education, and seen as a source of disadvantage, then rising levels of education and growing similarity with the core cultural group imply that upward mobility goes hand in hand with dispersion out of the immigrant niche.

Skill deficiencies are only one of the factors in my account of the first-generation niche, however. I place much greater weight on the role of ethnic networks and their impact on the actions of both workers and employers. Consequently, my view suggests a different scenario, in which the continuing importance of ethnic networks shapes a group's employment distribution into the second, and later, generations. Just as with the first generation, the second generation's search for advancement takes on a *collective* form. Starting out from an immigrant niche, the second generation is already embedded in a cluster of interlocking organizations, networks, and activities. Not only do these commonalities shape aspirations, they also create the organizational framework for the rapid diffusion of information and innovations. Thus, the social organization of the second generation serves as a mechanism for channeling people into the labor market; once a favorable niche develops, informal recruitment patterns can quickly funnel in new hires.

The Advantages of the Ethnic Niche

The process of niche formation turns ethnic disadvantage to good account, enabling social outsiders to compensate for the background deficits of their groups and the discrimination they encounter. The networks that span ethnic communities constitute a source of "social capital," providing social structures that facilitate action, in this case, the search for jobs and the acquisition of skills and other resources needed to move up the economic ladder. Networks among ethnic incumbents and job seekers allow for rapid transmission of information about openings from workplaces to the communities. And the networks provide better information within workplaces, reducing the risks associated with initial hiring. Once in place, ethnic hiring networks are self-reproducing, since each new employee recruits others from his or her own group.

While the development of an ethnic niche provides a group with privileged access to jobs, one classic example—that of small business—suggests that it can do far more. Ethnic businesses emerge

as a consequence of the formation of ethnic communities, with their sheltered markets and networks of mutual support. Individual firms may die off at an appalling rate, but business activity offers a route to expansion into higher profit and more dynamic lines. Retailers evolve into wholesalers; construction firms learn how to develop real estate; garment contractors gain the capital, expertise, and contacts to design and merchandise their own clothing. As the ethnic niche expands and diversifies, the opportunities for related ethnic suppliers and customers also grow.

With an expanding business sector comes both a mechanism for the effective transmission of skill and a catalyst for the entrepreneurial drive. From the standpoint of ethnic workers, the opportunity to acquire managerial skills through a stint of employment in immigrant firms both compensates for low pay and provides a motivation to learn a variety of different jobs. Employers who hire co-ethnics gain a reliable work force with an interest in skill acquisition—attributes that diminish the total labor bill and make for greater flexibility. Thus, a growing ethnic economy creates a virtuous circle: business success gives rise to a distinctive motivational structure, breeding a community-wide orientation toward small business and encouraging the acquisition of skills within a stable, commonly accepted framework.

Sociologist Suzanne Model coined the concept of "hierarchically organized niches" to denote ethnic economic concentrations in which employees not only work among their co-ethnics but are hired and overseen by co-ethnic owners and managers. These characteristics usually define the ethnic economy; they can also be found in the public sector. Along with small business, the civil service forms the other classic ethnic niche, even though it is governed by seemingly opposite principles. Moving into civil service has been an ethnic mobility strategy for over one hundred years, and not just because ethnic networks increase a group's access to jobs. Once in place, groups of ethnic workers repeatedly engage in bargaining games that shelter them from competition and exclude opportunities for promotion from all but insiders. Thus, the public sector comes under group pressures that make it a protected, self-regulating enclave. And that trait increases its attraction for stigmatized groups that fare poorly in the private market.

Job Competition

I have depicted niche formation as the unintended result of activities of which people are only partly aware. But once the niche is in place, different dynamics occur. The higher the level of concentration in the niche, the more frequent and more intense the interaction among group members. These interactions make them feel that they belong to a group. If the niche is one of the salient traits that group members share, it also helps define who they are. As a result, members pay greater attention to the boundaries of the niche and the characteristics of those who can and cannot cross those boundaries. As the niche strengthens group identity, it sharpens the distinction between insiders and outsiders.

Once established, the niche also takes on properties that make it difficult for outsiders to get in the door. A variety of factors incline ethnics toward working with others of their own kind whenever they can. Fearful that outsiders might undercut wages, workers prefer to train co-ethnic neophytes whom they trust; anxious about the reliability and performance of job applicants who walk in off the street, employers prefer to hire the friends and relatives of their key workers; concerned that a vendor might not deliver on time, or that a customer might delay in paying the bill, business owners look for known entities with track records of successful dealings with others. In effect, membership in an ethnic community serves as an index of trust in an economic transaction, telling co-ethnic actors that one can rely on another. The web of contacts within a community works in the same direction; the history of prior exchanges with members of an ethnic network provides a baseline against which future behavior can be assessed. Since relations among co-ethnics are likely to be many-sided rather than specialized, community effects go beyond their informational value, engendering both codes of conduct and the mechanisms for sanctioning those who violate norms.

The trust extended from one member of a community to another, though both efficient and efficacious, is not available to everyone. Outsiders lack the traits, histories, and relational ties conducive to collaboration or trust; on these grounds alone, rational considerations lead insiders toward economic exchanges with their own.

Since employers and employees in the niche tend to arrive at agreement over hiring practices and promotional rules, past practices operate with a similar, exclusionary effect. To be sure, the parties often fight with one another over the content of the rules. But the quarrels rarely get out of hand: in hierarchically organized niches, such as the civil service, managers and workers often come from the same group and identify with one another. In other cases, where higher management and the rank and file have little in common, the line managers who make key personnel decisions generally share the views, and often the origins, of the important workers with whom they interact.

Thus, over time, hiring practices and promotional rules get adapted to the needs of incumbent groups. Often, the entry criteria demand more exacting skills than the jobs require. As long as insiders and the members of their network furnish a steady stream of qualified applicants, however, employers have no incentive to relax their hiring criteria to ease the way in for outsiders. Once in place, the rules change slowly; the weight of tradition stands in their favor, sustaining incumbents' belief in the fairness of rules and the rule-making process.

All this is important because the labor market is not always home to a game of ethnic musical chairs, in which some groups move one rung up the ladder, allowing newcomers to take up the vacated rung. Although the queue metaphor suggests movement without friction, the structural properties of the labor queue can shift or stabilize in ways that either forestall or promote ethnic conflict over jobs.

Recall that outsider groups enter the economy in response to labor shortages and then gravitate toward the tier of labor-scarce jobs, remaining in that ambit as long as their (low) economic orientations match the (low) requirements and perquisites of the jobs. What happens next generally follows one of several scenarios. In the succession scenario, the shape of the labor queue can change if later economic expansion further tightens the supply of established groups, pulling the low-ranked group up the totem pole. In the leapfrogging scenario, the characteristics of the low-rank group—in particular, its schooling levels—substantially improve, making the group more desirable to employers and thereby reordering its position in the labor queue. in the persistence scenario, the preferences of the low-rank group remain unchanged, in which case its tolerance for low-level work stays more or less the same.

But one can also imagine a sequence of events ending in conflict, in which the preferences of low-rank groups change more quickly and more extensively than either the order or the shape of the labor queue. In this case, the ambitions of outsiders extend to higher-level jobs to which established groups remain firmly attached. But the allocation procedures exclude all those who do not meet hiring criteria, which have previously evolved in ways that fit the preferences of incumbents. Under these circumstances, competition becomes overt and leads to ethnic conflict, as newcomers seek to alter hiring and promotion rules and incumbents try to maintain the structures that have protected their group's jobs.

As the advent of ethnic conflict threatens the order of the queue, outcomes will depend on the resource-mobilization capacity of outsider and insider groups and on their ability to use those resources to effect changes in recruitment and promotional structures. Power makes such a difference because niches are ultimately not that easy to control. Employers may have a preference for hiring one of their own or may yield to the "tastes" of their employees. They can never totally ignore, however, the potential cost savings made possible by recruiting outside the niche or the desirability of gaining skills that the in-group cannot provide. Similarly, unions might block the front door that gives access to a trade; but the presence of ethnic entrepreneurs, who hire and train their co-ethnics, provides a back door through which a corps of skilled workers can be built. In the public sector, particular groups may control information about openings and exams but they cannot prevent the competitive exam process from allowing skilled outsiders to gain entrée.

There is more to job competition than the human or social capital of insider and outsider groups. Groups' resource-bearing capacities in the political realm often count for a great deal: shifts in the relative balance of *political* power between incumbents and outsiders can lead to policy changes that alter recruitment practices, opening up defended, previously closed ethnic niches. While political pressure can make a difference, the range of exposure to political forces varies with the characteristics of labor market arrangements. Government's instruments will be most effective in those segments of the economy where hiring and recruitment practices are most institutionalized, and thus most susceptible to internal and external monitoring. By contrast, political intervention will carry much less weight in small-firm sectors, which mainly rely on informal recruitment mechanisms.

Discrimination

This account of job competition provides an explanation of the activation, persistence, and possible decline of discrimination; because it stands at variance with established economic and sociological views, a comparison with the alternative, better-known accounts deserves attention. In economics, the most powerful statement explains the behavior of discriminators as a manifestation of their "tastes": thus, whites have a distaste for working with blacks. The economists' assumptions about whites' preferences have been subject to criticism on several grounds—don't whites really want to maintain social distance? Aren't they principally concerned with preserving status differences relative to blacks? But the most damaging criticism is simply that by assuming distinctive preferences, the economists beg the question at hand, namely, what causes whites' peculiar tastes? As the ethnic order becomes more complex, the import of this failure becomes increasingly grave, since whites seem to have a much stronger distaste for blacks than they do for the various foreign-born groups who are just as visibly identifiable.

But let us assume that whites do indeed have such a strong distaste for working alongside blacks; what difference would it make? White employers with a "taste for discrimination" would pay a premium to hire mainly white crews, deducting the costs of the psychic discomforts they must endure from the wages of any blacks they engage. Like any other preference, the taste for discrimination is not equally shared by all white employers; those employers who experience less psychic pain from proximity to blacks should be happy to hire an entirely black crew at bargain rates. In a competitive market, the lowest-cost, nondiscriminating producer would inevitably compel the discriminators to either swallow their distastes and hire more blacks or else go out of business.

By definition, the economic model thus predicts declining discrimination. The problem, of course, is that persistent discrimination is what requires explanation. Moreover, the economists' approach focuses almost entirely on wages, whereas occupational segregation and access to employment lie at the heart of black-white disparities.

Sociologists, by contrast, are wont to explain discrimination as the reaction of "high-priced" labor to competition from "lower-priced" competitors, as can be seen in William J. Wilson's highly influential book *The Declining Significance of Race.* In this account, black migrants entered the north as low-price labor: willing to work at rates below those acceptable to whites, blacks were used by employers in their efforts to "undercut the white labor force by hiring cheaper labor." These attempts fanned whites' antagonism toward blacks and efforts at either excluding African-Americans outright or else confining them to low-level jobs. As the American state expanded its role in regulating industrial and race relations from the New Deal on, the potential for wage competition between blacks and whites steadily diminished. With whites no longer having to fear displacement from low-priced blacks, they lost their motivation to discriminate.

The conventional economic approach predicts declining discrimination without, however, accounting for what activates discrimination in the first place. The conventional sociological framework goes one step better in addressing the question of motivation but, likewise, forecasts discrimination's decline. Unlike the economists' approach, the job-competition perspective provides an answer to the question of motivation; unlike the sociologists' approach, it also tells us why discrimination might persist.

The economists are certainly right in thinking that discrimination is in part a matter of tastes; as I contended above, however, those tastes are not exogenous but rather a consequence of the development of an ethnic niche. Moreover, the motivation to maintain boundaries around the niche does not just emanate from an abstract desire to be with others of one's own kind (or even to maintain social distance from some stigmatized other); rather, it derives from the process of serial migrant labor market incorporation, which in turn spurs the cycle of complementary and competitive relationships between old-timer and newcomer groups.

The instability of capitalist economies leads to a recurrent recourse to outsider groups, who enter the queue at the bottom, where they work in complementarity to higher-ranked insiders. But the initial situation of complementarity lasts only as long as the economic orientations of the two groups diverge; once the aspirations and orientations of the two groups converge, job competition ensues. Under these circumstances, a combination of economic and noneconomic factors impel insider groups to prevent outsiders from gaining access to the niche. The influx of a stigmatized other threatens the overall standing of the group's niche—itself often recently won. More important, incumbents in a good niche have a scarce commodity to protect. Even in the best of times, good jobs attract a surplus of applicants, which tells us that there are never enough truly desirable positions. The exclusion of outsiders keeps competition in check, serving the needs of incumbents while also preserving a resource for future cohorts of insiders not yet admitted to the niche. Finally, competition activates cultural and ideological sources of group affinity and exclusiveness, since incumbents' sense of group identity is embedded in stable networks and patterns of hiring, recruitment, and mobility.

Black-White Antagonism

Thus, discrimination can be seen as the consequence of job competition, with the niche taking the form of a kind of group property. Though perhaps Balkanized, the labor market is not yet the Balkans, with each group pitted against the next. On the contrary, as one black skilled-trades worker pointed out to me: "When the white workers are in the room, it's fuckin' guinea this, stinking kike that, polack this. When I come into the room, they're all white."

This statement pungently crystallizes the intellectual puzzle of why so much more antagonism characterizes the encounters between whites and blacks than those among the plethora of culturally distinctive, visibly identifiable groups that joust with one another over economically desirable slots.

The answer to that puzzle, I suggest, has several parts. First, race is a particularly convenient marker, with slightly more subtle ethnic criteria providing more difficult, and therefore more costly, means around which to organize exclusion. Second, in the American context race is far more than a marker: it is a characteristic suffused with meaning, adding an extraeconomic dimension to the entry of blacks into a dominant white niche. Third, conflict has been crucial to blacks' efforts to move into dominant white niches, and far more so than has been true for other outsider groups.

The persistence and intensity of black-white conflict reflects, in part, the mismatch between black economic ambitions and the thresholds needed to enter the jobs to which blacks aspire. Whereas African-American migrants accepted jobs that whites would no longer do, the migrants' children and grandchildren have sought positions in niches which whites have not left. In this quest, African-Americans resemble other outsider groups who began as migrants at the bottom. But earlier groups of outsiders like Italians or Jews, as well as contemporary counterparts like Chinese, Koreans, and even Jamaicans or Dominicans, have had access to resources—education, skills, capital, and most important, assistance from their co-ethnics—that have helped them find alternate routes into defended niches and improve their bargaining position with incumbent groups. Lacking these resources, African-Americans have been more likely than other outsider groups to pursue a directly competitive strategy for entering a niche. That strategy, in turn, has heightened the defensive orientations of whites, intensifying their concern with boundary maintenance and markers, and breeding a cycle of escalating conflict.

Slicing the Pie

Thus far, I have tried to explain why ethnic groups develop economic specializations and how those specializations evolve. But the problem is still more complex, because I need to provide an account of how the same opportunity—the vacancies created by the diminishing presence of whites—has had such different effects on immigrants and on African-Americans.

The answer lies in the framework developed above. A group's *prior* place in the ethnic division of labor exercises a crucial influence on its chances of benefiting from the opportunities that arise from succession. To inherit the positions abandoned by departing whites, one needs a recruitment network already in place. Since hiring works with a built-in bias toward incumbents, recruitment into an industry can become a self-feeding process; consequently, replacement processes will work to the advantages of those groups that most easily and quickly produce new recruits.

Timing also influences the outcome. When ethnic succession stirred up New York's ethnic division of labor, history had put African-Americans and new immigrants in different places. At the high tide of black migration to New York, whites were still solidly entrenched in the city's working class; even low-level, traditionally immigrant industries retained whites within their effective labor supply; in more skilled, manual jobs, whites maintained virtually complete control. In contrast to the circumstances under which the post-1965 immigrants entered the economy, African-Americans encountered a situation in which white ethnic incumbents held on to all but the bottom-most positions; the strength of these network-based tendencies toward social closure narrowed the scope of black employment and shaped their pattern of job concentration.

By the time compositional changes in the 1970s and 1980s produced widespread vacancies, African-Americans had developed alternative feeding points into the economy. These black niches were shaped by previous experience. Sectors that provided more and better opportunities gained a heavier flow of recruits. Where, by contrast, discrimination continued to prevail, the potential supply of African-American workers dwindled. Although the transitional nature of the migration experience had conditioned earlier cohorts of black workers to accept jobs in the traditional immigrant industries, the children and grandchildren of the southern migrants had taken on aspirations that precluded this type of work. Consequently, employers turned to immigrants to fill the vacancies created by the massive outflow of whites. Once a small cluster of "seedbed" immigrants implanted itself, networks among newcomers and settlers quickly directed new arrivals into the appropriate places in the job market. Given employers' preference for hiring through networks—and the ability of employees to pressure their bosses to do so—information about job openings rarely penetrated outside the groups that concentrated in a particular trade. As the newcomers built up their niches, they limited entry to members of the club. Thus, history became crucial in understanding who got which pieces of New York's pie and why.

Bibliography

The articles reprinted in this volume are drawn from a wide range of sources and reflect many different reference formats. I have provided some uniformity of reference style. Where the references are numbered in the original publication I have placed them at the end of each article ("Endnotes"). Where the system of identifying references by last name of author, year of publication, and page numbers (for example, Bonacich 1972:553) has been used, I have placed all reference sources in this bibliography. An asterisk (*) next to a citation in this bibliography indicates that the selection or portions of it are reprinted in this volume.

Ablon, Joan. 1964. "Relocated American Indians in the San Francisco Bay Area: Social Interactions and Indian Identity." *Human Organization.* 23.

———. 1965. "American Indian Relocation: Problems of Dependency and Management in the City." *Phylon.* 66.

———. 1971. "Retention of Cultural Values and Differential Urban Adaptation: Samoans and American Indians in a West Coast City." *Social Forces.* 49.

Abowd, J. M. and M. R. Killingsworth. 1985. "Employment, Wages, and Earnings of Hispanics in the Federal and Non-Federal Sectors: Methodological Issues and their Empirical Consequences. See Borjas and Tienda 1985.

Abramson, Harold J. 1973. *Ethnic Diversity in Catholic America.* New York: Wiley.

———. 1975. "The Religioethnic Factor and the American Experience: Another Look at the Three Generation Hypothesis." *Ethnicity.* 2.

———. 1980. "Assimilation and Pluralism." In Stephan Thernstrom, ed., *Harvard Encyclopedia of American Ethnic Groups.* Cambridge, MA: Harvard University Press.

Achor, Shirley. 1978. *Mexican Americans in a Dallas Barrio.* Tucson: U. of Arizona Press.

Acuña, Rudolfo. 1971. *Occupied America: The Chicano Struggle Toward Liberation.* San Francisco: Canfield Press.

Adam, Heribert and Kogila Moodley. 1993. *The Opening of the Apartheid Mind: Options for the New South Africa.* Berkeley: University of California Press.

Adamic, Louis. 1938. *My America.* New York: Harper and Row.

Adams, David Wallace. 1988. "Fundamental Considerations: The Deep Meaning of Native American Schooling, 1880–1900." *Harvard Educational Review.* 58.

Adams, June and Richard La Course. 1977. "Backlash Barrage Erupts Across U.S." *Yakima Nation Review.* July 18:12.

Alba, Richard D. 1976. "Social Assimilation among American Catholic National Origin Groups." *American Sociological Review.* 41.

———. 1981. "The Twilight of Ethnicity among American Catholics of European Ancestry." *Annals of the American Academy of Political and Social Science.* 454.

———. 1985. *Italian Americans: Into the Twilight of Ethnicity.* Englewood Cliffs, NJ: Prentice-Hall.

———. 1990. *Ethnic Identity: The Transformation of White America.* New Haven, CT: Yale University Press.

*———. 1995. "Assimilation's Quiet Tide." *The Public Interest.* 119. Spring.

Alba, Richard D. and Reid M. Golden. 1986. "Patterns of Ethnic Marriage in the United States." *Social Forces.* 65.

Alba, Richard D., and Ronald C. Kessler. 1979. "Patterns of Interethnic Marriage Among American Catholics." *Social Forces.* 57.

Alba, Richard D. and Gwen Moore. 1982. "Ethnicity in the American Elite." *American Sociological Review.* 47.

Aldrich, Howard and Jane Weiss. 1981. "Differentiation Within the U.S. Capitalist Class." *American Sociological Review.* 46.

Allport, Gordon W. 1958. *The Nature of Prejudice.* Garden City, NY: Doubleday.

Allworth, Edward. 1989. *Central Asia: 120 Years of Russian Rule.* Durham, NC: Duke University Press.

Almaguer, Tomas. 1974. "Historical Notes on Chicano Oppression: The Dialectics of Race and Class Domination in North America." *Aztlan.* 5.

Alvarez, Rodolfo. 1973. "The Psycho-Historical and Socioeconomic Development of the Chicano Community in the United States." *Social Science Quarterly.* 53.

Amado, Pablo Comesana. 1990. "Madres y sacerdotes solicitan trabajo para pandilleros de puerta en puerta." *La Opinion.* May 2.

Ambler, Marjane. 1990. *Breaking the Iron Bonds: Indian Control of Energy Development.* Lawrence: University Press of Kansas.

American Council on Education. 1988. *One Third of a Nation.* Washington, DC: American Council on Education.

———. 1993. "Educating One-Third of a Nation IV: Making our Reality Match our Rhetoric." Washington, DC: American Council on Education.

Anderson, Benedict. 1991. *Imagined Communities: Reflections on the Origin and Spread of Nationalism.* London: Verso.

Anderson, Charles H. 1970. *White Protestant Americans.* Englewood Cliffs, NJ: Prentice-Hall.

Anderson, Patrick. 1976. "On Working Closely with Jimmy Carter." *New York Times.* July 19.

Applebome, Peter. 1991. "Arab-Americans Fear a Land War's Backlash." *New York Times.* February 20.

———. 1997a. "In Shift, U.S. Tells Texas to Obey Court in Barring Bias in College Admissions." *New York Times.* April 15.

———. 1997b. "Schools See Re-Emergence of 'Separate but Equal.'" *New York Times.* April 8.

Archdeacon, Thomas J. 1983. *Becoming American: An Ethnic History.* New York: The Free Press.

Aronowitz, Stanley. 1973. *False Promises.* New York: McGraw-Hill.

Associated Press. 1990. "Pact Gives Indian Tribe Cash, Land, Hope for Jobs." *Kansas City Star.* March 24.

Au, K. H. 1981. "Participant Structure in a Reading Lesson with Hawaiian Children: Analysis of a Culturally Appropriate Instructional Event." *Anthropology and Education Quarterly.* 10:2.

Auster, Ellen and Howard Aldrich. 1984. "Small Business Vulnerability, Ethnic Enclaves, and Ethnic Enterprise." In Robin Ward, ed., *Ethnic Business in Britain.* Cambridge: Cambridge University Press.

Baca, Reynaldo and Dexter Bryan. 1983. "The 'Assimilation' of Unauthorized Mexican Workers: Another Social Science Fiction." *Hispanic Journal of Behavioral Sciences.* 5.

Bach, Robert L. 1980. "The New Cuban Immigrants: Their Background and Prospects." *Monthly Labor Review.* 103.

Bach, Robert L., Jennifer B. Bach, and Timothy Triplett. 1981. "The Flotilla 'Entrants': Latest and Most Controversial." *Cuban Studies.* 11.

Bahr, Howard M. 1972. "An End to Invisibility." In Howard M. Bahr, Bruce A. Chadwick, and Robert C. Day (eds.), *Native Americans Today: Sociological Perspectives.* New York: Harper and Row.

Bailey, Eric. 1988. "Tempers Flare Over Illegals in S.D. County." *Los Angeles Times.* June 6. San Diego County ed.

Bailey, Eric and H. G. Reza. 1988. "Illegals, Homeless Clash in S.D. County." *Los Angeles Times.* June 5. San Diego County ed.

Bailey, Thomas. 1987. *Immigrants and Native Workers: Contrasts and Competition.* Boulder: Westview.

Bailyn, Bernard. 1955. *The New England Merchants in the Seventeenth Century.* Cambridge, MA: Harvard University Press.

Bakalian, Anny. 1991. "From Being to Feeling Armenian: Assimilation and Identity Among Armenian-Americans." Paper presented at the annual meeting of the American Sociological Association, Cincinnati.

———. 1993. *Armenian-Americans: From Being to Feeling Armenian.* New Brunswick, NY: Transaction Books.

Baker, Ray Stannard. 1964. *Following the Color Line: American Negro Citizenship in the Progressive Era.* New York: Harper Torchbooks.

Baltzell, E. Digby. 1964. *The Protestant Establishment: Aristocracy and Caste in America.* New York: Vintage.

Bane, Mary Jo. 1986. "Household Composition and Poverty." In S. H. Danziger and D. H. Weinberg, eds., *Fighting Poverty: What Works and What Doesn't,* pp. 209–31. Cambridge, MA: Harvard University Press.

Banks, James A. and Geneva Gay. 1978. "Ethnicity in Contemporary American Society: Toward the Development of a Typology." *Ethnicity.* 5.

Banton, Michael. 1983. *Racial and Ethnic Competition.* Cambridge: Cambridge University Press.

Baratz, Stephen S. and Joan C. Baratz. 1970. "Early Childhood Intervention: The Social Science Base of Institutional Racism." *Harvard Educational Review.* 40.

Baron, Harold M. 1968. "Black Powerlessness in Chicago." *Transaction.* 6.

Barrera, Mario. 1979. *Race and Class in the Southwest: A Theory of Racial Inequality.* Notre Dame, IN: Notre Dame University Press.

*Barrett, James and David Roediger. 1997. "Inbetween Peoples: Race, Nationality and the 'New Immigrant' Working Class." *Journal of American Ethnic History.* 16:3. Spring.

Barringer, Felicity. 1991. "Census Shows Profound Change in Racial Makeup of the Nation." *New York Times.* March 11.

Barringer, H. and S. Cho. 1989. *Koreans in the United States: A Fact Book.* Honolulu: Center for Korean Studies, University of Hawaii at Manoa.

Barringer, H., R. W. Gardner, and M. J. Levin. 1993 *Asians and Pacific Islanders in the United States.* New York: Russell Sage Foundation.

Barsh, Russell Lawrence and James Youngblood Henderson. 1980. *The Road: Indian Tribes and Political Liberty.* Berkeley and Los Angeles: University of California Press.

Barth, Earnest A. T. and Donald L. Noel. 1972. "Conceptual Frameworks for the Analysis of Race Relations: An Evaluation." *Social Forces.* 50.

Barth, Frederik. 1962. *The Role of Entrepreneur in Social Change in Northern Norway.* Bergen: Norwegian Universities Press.

———. 1969. *Ethnic Groups and Boundaries.* Boston: Little, Brown.

Barton, Josef. 1975. *Peasants and Strangers.* Cambridge, MA: Harvard University Press.

Beale, Calvin. 1957. "American Tri-Racial Isolates: Their Status and Pertinence to Genetic Research." *Eugenics Quarterly.* 4.

*Bean, Frank D., E. Stephen, and W. Opitz. 1985. "The Mexican Origin Population in the United States: A Demographic Overview." In Rudolfo de la Garza, F. Bean, C. Bonjean, R. Romo, and R. Alvarez, eds., *The Mexican American Experience: An Interdisciplinary Anthology.* Austin: University of Texas Press.

Bean, Frank D. and Marta Tienda. 1987. *The Hispanic Population of the United States.* Russell Sage Foundation.

Bechofer, Frank, Brian Elliott, Monica Rushforth, and Richard Bland. 1974. "Small Shopkeepers: Matters of Money and Meanings." *Sociological Review.* 22.

Bell, Daniel. 1976. *The Cultural Contradictions of Capitalism.* New York: Basic Books.

Bell, Derrick. 1997. "A Commission on Race? Wow." *New York Times.* June 14.

Bellah, Robert N., Richard Madsen, William M. Sullivan, Ann Sidler, and Stephen M. Tipton. 1985. *Habits of the Heart: Individualism and Commitment in American Life.* New York: Harper & Row.

Belshaw, Cyril. 1955. "The Cultural Milieu of the Entrepreneur." *Explorations in Entrepreneurial History.* 7.

Bennett, Claudette E. 1995. "The Black Population in the United States, 1994 and 1993." U.S. Bureau of the Census. *Current Population Reports,* P20-480. Washington, DC: Government Printing Office.

Benokraitis, Nijole and Joe R. Feagin. 1986. *Modern Sexism: Blatant, Subtle and Covert Discrimination.* Englewood Cliffs: Prentice-Hall.

Berelson, Bernard, and Patricia J. Salter. 1946. "Majority and Minority Americans: An Analysis of Magazine Fiction." *Public Opinion Quarterly.* 10.

Berger, Peter L. and Thomas Luckmann. 1967. *The Social Construction of Reality: A Treatise on the Sociology of Knowledge.* Garden City, NJ: Anchor Books.

Berreman, Gerald D. 1969. "Caste in India and the United States." In J. Roach, L. Gross, and O. Gursslin, eds., *Social Stratification in the United States.* Englewood Cliffs, NJ: Prentice-Hall.

*———. 1972. "Race, Caste, and Other Invidious Distinctions in Social Stratification." *Race.* 12.

Berthoff, Rowland T. 1953. *British Immigrants in Industrial America.* Cambridge, MA: Harvard University Press.

Beveridge, Andrew A. and Anthony R. Oberschall. 1979. *African Businessmen and Development in Zambia.* Princeton, NJ: Princeton University Press.

Bierstedt, Robert. 1948. "The Sociology of Majorities." *American Sociological Review.* 13.

Blackman, Ann. "Lowell's Little Acre." *Time.* Fall 1993.

Blackstone, Kevin B. 1981. "Arab Entrepreneurs Take Over Inner City Grocery Stores." *Chicago Reporter.* 10.

Blackwell, James E. 1981. *Mainstreaming Outsiders: The Production of Black Professionals.* Bayside, NY: General Hall.

Blair, P. M. 1972. *Job Discrimination and Education: An Investment Analysis.* New York: Praeger.

Blalock, Hubert J., Jr. 1967. *Toward a Theory of Minority-Group Relations.* New York: Wiley.

Blanchard, Fletcher A., Teri Lilly, and Leigh Ann Vaughn. 1991. "Reducing the Expression of Racial Prejudice." *Psychological Science.* 2.

Blassingame, John W. 1972. *The Slave Community: Plantation Life in the Antebellum South.* New York: Oxford University Press.

Blau, Francine D. 1984. "The Use of Transfer Payments by Immigrants." *Industrial and Labor Relations Review.* 37.

Blauner, Robert. 1969. "Internal Colonialism and Ghetto Revolt." *Social Problems.* 16.

———. 1972. *Racial Oppression in America.* New York: Harper and Row.

———. 1989. *Black Lives, White Lives.* Berkeley: University of California Press.

Bloom, Jack M. 1987. *Class, Race and the Civil Rights Movement.* Bloomington, IN: Indiana University Press.

Bloom, Leonard. 1948. "Concerning Ethnic Research." *American Sociological Review.* 13.

Blumenfeld, Ruth. 1965. "Mohawks: Round Trip to the High Steel." *TransAction.* 3.

Blumer, Herbert. 1958. "Race Prejudice as a Sense of Group Position." *Pacific Sociological Review.* 1.

———. 1965. "Industrialization and Race Relations." In G. Hunger, ed., *Industrialization and Race Relations: A Symposium.* Institute of Race Relations. New York: Oxford University Press.

Bodnar, John R. 1985. *The Transplanted: A History of Immigrants in Urban America.* Bloomington, IN: Indiana University Press.

Bogen, Elizabeth. 1987. *Immigration in New York.* New York: Praeger.

Bohannan, P. 1957. *Justice and Judgment among the Tiv.* London: Oxford University Press.

Boissevain, Jeremy. 1984. "Small Entrepreneurs in Contemporary Europe." In Robin Ward, ed., *Ethnic Business in Britain.* Cambridge: Cambridge University Press.

Bonacich, Edna. 1972. "A Theory of Ethnic Antagonism: The Split Labor Market." *American Sociological Review.* 37.

———. 1973. "A Theory of Middleman Minorities." *American Sociological Review.* 38.

———. 1975a. "Abolition, the Extent of Slavery and the Position of Free Blacks: A Study of Split Labor Markets in the United States, 1830–1863." *American Journal of Sociology.* 81.

———. 1975b. "Small Business and Japanese American Ethnic Solidarity." *Amerasia Journal.* 3.

———. 1980. "Class Approaches to Ethnicity and Race." *Insurgent Sociologist.* 10.

———. 1984. "U.S. Capitalist Development: A Background to Asian Immigration." In Lucie Cheng and Edna Bonacich, eds., *Labor Migration under Capitalism.* Berkeley: University of California Press.

Bonacich, Edna, and Lucie Cheng. 1984. "Introduction: A Theoretical Orientation to International Labor Migration." In Lucie Cheng and Edna Bonacich, eds., *Labor Migration under Capitalism.* Berkeley: University of California Press.

Bonacich, Edna and Tae Hwan Jung. 1982. "A Portrait of Korean Small Business in Los Angeles: 1977." In Eeui-Young Yu, Earl H. Phillips, and Eun Sik Yang, eds., *Koreans in Los Angeles.* Los Angeles: Yoryo Research Institute and Center for Korean-American and Korean Studies. California State University.

Bonacich, Edna and Ivan H. Light. 1988. *Immigrant Entrepreneurs: Koreans in Los Angeles, 1965–1982.* Berkeley and Los Angeles: University of California Press.

Bonacich, Edna, Ivan Light, and Charles Wong. 1977. "Koreans in Business." *Society.* 14.

Bonacich, Edna and John Modell. 1981. *The Economic Basis of Ethnic Solidarity: Small Business in the Japanese-American Community.* Berkeley: University of California Press.

Bonilla, Frank. 1974. "Por que seguiremos siendo puertorriqueños." In Alberto Lopez and James Petras, eds., *Puerto Rico and Puerto Ricans.* Cambridge, MA: Schenkman.

Borhek, J. T. 1970. "Ethnic Group Cohesion." *American Journal of Sociology.* 76.

Borjas, George J. 1990. *Friends or Strangers: The Impact of Immigrants on the U.S. Economy.* New York: Basic Books.

———. 1991. "Immigrants in the U.S. Labor Market 1940–1980." *AEA Pap. Proc.* 81:2.

———. 1994. "The Economics of Immigration." *Journal of Economic Literature,* 32.

Borjas, George J. and Richard B. Freeman, (eds.). 1992. *Immigration and the Workforce: Economic Consequences for the United States and Source Areas.* Chicago: University of Chicago Press.

Borjas, George J. and Marta Tienda, eds. 1985. *Hispanics in the U.S. Economy.* Orlando, FL: Academic Press.

———. 1987. "The Economic Consequences of Immigration." *Science.* 235.

———. 1993. "The Employment and Wages of Legalized Immigrants. *International Migration Review.* 27:4.

Bosworth, Allen R. 1967. *America's Concentration Camps.* New York: W.W. Norton.

Bottomore, Thomas B. 1966. *Classes in Modern Society.* New York: Pantheon.

Bouie, A. 1981. *Student Perceptions of Behavior and Misbehavior in the School Setting: An Exploratory Study and Discussion.* San Francisco: Far West Laboratory for Educational Research and Development.

Bouvier, Leon F. and Anthony J. Agresta. 1987. "The Future Asian Population of the United States." In James T. Fawcett and Benjamin V. Carino, eds., *Pacific Bridges: The New Immigration from Asia and the Pacific Islands.* Staten Island: Center for Migration Studies.

Bouvier, Leon F. and Robert W. Gardner. 1986. "Immigration to the U.S.: The Unfinished Story." *Population Bulletin.* 41.

Boykin, A. W. 1986. "The Triple Quandary and the Schooling of Afro-American Children." In U. Neisser, ed. *The School Achievement of Minority Children: New Perspectives.* Hillsdale, NJ: Erlbaum.

Brass, Paul. 1985. "Ethnic Groups and the State." In P. Brass, ed., *Ethnic Groups and the State.* London: Croome-Heim.

Braverman, Harry. 1974. *Labor and Monopoly Capital: The Degradation of Work in the Twentieth Century.* New York: Monthly Review Press.

Breen, Timothy H. 1973. "The 'Giddy Multitude': Race and Class in Early Virginia." *Journal of Social History.* 7.

Briggs, Vernon M. 1990. "Immigration Policy Sends Blacks Back to South." *New York Times.* February 1.

Brimelow, Peter. 1995. *Alien Nation: Common Sense About America's Immigration Disaster.* New York: Random House.

Brimhall-Vargas, Mark. 1994. "Hispanic Elected Officials." Washington, DC: National Association of Latino Elected Officials Fund.

Brittan, Arthur and Mary Maynard. 1984. *Sexism, Racism and Oppression.* Oxford: Basil Blackwell.

Bronner, Ethan. 1998. "U. of California Reports Big Drop in Black Admissions." *New York Times.* April 1.

Brooke, James, 1988. "In Africa, Tribal Hatreds Defy the Borders of State." *New York Times.* August 28.

———. 1996. "Indians' Cruel Winter of Aid Cuts and Cold." *New York Times.* January 27.

Brooks-Gunn J., G. Duncan, P. K. Klebanov, and N. Sealand. 1993. "Do Neighborhoods Influence Child and Adolescent Development?" *American Journal of Sociology.* 99.

Broom, L. and J. H. Smith. 1963. "Bridging Occupations." *British Journal of Sociology.* 14.

Browning, Harley L. and Rudolfo de la Garza (eds.). 1986. *Mexican Immigrants and Mexican Americans: An Evolving Relation.* Austin: Center for Mexican American Studies, University of Texas.

Brubaker, William Rogers. 1989. "Membership Without Citizenship: The Economic and Social Rights of Noncitizens." In William Rogers Brubaker, ed., *Immigration and the Politics of Citizenship in Europe and North America.* Lanhan, MD: University Press of America.

Bryce-Laporte, Ray Simon. 1969. "The American Slave Planation and Our Heritage of Communal Deprivation." *American Behavioral Scientist.* 4.

———. 1972. "Black Immigrants: The Experience of Invisibility and Inequality." *Journal of Black Studies.* 3:1.

Bullivant, M. 1987. *The Ethnic Encounters in the Secondary Schools: Ethnocultural Reproduction and Resistance, Theory and Case Studies.* London: Falmer Press.

Burgess, M. Elaine. 1978. "The Resurgence of Ethnicity: Myth or Reality?" *Ethnic and Racial Studies.* 1:3.

Burkett, Elinor. 1997. "God Created Me to Be a Slave." *New York Times Magazine.* October 12.

Buroway, Michael. 1976. "The Functions and Reproduction of Migrant Labor: Comparative Material from Southern Africa and the United States." *American Journal of Sociology.* 81.

Burstein, Paul. 1991. " 'Reverse Discrimination' Cases in the Federal Courts: Legal Mobilization by a Countermovement." *Sociological Quarterly.* 32.

Butcher, K. F. and D. Card. 1991. "Immigration and Wages: Evidence from the 1980s." *AEA Pap. Proc.* 81:2.

Butterfield, Fox. 1996. "Old Fears and New Hope: Tale of Burned Black Church Goes Far Beyond Arson." *New York Times.* July 21.

———. 1997. "Many Black Men Barred From Voting, Study Shows." *New York Times.* January 30.

Butterworth, Douglas S. 1962. "A Study of the Urbanization Process Among Mixtec Migrants from Tilaltongo in Mexico City." *América Indigena.* 22.

Byers, P. and H. Byers. 1972. "Non-Verbal Communication and the Education of Children." In C. B. Cazden et al., eds., *Functions of Language in the Classroom.* New York: Teachers College Press.

Cafferty, Pastora San Juan, Barry R. Chiswick, Andrew M. Greeley, and Teresa A. Sullivan. 1985. *The Dilemma of American Immigration.* New Brunswick, NJ: Transaction Books.

Cahan, Abraham, 1917/1966. *The Rise of David Levinsky.* New York: Harper Torchbooks.

Calderon, Jose. 1992. " 'Hispanic' and 'Latino': The Viability of Categories for Panethnic Unity." *Latin American Perspectives.* 19:4.

California Assembly Office of Research. 1986. *California 2000: A People in Transition.* Sacramento Assembly Office of Research.

Camarillo, Albert. 1979. *Chicanos in a Changing Society.* Cambridge, MA: Harvard University Press.

Caplan, Nathan, M. H. Choy, and J. K. Whitmore. 1991. *Children of the Boat People: A Study of Educational Success.* Ann Arbor: University of Michigan Press.

Caplan, Nathan, J. K. Whitmore, and M. H. Choy. 1989. *The Boat People and Achievement in America: A Study of Family Life, Hard Work, and Cultural Values.* Ann Arbor: University of Michigan Press.

———. 1992. "Indochinese Refugee Families and Academic Achievement." *Scientific American.* 266:2. February.

Cardoso, Lawrence. 1980. *Mexican Emigration to the United States: 1897–1931.* Tucson: University of Arizona Press.

Carlson, Leonard A. 1981. *Indians, Bureaucrats, and Land.* Westport, CT: Greenwood Press.

Carmichael, Stokely and Charles Hamilton. 1967. *Black Power: The Politics of Liberation in America.* New York: Vintage.

Carnegie Foundation for the Advancement of Teaching. 1989. *Tribal Colleges: Shaping the Future of Native America.* Princeton, NJ: Princeton University Press.

Carnoy, M., H. M. Daley, and R. H. Ojeda. 1993. "The Changing Position of Latinos in the U.S. Labor Market since 1939." See Morales and Bonilla 1993, pp. 28–54.

Carpenter, Niles. 1927. *Immigrants and Their Children.* Washington, DC: Government Printing Office, Census Monograph VII.

Carter, Deborah J. and Reginald Wilson. 1991–1997. *Minorities in Higher Education: Annual Status Report.* Washington, DC: American Council on Education.

Casal, Lourdes and Andres Hernandez. 1975. "Cubans in the U.S.: A Survey of the Literature." *Cuban Studies.* 5.

Castells, Manuel. 1975. "Immigrant Workers and Class Struggles in Advanced Capitalism: The Western European Experience." *Politics and Society.* 5.

Castile, George. P. and G. Kushner, eds. 1981. *Persistent Peoples: Cultural Enclaves in Perspective.* Tucson: University of Arizona Press.

Center for Educational Statistics, U.S. Department of Education. 1987. *The American Indian in Higher Education 1975–76 to 1984–85.* Washington, DC: Government Printing Office.

Center for the Study of Sport and Society. 1998. *1997 Racial Report Card.* Boston: Center for the Study of Sport and Society, Northeastern University.

Centro de Estudios Puertorriqueños. 1979a. "The History Task Force." In *Labor Migration Under Capitalism.* New York: Monthly Review Press.

———. 1979b. *Labor Migration under Capitalism.* New York: Monthly Review.

Chadwick, Bruce A. and Joseph Strauss. 1975. "The Assimilation of American Indians into Urban Society: The Seattle Case." *Human Organization.* 34.

Chadwick, Bruce A. and L. C. White. 1973. "Correlates of Length of Urban Residence Among Spokane Indians." *Human Organization*. 34.

Champagne, Duane. 1989. *American Indian Societies— Strategies and Conditions of Political and Cultural Survival*. CS Report 32. Cambridge, MA: Cultural Survival, Inc.

——. 1990. "Culture, Differentiation, and Environment: Social Change in Tlingit Society." In J. Alexander and P. Colomy, eds., *Differentiation Theory and Social Change*. 88–118. New York: Columbia University Press.

Chan, Janet B. L. and Yuet-Wah Cheung, 1982. "Ethnic Resources and Business Enterprise: A Study of Chinese Businesses in Toronto." Paper presented at the annual meeting of the American Sociological Association, San Francisco. September.

Chan, S. 1991. *Asian Americans: An Interpretive History*. Boston: Twayne Publishers.

Chan, Sucheng. 1986. *This Bitter Sweet Soil: The Chinese in California Agriculture, 1860–1910*. Berkeley: University of California Press.

Chapman, Malcolm. 1979. *The Gaelic Vision in Scottish Culture*. London: Croome-Helm.

Cheng, Lucie and Edna Bonacich. 1984. *Labor Migration under Capitalism: Asian Workers in the United States before World War II*. Berkeley: University of California Press.

Child, Irwin L., 1943. *Italian or American? Second Generation in Conflict*. New Haven, CT: Yale University Press.

Chinoy, Ely. 1952. "The Tradition of Opportunity and the Aspirations of Automobile Workers." *American Journal of Sociology*. 57.

Chiswick, Barry. 1979. "The Economic Progress of Immigrants: Some Apparently Universal Patterns." In William Fellner, ed., *Contemporary Economic Problems*. Washington, DC: American Enterprise Institute.

——. 1982. "Immigrants in the U.S. Labor Market." *The Annals of the American Academy of Political and Social Sciences*. March.

——. 1983. "An Analysis of the Earnings and Employment of Asian American Men." *Journal of Labor Economics*. 1.

Chock, Phyllis P. 1981. "The Greek-American Small Businessman: A Cultural Analysis." *Journal of Anthropological Research*. 37.

Cingolani, Cindy. 1973. "Avoiding Management Pitfalls." *Bank of America Small Business Reporter*. 11.

Clark, Blue. 1988. "Bury My Heart in Smog: Urban Indians." In P. Weeks, ed., *The American Indian Experience. A Profile: 1524 to the Present*. 278–91. Arlington Heights, IL: Forum Press, Inc.

Clark, Kenneth B. 1965. *Dark Ghetto*. New York: Harper and Row.

Clark, Robert. 1984. *The Basque Insurgents: ETA, 1952–1980*. Madison: University of Wisconsin Press.

Cleaver, Eldridge. 1968. *Soul on Ice*. New York: McGraw-Hill.

Clifford, James. 1986. "Introduction: Partial Truths." In Clifford and George E. Marcus, eds., *Writing Culture: The Poetics and Politics of Ethnography*. Berkeley: University of California Press. 1–26.

——. 1988. *The Predicament of Culture: Twentieth Century Ethnography, Literature, and Art*. Cambridge, MA: Harvard University Press.

Clifford, James and George Marcus, eds. 1986. *Writing Culture: The Poetics and Politics of Ethnography*. Berkeley: University of California Press.

Clinton, Lawrence, Bruce A. Chadwick, and Howard M. Bahr. 1975. "Urban Relocation Reconsidered: Antecedents of Employment Among Indian Males." *Rural Sociology*. 40.

Cockcroft, James. 1983. *Mexico: Class Formation, Capital Accumulation, and the State*. New York: Grove.

——. 1986. *Outlaws in the Promised Land: Mexican Workers and America's Future*. New York: Grove Press.

Cohen, Abner. 1974. *Urban Ethnicity*. New York: Harper and Row.

——. 1981. "Variables in Ethnicity." In Charles F. Keyes, ed., *Ethnic Change*. Seattle, WA: University of Washington Press.

Cohen, Anthony P. 1985. *The Symbolic Construction of Community*. New York: Tavistock.

Cohen, M. 1988. *From Workshop to Office*. Urbana, IL: University of Illinois Press.

Cohen, Robin. 1986. *Endgame in South Africa?* Paris: UNESCO Press.

Cohen, Roger. 1994. "Yugoslavia's Ethnic Conflict Threatens Europe's Stability." *New York Times*. November 26.

Cohn, Bernard S. 1983. "Representing Authority in Victorian India." In E. Hobsbawm and T. Ranger, eds., *The Invention of Tradition*. Cambridge: Cambridge University Press.

Cole, Stewart G. and Mildred Wiese Cole. 1954. *Minorities and the American Promise*. New York: Harper.

Coleman, James. 1966. *Equality of Educational Opportunity*. Washington, DC: U.S. Government Printing Office.

Coleman, Kevin. 1995. "Latino Electoral Participation and Representation." *CRS Report to Congress*. Washington, DC: Congressional Research Service.

Collins, Sheila M. 1983. "The Making of the Black Middle Class." *Social Problems*. 30:4.

Connor, Walker. 1978. "A Nation Is a Nation, Is a State, Is an Ethnic Group, Is a." *Ethnic and Racial Studies*. 1.

——. 1991. "When Is a Nation?" *Ethnic and Racial Studies*. 13.

Conzen, Kathleen N., David A. Gerber, Ewa Morawska, George E. Pozzetta, and Rudolph J. Vecoli. 1992. "The Invention of Ethnicity: A Perspective from the U.S.A." *Journal of American Ethnic History*. 12.

Copage, Eric V. 1991. "The Seven Days of Kwanzaa." *New York Times.* December 1.

Corey, Lewish. 1966. "The Middle Class." In Reinhard Bendix and Seymour Lipset, eds., *Class, Status, and Power,* 2d ed. Glencoe, IL: Free Press.

Cornell, Stephen. 1988a. *The Return of the Native: American Indian Political Resurgence.* New York: Oxford University Press.

———. 1988b. "The Transformations of Tribe: Organization and Self-Concept in Native American Ethnicities." *Ethnic and Racial Studies.* 1:1.

*———. 1990. "Land, Labour, and Group Formation: Blacks and Indians in the United States." *Ethnic and Racial Studies.* 13:3. July.

Cornell, Stephen and Joseph P. Kalt. 1990. "Pathways from Poverty: Economic Development and Institution Building on American Indian Reservations." *American Indian Cultural Reservation Journal.* 14.

Cose, Ellis. 1993. *The Rage of a Privileged Class.* New York: HarperCollins.

Coser, Lewis A. 1978. "American Trends." In Tom Bottomore and Robert Nisbet, eds., *A History of Sociological Analysis.* New York: Basic Books.

Council of Jewish Federations. 1991. *Highlights of the CJF 1990 National Jewish Population Survey.* New York: Council of Jewish Federations.

Cox, Oliver Cromwell. 1948. *Caste, Class and Race: A Study in Social Dynamics.* New York: Doubleday.

Crane, J. 1991. "Effects of Neighborhoods on Dropping Out of School and Teenage Child-bearing." In C. Jencks and P. E. Peterson, eds., *The Urban Underclass.* pp. 299–320. Washington, DC: Brookings Inst.

Crèvecoeur, Hector St. John de. 1782/1957. *Letters from an American Farmer.* New York: E.P. Dutton.

Crossette, Barbara. 1991. "India's Descent." *New York Times Magazine.* May 19.

Cummings, Scott A. et al., eds. 1980. *Self-Help in Urban America.* Port Washington, NY: Kennikat.

Daedalus. 1965. "The Negro American."

———. 1981. "American Indians, Blacks, Chicanos, and Puerto Ricans."

Daley, Suzanne. 1997. "Blacks in South Africa Find New Wealth but Old Biases." *New York Times.* October 2.

Daniels, Roger. 1962/1966/1977. *The Politics of Prejudice: The Anti-Japanese Movement in California and the Struggle for Japanese Exclusion.* Berkeley: University of California Press.

———. 1972. *Concentration Camps USA: Japanese Americans and World War II.* New York: Holt, Rinehart and Winston.

———. 1975. *The Decision to Relocate the Japanese Americans.* Philadelphia: J. B. Lippincott Co.

———. 1977. "The Japanese-American Experience: 1890–1940." In Leonard Dinnerstein and F. C. Jaher, eds., *Uncertain Americans.* New York: Oxford University Press.

———. 1988. *Asian America: Chinese and Japanese in the United States since 1850.* Seattle: University of Washington Press.

———. 1990. *Coming to America: A History of Immigration and Ethnicity in American Life.* New York: HarperCollins.

———. 1993. *Prisoners Without Trial: Japanese Americans in World War II.* New York: Hill and Wang.

Daniels, Roger and Harry H. L. Kitano. 1970. *American Racism.* Englewood Cliffs, NJ: Prentice-Hall.

Danziger, Sheldon and P. Gottschalk, eds. 1993. *Uneven Tides: Rising Inequality in America.* New York: Russell Sage Foundation.

Dao, James. 1993. "Casino Issue Hotly Divides Mohawks as New York Reservation Arms Itself." *New York Times.* March 22.

Dashefsky, Arnold. 1972. "And the Search Goes On: The Meaning of Religio-Ethnic Identity and Identification." *Sociological Analysis.* 33.

Davidson, Miriam. 1990. "Immigrant Bashing: The Mexican Border War." *The Nation.* 12. November.

Davies, Charlotte. 1989. *Welsh Nationalism in the Twentieth Century: The Ethnic Option and the Modern State.* New York: Praeger.

Davis, Cary, Carl Haub, and Joanne Willette. 1983. "U.S. Hispanics: Changing the Face of America." *Population Bulletin.* 38.

Davis, David Brian. 1966. *The Problem of Slavery in Western Culture.* Ithaca, NY: Cornell University Press.

———. 1975. *The Problem of Slavery in the Age of Revolution.* Ithaca, NY: Cornell University Press.

Davis, F. James. 1991. *Who Is Black? One Nation's Definition.* University Park, PA: Pennsylvania State University.

Davis, L., R. Easterin, and W. Parker. 1972. *American Economic Growth: An Economist's History of the United States.* New York: Harper Row.

Davis, Mike. 1985. "Urban Renaissance and the Spirit of Postmodernism." *New Left Review.* 151.

———. 1986. *Prisoners of the American Dream: Politics and Economy in the History of the U.S. Working Class.* London: Verso.

———. 1987. "*Chinatown,* Part Two? The 'Internationalization' of Downtown Los Angeles." *New Left Review.* 164.

Day, Jennifer C. 1993. "Population Projections of the United States, by Age, Sex, Race, and Hispanic Origin: 1993 to 2050." U.S. Bureau of the Census. *Current Population Reports,* P25–1104. Washington, DC: U.S. Government Printing Office.

Dedman, Bill. 1989. "Blacks Turned Down for Home Loans from S & Ls Twice as Often as Whites." *Atlanta Constitution.* January 22.

DeFrietas, G. 1985. "Ethnic Differentials in Unemployment Among Hispanic Americans." See Borjas and Tienda 1985.

———. 1991. *Inequality at Work: Hispanics in the U.S. Labor Force.* New York: Oxford University Press.

Degler, Carl N. 1971. *Neither Black Nor White.* New York: Macmillan.

Delgado, Héctor L. *New Immigrants, Old Unions: Organizing Undocumented Workers in Los Angeles.* Philadelphia: Temple University Press.

Deloria, Vine, Jr. 1986. "The New Indian Recruits: The Popularity of Being Indian." *Americans Before Columbus.* 14:3.

Denton, Nancy A. 1994. "Are African Americans Still Hypersegregated?" In Robert D. Bullard, J. Eugene Grigsby III, and Charles Lee, eds. *Residential Apartheid: The American Legacy.* Los Angeles: CAAS Publications, UCLA.

Depres, Leo A. 1975. *Ethnicity and Resource Competition.* The Hague: Mouton.

Desai, Manisha. 1992. "The Demise of Secularism and the Rise of Majority Communalism in India." Paper presented at the annual meeting of the Midwest Sociological Society, Kansas City.

DeVos, George. A. 1984. "Ethnic Persistence and Role Degradation: An Illustration from Japan." Paper presented for the American-Soviet Symposium on Contemporary Ethnic Processes in the U.S.A. and the U.S.S.R. New Orleans. April.

DeVos, George and Hiroshi Wagatsuma. 1966. *Japan's Invisible Race: Caste in Culture and Personality.* Berkeley: University of California Press.

DeWolf, Evelyn. 1982. "Fund Pools Blocked by Postal Law." *Los Angeles Times.* February 21. VIII.

DiMaggio, Paul. 1982. "Cultural Capital and School Success: The Impact of Status Culture Participation on the Grades of U.S. High School Students." *American Sociological Review.* 47.

Diner, Hasia R. 1983. *Erin's Daughters in America: Irish Immigrant Women in the Nineteenth Century.* Baltimore, MD: Johns Hopkins Press.

Dinnerstein, Leonard, Roger L. Nichols, and David M. Reimers. 1979/1990/1996. *Natives and Strangers: A Multicultural History of Americans.* New York: Oxford University Press.

Dinnerstein, Leonard and David M. Reimers. 1975/1983/1987. *Ethnic Americans: A History of Immigration and Assimilation.* New York: Harper and Row.

DiPrete, Thomas A. and David B. Grusky. 1990. "Structure and Trend in the Process of Stratification for American Men and Women." *American Journal of Sociology.* 96.

Doane, Ashley W., Jr. 1992. "Class, Competition, and Capitalist Development: A Framework for Analyzing the Evolution of American Ethnic Identities." Paper presented at the 1992 annual meeting of the American Sociological Association. Pittsburgh, PA.

———. 1996a. "Rethinking the National Question: Toward a Theory of Ethnicity and Nationality in the New World Order." In Chronis Polychroniou and Harry R. Targ, eds., *Marxism Today: Essays on Capitalism, Socialism, and Strategies for Social Change.* Westport, CT: Praeger.

———. 1996b. "Contested Terrain: Negotiating Racial Understandings in Public Discourse." *Humanity and Society.* 20:4.

———. 1997a. "White Identity and Race Relations in the 1990s." In Gregg Lee Carter, ed., *Perspectives on Current Social Problems.* Boston: Allyn and Bacon.

*———. 1997b. "Dominant Group Ethnic Identity in the United States: The Role of 'Hidden' Ethnicity in Intergroup Relations." *The Sociological Quarterly.* 38:3. Summer.

Dollard, John. 1937. *Caste and Class in a Southern Town.* New Haven, CT: Yale University Press.

Domhoff, G. William. 1970. *The Higher Circles: The Governing Class in America.* New York: Random House.

Dominguez, Virginia R. 1986. *White by Definition: Social Classification in Creole Louisiana.* New Brunswick: Rutgers University Press.

Donato, Katharine M., Jorge Durand, and Douglas S. Massey. 1992. "Stemming the Tide? Assessing the Deterrent Effects of the Immigration Reform and Control Act." *Demography.* 29.

Dorris, Michael A. 1981. "The Grass Still Grows. The Rivers Still Flow: Contemporary Native Americans." *Daedalus.* 110.

———. 1989. *The Broken Cord.* New York: Harper & Row.

Doyle, Betram W. 1937. *The Etiquette of Race Relations in the South.* Port Washington, NY: Kennikat Press.

Dozier, E. P. 1966. "Problem Drinking Among American Indians: The Role of Socio-Cultural Deprivation." *Quarterly Journal of Alcohol Studies.* 27.

Drake, St. Clare and Horace Cayton. 1945. *Black Metropolis: A Study of Negro Life in a Northern City.* New York: Harcourt, Brace.

Duboff, R. 1989. *Accumulation and Power: An Economic History of the United States.* Armonk, New York: M. E. Sharpe.

DuBois, W. E. B. 1899/1967. *The Philadelphia Negro: A Social Study.* New York: Schocken.

———. 1903/1961/1986. *The Souls of Black Folk.* Greenwich, CT: Fawcett.

———. 1935/1946. *Black Reconstruction.* New York: S. A. Russell.

Dugger, Celia W. 1997. "Backlog Threatens Applicants for Citizenship." *New York Times.* March 3.

Duleep, H. and S. Sanders. 1992. "Discrimination at the Top: American-Born Asian and White Men." *Industrial Relations.* 31:3.

Dumont, Jr., R. V. 1972. "Learning English and How to Be Silent: Studies in Sioux and Cherokee Classrooms." In C. B. Cazden et al., eds., *Functions of Language in the Classroom.* New York: Teachers College Press.

The Economist. May 13, 1985.

Edmonston, Barry and Jeffrey Passel. 1991. "The Future Immigrant Population of the United States." Paper presented at the Conference on Immigration and Ethnicity, the Urban Institute. Washington, DC.

Edsall, Thomas Byrne with Mary D. Edsall. 1991. "Race." *The Atlantic Monthly.* May.

———. 1992. *Chain Reaction: The Impact of Race, Rights, and Taxes on American Politics.* New York: W. W. Norton.

Egan, Timothy. 1992. "Indians Become Foes in Bid for Tribal Rights." *New York Times.* September 6.

———. 1996. "Expelled in 1877, Indian Tribe is Now Wanted as a Resource." *New York Times.* July 22.

Ehrlich, Howard J. 1990. *Campus Ethnoviolence and Policy Options.* Baltimore: National Institute against Prejudice and Violence.

Eichenwald, Kurt. 1996. "Texaco Executives, on Tape, Discussed Impeding a Bias Suit." *New York Times.* November 4.

Eisenhower Foundation. 1998. *The Millenium Breach: Richer, Poorer, and Racially Apart.* Washington, DC: Milton S. Eisenhower Foundation.

Eitzen, D. Stanley and Norman R. Yetman. 1977. "Immune from Racism?" *Civil Rights Digest.* 9

Eitzen, D. Stanley and Maxine Baca Zinn. 1989. *The Reshaping of America: Social Consequences of the Changing Economy.* Englewood Cliffs, NJ: Prentice Hall.

Elkins, Stanley M. 1959. *Slavery: A Problem in American Institutional and Intellectual Life.* Chicago: University of Chicago Press.

Engelhardt, Tom. 1971. "Ambush at Kamikaze Pass." *Bulletin of Concerned Asian Scholars.* 3.

Enloe, Cynthia. 1973. *Ethnic Development and Political Conflict.* Boston: Little, Brown.

———. 1981. "The Growth of the State and Ethnic Mobilization: The American Experience." *Ethnic and Racial Studies.* 4.

Erdrich, Louise and Michael Dorris. 1988. "Who Owns the Land?" *New York Times Magazine.* September 4.

Erickson, Charlotte. 1972. *Invisible Immigrants: The Adaptation of English and Scottish Immigrants in Contemporary America.* Coral Gables, FL: University of Miami Press.

———. 1975. *American Industry and the European Immigrant, 1860–1885.* New York: Russell & Russell.

Erickson, F. and J. Mohartt. 1982. "Cultural Organization of Participant Structure in Two Classrooms of Indian Students." In G. D. Spindler, ed., *Doing the Ethnography of Schooling: Educational Anthropology in Action.* New York: Holt.

Eschbach, Karl. 1992. "Shifting Boundaries: Regional Variation in Patterns of Identification as American Indians." Ph.D. dissertation, Department of Sociology, Harvard University, Cambridge, MA.

———. 1995. "The Enduring and Vanishing American Indian: American Indian Population Growth and Intermarriage in 1990." *Ethnic and Racial Studies.* 18.

Escott, Paul D. 1979. *Slavery Remembered: A Record of Twentieth-Century Slave Narratives,* Chapel Hill: University of North Carolina Press.

Espenshade, Thomas J. 1995. "Unauthorized Immigration to the United States." *Annual Review of Sociology.* 21.

Espenshade, Thomas J. and Charles A. Calhoun. 1993. "An Analysis of Public Opinion Toward Undocumented Immigration." *Population Research and Policy Review.* 12.

Espenshade, Thomas J. and W. Ye. 1994. "Differential Fertility Within an Ethnic Minority: The Effect of Trying Harder Among Chinese American Women." *Social Problems.* 41:1.

Espiritu, Yen Le. 1992. *Asian American Panethnicity: Bridging Institutions and Identities.* Philadelphia: Temple University Press.

Essed, Philomena. 1991. *Understanding Everyday Racism.* Newbury Park, CA: Sage Publications.

Estrada, Leobardo F., F. Chris Garcia, Reynaldo Flores Macias, and Lionel Maldonado. 1981. "Chicanos in the United States: A History of Exploitation and Resistance." *Daedalus.* 110:2.

Evans-Pritchard, Deirdre. 1987. "The Portal Case: Authenticity, Tourism, Traditions, and the Law." *Journal of American Folklore.* 100.

Fain, T. Scott. 1980. "Self-Employed Americans: Their Number Has Increased." *Monthly Labor Review.* 103.

Fallows, James. 1983. "Immigration." *The Atlantic.* 252:5.

———. 1990. "Japan's Hidden Race Problems." *New York Times.* October 14.

Faludi, Susan. 1991. *Backlash: The Undeclared War Against American Women.* New York: Crown.

Fantasia, Rick. 1988. *Cultures of Solidarity.* Berkeley, CA: University of California Press.

Farley, Reynolds. 1977. "Trends in Racial Inequalities: Have the Gains of the 1960s Disappeared in the 1970s?" *American Sociological Review.* 42.

———. 1991. "The New Census Question about Ancestry: What Did It Tell Us?" *Demography.* 28.

———. 1993. "The Common Destiny of Blacks and Whites." In H. Hill and J. E. Jones, eds., *Race in America: The Struggle for Equality.* Madison: University of Wisconsin.

———. 1997. "Modest Declines in U.S. Residential Segregation Observed." *Population Today.* 25:2.

Farley, Reynolds and William Allen. 1987. *The Color Line and the Quality of Life: The Problem of the Twentieth Century.* New York: Russell Sage Foundation.

Farley, Reynolds and William H. Frey. 1994. "Changes in the Segregation of Whites From Blacks During the 1980s: Small Steps Toward a More Integrated Society." *American Sociological Review.* 59.

Feagin Joe R. 1978/1996. *Racial and Ethnic Relations.* Englewood Cliffs, NJ: Prentice Hall.

*——. 1991. "The Continuing Significance of Race: Antiblack Discrimination in Public Places." *American Sociological Review.* 56:1. February.

——. 1992. "The Continuing Significance of Racism: Discrimination Against Black Students at White Colleges." *Journal of Black Studies.* 22.

Feagin, Joe R. and Douglas Eckberg. 1980. "Prejudice and Discrimination." *Annual Review of Sociology.* 6.

Feagin, Joe R. and Clairece Booher Feagin. 1978/1986. *Discrimination American Style: Institutional Racism and Sexism.* Melbourne, FL: Krieger Publishing Co.

——. 1996. *Racial and Ethnic Relations.* 5th ed., Englewood Cliffs, NJ: Prentice-Hall.

Feagin, Joe R. and M. P. Sikes. 1994. *Living with Racism: The Black Middle-Class Experience.* Boston: Beacon Press.

Feagin, Joe R. and Hernan Vera. 1995. *White Racism: The Basics.* New York: Routledge.

Featherman, David and Robert Hauser. 1976. "Changes in the Socioeconomic Stratification of the Races, 1962–1973." *American Journal of Sociology.* 82.

Federal Reserve Bulletin. 1991. "Home Mortgage Disclosure Act: Expanded Data on Residential Lending." 77.

Feeney, Patrick G. 1992. "The 1990 Census and the Politics of Apportionment." *Footnotes.* Washington, DC: American Sociological Association. March.

Ferenczi, Imre. 1929. *International Migration,* Vol. 1, *Statistics.* New York: National Bureau of Economic Research.

Ferguson, F. N. 1968. "Navajo Drinking: Some Tentative Hypotheses." *Human Organization.* 27.

Fernandez-Kelly, Maria Patricia. 1987. "Economic Restructuring in the United States: The Case of Hispanic Women in the Garment and Electronics Industries in Southern California." Paper presented at the annual meeting of the American Sociological Association. Chicago.

Firebaugh, Glenn and Kenneth E. Davis. 1988. "Trends in Antiblack Prejudice 1972–1984: Region and Cohort Effects." *American Journal of Sociology.* 94.

Fischer, David Hackett. 1989. *Albion's Seed: Four British Folkways in America.* New York: Oxford University Press.

Fischer, Michael M. J. 1986. "Ethnicity and the Post-Modern Arts of Memory." In J. Clifford and G. Marcus, eds., *Writing Culture: The Poetics and Politics of Ethnography.* Berkeley: University of California Press.

Fitzpatrick, Joseph P. and Douglas M. Gurak. 1979. *Hispanic Intermarriage in New York City.* New York: Fordham University Hispanic Research Center.

Fixico, Donald L. 1986. *Termination and Relocation: Federal Indian Policy, 1945–1960.* Albuquerque: University of New Mexico Press.

Fogel, Robert William and Stanley L. Engerman. 1974. *Time on the Cross: The Economics of American Negro Slavery.* Boston: Little, Brown.

Fordham, S. 1985. *"Black Student School Success as Related to Fictive Kinship.* Final report to National Institute of Education. Washington, DC: National Institute of Education.

——. 1988. "Restlessness as a Factor in Black Students' School Success: Pragmatic Strategy or Pyrrhic Victory?" *Harvard Education Review.* 58:1.

Fordham, S. and John U. Ogbu. 1986. "Black Students' School Success: Coping with the Burden of 'Acting White.' " *The Urban Review.* 18:3.

Francis, E. K. 1976. *Interethnic Relations: An Essay in Sociological Theory.* New York: Elsevier.

Franco, Jean. 1985. "New York Is a Third World City: Introduction." *Tabloid* 9.

Frankenberg, Ruth. 1993. *White Women, Race Matters: The Social Construction of Whiteness.* Minneapolis: University of Minnesota Press.

Franklin, V. P. 1984. *Black Self-Determination: A Cultural History of the Faith of the Fathers.* Westport: Lawrence Hill.

Fraser, Steven. 1995. *The Bell Curve Wars: Race, Intelligence, and the Future of America.* New York: Basic Books.

Freedman, Maurice. 1959. "The Handling of Money: A Note on the Background to the Economic Sophistication of the Overseas Chinese." *Man.* 59.

Freeman, Gary P. 1986. "Migration and the Political Economy of the Welfare State." *The Annals of the American Academy of Political and Social Science.* 485.

Frey, William H. 1996. "Immigration, Domestic Migration, and Demographic Balkanization in America: New Evidence for the 1990s." *Population and Development Review.* 22:4. December.

Frey, William H. and Reynolds Farley. 1996. "Latino, Asian, and Black Segregation in U.S. Metropolitan Areas: Are Multiethnic Metros Different?" *Demography.* 33:1. February.

Friedman, Debra and Doug McAdam. 1987. "Collective Identity as a Selective Incentive." Paper presented at the annual meeting of the American Sociological Association.

——. 1992. "Collective Identity and Action: Networks, Choices, and the Life of a Social Movement." In A. D. Morris and C. M. Mueller, eds., *Frontiers in Social Movement Theory.* New Haven: Yale University Press.

Friedman, Thomas L. 1985. "Kahane Appeal to Oust Arabs Gains in Israel." *New York Times.* August 5.

——. 1996. "The Next Rwanda." *New York Times.* January 24.

Galbraith, John K. 1963. *The Affluent Society.* New York: Dutton.

Galens, Judy, Anna Sheets, and Robyn V. Young, eds. 1995. *Gale Encyclopedia of Multicultural America.* Detroit: Gale Research.

Gallagher, Charles A. 1994. "White Reconstruction in the University." *Socialist Review.* 24.

Gallup Poll Social Audit. 1997. *Black/White Relations in the United States.* Princeton, NJ: The Gallup Organization. June.

Gamson, William. 1982. "The Political Culture of the Arab-Israeli Conflict." *Conflict Management and Peace Sciences.* 5.

———. 1988. "Political Discourse and Collective Action." In B. Klandermans, B. Kriesi, and S. Tarrow, eds., *International Social Movements Research.* Greenwich, CT: JAI Press.

———. 1992. "The Social Psychology of Collective Action." In A. D. Morris and C. M. Mueller, eds., *Frontiers in Social Movement Theory.* New Haven: Yale University Press.

Gamson, William and Kathryn E. Lasch. 1983. "The Political Culture of Welfare Policy." In S. E. Spiro and E. Yuchtman-Yaar, eds., *Evaluating the Welfare State: Social and Political Perspectives.* New York: Academic Press.

Gamson, William and Andre Modigliani. 1987. "The Changing Culture of Affirmative Action." In R. G. Braungart, ed., *Research in Political Sociology.* Greenwich, CT: JAI Press.

Gans, Herbert. 1962. *The Urban Villagers.* New York: Free Press.

———. 1968. "Social Protest of the 1960's Takes the Form of the Equality Revolution." *New York Times Magazine.* November 3.

*———. 1979. "Symbolic Ethnicity: The Future of Ethnic Groups and Culture in America." *Ethnic and Racial Studies.* 2.

———. 1988. *Middle American Individualism: Political Participation and Liberal Democracy.* New York: Free Press.

———. 1992. "Comment: Ethnic Invention and Acculturation: A Bumpy-Line Approach." *Journal of American Ethnic History.* 12.

———. 1992. "Second-Generation Decline: Scenarios for the Economic and Ethnic Futures of the Post-1965 American Immigrants." *Ethnic and Racial Studies.* 15:2.

García, John A. 1981. "Yo Soy Mexicano: Self-Identity and Sociodemographic Correlates." *Social Science Quarterly.* 62.

Gardner, Bruce. 1977. *Bilingual Schooling and the Survival of Spanish in the United States.* Rowley, MA: Newbury House.

Gardner, Carol Brooks. 1980. "Passing By: Street Remarks, Address Rights, and the Urban Female." *Sociological Inquiry.* 50.

———. 1988. "Access Information: Public Lies and Private Peril." *Social Problems.* 35.

Gardner, Robert W., Bryant Robey, and Peter C. Smith. 1985. "Asian Americans: Growth, Change, and Diversity." *Population Bulletin.* 4.

Gay, J. and M. Cole. 1967. *The New Mathematics and an Old Culture: A Study of Learning among the Kpelle of Liberia.* New York: Holt.

Geertz, Clifford. 1963. *Old Societies and New States.* New York: Free Press.

———. 1988. *Works and Lives: The Anthropologist as Author.* Palo Alto: Stanford University Press.

Gelfand, Mitchell Brian. 1981. "Chuzpah in El Dorado: Social Mobility of Jews in Los Angeles, 1900–1920." Ph.D. Dissertation. Carnegie-Mellon University.

Gellner, Ernest. 1983. *Nations and Nationalism.* London: Basil Blackwell.

———. 1987. *Culture, Identity, and Politics.* Cambridge: Cambridge University Press.

Genovese, Eugene D. 1974/1976. *Roll, Jordon, Roll: The World the Slaves Made.* New York: Pantheon Books.

Gerner, Deborah J. 1991. *One Land, Two Peoples: The Conflict Over Palestine.* Boulder, CO: Westview.

Gerry, Chris and Chris Birkbeck. 1981. "The Petty Commodity Producer in Third World Cities: Petit-Bourgeois or Disguised Proletarian?" in Frank Bechofer and Brian Elliott, ed., *The Petite Bourgeoisie.* New York: St. Martin's Press.

Geschwender, James A. and Rita Carroll-Seguin. 1990. "Exploding the Myth of African-American Progress." *Signs.* 15:2.

Gibson, M. A. 1987. "The School Performance of Immigrant Minorities: A Comparative View." *Anthropology and Education Quarterly.* 18:4.

———. 1988. *Accommodation Without Assimilation: Punjabi Sikh Immigrants in an American High School and Community.* Ithaca: Cornell University Press.

Giddens, Anthony. 1973. *The Class Structure of the Advanced Societies.* New York: Harper and Row.

Gimenez, Marta E. 1992. "U.S. Ethnic Politics: Implications for Latin Americans." *Latin American Perspectives.* 19.

Gimenez, Marta E., Fred A. Lopez, and Carlos Munoz, Jr. 1992. *The Politics of Ethnic Construction: Hispanic, Chicano, Latino?* Beverly Hills, CA: Sage Publications.

Gittler, Joseph B. 1956. *Understanding Minority Groups.* New York: Wiley.

Glasgow, Douglas G. 1980. *The Black Underclass: Poverty, Unemployment and Entrapment of Ghetto Youth.* San Francisco: Jossey-Bass.

Glazer, Nathan. 1975. *Affirmative Discrimination.* New York: Basic Books.

———. 1985. *Clamor at the Gates: The New American Immigration.* San Francisco: Institute for Contemporary Studies Press.

———. 1987. "New Perspectives on American Jewish Sociology." In David Singer, ed., *American Jewish*

Yearbook, 1987. 87. Philadelphia: The American Jewish Committee.

Glazer, Nathan and Daniel P. Moynihan. 1963/1970. *Beyond the Melting Pot: The Negroes, Puerto Ricans, Jews, Italians, and Irish of New York City.* Cambridge, MA: MIT Press.

——. 1975. *Ethnicity: Theory and Experience.* Cambridge, MA: Harvard University Press.

Gleason, Philip. 1980. "American Identity and Americanization." In Stephan Thernstrom, ed., *Harvard Encyclopedia of American Ethnic Groups.* Cambridge, MA: Harvard University Press.

——. 1991. "Minorities (Almost) All: The Minority Concept in American Social Thought." *American Quarterly.* 43:3. September.

——. 1992. *Speaking of Diversity: Language and Ethnicity in Twentieth-Century America.* Baltimore, MD: Johns Hopkins University Press.

Glenn, Evelyn N. 1986. *Issei, Nisei, Warbride: Three Generations of Japanese American Women in Domestic Service.* Philadelphia: Temple University Press.

Goering, John M. 1971. "The Emergence of Ethnic Interests: A Case of Serendipity." *Social Forces.* 49.

Goffman, Erving. 1956. "The Nature of Deference and Demeanor." *American Anthropologist.* 58.

——. 1961. *Asylums.* New York: Doubleday.

——. 1963. *Behavior in Public Places.* New York: Free Press.

——. 1971. *Relations in Public.* New York: Basic Books.

Goldberg, J. J. 1997. "Interfaith Marriage: The Real Story." *New York Times.* August 3.

Goldberg, M. L. 1971. "Socio-Psychological Issues in the Education of the Disadvantaged." In A. Harry Passow, ed., *Urban Education in the 1970's.* New York: Teachers College Press.

Goldschneider, Calvin and Frances Kobrin. 1980. "Ethnic Continuity and the Process of Self-Employment." *Ethnicity.* 7.

Gomez, Laura. 1986. "What's in a Name: The Politics of Hispanic Identity." B. A. Honors Thesis, Harvard College, Cambridge, MA.

Gómez-Peña, Guillermo. 1987. "Wacha Esa Border, Son." *La Jornada Semanal* (Mexico City). October 25.

Gordon, David, Richard Edwards, and Michael Reich. 1982. *Segmented Work, Divided Workers.* New York: Cambridge University Press.

*Gordon, Milton M. 1961. "Assimilation in America: Theory and Reality." *Daedalus.* 90:2.

——. 1964. *Assimilation in American Life.* New York: Oxford University Press.

——. 1978. *Human Nature, Class, and Ethnicity.* New York: Oxford University Press.

Gould, Stephen Jay. 1981. *The Mismeasure of Man.* New York: Norton.

Graber, Doris A. 1980. *Crime News and the Public.* New York: Praeger.

Grant, Madison. 1916. *The Passing of the Great Race.* New York: Scribners.

Grasmuck, Sherri and Patricia R. Pessar. 1991. *Between Two Islands: Dominican International Migration.* Berkeley: University of California Press.

Graves, Theodore D. 1971. "Drinking and Drunkeness Among Urban Indians." In Jack O. Waddell and O. Michael Watson, eds., *The American Indian in Urban Society.* Boston: Little, Brown.

Grebler, Leo, Joan W. Moore, and Ralph Guzman. 1970. *The Mexican-American People, The Nation's Second Largest Minority.* New York: Free Press.

Greeley, Andrew M. 1971/1975. *Why Can't They Be Like Us?* New York: Dutton.

——. 1974. *Ethnicity in the United States: A Preliminary Reconnaissance.* New York: Wiley.

——. 1976. "The Ethnic Miracle." *The Public Interest.* 45.

Green, V. 1981. "Blacks in the United States: The Creation of an Enduring People." In G. P. Castile and G. Kushner, eds., *Persistent Peoples: Cultural Enclaves in Perspective.* Tucson: University of Arizona Press.

Greenhouse, Linda. 1996. "Race Statistics Alone Do Not Support a Claim of Selective-Prosecution, Justices Rule." *New York Times.* May 14.

Grenier, Gilles. 1984. "Shifts to English as Usual Language by Americans of Spanish Mother Tongue." *Social Science Quarterly.* 65.

Grier, Eunice, and Scott Grier. 1965. "Equality and Beyond: Housing Segregation in the Great Society." *Daedalus.* 95.

Griffen, Sally and Clyde Griffen. 1977. "Family and Business in a Small City: Poughkeepsie, N.Y., 1850–1880." In Tamara Hareven, ed., *Family and Kin in Urban Communities, 1700–1930.* New York: New Viewpoints.

Griffin, John Howard. 1961. *Black Like Me.* Boston: Houghton Mifflin.

Grimshaw, Allen D. 1959. "Lawlessness and Violence in America and Their Special Manifestations in Changing Negro-White Relationships." *Journal of Negro History.* 44.

Grodzins, Morton. 1956/1966. *American Betrayed: Politics and the Japanese Evacuation.* Chicago: University of Chicago Press.

Guillemin, Jeanne. 1975. *Urban Renegades: The Cultural Strategy of American Indians.* New York: Columbia University Press.

Gumperz, J. J. 1981. "Conversational Inferences and Classroom Learning." In J. Green and C. Wallat, eds., *Ethnographic Approach to Face-to-Face Interaction.* Norwood, NJ: ABLEX.

Gundlach, James H. and Alden E. Roberts. 1978. "Native American Indian Migration and Relocation: Success or Failure." *Pacific Sociological Review.* 12.

Gutiérrez, Carlos González. "The Mexican Diaspora in California: Limits and Possibilities for Mexican Government." In Abraham F. Lowenthal and Katrina

Burgess, eds., *The California-Mexico Connection.* Stanford, CA: Stanford University Press.

Gutman, Herbert G. 1976. *The Black Family in Slavery and Freedom, 1750–1925.* New York: Pantheon Books.

Gwartney, J. D. and J. E. Long. 1978. "The Relative Earnings of Blacks and Other Minorities." *Industrial and Labor Relations Review.* 31.

Haberman, Clyde. 1989. "Flow of Turks Leaving Bulgaria Swells to Hundreds of Thousands." *New York Times.* August 15.

Hacker, Andrew. 1992. *Two Nations: Black and White, Separate, Hostile, and Unequal.* New York: Charles Scribner's Sons.

Hagen, Everett. 1968. *The Economics of Development.* Homewood, IL: Richard D. Irwin.

Hagan, William T. 1976. "The Reservation Policy: Two Little and Too Late." In Jane F. Smith and Robert M. Kvasnicka, eds., *Indian-White Relations: A Persistent Paradox.* Washington, DC: Howard University Press.

———. 1979. *American Indians.* Chicago, IL: University of Chicago Press.

Halbfinger, David M. 1997. "New York Continues to be Shaped by New Immigrants." *New York Times.* December 1.

Hall, Peter Dobkin. 1977. "Family Structure and Economic Organization: Massachusetts Merchants, 1700–1850." In Tamara Hareven, ed., *Family and Kin in Urban Communities 1700–1930.* New York: New Viewpoints.

Hall, Thomas D. 1986. "Incorporation in the World-System: Toward a Critique." *American Sociological Review.* 51:3.

———. 1987. "Native Americans and Incorporation: Patterns and Problems." *American Indian Culture and Research Journal.* 11:2.

———. 1989. *Social Change in the Southwest, 1350–1880.* Lawrence, KS: University Press of Kansas.

Handlin, Oscar. 1941/1959. *Boston's Immigrants: A Study of Acculturation.* Cambridge, MA: Harvard University Press.

———. 1951. *The Uprooted: The Epic Story of the Great Migration That Made the American People.* New York: Grossett and Dunlap.

———. 1956. *The Newcomers: Negroes and Puerto Ricans in a Changing Metropolis.* Cambridge, MA: Harvard University Press.

———. 1957. *Race and Nationality in American Life.* Garden City, NY: Doubleday.

———. 1959. *The Newcomers: Negroes and Puerto Ricans in a Changing Metropolis.* Cambridge, MA: Harvard University Press.

———. 1961. "Historical Perspectives on the American Ethnic Group." *Daedalus.* 90.

Hansen, Kristin A., and Carol S. Faber. 1997. "The Foreign-Born Population: 1996." U.S. Bureau of the Census. *Current Population Reports.* P20-494. March.

Hansen, Marcus Lee. 1938. *The Problem of the Third Generation Immigrant.* Rock Island, IL: Augustana Historical Society.

———. 1940a. *The Atlantic Migration, 1907–1860.* Cambridge, MA: Harvard University Press.

———. 1940b. *The Immigrant in American History.* Cambridge, MA: Harvard University Press.

———. 1954. "The Problem of the Third Generation Immigrant." In Edward Saveth, ed., *Understanding the American Past.* Boston: Little Brown.

Hanson, H. Allan. 1995. "Testing, *The Bell Curve,* and the Social Construction of Intelligence." *Tikkun.* 10:1.

Harbison, Frederick. 1956. "Entrepreneurial Organization as a Factor in Economic Development." *Quarterly Journal of Economics.* 70.

Hardy-Fanta, Carol. 1993. *Latina Politics, Latino Politics: Gender, Culture, and Political Participation in Boston.* Philadelphia: Temple University Press.

Harris, David. 1994. "The 1990 Census Count of American Indians: What Do the Numbers Really Mean?" *Social Science Quarterly.* 75.

Harris, Marvin. 1964. *Patterns of Race in the Americas.* New York: Norton.

Harrison, Bennett and Barry Bluestone. 1988. *The Great U-Turn: Corporate Restructuring and the Polarization of America.* New York: Basic.

Harrison, R. J. and C. Bennett. 1995. "Racial and Ethnic Diversity." In R. Farley, ed., *State of the Union: America in the 1900s,* Vol. 2. *Social Trends.* New York: Russell Sage Foundation.

Hartwig, M. C. 1972. "Aborigines and Racism: An Historical Perspective." In F. S. Stevens, ed., *Racism: The Australian Experience.* vol. 2. New York: Taplinger.

Harvie, Christopher. 1977. *Scotland and Nationalism.* London: Allen and Unwin.

Hatton, Timothy J. and Jeffrey G. Williamson. 1992. "International Migration and World Development: A Historical Perspective," Historical Paper No. 41. Cambridge, MA: National Bureau of Economic Research.

Hauser, Robert M. 1995. "Review of *The Bell Curve. Contemporary Sociology.* 24:2. March.

Haycock, K. and M. S. Navarro. 1988. *Unfinished Business: Report from the Achievement Council.* Oakland, CA: The Achievement Council.

Hayes-Bautista, David E., Werner O. Schink, and Jorge Chapa. 1988. *The Burden of Support: Young Latinos in an Aging Society.* Stanford, CA: Stanford University Press.

Hechter, Michael. 1975. *Internal Colonialism.* Berkeley: University of California Press.

———. 1987a. *Principles of Group Solidarity.* Berkeley: University of California Press.

———. 1987b. "Nationalism as Group Solidarity." *Ethnic and Racial Studies.* 10.

——. 1992. "The Dynamics of Secession." *Acta Sociologica.* 35.

Hechter, Michael and Debra Friedman. 1984. "Does Rational Choice Theory Suffice? Response to Adam." *International Migration Review.* 18.

Hechter, Michael, Debra Friedman, and Malka Applebaum. 1982. "A Theory of Ethnic Collective Action." *International Migration Review.* 16.

Heer, David M. 1974. "The Prevalence of Black-White Marriage in the United States, 1960 and 1970." *Journal of Marriage and the Family.* 36.

Hein, Jeremy. 1991. "Do 'New Immigrants' Become 'New Minorities'?: The Meaning of Ethnic Minority for Indochinese Refugees in the United States." *Sociological Perspectives.* 31.

——. 1993. "Refugees, Immigrants and the State." *Annual Review of Sociology.* 19.

——. 1994. "From Migrant to Minority." *Sociological Inquiry.* 64.

Heisler, Barbara Schmitter. 1986. "Immigrant Settlement and the Structure of Emergent Immigrant Communities in Western Europe." *The Annals of the American Academy of Political and Social Sciences.* 485.

Henley, Nancy M. 1978. *Body Politics.* Englewood Cliffs, NJ: Prentice-Hall.

Henry, Frances. 1976. *Ethnicity in the Americas.* Chicago: Aldine.

Henry, Jeannette. 1967. "Our Inaccurate Textbooks." *The Indian Historian.* 1.

Herberg, Will. 1955/1960. *Protestant-Catholic-Jew.* New York: Doubleday.

Herman, Harry Vjekoslav. 1979. "Dishwashers and Proprietors: Macedonians in Toronto's Restaurant Trade." In Sandra Wallman, ed., *Ethnicity at Work.* London: Macmillan.

Herrnstein, Richard J. and Charles Murray. 1994. *The Bell Curve: Intelligence and Class Structure in American Life.* New York: Free Press.

Hershberg, Theodore, Alan N. Burstein, Eugene P. Ericksen, Stephanie Greenberg, and William L. Yancey. 1979. "A Tale of Three Cities: Blacks, Immigrants and Opportunity in Philadelphia: 1850-1890, 1930 and 1970." *The Annals of the American Academy of Political and Social Science.* 441.

Hertz, Rosanna. 1986. *More Equal Than Others.* Berkeley: University of California Press.

Hertzberg, Hazel. 1971. *The Search for an American Indian Identity: Modern Pan-Indian Movements.* Syracuse, NY: Syracuse University Press.

Hewitt de Alcántara, Cynthia. 1976. *Modernizing Mexican Agriculture: Socioeconomic Implications of Technological Change, 1940-1970.* Geneva: UN Research Institute for Social Development.

Higgs, Robert. 1977. *Competition and Coercion.* Cambridge: Cambridge University Press.

Higham, John. 1963. *Strangers in the Land: Patterns of American Nativism, 1896-1925.* New York: Atheneum.

——. 1975. *Send These To Me.* New York: Atheneum.

Hill, Robert B. 1981. "The Economic Status of Black Americans." In *The State of Black America.* New York: National Urban League.

Himes, Joseph. 1966. "The Functions of Racial Conflict." *Social Forces.* 46.

Hirschman, Charles. 1983. "America's Melting Pot Reconsidered." *Annual Review of Sociology.* 9.

Hirschman, Charles and Morrison G. Wong. 1981. "Trends in Socioeconomic Achievement among Immigrant and Native-Born Asian-Americans, 1960-1976." *Sociological Quarterly.* 22.

——. 1984. "Socioeconomic Gains of Asian-Americans, Blacks, and Hispanics: 1960-1976." *American Journal of Sociology.* 90.

——. 1986. "The Extraordinary Educational Attainment of Asian-Americans: A Search for Historical Evidence and Explanations." *Social Forces.* 65:1

Hobsbawm, Eric. 1983. "Introduction: Inventing Traditions." In *The Invention of Tradition,* eds. E. Hobsbawm and T. Ranger. Cambridge: Cambridge University Press.

——. 1990. *Nations and Nationalism Since 1780.* London: Cambridge University Press.

Hochschild, Arlie with Anne Machung. 1989. *The Second Shift: Working Parents and the Revolution at Home.* New York: Viking.

Hochschild, Jennifer L. 1995. *Facing Up to the American Dream: Race, Class and the Soul of the Nation.* Princeton: Princeton University Press.

Hodgkinson, Harold L., Janice Hamilton Outtz, and Anita M. Obarakpor. 1990. *The Demographics of American Indians.* Washington, DC: Institute for Educational Leadership.

Hodson, Randy, Dusko Sekulic, and Garth Massey. 1994. "National Tolerance in Yugoslavia." *American Journal of Sociology.* 99.

Hoffman, Abraham. 1974. *Unwanted Mexican Americans in the Great Depression: Repatriation Pressures 1929-1939.* Tucson: University of Arizona Press.

Hogeland, Chris and Karen Rosen. 1990. *Dreams Lost, Dreams Found: Undocumented Women in the Land of Opportunity.* San Francisco: Coalition for Immigrant and Refugee Rights and Services.

*Hollinger, David A. 1992. "Postethnic America." *Contention.* 2:1. Fall.

Holstein, James A. and Gale Miller, eds. 1993. *Perspectives on Social Problems: Reconsidering Social Constructionism* (Volume 5). New York: Aldine.

Holt, G. S. 1972. " 'Inversion' in Black Communication." In *Rappin' and Stylin' Out: Communication in Urban Black America.* Chicago: University of Illinois Press.

"Home Mortgage Disclosure Act: Expanded Data on Residential Lending." 1991. *Federal Reserve Bulletin.* 77.

Hondagneu-Sotelo, Pierrette. 1991. Family and Community in the Migration of Mexican Undocumented Immigrant Women. In M. T. Segal and V. Demos, eds., *Ethnic Women: A Multiple Status Reality.* Dix Hills, NY: General Hall.

*———. 1994. *Gendered Transitions: Mexican Experiences of Immigration.* Berkeley: University of California Press.

Hondagneu-Sotelo, Pierrette and Michael A. Messner. 1994. "Gender Displays and Men's Power: The 'New Man' and the Mexican Immigrant Man." In Harry Brod and Michael Kaufman, eds., *Theorizing Masculinities.* Newbury Park, CA: Sage Publications.

Horowitz, Donald. 1985. *Ethnic Groups in Conflict.* Berkeley: University of California Press.

Horowitz, Ruth. 1983. *Honor and the American Dream: Culture and Identity in a Chicano Community.* New Brunswick, NJ: Rutgers University Press.

Horsman, Reginald. 1981. *Race and Manifest Destiny: The Origins of American Racial Anglo-Saxonism.* Cambridge, MA: Harvard University Press.

Horton, John. 1966. "Order and Conflict Theories of Social Problems in Competing Ideologies." *American Journal of Sociology.* 71.

———. 1995. *The Politics of Diversity: Immigration, Resistance, and Change in Monterey Park, California.* Philadelphia: Temple University Press.

Horvat, Branko. 1982. *The Political Economy of Socialism.* Armonk, NY: M. E. Sharpe.

Hough, Joseph C., Jr. 1968. *Black Power and White Protestants: A Christian Response to the New Negro Pluralism.* New York: Oxford University Press.

Hout, Michael. 1988. "More Universalism, Less Structural Mobility: The American Occupational Structure in the 1980s." *American Journal of Sociology.* 93.

Hout, Michael and J. Goldstein. 1994. "How 4.5 Million Irish Immigrants Became 40 Million Irish Americans: Demographic and Subjective Aspects of the Ethnic Composition of White Americans." *American Sociological Review.* 59.

Howe, Irving. 1976. *World of Our Fathers.* New York: Harcourt, Brace, Jovanovich.

———. 1977. "The Limits of Ethnicity." *The New Republic.* June 25.

Hoxie, Frederick E. 1984. *A Final Promise: The Campaign to Assimilate the Indians, 1880–1920.* Lincoln, NE: University of Nebraska Press.

Hraba, Joseph. 1979. *American Ethnicity.* Itasca, IL: F. E. Peacock.

Hsu, Francis L. K. 1971. *The Challenge of the American Dream: The Chinese in the United States.* Belmont, CA: Wadsworth.

Huggins, Nathan Irvin. 1979. *Black Odyssey: The Afro-American Ordeal in Slavery.* New York: Vintage.

Hughes, Everett C. 1963. "Race Relations and the Sociological Imagination." *American Sociological Review.* 28.

Hughes, Everett C. and Helen M. Hughes. 1952. *Where People Meet: Racial and Ethnic Frontiers.* Glencoe, IL: The Free Press.

Human Rights Watch. 1992. *War Crimes in Bosnia-Herzegovina.* New York: Human Rights Watch.

Humphrey, Norman D. 1944. "The Changing Structure of the Detroit Mexican Family: An Index of Acculturation." *American Sociological Review.* 9.

Hune, Shirley. 1977. "Pacific Migration to the United States: Trends and Themes in Historical and Sociological Literature." *RIIES Bibliographic Studies.* 2. Washington, DC: Smithsonian Institution.

Hurh, Won Moo, and Kwang Chung Kim. 1983. "Korean Americans and the 'Success' Image: A Critique." *Amerasia Journal.* 10.

———. 1989. "The 'Success' Image of Asian Americans: Its Validity and Its Practical and Theoretical Implications." *Ethnic and Racial Studies.* 12.

Hurtado, Albert L. 1982. "Hardly a Farm House—A Kitchen Without Them: Indian and White Households on the California Borderland Frontier in 1860." *Western Historical Quarterly.* 13:3.

Hutchinson, Edward P. 1956. *Immigrants and Their Children, 1850–1950.* New York: Wiley.

———. 1981. *Legislative History of American Immigration Policy, 1798–1965.* Philadelphia: University of Pennsylvania Press.

Ignatiev, Noel. 1995. *How the Irish Became White.* New York: Routledge.

Isajiw, Wsevolod W. 1974. "Definitions of Ethnicity." *Ethnicity.* 1.

Ito-Adler, James. 1980. *The Portuguese in Cambridge and Somerville, Part II: 1977 Supplement.* Cambridge, MA: Department of Planning and Development.

Jackson, K. 1983. "The Old Minorities and the New Immigrants: Understanding a New Cultural Idiom in U.S. History." See M. M. Kritz 1983, pp. 317–35.

Jacobsen, Cardell K. 1984. "Internal Colonialism and Native Americans: Indian Labour in the United States from 1871 to World War II." *Social Science Quarterly.* 65:1.

Jaffe, A. J., Ruth M. Cullen, and Thomas D. Boswell. 1980. *The Changing Demography of Spanish Americans.* New York: Academic Press.

Jaffe, Amy Myers. 1994. "At Texaco, The Diversity Skeleton Still Stalks the Halls." *New York Times.* December 11.

Jaimes, M. Annette. 1992. "Federal Indian Identification Policy: A Usurpation of Indigenous Sovereignty in North America." In M. A. Jaimes, ed., *The State of Native America: Genocide, Colonization, and Resistance.* Boston, MA: South End Press.

James, David R. 1989. "City Limits on Racial Equality: The Effects of City-Suburban Boundaries on Public-School Desegregation, 1968–1976." *American Sociological Review.* 54.

*———. 1994. "The Racial Ghetto as a Race-Making Situation: The Effects of Residential Segregation on Racial Inequities and Racial Identity." *Law & Social Inquiry.* 19:2. Spring.

James, David R. and Karl E. Taeuber. 1985. "Measures of Segregation." In Nancy Tuma, ed., *Sociological Methodology 1985.* San Francisco: Jossey-Bass.

Jameson, Fredric. 1984. "Postmodernism, or the Cultural Logic of Late Capitalism." *New Left Review.* 146.

Jaret, Charles. 1995. *Contemporary Racial and Ethnic Relations.* New York: HarperCollins.

Jarvenpa, Robert and Walter P. Zenner. 1979. "Scot Trader/Indian Worker Relations and Ethnic Segregation: A Subarctic Example." *Ethnos.* 44.

Jasso, Guillermina and Mark R. Rosenzweig. 1990. *The New Chosen People: Immigrants in the United States.* New York: Russell Sage.

Jaynes, Gerald David and Robin M. Williams, Jr., eds. 1989. *A Common Destiny: Blacks and American Society.* Washington, DC: National Academy Press.

Jencks, Christopher. 1991. "Is the American Underclass Growing?" In C. Jencks and P. E. Peterson, eds., *The Urban Underclass.* Washington, DC: Brookings Institution.

———. 1992. *Rethinking Social Policy: Race, Poverty, and the Underclass.* Cambridge, MA: Harvard University Press.

Jencks, Christopher and S. E. Mayer. 1990. "The Social Consequences of Growing Up In a Poor Neighborhood." In L. E. Lynn and M. G. H. McGeary, eds., *Inner City Poverty in the United States.* Washington, DC: National Academy Press.

Jenkins, Richard. 1984. "Ethnicity and the Rise of Capitalism." In Robin Ward, ed., *Ethnic Business in Britain.* Cambridge: Cambridge University Press.

Jennings, Francis. 1976. *The Invasion of America: Indians, Colonialism, and the Cant of Conquest.* New York: W. W. Norton.

Jensen, Arthur A. 1969. "How Much Can We Boost I.Q. and Scholastic Achievement?" *Harvard Educational Review.* 39.

Jensen, Joan M. 1988. *Passage from India: Asian Indian Immigrants in North America.* New Haven: Yale University Press.

Johnson, Charles S. 1934. *Shadow of the Plantation.* Chicago: University of Chicago Press.

Johnson, Dirk. 1994. "Economies Come to Life on Indian Reservations." *New York Times.* July 3.

Johnston, Hank. 1991. *Tales of Nationalism: Catalonia: 1939–1979.* New Brunswick, NJ: Rutgers University Press.

Joint Center for Political Studies. 1997. Personal communication. May 19.

Jones, Charisse. 1995. "Crack and Punishment: Is Race the Issue?" *New York Times.* October 25.

Jones, Faustine C. 1981. "External Crosscurrents and Internal Diversity: An Assessment of Black Progress, 1960–1980." *Daedalus.* 110:2.

Jones, LeRoy and I. Sakong. 1980. *Government, Business and Entrepreneurship in Economic Development: The Korean Case.* Cambridge, MA: Harvard University Council on East Asian Studies.

Jones, Maldwyn Allen. 1960. *American Immigration.* Chicago: University of Chicago Press.

———. 1976. *Destination America.* New York: Holt, Rinehart, and Winston.

Jordan, Winthrop D. 1968. *White Over Black: American Attitudes Toward the Negro 1550–1812.* Baltimore: Penguin.

Jorgensen, Joseph G., Richard O. Clemmer, Ronald L. Little, Nancy J. Owens, and Lynn A. Robbins. 1978. *Native Americans and Energy Development.* Cambridge, MA: Anthropology Resource Center.

Kallen, Horace. 1915. "Democracy *versus* the Melting Pot." *The Nation.* February 18–25.

———. 1924. *Culture and Democracy in the United States.* New York: Boni and Liveright.

Kallenberg, Arne L. and Aage B. Sorenson. 1979. "The Sociology of Labor Markets." *Annual Review of Sociology.* 5.

Kalmijn, M. 1993. "Trends in Black/White Intermarriage." *Social Forces.* 72.

Kandiyoti, Deniz. 1988. "Bargaining with Patriarchy." *Gender and Society.* 2.

Kansas City Star. 1991. "Indian Art Protection Law May End Up Hurting the Artists." August 4:J-5.

Karner, Tracy X. 1991. "Ideology and Nationalism: The Finnish Move to Independence, 1809–1918." *Racial and Ethnic Studies.*

Karsh, Norman C. 1977. *What Is a Small Business?* Washington, DC: Small Business Administration.

Kasarda, John. 1985. "Urban Change and Minority Opportunities." In P. E. Peterson, ed., *The New Urban Reality.* Washington, DC: Brookings Institution.

Katz, Elaine N. 1976. *A Trade Union Aristocracy.* African Studies Institute Communication, No. 3. Johannesburg: University of the Witwatersrand.

Katzman, David M. 1973. *Before the Ghetto: Black Detroit in the Nineteenth Century.* Urbana: University of Illinois Press.

———. 1981. *Seven Days a Week: Women and Domestic Service in Industrializing America.* Urbana: University of Illinois Press.

Katznelson, Ira. 1976. *Black Men, White Cities: Race, Politics, and Migration in the United States, 1900–30, and Britain, 1948–68,* Chicago: University of Chicago Press.

*Kazal, Russell A. 1995. "Revisiting Assimilation: The Rise, Fall, and Reappraisal of a Concept in American Ethnic History." *American Historical Review.* 100:2. April.

Kearney, Michael. 1986. "From the Invisible Hand to Visible Feet: Anthropological Studies of Migration and Development." *Annual Review of Anthropology.* 15.

Kearney, Michael and Carole Nagengast. 1989. *Anthropological Perspectives on Transnational Communities in Rural California.* Working Paper 3, Working Group on Farm Labor and Rural Poverty. Davis, CA: California Institute for Rural Studies.

Keely, Charles B. 1979. *U.S. Immigration: A Policy Analysis.* New York: Population Council.

Keith, Verna M. and Cedric Herring. 1991. "Skin Tone and Stratification in the Black Community." *American Journal of Sociology.* 97.

Kelly, Mary. 1993. "Lithuanian-Americans in the United States and Lithuania." *Sociologija Lietuvoje: Praeitis ir Dabartis.* Kaunas Technological University, Lithuania. 3.

———. 1994. "Ethnic Pilgrimages: Lithuanian Americans in Lithuania." Paper presented at the annual meeting of the Midwest Sociological Society. St. Louis, MO.

Kemper, Robert V. 1977. *Migration and Adaptation: Tzintzuntzan Peasants in Mexico City.* Beverly Hills: Sage.

Kennedy, Ruby Jo Reeves. 1944. "Single or Triple Melting Pot? Intermarriage Trends in New Haven, 1870–1940." *American Journal of Sociology.* 49.

———. 1952. "Single or Triple Melting Pot? Intermarriage in New Haven, 1940–1950," *American Journal of Sociology.* 58.

Kenney, G. M. and D. A. Wissoker. 1994. "An Analysis of the Correlates of Discrimination Facing Young Hispanic Job Seekers." *American Economic Review.* 84:3.

Kerr, Peter. 1993. "Insurance Industry Bias Seen in National Study." *New York Times.* February 5.

Keyes, Charles F. 1981. "The Dialectics of Ethnic Change." In Charles F. Keyes, ed., *Ethnic Change.* Seattle, WA: University of Washington Press.

Khleif, Bud B. 1989. "Ethnicity as a Social Movement: The Case of Arab Americans." Paper presented at the 1989 annual meeting of the Society for the Study of Social Problems. Berkeley, CA.

———. 1992. "The Myth of Individualism: Some Observation on the Sociology of Culture." Paper presented at the 1992 meeting of the Association for Humanist Sociology. Portland, ME.

Kibria, N. 1994. "Household Structure and Family ideologies: The Dynamics of Immigrant Economic Adaptation Among Vietnamese Refugees." *Social Problems.* 41:1.

Kiernan, Ben. 1988. "Orphans of Genocide: The Cham Muslims of Kampuchea under Pol Pot." *Bulletin of Concerned Asian Scholars.* 20:4.

Kilborn, Peter T. 1995. "A Family Spirals Downward in Waiting for Agency to Act." *New York Times.* February 11.

———. 1997. "For Poorest Indians, Casinos Aren't Enough." *New York Times.* June 11.

Kiljunen, Kimmo. 1984. "Power Politics and the Tragedy of Kampuchea During the Seventies." *Bulletin of Concerned Asian Scholars.* 17:2.

Killian, Lewis M. 1968. *The Impossible Revolution.* New York: Random House.

———. 1970. *White Southerners.* New York: Random House.

Kim, Hyung-Chang. 1977. "Ethnic Enterprises among Korean Immigrants in America." In Hyung-Chang Kim, ed., *The Korean Diaspora.* Santa Barbara, CA: ABC:CLIO.

Kim, Illsoo. 1981. *New Urban Immigrants: The Korean Community in New York.* Princeton, NJ: Princeton University Press.

———. 1988. "A New Theoretical Perspective on Asian Enterprises." *Amerasia Journal.* 14.

Kindleberger, Charles P. 1967. *Europe's Postwar Growth: The Role of Labor Supply.* New York: Oxford University Press.

King, Martin Luther, Jr. 1964. *Why We Can't Wait.* New York: Harper and Row.

Kinton, Jack. 1977. *American Ethnic Revival.* Aurora, IL: Social Service and Sociological Resources.

Kirschenman, J. and K. M. Neckerman. 1991. "We'd Love to Hire Them, but . . .": The Meaning of Race for Employers. In C. Jencks and P. E. Peterson, eds., *The Urban Underclass.* Washington, DC: Brookings Institution.

Kitano, Harry H. L. 1969/1976. *Japanese Americans: The Evolution of a Subculture.* Englewood Cliffs, NJ: Prentice-Hall.

Kitano, Harry and Sue Stanley. 1973. "The Model Minorities." *The Journal of Social Issues.* 29.

Kivisto, Peter, ed. 1989. *The Ethnic Enigma: The Salience of Ethnicity for European-Origin Groups.* Philadelphia: The Balch Institute Press.

Klineberg, Otto. 1963. "Children's Readers: Life Is Fun in a Smiling, Fair-Skinned World." *Saturday Review.* February.

Kluegel, James R. 1990. "Trends in Whites' Explanations of the Black-White Gap in Socioeconomic Status." *American Sociological Review.* 55.

Kluegel, James R. and Lawrence Bobo. 1993. "Opposition to Race-Targeting: Self-Interest, Stratification Ideology, or Racial Attitudes?" *American Sociological Review.* 58:4. August.

Kluegel, James R. and Eliot R. Smith. 1982. "Whites' Beliefs About Black Opportunity." *American Sociological Review.* 47.

———. 1986. *Beliefs About Inequality.* New York: Aldine de Gruyter.

Kluger, Richard. 1975. *Simple Justice: The History of Brown v. Board of Education and Black America's Struggle for Equality.* New York: Vintage.

Knight, Rolf. 1978. *Indians at Work: An Informal History of Native Indian Labour in British Columbia, 1858–1930.* Vancouver: New Star.

Kochman, T. 1982. *Black and White Styles in Conflict.* Chicago: University of Chicago Press.

Kolata, Gina. 1989. "A New Toll of Alcohol Abuse: The Indians' Next Generation." *New York Times.* July 19.

Kopinak, Kathryn. 1996. *Desert Capitalism: Maquiladoras in North America's Western Industrial Corridor.* Tucson: University of Arizona Press.

Koptiuch, Kristin. 1989. "Third Worlding at Home." Manuscript. Austin: Dept. of Anthropology, University of Texas.

Kozol, Jonathan. 1991. *Savage Inequalities: Children in America's Schools.* New York: HarperCollins.

Kristof, Nicholas D. 1995. "Japanese Outcasts Better Off Than in Past, But Still Outcasts." *New York Times.* November 30.

Kritz, Mary M., ed. 1983. *U.S. Immigration and Refugee Policy: Global and Domestic Issues.* Lexington, MA: Lexington.

Kuhlmann, Annette. "Steelheads and Walleyes: Changes in Political Culture in and Around Indian Country and the Fishing Rights Struggle in the Pacific Northwest and the Great Lakes." In C. Ward and C. M. Snipp, eds., *Research in Human Capital and Development.* Greenwich, CT: JAI Press.

Kuhn, Thomas S. 1970. *The Structure of Scientific Revolutions.* 2nd edition. Chicago: University of Chicago Press.

Kuo, Wen H. 1995. "Coping with Discrimination: The Case of Asian-Americans." *Ethnic and Racial Studies.* 18.

LaBelle, T. J. 1976. "Anthropological Framework of Studying Education," In J. I. Roberts and S. Akinsanya, eds., *Schooling in the Cultural Context: Anthropological Studies of Education.* New York: David McKay.

Laitin, David D. 1985. "Hegemony and Religious Conflict: British Imperial Control and Political Cleavages in Yorubaland." In P. B. Evans, D. Rueschemeyer and T. Skocpol, eds., *Bringing the State Back In.* Cambridge: Cambridge University Press.

LaLonde, R. and R. H. Topel. 1991. "Immigrants in the American Labor Market: Quality Assimilation and Distributional Effects." *AEA Pap. Proc.* 81:2.

Lamm, Richard D. and Gary Imhoff. 1985. *The Immigration Time Bomb: The Fragmenting of America.* New York: Dutton.

Lancy, D. F. 1983. *Cross-Cultural Studies in Cognition and Mathematics.* New York: Academic Press.

Landry, Bart. 1987. *The New Black Middle Class.* Berkeley: University of California Press.

Larimore, Jim and Rick Waters. 1993. "American Indians Speak Out Against Ethnic Fraud in College Admissions." Paper presented at a conference sponsored by the American Council on Education: "Educating One-Third of a Nation IV: Making Our Reality Match our Rhetoric." Houston, TX.

Larrick, Nancy. 1965. "The All-White World of Children's Books." *Saturday Review.* September 11.

Lauwagie, Beverly. 1979. "Ethnic Boundaries in Modern States: Romano Lavo-Lil Revisted." *American Journal of Sociology.* 87.

Laws, Glenda. 1997. "Globalization, Immigration, and Changing Social Relations in U.S. Cities." *The Annals of the American Academy of Political and Social Science.* 551. May.

Layne, Linda L. 1989. "The Dialogics of Tribal Self-representation in Jordan." *American Ethnologist.* 16.

Lee, Sharon M. 1989. "Asian Immigration and American Race Relations: From Exclusion to Acceptance?" *Ethnic and Racial Studies.* 12:3.

———. 1993. "Racial Classification in the U.S. Census: 1890–1990." *Racial and Ethnic Studies.* 16.

Leff, Nathaniel. 1978. "Industrial Organization and Entrepreneurship in the Developing Countries: The Economic Groups." *Economic Development and Cultural Change.* 26.

Leland, John and Gregory Beals. 1997. "In Living Colors." *Newsweek.* May 7.

Lelyveld, Joseph. 1985. *Move Your Shadow: South Africa, Black and White.* New York: Penguin.

Lemann, Nicholas. 1991. *The Promised Land: The Great Black Migration and How It Changed America.* New York: A.A. Knopf.

Lemarchand, Rene. 1975. "Ethnic Genocide." *Society.* 12.

Lester, Julius. 1968. *Look Out Whitey! Black Power's Gon' Get Your Mama.* New York: The Dial Press, Inc.

Levine, Barry. 1987. "The Puerto Rican Exodus: Development of the Puerto Rican Circuit." In Barry Levine, ed., *The Caribbean Exodus.* New York: Praeger.

Levine, Gene N. 1989. "Review of *American Assimilation or Jewish Revival* by Steven M. Cohen." *Contemporary Sociology.* 18.

Levine, Lawrence W. 1977. *Black Culture and Black Consciousness: Afro-American Folk Thought from Slavery to Freedom.* New York: Oxford University Press.

Levitan, Sar A. and William B. Johnston. 1975. *Indian Giving: Federal Programs for Native Americans.* Baltimore: Johns Hopkins University Press.

Levy, Frank. 1987. *Dollars and Dreams: The Changing American Income Distribution.* New York: Russell Sage.

———. 1995. "Incomes and Income Inequality." In Reynolds Farley, ed., *State of the Union—America in the 1990s,* Vol. 1: *Economic Trends.* New York: Russell Sage.

Lewin, Tamar. 1997. "Seeking to Shield Schools from Tax Breaks." *New York Times.* May 21.

Lewis, Neil A. 1991. "Police Brutality Under Wide Review by Justice Department." *New York Times*. March 15.

——. 1997. "Nationwide Settles U.S. Lawsuit on Bias in Inner-City Areas." *New York Times*. March 11.

Lewis, Oscar. 1952. "Urbanization Without Breakdown: A Case Study." *Scientific Monthly*. 75.

Lewthwaite, Gilbert A. and Gregory Kane. 1996. "Witness to Slavery." *Baltimore Sun*. June 16.

Lichtenstein, Grace. 1976. "Custer's Defeat Commemorated by Entreaties of Peace." *New York Times*. June 25.

Lieberson, Stanley. 1961. "A Societal Theory of Race and Ethnic Relations." *American Sociological Review*. 26.

——. 1963. *Ethnic Patterns in American Cities*. New York: Free Press.

——. 1980. *A Piece of the Pie: Blacks and White Immigrants since 1900*. Berkeley: University of California Press.

——. 1985. "Unhyphenated Whites in the United States." *Ethnic and Racial Studies*. 8.

Lieberson, Stanley and Mary C. Waters. 1986. "Ethnic Groups in Flux: The Changing Ethnic Responses of American Whites." *Annals of the American Academy of Political and Social Sciences*. 487. September.

——. 1988. *From Many Strands: Ethnic and Racial Groups in Contemporary America*. New York: Russell Sage.

——. 1993. "The Ethnic Response of Whites: What Causes Their Instability, Simplification, and Inconsistency?" *Social Forces*. 72:2.

Light, Ivan. 1972. *Ethnic Enterprise in America: Business and Welfare Among Chinese, Japanese, and Blacks*. Berkeley: University of California Press.

——. 1977a. "The Ethnic Vice District, 1880–1944." *American Sociological Review*. 44.

——. 1977b. "Numbers Gambling: A Financial Institution." *American Sociological Review*. 43.

——. 1979. "Disadvantaged Minorities in Self-Employment." *International Journal of Comparative Sociology*. 20.

——. 1980. "Asian Enterprise in America." In Scott A. Cummings, ed., *Self-Help in Urban America*. Port Washington, NY: Kennikat.

*——. 1984. "Immigrant and Ethnic Enterprise in North America." *Ethnic and Racial Studies*. 7:2.

Light, Ivan and Edna Bonacich. 1988. *Immigrant Entrepreneurs: Koreans in Los Angeles, 1965–1982*. Berkeley: University of California Press.

Light, Ivan H. and Charles Wong. 1975. "Protest or Work: Dilemmas of the Tourist Industry in American Chinatowns." *American Journal of Sociology*. 80.

Lipset, Seymour Martin and Reinhard Bendix, eds. 1959. *Social Mobility in Industrial Society*. Berkeley and Los Angeles: University of California Press.

——. 1953/1966. "Social Mobility and Occupational Career." In Seymour Martin Lipset and Reinhard Bendix, eds., *Class, Status and Power*. Glencoe, IL: The Free Press.

Lipsitz, George. 1986–87. "Cruising Around the Hispanic Bloc: Postmodernism and Popular Music in Los Angeles." *Cultural Critique*. 5.

Litwak, Leon. 1961. *North of Slavery: The Negro in the Free States, 1790–1860*. Chicago: University of Chicago Press.

Litwack, Leon F. 1979. *Been in the Storm So Long: The Aftermath of Slavery*. New York: Vintage.

Lockwood, Charles and Christopher B. Leinberger. 1988. "Los Angeles Comes of Age." *Atlantic Monthly*.

Lodge, Henry Cabot. 1896. Speech in the United States Senate. *Congressional Record* 54th Congress, Second Session. March 16.

Loewen, James W. 1971. *The Mississippi Chinese: Between Black and White*. Cambridge, MA: Harvard University Press.

——. 1995. *Lies My Teacher Told Me: Everything Your American History Textbook Got Wrong*. New York: New Press.

Logan, Kathleen. 1984. *Haciendo Pueblo: The Development of a Guadalajaran Suburb*. Tuscaloosa: University of Alabama Press.

Logan, John R., Richard D. Alba, and Thomas L. McNulty. 1994. "Ethnic Economics in Metropolitan Regions: Miami and Beyond." *Social Forces*. 72.

Lomnitz, Larissa A. 1977. *Networks and Marginality: Life in a Mexican Shantytown*. Tr. Cinna Lomnitz. New York: Academic.

London, Robb. 1991. Judge's Overruling of Crack Law Brings Turmoil." *New York Times*. January 11.

Loomis, Charles P. 1974. "A Backward Glance at Self-Identification of Blacks and Chicanos." *Rural Sociology*. 39.

Lopez, Alberto. 1974. "The Puerto Rican Diaspora." In Alberto Lopez and James Petras, eds., *Puerto Rico and Puerto Ricans*. Cambridge, MA: Schenckman.

Louis Harris and Associates. 1989. *The Unfinished Agenda on Race in America*. New York: NAACP Legal Defense and Educational Fund.

Lovell-Troy, Lawrence A. 1980. "Clan Structure and Economic Activity: The Case of Greeks in Small Business Enterprise." In Scott Cummings, ed., *Self-Help in Urban America*. Port Washington, NY: Kennikat Press.

——. 1981. "Ethnic Occupational Structures: Greeks in the Pizza Business." *Ethnicity*. 8.

Luce, Henry R. 1941. "The American Century." *Life*. February 17.

Lupul, M. R. 1983. "Multiculturatism and Canada's White Ethnics." *Multiculturalism*. 6.

Lurie, Nancy Oestreich. 1965/1968. "The American Indian: Historical Background." In Stuart Levine and Nancy Lurie, eds., *The American Indian Today*. Deland, FL: Everett/Edwards.

Luttwak, Edwin. 1992. "The Third-Worldization of America." *New York Times*. January 10.

Lyman, Stanford M. 1974. *Chinese Americans.* New York: Random House.

———. 1991. "Race Relations as Social Process: Sociology's Resistance to a Civil Rights Orientation." In Herbert Hill and James E. Jones, eds., *Race in America: The Struggle for Equality.* Madison, WI: University of Wisconsin Press.

Lyman, Stanford M. and William A. Douglass. 1973. "Ethnicity: Strategies of Collective and Individual Impression Management." *Social Research.* 40.

Lynd, Robert S. and Helen M. Lynd. 1937. *Middletown in Transition.* New York: Harcourt Brace.

McBeth, Sally. 1989. "Layered Identity Systems in Western Oklahoma Indian Communities." Paper presented at the annual meeting of the American Anthropological Association. Washington, DC.

McBride, Teresa. 1976. *The Domestic Revolution: The Modernization of Household Service in England and France, 1820–1920.* New York: Holmes and Meier.

McDonnell, Patrick J. 1997. "Immigrants Net Economic Plus, Study Says." *Los Angeles Times.* May 18.

McIntosh, Peggy. 1989. "White Privilege: Unpacking the Invisible Knapsack." *Peace and Freedom.* July/August.

McKee, James B. 1993. Sociology and the Race Problem: The Failure of a Perspective. Urbana, IL: University of Illinois Press.

McLemore, S. Dale. 1973. "The Origins of Mexican American Subordination in Texas." *Social Science Quarterly.* 53. March.

———. 1983/1991/1998. *Racial and Ethnic Relations in America,* 2nd ed. Boston: Allyn and Bacon.

McMillan, Penelope. 1982. "Vietnamese Influx: It's Chinatown with Subtitles." *Los Angles Times.* February 14.

Maarseveen, Henc T. and Ger van der Tang. 1978. *Written Constitutions: A Computerized Comparative Study.* Dobbs Ferry, NY: Oceana Publications.

Madsen, William. 1964. *Mexican Americans of South Texas.* New York: Holt.

Malcolm X. 1966. *The Autobiography of Malcolm X.* New York: Grove Press.

Mar, Don. 1991. "Another Look at the Enclave Economy Thesis: Chinese Immigrants in the Ethnic Labor Market." *Amerasia Journal.* 17.

*Mar, Don and Marlene Kim. 1994. "Historical Trends." In Paul Ong, ed., *The State of Asian Pacific America: Economic Diversity, Issues and Politics.* Los Angeles: LEAP and UCLA Asian American Studies Center.

Marcuse, Herbert. 1964. *One Dimensional Man: Studies in the Ideology of Advanced Industrial Society.* London: Sphere.

Mare, R. D. and C. Winship. 1984. "The Paradox of Lessening Racial Inequality and Joblessness Among Black Youth: Enrollment, Enlistment and Employment, 1964–1981." *American Sociological Review.* 49:1.

Marger, Martin. 1978. "A Reexamination of Gordon's Ethclass." *Sociological Focus.* 11.

Marriott, Michael. 1991. "Slaying Divides a Neighborhood on Racial Lines." *New York Times.* September 3.

Marson, Wilfred G. and Thomas Van Valey. 1979. "The Role of Residential Segregation in the Assimilation Process." *The Annals of the American Academy of Political and Social Science.* 441.

Martin, Ben L. 1991. "From Negro to Black to African American: The Power of Names and Naming." *Political Science Quarterly.* 106.

Martin, Philip and Elizabeth Midgley. 1994. "Immigration to the United States: Journey to an Uncertain Destination," *Population Bulletin.* 49:2. September.

Martinez, Ramiro, Jr. 1996. "Latinos and Lethal Violence: The Impact of Poverty and Inequality." *Social Problems.* 43.

Massarik, Fred. n.d. "Intermarriage: Factors for Planning." National Jewish Population Study. New York: Council of Jewish Federation and Welfare Funds.

Massey, Douglas S. 1978. *Residential Segregation of Spanish Americans in United States Urbanized Areas.* Unpublished doctoral dissertation. Department of Sociology, Princeton University.

———. 1981. "Dimensions of the New Immigration to the United States and the Prospects for Assimilation." *Annual Review of Sociology.* 7.

———. 1981b. "Hispanic Residential Segregation: A Comparison of Mexicans, Cubans, and Puerto Ricans." *Sociology and Social Research.* 65.

———. 1981c. "Social Class and Ethnic Segregation: A Reconsideration of Methods and Conclusions." *American Sociological Review.* 46.

———. 1983. *The Demographic and Economic Position of Hispanics in the United States: The Decade of the 1970s.* Washington, DC: National Commission for Employment Policy.

———. 1985. "Ethnic Residential Segregation: A Theoretical Synthesis and Empirical Review." *Sociology and Social Research.* 60.

———. 1986a. "The Settlement Process Among Mexican Immigrants to the United States." *American Sociological Review.* 51.

———. 1986b. "The Social Organization of Mexican Migration to the United States." *The Annals of the American Academy of Political and Social Science.* 487.

———. 1987. "Understanding Mexican Migration to the United States." *American Journal of Sociology.* 92.

———. 1988. "Economic Development and International Migration in Comparative Perspective." *Population and Development Review.* 14.

———. 1990. "American Apartheid: Segregation and the Making of the Underclass." *American Journal of Sociology.* 96.

———. 1990a. "Social Structure, Household Strategies, and the Cumulative Causation of Migration." *Population Index.* 56.

———. 1990b. "The Social and Economic Origins of Immigration." *Annals of the American Academy of Political and Social Sciences.* 510.

*———. 1995. "The New Immigration and Ethnicity in the United States." *Population and Development Review.* 21:3. September.

Massey, Douglas S., Rafael Alarcon, Jorge Durand, and Humberto Gonzalez. 1987. *Return to Aztlan: The Social Process of International Migration from Western Mexico.* Berkeley: University of California Press.

Massey, Douglas S. and Brooks Bitterman. 1985. "Explaining the Paradox of Puerto Rican Segregation." *Social Forces.* 64.

Massey, Douglas S., Gretchen A. Condran, and Nancy A. Denton. 1987. "The Effect of Residential Segregation on Black Social and Economic Well-Being." *Social Forces.* 66:1.

Massey, Douglas S. and Nancy A. Denton. 1987. "Trends in the Residential Segregation of Blacks, Hispanics, and Asians: 1970–1980." *American Sociological Review.* 52.

*———. 1993. *American Apartheid: Segregation and the Making of the Underclass.* Cambridge, MA: Harvard University Press.

Massey, Douglas S. and Brendan P. Mullan. 1984. "Processes of Hispanic and Black Spatial Assimilation." *American Journal of Sociology.* 89:4.

Massey, Douglas S. and Audrey Singer. 1995. "New Estimates of Undocumented Mexican Migration and the Probability of Apprehension." *Demography.* 32.

Massey, Douglas S. et. al. 1993. "Theories of International Migration: A Review and Appraisal." *Population and Development Review.* 19.

———. 1994. "An Evaluation of International Migration Theory: The North American Case." *Population and Development Review.* 20.

Mathews, Fred H. 1964. "White Community and Yellow Peril." *Mississippi Valley Historical Review.* 50.

Mayer, Kurt B. and Walter Buckley. 1970. *Class and Society,* 3rd ed. New York: Random House.

Mazumdar, Partha. 1996. "Unfortunately It's Racist: The Ideological Construction of the 'Model Minority' Thesis." Unpublished Master's thesis. The University of Kansas.

Means, Gordon P. 1976. *Malaysian Politics.* London: Hodder and Stoughton.

Melson, Robert and Howard Wolpe, eds. 1971. *Nigeria: Modernization and the Politics of Communalism.* East Lansing: Michigan State University Press.

Mercer, John. 1978. *Scotland: The Devolution of Power.* London: Calder.

Meriam, Lewis, ed. 1928. *The Problem of Indian Administration.* Baltimore: Johns Hopkins University Press.

Merton, Robert K. 1949. "Discrimination and the American Creed." In Robert MacIver, ed., *Discrimination and the National Welfare.* New York: Institute for Religious and Social Studies and Harper and Row.

Metzger, L. Paul. 1971. "American Sociology and Black Assimilation: Conflicting Perspectives." *American Journal of Sociology.* 76.

Meyer, Kurt. 1947. "Small Business as a Social Institution." *Social Research.* 14.

———. 1953. "Business Enterprise: Traditional Symbol of Opportunity." *British Journal of Sociology.* 4.

Miller, Daniel R. and Guy E. Swanson. 1958. *The Changing American Parent.* New York: John Wiley.

Mills, C. Wright. 1951. *White Collar.* New York: Oxford University Press.

———. 1956. *Power Elite.* New York: Oxford University Press.

———. 1966. "The Middle Classes in Middle-Sized Cities." In Seymour Martin Lipset and Reinhard Bendix, eds., *Class, Status, and Power,* 2nd ed. New York: Free Press.

Min, P. G. 1990. "Problems of Korean Immigrant Entrepreneurs." *International Migration Review.* 24:3.

Mindel, Charles H. and Robert W. Habenstein. 1976. *Ethnic Families in America: Patterns and Variations.* New York: Elsevier.

Mines, Richard. 1981. *Developing a Community Tradition of Migration: A Field Study in Rural Zocatecas, Mexico, and in California Settlement Areas.* La Jolla, CA: Program in U.S.-Mexican Studies.

Mintz, Sidney W. 1971. "Toward an Afro-American History." *Journal of World History.* 13.

———. 1973. "Puerto Rico: An Essay in the Definition of National Culture." In Francesco Cordasco and Eugene Bucchioni, eds., *The Puerto Rican Experience.* Totowa, NJ: Rowan and Littlefield.

Model, Suzanne. 1988. "The Economic Progress of European and East Asian Americans." *Annual Review of Sociology.* 14.

Modell, John. 1977. *The Economics and Politics of Racial Accommodations: The Japanese of Los Angeles, 1900–1942.* Urbana, IL: University of Illinois Press.

Moerman, Michael. 1965. "Ethnic Identification in a Complex Civilization: Who Are the Lue?" *American Anthropologist.* 76.

———. 1974. "Accomplishing Ethnicity." In R. Turner, ed., *Ethnomethodology.* New York: Penguin Education.

Montero, Darrel. 1981. "The Japanese Americans: Changing Patterns of Assimilation Over Three Generations." *American Sociological Review.* 46.

Moore, Joan W. 1970. "Colonialism: The Case of the Mexican Americans." *Social Problems.* 17.

———. 1981. "Minorities in the American Class System." *Daedalus.* 110.

Moore, Joan and James Diego Vigil. 1993. "Barrios in Transition," In Joan Moore and Raquel Pinderhughes, eds., *Latinos and the Underclass Debate.* New York: Russell Sage Foundation.

Moore, Joan and Raquel Pinderhughes, eds. 1993. *Latinos and the Underclass Debate*. New York: Russell Sage Foundation.

Morales, R. and F. Bonilla, ed. 1993. *Latinos in a Changing U.S. Economy*. Newbury Park, CA: Sage.

Morawska, Ewa. 1990. "The Sociology and Historiography of Immigration." In Virginia Yans-McLaughlin, ed., *Immigration Reconsidered: History, Sociology, and Politics*. New York: Oxford University Press.

Morley, Jefferson. 1995. "Crack in Black and White," *Washington Post*. November 19.

Morris, Aldon. 1984. *The Origins of the Civil Rights Movement*. New York: Free Press.

Morris, Aldon D. and Carol M. Mueller, eds. 1992. *Frontiers in Social Movement*. New Haven, CT: Yale University Press.

Moss, E. Yvonne. 1990. "African Americans and the Administration of Justice." In Wornie L. Reed, ed., *Assessment of the Status of African-Americans*. Boston: University of Massachusetts. William Monroe Trotter Institute.

Moss, P. and C. Tilly. 1991. *Why Black Men Are Doing Worse in the Labor Market: A Review of Supply-Side and Demand-Side Explanations*. New York: Social Science Research Council.

Muller, Thomas. 1993. *Immigrants and the American City*. New York: New York University Press.

Muller, Thomas and Thomas J. Espenshade. 1985. *The Fourth Wave: California's Newest Immigrants*. Washington, DC: The Urban Institute.

Murguia, E. 1975. *Assimilation, Colonialism and the Mexican American People*. Austin: Center for Mexican-American Studies, University of Texas.

Murray, Janice. 1977. *Canadian Cultural Nationalism*. New York: New York University Press.

Musgrove, F. 1953. "Education and the Culture Concept." *Africa*. 23:2

Mydans, Seth. 1990. "Clash of Cultures Grows Amid American Dream." *New York Times*. March 26.

Myerson, Allen R. 1997. "As U.S. Bias Cases Drop, Employees Take Up Fight." *New York Times*. January 12.

———. 1997. "At Rental Counters, Are All Drivers Created Equal?" *New York Times*. March 18.

Myrdal, Gunnar. 1944/1962. *An American Dilemma: The Negro Problem and Modern Democracy*. New York: Harper and Row.

Nagel, Joane. 1982. "Political Mobilization of Native Americans." *Social Science Journal*. 19.

———. 1986. "The Political Construction of Ethnicity." In Susan Olzak and Joane Nagel, eds., *Competitive Ethnic Relations*. Orlando, FL: Academic Press.

*———. 1994. "Constructing Ethnicity: Creating and Recreating Ethnic Identity and Culture." *Social Problems*. 44:1. February.

———. 1995. "American Indian Ethnic Renewal: Politics and the Resurgence of Identity." *American Sociological Review*. 60. December.

———. 1996. *American Indian Ethnic Renewal: Red Power and the Resurgence of Identity and Culture*. New York: Oxford University Press.

Nagel, Joane and Susan Olzak. 1982. "Ethnic Mobilization in New States and Old States: an Extension of the Competition Model." *Social Problems*. 30:2.

Nagel, Joane, Carol Ward, and Timothy Knapp. 1986. "The Politics of American Indian Economic Development: The Reservation/Urban Nexus." In Matthew Snipp, ed., *American Indian Economic Development: Policy Impacts and Unresolved Problems*. Albuquerque: University of New Mexico Press.

Naples, Nancy A. 1991. "'Just What Needed to be Done': The Political Practice of Women Community Workers in Low-Income Neighborhoods." *Gender and Society*. 5.

Nash, Manning. 1962. "Race and the Ideology of Race." *Current Anthropology*. 3:3.

National Advisory Commission on Civil Disorders. 1968. *Report*. Washington, DC: Government Printing Office.

National Association of Hispanic Publications. 1995. *Hispanics–Latinos: Diverse People in a Multicultural Society*. Washington, DC: National Association of Hispanic Publications.

National Association of Latino Elected Officials. 1997. *National Directory of Latino Elected Officials*. Los Angeles: NALEO Educational Fund.

National Puerto Rican Coalition. 1985. *Puerto Ricans in the Mid '80s: An American Challenge*. Washington, DC: National Puerto Rican Coalition.

Nayar, Baldev Raj. 1966. *Politics in the Punjab*. New Haven, CT: Yale University Press.

Neary, Ian J. 1986. "Socialist and Communist Party Attitudes Toward Discrimination against Japan's *Burakumin*." *Political Studies*. 34.

Nee, Victor G. and Brett DeBary Nee. 1973. *Longtime Californ': A Documentary Study of an American Chinatown*. Boston: Houghton Mifflin.

Nee, Victor and Jimy Sanders. 1985. "The Road to Parity: Determinants of the Socioeconomic Attainments of Asian Americans." *Ethnic and Racial Studies*. 8.

Nee, Victor and Herbert Y. Wong. 1985. "Asian American Socioeconomic Achievement: The Strength of the Family Bond." *Sociological Perspectives*. 28.

Neidert, Lisa and Reynolds Farley. 1985. "Assimilation in the United States: An Analysis of Ethnic and Generation Differences in Status and Achievement." *American Sociological Review*. 50.

Nelson, Candace and Marta Tienda. 1985. "The Structuring of Hispanic Ethnicity: Historical and Contemporary Perspectives." *Ethnic and Racial Studies*. 8.

Newcomer, Mabel. 1961. "The Little Businessman: A Study of Business Proprietors in Poughkeepsie, N. Y." *Business History Review.* 35.

Newman, William M. 1973. *American Pluralism: A Study of Minority Groups and Social Theory.* New York: Harper and Row.

Newsweek. 1980. "The Mood of Ghetto America." June 2.

———. 1991. "The New Politics of Race." May 6.

———. 1995. "What Color Is Black?" February 15.

New York Times. 1990. "New York Town Finds Debt to Indians May Now Be Due." June 11.

Nisbitt, Richard. 1995. "Race, IQ, and Scientism." In Steven Fraser, ed. *The Bell Curve Wars: Race, Intelligence, and the Future of America.* New York: Basic Books.

Noel, Donald L. 1968. "A Theory of the Origin of Ethnic Stratification." *Social Problems.* 16.

———. 1972. *The Origins of American Slavery and Racism.* Columbus, OH: Charles E. Merrill.

Norton, Mary Beth, David M. Katzman, Paul D. Escott, Howard P. Chudacoff, Thomas G. Patterson, and William M. Tuttle, Jr. 1982/1994. *A People and a Nation: A History of the United States.* Boston: Houghton Mifflin.

Novak, Michael. 1971. *The Rise of the Unmeltable Ethnics.* New York: Macmillan.

———. 1975. "Black and White in Catholic Eyes." *New York Times Magazine.* November 16.

Nugent, Walter. 1992. *Crossings: The Great Transatlantic Migrations, 1870–1914.* Bloomington: Indiana University Press.

O'Brien, D. and S. Fugita. 1991. *The Japanese American Experience.* Bloomington: Indiana University Press.

O'Brien, Sharon. 1990. *American Indian Tribal Governments.* Norman: University of Oklahoma Press.

O'Brien, William V. 1968. "International Crimes." In D. L. Sills, ed., *International Encyclopedia of the Social Sciences.* New York: Macmillan.

O'Connor, James. 1973. *The Fiscal Crisis of the State.* New York: St. Martin's Press.

O'Hare, William P. and Judy C. Felt. 1991. "Asian Americans: America's Fastest Growing Minority Group." *Population Trends and Public Policy.* February.

O'Sullivan, Katharine and William J. Wilson. 1988. "Race and Ethnicity." In Neil J. Smelser, ed., *The Handbook of Sociology.* Newbury Park, CA: Sage.

Oates, Stephen B. 1982. *Let the Trumpet Sound: The Life of Martin Luther King, Jr.* New York: Mentor Books.

Oberschall, Anthony. 1973. *Social Conflict and Social Movements.* Englewood Cliffs, NJ: Prentice-Hall.

Obidinski, Eugene. 1978. "Methodological Considerations in the Definition of Ethnicity." *Ethnicity.* 6.

Ogbu, John U. 1974. *The Next Generation: An Ethnography of Education in an Urban Neighborhood.* New York: Academic Press.

———. 1978. *Minority Education and Caste: The American System in Cross-cultural Perspective.* New York: Academic Press.

———. 1982. "Cultural Discontinuities and Schooling." *Anthropology and Education Quarterly.* 13:4.

———. 1983. "Minority Status and Schooling in Plural Societies." *Comparative Education Review.* 27:2.

———. 1984. *Understanding Community Forces Affecting Minority Students' Academic Achievement Effort.* Unpublished manuscript. Oakland, CA: The Achievement Council.

———. 1985a. "Cultural-Ecological Influences on Minority Education." *Language Arts.* 62:8.

———. 1985b. "Schooling in the Ghetto: An Ecological Perspective on Community and Home Influences." ERIC ED.

———. 1986. "The Consequences of the American Caste System." In U. Neisser, ed., *The School Achievement of Minority Children: New Perspectives.* Hillsdale, NJ: Erlbaum.

———. 1987. "Variability in Minority School Performance: A Problem in Search of an Explanation." *Anthropology and Education Quarterly.* 18:4.

———. 1988. "Diversity and Equity in Public Education: Community Forces and Minority School Adjustment and Performance. In R. Haskins and D. MaCrae, eds., *Policies for America's Public Schools: Teachers, Equity, and Indicators.* Norwood, NJ: ABLEX.

———. 1989. "Minority Youth and School Success." In *Teaching At-Risk Youth,* conference proceedings of Council of State Chief School Officers. Baltimore. Washington, DC: Council of State Chief School Officers.

*———. 1990. "Minority Status and Literacy in Comparative Perspective." *Daedalus.* 119:2. Spring.

Ogbu, John U. and M. E. Matute-Bianchi. 1986. "Understanding Sociocultural Factors: Knowledge, Identity, and School Adjustment." In *Beyond Language: Social and Cultural Factors in Schooling Language Minority Students.* Sacramento: Bilingual Education Office, CA State Department of Education.

Okamura, Jonathan Y. 1981. "Situational Ethnicity." *Ethnic and Racial Studies.* 4.

Okihiro, Gary Y., Shirley Hune, Arthur A. Hansen, and John M. Liu, eds. 1988. *Reflections on Shattered Windows.* Pullman: Washington State University Press.

Oliver, Melvin L., C. Rodriguez, and R. A. Mickelson. 1985. "Brown and Black in White: The Social Adjustment and Academic Performance of Chicano and Black Students in a Predominantly White University." *The Urban Review.* 17:2.

Oliver, Melvin L. and Thomas M. Shapiro. 1989a. "Wealth of a Nation: A Reassessment of Asset Inequality in America." *American Journal of Economics and Sociology.* 48.

——. 1989b. "Race and Wealth." *Review of Black Political Economy.* 17:4.

——. 1995. *Black Wealth/White Wealth: A New Perspective on Racial Inequality.* New York: Routledge.

Olson, Mary. 1988. "The Legal Road to Economic Development: Fishing Rights in Western Washington." In C. Matthew Snipp, ed., *Public Policy Impacts on American Indian Economic Development.* Albuquerque: Institute for Native American Development, University of New Mexico.

Olzak, Susan. 1980. "Contemporary Ethnic Mobilization." *Annual Review of Sociology.* 9.

——. 1986. "A Competition Model of Ethnic Collective Action in American Cities, 1877–1889." In Susan Olzak and Joane Nagel, eds., *Competitive Ethnic Relations.* Orlando, FL: Academic Press.

——. 1989. "Labor Unrest, Immigration, and Ethnic Conflict in Urban America, 1880–1914." *American Journal of Sociology.* 94.

——. 1992. *The Dynamics of Ethnic Competition and Conflict.* Stanford: Stanford University Press.

Olzak, Susan and Joane Nagel, eds. 1986. *Competitive Ethnic Relations.* Orlando, FL: Academic Press.

Omi, Michael and Howard Winant. 1986. *Racial Formation in the United States.* New York: Routledge and Kegan Paul.

Ong, Paul. 1981. "An Ethnic Trade: The Chinese Laundries in Early California." *The Journal of Ethnic Studies.* 8:4. Winter.

Ong, Paul and Suzanne Hee. 1994. "The Growth of the Asian Pacific American Population: Twenty Million in 2020." In Paul Ong, ed., *The State of Asian Pacific America: Economic Diversity, Issues and Politics.* Los Angeles: LEAP and UCLA Asian American Studies Center.

Ong, Paul and J. Liu. 1994. "U.S. Immigration Policies and Asian Migration." In P. Ong, E. Bonacich, and L. Cheng, eds., *The New Asian Immigration.* Philadelphia: Temple University Press.

Opperman, Hubert. 1966. "Australia's Immigration Policy." Paper delivered to the Youth and Student Seminar. Canberra, Australia. May 28.

Orfield, Gary, Mark Bachmeier, David R. James, and Tamela Eitle. 1997. *Deepening Segregation in American Public Schools.* Cambridge, MA: Harvard Project on School Desegregation.

Orfield, Gary, and Franklin Monfort. 1988. "Racial Change and Desegregation in Large School Districts: Trends Through the 1986–1987 School Year." Report of the Council of Urban Boards of Education and the National School Desegregation Project of the University of Chicago.

Orfield, Gary, Franklin Monfort, and Melissa Aaron. 1989. "Status of School Desegregation, 1968–1986." Report of the Council of Urban Boards of Education and the National School Desegregation Research Project of the University of Chicago.

Padilla, E. 1958. *Up from Puerto Rico.* New York: Columbia University Press.

Padilla, Felix. 1985. *Latino Ethnic Consciousness: The Case of Mexican Americans and Puerto Ricans in Chicago.* Notre Dame, IN: University of Notre Dame Press.

——. 1986. "Latino Ethnicity in the City of Chicago." In Susan Olzak and Joane Nagel, eds., *Competitive Ethnic Relations.* New York: Academic Press.

Pardo, Mary. 1990. "Mexican American Women Grassroots Community Activists: 'Mothers of East Los Angeles.'" *Frontiers.* 11.

Paredes, Américo. 1978. "The Problem of Identity in a Changing Culture: Popular Expressions of Culture Conflict Along the Lower Rio Grande Border." In Stanley R. Ross, ed., *Views Across the Border: The United States and Mexico.* Albuquerque: University of New Mexico Press.

Parillo, Vincent N. 1994. "Diversity in America: A Sociohistorical Analysis." *Sociological Forum.* 9.

Parish, Peter J. 1989. *Slavery: History and Historians.* New York: Harper and Row.

Park, Robert E. 1928/1950. *Race and Culture.* Glencoe, IL: The Free Press.

Parsons, Talcott. 1966. "Full Citizenship for the Negro American?" In Talcott Parsons and Kenneth B. Clark, eds., *The Negro American.* Boston: Houghton Mifflin.

Passell, Peter. 1996. "Race, Mortgages and Statistics." *New York Times.* May 10.

Patterson, Orlando. 1975. "Context and Choice in Ethnic Allegiance: A Theoretical Framework and Caribbean Case Study." In Nathan Glazer and Daniel P. Moynihan, eds., *Ethnicity: Theory and Experience.* Cambridge: Harvard University Press.

——. 1977. *Ethnic Chauvinism: The Reactional Impulse.* New York: Stein and Day.

——. 1997. "The Race Trap." *New York Times.* July 11.

Peach, Ceri. 1981. "Ethnic Segregation and Ethnic Intermarriage: A Reexamination of Kennedy's Triple Melting Pot in New Haven, 1900–1950." In Ceri Peach, ed., *Ethnic Segregation in Cities.* London: Croom-Helm.

Pear, Robert. 1984. "Cuban Aliens, but Not Haitians Will Be Offered Residency Status." *New York Times.* February 12.

——. 1997. "Academy's Report Says Immigration Benefits the U.S." *New York Times.* May 18.

Pedraza-Bailey, Silvia. 1985. *Political and Economic Migrants in America: Cubans and Mexicans.* Austin: University of Texas Press.

Pedraza, Silvia. 1991. "Women and Migration: The Social Consequence of Gender." *Annual Review of Sociology.* 17.

——. 1992. "Ethnic Identity: Developing a Hispanic-American Identity." Paper presented at the 5th Congreso Internacional sobre las Culturas Hispanas de los Estados Unidos, Madrid, Spain.

Perlez, Jane. 1988. "Burundi's Army May Have Inflamed a Deadly Tribal Revenge Born in Fear." *New York Times*. August 19.

Perry, David C. and Paula A. Sornoff. 1973. *Politics at the Street Level*. Beverly Hills: Sage.

Petersen, William. 1966. "Success Story, Japanese-American Style." *New York Times Magazine*. January 9.

———. 1971. *Japanese Americans: Oppression and Success*. New York: Random House.

———. 1987. "Politics and the Measurement of Ethnicity." In William Alonso and Paul Starr, eds., *The Politics of Numbers*. New York: Russell Sage Foundation.

Petonito, Gina. 1991a. "Constructing 'Americans': 'Becoming American,' 'Loyalty' and Japanese Internment During World War II." In G. Miller and J. Holstein, eds., *Perspectives on Social Problems*. Greenwich, CT: JAI Press.

———. 1991b. "Racial Discourse, Claims Making and Japanese Internment During World War II." Paper presented at the meeting of the American Sociological Association. Cincinnati.

Petroni, F. A. 1970. "Uncle Sams: White Stereotypes in the Black Movement." *Human Organization*. 29:4.

Pettigrew, Thomas F. 1979. "Racial Change and Social Policy." *The Annals of the American Academy of Political and Social Science*. 441.

Philips, S. U. 1983. *The Invisible Culture: Communication in Classroom and Community on the Warm Springs Indian Reservation*. New York: Longman.

———. 1976. "Commentary: Access to Power and Maintenance of Ethnic Identity as Goals of Multi-Cultural Education." *Anthropology and Education Quarterly*. 7:4.

Phillips, George Harwood. 1980. "Indians in Los Angeles, 1781–1875: Economic Integration, Social Disintegration." *Pacific Historical Review*. 69. August.

Phillips, Kevin. 1990. *The Politics of Rich and Poor: Wealth and the American Electorate in the Reagan Aftermath*. New York: Random House.

Pido, A. 1986. *The Filipinos in America*. New York: Center for Migration Studies.

Piore, Michael J. 1979. *Birds of Passage: Migrant Labor and Industrial Societies*. Cambridge: Cambridge University Press.

Pitt-Rivers, Julian. 1967. "Race, Color, and Class in Central America and the Andes." *Daedalus*. 92:2.

Piven, Frances F. and Richard A. Cloward. 1971. *Regulating the Poor: The Functions of Public Welfare*. New York: Pantheon.

Plascov, Avi. 1981. *The Palestinian Refugees in Jordan, 1948–1957*. London: Frank Cass.

Polenberg, Richard. 1980. *One Nation Divisible: Class, Race and Ethnicity in the United States Since 1938*. New York: Viking.

Portes, Alejandro. 1969. "Dilemmas of a Golden Exile: Integration of Refugee Families in Milwaukee." *American Sociological Review*. 34.

———. 1978. "Migration and Underdevelopment." *Politics and Society*. 8:1.

———. 1979. "Illegal Immigration and the International System, Lessons from Recent Legal Mexican Immigrants to the United States." *Social Problems*. 26.

———. 1981. "Modes of Structural Incorporation and Present Theories of Labor Immigration." In Mary M. Kritz and Charles B. Keely, eds., *Global Trends in Migration: Theory and Research on International Population Movements*. New York: Center for Migration Studies.

Portes, Alejandro and Robert L. Bach. 1980. "Immigrant Earnings: Cuban and Mexican Immigrants in the United States." *International Migration Review*. 14.

———. 1985. *Latin Journey: Cuban and Mexican Immigrants in the United States*. Berkeley: University of California Press.

Portes, Alejandro, Juan M. Clark, and Robert L. Bach. 1977. "The New Wave: A Statistical Profile of Recent Cuban Exiles in the United States." *Cuban Studies*. 7.

Portes, Alejandro, Juan M. Clark, and Manuel M. Lopez. 1981–82. "Six Years Later: The Process of Incorporation of Cuban Exiles in the United States 1973–1979." *Cuban Studies*. 11–12.

Portes, Alejandro and Leif Jensen. 1987. "What's an Ethnic Enclave? The Case for Conceptual Clarity." *American Sociological Review*. 52.

———. 1989. "The Enclave and the Entrants: Patterns of Ethnic Enterprise in Miami Before and After Mariel." *American Sociological Review*. 54.

———. 1992. "Reply to Sanders and Nee: Disproving the Enclave Hypothesis." *American Sociological Review*. 57.

Portes, Alejandro and Robert D. Manning. 1986. "The Immigrant Enclave: Theory and Empirical Examples." In Susan Olzak and Joane Nagel, eds., *Competitive Ethnic Relations*. New York: Academic Press.

Portes, Alejandro and Rubén G. Rumbaut. 1990/1996. *Immigrant America: A Portrait*. Berkeley and Los Angeles: University of California Press.

Portes, Alejandro and Alex Stepick. 1985. "Unwelcome Immigrants: The Labor Market Experiences of 1980 (Mariel) Cuban and Haitian Refugees in South Florida." *American Sociological Review*. 50.

———. 1993. *City on the Edge: The Transformation of Miami*. Berkeley and Los Angeles: University of California Press.

Portes, Alejandro and Cynthia Truelove. 1987. "Making Sense of Diversity: Recent Research on Hispanic Minorities in the United States." *Annual Review of Sociology*. 13.

Portes, Alejandro and John Walton. 1981. *Labor, Class, and the International System*. Orlando, FL: Academic Press.

Portes, Alejandro and Min Zhou. 1992. "Gaining the Upper Hand: Economic Mobility Among Immigrant and Domestic Minorities." *Ethnic and Racial Studies.* 15:4.

*———. 1993. "The New Second Generation: Segmented Assimilation and Its Variants," *Annals of the American Academy of Political and Social Science.* 530. November.

Poston, Dudley L. 1988. "The Socioeconomic Attainment Patterns of Asian Americans." *Journal of Sociology.* 19.

———. 1994. "Patterns of Economic Attainment of Foreign Born Male Workers in the U.S." *International Migration Review.* 28:3.

Prebble, John. 1963. *The Highland Clearances.* London: Secker and Warburg.

Price, James A. 1968. "The Migration and Adaptation of American Indians to Los Angeles." *Human Organization.* 27.

Prosen, Rose Mary. 1976. "Looking Back." In Michael Novak, ed., *Growing Up Slavic in America.* Bayville, NY: EMPAC.

Prucha, Francis P. 1984. *The Great Father. The United States Government and the American Indians.* Lincoln: University of Nebraska Press.

Qian, Zenchao. 1997. "Breaking the Racial Barriers: Variations in Interracial Marriage Between 1980 and 1990." *Demography.* 34:2. May.

Quality Education for Minorities Project. 1990. *Education That Works: An Action Plan for the Education of Minorities.* Cambridge, MA: Massachusetts Institute of Technology.

Quinn, William W., Jr. 1990. "The Southeast Syndrome: Notes on Indian Descendant Recruitment Organizations and Their Perceptions of Native American Culture." *American Indian Quarterly.* 14.

Raboteau, Albert J. 1978. *Slave Religion: The 'Invisible Institution' in the Antebellum South.* New York: Oxford University Press.

Ramey, C. T. and F. A. Campbell. 1987. "The Carolina Abecedarian Project: An Educational Experiment Concerning Human Malleability." In J. J. Gallagher and C. T. Ramey, eds., *The Malleability of Children.* Baltimore: Paul H. Brooks.

Ramey, C. T. and J. J. Gallagher. 1975. "The Nature of Cultural Deprivation: Theoretical Issues and Suggested Research Strategies." *North Carolina Journal of Mental Health.*

Ramirez, Anthony. 1980. "Cubans and Blacks in Miami." *Wall Street Journal.* May 29.

Ramirez, M. and A. Castenada. 1974. *Cultural Democracy. Bicognitive Development and Education.* New York: Academic Press.

Raper, Arthur F. 1933. *The Tragedy of Lynching.* Chapel Hill: University of North Carolina Press.

Rawick, George P. 1972. *From Sundown to Sunup: The Making of the Black Community.* Westport, CT: Greenwood Press.

Rawley, James A. 1981. *The Transatlantic Slave Trade: A History.* New York: W. W. Norton.

Ray, Robert N. 1975. "A Report on Self-Employed Americans in 1973." *Monthly Labor Review.* 98.

Redfield, Robert. 1966. *The Little Community and Peasant Society and Culture.* Chicago: University of Chicago Press.

Reimers, C. W. 1985. "A Comparative Analysis of the Wages of Hispanics, Blacks, and Non-Hispanic Whites." In George J. Borjas and Marta Tienda, eds., *Hispanics in the U.S. Economy.* Orlando, FL: Academic Press.

Reitz, Jeffrey G. 1980. *The Survival of Ethnic Groups.* Toronto: McGraw-Hill.

———. 1982. "Ethnic Group Control of Jobs." Paper presented at the Annual Meeting of the American Sociological Association. San Francisco.

Research News. 1987. "The Costs of Being Black." 38.

Rhoodie, Eschel. 1983. *Discrimination in the Constitutions of the World.* Atlanta: Orbis.

Richardson, James and J. A. Farrell. 1983. "The New Indian Wars." *Denver Post.* Special reprint November 20–27. Denver, CO.

Richardson, Ken and David Spears, eds. 1972. *Race and Intelligence: The Fallacies Behind the Race-IQ Controversy.* Baltimore: Penguin.

Richman, Neal, and Ruth Schwarz. 1987. "Housing Homeless Families: Why L. A. Lags Behind." *Los Angeles Times.* May 24.

Rieff, David. 1993. "Multiculturalism's Silent Partner." *Harper's.* 287:1719. August.

Riesman, David. 1950. *The Lonely Crowd: A Study of the Changing American Character.* New Haven, CT: Yale University Press.

Ringer, Benjamin B. and Eleanor R. Lawless. 1989. *Race Ethnicity and Society.* New York: Routledge.

Robbins, Jim. 1997. "For Indians, Latest Fight Is Over the Environment." *New York Times.* February 2.

Roberts, Bryan. 1974. "The Interrelationships of City and Provinces in Peru and Guatemala." *Latin American Urban Research.* 4.

Roddy, Dennis B. 1990. "Perceptions Still Segregate Police, Black Community." *The Pittsburgh Press.* August 26.

Rodriguez, Clara. 1979. "Economic Factors Affecting Puerto Ricans in New York." In *Labor Migration Under Capitalism.* New York: Monthly Review Press.

Rodriguez, Nestor and Rogelio T. Nuñez. 1986. "An Exploration of Factors That Contribute to Differentiate Between Chicanos and Indocumentatos. In Harley L. Browning and Rudolfo O. de la Garza, eds., *Mexican Immigrants and Mexican Americans: An Evolving Relation.* Austin: Center for Mexican American Studies Publications, University of Texas Press.

Roediger, David R. 1991. *The Wages of Whiteness: Race and the Making of the American Working Class.* London: Verso.

———. 1994. *Towards the Abolition of Whiteness: Essays on Race, Politics, and Working Class History.* New York: Verso.

Rogg, Eleanor. 1971. "The Influence of a Strong Refugee Community on the Economic Adjustment of Its Members." *International Migration Review.* 5.

———. 1974. *The Assimilation of Cuban Exiles: The Role of Community and Class.* New York: Abergeen Press.

Rogg, Eleanor and Rosemary Cooney. 1980. *Adaptation and Adjustment of Cubans: West New York, N.J.* Hispanic Research Center Monograph. New York: Fordham University.

Rollins, Judith. 1985. *Between Women.* Philadelphia: Temple University Press.

Romero, Mary. 1988. "Chicanas Modernize Domestic Service." *Qualitative Sociology.* 11.

Roof, Wade Clark. 1979. "Race and Residence: The Shifting Basis of American Race Relations." *The Annals of the American Academy of Political and Social Science.* 441.

Roosens, Eugeen E. 1989. *Creating Ethnicity: The Process of Ethnogenesis.* Newbury Park: Sage Publications.

Root, Maria P. P., ed., 1992. *Racially Mixed People in America.* Newbury Park, CA: Sage Publications.

Rosaldo, Renato. 1988. "Ideology, Place, and People Without Culture." *Cultural Anthropology.* 3:1.

———. 1989. *Culture and Truth: The Remaking of Social Analysis.* Boston: Beacon.

Rose, Jerry D. 1976. *Peoples: The Ethnic Dimension in Human Relations.* Chicago: Rand McNally.

Rothman, Eric S. and Thomas J. Espenshade. 1992. "Fiscal Impacts of Immigration to the United States." *Population Index.* 58.

Rouse, Roger. 1987. "Migration and the Politics of Family Life: Divergent Projects and Rhetorical Strategies in a Mexican Transnational Migrant Community." Unpublished paper. Center for U.S.-Mexican Studies, University of California at San Diego.

———. 1989a. "Men in Space: Power and the Appropriation of Urban Form Among Mexican Migrants in the United States." Ann Arbor: Dept. of Anthropology, University of Michigan.

———. 1989b. "Mexican Migration to the United States: Family Relations in the Development of a Transnational Migrant Circuit." Unpublished doctoral dissertation. Stanford University.

———. 1990. "Men in Space: Power and Appropriation of Urban Form Among Mexican Migrants in the United States." Paper presented at the Residential College, University of Michigan. March.

*———. 1991. "Mexican Migration and the Social Space of Postmodernism." *Diaspora.* 1:1. Spring.

Roy, Prodipto. 1962. "The Measurement of Assimilation: The Spokane Indians." In Howard M. Bahr, Bruce A. Chadwick, and Robert C. Day, eds., *Native Americans Today: Sociological Perspectives.* New York: Harper and Row.

Rubel, Arthur J. 1966. *Across the Tracks: Mexican-Americans in a Texas City.* Austin: University of Texas Press.

Rubin, Lillian B. 1972. *Busing and Backlash: White Against White in a California School District.* Berkeley: University of California Press.

Rudolph, Lloyd and Susanne Rudolph. 1967. *The Modernity of Tradition: Political Development in India.* Chicago: University of Chicago Press.

Ruhlen, Merritt. 1987. "The First Americans: Voices From the Past." *Natural History.* 96.

Ruiz, Vicki L. and Susan Tiano, eds. 1987. *Women on the U.S.-Mexico Border: Responses to Change.* Boston: Allen and Unwin.

Rumbaut, Rubén G. 1989. "Portraits, Patterns, and Predictors of the Refugee Attainment Process: Results and Reflections from the IHARP Panel Study." In D. W. Haines, ed., *Refugees as Immigrants: Cambodians, Laotians, and Vietnamese in America.* Totowa, NJ: Rowman & Littlefield.

———. 1996. "Origins and Destinies: Immigration, Race, and Ethnicity in Contemporary America." In Silvia Pedraza and Rubén G. Rumbaut, eds., *Origins and Destinies: Immigration, Race, and Ethnicity in America.* Belmont, CA: Wadsworth Publishing.

Russell, Raymond. 1982. "Ethnic and Occupational Cultures in the New Taxi Cooperatives of Los Angeles." Paper presented at the annual meeting of the American Sociological Association. San Francisco.

Ryan, William. 1971. *Blaming the Victim.* New York: Pantheon Books.

Sack, Kevin. 1996. "Burnings of Dozens of Black Churches Across the South Are Investigated." *New York Times.* May 21.

Salamone, Frank A., ed. 1985. *Missionaries and Anthropologists, Part II.* Athens, GA: University of Georgia, Department of Anthropology.

Salzinger, Leslie. 1991. "A Maid by Any Other Name: The Transformation of 'Dirty' Work by Central American Immigrants." In Michael Buroway, et al., eds., *Ethnography Unbound: Power and Resistance in the Modern Metropolis.* Berkeley: University of California Press.

Samora, Julian. 1971. *Los Mojados: The Wetback Story.* Notre Dame, IN: University of Notre Dame Press.

Sandberg, Neil C. 1974. *Ethnic Identity and Assimilation: The Polish American Community.* New York: Praeger.

Sandefur, Gary D. and W. J. Scott. 1983. "Minority Group Status and the Wages of Indian and Black Males." *Social Science Research.* 15:347–71.

Sandefur, Gary D. and Trudy McKinnell. 1986. "American Indian Intermarriage." *Social Science Research.* 15.

Sanders, Jimy M. and Victor Nee. 1985. "The Road to Parity: Determinants of the Socioeconomic Achievements of Asian Americans." *Ethnic and Racial Studies.* 8.

———. 1987. "Limits of Ethnic Solidarity in the Ethnic Enclave." *American Sociological Review.* 52:6.

———. 1992. "Comment on Portes and Jensen: Problems in Resolving the Enclave Economy Debate." *American Sociological Review.* 57.

Sanneh, Lamin. 1989. *Translating the Message: The Missionary Impact on Culture.* New York: Orbis Books.

Santiago, Anne M. and Margaret G. Wilder. 1991. "Residential Segregation and the Links to Minority Poverty: The Case of Latinos in the United States." *Social Problems.* 38.

Saragoza, Alex. 1983. "The Conceptualization of the History of the Chicano Family." In Armando Valdez, Albert Camarillo, and Thomas Almaguer, eds., *The State of Chicano Research in Family, Labor and Migration: Proceedings of the Symposium of Work, Family, and Migration.* Palo Alto: Stanford Center for Chicano Research.

Sassen, Saskia. 1988. *The Mobility of Labor and Capital: A Study in International Investment and Labor Flow.* Cambridge: Cambridge University Press.

*———. 1989. "America's Immigration 'Problem.'" *World Policy Review.* VI:4. Fall.

———. 1991. *The Global City.* Princeton: Princeton University Press.

Sassen-Koob, Saskia. 1981. "Exporting Capital and Importing Labor: The Role of Caribbean Migration to New York City." New York: Center for Latin American and Caribbean Studies. Occasional Paper No. 28. New York University.

———. 1982. "Recomposition and Peripheralization at the Core." *Contemporary Marxism.* 5. Summer.

Saveth, Edward N. 1948. *American Historians and European Immigrants.* New York: Columbia University Press.

Saxton, Alexander. 1971. *The Indispensable Enemy: Labor and the Anti-Chinese Movement in California.* Berkeley: University of California Press.

———. 1990. *The Rise and Fall of the White Republic: Class Politics and Mass Culture in Nineteenth-Century America.* London: Verso.

Schermerhorn, Richard A. 1970. *Comparative Ethnic Relations: A Framework for Theory and Research.* New York: Random House.

———. 1974. "Ethnicity in the Perspective of Sociology of Knowledge." *Ethnicity.* 1.

———. 1978. *Ethnic Plurality in India.* Tucson: University of Arizona Press.

Schmitt, Eric. 1996. "Milestones and Missteps on Immigration." *New York Times.* October 26.

Schuman, Howard. 1969. "Sociological Racism." *Transaction.* 7.

Schuman, Howard, Charlotte Steeh, and Lawrence Bobo. 1985. *Racial Attitudes in America: Trends and Interpretations.* Cambridge, MA: Harvard University Press.

Schumpter, Joseph. 1934. *The Theory of Economic Development,* tr. Redvers Opie. Cambridge, MA: Harvard University Press.

Scott, James C. 1990. *Domination and the Arts of Resistance: Hidden Transcripts.* New Haven: Yale University Press.

See, Katherine O'Sullivan and William Julius Wilson. 1988. "Race and Ethnicity." In Neil J. Smelser, ed., *The Handbook of Sociology.* Newbury Park, CA: Sage.

Seller, Maxine S. 1977. *To Seek America: A History of Ethnic Life in the United States.* Englewood, NJ: Jerome S. Ozer.

Sengstock, Mary Catherine. 1967. "Maintenance of Social Interaction Patterns in an Ethnic Group." Ph.D. dissertation. Washington University.

Shack, W. A. 1970–1971. "On Black American Values in White America: Some Perspectives on the Cultural Aspects of Learning Behavior and Compensatory Education." Unpublished manuscript. Social Science Research Council, Subcommittee on Values and Compensatory Education.

Shade, B. J. 1982. "Afro-American Patterns of Cognition." Unpublished manuscript. Madison: Wisconsin Center for Educational Research.

Shibutani, Tamotsu and Kian Kwan. 1965. *Ethnic Stratification: A Comparative Approach.* New York: Macmillan.

Sidell, Scott. 1981. "The United States and Genocide in East Timor." *Journal of Contemporary Asia.* 11:1.

Simmons, Ron. 1982. *Affirmative Action: Conflict and Change in Higher Education After Bakke.* Cambridge, MA: Schenkman.

Simon, Julian L. 1984. "Immigrants, Taxes, and Welfare in the United States." *Population and Development Review.* 10.

———. 1989. *The Economic Consequences of Immigration.* Cambridge, MA: Basil Blackwell.

Simpson, George E. and J. Milton Yinger. 1954/1972/1985. *Racial and Cultural Minorities: An Analysis of Prejudice and Discrimination.* New York: Harper and Row.

Singelmann, Joachim and Marta Tienda. 1985. "The Process of Occupational Change in a Service Society: The Case of the United States, 1960–1980." In Bryan Roberts, Ruth Finnegan, and Duncan Gallie, eds., *New Approaches to Economic Life: Economic Restructuring, Unemployment and the Social Division of Labor.* Manchester, England: University of Manchester Press.

Sirola, Paula. 1992. "Beyond Survival: Latino Immigrant Street Vendors in the Los Angeles Informal Sector." Paper presented at the Seventeenth International Congress of the Latin American Studies Association. Los Angeles. September.

Sitkoff, Harvard. 1981. *The Struggle for Black Equality: 1945–1980.* New York: Hill and Wang.

Skidmore, Thomas E. 1993. "Bi-racial U.S.A. vs. Multi-Racial Brazil: Is the Contrast Still Valid?" *Journal of Latin American Studies.* 25:2.

Sklair, Leslie. 1989. *Assembling for Development: The Maquila Industry in Mexico and the United States.* Boston: Unwin Hyman.

Skocpol, Theda. 1985. "Bringing the State Back In: Strategies of Analysis in Current Research." In Peter B. Evans, Dietrich Rueschemeyer, and Theda Skocpol, eds., *Bringing the State Back In.* Cambridge: Cambridge University Press.

Skolnick, Jerome. 1969. *The Politics of Protest: A Staff Report to the National Commission on the Causes and Prevention of Violence.* Washington, DC: U.S. Government Printing Office.

Slade, M. 1981. "Aptitude, Intelligence or What?" *New York Times.* October 24.

Smith, Anthony D. 1986. *The Ethnic Origins of Nations.* New York: B. Blackwell.

———. 1992. *Ethnicity and Nationalism.* Leiden: E. J. Brill.

Smith, David N. 1995. "The Genesis of Genocide in Rwanda: The Fatal Dialectic of Class and Ethnicity." *Humanity and Society.* 19:4. November.

Smith, James P. 1988. "Poverty and the Family in the United States." In Gary D. Sandefur and Marta Tienda, eds., *Divided Opportunities: Minorities, Poverty, and Social Policy.* New York: Plenum.

Smith, James P. and Barry Edmonston, eds. 1997. *The New Americans: Economic, Demographic, and Fiscal Effects of Immigration.* Washington, DC: National Academy Press.

Smith, J. P. and F. R. Welch. 1989. "Black Economic Progress After Myrdal." *Journal of Economic Literature.* 27.

Smith, Tom W. 1980. "Ethnic Measurement and Identification." *Ethnicity.* 7.

———. 1992. "Changing Racial Labels: From Colored to Negro to Black to African American." Chicago: University of Chicago, General Social Survey Topical Report No. 22.

Smitherman-Donaldson, Geneva and Teun A. van Dijk. 1988. *Discourse and Discrimination.* Detroit: Wayne State University Press.

Snipp, C. Matthew. 1986. "American Indians and Natural Resource Development." *American Journal of Economics and Sociology.* 45.

———. 1988. "Public Policy Impacts on American Indian Economic Development." In C. Matthew Snipp, ed., *Public Policy Impacts on American Economic Development.* Albuquerque, NM: Institute for Native American Development, University of New Mexico.

———. 1989. *American Indians: The First of This Land.* New York: Russell Sage Foundation.

———. 1993. "Some Observations About the Racial Boundaries and the Experiences of American Indians." Paper presented at the University of Washington, April 22, Seattle, WA.

*———. 1996. "The First Americans: American Indians." In Silvia Pedraza and Ruben G. Rumbaut, eds. *Origins and Destinies: Immigration, Race, and Ethnicity in America.* Belmont, CA: Wadsworth.

———. 1997. "Some Observations About Racial Boundaries and the Experiences of American Indians." *Ethnic and Racial Studies.* 20:4. October.

Snipp, C. Matthew and Gary D. Sandefur. 1988. "Earnings of American Indians and Alaska Natives: the Effects of Residence and Migration." *Social Forces.* 66.

Snipp, C. Matthew and Gene F. Summers. 1991. "American Indian Development Policies." In Cornelia B. Flora and James A. Christenson, eds., *Rural Policies for the 1990s.* Boulder, CO: Westview Press.

Snow, D. A. and Robert D. Benford. 1988. "Ideology, Frame Resonance, and Participant Mobilization." In B. Klandermans, B. Kriesi, and S. Tarrow, eds., *International Social Movements Research.* Greenwich, CT: JAI Press.

———. 1992. "Master Frames and Cycles of Protest." In A. D. Morris and C. M. Mueller, eds., *Frontiers in Social Movement Theory.* New Haven: Yale University Press.

Snow, D. A., E. B. Rochford, Jr., S. K. Worden, and R. D. Benford. 1986. "Frame Alignment Processes, Micromobilization, and Movement Participation." *American Sociological Review.* 51.

Soja, Edward W. 1989. *Postmodern Geographics: The Reassertion of Space in Critical Social Theory.* London: Verso.

Sollors, Werner, ed. 1989. *The Invention of Ethnicity.* New York: Oxford University Press.

Solomon, Barbara. 1956/1965. *Ancestors and Immigrants.* New York: Wiley.

Sorensen, Annemette, Kari E. Taeuber, and L. J. Hollingsworth, Jr. 1975. "Indexes of Residential Segregation for 109 Cities in the United States: 1940–1970." *Sociological Focus.* 8.

Sorkin, Alan L. 1978. *The Urban American Indian.* Lexington, MA: Lexington Books.

Sowell, Thomas. 1978. *Essays and Data on American Ethnic Groups.* Washington, DC: Urban Institute.

———. 1980. *Ethnic America: A History.* New York: Basic Books.

———. 1981. *Markets and Minorities.* New York: Basic Books.

———. 1995. "Ethnicity and IQ." In Steven Fraser, ed. *The Bell Curve Wars: Race, Intelligence, and the Future of America.* New York: Basic Books.

Special Task Force to the Secretary of Health, Education, and Welfare. 1973. *Work in America.* Cambridge, MA: MIT Press.

Spector, Malcolm and John I. Kitsuse. 1977. *Constructing Social Problems.* New York: Aldine.

Spicer, Edward H. 1962. *Cycles of Conquest: The Impact of Spain, Mexico, and the United States on the Indians of the Southwest, 1533–1960.* Tucson: University of Arizona Press.

———. 1966. "The Process of Cultural Enclavement in Middle America." *36th Congress of International de Americanistas. Seville.* 3.

———. 1971. "Persistent Cultural Systems: A Comparative Study of Identity Systems that Can Adapt to Contrasting Environments." *Science.* 174. November 19.

Spickard, Paul R. 1989. *Mixed Blood: Intermarriage and Ethnic Identity in Twentieth Century America.* Madison, WI: University of Wisconsin Press.

Stalker, Peter. 1994. *The Work of Strangers: A Survey of International Labour Migration.* Geneva: International Labour Office.

Stampp, Kenneth M. 1956. *The Peculiar Institution: Slavery in the Ante-Bellum South.* New York: Random House.

Stampp, Kenneth M. et al. 1968. "The Negro in American History Textbooks." *Negro History Bulletin.* 31.

Stark, Oded. 1991. *The Migration of Labor.* Cambridge: Basil Blackwell.

Stauss, Joseph A. and Bruce A. Chadwick. 1979. "Urban Indian Adjustment." *American Indian Culture and Research Journal.* 3.

Steele, C. Hoy. 1975. "Urban Indian Identity in Kansas: Some Implications for Research." In J. W. Bennett, ed., *The New Ethnicity: Perspectives from Ethnology.* St. Paul, MN: West Publishing Company.

Steele, Claude M. 1997. "A Threat in the Air: How Stereotypes Shape Intellectual Identity and Performance." *American Psychologist.* 52:6. June.

Steele, Claude M. and Joshua Aronson. 1995. "Stereotype Threat and the Intellectual Test Performance of African Americans." *Journal of Personality and Social Psychology.* 69:5.

Stein, Judith. 1989. "Defining the Race, 1890–1930." In Werner Sollors, ed., *The Invention of Ethnicity.* New York: Oxford University Press.

Steinberg, Stephen. 1974. *The Academic Melting Pot: Catholics and Jews in American Higher Education.* New York: McGraw-Hill.

———. 1981/1989. *The Ethnic Myth: Race, Ethnicity, and Class in America.* New York: Atheneum.

———. 1995. *Turning Back: The Retreat from Racial Justice in American Thought and Policy.* Boston: Beacon Press.

Stevens, Gillian. 1985. "Nativity, Intermarriage, and Mother-Tongue Shift." *American Sociological Review.* 50.

Stolzenberg, Ross M. 1990. "Ethnicity, Geography, and Occupational Achievement of Hispanic Men in the United States." *American Sociological Review.* 55.

Stone, Irving. 1943. *Clarence Darrow For the Defense.* Garden City, NY.

Strodtbeck, Fred L. 1958. "Family Interaction. Values and Achievement." In Marshall Sklare, ed., *The Jews: Social Patterns in an American Group.* New York: Free Press.

Stuckey, Sterling. 1987. *Slave Culture: Nationalist Theory and the Foundations of Black America.* New York: Oxford University Press.

Suarez-Orozco, M. M. 1989. *Central American Refugees and U.S. High Schools: A Psychological Study of Motivation and Achievement.* Stanford: Stanford University Press.

Sullivan, John. 1988. *ETA and Basque Nationalism: The Fight for Euskadi, 1890–1986.* Rutledge: New York.

Summers, Gene F. n.d. "Social Characteristics of Reservations." Mimeo. Department of Rural Sociology, University of Wisconsin, Madison.

Sway, Marlene. 1983. "Gypsies as a Middleman Minority." Ph.D. dissertation, University of California, Los Angeles.

Swidler, Ann. 1986. "Culture as Action: Symbols and Strategies." *American Sociological Review.* 51.

Swinton, David H. 1990. "The Economic Status of Black Americans During the 1980s: A Decade of Limited Progress." *The State of Black America.* New York: National Urban League.

Szasz, Margaret C. 1988. *Indian Education in the American Colonies, 1607–1783.* Albuquerque, NM: University of New Mexico Press.

Taber, Charles R. 1991. *The World Is Too Much with Us: "Culture" in Modern Protestant Missions.* Macon, GA: Mercer University Press.

Taeuber, Karl. 1983. "Racial Residential Segregation, 28 Cities, 1970–1980." *CDE Working Paper 83–12.* University of Wisconsin, Madison.

———. 1990. "Race and Residence, 1619 to 2019." In Winston A. Van Horne and T. V. Tonnesen, eds., *Race: Twentieth Century Dilemmas—Twentieth-First Century Prognoses.* Milwaukee: University of Wisconsin Institute on Race and Ethnicity.

Taeuber, Karl E. and Alma F. Taeuber. 1965. *Negroes in Cities.* Chicago: Aldine.

Takaki, Ronald. 1989. *Strangers from a Different Shore: A History of Asian Americans.* Boston: Little, Brown.

———. 1993. *A Different Mirror: A History of Multicultural America.* Boston: Little, Brown.

Task Force on the Administration of Military Justice in the Armed Forces. 1972. *Report.* Washington, DC: U.S. Government Printing Office.

Taylor, D. Garth, Paul B. Sheatsley, and Andrew M. Greeley. 1978. "Attitudes toward Racial Integration." *Scientific American.* 238.

Taylor, Howard F. 1995. "Review of *The Bell Curve.*" *Contemporary Sociology.* 24:2. March.

Taylor, M. and S. Hegarty. 1985. *The Best of Both Worlds. . . .? A Review of Research into the Education of Pupils of South Asia Origin.* Windsor: NFER-Nelson.

Taylor, Philip. 1971. *The Distant Magnet: European Emigration to the U.S.A.* New York: Harper and Row.

Teague, Bob. 1968. "Charlie Doesn't Even Know His Daily Racism Is a Sick Joke." *New York Times Magazine.* September 15.

Terry, Robert W. 1981. "The Negative Impact on White Values." In Benjamin P. Bowser and Raymond G. Hunt, eds., *Impacts of Racism on White Americans.* Beverly Hills, CA: Sage.

Thernstrom, Abigail and Stephan Thernstrom. 1997. *America in Black and White.* New York: Simon and Schuster.

Thernstrom, Stephan. 1973. *The Other Bostonians: Poverty and Progress in the American Metropolis, 1880–1970.* Cambridge, MA: Harvard University Press.

——. ed. 1980. *Harvard Encyclopedia of American Ethnic Groups.* Cambridge, MA: Harvard University Press.

Thomas, Dorothy Swaine and Richard S. Nishimoto. 1969. *The Spoilage: Japanese American Evacuation and Resettlement.* Berkeley: University of California Press.

Thomas, Robert K. 1965/1968. "Pan-Indianism." In Stuart Levine and Nancy O. Lurie, eds., *The American Indian Today.* Deland, FL: Everett/Edwards.

Thompson, Richard H. 1979. "Ethnicity vs. Class: Analysis of Conflict in a North American Chinese Community." *Ethnicity.* 6.

Thorne, Barrie. 1993. *Gender Play: Girls and Boys in School.* New Brunswick, NJ: Rutgers University Press.

Thornton, Russell. 1987. *American Indian Holocaust and Survival.* Norman, OK: University of Oklahoma Press.

Thornton, Russell, Gary D. Sandefur, and Harold Grasmick. 1982. *The Urbanization of American Indians.* Bloomington, IN: Indiana University Press.

Thurston, Richard G. 1974. *Urbanization and Sociocultural Change in a Mexican-American Enclave.* San Francisco: R. & E. Research Associates.

Tienda, Marta. 1980. "Familism and Structural Assimilation of Mexican Immigrants in the United States." *International Migration Review.* 14.

——. 1981. "The Mexican American Population." In Amos Hawley and Sara Mills Mazie, eds., *Nonmetropolitan America in Transition.* Chapel Hill: University of North Carolina Press.

——. 1983a. "Nationality and Income Attainment Among Native and Immigrant Hispanic Men in the United States." *Sociological Quarterly.* 24.

——. 1983b. "Socioeconomic and Labor Force Characteristics of U.S. Immigrants: Issues and Approaches." In Mary Kritz, ed., *U.S. Immigration and Refugee Policy.* Lexington, MA: Lexington.

——. 1984. "The Puerto Rican Worker: Current Labor Market Status and Future Prospects." In National Puerto Rican Coalition, *Puerto Ricans in the Mid '80s: An American Challenge.* Washington, DC: National Puerto Rican Coalition.

Tienda, Marta, Katherine M. Donato, and H. Cordera-Guzman. 1992. "Schooling, Color and the Labor Force Activity of Women." *Social Forces.* 71:2.

Tienda, Marta and F. D. Wilson. 1992. "Migration and the Earnings of Hispanic Men." *American Sociological Review.* 57.

Tilly, Charles. 1986. *The Contentious French.* Cambridge, MA: Harvard University Press.

Time. 1987. "Racism on the Rise." February 2.

——. 1993. "The New Face of America." Fall.

Tinker, John N. 1973. "Intermarriage and Ethnic Boundaries: The Japanese American Case." *Journal of Social Issues.* 29:2.

Todaro, Michael P. 1976. *International Migration in Developing Countries.* Geneva: International Labor Office.

Todaro, Michael P. and Lydia Maruszko. 1987. "Illegal Migration and U.S. Immigration Reform: A Conceptual Framework." *Population and Development Review.* 13.

Tonkin, Elizabeth, Maryon McDonald, and Malcolm Chapman, eds. 1989. *History and Ethnicity.* New York: Routledge.

Trennert, Robert A. 1975. *Alternative to Extinction: Federal Indian Policy and the Beginnings of the Reservation System, 1846–51.* Philadelphia: Temple University Press.

Trevor-Roper, Hugh. 1983. "The Invention of Tradition: The Highland Tradition of Scotland." In *The Invention of Tradition,* eds. E. Hobsbawn and T. Ranger. Cambridge: Cambridge University Press.

Trillin, Calvin. 1986. "Black or White." *The New Yorker.* 62.

Trosper, R. L. 1974. *The Economic Impact of the Allotment Policy on the Flathead Reservation.* Ph.D. thesis. Harvard University.

——. 1994. "Who Is Subsidizing Whom?" In L. H. Letgers and F. J. Lyden, eds., *American Indian Policy: Self-Governance and Economic Development.* Westport, CT: Greenwood.

Tucker, M. Belinda and Claudia Mitchell-Kernan. 1990. "New Trends in Black American Interracial Marriage: The Social Structural Context." *Journal of Marriage and the Family.* 52.

Tumin, Melvin M. 1969. *Comparative Perspectives on Race Relations.* Boston: Little, Brown.

Turner, Frederick Jackson. 1894/1966. "The Significance of the Frontier in American History." In Ray Allen Billington, ed., *The Frontier Thesis: Valid Interpretation of American History?* New York: Holt, Rinehart, and Winston.

Turner, Jonathan H. and Edna Bonacich. 1980. "Toward a Composite Theory of Middleman Minorities." *Ethnicity.* 7.

Turner, Jonathan H., Royce Singleton, Jr., and David Musick. 1984. *Oppression: A Social History of Black Relations in America.* Chicago: Nelson-Hall.

Turner, Margery Austin, Michael Fix, and Raymond J. Struyk. 1991. *Opportunities Denied, Opportunities Diminished: Discrimination in Hiring,* Washington, DC: The Urban Institute.

Tuttle, William M., Jr. 1972. *Race Riot: Chicago in the Red Summer of 1919.* New York: Atheneum.

Uchitelle, Louis. 1993. "America's Newest Industrial Belt." *New York Times.* March 21.

Ugalde, Antonio. 1974. *The Urbanization Process of a Poor Mexican Neighborhood.* Austin: Institute of Latin American Studies, University of Texas.

U.S. Bureau of the Census. 1980. *Census of Population and Housing 1980. Summary Tape File 4A.*[MRDF] NPDC ed. Washington, DC: U.S. Bureau of the Census [producer]. Ithaca, NY: National Planning Data Corporation (NPDC) [distributor].

——. 1981e. "Population Profile of the United States: 1980," *Current Population Reports.* P-20:363. Washington, DC: U.S. Government Printing Office.

——. 1982c. *Statistical Abstract of the United States: 1982–83.* Washington, DC: U.S. Government Printing Office.

——. 1986. *1982 Survey of Minority-Owned Business Enterprises.* Washington, DC: U.S. Government Printing Office.

——. 1988a. "Educational Attainment in the United States: March 1987 and 1986." *Current Population Reports.* P-20:428. Washington, DC: U.S. Government Printing Office.

——. 1989. *Census of Population, Subject Reports, Characteristics of American Indians by Tribes and Selected Areas, 1980.* Washington, DC: Government Printing Office.

——. 1989b. "Money Income and Poverty Status in the United States: 1988." *Current Population Reports.* P-60:166. Washington, DC: U.S. Government Printing Office.

——. 1990. *1990 March Current Population Survey (CPS) file.*

——. 1990. "Household Wealth and Asset Ownership: 1988."

——. 1990a. "United States Population Estimates by Age, Sex, Race, and Hispanic Origin: 1980 to 1988." *Current Population Reports.* P-25:1045. Washington, DC: U.S. Government Printing Office.

——. 1990b. "The Hispanic Population of the United States: March 1989." *Current Population Reports.* P-20:444. Washington, DC: U.S. Government Printing Office.

——. 1990d. "Money Income and Poverty Status in the United States: 1989." *Current Population Reports.* P-60:168. Washington, DC: U.S. Government Printing Office.

——. 1991. "Census Bureau Releases 1990 Census Counts on Specific Racial Groups" (Census Bureau Press Release CB91–215. Wednesday, June 12). U.S. Bureau of the Census, Washington, DC.

——. 1992. *Minority Economic Profiles.* July 24.

——. 1992. *Statistical Abstract of the United States: 1992.* Washington, DC: Government Printing Office.

——. 1993. *Census of Population. 1990. Social and Economic Charateristics CP-2-1.* U.S. Department of Commerce. Washington, DC: U.S. Government Printing Office.

——. 1994. "Tables on Multiracial Responses and on Interracial and Interethnic Couples and Children." Unpublished report prepared for the OMB-NAS workshop on race and ethnicity, 17–18 February. Washington, DC.

——. 1995. *Current Population Reports.* Washington, DC, P-20:480. U.S. Government Printing Office.

——. 1996. "Money Income in the United States: 1995." *Current Population Reports.* P60:193. Washington, DC: U.S. Government Printing Office.

——. 1996. "Poverty in the United States, 1995." *Current Population Reports,* P60:194. Washington, DC: U.S. Government Printing Office.

——. 1996. *Statistical Abstract of the United States: 1996.* Washington, DC: Government Printing Office.

——. [Online]. 1997. "Asset Ownership of Households: 1993."

——. 1997. Historical Income Tables—Families [Online], "Race and Hispanic Origin of Householder-Families by Median and Mean Income: 1947 to 1995."

——. 1997. "Money Income in the United States: 1996." *Current Population Reports.* P60–197. Washington, DC: Government Printing Office.

——. 1997. Population Division, Release PPL-57 [Online], "United States Population Estimates, by Age, Sex, Race, and Hispanic Origin."

——. 1997. "Poverty in the United States: 1996." *Current Population Reports.* P60–198. Washington, DC: U.S. Government Printing Office.

U.S. Commission on Civil Rights. 1961. *Report: Justice 5.* Washington, DC: U.S. Government Printing Office.

——. 1976. *Puerto Ricans in the United States: An Uncertain Future.* Washington, DC: U.S. Government Printing Office.

——. 1988. *The Economic Status of Americans of Asian Descent.* Washington, DC: U.S. Government Printing Office.

——. 1990. *Intimidation and Violence: Racial and Religious Bigotry in America.* Washington, DC: U.S. Government Printing Office.

U.S. Congress. 1990. *United States at Large, 101st Congress, 2nd Session.* Volume 104, Part 6:4662–4665. Washington, DC: U.S. Government Printing Office.

U.S. Department of the Interior [Online]. 1997. Bureau of Indian Affairs home page.

U.S. General Accounting Office. 1997. *Tax Policy: A Profile of the Indian Gaming Industry.* May.

U.S. Immigration and Naturalization Service. 1991. *Statistical Yearbook of the Immigration and Naturalization Service, 1990.* Washington, DC: U.S. Government Printing Office.

——. 1994. *Statistical Yearbook of the Immigration and Naturalization Service, 1993.* Washington, DC: U.S. Government Printing Office.

——. 1997. *1995 Statistical Yearbook of the Immigration and Naturalization Service,* Washington, DC: U.S. Government Printing Office.

U.S. Small Business Administration, Office of Advocacy. 1980. *The Small Business Data Base.* Washington, DC: U.S. Small Business Administration.

USA Today. 1991. "Segregation: Walls Between Us." November 11.

Useem, Michael. 1980. "Corporations and the Corporate Elite." *Annual Review of Sociology.* 6.

Utley, Robert M. 1984. *The Indian Frontier of the American West, 1846–1890.* Albuquerque: University of New Mexico Press.

Uys, Pieter-Dirk. 1988. "Chameleons Thrive Under Apartheid." *New York Times.* September 23.

Valentine, Bettylou. 1978. *Hustling and Other Hard Work.* New York: Macmillan.

van den Berghe, Pierre L. 1966. "Paternalistic versus Competitive Race Relations: An Ideal-Type Approach." In Bernard E. Segal, ed., *Racial and Ethnic Relations.* New York: Crowell.

——. 1967/1978a. *Race and Racism: A Comparative Perspective.* New York: Wiley.

——. 1970. *Race and Ethnicity.* New York: Basic Books.

——. 1978. "Race and Ethnicity: A Sociobiological Perspective." *Ethnic and Racial Studies.* 1:4. October.

Vecoli, Rudolph J. 1964. "Contadini in Chicago: A Critique of the Uprooted." *Journal of American History.* 51.

Veltman, Calvin. 1988. "Modelling the Language Shift Process of Hispanic Immigrants." *International Migration Review.* 22.

Venable, Abraham S. 1972. *Building Black Business: An Analysis and a Plan.* New York: Earl G. Graves.

Vidich, Arthur and Joseph Bensman. 1960. *Small Town in Mass Society.* Garden City, NY: Doubleday Anchor Books.

Vincent, Joan. 1974. "The Structuring of Ethnicity." *Human Organization.* 33.

Vinje, David L. 1985. "Cultural Values and Economic Development on Reservations." In Vine Deloria, Jr., ed., *American Indian Policy in the Twentieth Century.* Norman, OK: University of Oklahoma Press.

Vogt, Ezra Z. 1957. "The Acculturation of American Indians." *Annals.* 311.

Wacquant, Loïc J. D. and William Julius Wilson. 1989. "The Cost of Racial and Class Exclusion in the Inner City." *The Annals of the American Academy of Political and Social Science.* 501.

Wagatsuma, Hiroshi. 1976. "Political Problems of a Minority Group in Japan: Recent Conflicts in Buraku Liberation Movements." In William A. Veenhoven and Winifred Crum Ewing, eds., *Case Studies on Human Rights and Fundamental Freedoms.* Vol. III. The Hague: Martinus Nijhoff.

Wagley, Charles and Marvin Harris. 1958. *Minorities in the New World.* New York: Columbia University Press.

Wagner, Roy. 1975. *The Invention of Culture.* Chicago: University of Chicago Press.

Waldinger, Roger. 1982. "Immigrant Enterprise and Labor Market Structure." Paper presented at the annual meeting of the American Sociological Association. San Francisco.

——. 1986. *Through the Eye of the Needle: Immigrants and Enterprise in New York's Garment Trades.* New York: New York University Press.

——. 1986/87. "Changing Ladders and Musical Chairs: Ethnicity and Opportunity in Post-Industrial New York." *Politics and Society.* 15.

——. 1989. "Structural Opportunity of Ethnic Advantage? Immigrant Business Development in New York." In *International Migration Review.* 23:1.

——. 1993. "The Ethnic Enclave Debate Revisited." *International Journal of Urban and Regional Research.* 17:3. September.

——. 1994. "The Making of an Immigrant Niche." *International Migration Review.* 28:1.

*——. 1996. *Still the Promised City: African-Americans and New Immigrants in Postindustrial New York.* Cambridge, MA: Harvard University Press.

Waldinger, Roger, H. Aldrich, R. Ward, et al. 1990. *Ethnic Entrepreneurs: Immigrant Business in Industrial Societies.* Newbury Park, NJ: Sage.

Walker, Charles and Robert Guest. 1952. *The Man on the Assembly Line.* Cambridge, MA: Harvard University Press.

Wallace, M. 1970–1971. "The Uses of Violence in American History." *American Scholar.* 40:1

Wallerstein, Immanuel. 1960. "Ethnicity and National Integration." *Cahiers d'Etudes Africaines.* 3.

——. 1976. *The Modern World-System.* New York: Academic Press.

——. 1979. *The Capitalist World Economy.* Cambridge: Cambridge University Press.

Wallman, Sandra, ed. 1979. *Ethnicity at Work.* London: Macmillan.

Walsh, James. 1993. "The Perils of Success." *Time.* Fall.

Walton, Anthony. 1996. *Mississippi: An American Journey.* New York: Knopf.

Warner, W. Lloyd and Leo Srole. 1945. *The Social Systems of American Ethnic Groups.* New Haven, CT: Yale University Press.

Warner, W. L., R. J. Havighurst, and M. B. Loeb. 1944. *Who Shall Be Educated? The Challenge of Equal Opportunity.* New York: Harper.

Warr, Mark. Forthcoming. "Dangerous Situations: Social Context and Fear of Victimization." *Social Forces.*

Warren, Robert and Ellen P. Kraly. 1985. *The Elusive Exodus: Emigration from the United States.* Population

Reference Bureau, Occasional Paper No. 8. Washington, DC: Population Reference Bureau.

Warren, Robert and Jeffrey S. Passel. 1987. "A Count of the Uncountable: Estimates of Undocumented Aliens Counted in the 1980 United States Census." *Demography.* 24.

Washburn, Wilcomb. 1964. *The Indian and the White Man.* New York: Anchor Books.

———. 1975. *The Indian in America.* New York: Harper and Row.

Waters, Mary C. 1988. "Ethnic Heterogeneity Within Racial Groups: Census Data on Blacks." Paper presented at the Population Association of America Annual Meeting. New Orleans.

———. 1990. *Ethnic Options: Choosing Identitites in America.* Berkeley, CA: University of California Press.

———. 1991. "The Intersection of Race and Ethnicity: Generational Changes Among Caribbean Immigrants to the United States." Paper presented at the annual meeting of the American Sociological Association. Cincinnati.

———. 1994. "West Indian Immigrants, African Americans and Whites in the Work-Place." Paper presented at annual meeting of the American Sociological Association. Los Angeles.

———. 1994. "The Social Construction of Race and Ethnicity: Some Examples from Demography." Paper presented at the conference "American Diversity: A Demographic Challenge for the 21st Century." State University of New York, Albany, NY.

*Waters, Mary C. and Karl Eschbach. 1995. "Immigration and Ethnic and Racial Inequality in the United States." *Annual Review of Sociology.* 21.

Wattenberg, Ben J. 1991. *The First Universal Nation.* New York: Free Press.

Watters, Ethan. 1995. "Claude Steele Has Scores to Settle." *New York Times Magazine.* September 17.

Wax, Murray L. 1971. *Indian Americans: Unity and Diversity.* Englewood Cliffs, NJ: Prentice-Hall.

Webber, Thomas L. 1978. *Deep Like the Rivers: Education in the Slave Quarter Community, 1831–1865.* New York: W.W. Norton.

Weber, Max. 1923/1968. *Economy and Society.* 3 volumes. New York: Bedminster Press.

———. 1958a. *The Protestant Ethnic and the Spirit of Capitalism.* New York: Scribner.

———. 1958b. "The Protestant Sects and the Spirit of Capitalism." In Hans H. Gerth and C. W. Mills, eds., *From Max Weber.* New York: Oxford University Press.

Weibel-Orlando, Joan. 1991. *Indian Country, L.A.: Maintaining Ethnic Community in Complex Society.* Champaign, IL: University of Illinois Press.

Weinberg, Meyer. 1983. *The Search for Quality Integration Education: Policy and Research on Minority Studies in School and College.* Westport, CT: Greenwood Press.

Whitaker, Mark. 1993. "White and Black Lies." *Newsweek.* November 15.

White, Jack E. 1997. "I'm Just Who I Am." *Time.* May 5.

White, Richard. 1983. *The Roots of Dependency: Subsistence, Environment and Social Change Among the Choctaws, Pawnees, and Navajos.* Lincon, NB: University of Nebraska.

White, Robert H. 1990. *Tribal Assets: The Rebirth of Native America.* New York: Henry Holt.

White, S. H. et al. 1973. *Goals and Standards of Public Programs for Children.* vol. 1, *Federal Programs for Young Children, Review and Recommendations.* Washington, DC: U.S. Government Printing Office.

Whitehorse, David. 1988. *Pow-Wow: The Contemporary Pan-Indian Celebration.* San Diego State University, Publications in American Indian Studies, No. 5.

Whiteman, Darrell L., ed. 1985. *Missionaries and Anthropologists. Part I.* Athens, GA: University of Georgia, Department of Anthropology.

Whitt, J. Allen. 1979. "Towards a Class-Dialectical Model of Power." *American Sociological Review.* 44.

Whorton, Brad. 1994. "The Transformation of American Refugee Policy in the 1970s and 1960s." Paper presented at the annual meeting of the Midwest Sociological Society. St. Louis.

Wieseltier, Leon. 1989. "Scar Tissue." *New Republic.* June 5.

Wilcox, Preston. 1970. "Social Policy and White Racism." *Social Policy.* 1.

Wilensky, Harold L. and Anne T. Lawrence. 1979. "Job Assignment in Modern Societies: A Reexamination of the Ascription-Achievement Hypothesis." In Amos H. Hawley, ed., *Societal Growth.* New York: Free Press.

Wilhelm, Sidney M. 1970. "Who Needs the Negro?" *Transaction.* 1.

Williams, Gregory Howard. 1995. *Life on the Color Line: The True Story of a White Boy Who Discovered He Was Black.* New York: Dutton.

Williams, Raymond. 1976. *Keywords.* London: Fontana/Croom Helm.

Williams, Robin M. 1964. *Strangers Next Door: Ethnic Relations in American Communities.* Englewood Cliffs: NJ: Prentice-Hall.

Williams, W. 1969. *The Roots of the Modern American Empire.* New York: Random House.

Willie, Charles V. 1983. *Race, Ethnicity, and Socioeconomic Status.* Bayside: General Hall.

———. 1996. "Dominant and Subdominant People of Power: A New Way of Conceptualizing Minority and Majority Populations." *Sociological Forum.* 11.

Wilson, Kenneth L. and W. Allen Martin. 1982. "Ethnic Enclaves: A Comparison of the Cuban and Black Economies in Miami." *American Journal of Sociology.* 88.

Wilson, Kenneth L. and Alejandro Portes. 1980. "Immigrant Enclaves: An Analysis of the Labor Market Experience of Cubans in Miami." *American Journal of Sociology.* 86.

Wilson, Reginald. 1996. "Special Focus: Affirmative Action and Higher Education." In Deborah J. Carter and Reginald Wilson, *Minorities in Higher Education.* Washington, DC: American Council on Education.

Wilson, William Julius. 1973. *Power, Racism, and Privilege: Race Relations in Theoretical and Sociohistorical Perspectives.* New York: Macmillan.

*———. 1978. *The Declining Significance of Race: Blacks and Changing American Institutions.* Chicago: University of Chicago Press.

———. 1981. "The Black Community in the 1980s: Questions of Race, Class, and Public Policy." *Annals of the American Academy of Political and Social Science.* 454.

———. 1987. *The Truly Disadvantaged: The Inner City, the Underclass, and Public Policy.* Chicago: University of Chicago Press.

*———. 1996a. "Work." *The New York Times Magazine.* August 18.

———. 1996b. *When Work Disappears: The World of the New Urban Poor.* New York: Knopf.

Wirth, Louis. 1928/1956. *The Ghetto.* Chicago: University of Chicago Press.

Wittke, Carl. 1940. *We Who Built America.* Englewood Cliffs, NJ: Prentice-Hall.

Woldemikael, Tekle Mariam. 1989. *Becoming Black American: Haitians and American Institutions in Evanston, Illinois.* New York: AMS Press.

Wolf, Diane L. 1992. *Factory Daughters: Gender, Household Dynamics, and Rural Industrialization in Java.* Berkeley: University of California Press.

Wolf, Eric. 1955. "Types of Latin American Peasantry: A Preliminary Discussion." *American Anthropologist.* 57.

Wolfe, Alan. 1995. "Has There Been a Cognitive Revolution in America? The Flawed Sociology of *The Bell Curve.*" In Steven Fraser, ed. *The Bell Curve Wars: Race, Intelligence, and the Future of America.* New York: Basic Books.

Wong, Charles Choy. 1977. "Black and Chinese Grocery Stores in Los Angeles' Black Ghetto." *Urban Life.* 5.

Wong, M. L. 1987. "Education versus Sports." Special project. University of California at Berkeley.

Wong, Morrison G. 1986. "Post-1965 Asian Immigrants: Where Do They Come From, Where Are They Now, and Where Are They Going?" *Annals of the American Academy of Political and Social Science.* 487.

———. 1989. "A Look at Intermarriage Among the Chinese in the United States in 1980." *Sociological Perspectives.* 32.

Wong, Morrison G. and Charles Hirschman. 1983. "The New Asian Immigrants." In William C. McCready, ed., *Culture, Ethnicity and Identity: Current Issues in Research.* New York: Academic Press.

Woo, Ofelia Morales. 1993. "Migracion internacional y movilidad transfronteriza: El caso de las mujeres

mexicanas que cruzan hacia Estados Unidos." *Mujer y frontera.* 8. Mexico: El Colegio de la Frontera Norte 7 Universidad Autonoma de Cuidad Juarez.

Wood, Peter H. 1974. *Black Majority: Negroes in Colonial South Carolina from 1670 through the Stono Rebellion.* New York: W. W. Norton.

Woodrow-Lafield, Karen A. 1993. "Undocumented Residents in the United States in 1989–1990: Issues of Uncertainty in Quantification." Paper presented at the annual meeting of the Population Association of America. Miami.

Woodrum, Eric, Colbert Rhodes, and Joe R. Feagin. 1980. "Japanese American Economic Behavior: Its Types, Determinants and Consequences." *Social Forces.* 58.

Woodward, C. Vann. 1957. *The Strange Career of Jim Crow.* New York: Oxford University Press.

Worsley, Peter. 1984. *The Three Worlds of Culture and World Development.* Chicago: University of Chicago Press.

Wren, Christopher S. 1996. "Study Poses a Medical Challenge to Disparity in Cocaine Sentences." *New York Times.* November 20.

Wright, Carole. 1977. "What People Have Formed Backlash Groups?" *Yakima Nation Review.* July 18.

Wright, Eric O., Cynthia Costello, David Hachen, and Joey Sprague. 1982. "The American Class Structure." *American Sociological Review.* 47.

Wright, Lawrence. 1994. "One Drop of Blood." *The New Yorker.* July 25.

Xenos, Peter S., Robert W. Gardner, Herbert R. Barringer, and Michael J. Levin. 1987. "Asian Americans: Growth and Change in the 1970s." In James T. Fawcett and Benjamin V. Carino, eds., *Pacific Bridges: The New Immigration from Asia and the Pacific Islands.* Staten Island, NY: Center for Migration Studies.

Yamanaka, K. and K. McClelland. 1994. "Earning the Model Minority Image: Diverse Strategies of Economic Adaptation by Asian American Women." *Ethnic and Racial Studies.* 17:1.

Yancey, William L., Eugene P. Eriksen, and Richard N. Juliani. 1976. "Emergent Ethnicity: A Review and Reformulation." *American Sociological Review.* 41.

Yetman, Norman R. 1970. *Life under the "Peculiar Institution."* New York: Holt, Rinehart and Winston.

———. 1975. "The Irish Experience in America." In Hal Orel, ed., *Irish History and Culture.* Lawrence, KS: University Press of Kansas.

———. 1983. "The 'New Immigrant Wave': Migration Pressures and the American Presence." Paper presented at the annual meeting of the American Studies Association. Philadelphia.

———. 1984. "Ethnic Pluralism in the 1970s." *American Studies in Scandinavia.* 16:2.

———. "Race and Ethnicity in 1980s America." In N. Yetman, ed., *Majority and Minority: The Dynamics of*

Race and Ethnicity in American Life. Boston: Allyn and Bacon.

Yetman, Norman R. and E. Stanley Eitzen. 1982. "Racial Dynamics in American Sport: Continuity and Change." In Norman R. Yetman, ed., *Majority and Minority: The Dynamics of Race and Ethnicity in American Life.* Boston: Allyn and Bacon.

Yinger, J. Milton, 1968. "Prejudice: Social Discrimination." In D. L. Sills, ed., *International Encyclopedia of the Social Sciences.* New York: Macmillan.

———. 1985. "Ethnicity." *Annual Review of Sociology.* 11.

Yinger, John. 1995. *Closed Doors, Opportunities Lost: The Continuing Costs of Discrimination.* New York: Russell Sage.

Young, Crawford. 1976. *The Politics of Cultural Pluralism.* Madison, WI: University of Wisconsin Press.

Young, Eva, and Mariwilda Padilla. 1990. "Mujeres undias en accion: A Popular Education Process." *Harvard Educational Review.* 60.

Young, Frank W. 1971. "A Macrosociological Interpretation of Entrepreneurship." In Peter Kilby, ed., *Entrepreneurship and Economic Development.* New York: Free Press.

Yu, Eui-Young. 1982. "Occupation and Work Patterns of Korean Immigrants." In Eui-Young Yu, Earl H. Phillips, and Eun-sik Yang, eds., *Koreans in Los Angeles.* Los Angeles: Koryo Research Institute and Center for Korean-American and Korean Studies, California State University.

Yu, E. 1987. Personal communication.

Zack, Naomi, ed., 1995. *American Mixed Race: The Culture of Microdiversity.* Lanham, MD: Rowman and Littlefield.

Zangwill, Israel. 1906. *The Melting Pot.* New York: Macmillan

Zenner, Walter P. 1982. "Arabic-Speaking Immigrants in North America as Middlemen Minorities." *Ethnic and Racial Studies.* 5.

Zhou, Min and John Logan. 1991. "Returns on Human Capital in Ethnic Enclaves: New York City's Chinatown." *American Sociological Review.* 54.

Zinn, Maxine Baca. 1989. "Family, Race, and Poverty in the Eighties." *Signs.* 14.

Zolberg, Aristide R. 1989a. "The Next Waves: Migration Theory for a Changing World." *International Migration Review.* 23.

———. 1989b. "The Politics of Immigration Reform." *Revue Française D'Etudes Americaines.* 4.

Zulaika, Joseba. 1988. *Basque Violence: Metaphor and Sacrament.* Reno: University of Nevada Press.

Statistical Appendix

Unless indicated otherwise, the data on which the tables, graphs, and figures in this Statistical Appendix have been based were derived from U.S. government publications (see especially http://www.census.gov or ins.usdoj.gov/stats). If you are interested in the precise sources of the data, please contact the editor at norm@falcon.cc.ukans.edu.

TABLE 1 *Racial Populations in the United States, 1970 to 1998*

	NUMBER (THOUSANDS)				PERCENT OF THE POPULATION			
	1970	*1980*	*1990*	*1998*	*1970*	*1980*	*1990*	*1998*
Total	203,212	226,546	249,398	269,073	100.0	100.0	100.0	100.0
White	177,749	188,341	209,173	222,412	87.5	83.2	83.9	82.6
Black	22,580	26,488	30,598	34,200	11.1	11.7	12.3	12.7
American Indian, Eskimo, and Aleut	827	1,418	2,073	2,343	0.4	0.6	0.8	0.9
Asian and Pacific Islander	1,539	3,501	7,554	10,225	0.8	1.5	3.0	3.8
Chinese	435	806	1,645	*	0.2	0.4	0.7	*
Filipino	343	775	1,407	*	0.2	0.3	0.6	*
Japanese	591	701	848	*	0.3	0.3	0.3	*
Asian Indian	*	362	815	*	*	0.2	0.3	*
Korean	69	355	799	*	0.0	0.2	0.3	*
Vietnamese	*	262	615	*	*	0.1	0.2	*
Hispanics[†]	9,073	14,609	22,558	29,960	4.5	6.4	9.0	11.1
Mexican American	4,532	8,740	13,496	*	2.2	3.9	5.4	*
Puerto Rican	1,429	2,014	2,728	*	0.7	0.9	1.1	*
Cuban	544	803	1,044	*	0.3	0.4	0.4	*
Other Hispanic	2,566	3,051	5,086	*	1.2	1.3	2.0	*

*Not available.

[†]Hispanics are also included in "White," "Black," and "Other Hispanic."

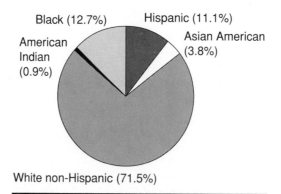

FIGURE 1 *Racial and Hispanic Population of the United States, 1998*

TABLE 2 *Resident Population Distribution, by Race and Hispanic Origin, for the United States, Regions, and States, 1990*

United States, Region, and State	Total	White	Black	American Indian, Eskimo, or Aleut	Asian or Pacific Islander	Other Race	Hispanic Origin*
United States	248,709,873	199,606,070	29,986,060	1,959,234	7,273,662	9,804,847	22,354,059
Northeast	50,809,229	42,068,904	5,613,222	125,148	1,335,375	1,666,580	3,754,389
Connecticut	3,287,116	2,859,353	274,269	6,654	50,698	96,142	213,116
Maine	1,227,928	1,208,360	5,138	5,998	6,683	1,749	6,829
Massachusetts	6,016,425	5,405,374	300,130	12,241	143,392	155,288	287,549
New Hampshire	1,109,252	1,087,433	7,198	2,134	9,343	3,144	11,333
New Jersey	7,730,188	6,130,465	1,036,825	14,970	272,521	275,407	739,861
New York	17,990,455	13,385,255	2,859,055	62,651	693,760	989,734	2,214,026
Pennsylvania	11,881,643	10,520,201	1,089,795	14,733	137,438	119,476	232,262
Rhode Island	1,003,464	917,375	38,861	4,071	18,325	24,832	45,752
Vermont	562,758	555,088	1,951	1,696	3,215	808	3,661
Midwest	59,668,632	52,017,957	5,715,940	337,899	768,069	828,767	1,726,509
Illinois	11,430,602	8,952,978	1,694,273	21,836	285,311	476,204	904,446
Indiana	5,544,159	5,020,700	432,092	12,720	37,617	41,030	98,788
Iowa	2,776,755	2,683,090	48,090	7,349	25,476	12,750	32,647
Kansas	2,477,574	2,231,986	143,076	21,965	31,750	48,797	93,670
Michigan	9,295,297	7,756,086	1,291,706	55,638	104,983	86,884	201,596
Minnesota	4,375,099	4,130,395	94,944	49,909	77,886	21,965	53,884
Missouri	5,117,073	4,486,228	548,208	19,835	41,277	21,525	61,702
Nebraska	1,578,385	1,480,558	57,404	12,410	12,422	15,591	36,969
North Dakota	638,800	604,142	3,524	25,917	3,462	1,755	4,665
Ohio	10,847,115	9,521,756	1,154,826	20,358	91,179	58,996	139,696
South Dakota	696,004	637,515	3,258	50,575	3,123	1,533	5,252
Wisconsin	4,891,769	4,512,523	244,539	39,387	53,583	41,737	93,194
South	85,445,930	65,582,199	15,828,888	562,731	1,122,248	2,349,864	6,767,021
Alabama	4,040,587	2,975,797	1,020,705	16,506	21,797	5,782	24,629
Arkansas	2,350,725	1,944,744	373,912	12,773	12,530	6,766	19,876
District of Columbia	606,900	179,667	399,604	1,466	11,214	14,949	32,710
Delaware	666,168	535,094	112,460	2,019	9,057	7,538	15,820
Florida	12,937,926	10,749,285	1,759,534	36,335	154,302	238,470	1,574,143
Georgia	6,478,216	4,600,148	1,746,565	13,348	75,781	42,374	108,922
Kentucky	3,685,296	3,391,832	262,907	5,769	17,812	6,976	21,984
Louisiana	4,219,973	2,839,138	1,299,281	18,541	41,099	21,914	93,044
Maryland	4,781,468	3,393,964	1,189,899	12,972	139,719	44,914	125,102
Mississippi	2,573,216	1,633,461	915,057	8,525	13,016	3,157	15,931
North Carolina	6,628,637	5,008,491	1,456,323	80,155	52,166	31,502	76,726
Oklahoma	3,145,585	2,583,512	233,801	252,420	33,563	42,289	86,160
South Carolina	3,486,703	2,406,974	1,039,884	8,246	22,382	9,217	30,551
Tennessee	4,877,185	4,048,068	778,035	10,039	31,839	9,204	32,741
Texas	16,986,510	12,774,762	2,021,632	65,877	319,459	1,804,780	4,339,905
Virginia	6,187,358	4,791,739	1,162,994	15,282	159,053	58,290	160,288
West Virginia	1,793,477	1,725,523	56,295	2,458	7,459	1,742	8,489

(continued)

TABLE 2 *(continued)*

United States, Region, and State	Total	White	Black	American Indian, Eskimo, or Aleut	Asian or Pacific Islander	Other Race	Hispanic Origin*
West	52,786,082	40,017,010	2,828,010	933,456	4,047,970	4,959,636	10,106,140
Alaska	550,043	415,492	22,451	85,698	19,728	6,674	17,803
Arizona	3,665,228	2,963,186	110,524	203,527	55,206	332,785	688,338
California	29,760,021	20,524,327	2,208,801	242,164	2,845,659	3,939,070	7,687,938
Colorado	3,294,394	2,905,474	133,146	27,776	59,862	168,136	424,302
Hawaii	1,108,229	369,616	27,195	5,099	685,236	21,083	81,390
Idaho	1,006,749	950,451	3,370	13,780	9,365	29,783	52,927
Montana	799,065	741,111	2,381	47,679	4,259	3,635	12,174
Nevada	1,201,833	1,012,695	78,771	19,637	38,127	52,603	124,419
New Mexico	1,515,069	1,146,028	30,210	134,355	14,124	190,352	579,224
Oregon	2,842,321	2,636,787	46,178	38,496	69,269	51,591	112,707
Utah	1,722,850	1,615,845	11,576	24,283	33,371	37,775	84,597
Washington	4,866,692	4,308,937	149,801	81,483	210,958	115,513	214,570
Wyoming	453,588	427,061	3,606	9,479	2,806	10,636	25,751

*Persons of Hispanic origin may be of any race.

TABLE 3 *Percent Distribution of the Resident Population, by Race and Hispanic Origin, for the United States, Regions, and States, 1990*

United States, Region, and State	Total	White	Black	American Indian, Eskimo, or Aleut	Asian or Pacific Islander	Other Race	Hispanic Origin*
United States	100.0	80.3	12.1	0.8	2.9	3.9	9.0
Northeast	100.0	82.8	11.0	0.2	2.6	3.3	7.4
Connecticut	100.0	87.0	8.3	0.2	1.5	2.9	6.5
Maine	100.0	98.4	0.4	0.5	0.5	0.1	0.6
Massachusetts	100.0	89.8	5.0	0.2	2.4	2.6	4.8
New Hampshire	100.0	98.0	0.6	0.2	0.8	0.3	1.0
New Jersey	100.0	79.3	13.4	0.2	3.5	3.8	9.6
New York	100.0	74.4	15.9	0.3	3.9	5.5	12.3
Pennsylvania	100.0	88.5	9.2	0.1	1.2	1.0	2.0
Rhode Island	100.0	91.4	3.9	0.4	1.8	2.5	4.6
Vermont	100.0	98.6	0.3	0.3	0.6	0.1	0.7
Midwest	100.0	87.2	9.6	0.6	1.3	1.4	2.9
Illinois	100.0	78.3	14.8	0.2	2.5	4.2	7.9
Indiana	100.0	90.6	7.8	0.2	0.7	0.7	1.8
Iowa	100.0	96.6	1.7	0.3	0.9	0.5	1.2
Kansas	100.0	90.1	5.8	0.9	1.3	2.0	3.8
Michigan	100.0	83.4	13.9	0.6	1.1	0.9	2.2
Minnesota	100.0	94.4	2.2	1.1	1.8	0.5	1.2
Missouri	100.0	87.7	10.7	0.4	0.8	0.4	1.2
Nebraska	100.0	93.8	3.6	0.8	0.8	1.0	2.3
North Dakota	100.0	94.6	0.6	4.1	0.5	0.3	0.7
Ohio	100.0	87.8	10.6	0.2	0.8	0.5	1.3
South Dakota	100.0	91.6	0.5	7.3	0.4	0.2	0.8
Wisconsin	100.0	92.2	5.0	0.8	1.1	0.9	1.9
South	100.0	76.8	18.5	0.7	1.3	2.8	7.9
Alabama	100.0	73.6	25.3	0.4	0.5	0.1	0.8
Arkansas	100.0	82.7	15.9	0.5	0.5	0.3	0.8
District of Columbia	100.0	29.6	65.8	0.2	1.8	2.5	5.4
Delaware	100.0	80.3	16.9	0.3	1.4	1.1	2.4
Florida	100.0	83.1	13.6	0.3	1.2	1.8	12.2
Georgia	100.0	71.0	27.0	0.2	1.2	0.7	1.7
Kentucky	100.0	92.0	7.1	0.2	0.5	0.2	0.6
Louisiana	100.0	67.3	30.8	0.4	1.0	0.5	2.2
Maryland	100.0	71.0	24.9	0.3	2.9	0.9	2.6
Mississippi	100.0	63.5	35.6	0.3	0.1	0.1	0.6
North Carolina	100.0	75.6	22.0	1.2	0.8	0.5	1.2
Oklahoma	100.0	82.1	7.4	8.0	1.1	1.3	2.7
South Carolina	100.0	69.0	29.8	0.2	0.6	0.3	0.9
Tennessee	100.0	83.0	16.0	0.2	0.7	0.2	0.7
Texas	100.0	75.2	11.9	0.4	1.9	10.6	25.5
Virginia	100.0	77.4	18.8	0.2	2.6	0.9	2.6
West Virginia	100.0	96.2	3.1	0.1	0.4	0.1	0.5

(continued)

TABLE 3 *(continued)*

United States, Region, and State	Total	White	Black	Indian, Eskimo, or Aleut	American Pacific Islander	Asian or Other Race	Hispanic Origin*
West	100.0	75.8	5.4	1.8	7.7	9.4	19.1
Alaska	100.0	75.5	4.1	15.6	3.6	1.2	3.2
Arizona	100.0	80.8	3.0	5.6	1.5	9.1	18.8
California	100.0	69.0	7.4	0.8	9.6	13.2	25.8
Colorado	100.0	88.2	4.0	0.8	1.8	5.1	12.9
Hawaii	100.0	33.4	2.5	0.5	61.8	1.9	7.3
Idaho	100.0	94.4	0.3	1.4	0.9	3.0	5.3
Montana	100.0	92.7	0.3	6.0	0.5	0.5	1.5
Nevada	100.0	84.3	6.6	1.6	3.2	4.4	10.4
New Mexico	100.0	75.6	2.0	8.9	0.9	12.6	38.2
Oregon	100.0	92.8	1.6	1.4	2.4	1.8	4.0
Utah	100.0	93.8	0.7	1.4	1.9	2.2	4.9
Washington	100.0	88.5	3.1	1.7	4.3	2.4	4.4
Wyoming	100.0	94.2	0.8	2.1	0.6	2.3	5.7

*Persons of Hispanic origin can be of any race.

TABLE 4 *Urban Population of the United States, 1790 to 1990 (in thousands)*

Year	Total Population	Urban Population	Percent Urban
1790	3,929	202	5.1
1800	5,308	322	5.1
1810	7,240	525	7.3
1820	9,638	693	7.2
1830	12,899	1,127	8.8
1840	17,069	1,845	10.3
1850	23,192	3,544	15.3
1860	31,443	6,217	19.8
1870	39,818	9,902	24.9
1880	50,156	14,130	28.2
1890	62,948	22,106	35.1
1900	75,995	30,160	39.7
1910	91,972	41,999	45.7
1920	105,711	54,158	51.2
1930	122,775	68,955	56.2
1940	131,669	74,424	56.5
1950	150,697	96,468	64.0
1960	179,323	125,269	69.9
1970	203,212	149,325	73.6
1980	226,505	167,000	73.7
1990	248,710	187,053	75.2

TABLE 5   *Population in 1990 for Cities with 100,000 or More Inhabitants in 1994*

City	Total (in thousands)	Percent Black	Percent American Indian, Eskimo, Aleut	Percent Asian, Pacific Islander	Percent Hispanic[1]
Abilene, TX	107	7.0	0.4	1.3	15.5
Akron, OH	223	24.5	0.3	1.2	0.7
Albany, NY	100	20.6	0.3	2.3	3.1
Albuquerque, NM	385	3.0	3.0	1.7	34.5
Alexandria, VA	111	21.9	0.3	4.2	9.7
Allentown, PA	105	5.0	0.2	1.3	11.7
Amarillo, TX	158	6.0	0.8	1.9	14.7
Anaheim, CA	266	2.5	0.5	9.4	31.4
Anchorage, AK	226	6.4	6.4	4.8	4.1
Ann Arbor, MI	110	9.0	0.4	7.7	2.6
Arlington, TX	262	8.4	0.5	3.9	8.9
Arlington, VA[2]	171	10.5	0.3	6.8	13.5
Atlanta, GA	394	67.1	0.1	0.9	1.9
Aurora, CO	222	11.4	0.6	3.8	6.6
Aurora, IL	100	11.9	0.2	1.3	23.0
Austin, TX	466	12.4	0.4	3.0	23.0
Bakersfield, CA	175	9.4	1.1	3.6	20.5
Baltimore, MD	736	59.2	0.3	1.1	1.0
Baton Rouge, LA	220	43.9	0.1	1.7	1.6
Beaumont, TX	114	41.3	0.2	1.7	4.3
Birmingham, AL	265	63.3	0.1	0.6	(Z)
Boise City, ID	126	0.6	0.6	1.6	2.7
Boston, MA	574	25.6	0.3	5.3	10.8
Bridgeport, CT	142	26.6	0.3	2.3	26.5
Brownsville, TX	99	0.2	0.1	0.3	90.1
Buffalo, NY	328	30.7	0.8	1.0	4.9
Cedar Rapids, IA	109	2.9	0.2	1.0	1.1
Chandler, AZ	90	2.6	1.2	2.4	17.3
Charlotte, NC	396	31.8	0.4	1.8	1.4
Chattanooga, TN	152	33.7	0.2	1.0	0.6
Chesapeake, VA	152	27.4	0.3	1.2	1.3
Chicago, IL	2,784	39.1	0.3	3.7	19.6
Chula Vista, CA	135	4.6	0.6	8.9	37.3
Cincinnati, OH	364	37.9	0.2	1.1	0.7
Cleveland, OH	506	46.6	0.3	1.0	4.6
Colorado Springs, CO	280	7.0	0.8	2.4	9.1
Columbia, SC	103	43.7	0.3	1.4	2.0
Columbus, GA[3]	179	38.1	0.3	1.4	3.0
Columbus, OH	633	22.6	0.2	2.4	1.1
Concord, CA	111	2.4	0.7	8.7	11.5
Corpus Christi, TX	257	4.8	0.4	0.9	50.4
Dallas, TX	1,008	29.5	0.5	2.2	20.9
Dayton, OH	182	40.4	0.2	0.6	0.7
Denver, CO	468	12.8	1.2	2.4	23.0
Des Moines, IA	193	7.1	0.4	2.4	2.4
Detroit, MI	1,028	75.7	0.4	0.8	2.8
Durham, NC	137	45.7	0.2	2.0	1.2
Elizabeth, NJ	110	19.8	0.3	2.7	39.1
El Monte, CA	106	1.0	0.6	11.8	72.5
El Paso, TX	515	3.4	0.4	1.2	69.0
Erie, PA	109	12.0	0.2	0.5	2.4
Escondido, CA	109	1.5	0.8	3.7	23.4
Eugene, OR	113	1.3	0.9	3.5	2.7
Evansville, IN	126	9.5	0.2	0.6	0.6
Flint, MI	141	47.9	0.7	0.5	2.9

(continued)

TABLE 5   (continued)

City	Total (in thousands)	Percent Black	Percent American Indian, Eskimo, Aleut	Percent Asian, Pacific Islander	Percent Hispanic[1]
Fontana, CA	88	8.7	0.9	4.5	36.1
Fort Lauderdale, FL	149	28.1	0.2	0.9	7.2
Fort Wayne, IN	184	16.7	0.3	1.0	2.7
Fort Worth, TX	448	22.0	0.4	2.0	19.5
Fremont, CA	173	3.8	0.7	19.4	13.3
Fresno, CA	354	8.3	1.1	12.5	29.9
Fullerton, CA	114	2.2	0.5	12.2	21.3
Garden Grove, CA	143	1.5	0.6	20.5	23.5
Garland, TX	181	8.9	0.5	4.5	11.6
Gary, IN	117	80.6	0.2	0.2	5.7
Glendale, AZ	148	3.0	0.9	2.1	15.5
Glendale, CA	180	1.3	0.3	14.1	21.0
Grand Prairie, TX	100	9.7	0.8	3.0	20.5
Grand Rapids, MI	189	18.5	0.8	1.1	5.0
Green Bay, WI	96	0.5	2.5	2.3	1.1
Greensboro, NC	184	33.9	0.5	1.4	1.0
Hampton, VA	134	38.9	0.3	1.7	2.0
Hartford, CT	140	38.9	0.3	1.4	31.6
Hayward, CA	111	9.8	1.0	15.5	23.9
Henderson, NV	65	2.7	1.0	2.0	8.1
Hialeah, FL	188	1.9	0.1	0.5	87.6
Hollywood, FL	122	8.5	0.2	1.3	11.9
Honolulu, HI[4]	377	1.3	0.3	70.5	4.6
Houston, TX	1,631	28.1	0.3	4.1	27.6
Huntington Beach, CA	182	0.9	0.6	8.3	11.2
Huntsville, AL	160	24.4	0.5	2.1	1.2
Independence, MO	112	1.4	0.6	1.0	2.0
Indianapolis, IN[3]	731	22.6	0.2	0.9	1.1
Inglewood, CA	110	51.9	0.4	2.5	38.5
Irvine, CA	110	1.8	0.2	18.1	6.3
Irving, TX	155	7.5	0.6	4.6	16.3
Jackson, MS	197	55.7	0.1	0.5	0.4
Jacksonville, FL[3]	635	25.2	0.3	1.9	2.6
Jersey City, NJ	229	29.7	0.3	11.4	24.2
Kansas City, KS	150	29.3	0.7	1.2	7.1
Kansas City, MO	435	29.6	0.5	1.2	3.9
Knoxville, TN	165	15.8	0.2	1.0	0.7
Lafayette, LA	97	27.2	0.2	1.3	1.7
Lakewood, CO	126	1.0	0.7	1.9	9.1
Lancaster, CA	97	7.4	0.9	3.7	15.2
Lansing, MI	127	18.6	1.0	1.8	7.9
Laredo, TX	123	0.1	0.2	0.4	93.9
Las Vegas, NV	258	11.4	0.9	3.6	12.5
Lexington-Fayette, KY	225	13.4	0.2	1.6	1.1
Lincoln, NE	192	2.4	0.6	1.7	2.0
Little Rock, AR	176	34.0	0.3	0.9	0.8
Livonia, MI	101	0.3	0.2	1.3	1.3
Long Beach, CA	429	13.7	0.6	13.6	23.6
Los Angeles, CA	3,486	14.0	0.5	9.8	39.9
Louisville, KY	270	29.7	0.2	0.7	0.7
Lubbock,TX	186	8.6	0.3	1.4	22.5
Macon, GA	107	52.2	0.1	0.4	0.6
Madison, WI	191	4.2	0.4	3.9	2.0
Memphis, TN	619	54.8	0.2	0.8	0.7
Mesa, AZ	289	1.9	1.0	1.5	10.9

(continued)

TABLE 5 *(continued)*

City	Total *(in thousands)*	Percent Black	Percent American Indian, Eskimo, Aleut	Percent Asian, Pacific Islander	Percent Hispanic[1]
Mesquite, TX	101	5.8	0.5	2.6	8.8
Miami, FL	359	27.4	0.2	0.6	62.5
Milwaukee, WI	628	30.5	0.9	1.9	6.3
Minneapolis, MN	368	13.0	3.3	4.3	2.1
Mobile, AL	196	38.9	0.2	1.0	1.0
Modesto, CA	165	2.7	1.0	7.9	16.3
Montgomery, AL	188	42.3	0.2	0.7	0.8
Moreno Valley, CA	119	13.8	0.7	6.6	22.9
Naperville, IL	86	2.1	0.1	4.8	1.8
Nashville-Davidson, TN[3]	488	24.3	0.2	1.4	0.9
Newark, NJ	275	58.5	0.2	1.2	26.1
New Haven, CT	130	36.1	0.3	2.4	13.2
New Orleans, LA	497	61.9	0.2	1.9	3.5
Newport News, VA	171	33.6	0.3	2.3	2.8
New York, NY	7,323	28.7	0.4	7.0	24.4
Norfolk, VA	261	39.1	0.4	2.6	2.9
Norwalk, CA	94	3.2	0.9	12.4	47.9
Oakland, CA	372	43.9	0.6	14.8	13.9
Oceanside, CA	128	7.9	0.7	6.1	22.6
Oklahoma City, OK	445	16.0	4.2	2.4	5.0
Omaha, NE	336	13.1	0.7	1.0	3.1
Ontario, CA	133	7.3	0.7	3.9	41.7
Orange, CA	111	1.4	0.5	7.9	22.8
Orlando, FL	165	26.9	0.3	1.6	8.7
Overland Park, KS	112	1.8	0.3	1.9	2.0
Oxnard, CA	143	5.2	0.8	8.6	54.4
Palmdale, CA	70	6.4	0.9	4.4	22.0
Pasadena, CA	132	19.0	0.4	8.1	27.3
Pasadena, TX	120	1.0	0.5	1.6	28.8
Paterson, NJ	141	36.0	0.3	1.4	41.0
Peoria, IL	114	20.9	0.2	1.7	1.6
Philadelphia, PA	1,586	39.9	0.2	2.7	5.6
Phoenix, AZ	984	5.2	1.9	1.7	20.0
Pittsburgh, PA	370	25.8	0.2	1.6	0.9
Plano, TX	128	4.1	0.3	4.0	6.2
Pomona, CA	132	14.4	0.6	6.7	51.3
Portland, OR	439	7.7	1.2	5.3	3.2
Portsmouth, VA	104	47.3	0.3	0.8	1.3
Providence, RI	161	14.8	0.9	5.9	15.5
Pueblo, CO	99	2.2	0.8	0.6	39.5
Raleigh, NC	212	27.6	0.3	2.5	1.4
Rancho Cucamonga, CA	101	5.9	0.6	5.4	20.0
Reno, NV	134	2.9	1.4	4.9	11.1
Richmond, VA	203	55.2	0.2	0.9	0.9
Riverside, CA	227	7.4	0.8	5.2	26.0
Rochester, NY	230	31.5	0.5	1.8	8.7
Rockford, IL	140	15.0	0.3	1.5	4.2
Sacramento, CA	369	15.3	1.2	15.0	16.2
St. Louis, MO	397	47.5	0.2	0.9	1.3
St. Paul, MN	272	7.4	1.4	7.1	4.2
St. Petersburg, FL	240	19.6	0.2	1.7	2.6
Salem, OR	108	1.5	1.6	2.4	6.1
Salinas, CA	109	3.0	0.9	8.1	50.6
Salt Lake City, UT	160	1.7	1.6	4.7	9.7
San Antonio, TX	935	7.0	0.4	1.1	55.6

(continued)

TABLE 5   (*continued*)

City	Total (in thousands)	Percent Black	Percent American Indian, Eskimo, Aleut	Percent Asian, Pacific Islander	Percent Hispanic[1]
San Bernardino, CA	164	16.0	1.0	4.0	34.6
San Diego, CA	1,111	9.4	0.6	11.8	20.7
San Francisco, CA	724	10.9	0.5	29.1	13.9
San Jose, CA	782	4.7	0.7	19.5	26.6
Santa Ana, CA	294	2.6	0.5	9.7	65.2
Santa Clarita, CA	118	1.5	0.6	4.2	13.4
Santa Rosa, CA	113	1.8	1.2	3.4	9.5
Savannah, GA	138	51.3	0.2	1.1	1.4
Scottsdale, AZ	130	0.8	0.6	1.2	4.8
Seattle, WA	516	10.1	1.4	11.8	3.6
Shreveport, LA	199	44.8	0.2	0.5	1.1
Simi Valley, CA	100	1.5	0.6	5.5	12.7
Sioux Falls, SD	101	0.7	1.6	0.7	0.6
South Bend, IN	106	20.9	0.4	0.9	3.4
Spokane, WA	177	1.9	2.0	2.1	2.1
Springfield, IL	105	13.0	0.2	1.0	0.8
Springfield, MA	157	19.2	0.2	1.0	16.9
Springfield, MO	140	2.5	0.7	0.9	1.0
Stamford, CT	108	17.8	0.1	2.6	9.8
Sterling Heights, MI	118	0.4	0.2	2.9	1.1
Stockton, CA	211	9.6	1.0	22.8	25.0
Sunnyvale, CA	117	3.4	0.5	19.3	13.2
Syracuse, NY	164	20.3	1.3	2.2	2.9
Tacoma, WA	177	11.4	2.0	6.9	3.8
Tallahassee, FL	125	29.1	0.2	1.8	3.0
Tampa, FL	280	25.0	0.3	1.4	15.0
Tempe, AZ	142	3.2	1.3	4.1	10.9
Thousand Oaks, CA	104	1.2	0.4	4.8	9.6
Toledo, OH	333	19.7	0.3	1.0	4.0
Topeka, KS	120	10.6	1.3	0.8	5.8
Torrance, CA	133	1.5	0.4	21.9	10.1
Tucson, AZ	409	4.3	1.6	2.2	29.3
Tulsa, OK	367	13.6	4.7	1.4	2.6
Vallejo, CA	109	21.2	0.7	23.0	10.8
Virginia Beach, VA	393	13.9	0.4	4.3	3.1
Waco, TX	104	23.1	0.3	0.9	16.3
Warren, MI	145	0.7	0.5	1.3	1.1
Washington, DC	607	65.8	0.2	1.8	5.4
Waterbury, CT	109	13.0	0.3	0.7	13.4
West Covina, CA	96	8.5	0.5	17.2	34.6
Wichita, KS	304	11.3	1.2	2.6	5.0
Winston-Salem, NC	151	39.3	0.2	0.8	0.9
Worcester, MA	170	4.5	0.3	2.8	9.6
Yonkers, NY	188	14.1	0.2	3.0	16.7

Z Less than .05 percent.

[1]Hispanic persons may be of any race.

[2]Data are for Arlington CDP (census designated place) which is not incorporated as a city but is recognized for census purposes as a large urban place. Arlington CDP is coextensive with Arlington County.

[3]Represents the portion of a consolidated city that is not within one or more separately incorporated places.

[4]The population shown in this table is for the CDP; the 1990 census population for the City and County of Honolulu is 836,231.

[5]Not incorporated.